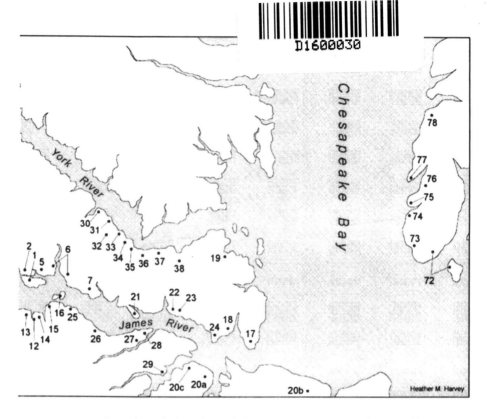

D1600030

VIRGINIA IMMIGRANTS AND ADVENTURERS, 1607-1635:

A Biographical Dictionary

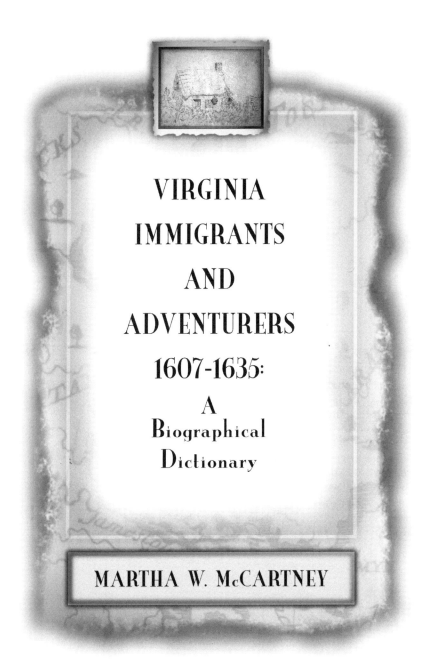

VIRGINIA IMMIGRANTS AND ADVENTURERS

1607-1635:

A Biographical Dictionary

MARTHA W. McCARTNEY

Genealogical Publishing Company

Published by Genealogical Publishing Co., Inc.
3600 Clipper Mill Road, Suite 260
Baltimore, MD 21211
Library of Congress Catalogue Card Number 2006940791
International Standard Book Number 978-0-8063-1774-8
Made in the United States of America

Index compiled by Carolyn Barkley

DEDICATED TO

MADELEINE, LAUREL, AND NICHOLAS

CONTENTS

PREFACE

In 1607 America's first permanent English colony was planted on Jamestown Island, in Virginia. Afterward, the Virginia Company of London's investors ventured funds in hope of reaping a handsome profit, and thousands of new immigrants flocked to Virginia's shores. This unprecedented flow of colonists and adventurers included prominent individuals whose names made their way into the colony's official records. However, the majority—the ordinary men, women, and children, whose efforts enabled the colony to become viable—simply escaped notice. As a result, 400 years later, we still yearn to know more about Virginia's earliest settlers. Who were they? Where did they live and what obstacles did they face in their attempts to survive? Was social and economic advancement possible? When did family life take root? What do we know about the texture of everyday life, locally and in the colony as a whole? In an attempt to answer these questions, this book brings together a broad variety of widely scattered primary sources that inform the reader about the Virginia colony's earliest inhabitants and the sparsely populated communities in which they lived.

Although the population of early seventeenth-century Virginia was highly mobile, most of the more than 5,500 men, women, and children included in this volume can be linked to the geographical settings with which they were associated. Maps that identify the sites at which Virginia's earliest plantations were located enable genealogists and students of colonial history to link people and events to the cultural landscape. An introductory chapter includes an overview of local and regional settlement and succinct histories of the various plantations established in Tidewater Virginia by 1635.

Early seventeenth-century records display the English colonists' ethnocentrism, for the non-English often were identified by the ethnic, cultural, or socio-economic group to which they belonged. This book includes biographies of Africans, Dutch, French, Germans, Irish, Italians, Native Americans, Poles, and others who made significant contributions to the early success of the Virginia colony. One individual was from Persia or Armenia, now Iran. Some of Virginia's early colonists were society's outcasts, former inmates of English prisons and penal institutions, who agreed to transportation overseas and a lengthy term of indentured servitude. Impoverished youngsters, rounded up from the streets of London, also were packed off to Virginia. Some early immigrants came from well-to-do families, younger sons eager to try their luck in the New World. The Virginia Company also recruited marriageable young women as prospective wives for the colonists.

Information has been drawn from a broad variety of primary sources, many of which are widely scattered and relatively inaccessible. Biographical information has been extracted from the Virginia Company's records, collections of private papers, diaries and journals, land patents, and records maintained by the overarching branches of government in the United States and Great Britain. The year 1635 was chosen as a cut-off point because it postdates by only a year formation of Virginia's county governments and the burgeoning of the colony's population.

INTRODUCTION

As Geography without History seemeth as carkasse without motion, so History without Geography wandereth as vagrant without a certaine habitation.

Captain John Smith, 1624 (CJS 2:338)

As Captain John Smith so astutely observed, whenever a link is forged between history and geography, everything we know becomes much more meaningful. With that thought in mind, most of the individuals whose personal histories appear in this volume have been linked to the geographic settings with which they were associated.

The sites at which Virginia's earliest settlements were located are shown on a two-part map that depicts the territory between the falls of the James River and the Eastern Shore. Each plantation has been assigned a number that appears on the map, signifying its location. These numbers also appear in specific biographies. For example, the site of the early seventeenth-century plantation known as Berkeley Hundred, arbitrarily designated number (**55**), is shown on a map of the countryside bordering the upper James River, while the biography of William Tracy notes that he lived at Berkeley Hundred (**55**). This simple technique allows the reader to link specific individuals to the areas with which they were associated. Basic background information and succinct outline histories of each settlement are found in the section entitled **Where They Were**.

Because early seventeenth-century spelling was phonetic and literacy was in relatively short supply, most people's names were spelled a variety of ways. Herein, the most readily recognized spelling is given first, followed by lesser known variations that are expressed parenthetically. Because serial marriage was commonplace during the early seventeenth century, women who wed more than once are cross-referenced with the spouses they married sequentially. Those who used aliases have been cross-referenced under their alternative surnames.

Sometimes, fathers and sons, mothers and daughters, successively utilized the same given name. For convenience of reference, they have been identified as generation I or II rather than Jr. or Sr. In accord with tradition, members of nuclear families are listed in descending order, that is, father, mother, then children, and (occasionally) grandchildren, set down in alphabetical, not chronological, order. Members of nuclear families have been clustered and are separated from solitary individuals' listings by a series of three asterisks (***). Likewise, three asterisks have been used to set off known members of extended families, that is, siblings whose biographies appear without those of their parents. People known only by their given names are listed alphabetically among

11

surnames, as are those identified exclusively by their surnames. Some individuals, notably Native Americans, Africans, and African Americans, known to the colonists by only one name, have been integrated in this manner.

The names of Virginia Company investors ("adventurers") to whom patents were issued have been included whenever Company records state that they were sending colonists to Virginia. Likewise, the names of English merchants and mariners who were shipping goods and servants to Virginia, or making the trip themselves, have been integrated into the text because quite a few made use of the headright system and acquired land in the colony. Merchants and mariners sometimes appeared before Virginia's court justices, giving testimony that sheds light upon trade networks and interaction with specific colonists.

The 1624 census, 1625 muster, and early court minutes exhibit the English colonists' ethnocentrism, often identifying the non-English only by the ethnic group to which they belonged. For example, we know that in 1624 there were four African men and two African women living at Flowerdew Hundred, but their personal names remain a mystery. Other examples abound. Therefore, references to the *totally* anonymous Africans, Dutch, French, Germans, Italians, Poles, French, and others who made significant contributions to the early success of the Virginia colony, and indeed to the history of the United States, have been omitted from this biographical work. However, they are enumerated in the seminal compilations of demographic records produced by John Camden Hotten and Peter Wilson Coldham.

Fortunately, relatively detailed information exists about the Walloons and French who in 1621 received the Virginia Company's permission to immigrate to Virginia. Likewise, the Ferrar Papers, on file at Cambridge University, contain an abundance of information about the young, marriageable women ("young maids") who were sent to Virginia as prospective wives for the colonists. At least 10 of these females who reached the colony remained single for several years. Many others undoubtedly arrived safely, wed, and upon assuming their husbands' names, quickly disappeared into the demographic and governmental records that were compiled

Whenever possible, references to individuals mentioned in sources such as the 1622 casualty list, the 1624 census, the 1625 muster, and the 1625 land list have been linked to patents and headrights and to material found in the records of the Virginia Company of London, the minutes of the General Court, and records of the Virginia assembly. In general, linkage has been made whenever data from two or more sources have been found to converge. This technique, called "triangulation," sometimes used by cultural anthropologists when analyzing oral history data, takes into account the laws of probability.

Immigrants' names have been carefully culled from land patents. In November 1618 the Virginia Company of London ratified its Great Charter, which made provisions for the private ownership of land. This ushered in what became known as the headright system, a land policy that enabled Virginia colonists and investors to acquire real estate and work for their own personal gain. Under the headright system, those who paid the cost of their own transportation to Virginia and met minimum residency requirements were entitled to 50 acres of land. So-called *ancient planters,* those who came to Virginia prior to Sir Thomas Dale's May 1616 departure, and lived in the colony at least three years, were awarded 100 acres of land. Virginia Company investors ("adventurers") who purchased a share of stock were entitled to 100 acres of land and another 100 acres when their first tract was planted. An individual also could acquire 50 acres of land by underwriting the cost of another person's transportation.

As land patents clearly demonstrate, the headright system, fueled by the discovery that tobacco was a highly marketable commodity, served as an important stimulus to settlement. It provided prospective immigrants with an incentive to seek their fortunes in Virginia, but it also encouraged wealthy investors to underwrite the cost of outfitting and transporting prospective colonists. The successful could import indentured servants to work their land, simultaneously using those servants' headrights to acquire additional acreage. Merchants and mariners also reaped a benefit, for they recruited prospective servants who could be sent to Virginia, where labor was in short supply, and sold profitably. They also could acquire land under the headright system. In time, headrights (in reality, land rights) were bought and sold, much like stock certificates are today.

The Virginia Company and, often, groups of private investors, tried to entice prospective colonists to go to Virginia as indentured servants or tenants by promising them land in exchange for labor. For instance, skilled workers, outfitted at the expense of the Society of Berkeley Hundred's investors, were sent to Berkeley Hundred. Their contracts required them to ply their trades for a certain number of years in exchange for a specific amount of land. A cooper, for example, might be expected to work for the Society for three years in exchange for 30 acres. Similar contracts were issued to those who settled at Martin's Hundred and Southampton Hundred, plantations whose investors included high-ranking Virginia Company officials. As the Company's fortunes waned, officials found it increasingly difficult to recruit servants and tenants. Therefore, they began offering more favorable working agreements, such as relatively generous sharecropping agreements. Bankruptcy and revocation of the Virginia Company's charter in May 1624 heralded a decade of confusion about ownership of Company land and livestock, the unexpired terms of Company servants and tenants, and other important legal issues. In general, most settlers, upon being reassured that the king would uphold their land rights, were pleased when Virginia became a crown colony.

FINDINGS

During the course of research, some illuminating discoveries were made. The names of at least 227 people were omitted from the February 16, 1624, census, individuals who came to Virginia prior to that date and were still alive in early 1625. While it could be argued that some colonists were away on the day demographic records were collected, it is unlikely that almost 18 percent of the population left briefly and then returned. The 1625 muster seems to have been compiled much more carefully, for only 44 people (3.5 percent) were missing. The men collecting information for the 1625 muster frequently listed the name of the ship on which a colonist came to Virginia, along with a specific date. Research has revealed that sometimes the date recorded denotes when a particular vessel left England; in other instances, it indicates the date of the ship's arrival in Virginia. Unless otherwise noted, the dates used herein are those listed in the muster. Notably, the muster-taker classified all indentured servants and tenants as "servants," even though tenants were free and therefore had more rights.

A considerable number of men, women, and children who spent time in English prisons and jails were deemed suitable for transportation to Virginia. It is unclear how many of these individuals actually left England, despite being selected. Many inmates undoubtedly were in such poor physical condition that they perished on the way to the colony or died shortly after their arrival. On the other hand, at least 42 former prisoners did indeed survive and a handful continued to run afoul of the law after they reached Virginia. Sometimes, people who wanted to acquire Virginia land by means of the headright system did so by paying for a prisoner's passage to the colony. Likewise, Virginia Company officials occasionally procured prisoners and sent them to Virginia. For example the 50 young males the Company sent to the colony in the *Duty* in 1620 (afterward dubbed the "*Duty* boys") were brought in from Bridewell Prison in London. The Virginia Company also sent large numbers of children to the colony, youngsters who had been rounded up from the streets of London specifically for that purpose. Just as numerous people's names were omitted from the 1624 census and 1625 muster, many of those listed as headrights never made it into contemporary demographic or court records. Likewise, relatively few of the literally hundreds of former prisoners selected for transportation to the colony show up in the census and muster. The omission of these people raises the possibility that during the early years the colony was a deathtrap, just as some of its harshest critics claimed.

Through research, the known number of ancient planters (that is, people who came to Virginia prior to Sir Thomas Dale's May 1616 departure) has increased modestly and the given name of one ancient planter has been corrected. Also discovered was an individual whose descendants incorrectly identified him as an ancient planter and attempted to patent the amount of land to which they assumed he was entitled. Through the use of a little known seventeenth-century text, a Virginia colonist's marriage to the daughter of an Indian king has been documented. Thus, the union of John Rolfe and Pocahontas was not the only early instance of legal marriage between a colonist and a Native. Sir Thomas Dale, whose wife, Elizabeth, was in England, unsuccessfully sought an Indian bride.

It has been learned that certain people, listed in the official account of those slain in the March 22, 1622, Indian attack, did in fact survive. In light of the chaos that followed the surprise assault upon the settlements sparsely scattered along the banks of the James River, this is understandable. The need to evacuate survivors to positions of greater safety and the abandonment of certain plantations undoubtedly added to the confusion. Listed among the casualties were 19 women captured by the Pamunkey Indians and taken to their homeland and one colonist and his household, who were spirited across the James River by the Nansemond Indians, but managed to escape to safety. Discrepancies can be found in the accounts compiled by the Virginia Company and Captain John Smith, who may have drawn upon the same sources. An alternative account of the 1622 Indian attack reveals that at least three Natives warned the colonists that an assault was imminent.

The May 1625 land list, compiled by William Claiborne, includes the names of those who held patents for acreage outside of Jamestown Island. It describes the location of patentees' property in general terms, and often lists the quantity of land to which they had laid claim. In many instances the acreage was described as "seated" or "planted," an indication that it had been partially cleared or developed. Claiborne's list includes the names of certain people known to have perished in the March 22, 1622, Indian attack or who died a year or so later. Therefore, he probably was documenting the decedents' land claims to preserve their heirs' hereditary rights.

The reader is invited to check the sources listed at the end of each biography. Although the research culminating in the production of this volume spans a period of more than 20 years, undoubtedly, as new record groups are discovered, more will be learned about Virginia's first settlers.

ABOUT THE SOURCES

Reliable transcriptions of primary sources (for example, Susan M. Kingsbury's *Records of the Virginia Company of London*) have been used throughout this volume. In many instances the original texts have been examined. Records generated in other North American colonies (for example, Maryland, Carolina, New York, Newfoundland, and Bermuda) were found to contain pertinent information. The early narratives produced by Captain John Smith, Ralph Hamor, John Rolfe, George Percy, David DeVries, and numerous others were used extensively. A copy of the DeVries journal, originally written and published in the Dutch language, was accessed so that it could be reviewed by a modern translator. Likewise, a translator examined pertinent portions of John Clark's interrogations in Cuba and Madrid, which were conducted and recorded in Spanish.

Throughout the research process, sources sometimes were used that required extensive travel, notably records preserved in the Huntington Library in San Marino, California; in the archives of Bermuda, Northern Ireland, and the Irish Republic; in England (the Smyth of Nibley Papers, the Ferrar Papers, and the Hartlib Papers); and the Ambler Papers, on file in the United States Library of Congress. Research, conducted under the auspices of the Colonial Williamsburg Foundation, was undertaken at Cambridge and Oxford Universities, the British Library, and the British Public Record Office at Kew (now called The National Archives).

The 1624 census and 1625 muster, which have been published, are part of The National Archives' Colonial Office papers. The 1624 census includes those reportedly living in the colony on February 16, 1624, and those known to have died since April 1623. Most, but not all, communities are listed by name. For example, in February 1624, those living on the lower side of the James River, within the corporation of James City, were attributed to areas vaguely described as "Over the River" and "Against James Cittie." Research has demonstrated that the settlers living "Over the River" were located on the west side of Gray's Creek, whereas those residing "Against James Cittie" inhabited plantations that were east of Gray's Creek. The dead of both areas, with the exception of Hog Island, were included in a solitary list headed "Against James Cittie." Government officials provided more descriptive information in early 1625 when the muster was compiled. However, virtually all of the dead on the lower side of the James River, within the corporation of James City, were listed under the heading "Over ye Watter." The 1625 muster provides much more explicit information.

In 1865, when the Confederate capital at Richmond burned, a vast quantity of eastern Virginia's colonial records were destroyed. The early court records of five of Virginia's eight original shires or counties, taken to the capital city for safekeeping, were destroyed at that time. Even so, the seventeenth-century records of Accomack County (and its descendant, Northampton), Isle of Wight County, Lower Norfolk County (a descendant of Elizabeth City County), Surry County (a descendant of James City), and York County have been preserved and are largely intact. Fortunately, fragmentary records exist for Elizabeth City, Warwick, James City, Charles City, and Henrico Counties. Throughout this volume, reliable transcriptions of early court records or the original records themselves have been utilized whenever appropriate.

Information has been culled from documents generated by the overarching branches of government. These records, which are interlaced with personal information, have been drawn upon in preparing Virginia settlers' biographies. Minutes of the assembly and those of the Council of State (the governor's council), though incomplete, were very useful, as both bodies often dealt with matters of a personal nature. In the beginning, when the Virginia colony was under the sway of the Virginia Company of London, the governor and his council were expected to handle important legal matters, although the local leader of each private plantation settled petty disputes and made most major decisions. Plantations established by the Virginia Company itself (for example, Bermuda Hundred and Elizabeth City) were under the command of local leaders selected by Company officials in England.

Throughout the seventeenth century, members of the governor's council sat regularly as justices of the Quarter Court. At first, they met monthly and handled legal matters that ranged from the lofty to the mundane. However, the population grew, as did the number of civil and criminal cases to be processed, with the result that the Quarter Court's workload became burdensome. In 1624, local justices, appointed to office by the Council of State, were authorized to settle petty disputes and punish minor offences. These local courts met monthly in the corporations of Elizabeth City and Charles City, both of which areas were a considerable distance from Jamestown, seat of the Quarter Court. A litigant could challenge the local justices' decision by filing an appeal with the Quarter Court, which at first convened monthly and then quarterly. A complainant, if dissatisfied by the Quarter Court's decision, could send an appeal to officials in England. This rudimentary justice system prevailed until 1634 when county government was established, along with county courts, which met monthly. In 1662 the Quarter Court was renamed the General Court, a judicial body that convened three times a year instead of four.

In 1924 H. R. McIlwaine's edition of the *Minutes of the Council and General Court of Colonial Virginia, 1622–1632, 1670–1676* was published, along with notes taken by attorney Conway Robinson during the 1840s. Robinson also included portions of notes taken by Thomas Jefferson when examining the original records. Information extracted from the notes of Robinson and Jefferson has been used in preparing certain biographies. When McIlwaine's *Minutes of the Council and General Court* was reprinted in 1979, an inventory of antebellum records was included. It hints at the abundance of legal records that were lost when Richmond burned.

The Established Church's influence permeated many aspects of daily life, and some of the dates that appear in very early court records and patents refer to feast days in the Anglican Church's calendar. For example, a tenant was told to pay his annual rent on Michaelmas, that is, September 29th. The Old Style calendar was in use and March 25th was New Year's Day. Thus, when an inebriated man fell overboard and drowned in the James River on New Year's Eve 1626, he died on March 24th. The first colonists celebrated what we would call Old Christmas, which occurred on January 6th of each year. The Virginia Company's court records are dated in accord with four legal "terms" or periods. They are Hilary, which began in January; Easter, which began the 15th day after Easter; Trinity, which ran from Trinity Sunday (56 days after Easter) to July; and Michaelmas, which began in October and ended in December. Sometimes, court records cite a regnal year, that is, the year in which a monarch's reign began. For example, April 12, 1625, might be described as the 12th of April in the first year of King Charles I. Sometimes months were referred to by number. Thus, the eighth month of 1634 (Old Style) was October, that is eight months after the new year began.

Virginia's land patents contain a wealth of information and are extremely useful in documenting familial relationships. They also document the spread of settlement and shed light upon each patentee's socio-economic status and success as an entrepreneur. Patents provide the names of those used as headrights, sometimes disclosing when they came to the colony. Research has demonstrated that Virginia colonists sometimes retained headrights for many years before using them to acquire land. For example, one man used all three of his wives as headrights, although it is safe to say that the marriages were consecutive. Headrights were bought and sold and were considered a marketable commodity. Colonists themselves could acquire headrights when they made a trip to England and then returned at their own expense.

There was an opportunity for fraud and sometimes it occurred. For example, in 1626 William Eppes patented some land using the headrights of three people who came on the *Ann* in 1623. In 1635, William's brother, Francis, when patenting another piece of land, used the same three people as headrights, citing their voyage on the *Ann* in 1623. Occasionally, the General Court's justices seem to have suspected wrongdoing, for they asked prospective patentees to *prove* that they had transported certain persons. As time went on, would-be patentees, who had covered the cost of transporting someone to Virginia, appeared before local court justices where they could obtain a land certificate, entitling them to a certain number of headrights. These land certificates could then be presented to the Secretary and redeemed, that is, used as headrights in the acquisition of land. In April 1699 Virginia's governing officials decided that Africans no longer could be used as headrights. This change occurred in response to the opening up of the slave trade.

It is notable that all of the patents issued before 1683 are transcriptions of the originals, which consisted of loose leaves of paper suspended on a string. Not surprisingly, many patents were lost, particularly during the early seventeenth century, and obvious errors were made by copyists. Sometimes, when patents were transcribed into books, they were placed slightly out of chronological sequence and then renumbered. Some original patents, particularly those of Patent Book 4, bear two sets of page numbers, a reflection of the documents' being transcribed one or more times. Copies of a few original patents, preserved among the Ambler Papers, make it readily apparent that clerks in the office of the Secretary of the Colony, when transcribing earlier patents, sometimes omitted headrights and other critical details. Listings of people used as headrights, and copies of some patents that have been lost or destroyed, occasionally can be found in the records of county courthouses. Abstracts of land patents, prepared by Nell M. Nugent and her successors (see Sources and Abbreviations), are an invaluable finding aid, but facsimiles of the originals, which are available on microfilm and online, should be consulted. Significantly, Nugent made no attempt to distinguish between Old Style and New Style calendar dates.

Virginia's patents, traditionally maintained by the Secretary of the Colony, sustained damage in the statehouse fires that occurred at Jamestown on September 19, 1676, when the rebel Nathaniel Bacon put the capital city to the torch, and on October 20, 1698, when an arsonist set ablaze the statehouse built after Bacon's Rebellion. Records were salvaged only because they were tossed out of the windows. They reportedly landed in heaps and some were carried off by bystanders. After Virginia's capital was moved from Jamestown to Williamsburg and a new statehouse was built, a separate structure, known as the Public Record Office, was erected so that legal documents could be preserved.

One of the most remarkable record groups that has come to light during modern times is the Ferrar Papers, which have been preserved in the Pepys Library at the University of Cambridge in England. They comprise the bulk of the "lost records" of the Virginia Company of London. Thanks to the diligent scholarship of David Ransome and the generosity of the University of Cambridge's Pepys Library, the Ferrar Papers have been made readily accessible to scholars. The hand list Dr. Ransome prepared more than a decade ago is an invaluable finding aid, for it provides easy access to the Ferrar Papers, which have been microfilmed and can be found at many major libraries.

As is evident in the list of Sources and Abbreviations, numerous record groups preserved in The National Archives in Kew, England, have been utilized. They include records generated by the Privy Council, Prerogative Court of Canterbury, Exchequer, High Court of the Admiralty, and Colonial Office Papers. Some record groups were accessed by means of the Virginia Colonial Records Project (VCRP) Survey Reports and W. Noel Sainsbury's *Calendar of State Papers* and then examined on microfilm or other facsimiles of the original. Probate records were identified through use of the published works of Coldham, McGhan, Morrison, Sherwood, Torrence, Waters, Withington, and the Index Society, and then accessed by means of the VCRP, microfilm, or photocopies of the original records.

Online access to certain primary sources that otherwise would require overseas travel are available to modern scholars. Likewise, the online availability of Virginia Colonial Records Project Survey Reports and the records of the Virginia Land Office have expanded our horizons tremendously, providing unprecedented opportunities for researchers to study the distant past.

ACKNOWLEDGMENTS

Without the able assistance and logistical support of several people, production of this text would have been much less successful, if indeed possible. Colonial Williamsburg Foundation reference librarian Susan Pattison Shames offered unflagging encouragement and selflessly provided tactical support by reading each chapter and providing useful, highly insightful comments. Susan also helped tremendously by transcribing certain sections of my early settlers database into an electronic format. Peggy Bowditch of Gloucester County graciously assisted by doing the same. Heather M. Harvey of the Department of

Archaeological Research fabricated the maps used to show where Virginia's very early settlements were located. Gregory J. Brown of Colonial Williamsburg Foundation's Digital Library Project was the "computer guru" to whom I often turned for advice. Dr. Marley R. Brown III and Andrew Edwards of the Department of Archaeological Research, David K. Hazzard of the Virginia Department of Historic Resources, and my husband, Carl Aschman, provided encouragement and logistical support throughout this project. Thanks also to Marian Hoffman of the Genealogical Publishing Company for her superb editing.

SOURCES AND ABBREVIATIONS

AHR: "Spanish Policy Toward Virginia." *American Historical Review* 25:448–472.

AMB: Ambler Papers 1636–1809. Library of Congress, Washington, D. C. Transcripts and microfilm, Rockefeller Library, Colonial Williamsburg Foundation, Williamsburg, Virginia.

AMES 1: Ames, Susie M., ed. *County Court Records of Accomack-Northampton, Virginia, 1632–1640.* Washington: American Historical Association, 1954.

AMES 2: Ames, Susie M., ed. *County Court Records of Accomack-Northampton, Virginia, 1640–1645.* Charlottesville: University Press of Virginia, 1973.

AP: Ancient Planters. *An Account of the Ancient Planters [1624].* In Colonial Records of Virginia. Richmond: Senate Document printed by Commonwealth of Virginia, 1871. Original in Colonial Office 3/21 ff 72–89.

BASS: Bass Family Bible Records 1613–1699. Digital images. Library of Virginia. http://www.lva.lib.va.us/ 2006.

BEV: Beverly, Robert II. *History of the Present State of Virginia (1705),* L.B. Wright, ed. Chapel Hill: University of North Carolina Press, 1947.

BL: British Library, London, England. Database and digital images. British Library. http://www.bl.uk/ 2006

BOD: Boddie, John B. *Seventeenth Century Isle of Wight County, Virginia.* 2 vols. Chicago: Chicago Law Printing Company, 1938; repr. Baltimore: Genealogical Publishing Company, 1980.

BRO: Brown, Alexander G. *The Genesis of the United States.* 2 vols. Boston and New York: Houghton, Mifflin and Company, 1890; repr. Bowie, MD: Heritage Books Inc., 1994.

BRU: Bruce, Philip A., ed. "Viewers of the Tobacco Crop." *Virginia Magazine of History and Biography* 5:119–123.

C: Chancery Records. Chancery Records, The National Archives, Kew, England. Survey Reports and photocopies, Rockefeller Library, Colonial Williamsburg Foundation, Williamsburg, Virginia.

CBE: Coldham, Peter W. *The Complete Book of Emigrants, 1607–1660.* Baltimore: Genealogical Publishing Company, 1987.

CELL: Cell, Gillian T., ed. *Newfoundland Discovered: English Attempts at Colonisation, 1610–1630.* London: Hakluyt Society, 1982.

CH: Coldham, Peter W. *Child Apprentices in America from Christ's Hospital, London, 1617–1778.* Baltimore: Genealogical Publishing Company, 1990.

CHE: Tyler, Lyon G., ed. "Two Tragical Events: Schepps-togt von Anthony Chester in Virginia, gedaan in het jaar 1620." *William and Mary Quarterly* (First Series) 9:203–214.

CJS: Barbour, Philip, ed. *Travels and Works of Captain John Smith, President of Virginia and Admiral of New England, 1580–1631.* 3 vols. Chapel Hill: University of North Carolina, 1986.

CO: Colonial Office Papers. The National Archives, Kew, England. Survey Reports and microfilms, Rockefeller Library, Colonial Williamsburg Foundation, Williamsburg, Virginia.

DEV: DeVries, David. *Voyages from Holland to America, Led 1632 to 1644 by David Peterson Devries*, Henry C. Murphy, trans. New York, 1853.

DOR: Dorman, John F., ed. *Adventurers of Purse and Person, Virginia 1607– 1624/5.* Fourth ed. 3 vols. Baltimore: Genealogical Publishing Company, 2004–2007.

DUNN: Dunn, Richard, ed. *Warwick County, Virginia, Colonial Court Records in Transcription.* Baltimore: Genealogical Publishing Company for Clearfield Company, 2000.

EAE: Coldham, Peter W. *English Adventurers and Emigrants, 1609–1660: Abstracts of Examinations in the High Court of Admiralty with Reference to Colonial America.* Baltimore: Genealogical Publishing Company, 1984.

EEAC: Coldham, Peter W. *English Estates of American Colonists.* Baltimore: Genealogical Publishing Company, 1980.

EEAE: Coldham, Peter W. *English Estates of American Colonists: American Wills and Administrations in the Prerogative Court of Canterbury, 1610– 1857.* Baltimore: Genealogical Publishing Company, 1989.

EXC: Exchequer Records. The National Archives, Kew, England. Survey Reports and microfilms, Rockefeller Library, Colonial Williamsburg Foundation, Williamsburg, Virginia.

FER: Ferrar Papers, 1590–1790. Pepys Library, Magdalen College, Cambridge University, Cambridge, England. Microfilms, Rockefeller Library, Colonial Williamsburg Foundation, Williamsburg, Virginia.

FLEE: Fleet, Beverley, comp. *Virginia Colonial Abstracts.* 3 vols. Baltimore: Genealogical Publishing Company, 1988.

FOR: Force, Peter, comp. *Tracts and Other Papers, Relating to the Origin, Settlement and Progress of the Colonies in North America.* 4 vols. 1836. Repr. Gloucester, MA: Peter Smith, 1963.

G&M: Grant, W. L. and James Munro, eds. *Acts of the Privy Council of England: Colonial Series Vol. 1 A.D. 1613–1680.* London: His Majesty's Stationery Office, 1908; repr. Nendeln, Liechtenstein: Kraus Reprint Ltd., 1966.

GEN: "The Virginia Massacre, 162–." *The Genealogists' Magazine* 2:51.

HAI: Haile, Edward W., ed. *Jamestown Narratives: Eyewitness Accounts of the Virginia Colony: The First Decade, 1607–1617.* Champlain, VA: Roundhouse, 1998.

HALL: Hall, Clayton C., ed. *Narratives of Early Maryland, 1633–1684.* New York: Charles Scribner's Sons, 1946; repr. Barnes and Noble, 1959.

HAR: Samuel Hartlib's Papers, 1600–1662. University of Sheffield, Sheffield, England. CD with facsimiles and transcriptions at University of North Carolina Library, Chapel Hill, North Carolina.

HCA: High Court of Admiralty Records. The National Archives, Kew, England. Survey Reports and photocopies, Rockefeller Library, Colonial Williamsburg Foundation, Williamsburg, Virginia.

HEN: Hening, William W., ed. *The Statutes at Large: Being a Collection of All the Laws of Virginia.* 13 vols. Richmond: Samuel Pleasants, 1809–1823; repr. Charlottesville: University Press of Virginia, 1969. Database and digital images. http://vagenweb.rootsweb.com/hening/ 2006

HLOP: House of Lords Record Office Papers, 1625–1641. House of Lords Record Office, The National Archives, Kew, England. Survey Reports and photocopies, Rockefeller Library, Colonial Williamsburg Foundation, Williamsburg, Virginia.

HOT: Hotten, John Camden. *The Original Lists of Persons of Quality . . . and Others Who Went from Great Britain to the American Plantations, 1600–1700.* London, 1874; repr. Baltimore: Genealogical Publishing Company, 1974.

HUME: Hume, Robert. *Early Child Immigrants to Virginia, 1618–1642, Copied from the Records of Bridewell Royall Hospital.* Baltimore: Magna Carta Book Company, 1986.

JAM: Jameson, J. Franklin, ed. *Narratives of New Netherland, 1609–1664.* New York: Charles Scribner's Sons, 1909; repr. Barnes and Noble, 1959.

JHB: McIlwaine, H. R. et al., eds. *Journals of the House of Burgesses, 1619–1776.* 13 vols. Richmond: Virginia State Library, 1905–1915.

LEF: Lefroy, J. H., comp. *Memorials of the Discovery and Early Settlement of the Bermudas or Somer Islands, 1511–1687.* Toronto: Bermuda Historical Society, University of Toronto Press, 1981.

LEO: Leonard, Cynthia M., comp. *The General Assembly of Virginia, July 30, 1619–January 11, 1978, A Bicentennial Register of Members.* Richmond: Virginia State Library Board, 1978.

LNC: Walter, Alice Granbery, comp. *Lower Norfolk County Court Records: Book A 1637–1646 and Book B 1646–1651/2.* Virginia Beach: privately published, 1978; repr. Baltimore: Genealogical Publishing Company for Clearfield Company, 1994.

MCGC: McIlwaine, H. R., ed. *Minutes of the Council and General Court of Colonial Virginia.* Richmond: The Library Board, 1924; repr. Richmond: Virginia State Library, 1979.

MCGH: McGhan, Judith, indexer. *Virginia Will Records from The Virginia Magazine of History and Biography, The William and Mary College Quarterly,* and *Tyler's Quarterly.* Baltimore: Genealogical Publishing Company, 1982.

MEY: Meyer, Virginia M. and John F. Dorman, eds. *Adventurers of Purse and Person, Virginia 1607–1624/5.* Third ed. Richmond: Dietz Press, 1987.

MHS: Aspinall, Thomas et al. *Collections of the Massachusetts Historical Society.* (Fourth Series) 9:1–164.

MOR: Morrison, J. H., comp. *Prerogative Court of Canterbury: Letters of Administration 1620–1630 (Inclusive), Abstracts Translated from the Original Latin.* London: privately published, 1935.

NEAL: Neal, Rosemary C., comp. *Elizabeth City County, Virginia (Now the City of Hampton), Deeds, Wills, Court Orders, Etc. 1634, 1659, 1688–1701.* Bowie, MD: Heritage Books, 1987.

NEI: Neill, Edward D. *Virginia Carolorum: The Colony Under the Rule of Charles the 1st and 2nd.* New York: J. Munsell's Sons, Albany, 1886; repr. Bowie, MD: Heritage Books, 1996.

NUG: Nugent, Nell M. et al. *Cavaliers and Pioneers: Abstracts of Virginia Land Patents and Grants [1623–1732].* 3 vols. Vol. 1: 1623–1666. Richmond: Dietz Printing Company, 1934 (repr. Genealogical Publishing Company, 1963); Vol. 2: 1666–1695. Richmond: Virginia State Library, 1977; Vol. 3: 1695–1732. Richmond: Virginia State Library, 1979.

OCAL: O'Callaghan, E. B., ed. *Documents Relative to the Colonial History of the State of New York, Procured in Holland, England and France.* Vol. 1. Albany: Weed, Parsons and Co., 1856.

PB: Virginia Land Office Patent Books 1619–1660. Microfilm on file at Library of Virginia, Richmond, and Rockefeller Library, Colonial Williamsburg Foundation, Williamsburg, Virginia. Database and digital images. Library of Virginia. http://ajax.lva.lib.va.us/

PC: Privy Council Office. The National Archives, Kew, England. Survey Reports and photocopies, Rockefeller Library, Colonial Williamsburg Foundation, Williamsburg, Virginia.

PCC: Prerogative Court of Canterbury. The National Archives, Kew, England. Survey Reports and microfilm, Rockefeller Library, Colonial Williamsburg Foundation, Williamsburg, Virginia.

POR: Pory, John. *John Pory, 1572–1636, The Life and Letters of a Man of Many Parts.* Chapel Hill: University of North Carolina Press, 1977.

PRO: Public Record Office. Public Record Office, Kew, England (now called The National Archives). Survey Reports and photocopies, Rockefeller Library, Colonial Williamsburg Foundation, Williamsburg, Virginia. Database and digital images. Public Record Office. http://nationalarchives.gov.uk/ 2006

PPR: Principal Probate Register. The National Archives, Kew, England. Survey Reports and photocopies, Rockefeller Library, Colonial Williamsburg Foundation, Williamsburg, Virginia.

S of N: Smyth of Nibley Papers. New York Public Library, New York, New York, and Gloucestershire Library, Gloucester, England. Survey Reports and microfilms, Rockefeller Library, Colonial Williamsburg Foundation, Williamsburg, Virginia.

SAIN: Sainsbury, William Noel et al. *Calendar of State Papers, Colonial Series, America and the West Indies.* 22 vols. Vaduz: Kraus Reprint, 1964.

SAL: Salley, Alexander S., comp. *Narratives of Early Carolina.* New York: Charles Scribner's Sons, 1911; repr. Barnes and Noble, 1967.

SH: Sherwood, George. *American Colonists in English Records: A Guide to Direct References in Authentic Records, Passenger Lists Not in Hotten, etc.* Repr. Baltimore: Genealogical Publishing Company, 1961.

SMITH: Smith, Annie L., comp. *The Quitrents of Virginia.* Gloucester County, Virginia: privately published, 1957; repr. Baltimore: Genealogical Publishing Company, 1980.

SP: State Paper Office. The National Archives, Kew, England. Survey Reports and photocopies, Rockefeller Library, Colonial Williamsburg Foundation, Williamsburg, Virginia.

SR: Virginia Colonial Records Project Survey Reports. Rockefeller Library, Colonial Wlliamsburg, Virginia. Database and digital images. Library of Virginia. http://ajax.lva.va.us/

STAN: Stanard, William G. and Mary Stanard, comps. *Colonial Virginia Register.* Albany: privately published, 1902; repr. Baltimore: Genealogical Publishing Company, 1965.

T: Treasury. The National Archives, Kew, England. Survey Reports and photocopies, Rockefeller Library, Colonial Williamsburg Foundation, Williamsburg, Virginia.

VCR: Kingsbury, Susan M., ed. *Records of the Virginia Company of London.* 4 vols. Washington: Government Printing Office, 1906–1935.

WAT: Waters, Henry F. *Genealogical Gleanings in England, New Series.* 2 vols. Boston: New England Historic Genealogical Society, 1901, 1907; repr. Baltimore: Genealogical Publishing Company, 1969.

WITH: Withington, Lothrop. *Virginia Gleanings in England.* Baltimore: Genealogical Publishing Company, 1980.

Note: whenever original county court records have been used, references to specific record books have been provided.

GLOSSARY

Ancient Planter: someone who came to Virginia prior to Sir Thomas Dale's May 1616 departure and had lived in the colony at least three years when applying for a patent. Ancient planters were eligible for 100 acres of land and had a few other privileges.

Administrator: the person appointed by court officials to settle an estate. A female administrator sometimes was termed an **administratrix**.

Burgess: an elected official who represented his community in the legislature.

Cape Merchant: the Virginia Company's official merchant in the Virginia colony.

Caveat: an instrument filed by a party intent upon halting the patenting process until his opposition could be entered.

Churchwarden: the "chairman" or headman of a parish vestry.

Court Commissioner or Justice: local officials who performed judiciary functions.

Decedent: a legal term used in reference to a deceased person.

Escheat: the reversion of land to the Crown or other granting party (in the case of Proprietary territories) when a patentee failed to leave heirs or was found guilty of a major crime.

Established Church: the Anglican Church, which was the Virginia colony's state church until the time of the American Revolution.

Executor: an individual designated by the maker of a will to settle his/her estate. A female executor sometimes was termed an executrix.

Factor: a merchant's agent or representative.

Fee Simple Ownership: outright ownership of a piece of property, including the right to sell.

First (1st) Supply: the first group of new colonists to arrive at Jamestown after the initial establishment of settlement. They landed in January 1608.

Freedom Dues: the allotment of corn and clothes usually provided to a newly freed servant who has completed his/her agreed-upon term of service.

Guardian: a person appointed to oversee the general welfare and material assets of an underage orphan.

Headright: an entitlement to 50 acres of land, awarded to someone who paid for his own (or another person's) transportation to Virginia.

Hogshead: the large cask or barrel-like containers into which dried tobacco leaves were packed and then shipped out of the colony.

Hundreds: a seventeenth-century term used in reference to a large plantation. Prior to the formation of county government, the leaders of Hundreds were authorized to settle petty disputes and perform other functions associated with leadership.

Indenture: a service contract or agreement made between a master and servant.

Indentured Servant: a person of either sex who agreed to work for a specified amount of time in exchange for transportation, food, shelter, and clothing. A guardian could sign a contract on a minor child's behalf.

Intestate: someone who died before making a will.

Lady Day: March 25th in the calendar of the Anglican Church.

Legatee: an heir.

Life-rights: the right to possession for one's lifetime.

Michaelmas: September 29th in the calendar of the Anglican Church.

Nuncupative Will: a will made verbally in the presence of witnesses.

Old Christmas: during the seventeenth century, Christmas was celebrated on January 6th of each year. The Christmas season traditionally lasted for twelve days, ending on Epiphany.

Old Style and New Style Calendar Dates: The Old Style, or Julian, Calendar was in general use in England until 1752. With the Old Style Calendar, March 25th was the first day of the new year: New Year's Day.

Parish: the geographic area served by a church.

Particular Plantation: a settlement whose cost was underwritten by private investors who usually outfitted and sent a group of prospective colonists to Virginia.

Patentee: a person to whom a tract of un-owned land was assigned by means of a patent.

Pentecost: Whit Sunday or 50 days after Easter in the ecclesiastical calendar.

Plant: to clear, develop, or settle upon unclaimed or vacant land, a requirement for validating one's title; synonymous with "seat."

Probate: the process whereby the real and/or personal assets of a deceased person are documented, his/her just debts are paid, and distribution is made to legitimate decedent's heirs.

Reversionary Heir: the individual or individuals to whom a decedent's estate would revert if the primary heirs were deceased.

Seat: to clear, develop, or settle upon un-owned or vacant land, thereby validating one's claim; synonymous with "plant."

Second (2nd) Supply: the second group of new colonists to arrive at Jamestown after the initial establishment of settlement. They landed during the latter part of 1608.

Son-in-Law, Daughter-in-Law: this term often was applied to stepchildren but also could refer to members associated with a family through marriage.

Testator: the maker of a will.

Third (3rd) Supply: the third group of new colonists to arrive at Jamestown after the initial establishment of settlement. Some of these people reached Virginia in 1609 and the remainder, who were shipwrecked in Bermuda, landed in May 1610.

Tobacco Inspector: an appointed official authorized to examine casks or hogsheads of tobacco that had been prepared for export. His job was to assure that the tobacco being sent out of the colony was of saleable quality and did not include trash.

Tobacco Note: a certificate obtained from a tobacco inspector certifying that an individual had available a certain number of hogsheads of saleable tobacco. Tobacco notes were used as a medium of exchange, much like currency.

Vestry: a small committee of elected church officials who were responsible for overseeing the business of their parish. Colonial vestries, always male, were responsible for maintaining church property, and during the early seventeenth century they were to see that moral laws were enforced. Vestrymen also were responsible for public welfare.

Whit Sunday: Pentecost or 50 days after Easter in the calendar of the Anglican Church.

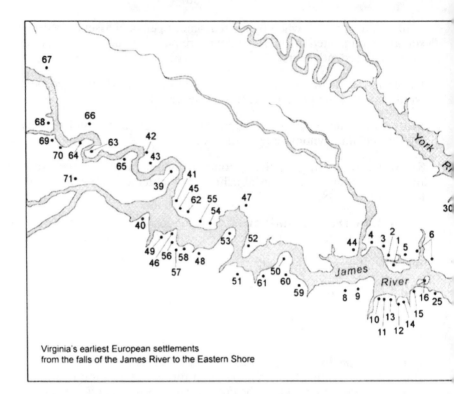

Virginia's earliest European settlements
from the falls of the James River to the Eastern Shore

1. Jamestown Island
2. Glasshouse
3. Governor's Land (The Maine and Pasbehay)
4. Company Land in James City
5. Neck O'Land
6. Archer's Hope
7. Martin's Hundred
8. Burrows Hill (Burrows Mount, Smith's
   Mount)
9. Paces Paines
10. Captain Roger Smith's Plantation
11. Treasurer's Plantation
12. Hugh Crowder's Plantation
13. William Ewen's Plantation
14. Captain William Powell's Plantation
15. Captain Samuel Mathews' Plantation
16. Hog Island
17. Old Point Comfort, the Company Land,
    and the Common Land in Elizabeth City
18. Elizabeth City (west side of the Hampton
    River)
19. Elizabeth City (near the mouth of the York
    River)

20. Elizabeth City (lower side of the James River):
    20 a: Elizabeth River
    20 b: Lynnhaven area
    20 c: Nansemond River area
21. Mulberry Island
22. Blunt Point and Stanley Hundred
23. Mathews Manor (Denbigh)
24. Newportes News (Marie's Mount)
25. Captain Christopher Lawne's Plantation
26. Bennett's Welcome (Warresqueak)
27. Basses Choice
28. Giles Jones's Plantation at Day's Point
29. Nansemond
30. Kings Creek Plantation
31. Ringfield
32. The Indian Field Plantation
33. Francis Morgan's Plantation
34. William Prior's Plantation
35. Richard Townsend's Plantation
36. Martiau's Plantation
37. York Plantation
38. Wormeley Creek

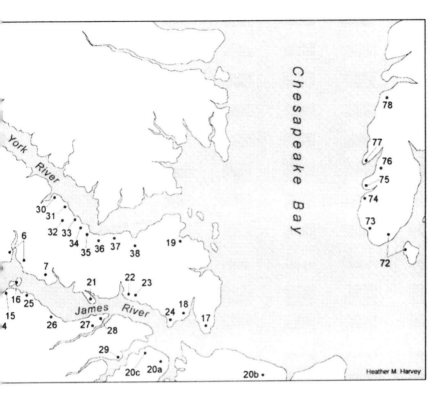

WHERE THEY WERE

PLANTING THE COLONY

On May 13, 1607, Virginia's first colonists came ashore on what became known as Jamestown Island. The next day, they commenced establishing an outpost they called James Cittie or Jamestown, the first permanent English settlement in the United States. The 104 colonists were unaware that they had arrived at the close of the most severe period of drought to strike tidewater Virginia in 500 years. Moreover, they paid little heed to the fact that they had intruded upon the homeland of Natives whose culture was well developed. The men the Virginia Company had named to the colony's Council elected a president. Soon, sickness, bickering, and food shortages began taking a deadly toll. After successive changes in leadership, Captain John Smith became president. A vigorous but controversial leader, he imposed military discipline and forced the colonists to plant crops, build houses and fortifications, and work toward their own support. His ability to negotiate with the Indians proved invaluable.

In early January 1608, 120 weak and famished immigrants (the 1st Supply) came ashore. Approximately nine months later, 70 more colonists landed in the 2nd Supply. Among them were two women, the first to arrive. Finally, in May 1609, a 3rd Supply of colonists set sail for Virginia. The fleet of nine ships got caught in a hurricane and in August seven of them limped into Jamestown, with 200 to 300 passengers. One small vessel went down at sea. Also missing was the flagship *Seaventure*, which had run aground in Bermuda, stranding the men chosen to serve as the colony's principal leaders. Samuel Argall arrived in Virginia in July 1609, spreading word of the Virginia Company's plan to change the way the colony was governed. This sparked dissention and Captain John Smith, ousted as president and injured by a gunpowder explosion, left the colony. George Percy took his place.

At Jamestown, the struggle to survive proved so arduous that the winter of 1609–1610, termed the "Starving Time," nearly led to the colony's extinction. In May 1610, Sir Thomas Gates, Sir George Somers, and other members of the 3rd Supply reached Virginia in two vessels fashioned from Bermuda's native cedar wood. Gates, who was ill-prepared for the dire conditions he found, resolved to evacuate the surviving colonists to Newfoundland, where they could secure passage to England. Only the timely arrival of Lord De La Warr's three ships in June, with provisions and 250 new immigrants, averted the Virginia colony's abandonment. De La Warr immediately put the colonists to work, cleansing and strengthening their settlement, and he dispatched Gates and Somers to Bermuda, to bring back food. As it turned out, Somers died and Gates returned to England.

In May 1611 Sir Thomas Dale arrived with 300 new settlers. He was joined in August by Sir Thomas Gates, Virginia's lieutenant governor, who brought an additional 300 people and new instructions from the Virginia Company. Together, Gates and Dale, former comrades-in-arms, fabricated a strict code of justice known as *The Lawes Divine and Martiall*, which required the colonists to work toward their own support and imposed severe penalties upon the disobedient. In response to the Company's orders to build the colony's principal town in a healthier, more defensible location than Jamestown Island, Dale, as marshal, established several new settlements near the head of the James River, in territory that became known as Charles City and Henrico. In 1614 he sent some colonists to the Eastern Shore to extract salt from seawater, so that fish could be preserved. Sir Thomas Dale, as deputy-governor, introduced several innovative policies that fostered the colony's development. During his administration John Rolfe developed a strain of sweet-scented tobacco that quickly became a highly marketable money crop and fueled the spread of settlement. Deputy Governor Samuel Argall, who took over in 1617–1618, pursued many of the strict policies that Dale had established.

A CHANGE IN GOVERNMENT

In April 1619 incoming Governor George Yeardley suspended martial law and in accord with his instructions, subdivided the colony into four corporations: *James City, Elizabeth City, Charles City,* and *Henrico*. Each was vast in size and vaguely defined, but encompassed both sides of the James River. In July 1619 delegates from all but one of the colony's plantations went to Jamestown, where they convened in America's first legislative assembly. The following month another momentous event occurred. A Dutch frigate and a ship called the *Treasurer* sailed into the mouth of the James River with Virginia's first Africans aboard.

The Virginia Company's Great Charter, which Governor Yeardley implemented, introduced a land policy known as the headright system. In synch with the fledgling tobacco economy, it was an enormous stimulus to settlement, for it provided prospective immigrants with an incentive to seek their fortunes in Virginia. It also encouraged groups of wealthy investors to underwrite the cost of outfitting and transporting prospective colonists to establish large "particular" (private) plantations sometimes known as "hundreds." Because an individual could acquire 50 acres of land by underwriting the cost of another's transportation, successful planters could bring indentured servants to Virginia to work their land, simultaneously accumulating acreage and fulfilling their need for labor. In essence, the headright system enabled Virginia colonists to acquire real estate and work toward their own personal gain.

During Sir George Yeardley's first term as governor (1619 to 1621), 18 or 19 new private plantations were established. Most were thinly scattered along both sides of the James River, west of the Chickahominy River's mouth. After Sir Francis Wyatt became governor (1621 to 1626), at least a dozen new plantations were established along the James River, within largely vacant territory that was close to Jamestown Island. Unfortunately, many of the plantations seated while Governors Yeardley and Wyatt held office lay within what scientists call the oligohaline zone, an area within the James River basin where salt concentrations are especially high in summer and tidal action fails to flush away contaminants. The result was a high mortality rate. Even so, the Virginia colony grew and flourished and by March 1620 there were 928 people living within the colonized areas: 892 Europeans, 32 Africans (17 women and 15 men), and four Indians. All of the Indians and Africans were described as being "in ye service of severall planters."

On March 22, 1622, the Native population, threatened by the inroads of expanding settlement, launched a carefully orchestrated attack upon the sparsely inhabited plantations along the James River. It was a vigorous attempt to drive the colonists from their soil. At the end of the day, an estimated 347 men, women, and children reportedly were dead, just over a third of the colony's population. Although the survivors withdrew to eight settlements that were strengthened and held, by autumn 1623 many colonists had begun reoccupying the outlying plantations they had abandoned. Again, settlement began to spread and by the mid-1620s the Virginia colony had become well established. In February 1624 when a community-by-community census was made of the colony's inhabitants, at least 906 people were living within the settled area and another 371 colonists had died since April 1623. By January and February 1625 the number of living colonists had soared to 1,232.

In May 1624 the Virginia Company's charter was revoked and Virginia became a Crown colony. Although the settlers weathered a period of uncertainty, their concern about their land titles' validity was quickly put to rest. However, the legal dilemma posed by the defunct Virginia Company's ownership of land proved to be more troublesome. Surviving land patents reveal that for the first decade after the Company's dissolution, the tracts of land its leaders had set aside to generate income for investors were let to leaseholders. Despite some half-hearted attempts to revive the Virginia Company, by the early-to-mid 1630s patents were issued for those parcels.

In 1634 the colony was subdivided into eight shires or counties, each of which was to have a local court with justices, a sheriff, a clerk, and other functionaries. *It was then that James City, Charles City, Elizabeth City (Kecoughtan), Henrico, Warwick, York (Charles River), Isle of Wight (Warresqueak), and Accomack Counties were formed, replacing the four corporations that previously existed.* The establishment of county courts, whose authority increased over time, relieved the Quarter Court of many routine matters, freeing it to handle important cases and function as an appellate body. In 1634 the colony had a population of 4,914, and new immigrants were arriving constantly. In the discussion that follows, the settlements established between 1607 and 1635 are clustered geographically, within the political units in which they lay in 1634.

JAMES CITY

In 1618 the Virginia Company of London decided to set aside four tracts of publicly-owned land within James City. One was the 3,000-acre tract known as the Governor's Land, located on the north side of the James River. Another was a neighboring 3,000-acre tract designated the Company Land. A third area, 1,500 acres called the Common Land, was set aside for the grazing of livestock. Although the Common Land's location is uncertain, it probably encompassed the eastern end of Jamestown Island, an area traditionally used for grazing livestock and agricultural purposes. The fourth tract of publicly-owned land in James City was the parish glebe, a 100-acre parcel that was part of the incumbent clergyman's stipendiary support.

By 1619 settlers had begun laying claim to land on the lower side of the James River within what was then the Corporation of James City. In February 1624 when a census was made of the colony's inhabitants, the territory on the lower side of the James River, in James City, was thickly settled. In 1625 a substantial portion of the Corporation of James City's population was living within that area.

In 1634 James City County, the colony's most populous county, was home to 886 men, women, and children. It spanned both sides of the James River and encompassed all of the territory formerly known as the Corporation of James City. On the north side of the river, James City County was bound on the east by Skiffs Creek. It extended in a westerly direction to a point just above the Chickahominy River's mouth. On the lower side of the James River, James City County spanned the territory between Lawnes Creek (on the east) and Upper Chippokes Creek (on the west). In 1652 James City County's territory on the lower side of the James became Surry County.

Jamestown Island (1)

Virginia's first colonists planted a settlement, "James Cittie" (Jamestown), on May 14, 1607. Despite a precarious beginning, the community, situated in the western end of Jamestown Island, survived. In fact, Jamestown served as the colony's capital until 1699. In 1616 John Rolfe said that there were 50 people living at Jamestown who were under the command of Lieutenant Sharpe, in the absence of Captain Francis West, brother of Thomas West, Lord De La Warr. Of those 50 people, 32 were farmers. Surviving patents reveal that much of Jamestown Island's eastern end had been laid out into tracts of 12 acres or less that were occupied by *ancient planters*. That raises the possibility that the area had been purposefully carved up into small parcels for the use of subsistence farmers. By March 1620, the area defined as James City was home to 117 people (84 men, 24 women, and 9 children or young people), who probably lived upon Jamestown Island and in its immediate vicinity. In 1624 there were 222 men, women, and children living upon Jamestown Island, 183 of whom lived within the urbanized area at the western end of the island. By early 1625 Jamestown Island's population had declined to 175 (CBE 37-40, 54-56; FER 138, 139; HAI 874).

The Glasshouse (2)

In autumn 1608, when Captain John Smith was president of the colony, a small group of men undertook glass production at a site about a mile above Jamestown, on the western end of the isthmus then connecting the island to the mainland. There, at Glasshouse Point, some Dutchmen (actually, Germans) and Poles who came in the 2nd Supply of new settlers produced "a tryall of glass," a sample of which was sent back to England. Glassmaking probably ceased during the winter of 1609–1610, the "Starving Time." In 1621, when Virginia Company officials were trying to demonstrate the colony's potential for producing marketable commodities, some investors underwrote the cost of a glassmaking operation. A small group of Italian artisans, accompanied by their families and co-workers, were outfitted with clothing, provisions and equipment and sent to the colony. They were supposed to work under the supervision of Captain William Norton, who died shortly after his arrival in Virginia. Oversight of the glassmaking project was delegated to Treasurer George Sandys. Artisans Bernardo and Vincentio (Vincencio) built a glass furnace that was destroyed shortly after its construction. Although it was repaired, the glassworkers continuously complained about their materials and working conditions. In 1624 they were living at the Glasshouse, but by 1625 they had moved to Treasurer Sandy's plantation on the lower side of the James River and were clamoring to go home. During the 1630s Governor John Harvey, a strong advocate of industrial development, came into possession of the Glasshouse tract, 24 acres that abutted the Governor's Land but never was part of it (CJS 1:180-181, 233-234; CBE 41, 60; VCR 1:498, 511; PB 3:26).

The Governor's Land (The Maine and Pasbehay) (3)

Governor George Yeardley's November 1618 instructions from the Virginia Company stipulated that a 3,000-acre tract be set aside in Pasbehay toward the support of the colony's highest ranking official. The Governor's Land, located upon the north side of the James River, extended from Powhatan Creek (just above Jamestown Island), westward to Deep Creek (now Lake Pasbehay). In April 1619 when Governor Yeardley arrived in Virginia with servants supplied by the Virginia Company, he discovered that his predecessor, Deputy Governor Samuel Argall, already had seated some of his own servants and the Society of Martin's Hundred's settlers upon the Governor's Land, calling his community Argall Town. Yeardley ordered them to move. In January 1620 John Rolfe indicated that Yeardley had laid out the public properties within each of the colony's four corporations. In March 1620, 50 men were seated upon the Governor's Land. In February 1624 when a census was made of the colony's inhabitants, 88 people reportedly were living in The Maine or mainland. Most (if not all) of those individuals were residing upon the Governor's Land. In January 1625, when a muster was made, the Governor's Land was home to two communities of settlers who lived in areas identified as The Maine and Pasbehay. The Maine, which was situated just west of Jamestown Island (1), had a population of 37, which included 30 men, 6 women, and an infant. One household included eight servants belonging to Dr. John Pott, a resident of Jamestown Island and the colony's physician-general. A second group, 30 people described as residents of Pasbehay, were clustered with a dozen males identified as the Governor's Men, servants to incumbent Governor Francis Wyatt. They, like the people who occupied The Maine, were residing upon the Governor's Land. Throughout the colonial period, the 3,000-acre tract known as the Governor's Land was reserved for the use of the colony's highest ranking official. Most governors leased portions of their office land to tenants but placed some of their own servants upon the property. After the close of the American Revolution, the Governor's Land passed into private hands (VCR 3:99-101, 245, 287, 310; CBE 39-40, 57-58; FER 138, 139).

The Company Land in James City (4)

Shortly after Governor George Yeardley arrived in Virginia in April 1619, he saw that a 3,000-acre tract of Company Land was laid out in each of the colony's four corporations. Later, one was set aside on the Eastern Shore. The

Virginia Company intended to place its own servants and tenants upon its corporate holdings so that they could generate income for Company investors. Company servants were obliged to serve for seven years, during which time they were sharecroppers who retained half of what they earned. The Company Land within the Corporation of James City was located upon the north side of the James River, immediately upstream from the Governor's Land (3). It extended from Deep Creek (now Lake Pasbehay) westward to the mouth of the Chickahominy River. In early November 1619 a hundred men sent to the colony as Company servants arrived at Jamestown. Half were supposed to settle upon the Company's Land in James City, under the command of Lieutenant Jabez Whittaker. A suitable site was found approximately four miles above Jamestown Island, near the mouth of the Chickahominy River.

By June 1620 an estimated 100 Company men were residing upon the Company's acreage in James City. In May 1621 Captain Whitaker reported that he had built a guesthouse in which newly-arrived settlers could recover from their voyage and become acclimated to living in the colony. In 1621 when a group of Italian glassmakers arrived in the colony, they convalesced at Captain Whitaker's guesthouse and then went to the Glasshouse site (2). When the Indians attacked the settlements along the James River in March 1622, it is probable that some of the Company Land's residents perished, for one of Captain Jabez Whitaker's servants was among those slain. Several months after the Indian onslaught, Virginia Company officials tried to encourage private individuals to seat upon the tracts of Company Land, promising them long-term use of the acreage and compensation for any improvements they made. However, Captain Whitaker took his men to the Company Land (17) in Elizabeth City and seated them there. The dissolution of the Virginia Company in May 1624 probably led to the abandonment of the Company's property in the Corporation of James City. By the 1630s, portions of the Company Land were in private hands (PB 3:307; VCR 3:99-101, 441-442, 477, 489, 494, 571, 670; 4:107).

Neck O'Land (5)

During the second decade of the 1600s, a loosely defined community of settlers became established upon the mainland directly behind Jamestown Island (1), on the north side of the Back River, between Mill and Powhatan Creeks. The Rev. Richard Buck, who arrived in Virginia in May 1610, having been shipwrecked in Bermuda with Sir Thomas Gates and Sir George Somers, laid claim to 750 acres of land on Mill Creek, across from the James City Parish Glebe, which consisted of 100 acres. In 1620 Buck, who was minister of the church at Jamestown, purchased a dwelling in the eastern end of Jamestown Island and probably intended to place servants upon his property in the Neck O'Land. Buck and his wife died between December 1622 and April 1623 and Richard Kingsmill, a Jamestown Island planter and one of the Rev. Buck's executors, moved to his acreage in the Neck O'Land. He probably did so as a means of preserving the Buck orphans' claim to the land they stood to inherit. In February 1624 a total of 25 people, members of at least four households, were living in the Neck O'Land. By 1625 the area's population had declined to 17. One of the people living in the Neck O'Land in 1625 was an African servant named Edward. The settlement was relatively well provisioned and livestock was plentiful. By 1626 John Burrows, one of the Buck orphans' guardians, received permission to move to the Neck O'Land and in 1628 Thomas Harwood (a tenant) was living there. The Buck estate remained intact and in 1636 when the Rev. Richard Buck's eldest son, Gercian, came of age, he took possession of the property and combined it with 500 acres he bought from his brother-in-law. Meanwhile the James City Parish glebe passed through the hands of a succession of clergymen, only becoming private property after the American Revolution and the disestablishment of Virginia's state church (MCGC 109, 117, 159; VCR 4:555; PB 1 Pt. 2:532-533; CBE 58).

Archer's Hope (6)

In May 1607, when the first Virginia colonists sailed up the James River in search of a suitable location to plant their settlement, they took note of a point of land on the east side of the mouth of a navigable creek that entered the James from the north. They called the promontory Archer's Hope, in recognition of Gabriel Archer, who favored seating there. Although the colonists continued on upstream and seated upon Jamestown Island, in time the territory flanking both sides of the promontory became known as Archer's Hope. By 1619 several colonists had received patents for land in that vicinity. In March 1622 when the Indians attacked the settlements sparsely scattered along the banks of the James River, several people were killed in Archer's Hope, on the west side of Archer's Hope (later College) Creek. Although the area was not among those strengthened and held in the wake of the assault, by February 1624 a small community had become established there. It consisted of 14 people, who comprised at least three households. A year later, the population was essentially the same. The residents of Archer's Hope were relatively well armed and had an adequate food supply. In May 1625, when a list of patented land was sent back to England, several people (some of whom owned homesteads on Jamestown Island) were credited with land in Archer's Hope. However, only three parcels were identified as "planted," all of which were on the west side of Archer's Hope Creek. Although land on the east side of the creek had been patented, none of those parcels had been seated. During the 1620s and '30s most of the patents in Archer's Hope were in the hands of tenants. By May 1626 Richard Kingsmill, who claimed 500 acres in what became known as Kingsmill Neck, had begun to clear and plant his acreage, and as time went on he acquired more land in that area. William Claiborne, George Sandys, and John Uty, all of whom were members of the Council of State, also acquired patents on the east side of Archer's Hope Creek (PB 1 Pt. 2:648; VCR 4:556; MCGC 102; CBE 41, 58).

Martin's Hundred (7)

The Society of Martin's Hundred dispatched its first settlers to Virginia in October 1618. When the 250 people aboard the *Gift of God* reached the colony in January 1619, Deputy Governor Samuel Argall seated them upon the mainland just west of Jamestown Island instead of sending them to the acreage allocated for their use. On April 19, 1619, when incoming Governor George Yeardley arrived, he learned that the Martin's Hundred settlers were occupying part of the tract the Virginia Company had selected as the Governor's Land (3). Despite the fact that the Society of Martin's Hundred's people had not settled upon their own property, in July 1619 they sent delegates to the colony's assembly. In January 1620 John Rolfe reported that the Society of Martin's Hundred's colonists, who still were residing upon the Governor's Land, were in good health although there had been some deaths. By March they had moved to the acreage assigned to their sponsors. It was located on the upper side of the James River between Grove and Skiffs Creeks. Within a short time, the Society of Martin's Hundred tried to extend its holdings westward to Archer's Hope (later College) Creek and northward into the territory of the Chiskiack Indians. In March 1620 there were 45 men, 14 women, and 13 children living at Martin's Hundred. In March 1622 the Indians of the Powhatan Chiefdom attacked Martin's Hundred. Although 73 people were first thought to have been slain, later it was discovered that 19 women had been captured by the Pamunkey Indians and detained at their village. Most (perhaps all) of these women were from Martin's Hundred. In 1625 there were only 27 people residing at Martin's Hundred. During the 1630s, the Society of Martin's Hundred's land was broken up into smaller parcels and patented by numerous individuals (FER 138, 139; VCR 1:561; 3:553, 565, 587, 643; PB 1:12, 62, 78; 8:125; CBE 42, 61-62).

Burrows Hill (Burrows Mount, Smith's Mount) (8)

John Burrows patented 150 acres of land and developed it as a plantation he called Burrows Hill or Burrows Mount. Burrows' property was located upon the lower side of the James River and abutted east upon Paces Paines (9) and extended west toward Martin's Brandon (59). In early 1625, when a muster was made, John and Susanna Smith, their baby boy, and a servant named John Elliott were living at Burrows Hill. Also present were John Burrows and six of his men who sometimes resided at Jamestown (1). John Burrows married Bridget, one of the late Rev. Richard Buck's daughters, and eventually moved to the Neck O'Land (5). Although Burrows received his Burrows Hill patent in February 1625, he probably seated his property a year or so earlier. In 1626 he was ordered to see that his plantation was well manned. It was then leased to John Smith. After John Burrows's sudden death in 1629, his widow sold Burrows Hill to leaseholder John Smith, who called it Smith's Mount. In 1634 Burrows Hill (then described as 250 acres that had been owned by the late John Smith) was part of the 2,250-acre tract acquired by Captain Henry Browne, who developed his acreage into the plantation known as Four Mile Tree (PB 1 Pt. 1:62, 441, Pt. 2:929; CBE 59; MCGC 131).

Paces Paines (9)

Richard and Isabell (Izabell) Pace, who were ancient planters, were granted 200 acres of land on the lower side of the James River. They developed their holdings into a plantation they called Paces Paines. The Pace property abutted west upon John Burrows' plantation (Burrows Mount or Burrows Hill), and east upon the acreage that belonged to Francis Chapman. In March 1622 an Indian named Chanco, who was living in the Pace household and had been converted to Christianity, warned Richard Pace that the Natives were planning to attack. Pace rowed his boat across the river to Jamestown, where he alerted the authorities. In the wake of the Indian assault, the Pace household moved to Jamestown Island, where they lived for several months. Later, the Paces reoccupied their property. After Richard Pace's death, his widow, Izabell, married William Perry and moved to Jamestown. In 1625 there were three households living at Paces Paines, all of which were headed by ancient planters. One couple, John and Alice Proctor, formerly lived upon their own plantation in Henrico, but withdrew after the 1622 Indian attack. Just east of Paces Paines was the 100-acre patent that belonged to ancient planter Francis

Chapman. His land abutted east upon a nameless tributary of the James River located to the east of the nineteenth-century mansion known as Mount Pleasant. In 1628 Izabell Pace Perry, who was in possession of the western part of Paces Paines, purchased the Chapman acreage and added to her holdings. Meanwhile, son George Pace owned the 100 acres he had inherited from his father plus 300 acres he acquired on the basis of headrights. The Pace and Chapman tracts were located within the boundaries of the eighteenth-century Surry County plantation known as Mount Pleasant. Sometime prior to 1629 William Perry, who had moved to his wife's property at Paces Paines and may have expanded his holdings in that vicinity, was placed in command of the settlers there and at Smith's Mount (Burrows Hill) **(8)**. Three years later he became a burgess. By 1635 the Perrys had moved to Buckland in Charles City, and William Swann patented a 1,200-acre tract that included Paces Paines and extended eastward, taking in Swann's Point, which in 1632 was known as Perry's Point (VCR 3:555, 682; CBE 40, 59; PB 1 Pt.1:62, 64, 293; MCGC 63, 65; HEN 1:178).

Captain Roger Smith's Plantation (10)

Captain Roger Smith, a respected military leader with experience in the Low Countries, came to Virginia in 1618 in the fleet that brought Lord De La Warr. For a time, Smith was responsible for a company of men seated upon the Governor's Land **(3)**. After the 1622 Indian attack he was placed in charge of several communities and in 1623 he was hired to build a fort in Warresqueak **(26)**, overlooking what became known as Burrells Bay. By February 1624 Roger Smith had married the former Joan Peirce, the widow of John Rolfe, who died in 1622. Therefore, Smith had use of the 400 acres that Joan's young stepson, Thomas Rolfe, had inherited from his parents, Pocahontas and John Rolfe. The Rolfe plantation, located between Gray's and Crouches Creeks, encompassed the site upon which Captain John Smith and his men had constructed a fort in 1609, a refuge to which the colonists could flee if a foreign invasion occurred. In early 1625 Roger Smith had nine male servants on the Rolfe property. In time, the Rolfe acreage became known as the Smith's Fort Plantation in Surry County. In May 1625 Roger Smith was credited with 100 acres of land in Archer's Hope **(6)**, land he acquired by means of a court order, and he also had some property near Blunt Point **(22)** (VCR 3:70; 4:551, 555, 556; MCGC 130; MCGH 821; CBE 59; SR 3960).

The Treasurer's Plantation (11)

In December 1624 George Sandys, the colony's treasurer, received a patent for 650 acres of riverfront land on the lower side of the James River, within today's Surry County. The Treasurer's Plantation included three parcels: Sandys' original 300 acres, a 200-acre tract on the east side of Crouches Creek's mouth that had been assigned to John Bainham in January 1619, and a 150-acre parcel on the east that had been in the possession of Edward Grindon since December 1620. In 1625, when a muster was made of each component of the Treasurer's Plantation, there were 5 men in residence upon the former Bainham property; 15 men and 2 women on the old Grindon patent, including the Italian glassblowers from Jamestown; and 16 men and a woman, including a Frenchman skilled in making wine and producing silk, on the 300 acres that George Sandys patented in late 1624. The settlers had use of two houses, two storehouses, a silkworm house, and some "other cabins."

As one of Treasurer George Sandys' responsibilities was overseeing the Virginia Company's industrial activities, it is understandable that some of the Company's skilled workers were in his custody. In 1649, Edward Grindon's son, Thomas, who had come into possession of the 650-acre Treasurer's Plantation, sold it to Captain George Evelin, who gave it to his son, Monjoy, in 1650. In 1657 William Edwards acquired 490 acres of the Treasurer's Plantation (PB 1 Pt. 1:12; 4:435; DOR 1:41-42; CBE 60; VCR 2:95).

Hugh Crowder's Plantation (12)

Hugh Crowder came to Virginia in 1619 and by 1622 had become involved in clearing land on the lower side of the James River, within the Indian territory known as Tappahanna. In February 1624 he was living upon the east side of Gray's Creek, most likely on land to which he had laid claim, acreage that had belonged successively to Captain William Powell and Captain John Hurleston. In 1625 Hugh Crowder was credited with his own plantation, which had two dwellings and was home to six males. The Crowder homestead was fortified or had at least one palisaded building. In November 1626 Hugh Crowder and his men vacated his plantation, which he claimed was infertile, and moved to Captain Francis West's acreage on the west side of Lower Chippokes Creek. Crowder died sometime prior to April 1628. He may have been the son of Hugh Crowder, a wealthy Virginia colonist who died prior to 1623 (VCR 2:457; CBE 60; MCGC 63, 123, 171).

William Ewen's Plantation (13)

In September 1619 William Ewen received a patent for 400 acres of land located on the lower side of the James River. His property abutted northwest upon the land of Edward Grindon (Grindon's Hill), which later became part of the Treasurer's Plantation (11). In January 1621 Ewen received a patent for an additional 1,000 acres fronting upon Cobham Bay and located upon the west side of a stream that became known as the Sunken Marsh or College Run. Refugees from the College land (66) in Henrico were taken to the Ewens property in the wake of the March 1622 Indian attack. The people sent to establish the East India School were placed there, too. By the mid-1630s the Ewen plantation had become known as The College. In 1648 it came into the hands of William Edwards and Rice Davis (MCGC 60; PB 1 Pt. 2:143, 775).

Captain William Powell's Plantation (14)

Captain William Powell's 550-acre plantation was located on the south side of the James River between College Run and Lower Chippokes Creek. Powell and John Smith (not the famous captain) had tried to obtain 100 acres in that vicinity in 1619, along with 300 acres on Hog Island (16). In May 1625 Powell's 550-acre tract was described as seated. He also was credited with 200 acres of land on Crouches Creek, to the south of the Treasurer's Plantation (11). After Captain William Powell's death in February 1623, his widow, Margaret, married Edward Blaney, a Jamestown (1) merchant. He quickly shifted seven of his own male servants to his new wife's plantation, which she held in trust for her late husband's son, George. When a muster was made in early 1625 Edward Blaney had 15 men residing on the Powell property. George Powell eventually inherited his late father's property. As he died in 1643 without heirs, his plantation escheated to the Crown. Later, the Powell plantation was patented by Sir William Berkeley, who conveyed it to Colonel Henry Bishop. Captain William Powell's plantation is located within Surry County's Chippokes State Park (VCR 1:308; PB 2:81; Surry County Deeds, Wills, Etc. 1 [1652–1672]:176-178; CBE 59).

Captain Samuel Mathews' Plantation (15)

Samuel Mathews, who came to Virginia in 1618 and, with Deputy Governor Samuel Argall's permission, seated some land at Arrohattock (66), transported 100 people to the colony in 1622. He became interested in Captain William Powell's cleared land near Hog Island (16) and secured the right to occupy the property and let his servants use "the howses of the upper fort." In February 1625 there were 25 people living at the Mathews plantation. In May 1625 when a list of patented land was sent back to England, Samuel Mathews was in possession of a "Divident planted" in Tappahanna (seemingly part of the Powell property) and some acreage on the upper side of the James River at Blunt Point. By 1626 he had vacated the Powell property and established his plantation, Mathews Manor (23), near Blunt Point (22) (VCR 4:555; CBE 59-60).

Hog Island (16)

This low-lying marshy peninsula, which protrudes from the lower side of the James River, was the site of a fort or blockhouse Captain John Smith and his men built in 1609. Prior to that time, colonists had begun using Hog Island for the pasturing of swine. In March 1619 Deputy Governor Samuel Argall declared that Hog Island was open to settlement by the inhabitants of Jamestown Island (1). By that time, Captain William Powell and John Smith already had tried to claim 300 acres there. Powell later made arrangements to trade some property on Crouches Creek for some acreage near the neck of Hog Island. He had his servants clear some land, which he allowed Captain Samuel Mathews to use.

On February 20, 1620, Mary Bayly, the orphan of ancient planter John Bayly, was awarded 490 acres on Hog Island. Her patent stipulated that if the island were somewhat larger, she had the right to purchase the excess acreage. Her guardians did so with the use of headrights. Sometime prior to March 1622 Ralph Hamor obtained a patent for 250 acres at Hog Island, a land title he later claimed was burned during the Indian attack. He became embroiled in a suit with Robert Evers, Mary Bayly's guardian, and insisted that her land be surveyed. As it turned out, some of the structures Hamor built at Hog Island were on the Bayly property. Although Ralph Hamor placed some indentured servants on his land at Hog Island, he resided in urban Jamestown almost continuously. Around 1624 Mary Bayly's guardians began leasing her acreage to Sir George Yeardley.

Another person who established a plantation on Hog Island was Ensign John Uty, who was living there with 30 other people when a census was compiled in February 1624. By November he had received a patent for 100 acres that abutted east upon Lower Chippokes Creek and extended northward within the neck of Hog Island. Uty called his plantation "Utopia." By February 1625, 53 people were living upon Hog Island in a number of households. The community included two households of indentured servants who belonged to Ralph Hamor and George Yeardley. Also present were households headed by Lieutenant Edward Berkeley, John Uty, and John Chew. Lieutenant Berkeley was responsible for some of the Society of Southampton Hundred's settlers, who had abandoned their own plantation (44) and cleared and seated some land at Hog Island, making it their temporary home. Around 1630 the heiress Mary Bayly married Randall Holt, at which point Hog Island in its entirety came into the hands of the Holt family (PB 1 Pt. 1:14; Pt. 2:880; MCGC 17, 44, 63-65; VCR 4:482-483, 551, 556; M&D 44; CBE 41-42, 61).

ELIZABETH CITY (KECOUGHTAN)

In 1607 the first colonists paused at the promontory they called Point Comfort and encountered the Kecoughtan Indians, but moved further inland to establish their settlement. Captain John Smith returned to Kecoughtan to trade for corn and it was there, in early January 1608, that he and a party of explorers celebrated Christmas, the first recorded in the annals of the colony's history. In October 1609 then-President George Percy sent a detachment of men to Point Comfort to build Algernone Fort, a fortified position from which incoming ships could be sighted. When Lord De La Warr arrived in mid-June 1610, he authorized Sir Thomas Gates to drive the Natives from their village at Kecoughtan, where he had two additional strongholds built: Forts Henry and Charles. Both positions were strengthened by Sir Thomas Dale, who came in May 1611. Settlement slowly took root at Kecoughtan and in 1616 John Rolfe reported that the area was home to 20 people, who were under the command of Captain George Webb. When Governor George Yeardley reached Virginia in mid-April 1619, he found a community of settlers at Kecoughtan. Some were seated on the east side of the Southampton (Hampton) River, on land Yeardley had been ordered to declare public property. The inhabitants of Kecoughtan were authorized to build homesteads within the territory that extended up the James River as far as Skiffs Creek.

During summer 1619, when the first assembly convened, the delegates from Kecoughtan asked that the area be renamed. It was then that the Corporation of Elizabeth City was created. In March 1620 there were 28 men, 12 women, and 14 children or young people living in Kecoughtan. Although the 1622 Indian attack apparently did not claim many settlers' lives in Elizabeth City, the people residing there suffered from the severe food shortages that other communities experienced. In time, Elizabeth City became one of the Virginia colony's most populous areas. In February 1624, there were 349 people living in Elizabeth City, but 101 men, women, and children had died since April 1623. In 1625 when a muster was made of the colony's inhabitants, a total of 359 people were residents of Elizabeth City. Approximately 25 percent of them lived on the east side of the Hampton River, on the Virginia Company's land. In May 1625 when a list of patented land was sent back to England, approximately 5,650 acres within the Corporation of Elizabeth City had been claimed by private individuals, most of whom had seated their land. An additional 4,500 acres had been assigned to public use: 3,000 acres of Company Land and 1,500 acres of Common Land.

By the 1630s colonists had begun claiming land in the vicinity of the Old and New Poquoson Rivers and the Back River and along Harris and Brick Kiln Creeks. Settlers also began taking an interest in land on the lower side of the James River, within the Corporation of Elizabeth City. Although at least seven patentees had secured land in that area by early 1625, none of those tracts were seated. Displacement of the Native population began in the aftermath of the

1622 Indian assault, when Sir George Yeardley led an expedition against the Nansemond Indians. However, there was a lingering Native presence and settlers knew that they were beyond the reach of assistance if the Indians attacked. By 1630 colonists had begun patenting land on Lynnhaven Bay, and in 1635 several people claimed land on the Elizabeth and Nansemond Rivers. Early patents for land on the south side of Hampton Roads frequently made reference to Indian fields and other features associated with Native occupation.

In 1634 when Elizabeth City County was formed from the eastern part of the Corporation of Elizabeth City's territory, it spanned both sides of the James River and was home to 859 people. The Poquoson River (in colonial times known as the New Poquoson) then became the dividing line between Elizabeth City and Charles River (York) Counties. The northern portion of Elizabeth City County (on the upper side of the James River) extended from Old Point Comfort (on the east) **(17)** to Marie's Mount or Newportes News (on the west) **(24)** and ran inland to include Fox Hill and the countryside along the Back and Old Poquoson Rivers **(19)**. The size of Elizabeth City County was reduced dramatically in 1636 when its territory on the south side of the James River was split off and New Norfolk County was formed. Today, Elizabeth City County's territory is coterminous with the City of Hampton (VCR 4:558; CBE: 43-45, 76; PB 1 Pt. 1:45-47, 152, 156, 158, 165-166, 169, 171-172, 179, 383; CO 8/55 f 155).

Old Point Comfort, the Company Land, and the Common Land in Elizabeth City (17)

During 1619 Governor George Yeardley, in accord with his instructions, saw that a 3,000-acre tract on the east side of the Hampton River was set aside as Company Land, acreage that was supposed to produce income for the Virginia Company's investors. Unfortunately, prior to the time Yeardley claimed that area on the Virginia Company's behalf, settlers already had built homesteads there. He evicted them but assigned them land elsewhere. The Company Land remained intact until around 1635, more than a decade after the Virginia Company's demise. Also located on the east side of the Hampton River were 1,500 acres set aside as Common Land, probably for the grazing of livestock, and 100 acres as a glebe for Elizabeth City's clergyman. In 1620 the Virginia Company sent some French workers to Virginia to produce marketable commodities. They were seated at Buckroe, where they were engaged in planting mulberries (for silk culture) and growing vines (for wine-making). In 1621 Captain Thomas Newce (Nuce) came as manager of the Company Land and the Company's employees. He built two guesthouses for the reception of new immigrants and constructed a brick-lined well. His property, which was located on the east side of the Hampton River's mouth, between Johns Creek and the Strawberry Banks, was known as the fort field or Fort Henry field and was occupied in succession by Thomas Purfoy, Francis Hooke, Francis West, and others responsible for the fortifications at Point Comfort, later known as Old Point Comfort. During this period, the Rev. Jonas Stockton was the area's minister. In 1624 there were 30 people living at Buckroe and 12 at "the Indian Thickett" or "Indian House Thickett." By 1625 a fourth of the Corporation of Elizabeth City's population was living on the east side of the Hampton River, where there were 89 houses, 24 of which were fortified. The area was home to some prominent citizens who had a longstanding association with the Virginia Company.

In September 1628 Dictoris Christmas, who resided at the Strawberry Banks, overlooking Hampton Roads, assigned his acreage to his neighbor, Lyonel Raulston, who moved to Chiskiack a couple years later. Roulston assigned his land at Strawberry Banks to John Neale. Meanwhile, the Rev. William Hampton procured some land at Buckroe, as did James Bonall, a Frenchman. Several people (notably the Rev. Jonas Stockden, Thomas Flint, and Edward Waters) leased land within the Indian House Thicket and at the Strawberry Banks, acreage that had been part of the Virginia Company's land. Although the Virginia Company's charter was revoked in May 1624, questions lingered about the Company's legal interest in the land that they had developed prior to that time. In 1632 James Knott of Accomack leased acreage on the east side of the Hampton River's mouth, where he intended to operate a house of entertainment or inn. He may have been leasing the property on which Captain Thomas Nuce had built guesthouses in 1622. A 1637 patent suggests that Knott's inn was located on Johns Creek. Additional commercial development was located near the mouth of the Hampton River (PB 1 Pt. 1:77-79, 85, 88, 90, 93, 96, 133-136, 139-142, 147, 323; Pt. 2:675; 2:128, 473; CBE 42-43, 45, 67-68; MCGC 62, 468).

Elizabeth City (West Side of the Hampton River) (18)

During the early 1620s several households resided in the area between the Hampton River and Newport News Point. In 1625 Captain William Tucker and Thomas Dunthorne had Indian servants living in their homes on the west side of the Hampton River. The Dunthorne property abutted the river's mouth and fronted upon the James. Tucker's Indian servant, who had been given an English name, had been baptized. By 1620 William Capps owned some land between Sunset and Salters Creeks, acreage first known as Capps Point and later, Little England. William Claiborne patented land north of Salters Creek sometime prior to 1624. His property later became the site of Hampton Town. John Gundry, William Ganey, William Landsell and others had patents on the west side of the Hampton River (PB 1 Pt.1:38-43, 476; Pt. 2:76; CBE 43-45, 63, 66-67).

Elizabeth City (Near the Mouth of the York River) (19)

In 1624, Peter Arundell (a French silkmaker) and Bartholomew Hoskins, both of whom were residents of Buckroe, secured patents for some land on the Back River. Four years later, Elias LaGuard, a French vine grower, acquired a leasehold on the west side of Harris Creek. In 1625 Raleigh Croshaw had a patent for 500 acres at Fox Hill, but he may have failed to seat it. In 1627 Thomas Flint asked the Council of State for permission to take up some land at Fox Hill, if it were not part of the Virginia Company's land. During the early 1630s, after European settlement had spread up the lower side of the York River, to the east of Queens Creek, at least eleven men (William Conner, Hugh Bullock, Nicholas Brown, Thomas Eaton, Adam Thorogood, Thomas Seawell, Richard Robinson, John Watson, Christopher Calthrop, Christopher Stokes, and Gilbert Symonds) patented land at the head of the Hampton River, on the Back River and its Northwest Branch, and close to the Poquoson River. Elmer Philips was credited with acreage at the Indian Spring near Fox Hill in 1633, where Thomas and Mary Flint had acquired land earlier on. All of these people claimed land by means of the headright system, unlike the groups of investors who had banded together when establishing large plantations on the James River a decade or so earlier (PB 1 Pt. 1:44-45, 99, 101, 116-117, 123, 152-153, 156, 158-161, 164, 167, 225, 227, 264-265; MCGC 137-138; VCR 4:558).

Elizabeth City (Lower Side of the James River) (20 a, b, c)

By September 1624 patents had been issued to John Sipsey, Captain William Tucker, and Lieutenant John Chisman for land on the south side of the James River. All three men were residents of Kecoughtan when they laid claim to parcels on the opposite shore. In May 1625 when a list of patented land was sent back to England, all three men were credited with their acreage. Thomas Willoughby, Thomas Chapman, John Downman, and Thomas Brewood had tracts located on the Elizabeth River, where William Ramshaw also had a patent (**20 a**). In May 1625 none of these parcels was described as seated. By 1630 Thomas Allen had laid claim to land on Lynnhaven Bay (**20 b**). Captain Adam Thorogood also patented a massive tract on the Lynnhaven, land that eventually became his family seat. In 1635 Francis Hough, George White, James Knott, John Parrott, John Wilkins, Robert Newman, Richard Bennett, and others moved into the territory along the east side of the Nansemond River (**20 c**), which separated Elizabeth City County from Warresqueak (Isle of Wight) County. Meanwhile, Thomas Burbage and Francis Bullock patented land on the banks of the James River, between the Nansemond River and the Elizabeth River's Western Branch. In 1636 New Norfolk County was formed from Elizabeth City County's territory on the south side of the James River. Thanks to dramatic population growth, within a year New Norfolk was subdivided into Upper and Lower Norfolk Counties and Bullock's Creek became the boundary line between the two jurisdictions. By 1646 Upper Norfolk County had been renamed Nansemond County (PB 1 Pt. 1:45-47, 170-171, 179, 186, 240, 305, 381-382).

WARWICK RIVER (WARWICK)

The shire or county of Warwick River (Warwick), created in 1634, and located on the upper side of the James River, comprised the northwestern portion of the Corporation of Elizabeth City (Kecoughtan), established in 1619. It extended Marie's Mount and Newportes News Point (**24**) (on the east) to Skiffs Creek and Mulberry Island (on the west) (**21**). It had 811 inhabitants and was the third most populous shire in the colony. Between 1619 and 1625 colonists developed land at Newportes News (Newports News), Blunt Point, and Mulberry Island, and along the Warwick River, Skiffs Creek, and other navigable streams. In 1643 the Grand Assembly passed an act whereby the name Warwick River County was shortened to Warwick County. At that time, the county's original boundaries were reaffirmed and described more fully. Eventually, all of Warwick County was incorporated as the City of Newport News (CBE 43-45, 63-68; CO 8/55 f 155; HEN 1:249-250).

Mulberry Island (21)

Mulberry Island's southernmost tip, Mulberry Point, was identified by Captain John Smith on his well known map of Virginia. However, it was not until June 1610, when Sir Thomas Gates and the departing Jamestown colonists encountered Lord De La Warr's longboat at Mulberry Island, that it became an important landmark. By 1619 Captain William Peirce, who resided in urban Jamestown (**1**), had patented 650 acres on Mulberry Island and developed his property. Peirce's famous son-in-law, John Rolfe, and some others also were in possession of acreage on Mulberry Island. On March 22, 1622, when the Indians attacked the settlers living on Mulberry Island, William Peirce's son, Thomas, and several members of his household were killed. Mulberry Island was abandoned briefly, but it probably was reoccupied within a year or so. On January 25, 1625, Mulberry Island was home to 25 men and 5 women. The community, which consisted of several households, was relatively well armed and provisioned. Some of these people lived on the mainland behind Mulberry Island and further up Skiffs Creek. Nearby were settlers living along the east side of the Warwick River, in the vicinity of Blunt Point (VCR 2:106; 3:570; CJS 2:302; CBE 56-57).

Blunt Point and Stanley Hundred (22)

Edward Waters, who had been shipwrecked in Bermuda with Sir Thomas Gates and Sir George Somers in 1609, accompanied them to Virginia a year later. He was among those sent back to Bermuda, with Sir Thomas Gates and Sir George Somers, to procure hogs for the Virginia colony, but did not return until around 1617. By March 1622 Waters and his wife, Grace, had established a plantation about two miles below Blunt Point in the vicinity of what became known as Waters Creek, now Lake Maury, and were residing there when the Indians attacked. Three of Edward Waters' men were killed, but he and his wife and child and two servants were captured by the Nansemond Indians, who took them across the James River. Fortunately, the Waters' found a boat and managed to escape, reaching safety at Kecoughtan. Afterward, the Waters' moved to Strawberry Banks (17), near the mouth of the James River.

In April 1623 Captain Samuel Each proposed building a blockhouse on some oyster banks at Blunt Point, but he died and afterward his proposal was deemed unfeasible. In August 1624 Edward Waters obtained a patent for 100 acres at Blunt Point, and several months later patents were issued to several other colonists, some of whom were ancient planters. Maurice Thompson, a London merchant, was awarded 150 acres there, land that may have been in his possession by 1621. By May 1625 approximately 2,200 acres had been patented at Blunt Point, along with another 1,390 acres "belowe Blunt Point." In 1626 Thomas Harwood patented 100 acres at or near Blunt Point, on the south bank of the Warwick (Blunt Point) River, and by 1632 he had acquired land on the east side of Skiffs Creek, where he established his home plantation, Queen Hithe. Another settler whose homestead was located on the east side of the Warwick River was Lieutenant Gilbert Peppett, who had obtained his land from Captain Samuel Mathews. Sir George Yeardley received a patent for 1,000 acres in this vicinity, a plantation he called Stanley Hundred (CBE 44, 65; VCR 3:571; 4:557; MCGC 103, 129-130, 180; PB 1 Pt. 1:1, 18, 20-25, 50, 59, 110, 347; 2:34; 5:349; CJS 2:301, 308-309).

Mathews Manor (Denbigh) (23)

In May 1625 Captain Samuel Mathews was credited with some acreage at Blunt Point. Although he was then residing on the lower side of the James River upon property that belonged to the late William Powell's estate (14), by December 1626 he had moved to Blunt Point and commenced developing his well known plantation, Mathews Manor, or Denbigh. In 1627 when there was a perceived threat of foreign invasion, plans were made to use Mathews' plantation as a safe haven. In 1649 Mathews Manor was described as a showcase of industry. Not only were agricultural crops and livestock raised on a grand scale, Samuel Mathews had a tan house, where leather was produced, and he employed eight shoemakers. He also had weavers who processed flax and wove it into cloth. So productive was the Mathews plantation that ships often stopped there to be victualed and commodities were exported to other colonies (PB 1 Pt. 1:50; VCR 4:555, 557; MCGC 63, 65, 83, 135; FOR 2:Bk 8:14-15).

Newportes News (Marie's Mount) (24)

The earliest dated reference to Newportes (Newports, Newport) News Point as a topographic feature occurs in a November 1619 legal document authorizing colonists to seat land along the banks of the James, from there to Kecoughtan (17, 18). Captain Daniel Gookin, who agreed to transport a shipment of livestock and other commodities to Virginia, received permission to establish a settlement in the colony. He sold his 500-acre estate in County Longford, Ireland, and arrived in Virginia in November 1621 with a shipload of colonists and cattle. The plantation Gookin established at Newportes News Point probably was fortified, for it seems to have escaped harm during the March 1622 Indian attack. According to Captain John Smith, Gookin, despite orders to the contrary, refused to vacate his plantation in favor of a more secure position. When summer came, Daniel Gookin returned to England, where he recruited more settlers, loaded a ship with supplies, and secured a patent for his plantation, calling it Marie's Mount. While Gookin was away, the Indians continuously harassed his settlers at Newportes News and by June 1623 only seven people were left. When a census was taken in February 1624 the inhabitants of Newportes News were listed among the other residents of the Corporation of Elizabeth City, west of the Hampton River. In early 1625, when more detailed demographic records were compiled, Daniel Gookin was credited with 20 servants and four houses at Newportes News, a plantation that was relatively well provisioned and fortified. In May 1625, when a list of patented land was sent back to England, 1,300 acres called Newportes News were attributed to Daniel Gookin, whose acreage was described as planted. Gookin's son, Daniel II, came to Virginia and took up residence at Newportes News, where he was living in 1631. A patent assigned to William Cole in 1635 reveals that Daniel Gookin II sold all but 250 acres of his father's land to John Chandler. A survey of Gookin's Newportes News tract, done in 1769 as part of a boundary dispute, revealed that it contained more than 1,400 acres and extended from Waters Creek (now Lake Maury) eastward to Newport News Point, interfacing with the western boundary of Elizabeth City County. By 1629 the territory between Marie's Mount and Waters Creek had become populous (VCR 1:553-554, 618; 2:89, 584; 3:587, 612; 4:105, 229; CBE 63; CJS 2:287, 301-302; PB 7:466).

WARRESQUEAK (ISLE OF WIGHT)

In 1608 Captain John Smith and a party of explorers visited the village of the Warresqueak (Warascoyak, Warisqueak) Indians, which was located on the banks of Warresqueak (later Burwell's) Bay. Another village, Mokete, was situated at Pagan Point. Smith indicated that the Warresqueak Indians' hunting grounds extended approximately 20 miles inland from the banks of the James and encompassed an estimated five miles of river frontage. By 1619, Giles Jones, Captain Nathaniel Basse, and an Ensign Washer had patented land close to the Pagan River. Then, Captain Christopher Lawne seated land on the east side of Lawnes Creek's mouth and in 1621–1622 the Bennett family established a plantation in the mouth of Burwell's Bay. The presence of these Europeans impelled the Natives to attempt to drive them out. Their efforts were somewhat successful, but in 1624–1625 there were around 30 colonists living there. By the late 1620s and early 1630s settlers began seating there in substantial numbers and were prepared to defend themselves. Two Indian maidens, having converted to the Christian faith, intermarried with Nathaniel Basse's sons.

In 1634 when Virginia was subdivided into eight shires or counties, Warresqueak's territory, which was located on the south side of the James River, extended from the Nansemond River (on the east) to Lawnes Creek (on the west). The county had a population of 522 people. In 1637 Warresqueak County's aboriginal name was changed to Isle of Wight. Isle of Wight County continued to have a sizeable Native population. By the mid-seventeenth century it also was home to a substantial number of Puritans (VCR 1:534; 3:226-229; PB 1 Pt 1:160; CJS 2:266, 296; CBE 42-43, 62-63; CO 8/55 f 155).

Captain Christopher Lawne's Plantation (25)

The first European settlement in what became Isle of Wight County was established in 1619 by Captain Christopher Lawne, Sir Richard Worsley, and their associates. Lawne's ship, the *Marigold,* left England in March 1619 and arrived in the colony in mid-May. Aboard were people he intended to seat upon his own land, plus 15 male Virginia Company servants. By July 1619 Captain Christopher Lawne had established a plantation on the lower side of the James River in Warresqueak (now Isle of Wight County), in Lawnes Neck, just east of the mouth of what became known as Lawne's Creek. When the colony's officials expressed concern about Lawne's seating his people in such a remote location, he reminded them that his plantation was near those to be established by Lieutenant Nathaniel Basse and Ensign Washer. Many of the inhabitants of Captain Christopher Lawne's plantation became ill during the summer of 1619 and by November 1619 the survivors abandoned their settlement and moved to Charles City **(39)**, where Lawne himself died. Later, Captain Christopher Lawne's heirs and co-investors tried to preserve their legal claim to the land they had seated in Warresqueak. In March 1620 the Lawne plantation was credited with a population of 89 men, 12 women and 9 children, even though the property itself had been vacated (VCR 1:255-256, 268, 381, 414; 3:162, 217, 227, 246; 4:94; MCGC 90; CJS 2:266; FER 138, 139).

Bennett's Welcome (Warresqueak) (26)

London merchant Edward Bennett and his family established a plantation known as Bennett's Welcome (Warresqueak), on the lower side of the James River, to the west of the Pagan River and within the mouth of Burwells Bay. Bennett, a member of the Virginia Company, obtained his patent at the close of 1621 and immediately prepared to send 100 people to Virginia. Documentary records suggest that the Bennett plantation was well established by March 22, 1622, when the Indians attacked. A total of 53 men, women, and children were slain at Bennett's Welcome, including the settlement's commander,

Thomas Brewood. Captain John Smith later described the assault in vivid detail, which suggests that he had interviewed an eyewitness. Captain Ralph Hamor evacuated the surviving settlers to Jamestown (1), a position of safety. By October 1622 Edward Bennett received permission for his people to return to Bennett's Welcome, but several more months passed before they actually did. In spring 1623 construction of a fort got underway at the site, which provided a commanding view of the James River's shipping lanes. Then, in July, Sir George Yeardley led an expedition against the Warresqueak Indians, putting their villages to the torch. The inhabitants of Bennett's Welcome began returning to their homes, but the Indians harassed them constantly and sickness took a severe toll. In February 1624 there were 33 people at Bennett's Welcome, but another 26 had died. By early 1625 only 19 people were living there. In May 1625 an estimated 1,750 acres in Warresqueak had been patented, including the 300 acres claimed and seated by Nathaniel Basse. In 1632 tensions with the Indians began to ease and, within a year, colonists began patenting modest sized tracts in Warresqueak (VCR 1:553-554, 561-562; CJS 2:296, 301; CBE 42, 62; PB 1 Pt. 1:126-128).

Basses Choice (27)

In November 1621 the Virginia Company gave a patent to Nathaniel Basse, Arthur Swayne, and their associates, who intended to transport 100 people to Virginia. The investors received confirmation of their patent in January 1622. When Nathaniel Basse reached Virginia later that year, he established a plantation at a site several miles southeast of Bennett's Welcome (26) and fronting upon the Pagan River. According to Captain John Smith, when the Indians attacked the Basse settlement in March 1622, one house was burned and everyone perished. Nathaniel Basse represented the community of 20 settlers at Basses Choice in the 1624 assembly meeting. By 1625 the population had dwindled to only 12. The list of patented land compiled in May 1625 indicates that the Basse plantation encompassed 300 acres. In 1643 Peter Knight lay claim to 255 acres then known as Basses Choice (CJS 2:296; PB 1 Pt. 1:66; 2:86; VCR 1:561-562, 575; 4:556; CBE 46, 62-63).

Giles Jones's Plantation at Day's Point (28)

On December 14, 1619, Giles Jones received a patent for 150 acres of land in Warresqueak near the acreage of John Day, for whom Day's Point is named. Jones's property, which was at the eastern edge of Warresqueak (Burwell's) Bay, was at the head of what became known as Polentines Swamp. In May 1625 the Jones patent was described as "seated." In early 1625 Giles Jones' wife, Elizabeth, an ancient planter, was living on the east side of the Hampton River on the Virginia Company's land in Elizabeth City (17). As she was identified as a servant in Thomas Dunthorne's house, indebtedness may have forced Mrs. Jones's to seek employment. In October 1628 Giles Jones sold 100 acres of his land in Warresqueak, exclusive of the northernmost 50 acres containing his "late mansion house," to Justinian Cooper, who less than a year later conveyed it to Wassell Weblin and George Fadden. Later the land passed through the hands of Robert Sabine and several others (VCR 4:556; PB 1 Pt. 1:60; Pt. 2:564; 7:417; Isle of Wight Deed Book A:102; MCGC 138).

Nansemond (29)

In late summer 1609 Captain John Smith sent Captain John Martin, George Percy, and 60 other men to a Nansemond River islet now known as Dumpling Island, hoping to relieve the food shortages at Jamestown (**1**). The Indians attacked the colonists and eventually the survivors returned to Jamestown. A substantial Native presence in the region discouraged colonists from returning to the area until the 1630s. By 1636 Dumpling Island was surrounded by patented land. Among the early patentees along the Nansemond River were Richard Bennett, Francis Bullock, Francis Hough, John Parrott, Thomas Burbage, and John Wilkins. In April 1644 when a second major Indian attack occurred, settlers living on the lower side of the James River were especially hard hit. Retaliatory raids were undertaken against the Nansemond Indians and by 1648 so many colonists were living in the Natives' territory that it was subdivided into three parishes (CJS 2:103, 178-179, 220-221; PB 1 Pt. 1:126, 170, 186, 193-195, 233, 305, 362; HEN 1:315, 323, 326-327; NUG 1:42, 174).

CHARLES RIVER (YORK)

In 1607 when Captain Christopher Newport and his men explored the York River and its major tributaries, they took note of the numerous Indian villages along the shore. Later, when Captain John Smith prepared his well known map of Virginia, he indicated that the Chiskiack Indians' village was located on the west side of the mouth of Chiskiack (later, Indian Field) Creek. The Chiskiacks' territory extended eastward along the south side of the York River, probably meeting that of the Kecoughtan Indians. After the March 1622 Indian attack, the Chiskiacks, like other Natives in the Powhatan Chiefdom, were subjected to the retaliatory raids the colonists undertook in an attempt to drive them from their homeland. Undoubtedly, the Chiskiacks' presence, to the north of Jamestown (**1**) and Martin's Hundred (**7**), made the colonists uneasy. In 1624 Virginia's governing officials considered building a palisade from Martin's Hundred to Chiskiack, but no action was taken. They revisited the issue in 1627, but again nothing was done. Finally, in 1630 an earnest effort was made to colonize the territory known as Chiskiack. In 1633 work commenced on the construction of a palisade between the heads of Archer's Hope (College) and Queens Creeks, and land was offered to those establishing homesteads in the Chiskiacks' territory on the York River frontier. The Chiskiack Indians probably withdrew to the Middle Peninsula around the time Captains John Uty, Robert Felgate, John West, and others moved into the region and began establishing their plantations. Soon, settlers flocked into the newly opened territory. In 1634 when the Virginia colony was subdivided into eight shires or counties, Charles River County was formed from the land bordering the York River, from the New Poquoson River (by 1670 known as the Poquoson) on the east, westward to the limits of the colony. Included were the plantations of Chiskiack and York and those on the west side of the New Poquoson River. In 1634 the newly formed county had a population of 510 men, women, and children. In 1636 the name of Charles River County was changed to York County (PB 1 Pt. 1:369; CO 8/55 f 155).

Kings Creek Plantation (30)

On October 8, 1630, Captain John Uty received a patent for 1,250 acres, half of which was an award for seating at Chiskiack. Uty's patent fronted upon the York River and extended from the mouth of Queens Creek eastward to what became known as Utimaria Point, at the mouth of Kings Creek. In April 1640, Colonel William Tayloe (Taylor) bought a 1,200-acre tract from John Uty II, son and heir of the original patentee. Tayloe disposed of part of the Uty tract but bequeathed the remainder to his wife, the former Elizabeth Kingsmill, who wed Colonel Nathaniel Bacon (PB 1 Pt. 1:174; Pt. 2:569, 717; York County Deeds, Orders, Wills 1:71, 153; 9:113).

Ringfield (31)

On December 7, 1630, Captain Robert Felgate received a court order entitling him to land in Chiskiack. Less than two years later he obtained a 350-acre patent for acreage that fronted upon the York River and abutted west upon Kings Creek. Meanwhile, Captain Tobye (Tobias) Felgate, also a mariner, patented 150 acres in Chiskiack, acreage that reportedly abutted east upon the land of his brother, Robert. The Felgate brothers' patents formed the core of what became known as the Ringfield plantation. In time, Robert Felgate accumulated 1,000 acres in that vicinity. The eastern branch of Kings Creek, which became known as Felgates Creek, bears their name (PB 1 Pt. 1:104; Pt. 2:475, 569, 714).

The Indian Field Plantation (32)

On October 8, 1630, Captain John West, one of the first adventurers to seat land at Chiskiack, received a patent for 600 acres. His land extended in an easterly direction from the mouth of Kings Creek's easternmost branch (Felgates Creek, formerly known as West's Creek) along the York River to a point just west of Morgan's Creek, which separated it from Captain Francis Morgan's plantation. In 1632 Captain John West was awarded 2,000 acres of land for having fathered "the first born Christian at Chiscaysck." It is uncertain where West's dwelling was located within his original 600-acre patent. He may have established a home near the mouth of Indian Field Creek in an area previously cleared by the Chiskiack Indians, or he may have settled near his neighbor, Captain Robert Felgate. In September 1650 West sold his 1,250-acre plantation at Chiskiack to Edward Digges I, whose successors called the property Bellefield (PB 1 Pt. 2:475; PB 2:316; MCGC 11, 279, 479, 481; VCR 3:89, 335-336).

Francis Morgan's Plantation (33)

In 1637 Captain Francis Morgan obtained a patent for 100 acres of land that extended from the eastern limits of Captain John West's property at Morgan's Creek, downstream to the small dammed York River tributary now known as Bracken's Pond, in Morgan's day called Prior's Creek. In 1638 Francis Morgan patented an additional 100 acres. He was among the first to settle in the territory known as Chiskiack (PB 1 Pt. 2:484, 591).

William Prior's Plantation (34)

In 1636 William Prior (Pryor), who had been in Virginia for at least a decade, received 300 acres on account of his adventure to Chiskiack plus another 300 acres on the basis of headrights. Prior's land, which fronted upon the York River, abutted west upon Prior's Creek, now known as Bracken's Pond, and east upon Townsend's Creek, today known as Ballards Creek. Prior, a successful planter, became a county justice and sometimes hosted court sessions. In 1646 he laid claim to 650 acres of additional land on the basis of headrights. When he died in 1647 he bequeathed his property to his daughters. Later, the Prior tract came into the hands of Thomas Ballard I (PB 1 Pt. 1:223, 427, 447; Pt. 2:591; MCGC 72; EEAC 47; WITH 107-108).

Richard Townsend's Plantation (35)

In 1636 Richard Townsend, who came to Virginia in the *Abigail* in 1620 and was one of Dr. John Pott's former servants at Jamestown (1), acquired 650 acres of land that extended along the banks of the York River between Prior's (Ballards) Creek and Martiau's (Yorktown) Creek. He received 350 acres because of his household's adventure to Chiskiack and another 300 acres on the basis of headrights. Richard Townsend's land descended to his son, Robert, and eventually became the property of Augustine and Mildred Warner (PB 1 Pt. 1:447, Pt. 2:705; MCGC 117).

Martiau's Plantation (36)

In 1630 Captain Nicholas Martiau patented 600 acres on the lower side of the York River, land he was awarded for establishing a homestead in Chiskiack. His property extended eastward from Martiau's (Yorktown) Creek to Sir John Harvey's York Plantation (37), which it adjoined. In 1639 Martiau's patent, which encompassed the site upon which Yorktown was built, was enlarged to 1,300 acres. The Martiau property eventually came into the hands of Benjamin Read, Nicholas Martiau's grandson (PB 1 Pt. 2:709).

York Plantation (37)

Sometime prior to 1639, when Captain Nicholas Martiau patented 1,300 acres on the York River, Sir John Harvey acquired a 750-acre tract that extended eastward to Wormeley Creek. In April 1639 Harvey, who had fallen deeply into debt and become embroiled in political controversy, was ordered to sell his landholdings in accord with a court decree. Although he retained life-rights in the home he occupied at Jamestown (1) and a limited amount of personal property, on May 6, 1640, he was ordered to sell his real estate in York County. On June 14, 1642, Sir John Harvey mortgaged his York Plantation to George Menefie, who sold it to George Ludlow. Ludlow enhanced the size of the tract, amassing 1,452 acres in all (PB 1 Pt. 2:709; 2:51, 74; MCGC 482, 497).

Wormeley Creek (38)

In January 1638 Captain Christopher Wormeley patented 1,420 acres on the east side of what already had become known as Wormeley Creek. By that date, Wormeley was serving as a York County justice and sometimes hosted court sessions. Christopher Wormeley served as the governor of Tortuga from 1632 to 1635 and as Virginia's secretary of state from 1635 to 1639. His daughter, Elizabeth, married Richard Kemp (PB 1 Pt. 2:607; York County Deeds, Orders, Wills 1:37; MCGH 775; WITH 323; MCGC 498).

CHARLES CITY

In 1609, officials of the Virginia Company of London instructed Sir Thomas Gates to establish several new settlements in the upper reaches of the James River, away from the unhealthy marshes of Jamestown. Sir Thomas Dale, who arrived in Virginia in 1611, commenced carrying out the Company's directives, using martial law to exert his will. By Christmas 1613 (Old Style) or January 6, 1614 (New Style), Dale reportedly had established a cluster of settlements he called the New Bermudas or Bermuda Incorporation. These communities, close to the mouth of the Appomattox River, included Bermuda City and Bermuda (Nether) Hundred, Digges Hundred, the Upper Hundred (or Curles), Rochdale Hundred, and West and Shirley Hundred and Island. Sir Thomas Dale divided the main body of planters into three groups: officers, laborers, and farmers. Officers were assigned a leadership role that included military defense, whereas laborers were those who performed routine manual tasks or plied specialized trades, such as carpenters, tailors, smiths, and tanners. Farmers were obliged to till the soil and raise provisions for the community, but were allocated a small plot of ground for their own personal use and excused from public service for 11 months a year, emergencies excepted. Through this means Dale enabled the colonists to reap a reward for their own hard work and provided them with an incentive to succeed. Some of the Bermudas' settlers signed special contracts, agreeing to serve the corporation for three consecutive years. Although Sir Thomas Dale said relatively little about what these settlements actually were like, Ralph Hamor and John Rolfe described them.

The Corporation of Charles City, established by law in 1619, spanned both sides of the James River. On the north, its territory extended in a westerly direction from a point just west of the Chickahominy River's mouth and encompassed West and Shirley Hundred. On the lower side of the James, the Corporation of Charles City ran from Upper Chippokes Creek (on the east) to the mouth of the Appomattox River (on the west). Within the shire or county of Charles City were two publicly-owned tracts of land set aside by the Virginia Company of London. One was the 3,000-acre parcel known as the Company Land. The other was the 100-acre glebe set aside toward the support of the corporation's incumbent clergyman. In 1634 when the colony's four corporations were subdivided to form counties or shires, Charles City County was created. Its boundaries were identical to those of the Corporation of Charles City and encompassed both sides of the James River. In 1634 Charles City County was home to 511 men, women, and children. In 1702 Prince George County was formed from Charles City County's territory on the lower side of the James River (CO 8/55 f 155; HAI 870-872; FER 40).

Bermuda Hundred (Charles Hundred, the Nether Hundred, the Neck of Land in Charles City) (39)

During 1613 Sir Thomas Dale and his men drove the Appomattox Indians from their habitation near the mouth of the river that still bears their name. By January 1614 Dale had established the New Bermudas or Bermuda Incorporation. According to Ralph Hamor, when initial settlement occurred, Dale's men built a two-mile-long palisade across the elongated peninsula that became known as Bermuda Hundred, sometimes called Charles Hundred, the Nether

Hundred, and the Neck of Land in Charles City. The Bermuda Hundred promontory, which now lies within Chesterfield County, is on the west side of the
Appomattox River's mouth. It protrudes deeply into the James River and in-
cludes the low-lying area now known as Turkey Island. Ralph Hamor stated that
Bermuda Hundred's settlers were seated along the riverfront and the palisade.
Although many of the plantations Dale established were abandoned soon after
his May 1616 departure from the colony, Bermuda Hundred endured. According to John Rolfe, the community was home to Sir Thomas Dale and Captain
George Yeardley; the Rev. Alexander Whitaker served as clergyman. In 1616
Bermuda Hundred had 119 inhabitants, some of whom were engaged in making pitch and tar, potash, charcoal, and other useful commodities. By April 1619
the fortifications at Bermuda Hundred were weak and in disrepair.

In March 1620 Bermuda Hundred had 184 residents: 123 men, 30 women,
and 31 children and young people. The population was inflated by refugees
from Captain Christopher Lawne's plantation, who by November 1619 had
moved there to recover their health. Some parcels in Bermuda Hundred had
been assigned to individual landowners by 1620. Samuel Jordan, who later established the plantation called Jordan's Journey **(46)**, received a 50-acre tract on
the riverfront. Abraham Peirsey's plantation, called Peirseys Toile, was on the
west side of the Appomattox River, near Swift's Creek. In March 1622 when an
Indian attack occurred, seven people were killed in the immediate vicinity of
Bermuda Hundred, though perhaps not within the main settlement. Later, the
Natives returned and burned some settlers' abandoned houses. In February 1624
there were 41 people residing in Bermuda Hundred, and a year later the population consisted of 44 individuals who lived in 16 households. Some of these
people may have been living at Abraham Peirsey's plantation. Demographic
records suggest that Bermuda Hundred's population was relatively stable. By
the 1630s new settlers began streaming into the area (FER 40, 138-139; HAI 825-826,
872, 874; CBE 35-36, 53-54; PB1 Pt. 2:467, 525, 557; 2:26-27; 5:483; 8:125).

Bermuda City (Charles City) (40)

In late 1613 when Sir Thomas Dale established the New Bermudas, he seated
a group of colonists on the east side of the Appomattox River's mouth at a site
he called Bermuda City. In time, that area became known as Charles City and,
eventually, City Point. It is uncertain how the community at Charles City fared
after Dale's May 1616 return to England, but in April 1619 when incoming
Governor George Yeardley arrived in Virginia, there reportedly were only "sixe
Houses much decayed" at Charles City. In March 1620 there were 27 men, 7
women, and 3 children or young persons residing at Bermuda City. When the
Indians attacked in March 1622, 10 people were killed at William Farrar's plantation, which was located somewhat inland from Bermuda City and on the east
side of the Appomattox River. Bermuda City is located in Prince George County
(FER 40, 138-139; HAI 825-826, 872, 874; PB 1 Pt. 1:439; AP 80; CJS 2:301).

West and Shirley Hundred and West and Shirley Hundred Island (41)

In late 1613-early 1614 Sir Thomas Dale seated colonists at three sites on the
north side of the James River: Digges Hundred **(43)** (across the James from
Rochdale **[65]**), the Upper Hundred (Curles) **(42)**, and West and Shirley Hundred. All three communities were part of the settlements known as the New

Bermudas. West and Shirley Hundred, which lay directly across the James River from Bermuda Hundred, included the mainland later known as Shirley Plantation and West and Shirley Hundred (now Eppes) Island. West and Shirley Hundred's name is derived from two Virginia Company investors, Sir Thomas West (Lord De La Warr, Virginia's governor from 1610 to 1618) and his father-in-law, Sir Thomas Shirley. Because Lord De La Warr held at least 65 shares of Virginia land and was entitled to 50 acres per share, West and Shirley Hundred probably encompassed at least 3,250 acres. West and Shirley Hundred enveloped the territory between Causey's Care (**45**) (on the east) and Digges Hundred (on the west). Lord De La Warr's land also took in at least part of West and Shirley Hundred Island. According to John Rolfe, in 1616 West and Shirley Hundred was home to 25 people who were employed in the cultivation of tobacco. By 1617 Captain Isaac Madison had begun clearing land on West and Shirley Hundred Island. This sparked a formal protest from the people of Bermuda Hundred who asserted that the island belonged to their corporation. In March 1620 West and Shirley Hundred had an all-male population of 45. Some may have been settlers Sir William Throgmorton sent over in September 1619 to seat Berkeley Hundred. Thomas West, Lord De La Warr, died in 1618 and his widow and sons gradually disposed of his land rights. After Sir Thomas Dale's death in 1619, his widow, Lady Elizabeth, inherited his acreage in Virginia, part of which was located in the eastern end of West and Shirley Hundred Island. In 1640 Lady Elizabeth Dale bequeathed her land and buildings in Shirley Hundred to one of her heirs.

On March 22, 1622, when the Indians attacked the settlers living in the vicinity of West and Shirley Hundred, several people were killed. By February 1624 there were 22 poorly armed people living on Lady Dale's property on West and Shirley Hundred Island who were responsible for guarding a large herd of cattle. In mid-February 1624 there were 45 people living on the mainland at West and Shirley Hundred and 24 on the island. However, a total of 11 people (including an African and two Native Americans) had died in the community since April 1623. In January 1625, there were 61 people (38 men, 10 women, and 13 children) residing at West and Shirley Hundred, then defined as the mainland and the island. At least six male residents had arrived in Virginia in 1609–1610 and therefore were experienced planters. Six of the community's 17 households were nuclear families, three of which were headed by widows. The community had 17 houses and an ample supply of provisions, livestock, and defensive weaponry. The abundance of military equipment may reflect the settlement's being strengthened and held in the wake of the March 1622 Indian attack. It is certain that 16 of the Berkeley Hundred Company's men were placed briefly at Shirley Hundred in the aftermath. Other temporary residents of West and Shirley Hundred were the Truelove Company's people, who arrived in Virginia right after the Indian attack. Violent crime and infractions of ecclesiastical law resulted in several of West and Shirley Hundred's residents being summoned before the General Court, and one man was executed for rape. Collectively, the early court records associated with West and Shirley Hundred reveal that life on the Virginia frontier was stressful and turbulent. The Indians harassed West and Shirley Hundred's inhabitants almost continuously until at least 1627. West and Shirley Hundred and the island are located in Charles City County (FER 40, 138, 139; CJS 2:242; PB 2:78; 3:379; 4:450; 5:635; 6:1438; VCR 3:76; EEAC 17; VCR 3:612; 4:9-12; MCGC 51, 116, 142, 149-151, 153; CBE 36, 52-53; M&D 12-16; HAI 825-826, 870, 874).

The Upper Hundred (Curles) (42)

This area, on the north side of the James River across from Bermuda Hundred (39), was one of the communities included in the New Bermudas. Settlement occurred at the Upper Hundred, in the "curls" of the James River, in 1613. Very little is known about how extensively this plantation was developed or how long it endured after Sir Thomas Dale's May 1616 return to England. In 1619 Edward Gurganay's widow, Ann, bequeathed her late husband's 400 acres, called the Longfield or Curles, to Captain Thomas Harris. Harris's 1636 and 1637 patents for the Gurganay parcel and an additional 300 acres note that the late Edward Gurganay had received his acreage from the Virginia Company in 1617. In 1636 Elizabeth Ballhash, a widow, also patented 450 acres at Curles, in what was then Henrico County. Later, Curles Neck was home to Nathaniel Bacon, who during the mid-1670s led a popular uprising (PB 1 Pt. 1:337, 412, 438).

Digges Hundred (43)

This plantation, like Curles or the Upper Hundred, was one of several that Sir Thomas Dale seated in 1613–1614 and annexed to the New Bermudas. It was located on the north side of the James River, just west of Curles. It is uncertain how long this plantation existed after Sir Thomas Dale's May 1616 departure from Virginia. However, the July 1622 patent issued to Samuel Jordan for some land previously owned by Virginia Company investor Mary Tue suggests strongly that there was ongoing activity at "Digges His Hundred." It is uncertain whether Jordan ever seated his newly patented land. In 1635 Thomas Harris, an ancient planter, patented 750 acres within Digges Hundred. Three years later, Joseph Royal laid claim to 200 acres located there (PB 1 Pt. 1:304; Pt. 2:631; VCR 2:74).

Smith's or Smyth's (Southampton) Hundred (44)

The Society of Smith's (Smyth's) Hundred's members included several high-ranking Virginia Company officials. Governor George Yeardley was a Society investor and its business manager in Virginia. The November 18, 1618, instructions he received as incoming governor required him to seat the Smith's Hundred settlers near the mouth of the Chickahominy River. By that date, the *William and Thomas* already had left England with 150 of the Society's people and in April 1619 Yeardley and some associates brought another 35. By January 1620 the plantation called Smith's Hundred had been established at Dancing Point, where the Chickahominy River meets the James. It extended up the James River toward Westover (54) and encompassed 100,000 acres, wholly within the Corporation of Charles City County. According to one official, the settlers living at Dancing Point were troubled by sickness. Among them were several skilled workers capable of undertaking industrial activities such as brick making, blacksmithing, iron manufacturing, and milling. Plans were made for construction of a church at Smith's Hundred, which in March 1620 was home to 75 men, 8 women, and 22 children or young people.

On May 17, 1620, outgoing Virginia Company treasurer Sir Edwin Sandys informed the Company court that 310 people had been sent to the plantation. By that time, Sir Thomas Smith had surrendered his legal and financial interest in the project to the Earl of Southampton, at which point the plantation became known as Southampton Hundred. Governor George Yeardley had built a "mansion house" at Southampton Hundred sometime prior to spring 1621 when Jeremy Clements had patented some land directly across the James River, on the east side of Upper Chippokes Creek. The March 22, 1622, Indian attack dealt Southampton Hundred a reeling blow. Afterward, the plantation was among those strengthened and held, but the Indians continued to harass the colonists, who ultimately withdrew to a position of greater safety. In 1625 some of the Society of Southampton Hundred's cattle were at Hog Island (**16**), along with some of the plantation's inhabitants. In 1627 when Sir George Yeardley died, his widow was obliged to account for the cattle, land rent, and property that belonged to Southampton Hundred. By the mid-1630s patentees had begun to claim portions of the Society of Southampton Hundred's vast plantation (FER 92, 138-139; VCR 1:287, 347, 350; 3:95-96, 98, 246-247, 433, 612, 652-653; 4:94, 482; PB 1 Pt. 1:124; MCGC 17, 55, 74, 167).

Causey's Care (Cleare) (45)

Nathaniel Causey, who came to Virginia in 1608 in the 1st Supply of new settlers, by December 1620 had received a patent for 200 acres on the upper side of the James River. The property, variously known as Causey's Care or Causey's Cleare, lay just east of West and Shirley Hundred (**41**), behind the eastern end of Eppes Island. The Causey land abutted east upon the Virginia Company's 3,000-acre tract of Company Land (**62**) in Charles City and south upon what became Eppes Creek, which flows behind Eppes Island. Thus, the plantation was somewhat set back from the James River. Nathaniel Causey and his wife were "ancient planters." In March 1622 when the Indians attacked, he was seriously wounded but managed to defend his homestead and ultimately the Indians fled. In February 1624 the Causey couple was living across the river at Jordan's Journey (**46**), one of the settlements strengthened and held after the Native assault. The Causeys were still there in 1625, but probably secured their land claim by placing some of their servants at Causey's Care. It descended to their heir, John Causey, who in 1634 sold it to Walter Aston I, owner and occupant of some contiguous property. After Aston expanded his holdings, he called his enlarged plantation Causey's Care. The tract descended to his son, Walter Aston II, and widow, Hannah, who married Edward Hill of Shirley (**41**) (PB 1 Pt. 2:578; PB 2:12, 78).

Jordan's Journey (Beggars Bush) (46)

Jordan's Journey was located on a wedge-shaped peninsula between Jenny and Billy Creeks, on the lower side of the James River. The plantation's name is derived from its founder, Samuel Jordan, an ancient planter whose patent encompassed a 450-acre tract that in May 1625 was described as "planted" or seated. Earlier on, Samuel Jordan owned a plot of ground at Bermuda Hundred (**39**), whose inhabitants he represented in the colony's 1619 assembly meeting. In 1622 he acquired 100 acres in Digges Hundred (**43**). After the March 1622 Indian attack, Jordan's Journey was one of the settlements fortified and held. Samuel Jordan died before April 1623. Shortly thereafter, his widow, Ciseley, became involved with Captain William Farrar, who vacated his own plantation on the east side of the Appomattox River and moved to Jordan's Journey. In 1624 there were 42 people living at Jordan's Journey and by 1625 the population consisted of 55 people: 36 males and 19 females. The community, which reportedly had 22 buildings, was well supplied with provisions and military equipment. By May 1625 Ciseley Jordan had married William Farrar. Although Samuel and Ciseley Jordan's heirs seem to have retained legal possession of Jordan's Journey during the 1630s and 1640s, by the 1650s the property had come into the possession of Benjamin and Mary Siddway, who in 1657 conveyed it to John and Theodorick Bland. Today, Jordan's Journey lies in Prince George County (PB 1 Pt. 2:467, 580; 8:125; VCR 2:74; 3:154; 4:554; CJS 2:303; CBE 36-37, 51-52; Surry County Records 1652-1663:107).

Swinehowe's Plantation (47)

Thomas Swinhow came to Virginia on the *Diana* sometime prior to 1621 and established a plantation on the north side of the James River. Although his original patent has been lost, in May 1625 he was credited with 300 acres in the Corporation of Charles City, but the acreage does not appear to have been seated (developed). Subsequent land transactions indicate that Swinhow's property was located between Buckland and Queens Creeks. From the seventeenth century on, that area was known as Swinehows (Swyneards, Swiniares, Swineherds, Swineyards), and in the 1660s Queens Creek was called Swinhows Creek. In March 1622 when the Swinhow plantation was attacked by Indians, Thomas Swinhow's wife, two sons, and four servants were killed. Thomas Swinhow abandoned his property and in 1624 and 1625 he and one of his servants were living upon the Governor's Land (3) in James City. By March 27, 1626, Thomas Swinhow was dead. When he made his will, disposing of his personal effects, he made no reference to the plantation he had attempted to establish, thereby suggesting that he had vacated his claim. By 1633 William Perry had acquired a 2,000-acre tract (Buckland) that included the acreage formerly belonging to Thomas Swinhow (VCR 2:88; 3:568; 4:257; HEN 1:472; 3:58, 470, 553; 6:176; PB 1 Pt. 2:510; CBE 39, 57; MCGC 98-99, 103).

Maycock's (Macock's) Plantation (48)

Samuel Maycock (Macock), who came to Virginia around 1618, was a Cambridge University scholar and highly respected man who in 1619 was named to the Council of State. Although he was living at Bermuda Hundred (39) in late 1620, he appears to have established his own plantation during 1621. Maycock's settlement was located on the lower side of the James River, on the east side of Powell's Creek's mouth, to the west of Flowerdew Hundred (53). On March 22, 1622, when the Indians attacked the Maycock settlement, four people were killed, including Samuel Maycock. In May 1625 when a list of patented land was sent to England, "Macocks Divident" in the Corporation of Charles City was included, but no quantity of acreage was listed. Samuel Maycock's daughter, Sara, inherited his property and in May 1626 received 200 acres of land on account of the four servants her late father transported to Virginia in 1622. In August 1650 George Pace, son of the late Richard Pace of Paces Paines (9), patented 1,700 acres called "Matocks" (Maycock's) on the south side of the James River, between the east side of Powell's Creek's mouth and a small creek that separated it from Flowerdew Hundred. As George Pace had married Samuel Maycock's daughter, Sara, the plantation she inherited from her late father came into his hands. Today, the Maycock plantation lies within the boundaries of Prince George County (VCR 3:92, 118-119, 482, 555, 568; 4:554; CJS 2:266, 301; PB 2:252; MCGC 102; Charles City County Court Orders 1655-1665:179).

Captain John Woodlief's Plantation (49)

In June 1619 John Woodlief (Woodliffe), a merchant and gentleman, asked the Virginia Company for a patent. He said that he had invested in the Company in 1608 and had lived in Virginia for 11 years. Woodlief indicated that he and his associates intended to seat 200 people upon their land within six years. When Company officials approved John Woodlief's request in July 1619, they stipulated that the patent was to be listed under the name of Sir Thomas Wainman and associates. Woodlief invested in Berkeley Hundred (55) and in September 1619 took a group of settlers there. He was placed in command of the plantation and served for approximately a year, while pursuing his own financial interests. The Society of Berkeley Hundred's investors warned Woodlief not to seat his people within ten miles of their settlement. He heeded their orders and by December 1620 Woodlief was in possession of some land on the south side of the James River a considerable distance from Berkeley Hundred. In May 1625 John Woodlief was credited with 350 acres of unplanted land within the Corporation of Charles City. His plantation was located just west of Jordan's Journey (46) from which it was separated by Billy Creek. The Woodlief property was situated within today's Prince George County. (PB 1 Pt. 2:467, 580, 788; 8:125; CJS 2:268; VCR 1:232, 252; 3:188, 193-195, 197, 207, 248-249; 4:554).

Powle-Brooke or Merchants Hope (50)

Captain Nathaniel Powell, who came to Virginia in 1607, served as acting governor between the time of Deputy Governor Samuel Argall's April 2, 1619, departure and Governor George Yeardley's April 19, 1619, arrival. The Powell plantation, known as Powle-Brooke, was seated around 1619. It was located midway between Chappell and Powell Creeks, on the lower side of the James River. Powle-Brooke encompassed 600 acres and was located deep within the mouth of Bikars (Tar) Bay. It was just east of William Bikers' plantation, which was situated upon a point of land on the east side of Chappell Creek's mouth. In March 1622 when the Indians attempted to drive the Virginia colonists from their soil, Captain Nathaniel Powell and his wife, Joyce, daughter of William Tracy of Berkeley Hundred (55), were brutally slain at their plantation as were ten other settlers. Captain Powell's brother, Thomas, of Suffolk, England, inherited the property and sold it to a group of investors, who acquired some additional land that extended in an easterly direction to Powell Creek. The enlarged plantation, which became known as Merchants Hope, encompassed 1,850 acres. Today, Powle-Brooke or Merchants Hope is located in Prince George County (PB 1 Pt. 1:151, 320; Pt. 2:609; CJS 2:302; VCR 3:555, 569).

Captain Henry Spellman's Dividend (51)

Henry Spellman or Spillman, who came to Virginia as a youth in 1609, lived with the Indians and in time became the colony's most skillful interpreter. Although he attained the rank of captain, in 1619 he was stripped of his status on account of making unfavorable comments about Governor George Yeardley. Sometime prior to the March 1622 Indian attack, Henry Spellman established a plantation that abutted the west side of Ward's Creek and extended up the James River toward Flowerdew Hundred. When the Indians descended upon Spellman's settlement, at least two men were slain. According to Captain John

Smith, seven people lost their lives there. Henry Spellman was away at the time and escaped harm, but he was killed by the Anacostan Indians in 1623, while on a trading voyage to the Potomac River. The Spellman plantation, though abandoned, was included in the May 1625 land list. However, the amount of acreage Spellman had owned was left blank. Henry Spellman's land was included in a 2,000-acre tract that Captain Francis Hooke patented in 1634 (PB 1 Pt. 2:485; VCR 3:569; CJS 2:302).

Weyanoke (Tanks or Tanx Weyanoke) (52)

In 1617 the Native chief Opechancanough presented Captain George Yeardley with a large tract of land known as Tanks (Tanx or Little) Weyanoke, located upon the north side of the James River. It encompassed a large, roughly triangular peninsula still known as Weyanoke. A year later, the Virginia Company gave Yeardley a legally binding title to Weyanoke, which encompassed 2,200 acres. Simultaneously, he acquired 1,000 acres on the lower side of the James at Tobacco Point, where he established the plantation called Flowerdew Hundred (53). Documentary sources suggest that Yeardley seated some of his people at Weyanoke before he had secured the Virginia Company's official approval. Shortly after Governor George Yeardley's April 1619 arrival in Virginia, he placed some of his indentured servants upon his Weyanoke property. In March 1622 when the Indians attacked Weyanoke, 21 people were killed. In October 1624, Yeardley sold Weyanoke and Flowerdew Hundred to Abraham Peirsey. By 1636 Peirsey's properties had descended to his daughters. By the late 1630s, portions of Weyanoke had come into the hands of Joseph Harwood, David Jones, and others. Weyanoke is located in Charles City County (VCR 1:229; 3:103, 162, 301; CBE 37, 50-51; MCGC 157; FER 138-139; PB 1 Pt. 1:395; Pt. 2:484; 5:434-435).

Flowerdew (Peirsey's) Hundred (53)

Late in 1618 Sir George Yeardley acquired 1,000 acres on the lower side of the James at Tobacco Point, a triangular landform that protrudes northward into the James River just west of Weyanoke (52). Yeardley and his wife, the former Temperance Flowerdew, set sail for Virginia in the *Diana* in January 1619 and arrived on April 19th. Afterward, Yeardley established the settlement known as Flowerdew Hundred. In July 1619 Edmund Rossingham, Lady Temperance Yeardley's nephew, served as one of the community's delegates to the assembly. In March 1620 there were 68 men, 5 women, and 4 children or young people at Flowerdew Hundred. During the March 1622 Indian attack, six people reportedly were killed there. In February 1624 the settlement had a population of 63, including 11 Africans. The following October the Yeardleys sold Flowerdew to cape merchant Abraham Peirsey. By the time a muster was made in early 1625, the plantation was known as Peirsey's Hundred and was home to 57 people who had use of a dozen houses, three storehouses, four tobacco houses, and a windmill. The settlement also was strongly fortified against a potential Indian attack. After Abraham Peirsey's death, Flowerdew Hundred and Weyanoke descended to his daughters as co-heirs. In 1636 daughter Elizabeth Stephens repatented Flowerdew Hundred, noting that it was part of her inheritance. Flowerdew Hundred is in Prince George County (VCR 1:229; 3:103, 162, 301; CBE 37, 50-51; MCGC 157; FER 138, 139; PB 1 Pt. 1:395; Pt. 2:484).

Westover (54)

Around 1619 Captain Francis West appears to have laid out a plantation he called Westover. Although no colonists seem to have been seated there in March 1620 when demographic records were compiled, Governor George Yeardley's January 1620 reference to the West property suggests that he was acknowledging the validity of the late Lord De La Warr's land claim despite its uncertain boundaries. On March 22, 1622, the Indians attacked the plantations established by John West, Captain Francis West, and Captain Nathaniel West, the late Lord De La Warr's brothers. Two people were killed at each of the West brothers' plantations, which were collectively known as Westover. Lieutenant John Gibbs' dividend, part of the same community, also came under attack. The nearby plantations of Owen Macar and Richard Owen appear to have been part of Westover. In May 1625 Captain Francis West was credited with 500 acres that were "planted." This raises the possibility that he reoccupied his property after the Indian assault, although his brothers may have failed to do so (FER 138-139; VCR 3:567-568; 4:554; CJS 2:301).

Berkeley Hundred (55)

Richard Berkeley, Sir William Throgmorton, and their associates, who intended to establish a plantation called Berkeley Hundred, outfitted 50 men and sent them to Virginia in the Bristol ship *Margaret*. They left England on September 16, 1619, and arrived at Old Point Comfort on November 30. The group of 35-45 people, who were under the command of Captain John Woodlief, included several artisans outfitted with the tools of their trade. Within a month of their arrival, the Berkeley Hundred colonists set out for the land they were supposed to seat. It was on the north side of the James above Westover (54) but below West and Shirley Hundred (41), in the immediate vicinity of the plantation still known as Berkeley. When the settlers reached their destination, they gave thanks for their safe arrival and promised to observe an annual day of thanksgiving; it was America's first. Captain John Woodlief, as commander of Berkeley Hundred, was given instructions on the types of houses the colonists were supposed to build and he was ordered to see that 400 acres of grazing land were enclosed with a palisade. During 1620 there was a change in Berkeley Hundred's leadership, for William Tracy was assigned Sir William Throgmorton's interest in the plantation and he and George Thorpe set out for Virginia with some additional settlers and supplies. Berkeley was well established by the time of the Indians' March 1622 attack, at which time 11 people were killed. The survivors were evacuated to safety and 16 men were briefly placed at West and Shirley Hundred Island. In 1624 and 1625 when demographic records were compiled, there was no mention of settlers living at Berkeley Hundred, which had been abandoned. Official records indicate that the cattle belonging to the Society of Berkeley Hundred were kept at Flowerdew (53) and at Shirley Hundred (VCR 1:311; 3:110, 114-115, 136, 190, 212, 230, 247-248, 385-393; 3:248-249; MCGC 11, 43, 134).

Chaplin's Choice (56)

Isaac Chaplin, an ancient planter, sent 40 people to the colony. They left England in September 1619 and arrived in Virginia in November. By February 1624 Chaplin and 23 others were living at his plantation, Chaplins Choice, which was located on the west side of Tar Bay, between Chappell and Bickers Creeks, in what is now Prince George County. In May 1625 Isaac Chaplin was credited with 200 acres of land in "the Territory of Greate Weyanoke," land that was described as "planted." In February 1624 when demographic records were compiled, there were 24 people at Chaplin's Choice, but by early 1625 there were only 17 settlers living there, some of whom were members of Truelove's Company. In 1625 the colonists at Chaplin's Choice occupied two houses and reportedly had a fort. They also were relatively well provisioned and supplied with military equipment. By 1640 some of the land called Chaplin's had come into the hands of Richard Williams (VCR 1:345, 351-352; 4:402; CBE 37, 51; FER 138, 139; PB 1 Pt. 1:151; Pt. 2:475, 579, 781).

William Bikar's Plantation (57)

Very little is known about the plantation established by William Bikar or Bykar, except that it was located on a small point of land on the east side of Chappell Creek's mouth, overlooking what became known as Bikars or Tar Bay. On March 22, 1622, when the Indians attacked the settlers living along the James River, William Bikar and four others were slain at his house. Bikar's property, which appears to have been abandoned after the massacre, abutted east upon Captain Nathaniel Powell's plantation, which in 1637 was encompassed by William Barker's 600-acre patent that eventually became part of Merchants Hope **(50)** (VCR 3:568; PB 1 Pt. 1:151; Pt. 2:475, 837).

Truelove's Plantation (58)

Early in 1621 London cloth worker Rowland Truelove received a patent for some land. He and his associates made plans to bring 100 settlers to Virginia. Despite the March 1622 Indian attack, Truelove and his group resolved to proceed with establishing their plantation. Their patent, which was acquired with some land rights obtained from Lady De La Warr, was renewed in 1623. Rowland Truelove and his fellow investors agreed to supply their plantation with food, clothing, and other necessities. During summer 1623, they outfitted 25 new immigrants and sent them to Virginia. The settlement apparently never became successful, for in January 1624 Nathaniel Causey, owner of Causey's Care **(45)**, was ordered by the General Court to take custody of the goods belonging to the Truelove plantation. In 1625, when a muster was taken of the colony's inhabitants, the surviving settlers associated with the Truelove plantation were living at Chaplain's Choice **(56)**, which was nearby (CBE 37, 51, 79; VCR 1:523, 534, 553-554, 561-562; 2:93; 3:643).

Captain John Martin's Plantation (Martin's Brandon) (59)

In January 1618 Captain John Martin, a Virginia Company member and one of the first colonists, received a patent for a large tract of land on the lower side of the James River, between Ward's and Upper Chippokes Creeks. His acreage was in the immediate vicinity of the eighteenth-century plantation known as Upper Brandon, in Prince George County. Martin arrived in Virginia in May 1618 and established the plantation known as Martin's Brandon. Martin's original patent entitled him to privileges that were unprecedented in the Virginia colony. Martin formed a business partnership with Captain John Bargrave, who also was entitled to shares of Virginia land. In April 1619, when Sir George

Yeardley arrived in Virginia as governor, Martin's Brandon was one of the eight plantations then in existence. In July 1619, when the colony's first assembly convened, Captain John Martin's settlement was refused representation because his land title was thought to convey immunity to the colony's laws. Therefore, Martin was told that he had to relinquish his patent if his plantation's representatives were to have a seat and voice in the assembly. Although Captain Martin tried to retain his original patent, ultimately he accepted a new one and retained Martin's Brandon. In March 1620, Captain Martin's plantation reportedly had 21 inhabitants, one of whom was a woman. Martin left for England in spring 1621, entrusting his plantation to the care of Lieutenant Edward Saunders. On March 22, 1622, when the Indians attacked, six men and a woman were slain at Martin's Brandon. The plantation may have been abandoned for a time, but in May 1625 when a list of patents was sent back to England, Captain John Martin was credited with 100 acres called Martin's Brandon, land that had been seated. Martin was outspoken and controversial and sometimes voiced opinions that led to his being summoned to court. In 1625 several prominent people accused him of being a liar. For instance, he was said to have spread rumors in England that the houses at Jamestown (1) were daubed with gold. One witness against Martin claimed that he had said that his house at Martin's Brandon was quite grand and had a crystal mantle, whereas it really was a crude blockhouse with two small windows. Captain Martin weathered the controversy and continued to seat new settlers upon his property, sometimes leasing parcels to tenants, and until at least 1627 he took an active role in management of his property. In March 1636 a colonist named Simon Sturges (or Turges) and two London merchants patented Martin's Brandon, which they had purchased from Captain Robert Bargrave. The tract then extended from Upper Chippokes Creek to Ward's Creek and took in 4,550 acres. Jeremy Clements' patent was located at the mouth of Upper Chippokes Creek (FER 138, 571; AP 73, 80; CBE 75; VCR 3:162-163, 599; PB 1 Pt. 1:415; Pt. 2:549, 910).

Captain John Bargrave's Plantation (60)

On May 12, 1619, Captain John Bargrave's pinnace, the *Edwin,* arrived in Virginia with men he planned to seat upon his land on the lower side of the James River, near Captain John Martin's plantation. Bargrave's settlement was not represented in the assembly meetings held between July 30 and August 4, 1619, although its existence was acknowledged. In March 1620 Captain John Bargrave's plantation was home to 37 men. Bargrave and his associates received a patent for their land on May 17, 1620. By 1621 he had become embroiled in a dispute with his volatile neighbor, Captain John Martin, and he began making many complaints about the Virginia Company. Company officials retaliated by claiming that Bargrave's patent was invalid. Later, he claimed that he had suffered financial ruin because of his work on behalf of the colony. John Bargrave's land eventually became part of Martin's Brandon (VCR 1:309, 312, 347; 3:118, 242, 444, 517-520, 608; 4:95; CJS 2:266; PB 8:125, 415; CBE 48).

Captain John Ward's Plantation (61)

Captain John Ward's ship, the *Sampson,* arrived in Virginia in April 1619 with 50 settlers. They were headed for the Corporation of Charles City, where Ward and his associates intended to establish a plantation. Ward's land was located just west of Martin's Brandon (59) and abutted west upon what became known as Ward's Creek. John Rolfe indicated that in May 1619 Ward went north on a fishing voyage but returned around the end of July. Lieutenant John Gibbs and Captain John Ward represented the Ward plantation in the July–August 1619 assembly meetings, although Ward then lacked a formal commission. Mariner and cartographer Thomas Dermer stayed at Captain John Ward's plantation during November and December 1619 while repairing his ship. According to John Rolfe, Ward returned from a trading voyage to the Potomac River at the end of December 1619. In March 1620 Captain John Ward's plantation had a population of 26 men. Ward and his fellow investors received a patent for their acreage on May 17, 1620. He rented his plantation and indentured servants to Captain William Eppes sometime prior to the March 22, 1622, Indian attack. After Eppes evacuated the servants to safety, the Indians returned and put the plantation's buildings to the torch. In March 1636 a colonist named Simon Sturges (or Turges) and two London merchants patented the 4,550 acres that became known as Martin's Brandon. The tract then extended from Upper Chippokes Creek to Ward's Creek, taking in Captain John Ward's land (VCR 1:347; 3:94, 118, 242, 247; 4:95; CJS 2:266; PB 1 Pt. 1:338, 415; Pt. 2:485, 549, 910; FER 138-139; MCGC 138-139).

The Company Land in Charles City (62)

Within the Corporation of Charles City, the Virginia Company's 3,000-acre tract of Company Land was located on the upper side of the James River just east of Shirley Hundred (Eppes) Island. If the tract extended inland for a mile, as early riverfront patents usually did, the Company Land in Charles City would have run from the east side of Eppes Creek to the west side of Kimoges Creek. In June 1620 Virginia Company officials indicated that they intended to send 100 new tenants to the Company Land in each corporation. It is uncertain how extensively the Company Land in Charles City was developed. However, in December 1620 Captain Roger Smith asked Company officials to place him in charge of its tenants. On March 22, 1622, when the Indians attacked, several members of Captain Smith's group in Charles City were killed. Afterward, he was briefly given command of the people in the Corporation of Charles City. By 1635 a settler named Hugh Cox was in possession of 500 acres that comprised the westernmost part of the Company Land (VCR 1:433-434; 3:101, 245, 313, 566, 609; 4:554; PB 1 Pt 1:282; 2:78; CJS 2:301).

HENRICO

Toward the close of 1611, Sir Thomas Dale established several settlements near the head of the James River. Having laid out a cluster of communities he called the New Bermudas, he moved upstream and established another group of settlements. In 1614 there were 38 men and boys within the territory called Henrico, which included four small communities. The city of Henrico or Henricus was situated on the upper side of the James River, on a small peninsula now known as Farrar Island. Three miles to the west another group of colonists was seated at Arrohattock, the former site of a Powhatan Indian village. On the lower side of the James River, opposite Henricus, was Hope in Faith or Coxendale. To the east was Rochdale (Rochen Dale), which encompassed Jones Neck and the land abutting Rochdale Creek. According to an account written by a group of ancient planters, when Sir Thomas Dale left Virginia in May 1616, many of the settlements he had established had gone to ruin.

In 1619 Governor George Yeardley, in accord with his instructions, had the colony subdivided into four corporations. It was then that the Corporation of Henrico, which spanned both sides of the James River, was established. It extended from the Appomattox River (on the east) westward to the limits of the colony and included the settlements Sir Thomas Dale had established in that area. Within the Corporation of Henrico were three tracts of publicly-owned land that had been set aside by the Virginia Company of London. One parcel was the 3,000-acre tract known as the Company Land. Another was the 100-acre glebe assigned to the incumbent clergyman. The third consisted of 10,000 acres set aside toward the support of a College and University. That parcel, which was located on the upper side of the James River, encompassed the sites that Sir Thomas Dale originally developed as the city of Henrico and Arrohattock. On November 15, 1619, 25 Virginia Company servants were taken up to Arrohattock, and the settlers Deputy Governor Samuel Argall (1617–1618) had authorized to seat there were ordered to move. In March 1620 there were 103 people in the communities collectively known as Henrico: 77 men, 9 women, and 17 children or young people. In March 1622 when the Indians attacked the settlers living near the head of the James River, many people were slain. Although the area was reoccupied, in January 1625 only 22 people were living there, occupying the College land, which included Arrohattock. In 1634 when the Virginia colony was divided into eight shires or counties, Henrico's territory spanned the James River and included the land from Arrohattock down to (but not including) Shirley Hundred (Eppes) Island. At that time the area had a population of 419 (FER 40, 138-139; CJS 2:242-247; PB 1:69, 326, 351, 436, 519, 836; VCR 1:226, 234, 268; 3:101-102, 226-227, 229, 245, 262, 264; CO 8/55 f 155; HAI 761, 763, 765, 824-825, 870, 872).

City of Henrico (Henricus Island) (63)

In September 1611 Sir Thomas Dale reached a high, narrow-necked peninsula that jutted southward into the James River. There, he decided to establish a new settlement he called Henrico. Dale had his men build a palisade across the neck of the peninsula, isolating it from the mainland, and he had them enclose seven acres for livestock. According to Ralph Hamor's 1614 narrative, the City of Henrico had three streets, a handsome church, good houses, some storehouses, watchtowers, and five blockhouses. In 1616, when Dale left the colony, John Rolfe reported that there were 38 men and boys at Henrico, 22 of whom were farmers. By 1619 the City of Henrico had fallen into disrepair and only a few deteriorated buildings survived. Around that time it became part of the College (66) tract. Some of the sites first seated by Sir Thomas Dale's men were opened to private use soon after his departure. For instance, John Laydon obtained 100 acres in Henrico Island and Coxendale in 1619 or 1620. In March 1622 when the Indians attacked the settlements along the James River, 17 people were slain on the College property, probably at Arrohattock. In 1628 Laydon exchanged his property for some land at Blunt Point (22) because "of the great danger of planting" in his original location. Nearly a decade later, William Farrar II, the son and heir of William Farrar I of Jordan's Point (46), patented a 2,000-acre tract that included Henrico (now Farrar) Island. During 1864 the Union Army tried to cut a channel through the neck of the Farrar Island peninsula. The dredging of this ditch was completed in 1871–1872, effectively separating the "island" from the mainland. Today, Farrar's Island lies in Chesterfield County (HAI 761, 765, 824-825; AP 50, 69, 74-75; VCR 3:566; PB 1 Pt 1:69, 436).

Coxendale (64)

In 1613 Sir Thomas Dale established a settlement he called "Hope in Faith" or Coxendale, a large expanse of land on the lower side of the James River across from the City of Henrico. He secured the acreage with a line of four forts (Charity, Elizabeth, Patience, and Mount Malado), placing them under the command of Captain James Davis, and he built a retreat or guesthouse for the sick. The Rev. Alexander Whitaker selected a portion of Coxendale as his glebe and built a parsonage there, calling it Rocke Hall. Coxendale, like the City of Henrico, was opened to private settlement shortly after Sir Thomas Dale left Virginia. By early 1619 or 1620 ancient planter John Laydon had obtained a patent for 100 acres of land in both locations, although he relinquished his land in 1628. In April 1619 when Governor George Yeardley arrived in the colony, Coxendale was still considered a viable community. Yeardley gave Thomas Read a 100-acre patent in Coxendale, acreage that included Mount Malado (Mount My Lady), in recognition for his service to the colony. In July 1622 Read conveyed his property to merchant Edward Hurd. In the wake of the March 1622 Indian attack, those who lived in the City of Henrico and Coxendale were ordered to withdraw to a position of greater safety. Among those who had servants at Coxendale at the time of the assault was Lady Elizabeth Dale, who had inherited her late husband's interest to his Virginia land. In May 1625 when a list of patented land was sent back to England, eight parcels, totaling 802 acres, were attributed to Coxendale; none was then seated. Coxendale is located in Chesterfield County (PB 1 Pt 1:69; HAI 765, 778-779, 825-827; VCR 2:91; 3:565-566; 4:552; GEN 2:51).

Rochdale (Roxdale) Hundred (65)

Just west of Bermuda Hundred and on the south side of the James River was Rochdale Hundred, a settlement established by Sir Thomas Dale around 1613–1614. A four-mile-long palisade enclosed Rochdale Hundred, which was vast in size and intended as pasturage for livestock. Although the area probably was abandoned shortly after Sir Thomas Dale's 1616 return to England, in 1623 Sir John Zouch I received a patent for some acreage in Rochdale Hundred and made elaborate plans to build an ironworks. He sold Codnor Castle in Derbyshire, England, and around 1634 moved his son, John II, and his daughter, Isabella, to Virginia. Although he invested heavily in his plantation and the ironworks project, his efforts proved unsuccessful. In August 1636 when Sir John Zouch made his will, he left his Virginia land to his son, John Zouch II. He noted that he had invested £1,200 in his plantation and that his partners had failed to provide the necessary support. John Zouch I died in 1639 and his land eventually escheated to the Crown. Zouch's Rochdale Hundred property, which now lies in Chesterfield County, eventually came into the hands of William Byrd I. By the eighteenth century Rochdale Creek had become a well known local landmark (HAI 825-827; CJS 2:242; VCR 3:339; 4:221; PB 1: Pt 2:567, 839; 6:84; 7:127; Henrico County Deeds and Wills 1677–1692:36-37, 156, 202; 1725–1737:134; WITH 67-68; SR 3987).

College Land and Arrohattock (Sir Thomas Smith's Hundred) (66)

In 1613 when Sir Thomas Dale planted settlements at Henricus Island **(63)** and Coxendale **(64)**, he indicated that he hoped to impale Arrohattock, a site he intended to call Sir Thomas Smith's Hundred. Arrohattock, like Bermuda Hundred, had been the site of an Indian village in 1607, when the first colonists arrived. When Governor George Yeardley reached Virginia in April 1619, he brought orders to lay out 10,000 acres on the north side of the James River, between the falls and the City of Henrico, land that was to be used toward the support of a College and University. Part of this vast tract included Arrohattock, which is located in a bend of the James River. In early August 1619 the Virginia Company sent 100 male servants and tenants to Virginia on the *Bona Nova*. Half were supposed to be assigned to the College land in Henrico. However, because the ship arrived in the dead of winter, and the newcomers were inexperienced at living in a wilderness environment, only 25 Company men were sent to the College property. The remaining 25 were hired out to established planters, as were the residual 50. When William Weldon and the Virginia Company's men arrived at Arrohattock, they discovered that Captain Samuel Mathews and Thomas Dowse already were seated there on land that had been granted to them by Deputy Governor Samuel Argall (1617–1618). Weldon left the College men with Mathews, who shortly thereafter was ordered to move.

On March 22, 1622, when the Indians attacked the settlements at the head of the James River, 18 people were killed at the College, including George Thorpe, the Virginia Company's deputy, who lived at Berkeley Hundred **(55)**. The survivors were evacuated to safety and seated upon William Ewin's plantation **(13)** across the James River from Jamestown Island **(1)**. By spring 1623 the College people had returned to their property at Arrohattock. Their ranks were reinforced by newcomers sent to establish the East India School, which was supposed to be associated with the College but located in Charles City. In 1624 there were 29 people living upon the College land, but by 1625 there were only 22, who occupied eight houses. The small community was relatively well armed, but unfortified, and there was a shortage of food. Revocation of the Virginia Company's charter in May 1624 heralded the abandonment of the College as a project. However, a small number of settlers were still residing there in 1629. By 1635 colonists had begun patenting portions of the College property, including the site of Arrohattock (VCR 1:255-256, 268, 538-541; 3:226-227, 245, 262; CJS 2:268; PB 1 Pt. 1:351, 403; Pt. 2:599; MCGC 64, 151, 189; CBE 35, 53; HAI 777-783).

The Falls (West Fort and Nonsuch) (67)

In late May 1607 Captain Christopher Newport and a small party of explorers visited the falls of the James River, where they planted a cross bearing King James' name. In late summer 1609 Captain Francis West set out for the falls, where he intended to establish a settlement, West Fort. He brought along 140 men and a food supply that was supposed to last six months. When Captain John Smith visited the area, he concluded that the lowland site West had selected would be subject to flooding. Therefore, Smith negotiated with the Indians, obtained use of a high point of land containing 300 acres (Nonsuch), and shifted the settlement to the new location. However, when West returned, he angrily moved the settlers back to their original location. The Indians attacked, and afterward Captain Francis West and the survivors returned to Jamestown

(1). Captain West's brother, Thomas West, Lord De La Warr, visited the falls of the James River in 1610 and built a fort that he intended to use as a base of operations while searching for minerals. However, illness forced De La Warr and his men to return to Jamestown. Land at the falls remained deserted until 1634, when it was granted to merchant George Menefie, who conveyed it to Captain Mathew Gough. The sites at the falls upon which Captain John Smith and the Wests attempted to establish settlements (probably My Lords Island, Prince's Island, and the adjacent land) were located within what became Henrico and Chesterfield Counties and, later, the cities of Richmond and Manchester (HAI 320, 329, 481-483, 502-503, 531, 614).

Falling Creek (68)

In 1619 workmen with specialized skills were sent to a 100-acre tract on Falling Creek (in today's Chesterfield County), where they were supposed to set up an ironworks in an area known to have good ore. Captain Blewitt, an experienced artisan, was placed in charge of the project and the ironworks that were to be built there and at Southampton Hundred **(44)**. However, because Blewitt died shortly after his arrival in Virginia, the project was postponed. In May 1621 Virginia Company officials hired John Berkeley, an experienced ironworker, to oversee the facilities to be built at Falling Creek. Berkeley, his son Maurice, three servants, and 20 workmen set out for Virginia. The group also included 8 furnace men and 12 others. John Berkeley was pleased by what he found at Falling Creek and informed Company officials that he expected to be producing good quantities of iron by late spring 1622. However, the March 1622 Indian attack claimed 27 lives (including John Berkeley's) at Falling Creek and led to the destruction of the ironworks. Maurice Berkeley concluded that it was unfeasible to re-establish the ironworks and eventually it was abandoned. The land selected as the site of the Falling Creek ironworks originally had been assigned to John Blower, who surrendered his patent and took up land on the Eastern Shore (VCR 1:379, 475-476, 479, 587-588; 3:128, 452-453; 4:552; FER 184, 268).

Thomas Sheffield's Plantation (69)

Sometime prior to March 1622 Thomas Sheffield obtained a patent for 150 acres approximately three miles below Falling Creek **(68)** and two miles above Henrico (Farrar) Island **(63)**. His plantation, on the lower side of the James and west of Arrohattock **(66)**, was northwest of Proctor's Creek and probably was just above Kingsland Creek's mouth. Thomas Sheffield, his wife Rachael, and at least 11 other people were killed on March 22, 1622, when the Indians attacked. In August 1622 the late Thomas Sheffield's father sought to settle his estate, at which time the decedent's young son, Samuel, was identified as the principal heir. In May 1625 the late Thomas Sheffield was credited with 150 acres of land. The site of the Sheffield plantation lies in Chesterfield County (VCR 3:565; 4:552; EEAC 52; PB 1 Pt. 1:155, 326; Pt. 2:553, 634; VCRP 4328; CBE 28).

John and Alice Proctor's Plantation (70)

John Proctor, who came to Virginia sometime prior to 1610, patented 200 acres on the lower side of the James River. His land abutted north upon the stream that became known as Proctor's Creek. John Proctor developed his property sometime prior to the March 1622 Indian attack. According to Captain John

Smith, John Proctor's wife, Alice, "a proper and civill gentlewoman," stoutly defended the family home. Three or four weeks after the Indian assault, government officials ordered the Proctors to leave their plantation and move to a position of greater safety. The Indians reportedly returned and burned the Proctor home. There is no evidence that John and Alice Proctor ever attempted to reoccupy their property near the head of the James River. In February 1624 they were living upon the south side of the James River, across from the western end of Jamestown Island, at the settlement known as Paces Paines **(9)**. The Proctors, who probably were tenants, were still there in 1625. By July 1627 John Proctor was dead. Within a decade his land in Henrico, near Coxendale **(64)** and Mount Malado, had come into the hands of Captain Thomas Osborne. Today, the site of the Proctor plantation is located in Chesterfield County (PB 1 Pt. 1:381; Pt. 2:836; PB 5:337; MCGC 150; CJS 2:303).

Peirsey's Plantation (Peirsey's Toile) (71)

Sometime prior to the March 1622 Indian attack, cape merchant Abraham Peirsey seated some settlers at his plantation on the west side of the Appomattox River. During the Indian assault, four people were killed. In May 1625 when a list of patented land was compiled, Peirsey was credited with 1,150 acres of land on the Appomattox River, perhaps the acreage he had been awarded in recognition of his long service to the Virginia Company. The historic name of a creek on the upper side of the Appomattox River, "Pearse his stile" or "Peircies Toyle," a local landmark in 1636, probably is attributable to the presence of the Peirsey plantation, which was near Swift Creek. Today, that location is in Chesterfield County (PB 1 Pt. 1:353, 355, 438; CJS 2:301; VCR 4:556).

ACCAWMACK (ACCOMACK AND NORTHAMPTON)

When the first colonists sailed into the Chesapeake Bay in spring 1607 they took note of the Eastern Shore, which is bound on the east by the Atlantic Ocean. In June 1608 when Captain John Smith toured the bay, he set foot upon the peninsula itself. A small group of men was sent to Smith's Island in 1614 to extract salt from seawater, but the little outpost was abandoned within three years. In early 1619, shortly before the arrival of incoming governor Sir George Yeardley, Thomas Savage (an experienced Indian interpreter) visited the Eastern Shore and found the Natives hospitable. Within a year small settlements were established at Smith's Island, Dale's Gift, and Old Plantation Creek, and shortly thereafter on special tracts set aside for the Virginia Company and the colony's Secretary. The king of the Eastern Shore's Indians enjoyed a friendly relationship with the colonists. He gave land to Thomas Savage sometime prior to 1621 and presented some acreage to Sir George Yeardley around 1622. In February 1624 when a census was made of the colony's inhabitants there were 76 men, women, and children living on the Eastern Shore, but a year later the population was only 51. In May 1625 when a list of patented land was sent back to England, several plantations were attributed to the Eastern Shore. They included John Blower's 140 acres (on Old Plantation Creek), Thomas Savage's land, and 3,700 acres that had been assigned to Sir George Yeardley "at Hangers" or Hungers via a court order. Surveyor William Claiborne, who compiled the land list, noted that the Secretary's Land and the Company's Land had been seated, as had a few other parcels for which no patents had been granted. In 1634 when the colony was divided into eight shires or counties, one was called Accawmack (Accomack). There were then 396 European colonists living upon the Eastern Shore. In 1643, the southerly part of Accomack County was renamed Northampton County (CBE 46, 68-69, 76; VCR 4:556, 559; MCGC 481; CO 8/55 f 155).

Smith's Island and The Golden Quarter (Dale's Gift) (72)

In June 1608 Captain John Smith and a party of explorers landed upon Virginia's Eastern Shore and established friendly relations with the Natives. Captain Samuel Argall visited the area in 1613 and explored some of the islands along the seacoast. He concluded that salt might be produced easily if ponds were dug. After Sir Thomas Dale became deputy governor, he sent a detachment of 20 men to the Eastern Shore to establish a salt works. The site he selected was on Smith's Island's periphery and became part of the area known as Dale's Gift or the Golden Quarter. In 1616 John Rolfe reported that there were 17 men at Dale's Gift "upon the sea neere unto Cape Charles," who were under the command of Lieutenant Craddock. Their job was to make salt and catch fish, which could be preserved and used to supply the settlements on the mainland. Although the salt works were abandoned around the time Samuel Argall left Virginia in 1619, they were re-established in 1620–1621 (HAI 254, 262, 753, 817).

Old Plantation Creek (73)

By 1624–1625 colonists had begun building homesteads on small tracts of land that bordered both sides of Old Plantation Creek. On the north side of the creek were plantations that belonged to John Blower, Henry Fleet, and Thomas Graves. A little earlier, a vast tract that abutted the south side of Old Plantation Creek and straddled the Eastern Shore from bay to ocean was confirmed to Lady Elizabeth Dale, Sir Thomas Dale's widow and heir. The nearly 4,000 acres of land she was awarded in right of her late husband seems to have included the plantation called Dale's Gift (72) that had been seated at an earlier date. Probably for this reason, the creek that formed the northerly boundary of Lady Dale's property became known as the Old Plantation Creek. In 1627 officials at Jamestown expressed their concern that planters on the Eastern Shore were establishing homes in remote locations, especially along Old Plantation Creek and at Magothy Bay. However, settlement continued to spread and planters such as Thomas Savage, William Andrews, Lewin Denwood, and others flocked into the region (MCGC 156, 179; VCR 1:483, 491-492; 3:240, 268; PB 2:68, 167; 4:504).

Captain William Eppes's Plantation (74)

Captain William Eppes, who came to Virginia in 1618 and was placed in command of Smith's or Southampton Hundred in 1619, moved to the Eastern Shore sometime after he was found guilty of manslaughter. In February 1624 Eppes and his wife were living there and he was listed as a household head. In early 1625 his plantation contained two houses and a fort. By February 1626 Eppes had patented 450 acres of land on the south side of Kings Creek's mouth, staking his claim on the basis of nine headrights. He continued to have trouble with some of his contemporaries, who termed him "a mad, ranting fellow." In 1627 or 1628 Captain William Eppes moved to the West Indies, placing his landholdings in the hands of a tenant. After the tenant died, James Knott occupied the property as a squatter. In 1653 the Eppes property was awarded to Anthony Hodgkins (Hoskins), for it was considered abandoned land (CBE 46, 68; PB 1 Pt. 1:49; 3:286; DOR 1:68, 854-855).

The Secretary's Plantation (75)

In May 1620 the Virginia Company authorized Secretary of the Colony John Pory to lay out 500 acres on the Eastern Shore as office land. The income he and his successors earned from renting or farming the acreage, which was on the north side of Kings Creek, was to serve as their stipend. The Virginia Company sent 10 male tenants to Pory's property in 1620 and 10 more the following year. Their rent was to serve as Pory's salary. By 1622, however, only nine of the men remained and Company officials agreed to supplement the Secretary's salary with fees he earned by performing official duties, such as seeing that patents and other legal documents were recorded. In 1625 William Claiborne, an experienced surveyor, became the colony's secretary and held office for many years. When a list of patented land was sent to England in May 1625, Claiborne noted that "the Companyes and the Secretares Tennants were also seated but no land ordered to be laid out for them, as [had been] in the other 4 corporations." In 1631 Claiborne was authorized to select a tract near Jamestown (1) as his office land, but he failed to do so. Then, in 1633 he was given the right to subdivide and lease portions of the Secretary's Land (on the Eastern Shore) to tenants for 21 years. In 1637 Claiborne's successor, Richard Kemp, chose a tract near Jamestown as the Secretary's Land (VCR 1:332, 349; 3:477, 585; MCGC 111, 148, 165, 480; PB1 Pt. 1:49, 86-87; Pt. 2:110, 496).

The Company Land (76)

The Eastern Shore was not included within the four corporations the Virginia Company of London established in 1619, each of which was supposed to have a tract of Company Land. However, a letter written by Secretary of the Colony John Pory in 1620 indicates that Captain John Wilcox already had seated the Company Land on the Eastern Shore. Moreover, a May 1625 reference to the Company's property and a February 1626 lease granted to Clement Dilke make it clear that such a tract did exist. Dilke's 1626 lease allowed him 10 years' use of the houses and 20 acres that were "part of the late Companies land," noting that it was formerly occupied by Captain John Wilcox. Then, on September 20, 1628, when John Howe or Home received a lease for acreage abutting south upon the Secretary's Plantation, it was noted that Howe's property abutted north upon a creek separating it from "the land belonging to the late Company & granted by lease to Captain Clement Dilke." Another tenant living on the Company Land during the late 1620s was Nicholas Fiskins. These patents indicate that the Company Land in Accomack was located at the head of Cheriston Creek and extended southward toward Kings Creek, abutting the Secretary's Land (PB 1 Pt. 1:76, 87; 2:110; CJS 2:288; VCR 4:556, 559).

Savage's Neck (77)

Prior to 1621 Thomas Savage, who had been an Indian interpreter for at least a decade, seated a large tract of land between Kings and Cheriton Creeks, acreage that became known as Savage's Neck. Savage received his property, which the Natives called Esmy Shichans, from the king of the Eastern Shore Indians.

In 1624 he established a plantation on the Eastern Shore and in 1625 he was residing there with his wife, Hannah, sometimes identified as Ann. In May 1625 Thomas Savage was credited with a dividend of land in Accomack. He died in July 1626. In December 1627 Thomas's widow, Hannah, patented some land adjacent to the home they had shared on property sometimes known as Savage's Choice. She probably relocated because Thomas Savage's son, John, inherited his late father's land, which he repatented in 1637 (CBE 46, 68; VCR 4:559; MCGC 122; PB 1 Pt.1:57, 189, 275; Pt. 2:499).

Sir George Yeardley's Plantation (78)

Around 1622 the king of the Indians on the Eastern Shore gave land to Sir George Yeardley. In May 1625 when a list of patented land was sent back to England, Yeardley's 3,700 acres "at Hangers" or Hungars was among the properties listed. A 1638 patent awarded to Argall Yeardley indicates that the acreage had been "granted to Sir George Yeardley, Knight, father to the said Argall by patent from the late Treasurer & Company." It also indicated that the title to Sir George Yeardley's property on the Eastern Shore had been confirmed to him by a court order dated May 9, 1623, and had descended to his son, Argall Yeardley, who retained it and enhanced his holdings. The Yeardley property was on the lower side of Hungars Creek's mouth (CBE 76; VCR 4:556, 559; MCGC 481; PB 1 Pt. 2:595; 3:269).

VIRGINIA IMMIGRANTS
AND ADVENTURERS, 1607-1635:

A Biographical Dictionary

A

THOMAS ABBAY

Thomas Abbay, a gentleman, came to Virginia in 1608 in the 2nd Supply of new settlers to Jamestown (1). Captain John Smith described him as a diligent observer of the colony's early beginnings and drew from Abbay's writings, which he included in his *Proceedings* (CJS 1:135, 197, 202, 241; 2:190).

THOMAS ABBE (ABBES)

Thomas Abbe (Abbes) came to Virginia on the *Southampton* in 1623. On January 20, 1625, he was living at Flowerdew Hundred (53) and was identified as a 20-year-old servant in Abraham Peirsey's household (CBE 50).

EDWARD ABBES

When Edward Abbes, a Virginia colonist, made his will on August 24, 1636, it was witnessed by Henry and William Batt. He bequeathed money to Nicholas Browne's daughter, Sarah, and his own nephew, Thomas Abbes, so that each of them could buy a cow, and he reduced the term of his manservant, William Goulder, by a year and a half. Edward designated his wife, Sarah, as his executrix and primary heir and appointed his friends Nicholas Browne and Robert Todd of Elizabeth City (17) as overseers of his estate. On May 23, 1637, Sarah Abbes, who was in England, presented her late husband's will to probate officials, noting that he had died in Virginia. Since Nicholas Browne, Robert Todd, and Henry Batt were all associated with Elizabeth City, it is probable that Edward Abbes was connected with that area too (SR 3978).

ELIZABETH ABBOTT
(ABBITT, ABBOT)

On September 19, 1618, the Bridewell court decided to send Elizabeth Abbott (Abbitt, Abbot), a young vagrant from Lombard Street in St. Tholeyes, to Virginia. By February 16, 1624, she had become an indentured servant in John and Alice Proctor's household at Paces Paines (9) on the lower side of the James River, just west of Gray's Creek. Elizabeth died prior to October 10, 1624, probably as a result of flesh wounds she received during an especially severe beating administered by one of the Proctors' employees. Court testimony reveals that Elizabeth, a habitual runaway, was beaten many times, on one occasion receiving 500 lashes. The beating that proved fatal was inflicted with a stout cord containing fishhooks. At the inquest held after Elizabeth's death, a fellow servant described her as "a very lewd wench" (CBE 9-10, 40; MCGC 22-24).

JEFFREY ABBOTT (ABBOT)

Jeffrey Abbott (Abbot), a gentleman, came to Virginia in the 1st Supply of new colonists and arrived in Jamestown (1) in January 1608. In late December 1608, when Abbott accompanied Captain John Smith and others on a voyage to Werowocomoco, Powhatan's principal village, he held the rank of sergeant. In 1609 Jeffrey Abbott was one of two men sent to kill some disobedient Dutchmen who had fled to the Indians. In 1610 he was identified as Lieutenant Abbott when President George Percy dispatched him to the blockhouse at the entrance to Jamestown Island, to assist Captain Puttocke in a fight against the Pasbehay Indians. Sometime prior to 1611 Jeffrey Abbott was executed for formulating a dangerous plot. Captain John Smith later said that he had been a good soldier and an intelligent, hardworking man, who had served in Ireland and in the Netherlands. Smith considered Abbott to be loyal and said that he was severely punished for his offenses but not rewarded for his good deeds. Abbott supplied some of the information that Smith used in his *Proceedings* (CJS 1:197, 222, 244, 267; 2:136, 161, 193, 216, 240; HAI 513, 822).

NICHOLAS ABBOTT

Nicholas Abbott set sail from England on the *William and Thomas* and arrived in Virginia in 1621. When William Julian patented some land on September 20, 1624, he identified Nicholas as one of his servants and used his headright when patenting some land. Nicholas and his master probably lived in Elizabeth City (**18**) (PB 1 Pt. 1:32).

ABOCHANCANO
(SEE OPECHANCANOUGH)

***

GEORGE ACKLAND

On February 16, 1624, George Ackland, a young boy, was living in Elizabeth City (**18**) in the household of John and Amity (Amyte, Ann) Waine (Wayne). In early 1625 he was still living in the Waine household. George, who was then 7 years old, was Virginia-born. Also living in the household was 4-year-old Mary Ackland, who probably was George's sister. They may have been Amity Waine's children by a former marriage (CBE 44, 65).

MARY ACKLAND

On February 16, 1624, Mary Ackland, a young girl, was living in Elizabeth City (**18**) in the household of John and Amity (Amyte, Ann) Waine (Wayne). In early 1625 she was still living with the Waines and was identified as Virginia-born and 4 years old. Also living in the Waine household was 7-year-old George Ackland, probably Mary's brother. The children may have been Amity Waine's by a former marriage (CBE 44, 65).

***

[NO FIRST NAME] ACOURT

On August 30, 1628, officials decided that Mrs. Acourt's son would be released from Bridewell so that he could accompany Isaac Fletcher to Virginia (CBE 84).

GEORGE ACRIG

In 1608 Captain John Smith said that George Acrig was one of the men sent overland to build a house for Powhatan. On December 29, 1608, Smith described Acrig as a gentleman and soldier who accompanied him on a voyage to Werowocomoco, Powhatan's village (CJS 1:244; 2:193).

SAMUEL ACTON

In June 1626 the General Court learned that Captain William Tucker of Elizabeth City (**17, 18**) had ordered Samuel Acton to go to Warresqueak (**26**). Acton, one of Captain John Stone's servants, was supposed to decide where he was to go when his master (a mariner) arrived in Virginia (MCGC 134).

[NO FIRST NAME] ADAMS

On January 16, 1620, William Weldon sent word to Virginia Company officials that he wanted to claim the headright of Captain Whitaker's man, Adams. Weldon had brought George Eden (Eaden, Aden) to the colony and was planning to use his headright. However, Weldon allowed the Society of Southampton Hundred (**44**) to have Eden and, therefore, wanted to use Whitaker's man, Adams, as a headright instead (VCR 3:254).

[NO FIRST NAME] ADAMS
(ADDAMS, ADDAMES)

On July 15, 1610, Captain Adams (Addams, Addames), a mariner, arrived at Old Point Comfort (**17**) with two Indians who had been captured. One of the natives Adams was transporting to England on the *Blessing* was a son of the Warresqueak Indians' king. In 1611 Captain Adams returned to Virginia on the *Blessing* and reported that Sir Thomas Dale would be arriving soon (HAI 438, 514).

[NO FIRST NAME] ADAMS

On February 16, 1624, Mr. Adams was living in the Jamestown (**1**) household of Goodman Stoiks, probably John Stoaks (Stoiks, Stokes) (CBE 40).

ANN ADAMS (ADDAMS)

Ann Adams, who was living in urban Jamestown (**1**) on February 16, 1624, was a servant in Ralph Hamor's household. She was still there on January 24, 1625, and was identified as a servant (CBE 38, 55).

IAN ADAMS (ADDAMS)

On August 30, 1628, the justices of Bridewell Court decided to send a boy named Ian Adams (Addams) to Virginia. When he was apprehended he was working with a woman named Anne, reputedly a "great pickpocket" (HUME 34).

JOHN ADAMS

On August 21, 1625, the justices of Bridewell decided to send John Adams, who had been brought in from Coleman Street, to Virginia. He appears to have been a vagrant (CBE 47).

RALPH ADAMS

On February 16, 1624, Ralph Adams was living in Elizabeth City (**17, 18**) (CBE 43).

RICHARD ADAMS

On January 29, 1620, Richard Adams, who had been detained at Bridewell, was among those being sent to Virginia (CBE 18).

***

ROBERT ADAMS

Robert Adams came to Virginia on the *Bona Nova* and was sent to Martin's Hundred (**7**), where he was living at the time of the March 22, 1622, Indian attack. Afterward, Robert, who identified himself as one of Richard Smith's servants, was among those sent to Jamestown Island (**1**), then considered a position of safety. While he was there he was accused of killing a hog that belonged to Jamestown resident George Graves. By 1623 Robert Adams, then a married man, had been sent back to Martin's Hundred by the colony's governing officials. He was given the late Richard Staples' ruined house and cleared ground and was told to associate himself with the settlement's leader, William Harwood. Because of severe food shortages and harassment by the Indians, living conditions at Martin's Hundred were harsh. Robert Adams wanted to leave, but Mr. Emmerson persuaded him to stay. When Indians bearing firearms attacked Martin's Hundred in 1623, Robert Adams was shot in the leg. He later sent word to England that during the attack he and his wife had been forced to hide in the fortified settlement's watch-house because Mr. Harwood refused to let them take refuge in his house. In February 1624 Robert Adams served as one of the burgesses representing Martin's Hundred. He was among those who signed the assembly's rebuttal to Alderman Johnson's claim that conditions in the colony were tolerable. Later in the year he testified about a matter involving James Davis and Mr. Emmerson. On February 4, 1625, Robert Adams was living at Martin's Hundred, where he and his partner, Augustine Leake, headed a household that was relatively well supplied with stored food and defensive weaponry. They also had a servant. On June 15, 1625, Robert sent request for supplies to some of the Society of Martin's Hundred's investors. On January 11, 1627, he appeared before the Council of State and testified that he had been at Mr. Harwood's house when he heard Richard Crocker accuse Mr. Percy and Captain Hamor of price gouging. At the same court session, Robert Adams was accused of drunkenness and fined. He and his wife stayed on at Martin's Hundred, and in April 1627 he served as the guarantor of Giles Allington, who was settling Caleb Page's estate. Robert Adams died sometime prior to January 21, 1629, when his wife was authorized to settle his estate and pay John Wareham for a servant he had purchased. The Rev. John Lyford presented the decedent's will (FER 572; HEN 1:128-129; HAI 915; MCGC 30, 54, 132-133, 147, 196; CBE 62; DOR 1:45).

MRS. ROBERT ADAMS

When Robert Adams of Martin's Hundred (**7**), formerly one of Richard Smith's servants, sent a letter on June 15, 1625, to some of the Society of Martin's Hundred's investors, he complained about the harsh living conditions at the plantation and the shortage of supplies. He also said that when Indians attacked the settlement with firearms in 1623, he and his wife had to take refuge in a watch-tower because the community's leader, William Harwood, refused to let them into his house. On January 21, 1629, Mrs. Robert Adams of Martin's Hundred was given a letter of administration authorizing her to settle her late husband's estate, and she was ordered to pay John Wareham for a servant her late husband had purchased (FER 572; MCGC 181).

***

DAMARIS ADDERTON

On September 28, 1628, Damaris Adderton was among several men delivered to the Rev. Lewis Hughes so that they could be sent to Virginia (CBE 84).

THOMAS ADDISON

On May 20, 1622, Thomas Addison of Lincolne Inn in Middlesex County, England, acquired some land from Francis Carter, who had purchased it from Lady Cecily Delaware, the widow of Thomas West, Lord Delaware. Addison came to Virginia and on February 16, 1624, was living in Elizabeth City **(17, 18)**. On February 23, 1636, reference was made to a will that Anthony Younge of Kecoughtan left with Thomas Addison—a document then described as null and void (VCR 2:17, 25; CBE 43; WITH 195).

LUKE ADEN
(SEE LUKE EDEN, EADEN)

JOHN ADIS

On July 29, 1626, Bridewell's justices decided that John Adis, an apprentice to haberdasher Thomas Ridiard, would be sent to Virginia. Adis had been found guilty of having a sexual relationship with Katherin Bukill (CBE 72-73).

HENRY ADLING

Henry Adling came to Virginia in 1607 in the first group of colonists who settled in Jamestown **(1)** (CJS 2:142).

ROBERT ADWARDS (EDWARDS?)

Sometime after April 1623 but before February 16, 1624 Robert Adwards (Edwards?) died at one of the plantations on the lower side of the James River **(8-15)**, within the corporation of James City (CBE 41).

ANTHONY AFTON

Sometime prior to January 10, 1627, Anthony Afton, who was visiting Kecoughtan **(17)**, sent Thomas Sauvage (Savage), a young servant, across a creek to retrieve his canoe. Because the youth drowned, Afton was summoned to court and interrogated. The General Court's justices noted that he could have gone into the water to assist the boy but failed to do so. Moreover, Afton had failed to ask the boy's master's permission to send him to get the canoe. Anthony Afton was ordered to pay William Gayney and Humphrey Rastell what Thomas Sauvage was worth as a servant (MCGC 131-132).

ROBERT ALBERTON (ALBERTOON)

Robert Alberton (Albertoon), a perfumer, came to Virginia in 1608, in the 1st Supply of new colonists. He would have lived in Jamestown **(1)** (CJS 1:222; 2:162).

EDWARD ALBORNE
(SEE EDWARD AUBORNE)

RICHARD ALDER (ALDON)

Richard Alder (Aldon) came to Virginia on the *George* in 1620 and on February 16, 1624, was a servant in William Peirce's household in urban Jamestown **(1)**. By January 25, 1625, Richard had moved to Mulberry Island **(21)**, where he was identified as a 19-year-old servant in Peirce's household (CBE 38, 57).

ROBERT ALDRIDGE

Sometime after February 16, 1624, but before early 1625, Robert Aldridge died at one of the plantations on the lower side of the James River, to the east of Gray's Creek **(10-16)** and within the corporation of James City (CBE 60).

MICHAEL ALEWORTH

When the Indians attacked Westover **(54)** on March 22, 1622, Michael Aleworth, a member of Captain Nathaniel West's household, was killed (VCR 3:567).

ALEXANDER

On December 27, 1625, a man named Alexander was identified as one of Luke Eden's (Aden's, Eaden's) servants. He may have lived with his master in Elizabeth City **(17, 18)** (MCGC 94).

JONAS ALFORD

On February 27, 1619, Jonas Alford, a boy, was identified as one of the children the

Bridewell court decided to send to Virginia (CBE 12).

RICHARD ALFORD

On February 4, 1625, Richard Alford, a 26-year-old indentured servant, was living on the lower side of the James River on Captain Roger Smith's plantation (**10**). However, throughout much of 1625 and 1626 Richard lived in urban Jamestown (**1**), probably in Captain Roger Smith's home. Richard Alford appeared in court on April 25, 1625, and testified in a legal case involving some Jamestown Island land that was in Robert Marshall and Thomas Grubb's possession. On January 3, 1626, he testified about a weapon that Jamestown gunsmith John Jefferson had repaired unsatisfactorily. On August 21, 1626, Richard was sued by Robert Marshall, who claimed that he was owed eleven days of work. Ultimately, the General Court ordered Richard Alford to work for Robert Marshall for four days and pay him for the remaining seven. On January 12, 1627, Richard was identified as a Virginia Company tenant who had been assigned to Captain Samuel Mathews. A year later, he was arrested by Mr. John Gill, a Jamestown merchant (CBE 59; MCGC 56, 84, 107-108, 136, 159; DOR 1:39).

JEREMY (HEROME) ALICOCK (ALLICOCK)

Jeremy (Herome) Alicock (Allicock), a gentleman, came to Virginia in 1607 in the first group of colonists to Jamestown (**1**). George Percy indicated that Alicock died on August 14, 1607, after being wounded. In 1608 Edward Maria Wingfield spoke appreciatively of Jeremy Alicock and said that Alicock had maintained cordial relations with members of the council and not reviled them (CJS 1:20, 208; 2:141; HAI 99, 199).

ALLEN

On February 16, 1624, a man known only as Allen was living in the Neck O'Land (**5**), where he was one of Mr. Perse's (Peirce's) servants (CBE 35).

EDWARD ALLEN (ALLYN)

On January 22, 1620, the justices of Bridewell court decided that Edward Allen (Allyn), a vagrant, would be sent to Virginia.

On February 7, 1628, he was identified as one of Edward Grindon's servants who lived at his plantation (**11**) on the lower side of the James River. Allen informed the General Court that he was visiting John Tios's house when another man brought in some stolen goods (CBE 17; MCGC 163).

GEORGE ALLEN

On February 27, 1626, George Allen, Thomas Dunthorne's servant, testified that he had been sick with the flux for two months before he went to work for John Woolrich, a tenant on the Governor's Land (**3**). George claimed that Dunthorne, whose plantation was in Kecoughtan (**18**), told him to conceal his illness (MCGC 96).

JOHN ALLEN

On March 22, 1622, when the Indians attacked the settlers living on the College Land at Arrohattock (**66**), John Allen was killed (VCR 3:566).

JOHN ALLEN

On May 8, 1626, John Allen was identified as a servant who had been transported to Virginia at the expense of Thomas Harwood. Harwood received a patent for land at Blunt Point (**22**), using Allen and himself as headrights (MCGC 103).

MATHEW ALLEN (ALLIN)

In January 1620 Mathew Allen (Allin) was reprieved by the Middlesex Sessions so that he could be sent to Virginia. On February 26, 1620, he was among those being detained at Newgate until he could be sent to the colony (CBE 16, 19).

NATHANIEL ALLEN (ALLIN)

On February 26, 1620, it was decided that Nathaniel Allen (Allin), a boy brought in from Newgate, would be detained until he could be sent to Virginia (HUME 28).

OLIVER ALLEN (ALLIN)

On January 22, 1620, the court at Bridewell decided that Oliver Allen (Allin), a long-time prisoner from Crutched Friars, would be sent to Virginia (CBE 17).

WILLIAM ALLEN

William Allen came to Virginia on the *Southampton* in 1623 and on February 16, 1624, was living in Elizabeth City (**17, 18**). By January 20, 1625, he had moved to Flowerdew Hundred (**53**), where he was one of Abraham Peirsey's servants and was age 22. When the colony's assembly convened on October 16, 1629, William Allen, then a free man, served as the burgess for Henry Throgmorton's plantation at Shirley Hundred (**41**) (CBE 43, 50; HEN 1:138).

***

LEONARD ALLENSON

On July 31, 1622, Leonard Allenson and his wife, Christian, were among those who set sail for Virginia on the *James* (FER 400).

CHRISTIAN ALLENSON (MRS. LEONARD ALLENSON)

On July 31, 1622, Christian, the wife of Leonard Allenson, went to Virginia on the *James* (FER 400).

***

ANN ALLERSON

On June 24, 1635, when Adam Thorogood patented some land, he used Ann Allerson as a headright and indicated that he had paid for her transportation on the *Africa* (PB 1 Pt. 1:179).

CHRISTOPHER ALLETT

In 1629 Christopher Allett, a 25-year-old planter, testified that when he had been at Mr. John Cheeseman's house in Elizabeth City (**18**) a month or six weeks earlier, William Carter's wife had called Goodwife Gray a whore (MCGC 197).

***

GILES (GYLES) ALLINGTON

On December 1, 1624, when Lieutenant Giles (Gyles) Allington of Kecoughtan (**17, 18**) patented 100 acres between Newportes News (**24**) and Blunt Point (**22**), he was identified as a gentleman and ancient planter. On March 12, 1625, he participated in a coroner's inquest, and in mid-Decem-

ber he was mentioned in court testimony. When a list of patented land was sent to England in May 1625, Giles Allington's 100 acres "below Blunt Point" were included. Allington got married sometime prior to September 11, 1626, for he testified in court that although he had asked Mrs. Joan Wright to serve as his wife's midwife, his wife had preferred a Mrs. Grave. Because Giles Allington and his wife became ill and their newborn died, he suspected Mrs. Wright—who was angry that the other midwife had been chosen—of witchcraft. He said that Mrs. Wright had put a curse on Sergeant Booth, with whom she also had become angry. Allington returned to court on October 12, 1626, and testified in the dispute between John Butterfield and Margaret Jones, who lived on the Governor's Land (**3**). He apparently was a respected member of the community, for on April 3, 1627, he was given a letter of administration for the late Caleb Page's estate and was ordered to make an inventory, which he did by July 4, 1627. Lieutenant Giles Allington died sometime before the end of 1629, when Captain Robert Felgate was named his administrator (PB 1 Pt. 1:23; VCR 4:557; MCGC 53, 81, 111-112, 119, 147, 151, 197).

MRS. GILES (GYLES) ALLINGTON

On September 11, 1626, Giles (Gyles) Allington of the corporation of Elizabeth City (**17, 18**) testified that his pregnant wife wanted Mrs. Grave to be her midwife instead of Mrs. Joan Wright, a midwife who was suspected of witchcraft. He said that after the child was born, he and his wife became ill and their child died. Allington believed that Mrs. Wright was responsible for his family's illnesses (MCGC 111-112).

***

ANDREW ALLISON (ALLINSON)

Andrew Allison (Allinson) died in Elizabeth City (**17, 18**) sometime after April 1623 but before February 16, 1624 (CBE 45).

***

THOMAS ALLNUTT (ALNUTT)

Thomas Allnutt, who came to Virginia on the ship *Gift*, served on a jury in Jamestown on August 4, 1623. On February 16, 1624, he and his wife were living on the mainland behind Jamestown Island, within the Neck O'Land (5), where he had a patent. On June 24, 1624, Allnutt was summoned to court and fined for saying that the Rev. David Sandys (Sands, Sanders) was trying to take advantage of 13-year-old Mara Buck, a wealthy orphan who reportedly was slow-witted. Allnutt was punished because the General Court's justices (one of whom was the minister's brother) believed that he had sullied the clergyman's reputation by making the statement. By January 24, 1625, Thomas Allnutt and his wife were living in urban Jamestown (1), where they were in possession of a house and a boat. By that date Allnutt and a servant already had seated his acreage in the Neck O'Land. In early 1625 Thomas Allnutt served on a jury, authenticated a will, and ordered some hats from England. He was responsible for some of the Rev. Richard Buck's orphans' cattle, and in 1626 the orphaned Peleg Buck was living in the Allnutt household. In early 1625 Thomas Allnutt made a wager with his servant, Roger Rodes (Redes, Roeds), about the date of Easter and agreed to free Rodes a year early if he won. Thomas Allnutt died sometime prior to August 21, 1626, at which time his will was proved. Several months later his widow married Thomas Bagwell (CBE 35, 55; MCGC 4-5, 18, 38-39, 46, 53, 70, 85-86, 96-97, 107-108, 117, 137; DOR 1:32).

JOAN (JOANE) ALLNUTT (ALNUTT) (MRS. THOMAS ALLNUTT [ALNUTT]; MRS. THOMAS BAGWELL)

Joan (Joane), who married Thomas Allnutt (Alnutt), came to Virginia on the *Marigold* sometime prior to early August 1623. On February 16, 1624, the Allnutts were living in the Neck O'Land (5) behind Jamestown Island. On June 24, 1624, Mrs. Allnutt testified in court about the orphaned Mara Buck's innate lack of acuity. By January 24, 1625, Joan and Thomas Allnutt had moved to urban Jamestown (1). He died there sometime prior to August 21, 1626, and by February 5, 1627, Joan had married ancient planter Thomas Bagwell of West and Shirley Hundred (41), who used her as a headright when patenting some land on the Appomattox River in 1638 (CBE 35, 55; MCGC 16, 137; PB 1 Pt. 1:550).

***

JONAS ALPART

When the Indians attacked Weyanoke (52) on March 22, 1622, Jonas Alpart, one of Sir George Yeardley's servants, was killed (VCR 3:569).

JOHN ALPORT (ALPORTE)

On June 24, 1635, when Adam Thorogood patented some land, he used the headright of John Alport (Alporte) and indicated that he had paid for Alport's transportation to Virginia on the *John and Dorothy* in 1634 (PB 1 Pt. 1:179).

JOHN ALSOPP

In 1619 John Alsopp went to Virginia at the expense of the Ferrars, who were important Virginia Company investors (FER 296).

RICHARD ALTHROPE

On February 16, 1624, Richard Althrope was living at Buckroe (17), within the corporation of Elizabeth City (CBE 45).

AMBROSE

On February 7, 1625, a man known as Ambrose, who came to Virginia on the *Marmaduke* in 1621, was living at Warresqueak (26). He was a servant in the household headed by Henry Woodward and John Browning (CBE 62).

FRANCIS AMCOTTO

On July 21, 1627, Francis Amcotto, who was being detained at Bridewell, agreed to go to Virginia to be a servant for seven years (CBE 79).

EDWARD AMES

Edward Ames came to Virginia in a Spanish frigate in 1629. Captain Francis Eppes used him as a headright in 1638 when patenting some land (PB 1 Pt. 2:537).

***

FRANCIS AMIAS

When Francis Amias—a gentleman from Gosnarch, in Lancashire, England—made his will on November 28, 1620, he identified himself as an adventurer to Virginia and named his brother Paul as his executor and one of his heirs. Francis left his brothers, Paul and Thomas, halves of his interest in Virginia (EEAC 2; WITH 36-37).

PAUL AMIAS

In July 1622 Paul Amias was identified as the brother and executor of Francis Amias, who died in Virginia. He also was one of Francis's heirs (EEAC 2; WITH 36-37).

THOMAS AMIAS

When Francis Amias—a gentleman from Gosnarch, in Lancashire, England—made his will on November 28, 1620, he left his brothers, Thomas and Paul, halves of his adventure in Virginia. Francis died prior to July 1622 (EEAC 2; WITH 36-37).

***

THOMAS ANDERSON

On February 26, 1620, Thomas Anderson was among those brought in from Newgate so that they could be sent to Virginia (CBE 19).

ANTHONY ANDREW

Anthony Andrew died in Elizabeth City (17, 18) sometime after April 1623 but before February 16, 1624 (CBE 45).

THOMAS ANDREWE

On January 22, 1620, Thomas Andrewe, a vagrant, was detained at Bridewell until he could be sent to Virginia (CBE 17).

ANDREW ANDREWES ALIAS JOHNSON (SEE ANDREW JOHNSON)

***

JOACHIM (JOCOMB, JOAKIM, JOCKEY, JENKIN) ANDREWES (ANDREWS, ANDRUS)

Sometime prior to February 20, 1619, Joachim (Jocomb, Joakim, Jockey, Jenkin) Andrewes (Andrews, Andrus), an ancient planter, patented 12 acres in the eastern end of Jamestown Island (1), south of William Fairfax's patent. Andrewes may have shared his acreage with John Grubb. Joachim Andrewes also had a 100-acre patent in the territory known as Archer's Hope (6), acreage that eventually became the eighteenth-century plantation known as Jockey's Neck. On February 16, 1624, Andrewes and his wife were living in urban Jamestown, where they were members of Captain William Peirce's household. However, in early 1625 Joachim Andrewes' name was listed among those who had died in Pasbehay (3), the mainland just west of Jamestown Island. Although no evidence has come to light suggesting that Andrewes or his wife produced heirs, an August 1650 patent for some acreage in the Neck O'Land makes reference to the tract "lately belonging to Jenkin Andrews" (PB 1 Pt 2:648-649; 2:240; VCR 4:551, 556; CBE 38, 58).

MRS. JOACHIM (JOCOMB, JOAKIM, JOCKEY, JENKIN) ANDREWES (ANDREWS, ANDRUS)

On February 16, 1624, Mrs. Joachim (Jocomb, Joakim, Jockey, Jenkin) Andrewes (Andrews, Andrus) and her husband were living in urban Jamestown (1), where they were members of Captain William Peirce's household. By early 1625 Mrs. Andrewes was widowed. Although there is no documentary evidence that Mr. and Mrs. Joachim Andrewes produced heirs, in August 1650 a patent for some acreage in the Neck O'Land (5) behind Jamestown Island, where Joachim had owned a 100-acre tract, makes reference to the parcel "lately belonging to Jenkin Andrews." This raises the possibility that the couple had produced an heir (CBE 38, 58; VCR 4:556; PB 2:240).

***

***

JOHN ANDREWES I

On September 7, 1608, when John Andrewes I of Cambridge, England, a merchant, made his will in preparation for a trip to Ireland, he indicated that he was the owner of some Virginia Company stock. He named as his heirs his wife, Hester; his sons, John II, William, and Peter; and his daughters, Hester and Elizabeth. John Andrewes I added a codicil to his will on March 21, 1609, indicating that his son John Andrewes II had died in Virginia. The will of John Andrewes I was presented for probate on June 4, 1616 (SR 3111; SH 2; EEAC 2).

HESTER ANDREWES (MRS. JOHN ANDREWES I)

On September 7, 1608, when John Andrewes I of Cambridge, England, a merchant and owner of Virginia Company stock, made his will in preparation for a trip to Ireland, he named his wife, Hester, as executrix and one of his heirs. The will of John Andrews I was presented for probate on June 4, 1616 (SR 3111; SH 2; EEAC 2).

JOHN ANDREWES II

John Andrewes II was a son and heir of John Andrewes I of Cambridge, England, a merchant and owner of Virginia Company stock. When the elder man made his will on September 7, 1608, he named his wife, sons, and daughters as his heirs. The testator added a codicil to his will on March 21, 1609, indicating that his son, John Andrewes II, had died in Virginia (SR 3111; SH 2; EEAC 2).

PETER ANDREWES (ANDREWS)

Peter Andrewes (Andrews) was a son and heir of John Andrewes I of Cambridge, England, a merchant and Virginia Company investor. On September 7, 1608, the elder Andrewes made his will, which was presented for probate on June 4, 1616. Peter Andrewes may have been the mariner who made many trips to Virginia during the 1620s (SR 3111; SH 2; EEAC 2).

WILLIAM ANDREWES

William Andrewes was a son and heir of John Andrewes I of Cambridge, England, a merchant and Virginia Company investor. The elder man's September 7, 1608, will was proved on June 4, 1616 (SR 3111; SH 2; EEAC 2).

***

PETER ANDREWES (ANDREWS)

On March 12, 1627, Peter Andrewes (Andrews), a mariner then in Virginia, testified that he saw no fighting between Robert Cooke and Thomas Lawley while he was at sea. Robert Middleton, a bachelor who died in Virginia, left Andrewes his plantation sometime prior to April 3, 1627. Peter Andrewes returned to England and in July 1627 went to Virginia as master of the *Anne* of London. At the same time, he sent goods from London to Virginia on the *Thomas and John* and the *Robert and John*. In October 1628 Andrewes returned to England on the *Anne*, transporting a shipment of tobacco intended for London merchant Samuel Vassall. He returned to the colony in October 1629 on the *Susan*, with passengers and goods he took for Vassall. Several months later Peter Andrewes, who was called on to testify before an English court, gave his age as 33 and said that he was from Ratcliffe in Middlesex. He indicated that he had gone to Virginia in October and November 1629 as master of the *Susan* of Alborowe, a vessel chartered by Samuel Vassall. He added that the ship was leaky and rotten and said that the passengers had a difficult voyage. Andrewes said that after he arrived in Virginia, he had the *Susan* caulked and outfitted with rope taken from a ship leased to Jamestown (1) merchant Richard Stephens. In September 1634, when a complaint was filed against Peter Andrewes for refusing to transport Edward Kingswell to Carolina, Andrewes was identified as the ship's master and brother-in-law of Samuel Vassall (MCGC 144; SH 8; CBE 79, 83, 91; EAE 19, 24; G&M 205; SR 4001; HCA 13/49).

PETER ANDREWES (ANDREWS)

In November 1634 Peter Andrewes (Andrews) was identified as master of the *Mayflower.* He was a 39-year-old mariner from Limehouse, in Middlesex. He testified that he had made a voyage from London to Virginia in 1633–34 (CBE 119).

PETER ANDREWES (ANDREWS)

On December 31, 1645, Captain Peter Andrewes (Andrews), who was identified as someone who had had business dealings with the late George Menefie of Jamestown (1), was ordered to pay Humphrey Adington, overseer of Menefie's will. This mariner may have been the same man employed by Samuell Vassall, or he may have been the son of merchant John Andrewes I (WITH 180-181).

RICHARD ANDREWES (ANDREWS)

On June 23, 1627, when John Throgmorton of Shirley Hundred (41) made a nuncupative will, he bequeathed to Richard Andrewes (Andrews), "the old cooper," his share of Andrewes' service after the end of the year (MCGC 153).

THOMAS ANDREWES (ANDREWS)

Thomas Andrewes (Andrews), who was in Virginia, witnessed the January 6, 1635, will of Jamestown (1) merchant Thomas Whaplett (WITH 77).

***

WILLIAM ANDREWES (ANDREWS, ANDROS)

William Andrewes (Andrews, Andros) came to Virginia in 1617 on the *Treasurer* and on February 16, 1624, was living on the Eastern Shore. In early 1625 Andrewes, who was age 25, was living in Thomas Gaskoyne's house, which probably was located at Sir George Yeardley's plantation (78). On March 14, 1628, William Andrewes, who was identified as an Accomack planter, patented 100 acres of land, utilizing two headrights that had been transferred to him. He continued to accumulate land and on June 25, 1635, acquired 100 acres between Old Plantation (73) and Kings Creeks (74)—where Captain William Eppes's plantation was located— and 200 acres on Hungars Creek, using the headright of his wife, Susanna. William Andrewes became a commissioner of Accomack's monthly court and a vestryman. He was alive in December 1644. His name appeared frequently in the Accomack-Northampton court records, sometimes as a county official and occasionally as a wrongdoer. In 1644 he was accused of illegally trading with the Indians. He became a militia captain and later a major, and was Northampton County's high sheriff in 1655. He died sometime prior to February 28, 1656, when his will was presented at court (CBE 46, 69; PB 1 Pt. 1:71, 181-182; AMES 1:7,

36, 39, 49, 63, 141-142; 2:5, 33-34, 56, 66, 88, 202, 386, 418; DOR 1:75-76).

SUSANNA ANDREWES (ANDREWS, ANDROS) (MRS. WILLIAM ANDREWES [ANDREWS, ANDROS])

On June 25, 1635, when William Andrewes (Andrews, Andros) patented some land in Accomack, bordering Hungars Creek, he listed his wife, Susanna, as a headright. She died prior to March 1644, by which time he had married a woman named Mary (PB 1 Pt. 1:182; AMES 2:356).

***

WILLIAM ANDREWES (ANDREWS)

William Andrewes (Andrews), who was age 25, testified before the General Court sometime prior to January 9, 1624. He indicated that Thomas Harris of Bermuda Hundred (39) had loaned some corn to Captain Nathaniel West and that he (Andrewes) had transported it. West lived at Westover (54) prior to the 1622 Indian attack but later moved to West and Shirley Hundred (41) (MCGC 11).

ANGELO

Angelo, an African woman, came to Virginia on the *Treasurer*, probably in 1619. On February 16, 1624, she was living in urban Jamestown (1) in the household of Captain William Peirce, and she was still residing there on January 24, 1625. Peirce and his son-in-law, John Rolfe, met the *Treasurer* when it arrived at Old Point Comfort (17) in late August or early September 1619. Afterward the ship went to Bermuda, where it also left some Africans (CBE 38, 55).

ANN

On February 16, 1624, a maidservant named Ann was living at Chaplin's Choice (56) (CBE 37).

[NO FIRST NAME] ANNOT

On October 25, 1629, the justices of Bridewell decided that a boy named Annot, who was being detained, would be sent to Virginia (HUME 35).

JOHN ANTHONIE (ANTHONY)

John Anthonie (Anthony) came to Virginia on the *Swan* in 1624 and in early 1625 was living in Elizabeth City (**17**) on the Virginia Company's land. He was then age 23 and lived in Captain John Martin's household (CBE 67).

ANTHONY

Anthony came to Virginia on the *Catherine* in 1621 at the expense of William Spencer of Jamestown Island (**1**), who used Anthony's headright when patenting some land in 1629. He probably was one of Spencer's servants (MCGC 200).

ANTHONY (ANTONIO)

Anthony (Antonio), an African, left England in July 1621 and came to Virginia on the *James*. On February 16, 1624, he was living at Warresqueak (**26**). He was still there on February 7, 1625, and was described as a servant in Edward Bennett's household. Mary, an African who arrived at Warresqueak in 1622, probably became his wife (CBE 42, 62).

ANTHONY

On February 16, 1624, Anthony, an African, was living in Elizabeth City (**18**) in Captain William Tucker's household. He was still there in early 1625, at which time he was identified as a servant. Listed with Anthony in 1624 was his wife, an African woman servant named Isabella (Isabell). By early 1625 Anthony and Isabella had a child, William, and all three had been baptized (CBE 43, 63).

ANTHONY

On February 16, 1624, an African named Anthony was living at Flowerdew Hundred (**53**) (CBE 37).

ARTHUR ANTHONY (ANTHONYE)

Sometime prior to May 1625, Arthur Anthony (Anthonye) patented 150 acres on the Appomattox River (**39**). His land, located in what eventually became Chesterfield County, was mentioned in a June 10, 1639, patent (VCR 4:554; PB 1 Pt. 2:665).

***

CHARLES ANTHONY

Charles Anthony, a goldsmith and Virginia Company investor from St. John Zachary's Parish in London, made his will on October 24, 1615, indicating that he had invested money in the colonization of Virginia and Bermuda. The testator, who was "chief graver" of the king's mint, named his eldest son, Thomas, as his principal heir and left him all of the tools of his trade. He also made bequests to several other children and made reference to his brother, Francis. Charles Anthony died soon after making his will, which was presented for probate on November 21, 1615. Because his estate had not been settled by September 15, 1623, by which time son Thomas was dead, Charles Anthony's widow, Elizabeth, was named executrix (WITH 98-99; CBE 34; EEAC 3; SH 3).

FRANCIS ANTHONY

When Dr. Francis Anthony made his will in June 1623, he identified himself as a physician and resident of St. Bartholomew the Great, London. He indicated that he was an investor in the Virginia Company and had goods in Virginia. Dr. Anthony also stated that he had an interest in some buildings in Southampton Hundred (**44**). He was the brother of goldsmith Charles Anthony, also a Virginia Company adventurer (CBE 33; EEAC 3; WAT 86-87; WITH 99).

***

EDWARD AP-EVAN

On December 24, 1619, the justices of Bridewell decided that Edward ap-Evan, a boy, would be detained until he could be sent to Virginia (CBE 14; HUME 13).

DAVID AP-RICHARD

In December 1619 David ap-Richard—who was being detained at Bridewell Prison and was to be sent to Virginia—escaped. It is uncertain whether he was apprehended and taken to the colony (CBE 14).

THOMAS AP-RICHARD

On March 22, 1622, when the Indians attacked Weyanoke (**52**), Thomas ap-Richard was slain. He was one of Sir George Yeardley's men (VCR 3:569).

JOHN AP-ROBERTS

John ap-Roberts died at Flowerdew Hundred (53) sometime after April 1623 but before February 16, 1624 (CBE 37).

RICE AP-WILLIAMS

On February 16, 1624, Rice ap-Williams was living on one of the plantations on the lower side of the James River, just east of Gray's Creek (10-16) and within the corporation of James City (CBE 40).

PETER APPLEBY (APLEBY)

On February 27, 1619, it was decided that Peter Appleby (Apleby), a boy, would be sent to Virginia. He was among the children rounded up from the streets of London so that they could be shipped to the colony (CBE 12).

WILLIAM APPLEBY (APLEBY)

William Appleby (Apleby), who came to Virginia on the *Furtherance*, died in Jamestown (1) sometime after April 1623 but before February 16, 1624 (CBE 39).

RICHARD APPLETON (APLETON)

Richard Appleton (Apleton) came to Virginia on the *James* in 1622 and on February 16, 1624, was living in Elizabeth City (18). In early 1625 he was identified as a 19-year-old servant in the household of Captain William Tucker of Elizabeth City (CBE 43, 63).

APOCHANCANO
(SEE OPECHANCANOUGH)

***

GABRIEL ARCHER

Gabriel Archer—a gentleman from Essex, England, who was educated at Cambridge and Gray's Inn—came to Virginia in 1607 in the first group of settlers. When the inbound colonists arrived at Cape Henry, Archer was wounded by an Indian who fired a pistol at him. He recovered and when the colonists sailed up the James River, he urged them to plant their settlement on a promontory located on the east side of College Creek's mouth, a site that Captain John Smith dubbed Archer's Hope. Gabriel Archer began a narrative that described the colonists' first few weeks on Jamestown Island (1) and the construction of their fortifications. He also accompanied Captain Christopher Newport on an exploratory voyage toward the head of the James River. Afterward, he described their journey and the Natives they encountered. Archer clashed openly with President Edward Maria Wingfield. In September 1607 he was made secretary of the colony and in January 1608 was named a councilor. Later in the year Captain Gabriel Archer returned to England with Christopher Newport, who had brought the 1st Supply of new settlers. However, he was back in the colony by 1609 and, according to Captain John Smith, caused problems. Gabriel Archer reportedly died in Virginia during the winter of 1609–10. In January 1620 John, Gabriel's brother and heir, asked the Virginia Company to give him the decedent's stock (CJS 1:xxix, 27, 61, 128, 205, 208, 212, 217; 2:141, 145, 158-159, 219, 222-223, 271; HAI 101-102, 115-116, 118, 122, 184, 188-189, 191, 196, 200, 352-353; VCR 1:300; STAN 21, 27).

JOHN ARCHER

On January 26, 1620, John Archer, the brother and heir of Captain Gabriel Archer, indicated that he wanted the decedent's Virginia Company stock (VCR 1:300).

***

JOSEPH ARCHER

Joseph Archer died in Virginia sometime after April 1623 but before February 16, 1624. He lived on the lower side of the James River, within the corporation of James City (8-15) (CBE 41).

RALPH ARDEN
ALIAS LITTLE TOM

On November 20, 1622, Ralph Arden, otherwise known as Little Tom, a Newgate inmate, was among those pardoned and selected to be sent to Virginia (CBE 29).

SAMUEL ARGALL
(ARGAL, ARGOLL, ARGYLE)

Sir Samuel Argall (Argal, Argoll, Argyle), who was from East Sutton in Kent, England, was considered a capable mariner and in March 1610 conducted Lord Delaware to Virginia. Argall and Sir George Somers left Jamestown (1) in June 1610 and set out for Bermuda to bring food back to the starving Virginia colonists. Afterward, Argall made an exploratory voyage to the New England coast, undertaking the first of numerous fishing voyages. He explored the Chesapeake Bay and its tributaries during the autumn and winter 1610 and accompanied Lord Delaware when he left Virginia in June 1611, having been designated captain of a company of men. When word reached England that French missionaries had been sent to North Virginia, Argall was sent out on the *Treasurer* to oust them. He reached Virginia in September 1612 and helped Sir Thomas Dale subdue the Indians. He also reported that the colony was in good condition at the time of his arrival. In March 1613 Argall was involved in the plot to capture Pocahontas. Argall set sail from Virginia in June 1613 and headed north. He destroyed the French Jesuit colony on Mount Desert Island (in Maine) and returned with prisoners. He also attacked the Dutch colony on the Hudson. Argall was employed in Virginia from December 1613 to June 1614. He returned to England but was sent back to the colony in February 1615.

In early 1617 Samuel Argall, who again was in England, was appointed deputy governor and admiral of Virginia and given a patent for a plantation. Soon after, he set sail for the colony and arrived on May 15, 1617, with 100 settlers. He appears to have considered himself the owner of a portion of West and Shirley Hundred (Eppes) Island (41), land to which Lord Delaware, Lady Elizabeth Dale, and others already had laid claim. Argall, as deputy governor, favored martial law and attempted to continue the policies and strict military code of justice established by Sir Thomas Gates and Sir Thomas Dale. On June 7, 1617, he informed Virginia Company officials that the colony was in poor condition. His solution was to strengthen Jamestown instead of Bermuda (39) and to expand the colonized territory. He asked for 100 men outfitted with the tools of their trade, and said that he expected hemp and flax to thrive. He also told Company officials that English grains could be grown in soil worn out by the cultivation of tobacco, and that cattle thrived in Virginia. He recommended

that the Company's magazine ship be sent to the colony every September, at harvest season, and reported that he had authorized people to trade with the Indians. He also confirmed ownership of the colony's leaders' cattle. After Samuel Argall had been in Virginia for a year, he asked to be replaced, claiming that he had greatly improved conditions while in office. He asked for ships' carpenters and 50 men outfitted with tools, plows, and clothing. When the Chickahominy Indians attacked and killed some colonists, he failed to seek revenge, a decision that later yielded criticism. In May 1618 Argall forbade private trade with the Indians, and he ordered the colonists to plant crops and bear arms at all times. No one was allowed to dismantle palisades or teach Indians how to shoot firearms. Argall had a frame church built in Jamestown, and he saw that a boat was built.

When the late Lord Delaware's ship, the *Neptune*, arrived in Virginia on August 14, 1618, in consort with the *Treasurer*, Argall commandeered the deceased governor's goods and servants. When Captain Edward Brewster, one of Lord Delaware's men, protested, Argall had Brewster tried at a court martial hearing and sentenced to death; later he suspended the sentence but banished Brewster from Virginia. Argall left for England in early April 1619, shortly before Governor George Yeardley's arrival. However, he had sent out the *Treasurer*, which captured some Africans under questionable circumstances and brought them to Virginia in late summer 1619. Samuel Argall eventually was subjected to a considerable amount of criticism. He had been given use of some public land known as the Common Garden, acreage tended by Company servants, but he reportedly diverted both ground and servants to his own use. He also placed the Society of Martin's Hundred's settlers on the acreage tentatively set aside as the Governor's Land (3), put the late Lord Delaware's servants to work on his own projects, and misappropriated their goods. He was accused of using the Virginia Company's frigate for Indian trade, which he monopolized, and he allegedly sold the Company's cattle, pocketing the proceeds. Argall refused to free the ancient planters, even though their time had expired, and he allowed people to ship tobacco and sassafras at the same rates the Company used, thereby making them competitors. He also received criticism for failing to punish the Chickahominy Indians for killing some colonists. Despite his detractors, Samuel Argall was knighted at Rochester in 1622 and was involved in the attack on Cadiz. Eventually, however, he was made to account for his actions in Virginia and the Company assets under his control. He was sued by the widow of Robert Smalley of Bermuda Hundred and by Lady Cecily West, the widow of Lord Delaware. When Argall died in 1625–26, he was under a persistent cloud of suspicion. Sometime prior to June 1631 his heirs sold his Virginia landholdings to John Woodall, a former investor in the Virginia Company (WITH 664; HAI 433-434, 509, 752-756, 801-802, 829-830, 902, 905, 907-908, 904-905; PRO 30/15/2 f 205; C 24/490; VCR 1:217, 219, 222, 224, 255-257, 264, 284-286, 323, 337, 350-351, 360-364, 372-374, 387; 2:27, 51-55, 79-80, 393-397, 400; 3:68-69, 73-74, 76, 78-79, 92-93, 175-176, 231-232, 249, 255, 298, 522; 4:4-5, 562-567; STAN 14, 28; SH 4; SR 3112, 10376; POR 72, 80; AP 78; FER 522, 523, 524; CBE 31, 71, 94-95; EAE 12; MCGC 44, 55, 132; EEAC 3; WAT 919-920).

SYMON ARMESTED

On May 23, 1625, Symon Armested testified before the General Court about some business dealings that occurred in England and involved Mr. Welch and Mr. Beaumont, master of a ship bringing some servants to Virginia (MCGC 59-60).

[NO FIRST NAME] ARMESTRONGE

On February 7, 1625, the muster-taker noted that someone named Armestronge had died in Newportes News (24) sometime after February 16, 1624 (CBE 63).

JOCKY [JOACHIM?] ARMESTRONGE

Jocky [Joachim?] Armestronge reportedly died in Elizabeth City (17, 18) sometime after April 1623 but before February 16, 1624 (CBE 63).

***

JOHN ARMY (ARMIE)

John Army (Armie) came to Virginia in 1622 on the *Furtherance* and on February 16, 1624, was living at Basses Choice (27)

in Warresqueak. On January 3, 1625, he was fined for disobeying Captain Nathaniel Basse, the settlement's commander, and for failing to attend church. On February 7, 1625, John Army and his partner, William Newman, were living in Basses Choice and were sharing a dwelling. They were amply supplied with stored food and defensive weaponry. On March 4, 1629, John Army was summoned before the General Court, where he acknowledged his indebtedness to Thomas Flint and was ordered to pay what he owed. On June 26, 1635, Army patented 400 acres in Warresqueak (later Isle of Wight) County, using the headrights of his wife, Marie, and son, William. His acreage adjoined that of Richard and Robert Bennett. On November 11, 1636, John Army witnessed the will of Edward Dewell of Warresqueak, one of Simon Curnock's servants (CBE 46, 62; MCGC 39, 189; PB 1 Pt. 1:185; SH 27; DOR 1:49).

MARIE ARMY (ARMIE) (MRS. JOHN ARMY [ARMIE])

On June 26, 1635, when John Army (Armie) patented 400 acres of land in Warresqueak (Isle of Wight) County, he used the headrights of his wife, Marie, and son, William (PB 1 Pt. 1:185).

WILLIAM ARMY (ARMIE)

When John Army (Armie) patented 400 acres of land in Warresqueak (Isle of Wight) County on June 26, 1635, he listed his son, William, as a headright (PB 1 Pt. 1:185).

***

WILLIAM ARNALL

On August 14, 1624, when Edward Waters patented some land, he used William Arnall as a headright and indicated that Arnall had come to Virginia on the *Seaflower* in 1621 (PB 1 Pt. 1:18).

JOHN ARNOLD

In July and August 1630 John Arnold testified that the ship *Susan* was caulked for the first time in Virginia. He indicated that the vessel had needed extensive repairs and therefore had stayed in the colony for six weeks (EAE 24).

NICHOLAS ARRAS

On February 16, 1624, Nicholas Arras was living on the lower side of the James River. He resided at one of the plantations east of Gray's Creek (**11-16**), within the corporation of James City (CBE 41).

ELIZABETH ARRUNDELL (ARUNDEL, ARUNDELLE, ARUNDELL, ARONDELL, ARNDELL)

Elizabeth Arrundell (Arundel, Arundelle, Arundell, Arondell, Arndell), who came to Virginia in 1620 on the *Abigail*, was living in Elizabeth City at Buckroe (**17**) on February 16, 1624. By January 24, 1625, she had moved to urban Jamestown (**1**), where she was a servant in Sir George Yeardley's household. She may have been related to Richard Arrundell, who also was a Yeardley servant. On September 11, 1626, Daniel Watkins testified in court that Mrs. Joan Wright, who was accused of practicing witchcraft while she lived in Elizabeth City, had predicted that Elizabeth Arrundell would die before receiving some hens promised to her by Robert Thresher, a resident of Elizabeth City. A few days later, Thresher confirmed the allegations against Mrs. Wright (CBE 45, 54; MCGC 111-112, 114).

JOHN ARRUNDELL (ARUNDEL)

According to Captain John Smith, John Arrundell (Arundel) was among those who left Plymouth, England, with Sir Richard Grenville on April 9, 1585. He said that as soon as the group arrived in the vicinity of Roanoke Island, they explored the mainland and then went to Croatan. In 1620 Smith identified Arrundell as an investor in the Virginia Company (CJS 1:68; 2:69, 273).

MARGARET ARRUNDELL (ARUNDEL, ARUNDELLE, ARUNDELL, ARONDELL, ARNDELL)

Margaret Arrundell (Arundel, Arundelle, Arundell, Arondell, Arndell) came to Virginia in 1621 on the *Abigail* and may have been related to John and Peter Arrundell, who also were aboard. On February 16, 1624, Margaret was living at Buckroe (**17**) in Elizabeth City. However, by January 20, 1625, she had been moved to Flowerdew Hundred (**53**), where she was a member of Humphrey Kent's household. Margaret was then 9 years old (CBE 45, 50).

***

PETER ARRUNDELL (ARUNDEL, ARUNDELLE, ARUNDELL, ARONDELL, ARNDELL)

On February 16, 1620, Peter Arrundell (Arundel, Arundelle, Arundell, Arondell, Arndell), a Virginia Company investor and a silk-maker, asked Company officials to double the number of shares he owned. On June 27, 1621, after Arrundell had arrived in Virginia, Governor George Yeardley recommended him to Captain Nuce, the commander of Elizabeth City. Peter Arrundell wrote to Virginia Company treasurer Edwin Sandys on December 15, 1621, stating that his son-in-law, Captain Mansell, who was supposed to assist him by hunting and fishing, was dead. He added that although Captain Nuce had offered to help, the Virginia Company's promises of support were unfulfilled, for his household had scanty provisions and poor housing, lacked cattle, and lived in a dangerous place. Two weeks later Arrundell sent word to John Smyth of Nibley that people had begun living along the Chickahominy River, perhaps referring to the Virginia Company servants seated on the tract of Company Land (**4**) in James City. Peter Arrundell was in Elizabeth City on September 10, 1622, when he witnessed Captain John Wilcocks' will. In mid-April 1623 he informed Company officials that he was living at Buckroe (**17**) and that the governor had seen his new silk house. He said that his household was experiencing severe food shortages and that his late son-in-law's corn crop had been confiscated and taken to Jamestown. He added that meal was in such short supply that he had to exchange a silver bowl for some, and that old planters died daily. Arrundell complained about the cost of supplies and the problems the colonists were having with the Indians. He said that Captain Whitaker's chief man (or overseer) had had a dispute with Anthony Bonall (another silk-maker), who had gathered mulberry leaves on Whitaker's land. On February 16, 1624, when a census was made of the colony's inhabitants, Peter Arrundell was still living at Buckroe on the Virginia Company's land. When he received 200 acres in that vicinity on November 8, 1624, he was described as a gentleman. By early 1625, however, he was dead. When a list of patented land was sent back to England in May 1625, he was credited with 200 acres in Elizabeth City. On September 7, 1632, John Arrundell, Peter's son and heir, claimed some Virginia land on the basis of his late father's bill of adventure (VCR 1:309; 3:462-464, 534, 589; 4:89, 92-93, 230, 558; SH 5; CBE 45, 68; PB 1 Pt. 1:116).

JOHN ARRUNDELL (ARUNDEL, ARUNDELLE, ARUNDELL, ARONDELL, ARNDELL)

John Arrundell (Arundel, Arundelle, Arundell, Arondell, Arndell) came to Virginia in 1621 on the *Abigail,* the vessel that brought 5-year-old Margaret Arrundell, perhaps a relative. John's father, Peter Arrundell, a Virginia Company investor and silkworker, wrote a letter on April 15, 1623, in which he indicated that his son, John, also had been trained in silk-making. On February 16, 1624, John Arrundell was residing at Buckroe (17), where his father also lived. He was still there in early 1625 and was identified as a member of William Hampton's household, which was located on the Virginia Company's land. John Arrundell was age 22; his father, Peter, who also had come to the colony, was dead. On April 11, 1625, John Arrundell was summoned to Jamestown to testify at an inquest concerning John Verone's possible suicide. On November 10, 1627, he was identified as a gentleman when he informed the General Court that Thomas Hunter's will, presented by Edward Waters, was authentic. On December 12, 1627, John Arrundell was granted a 12-acre leasehold in Buckroe, opposite Old Point Comfort Island. Sometime prior to January 29, 1629, he came into possession of a 50-acre leasehold that he assigned to Elias LaGuard. In September 1632 Arrundell received a patent for 100 acres on the Back River in Elizabeth City (19), land to which he was entitled as his father's heir. In September 1632 John Arrundell was identified as a commissioner of Elizabeth City's local court, and in February 1633 he served as a burgess for the lower parish of Elizabeth City. In late 1634 he purchased some of the late Thomas Lee's goods, which were sold by Bartholomew Hopkins (VCR 4:230; CBE 45, 208; MCGC 53, 130; PB 1 Pt. 1:80-82, 109, 116, 141; HEN 1:170, 187, 203).

***

RICHARD ARRUNDELL (ARUNDEL, ARUNDELLE, ARUNDELL, ARONDELL, ARNDELL)

Richard Arrundell (Arundel, Arundelle, Arundell, Arondell, Arndell), who came to Virginia on the *Abigail,* was living in urban Jamestown (1) on February 16, 1624, and was a servant in Sir George Yeardley's household. He was still residing there on January 24, 1625. He may have been related to Elizabeth Arrundell, who also was a servant in the Yeardley household in 1625 (CBE 38, 54).

RICHARD ARTHUR

On January 31, 1625, Richard Arthur, who was in Jamestown (1), testified before the General Court in litigation involving Captain Wilcox (Wilcocks) and John Crowdick (MCGC 45-46).

JOHN ASBIE

John Asbie was in the first group of Jamestown (1) colonists who came to Virginia in 1607. However, he was not included in the list of settlers compiled by Captain John Smith. According to George Percy, Asbie died of the bloody flux on August 9, 1607 (CJS 1:19; HAI 99).

JOHN ASCAM (ASCOMB, ASCOMBE)

John Ascam (Ascomb, Ascombe) came to Virginia on the *Charles* in 1624. On February 16, 1624, he was living on the Eastern Shore in the household headed by Charles Harmar, who lived on Old Plantation Creek (73) and was overseer of Lady Elizabeth Dale's property in Virginia. In early 1625 John was still living in the Harmar home and was 22 years old. He may have been the same man identified as John Ashcome, who was living on the Eastern Shore in the early 1630s (CBE 46, 69; AMES 1:37-38, 41, 58).

***

PETER ASCAM (ASCOMB, ASCOMBE) I

Peter Ascam (Ascomb, Ascombe) I came to Virginia sometime prior to December 1621, when he was ordered to release Hugh Hughs, whom he was detaining as a servant. In February 1623 Peter served on a jury that convened in urban Jamestown (**1**), his household's place of residence. He was identified by the title "Goodman," an indication that he was considered a respectable citizen though not a "gentleman," a person of higher social standing. Peter Ascam died sometime after August 5, 1623, but before February 16, 1624. He was survived by his widow, Mary, and their two children: 1-year-old Peter and 4-year-old Abigail (Abigall) (MCGC 4-5; CBE 39; FER 339).

MARY ASCAM (ASCOMB, ASCOMBE) (MRS. PETER [ASCOMB, ASCOMBE]) (SEE MRS. PETER LANGMAN)

On February 16, 1624, Mary, the widow of Peter Ascam (Ascomb, Ascombe) I, headed a household in urban Jamestown (**1**) that included her daughter. On October 4, 1624, when Mary testified that she witnessed Sybil (Sybil, Sybill) Royall's will, she indicated that she was 40 years old. By January 24, 1625, Mary Ascam had married Peter Langman. She and her children, 1-year-old Peter II and 4-year-old Abigail (Abigall), and her new husband, Peter Langman, shared a home in Jamestown (CBE 38-39, 55; MCGC 4, 21).

PETER ASCAM (ASCOMB, ASCOMBE) II

On January 24, 1625, Peter Ascam (Ascomb, Ascombe) II, the 1-year-old son of Peter and Mary Ascam, was living in urban Jamestown (**1**) in the household of his mother, Mary, and stepfather, Peter Langman. As young Peter's name was not included in the February 16, 1624, census, he may have been somewhat younger than presumed (CBE 55).

ABIGAIL (ABIGALL) ASCAM (ASCOMB, ASCOMBE)

On February 16, 1624, Abigail (Abigall) Ascam (Ascomb, Ascombe), whose father, Peter, was deceased, was living in urban Jamestown (**1**) with her mother, Mary Ascam. On January 24, 1625, Abigail, who was then 4 years old, was still residing in Jamestown with her mother, her 1-year-old brother, Peter Ascam II, and her stepfather, Peter Langman (CBE 38-39, 55).

***

***

CHRISTOPHER ASH

Christopher Ash, his wife, and their infant died at Warresqueak (**26**) sometime after April 1623 but before February 16, 1624 (CBE 42).

MRS. CHRISTOPHER ASH

Mrs. Christopher Ash, her husband, and their infant died at Warresqueak (**26**) sometime after April 1623 but before February 16, 1624 (CBE 42).

[NAMELESS INFANT] ASH

Mr. and Mrs. Christopher Ash and their infant died at Warresqueak (**26**) sometime after April 1623 but before February 16, 1624 (CBE 42).

***

JAMES ASHBEE

On August 30, 1628, Bridewell officials decided that James Ashbee, a vagrant boy from St. Sepulcher's Parish, would be sent to Virginia (CBE 84; HUME 34).

DANIELL ASHE

On October 21, 1629, the justices of Bridewell decided that Daniell Ashe, a boy, would be sent to Virginia (HUME 35).

PETER ASHELEY

On September 7, 1632, when John Robins I obtained a patent using Peter Asheley as a headright, he identified Peter as one of his servants and said that in 1622 he had paid for Asheley's transportation to Virginia on the *Margaret and John* (PB 1 Pt. 1:116).

ANN ASHLEY

On February 16, 1624, Ann Ashley, a maidservant, was living in John Burrows' household in Jamestown (**1**). She was still there on January 24, 1625, and was 19 years old (CBE 38, 56).

RICHARD ASHMAN

On November 15, 1615, it was decided that Richard Ashman, a convicted felon and prisoner in the White Lyon in Southwark Parish, would be delivered to Sir Thomas Smith so that he could be transported to Virginia (PC 2/29 f 167; SR 4525).

WALTER ASHTON (ASTON?) (SEE WALTER ASTON)

On July 19, 1627, Walter Ashton shipped goods from London to Virginia on the *James*. He may have been the Virginia colonist Walter Aston, who came to Virginia in 1628 and settled in Charles City County near Causey's Care (**45**) (CBE 79).

JOHN ASKEW (ASCUE)

On August 19, 1618, the justices of Bridewell Court decided to send John Askew (Ascue), a vagrant from the Bridge Ward, to Virginia (CBE 10).

JOHN ASKEW (ASCUE)

On February 27, 1619, it was decided that John Askew (Ascue), one of the youngsters rounded up from the streets of London, would be sent to Virginia (CBE 13).

WILLIAM ASKEW

William Askew, an ancient planter, came to Virginia on the *Prosperous* in May 1610 and on February 16, 1624, was living at West and Shirley Hundred (**41**). He was still there a year later and was a solitary household head. William was then 30 years old and had a dwelling of his own and an ample supply of food and defensive weaponry (CBE 36, 52; DOR 1:14).

JOHN ASLEY

On June 24, 1635, when John Russell patented some land, he used John Asley as a headright (PB 1 Pt. 1:177).

PETER ASTLEY

Virginia Company records dated May 17, 1622, indicate that Peter Astley was compensated for going to Virginia. This suggests that he was a skilled worker (FER 376).

THOMAS ASTLEY

According to records maintained by the Drapers Company in London, Thomas

Astley, a linen draper, settled in Virginia in 1618 (SR 879).

ANTHONY ASTON

In July 1626 Anthony Aston borrowed Mr. William Gainey's servant boy, Thomas Savage, who drowned while he was in Aston's custody and visiting the home of Mr. William English in Elizabeth City (**18**) (MCGC 122).

EDWARD ASTON

On February 16, 1624, Edward Aston was living in Elizabeth City (**17, 18**) (CBE 44).

MANUEL ASTON

Manuel Aston, a bricklayer, went to Virginia on the *Garland* in 1619 and appears to have been sent to Southampton Hundred (**44**) (FER 137).

ROBERT ASTON

On January 25, 1625, Robert Aston, who came to Virginia on the *Treasurer*, was living on Mulberry Island (**21**), where he was a 29-year-old servant in the household of William Peirce (CBE 56).

WALTER ASTON

Walter Aston, according to his own epitaph, came to the colony in 1628 when he was 21 years old. He may have been the individual identified as Walter Ashton who on July 19, 1627, shipped goods from London to Virginia on the *James*. When Walter Aston first arrived in the colony, he probably lived in the vicinity of West and Shirley Hundred (**41**), for in March 1630 he served as the burgess for Shirley Hundred (Eppes) Island. In the February 1632 session of the assembly, he represented the settlers living at Shirley Hundred and the Island, at Chaplin's Choice (**56**), and at Mr. Farrar's (Ferrar's, Ferrer's) plantation, Jordan's Journey (**46**). A year later he was described as a resident of Causey's Care (**45**), a name given to the territory between Shirley Hundred and the defunct Virginia Company's tract of company land, which lay to the east (**62**). On February 6, 1634, Walter Aston purchased a 200-acre tract—the plantation known as Causey's Care—from the late Nathaniel Causey's son, John. In July 1638, when Walter Aston patented the 590 acres on which he was living, he did so on the basis of headrights. He indicated that he was entitled to 50 acres for his own personal adventure and that of his wife, Warbowe. By 1638 Walter had married a second time, taking as his wife a woman named Hannah. He continued to acquire acreage in Charles City, close to the land he already owned. In 1639 Walter Aston was appointed one of Charles City's tobacco viewers (or inspectors), and he served as a justice of the county court. In 1641 he and three other men obtained the assembly's permission to undertake explorations at the head of the Appomattox River. On December 31, 1645, Walter Aston was identified in Jamestown (1) merchant George Menefie's will as a debtor. Aston died on April 6, 1656, at age 49 and was buried in the graveyard of Westover Church in Charles City County. His son, Walter Aston II, was his primary heir (HEN 1:147, 154, 168, 178, 202, 239; WITH 180-181; PB 2:78; CBE 79).

[NO FIRST NAME] ATKINS

On March 22, 1622, when the Indians attacked Henricus Island (63), someone named Atkins was killed (VCR 3:565).

[NO FIRST NAME] ATKINS

Sometime prior to April 1623, Virginia Company officials learned that Mr. Atkins had told the servants he was bringing to Virginia that living conditions were good. However, two for whom he was responsible, Thomas Best and Henry Brigg, claimed that they were starving and that Atkins had sold them as soon as they arrived in the colony. Both servants lived in Elizabeth City (17, 18) (VCR 4:236).

JOHN ATKINS (ATTKINS)

John Atkins (Attkins) came to Virginia on *Gifte* in 1623 and on February 16, 1624, was living in Warresqueak (26). When a muster was made of that area's inhabitants on February 7, 1625, John was identified as a servant in the household of Edward Bennett, whose plantation was known as Bennett's Welcome. On March 25, 1629, when John Atkins testified before the General Court, he indicated that he was 29 years old. When he was questioned about Thomas Hall, a hermaphrodite, he denied that Hall was his servant. When the assem-

bly convened in March 1630, John Atkins served as a burgess for Warresqueak (CBE 42, 612; MCGC 195; HEN 1:149).

JOHN ATKINS

John Atkins, who made his will on September 3, 1623, probably resided near Jamestown (1). He asked to be buried "in the usual place" in Jamestown, and his will was witnessed by Christopher Davison, Edward Sharples, and Peter Stafferton, all of whom resided in the capital city. John Atkins seems to have been a planter, for he asked Luke Boyse of Bermuda Hundred (39) to see that his tobacco crop was harvested and his debts paid. He made bequests to the three men who witnessed his will and to his brother William, who lived in England at Bassinghall. On October 2, 1624, when English officials appointed an administrator for John Atkins' estate, he was described as a bachelor who had died in Virginia. In time, John's brothers—William, Richard, and Humphrey—served as administrators (WITH 35-36; EEAC 3-4; CBE 39, 48).

JOHN ATKINS I

In November 1636, when John Atkins Sr. of Chard, in Somerset, made his will, he made reference to his son and grandson, both of whom were named John Atkins and were then in Virginia. The testator designated his widow, Katherine Atkins, as his executrix (EEAC 4; WITH 32-33).

***

RICHARD ATKINS

Richard Atkins and his child died in Jamestown (1) sometime after April 1623 but before February 16, 1624 (CBE 39).

[NO FIRST NAME] ATKINS

Richard Atkins' child died in Jamestown (1) sometime after April 1623 but before February 16, 1624 (CBE 39).

***

***

RICHARD ATKINS

When Richard Atkins patented some land in 1632, he indicated that he had come to Virginia on the ship *Abigail* in 1621 and that his transportation costs had been paid by Captain William Peirce. On February 16, 1624, Richard and his wife were living on the Governor's Land (3), where he was a household head and probably occupied Peirce's leasehold. By January 24, 1625, he and his wife, Abigail, had relocated to Mulberry Island (21), where they were described as Captain William Peirce's servants. Richard, who was then 24 years old, was said to have come to the colony on the *London Merchant*. His Mulberry Island household was well supplied with stored food and defensive weaponry. Richard Atkins returned to England on the *Hopewell* and when he appeared before the High Court of the Admiralty on May 25, 1630, he identified himself as a 29-year-old Virginia planter. He testified about the *Gift of God*, which was bound for London when it was lost in a storm off Cape Hatteras. Richard Atkins returned to Virginia and on May 6, 1632, when he received a patent for 100 acres at the head of Skiffs Creek, was identified as a Mulberry Island planter. When obtaining land under the headright system, Richard indicated that although Captain Peirce had paid for Richard's transportation to the colony, he (Richard) had underwritten the cost of bringing his own wife, Abigail, who had arrived aboard the *Tiger* in 1621. On August 31, 1636, when yeoman John Ring, a former resident of London, made his will, he bequeathed Richard Atkins (whom he described as a merchant) a gold signet ring and some tobacco. He also left Richard's wife, Abigail, a silver drinking cup (CBE 39, 56, 96; EAE 23; HCA 13/49; PB 1 Pt. 1:75; SR 4001, 3977; EEAC 48, WITH 152).

ABIGAIL (ABIGALL) ATKINS (MRS. RICHARD ATKINS)

Abigail (Abigall), Richard Atkins' wife, came to Virginia in 1621 on the *Tiger* at her husband's expense. On February 16, 1624, the Atkins couple was living on the Governor's Land (3), where he was a household head. By January 24, 1625, Richard and Abigail Atkins had been moved to Mulberry Island (21), where they were described as Captain William Peirce's servants. Abigail was then said to have come to the colony on the *Abigail*. On May 6, 1632, when Richard Atkins patented some land at the head of Skiffs Creek, he used

Abigail as a headright. She apparently was still alive on August 31, 1636, for John Ring, a yeoman from London, bequeathed her a silver drinking cup (CBE 39, 56; PB 1 Pt. 1:75; SR 3977; EEAC 48; WITH 152).

***

WILLIAM ATKINS

On April 25, 1625, William Atkins testified that John Stephens was of sound mind when he prepared his will and gave it to Tobias Felgate. Atkins added, however, that he did not see Stephens sign the will or affix his seal to it. On March 27, 1626, when William Atkins made a nuncupative will stating that he was sick and weak, he was staying at the home of Thomas Bunn, a surgeon who lived at the Governor's Land (3). Atkins made reference to his wife and children, who were in England, but he failed to identify them (MCGC 56, 98).

WILLIAM ATKINS

On June 24, 1635, when Adam Thorogood patented some land, he used William Atkins as a headright, indicating that he had transported him to the colony (PB 1 Pt. 1:179).

ANN ATKINSON

On February 16, 1624, Ann Atkinson was living in Elizabeth City (17, 18) (CBE 43).

CHARLES ATKINSON

On October 7, 1622, Charles Atkinson was identified as a Virginia Company tenant when he was asked to account for the Company's goods in Elizabeth City (17). On February 16, 1624, Charles was still living in Elizabeth City (VCR 2:104; CBE 43).

FRANCIS ATKINSON

Francis Atkinson died at Martin's Hundred (7) sometime after April 1623 but before February 16, 1624. Francis may have been related to the Robert Atkinson who also died then at Martin's Hundred (CBE 42).

RICHARD ATKINSON

On June 29, 1608, when Hugh Willastone made an investment in the Virginia Company, Richard Atkinson served as a witness (MCGC 49).

ROBERT ATKINSON

Robert Atkinson died at Martin's Hundred (**7**) sometime after April 1623 but before February 16, 1624. Robert may have been related to Francis Atkinson, who also died then at Martin's Hundred (CBE 42).

WILLIAM ATKINSON

On May 5, 1609, when William Atkinson of St. Vedast, Foster Lane, London, made his will immediately prior to his departure for Virginia, he identified himself as the younger man of that name and a gentleman. William named his father, William Sr., as his principal heir and acknowledged that he was indebted to him. He also mentioned his brothers, Thomas and Ralph, who were in England. William Atkinson's will was proved on August 27, 1613 (WITH 99; SH 1; EEAC 3; SR 3108).

THOMAS ATMORE

On June 24, 1635, when Adam Thorogood patented some land, he used Thomas Atmore as a headright and indicated that in 1634 he had paid for Atmore's transportation to Virginia on the *John and Dorothy* (PB 1 Pt. 1:179).

NICHOLAS ATWELL

On January 21, 1629, Nicholas Atwell informed the General Court that he had heard John Lightfoot bequeath his entire estate to William Spencer. Since Lightfoot and Spencer resided in the eastern end of Jamestown Island (**1**), Nicholas also may have been associated with that area (MCGC 181).

THOMAS ATWELL

On July 15, 1631, Thomas Atwell, a Virginia planter, was among those who petitioned royal officials for relief from the customs duties on tobacco. He indicated that his hogsheads of tobacco bore the mark *HL* (G&M 164).

EDWARD AUBORNE (AUBORINE, ALBORNE, AWBORN)

Edward Auborne (Auborine, Alborne, Awborn) came to Virginia on the *Jonathan* in 1620 and on February 16, 1624, was living at Flowerdew Hundred (**53**). He was still resid-ing there on January 20, 1625, and was a solitary household head who had an adequate supply of provisions and defensive weaponry. By late June 1627 Edward Auborne had relocated to Shirley Hundred (**41**). On September 17, 1627, he testified that he had been present on June 23rd when Indians attacked John Throgmorton while he was working in the field. He said that John lived only a short time after being wounded but made a nuncupative will. On March 4 and March 7, 1629, Edward Auborne was summoned before the General Court to testify in a dispute that involved the Rev. Grivel Pooley (CBE 37, 50; DOR 1:22; MCGC 153, 189, 192).

ROBERT AUKLAND

When a list of patented land was sent back to England in May 1625, Robert Aukland was credited with 200 acres in Coxendale (**64**), within the corporation of Henrico (VCR 4:552).

ROBERT AUSLEY (AUSTYE)

On February 12, 1620, it was decided that Robert Ausley (Austye), who had been brought in from Cheapside, would be detained at Bridewell until he could be sent to Virginia (CBE 18).

AMBROSE AUSTIN

On July 18, 1620, Ambrose Austin of High Holborne, England, asked the Virginia Company for an appropriation of Virginia land in exchange for his bill of adventure (VCR 1:407).

ROBERT AUSTIN (AUSTINE, ASTON, AUSTEN)

On February 16, 1624, Robert Austin (Austine, Aston, Austen) was living in urban Jamestown (**1**), where he was a servant in William Peirce's household. By January 24, 1625, he had moved to Mulberry Island (**21**), where he lived in a household headed by Richard Atkins, who also was one of Peirce's servants. Robert, who was age 29, reportedly came to the colony on the *Abigail*, which transported some of Peirce's other servants. When Robert Austen made his will on September 18, 1626, he named Captain Peirce as his executor. Robert Austen died, and on October 2, 1626, John

Lightfoot, John West, and Thomas Smith came into court to prove his will. When an inventory of his estate was presented in court on January 10, 1627, he was identified as a resident of Mulberry Island and one of Captain William Peirce's servants (CBE 38, 56; MCGC 115, 130).

TABITHA AUSTIN (AUSTYN)

On January 22, 1620, the court of Bridewell decided that Tabitha Austin (Austyn) would be sent to Virginia (CBE 17).

TOBIAS AUSTIN (AUSTYN)

On January 22, 1619, it was decided that Tobias Austin (Austyn), a boy, would be detained so that he could be sent to Virginia (HUME 21).

WILLIAM AUSTIN (AUSTINE, ASTON, AUSTEN)

In 1619 the Ferrars, who were important Virginia Company investors, paid for the transportation of William Austin (Austine, Aston, Austen) to Virginia (FER 296).

ABRAHAM (ABRAM) AVELIN (AVELINGE, AVELING)

Abraham (Abram) Avelin (Avelinge, Aveling) came to Virginia in 1620 on the *Elizabeth* and on February 16, 1624, was residing on the Eastern Shore (**72-78**). However, by early 1625 he had relocated to Elizabeth City (**18**) and was living in the household headed by William Gayne and Robert Newman. Abraham was then 23 years old. He may have been a kinsman of Arthur Avelin, who also came to the colony on the *Elizabeth* in 1620 (CBE 46, 65).

ARTHUR AVELIN (AVELINGE, AVELING)

In 1620 Arthur Avelin (Avelinge, Aveling) came to Virginia on the *Elizabeth* and in early 1625 was living in the Elizabeth City (**18**) household of William Gayne and Robert Newman. Arthur was then 26 years old and appears to have been a servant. On November 21, 1625, Arthur Avelin testified that he had done some work for Robert Newman. A month later, when he was summoned to court again on December 19,

1625, he appeared with his masters, Richard Evans of Basses Choice (**27**) and Robert Newman. On January 3, 1626, Avelin testified that Evans, as his master, had prevented him from obeying a previous summons to court. He was called on to answer questions about the statements Edward Nevell had made in Canada about Richard Cornish's being wrongfully hanged. Arthur indicated that he had gone to Canada on the *Swann*. By November 1628 Arthur Avelin appears to have gained his freedom and moved to Archer's Hope (**6**). It was then that he co-signed Joseph Johnson's peace bond, a guarantee that Johnson would not disturb his neighbor, Thomas Farley (CBE 65; MCGC 75, 81-83, 85, 178).

JACOB AVERY (AVERIE)

On February 2, 1630, Jacob Avery (Averie), a gentleman, obtained a 21-year lease for 500 acres on Skiffs Creek, near Martin's Hundred (**7**), and another 250 acres at the head of the creek. He had acquired his property by means of a July 8, 1629, court order. On June 29, 1631, Avery's acreage was described as being near Hugh Heyward's land (PB 1 Pt. 1:102, 111, 144).

GEORGE AYRES

On December 15, 1628, when Tobias Boxe made his will, he identified George Ayres as a Virginia planter (WITH 55).

B

ELIZABETH KINGSMILL BACON (MRS. WILLIAM TAYLOR [TAYLOE, TAYLER], MRS. NATHANIEL BACON) (SEE ELIZABETH KINGSMILL)

HENRY BACON

On February 15, 1619, Virginia Company officials noted that Henry Bacon, master of Sir Edward Zouch's ship, the *Silver Falcon,* would be taking the ship to Virginia (VCR 3:135).

THOMAS BACON

When the Indians attacked Edward Bennett's plantation in Warresqueak (**26**) on March 22, 1622, Thomas Bacon was killed (VCR 3:571).

JOHN BADSTON (BADELEY)

John Badston (Badeley) came to Virginia on the *Hopewell* in 1623 and on February 16, 1624, was living on the Maine (**3**). However, by February 4, 1625, he had moved to Archer's Hope (**6**), where he was a 24-year-old servant in John Ellison's household (CBE 39, 58).

JOHN BAFFE (BASSE?)

On August 23, 1631, the justices of Bridewell Court decided that John Baffe (Basse?), a boy from Langborne, would be sent to Virginia (HUME 36).

HENRY BAGFORD

Henry Bagford died at Martin's Hundred (**7**) sometime after April 1623 but before February 16, 1624 (CBE 42).

THOMAS BAGLEN

Thomas Baglen was a resident of Jamestown Island (**1**) on January 24, 1625 (CBE 56).

ROGER BAGNALL

On November 16, 1635, Roger Bagnall patented some acreage in Warresqueak (**26**) that he had purchased from William Clapham (PB 1 Pt. 1:308).

ANTHONY BAGNESS (BAGLEY)

Anthony Bagness (Bagley) was one of the first Jamestown (**1**) colonists. According to Captain John Smith, during the summer of 1608 some Nansemond and Chesapeake Indians shot at Bagness and struck his hat. Later in the year Bagness went with Smith on his second exploratory voyage in the Chesapeake Bay. Smith said that Bagness and another man killed nearly 150 waterfowl when they were at Kecoughtan (**17**) during Christmas 1608 (that is, early January 1609). Anthony Bagness was coauthor of an account that Smith included in some of his published narratives (CJS 1:197, 244-245; 2:170, 179-180, 194).

HENRY BAGNESS

On August 6, 1635, Henry Bagness was in possession of some land in Accomack in the vicinity of Old Plantation Creek (**73**), adjacent to William Berriman's acreage (PB 1 Pt. 1:270).

HENRY BAGWELL

Henry Bagwell, an ancient planter, was shipwrecked in Bermuda with Sir Thomas Gates and Sir George Somers in 1609. He reached Virginia in 1610 on the *Deliverance*, which had been fashioned from Bermuda's native cedar wood. On February 16, 1624, Henry was living at West and Shirley Hundred (**41**); he was still there on January 22, 1625, heading a household with his partner, Simon (Symon) Sturgis (Turgis). Henry Bagwell was then 35 years old. The two men had an ample supply of stored food and defensive weaponry and some livestock. When a list of patented land was sent back to England in May 1625, Henry Bagwell was credited with 50 acres within the corporation of Charles City. On December 22, 1628, the General Court ordered him to pay the remainder of his debt to Hugh Hawkridge. Bagwell moved to the Eastern Shore and in 1630 and 1632 served as a burgess for Accomack. By 1637 he had married Alice, the widow of Benjamin Stratton. Henry Bagwell continued to play an active role in public life and became clerk of the local court. He was still alive in April 1645 (CBE 36, 52-53; VCR 4:555; MCGC 180; HEN 1:149, 179; AMES 1:67, 96, 146; 2:437; PB 3:289; DOR 1:15, 90-91).

ROBERT BAGWELL

When information was compiled on the inhabitants of Shirley Hundred (**41**) on January 22, 1625, the name "Robert Bagwell" appeared in the list directly over those of household head Henry Bagwell and his partner, Simon (Symon) Sturgis (Turgis). It is unclear whether Henry and Robert Bagwell were one and the same, or whether Robert was a sponsor who was perhaps absent or deceased when demographic records were compiled (DOR 1:15).

***
THOMAS BAGWELL

Thomas Bagwell, an ancient planter, came
to Virginia sometime prior to May 1616 and
on February 16, 1624, was living at West
and Shirley Hundred (**41**). By February 4,
1625, he had moved to the Neck O'Land
(**5**), where he headed a household that had
a modest supply of stored food and defensive weaponry. When Thomas Bagwell testified before the General Court on March
13, 1626, he said that Allen Keniston had
wanted Richard Peerce to free him and that
he (Bagwell) had spoken with Peerce on
Keniston's behalf. By February 5, 1627,
Thomas Bagwell had married Thomas
Allnutt's widow and represented her in a
dispute with Thomas Harwood. In March
1629 Bagwell served on a jury and later in
the year was a burgess for Pasbehay (**3**).
When Thomas Bagwell received a patent
for 450 acres on the Appomattox River on
May 12, 1638, he was identified as an ancient planter and used his wife, Joan
(Joane), as a headright (CBE 36, 58; MCGC
96-97, 137, 190; HEN 1:138; PB 1 Pt. 2:550;
DOR 1:37).

JOAN (JOANE) BAGWELL (MRS. THOMAS BAGWELL) (SEE MRS. THOMAS ALLNUTT [ALNUTT])

Ancient planter Thomas Bagwell married
Thomas Allnutt's widow sometime prior to
February 5, 1627, and represented her in a
dispute with Thomas Harwood. On May 12,
1638, when Bagwell patented some land on
the Appomattox River in Charles City, he
used his wife, Joan (Joane), as a headright
(MCGC 137; PB 1 Pt. 1:550).

***

ALICE BAILEY (BAYLIE)

On September 11, 1626, Alice Bailey
(Baylie) testified before the General Court
when Mrs. Joane Wright was accused of
witchcraft. She said that she had asked Mrs.
Wright whether she (Alice) or her husband
would die first. Although Mrs. Wright refused to say, she admitted that she could
make an accurate prediction if she wanted
to (MCGC 112).

GEORGE BAILEY (BAILYE)

In November and December 1631 George
Bailey (Bailye) shipped some goods from
Barnstaple to Virginia on the *Exchange* of
Bideford and the *Delight* (CBE 96-97).

***

JOHN BAILEY (BAILY, BAYLY, BAYLEY, BAILIE, BAILE)

John Bailey (Baily, Bayly, Bayley, Bailie,
Baile), an ancient planter and resident of
Hog Island (**16**), acquired some land in the
eastern end of Jamestown Island (**1**) prior to
1618. He probably was one of the men to
whom Sir Thomas Dale or Deputy Governor
Samuel Argall gave land before the headright system was established. At John's death
(before February 20, 1620) his Virginia land
descended to his daughter and sole heir,
Mary, who also was an ancient planter. John
Bailey reportedly brought five servants to
Virginia on the *William and Thomas* in August 1618 (PB 1 Pt. 2:880; MCGC 122; VCR
4:556; DOR 1:215-216; 2:311).

MARY BAILEY (BAILY, BAYLY, BAYLEY, BAILIE, BAILE) (MRS. RANDALL HOLT [HOWLETT]) (SEE MARY BAYLY [BAILEY] HOLT [HOWLETT])

Mary Bailey, an ancient planter and the
daughter and heir of ancient planter John
Bailey (Baily, Bayly, Bayley, Bailie, Baile),
inherited her father's Hog Island (**16**) and
Jamestown Island (**1**) acreage sometime
prior to February 20, 1620. In 1624 Mary's
guardians, Robert Evers and Richard Bailey
(and Richard's surrogate, Edward Grindon),
preserved her legal interest in her late
father's real estate by placing it in the hands
of tenants. Evers personally occupied one
of Mary's patents on Jamestown Island, and
in 1626 Grindon leased her Hog Island
acreage to Sir George Yeardley. When a list
of patented land was sent back to England
in May 1625, Mary Bailey was credited
with 500 acres at Hog Island, property that
had been planted or seated. Mary married
Randall Holt I sometime prior to 1629 and
produced a son and heir, Randall Holt II.
She died sometime prior to August 1643
(PB 1 Pt. 2:648, 880; 2:240; MCGC 17, 122,
153; VCR 4:551, 556; DOR 1:215-216; 2:311).

***

JOHN BAILEY
(BAILY, BAYLY, BAYLEY)

In September 1620 John Bailey (Baily, Bayly, Bayley) was among those who set sail from Bristol, England, on the ship *Supply* with William Tracy, who was bound for Berkeley Hundred (**55**). Bailey was supposed to serve the Society of Berkeley Hundred's investors in exchange for some land. Governor George Yeardley, in a letter to the Virginia Company, indicated that John Bailey arrived at his destination on January 29, 1621, but died within a short time (CBE 21; VCR 3:396, 426).

JOHN BAILEY (BAILY, BAYLY, BAYLEY)

John Bailey (Baily, Bayly, Bayley) died in Jamestown (**1**) sometime after April 1623 but before February 16, 1624 (CBE 39).

LEWIS BAILEY
(BAILY, BAYLY, BAYLEY)

Lewis Bailey (Baily, Bayly, Bayley) came to Virginia on the *Marmaduke* in 1621. On November 20, 1623, Thomas Bilby, who was very ill, made a nuncupative will. He named Bailey as his heir, making the statement in William Hall's presence. On February 16, 1624, Lewis Bailey was living at one of the plantations on the lower side of the James River, east of Gray's Creek (**10-16**), within the corporation of James City. On January 21, 1628, he brought suit against John Cooke and had him jailed. A few months later George Pace used Lewis Bailey as a headright when patenting some land. This raises the possibility that Bailey was associated with Paces Paines (**9**) (CBE 40; MCGC 8, 159; PB 1 Pt. 1:64).

MARY BAILEY
(BAYLEY, BAYLY, BAILIE, BAILE)

On February 27, 1619, the Bridewell Court decided that Mary Bailey (Bayley, Bayly, Bailie, Baile), a wench, would be sent to Virginia. She was part of a large group of young people rounded up from the streets of London so that they could be sent to the colony (CBE 13).

***

NICHOLAS BAILEY (BALY, BALEY)

Nicholas Bailey (Baly, Baley), an indentured servant, came to Virginia in 1620 aboard the *Jonathan*. On February 16, 1624, he and his wife were living in West and Shirley Hundred (**41**). However, by January 20, 1625, Nicholas and wife, Ann, were residing in Flowerdew Hundred (**53**), where he headed a household that had an ample supply of stored food and defensive weaponry. On January 3, 1625, Nicholas Bailey agreed to reimburse cape merchant Abraham Peirsey for buying his freedom from Sir George Yeardley and John Pountis. If he failed to repay Peirsey, Bailey would have to work for him as a sawyer (CBE 36, 50; MCGC 38-39; DOR 1:23).

ANN BAILEY (BALY, BALEY)
(MRS. NICHOLAS BAILEY [BALY, BALEY])

Ann, who married Nicholas Bailey (Baly, Baley), came to Virginia in 1621 on the *Marmaduke*. On February 16, 1624, the Baileys were living at West and Shirley Hundred (**41**), but by January 20, 1625, they had moved to Flowerdew Hundred (**53**), where Nicholas was listed as a household head (CBE 36, 50).

***

RALPH BAILEY
(BAYLIE, BALY, BALEY)

On October 7, 1622, Virginia Company officials noted that Ralph Bailey (Baylie, Baly, Baley) and John Stephens wanted Virginia's governor to lay out their land (VCR 2:107).

RICHARD BAILEY
(BAYLIE, BALY, BALEY)

On December 31, 1619, officials at Bridewell decided that Richard Bailey (Baylie, Baly, Baley), who was being detained in the Middlesex House of Correction, would be sent to Virginia (CBE 14).

RICHARD BAILEY
(BAYLIE, BALY, BALEY)

On October 23, 1626, Richard Bailey (Baylie, Baly, Baley)—the guardian of Mary, orphan and heir of ancient planter John Bailey—authorized Edward Grindon to decide how Mary's land at Hog Island (16) would be used. Grindon leased it to Sir George Yeardley (MCGC 122).

TEMPERANCE BAILEY
(BAYLIE, BALY, BALEY, BAYLISE)

On September 20, 1620, Temperance Bailey (Baylie, Baly, Baley, Baylise), who was only around 2 or 3 years old and Virginia-born, received a patent for 100 acres of land. This suggests that she was the child of an ancient planter. When a list of patented land was sent back to England in May 1625, Temperance Bailey was credited with 200 acres of land in the Great Weyanoke (52), acreage that had been planted. On February 16, 1624, Temperance was living at Jordan's Journey (46). She was still there on January 21, 1625, at which time she was identified as a 7-year-old child who had been born in the colony. Temperance was then living in the household headed by William Farrar and Mrs. Cisley Jordan, the widow of Samuel Jordan, and may have been her daughter from a previous marriage. Half of the land for which Temperance Bailey received a patent in September 1620 was encompassed by a tract Richard Cocke patented on October 10, 1652 (CBE 36, 51; VCR 4:554; DOR 1:120-121; PB 3:133).

WILLIAM BAILEY
(BAYLIE, BALY, BALEY)

In 1608 William Bailey (Baylie, Baly, Baley), a gentleman, arrived in Jamestown (1) as part of the 1st Supply of new settlers (CJS 1:222; 2:161).

***

WILLIAM BAILEY
(BAYLIE, BALY, BALEY)

William Bailey (Baylie, Baly, Baley), an ancient planter, came to Virginia in 1610 on the *Prosperous*. On January 22, 1625, he was heading a household at West and Shirley Hundred (41) that included his wife, Mary, and 4-year-old son, Thomas. The Baileys had an ample supply of stored food and defensive weaponry. William was then age 41. On April 7, 1625, William Bailey informed the justices of the General Court that he had seen Indians attack and

kill Andrew Dudley at Shirley Hundred. When a list of patented land was sent to England in May 1625, William Bailey was credited with 50 acres in Great Weyanoke (52) and 100 acres in Charles City, near Bailey's Creek. William died sometime prior to July 9, 1635, at which time his son, Thomas, patented 150 acres, 50 of which he had inherited from his late father (CBE 52; MCGC 51; VCR 4:553-554; PB 1 Pt. 2:214; DOR 1:12).

MARY BAILEY (BAYLIE, BALY, BALEY) (MRS. WILLIAM BAILEY [BAYLIE, BALY, BALEY])

Mary, who became the wife of ancient planter William Bailey (Baylie, Baly, Baley), came to Virginia in 1617 on the *George*. On January 22, 1625, she was living at West and Shirley Hundred (41) with her husband and 4-year-old son, Thomas. Mary was then age 24 (CBE 52).

THOMAS BAILEY
(BAYLIE, BALY, BALEY)

Thomas Bailey (Baylie, Baly, Baley), who was born in Virginia, was the son of William and Mary Bailey. On January 22, 1625, when Thomas was 4 years old, the Baileys were living at West and Shirley Hundred (41). On July 9, 1635, Thomas Bailey received a patent for 150 acres in Charles City, 50 acres of which he had inherited from his late father, William Bailey (CBE 52; PB 1 Pt. 1:214).

***

***

WILLIAM BAILEY
(BAYLIE, BALY, BALEY)

In 1619 William Bailey (Baylie, Baly, Baley), a bricklayer from Northampton-shire, went to Virginia on the *Bona Nova*. His transportation costs and those of his wife were paid by the Ferrars, who were Virginia Company investors (FER 295, 296).

MRS. WILLIAM BAILEY
(BAYLIE, BALY, BALEY)

Mrs. William Bailey (Baylie, Baly, Baley) and her husband, a bricklayer from

Northamptonshire, went to Virginia in 1619 at the expense of the Ferrars (FER 295, 296).

***

WILLIAM BAILEY (BAYLIE, BALY, BALEY)

On March 22, 1622, when the Indians attacked the College Land (**66**), William Bailey (Baylie, Baly, Baley) was killed (VCR 3:566).

GEORGE BAILIFE (BAYLEY)

In 1621 George Bailife (Bayley) came to Virginia on the *George* and on February 16, 1624, was living at one of the plantations east of Gray's Creek on the lower side of the James River, within the corporation of James City. On February 4, 1625, he was residing at the Treasurer's Plantation (**11**), where he was an indentured servant (CBE 41, 60).

FRANCIS BAINBRIG

Francis Bainbrig, a 36-year-old yeoman from Durham, England, arrived in Jamestown in 1619 on the *Bona Nova* (FER 295).

[NO FIRST NAME] BAINE

On March 24, 1621, Mr. Baine was identified as someone who had exported tobacco from Virginia with Mr. Felgate (VCR 3:435-436).

ROBERT BAINES

Robert Baines died at one of the settlements on the lower side of the James River, within the corporation of James City (**8-15**), sometime after April 1623 but before February 16, 1624 (CBE 41).

GEORGE BAKER

On October 16, 1618, officials at Bridewell decided that George Baker, a vagrant, would be transported to Virginia (CBE 11).

JOHN BAKER

On September 19, 1618, the Bridewell court decided that John Baker, a vagrant, would be sent to Virginia. He was killed in Elizabeth City (**17, 18**) sometime after April 1623 but before February 16, 1624. The cause of his death is unknown (CBE 9, 45).

JOHN BAKER

John Baker, a 17-year-old joiner from London, arrived in Jamestown on September 5, 1623, on the *Ann* and took the oath of supremacy. By January 1625 he was living on the Eastern Shore, where he was a 20-year-old servant in Captain William Eppes's (**74**) household (CBE 68; MCGC 6).

MARTHA BAKER

Martha Baker, a young marriageable maid, came to Virginia in 1621 on the *Warwick* (FER 309).

MARTIN BAKER

On April 24, 1635, Martin Baker patented 600 acres adjacent to Captain John Martin's land (**59**) (PB 1 Pt. 1:168).

MORICE (MAURICE) BAKER

Morice (Maurice) Baker died at one of the settlements on the lower side of the James River, within the corporation of James City (**8-15**) sometime after April 1623 but before February 16, 1624 (CBE 41).

RICHARD BAKER

Richard Baker, one of Sir George Yeardley's servants, died at Hog Island (**16**) sometime after February 16, 1624, but before February 4, 1625 (CBE 61).

ROBERT BAKER

In September 1620 Robert Baker set sail from Bristol, England, with William Tracy on the ship *Supply* and was bound for Berkeley Hundred (**55**). Baker was supposed to serve the Society of Berkeley Hundred's investors for a certain number of years in exchange for some land. Governor George Yeardley, in a letter to the Virginia Company, indicated that Robert Baker arrived at his destination on January 29, 1621, but died within a short time (CBE 21; VCR 3:397, 426).

THOMAS BAKER

Thomas Baker, a 22-year-old skinner from Staffordshire, arrived in Jamestown in 1619 on the *Bona Nova*. He probably was a Virginia Company tenant or servant (FER 295).

WILLIAM BAKER

William Baker, an ancient planter, came to Virginia in 1609 on the *Jonathan* and on February 16, 1624, was living at Flowerdew Hundred (53). He was still residing there on January 20, 1625, and was occupying his own house. Baker was amply outfitted with defensive weaponry and had a good supply of stored food (CBE 37, 50; DOR 1:23).

WILLLIAM BAKER

William Baker came to Virginia on the *Abigail* and on February 16, 1624, was living on the Maine (3), where he was listed as one of William Peirce's servants. By January 20, 1625, he had moved to Mulberry Island (21), where he was described as a 20-year-old Peirce servant (CBE 39, 56).

WILLIAM BAKER

On February 4, 1625, William Baker was living at Captain Roger Smith's plantation (10) on the lower side of the James River. He was then described as a 24-year-old servant (CBE 59; DOR 1:39).

WILLIAM BAKER

In early 1627 William Baker, a tenant of the defunct Virginia Company, was assigned to the governor. On March 12, 1627, he was identified as a planter and tenant when he was fined for failing to perform sentry duty. William and fellow planter Jonas Raley of Jamestown Island (1) reportedly had stayed at Hog Island (16) for nine days instead of standing watch (MCGC 136, 143).

***

[NO FIRST NAME] BALDWIN

On March 22, 1622, the Indians attacked the settlers at Warresqueak (26), but they fled when Mr. Baldwin fired his gun. According to Captain John Smith, Mr. Baldwin saved his house, which was a half-mile from Mr. Harrison's (CJS 2:295-296).

[NO FIRST NAME] BALDWIN

On March 22, 1622, when the Indians attacked Warresqueak (26), Mrs. Baldwin was wounded and left for dead. Her husband fired his gun and the Natives fled (CJS 2:295-296).

***

FRANCIS BALDWIN (BALDEN, BALDWINE)

On April 3, 1620, the Virginia Company sent a petition they had received from Francis Baldwin (Balden, Baldwine) to Governor George Yeardley. In November 1622 Company officials noted that Baldwin wanted a patent because he was taking 100 people to Virginia. Francis Baldwin shipped goods from London to Virginia on the *Samuel* in September 1627. In October 1628 he agreed to serve as the late John Moseley's attorney at the request of the decedent's widow and son. On July 16, 1631, Captain Francis Baldwin was identified as a Virginia planter when he requested relief from customs duties (VCR 1:334; 2:132; CBE 80; MCGC 176; G&M 166).

***

HUGH BALDWIN (BALDWINE, BALDEN)

Hugh Baldwin (Baldwine, Balden) came to Virginia on the *Trial*, and on February 16, 1624, he and his wife, Susan, were living on the Maine (3). On January 30, 1625, they were still there and were identified as Thomas Swinhowe's servants (CBE 39, 58; DOR 1:27).

SUSAN BALDWIN (BALDWINE, BALDEN) (MRS. HUGH BALDWIN [BALDWINE, BALDEN])

On February 16, 1624, Susan Baldwin (Baldwine, Balden) and her husband, Hugh, were living on the Maine (3). They were still there on January 30, 1625, at which time they were identified as servants of Thomas Swinhowe. On December 8, 1628, Susan informed the justices of the General Court that on the night Leonard Huett died, he made a nuncupative will, leaving his chest and its contents to Goodman George Fryer (CBE 39, 58; MCGC 179).

***

JOHN BALDWIN (BALDWINE)

John Baldwin (Baldwine), who came to Virginia on the *Tyger* in 1622, was a free man with friends or family members in Bermuda. From at least 1623 to February 4, 1625, he resided on the lower side of the James River on the Treasurer's Plantation (**11**), a tract that belonged to the colony's treasurer, George Sandys. A letter Baldwin sent to a friend in Bermuda around 1623 described the hardships he endured while living at the Treasurer's Plantation. He claimed that even though he and his comrades were free men, Sandys dealt harshly with them and compelled them to serve him. Baldwin indicated that four fellow servants had been ambushed and killed by Indians and that others at the Sandys plantation had perished from ill treatment and lack of food and medical care. He claimed that the sick were isolated and allowed to starve to death. On May 20, 1637, when John Baldwin disposed of a plot of ground in the eastern end of Jamestown Island (**1**), he was described as a gentleman. In 1653 he served as a burgess in the colony's assembly, perhaps representing Jamestown. By 1656 he had patented a 15-acre parcel in the western end of Jamestown Island, adjacent to the isthmus that extended to the mainland. He also became involved in a lawsuit in Surry County. When John Baldwin made his will, he designated John Fulcher as his heir (CBE 40, 60; LEF 264-265; JHB 1619-1659:88; PB 1 Pt. 1:423; 4:88; 7:97; AMB 5; Surry County Deeds and Wills 1652-1672:100).

NICHOLAS BALDWIN

Nicholas Baldwin came to Virginia on the *Truelove* in 1622. He was killed at Chaplin's Choice (**56**) when the Indians attacked in 1625 (CBE 51).

SILVESTER BALDWIN (BALLDWIN)

On December 11, 1623, Silvester Baldwin (Balldwin) testified that Captain Baldwin had little personal property of his own, but that he had sold goods to Captain Wilcocks, Richard Kingsmill, Richard Taylor, and Sergeant Williams, and had been paid (MCGC 9).

THOMAS BALDWIN

On February 16, 1624, Thomas Baldwin was living in Elizabeth City (**17, 18**) (CBE 44).

THOMAS BALDWIN (BALDWYN)

On February 16, 1624, Thomas Baldwin (Baldwyn) was living at Chaplin's Choice (**56**) (CBE 37).

WILLIAM BALDWIN

On February 16, 1624, William Baldwin was living in Elizabeth City (**17, 18**) (CBE 44).

WILLIAM BALDWIN (BAULDWIN)

On February 16, 1624, William Baldwin (Bauldwin) was living in Elizabeth City (**18**). He was still there in early 1625 and was a servant in Thomas Purfoy's household (CBE 44, 64).

LORD BALTIMORE (SEE GEORGE CALVERT, CECIL CALVERT, LEONARD CALVERT)

ALEXANDER BALE

On March 22, 1622, when the Indians attacked Ensign Spence's house in Archer's Hope (**6**), Alexander Bale was killed (VCR 3:570).

MARY BALL

On September 19, 1618, the justices of Bridewell Court decided that Mary Ball, a vagrant from Cripplegate, would be sent to Virginia (CBE 10).

NICHOLAS BALL

In 1619 officials at Bridewell decided that Nicholas Ball, a thief from London who was being detained at Newgate Prison, would be sent overseas (CBE 12).

RICHARD BALL (BAULE)

Richard Ball (Baule) came to Virginia in 1617 on the *George*. On August 9, 1617, his father was censured by the justices of Middlesex Court for sending him to the colony without providing his pregnant wife, Elizabeth, with a means of maintenance and support. On February 4, 1625, Richard Ball, an indentured servant, was living at Hugh Crowder's plantation (12) on the lower side of the James River. He was still there in April when he testified at the inquest held after John Verone's death. By December 1627 Richard had obtained his freedom and was in possession of a 6-acre leasehold at Buckroe (17). At that time he was described as a planter (CBE 8, 60; PB 1 Pt. 1:80, 84; MCGC 53).

***

ROBERT BALL

Robert Ball went to Virginia on the *London Merchant* in 1619. His wife, identified only as Mrs. Robert Ball, died in Elizabeth City (17, 18) between April 1623 and mid-February 1624. On February 16, 1624, Robert and his new wife (identified only as Goodwife Ball) were living on the Eastern Shore. In early 1625 Robert, who was then 27 years old, was part of the community of settlers on Old Plantation Creek (73). He was a solitary household head who had an ample supply of stored food and defensive weaponry (CBE 46, 69; DOR 1:70).

MRS. ROBERT BALL

Mrs. Robert Ball died in Elizabeth City (17, 18) between April 1623 and February 16, 1624. She most likely was the late wife of Robert Ball, who by mid-February 1624 had remarried and was living on the Eastern Shore (CBE 45).

MRS. ROBERT BALL

On February 16, 1624, Goodwife Ball and her husband, Robert, were living on the Eastern Shore, probably in the vicinity of Old Plantation Creek (73), where he was living alone a year later. She probably was a successor to the Mrs. Robert Ball who died in Elizabeth City (17, 18) between April 1623 and February 16, 1624 (CBE 46).

***

JOHN BAMFORD
(BRAMFORD, BRAMPFORD)

John Bamford (Bramford, Brampford), who set out for Virginia on the *James* with cape merchant Abraham Peirsey, arrived in Jamestown (1) on July 31, 1622. On February 16, 1624, John was living at Flowerdew Hundred (53). He was still there on January 20, 1625, at which time he was 23 years old and was identified as one of Peirsey's servants (FER 400; CBE 37, 50).

JANE BAMPFORD (BAMFORD)

Jane Bampford (Bamford) came to Virginia with Edward Grindon on the *James* and arrived in Jamestown (1) on July 31, 1622 (FER 400).

PHILLIP BANDAGE

Phillip Bandage, a 23-year-old cook from Somersetshire, arrived in Jamestown (1) in 1619 aboard the *Bona Nova*. He probably was one of the Virginia Company servants or tenants who reached Virginia in November 1619 (FER 295).

JOHN BANCKTON (BANKTON?)

John Banckton (Bankton?) came to Virginia with William Felgate on the *James* and arrived in Jamestown (1) on July 31, 1622 (FER 400).

WILLIAM BANK
("COUNTRY WILL")

On November 20, 1622, officials at Bridewell decided that Newgate Prison inmate William Bank, commonly known as "Country Will," would be transported overseas (CBE 29).

CHRISTOPHER BANKS (BANCKS)

On July 16, 1631, Christopher Banks (Bancks) was identified as a Virginia planter when he requested relief from customs duties. He may have been the former indentured servant Christopher Bankus (G&M 166).

EDWARD BANKS

Edward Banks died at Warresqueak (26) sometime after April 1623 but before February 16, 1624 (CBE 42).

FRANCIS BANKS

Francis Banks came to Virginia on the *Gift* in 1623 and on February 16, 1624, was living in Warresqueak (**26**), at the Bennett plantation. On February 7, 1625, he was identified as a servant in Edward Bennett's house. When Francis Banks testified before the General Court on January 24, 1625, he stated that Jamestown (**1**) merchant John Chew had taken one of the sentinels from the capital city's fort with him to the store at Warresqueak. In May 1627 Banks verified John Uty's allegation that Richard Bickley had refused to perform military duty (CBE 42, 62; MCGC 44, 148).

GEORGE BANKS (BANCKES)

George Banks (Banckes) came to Virginia on the *Swann* in 1624. In early 1625 he was living in Elizabeth City (**18**), where he was a 15-year-old servant in Thomas Dunthorne's house (CBE 66).

THOMAS BANKS

On February 16, 1624, Thomas Banks was living on the Maine (**3**) (CBE 39).

***

WILLIAM BANKS (BANCKS, BINKS, BYNCKS, BINCKS)

Goodman William Banks (Bancks, Binks, Byncks, Bincks) and his wife, Ann, came to Virginia on the *George*. On February 16, 1624, they were living on the lower side of the James River, within the corporation of James City and across from Jamestown (**10-16**). However, on December 18, 1624, William made a legally binding agreement with John Lightfoot to rent a house and land on Jamestown Island (**1**). Despite that lease, on January 30, 1625, William Banks and his wife, Ann, were residing on the Governor's Land (**3**) and were identified as Thomas Swinhowe's servants. In October 1625 William testified in court that the late Captain William Norton had failed to pay two men who sought compensation for their labor. In March 1626 the General Court heard testimony that Mr. Swift gave some of William Banks's corn to another man. These statements about Norton and Swift suggest that Banks formerly lived at the Treasurer's Plantation (**11**) on the lower side of the James River (CBE 40, 58; MCGC 36, 41, 43, 72-73, 96; DOR 1:27).

ANN BANKS (BANCKS, BINKS, BYNCKS, BINCKS) (MRS. WILLIAM BANKS [BANCKS, BINKS, BYNCKS, BINCKS])

Ann, the wife of Goodman William Banks (Bancks, Binks, Byncks, Bincks), came to Virginia on the *George* with her husband. On February 16, 1624, they were living on the lower side of the James River, across from Jamestown (**10-16**). Although the Banks family made plans to live on rented property on Jamestown Island (**1**), on January 30, 1625, they were residing in Pasbehay, on the Governor's Land (**3**), and were identified as Thomas Swinhowe's servants (CBE 41, 58; MCGC 41).

***

CHRISTOPHER BANKUS

Christopher Bankus came to Virginia aboard the *Abigaile* in 1622. On January 24, 1625, he was a 19-year-old indentured servant in the urban Jamestown (**1**) household of Captain Roger Smith. He may have been the Virginia planter named Christopher Banks (Bancks) who in 1631 tried to get relief from customs duties (CBE 55).

IVY (IVIE) BANTON

Ivy (Ivie) Banton came to Virginia on the *James* in 1622. On January 21, 1625, she was living in the household of Isaac Chaplin at Chaplin's Choice (**56**), where she was a servant (CBE 51).

JOHN BANTON

John Banton came to Virginia at the expense of John Parrott. On May 29, 1635, when Parrott patented some land on the Nansemond River (**20 c**), he listed Banton as a headright (PB 1 Pt. 1:170).

ANTHONY BANHAM

On July 31, 1622, Anthony Banham and three others came to Virginia on the *James* at the expense of Virginia Company investors (FER 400).

GEORGE BANUM

George Banum, an indentured servant, arrived at Martin's Hundred (**7**) in January

1623 and resided in the home of William Harwood, the settlement's leader. He died at Harwood's prior to March or April 1623 (VCR 4:60).

***

JOHN BANUM (BAYNHAM, BAINHAM, BAYNAM, BAINEHAM) I

John Banum (Baynham, Bainham, Baynam, Baineham) I, an ancient planter, came to Virginia in 1616 on the *Susan*. He brought his son, John II, to Virginia in 1621 on the *Charles*. On February 16, 1624, John I and his wife were living in Elizabeth City (**18**). In October 1624 he told the General Court that Captain Nathaniel Butler had asked for a list of Treasurer George Sandys' wrongdoings. In December 1624 John Banum, who was described as a gentleman of Kecoughtan, patented 300 acres near the land of George Sandys. In early 1625 John and his wife, Elizabeth, were living in Elizabeth City, where he and her partner, Robert Sweete, headed a household that was amply supplied with stored food and defensive weaponry. They also had a small herd of livestock. John Banum was then age 54 and his wife was 43.

When a list of patented land was sent back to England in May 1625, John Banum was credited with 200 acres of land in Tappahannah, acreage that already had become part of George Sandys' office land, the Treasurer's Plantation (**11**). John also was credited with 200 acres of unimproved land at Blunt Point (**22**), property he had gotten from George Sandys. This raises the possibility that Banum and Sandys swapped land. On February 20, 1626, John Banum was ordered to bring certain accounts to merchant Thomas Weston, who was to make an inventory. John was made a commissioner of Elizabeth City's monthly court later that year. In March 1627 he mistakenly gave a man's tobacco to one ship captain instead of another. He apparently was a successful planter, for he continued to acquire servants. John Banum died sometime prior to February 9, 1629, at which time his widow, Elizabeth, was named his administrator; his partner, Robert Sweete, brought in an inventory of John's estate (CBE 44, 64; MCGC 24, 39, 79, 96, 103, 106, 118, 132-133, 145, 185-186; PB 1 Pt. 1:12, 17; VCR 4:555, 557; DOR 1:56).

ELIZABETH BANUM (BAYNHAM, BAINHAM, BAYNAM, BAINEHAM) (MRS. JOHN BANUM [BAYNHAM, BAINHAM, BAYNAM, BAINEHAM] I)

Elizabeth, who married ancient planter John Banum (Baynham, Bainham, Baynam, Baineham) I, came to Virginia on the *Bona Nova* in 1620. On February 16, 1624, John and Elizabeth were residing in Elizabeth City (**18**), and they were still there in early 1625. Elizabeth Banum, who was age 43, resided in a household that was headed by her husband, John, and his partner, Robert Sweete. John died sometime after March 1627 but before February 1629, at which time his widow, Elizabeth, was named administrator of his estate. She replaced her late husband's executor, Robert Sweete, who renounced his executorship (CBE 44, 64; MCGC 145, 185).

JOHN BANUM (BAYNHAM, BAINHAM, BAYNAM, BAINEHAM) II

John Banum (Baynham, Bainham, Baynam, Baineham) II came to Virginia on the *Charles* in 1621. He died sometime prior to December 1, 1624, when his father, John Banum (Baynham, Bainham, Baynam) I, used him as a headright when patenting some land (PB 1 Pt. 1:17).

***

RICHARD BANUM (BAYNHAM, BAINHAM, BAYNAM)

On June 28, 1620, Richard Banum (Baynham, Bainham, Baynam), a London goldsmith, acquired two shares of Virginia land from John Grey (VCR 1:381).

ADRIAN BARBE

Dyer Adrian Barbe, his wife, and their four children were among the Walloons and French who indicated their willingness to go to Virginia. In August 1621 the Virginia Company agreed that they could immigrate (CBE 25).

ANN BARBER

Ann Barber reportedly died in Elizabeth City (**17, 18**) sometime after April 1623 but before February 16, 1624. However, she also was listed among Elizabeth City's living on February 16, 1624. This raises the possibility that she died while the census was being compiled or that two women with identical names lived in Elizabeth City (CBE 44-45).

GABRIEL BARBER
(BARBOUR, BARBOR)

On August 11, 1619, London merchant Gabriel Barber (Barbour, Barbor) recommended Mr. Newland, a merchant who had assisted Captain Christopher Lawne in his attempt to establish a plantation (**25**) in Virginia. On February 5, 1623, Gabriel, who was associated with the *Bonny Bess*, asked the Virginia Company for permission to transport some settlers to the colony and then undertake a fishing voyage. In May the Company noted that Gabriel Barber had outfitted Anthony Hinton to go on the *Bonny Bess* and that he had agreed to send his surplus supplies to Martin's Hundred (**7**) (VCR 2:262; 3:190; 4:164, 245-246).

HENRY BARBER

On February 16, 1624, Henry Barber was living in Elizabeth City (**17, 18**) (CBE 44).

SUSAN BARBER

On February 16, 1624, Susan Barber was living on the lower side of the James River in the corporation of James City, on one of the plantations west of Gray's Creek (**8, 9**) (CBE 40).

VINCENT BARBER

On November 28, 1625, the General Court ordered Captain William Tucker to give Mr. Vincent Barber's goods to Marmaduke Rayner. On October 11, 1626, the administrator of the late Luke Eden (Aden, Eaden) was ordered to pay the decedent's debt to Vincent Barber. The setting in which these transactions occurred suggests that Barber was associated with Elizabeth City (**17, 18**) (MCGC 77, 117-118).

WILLIAM BARBER

On July 29, 1626, the Bridewell Court decided that William Barber, a boy, would be detained and sent to Virginia (HUME 31).

RICHARD BARD

On December 31, 1619, the Bridewell Court decided that Richard Bard, who had been brought in by the marshal of Middlesex, would be sent to Virginia (CBE 14).

RICHARD BAREFOOT

Richard Barefoot, a passenger for Virginia, arrived in Jamestown (**1**) on April 17, 1619 (FER 107).

GEORGE BARGRAVE

Captain George Bargrave's pinnace arrived in Virginia on April 12, 1619. He appeared before the General Court on February 4, 1625, at which time he was authorized by Governor George Yeardley to take Captain Edward Stallings' men and ship to Kecoughtan (**17, 18**) so that Captain William Tucker could inventory the goods that were aboard (CJS 2:266; VCR 4:511-512).

***

JOHN BARGRAVE

John Bargrave began making plans to establish a plantation in Virginia in January 1618. He later claimed that he had been given the right to free trade along the Chesapeake Bay. On May 12, 1619, Bargrave's pinnace, the *Edwin*, arrived in Virginia with men he planned to seat on his land (**60**), which was located on the lower side of the James River near Martin's Brandon (**59**). Bargrave's settlement was not represented in the assembly meetings held in July and August 1619, although his plantation's existence was acknowledged. In March 1620 the Bargrave plantation was home to 37 men. He and his associates received a patent for their land on May 17, 1620. Within a very short time, Bargrave clashed with his neighbor, Captain John Martin, over the ownership of some livestock, a long-term quarrel that culminated in a lawsuit. In 1621 Bargrave sued Sir Thomas Smith and several other Virginia Company officials, whom he accused of corruption, and they, in turn, claimed that he failed to pay his debts. Bargrave also complained about Governor George Yeardley. In 1622 he urged English officials to make Virginia a royal colony and claimed that four years earlier he had established Virginia's first private plantation, investing heavily in public service and the colony's defense. In June 1623 Captain John Bargrave was appointed marshal of Virginia, replacing the late William Nuce. He received a letter from Sir Nathaniel Rich containing recommendations about how the colony should be managed. Bargrave went to England in 1625 to pursue his suit against John Martin. He died sometime prior to January 12, 1627, at which time his widow was identified as Captain William Tucker's and Mrs. Alice Boyse's relative (VCR 1:223, 230-231, 309, 312, 330, 345, 441, 501, 522, 525, 570, 573; 2:119-120, 242, 448; 3:118, 125, 168, 444, 517-521, 598-602, 605-608, 637-638, 644, 653; 4:81-84, 223-224, 408-440, 448, 487-488, 511, 517-518; FER 138, 139, 184, 278; CBE 23, 26-27, 47-48; MCGC 37, 62, 134; PB 8:125, 415).

MRS. JOHN BARGRAVE

On January 12, 1627, the General Court decided to permit Captain William Tucker to serve as security for the widowed Mrs. John Bargrave, who was identified as his kinswoman. Tucker took custody of some cattle whose ownership had been the object of a dispute between the decedent and Captain John Martin. Mrs. Alice Boyse, who also was related to Mrs. Bargrave, brought in an account of the cattle (MCGC 134).

***

THOMAS BARGRAVE

According to Captain John Smith, in 1620 the Rev. Thomas Bargrave bequeathed his library to the College (66) that was to be built in Henrico. Virginia Company records from May 1622 indicated that Bargrave had been a minister in Virginia (CJS 2:288; VCR 3:643).

***

ANTHONY BARHAM (BARAM, BARRAM)

Anthony Barham (Baram, Barram) came to Virginia on the *Abigail* sometime prior to 1624 and became a planter. In October 1624 he testified before the General Court about the cruel beatings servants Elizabeth Abbott and Elias Hinton had received from their master, John Proctor of Paces Paines (9). By January 25, 1625, Anthony Barham

had taken up residence on Mulberry Island (21), where he headed a well-equipped household that included his wife, Elizabeth. In May 1625 he was credited with 100 acres of land in Warresqueak (26). Anthony Barham continued to live on Mulberry Island and in 1630 served as a burgess. In July 1640 he was identified as a kinsman of Anne Barham of Canterbury, Kent, England. On September 6, 1641, when Anthony Barham prepared his will, he indicated that he resided on Mulberry Island but was then in England. He made bequests to his brother-in-law Richard Bennett and his mother, and to Joan Peirce (Captain William Peirce's wife), Martha and Edward Major, William Butler, and several people in England. His will was proved on September 13, 1641 (EAE 89; MCGC 23; CBE 57; VCR 4:556; HEN 1:148; EEAC 5; SH 37; SR 3989; DOR 1:47).

ELIZABETH BARHAM (BARAM, BARRAM) I (MRS. ANTHONY BARHAM [BARAM, BARRAM])

Elizabeth I, who married Anthony Barham (Baram, Barram), came to Virginia on the *William and Thomas*. On January 25, 1625, she was living with her husband at Mulberry Island (21). When Anthony made his will on September 6, 1641, he named his wife, Elizabeth, as his executrix and one of his heirs (CBE 57; SH 37; SR 3989).

ELIZABETH BARHAM (BARAM, BARRAM) II

On September 6, 1641, when Anthony Barham (Baram, Barram) made his will, he named his daughter, Elizabeth II, who was in Virginia, as one of his heirs (SH 37; SR 3989).

***

FRANCES BARKE [BARKER?]

Frances Barke (Barker?) died at one of the settlements on the lower side of the James River, within the corporation of James City (8-15), sometime after April 1623 but before February 16, 1624 (CBE 41).

CHRISTOPHER BARKER

Christopher Barker came to Virginia sometime prior to the March 22, 1622, Indian offensive. Several years later, he testified that he had been one of Captain John Ward's servants and that Captain William Eppes had gotten some tobacco from Ward's plantation (61) shortly before the Indians attacked. He said that Eppes returned to evacuate Ward's surviving servants to safety on the Eastern Shore. Barker said that he left Ward's employ in November 1622. On January 31, 1625, Christopher Barker was identified as one of Thomas Allnutt's servants in Jamestown (1). He was accused of leaving Allnutt without cause. In January 1626 Barker testified before the General Court about an incident that had taken place at Kecoughtan. A month later he informed the court that he had come to Virginia to serve Captain Ward for four years and that he had fulfilled his contractual obligation. The General Court's justices decided that Barker, like Ward's other servants, was to be freed if he posted a bond (MCGC 46, 89, 96, 138-139).

EDWARD BARKER

On December 19, 1625, Edward Barker testified before the General Court about the *Swann's* being moored safely at Dambrells Cove in Canada. He said that after Mr. Nevill moved the ship to another location, it sustained damage and became leaky (MCGC 82).

EDMUND BARKER

On December 19, 1625, Edmund Barker testified before the General Court about the circumstances under which Arthur Aveling received a summons. In 1628 the General Court ordered Barker to return Mr. Perry's shallop, a vessel that he (Barker) had sold to Mr. Rastell's men (MCGC 81, 173).

HENRY BARKER

On February 16, 1624, Henry Barker was living in urban Jamestown (1) in Captain William Holmes's household (CBE 38).

JOHN BARKER

On February 27, 1619, the Bridewell Court decided that John Barker, a boy, would be sent to Virginia. He was part of a large group of youngsters rounded up from the streets of London so that they could be transported to the colony. On March 22, 1622, when the Indians attacked Abraham Peirsey's plantation on the Appomattox

River near Bermuda Hundred (39), a boy named John Barker was killed (CBE 12; VCR 3:566).

JOHN BARKER

Between July and September 1619 Virginia Company officials mentioned John Barker in connection with Berkeley Hundred (55) (VCR 3:183).

JOHN BARKER

John Barker came to Virginia in 1623 on the *Anne*. On February 3, 1626, William Eppes used him as a headright when patenting some land (PB 1 Pt. 1:49).

ROBERT BARKER

Robert Barker came to Virginia in 1619 at the expense of the Ferrars, who were important Virginia Company investors. He probably was a Company servant or tenant (FER 296).

STEPHEN BARKER

Stephen Barker, who came to Virginia aboard the *James* at his own expense, arrived in Jamestown (1) on July 31, 1622. On February 4, 1625, he was living at Martin's Hundred (7), where he and his partner, Humphrey Walden, headed a household that had an abundant supply of stored food and defensive weaponry. On January 14, 1628, he was arrested by merchant Edward Sharples, one of his creditors. On March 2, 1629, Stephen Barker, who indicated that he was then living at the Neck O'Land (5), stated under oath that Abraham Porter, when making a nuncupative will, forgave John Rodis's debt. Later in the year, Barker agreed that Edward Wigg could marry his maidservant, if Wigg reimbursed him for the woman's transportation costs. However, because Wigg failed to uphold his end of the bargain, Barker took him to court so that he could recover the sum he was owed. On May 26, 1634, Stephen Barker and some other planters, who said that they had families in Virginia, claimed that Governor John Harvey and his council intended to make Maurice Thompson the sole source of shipping. They asserted that they feared ruin if that were to occur (FER 400; CBE 62, 115-116; MCGC 158, 188, 197; G&M 187-188; DOR 1:46).

WILLIAM BARKER

On July 29, 1626, the Bridewell Court decided that William Barker, a vagrant, would be sent to Virginia (CBE 72).

WILLIAM BARKER

William Barker, a mariner from Ratcliffe in Middlesex, came to Virginia sometime prior to January 1626, at which time he was in Kecoughtan **(17, 18)**. In 1628 he was arrested by Lady Temperance Yeardley who claimed that he owed her a sum of money. In 1628 and 1630 he was identified as an importer of Virginia tobacco. William Barker testified before the Admiralty Court in 1630, indicating that he had been mate of the *Hopewell*, which left Virginia on New Year's Eve 1629 in consort with the *Gift* of London, which was lost in a storm off Cape Hatteras. In 1633, when Barker was master of the *America* of London, he transported 40 beaver skins from Virginia along with his own tobacco crop. He was among those who strenuously objected to Governor John Harvey's appointment of Maurice Thompson and his associates as the sole importers of Virginia tobacco. By 1634 William Barker had come into possession of Captain Nathaniel Powell's 600-acre plantation, Powle-Brooke **(50)**, in Charles City. On November 26, 1635, Barker joined merchants John Sadler and Richard Queyney in patenting some adjacent acreage, calling their 1,250 acres Merchants Hope. Then, in August 1637 Barker patented 600 acres called Bikar's **(57)**, which he added to the Merchants Hope grant in February 1638. William Barker made numerous trips across the Atlantic, taking tobacco to England and returning with goods. In 1638 he bought a waterfront lot in urban Jamestown **(1)**. Although it is uncertain to what extent Barker developed his property, he was tied into a mercantile network that would have made it very desirable to own a piece of real estate in the colony's capital city and sole port of entry. Between June and December 1654, William Barker purchased 150 acres of land on the lower side of the James River at "Smith's Fort," part of the land "due unto the said [Thomas] Rolfe by Guift from the Indyan King." Barker quickly conveyed the parcel to Roger Gilbert (MCGC 85, 159, 184; SR 2851, 3466, 3490, 3498, 3566, 3784, 4001; HCA 13/49; E 190/38/5; 190/44/1; EAE 23; G&M 187-188; PB 1 Pt. 1:151, 320-321; Pt. 2:622; CBE 115-116; SH 28; Surry County Deeds, Wills &c. 1652-1672:54-55).

[NO FIRST NAME] BARKHAM

On July 17, 1622, Virginia Company officials noted that a Mr. Barkham, whose first name is unknown, had been given a patent by Governor George Yeardley, but it was contingent on Opechancanough's approval. Company officials strongly disapproved of Yeardley's acknowledging the Indians' land rights by dealing with their principal leader (VCR 2:94-95).

***

EDWARD BARKLEY

Edward Barkley came to Virginia on the *Unity* and on February 16, 1624, was living in Elizabeth City **(17, 18)** with Captain William Tucker. Edward was then a lieutenant. By February 4, 1625, he had moved to Hog Island **(16)**, where he headed a well-equipped household that included his wife and daughter (both of whom were named Jane) and four servants. On March 12, 1625, Lieutenant Edward Barkley served on the jury that conducted John Verone's inquest. In May 1625, when a list of patented land was sent back to England, he was credited with 12 acres of land in Coxendale **(64)**. This raises the possibility that he may have been associated with Coxendale when Sir Thomas Dale was deputy-governor (CBE 43, 61; MCGC 53; VCR 4:552; DOR 1:43).

JANE BARKLEY I
(MRS. EDWARD BARKLEY)

Jane I, who became Lieutenant Edward Barkley's wife, went to Virginia on the *Seaflower*. On February 4, 1625, she and her husband and their daughter, Jane II, were living at Hog Island **(16)** (CBE 61).

JANE BARKLEY II

On February 4, 1625, Jane II, the daughter of Lieutenant Edward Barkley and his wife, Jane I, was living with her parents at Hog Island **(16)** (CBE 61).

***

HENRY BARLOW

On February 16, 1624, Henry Barlow was living on the lower side of the James River, within the corporation of James City and east of Gray's Creek (**10-16**) (CBE 40).

[NO FIRST NAME] BARNABY

On July 15, 1631, Mrs. Barnaby was among the Virginia planters who asked for relief from customs duties. She may have been the wife of Virginia colonist John Barnaby (Barnabe) (G&M 166).

JOHN BARNABY (BARNABE)

John Barnaby (Barnabe) came to Virginia on the *London Merchant* in 1621. He later testified that he was a servant in Governor George Yeardley's house in Jamestown (**1**) for two years and afterward kept in touch with him. On February 16, 1624, Barnaby was living in Elizabeth City (**18**). He was still there in early 1625 and was a 21-year-old household head with a modest supply of stored food and defensive weaponry. In May 1630 John Barnaby, who had gone to England temporarily and was living on Lombard Street, London, testified in a chancery case that involved Edmund Rossingham's claim against Sir George Yeardley's estate. In September 1630 John Barnaby identified himself as a 27-year-old Virginia planter when he and George Rookes, a London merchant, requested permission to trade in the king's dominions. In July 1636 John was identified as the brother of Richard Barnaby of All Hallows, Lombard Street; his sister was Elizabeth Rookes (CBE 44, 64, 92; SR 9963; C 24/561; EEAC 5; DOR 1:54).

JOHN BARNARD

On January 10, 1627, the General Court noted that Captain John Harvey of urban Jamestown (**1**) owed money to John Barnard for his services. It is uncertain what kind of special skills Barnard had; however Harvey, as a colonist and Virginia governor, demonstrated a long-term interest in industrial activities (MCGC 130-131).

WILLIAM BARNARD

William Barnard came to Virginia on the *Furtherance* in 1622 and on February 16, 1624, was living at Basses Choice (**27**). He was still there on February 7, 1625, at which time he was age 21, free, and living in one of Nathaniel Basse's houses. William Barnard, a successful planter, continued to reside in what became known as Warresqueak (**26**) or Isle of Wight County and on August 10, 1642, patented 1,200 acres of land at the head of Lawne's Creek (CBE 46, 62; PB 1 Pt. 1:798).

JOHN BARNARDS

John Barnards came to Virginia in 1628 on the *Hopewell* at the expense of Adam Thorogood. On June 24, 1635, when Thorogood secured a patent, he listed Barnards as a headright (PB 1 Pt. 1:179).

EDWARD BARNES

On October 31, 1621, Virginia Company officials reviewed a petition submitted to them by Alice, the widow of Dr. Lawrence Bohunne. She asked that her son, Edward Barnes, be freed from his seven years' service. Mrs. Bohunne's request was denied, for it was determined that Edward Barnes was a Virginia Company servant, not one of the late Dr. Bohunne's men. On February 16, 1624, Edward Barnes was living in Elizabeth City (**17**) (VCR 1:544; CBE 43).

LANCELOT (LAUNCELOTT) BARNES

Lancelot (Launcelott) Barnes came to Virginia sometime prior to 1628 and was associated with Elizabeth City (**17, 18**). In 1628 he and Gabriel Holland were authorized to settle merchant Humphrey Rastell's estate, which included paying Captain William Johnson, master of the *Anne*. In March 1630 Lancelot Barnes served as a burgess for the lower part of the corporation of Elizabeth City. In February 1632 he patented a 100-acre tract that he acquired from Captain William Tucker. A year later Lancelot, who was identified as a gentleman, obtained a 100-acre leasehold in the Indian Thicket (**17**), acreage on the east side of the Hampton River that formerly was part of the Virginia Company's land in Elizabeth City. He died sometime prior to May 30, 1634 (MCGC 174; HEN 1:149; PB 1 Pt. 1:123, 142, 149).

MATHEWE BARNES

In 1624 Mathewe Barnes witnessed Richard Domelawe's will, which was made in Virginia (SH 6).

PHILLIP BARNES

On March 22, 1622, when the Indians attacked Captain John Berkeley's plantation at Falling Creek **(68)**, Philip Barnes was killed (VCR 3:565).

RICHARD BARNES

Richard Barnes, who criticized the colony's governor, was brutally punished and then banished from Jamestown Island **(1)**, unarmed. Sometime prior to May 5, 1624, he sent a petition to Governor Francis Wyatt, pleading for mercy (VCR 4:480; MCGC 14).

ROBERT BARNES

In 1608 Robert Barnes, a gentleman, arrived in Virginia in the 1st Supply of colonists to reach Jamestown **(1)** (CJS 1:222; 2:161).

ROBERT BARNES

On November 20, 1622, Robert Barnes, an inmate being detained in Newgate Prison where there was an outbreak of jail fever, was pardoned and sentenced to transportation overseas, probably to Virginia (CBE 29).

WILLIAM BARNES

On July 20, 1625, William Barnes, who indicated that he was from Fawley, in England, appeared before the General Court to testify about Captain John Powell. On June 25, 1627, William was fined for being negligent while on sentry duty. On March 4, 1629, he was arrested and sued by Thomas Crump of Jamestown Island **(1)**. William Barnes died later in the year. Thomas Phillips, who presented an inventory of his estate, was given letters of administration (MCGC 66-68, 150, 189, 200).

JOHN BARNETT

John Barnett immigrated to Virginia in 1620 on the *Jonathan*. On February 16, 1624, he was living on the Eastern Shore in Captain William Eppes's household **(74)**. Around that time he presented a petition to

Governor Francis Wyatt on behalf of John Clarke's heirs. By January 24, 1625, John Barnett had moved to Jamestown **(1)**, where he headed a household that was well supplied with stored food, defensive weaponry, and livestock. By October 13, 1627, Barnett had married Samuel Kennell's widow, who ran afoul of the law by disposing of her late husband's estate before she satisfied his debt to Mr. Abraham Peirsey. The General Court decided that John Barnett was not at fault (CBE 46, 56; VCR 4:456-457; MCGC 156; DOR 1:34).

***

THOMAS BARNETT (BARNET)

Thomas Barnett (Barnet) came to Virginia in 1620 on the *Elizabeth*. On February 16, 1624, he was living at Sir George Yeardley's plantation, Flowerdew Hundred **(53)**, where he was a servant. By January 24, 1625, he had moved to urban Jamestown **(1)**, where he was a 16-year-old servant in the Yeardley household. On October 12, 1626, Thomas Barnett testified before the General Court about a tobacco bill that he had seen in Gravesend, England. In September 1632 Thomas Barnett served as a burgess for the Stanley Hundred area **(22)**, where the late George Yeardley had owned property. On November 20, 1636, the Rev. Thomas Butler of Elizabeth City **(17, 18)** named Thomas Barnett as overseer of his will and made a bequest to Thomas's wife, Mary (CBE 37, 54; MCGC 119; HEN 1:179; WITH 49).

MARY BARNETT (BARNET) (MRS. THOMAS BARNETT [BARNET])

On November 20, 1636, when the Rev. Thomas Butler of Elizabeth City **(17, 18)** prepared his will, he made a bequest to Mary Barnett (Barnet), the wife of Thomas Barnett, whom he had named as overseer of his estate (WITH 49).

***

WILLIAM BARNETT (BARNET)

William Barnett (Barnet) came to Virginia on the *Truelove* in 1623. He died at Chaplin's Choice **(56)** sometime after February 16, 1624, but before January 21, 1625 (CBE 51).

WILLIAM BARNETT (BARNET)

In 1629 Captain John Smith said that William Barnett (Barnet) was one of several colonists he had interviewed in England about conditions in Virginia (CJS 3:219).

WILLIAM BARNWELL

William Barnwell, a 24-year-old miller from Staffordshire, England, arrived in Jamestown in 1619 aboard the *Bona Nova*. He probably was a Virginia Company tenant or servant (FER 295).

HUGH BARRAGE

In 1619 officials at Bridewell decided that Hugh Barrage, an inmate at Newgate Prison who had stolen a mare from Middlesex, would be transported overseas. He probably was sent to Virginia (CBE 12).

NICHOLAS BARRAN

On April 4, 1625, Nicholas Barran testified before the General Court that he had inspected Sir George Yeardley's tobacco while it was aboard an outbound ship (MCGC 51).

[NO FIRST NAME] BARRETT

On January 16, 1622, Virginia Company officials learned that a Mr. Barrett, who reputedly was a good shipwright, was planning to go to Virginia, taking along some good boatwrights and carpenters (VCR 1:576).

FRANCIS BARRETT

Francis Barrett came to Virginia on the *Bona Nova*. On February 16, 1624, he was living in Elizabeth City (**17, 18**), where he was a member of Lieutenant Edward Barkley's household. By February 4, 1625, he had moved to Hog Island (**16**), where he was identified as a servant in the Barkley household (CBE 43, 61).

HUMPHREY BARRETT (BARRET)

On February 5, 1628, Humphrey Barrett (Barret) was identified as a mariner to whom John Gunnery owed money. In September 1630 he was described as the overseer of the will made by John Raymond, who died while on a voyage to Virginia (MCGC 161; EAE 26).

THOMAS BARRETT (BARRET)

In 1619 Thomas Barrett, a 20-year-old weaver from Lancastershire, arrived in Jamestown (**1**) aboard the *Bona Nova*. He came to the colony at the expense of the Ferrars, who were major Virginia Company investors, and probably was a Company servant or tenant (FER 295, 296).

THOMAS BARRETT (BARRET)

Captain John Smith said that in 1619, incoming governor George Yeardley freed Thomas Barrett (Barret), an ancient planter and sergeant, and some others who formerly had been indentured servants. Smith said that they were the first farmers to go forth to their own land (CJS 2:268).

WALTER BARRETT

Walter Barrett came to Virginia in 1620 on the *Bona Nova*. In early 1625 he was living in Elizabeth City (**18**) in the home of the Rev. Jonas Stockton. Barrett, who was 26 years old and free, had accompanied Stockton to the colony (CBE 66).

WILLIAM BARRETT

On February 16, 1624, William Barrett was living at Flowerdew Hundred (**53**) (CBE 37).

ROBERT BARRINGTON

In July 1628 Robert Barrington patented 250 acres of land on the Back River, abutting Powhatan Swamp. He also was appointed clerk of the Council and took the oath of office. During 1629 and 1630 Barrington served as a burgess, representing Jamestown Island (**1**). The following year he repatented the acreage he had acquired in 1628. However, in April 1641 Robert Barrington was obliged to relinquish his 250 acres because it was determined that Sir John Harvey, while governor, had wrongfully given him a patent for part of the Governor's Land (**3**). Barrington received a 500-acre patent in exchange for the other land, in payment for his expenses in building and clearing his original acreage (PB 1 Pt. 1:108; MCGC 174, 497-498; HEN 1:148).

HENRY BARRONE

According to Virginia Company records, in 1623 Henry Barrone left Martin's Hundred (**7**) (FER 572).

THOMAS BARROW

Thomas Barrow died at one of the settlements on the lower side of the James River, within the corporation of James City (**8-15**), sometime after April 1623 but before February 16, 1624 (CBE 41).

DAVID BARRY

On March 22, 1622, David Barry was killed at Warresqueak (**26**) when the Indians attacked. On November 30, 1624, his partners were identified as James Harrison and John Costard (VCR 3:571; MCGC 35).

WILLIAM BARRY

William Barry, a husbandman from Yorkshire, England, came to Virginia in 1619 on the *Bona Nova*. On February 16, 1624, he was residing at Buckroe (**17**), part of the Virginia Company's land in Elizabeth City. He was still there in early 1625, at which time he was identified as a sergeant. Barry headed a household that was abundantly supplied with stored food and defensive weaponry and included 15 servants. In November 1625 he had a dispute with Henry Geny and a month later, the General Court ordered him to pay William Harwood of Martin's Hundred (**7**) for some corn he had purchased on behalf of the Company. Later in December William Barry gave Lawrence May a receipt for a debt incurred by the Virginia Company. These actions suggest that Lieutenant Barry was serving as one of the Virginia Company's principal agents in Virginia. In January 1626 Humphrey Rastell was ordered to refund William Barry's tobacco, for he had failed to deliver the indentured servants he had promised (FER 295; CBE 45, 68; MCGC 42-43, 77-78, 87, 90; DOR 1:66).

MILES BARTE

Miles Barte, a mason, immigrated to Virginia in April 1619. He probably was a Virginia Company tenant or servant (FER 107).

[NO FIRST NAME] BARTLETT

Lieutenant Bartlett of Bermuda Hundred (**39**), whose given name is unknown, was mentioned in the will made by Captain Robert Smalley. On November 11, 1619, Virginia Company officials noted that Bartlett would take the eleven Company men who came with Captain Christopher Lawne (SH 4; VCR 3:226-229).

RICHARD BARTLETT

On August 21, 1624, officials at Bridewell decided that Richard Bartlett, a vagrant from Cordwainer Ward, would be sent to Virginia (CBE 47).

RICHARD BARTLETT

On February 16, 1624, Richard Bartlett was residing in Warresqueak (**26**). He was still living there on February 7, 1625. In April 1625 he agreed to build a house for Mr. John Chew, a merchant. It is unclear whether Bartlett was going to construct a dwelling on Chew's lot in urban Jamestown (**1**), on his property at Hog Island (**16**), or in Warresqueak, where he had a store (CBE 42; MCGC 51).

EDWARD BARTLEY (BARTLETT?)

On July 5, 1627, Mrs. Jane Martiau delivered an inventory of Lieutenant Edward Bartley's estate. He may have been the individual identified as Lieutenant Bartlett of Bermuda Hundred (**39**) (MCGC 151).

JOHN BARTLEY (BERKELEY?)

In May 1620 John Bartley (Berkeley?) and his associates were assigned a patent by the Virginia Company (VCR 1:341, 345).

***

THOMAS BARWICK

In June 1622 Captain Thomas Barwick and 25 men were outfitted and sent to Virginia by the Company of Shipwrights, who intended for them to build watercraft. They were to be given 1,200 acres and 4 oxen and were supposed to settle as a community. When Barwick and his men arrived in the colony, they decided to live on Jamestown Island (**1**) and commenced building homes there. Treasurer George Sandys indicated that Barwick and his workers, who were motivated by the opportunity to reap handsome profits, built a few shallops. However, Captain Barwick became mortally ill, as did six or seven of his principal workmen. After Barwick's death, which occurred sometime prior to December 1623, Thomas Nunn testified about some of the decedent's purchases and the bequests he had intended to make. The November 1624 minutes of the General Court made reference to Barwick's house on Jamestown Island, noting that he had procured timber from John Danes for use in shipbuilding. In March 1626 the General Court's justices acknowledged that Captain Thomas Barwick and Thomas Nunn had overseen the construction of a vessel in Jamestown. When Barwick died he was indebted to Treasurer George Sandys, who was responsible for many of the Virginia Company's money-making projects that involved the use of skilled artisans. In July 1629 Thomas Barwick's widow, Elizabeth, asked Virginia's governor to see that his estate be inventoried. She also said that he had died six years earlier, around Christmas, probably in January 1623 (VCR 3:649-650; 4:9, 22-26; CJS 2:292; FER 382; MCGC 8, 33, 98-100; CBE 88; G&M 136).

ELIZABETH BARWICK (MRS. THOMAS BARWICK)

On July 29, 1629, Elizabeth, the late Thomas Barwick's widow, asked Virginia's governor to see that his estate be inventoried. She said that Thomas had died six years earlier around Christmas (MCGC 8; G&M 136).

***

THOMAS BARYHARD

Thomas Baryhard and Thomas Locke witnessed the will made by William Beard on December 20, 1636 (SH 28).

RICHARD BASCOUGH (BOSCOUGH)

On March 22, 1622, when the Indians attacked Captain John Berkeley's plantation at Falling Creek (68), Richard Bascough (Boscough) was killed (VCR 3:565).

JOHN BASINGTHWAYTE

John Basingthwayte was killed on March 22, 1622, when the Indians attacked Captain Henry Spellman's plantation (51) in the corporation of Charles City (VCR 3:569).

***

NATHANIEL BASSE (BASS, BASE)

Nathaniel Basse (Bass, Base) came to Virginia sometime prior to November 1619 and established a plantation called Basses Choice (27) at a site fronting on the Pagan River and several miles southeast of Bennett's Welcome (26). He also invested funds with Captain Christopher Lawne, who intended to establish a settlement of his own (25). According to genealogical records compiled in the seventeenth century by a member of the Basse family, Nathaniel Basse and his wife, Mary Jordan, married on May 21, 1613. It is uncertain whether they wed in England or after they reached Virginia. They had at least seven children, who were born between 1615 and 1624.

In October 1620 Nathaniel Basse testified that he had witnessed a wager made by Thomas Hamor of Warresqueak and Captain William Sampson of the *Furtherance*. By March 1621 Nathaniel Basse had begun exporting tobacco from Virginia. The Virginia Company gave Basse and his associates a patent in November 1621, for they intended to transport 100 people to Virginia. According to Captain John Smith, when the Indians attacked Basses Choice on March 22, 1622, Nathaniel Basse's house was burned and several people were killed. Basse's son, Humphrey, who was 7 years old, was among those slain. Mary Jordan Basse was pregnant at the time with her son Edward. Nathaniel Basse went to England but returned to the colony on the *Furtherance* later in the year and in 1623 testified about a bargain two men made. In March 1624 Nathaniel Basse represented the Basses Choice community in the assembly meeting. As the community's commander, Captain Basse was responsible for enforcing the law. The General Court awarded him use of George Grymes's land in Bermuda Hundred (39) to satisfy a debt. On February 7, 1625, when a muster was made of Basses Choice's inhabitants, Nathaniel Basse was described as a 35-year-old household head, who shared his home with two other men. He had an ample supply of stored food and defensive weaponry, but lacked indentured servants. During 1625 and 1626 he tried to fulfill that need by purchasing them from mariners. He tried to buy a black male Portuguese servant but the man was awarded to Governor Francis Wyatt. The 1625 list of patented land indicates that the Basse plantation encompassed 300 acres. During 1626 and 1627 Captain Nathaniel Bass made several appearances before the General Court, where he testified and helped in settling disputes. In 1626 he and three other men were authorized to function as court justices at Basses Choice, trying all cases except capital offences. In 1627 he was ordered to ransom some English prisoners from the Nansemond Indians and lead an offensive against those Natives in July. As time went on, Nathaniel Basse rose in prominence. In 1629 he served as a burgess for Warresqueak and in 1632 became a court commissioner. Finally, in February 1632 he was named to the Council of State. On August 14, 1638, Nathaniel and Mary Basse's son John married Elizabeth, a daughter of the King of the Nansemond Indians, who had been converted to the Christian faith (VCR 1:414, 561-562, 575; 3:226-229, 435-436, 695; 4:556; CJS 2:296; MCGC 39-40, 69, 71, 73, 84, 90, 120, 127, 134, 141, 195-196, 483; CBE 46, 62; HEN 1:128-129, 139-140, 153, 169; PB 1 Pt. 1:66; DOR 1:48; Bass Family Bible Records 1613-1699).

MARY JORDAN BASSE (BASS, BASE) (MRS. NATHANIEL BASSE (BASS, BASE)

Mary Jordan married Nathaniel Basse (Bass, Base) on May 21, 1613. It is uncertain whether they were living in the colony at the time they wed. They had at least seven children, some of whom most likely were born in Virginia. Mary gave birth to a pair of twin girls on October 9, 1624. It is unclear how long she lived thereafter. However, the muster that was taken at Basses Choice (**27**) on February 7, 1625, did not include her name or the names of her children (Bass Family Bible Records 1613-1699).

ANNE BASSE (BASS, BASE)

Anne, the daughter of Nathaniel and Mary Jordan Basse (Bass, Base), was born on October 9, 1624, probably at Basses Choice (**27**). She was the firstborn of a pair of twins. Anne's sister, Genevieve, arrived 10 minutes later (Bass Family Bible Records 1613-1699).

ANTHONY BASSE (BASS, BASE)

Anthony, the son of Nathaniel and Mary Jordan Basse (Bass, Base), was born on March 13, 1620. It is unclear whether he was born in England or Virginia (Bass Family Bible Records 1613-1699).

EDWARD BASSE (BASS, BASE)

Edward, the son of Nathaniel and Mary Jordan Basse (Bass, Base), was born on May 8, 1622, about six weeks after the March 22, 1622, Indian attack on Basses Choice (**27**). In 1644 he married Mary Tucker, an Indian girl, who was a member of the Christian faith (Bass Family Bible Records 1613-1699; CJS 2:296).

GENEVIEVE BASSE (BASS, BASE)

Genevieve, the daughter of Nathaniel and Mary Jordan Basse (Bass, Base), was born on October 9, 1624, probably at Basses Choice (**27**). She arrived 10 minutes after the birth of her twin sister, Anne (Bass Family Bible Records 1613-1699).

HUMPHREY BASSE (BASS, BASE)

Humphrey, the son of Nathaniel and Mary Jordan Basse (Bass, Base), was born on July 15, 1615. It is unclear whether he was born in England or Virginia. Humphrey died on March 22, 1622, probably at Basses Choice (**27**), where attacking Indians killed several people (Bass Family Bible Records 1613-1699; CJS 2:296).

JOHN BASSE (BASS, BASE)

John, the son of Nathaniel and Mary Jordan Basse (Bass, Base), was born on September 7, 1616. He made notes about his parents' and siblings' births and marriages in a book of sermons. On August 14, 1638, John Basse married Elizabeth, the daughter of the King of the Nansemond Indian nation. She had been baptized and converted to Christianity. John Basse died in 1699 (Bass Family Bible Records 1613-1699).

WILLIAM BASSE (BASS, BASE)

William, the son of Nathaniel and Mary Jordan Basse (Bass, Base), was born on February 3, 1618. It is unclear whether Mary gave birth to him in England or Virginia. William married Sarah Batton on September 20, 1641 (Bass Family Bible Records 1613-1699).

***

WILLIAM BASSETT

On March 22, 1622, when the Indians attacked the College Land (66), William Bassett was killed (VCR 3:566).

JOHN BATE (BATES, BATT)

John Bate (Bates, Batt) came to Virginia on the *Adam* in 1621. On February 16, 1624, he was living in Warresqueak (26). He was still there on February 7, 1625, and was a servant in Edward Bennett's household. In January 1625 he received high praise for reacting quickly in an emergency at the Warresqueak fort. In March 1625 Mr. John Bate was described as a merchant when he served on a jury investigating John Verone's death. In April 1625 he was identified as one of the men who had inspected Sir George Yeardley's tobacco, which was loaded aboard a ship and sent to London merchant Edward Bennett. John Bate died sometime prior to April 20, 1626, at which time the General Court decided that his clothing and trunk were to be sold to settle his debts to John Southern and Nicholas Skinner (CBE 42, 62; MCGC 44, 51, 53, 60, 101).

HASTINGS BATEMAN

On July 31, 1622, Hastings Bateman set out for Virginia on the *James,* accompanied by merchant Richard Stephens. They arrived in Jamestown (1) on July 31, 1622 (FER 400).

JOHN BATEMAN

John Bateman went to Virginia with merchant Richard Stephens on the *James* and arrived in Jamestown (1) on July 31, 1622 (FER 400).

RALPH BATEMAN

On July 17, 1622, Virginia Company officials noted that Ralph Bateman had acquired some Virginia land from Richard Bull, who had obtained it from Henry Rowland and John Budge of London (VCR 2:93).

THOMAS BATEMAN

On July 21, 1627, officials at Bridewell noted that Thomas Bateman was willing to go to Virginia as an indentured servant and would serve for 8 years (CBE 79).

JOHN BATES

John Bates came to Virginia in 1623 on the *Southampton.* On January 20, 1625, he was living at Flowerdew Hundred (53) where he was a 24-year-old servant in cape merchant Abraham Peirsey's household. In September 1655 he patented 50 acres of land at the Middle Plantation, later the site of Williamsburg. In May 1660 Bates was identified as an "ancient inhabitant" who was age 62 and unable to work. Therefore, he was relieved of the need to pay taxes (CBE 50; PB 3:377; DOR 1:206).

JOHN BATH (BUTH, BOOTH?)

John Bath (Buth, Booth?), a leather-fellow from London, came to Virginia on the *Bonny Bess.* He arrived in Jamestown (1) on September 12, 1623, and took the oath of supremacy. Bath became ill while staying in Richard Stephens' house in urban Jamestown and died sometime prior to February 16, 1624. On January 24, 1625, Wassell Rayner, one of Stephens' servants, testified that John Bath made a written will, bequeathing his estate to a woman in England. However, after further reflection, Bath had James (another Stephens servant) destroy the will and asked Richard Stephens to serve as his administrator. The testator reportedly told Stephens that after his just debts were paid, he wanted the residue of his estate sent to his father in England. John Bath may have been a leather merchant or had specialized knowledge of the processing of leather (MCGC 6, 45; CBE 39).

THOMAS BATS

On March 22, 1622, when the Indians attacked Martin's Hundred (7), Thomas Bats was killed (VCR 3:570).

***

MICHAEL BATT

Michael Batt, an indentured servant, came to Virginia on the *Hercules*. On February 16, 1624, he and his wife, Ellen (Ellin), were living in a household on the Governor's Land (3). They were still there on January 24, 1625, and were listed among Thomas Swinhowe's servants. On January 10, 1627, Michael Batt received permission to move to Burrows or Smith's Mount (8) on the lower side of the James River. His wife was still alive in February 1629. On September 20, 1643, Michael patented 1 acre of land on Jamestown Island (1) near the Back River (CBE 39, 58; MCGC 131; PB 1 Pt. 2:890; SH 11-12; DOR 1:27).

ELLEN (ELLIN) BATT
(MRS. MICHAEL BATT)

Ellen (Ellin), who married Michael Batt, came to Virginia on the *Warwick*. On February 16, 1624, she and her husband were living on the Maine or Governor's Land (3). They were still there on January 24, 1625, and were listed among Thomas Swinhowe's servants. In January 1627 Michael Batt received permission to move to Smith's Mount (8) on the lower side of the James River. Ellen was still alive on February 13, 1629, when Jamestown (1) merchant Thomas Warnett named her as one of his beneficiaries (CBE 39, 58; MCGC 131; PB 1 Pt. 2:890; SH 11-12).

***

[NO FIRST NAME] BATTERS

Lieutenant Batters received land in the eastern end of Jamestown Island (1) during Deputy Governor Samuel Argall's government, 1617–1618. Sometime prior to January 24, 1625, he sold his acreage to David Ellis (MCGC 44).

FRANCIS BATTERSEA
(BATHURST)

On November 20, 1622, Francis Battersea (Bathurst), a yeoman from Islington, Middlesex, who was being detained at Newgate, was pardoned so that he could be transported overseas. He was among those freed and sent abroad on account of jail fever (CBE 29).

ELIZABETH SHARPE PACKER
[PARKER] BAUGH
(MRS. WILLIAM BAUGH)
(SEE MRS. WILLIAM SHARPE
[SHARP], MRS. THOMAS PACKER
[PARKER])

Elizabeth, the widow of William Sharpe (Sharp), married Thomas Packer (Parker), whom she also outlived. Afterward, she wed William Baugh of London, who went to Virginia prior to June 5, 1639. Elizabeth died prior to February 1, 1651 (MEY 555-557).

THOMAS BAUGH

In September 1620 Thomas Baugh set sail from Bristol, England, on the *Supply* and accompanied William Tracy, who was bound for Berkeley Hundred (55). Baugh was supposed to serve the Society of Berkeley Hundred's investors for a certain number of years in exchange for some land. Governor George Yeardley, in a letter to the Virginia Company, indicated that Thomas Baugh arrived at his destination on January 29, 1621. In August 1622 he was listed among the surviving Berkeley servants who were still residing in Virginia. On February 16, 1624, Baugh was living at West and Shirley Hundred (41). However, by January 23, 1625, he had relocated to the College (66), where he was a household head who was relatively well supplied with stored food and defensive weaponry (CBE 21, 28, 36, 53; VCR 3:396-397, 426, 674; DOR 1:8).

ISAAC (ISACKE) BAUGHTON

On February 16, 1624, Isaac (Isacke) Baughton was living at Chaplin's Choice (56) (CBE 37).

RICHARD BAULE
(SEE RICHARD BALL)

RANDALL BAWDE

Randall Bawde came to Virginia on the *Due Return* in 1623. On January 22, 1625, he was living at West and Shirley Hundred (41), where he was a 30-year-old servant in Robert Bagwell's house (CBE 53).

MARY BAWDREYE

Mary Bawdreye died in Jamestown (1) sometime after April 1623 but before February 16, 1624 (CBE 39).

PHILLIP BAYNES

In 1619 Phillip Baynes came to Virginia at the expense of the Ferrars, who were major Virginia Company investors. He probably was a Company servant or tenant (FER 296).

RICHARD BAYNES

On February 24, 1622, Richard Baynes, who was age 35 or 36, was summoned to court and accused of being involved in killing a calf. Richard was a servant in Dr. John Pott's household in urban Jamestown (1) (MCGC 3-4).

THOMAS BAYWELL

Thomas Baywell, an ancient planter, patented 450 acres on the upper side of the Appomattox River (39) on November 7, 1635. He listed his wife as a headright but failed to provide her given name (PB 1 Pt. 1:300).

[NO FIRST NAME] BEADLE

According to William Strachey, a man named Beadle (perhaps Gabriel or John Beadle) was Captain Davies' lieutenant. In his July 1610 account, Strachey said that Beadle had spread false tales in Jamestown (1) (HAI 440).

GABRIEL BEADLE

In 1608 Gabriel Beadle, a gentleman and Virginia Company investor, arrived in Jamestown (1) as part of the 2nd Supply. Captain John Smith that he had assisted in felling trees and making clapboard (CJS 1:241; 2:185, 190, 274).

GRIFFIN BEADLE

On January 29, 1620, the Bridewell court decided that Griffin Beadle would be sent to Virginia (CBE 18).

JOHN BEADLE

John Beadle, a gentleman and Virginia Company investor, arrived in Virginia in 1608 in the 2nd Supply of Jamestown (1) colonists (CJS 1:241; 2:185, 190, 274).

GEORGE BEALE

In 1619 George Beale, a 22-year-old blacksmith from Staffordshire, England, came to Virginia on the *Bona Nova* and took the oath of allegiance in Jamestown (1). He probably was a Virginia Company tenant or servant (FER 295).

EDWARD BEALE

In July 1631 Edward Beale was identified as master of the *Gift of God*, which made a trip from Virginia to London in 1629 (CBE 96).

GRIFFIN BEALE (BEADLE?)

On August 24, 1618, officials at Bridewell decided that Griffin Beale, a vagrant born in Shoe Lane and incarcerated in the Middlesex jail, would be transported to Virginia. He may have been the same individual identified on January 29, 1620, as Griffin Beadle, who was in a group being detained until they could be sent to Virginia (CBE 9, 18).

STEPHEN BEALE

On July 19, 1627, Stephen Beale was said to have shipped goods from London to Virginia on the *James* (CBE 79).

JOHN BEANAM

John Beanam died at Martin's Hundred (7) sometime after April 1623 but before February 16, 1624. He also may have been the man identified as John Beman, who died in the same area around the same time (CBE 42).

CHRISTOPHER BEANE

Christopher Beane came to Virginia on the *Neptune* in 1618 and on February 16, 1624, was living at West and Shirley Hundred (41). However, by January 20, 1625, he had moved to Flowerdew Hundred (53), where he was a 40-year-old servant in the household of Humphrey Kent (CBE 36, 50).

WILLIAM BEANE

William Beane came to Virginia on the *Diana* in 1618 and on February 16, 1624, was living on the Eastern Shore (77). By early 1625, he had relocated to Elizabeth City (18) and was living in Richard Mintrene I's house. William Beane was then age 25 (CBE 46, 65).

JOHN BEARD

On February 10, 1629, Leonard Peddock, a merchant, was named the administrator of John Beard's estate. Beard died in Accomack (72-78) (MCGC 186).

***

WILLIAM BEARD

In June 1635 William Beard patented some land in Pasbehay, adjacent to his leasehold in the Governor's Land (3), using as a head-right his late wife, Joan (Joane). Beard's patent was adjacent to Robert Barrington's, whose acreage abutted the Back River. William Beard quickly surrendered his newly acquired 450 acres, which had not been seated, probably because it (like the Barrington land) was found to be part of the Governor's Land that Governor John Harvey had assigned to patentees. William Beard made his will on December 20, 1636, but survived for another decade. He made bequests to several people, including his sister, Dorothy Beard, in Rye, England. He also left £5 and a bed to his "wicked wife Margaret," whom he termed a whore. William Beard's personal effects indicate that he was relatively wealthy (PB 1 Pt. 1:252; WITH 30; SH 28; SR 3992; EEAC 6; MCGC 475).

JOAN (JOANE) BEARD (MRS. WILLIAM BEARD)

On June 19, 1635, when William Beard patented some land in Pasbehay (3), he used the headright of his wife, Joan (Joane) (PB 1 Pt. 1:252).

MARGARET BEARD (MRS. WILLIAM BEARD)

Margaret, who had become William Beard's wife by 1636, was accused of adultery on several occasions and reportedly had had sex with a servant named Thomas Bates. When William Beard of Pasbehay (3) made his will on December 20, 1636, he called Margaret a whore and left her very little. He also ordered her to vacate their house within three months of his death. As it turned out, he didn't die until 1646. Margaret Beard ran afoul of the law in July 1640 for becoming pregnant as a result of her adulterous behavior. Later in the year she got into trouble for failing to report some runaway servants. As a result, she received a whipping in Jamestown (1). It is uncertain how long Margaret Beard survived (WITH 30; MCGC 467, 475).

***

WALTER BEARE

Walter Beare came to Virginia on the *Abigail* in 1620. On January 30, 1625, he was living on the Maine (3), where he was a 28-year-old servant in the household of Dr. John Pott (CBE 58).

WILLIAM BEARE

On May 2, 1622, officials at Bridewell decided that William Beare, a prisoner being detained in the White Lion in Southwark, would be sent to Virginia (CBE 27).

THEOPHILUS BEASTON (BEASTONE, BERISTON, BERRISTONE, BORISTON)

Theophilus Beaston (Beastone, Beriston, Berristone, Boriston) came to Virginia on the *Treasurer* in 1614 and was an ancient planter. On February 16, 1624, he was an indentured servant in Sir George Yeardley's household at Flowerdew Hundred (53). By January 22, 1625, he was residing at Shirley Hundred (41) on behalf of the Society of Berkeley Hundred (55). However, on January 24, 1625, when a muster was taken of the colony's inhabitants, he was living in urban Jamestown (1), where he was a member of the Yeardley household. Theophilus was then age 23. In May 1625 Theophilus Beaston was credited with 100 acres of land in Charles City. He died sometime prior to February 9, 1633, when it was reported that he had bequeathed Theophilus Stone, an orphan, some tobacco (CBE 37, 54; MCGC 42, 202; VCR 4:553).

GILES BEAUMONT (BELMONT, BEWMONT, BEWMOUNT, BOMOUNTE, BOMONTE)

In December 1624 Giles Beaumont (Belmont, Bewmont, Bomounte, Bomonte), a Frenchman, was granted denization and allowed to take some people to Virginia. On May 23, 1625, he was identified as the master of John Smith, who testified in court. Others spoke about servants that Mr. Beaumont turned away or released before they had set sail for Virginia. Mr. Beaumont arrived in the colony sometime prior to June 15, 1625. Afterward, Virginia Company officials were informed that the governor had given him the best accommodations he could. On August 22, 1625, Mr. Beaumont was authorized to settle on the Eastern Shore (**72-78**), as long as he seated 5 miles from other colonists' plantations (CBE 14; MCGC 59-60, 69; VCR 4:562-567).

RICHARD BEAUMONT (BEWMOUNT, BEWMONT, BOMOUNTE, BOMONTE, BEDMONT)

In 1618 when Thomas West, Lord Delaware, set sail for Virginia, he traveled on the *Neptune*, with Richard Beaumont (Bewmount, Bewmont, Bomounte, Bomonte, Bedmont) as master. Aboard were goods belonging to Delaware, Brewster, and cape merchant Abraham Wilkie, who had provided them in accord with a Virginia Company contract. On May 3, 1623, Beaumont, who identified himself as a 43-year-old mariner from Ratcliffe in Middlesex, testified in the Earl of Warwick's suit against Edward Brewster involving the ships *Neptune* and *Treasurer* (EAE 13; HCA 13/44 f 124ro; SR 10376).

GEORGE BEAVA

Porter George Beava, his wife, and his child were among the Walloons and French who indicated their willingness to go to Virginia. In August 1621 the Virginia Company agreed that they could immigrate (CBE 24).

[NO FIRST NAME] BECGAM (BECKHAM?)

On January 9, 1624, John Howbeck told the General Court that Mr. Weston, owner of the *Sparrow*, had bought a servant named Becgam (Beckham?) before the ship left Plymouth (MCGC 10).

***

[NO FIRST NAME] BECKHAM

In late 1623 or early 1624 Carsten Beckham sent a petition to the governor, indicating that his father and Maurice Holsten, who were skilled workers, had come to Virginia but died shortly after their arrival. The given name of Carsten Beckham's father is unknown (VCR 4:287).

CARSTEN BECKHAM

Carsten Beckham and his father came to Virginia with Maurice Holsten. In late 1623 or early 1624 Carsten presented a petition to the governor, requesting permission to return to England. He said that his father and Holsten were skilled workers who died shortly after their arrival in the colony. He added that he personally was unskilled. Carsten Beckham was given permission to leave (VCR 4:287).

***

WILLIAM BECKWITH

William Beckwith, a tailor, arrived in Virginia in 1608 and was in the 1st Supply of new colonists. He would have resided in Jamestown (**1**) (CJS 1:223; 2:162).

JOHN BEDDINGFIELD

On November 20, 1622, officials at Bridewell pardoned John Beddingfield, an inmate at Newgate Prison, on account of an outbreak of jail fever. They sentenced him to transportation overseas, probably to Virginia (CBE 29).

WILLIAM BEDFORD

William Bedford came to Virginia in 1621 on the *James* and on February 16, 1624, was living on the lower side of the James River at Paces Paines (**9**). On February 4, 1625, he was still there and was living in Thomas Gates's home. In 1628 when William Enry made a nuncupative will, he designated William Bedford as his sole heir. Afterward Bedford was designated the decedent's administrator (CBE 40, 59; MCGC 174).

***
ROBERT BEHEATHLAND (BEHETHLEM)

Robert Beheathland (Behethlem), a gentleman and ancient planter, came to Virginia in 1607 in the first group of Jamestown **(1)** colonists. In 1608 he accompanied Captain John Smith to Werowocomoco, Powhatan's village on the York River, and to the Pamunkey Indians' territory. He also went with Smith on a voyage of discovery within the Chesapeake Bay. Smith later said that Beheathland guarded the door when he was negotiating with Opechancanough. In 1620 Captain Robert Beheathland identified himself as an associate of Thomas West, Lord Delaware, when he signed a petition in England asking that Sir George Yeardley be removed as governor. By 1627 Robert Beheathland was dead. He was survived by his daughter, Dorothy, and his widow, Mary, who married Thomas Flint of Elizabeth City **(18)** (CJS 1:208, 216, 231, 243; 2:141, 192, 200, 202, 252-253, 404; VCR 3:231-232; MCGC 177; DOR 1:217-218).

MARY BEHEATHLAND (BEHETHLEM) (MRS. ROBERT BEHEATHLAND [BEHETHLEM], MRS. THOMAS FLINT [FLYNT]) (SEE MRS. THOMAS FLINT [FLYNT])

Mary, the wife of Robert Beheathland (Behethlem), was widowed by 1627. Afterward she married Thomas Flint (Flynt), who was then living in Elizabeth City **(18)**, near the Warwick River. Mary Flint was identified as an ancient planter in 1628 when she patented 100 acres in Elizabeth City **(19)** called Fox Hill. In November 1628 she complained to the governor about her new husband's inappropriate behavior with Dorothy Beheathland, his stepdaughter, and threatened to discuss it with Dorothy's grandmother when she arrived from England. Despite the Flint couple's tumultuous behavior, Mary Flint asked the governor to release her husband, who had been arrested and detained. He refused to accompany her home (PB 1 Pt. 1:73; MCGC 177, 180; DOR 1:218).

DOROTHY BEHEATHLAND (BEHETHLEM) (MRS. RANDALL CREW) (SEE DOROTHY BEHEATHLAND [BEHETHLEM] CREW)

Dorothy Beheathland (Behethlem) was the daughter of ancient planter Robert Beheathland who died sometime prior to 1627. On September 11, 1626, Dorothy testified before the General Court against Joane Wright, an accused witch. She repeated a conversation she had with Mrs. Isabella Perry of Paces Paines **(9)** concerning Mrs. Wright's behavior and described what the accused witch had said about her life in England. By November 1628 the propriety of Dorothy Beheathland's behavior was questioned because she was suspected of having an inappropriate relationship with her stepfather, Thomas Flint of Elizabeth City **(18)**. By 1638 Dorothy had wed Randall Crew (MCGC 112, 177; PB 1 Pt. 2:584; DOR 1:218-219).

***

ANN BEHOUTE

Ann Behoute, one of Gabriel Holland's servants, arrived in Virginia in 1625 and resided in his house on Jamestown Island **(1)**. In January 1627 Holland, a court-appointed administrator, presented an inventory of her goods (MCGC 137).

RICHARD BELFIELD

Richard Belfield, a goldsmith, arrived in Jamestown **(1)** in 1608, as part of the 1st Supply of new colonists (CJS 1:222; 2:162).

HENRY BELL

Henry Bell, a tradesman, came to Virginia in 1608 as part of the 2nd Supply of new colonists. He would have lived in Jamestown **(1)** (CJS 1:241; 2:191).

JOHN BELL (BEL)

John Bell (Bel), an 18-year-old husbandman from Yorkshire, England, came to Virginia in 1619 on the *Bona Nova* and landed in Jamestown **(1)**. On March 22, 1622, when the Indians attacked William Farrar's house on the Appomattox River **(39)**, John Bell, an indentured servant, and his master, John England, were killed (FER 295; VCR 3:566).

RICHARD BELL

Sometime prior to June 27, 1635, Richard Bell purchased 200 acres of James City County land from Alexander Stonar (PB 1 Pt. 1:254).

JAMES BELLY

James Belly came to Virginia in 1634 on the *Bonaventure* at the expense of Adam Thorogood. On June 24, 1635, when Thorogood secured a patent, he listed Belly as a headright (PB 1 Pt. 1:179).

ANN BELSON

On October 9, 1640, Ann Belson, an indentured servant who had served Theodore Moses since 1633, asked to be freed from her remaining year of service. She claimed that Moses had promised to teach her to read and to instruct her in religion but instead had put her to work at hard labor. He also kept the legacy she had received in 1635. After hearing the testimony of two witnesses, the General Court decided to free Ann Belson and give her custody of her inheritance (MCGC 465).

THOMAS BELSON

In early 1625 Thomas Belson, a 12-year-old servant, was living on the Eastern Shore in Thomas Savage's house (77) (CBE 68).

JOHN BEMBRIDGE

John Bembridge came to Virginia at the expense of Maurice Thompson, who used him as a headright when patenting some land on March 4, 1621 (PB 1 Pt. 1:20).

JOHN BEMAN

John Beman died at one of the settlements on the lower side of the James River, within the corporation of James City (8-15) sometime after April 1623 but before February 16, 1624. He also may have been listed as John Beanam (CBE 41).

JOHN BENBRICKE

John Benbricke died in Elizabeth City (17, 18) sometime after April 1623 but before February 16, 1624 (CBE 45).

EDWARD BENDIGE

Edward Bendige died in Elizabeth City (17, 18) sometime after April 1623 but before February 16, 1624 (CBE 45).

WILLIAM BENGE

William Benge came to Virginia on the *Marigold* in 1619. On February 4, 1625, he was living on the Treasurer's Plantation (11), where he may have been a tenant (CBE 60).

JOHN BENNER

On March 22, 1622, when the Indians attacked Martin's Hundred (7), John Benner was killed (VCR 3:570).

EDWARD BENNETT

Edward Bennett, a London merchant with extensive trading interests in the Netherlands and Virginia, was the Virginia Company's largest investor. He and some associates, who intended to bring 100 to 200 people to Virginia in 1621, founded the plantation called Bennett's Welcome or Warresqueak (26), for which they held a patent. Approximately 50 people were killed there during the March 22, 1622, Indian attack. Even so, on July 31, 1622, Edward Bennett sent some people to Virginia on the *James*. His brother, Richard, already was in the colony. By October 1622 Edward Bennett began insisting that his people be allowed to return to Warresqueak and in April 1623 he made plans to send some additional settlers on the *Gift of God*. He sent two men on the *Hopewell* in 1623, and he paid for the transportation of John Inman, a surgeon. An agreement Edward Bennett made with one man suggests that he placed his land in the hands of tenants, who paid their rent with money and labor. Some of his indentured servants were obliged to serve for four years. Bennett had a land dispute with Jamestown (1) merchant Ralph Hamor, which resulted in his making a claim against Hamor's estate. He also had some business dealings with Sir George Yeardley. On February 7, 1625, when a muster was made of Bennett's Welcome, the plantation was well populated and provisioned and had a good supply of stored food and defensive weaponry. Edward Bennett, a burgess in 1628, went to England to seek a more favorable tobacco contract from the king. He seems to have stayed there, for he died in England sometime prior to June 3, 1651. Edward Bennett was the uncle of Richard Bennett, who served as Virginia's governor during the Commonwealth period (WITH 448; VCR 1:534, 553-554, 561-562; 2:104-105, 388-389; 3:643; FER 400; CJS 2:301; MCGC 60, 71, 97, 120, 124, 169-171, 187; CBE 62; DOR 1:48, 228-229).

ELIZABETH BENNETT

On March 22, 1622, when the Indians attacked Flowerdew Hundred (53), Elizabeth Bennett was killed (VCR 3:568).

JOHN BENNETT

On February 16, 1624, John Bennett was living at Warresqueak (26), the Bennett plantation. On January 24, 1625, he testified that he was supposed to serve as a sentinel at the Warresqueak fort. When he asked Henry Pinck to serve as his substitute, Pinck refused to do so (CBE 42; MCGC 44).

NICHOLAS BENNETT (BENNIT)

Nicholas Bennett (Bennit), who was marooned in Bermuda with Sir Thomas Gates and Sir George Somers, was a skillful carpenter and helped Gates build the pinnace they used to reach Virginia. Besides being a carpenter, Nicholas professed knowledge of the Bible (HAI 405-406).

RICHARD BENNETT

Richard Bennett, the brother of London merchant Edward Bennett, came to Virginia around 1621–1622 and resided at Warresqueak (26), also known as Bennett's Welcome. He died intestate in Virginia on August 28, 1626, failing to leave instructions about the disposition of his goods or those of his brother, Edward. An inventory was made of his estate, which was entrusted to Lodwick Pearle. English probate officials noted that Richard Bennett was from St. Bartholomew by Exchange, in London (MCGC 120; CBE 78; EEAC 6; MOR 10).

RICHARD BENNETT

Richard Bennett, a nephew of British merchant Edward Bennett, came to Virginia prior to March 1628, when he was involved in some litigation concerning the delivery of three young servants to John Burland. Richard Bennett settled in Warresqueak (26) and in 1629 commenced serving as a burgess. He also became a commissioner of the Warresqueak (later Isle of Wight) court. He became a very successful merchant and planter. During the 1630s, as his wealth and power increased, he began patenting vast tracts of land along the Nansemond and Elizabeth Rivers (20 a, c). He continued to deal with the family-owned mercantile group with which he was associated and had business dealings with Jamestown (1) merchant George Menefie, whose will he oversaw in 1645. The two men were given the responsibility of importing powder and shot into the colony for its defense. In 1639 when Bennett was named to the Council of State, he was residing in Nansemond County. Official records indicate that he served until 1651. In 1652 when Governor William Berkeley surrendered the Virginia colony to a Parliamentary fleet, Richard Bennett, Thomas Stegg I, and William Claiborne were among those representing the Commonwealth government. On March 24, 1652, Bennett was elected Virginia's governor. He was known for taking a strong stand against religious dissenters. On March 30, 1655, Sir William Berkeley sold to then-Governor Richard Bennett the westernmost of the three brick row houses he had built in Jamestown (1). The previous summer, Bennett had sold the 24-acre Glasshouse tract (2) to Francis Moryson.

After the Commonwealth era ended and Sir William Berkeley again became governor, Richard Bennett was appointed to the Council of State. He served in that capacity from 1665 through 1667 and in 1666 held the rank of major-general when the colony was threatened by a Dutch invasion. He was among the leaders who informed Lord Arlington that it was futile to build a fort at Old Point Comfort. On March 15, 1674, when Richard Bennett prepared his will, he bequeathed money to several people, including his daughter, Anna, the wife of Theodorick Bland. He also made a charitable bequest to his parish in Nansemond County and left some land in Virginia and Maryland to his grandchildren. Richard Bennett died within a year of making his will, which was recorded in England on April 12, 1675 (MCGC 169-170, 173, 181, 187, 193-194, 484, 488, 490-491, 498, 503, 516; HEN 1:139-140, 169, 187, 297, 370, 407; CBE

97; PB 1 Pt. 1:186; HCA 13/52; CO 1/20 f 119; EAE 73-74, 156; STAN 15, 34; SR 3989, 3997; SH 37; WITH 107, 180-181; FOR 2:8:14; 2:9:14, 19; 3:14:23; AMB 78; MCGH 197, 672; Lower Norfolk County Book A:246; B:87, 174; JHB 1619-1660:97; DOR 1:228-229).

ROBERT BENNETT

In November 1622 the Virginia Company authorized Robert Bennett, master of the *Samuel*, to trade in Virginia. By June 9, 1623, he was living at Bennett's Welcome **(26)** in Warresqueak. He sent word to his brother, London merchant Edward Bennett, that a new fort was being built in Warresqueak, that the people at Bennett's Welcome were in good health, and that trade was brisk. Robert Bennett ran afoul of Virginia law when he sold Sir George Yeardley some sack (a wine) that he had obtained from Thomas Edwards, failing to heed the trading restrictions on imported goods. In early June 1623 Robert sent a letter to his brother, Edward Bennett, inquiring whether Captain Nathaniel Bass or Lieutenant Barkley had claimed land within Warresqueak. He then described a shipment of goods he had received and expressed his desire to plant more land. Robert Bennett died sometime prior to November 20, 1623, at which time John Chew, a Jamestown **(1)** merchant, was named his administrator. On May 23, 1625, Robert Bennett's account book was produced in court by James Carter. At the time of his death, Robert owed the Rev. William Bennett, Warresqueak's clergyman, two years' salary (VCR 3:700; 4:220-222, 402; MCGC 5, 35, 60-61, 64; SR 1207).

ROBERT BENNETT

Robert Bennett died on Jamestown Island **(1)** sometime after April 1623 but before February 16, 1624 (CBE 39).

ROBERT BENNETT

On February 16, 1624, Robert Bennett reportedly was residing on Jamestown Island **(1)** in Ensign William Spence's household. He may have been erroneously listed as dead (CBE 39).

ROBERT BENNETT

On January 21, 1629, Robert Bennett, who was age 18, verified the statements made by

John Burland and Richard Bennett. He told the General Court that Burland had wanted three male servants and that Bennett's uncle had offered him three who were 17 years old—youths Burland refused to accept. On June 6, 1635, Robert Bennett patented some land in Warresqueak (later Isle of Wight) County. Later he procured a patent for acreage on the Nansemond River **(29)**. In March 1648 he was named a councilor (MCGC 181; PB 1 Pt. 1:185, 188; Lower Norfolk Book B:70).

ROBERT BENNETT

Robert Bennett came to Virginia on the *Jacob* in 1624. In early 1625 he was living in Elizabeth City **(18)** where he was a 24-year-old servant in Thomas Willoughby's household. On May 30, 1635, when John Slaughter patented some land in Elizabeth City, he identified Robert Bennett as one of his servants and said that he had paid for his transportation to Virginia (CBE 64; PB 1 Pt. 1:169).

***

SAMUEL BENNETT

Samuel Bennett and his wife came to Virginia on the *Providence* in 1622. On February 16, 1624, he was living in Elizabeth City **(17)** with his wife and two sons. In early 1625 Samuel and his wife, Joan, who were 40 years old, were living on the Virginia Company's land in Elizabeth City and were servants in the home of William Tiler (Tyler). On April 12, 1633, Samuel Bennett was credited with 50 acres in the Indian Thicket, part of a 100-acre leasehold that Lancelott Barnes had acquired on the east side of the Hampton River. On June 17, 1635, Samuel patented some land of his own in Elizabeth City (CBE 43, 67; PB 1 Pt. 1:142, 309; DOR 1:242).

JOAN BENNETT
(MRS. SAMUEL BENNETT)

Joan, the wife of Samuel Bennett, came to Virginia on the *Providence* in 1622. On February 16, 1624, they were living in Elizabeth City **(17)** with their two sons. In early 1625 Joan and Samuel Bennett, who were 40 years old, were living on the Virginia Company's land in Elizabeth City and were servants in the home of William Tiler (Tyler). Their sons' whereabouts are uncertain. Joan Bennett, after being widowed, married Thomas Chapman (CBE 43, 67; DOR 1:250).

[NO FIRST NAME] BENNETT

On February 16, 1624, Samuel Bennett's sons, whose given names are unknown, were living with him and his wife on the east side of the Hampton River in Elizabeth City (**17**) (CBE 43).

[NO FIRST NAME] BENNETT

On February 16, 1624, Samuel Bennett's sons, whose given names are unknown, were living with him and his wife on the east side of the Hampton River in Elizabeth City (**17**) (CBE 43).

***

***

THOMAS BENNETT

Thomas Bennett and his wife, Alice, were living at Burrows Hill (**8**) in 1624. On October 10, 1624, he testified about seeing the injuries sustained by Elizabeth Abbott, a maidservant who had been whipped. He said that he had taken Elizabeth to her master, John Proctor, so that she could receive medical attention (MCGC 23, 27).

ALICE BENNETT
(MRS. THOMAS BENNETT)

Alice, the wife of Thomas Bennett, was living at Burrows Hill (**8**) in October 1624. On October 10, 1624, she informed the General Court that she had seen the grievous injuries sustained by one of John Proctor's servants, Elizabeth Abbott, who had taken refuge behind a boat at Burrows Hill. Elizabeth told Alice that her wounds were the result of a severe beating she had received from her mistress. Alice Bennett said that she and her husband and Richard Richards carried Elizabeth to her master so that she could receive medical treatment (MCGC 23).

***

THOMAS BENNETT

On November 1, 1624, Thomas Bennett was identified as the father-in-law (stepfa-

ther) of Elizabeth Peirsey, the late John Phillimore's fiancé, when he was ordered to take care of Elizabeth's inheritance. Thomas Bennett may have been the individual who in October 1624 was living at Burrows Hill (**8**), for the late John Phillimore had resided on the lower side of the James River (MCGC 27).

***

THOMAS BENNETT (BENETT)

Thomas Bennett (Benett) came to Virginia on the *Bona Nova*, a vessel that brought numerous Virginia Company tenants and servants. On February 4, 1625, he was living on the Neck O'Land (**5**) with his wife, Margery, and 2-year-old Sara Bromedg (Bromage). Thomas's household was adequately supplied with stored food and defensive weaponry and had some livestock. On November 21, 1625, the General Court decided to reduce Thomas Bennett's rent on account of the heavy expenditures he had made. In 1627 he was identified as a tenant of the defunct Virginia Company when he was assigned to the governor (CBE 58; MCGC 76, 136; DOR 1:37).

MARGERY BENNETT (BENETT)
(MRS. THOMAS BENNETT
[BENETT])

Margery, who became the wife of Thomas Bennett (Benett), came to Virginia on the *Gift*. On February 4, 1625, she and her husband were living on the Neck O'Land (**5**) with 2-year-old Sara Bromedg (Bromage), who may have been related to Mr. and Mrs. Henry Bromage, killed at Martin's Hundred (**7**) in the March 22, 1622, Indian attack (CBE 58).

***

***

THOMAS BENNETT

Thomas Bennett came to Virginia in 1618 on the *Neptune*, the ship that brought Lord Delaware to the colony. On February 7, 1625, Thomas, who was age 38, was living at Basses Choice (**27**), where he headed a household that included his 18-year-old wife, Mary, and two other adults. The household was well supplied with stored food and defensive weaponry (CBE 62; DOR 1:49).

MARY BENNETT
(MRS. THOMAS BENNETT)

Mary, who married Thomas Bennett, came to Virginia on the *Southampton* in 1622. On February 7, 1625, she was age 18 and living at Basses Choice (27) in a household her husband headed (CBE 62).

***

THOMAS BENNETT

In September 1632 Thomas Bennett served as a burgess for Mulberry Island (21) (HEN 1:179).

***

WILLIAM BENNETT (BENET) I

The Rev. William Bennett (Benet) I, came to Virginia on the *Seaflower* in 1621 and became the minister at Warresqueak (26), the Bennett plantation. In November 1623 the General Court determined that the late Robert Bennett owed him two years' back pay. On January 7, 1624, the Rev. Bennett witnessed an agreement between Thomas Hamor and Lieutenant John Gibbs. He moved to West and Shirley Hundred (41) and died there sometime after February 16, 1624, but before January 22, 1625. He was survived by his wife, Katherine, and their 3-week-old son, William (VCR 4:402; MCGC 9-10, 91; CBE 53; SR 1207).

KATHERINE BENNETT (BENET)
(MRS. WILLIAM BENNETT
[BENET])

Katherine, who married the Rev. William Bennett (Benet) I, came to Virginia on the *Abigail* in 1622. On January 22, 1625, she and her 3-week-old son, William, were living at West and Shirley Hundred (41). Katherine Bennett was then a 24-year-old widow. By January 20, 1626, she had prepared an inventory of her late husband's estate. When it was presented to the General Court, she was represented by Captain William Eppes (CBE 53; MCGC 91).

WILLIAM BENNETT (BENET) II

On January 22, 1625, William II, the infant son of the late Rev. William Bennett (Benet) I and his wife, Katherine, was living at West and Shirley Hundred (41). He was 3 weeks old (CBE 53).

***

WILLIAM BENNETT

William Bennett, a boat-builder, came to Virginia sometime prior to March 23, 1624, and obtained bedding and other household items from Jamestown (1) merchant John Chew. On December 24, 1627, William was residing in the household of Dr. John Pott in urban Jamestown, where he received medical treatment, room, and board. He agreed to make Pott a boat like the one he had fabricated for Edward Sharples (MCGC 13, 158).

WILLIAM BENNETT

William Bennett came to Virginia on the *Gift of God* and died in Jamestown (1) sometime after April 1623 and before February 16, 1624 (HOT 196).

WILLIAM BENNETT

On August 8, 1628, officials at Bridewell decided that William Bennett, a vagrant from Queenhith, would be sent to Virginia (CBE 83).

RICHARD BENNINGTON
(BERINGTON)

On May 10, 1611, shortly before Richard Bennington (Berington), carpenter of the ship *Unicorn*, set sail for Virginia, he made his will, naming his friend Robert Arnold as executor. Richard Bennington died sometime prior to February 1612 (SH 2; EEAC 6; SR 3107).

HENRY BENSON

Henry Benson came to Virginia on the *Francis Bonaventure* in August 1620 and on February 16, 1624, was living at West and Shirley Hundred (41). He was still there on January 22, 1625. Henry and his partner, Nicholas Blackman, headed a household that had a substantial supply of stored food and defensive weaponry. Henry was then age 40 (CBE 36, 52; DOR 1:14).

WILLIAM BENTLEY

William Bentley came to Virginia in the 1st Supply of new colonists who landed in Jamestown (1) in 1608. Captain John Smith identified Bentley variously as a gentleman, a soldier, and a laborer. In late December 1608 William Bentley, who was then described as a soldier, accompanied Smith on a journey to Pamunkey. Later, Smith called him a fugitive who (like the runaway Dutchmen) fled to the Indians (CJS 1:223, 243, 266; 2:161, 193, 215).

WILLIAM BENTLEY
(BENTLY, BENTLIE)

William Bentley (Bently, Bentlie), a tailor, came to Virginia on the *Jacob* in 1624, at his own expense. He patented 50 acres of land in Elizabeth City, at Blunt Point (22) on December 1, 1624. He was living in Elizabeth City (18) in early 1625 in the household headed by Pharaoh Flinton. Bentley was then age 36. In May 1625 when a list of patented land was sent back to England, he was credited with 50 acres at Blunt Point. On December 19, 1625, William Bentley was summoned to appear in court in a matter involving his host, Mr. Flinton, and Mr. Allington. On February 8, 1629, he made another appearance in court, this time as a defendant. William Bentley, who had borrowed Mr. Conges's boat, ran aground near William Parker's house at Merry Point. Thomas Godby and some others, who were inside the dwelling, ignored his cries for help. When William Bentley reached the Parker home, he and Thomas Godby (his neighbor) exchanged insults, then came to blows. Afterward Bentley was indicted for killing Godby. In March 1629 a jury found William Bentley guilty of manslaughter. He received benefit of clergy and was freed. In October 1629 William was elected a burgess for Nutmeg Quarter (CBE 65; PB 1 Pt.1:24-25; VCR 4:557; MCGC 81, 190-192; HEN 1:139).

JOHN BERBYE

On July 31, 1622, John Berbye set sail for Virginia aboard the *James*, at the expense of Edward Bennett. He probably was bound for Bennett's Welcome or Warresqueak (26), the Bennett plantation (FER 400).

***

GEORGE BERKELEY

George Berkeley, a Virginia Company investor, died sometime prior to November 1620. His widow and heir, Elizabeth, asked Company officials to transfer his legal rights to her, noting that he had invested £400 and had transported men and cattle to Virginia. On February 13, 1622, Company officials acknowledged that George Berkeley was dead and that his widow was entitled to his 5½ shares of Virginia land (VCR 1:428, 598-599).

ELIZABETH BERKELEY
(MRS. GEORGE BERKELEY)

In mid-November 1620 Elizabeth, George Berkeley's widow and heir, asked Virginia Company officials for her late husband's shares of Virginia land. She said that he had transported men and cattle to Virginia and had invested £400 in the colony. On February 13, 1622, Company officials transferred the late George Berkeley's 5½ shares of Virginia land to the widowed Elizabeth (VCR 1:401, 418-419, 428, 598-599).

***

***

JOHN BERKELEY

In June 1621 John Berkeley went to Virginia to build an ironworks on behalf of the Virginia Company. He was accompanied by his son, Maurice, and 20 others, including a skillful salt-maker and a man capable of making iron pots and brewing vessels. Virginia Company officials agreed to provide free transportation and provisions for the Berkeleys and three of their servants and instructed Governor Francis Wyatt to find land for John Berkeley and his group. They also appointed him to the Council of State. In January 1622 John Berkeley was supposed to report on the feasibility of erecting an ironworks in Virginia. In early March, Treasurer George Sandys sent word that an ironworks was being built at Falling Creek (68) and that it was expected to be operational by Whitsuntide, that is, Pentecost, the 7th Sunday after Easter. John Berkeley asked the Virginia Company for additional provisions and they complied. However, on March 22, 1622, when the Indians attacked the Falling Creek ironworks, 22 people (including John Berkeley) were killed (VCR 1:475-476, 483, 622-623, 629; 3: 482, 486, 548, 555, 566, 586, 588, 651; CJS 2:301).

MAURICE BERKELEY

Maurice Berkeley, John Berkeley's son, was sent to Virginia by the Company of Mercers in 1621. He was supposed to make iron for seven years and supervise Miles Prickett, who was building a salt-works. After John Berkeley's death in the March 1622 Indian attack, Maurice Berkeley was put in charge of the survivors who had been involved in constructing the Falling Creek (**68**) ironworks. On January 20, 1623, he sent a report to Virginia Company officials on the status of the ironworks and in November informed Company officials that he had received the salt pans they sent. He also asked to be released from the Company's service and given some land of his own. On February 2, 1624, Maurice Berkeley was awarded a patent for the 800 acres of land to which he and his late father were entitled. His request for additional salt pans was forwarded to the governor (FER 297; VCR 1:476; 2: 497, 508-509; 3:586, 670; 4:9).

***

RICHARD BERKELEY

On February 3, 1619, Richard Berkeley was identified as one of several investors involved in the establishment of Berkeley Hundred (**55**), a private plantation. In an April 1619 letter he mentioned his kinsman, a Bristol surgeon named William Chester, who was interested in going to Virginia. On September 16, 1619, Richard Berkeley and his fellow investors sent a group of people to the colony with Captain John Woodlief (VCR 3:110, 130-134, 137-138).

MARGARET BERMAN

On February 16, 1624, Margaret Berman was living at Bermuda Hundred (**39**) (CBE 35).

DANIEL BERMOND

In 1621 the Society of Martin's Hundred sent Daniel Bermond, who was age 17, to Martin's Hundred (**7**) to be Mr. Limbrough's servant (FER 343).

JOHN BERNARD (BARNARD)

Between January 1618 and January 1620 the Virginia Company sent Captain John Bernard (Barnard) some of his books. He died in the colony sometime prior to April 26, 1624, at which time his patent was mentioned. Virginia Company officials noted that the decedent had married John James's widow and acquired his Company shares. John Bernard assigned his land in Martin's Hundred (**7**) to George Furzman. The location of Bernard's acreage reportedly was shown on the Society of Martin's Hundred's map of their plantation (FER 141; VCR 2:532-533).

STEPHEN BERNARD

Stephen Bernard came to Virginia in 1628 on the *Hopewell* at the expense of Adam Thorogood. On June 24, 1635, when Thorogood secured a patent, he listed Bernard as a headright (PB 1 Pt. 1:179).

***

[NO FIRST NAME] BERNARDO

Mr. Bernardo, an Italian artisan, was outfitted by the Virginia Company and sent to Virginia to produce glass that could be sold profitably. On February 16, 1624, he and his wife were living at Glass House Point (**2**), where a glass furnace had been built. By February 4, 1625, the Bernardo couple and their child had moved to the Treasurer's Plantation (**11**) on the lower side of the James River. Later in the year, he received a pass to go to England, but was obliged to post a bond with the investors in the glassworks. His wife, Peirce, stayed on in Virginia (CBE 41, 60; MCGC 56).

MRS. PEIRCE BERNARDO (MRS. [NO FIRST NAME] BERNARDO)

Mrs. Bernardo, the wife of an Italian artisan sent to Virginia to produce glass, was living with her husband at Glass House Point (**2**) on February 16, 1624. By February 4, 1625, the Bernardos and their child had moved to the Treasurer's Plantation (**11**), the office land of Treasurer George Sandys. Court testimony taken on October 7, 1625, reveals that Mrs. Bernardo's first name was Peirce and that she stayed on in the colony despite her husband's return to England. In October 1627 Mrs. Bernardo testified that she had lived with Captain William Norton, late overseer of the glassworks, and that he had not paid Thomas Wilson for his work (CBE 41, 60; MCGC 56, 72).

[NO FIRST NAME] BERNARDO

On February 4, 1625, when Mr. Bernardo and his wife, Peirce, were living at the Treasurer's Plantation (**11**), they shared their home with their child (CBE 60).

***

JOHN BERRY

On June 19, 1622, John Berry informed the Virginia Company that Deputy Governor Samuel Argall had given Adam Dixon and him some wooded ground. He said that he and Dixon, assisted by their four servants, cleared their land and built a house. Berry said that when Sir George Yeardley came in as governor in April 1619, he evicted them from their land and gave them no compensation. These statements indicate that John Berry and Adam Dixon had been occupying some of the acreage on the east side of the Hampton River (**17**) that was designated the Virginia Company's land. On January 21, 1624, John Berry claimed that Sir Samuel Argall forced him to sign away his pay. In May 1625 when a list of patented land was sent back to England, John Berry was credited with 100 acres in Warresqueak (**26**) (VCR 2:43-44; 4:556; FER 524).

TOBIAS BERRY

On December 24, 1634, when Tobias Felgate of Westover (**54**) made his will, he made a bequest to a youth named Tobias Berry (SH 19).

ANDREW BERRYMAN

On February 10, 1632, Andrew Berryman shipped goods from Barnstaple to Virginia on the *Merlyn* (CBE 100).

WILLIAM BERRYMAN (BERRIMAN)

William Berryman (Berriman) moved to the Eastern Shore sometime prior to 1633 and became a churchwarden. He patented 150 acres near Old Plantation Creek (**73**) in August 1635. Throughout the years he was plagued by financial problems. He was obliged to use half of his plantation as collateral in order to secure his debts, and in 1638 he had to mortgage virtually all of his possessions. Berryman was literate and reportedly prepared wills and other documents for submission to the Council of State. He was still in residence on the Eastern Shore in 1644 (PB 1 Pt. 1:270; AMES 1:5, 9, 26, 33, 37, 47, 50; 2:28-29, 437).

MILES BERTE

Miles Berte, a mason, set sail for Virginia on April 17, 1619, and may have been a Virginia Company tenant or servant (FER 107).

BESS

On March 25, 1629, when the General Court was trying to determine whether Thomas Hall, a hermaphrodite, should be legally classified as male or female, one witness testified that he had had a sexual encounter with a servant known as Great Bess. As Thomas was a resident of the Treasurer's Plantation (**11**) and later, Warresqueak (**26**), Bess may have lived there too (MCGC 194).

***

WILLIAM BESSE

In June 1619 William Besse, who described himself as a 35-year-old yeoman, testified that he had lived in Bermuda for 6 years before returning to England on the *Garland*. In a deposition he gave the following year, he said that he was a girdler originally from St. Mildred Poultry in London. Besse moved to Virginia sometime after 1621 but before February 16, 1624, when he and his wife were living at Jordan's Journey (**46**). Their names were not included in the 1625 muster, probably because they had gone to England. In April 1625 the General Court ordered Mr. Palmer to give John Kennell (a servant) to Rice Hoe, in accord with the written instructions William Besse sent to Virginia on the *Ann*. Court testimony dating to December 4, 1626, reveals that William Besse, though still in England, considered himself a resident of Jordan's Journey and a Virginia planter. Rice Hoe of nearby West and Shirley Hundred (**41**) was ordered to collect some documents belonging to Besse and to make an accounting of his tobacco crop. Besse's young male servant was entrusted to the care of Mrs. Alice Boyce, who had the right to hire him for a year or purchase his contract. William Besse returned to Virginia sometime prior to 1628 and brought suit against Mrs. Boyce, who had married Mathew Edloe. William Besse survived until at least 1640, at which time he shipped some tobacco from Virginia to Rotterdam (EAE 7; CBE 36; MCGC 51, 126, 173; SR 3506, 3807; PB 3:170).

MRS. WILLIAM BESSE

On February 16, 1624, Mrs. William Besse and her husband were living at Jordan's Journcy (**46**) (CBE 36).

***

BENJAMIN BEST (BEAST)

Benjamin Best (Beast), a gentleman, who was one of the first Jamestown (**1**) colonists, died on September 5, 1607 (CJS 1:20; 2:141; HAI 99).

CHRISTOPHER BEST

On April 1, 1623, Christopher Best, a surgeon and indentured servant then in Virginia, sent a letter to his master, John Woodall, who was in England, informing him that many of his cattle were dead. On February 16, 1624, Best was living in urban Jamestown (**1**) in the household headed by John Pountis. In early November 1624 John Woodall dispatched word to Best that he was sending him a chest of surgical supplies and medical goods. Best apparently practiced his profession in the capital city, for he dressed Lieutenant George Harrison's wound, tended to Rowland Loftis's medical needs, and assisted several other Jamestown residents. During 1625 the General Court mentioned some of the people who were indebted to Christopher Best for the medical care they had received. He apparently died sometime prior to September 19, 1625, for the General Court discussed the disposition of the recently arrived medical supplies that John Woodall had sent to him (VCR 4:238; CBE 38; MCGC 38-40, 44, 71-72).

THOMAS BEST

On April 12, 1623, Thomas Best sent a letter to his brother and his cousin saying that he was famished to the point of starvation. On February 16, 1624, Best was living in Elizabeth City (**18**) (VCR 4:235; CBE 44).

WILLIAM BEST

On April 21, 1624, when William Best asked for tax relief on account of the 1622 Indian attack, he described himself as a poor Virginia planter (VCR 2:519).

SAMUEL BETTON

Sometime after April 1623 but before February 16, 1624, Samuel Betton died at one of the settlements on the lower side of the James River, within the corporation of James City (**8-15**) (CBE 41).

RICHARD BEVERLEY

On January 29, 1620, officials at Bridewell decided that Richard Beverley would be sent to Virginia (CBE 17-18).

ROBERT BEW

Robert Bew came to Virginia on the *Duty.* On February 16, 1624, when census records were compiled, he was identified as a resident of urban Jamestown (**1**) but also was attributed to the territory on the lower side of the James River, east of Gray's Creek (**10-16**). Bew probably was listed in both locations because Edward Blaney, who had married Captain William Powell's widow, Margaret, moved his and his stepchildren's servants back and forth between the Powell plantation (**14**) and Jamestown. On January 24, 1625, Robert Bew was identified as a 20-year-old servant who lived in the urban Jamestown home of merchant Edward Blaney (CBE 40, 55).

CHARLES BEWSE

On January 22, 1620, it was decided that Charles Bewse, a vagrant from Old Jewry, would be detained at Bridewell until he could be sent to Virginia (CBE 17).

PIERRE BIARD

Father Pierre Biard, a Jesuit priest from New France, described his experiences in Virginia during 1613 and 1614. He and two other Jesuits were among the 15 men captured by Samuel Argall in July 1613 at

Mount Desert, a fledgling Catholic colony in what is now Maine. Argall took them to Jamestown (1), where they were detained aboard ship. Biard said they were in constant fear of being hanged by Sir Thomas Dale, who frequently threatened their lives. Finally, Argall persuaded Dale to let him take the men to England, so that they could return to their native country. He transported Father Biard to Wales, where he was released after 9½ months of living in captivity (JAM 227-228).

THOMAS BIBBIE

On July 31, 1622, Thomas Bibbie set sail from England on the *James* and accompanied William Rowley to Virginia (FER 400).

***

WILLIAM BIBBIE (BRIBBIE, BIBBY)

William Bibbie (Bribbie, Bibby) came to Virginia on the *Swan* in 1621 and on February 16, 1624, was living on the Eastern Shore. He was still there in early 1625 and headed a household with his partner, Thomas Sparkes. Bibbie was age 22. The two men were in possession of a house, a storehouse, an ample supply of stored food, and a defensive weapon. In 1625 William Bibbie inherited Thomas Parke's (Sparkes?) corn. When Bibbie testified in court in October 1633 he gave his age as 33, and two years later he said that he was 35 years old. In June 1636 he received a patent for 400 acres of land between King's and Old Plantation Creeks, using his wife, Mary, as a headright. William Bibbie's will was proved on September 25, 1637, and his widow died two months later (CBE 46, 69; MCGC 46; PB 1 Pt. 1:367; AMES 1:6, 28, 85; 2; 117, 249-250; DOR 1:71, 311).

MARY BIBBIE (BRIBBIE, BIBBY) (MRS. WILLIAM BIBBIE [BRIBBIE, BIBBY])

In June 1636, when William Bibbie (Bribbie, Bibby) patented some land on Old Plantation Creek (73), he used his wife, Mary, as a headright. William died prior to September 25, 1637, and Mary's death occurred two months later (PB 1 Pt. 1:436; AMES 1:43, 104; 2:117, 249-250; DOR 1:311).

***

WILLIAM BICKAR (BYKAR)

On March 22, 1622, when the Indians attacked William Bickar's (Byckar's) plantation (57), he and four others were killed at his house. Bickar's property was located on a small point of land on the east side of Chappell Creek's mouth, overlooking what became known as Bikars or Tar Bay. The plantation, now located in Prince George County, seems to have been abandoned after the 1622 Indian assault (CJS 2:302; VCR 3:568; PB 1 Pt. 1:151; Pt. 2:475, 837).

RICHARD BICKLEY

Richard Bickley came to Virginia on the *Return*. On February 4, 1625, he was living at Hog Island (16), where he was a servant in John Uty's household. On May 7, 1627, Bickley was punished because he refused to perform military duty in response to Ensign Uty's orders (CBE 61; MCGC 148).

DANIEL BIDEL (BEDDELL)

During the March–May 1630 court session, Daniel Bidel (Beddell), a 34-year-old mariner from All Hallows, Barking, London, testified about events that occurred when he was in Canada in May 1628. He said that he had been hired by Joseph Page, merchant of the ship *Sun*, to go to Virginia, and that although the vessel was leaky, it reached its destination. Bidel said that he returned to England on the *London Merchant* (EAE 21-22).

HENRY BIGGE

On January 30, 1635, when John Bigge of Whitechapel, Middlesex, made his will, he made a bequest to Henry Bigge, a tailor then living in Virginia (EEAC 7; WAT 627-628).

***

RICHARD BIGGS I

Richard Biggs I, an ancient planter, came to Virginia on the *Swan* in 1610. He was among those who inventoried the estate of George Thorpe, killed on March 22, 1622. Biggs signed the document with a mark, suggesting that he was not literate. On February 16, 1624, Biggs was living at West and Shirley Hundred (41) with his wife, Sarah (Sara), and their sons, Richard II and

William. The household also included another boy. On February 20, 1624, Richard Biggs, then a burgess, signed the General Assembly's rebuttal to a Virginia Company official's claims that conditions in the colony were good prior to 1619. On January 22, 1625, when a muster was compiled, Richard Biggs I was age 41. He headed a household that included wife Sarah, son Richard II, and two other children who were identified as cousins: Thomas Turner (age 11) and Susan Old (age 10). Also present were four servants: three males and a female. Biggs had possession of three houses, some livestock, a boat, and an abundance of stored food and defensive weaponry. In May 1625 when a list of patented land was sent back to England, Richard Biggs I was credited with 150 acres in Charles City that had been planted. On September 10, 1625, Richard made his will. He bequeathed most of his real and personal possessions to his wife, Sarah, and son, Richard II. He left 6 acres of land to Rebecca Rose, whom he identified as his sister, and he bequeathed some tobacco to his friend Samuel Sharpe. Richard Biggs I died sometime prior to April 20, 1626, at which time the General Court reviewed his will. His widow was ordered to take possession of the family's new home and the 9 acres on which it was situated, and to take custody of the decedent's livestock. However, she was to relinquish all real and personal property to son Richard II when he reached the age of 21. Samuel Sharpe and Sarah Biggs went to England to present Richard Biggs I's will to the authorities, who appointed Sarah the administrator of her late husband's estate (S of N 43; HAI 915; HEN 1:128-129; VCR 4:553; CBE 36, 52, 73; MCGC 100-101; SR 3114; SH 6; WITH 53-54; EEAC 7; DOR 1:12).

SARAH (SARA) BIGGS (MRS. RICHARD BIGGS I)

Sarah (Sara), who married Richard Biggs I, came to Virginia on the *Marigold,* which arrived in May 1618. On February 16, 1624, she was living at West and Shirley Hundred (**41**) with her husband, an ancient planter. The Biggs family shared their home with their two sons, Richard II and William, and another boy. On January 22, 1625, when a muster was taken of the plantation's inhabitants, Sarah was then age 35 and her son, Richard II, was age 3. Also present were two

other children, 11-year-old Thomas Turner and 10-year-old Susan Old, both of whom had come to the colony on the *Marigold* and were Richard Biggs I's cousins. On January 9, 1625, the General Court noted that church services were going to be held in the Biggs home at West and Shirley Hundred. On September 10, 1625, when Richard Biggs I made his will, he left the bulk of his land and goods to his wife, Sarah, and son, Richard II. He also made modest bequests to his sister, Rebecca Rose, and his friend Samuel Sharpe. On April 20, 1626, the General Court noted that Sarah Biggs was responsible for the house and 9 acres of land her son, Richard II, stood to inherit when he came of age. Sarah also was to accompany Samuel Sharpe to England so that the decedent's estate could be settled. On August 9, 1626, Sarah was named the administrator of her late husband's Virginia estate (CBE 36, 52, 73; MCGC 88-89, 100-101; SR 3114; EEAC 7; SH 6; WITH 53-54).

RICHARD BIGGS II

On February 16, 1624, Richard Biggs II was living with his parents, Richard and Sarah Biggs, and brother, William, at West and Shirley Hundred (**41**). When a muster of the community was taken on January 22, 1625, Richard II was said to be 3 years old. His brother, William, apparently was deceased. Also living in the Biggs home were Susan Old and Thomas Turner, Richard II's cousins. When Richard Biggs I made his will on September 10, 1625, he named his son, Richard II, as his principal heir. On April 20, 1626, the General Court acknowledged that the widowed Sarah Biggs would have custody of her late husband's house and 9 acres of land until Richard II turned 21 (CBE 36, 52; MCGC 101; SR 3114).

WILLIAM BIGGS

On February 16, 1624, William Biggs was living at West and Shirley Hundred (**41**) with his parents, Richard and Sarah Biggs, and brother, Richard II (CBE 36).

***

THOMAS BIGGS

Between April 1623 and February 16, 1624, Thomas Biggs died at one of the plantations on the lower side of the James River, within the corporation of James City (**8-15**) (CBE 41).

MARGARET BILBIE (BILBY)

Margaret Bilbie (Bilby) came to Virginia in 1628 on the *Hopewell* at the expense of Adam Thorogood. On June 24, 1635, when Thorogood secured a patent, he listed Margaret as a headright (PB 1 Pt. 1:179).

THOMAS BILBY (BILBIE)

On November 20, 1623, the General Court's justices heard testimony about the nuncupative will of Thomas Bilby (Bilbie). Phetiplace Close said that he advised Bilby, who had became very ill, to make a will. Bilby then stated that he planned to bequeath his goods to Lewis Bailey (Bayly). William Hall and Lewis Bailey (Bayly), who also were present when Thomas Bilby expressed his last wishes, verified the fact that he had named Bailey (Bayly) as his sole heir. As Phetiplace Close, William Hall, and Lewis Bailey (Bayly) lived on the lower side of the James River, within the corporation of James City (**8-16**), it is probable that Thomas Bilby resided there too, most likely at Paces Paines (**9**) (MCGC 8).

JOHN BILLIARD

On February 16, 1624, John Billiard was living in Elizabeth City (**17, 18**). In May 1625 when a list of patented land was sent back to England, he was credited with 100 acres of land in Henrico, on the south side of the James River, below The Falls (**67**) (CBE 44; VCR 4:552).

***

WILLIAM BINKS (SEE WILLIAM BANKS)

ANN BINKS (MRS. WILLIAM BINKS) (SEE ANN BANKS)

***

SUSAN BINN (BINX)

In 1621 Susan Binn (Binx), one of the young maids sent to be colonists' wives, went to Virginia on the *Marmaduke*. Susan, who was 20 years old, was born on Seaside Lane in St. Sepulcher's Parish. Virginia Company officials noted that her parents were still alive and that her aunt was Mrs. Gardiner, a widow. Susan, who had been placed in service and was recommended by her employer, Mrs. Patten, was said to be honest and of good character (FER 306, 309).

***

THOMAS BINION

On June 13, 1621, Virginia Company officials noted that Thomas Binion had died in Virginia and that his daughter, Katherine, wanted the money he was owed by Captain John Martin, owner of Martin's Brandon (**59**). This raises the possibility that Thomas Binion had invested in Martin's plantation or perhaps resided there (VCR 1:491).

KATHERINE BINION

Virginia Company records dating to June 13, 1621, indicate that Thomas Binion had died in Virginia and that his daughter, Katherine, wanted to recover the funds he was owed by Captain John Martin of Martin's Brandon (**59**) (VCR 1:491).

***

WILLIAM BINSLEY

In 1624 William Binsley came to Virginia on the *Jacob*. In early 1625 he was living in Elizabeth City (**17**) in Anthony Bonall's household. William was then age 18 and free (CBE 58).

ABRAHAM BINSTEAD (BINSTEED)

On March 12, 1627, Abraham Binstead (Binsteed) testified that three or four weeks before he arrived in Virginia, he saw Robert Cooke and Thomas Lawley fighting while they were aboard the ship *Plantation* (MCGC 144).

RICHARD BIRCHETT (BURCHER?)

On January 20, 1624, when Thomas Boulding patented 200 acres of land in Elizabeth City (**18**), he indicated that he had purchased half of it from Richard Birchett, an ancient planter (PB 1 Pt. 1:43).

***

ROBERT BISAKER (BYSAKER)

On September 1, 1620, Robert Bisaker (Bysaker) signed a contract with the Society of Berkeley Hundred (**55**), agreeing to serve the Society's investors in exchange for the Society's transporting Robert, his wife, Faith, and Richard Hopkins to Virginia. Bisaker and Hopkins were supposed to receive some support when they first arrived in the colony, but then were to become sharecroppers. Later in September the Bisaker couple set sail from Bristol, England, on the ship *Supply* and accompanied William Tracy to Berkeley Hundred (CBE 21; VCR 3:393-394).

FAITH BISAKER (BYSAKER) (MRS. ROBERT BISAKER [BYSAKER])

In September 1620, Faith, the wife of sharecropper Robert Bisaker (Bysaker), set sail from Bristol, England, on the ship *Supply* and accompanied William Tracy to Berkeley Hundred (**55**). The Bisakers went to Virginia with Richard Hopkins and were supposed to receive some support in exchange for crop shares (CBE 21; VCR 3:393-394).

***

JAMES BLACKBORNE (BLACKBOURNE)

James Blackborne (Blackbourne) came to Virginia in 1619 on the *Sampson*. In early 1625 he was living on the Eastern Shore, where he was a 20-year-old servant in the household of Captain William Eppes (**74**). On January 30, 1626, when Blackborne appeared before the General Court, he was given his freedom after he posted a bond guaranteeing to serve Captain Ward if Ward could prove that he was owed more time. Two other men posted security with Captain Eppes to cover any time they might owe Captain Ward. James Blackborne returned to court the following month and testified that he had heard Captain Ward say that Christopher Barker was to serve for four years and that he had done so (CBE 68; MCGC 91, 96).

THOMAS BLACKLOCKE

On February 16, 1624, Thomas Blacklocke was living on the Eastern Shore (**72-78**) (CBE 46).

JEREMY BLACKMAN

In December 1633 Jeremy Blackman testified about his voyage from London to Virginia as master of the *Expedition*, which carried 100 passengers. In 1634 he was accused of illegal trading and torturing a ship's boy. On December 24, 1634, when mariner Tobias Felgate of Westover (**54**) prepared his will, he made a bequest to Jeremy Blackman. The following year, Blackman, as master of the *Globe* of London, brought 161 passengers to Virginia. He exported tobacco from the colony in 1639–1640 and also attempted to transport four deer to England, which died during the journey. In 1640 he and Virginia merchant Thomas Stegg were authorized to import horses into the colony (CBE 108, 113, 117; EAE 42; SH 19; SR 3466, 3506, 4546; EXC 190/44 f 1; SAIN 1:285).

***

NICHOLAS BLACKMAN

Nicholas Blackman came to Virginia in August 1620 on the *Francis Bonaventure* and on February 16, 1624, was living at West and Shirley Hundred (**41**). He was still there on January 22, 1625, when he and his partner, Henry Benson, headed a household. The men, who were 40 years old, had a substantial supply of stored food and were outfitted with defensive weaponry. Nicholas got married sometime prior to June 1627 (CBE 36, 52; MCGC 149).

GOODWIFE BLACKMAN (MRS. NICHOLAS BLACKMAN)

On June 4, 1627, the General Court ordered William Farrar to interview Goodwife Blackman and two other women about some immoral conduct that had occurred at West and Shirley Hundred (**41**), where a young male servant had had sex with a young girl (MCGC 149).

***

WILLIAM BLACKWELL

When William Blackwell testified in 1624 in the suit involving the ships *Neptune* and *Treasurer*, he was identified as a 51-year-old gentleman of Grays Thurrock near Henley in Oxfordshire. On January 4, 1625, he testified on behalf of Edward Brewster, who was being sued by the Earl of Warwick. William Blackwell's firsthand knowledge of these events and his perspective suggest that he was in Virginia in 1618–1619 and that he may have been one of Lord Delaware's men (EAE 14; HCA 13/44 ff 327ro-328ro).

SUSAN BLACKWOOD

Susan Blackwood came to Virginia in 1622 on the *Abigail* and on February 16, 1624, was living on the Maine (3), where she was one of Dr. John Pott's servants. On January 24, 1625, Susan was living in urban Jamestown (1) in the Pott household (CBE 39, 55).

PATRICK BLACOCK (BLALOCKE)

On July 19, 1633, Patrick Blacock (Blalocke), who was brought in from Whitefriars and detained at Bridewell, agreed to go to Virginia. On June 24, 1634, when Adam Thorogood patented some land, he listed Patrick as a headright and said that he had paid for his transportation on the *Bonaventure* in 1634 (CBE 108; PB 1 Pt. 1:179).

ABIGAIL BLAKE

According to records at Christ Church Hospital, on July 19, 1633, Abigail Blake "broke the union" and departed. It is probable that she violated or nullified some sort of agreement that was considered binding, perhaps one that required her to go overseas (HUME 38).

BARTHOLOMEW BLAKE

Bartholomew Blake, a smith sent to Virginia in 1621 by the Company of Shipwrights, was promised 25 acres of land on completion of his 5-year contract. He reportedly received money, provisions, bedding, and clothing from his sponsors, along with some butter and aqua-vitae. In 1623 Blake was described as a carpenter. On December 11, 1623, Bartholomew Blake testified that Captain Wilcocks had sold Captain Barwick's goods to Sergeant Williams. Although he acknowledged that he had gotten a bed and apparel from his sponsors, he indicated that he had received neither a dish nor a spoon. It is probable that Bartholomew Blake (like others who came to Vir-

ginia on behalf of the Company of Shipwrights) resided on Jamestown Island (1). He died there sometime after February 16, 1624, but before January 24, 1625 (FER 378, 390; MCGC 8; CBE 56).

MARTHA BLAKE

In September 1621 Martha Blake, a young maid born at Ilford, came to Virginia on the *Warwick*. She was 20 years old and was skilled at weaving and making silk points. Virginia Company records indicate that Martha was in service to Vandall, a stationer, who had recommended her. She also was approved by the wife of the clerk of the Minories (FER 309).

WALTER BLAKE

Walter Blake came to Virginia on the *Swan* and on February 16, 1624, was living at Flowerdew Hundred (53) and was one of Sir George Yeardley's men. On February 4, 1625, when a muster was made of Hog Island's (16) inhabitants, Walter Blake was identified as one of Yeardley's men and described as a "dweller." Blake died sometime prior to January 10, 1627, at which time blacksmith John Stone, also a resident of Hog Island, presented an inventory of his estate (CBE 37, 61; MCGC 130).

JOHN BLANCHARD

On September 15, 1619, John Blanchard, a gentleman, set sail for Virginia on the *Margaret* of Bristol and was among those being sent to Berkeley Hundred (55) to work under Captain John Woodlief's supervision. Blanchard was supposed to serve the Society of Berkeley Hundred's investors for three years as steward and clerk of the store of bedding and apparel. In exchange, he was to get 50 acres of land and receive monetary compensation. In June 1620 John Smyth of Nibley reported that he had heard nothing from John Blanchard (CBE 13-14; VCR 3:197, 199, 210, 213, 293).

JAMES BLANCHER

On October 7, 1622, Virginia Company officials were informed that James Blanchard had died in Virginia and his widow, Joane, who resided in England, wanted his estate to be inventoried. She also wanted the proceeds of his estate (VCR 2:106).

THOMAS BLANCKS

On January 30, 1625, Thomas Blancks, a 17-year-old servant, was living on the Governor's Land (3), where he was one of the governor's men. Blancks came to Virginia on the *Francis Bonaventure* (CBE 57).

***

JOHN BLAND I

John Bland I (a Virginia Company investor) was a London merchant who sent family members, indentured servants, and saleable goods to Virginia. His wife, Mary, was the daughter of Francis Emperour. On January 30, 1622, John Bland became an investor in Martin's Hundred (7). He and his business partners—John Newman, Robert Watson, and Richard Perry—owned the ship *Abigail*. In April 1623 John Bland I indicated that he had transported his brother (probably brother-in-law) Thomas Finch to Virginia. In July 1623 he agreed to send surplus goods to the colony, and in September 1627 he dispatched a shipment on the *Samuell* of London. John Bland I was mentioned in the July 1631 will of his brother, Thomas, and he was the father of John II, Edward, Richard, Adam, and Theodorick Bland I. He also was the grandfather of Richard, Giles, and Theodorick Bland II (EAE 8; FER 322, 398; VCR 2:455; 4:115-116, 245-246; 3:593; DOR 1:323-324; WITH 257, 638).

JOHN BLAND II

During the second and third quarters of the seventeenth century, John Bland I's son, John Bland II, owned a lot in urban Jamestown (1), probably the waterfront parcel on which archaeologists have found the remains of a large warehouse. In 1644 John Bland II's brother Adam received a large shipment of goods in Jamestown, which were described in detail in his bill of lading. Another Bland brother, Theodorick, received high praise from the assembly in 1663 for working closely with John Bland II in obtaining substantial quantities of items essential to the colony's wellbeing. Bland was still in possession of his Jamestown lot in 1679 when his wife, Sarah, came to Virginia to conduct business on his behalf and identified the various properties he owned (Surry County Deeds, Wills &c. 1671-1684:229; DOR 1:325-326; HEN 2:199; CBE 7).

***

***

EDWARD BLANEY (BLANY, BLANYE, BLANIE, BLAINY, BLAYNY)

Edward Blaney (Blany, Blanye, Blanie, Blainy, Blayny), a merchant, came to Virginia on the *Francis Bonaventure* in 1621. As the Virginia Company's factor during 1621 and 1622, he was authorized to deal with the Indians for furs and was responsible for the Company's magazine or store of goods. He also brought along shipments that belonged to others. Blaney was responsible for accepting payment on the Company's behalf from those who wed the 50 young marriageable women who came to the colony on the *Warwick* and *Tyger*. In 1622 he also received a shipment of goods on the *Abigail*, a vessel owned in part by John Bland I, a prominent London merchant. Blaney was supposed to send home glass, furs, and tobacco and any funds derived from the employment of the shipwrights who had been sent to Virginia. He was well liked and respected by Sir George Yeardley. On April 11, 1623, Treasurer George Sandys sent word to England that Edward Blaney had married the late Captain William Powell's widow, Margaret, and aspired to being a planter. Blaney served as a burgess for James City during 1623 and 1624 and on at least one occasion was identified as the merchants' burgess in the assembly. In January 1624, when Blaney testified in court about a bargain he had witnessed, he said that he was age 28. Later in the year he signed a document that described conditions in Virginia. During 1624 Edward Blaney tried to recover debts owed to the Virginia Company's magazine, including some attributable to the estates of people killed in the 1622 Indian attack. This was one of his obligations as the Company's former agent.

On February 16, 1624, when a census was made of the colony's inhabitants, Edward Blaney headed an urban Jamestown (1) household that included 18 people, most of whom were servants. However, on January 24, 1625, when a muster was compiled, Blaney headed a Jamestown household that included only two servants, for most of his people had been shifted to the late Captain William Powell's plantation (14) on the lower side of the James River. The land Edward Blaney occupied in Jamestown was next door to Dr. John Pott's lot, an indication that he was occupying the urban parcel that belonged to the Powell estate. Blaney and his men shared two dwellings, were well provisioned, and had two boats. The muster-taker credited Blaney with six buildings, 15 servants, and some livestock that were on the Powell plantation, which belonged to the Powell orphans, Blaney's stepchildren. The herd of livestock Edward Blaney had on Jamestown Island was uncommonly large, perhaps because it included some animals that belonged to the Virginia Company. Some of Blaney's neighbors sued him over his wandering swine and the ownership of his cattle. The Blaneys also were involved in litigation with Captain Samuel Mathews, who tried to claim part of the Powell orphans' land on Hog Island (16). In May 1625 Margaret Blaney sued her neighbor, Dr. John Pott, alleging that while she was still married to Captain William Powell, Pott's refusal to share some pork had led to her having a miscarriage. Although Edward Blaney realized his ambition of becoming a planter, he never ceased being a merchant; however, he conducted business on his own behalf rather than the Virginia Company's. In January 1626 Blaney was named to the Council of State. By February 6, 1626, he was dead and his remarried widow, Margaret, who had become the wife of Francis West, was named his administrator. At the time of his death, Edward Blaney was indebted to the Virginia Company's magazine, unpaid sums that Francis and Margaret West were obliged to satisfy (FER 322, 538; VCR 1:514-515; 3:448-449, 503-505, 508, 582, 666, 668, 683-690; 4:106-107, 111, 263-265, 450, 453, 562-567, 585; HAI 915; MCGC 9, 11, 32, 36, 39-40, 46-47, 58-59, 64-66, 79-80, 82, 93, 97, 121-122; NEI 40; STAN 31, 53; CBE 38, 46, 55, 59, 71-72; HEN 1:128-129; PB 1 Pt. 1:61; DOR 1:31, 40).

MARGARET POWELL BLANEY (BLANY, BLANYE, BLANIE, BLAINY, BLAYNY) (MRS. EDWARD BLANEY [BLANY, BLANYE, BLANIE, BLAINY, BLAYNY], MRS. WILLIAM POWELL, MRS. FRANCIS WEST) (SEE MRS. WILLIAM POWELL, MRS. FRANCIS WEST)

Margaret, the widow of Captain William Powell, a resident of urban Jamestown (1), married merchant Edward Blaney (Blany,

Blanye, Blanie, Blainy, Blayny) sometime prior to April 1623. She reportedly made a trip to England specifically to assert a claim to part of her late husband's estate. In dispute was Powell's land on the lower side of the James River on Hog Island (16), property to which Samuel Mathews asserted a claim. The Blaneys also were in possession of the late Captain Powell's plantation (14), which his orphans stood to inherit. In May 1625 Mrs. Margaret Blaney brought suit against her next-door neighbor, Dr. John Pott, concerning an incident that had occurred prior to the death of Captain Powell. She claimed that she had miscarried because Pott refused to share the meat of a hog he had killed. She also indicated that she had asked Mrs. Joan Peirce to obtain the pork from Pott. After Edward Blaney's death in early 1626, Margaret quickly remarried, this time taking Captain Francis West (the late Lord Delaware's brother) as her husband. She died sometime prior to March 1628, by which time West (then interim-governor) had married Sir George Yeardley's widow, Lady Temperance (MCGC 58, 65, 93; CBE 72; VCR 4:562-567; PB 1 Pt. 1:61; 2:81; 4:120).

***

JOHN BLESSE (BLISS)

John Blesse (Bliss), a 19-year-old smith from Sussex, England, came to Virginia in 1619 aboard the *Bona Nova*. On April 7, 1623, he was described as a Virginia Company servant and smith who had been assigned to Sir Francis Wyatt (FER 295; VCR 4:104-106).

MOSES (MOYSES) BLESSE (BLISSE)

On August 12, 1620, officials at Bridewell decided that Moses (Moyses) Blesse (Blisse), a vagrant, would be sent to Virginia (CBE 20).

[NO FIRST NAME] BLEWITT (BLUETT, BLEWETT, BLUETT, BLUET)

According to Virginia Company records, Captain Blewitt (Bluett, Blewett, Bluett, Bluet) came to Virginia in 1619 but died shortly after his arrival. He brought along

80 men for employment in the ironworks that was to be built at Southampton Hundred (**44**). Blewitt had been appointed to the Council of State, and a case of pistols was sent to him on the *Elizabeth*. Captain Blewitt may have been Captain Benjamin Blewitt, the father of Elizabeth, a young, marriageable maid who came to Virginia in 1621 (VCR 1:379, 475-476, 479, 587-588; 3:128, 452-453; FER 184, 268).

***

BENNETT BLEWITT (BLUETT, BLEWETT, BLUETT, BLUET)

On February 15, 1635, when Bennett Blewitt (Bluett, Blewett, Bluett, Bluet) patented 50 acres of land in Warresqueak (**26**), he used the personal adventure of his wife, Elizabeth (PB 1 Pt. 1:333).

ELIZABETH BLEWITT (BLUETT, BLEWETT, BLUETT, BLUET) (MRS. BENNETT BLEWITT [BLUETT, BLEWETT, BLUETT, BLUET])

Bennett, the husband of Elizabeth Blewitt (Bluett, Blewett, Bluett, Bluet), used her as a headright when patenting some land in Warresqueak (**26**) (PB 1 Pt. 1:333).

***

ELIZABETH BLEWITT (BLUETT, BLEWETT, BLUETT, BLUET)

Elizabeth Blewitt (Bluett, Blewett, Bluett, Bluet), a young maid, came to Virginia in 1621 on the *Bona Nova* and was identified as the daughter of Captain Benjamin Blewitt. He may have been the Captain Blewitt who was sent to Virginia in 1619 to build an ironworks at Southampton Hundred (**44**) but died shortly after his arrival (FER 309).

JOHN BLEWITT (BLUETT, BLEWETT, BLUETT, BLUET)

On March 22, 1622, when the Indians attacked Weyanoke (**52**), John Blewitt (Bluett, Blewett, Bluett, Bluet), one of Sir George Yeardley's men, was killed. He may have been related to Margery Blewitt, who also was slain there (VCR 3:569).

MARGERY BLEWITT (BLUETT, BLEWETT, BLUETT, BLUET)

On March 22, 1622, when the Indians attacked Weyanoke (**52**), Margery Blewitt (Bluett, Blewett, Bluett, Bluet) was killed. She may have been John Bluett's wife or kinswoman (VCR 3:569).

GILBERT BLIGHT

On March 2, 1629, Mr. Gilbert Blight appeared before the General Court and released David Dixon from all debts (MCGC 187).

JOHN BLOCKSON (BLOXON)

The March 12, 1627, minutes of the General Court indicate that John Blockson (Bloxon) was supposed to go to Virginia as one of George Sandys' servants. Because Sandys failed to prepay his passage, Blockson told Captain John Preene that if payment was not forthcoming once they reached Virginia, Preene could hire him out. The General Court authorized Captain Preene to place John Blockson at hire, but Preene was obliged to reimburse George Sandys' representative for outfitting him to come to the colony (MCGC 144).

***

JOHN BLORE (BLOAR, BLOWER) I

John Blore (Bloar, Blower) I, an ancient planter, came to Virginia in 1610 on the *Starr*. On February 16, 1624, he was living on the Eastern Shore with his wife, Francis (Frances), identified as Goodwife Blore, and their son, John II. In early 1625 John and Francis Blore were still living on the Eastern Shore, in a community of settlers along Old Plantation Creek (**73**). John, who was age 27, headed a household that included his wife and two male servants, but his child, John II, no longer was present, probably because he was dead. The Blores had a dwelling, a storehouse, and a boat, and an ample supply of stored food and defensive weaponry. Early on, John Blore received a patent for 140 acres of land. In May 1625, when a list of patented land was sent back to England, it was noted that Blore had claimed 100 acres on the south side of the James River near the falls, land he had surrendered so that an ironworks could be built at Falling Creek (**68**). In exchange, John Blore was given 140 acres on the Eastern Shore, on Old Plantation Creek (**73**). He died sometime prior to March 14, 1628 (CBE 46, 69; PB 1 Pt. 1:3, 98, 157; AMES 1:48; DOR 1:70).

FRANCIS (FRANCES) BLORE (BLOAR, BLOWER) (MRS. JOHN BLORE [BLOAR, BLOWER], MRS. ROGER SANDERS [SAUNDERS], MRS. WILLIAM BURDETT)

Francis (Frances), who married ancient planter John Blore (Bloar, Blower), came to Virginia in 1620 on the *London Merchant*. On February 16, 1624, she was living on the Eastern Shore in a household headed by her husband. Also present was their child, John II. In early 1625 John and Francis Blore were still living on the Eastern Shore, on Old Plantation Creek (**73**). The household included two servants, but the Blores' child, John II, was no longer present, probably because he was deceased. In 1625 Francis Blore was age 25. Sometime prior to March 14, 1628, Francis was widowed. She married mariner Roger Sanders (Saunders), whom she also outlived, and sometime after September 16, 1633, she wed William Burdett, who executed a prenuptial agreement. When Francis Blore Sanders Burdett made her will on March 23, 1641, she made bequests to several individuals (CBE 46, 69; PB 1 Pt. 1:98; AMES 1:xxxii, 11; 2:126-127).

JOHN BLORE (BLOAR, BLOWER) II

On February 16, 1624, John Blore (Bloar, Blower) II, the son of John and Francis (Frances) Blore, was living with his parents on the Eastern Shore (**73**). He apparently died sometime prior to early 1625, when a muster was taken of that area's inhabitants (CBE 46, 69).

***

HENRY BLUNT

According to Captain John Smith, on July 6, 1610, Henry Blunt, one of Sir Thomas Gates's men, went to the lower side of the James River, below Weroscoick or Warres-

queak (**26**) to recover a longboat. When he reached his destination, he was captured and killed by the Indians (HAI 434-435).

JOHN BLYTHE

On May 14, 1623, the Virginia Company gave John Blythe a patent for some Virginia land (VCR 2:428).

WILLIAM BLYTHE

On March 22, 1622, when the Indians attacked the Swinehow plantation (**47**), William Blythe was killed (VCR 3:568).

JAMES BOATE

James Boate was killed on March 22, 1622, when the Indians attacked Weyanoke (**52**). He was one of Sir George Yeardley's men (VCR 3:569).

HUMPHREY BOCK

Humphrey Bock came to Virginia on the *James* with a Mr. Spencer, probably William Spencer of Jamestown Island (**1**). They left England on July 31, 1622 (FER 400).

JOHN BODIN

On May 29, 1635, when John Parrott patented some land, he used John Bodin as a headright (PB 1 Pt. 1:170).

CHRISTIANA BOCKHOLT

On November 20, 1622, officials at Bridewell decided that Christina Bockholt, who was being detained at Newgate, would be transported overseas (CBE 29).

***

LAWRENCE BOHUN (BOHUNE, BOHUNNE)

Dr. Lawrence Bohun (Bohune, Bohunne), a London physician, came to Virginia in 1610 with Thomas West, Lord Delaware, having formerly been with West in the Netherlands. In 1619 Dr. Bohun was granted a patent for some Virginia land because he and some co-investors were planning to transport 300 people to the colony. In 1620 he was appointed the colony's physician-general and a member of the Council of State. As physician-general he was to be assigned an apothecary, surgeons, 20 tenants, and 500 acres of office land. Dr. Bohun disliked Governor George Yeardley and was among those who petitioned for his removal. He made his will on March 10, 1620, and left England with Captain Arthur Chester in mid-December 1620. Dr. Bohun was killed in the West Indies on March 19, 1621, when the Spanish attacked the *Margaret and John* (WITH 317; HAI 463; VCR 1:296-297, 421, 428, 431, 508-509, 512, 515-516; 3:118, 231-232, 240; STAN 30).

ALICE BOHUN (BOHUNE, BOHUNNE)
MRS LAWRENCE BOHUN [BOHUNE, BOHUNNE])

On October 31, 1621, Mrs. Alice Bohun (Bohune, Bohunne), the widow of Dr. Lawrence Bohun, asked to be compensated for her late husband's substantial investment in the Virginia Company. She also wanted Company officials to free her son, Edward Barnes, from his seven years of service. They refused to free Barnes because he was a Company servant, not one of the late physician-general's servants (VCR 1:544).

***

AMIAS (ANNIS) BOLT (BOULT)

According to the 1625 muster, Amias (Annis) Bolt (Boult) came to Virginia on the *Neptune*, arriving in August 1619. It is more likely that he reached Virginia in August 1618, when the *Neptune*, Lord Delaware's ship, is known to have landed in Jamestown (**1**). On February 16, 1624, Amias was living at Flowerdew Hundred (**53**). However, by January 22, 1625, he had moved to West and Shirley Hundred (**41**), where he was a 23-year-old household head. Bolt had an ample supply of stored food and defensive weaponry and some poultry and swine (CBE 37, 52; DOR 1:13).

ELLEN BOLTER (BOULTER)

On August 4, 1620, officials at Bridewell decided that Ellen Bolter (Boulter), a vagrant who refused to be controlled by her father or friends, would be sent to Virginia (CBE 20).

ANN BOLTON (BOULTON)

Ann Bolton (Boulton) came to Virginia in 1634 on the *Bonaventure* at the expense of Adam Thorogood. On June 24, 1635, when Thorogood secured a patent, he listed Ann as a headright (PB 1 Pt. 1:179).

***

FRANCIS BOLTON (BOULTON)

In July 1621 Virginia Company officials noted that the Rev. Francis Bolton (Boulton) was going to Virginia with Captain Nuce and that he was being sent a chest of books. Bolton, who was accompanied by his brother, Joseph, was to be the minister for Elizabeth City (**17, 18**), replacing the Rev. Jonas Stockton. On November 21, 1623, Governor Francis Wyatt granted the Rev. Bolton a warrant for his salary, which consisted of corn and tobacco collected from the communities on the Eastern Shore. Bolton and his brother, Joseph, may have come to Virginia in 1621 with Wyatt. The Rev. Bolton made three appearances before the General Court in 1625 and 1626, twice in connection with matters pursued by others and once on his own behalf. He indicated that he had an account with Jamestown (**1**) merchant John Chew. Although the Rev. Francis Bolton had some land in Elizabeth City, in 1628 he became the rector of James City Parish. He was authorized to lease the parish glebe in Archer's Hope (**6**) to tenants in order to generate income. In 1629 Bolton was one of Jamestown merchant Thomas Warnett's beneficiaries. He may have returned to Elizabeth City, for in 1632 he witnessed a land transfer that occurred there, and in February 1633 he sued a parishioner who failed to pay his tithes (FER 297, 322; VCR 1:506; 3:485; 4:404; SR 1207; MCGC 44, 98, 115, 173-174; SH 11-12; PB 1 Pt. 1:65, 123).

JOSEPH BOLTON (BOULTON)

In 1621 Joseph Bolton (Boulton), brother of the Rev. Francis Bolton of Elizabeth City (**17, 18**), came to Virginia, with the sponsorship of the Company of Mercers. He was supposed to be his brother's servant (FER 297).

***

RICHARD BOLTON
(BOULTON, BOULTEN)

Richard Bolton (Boulton, Boulten), an ancient planter, came to Virginia in 1610 on the *Mary and James* and on February 16, 1624, was living in Elizabeth City (**18**). In early 1625 he and Bartholomew Wethersby headed an Elizabeth City household that was amply supplied with stored food and defensive weaponry and had some livestock. In 1625 Bolton was 28 years old. On May 1625, when a list of patented land was sent back to England, Richard Bolton was credited with 100 acres in Coxendale (**64**) and 100 acres in Elizabeth City (**18**); the latter acreage had been planted (CBE 44, 65; VCR 4:552, 557).

THOMAS BOLTON (BOULTON, BOLDEN)

Thomas Bolton (Boulton, Bolden) came to Virginia in 1628 on the *Hopewell* at the expense of Adam Thorogood. On June 24, 1635, when Thorogood secured a patent, he listed Thomas as a headright (PB 1 Pt. 1:179).

ANTHONY BONALL (BONNALL)

Anthony Bonall (Bonnall) came to Virginia on the *Abigail* in 1621 and on February 16, 1624, was living at Buckroe (**17**) with James Bonall, probably a kinsman. In early 1625 Anthony, who was 42 years old, was living on the east side of the Hampton River, on what was considered the Virginia Company's land. He headed a household that included five other adults and two children, all of whom were free. The Bonall household was well supplied with stored food and defensive weaponry and also had three storehouses and a palisade. Anthony Bonall was a French silk maker and vigneron and probably was one of the men from Languedoc sent to the colony in 1621 by John Bonall, keeper of the king's silkworms (CBE 45, 68; VCR 1:459; DOR 1:67).

JAMES BONALL (BONNALL)

On February 16, 1624, James Bonall (Bonnall) was living at Buckroe (**17**) with Anthony Bonall, most likely a kinsman. In December 1627 James was described as a French vigneron who held a 10-year lease for 50 acres of land at Buckroe. In May 1633 the duration of James's lease was described as being 21 years. James Bonall probably was one of the men from Languedoc sent to the colony in 1621 by John Bonall, keeper of the king's silkworms (CBE 45; PB 1 Pt. 1:81-82, 84, 136, 139, 153).

JOHN BONALL ((BONNALL, BOURNALL, BONOVILL, BONOEIL)

In April 1621 the Virginia Company noted that John Bonall (Bonnall, Bournall, Bonovill, Bonoeil), keeper of the king's silkworms, was author of a published treatise on producing silk, wine, and citrus. Officials said that he had procured mulberry trees and some Frenchmen from Languedoc—probably Anthony and James Bonall—and dispatched them to Virginia. John Bonall, who lived in London, sent instructions to Virginia's governor and his council on how to make silk and wine. During 1622 John Bonall was granted 50 acres of land in Buckroe (**17**), the destination to which he sent men and supplies. In 1623 Treasurer George Sandys asked Bonall to send him two Frenchmen skilled in working with silkworms and planting vines. In December 1627 he was identified as the master of David Poole, a French vigneron, who received a 10-year lease for 50 acres that were to be used for John Bonall's benefit (VCR 1:459, 543; 3:634, 651, 661-663; 4:68; PB 1 Pt. 1:80).

WILLIAM BONHAM

In July 1627 William Bonham shipped goods from London to Virginia on the *Ann*, the *James*, and the *Thomas and John* (CBE 78-79).

JAMES BONNER

James Bonner came to Virginia in 1623 on the *Truelove* and on January 21, 1625, was living at Jordan's Journey (**46**), where he was a 20-year-old servant in Nathaniel Causey's household. He probably was one of the settlers sent to the colony by the Truelove's Company (CBE 52).

DAVID BONNS

On March 22, 1622, when the Indians attacked Martin's Hundred (**7**), David Bonns was killed (VCR 3:570).

MICHAEL BOOKER

On March 22, 1622, when the Indians attacked Lieutenant John Gibbs's plantation at Westover (**54**), Michael Booker was killed (VCR 3:567).

FRANCIS BOOT

On February 16, 1624, Francis Boot was living at the College (**66**) (CBE 35).

[NO FIRST NAME] BOOTH (BOOTHE)

According to Captain John Smith, Sergeant Booth (Boothe), who would have resided in Jamestown (**1**), was involved in a march against Natives known as the Ozinies, and he later wrote an account of that event. According to Smith's map, the village of the Ozinies was on the east side of the mouth of Diascund Creek, in what is now James City County. Sergeant Booth may have been John Booth, a laborer who came to Virginia in 1608 in the 1st Supply (CJS 2:257-258).

HENRY (HENERY) BOOTH (BOWTH)

On December 31, 1619, officials at Bridewell decided that Henry (Henery) Booth (Bowth), a thief from Holborn, would be detained until he could be sent to Virginia. Later, he went to the colony on the *Duty*. On February 16, 1624, Booth was living on the Maine (**3**), where Captain Roger Smith had some servants. Simultaneously, he was attributed to Smith's household in urban Jamestown (**1**). He probably was listed twice because Smith had servants in both locations. On January 24, 1625, Henry Booth was identified as a 20-year-old servant in Captain Roger Smith's household in Jamestown. On January 3, 1626, the General Court censured gunsmith John Jefferson for inadequately repairing a gun that resulted in Henry Booth's receiving an eye injury. Booth was then described as a poor Virginia Company man who was unable to pay his own doctor bill. Henry Booth eventually gained his freedom. By July 13, 1630, he had at least one indentured servant of his own, William Mathews, who was found guilty of petty treason and sentenced to be drawn and hanged (CBE 15, 38, 39, 55; MCGC 84, 479; HEN 1:146).

JOHN BOOTH (BOUTH)

John Booth (Bouth), a laborer, arrived in Virginia in 1608 in the 1st Supply of new settlers in Jamestown (**1**). He may have been the Sergeant Booth who joined Captain John Smith in fighting against the Ozinies, an Indian tribe (CJS 1:223; 2:161, 256).

JOHN BOOTH (BUTH)

John Booth (Buth), a member of Ensign Spence's household, died on Jamestown Island (**1**) sometime after April 1623 but before February 16, 1624. Simultaneously, he was listed among the living (CBE 39-40).

***

REYNOLD BOOTH

Reynold Booth, an ancient planter, came to Virginia in 1609 on the *Hercules*. On July 23, 1620, when he testified before a court in England, he indicated that he was a 26-year-old gentleman from Reigate, in Surrey. He stated that he had known Daniel Elfirth for ten years and that in 1619 he went from Virginia to Bermuda on the *Treasurer*. He also said that at the end of June 1619, while the *Treasurer* was in the West Indies, it was compelled to consort with a Flemish man-of-war, the *White Lion* of Flushing, which was commanded by Captain Chope (Jope). According to Reynold Booth, Chope had permission to seize Spanish ships and in mid-July 1619 took 25 men from his and Elfirth's ship and sailed away in a pinnace. Three days late he brought back the Spanish frigate he had captured and gave Elfirth some tallow and grain. Afterward, Booth said that he left the *Treasurer* and boarded the *Seaflower*, which took him to Bermuda where he found passage back to England. On February 16, 1624, Reynold Booth was living in Elizabeth City (**18**), where he shared a home with wife, Elizabeth, and daughter, Mary. The Booths were still residing in Elizabeth City in early 1625. Reynold, who was age 32, headed a household that had an ample supply of stored food and defensive weaponry. Also present were two male servants. On September 11, 1626, Sergeant Reynold Booth testified before the General Court against Joan Wright, an accused witch. He claimed that he was unable to shoot game successfully because Mrs. Wright had put a curse on him (CBE 44, 66; EAE 182; MCGC 111-112; DOR 1:61).

ELIZABETH BOOTH
(MRS. REYNOLD BOOTH)

Elizabeth, who wed ancient planter Reynold Booth, came to Virginia on the *Ann* in 1623. On February 16, 1624, the Booths and their daughter, Mary, were living in Elizabeth City (**18**). In early 1625 the Booth couple was still in Elizabeth City but daughter Mary no longer was listed. Elizabeth Booth was then age 24 (CBE 44, 66).

MARY BOOTH

On February 16, 1624, Mary, the daughter of Reynold and Elizabeth Booth, was living in Elizabeth City (**18**) with her parents (CBE 44).

***

WILLIAM BOOTHEBY

On July 19, 1627, William Bootheby was identified as someone having shipped goods from London to Virginia on the *James* (CBE 79).

MARGARET BORDMAN

In 1621 Margaret Bordman, a young, marriageable maid, came to Virginia on the *Marmaduke*. She was 20 years old and was born in Bilbon, in Yorkshire. Both of Margaret's parents were dead. Sir John Gypson of Yorkshire was identified as a maternal uncle. Prior to setting sail for Virginia, Margaret Bordman had been in service to Captain Wood. Wood's wife and a Mrs. Kilbancks vouched for Margaret's character (FER 309).

ELLEN BORNE

Ellen Borne, a young maid, set sail for Virginia on the *Warwick* in September 1621 and was among the marriageable women sent to the colony to be wives. Ellen, who was a 19-year-old orphan, was born in Ay, in Suffolk. She was recommended to the Virginia Company by a Mr. and Mrs. Hobson, who said that she had many useful skills (FER 309).

JOHN BOTTOM (BOTTAM)

On February 16, 1624, John Bottom (Bottam) was attributed to two communities of settlers. He was grouped among those living west of Gray's Creek (**8, 9**) on the lower side of the James River, but he also was listed among those at Archer's Hope (**6**) on the upper side of the river. On January 28, 1627, John Bottom had John Davys (Davies, Davis), a Hog Island (**16**) planter, arrested for indebtedness. The matter was aired before the General Court on February 8, 1628 (CBE 40-41; MCGC 160, 165).

DANIEL BOUCHER

On November 13, 1633, William Parke of Virginia identified Daniel Boucher as purser of the ship *Blessing* (SH 15).

JOHN BOUCHER (BOUCHIER)

On June 13, 1621, John Boucher (Bouchier) was given a patent by Virginia Company officials. On June 10, 1622, he was identified as Sir John Bouchier when he was credited with a patent for a particular (private) plantation (VCR 1:491-492; 3:643).

ELIZABETH BOUISH

Elizabeth Bouish, a 20-year-old, marriageable young maid, came to Virginia in 1621 on the *Warwick*. Her father was dead, but her mother, Edith Smith, recommended her to the Virginia Company and vouched for her character (FER 309).

***

THOMAS BOULDING (BOULDIN, BOULDINGE)

Thomas Boulding (Bouldin, Bouldinge) came to Virginia on the *Swan* in 1610 and was an ancient planter. On January 20, 1624, he patented 200 acres in Elizabeth City (**18**), part of which abutted the acreage of his wife, Mary, also an ancient planter. In early 1625 when a muster was made of Elizabeth City's inhabitants, Thomas Boulding, who was age 40, headed a household that included his Virginia-born son, William, and three adult males, all of whom were free. Boulding's household had an abundant supply of stored food and defensive weaponry and was defended by a palisade. In May 1625, when a list of patented land was sent back to England, Boulding was credited with 200 acres in Elizabeth City, acreage that had been planted. In 1635 his land was described as being in the vicinity of the Old Poquoson and the Back River (**19**). On September 27, 1638, Thomas Boulding patented an additional 200 acres in Elizabeth City, acquiring his land on the basis of four headrights (CBE 66; PB 1 Pt. 1:43, 160, 164, 202; Pt. 2:601; DOR 1:61).

MARY BOULDING (BOULDIN, BOULDINGE)
(MRS. THOMAS BOULDING [BOULDIN, BOULDINGE])

Mary, who became the wife of ancient planter Thomas Boulding (Bouldin, Bouldinge), was an ancient planter. On December 12, 1624, she received a patent for 100 acres in Elizabeth City (**18**), land that adjoined her husband's. It was her first dividend. In May 1625, when a list of patented land was sent back to England, Mary Boulding was credited with 200 acres in Elizabeth City. She may have been the mother of Thomas Boulding's Virginia-born son, William (PB 1 Pt. 1:42; VCR 4:558).

WILLIAM BOULDING (BOULDIN, BOULDINGE)

In early 1625 William Boulding (Bouldin, Bouldinge), a Virginia-born child, was living in Elizabeth City (**18**) in the household headed by his father, Thomas Boulding, an ancient planter. His mother may have been ancient planter Mary Boulding, Thomas's wife (CBE 66).

***

EDWARD BOURBICTH

Edward Bourbicth came to Virginia on the *London Merchant* and on January 30, 1625, was living in Pasbehay (**3**) where he was a household head. He had a modest supply of stored food and defensive weaponry (CBE 57; DOR 1:25).

GEORGE BOURCHER

On August 8, 1626, George Bourcher testified about a conversation he overheard while at George Menefie's forge in urban Jamestown (**1**) (MCGC 107).

JAMES BOURNE

In June 1608 James Bourne, a gentleman and one of the first Jamestown (**1**) settlers, accompanied Captain John Smith on two exploratory voyages within Chesapeake Bay. In late December 1608, when Bourne went with Smith on a trip to the Pamunkey Indians' territory, he was described as a soldier (CJS 1:224, 230, 244; 2:170, 193).

ROBERT BOURNE (BOWINE, BOWEN?)

In May 1625, when a list of patented land was sent back to England, Robert Bourne (Bowine, Bowen?) was credited with 250 acres of land in Charles City (VCR 4:553).

CHRISTOPHER BOURTON

On September 15, 1619, Christopher Bourton, a tailor, set sail for Virginia on the *Margaret* of Bristol and went to Berkeley Hundred (**55**) to work under Captain John Woodlief's supervision. Bourton was supposed to serve the Society of Berkeley Hundred's investors for four years in exchange for 20 acres of land (CBE 14; VCR 3:198, 213).

JOHN BOWATER

On March 27, 1622, the Virginia Company noted that John Bowater, a merchant, had acquired some shares of Virginia land from Francis Carter, who had procured them from Lord Delaware's heirs (VCR 1:625).

[NO FIRST NAME] BOWEN

In September 1623 the General Court learned that a man named Bowen, formerly a sailor on the ship *Everett*, had hired himself out after reaching Virginia (MCGC 7).

BENJAMIN (BENIAMEN) BOWER

Benjamin (Beniamen) Bower, a 27-year-old laborer from Yorkshire, England, came to Virginia in 1619 on the *Bona Nova* and probably was a Virginia Company tenant or servant (FER 295).

RICHARD BOWER

Richard Bower, a 23-year-old cutler from Yorkshire, England, went to Virginia in 1619 on the *Bona Nova* and probably was a Virginia Company tenant or servant (FER 295).

SARAH BOWMAN

On February 6, 1626, Sara Bowman was identified as a servant of John Burrows, who listed her as a headright. Burrows had property on Jamestown Island (1) and on the lower side of the James River at Burrows Hill (8) (MCGC 93).

***

JOHN BOX (BOXE)

John Box (Boxe) came to Virginia on the *Truelove* in 1622 and on January 21, 1625, was living at Chaplin's Choice (56), where he was a 23-year-old household head. He probably was a member of the group of settlers known as Truelove's Company. John Box's household had an ample supply of stored food and three "murderers" or cannon for the settlement's defense. In June 1636, when John Box's widow, Mary, patented some land in Henrico County, she misidentified her late husband as an ancient planter. The couple had a daughter who also was named Mary (CBE 51; PB 1 Pt. 1:355).

MARY BOX (BOXE)
(MRS. JOHN BOX [BOXE])

On June 1, 1636, Mary, who identified herself as the widow of John Box (Boxe), patented 300 acres in Henrico County, on the north side of the Appomattox River. She claimed that that she was entitled to 100 acres, land accruable to her late husband as an ancient planter. She asserted a claim to the remainder on the basis of four headrights, one of which was her own. Later, Mary's daughter, Mary, renewed the patent (PB 1 Pt. 1:355).

***

JOHN BOX (BOXE)

John Box (Boxe) reportedly died in Elizabeth City (17, 18) sometime after April 1623 but before February 16, 1624. He may have been the same man who was living at Chaplin's Choice (56) in January 1625 (CBE 41).

TOBIAS BOX (BOXE)

In December 1628 the will of Tobias Box (Boxe) was presented to probate officials in England. He was said to have died abroad, leaving goods in Virginia (CBE 88).

WILLIAM BOX (BOXE)

William Box (Boxe) came to Virginia in the 3rd Supply of new settlers, who reached Jamestown (1) in 1609. Captain John Smith said that he was an honest gentleman and that he wrote a narrative in which he described his voyage to the colony. According to Smith, when Lord Delaware departed from Virginia in 1611, William Box accompanied him (CJS 2:219-220, 237).

ANDREW BOYER

Andrew Boyer came to Virginia in 1628 on the *Truelove* at the expense of Adam Thorogood. On June 24, 1635, when Thorogood secured a patent, he listed Andrew as a headright (PB 1 Pt. 1:179).

THOMAS BOYER

Thomas Boyer came to Virginia in 1628 on the *Truelove* at Adam Thorogood's expense. On June 24, 1635, when Thorogood secured a patent, he listed Thomas as a headright (PB 1 Pt. 1:179).

NAAMY BOYLE

Naamy Boyle died at one of the settlements on the lower side of the James River, within the corporation of James City (8-15), sometime after April 1623 but before February 16, 1624 (CBE 41).

***

CHENEY (CHYNA, CHENE, CHEYNEY) BOYSE (BOISE, BOYS, BOICE, BOYCE)

Cheney (Chyna, Chene, Cheyney) Boyse (Boise, Boys, Boice, Boyce) came to Virginia sometime prior to May 1616 and was an ancient planter. He returned to England but in May 1617 came back to the colony on the *George*. On January 22, 1625, he was living at West and Shirley Hundred (41) in a well-equipped home that he shared with John Throgmorton and three servants. Boyse was then age 26. In 1629, 1630, and 1632 Cheney Boyse served as a burgess for West and Shirley Hundred (now Eppes) Island. In May 1636 he was identified as an ancient planter when he patented a large tract of land on the lower side of the James River, on the east side of Merchant's Hundred (Powell's) Creek, in the immediate vicinity of what had been Samuel Macock's 2,000-acre plantation, "Macock's Divident" (**48**). He repatented his land in 1637. In 1641 Boyse was among those who testified before the General Court in a case accusing former Governor John Harvey of illegally allowing Robert Barrington to patent part of the Governor's Land (**3**) (CBE 53; HEN 1:138, 147, 178; PB 1 Pt. 1:352, 468; Pt. 2:893, 896; 2:199; 4:26; MCGC 498; DOR 1:355).

JOYCE BOYSE (BOISE, BOYS, BOICE, BOYCE) (MRS. CHENEY [CHYNA, CHENE, CHEYNEY] BOYSE [BOISE, BOYS, BOICE, BOYCE], MRS. RICHARD TYE, MRS. JOHN COGAN)

Joyce, the wife of Cheney (Chyna, Chene, Cheyney) Boyse (Boise, Boys, Boice, Boyce), was widowed by 1641 and within three years time married Captain Richard Tye. He repatented her former husband's land on Powell's Creek in October 1649. By June 1659 Joyce had been widowed again and had married Dr. John Cogan, a surgeon (Charles City County Order Book 1655-1665:164, 170, 355; PB 2:199; DOR 1:355-356).

***

HUMPHREY (HUMPRY) BOYSE (BOISE, BOYS, BOICE, BOYCE)

Humphrey (Humpry) Boyse (Boise, Boys, Boice, Boyce) died on Jamestown Island (**1**) sometime after April 1623 but before February 16, 1624 (CBE 39).

***

JOHN (JOHNNY) BOYSE (BOISE, BOYS, BOICE, BOYCE)

John (Johnny) Boyse (Boise, Boys, Boyce, Boice) served as a burgess for Martin's Hundred (**7**) in the July 1619 session of the assembly. When he first arrived in the colony, he, like the others sent to establish the Society of Martin's Hundred's plantation, would have lived on the Governor's Land (**3**). On May 16, 1621, Boyse, who

was identified as the warden of Martin's Hundred, was entrusted with the care of the servants belonging to Sir Lawrence Hyde and his brother, Nicholas. He informed Company officials that plots of land at Martin's Hundred had not yet been assigned to specific people. On March 22, 1622, when the Indians attacked Martin's Hundred, John Boyse and his wife erroneously were listed among those slain. In fact, John survived and his wife was captured by the Indians. In April 1624 John Boyse was one of the "poor planters" who asked the king for tax relief on account of the 1622 Indian attack. A year later he asked the king to raise the price of tobacco. He apparently was a relatively successful planter, for in 1627 he exported a substantial quantity of tobacco to England. In February 1628 the General Court noted that John had been paid by Martin's Hundred's leader, William Harwood, to clear some of the plantation's ground. John Boyse went to England where he made his will on August 7, 1649, on the eve of his return to Virginia. John's will, which makes no reference to a wife or living children, was proved in May 1650 (VCR 2:519; 3:154, 450-451, 570; 4:98-101; CJS 2:593; MCGC 166; E 190/32/8 f 6; EEAC 8; WAT 312).

SARA (SARAH) BOYSE (BOISE, BOYS, BOICE, BOYCE) (MRS. JOHN [JOHNNY] BOYSE (BOISE, BOYS, BOICE, BOYCE)

Sara (Sarah), the wife of John (Johnny) Boyse (Boise, Boys, Boice, Boyce), took up residence at Martin's Hundred (**7**) sometime prior to the March 22, 1622, Indian attack. She was reported dead but was, in fact, one of the 19 women captured by the Indians and detained at Pamunkey. In March 1623 the Indians sent word that they would return their captives if they would be allowed to plant their corn in peace. A week later, Sara, whom the Indians considered "chief of the prisoners," was returned, attired like a native queen. She probably was accorded that distinction because her husband was the "warden" of Martin's Hundred and a burgess. Sara Boyse, like the other English captives, reportedly endured great misery while a prisoner of the Indians (VCR 3:570; 4: 98-101, 228-229; CJS 2:309-310, 315, 593).

***

***

LUKE BOYSE (BOISE, BOYS, BOICE, BOYCE)

Luke Boyse (Boise, Boys, Boice, Boyce) came to Virginia on the *Edwin*, one of the ships that brought the Society of Martin's Hundred's settlers. On April 3, 1620, Virginia Company officials noted that although Mr. Boyse was supposed to be the bailiff of Martin's Hundred (7), he had broken his contract and settled elsewhere. On September 3, 1623, when John Atkins, a Virginia planter, made his will, he asked Luke Boyse of Bermuda Hundred (39) to harvest his tobacco crop and pay his debts. On February 16, 1624, Luke and his wife, Alice, were living at Bermuda Hundred. He served as a burgess for that community and signed the General Assembly's rebuttal to Alderman Johnson's claim about conditions in the colony between 1607 and 1619. In November 1624 Luke was ordered to pay Captain John Martin's debt to merchant Humphrey Rastell. A month later he was ordered to surrender the cattle in his possession. On December 27, 1624, Luke Boyse was mentioned in court testimony involving a suit that was pending. On January 24, 1625, Luke, who was age 44, headed a household at Bermuda Hundred. The following month he appeared before the General Court to testify in a suit involving Captain John Martin and Sir George Yeardley. In July 1625 the General Court decided that a Spaniard who arrived on Captain John Powell's ship would be sent to Bermuda Hundred to stay with Luke Boyse until a decision was made about what to do with him. In 1625 Luke sent John Croodicke to Accomack to collect Captain William Eppes's debt to Mr. Chamberlaine at Kecoughtan (17, 18). In January 1626 he was summoned to court in a matter involving Henry Williams. Luke Boyse became ill and died at his Bermuda Hundred home on June 21, 1626. When making a nuncupative will, he left his real and personal property to his wife, Alice, and their child. Court testimony taken after Luke's demise indicates that he had given tobacco to William Besse and that he used to have possession of a cow that belonged to Captain John Martin, an animal the Indians killed. In February 1627 Alice, Luke Boyse's widow and administrator, presented the General Court with an inventory of his estate. She remarried before the estate had been settled, taking as her new husband Matthew Edloe (Edlowe). In 1635 when Luke and Alice Boyse's daughter, Hannah, patented some land, she identified herself as their child (VCR 1:331-332; WITH 35-36; CBE 35, 53; HAI 915; HEN 1:128-129; MCGC 32, 37, 69, 86, 126, 129, 131-132, 140, 193; PB 1 Pt. 1:351; DOR 1:8).

ALICE BOYSE (BOISE, BOYS, BOICE, BOYCE) (MRS. LUKE BOYSE [BOISE, BOYS, BOICE, BOYCE], MRS. MATHEW EDLOE [EDLOWE]) SEE ALICE BOYSE EDLOE [EDLOWE])

Alice, who wed Luke Boyse (Boise, Boys, Boice, Boyce), came to Virginia on the *Bona Nova* in April 1622. By February 16, 1624, the Boyses were living at Bermuda Hundred (39). On November 25, 1624, Alice appeared before the General Court to accuse her neighbor, Joan Vincent (Vincine), of slander. In a counter-claim, Joan accused Alice of bastardry and said that she had interfered in Samuel and Cisley Jordan's marriage. On January 24, 1625, Alice Boyce and her husband were still living at Bermuda Hundred, where he was a household head. When Luke died in the family home on June 21, 1626, he named Alice and their child as heirs. In early December 1626 Alice Boyse, who was in possession of William Besse's servant boy, was ordered to pay for the youth's time if Besse decided to sell him. In January 1627 the General Court appointed Alice the administrator of her late husband's estate, since she and their child were his sole heirs. She successfully brought suit against tailor Joseph Royall, her late husband's servant, who was ordered to make clothes for her household. Alice Boyse, who was said to be related to the widowed Mrs. John Bargrave, presented an account of the cattle whose ownership was disputed by Captain John Martin and Captain Bargrave. She asked the General Court to assign them to someone else, as she was unable to post security. In February 1627 Alice presented an inventory of her late husband's estate. That same month she ran afoul of the law when she was accused of having sex with Captain William Eppes in James Slight's house at Martin's Brandon (59). Despite the testimony of several witnesses who supported the allegations, the charges against her were dismissed. Sometime prior to March 7, 1629, the widowed Alice Boyse married Mathew Edloe (Edlowe) of the College or Arrohattock (**66**). Together they presented the General Court with an account of the late Luke Boyse's estate. Alice was widowed again sometime prior to November 1635, for her marital status was mentioned when she patented some land (MCGC 31, 126, 132, 134, 139-140, 148, 193; CBE 35, 53; PB 1 Pt. 1:351).

HANNAH BOYSE (BOISE, BOYS, BOICE, BOYCE)

On November 11, 1635, when Hannah Boyse (Boise, Boys, Boice, Boyce) patented 300 acres of land in Henrico, she identified herself as the daughter of Luke and Alice Boyse. She probably was the child who was living in their Bermuda Hundred (**39**) home on January 24, 1625 (PB 1 Pt. 1:351).

***

***

THOMAS BOYSE (BOISE, BOYCE, BOYS, BOICE)

On March 22, 1622, when the Indians attacked Martin's Hundred (**7**), Thomas Boyse (Boise, Boyce, Boys, Boice), his wife, and his baby were killed (VCR 3:570).

MRS. THOMAS BOYSE (BOISE, BOYCE, BOYS, BOICE)

Mrs. Thomas Boyse (Boise, Boyce, Boys, Boice) was slain on March 22, 1622, when the Indians attacked Martin's Hundred (**7**). Her husband and infant also were killed (VCR 3:570).

[NO FIRST NAME] BOYSE (BOISE, BOYCE, BOYS, BOICE)

During the March 22, 1622, Indian attack on Martin's Hundred (**7**), the infant belonging to Mr. and Mrs. Thomas Boyse (Boise, Boyce, Boys, Boice) was slain (VCR 3:570).

***

THOMAS BRABANDER

On January 22, 1620, officials at Bridewell decided to send Thomas Brabander, a vagrant, to Virginia (CBE 17).

***

STEPHEN BRABY

On February 16, 1624, Stephen Braby and his wife, Elizabeth, were living at West and Shirley Hundred (now Eppes) Island (**41**) (CBE 36).

ELIZABETH BRABY (MRS. STEPHEN BRABY)

On February 16, 1624, Elizabeth, Stephen Braby's wife, was living with her husband at West and Shirley (Eppes) Hundred Island (**41**) (CBE 36).

***

JANE BRACKLEY

On February 16, 1624, Jane Brackley was living in Elizabeth City (**17, 18**) (CBE 43).

HENRY BRADFORD (BRODSUL)

Henry Bradford (Brodsul) came to Virginia on the *Abigail* and on January 24, 1625, was living in urban Jamestown (**1**) in William Peirce's household. Henry, who was 35 years old, was a Peirce servant. In May 1625 he testified about the ownership of an unmarked calf claimed by Robert Partin of Shirley Hundred (**41**). In January 1627 Henry Bradford was fined for being intoxicated. He may have been a cow-keeper, for on February 26, 1627, he testified in the General Court about the number of cattle John Pountis owned and said that Pountis had sold some of them to William Peirce. Henry also testified about how many cattle Governor Yeardley had slaughtered and said that Richard Peirce had killed a calf. By December 9, 1628, Henry Bradford was dead, at which time Ester Clariett presented an inventory of his estate (CBE 55; MCGC 59-60, 130, 141, 179).

JAMES BRADFORD

On April 26, 1624, Virginia Company officials noted that James Bradford, a servant, had been sent to Virginia by Garrett Weston. He accompanied Garrett's brother, Francis Weston (VCR 2:532).

JOHN BRADFORD (BRAFORD?)

John Bradford (Braford?) came to Virginia in 1621 on the *Temperance* at the expense of Sir George Yeardley. By September 20, 1628, John Bradford's headright had been assigned to Thomas Flint. He probably was the man identified as John Braford, who was killed in the March 22, 1622, Indian attack on Flowerdew Hundred **(53)** (PB 1 Pt. 1:59).

THOMAS BRADLEY

In 1608 Thomas Bradley, a tradesman, arrived in Jamestown **(1)** as part of the 2nd Supply of new settlers (CJS 1:241; 2:191).

***

GILES BRADSHAW
(BRADSHAWE)

On March 22, 1622, when the Indians attacked Captain Berkeley's plantation at Falling Creek **(68)**, Giles Bradshaw (Bradshawe), his wife, and his child were killed (VCR 3:565).

MRS. GILES BRADSHAW
(BRADSHAWE)

Mrs. Giles Bradshaw (Bradshawe) was killed at Captain John Berkeley's plantation at Falling Creek **(68)** during the March 22, 1622, Indian attack. Her husband and child also lost their lives (VCR 3:565).

[NO FIRST NAME] BRADSHAW
(BRADSHAWE)

When the Indians attacked Captain John Berkeley's plantation at Falling Creek **(68)**, Mr. and Mrs. Giles Bradshaw's (Bradshawe's) child was killed (VCR 3:565).

***

RICHARD BRADSHAW
(BROADSHAW)

In 1621 Richard Bradshaw (Broadshaw) came to Virginia on the *Temperance*. On February 16, 1624, he was living at Flowerdew Hundred **(53)**. On January 20, 1625, he was still residing at Flowerdew and was identified as a 20-year-old servant in Abraham Peirsey's home (CBE 37, 50).

ROBERT BRADSHAW
(BRADSHAWE)

On July 31, 1622, Robert Bradshaw (Bradshawe) set sail for Virginia on the *James* and accompanied John Harryson (Harrison) (FER 400).

JOHN BRADSTON

On February 16, 1624, John Bradston was living in Elizabeth City in the household of Lt. Sheppard **(17, 18)**. By January 24, 1625, Bradston, who was age 18, was a servant in the household of John and Bridget Burrows on eastern Jamestown Island **(1)** (CBE 43; HOT 226).

JOHN BRADSTON

John Bradston came to Virginia in 1628 on the *Hopewell* at the expense of Adam Thorogood. On June 24, 1635, when Thorogood secured a patent, he listed John Bradston as a headright. He may have been the same individual who in 1625 was a servant in John Burrows' household (PB 1 Pt. 1:179).

***

ALEXANDER (ALEX) BRADWAY
(BRODWAY, BROADWAY)

In September 1620 Alexander (Alex) Bradway (Brodway, Broadway) was among those who set sail from Bristol, England, on the ship *Supply* and went with William Tracy to Berkeley Hundred **(55)**. In a letter to the Virginia Company, Governor George Yeardley indicated that Alexander arrived at his destination on January 29, 1621. On February 16, 1624, Alexander Bradway and his wife, Sisley, were living at Bermuda Hundred **(39)**. They were still there on January 24, 1625, at which time their household included their 9-month-old infant, Adria. Alexander Bradway was then age 31 and headed a household that had a modest supply of stored food and defensive weaponry (CBE 21, 28, 35, 54; VCR 3:427, 674; DOR 1:11).

SISLEY BRADWAY (BRODWAY, BROADWAY) (MRS. ALEXANDER [ALEX] BRADWAY [BRODWAY, BROADWAY])

Sisley, who married Alexander (Alex) Bradway (Brodway, Broadway), one of the Society of Berkeley Hundred's (55) settlers, went to Virginia on the *Jonathan* in May 1620. On February 16, 1624, she was living with Alexander at Bermuda Hundred (39). She was still there on January 24, 1625, with her husband and 9-month-old daughter, Adria. At that time Sisley Bradway was age 28 (CBE 35, 54; VCR 3:427).

ADRIA BRADWAY (BRODWAY, BROADWAY)

On January 24, 1625, Adria, the 9-month-old daughter of Alexander (Alex) and Sisley Bradway (Brodway, Broadway), was living with her parents at Bermuda Hundred (39), where her father was a household head (CBE 54).

***

GILES BRADWAY (BRODWAY, BROADWAY)

In September 1620 Giles Bradway (Brodway, Broadway) was among those who set sail from Bristol, England, on the ship *Supply* and went with William Tracy to Berkeley Hundred (55). In a letter to the Virginia Company, Governor George Yeardley indicated that Giles arrived at his destination on January 29, 1621. He was supposed to serve a certain number of years in exchange for some acreage. On March 22, 1622, when the Indians attacked Berkeley Hundred, Giles Bradway was killed (CBE 21; VCR 3:397, 426, 567).

JOHN BRADWELL

On May 20, 1637, John Bradwell and John Radish, who came to Virginia in 1619, patented 16 acres in the eastern end of Jamestown Island (1), adjacent to Mary Holland (PB 1 Pt. 1:423).

JOHN BRAFORD

On March 22, 1622, John Braford was killed when the Indians attacked Flowerdew Hundred (53). He probably was the man known as John Bradford whom Sir George Yeardley brought to Virginia on the *Temperance* in 1621 (VCR 3:568).

WILLIAM BRAKLEY

William Brakley died at Hog Island (16) sometime after April 1623 but before February 16, 1624 (CBE 41).

JOHN BRAMBLE

On January 22, 1619, officials at Bridewell decided that John Bramble, a boy who had been brought in, would be detained until he could be sent to Virginia (HUME 21).

FRANCIS BRAMLEY

Francis Bramley came to Virginia in 1628 on the *Ark* at the expense of Adam Thorogood. On June 24, 1635, when Thorogood secured a patent, he listed Francis Bramley as a headright (PB 1 Pt. 1:179).

JOHH BRAMPFORD

John Brampford set sail for Virginia with Abraham Peirsey on July 31, 1622, aboard the *James* (FER 400).

CHARLES BRANCH

On September 19, 1618, the Bridewell court decided that Charles Branch, a vagrant from Cheapside, would be sent to Virginia (CBE 10).

CHARLES BRANCH

On February 27, 1619, officials at Bridewell agreed that Charles Branch, a boy from St. Andrew's, would be sent to Virginia (CBE 13).

***

CHRISTOPHER BRANCH

Christopher Branch came to Virginia on the *London Merchant* and on February 16, 1624, was living at the College or Arrohattock (66). He was still there on January 23, 1625, and headed a household that included his wife, Mary, and their 9-month-old son,

Thomas. The Branch household had an ample supply of stored food and defensive weaponry. On October 20, 1634, Christopher Branch was identified as a planter and resident of Arrohattock when he secured a lease for a 100-acre tract that he was authorized to occupy for 21 years. On December 8, 1635, he patented 250 acres on the lower side of the James River, across from Arrohattock, in an area called Kingsland. He claimed the land on the basis of his own personal adventure and four servants whose transportation he had paid to the colony. In time, he expanded his holdings in the same area. In February 1640 Christopher Branch testified about the estate of Thomas Sheffield, who died in the March 1622 Indian attack. In 1640 Branch was a tobacco viewer, and a year later he began serving as a burgess. He made his will in June 1678 and was living on his Kingsland property at that time (CBE 35, 53; PB 1 Pt. 1:155, 326, 381, 527, 634; SR 11329; DOR 1:7, 366-367).

MARY ADDY BRANCH
(MRS. CHRISTOPHER BRANCH)

Mary Addy, the daughter of Francis Addy of Darton, Yorkshire, married Christopher Branch and came to Virginia on the *London Merchant*. On January 23, 1625, Mary and Christopher were living at the College **(66)** with their 9-month-old infant, Thomas (CBE 53; DOR 1:366-367).

THOMAS BRANCH

On January 23, 1625, Thomas, the 9-month old son of Mary and Christopher Branch, was living at the College **(66)** with his parents (CBE 53; DOR 1:367).

***

JOHN BRANCKSON

On January 22, 1620, officials at Bridewell decided that John Branckson, a vagrant from Lombard Street, would be sent to Virginia (CBE 17).

***

WILLIAM BRANLIN

William Branlin came to Virginia on the *Margaret and John* in 1620. On January 21, 1625, he was living at Jordan's Journey **(46)**, where he headed a household that included his wife, Ann. The Branlins had an abundant supply of stored food and defensive weaponry (CBE 51; DOR 1:18).

ANN BRANLIN
MRS. WILLIAM BRANLIN)

Ann, who wed William Branlin, came to Virginia in 1622 on the *Truelove*. On January 21, 1625, she was living at Jordan's Journey **(46)** in a household headed by her husband (CBE 51).

***

THOMAS BRANSBY

Thomas Bransby came to Virginia on the *Charity* sometime prior to February 16, 1624, when he was living at Hog Island **(16)**. On August 16, 1624, the General Court heard testimony about some tobacco that Thomas and another man took to Captain Hamor's house. On February 4, 1625, Thomas Bransby was living in Archer's Hope **(6)**, where he headed a household that included three servants. Bransby, who was in command of the settlers at Archer's Hope, had a large supply of stored food and defensive weaponry and some livestock. In August 1625 Thomas Bransby testified before the General Court about the frequent need to stop Joseph Johnson from beating his wife. Cadwallader Jones and Thomas Crews, then identified as Bransby servants, were witnesses to the Johnsons' physically violent domestic disputes. In November 1626 Thomas Bransby reported Thomas Farley to the authorities for stating that the fine levied on him was comparable to stealing money from his pocket. In January 1627 Bransby appeared before the General Court, where he acknowledged a debt to John Harrison of London. Thomas Bransby was then identified as a gentleman and resident of Archer's Hope (CBE 41, 58; MCGC 19, 70, 123, 133; DOR 1:37).

THOMAS BRASINGTON

On March 22, 1622, when the Indians attacked Captain Berkeley's plantation at Falling Creek **(68)**, Thomas Brasington was killed (VCR 3:565).

BRASS

On October 3, 1625, the General Court decided that Brass, a Portuguese African man would remain in the possession of Governor Francis Wyatt, a resident of urban Jamestown (1). This occurred despite the fact that Captain Jones had sold him to Captain Nathaniel Basse of Basses Choice (37), who had provided Brass with clothing (MCGC 73).

RICHARD BRATHWAITE

On October 15, 1630, officials at Bridewell decided that a boy named Richard Brathwaite would be sent to Virginia (HUME 35).

[NO FIRST NAME] BRAY

When the Indians attacked Powle-Brooke (50) on March 22, 1622, Mrs. Bray was slain. She may have been Cicley Bray (VCR 569).

CISLEY BRAY

Cicley Bray, a marriageable young maid, came to Virginia on the *Warwick* in September 1621. According to Virginia Company records, Cisley, who was age 25, was born in Gloucestershire. Her parents were gentlefolk and she was related to Sir Edwin Sandys. Cisley Bray was recommended to the Company by Mr. Hall (FER 309).

EDWARD BRENT

Edward Brent came to Virginia prior to February 1, 1624, at which time he made his will. He bequeathed his goods in the colony to his brothers Giles and John. He also instructed his executors to see that some of his goods were sold so that the proceeds could be given to merchant Richard Bennett or, if Bennett was deceased, to Maurice Thompson. The General Court noted that Sir George Yeardley had owed Edward Brent some tobacco but had satisfied his debt. Brent's will was proved in England in August 1625 (EEAC 9; WAT 1090-1091; MCGC 60; CBE 70).

HUGH BRETT

On February 9, 1625, Roger Webster informed the General Court that in early 1624 Captain Croshaw hired Hugh Brett for a year and promised to take him to England at his expense when his term of service was over (MCGC 470).

***

JAMES BRETT

James Brett, a mariner, went to Virginia to trade and allowed others to invest with him in saleable goods. According to one man, Brett left for the colony on the *Edwin* (also known as the *Sampson*) around October 1618. Although Brett sent some tobacco back to England on the *Bona Nova*, he died in Virginia. As a result, in May 1622 some of those who had invested in his cargo of trade goods tried to recover funds from his estate, which was in the hands of his widow, Elizabeth, and her new husband, Richard Page (SR 9947, 9963; C 24/289; 24/561).

ELIZABETH BRETT (MRS. JAMES BRETT, MRS. RICHARD PAGE)

Elizabeth, the wife of mariner James Brett, was widowed sometime prior to May 1622. The decedent died in Virginia, leaving his business affairs in the hands of Elizabeth, who married Richard Page, another mariner (SR 9947; C 24/489).

***

WILLIAM BRETT

On November 20, 1622, officials at Bridewell decided that William Brett, an inmate being detained in Newgate Prison, would be sent to Virginia (CBE 29).

***

JOHN BREWER I

John Brewer I came to Virginia sometime prior to 1622 and was a citizen and grocer of London and the son of Thomas Brewer. In 1622 he identified himself as an ancient planter and an adventurer in New England when he asked the king to set a reasonable price for some of the tobacco imported each year. In January 1629 John Brewer was identified as a merchant when he purchased 1,000 acres called Stanley Hundred (22) from Thomas and Mary Flint. He also testified before the General Court about a debt

Captain Peirce owed to Mrs. Flint. In 1629 John Brewer was fined for not giving four days' work to the churchwardens of Stanley Hundred. A year later, he was elected a burgess for the community of settlers along the Warwick River. In September 1631 he was among the Virginia planters asking for relief from customs duties. John Brewer may have become seriously ill while contemplating a trip to England, for on September 4, 1631, he made his will, making bequests to his wife, Marie (Mary), sons John and Roger, daughter Margaret, and brother Thomas. However, he continued to live and in 1632 served as a justice of the Warwick River court and in February 1633 became a member of the Council of State. John Brewer I died in Virginia sometime prior to July 11, 1635, by which time his widow had married the Rev. Thomas Butler of Denbigh (**23**). In May 1636 she was appointed her late husband's administrator when his will was proved (CBE 29; VCR 3:580; MCGC 180; HEN 1:148, 187, 202; G&M 165; SR 3974; SH 14; EEAC 9; WAT 715; PB 1 Pt. 1:222).

MARIE (MARY) BREWER (MRS. JOHN BREWER I, MRS. THOMAS BUTLER)

On September 4, 1631, when John Brewer I of Stanley Hundred (or Brewer's Burrough) made his will, he named his wife, Marie (Mary), as a beneficiary. Although John survived until at least February 1633, he died sometime prior to July 11, 1635, by which time she had married the Rev. Thomas Butler of Denbigh. In May 1636 Marie was identified as the administrator of the late John Brewer, a citizen and grocer of London and owner of Stanley Hundred (**22**) in Virginia (SH 14; PB 1 Pt. 1:222; EEAC 9; WAT 715).

JOHN BREWER II

In September 1631 John Brewer II, the son of John Brewer I, was identified as a minor child and one of his late father's heirs. He was the brother of Margaret and Roger, who also were minors. John Brewer II inherited his father's acreage called Stanley Hundred (**22**) and enhanced its size on March 18, 1663, by patenting an additional 300 acres (EEAC 9; SH 14; WAT 715; PB 5:349).

MARGARET BREWER

In September 1631 Margaret Brewer, the daughter of John Brewer I, was identified as a minor child and one of her late father's heirs. Her brothers, John II and Roger, also were minors (EEAC 9; SH 14; WAT 715).

ROGER BREWER

In September 1631 Roger Brewer, the son of John Brewer I, was identified as a minor child and one of his late father's heirs. He was the brother of Margaret and John II, who also were minors (EEAC 9; SH 14; WAT 715).

***

JOSEPH BREWER

On July 15, 1631, Joseph Brewer was among the Virginia planters who asked for relief from customs. He indicated that his hogsheads of tobacco were marked *JB* (G&M 164).

THOMAS BREWER

On June 19, 1622, Virginia Company officials learned that Deputy-Governor Samuel Argall (1617–1618) had given Thomas Brewer some land in Elizabeth City on which he had built four houses. The buildings burned and he replaced them. In April 1619, when Governor George Yeardley arrived, he evicted Thomas Brewer from his acreage, which was designated part of the Virginia Company's land in Elizabeth City (**17**) (VCR 2:45).

WILLIAM BREWERE

On December 5, 1625, the General Court noted that William Brewere was owed money by the late Richard Page (MCGC 78).

JOHN BREWTON

John Brewton came to Virginia in 1634 on the *John and Dorothy* at the expense of Adam Thorogood. On June 24, 1635, when Thorogood secured a patent, he listed John Brewton as a headright (PB 1 Pt. 1:179).

EDWARD BREWSTER

On March 22, 1622, when the Indians attacked Edward Bennett's plantation in

Warresqueak (**26**), Edward Brewster was killed (VCR 3:571).

EDWARD BREWSTER

Edward Brewster came to Virginia with Thomas West, Lord Delaware, in 1610 and was present when he landed in Jamestown (**1**) on June 10th. Delaware designated him captain of his company and sent him to the falls of the James River (**67**), where he was supposed to wait for Delaware to arrive. The group was attacked by Indians, but Brewster escaped unharmed. In October 1610 Delaware had Brewster and Captain George Yeardley lead an expedition to the mountains, but they did not venture above the falls of the James. In May 1611, after Sir Thomas Dale took over, he had Brewster and his workers repair the church in Jamestown. During 1612 Brewster and a group of men went overland toward the head of the James, so that they could meet up with Sir Thomas Dale at the place on which Henricus (**63**) was to be built. Captain Edward Brewster left Virginia and returned in August 1618 on the *Neptune* as one of Lord Delaware's officers. Brewster later claimed that when the *Neptune* was on its way to Virginia, it encountered the *Treasurer*, aboard which Lord Delaware put some of his men and goods. Delaware died on the way to the colony, and Brewster tried to take custody of his goods as soon as the *Neptune* reached Jamestown. According to numerous witnesses, Edward Brewster immediately clashed with Deputy-Governor Samuel Argall, who seized Lord Delaware's goods and put his men (including skillful artisans, such as carpenters, smiths, and masons) to work on his own projects. Argall also refused to provide Delaware's men with food and shelter, which they lacked. When Brewster protested, Argall reportedly retaliated by having him tried at a court martial hearing. He was condemned to death for accusing Argall of destroying the plantation Lord Delaware tried to establish. Ultimately, Argall offered Brewster a reprieve if he agreed to leave the colony and never speak of him unfavorably. Brewster reached England and on May 12, 1619, appealed his sentence to officials of the Virginia Company. He alleged that he had been tried in a military court after the colony was no longer under marital law, and that he was entitled to a new trial. The widowed Lady Cisley Delaware also brought suit against

Argall. Company officials, anxious to settle the dispute, sought more information. In April 1622 Edward Brewster, who was age 40, claimed that Deputy Governor Argall had imprisoned him and misappropriated Lord Delaware's goods, which were given to cape merchant Abraham Peirsey but eventually placed in a storehouse. He also alleged that Argall refused to release Lord Delaware's men so that they could be sent to his landholdings and put to work on Lady Delaware's behalf. Instead, he had them work on the church and his own house and garden. Brewer said that Argall refused to allow him to trade with the Indians even though he had brought a supply of trade goods, and he stated that 10 people sent over by Lord Delaware in 1617 also had been put to personal use by Argall. In May 1623 the allegations against Sir Samuel Argall were still being debated (HAI 433, 458, 512-513, 517, 523, 898; SR 1957, 5860, 9946, 10376, 11699; CJS 2:265; HCA 13/44; C 24/486, 24/490; VCR 1:219, 222, 224, 230, 309, 360-364, 418-419; 2:400, 442; EAE 12).

HENRY BREWSTER

On February 6, 1637, when Richard Brewster patented some land in Archer's Hope (**6**), he used the headright of his brother, Henry (PB 1 Pt. 2:520).

***

RICHARD BREWSTER

Richard Brewster, an ancient planter, who was in England on May 4, 1622, identified himself as Captain Edward Brewster's kinsman and a 27-year-old Virginia planter. He said that he had known Samuel Argall for seven years and that although he was a resident of Jamestown (**1**), he was not present in August 1618 when Lord Delaware's ship, the *Neptune*, arrived. He indicated that he was aware that Argall had employed the late Lord Delaware's men in his kitchen and garden and had some of them build him a house. He added that Argall also had sent some of Delaware's men to the West Indies on the *Treasurer*. He said that Argall quickly took possession of the late Lord Delaware's goods, failing to provide a storehouse. He mentioned Argall's trial of Edward Brewster in a court martial hearing and said that he felt his kinsman had been mistreated. Richard Brewster returned to

Virginia on the *Margaret and John* and sent a petition to the governor. He served on a jury on August 4, 1623, and on April 21, 1624, asked to be relieved from paying taxes because of the losses he had sustained during the 1622 Indian attack. In April 1625 Brewster brought Robert Mansteed's will to the General Court, and he testified that John Stephens had given his will to Tobias Felgate. When a list of patented land was sent back to England in May 1625, Richard Brewster was credited with 100 acres in Archer's Hope (**6**). However, in December 1626 he was living in a house in Pasbehay (**3**) and paying rent to the governor. In October 1629 and March 1630 he was a burgess for the settlers living in the Neck O'Land (**5**), and in February 1633 he represented the territory between Harrop, on the east side of Archer's Hope (or College) Creek, and Martin's Hundred (**7**). In February 1637, when Richard Brewster patented some land in Archer's Hope, he used the headrights of his wife and two children and his brother, Henry (C 24/486; 24/490; SR 9946; VCR 2:519, 524-525; 4:127-128, 556; MCGC 4-5, 51, 56, 126; STAN 55; HEN 1:138, 148, 203; PB 1 Pt. 2:520).

MRS. RICHARD BREWSTER

On February 6, 1637, when Richard Brewster patented some land in Archer's Hope (**6**), he used the headrights of his wife and two children but failed to mention their names (PB 1 Pt. 2:520).

***

WILLIAM BREWSTER

William Brewster, a gentleman, came to Virginia in 1607 and was one of the first Jamestown (**1**) settlers. Sometime prior to June 22, 1607, he sent a letter back to England, and on August 7, 1607, he was wounded by the Indians. He died in or near Jamestown, where he was buried. In 1608 Edward Maria Wingfield spoke highly of Mr. Brewster and said that he had not reviled him as some of the other settlers had (CJS 1:20, 208; 2:141; HAI 99, 127, 199).

***

THOMAS BREWOOD

During 1621 Thomas Brewood of Kecoughtan (**17, 18**) and other area residents made an agreement with the captain of the *Falcon* to transport a shipload of sassafras to London. Three years later, a dispute over the cargo was aired before the Admiralty Court. On March 22, 1622, when the Indians attacked the Bennett plantation at Warresqueak (**26**), Thomas Brewood was killed, as were his wife and child. It is uncertain whether they were visiting the Bennett settlement at the time of the assault or had relocated. In May 1625, when a list of patented land was sent back to England, Thomas Brewood was credited with 200 acres on the south side of the James River, opposite Elizabeth City (**20 a, b, c**) (EAE 11; VCR 3:571; CBE 69-70; HCA 30/545; SR 14589).

MRS. THOMAS BREWOOD

On March 22, 1622, when the Indians attacked Edward Bennett's plantation in Warresqueak (**26**), Mrs. Thomas Brewood was killed (VCR 3:571).

[NO FIRST NAME] BREWOOD

Thomas Brewood's child was killed on March 22, 1622, when the Indians attacked Edward Bennett's plantation in Warresqueak (**26**) (VCR 3:571).

***

THOMAS BRICE

On July 27, 1634, it was decided that Thomas Brice, a prisoner at Newgate, would be sent to Virginia. His father, Ralph Brice, gave his consent (CBE 118).

EDWARD BRICKE (BRITT)

On February 16, 1624, Edward Bricke (Britt) was living in urban Jamestown (**1**). Court testimony taken on March 29, 1626, indicates that in 1620 he made an account of some tobacco received by John Rolfe. Bricke was then identified as one of Captain William Peirce's servants (CBE 38; MCGC 99).

JOHN BRIDE

On August 18, 1628, John Bride was identified as master of the *Thomas*, which was making a voyage from Bristol to Virginia (CBE 88).

HENRY BRIDGES

Henry Bridges died in Elizabeth City (**17, 18**) sometime after April 1623 but before February 16, 1624 (CBE 45).

JOHN BRIDGES

On January 24, 1629, John Bridges was among those serving on the jury that tried William Reade, who had stabbed John Burrows. Bridges returned to court on February 10, 1629, at which time he served as the attorney for John Haier's (Hayes's) estate, which successfully brought suit against Governor Francis West. In March 1629 John Bridges again served on a jury. He was still living in Virginia in March 1637 when he was named the administrator of his kinsman, George Warren (MCGC 184, 186-187, 192; EEAC 9).

THOMAS BRIDGES

Thomas Bridges came to Virginia on the *Marmaduke* in 1623. On February 4, 1625, he was a 12-year-old servant living on Captain Samuel Mathews' plantation (**15**) on the lower side of the James River (CBE 60).

***

RICHARD BRIDGEWATER

Richard Bridgewater came to Virginia on the *London Merchant*. On February 16, 1624, he and his wife, Isabell, were living on the Maine (**3**) or Governor's Land. On January 30, 1625, the Bridgewaters, who appear to have been free, were still residing there. Richard headed a household that had an ample supply of stored food and some defensive weaponry. He probably was one of the governor's tenants (CBE 39, 57; DOR 1:25).

ISABELL BRIDGEWATER (MRS. RICHARD BRIDGEWATER)

Isabell, the wife of Richard Bridgewater, came to Virginia on the *London Merchant*. On February 16, 1624, she and her husband were living on the Maine or Governor's Land (**3**), and they were still there on January 30, 1625. Richard, who was a household head, probably was one of the governor's tenants. On August 21, 1626, Isabell Bridges testified that Thomas Jones, Robert

Hutchinson, and John Osborn (all of whom lived on the Governor's Land) had been drunk and disorderly (CBE 39, 57; MCGC 108).

***

HENRY BRIGG

In April 1623 Henry Brigg sent a letter to his brother, Thomas, an English merchant at Customhouse Key, complaining about conditions in Virginia. He said that his master, Mr. Atkins, had misled him and that he was starving and miserable. He also said that Mr. Atkins had sold him and that he lived in constant fear of an Indian attack. Henry and Mr. Atkins appear to have been living in Elizabeth City (**17, 18**) (VCR 4:236).

[NO FIRST NAME] BRIGGS (BIGGS?)

On January 9, 1625, the General Court noted that church services would be held at the home of Mrs. Briggs, probably Mrs. Richard Biggs of West and Shirley Hundred (**41**) (MCGC 88-89).

ROBERT BRIGGS

On March 29, 1620, the Virginia Company noted that Robert Briggs had procured two shares of Virginia land from Captain John Bargrave. Bargrave was the owner of a plantation (**60**) in the colony (VCR 1:330).

HENRY BRIGHTON

On July 29, 1626, officials at Bridewell noted that Henry Brighton, who had been diseased, had been cured at St. Thomas Hospital. He was to be sent to Clerkenwell or to Virginia (HUME 32).

EDWARD BRINTON (BRYNTON)

Edward Brinton (Brynton), a mason, arrived in Virginia in 1607 and was one of the first Jamestown (**1**) settlers. According to Captain John Smith, in 1608 Brinton went with Powhatan on a hunting trip to kill some fowl. He also accompanied Smith to Werowocomoco, Powhatan's village on the York River, and to the Pamunkey Indians' territory. Smith described Brinton as a soldier. He said that when Brinton realized that the Dutchmen sent to build a house for

Powhatan were furnishing the Indians with weapons, he tried to reach Jamestown so that he could inform the authorities. However, he was caught and killed by the Indians on his way home (CJS 1:209; 2:142, 182, 193, 199-200).

PETER (PEETER) BRISHITT (BRISKITT)

Peter (Peeter) Brishitt (Briskitt) died in Jamestown (1) sometime after April 1623 but before February 16, 1624 (CBE 39).

RICHARD BRISLOW

Richard Brislow, a laborer, arrived in Jamestown (1) in 1608 as part of the 1st Supply (CJS 1:223; 2:161).

PETER BRISTOW

Peter Bristow went to Virginia with Mr. Spencer on the *James* and departed from England on July 31, 1622 (FER 400).

***

ROBERT BRITTIN (BRITTAINE)

Robert Brittin (Brittaine) went to Virginia in 1618 on the *Edwin* and on February 16, 1624, was living in Elizabeth City (18). He was still there in early 1625, at which time he was a 30-year-old household head who had an ample supply of stored food and defensive weaponry. In 1628 Robert Brittin and John Hill were given letters of administration so that they could settle Nicholas Thredder's estate. Robert died prior to April 9, 1629, at which time his widow, Eleanor, who had remarried, was named his administrator and presented an inventory of his estate (CBE 43, 64; MCGC 174, 196; DOR 1:53).

ELEANOR BRITTIN (BRITTAINE) (MRS. ROBERT BRITTIN [BRITTAINE], MRS. EDWARD PRICE [PRISE]) (SEE MRS. EDWARD PRICE [PRISE]

Sometime prior to April 9, 1629, Eleanor, who was Robert Brittain's (Brittaine's) widow and the administrator of his estate, married Edward Price. She outlived him

too, and on April 9, 1629, the General Court ordered her to make an inventory of both men's estates (MCGC 196).

***

FRANCES BROADBOTTOM

Frances Broadbottom, a marriageable young maid, came to Virginia in September 1621 on the *Warwick*. Virginia Company records reveal that she was the 19-year-old daughter of London cutler Robert Broadbottom and had been living in Lothebury (FER 309).

EDWARD BROCK (BROCKE)

Edward Brock (Brocke), a 14-year-old smith, came to Virginia in 1619 on the *Bona Nova*. He probably was a Virginia Company servant or tenant (FER 295).

JOHN BROCK (BROCKE)

John Brock (Brocke), a 13-year-old smith, came to Virginia in 1619 aboard the *Bona Nova*. In early 1625 he was residing on the Virginia Company's land in Elizabeth City (17) in the household of Thomas Flint. John was then age 19 and probably was a Virginia Company servant or tenant (FER 295; CBE 67).

RICHARD BROCK (BROCKE)

Richard Brock (Brocke), a 48-year-old smith from Shropshire, England, went to Virginia in 1619 aboard the *Bona Nova* and probably was a Virginia Company servant or tenant. Edward and John Brock, who accompanied him, may have been his sons (FER 295).

WILLIAM BROCK (BROCKE)

William Brock (Brocke) came to Virginia on the *Margaret* in May 1622 and on February 16, 1624, was living on West and Shirley Hundred Island (41). By January 22, 1625, he had moved to the mainland of West and Shirley Hundred and was living in Richard Biggs's household, where he was a 26-year-old servant (CBE 36, 52).

MATHEW BROCKBANKE

Mathew Brockbanke, who was from Wapping in Middlesex, went to Virginia on the *Margaret and John* in 1623 and was accompanied by his servant, Valentine Osserby. Mathew died before he reached the colony (VCR 4:95-96).

THOMAS BRODBANKE

Thomas Brodbanke died in Elizabeth City (17, 18) sometime after April 1623 but before February 16, 1624 (CBE 45).

THOMAS BRODSIL

On August 22, 1625, Thomas Brodsil testified that he witnessed a bargain between John Hall and Thomas Passmore, both of whom were residents of eastern Jamestown Island (1). This raised the possibility that Brodsil lived there too (MCGC 69).

JOHN BROGDEN

John Brogden died in Martin's Hundred (7) sometime after April 1623 but before February 16, 1624 (CBE 42).

***

HENRY BROMAGE (BROMEDG)

Henry Bromage (Bromedg) and his wife and child were killed on March 22, 1622, when the Indians attacked Martin's Hundred (7) (VCR 3:570).

MRS. HENRY BROMAGE (BROMEDG)

On March 22, 1622, when the Indians attacked Martin's Hundred (7), Mrs. Henry Bromage (Bromedg) was killed, as were her husband and child (VCR 3:570).

[NO FIRST NAME] BROMAGE (BROMEDG)

On March 22, 1622, when the Indians attacked Martin's Hundred (7), Mr. and Mrs. Henry Bromage's child reportedly was killed. However, the youngster or a sibling may have lived, for 2-year-old Sarah Bromage was alive in early February 1625 (VCR 3:570).

***

SARAH BROMAGE (BROMEDG)

On February 4, 1625, Sarah Bromage (Bromedg), who was 2 years old, was living at the Neck O Land (5), where she resided in the household headed by Thomas Bennett. If Sarah's age was reported inaccurately, she may have been the daughter of Mr. and Mrs. Henry Bromage, who were killed in the March 1622 Indian attack on Martin's Hundred (7) (CBE 58).

JOHN BROMLEY

On August 8, 1618, officials at Bridewell decided that John Bromley, a vagrant, would be sent to Virginia (CBE 9).

SIR JOHN BROOKE

On June 10, 1622, Sir John Brooke was identified as the holder of a patent for a particular plantation in Virginia (VCR 3:643).

CUTBERT (CUTHBERD) BROOKS (BROOKES)

Cutbert (Cuthberd) Brooks (Brookes) came to Virginia on the *Southampton* in 1622 at the expense of John Cheesman. He died in Elizabeth City (18) sometime after April 1623 but before February 16, 1624. On September 2, 1624, Cheesman used Brooks as a headright when patenting some land (CBE 45; PB 1 Pt. 1:47).

EDWARD BROOKS (BROOKES)

Edward Brooks (Brookes), a gentleman, came to Virginia in 1607 and was one of the first Jamestown (1) colonists (CJS 208; 2:141).

EDWARD BROOKS (BROOKES)

On February 27, 1619, Edward Brooks (Brookes), a boy from St. Bridges Parish, was detained so that he could be sent to Virginia (CBE 12).

HUGH BROOKS (BROOKES)

Sometime prior to September 19, 1625, William Webb, purser of the *Elizabeth*, which had been detained for the king's service, assigned three indentured servants to Abraham Peirsey as substitutes for the servants he lost. One was those assigned was Hugh Brooks (Brookes) (MCGC 71).

JAMES BROOKS (BROOKES)

In 1619 James Brooks (Brookes) came to Virginia on the *Jonathan*. On February 16, 1624, he was living in Elizabeth City (**17**) at Buckroe, part of the Virginia Company's land. In early 1625 he was still there and was a 19-year-old servant in Thomas Flint's household (CBE 45, 67).

JAMES BROOKS (BROOKES)

On January 29, 1620, officials at Bridewell decided that James Brooks (Brookes) would be sent to Virginia (CBE 18).

JAMES BROOKS (BROOKES)

On July 31, 1622, James Brooks (Brookes) set sail for Virginia on the *James* and accompanied John Harryson (Harrison) (FER 400).

JOHN BROOKS (BROOKES)

John Brooks (Brookes) came to Virginia in 1607 and was one of the first Jamestown (**1**) settlers. On May 20, 1607, he accompanied Captain Christopher Newport on an exploratory voyage in the James River (HAI 102).

THOMAS BROOKS (BROOKES)

Thomas Brooks (Brookes) came to Virginia on the *Southampton* in 1623 and on February 16, 1624, was living at Jordan's Journey (**46**). However, by January 20, 1625, he had moved to Flowerdew Hundred (**53**), where he was a 23-year-old servant in Abraham Peirsey's household (CBE 36, 50).

THOMAS BROOKS (BROOKES)

Thomas Brooks (Brookes) came to Virginia in 1628 on the *Hopewell* at the expense of Adam Thorogood. On June 24, 1635, when Thorogood secured a patent, he listed Thomas Brooks as a headright (PB 1 Pt. 1:179).

WILLIAM BROOKS (BROOKE)

William Brooks (Brooke) came to Virginia in 1621 on the *Temperance* at the expense of Sir George Yeardley. By September 20, 1628, William's headright had been assigned to Thomas Flint, who used it when patenting some land (PB 1 Pt. 1:59).

WILLIAM BROOKS (BROOKES)

On November 20, 1622, officials at Bridewell decided that William Brooks (Brookes), who was being detained in Newgate Prison, would be sent to Virginia (CBE 29).

***

WILLIAM BROOKS (BROOKES, BROOCKES) ALIAS MORGAN ALIAS JONES (SEE WILLIAM MORGAN)

SIBILE BROOKS (BROOKES, BROOCKES) ALIAS MORGAN ALIAS JONES (MRS. WILLIAM BROOKS [BROOKES, BROOCKES] ALIAS MORGAN ALIAS JONES) (SEE SIBILE MORGAN)

WILLIAM BROOKS (BROOKES, BROOCKES) II ALIAS MORGAN ALIAS JONES) (SEE WILLIAM MORGAN II)

***

WILLIAM BROOMEMAN

On March 6, 1620, Governor George Yeardley granted some land to George Harrison of Charles City on the basis of three headrights. One of the people Harrison transported was William Broomeman (CBE 19).

WILLIAM BROOMLEY

On October 21, 1629, officials at Bridewell decided that William Broomley, a boy, would be sent to Virginia (HUME 35).

GILLAIN BROQUE

Laborer Gillain Broque, a young man, was among the Walloons and French who indicated their willingness to go to Virginia. In August 1621 the Virginia Company agreed that he could immigrate (CBE 24).

LOUIS BROQUE

Laborer Louis Broque, his wife, and two children were among the Walloons and French who indicated their willingness to go to Virginia. In August 1621 the Virginia Company agreed that they could immigrate (CBE 25).

ROBERT BROQUE

Laborer Robert Broque, a young man, was among the Walloons and French who indicated their willingness to go to Virginia. In August 1621 the Virginia Company agreed that he could immigrate (CBE 24).

BRIGETT (BRIDGETT) BROWE

On February 5, 1620, it was decided that Brigett (Bridgett) Browe, who had been brought in from the Bridge and was being detained at Bridewell, would be sent to Virginia (CBE 18).

[NO FIRST NAME] BROWN

Sometime prior to the March 22, 1622, Indian attack, an interpreter named Brown, who was employed by Mr. Hamor of Warresqueak (26), was sent home to his master. He had been living with the Warresqueak Indians so that he could learn their language and had traded with them (VCR 3:550; CJS 2:294).

[NO FIRST NAME] BROWN

On June 12, 1610, Thomas West, Lord Delaware, designated Mr. Brown as clerk of the council. Therefore, he would have lived in Jamestown (1) (HAI 433).

[NO FIRST NAME] BROWNE

On July 10, 1635, Captain Brown was identified as the owner of Halfway Tree Neck or Perry's (later, Swann's) Point in what became Surry County (PB 1 Pt. 1:221).

ANTHONY BROWN

On April 3, 1620, the Virginia Company was informed that Anthony Brown had received 25 shares of land from Lady Delaware and that he intended to go to Virginia to establish a plantation (VCR 1:333).

BENJAMIN BROWN (BROWNE)

On November 19, 1627, the General Court learned that Benjamin Brown (Browne), a deceased mariner from Lyme in County Dorset who became ill on the way to Virginia, made a nuncupative will that was witnessed by John Southern of Jamestown Island (1). Southern said that Brown owed money to Valentine Oldis, a merchant, and had agreed to work on the voyage in order to repay his debt. However, as Benjamin Brown was too ill to work, he bequeathed £20 to Oldis and asked John Southern to see that he was paid (MCGC 157-158).

CHRISTOPHER BROWN (BROWNE)

On December 31, 1619, officials at Bridewell decided that Christopher Brown (Browne), who was being detained at the Middlesex House of Correction, would be sent to Virginia. He was transported to the colony on the *Duty* in May 1620 and on February 16, 1624, was living at Bermuda Hundred (39). He was still there on January 24, 1625, at which time he was identified as an 18-year-old servant in Richard Taylor's household (CBE 14, 36, 54).

EDWARD BROWN (BROWNE)

Edward Brown (Browne), a gentleman, came to Virginia in 1607 and was one of the first Jamestown (1) settlers. He died there on August 15, 1607 (CJS 1:20; 2:141; HAI 99).

ELIZABETH BROWN [BROWNE]

Elizabeth Brown (Browne), a young marriageable maid, came to Virginia on the *Tiger* in 1621. She was 16 years old and had been born in London. Virginia Company records indicate that Elizabeth's parents were alive and resided in the Blackfriars (FER 309).

GEORGE BROWN (BROWNE)

On December 24. 1619, officials in the Bridewell court decided that George Brown (Browne), a boy, would be detained so that he could be sent to Virginia (CBE 14; HUME 13).

JANE BROWN (BROWNE)

On November 20, 1622, Jane Brown (Browne), an inmate at Newgate Prison, was among those pardoned after an outbreak of jail fever so that they could be sent overseas (CBE 29).

JOHN BROWN (BROWNE)

On February 16, 1624, John Brown (Browne) was living at Flowerdew Hundred **(53)** (CBE 37).

***

JOHN BROWN (BROWNE)

John Brown (Browne) died sometime prior to June 5, 1632, at which time his widow, who had married Richard Cocke, agreed to pay the debts against his estate and keep the residue for the decedent's children (MCGC 200).

MRS. JOHN BROWN (BROWNE) (MRS. RICHARD COCKE)

On June 5, 1632, the General Court noted that the widow of John Brown (Browne), who had wed Richard Cocke, agreed to pay the decedent's debts. She and her new husband also agreed to keep the remainder of Brown's estate intact for his children (MCGC 200).

***

JOHN BROWN (BROWNE)

On February 27, 1619, officials at Bridewell decided that John Brown (Browne), a boy, would be detained until he could be sent to Virginia (CBE 12; HUME 11).

JOHN BROWN (BROWNE)

On December 31, 1619, it was decided that John Brown (Browne), a boy brought in from the Mids, would be kept until he could be sent to Virginia (HUME 14).

JOHN BROWN (BROWNE)

On February 16, 1624, John Brown (Browne) was living on Hog Island **(16)** (CBE 41).

JOHN BROWN (BROWNE)

John Brown (Browne) left England in April 1621 and came to Virginia on the *Bona Nova*. On February 16, 1624, he was living at Chaplin's Choice **(56)**. He was still there on January 21, 1625, and was described as a

28-year-old household head. On December 4, 1626, John was identified as a servant of Rowland Truelove and Company. He already had served for five years and was freed of the two additional years he was supposed to serve. On October 16, 1629, John Brown served as the burgess for West and Shirley Hundred (Eppes) Island **(41)** (CBE 37, 51; MCGC 126; HEN 1:138; DOR 1:21).

JOHN BROWN (BROWNE)

On July 29, 1626, officials at Bridewell noted that John Brown (Browne), who had been diseased, had been cured at St. Thomas Hospital and would be sent to Clerkenwell or Virginia. The matter was discussed again on August 26, 1626 (HUME 32; CBE 73).

MARGARET BROWN (BROWNE)

On February 5, 1619, it was decided that Margaret Brown (Browne), a girl who had been brought in, would be kept until she could be sent to Virginia (HUME 14).

NICHOLAS BROWN (BROWNE)

Nicholas Brown (Browne) came to Virginia on the *Charles* in 1621 and on February 16, 1624, was living in the corporation of Elizabeth City **(18)**. He was still there in early 1625 and was an 18-year-old servant in Edward Waters' household near Blunt Point **(22)**. In early June 1632 Nicholas Brown, who was identified as a planter, acquired a 21-year lease for 50 acres of land on the Hampton River near Walter Heeley's property. In November 1634 Nicholas was among the several Virginia men who certified that certain goods had been brought to the colony by the recently arrived but now deceased Thomas Lee (CBE 44, 66, 208; MCGC 201; PB 1 Pt. 1:101).

OLIVER (OLYVER) BROWN (BROWNE)

On May 20, 1607, Oliver (Olyver) Brown (Browne), a sailor, left Jamestown **(1)** and went with Captain Christopher Newport on an exploratory voyage up the James River (HAI 102).

REBECCA BROWN (BROWNE)

Rebecca Brown (Browne), who probably was the wife or kinswoman of Robert

Brown (Browne), came to Virginia in 1623 on the *Southampton*. In early 1625 she and Robert were living in Elizabeth City (**18**), where they were listed together as servants in the household of Thomas Spellman. Rebecca was then age 24 (CBE 65).

RICHARD BROWN (BROWNE)

In 1621 Richard Brown (Browne) was identified as part of the company of the *Falcon*, which was going to Jamestown (**1**) (EAE 11).

ROBERT BROWN (BROWNE)

Robert Brown (Browne) went to Virginia on the *Marigold* in 1618, at the expense of Robert Gire. William Ganey (Gainey) paid for his transportation and on January 12, 1624, used him as a headright when patenting some land. On February 16, 1624, Brown was residing in Elizabeth City (**18**). In November 1624 he testified in a suit involving William Ganey and Mr. Whittaker. In early 1625 25-year-old Robert Brown and his 24-year-old wife or kinswoman, Rebecca Brown, were living in Elizabeth City where they were listed as servants in Thomas Spellman's household. Robert Brown apparently moved to the Eastern Shore, for on February 8, 1628, the General Court learned that he and Samuel Woolves had been interrogated by Thomas Graves, commissioner of Accomack, about whether they had sold glass bottles to the Indians. On September 20, 1628, Robert Brown was identified as an Accomack planter when he procured a lease for 20 acres of land adjacent to the Secretary's Plantation (**75**) (CBE 44, 65; PB 1 Pt. 1:39, 86; MCGC 31-32, 165).

ROBERT BROWN (BROWNE)

On June 7, 1619, Virginia Company officials identified Robert Brown (Browne) as an adventurer who went to Virginia with Lord Delaware and died in the colony. His estate was to be credited with the 100 acres for which he had paid (VCR 1:232).

THOMAS BROWN (BROWNE)

On March 22, 1622, when the Indians attacked Samuel Macock's plantation (**48**), Thomas Brown (Browne) reportedly was killed. If he survived, he may have been the

Thomas Brown who died in Jamestown (**1**) or in Elizabeth City (**17, 18**) sometime after April 1623 but before February 16, 1624 (VCR 3:568).

THOMAS BROWN (BROWNE)

Thomas Brown (Browne) died on Jamestown Island (**1**) sometime after April 1623 but before February 16, 1624 (CBE 39).

THOMAS BROWN (BROWNE)

Thomas Brown (Browne) died in Elizabeth City (**17, 18**) sometime after April 1623 but before February 16, 1624 (CBE 45).

THOMAS BROWN (BROWNE)

On July 6, 1632, Thomas, the son of London wood-monger Thomas Brown, was sent to Virginia as an indentured servant. He was to serve a Thomas Brown, who was a bricklayer and citizen of London (HUME 37).

THOMAS BROWN (BROWNE)

In May 1635 Thomas Brown (Browne) was among the Virginia planters who claimed that if Governor John Harvey and his council were to make Maurice Thompson and his associates the sole source for shipping tobacco from the colony, they would sustain great losses. In 1638–1639 Thomas Brown, who identified himself as a 33-year-old Virginia planter of Kingsman (Kingsmill) Neck in Archer's Hope (**6**), stated that he and his wife were on the *Elizabeth* when it was captured and taken to Cadiz. He said that they lost their goods (CBE 115-116; G&M 187-188; EAE 90).

WESTON BROWN (BROWNE)

On February 16, 1624, Weston Brown (Browne) was living in Elizabeth City (**17, 18**). He was buried there on April 20, 1624 (CBE 43, 67).

WILLIAM BROWN (BROWNE)

On September 12, 1625, the General Court ordered William Brown (Browne), boatswain of the *Elizabeth*, who had sold three hats at Kecoughtan (**17,18**) that were intended for Thomas Allnutt, to see that they were returned (MCGC 70).

WILLIAM BROWN (BROWNE)

William Brown (Browne) went to Virginia on the *Southampton* in 1622 and on February 16, 1624, was living in Elizabeth City (**18**). He was still there in early 1625 and was living in the household of Richard Mintrene. William was then age 14 (CBE 43, 65).

WILLIAM BROWN (BROWNE)

William Brown (Browne) came to Virginia on the *Providence* in 1622. In early 1625 he was living in Elizabeth City (**17**) on the Virginia Company's land and was a 26-year-old servant in William Tyler's household (CBE 67).

WILLIAM BROWN (BROWNE)

William Brown (Browne) died in Archer's Hope (**6**) sometime after February 16, 1624, but before February 4, 1625 (CBE 58).

GEORGE BROWNING

On December 4, 1634, when Hugh Cox received a court order entitling him to a patent, he listed George Browning as a headright (PB 1 Pt. 1:282).

***

JOHN BROWNING (BROWNINGE)

John Browning (Browninge) came to Virginia in 1621 on the *Abigail*. On February 7, 1625, he was living at Basses Choice (**27**), where he and partner Henry Woodward headed a household that had an ample supply of stored food and defensive weaponry. John was then age 22. Sometime prior to February 1629, he got married. In October 1629 John Browning served as a burgess for the corporation of Elizabeth City, an indication that he owned property in that area. However, a month later he purchased 250 acres in Archer's Hope (**6**), acreage on the east side of Archer's Hope (College) Creek in what became known as Kingsmill Neck. In March 1630 John served as burgess for the territory between Archer's Hope and Martin's Hundred (**7**), an area that included Harrop (CBE 62; HEN 1:139, 148, 179; PB 2:100; DOR 1:49; SH 11-12; WAT 39).

MRS. JOHN BROWNING (BROWNINGE)

On February 13, 1629, when Jamestown (**1**) merchant Thomas Warnett made his will, he named Mrs. John Browning (Browninge) as a beneficiary and left her a thousand pins, some starch, and a pair of knives with carved handles. Mrs. John Browning probably lived in Archer's Hope (**6**) with her husband (SH 11-12; WAT 39).

***

WILLIAM BROWNING (BROWNINGE)

William Browning (Browninge), a 21-year-old glover from Kent, England, came to Virginia in 1619 on the *Bona Nova* and on February 16, 1624, was residing on the College Land (**66**) in Henrico. He was still there on January 23, 1625, and was a household head who had a modest supply of stored food and defensive weaponry. In April 1646 William Browning patented 650 acres in Archer's Hope (**6**), in what became known as Kingsmill Neck, land that John Browning had purchased in 1629. He died in Virginia sometime prior to September 1651, at which time administration was granted to a John Browning, who was described as his paternal uncle (FER 295; CBE 35, 53; PB 2:100; SR 4130; EEAC 10; DOR 1:7).

JAMES BRUMFIELD

James Brumfield, a boy, came to Virginia in 1607 in the first group of Jamestown (**1**) settlers (CJS 1:209; 2:142).

***

EDMUND BRUNDELL

On March 27, 1622, the Virginia Company noted that the two shares of land formerly owned by Edmund Brundell had been transferred to his son, Francis Brundell (VCR 1:624).

FRANCIS BRUNDELL

On March 27, 1622, the Virginia Company transferred to Francis Brundell two shares of Virginia land that formerly had belonged to his father, Edmund Brundell (VCR 1:624).

***

JOHN BRUNNET

On September 15, 1619, John Brunnet went to Virginia, probably on the *Margaret* of Bristol, and was among the people being sent to Berkeley Hundred (**55**) to work under Captain John Woodlief's supervision. According to Virginia Company records John Brunnet survived for four years, but died before fulfilling his obligation to the Society of Berkeley Hundred (CBE 14; VCR 3:198).

EDWARD BRYAN

Edward Bryan came to Virginia on the *Bona Nova* in 1620 at the expense of Edward Waters, who used him as a headright when patenting some land on August 14, 1624. On February 16, 1624, Edward Bryan was living in Elizabeth City (**18**) in the Waters home (CBE 44; PB 1 Pt. 1:18).

JOHN BRYAN

On July 31, 1622, John Bryan came to Virginia on the *James* with Isaac Chaplin and probably resided at Chaplin's plantation, Chaplin's Choice (**56**) (FER 400).

***

RICHARD BUCK

The Rev. Richard Buck, a graduate of Cambridge University, married his second wife, Maria Thorowgood, in London on December 21, 1608. The couple left England in June 1609 in the 3rd Supply of new colonists and were with Sir Thomas Gates and Sir George Somers aboard the *Seaventure* when it wrecked in Bermuda. In May 1610 the Rev. Buck arrived in Jamestown (**1**), where he replaced the late Rev. Robert Hunt as minister. When the *Neptune* reached Jamestown carrying some of the late Lord Delaware's skilled workers in August 1618, Buck offered to hire some of them. Buck served as chaplain in July 1619 when the colony's first assembly was held. As rector of the church in Jamestown, he had use of the James City glebe, which contained 100 acres and was laid out during 1619. He also patented 750 acres in Archer's Hope (**6**), part of which accrued to him and his wife as ancient planters. Although both parcels were planted (or seated), the Bucks preferred to live on Jamestown Island, and on December 18,

1620, they purchased William Fairfax's 12-acre homestead, which had two houses. While they were residing there, their household included their four young children and some indentured servants. When John Rolfe made his will in March 1622, he named the Rev. Buck, a witness, as one of his heirs. Buck considered Governor George Yeardley to be a good, religious man and said that he was supportive.

During the years 1621 and 1622 Buck repeatedly sent word to Virginia Company officials that he had not received his pay as a clergyman. He also indicated that all but one of his servants' time had expired and that he needed funds to procure more workers. References to Buck's business transactions reveal, however, that he was deriving a substantial amount of income from the cultivation of tobacco. The Rev. Richard Buck, a widower, died sometime after December 1622 but before April 1623. On February 16, 1624, when a census was made of the colony's inhabitants, all of Buck's minor children (Mara, Beomi, Gercian, and Peleg) were living in Jamestown in a foster home belonging to the widowed Mary Astomb (Ascomb). In December 1624 Buck was identified as one of the late George Thorpe's creditors but also as one of his debtors. From ca. 1623 to 1654 the Rev. Richard Buck's real estate was kept intact, apparently following the terms outlined in his will. His personal estate, which included livestock, was appraised by provost marshal Randall Smallwood and Nathaniel Reignolds (both of Jamestown) in April 1626, and his library was evaluated by John Pountis. Richard Kingsmill and John Jackson served as guardians of the Buck couple's minor children. Kingsmill, who presented the Rev. Buck's will to the General Court, also served as the estate's overseer. Documents associated with a 1655 court case reveal that Buck's eldest and only surviving daughter, Elizabeth, had life-rights in her father's property, but sons Benomi, Gercian, and Peleg were his reversionary heirs. In late 1654, when the last of the Buck brothers died, the Rev. Richard Buck's only grandson became the ultimate heir (LEF 1:694; HAI 412, 419, 432, 707; VCR 1:601-604; 3:155, 443, 461; 4:551, 555; PB 1 Pt 1:287; Pt. 2:650; SH 5; MCGH 861; FER 241, 267; C 24/490; MCGC 36, 47, 55, 100, 102-103, 117, 164; HEN 1:405; DOR 1:426-429; *Magazine of Virginia Genealogy* 40:259).

MARIA THOROWGOOD BUCK (MRS. RICHARD BUCK)

Maria Thorowgood married the Rev. Richard Buck in London on December 21, 1608, and accompanied him to Virginia in 1609. Like her husband, she was shipwrecked in Bermuda and arrived in the colony in May 1610. Mrs. Buck died in Jamestown (1), perhaps around 1620 when her youngest known child, Peleg, was born. She probably was the mother of Mara (born in 1611), Gercian (born in 1613), and Benomi (born in 1616), all of whom were Virginia-born, and would have been the stepmother of Elizabeth (CBE 55-56; *Magazine of Virginia Genealogy* 40:259).

BENOMI (BENOMY) BUCK

Benomi (Benomy) Buck, the Virginia-born son of the Rev. Richard Buck and his wife, Maria, was orphaned at an early age, for his parents died during the early 1620s. On February 16, 1624, Benomi and his older brothers and sister, Mara, were living in the home of the widowed Mrs. Mary Ascombe, a resident of Jamestown (1). By January 24, 1625, Mrs. Ascombe had married Peter Langman, but she continued to provide foster care to Benomi Buck, then age 8. Later, Benomi went to live with Richard and Jane Kingsmill, whose plantation was in the western end of Jamestown Island. After Richard Kingsmill's death and Jane's marriage to Ambrose Harmer, the issue arose of providing custodial care to Benomi Buck, who in 1637 came of age but was considered mentally incompetent. English officials designated Ambrose Harmer as Benomi's legal guardian, but Virginia governor John Harvey refused to implement the authorization because he felt that he had the right to choose custodians for mentally incapacitated adults. Therefore, he devised a plan whereby Benomi was to divide his time between the households of Richard Kemp and George Donne, each of whom was entitled to a fee as caregiver. When Ambrose Harmer went to England to protest that course of action, Governor Harvey was overruled. Meanwhile, official records reveal that Richard Kemp took care of Benomi for a year and then turned him over to the county sheriff until George Donne returned from overseas. Ambrose Harmer reached Virginia with his renewed commission for guardianship, but shortly thereafter

Benomi Buck, who was in Mrs. Jane Harmer's custody, died (CBE 38, 55; G&M 234; SAIN 1:251, 294; CO 1/9 ff 129-130; 1/10 f 65-68; PC 2/49 f 344).

ELIZABETH BUCK (MRS. THOMAS CRUMP, MRS. MATHEW PAGE) (SEE ELIZABETH BUCK CRUMP)

Elizabeth Buck, who appears to have been the daughter of the Rev. Richard Buck and his first wife, came to Virginia around 1625. She married Sergeant Thomas Crump, with whom she produced a son, John. After Thomas Crump's death, Elizabeth married Mathew Page. Elizabeth Buck Crump Page inherited life-rights to her late father's acreage in Archer's Hope (6), which she occupied (DOR 1:428; HEN 1:405; PB 6:298; 7:228).

GERCIAN (GERCION, GERCYON) BUCK

Gercian (Gercion, Gercyon) Buck, the Virginia-born son of the Rev. Richard Buck and his wife, Maria, resided in Jamestown (1) after his parents' deaths. On February 16, 1624, he and brothers, Peleg and Benomi, and sister, Mara, were living in urban Jamestown in the home of Mrs. Mary Ascomb, a widow. Sometime prior to January 24, 1625, 10-year-old Gercian went to live with John Jackson, also a resident of urban Jamestown. On September 1, 1636, when Gercian Buck purchased 500 acres in the Neck O'Land (6) from his brother-in-law Thomas Crump, he was described as a resident of Jamestown Island. Gercian died sometime prior to May 29, 1638, having named his brother, Peleg, as his heir (CBE 38, 55; PB 1 Pt. 2:532; 3:306).

MARA BUCK

Mara Buck, the Virginia-born daughter of the Rev. Richard Buck and his wife, resided in urban Jamestown (1) after her parents' deaths, as did her younger siblings. On February 16, 1624, Mara and her brothers, Benomi, Gercian, and Peleg, were living in the home of Mrs. Mary Ascomb, a widow. However, by January 24, 1625, Mara, who was 13 years old, had gone to live with Jamestown residents John and Bridget (Bridgett) Burrows. General Court records dating to June 1624 indicate that the Rev. David Sandys (Treasurer George Sandys' brother) was rumored to have a romantic interest in young Mara, presumably because she was an heiress. Bridget Burrows, who testified that she had tried in vain to teach Mara how to read, described her as slow-witted and uneducable. Some of the cattle on the Buck orphans' property in the Neck O'Land (5) belonged to Mara Buck (CBE 38, 55; MCGC 15-16, 109).

PELEG BUCK

Peleg Buck, the son of the Rev. Richard Buck and his wife, resided in urban Jamestown (1) after his parents' deaths. On February 16, 1624, he and his brother, Benomi, were living in the home of Mrs. Mary Ascomb, a widow, who by January 24, 1625, had married Peter Langman. For a time, they continued to provide the Buck boys, Peleg (age 4) and Benomi (age 8), with a home. However, Peleg later went to live with Thomas Allnutt and by October 10, 1626, was staying with Richard Kingsmill, a resident of the western end of Jamestown Island. By May 29, 1638, Peleg Buck, as his father's surviving male heir, had inherited 500 acres in the Neck O'Land (5) from his brother, Gercian. At Peleg's death, which occurred sometime prior to November 29, 1654, his nephew, John Crump, inherited the Buck family property (CBE 38, 55; MCGC 117; PB 1 Pt. 2:532; 3:306).

***

RICHARD BUCKAM

On May 1635 it was reported that Richard Buckam, master of the *Plaine Joane,* had brought 84 passengers to Virginia (SR 3466).

JOHN BUCKMASTER (BUCKMUSTER)

John Buckmaster (Buckmuster) came to Virginia on the *Great Hopewell* in 1623 and on August 14, 1624, was identified as one of Thomas Passmore's servants. Passmore used John's headright when patenting some land. On January 24, 1625, when a muster was made of Jamestown Island's inhabitants, John Buckmaster was described as a 20-year-old servant in Thomas Passmore's household. On March 22, 1625, John in-

formed the General Court that fellow servant Christopher Hall rarely worked a full day (PB 1 Pt. 1:10; HOT 227; MCGC 69).

[NO FIRST NAME] BUCKINGHAM

On March 22, 1622, when the Indians attacked Weyanoke (52), someone named Buckingham, one of Sir George Yeardley's people, was killed (VCR 3:569).

EDWARD BUCKINGHAM

On December 24, 1619, the Bridewell Court decided that Edward Buckingham would be transported to Virginia. He may have been the Yeardley servant named Buckingham who was killed at Weyanoke (52) during the March 22, 1622, Indian attack (CBE 14).

ANDREW BUCKLER

In 1608 Andrew Buckler accompanied Captain John Smith and some others on a visit to Werowocomoco. Therefore, Buckler would have resided in Jamestown (1) (CJS 1:235; 2:182).

RALPH BUCKRIDGE

Ralph Buckridge, a gentleman from Sutten in Berkshire, arrived in Jamestown (1) on September 5, 1623, aboard the *Ann* and took the oath of supremacy (MCGC 6).

JAMES BUDWORTH

Nathaniel Jeffreys agreed to let James Budworth, one of his indentured servants, serve John Southern for four years commencing on the feast day of St. Thomas the Apostle 1626, that is, December 21, 1626. However, Jeffreys, who like Southern was a resident of Jamestown (1), failed to deliver Budworth on time. Therefore, on January 22, 1629, the General Court decided that Nathaniel Jeffreys was to provide Southern with two years' use of another servant, and that James Budworth was to serve Southern for two years before being freed (MCGC 182).

ANN BUERGEN

Ann Buergen, a young maid, arrived in Jamestown (1) in 1621 aboard the *Marmaduke* (FER 309).

[NO FIRST NAME] BULDHAM

In 1628 the General Court noted that the late Thomas Gregory had owed money to Mr. Buldham on behalf of Captain William Saker (MCGC 174).

***

SIR RICHARD BULKELEY

In April 1621 Sir Richard Bulkeley, who owned some shares of Virginia land, received a patent that authorized him to establish a particular plantation. His land title was confirmed the following month. In June, Sir Richard asked for land in Cape Cod, Massachusetts, but was given land in Virginia in the corporation of Elizabeth City (17, 18). He died sometime prior to February 13, 1622, at which time his land descended to his son and heir, Thomas (VCR 1:448, 462, 468, 484; 3:643).

THOMAS BULKELEY

On February 13, 1622, Virginia Company officials noted that Thomas Bulkeley, the son of Sir Richard Bulkeley, had inherited his shares of Virginia land (VCR 1:597; 3:643).

***

JOSEPH BULL

Joseph Bull came to Virginia on the *Abigail* in 1622 and on January 21, 1625, was living alone at Jordan's Journey (46) in his own home. Bull had an abundant supply of stored food, a few chickens, and some defensive weaponry (CBE 52).

NICHOLAS BULL

On November 20, 1622, officials at Bridewell decided that Nicholas Bull, who was being detained in Newgate Prison, would be transported overseas (CBE 29).

RICHARD BULL

In June 1619 Richard Bull of London, a 28-year-old fishmonger, testified about the losses incurred by the Virginia Company. On July 17, 1622, Virginia Company officials noted that Ralph Bateman had acquired some Virginia land from Bull, who

had obtained it from Henry Rowland and John Budge of London (EAE 9; VCR 2:93).

THOMAS BULL

Thomas Bull died at Jordan's Journey (46) sometime after April 1623 but before February 16, 1624. He may have been a kinsman of Joseph Bull, who also lived there (CBE 37).

[NO FIRST NAME] BULLEN

In 1619 a carpenter named Bullen went to Virginia on the *Garland*, probably on behalf of the Society of Southampton Hundred (44). He may have been Silvester Bullen who in 1624 and 1625 was living on Jamestown Island (1) (FER 137).

SILVESTER (SYLVESTER) BULLEN

On November 30, 1624, Silvester (Sylvester) Bullen testified that John Danes transported timber to Captain John Barwick, overseer of the men whom the Company of Shipwrights sent to Virginia. On January 24, 1625, Silvester was living in the eastern end of Jamestown Island (1) in the household of carpenter Richard Tree and was a 28-year-old servant. In January 1625 Silvester Bullen testified about Robert Marshall's payment to Daniel Lacy for a sow (CBE 56; MCGC 33, 44).

NICHOLAS BULLINGTON

On February 16, 1624, Nicholas Bullington was living on the Maine (3) (CBE 39).

[NO FIRST NAME] BULLMAN

On January 3, 1625, a man named Bullman was described as one of the people who had been living at Shirley Hundred (41) on behalf of the Society of Berkeley Hundred (55) (MCGC 42).

[NO FIRST NAME] BULLOCK (BULLOCKE)

On March 22, 1622, when the Indians attacked Edward Bennett's plantation in Warresqueak (26), someone named Bullock (Bullocke) was killed (VCR 3:571).

HUGH BULLOCK (BULLOCKE)

Hugh Bullock (Bullocke) came to Virginia sometime prior to February 9, 1633, at which time he was ordered to pay the Rev. Francis Bolton his church dues, which were in arrears. In March 1634 Captain Hugh Bullock patented 2,250 acres of land in Elizabeth City (18). He returned to England on the *John and Dorothy*, which continued on to Ireland. In 1636–1638 Bullock identified himself as a 59-year-old resident of All Hallows Barking in London, and also as a Virginia planter. In July 1637 he agreed to give half of his Virginia plantation and his corn and sawmills to his son, William, who resided in London, if he (William) would pay Hugh's wife, Mary, a stipend of £50 a year. On October 22, 1649, when Hugh Bullock made his will, he said that he was "dim sighted." He divided his estate between his son (William) and grandson (Robert). He gave his age as 72 and said that he was a resident of All Hallows Barking (MCGC 202; PB 1 Pt. 1:158; EAE 59; WITH 280-281; York County Record Book 1 [1633-1646]:135).

MARY BULLOCK (BULLOCKE) (MRS. HUGH BULLOCK [BULLOCKE])

On July 8, 1637, Mary Bullock (Bullocke) was identified as the wife of Hugh Bullock, a former resident of All Gallows Barking, London. Mary was to receive an annual payment of £50 from Hugh's son, William, who inherited half of his father's Virginia plantation and his corn and sawmills (York County Record Book 1 [1633-1646]:135).

WILLIAM BULLOCK (BULLOCKE)

William Bullock (Bullocke), the son of Captain Hugh Bullock, came to Virginia on the *Jonathan* sometime prior to February 16, 1624, at which time he was living on one of the plantations west of Gray's Creek (8, 9) within the corporation of James City. On October 10, 1624, he testified that he had seen John Proctor beat his servant, Elias Hinton, with a rake, and he also spoke of the thrashing that Elizabeth Abbott, a maidservant, had received right before her death. On January 25, 1625, William Bullock was living at Mulberry Island (21), where he headed a household that had an ample supply of stored food and some defensive weaponry. On July 8, 1637, Hugh Bullock executed a document whereby his son, William, was to get half of his Virginia plantation and his corn and sawmills. William Bullock, of Barking in Essex, died sometime prior to February 7, 1650, leaving his widow and executrix, Elizabeth, son Robert, and daughter Frances. He appears to have died while returning to Virginia (MCGC 24; CBE 40, 57; DUNN 171, 174; WITH 281; EEAC 10; York County Record Book 1 [1633-1646]:135; DOR 1:47).

***

JAMES BULLOCKE

On July 31, 1622, James Bullock (Bullocke) came to Virginia on the *James* with Lieutenant John Gibbs. He probably was supposed to live at Gibbs's plantation, near Westover (54) (FER 400).

JANE BULLOCK (BULLOCKE)

Jane Bullock (Bullocke) on July 31, 1622, set sail for Virginia with William Rowley on the *James* (FER 400).

RICHARD BULLOCK (BULLOCKE)

In February 1633 Captain Richard Bullock (Bullocke) was a member of the Council of State (HEN 1:202).

WILLIAM BULLOCK (BULLOCKE)

On February 27, 1619, officials at Bridewell decided that William Bullock (Bullocke), a boy who had been brought in on September 26, 1618, would be detained until he could be sent to Virginia (CBE 12; HUME 5, 10).

JAN BULLT

Laborer Jan Bullt, his wife, and four children were among the Walloons and French who indicated their willingness to go to Virginia. In August 1621 the Virginia Company agreed that they could immigrate (CBE 24).

JOHN BUNCHER

On May 23, 1625, John Buncher testified before the General Court about Mr. Giles

Bewmount (a naturalized Frenchman), who had brought some servants to Virginia. Specifically, John mentioned five maidservants who had been allowed to disembark prior to the trans-Atlantic crossing (MCGC 59-60).

***

THOMAS BUNN I

In 1620 Thomas Bunn I, a surgeon, was outfitted by the Virginia Company of London and sent to Virginia as one of the men assigned to Captain Roger Smith. The Company agreed to pay Bunn's ground rent while he was in their employ. On February 16, 1624, Bunn headed a household on the Governor's Land **(3)**, where he was a tenant. He and his wife then shared their home with two servants. On October 10, 1624, Thomas Bunn testified at an inquest held in connection with the death of Elizabeth Abbott, one of John and Alice Proctor's indentured servants at Paces Paines **(9)**. Bunn reportedly tended to the Proctor servants' medical needs, sometimes taking them into his home while providing care. His skills seemingly were in demand throughout the region. In March 1625 he provided treatment to Mr. John Roe, who lay dying in Captain Samuel Mathews' house at Hog Island **(16)**. Roe rewarded Bunn with a legacy. In October 1624 Thomas Bunn was among those who received permission to move from the Governor's Land to more fertile ground on the College tract **(66)** within the corporation of Henrico, where he would have a 5-year lease. However, he apparently decided not to relocate or simply postponed his departure, for on January 30, 1625, he and his wife and 1-year-old son, Thomas II, were still living on the Governor's Land. In the Bunn household were five male servants, two of whom had been there the year before. The household had an ample supply of stored food and defensive weaponry and some swine. In March 1625 Thomas Bunn brought suit against Charles Harmer, a debtor and one of Lady Elizabeth Dale's men. In January 1626 he sued John Smith, an indentured servant, who was compelled to serve an additional month. The disharmony apparently continued, for several months later Smith was forced to apologize to Bunn and others for making some false accusations. In March 1626

Thomas Bunn testified that he had witnessed William Atkins' nuncupative will, and a month later he indicated that he had provided medical treatment to Andrew Waters, Richard Stephens' man. Thomas Bunn died sometime prior to January 28, 1628, at which time his widow, Bridget, tried to collect a debt from Thomas Ironmonger (CBE 39, 57; MCGC 22-25, 46, 48, 50, 89, 98, 101, 108; FER 215; EAE 89; DOR 1:27).

BRIDGET (BRIDGETT) BUNN (MRS. THOMAS BUNN I)

On February 16, 1624, Bridget (Bridgett), the wife of surgeon Thomas Bunn I, was living in Pasbehay on the Governor's Land **(3)**, in a home she shared a home with her husband and two servants. She was still there on January 30, 1625, by which time son Thomas II had been born. On January 28, 1628, Bridget Bunn, then a widow, went to court and had Thomas Ironmonger arrested for debt (CBE 39, 57; MCGC 160).

THOMAS BUNN II

Thomas Bunn II, who on January 30, 1625, was age 1, was the son of surgeon Thomas Bunn and his wife, Bridget (Bridgett). The family lived in Pasbehay, on the Governor's Land **(3)** (CBE 57).

***

THOMAS BURBAGE (BURBIDGE)

Thomas Burbage (Burbidge) came to Virginia sometime prior to June 26, 1628, when he witnessed the will made by John Perry, a London merchant, at Perry's (later, Swann's) Point **(9)**, across the James River from Jamestown **(1)**. In August 1630 Burbage, who was then in England, testified that in May 1630 he had sent Virginia tobacco to England on the *Vintage* and had returned on the ship. He indicated that he was a 22-year-old merchant tailor from St. Antholin, London. Later, when Burbage was deposed on behalf a Mr. Slayne, he said that in December 1629 some tobacco had been loaded aboard the *Gift of God* in Kecoughtan **(17, 18)** for Captain William Peirce and himself. In 1637–1639 Thomas Burbage was ordered to make an account of the late William Hutchinson's estate and then dispose of his belongings. Thomas apparently was a very successful planter, for in 1635 he patented 1,250 acres of land in Accomack (property that formerly belonged to William Ganey of Elizabeth City), and in 1638 he acquired 300 acres in Elizabeth City on the lower side of the James River, bordering the Nansemond River (**20 c**), and 200 acres in Warresqueak (**26**). In 1642 Thomas Burbage sued Edward Stogdell in Accomack's monthly court, claiming that the defendant had seated on his land. In March 1643 a jury agreed, and Stogdell was ordered to leave the premises. However, Burbage was obliged to compensate Stogdell for the buildings he had erected (SH 10; EAE 23, 25, 73; PB 1 Pt. 1:286, 385; Pt. 2:652; AMES 2:81, 213, 260).

NATHANIEL BURCH

On January 8, 1620, Nathaniel Burch, who had been brought in by the constable and detained at Old Bailey, was reprieved so that he could be sent to Virginia (CBE 16).

BARBARA BURCHENS (BURGENS?)

Barbara Burchens (Burgens?), a young, marriageable maid, came to Virginia in September 1621 on the *Warwick*. She was born in Denby and was the daughter of cloth-worker John Burchens and his wife, Margaret. Barbara was recommended to the Virginia Company by Jeane, the wife of John Brewer, a yeoman of the King's Guard. Barbara Burchens may have been the woman identified as Barbara Burgens, who was a casualty of the March 22, 1622, Indian attack on Powle-Brooke (**50**) (FER 309).

***

GEORGE BURCHER (BURTCHER)

On July 3, 1635, when George Burcher (Burtcher) patented 200 acres of land between Hog Island Creek and Lawnes Creek, he used his own headright and those of his wife, Ann (Anne) and his daughter, Jane, and stepson, John Jefferson, who were described as children (PB 1 Pt. 1:203).

ANN (ANNE) BURCHER (MRS. [NO FIRST NAME] JEFFERSON, MRS. GEORGE BURCHER [BURTCHER])

On July 15, 1631, Ann (Anne) Burcher (Burtcher) was among the Virginia planters who exported tobacco from Virginia and asked for relief from customs duties. Her hogsheads bore the mark *GB*. On July 3, 1635, when George Burcher patented some land in what became Surry County, he listed his wife, Ann, as a headright, along with his daughter, Jane, and stepson, John Jefferson (G&M 164-166; PB 1 Pt. 1:203).

JANE BURCHER (BURTCHER)

On July 3, 1635, when George Burcher patented some land in what became Surry County, he used the headright of his daughter, Jane (G&M 164-166; PB 1 Pt. 1:203).

***

JOHN BURCHER

On February 16, 1624, John Burcher was living at Hog Island (**16**) (CBE 41).

WILLIAM BURCHER

On February 16, 1624, William Burcher was living at Hog Island (**16**) (CBE 41).

ROBERT BURDE (BYRD, BIRD)

Robert Burde (Byrd, Bird) on February 5, 1628, was described as a servant of Edward Sharples of Jamestown (**1**) (MCGC 160-161).

JOHN BURDELY

John Burdley went to Virginia in August 1622 on the *Margaret and John* at his own expense, perhaps before he received word of the March 22, 1622, Indian attack (CBE 28; VCR 3:674).

LUKE BURDEN

On July 12, 1620, Virginia Company officials learned that Virginia officials had detained Luke Burden because he had taken goods from the Indians. Captain Ward, who disagreed with that decision, asked that Burden be freed (VCR 1:400).

***

WILLIAM BURDETT (BURCHITT, BURDITT)

William Burdett (Burchitt, Burditt), an ancient planter, came to Virginia on the *Susan* in 1615. In early 1625 he was living on the Eastern Shore, where he was a 25-year-old servant on Captain William Eppes's plantation (**74**). Sometime prior to 1634 he obtained a leasehold on Old Plantation Creek (**73**) and, as time went on, accumulated massive amounts of land by means of the headright system. In January 1634 William Burdett was appointed a commissioner of Accomack's monthly court, and a year later he became a vestryman. In 1639 he was elected a burgess. When he made his will on July 22, 1643, he identified himself as a resident of Northampton County and made bequests to his wife, Alice, and Thomas Burdett, his only son. By early October he was dead (CBE 68; PB 1 Pt. 1:157; Pt. 2:657, 713; AMES 1:8, 39, 153; 2:293-295, 307-308).

FRANCIS (FRANCES) BLORE [BLOAR, BLOWER] SAUNDERS BURDITT (MRS. WILLIAM BURDETT [BURCHITT, BURDITT]) (SEE FRANCIS [FRANCES] BLORE)

***

JOHN BURFITT

In 1621 John Burfitt was identified as part of the company of the *Falcon*, which was headed for Virginia (EAE 11).

WILLIAM BURFOOT

William Burfoot was identified on February 6, 1626 as an indentured servant of John Burrows of Jamestown Island (**1**), who used him as a headright (MCGC 93).

WILLIAM BURFORD

On December 31, 1619, officials at Bridewell decided that William Burford, who was being detained at Newgate, would be sent to Virginia (CBE 15).

ALICE (ALLICE) BURGES

Alice (Allice) Burges, a marriageable young maid whose parents were dead, came to Virginia in 1621 on the *Marmaduke*. She was 28 years old and was born in Linton, in Cambridgeshire. Alice's late father and one of her brothers were husbandmen, and another brother was a soldier. Prior to setting sail for Virginia, Alice lived with Mr. Collins, a silk-weaver at White Chapel Church, and with Mr. Demer, a goldsmith in Trinity Lane. Virginia Company records indicate that Alice Burges could brew, bake, and make malt, and was skillful in "country work"—probably chores such as milking and tending livestock (FER 309).

BARBARA BURGES (BURCHENS?)

On March 22, 1622, when the Indians attacked Powle-Brooke (**50**), Barbara Burges (Burchens?) was killed. She may have been the young, marriageable maid named Barbara Burchens who came to the colony in 1621 (VCR 3:569).

FRANCIS (FRANCES) BURGES

On February 27, 1619, the Bridewell Court decided that Francis (Frances) Burges, a boy, would be sent to Virginia. He was part of a large group of young people being sent to the colony (CBE 12).

THOMAS BURGESS

On February 10, 1629, Thomas Burgess testified that he had not authorized Mr. John Moone to move Mrs. Polentine's servants or any part of her estate. Three days later, when Jamestown merchant Thomas Warnett prepared his will, he made a bequest to Thomas Burgess. A year later Thomas Burgess served as a burgess for Warresqueak (**26**) (Isle of Wight) (MCGC 186; SH 11-12; HEN 1:149).

RICHARD BURKET

Richard Burket, a laborer, arrived in Jamestown (**1**) in 1608 as part of the 1st Supply of new settlers (CJS 1:223; 2:161).

JOHN BURLAND

John Burland, a 26-year-old vintner from Yorkshire, England, came to Virginia in

1619 on the *Bona Nova*. On April 7, 1623, he was described as a Virginia Company servant who had been rented to Captain William Norton, a sometime resident of Jamestown Island (1) who oversaw the glassworks and some of the Company's other industrial activities. On February 16, 1624, John Burland was living on the lower side of the James River at the Treasurer's Plantation (11). In October 1625 he went to court in an attempt to recover the funds he was owed by Captain Norton's estate. John Burland agreed to pay Thomas Smythe in December 1628 for two male servants who were supposed to be delivered to him. In January 1629 the General Court decided that Richard Bennett would give Burland three young male servants as soon as the *London Merchant* arrived; if Bennett failed to comply, Burland was to be compensated. On May 20, 1634, John Burland leased from Michael Ratcliff 25 acres of land in Chiskiack (30, 31), near Uty's (King's) Creek (FER 295, 296; VCR 4:104-106; CBE 40; MCGC 73, 178, 181; PB 1 Pt. 2:525).

PHILLIP BURLEMACH

On September 26, 1626, Phillip Burlemach sent goods from London to Virginia on the *Plantation* (CBE 74).

JOHN BURLEY

On September 28, 1628, John Burley was delivered to the Rev. Lewis Hughs, who was planning to send him to Virginia (CBE 84).

TIMOTHY BURLEY

Timothy Burley died in Elizabeth City (17, 18) sometime after April 1623 but before February 16, 1624 (CBE 45).

EDWARD BURNELL

On September 2, 1631, officials at Bridewell noted that Edward Burnell, a boy who was being detained, would be sent to Virginia by a merchant (CBE 96).

WILLIAM BURNHOUSE

William Burnhouse died in Elizabeth City (17, 18) sometime after April 1623 but before February 16, 1624 (CBE 45).

ANNE (ANN) BURRAS (BURAS) (MRS. JOHN LAYDON [LAYDEN, LEYDON, LAYTON]) (SEE ANNE [ANN] BURRAS LAYDON [LAYDEN, LEYDON, LAYTON])

In 1608 Anne (Ann) Burras (Buras) arrived in Jamestown (1) in the 2nd Supply of new settlers, thereby becoming the first maidservant to reach Virginia and one of the first female colonists. Anne, who was Mrs. Thomas Forrest's maid, wed laborer/carpenter John Laydon (Layden, Leydon, Layton) in the colony's first marriage (CJS 1:184, 238, 242; 2:191-192).

HUGH BURRAGE

In 1619 Hugh Burrage—who was found guilty of stealing a mare in Middlesex and was being detained in Newgate Prison—was reprieved and sentenced to transportation to Virginia (CBE 12).

JAMES BURRE (BURNE)

James Burre (Burne), a laborer, arrived in Jamestown (1) in 1608 as part of the 1st Supply of new settlers (CJS 1:223; 2:161, 163).

[NO FIRST NAME] BURREN

On February 16, 1624, Mr. Burren was living at Martin's Hundred (7) (CBE 42).

ANTHONY BURRIN (BURROWS?)

On February 16, 1624, Anthony Burrin (Burrows?) was living on the lower side of the James River, in one of the plantations west of Gray's Creek (8, 9). Since John Burrows' plantation, Burrows Hill (8), was in that area, Anthony may have been the Anthony Burrows simultaneously attributed to John Burrows' household in Jamestown (1) (CBE 40).

ANN BURROWS (BURROUGHS)

Ann Burrows (Burroughs) came to Virginia at the expense of Adam Thorogood, who on June 24, 1635, listed her as a headright when patenting some land (PB 1 Pt. 1:179).

ANTHONY BURROWS (BURROES)

Anthony Burrows (Burroes) came to Virginia in 1617 on the *George*. By early 1625 he was living in Elizabeth City (**18**), where he was a 44-year-old household head who had an ample supply of stored food and defensive weaponry. In January 1626 Anthony Burrows, who was identified as a gentleman, testified before the General Court in a case involving John Heney, who had illegally boarded a ship in Elizabeth City. In December 1628 Anthony Burrows and William Harris obtained a leasehold on Blunt Point Creek (**22**) (CBE 65; MCGC 85; PB 1 Pt. 1:69; DOR 1:56).

ANTHONY BURROWS (BURROWES)

On February 16, 1624, Anthony Burrows (Burrowes) was living in Jamestown (**1**) and was a member of John Burrows' household (CBE 38).

ANTHONY BURROWS (BURROWES)

On February 16, 1624, Anthony Burrows (Burrowes) was living at West and Shirley Hundred (**41**) (CBE 36).

***

JOHN BURROWS (BURROUGH, BURRAS, BURROWES, BOURROWS)

Ancient planter John Burrows (Burrough, Burras, Burrowes, Bourrows), a tradesman, arrived in Jamestown (**1**) in 1608 and was part of the 2nd Supply of new settlers. Robert Gaile, an English investor, provided Burrows with food, clothing, armor, bedding, copper, and money. Burrows failed to repay his sponsor, and in October 1621 the Virginia Company instructed Virginia officials to investigate, noting that 13 years had passed without Gaile's receiving his moiety. In April 1622 John Burrows was identified as one of several Jamestown Island residents who in 1618 had offered to hire the late Lord Delaware's servants so that they could support themselves.

On February 16, 1624, John Burrows and his wife were living on Jamestown Island, and they were still there on January 24, 1625. The household, which occupied the late Rev. Richard Buck's homestead, consisted of John Burrows, his wife Bridget (Bridgett), 13-year-old Mara Buck (one of the Buck orphans), and seven servants. The Burrows household had an abundant supply of stored food, defensive weaponry, livestock, and a boat. John Burrows, by January 24, 1625, had patented and seated a 150-acre tract he called Burrows Hill or Burrows Mount (**8**), on the lower side of the James River. In 1626 he placed his plantation in the hands of a tenant, John Smith, and sought to patent another 150-acre tract. In August 1626 Burrows was authorized to relocate to the Neck O'Land (**5**) so that he could tend to the orphaned Mara Buck's cattle. It may have been around that time that the Burrows household vacated the Rev. Richard Buck's homestead on Jamestown Island, but Burrows kept some servants there to care for the large herd of livestock that was left behind. General Court minutes suggest that Mara Buck, a young heiress who had a serious learning disability or was mentally impaired, was a sought-after marriage partner and that the Rev. David Sandys was a persistent suitor.

During the mid-1620s John Burrows, who was termed a gentleman, made several appearances before the General Court. In June 1624 he testified at the inquest held in connection with the death of John and Alice Proctor's maidservant at Paces Paines (**9**). Then, in March 1625 he served on a coroner's jury that investigated a young servant's suicide at Hugh Crowder's (Crowther's) plantation (**12**). Finally, in April 1625 he was summoned to court and ordered to pay Mr. Emmerson for the services of Mr. Patrick Copeland's apprentice, Elias Gaile, who was then living in his household. Late in 1628 John Burrows died as the result of a stab wound he received during an altercation with a servant boy at Blunt Point (**22**). His widow, Bridget, married William Davis sometime prior to March 27, 1643, and then, after Davis's death, wed John Bromfield. After Bridget's death in 1655, her widower, John Bromfield, sued Elizabeth Buck Crump in an attempt to recover Bridget's presumed legal interest in the late Rev. Richard Buck's property in the Neck O'Land. It was then determined that Bridget and John Burrows had only a life-interest in the Buck property (CJS 1:241; 2:191; VCR 1:535-536; 4:551, 555; CBE 38, 56; C 24/490; MCGC 15, 22, 52-53, 89, 109, 183-184; HEN 1:405; PB 4:55 [81]; DOR 1:33, 38, 426-429).

BRIDGET (BRIDGETT) BURROWS (BURROUGH, BURRAS, BURROWES, BOURROWS) (MRS. JOHN BURROWS [BURROUGH, BURRAS, BURROWES, BOURROWS], MRS. WILLIAM DAVIS, MRS. JOHN BROMFIELD)

Bridget (Bridgett), who became the wife of ancient planter and tradesman John Burrows (Burrough, Burras, Burrowes, Bourrows), probably married him sometime prior to February 16, 1624, when Mr. and Mrs. John Burrows were living in Jamestown (1). In June 1624 Bridget Burrows testified before the General Court that Mara Buck was "dull" and unable to learn to read. She also claimed that the Rev. David Sandys was trying to lure Mara into marriage. On January 24, 1625, Bridget and John Burrows, 13-year-old Mara Buck, and seven servants, were living together in Jamestown. Around 1626 they moved to the Neck O'Land (5), where the Rev. Richard Buck's orphans had inherited property. After John Burrows' sudden death in 1628, Bridget wed William Davis, who died sometime prior to March 1643. Bridget went to court in 1642, after Benomi and Gercian Buck's deaths, in an attempt to acquire a legal interest in the Rev. Richard Buck's estate. She married John Bromfield, who in 1654—after Bridget's death—sued Elizabeth Buck Crump in a vain attempt to recover Bridget's presumed legal interest in the Buck property in the Neck O'Land. It was then determined that Bridget had had only a life interest in the Buck estate. If the Rev. Buck bequeathed his land to his male heirs, leaving life-rights to his daughters, Bridget may have been one of the decedent's heirs (CBE 38, 56; MCGC 15; PB 4:55; HEN 1:405; DOR 1: 426-429).

***

ROBERT BURROWS

On September 19, 1625, Robert Burrows, one of Captain Richard Page's servants, was delivered to Abraham Peirsey in exchange for two men that Page failed to deliver to Peirsey (MCGC 71, 77).

WILLIAM BURROWS (BURROUGHS)

William Burrows (Burroughs) came to Virginia at the expense of Adam Thorogood, who on June 24, 1635, listed him as a headright when patenting some land (PB 1 Pt. 1:179).

JOHN BURSUCK

On February 20, 1626, John Bursuck testified before the General Court about some cargo on the *Deal* that was lost when the vessel ran aground (MCGC 95).

ANTHONY BURT

Anthony Burt came to Virginia on the *Hopewell* in 1622. In early 1625 he was living on the Virginia Company's land in Elizabeth City (17) and was an 18-year-old servant in William Tiler's (Tyler's) household (HOT 259).

ROBERT BURT (BURTE)

Robert Burt (Burte), an indentured servant, was brought to Virginia on the *Edwin* in 1617 at the expense of Richard Kingsmill (MCGC 44).

WILLIAM BURT (BURTT)

William Burt (Burtt) came to Virginia on the *Bonny Bess* in 1623 and on February 16, 1624, was living on the Maine (3), just west of Jamestown Island. However, by February 4, 1625, he had moved to Hog Island (16), where he was a servant in John Uty's household. When Uty patented some land on November 3, 1624, he used William Burt as a headright (CBE 39, 61; PB 1 Pt. 1:14).

GEORGE BURTON

George Burton came to Virginia as part of the 2nd Supply of new settlers and arrived in Jamestown (1) in 1608. Captain John Smith described him as a gentleman and soldier. When Smith went to Pamunkey in late 1608, Burton accompanied him. In 1620 George Burton was identified as a Virginia Company investor (CJS 1:241, 244; 2:190, 193, 274).

JOHN BURTON

On March 22, 1622, when the Indians attacked Edward Bennett's plantation in Warresqueak (26), John Burton was killed (VCR 3:571).

RICHARD BURTON

Richard Burton came to Virginia on the *Swann* in 1624. In early 1625 he was living in Elizabeth City (18), where he was a 28-year-old servant in Francis Chamberlin's household (CBE 66).

JANE BURTT

On February 16, 1624, Jane Burtt was living in urban Jamestown (1), where she was a servant in Governor Francis Wyatt's household (CBE 38).

EDWARD BUSBY (BUSBEE)

On February 26, 1620, Edward Busby (Busbee), who was being detained at Newgate Prison, was deemed by the chief justice of Bridewell Court as suitable for transportation to Virginia. On February 16, 1624, Edward was living on the Maine, otherwise known as the Governor's Land (3) (CBE 19, 39).

PETER BUSBY (BUSBEY)

On December 5, 1625, Peter Busby (Busbey) testified before the General Court about the accidental destruction of Mr. Peirce's shallop, which ran aground while loaded with passengers and tobacco. Mr. Proctor of Paces Paines (9) was ordered to pay for the shallop, which suggests that Busby was one of his servants (MCGC 78).

***

[NO FIRST NAME] BUSH

John Bush's brother, whose given name is unknown, was married to Susan, who came to Virginia on the *George* in 1617. The couple and John and Elizabeth Bush lived on the east side of the Hampton River in an area the Virginia Company chose for its own use (17). Mrs. Susan Bush, who was pregnant, was one of the settlers Governor George Yeardley evicted shortly after his April 1619 arrival in the colony. By the time she was turned out of her home, she had been widowed. Afterward she lived on the west side of the Hampton River, in Elizabeth City (18) (DOR 1:55, 454-455; MEY 147; VCR 1:229; 2:44).

SUSAN BUSH
(MRS. [NO FIRST NAME] BUSH)

Susan Bush, who married John Bush's brother, came to Virginia on the *George* in 1617. She and her husband, whose given name is unknown, lived on the east side of the Hampton River in an area the Virginia Company chose for its own use (17). Mrs. Susan Bush, who was pregnant and widowed, was one of the settlers Governor George Yeardley evicted shortly after his April 1619 arrival in the colony. On January 10, 1625, Susan Bush was described as a widow and the guardian of young Sara Spence, the orphan of the late Ensign William Spence and his wife. The General Court ordered Mrs. Bush, as Sara's guardian, to have Ensign Spence's acreage in Archer's Hope (6) surveyed, for it was in the hands of a tenant. In January 1625 Mrs. Susan Bush was living in Elizabeth City (18), where she was described as a 20-year-old household head. Susan's household included 4-year-old Sara Spence and several servants, one of whom John Bush had brought to Virginia and used as a headright. The Rev. George Keith and Mrs. Susan Bush were ordered to appear before the General Court on May 16, 1625, and on November 21, 1625, Susan placed the Spence land in the hands of Thomas Farley, a tenant. By April 3, 1627, Mrs. Susan Bush may have been dead, for the Rev. George Keith was then responsible for the Spence estate (CBE 64; MCGC 27, 42, 57, 76, 147; DOR 1:55, 64, 454-455; MEY 147; VCR 1:229; 2:44).

JOHN BUSH

John Bush came to Virginia in 1618 on the *Neptune*, the ship that brought Lord Delaware to the colony. His wife, Elizabeth I, and daughters, Mary and Elizabeth II, arrived on the *Gift* in 1619. The Bush household resided in Elizabeth City (17) on the east side of the Hampton River. Because Virginia Company officials decided to take that area for the Company's use, incoming

Governor George Yeardley had to evict the settlers living there. John and Elizabeth Bush and their daughters were turned out of the two houses he had built there, and Mrs. Bush was so traumatized that she had a miscarriage. On February 16, 1624, John Bush, his wife, and their two children were still living in Elizabeth City (**18**) but had moved to the west side of the Hampton River. On November 30, 1624, he and the Rev. George Keith were named administrators of an orphan's estate. On December 1, 1624, John Bush patented 300 acres of land in Elizabeth City on the basis of headrights, including those of two men he had transported to the colony in 1621. John Bush made his will on December 9, 1624, and died sometime prior to early January 1625. When a list of patented land was sent back to England in May 1625, he was credited with 300 acres in Elizabeth City, acreage that had been planted. The decedent's will was presented to the General Court on January 13, 1627 (VCR 2:44; 4:558; CBE 44, 67; PB 1 Pt. 1:31-32; MCGC 34, 137; DOR 1:64, 454-455).

ELIZABETH BUSH I
(MRS. JOHN BUSH)

Elizabeth I, John Bush's wife, came to Virginia on the *Gift* in 1619 with her daughters, Mary and Elizabeth II. The Bush household initially lived on the east side of the Hampton River in Elizabeth City (**17**), within an area the Virginia Company purportedly had reserved for its own use. When Governor George Yeardley evicted the family, Mrs. Elizabeth Bush was so upset that she had a miscarriage. On February 16, 1624, the Bush family was living in Kecoughtan (**18**) on some land that John patented a few months later (VCR 2:44; PB 1 Pt. 1:31; CBE 44; DOR 1:454-455).

ELIZABETH BUSH II

Elizabeth II, John Bush's daughter, came to Virginia with her mother, Elizabeth I, and her sister, Mary, on the *Gift* in 1619 and lived on the east side of the Hampton River in Elizabeth City (**17**). On December 1, 1624, John Bush listed himself and his family members as headrights when patenting some land in the western part of Elizabeth City (**18**) (PB 1 Pt. 1:31; DOR 1:454-455).

MARY BUSH

John Bush's daughter, Mary, came to Virginia with her mother, Elizabeth I, and her sister, Elizabeth II, on the *Gift* in 1619 and lived on the east side of the Hampton River in Elizabeth City (**17**). On December 1, 1624, John Bush listed himself and his family members as headrights when patenting some land in Elizabeth City (**18**) on the west side of the Hampton River (PB 1 Pt. 1:31).

***

HENRY BUSHEL

On March 22, 1622, when the Indians attacked Captain Smith's plantation at Bermuda Hundred (**39**), Henry Bushel was killed (VCR 3:566).

NICHOLAS BUSHELL

Nicholas Bushell died between April 1623 and February 16, 1624, at one of the plantations on the lower side of the James River, within the corporation of James City (**8-15**) (CBE 41).

MABEL BUSHER

When the Rev. Willis Hely (Heeley, Heyley, Heley), the rector of Mulberry Island Parish, patented some land on December 8, 1635, he used Mabel Busher as a headright (PB 1 Pt. 1:325).

DANIEL BUTCHER

In June 1635 Daniel Butcher was identified as one of Captain John Prynn's mariners (EAE 53-54).

FRANCIS BUTCHER

On February 16, 1624, Francis Butcher was living on the Maine (**3**) (CBE 39).

JOHN BUTCHER

According to a letter Richard Frethorne wrote from Martin's Hundred (**7**) between late March 1623 and April 1623, John Butcher arrived at the plantation at Christmas (that is, early January 1623) and died at the house of Mr. William Harwood, the settlement's leader (VCR 4:60).

EDWARD BUTLER

On February 16, 1624, Edward Butler was living at Chaplin's Choice (**56**) (CBE 37).

FRANCIS BUTLER

Francis Butler came to Virginia on the *Francis Bonaventure*. On January 30, 1625, he was living on the Governor's Land (**3**) and was one of the governor's servants. Francis was then age 18 (CBE 57).

JOHN BUTLER

On December 31, 1619, it was decided that John Butler, who was being detained at Old Bailey, would be sent to Virginia. He was killed in the March 22, 1622, Indian attack on Martin's Hundred (**7**) (CBE 15; VCR 3:570).

NATHANIEL BUTLER

Captain Nathaniel Butler, who served as Bermuda's governor from 1619 to 1622, visited Virginia in winter 1622 and stayed for approximately three months. He later wrote a scathing account of life in the colony, which he called the "Unmasking of Virginia." A number of burgesses and ancient planters responded by rebutting Butler's allegations (LEF 1:149, 706; CO 1/3 ff 36-37; VCR 2:408; 4:130-151; MCGC 24).

THOMAS BUTLER

On December 4, 1621, Virginia Company officials noted that according to Company records, Thomas Butler lacked one share of the Virginia land to which he was entitled (VCR 1:570).

***

THOMAS BUTLER

On July 11, 1635, the Rev. Thomas Butler, the rector of Denbigh Parish, patented 1,000 acres of land in Warresqueak (**26**). Among those he used as headrights was his wife, Mary (Marie) Butler, the widow of John Brewer. When the Rev. Butler made his will on November 20, 1636, he mentioned several residents of Kecoughtan (**18**), two of whom he appointed overseers. On July 25, 1637, when the decedent's will

was proved in England, his widow, Mary, was named executrix (PB 1 Pt. 1:222, 278; WITH 49; EEAC 11).

MARY (MARIE) BREWER BUTLER (MRS. THOMAS BUTLER, MRS. JOHN BREWER)

When the Rev. Thomas Butler, the rector of Denbigh Parish, patented 1,000 acres of land in Warresqueak (**26**) on July 11, 1635, he used as a headright his wife Mary (Marie) Butler, whom he described as the widow of John Brewer. On November 20, 1636, when the Rev. Butler made his will, he mentioned several residents of Kecoughtan (**18**). When the decedent's will was proved in England on July 25, 1637, his widow, Mary, was named executrix (PB 1 Pt. 1:222; WITH 49; EEAC 11).

***

JOHN BUTTERFIELD

John Butterfield came to Virginia prior to February 16, 1624, at which time he was living on the Eastern Shore (**72-78**). On February 4, 1625, he was identified as a 23-year-old servant who lived at Captain Roger Smith's plantation (**10**). John Butterfield was then a household head and had an ample supply of stored food and some defensive weaponry. Sometime prior to October 12, 1626, John Butterfield moved to Pasbehay (**3**), where he had an unpleasant encounter with his neighbor, Mrs. Margaret Jones, who attacked him while he was working in his own garden. On January 12, 1627, John was identified as a Virginia Company tenant who had been assigned to Captain Samuel Mathews (CBE 46, 59; MCGC 119, 136; DOR 1:39).

RICHARD BUTTERY

In May or June 1622, Richard Buttery (Buttry), a servant and tailor, went to Virginia on the *Furtherance*, which departed from the Isle of Wight in England. Richard died in Virginia sometime after April 1623 but before February 16, 1624, at one of the plantations on the lower side of the James River (**8-15**), within the corporation of James City (VCR 3:618-619, 674; CBE 41).

THOMAS BUTTON

On February 16, 1624, Thomas Button was living on the lower side of the James River, within the corporation of James City (**8-15**) (CBE 40).

WILLIAM BUTTON

On February 20, 1633, Governor John Harvey informed his superiors that Captain William Button would be able to report on current conditions in Virginia. In July 1634 Button presented a petition on behalf of the colony's planters, asking that they be entitled to the same privileges they had before their patents were withdrawn. Button asked for some land on both sides of the Appomattox River. On July 22, 1634, the Privy Council commended Captain William Button for the services he had performed and awarded him property on the Appomattox. A patent issued on December 21, 1636, for some land on the upper side of the Appomattox River, a considerable distance inland from Bermuda Hundred (**39**), makes reference to Captain Button's acreage (CBE 106, 117-118; PB 1 Pt. 2:590).

THOMAS BUWEN

Thomas Buwen died in Elizabeth City (**17, 18**) sometime after April 1623 but before February 16, 1624 (CBE 45).

MARGARET BYARD (BIARD)

Margaret Byard (Biard) reportedly died aboard the *Furtherance* around August 3, 1622, while on her way to Virginia. Nathaniel Basse took charge of her goods, which William Newman inventoried. Margaret may have been headed for Nathaniel Basses's plantation, Basses Choice (**27**) (MCGC 141).

ELIZABETH BYGRAVE

Elizabeth Bygrave came to Virginia on the *Warwick* and on February 16, 1624, was living at Martin's Hundred (**7**). She was still there on February 4, 1625, at which time she was described as a 12-year-old servant in the home of William Harwood, the settlement's leader (CBE 42, 61).

WILLIAM BYKAR (BIKAR)

On March 22, 1622, when the Indians attacked Martin's Hundred (**7**), William Bykar (Bikar) was killed (VCR 3:568).

HENRY BYSANT

On January 12, 1627, Henry Bysant, boatswain of the *Marmaduke*, testified before the General Court. He stated that on the way to Virginia, William Capps's young male servant went ashore from time to time but always came back to the ship, and that surgeon Richard Hewes guaranteed his return (MCGC 134).

C

WILLIAM CADWELL

On January 11, 1627, William Cadwell appeared before the General Court in Jamestown (**1**). He substantiated Robert Dennys' claim that the will Edward Pritchard made aboard the *Marmaduke* was authentic (MCGC 133).

DANIEL CAGE

In 1615 Daniel Cage, a gentleman, accompanied Captain John Smith on a voyage to New England and later coauthored an account of that trip. On August 20, 1630, Daniel Cage was in Elizabeth City (**18**), where he witnessed Edward Waters' will. He may have been related to Philip Cage, who also served as one of Waters' witnesses (CJS 1:351, 356; 2:428, 431; SH 13).

EDWARD CAGE (CADGE)

Edward Cage (Cadge), a Virginia Company investor, came to the colony on the *Marmaduke* sometime prior to March 12, 1624, when he testified before the General Court in a case involving one of Lieutenant James Harrison's servants. On January 24, 1625, Edward was residing in urban Jamestown (**1**) in a household he and his partner, Nathaniel Jefferys (Jeffries, Jeffreys), jointly headed. They shared a dwelling and were well supplied with stored food and defensive weaponry. On April 25, 1625, Edward Cage was ordered to inventory the estate of the late John Pountis of Jamestown, and on September 12, 1625, he was compensated by the Rev. Jonas Stogden of Elizabeth City (17). Cage was in Elizabeth City on September 28, 1628, and witnessed Dictoris Christmas transfer his lease to Lyonell Roulston. In March 1629 Edward Cage served on a jury, and on November 7, 1634, he was among those certifying a list of goods that the newly arrived but deceased Thomas Lee had brought to Virginia. In 1638 he was described as one of Virginia's chief merchants and planters (CJS 2:275; MCGC 13, 55, 70, 190; CBE 55, 208; PB 1 Pt. 1:134; SR 7292; DOR 1:32).

PHILIP CAGE

On August 20, 1630, Philip Cage witnessed Edward Waters' will in Elizabeth City (18). As Daniel Cage also served as one of Waters' witnesses, he and Philip may have been related (SH 13).

***

MR. CALCKER (CALCAR)

On February 16, 1624, Mr. Calcker (Calcar), his wife, and their child were living in urban Jamestown (1) in the household of Captain William Holmes. On March 23, 1624, the General Court was informed that Mr. Calcker had sold his bed, bedclothes, and pewter to John Chew, a Jamestown merchant (CBE 38; MCGC 13).

MRS. CALCKER (CALCAR)

On February 16, 1624, Mrs. Calcker (Calker), her husband, and their child were living in urban Jamestown (1) in the household of Captain William Holmes (CBE 38).

[NO FIRST NAME] CALCKER (CALCAR)

On February 16, 1624, Mr. and Mrs. Calcker (Calcar) and their child were living in Captain William Holmes's household in urban Jamestown (1) (CBE 38).

***

THOMAS CALDER

Thomas Calder, a shoemaker from Buckinghamshire, arrived in Jamestown (1) in 1619 on the *Bona Nova*. By early 1625 he was living in Elizabeth City (17) on the Virginia Company's land. He was described as a 24-year-old servant in the household of William Barry and probably was a Company servant (FER 295; CBE 68).

EDWARD CALEY

On August 26, 1626, the court of Bridewell decided that Edward Caley, a vagrant, would be sent to Virginia (CBE 73).

CHARLES CALTHROP

On February 16, 1624, Charles Calthrop was living in Elizabeth City (17) (CBE 43).

CHRISTOPHER CALTHROP (COLETHORPE)

Christopher Calthrop (Colethorpe), a young gentleman, came to Virginia on the *Furtherance* in 1622. On March 28, 1623, Virginia Company officials were informed that Treasurer George Sandys had offered him accommodations but that he declined because of Sandys' frequent absences. Sandys indicated that Calthrop had gone to Kecoughtan to live with Captain Isaac Whittaker and that he tended to squander his liquor by serving it to his inferiors. On February 16, 1624, he was still in the Whittaker home in Elizabeth City (17). In early 1625, when a muster was made of Elizabeth City's inhabitants, Christopher Calthrop was living in the home of Lieutenant Thomas Purfoy, on the west side of the Hampton River (18), and was described as 18 years old. However, as he was baptized in April 1605, he probably was at least age 20. On September 20, 1628, Christopher obtained a leasehold for some land near Purfoy's and the fields called Fort Henry and was still in possession of the property in June 1635. On July 13, 1635, Christopher Calthrop received a patent for 500 acres in the New Poquoson (19) on the basis of the headright system, an indication that he was a successful planter. In 1646 Captain Christopher Calthrop was among those fined for failing to render accounts as guardians. By 1661 he had left the New Poquoson area and gone to Carolina. He died in 1662 and was survived by his widow, Ann (CBE 43, 64; VCR 4:67-68; PB 1 Pt. 1:88-89, 227, 309; DOR 1:456-458).

STEPHEN CALTHROP
(GALTHORP, HALTHROP)

According to George Percy, Stephen Calthrop (Galthorp, Halthrop) died in Jamestown (1) on August 15, 1607. Captain John Smith later said that Edward Maria Wingfield claimed that Calthrop had led a mutiny (CJS 1:20; 2:139).

JAMES CALVER

On January 3, 1625, Bryan Caught informed the General Court that James Calver and John Gill said that they had given Captain Hamor's tobacco note to "Toby," probably Tobias Felgate (MCGC 40).

***

GEORGE CALVERT I
(LORD BALTIMORE I)

Sir George Calvert (I), the first Lord Baltimore and a graduate of Oxford University, was a member of the Virginia Company. He was knighted in September 1617. He was admitted to the New England Company in 1622 and received a grant to Newfoundland on April 7, 1623, a little over a year and a half after the death of his first wife, Anne Mynne. Calvert became a Roman Catholic and was elevated to the Irish peerage. In 1622 he married his second wife, Joane, and some of his children joined him in Newfoundland in 1628. However, Lord Baltimore, his wife, and some of his colonists found the climate severe and inhospitable and decided to leave. He sent word to England, requesting some Virginia land with the same privileges he enjoyed in Newfoundland. Sir George, Lady Joane, their family, and 40 members of their household left Newfoundland in August 1629 and arrived in Virginia in October. Sir George's refusal to take the oaths of allegiance and supremacy and his Catholic religion sparked controversy. Calvert and his group stopped off in Jamestown (1) while on the way to England. He continued on to England in response to a summons by the king, and sent a letter to the Privy Council asking that Virginia's governor, Sir John Harvey, be ordered to assist his wife in col-

lecting debts, securing safe passage to England, and disposing of her servants, if she saw fit. It is likely that she was a guest in Governor Harvey's home in urban Jamestown (1). In 1632 Sir George Calvert received a charter for what became Maryland. However, he died in April 1632, leaving as his primary heir, Cecil, Lord Baltimore (POR 148; CELL 55, 287, 293, 294-295, 299; CBE 32, 88; SR 626, 3970; NEI 98; SH 19; MCGC 481; EEAC 11; CO 1/5 ff 101-102; 1/9 f 135; DOR 1:468-469).

ANNE MYNNE CALVERT
(MRS. GEORGE CALVERT,
LADY BALTIMORE I)

On November 22, 1604, George Calvert I, who was knighted in 1617, married Anne Mynne, his first wife. She died on August 8, 1621, having produced at least a dozen children (DOR 1:468-469).

JOANE CALVERT
(MRS. GEORGE CALVERT,
LADY BALTIMORE I)

Joane, who married the widowed Sir George Calvert, Lord Baltimore, in 1622, accompanied him and some of his children to Newfoundland in the summer of 1628. She found the winter weather harsh and disagreeable, as did many of the other colonists. Lord and Lady Baltimore and her servants, and some of his children and colonists, left Newfoundland in August 1629. They arrived in Jamestown (1) in October and probably were guests in Governor John Harvey's home. Sir George Calvert went on to England, and his wife and the rest of the group followed a few months later on the *St. Claude*, which King Charles I had loaned to him for 6 months. The *St. Claude* was wrecked off the English coast and all aboard were lost (DOR 1:469; CELL 55, 276, 287).

CECIL (CECILIUS, CECILL)
CALVERT
(LORD BALTIMORE)

Cecil (Cecilius, Cecill) Calvert, the second Lord Baltimore, set out to plant a colony in Maryland. He arrived at Old Point Comfort on February 24, 1634. He expressed his appreciation to Virginia governor John Harvey for assisting him in the eviction of

William Claiborne from Kent Island and for being sympathetic to his colony's interests. Harvey's opponents, however, contended that Lord Baltimore was being given part of Virginia's land and ultimately ousted him from office. Calvert proved loyal, for in December 1635 he asked English authorities to reinstate then-ousted Harvey as governor. He died in England in 1675 (NEI 98; CBE 119; SAIN 1:190, 217; CELL 294; DOR 1: 469-470).

GEORGE CALVERT II

George Calvert II, the son of the first Lord Baltimore and his first wife, Anne, drowned during a heavy storm in Maryland in 1634. His will, prepared on July 10, 1634, was proved on January 19, 1635 (SR 3970; CELL 294; DOR 1:469).

LEONARD CALVERT

Leonard Calvert, Sir George Calvert's second oldest son, went to Newfoundland but returned to England with his father in August 1628. He and his elder brother, George II, set out from England in October 1633 and reached Maryland, the Baltimore family's new proprietary territory, in March 1634. They established their settlement at what they called St. Mary's City. On December 8, 1634, Leonard Calvert was identified in Virginia's General Court records as Maryland's incumbent governor (actually, lieutenant-general) when he summoned William Claiborne to appear before him. Leonard was George Calvert I's son and George Calvert II's brother and successor as Maryland's governor, taking office in 1637. He came to Virginia a few months after an Indian attack that occurred on April 18, 1644 and, according to Secretary of the Colony Richard Kemp, assisted the colonists by taking his ship into the Chickahominy River and attacking the Chickahominy Indians in their homeland (MCGC 481; CELL 294; DOR 1:470-471; SR 7377).

***

NICHOLAS CAME (CAMME, CAMBE)

On September 10, 1620, Nicholas Came (Camme, Cambe), a gentleman, set sail from Bristol on the *Supply* and was one of the new colonists William Tracy brought to

Berkeley Hundred (**55**). Came had agreed to serve the Society of Berkeley Hundred for three years in exchange for 50 acres of land. Nicholas Came arrived at Berkeley Hundred on January 29, 1621. He quickly became dissatisfied and returned to England in June 1621 aboard the same ship that had brought him to the colony. In March 1621 George Thorpe of Berkeley Hundred noted that Came had shipped some freight from Virginia with Mr. Felgate (CBE 21; VCR 3:396, 426, 435-436).

JOHN CAMINGE (CANING)

On February 16, 1624, John Caminge (Caning) was living at Jordan's Journey (**46**) (CBE 36).

WILLIAM CAMPE

On February 12, 1620, William Campe was brought in from Cheapside and detained at Bridewell so that he could be sent to Virginia (CBE 18).

JEAN CAMPION

Wool carder Jean Campion, his wife, and their four children were among the Walloons and French who indicated their willingness to go to Virginia. In August 1621 the Virginia Company agreed that they could immigrate (CBE 24).

PHILIPPE CAMPION

Draper Philippe Campion and his wife and child were among the Walloons and French who indicated their willingness to go to Virginia. In August 1621 the Virginia Company agreed that they could immigrate (CBE 24).

RICHARD CAMPION

Richard Campion, a 22-year-old husbandman from Leicestershire, England, arrived in Jamestown in 1619 aboard the *Bona Nova* and probably was a Virginia Company servant or tenant. His transportation costs were paid by the Ferrars, important Virginia Company investors. On March 22, 1622, when the Indians attacked one of the settlements on the upper side of the James River, opposite Flowerdew Hundred (**53**), Richard Campion was killed (FER 295; VCR 3:568).

ROBERT CAMPION

Robert Campion, a 25-year-old husband-man from Leicestershire, England, arrived in Jamestown (1) in 1619 aboard the *Bona Nova* and probably was a Virginia Company servant or tenant. His transportation costs were paid by the Ferrars, major investors in the Company. On January 23, 1625, Robert Campion was living at the College (66) in the corporation of Henrico and was the sole occupant of a dwelling. He was adequately supplied with stored food and defensive weaponry (FER 295, 296; CBE 53; DOR 1:8).

WILLIAM CAMPION

On August 23, 1631, it was decided that William Campion, a boy from Langborne who was being detained at Bridewell, was to be sent to Virginia (HUME 36).

PATRICK CANADA

On February 10 and March 2, 1629, Richard Cocke acted as the attorney of mariner Patrick Canada when trying to recover some funds from the Virginia estate of the late Thomas Hunter (MCGC 186).

GEORGE CANE

George Cane died at Warresqueak (26) sometime after April 1623 but before February 16, 1624 (CBE 42).

MAUDELIN (MANDELIN) CANE (CAVE) (MRS. EDWARD SPARSHOTT) (SEE MAUDELIN [MANDELIN] CANE [CAVE] SPARSHOTT)

On November 20, 1635, Edward Sparshott identified the former Maudelin (Mandelin) Cane (Cave) as his wife and used her as a headright (PB 1 Pt. 1:314).

[NO FIRST NAME] CANN

On February 16, 1624, Mr. Cann's boy was living on the Eastern Shore (72-78). He probably was the son or servant of Mr. Delpheus Cann, a merchant in Jamestown (1) (CBE 46).

DELPHEUS CANN

On February 16, 1624, Mr. Delpheus Cann was living in urban Jamestown (1). On March 12, 1625, he was identified as a merchant when he served on the jury investigating John Verone's death. On May 30, 1625, Mr. Cann was mentioned in litigation that involved Robert Bennett and Thomas Edwards (CBE 38; MCGC 53, 64).

PHOEBUS CANNER (CANER)

In April 1623 Phoebus Canner (Caner), a Virginia colonist, sent word to Lawrence Lay, an English merchant, that living conditions were harsh and that he was eager to return home. He said that people had suffered from famine, fire, and the sword, presumably a reference to the 1622 Indian attack and the hardships of its aftermath (VCR 4:235).

RALPH CANNION

On February 5, 1628, Ralph Cannion was identified as a servant of Edward Sharples of Jamestown (1) (MCGC 160-161).

JOHN CANNON (CANON)

John Cannon (Canon) came to Virginia in 1622 on the *Abigail*. On January 22, 1625, he was living at West and Shirley Hundred (41), where he was one of Christopher Woodward's servants. John was then 20 years old (CBE 52).

RALPH (RAPHE) CANNON (CANNION?)

According to records maintained by the Drapers Company in London, Ralph (Raphe) Cannon, a point-maker, settled in Virginia in 1620. He may have been the Ralph Cannion who in 1628 was identified as Edward Sharples' servant (SR 879).

HENRY CANTRELL

In 1631 Henry Cantrell, a Virginia planter, sent some tobacco to his brother, William, then in England. Henry and his shipment of tobacco crossed the Atlantic on the *Unicorn* (CBE 108; EAE 41).

WILLIAM CANTRELL (CANTRILL)

William Cantrell (Cantrill), a gentleman and Virginia Company investor, came to Virginia in 1608 in the 1st Supply of new Jamestown (1) settlers. Later in the year he accompanied Captain John Smith on a voyage of discovery within the Chesapeake Bay. In 1611 Cantrell was identified as co-author of an account that Smith included in his writings (CJS 1:222, 224; 2:161, 163, 258, 275).

JOHN CANTWELL

Sometime after April 1623 but before February 16, 1624, John Cantwell died at one of the settlements on the lower side of the James River, within the corporation of James City (8-15) (CBE 41).

JOHN CAPPER

On September 17, 1607, John Capper, one of the first Jamestown (1) colonists, supported Mr. Croft's claim that Edward Maria Wingfield had given him a copper kettle and that Croft had not acquired it through wrongdoing (HAI 193).

***

WILLIAM CAPPS
(CAPS, CAPPE, CAPP)

William Capps (Caps, Cappe, Capp), an ancient planter, came to Virginia in the 3rd Supply in the fleet that brought Sir Thomas Gates and Sir George Somers. It is unclear whether he was marooned with them in Bermuda and arrived in the colony in 1610 or was aboard one of the vessels that reached Virginia in 1609. Capps said that he could have held office while Sir Thomas Gates and Sir Thomas Dale were in charge but had declined. He was fiercely critical of Governor George Yeardley and philosophically seems to have been aligned with Captain Nathaniel Butler, one of the Virginia government's harshest critics. William Capps resided in Elizabeth City (17), on the east side of the Hampton River, throughout his first decade in the colony. In July 1619 when Virginia's assembly first met, William Capps represented the settlers at Kecoughtan. However, on February 20, 1619 (1620, New Style), he was awarded some land in

Archer's Hope (6), acreage that he seemingly failed to seat. During 1621 he made an agreement with Thomas Jones of the *Falcon*, who took a load of sassafras to London. In 1621 and 1622 Capps sent letters to the Virginia Company demanding satisfaction for the Elizabeth City land that Governor Yeardley seized on behalf of the Company, acreage that he previously had cleared and seated. Although the matter was referred to incumbent Governor Francis Wyatt, the Virginia Company awarded Capps free transportation for five men, in recognition of his service to the colony and his risking his life by fighting against the Indians.

In 1622 William Capps was among those who asked the king to pay a reasonable price for Virginia tobacco. He also was invested in the colonization of New England. During 1622 and 1623 Capps sent several letters to Virginia Company officials in which he offered to build guesthouses for newly arrived immigrants in Elizabeth City and Jamestown (1) if he was given two oxen and a horse. He also asked for men who could be used to fight the Indians. He claimed that Captain John Martin's plantation (59) was a refuge for debtors and renegades, and that Sir William Nuce (of Kecoughtan) had failed to deliver the five male servants to whom Capps was entitled. In one letter William Capps said that he had toiled for seven years breeding swine for the colony, and that Captain Nuce and his men had devoured them. Although he continued to grumble about public policies, he insisted that Virginia planters who complained about living conditions were exaggerating and that an honest man could raise much more tobacco than had been reported by Richard Brewster. As evidence of the colony's potential for agricultural productivity, he said that he had sold his excess corn to Captain Whittaker and had sent another shipment of sassafras to England.

On February 16, 1624, William Capps was living in Elizabeth City and his wife, Catherine, was recently deceased. Several months later Capps received a patent for some land on the west side of the Hampton River in Elizabeth City (18), acreage that in May 1625 was identified as planted. In January 1627 he testified before the General Court about a servant boy, Thomas Day, who arrived on the *Marmaduke*. On March 29, 1628, he told the General Court's justices that he had paid for Day's transportation to Virginia and that Day was supposed to go with Captain Bullock, offsetting part of the cost of his passage with labor at sea. Capps said that Captains Stone and Preen had refused to honor that arrangement, insisting on the full fare. The same day that William Capps filed a complaint about Stone and Preen, he admitted to slandering Adam Thorogood and apologized. On April 1, 1628, Capps was authorized to go to the Eastern Shore to search for suitable places to experiment with making salt by utilizing the heat of the sun. On April 8, 1629, he was fined for failing to attend his parish church in the lower part of Elizabeth City. He was still alive on March 21, 1634, at which time he received a patent for some land on the Back River in Elizabeth City (**19**) (PB 1 Pt. 1:41, 160; Pt. 2:648; VCR 1:461-462, 471, 608, 616; 2:43, 105, 524-525; 3:154, 580; 4:37-39, 76-79, 235, 558; EAE 11; CBE 29, 44, 69-70; MCGC 134, 169, 174, 194).

CATHERINE CAPPS
(CAPS, CAPPE, CAPP)
(MRS. WILLIAM CAPPS
[CAPS, CAPPE, CAPP])

Catherine, the wife of ancient planter William Capps (Caps, Cappe, Capp), died in Elizabeth City (**18**) sometime after April 1623 but before February 16, 1624 (CBE 45).

***

[NO FIRST NAME]
CARELEFF (CARELESS)

On June 15, 1625, the Council of State informed the Virginia Company that contrary to their recommendations, Mr. Careleff (Careless), who was associated with the East India School, had refused to seat his people at Martin's Hundred (**7**). They also expressed doubts that Mr. Careleff's age would overcome his inadequacy, but they failed to describe his shortcomings (VCR 4:562-567).

GEORGE CARELESS

On July 17, 1633, George Careless, a boy from Greene Cloth, was pardoned by the officials at Bridewell and selected for transportation to Virginia (HUME 38).

HENRY CARELESSE

On March 7, 1629, Henry Carelesse was the commander of Peirseys Hundred, formerly known as Flowerdew Hundred (**53**) (MCGC 192).

***

HENRY CARELEY
(CARSLEY, CAURSLEY)

Henry Careley (Carsley, Caursley) came to Virginia on the *Providence* in 1623. On February 7, 1625, he was living at Newportes News (**24**), where he was a 23-year-old servant in the household of Daniel Gookin, who later claimed his headright. Careley was living on the Eastern Shore on September 16, 1633, when he witnessed William Burdett's wedding contract, and several months later he procured a lease for 50 acres of land on Old Plantation Creek (**73**). Sometime prior to February 19, 1634, he married Elizabeth Berriman, and on August 6, 1635, he acquired some land in Accomack County, adjacent to William Berriman's. Henry Careley died sometime prior to November 26, 1635, when his widow, Elizabeth, functioned as his executrix. He was mentioned in a January 7, 1639, court order (CBE 63; AMES 1:11, 17-18, 33, 63, 132; 2:127; PB1 Pt. 1:270; Pt. 1:511; DOR 1:486).

ELIZABETH BERRIMAN CARELEY
(CARSLEY, CAURSLEY)
(MRS. HENRY CARELEY
[CARSLEY, CAURSLEY])

Henry Careley (Carsley, Caursley) and Elizabeth Berriman were wed sometime prior to February 19, 1634. On November 26, 1635, Elizabeth identified herself as Henry Careley's widow when she executed a deed of gift, transferring her plantation, along with two male servants and some household furnishings she had received from William Berriman, to her two children, Frances and Agnis Careley, (AMES 1:63; DOR 1:486).

***

NATHANIEL (NATHANIELL)
CARES

On September 2, 1631, the court of Bridewell decided that Nathaniel (Nathaniell) Cares, a boy, would be sent to Virginia. His transportation costs were to be covered by a merchant, whose name was not disclosed (CBE 96).

ROBERT CARLES (CHARLES)

In July 1622 the Virginia Company gave Robert Carles (Charles) some land in Virginia. He reputedly was capable of curing rice and producing cotton-wool, sugar, and indigo, and was described as highly experienced in agriculture. On April 3, 1623, Richard Frethorne, a young servant at Martin's Hundred (7), described Mr. Carles as a kinsman of the settlement's headman, William Harwood. On May 23, 1625, the General Court noted that Robert Carles and his people were supposed to seat at Martin's Hundred (VCR 4:73).

EDWARD CARLOWE

Edward Carlowe died at Flowerdew Hundred (53) sometime after February 16, 1624, but before January 20, 1625 (CBE 51).

HENRY CARMAN

On December 31, 1619, Henry Carman, a youth being detained at Bridewell, was among those chosen to be sent to Virginia. He arrived in the colony aboard the *Duty* in 1620 and was one of the so-called "*Duty* boys," who were obliged to serve for seven years. On February 16, 1624, Henry was living at West and Shirley Hundred (41) but by January 20, 1625, he had been moved across the river to Flowerdew or Peirsey's Hundred (53), where he was described as a 23-year-old servant in Samuel Sharpe's household. Henry Carman soon ran afoul of the law, for on October 11, 1626, he was found guilty of getting Alice Chambers pregnant. Alice, who was one of Abraham Peirsey's maidservants in James town (1), was accused of whoredom. As punishment, Henry and Alice were ordered to serve their respective masters for an additional seven years. Because Samuel Sharpe was not in Virginia when his servant Henry Carman was convicted and sentenced, Henry was placed in the custody of William Farrar of Jordan's Journey (46) and put to work on his master's behalf (CBE 15, 36, 50; MCGC 117).

JOHN CARNING

On February 16, 1624, John Carning was living at Buckroe, part of the Virginia Company's land in Elizabeth City (17) (CBE 45).

DIXI CARPENTER

Dixi Carpenter died at Flowerdew Hundred (53) sometime after April 1623 but before February 16, 1624 (CBE 37).

ANNE CARTER

On February 27, 1619, it was decided that Anne Carter, a young wench, would be sent to Virginia. She was one of the children rounded up from the streets of London so that they could be sent to the colony (CBE 13).

BENJAMIN CARTER

On August 23, 1631, Benjamin Carter, a boy from Langborne, was chosen by Bridewell's officials as one of those to be sent to Virginia (HUME 36).

CHRISTOPHER CARTER (CARRTER)

On February 16, 1624, Christopher Carter (Carrter) was living on the Eastern Shore (72-78). On September 22, 1645, he acquired 250 acres of land in Accomack, acreage he was assigned by several people (CBE 46; AMES 2:457-458).

EDMOND CARTER (CARTTER)

Edmond Carter (Cartter), who was living in Elizabeth City (17, 18), reportedly died sometime after April 1623 but before February 16, 1624 (CBE 45).

***

ERASMUS (ROSAMUS) CARTER

In 1621 Erasmus (Rosamus) Carter came to Virginia on the *George*. On February 16, 1624, he was living on the lower side of the James River, on the Treasurer's Plantation (11), where he was one of George Sandys' servants. Erasmus eventually gained his freedom and on July 10, 1635, patented 100 acres of land a relatively short distance upstream, at what was known as Halfway Tree

Neck or Swann's Point. He used as headrights the personal adventure of his wife, Phyllis (Phillis), and one indentured servant (CBE 40, 60; PB 1 Pt. 1:221).

PHYLLIS (PHILLIS) CARTER (MRS. ERASMUS [ROSAMUS] CARTER)

On July 10, 1635, when Erasmus (Rosamus) Carter patented some land on the lower side of the James River, he used his wife, Phyllis (Phillis), as a headright (PB 1 Pt. 1:221).

***

FRANCIS CARTER

In June 1619, Francis Carter, a 54-year-old barber surgeon from London, asked the Virginia Company for some shares of land in compensation for his services. Four years passed before his request was granted. By that time, Francis had obtained some shares of Virginia land from the widowed Lady Ciceley Delaware and assigned them to Thomas Addison, who was then in Virginia (EAE 8; VCR 1:347; 2:17, 383).

GILES (GYLES) CARTER

On September 10, 1620, Giles (Gyles) Carter set sail from Bristol on the *Supply* and was one of the new colonists brought by William Tracy, who was heading for Berkeley Hundred (**55**). Giles was supposed to serve the Society of Berkeley Hundred for three years in exchange for 50 acres of land. One Virginia Company document indicates that Giles Carter arrived at Berkeley Hundred on January 29, 1621, whereas another states that he died in England (CBE 21; VCR 3:396, 426).

HENRY CARTER

Henry Carter came to Virginia on the *James* in 1624. On February 3, 1626, William Eppes used his headright when patenting some land (PB 1 Pt. 1:49).

JAMES CARTER

Sometime after April 1623 but before February 16, 1624, James Carter died at one of the settlements on the lower side of the

James River, within the corporation of James City (**8-15**) (CBE 41).

JAMES CARTER (CARRTER)

James Carter (Carrter) of White Chapel, in Middlesex, England, who was a mariner, seems to have made several trips to Virginia. On April 30, 1623, he was identified as master of the *Truelove* when he signed a rebuttal to Captain Nathaniel Butler's allegations about conditions in the colony. In June 1623 he received permission to take passengers to the colony and then go on a fishing voyage. He also was identified as a subscriber for the relief of the colony. However, in January 1624 James Carter of the *Truelove* was detained in Elizabeth City (**17, 18**) and then brought before General Court, which fined him for illegal trading. By late May 1625 Carter was back in Virginia. This time, he produced merchant Robert Bennett's account book and testified in court. On March 27, 1626, James Carter made some sworn statements about the late Thomas Swinhowe's deathbed instructions and acknowledged that the decedent had bequeathed him a ring. On September 5, 1626, when Carter made his own will, he bequeathed the 50 acres in Shirley Hundred (**41**) that he had bought from Lady Elizabeth Dale to the Rev. Proby, the parish minister, and his successors, perhaps intending to establish a glebe. He also asked Nathaniel Causey and Richard Lowe to oversee shipment of his goods in the uplands, and called on Robert Sweete and Richard Lowe to see that his goods in the lowlands were sent home. The testator gave his servant, James Ostin (Osten), a year of his time and named his widow, Susan, as his executrix in England. Within two weeks of making his will, James Carter deeded some of his property to Richard Lowe. Carter died sometime prior to December 11, 1626, probably in Virginia. He was identified as the former master of the *Anne* of London and was held responsible for the loss of John Trehern's tobacco. James Carter's will was proved in England in April 1627 (VCR 2:385, 449; 4:245-247; MCGC 10, 60, 64, 98-99, 114, 126, 133; WAT 1016-1017; EEAC 12; CBE 77).

JOHN CARTER

In August 1612 John Carter was named the administrator of the estate of his nephew, Nicholas Glover, a bachelor who had died in Virginia (EEAC 24).

JOHN CARTER

On April 25, 1622, John Carter sent a letter to his uncle in Middlesex, saying that he had recently arrived at Southwark, having just come from Virginia. Carter said that he expected to return to his business in Jamestown **(1)** (CBE 26).

JOHN CARTER

On September 1, 1622, John Carter, who had been charged with stealing a horse and jailed, was tried and convicted by the London and Middlesex court. Afterward he asked the Privy Council to send him to Virginia. John's plea indicates that he was a poor man and that horse-stealing was his first offense. The Privy Council apparently agreed, for a warrant was issued to send him to Virginia or Bermuda (VCR 3:675; CBE 28-29).

JOHN CARTER

On April 24, 1623, John Carter, who had been a passenger on the *Margaret and John,* sent a petition to the governor, complaining about shipboard conditions (VCR 1:127-128).

JOHN CARTER

In 1624 John Carter gave a tobacco note to William Holmes, a Jamestown **(1)** merchant, who passed it along to Samuel Mathews and Abraham Peirsey (EAE 89).

JOHN CARTER (CARRTER)

On February 16, 1624, John Carter (Carrter) was living at West and Shirley Hundred **(41)** in the corporation of Charles City. In May 1625, when a list of patented land was sent back to England, John was credited with two tracts of land in Charles City: a 40-acre one and a 100-acre one (CBE 36; VCR 4:553).

JOHN CARTER

John Carter came to Virginia on the *Prosperous* and on February 16, 1624, was living on the Maine or Governor's Land **(3)**. On January 30, 1625, John was still there and was described as a servant in Thomas Swinhow's household. He may have been the former horse thief who in 1622 asked to be sent to the colony (CBE 39, 58; DOR 1:27).

JOHN CARTER

On May 30, 1625, the General Court ordered John Carter to post a bond, guaranteeing that by November he would pay John Tuke the duties he owed (MCGC 63).

JOHN CARTER

In May 1625, when a list of patented land was sent back to England, John Carter was credited with 100 acres in Warresqueak **(26)** (VCR 4:556).

JOHN CARTER

When Anthony Younge prepared his will on February 23, 1636, he made a bequest to John Carter, a surgeon in New Poquoson **(19)** (WITH 195).

THOMAS CARTER

In February or March 1620, Thomas Carter set out for Virginia on the *London Merchant.* He was associated with Mr. George Thorpe and was bound for Berkeley Hundred **(55)** or the Woodlief plantation **(49)**. Virginia Company records suggest that he died shortly after leaving for Virginia (CBE 14; VCR 3:199, 260-261).

THOMAS CARTER

Thomas Carter, an ancient planter, assigned 150 acres of land in Archer's Hope **(6)** to Richard Kingsmill. On May 8, 1626, the General Court transferred 100 acres of the Carter patent to Kingsmill along with some additional land that Kingsmill purchased from another individual (MCGC 102).

***

WILLIAM CARTER

William Carter, who in February 1623 was living in Dr. John Pott's house in urban Jamestown **(1)**, was involved in killing one of Sir George Yeardley's calves. Afterward, Carter and his associates were brought before the General Court and questioned. On June 24, 1624, William Carter testified about certain events that occurred at the Jamestown fort in June 1623 while he stood watch. On January 24, 1625, when a muster was taken of Jamestown's inhabitants, William Carter was living in the rural part of the island. He may have married later in the year, for a reference was made to Goodwife Carter's house. On at least one occasion during 1625, he assisted Jamestown gunsmith John Jefferson in repairing a weapon. Later in the year he treated a sick cow that belonged to the Rev. Richard Buck's orphans and was in the custody of Thomas Allnutt. On August 14, 1626, William Carter was described as one of George Menefie's servants and was then employed in his forge in Jamestown. Martin Turner, a co-worker at the forge, bequeathed his bed to William, who later claimed that Captain Hamor tried to seize it. In 1629 William Carter was identified as a married man. In 1636, when he patented 700 acres of land on the lower side of the James River, he used the headrights of his first, second, and third wives: Avis Turtley, Ann Mathis, and Alice Croxon (MCGC 3-4, 15, 59, 84-85, 107, 197-198; CBE 56; PB 1 Pt. 1:359, 451; DOR 1:511).

ALICE CROXON CARTER
MRS. WILLIAM CARTER)

In 1636, when William Carter patented some land on the lower side of the James River, he used the headright of his third wife, Alice Croxon (PB 1 Pt. 1:359, 451; DOR 1:511).

ANN MATHIS CARTER
(MRS. WILLIAM CARTER)

In 1636, when William Carter patented some land on the lower side of the James River, he used the headright of his second wife, Ann Mathis (PB 1 Pt. 1:359, 451; DOR 1:511).

AVIS TURTLEY CARTER
(MRS. WILLIAM CARTER)

On May 9, 1625, when Robert Fitts testified in court, he made reference to Goodwife Carter's house on rural Jamestown Island (1). In 1629 Mrs. William Carter ran afoul of the law by slandering Goodwife Gray, whom she called a whore. The women, who were cousins and Jamestown Island residents, were visiting Mr. Cheesman's house in Elizabeth City (18) when the offense occurred. Mrs. Carter, for her misbehavior, was ordered to apologize to Goodwife Gray in open court. She may have been William's first wife, the former Avis Turtley, whom he

used as a headright in 1636 (MCGC 59, 197-198; PB 1 Pt. 1:359, 451; DOR 1:511).

***

JOHN CARTWRIGHT

On March 10, 1622, John Cartwright witnessed John Rolfe's will. On February 16, 1624, when a census was taken of the colony's inhabitants, Cartwright was a servant in the urban Jamestown (1) household of Captain William Peirce, the late John Rolfe's father-in-law (CBE 38; SH 5; MCGH 861).

RICHARD CARWITHEY

On March 12, 1627, Richard Carwithey, a sailor, testified before the General Court in Jamestown (1) about an incident that occurred in the West Indies and involved the ship *Saker* (MCGC 143).

***

MR. CARYMBER

Mr. Carymber, his wife, and their son were sent to Virginia in 1621 by the Company of Mercers in 1621 (FER 297).

MRS. CARYMBER

Mrs. Carymber accompanied her husband and their son to Virginia in 1621 at the expense of the Company of Mercers (FER 297).

[NO FIRST NAME] CARYMBER

In 1621 the son of Mr. and Mrs. Carymber went with them to Virginia at the expense of the Company of Mercers (FER 297).

***

JAMES CASSE

On November 20, 1622, James Casse was among the Newgate inmates pardoned so that they could be sent to Virginia. They were sentenced to transportation on account of an outbreak of jail fever (CBE 29).

GEORGE CASSEN

George Cassen, a laborer, was one of the first Jamestown (1) colonists. He was involved in Indian trade and was ambushed by the Natives while in his boat. According to William White, George Cassen was tortured by the Indians before they executed him (CJS 1:212; 2:127, 142, 146; HAI 141).

THOMAS CASSEN

Thomas Cassen, one of the first Jamestown (1) colonists, was a laborer (CJS 209; 2:142).

WILLIAM CASSEN

According the Captain John Smith, William Cassen, a laborer, was one of the first Jamestown (1) colonists (CJS 209; 2:142).

***

VINCENCIO (VICENTIO) CASTINE (CASTILLIAN)

In 1621 Vincencio or Vicentio Castine (Castillian), an Italian glassmaker, was outfitted with provisions and the tools of his trade and sent to Virginia. He was part of a small group of glassworkers Virginia Company investors sent to make drinking glasses and to produce glass beads that could be used in trading with the Indians. The glassmakers and their families were entrusted to the care of Captain John Norton of Jamestown (1). Although the glassworkers built a furnace at Glasshouse Point (2), on the mainland just west of Jamestown Island, it exploded within two weeks. Vincencio was suspected of cracking it with an iron crowbar. The glassmaking venture proved unsuccessful, for the workers were dissatisfied with the conditions they found in the colony and clamored to go home. In March 1623 the roof was blown off of the glasshouse, which had to be repaired. After Captain Norton died, Treasurer George Sandys took over management of the glassmaking venture. The furnace was rebuilt but the Italians complained that their sand wouldn't liquefy, prompting Sandys to send men to the lower side of Hampton Roads to procure a different type. By June 15, 1623, one of the principal workmen at the Glasshouse had died and the other, who was ill, obtained permission to return to England. On February 16, 1624, Vincencio, whom the census-taker identified as Italian, was residing at Glasshouse Point. However, by February 4, 1625, he was living in the household of George

Sandys at the Treasurer's Plantation (11) on the lower side of the James River (CBE 41, 60; FER 290, 294, 301, 302; VCR 3:468, 485, 492, 646; 4:22, 562; MCGC 56).

VENCENTIA (VICENTIA) CASTINE (CASTILLIAN) (MRS. VICENCIO [VICENTIO] CASTINE [CASTILLIAN])

On May 23, 1625, Mrs. Vencentia (Vicentia) Castine (Castillian), the wife of Vincencio (Vicentio), one of the Italian glassworkers employed at Glasshouse Point, testified before the General Court about John Clever's demise at the Treasurer's Plantation (11). It is probable that she was living with her husband at the Treasurer's Plantation on February 4, 1625, but that her name was omitted from the muster. She also may have accompanied him to Virginia in 1621 and shared a home at Glasshouse Point (2). On February 20, 1626, Vencentia went to court in an attempt to recover the tobacco owed to her by Thomas Swift (Swyft), another resident of the Treasurer's Plantation (MCGC 60-61, 94).

***

ENOKE (ENOCH) CASTLE

On December 31, 1619, officials at Bridewell decided that Enoke (Enoch) Castle, a former inmate from the Middlesex House of Correction, would be sent to Virginia (CBE 14).

ROBERT CASTLE

On October 31, 1621, Robert Castle asked the Virginia Company for part of the late Anthony Gosnold's shares of land (VCR 1:541-542).

RICHARD CASWELL

In June 1619 Virginia Company officials acknowledged that Richard Caswell, a London baker, owned shares in the company (EAE 9).

HENRY CATELYNE

On January 28, 1628, Henry Catelyne, a merchant, sued Robert Eedes, surgeon of the ship *Hopewell*, in the General Court. He was attempting to recover the transportation costs of a maidservant Eedes had wed (MCGC 160).

DORCAS CATESBIE

Dorcas Catesbie came to Virginia with William Rowley on the *James*, which set sail from England on July 31, 1622 (FER 400).

JOHN CATESBY

John Catesby died at Martin's Hundred (7) sometime after April 1623 but before February 16, 1624 (CBE 42).

ERNOU CATOIR

Wool carder Ernou Catoir, his wife, and four children were among the Walloons and French who indicated their willingness to go to Virginia. In August 1621 the Virginia Company agreed that they could immigrate (CBE 25).

BRYAN CAUGHT (CAWT)

Bryan Caught (Cawt), who was living in Richard Stephens' household in urban Jamestown (1) on February 16, 1624, was a boat builder. In early January 1625, he agreed to build an 18½ foot shallop for John Uty, for whom he already had fabricated a boat. On January 3, 1625, Caught testified that John Gill and James Calver were to give him a tobacco note as payment from Captain Hamor (CBE 38; MCGC 39-40).

ROBERT CAUNTRIE (CHANTRY, CHANNTREE)

Robert Cauntrie (Chantry, Channtree) came to Virginia on the *George*. On February 16, 1624, when a census was taken of the colony's inhabitants, his name was listed in two locations: in Edward Blaney's household in urban Jamestown (1) and on the lower side of the James River at Captain William Powell's plantation (14), which was then in Blaney's hands. After Edward Blaney married the widowed Mrs. Powell, he moved some of his new wife's servants to the Powell plantation on the lower side of the James River. Therefore, Robert Cauntrie probably was one of the late Captain Powell's servants. On February 4, 1625, Robert Cauntrie was living on the Powell/Blaney plantation and was described as a 19-year-old indentured servant (CBE 38, 40, 59).

***

NATHANIEL CAUSEY (CAWSEY)

Nathaniel Causey (Cawsey), a gentleman and ancient planter, arrived in Jamestown (1) on the *Phoenix* in 1608 in the 1st Supply of new settlers. Although very little is known about his early years in the colony, on December 10, 1620, he received a patent for 200 acres of land on the north side of the James River, just east of the plantation known as West and Shirley Hundred (41). Causey and his wife, Thomasine, also an ancient planter, were living on their plantation, Causey's Cleare or Causey's Care (45), on March 22, 1622, when the Indians attacked. According to Captain John Smith, Nathaniel Causey, "being cruelly wounded, and with the Savages about him, with an axe did cleave one of their heads, whereby the rest fled and he escaped." Afterward, Causey and his wife took refuge at nearby Jordan's Journey (46), Samuel Jordan's plantation, which was made defensible and maintained, and they were living there on February 16, 1624. In March 1624 Nathaniel Causey served as a burgess for Jordan's Journey. He was among those who sent a petition to England describing the harsh treatment Virginia planters received while the colony was under martial law. Causey stayed on at Jordan's Journey, where he, wife Thomasine, and their five servants were living on January 21, 1625, in a household that was relatively well supplied with stored food and defensive weaponry. However, Causey still had legal possession of his own property, Causey's Care. On January 3, 1625, Nathaniel Causey testified about the relationship between the widowed Cisley Jordan and William Farrar, an unmarried couple living together at Jordan's Journey. Later in the month, Causey was ordered to take possession of the goods that belonged to the Society of Truelove's plantation (58). He also was allowed to take custody of three male servants left with him by William White, overseer of the Truelove Company, as long as he replaced them with three other men.

In May 1625 Nathaniel Causey was credited with 200 acres of land in the corporation of Charles City. He was summoned to court, where he agreed to pay a debt to Dr. John Pott. A document Causey witnessed on behalf of John Haule (Hall) of Jamestown Island (1) was presented at court in January 1626. On September 5, 1626, he testified on behalf of two men accused of making mutinous statements. Nathaniel Causey and Richard Lowe were made responsible for seeing that the late James Carter's goods were sent home, and Causey indicated that he had witnessed a deed Carter gave to Lowe. In August 1626 Causey was named a commissioner for the monthly court serving the communities along upper James River. As overseer of the Truelove Company's property in Virginia, Causey, on December 6, 1626, asked the General Court's permission to free one of the Truelove group's servants, John Brown. In early December 1628, Nathaniel Causey was fined for going aboard an incoming ship, the *William and Thomas*, without official authorization. A year later, his description of Virginia was used in an account written by Captain John Smith. He died sometime prior to February 7, 1634, at which time his heir, John Causey, disposed of the 200-acre Causey's Care plantation. (CBE 37, 52; CJS 1:222; 2:161, 222, 295; 3:215, 219; MCGC 41, 43, 60, 92, 106, 113-114, 126-127, 179; PB 2:78; HEN 1:128-129; VCR 4:553, 555, 585; HAI 915; WAT 1016-1017; DOR 1:20).

THOMASINE CAUSEY (CAWSEY) (MRS. NATHANIEL CAUSEY [CAWSEY])

Thomasine Causey (Cawsey), an ancient planter who came to Virginia in 1609 aboard the ship *Lyon,* was the wife of Nathaniel Causey (Cawsey), a gentleman and ancient planter who had arrived in the colony in 1608. At the time of the March 1622 Indian attack, the Causeys were living on their 200 acres at Causey's Cleare or Causey's Care (**45**), on the north side of the James River, within the corporation of Charles City. Nathaniel Causey successfully defended the couple's homestead from the Indians while other household members fled to safety. Afterward, the Causeys and their servants moved to nearby Jordan's Journey (**46**), one of the plantations that had been made defensible and held. The Causeys were still living there on February 16, 1624, and on January 21, 1625, when demographic records were compiled (CBE 37, 52; CJS 2:161, 222, 295; PB 2:78; DOR 1:20).

JOHN CAUSEY (CAWSEY)

On February 7, 1634, John Causey (Cawsey), who identified himself as a planter in the corporation of Charles City and Nathaniel Causey's heir, sold the plantation known as Causey's Care (**45**) to Walter Aston. The exact nature of John Causey's relationship to Nathaniel Causey is unclear (PB 2:78).

***

THOMAS CAUSEY (CAWSEY)

Thomas Causey (Cawsey) came to Virginia in 1620 on the *Francis Bonaventure* and on February 16, 1624, was living on Hog Island (**16**). However, by January 21, 1625, he had moved to Jordan's Journey (**46**), where he was a household head who was relatively well supplied with stored food and defensive weaponry. On April 18, 1635, Thomas patented 150 acres called the Indian Field, acreage that abutted Jordan's Journey and Chaplain's Choice (**56**). On May 2, 1636, he doubled his landholdings, with the result that he was in possession of 300 acres near the Appomattox River's mouth, on the west side of Jordan's Journey. On July 14, 1637, through the use of the headright system, he further enhanced the amount of property he owned. These land acquisitions suggest that Thomas Causey was a highly successful planter (CBE 41, 52; PB 1 Pt. 1:162, 336, 440).

ROBERT CAVE (CANE)

On December 18, 1635, Robert Cave (Cane) patented 200 acres adjacent to Mr. Wilkeson's land. The location of Cave's land is uncertain (PB 1 Pt. 1:327).

***

MATHEW CAVELL

On November 15, 1619, the Virginia Company, at the recommendation of Sir Samuel Argall, granted Mathew Cavell, master of the *William and Thomas*, his freedom on account of his service to the colony. They also promised him a reward. Two days later, Company officials gave Mathew Cavell 100 acres land in the colony. On March 4, 1629, the General Court learned that Mathew Cavell was dead and that his son, Thomas, wanted to take up the acreage that his father had obtained from the Virginia Company. This time, the parcel was described as 50 acres, not 100 (VCR 1:264, 273-274; MCGC 189).

THOMAS CAVELL

On March 4, 1629, Thomas Cavell, son and heir of Mathew Cavell, who had been master of the *William and Thomas*, asked the General Court for the 50 acres that his father had received from the Virginia Company. Thomas was told that he would be given the land if he could prove that he was Mathew's heir (MCGC 189).

***

THOMAS CAVENDISH

On June 26, 1621, Thomas Cavendish was identified as the cousin of Michael Lapworth, a Virginia colonist (FER 268).

GEORGE CAWCOTT

In May 1625, when a list of patented land was sent back to England, George Cawcott was credited with 100 acres of land in the corporation of Charles City. The precise location of Cawcott's acreage is uncertain (VCR 4:553).

THOMAS CEELY (SEELY, SEELIE)

On October 16, 1629, Thomas Ceely (Seely, Seelie) commenced serving as a burgess for the Warwick River communities, then in the western part of the corporation of Elizabeth City (**18**). He was among those ordered to find men to plant at Chiskiack (**30-38**), on the York River, and was promised land in exchange for doing so. In March 1630 Thomas Ceely served as a burgess for the Denbigh (**23**) area, and in 1632 he represented the settlers along the Warwick River. Simultaneously, he was named a commissioner of the Warwick River court (HEN 1:139-140, 148, 154, 187).

CENSA-BELS

In August 1621, Virginia Company officials made note of the cost of supplying food to Censa-bels, whose gender and ethnicity are uncertain. Company records suggest that Censa-bels came to the colony (FER 302).

HENRY CENY

In March 1630, September 1632, and February 1633 Henry Ceny served as a burgess for the settlers living in Archer's Hope (**6**), which included the James City Parish glebe (HEN 1:148, 178, 203).

WILLIAM CERRELL

According to a letter Richard Frethorne sent to England in March 1623, William Cerrell arrived at Martin's Hundred (**7**) at Christmastime, that is, in early January 1623. He died there at the home of Mr. William Harwood, the settlement's headman (VCR 4:60).

BRYAN CHALLICE (CHALLIS)

On October 18, 1620, Bryan Challice (Challis), a laborer from Roysdon or Saffron Walden, Herts, was found guilty of burglary and sentenced to transportation to Virginia (CBE 21).

CHACROW
(SEE SHACROW)

MORRIS CHALONER

Sometime after April 1623 but before February 16, 1624, Morris Chaloner died at one of the settlements on the lower side of the James River, within the corporation of James City (**8-15**) (CBE 41).

[NO FIRST NAME] CHAMBERLIN

On March 22, 1622, when the Indians attacked Edward Bennett's plantation in Warresqueak (**26**), Mrs. Chamberlin was killed (VCR 3:571).

***

FRANCIS CHAMBERLIN (CHAMBERLAYNE, CHAMBERLAINE) I

Francis Chamberlin (Chamberlayne, Chamberlaine) I came to Virginia on the *Marmaduke* in 1621, and on February 16, 1624, he and his wife were living in Elizabeth City (**18**). They were still residing there a year later, and he was identified as Mr. Francis Chamberlin, a 45-year-old household head who shared a dwelling with his wife, Rebecca, 3-year-old son, Francis II, and four adult male servants. The household had an adequate supply of stored food and defensive weaponry. In April 1625 Francis Chamberlin was sued by Ann Wood, who succeeded in recovering a debt owed to her husband, Percival. Chamberlin was still at Kecoughtan on January 10, 1627, when he was authorized to receive Luke Boyse's tobacco from John Croodicke. On April 3,

1627, Francis Chamberlin was required to post a bond, guaranteeing that he would pay a debt to Sir Francis Wyatt (CBE 44, 66; MCGC 51, 56, 131, 146; DOR 1:60).

REBECCA CHAMBERLIN (CHAMBERLAYNE, CHAMBERLAINE) (MRS. FRANCIS CHAMBERLIN [CHAMBERLAYNE, CHAMBERLAINE] I)

Rebecca, the wife of Francis Chamberlin (Chamberlayne, Chamberlaine) I, came to Virginia on the *Bona Nova* in 1622. On February 16, 1624, she and her husband were living in Elizabeth City (18). They were still there in early 1625 and shared a home with their 3-year-old son, Francis II, and four male servants. Rebecca Chamberlin was then age 37 (CBE 44, 66).

FRANCIS CHAMBERLIN (CHAMBERLAYNE, CHAMBERLAINE) II

In early 1625, 3-year-old Francis Chamberlin (Chamberlayne, Chamberlaine) II, the son of Rebecca and Francis Chamberlin I, was living in Elizabeth City (18) in a household his father headed. Little Francis was Virginia-born (CBE 66).

***

FRANCIS CHAMBERLINE

On July 31, 1622, Francis Chamberline, who was sent to Virginia by Mr. Ryder, set sail for the colony on the *James*. He died in Elizabeth City (17, 18) sometime after April 1623 but before February 16, 1624 (FER 400; CBE 67).

JAMES CHAMBERLIN

James Chamberlin died in Elizabeth City (17, 18) sometime after February 16, 1624, but before the first part of 1625 (CBE 67).

ALICE CHAMBERS

Alice Chambers came to Virginia on the *Southampton* in 1623. On January 24, 1625, she was residing in urban Jamestown (1) and was a servant in cape merchant Abraham Peirsey's household. Alice became pregnant and on October 10, 1626, was arrested on a charge of whoredom. She was found guilty of committing fornication with Henry Carman, one of Samuel Sharpe's servants and a resident of West and Shirley Hundred (41). Alice and Henry were ordered to serve their masters an additional seven years (CBE 55; MCGC 117).

GEORGE CHAMBERS

On June 28, 1617, George Chambers, an investor in the Virginia Company, made a complaint on behalf of the Society of Martin's Hundred (7) (VCR 1:239).

JAMES CHAMBERS

On January 8 1620, James Chambers was brought in by the marshal of Middlesex and detained at Bridewell until he could be transported to Virginia. Later in the year he set sail on the *Duty*. On February 16, 1624, James was living on the Eastern Shore (72-78). However, by February 4, 1625, he had been transferred to the Treasurer's Plantation (11), on the lower side of the James River. On April 11, 1625, James Chambers testified at John Verone's inquest. Then, on March 2, 1626, he returned to court and reported that Mr. Thomas Swift had allowed Thomas Hall to keep William Banks's corn. Almost exactly a year later, James received permission to plant at Hog Island (16) (CBE 16, 46, 60; MCGC 53, 96, 143).

JOHN CHAMBERS

John Chambers came to Virginia in 1622 on the *Bona Nova*. On January 20, 1625, he was living in Flowerdew Hundred (53), where he was a 21-year-old servant in the Rev. Grivel Pooley's house. On March 13, 1626, John served as a witness in William Vincent's suit against Thomas Harris and his wife (CBE 50; MCGC 97).

ROWLAND CHAMBERS

On July 10, 1635, when Rowland Chambers received a patent at Piney Point, at the mouth of the Chickahominy River in James City County, he received it under an agreement he had made with his former master, Thomas Phillips (PB 1 Pt. 1:216).

THOMAS CHAMBERS

Thomas Chambers came to Virginia on the *Southampton* in 1621. On January 20, 1625, he was living at Flowerdew Hundred (53), where he was a 24-year-old servant in cape merchant Abraham Peirsey's household (CBE 50).

ROBERT CHAMBLY (CHAMBLEY)

Robert Chambly, a gentleman, served on the December 21, 1624, jury that investigated the drowning death of George Pope, a Jamestown Island (1) youngster. In January 1625 Chambly was fined for neglecting jury duty (MCGC 38, 40).

JOHN CHAMP

Sometime after April 1623 but before February 16, 1624, John Cantwell died at one of the settlements on the lower side of the James River, within the corporation of James City (8-15) (CBE 41).

ROBERT CHAMPER

On February 16, 1624, Robert Champer was living at the College (66) within the corporation of Henrico (CBE 35).

PASCOE (PASTA) CHAMPION (CHAMPIN)

Pascoe (Pasta) Champion (Champin) came to Virginia in 1621 on the *Elleanor* and on February 16, 1624, was living in Elizabeth City (18). He was there in early 1625 and was identified as a 23-year-old servant in Captain William Tucker's household (CBE 43, 63).

***

PERCIVALL CHAMPION

Percivall Champion's adulterous wife, Jane, was sentenced to death on June 14, 1632, after she and William Gallopin were found guilty of murdering their illegitimate child and concealing the death. On July 8, 1635, Percivall Champion and John Slaughter were leasing land adjacent to Joseph Stratton's acreage in Nutmeg Quarter near Denbigh (23), in what became Warwick County (PB 1 Pt.1:212; MCGC 480).

JANE CHAMPION (MRS. PERCIVALL CHAMPION)

On June 14, 1632, Jane, Percivall Champion's wife, was sentenced to be hanged, as was her lover, William Gallopin. Both were found guilty of murdering their illegitimate child and concealing the death (MCGC 480).

***

JAMES CHAMPLE

James Chample came to Virginia with Lieutenant Gibbs on the *James*, which set sail from England on July 31, 1622 (FER 400).

CHANCO (CHAUCO)

Chanco (Chauco), an Indian youth who had been converted to the Christian faith, lived at Richard Pace's Paces Paines (9) plantation, directly across the James River from the western end of Jamestown Island (1). Although relatively little is known of Chanco's personal history, Virginia Company records describe him as a servant to William Perry, one of Pace's friends and business associates. They also credit the young Indian with saving many colonists' lives during the March 22, 1622, Indian assault. Chanco's brother reportedly told him about the plan to mount a surprise attack on the settlements and urged him to kill his master. But because Richard Pace had treated Chanco kindly, like a son, the youth warned Pace about the impending attack. Pace quickly rowed his boat across the river to Jamestown and notified the governor of the impending danger. That warning allowed some colonists to take defensive measures. Natives living in colonists' homes in Elizabeth City (18) and Newportes News (24) also gave warning of the attack. Afterward, the colonists undertook retaliatory raids, in an attempt to eradicate the Indians. Although the Natives did what they could to fight back, by early April 1623 they were suffering. It was then that Chanco and Comahum, as emissaries from the paramount chief Opechancanough, came to Martin's Hundred (7), where they made an overture for peace. Comahum and Chanco were taken into custody and brought up to Jamestown. The Indians said that Opechancanough was offering to return some colonists he was detaining in exchange for his people's being allowed to plant their crops in peace (VCR 3:554-557, 652-653; 4:6, 75, 98-101, 221, 223; CJS 2:297-298).

CHARLES CHANCY

Laborer Charles Chancy, his wife, and two children were among the Walloons and French who indicated their willingness to go to Virginia. In August 1621 the Virginia Company agreed that they could immigrate (CBE 24).

ARTHUR (ARTHURE) CHANDLER

On October 10, 1618, when Arthur (Arthure) Chandler was brought before the authorities at Bridewell, they decided that he would be detained until he could be sent to Virginia. However, his transportation to the colony was delayed until sometime after February 12, 1620. He set sail on the *Jonathan* and on February 16, 1624, was living on the Governor's Land or Maine (3). On January 30, 1625, Arthur was still there and was identified as one of the governor's servants. He was age 19 (CBE 10, 18, 39, 57).

JOHN CHANDLER (CHAUNDLER, CHANDELER)

John Chandler (Chaundler, Chandeler), an ancient planter, came to Virginia in 1609 on the *Hercules*, a vessel in the fleet that set out from England with Sir Thomas Gates and Sir George Somers. On February 16, 1624, John was living in Elizabeth City (18). He was still there in early 1625 and was a 24-year-old servant in Thomas Willoughby's household. By August 1632 John Chandler had attained his freedom and was living on some land on the Back River in Elizabeth City (19), acreage that he was leasing from Captain Richard Stephens (CBE 44, 64; PB 1 Pt. 1:109, 116).

RICHARD CHANDLER

On March 22, 1622, when the Indians attacked Edward Bennett's plantation in Warresqueak (26), Richard Chandler was killed (VCR 3:571).

THOMAS CHANDLER

On June 24, 1635, when Adam Thorogood patented some land, he used Thomas Chandler as a headright and stated that he had paid for his transportation to Virginia in 1628 on the *Hopewell* (PB 1 Pt. 1:179).

ANDREW CHANT

When Adam Thorogood patented some land on June 24, 1635, he used Andrew Chant as a headright and indicated that he had paid for Andrew's transportation to Virginia on the *Hopewell* in 1628 (PB 1 Pt. 1:179).

[NO FIRST NAME] CHANTERTON

On June 12, 1620, John Pory informed Virginia Company officials that Mr. Chanterton, who was then in the colony, was capable of finding good grapes, probably for wine-making. Pory noted that Chanterton was loyal to Rome (that is, a known Roman Catholic) and therefore might be a spy (VCR 3:302).

***

ISAAC (ISAAK) CHAPLIN (CHAPLINE, CHAPLAIN, CHAPLAINE, CHAPLYN)

Isaac (Isaak) Chaplin (Chapline, Chaplain, Chaplaine, Chaplyn), an ancient planter, came to Virginia on the *Starr* in 1610–1611. Although little is known about his first years in the colony, he may have been associated with Bermuda Hundred (39), one of the communities established by Sir Thomas Dale. When Captain Robert Smalley of Bermuda Hundred made his will on December 19, 1617, he mentioned his debtors, one of whom was Ensign Isaac Chaplin. Virginia Company records indicate that Chaplin, who was then in England, intended to bring 40 people to his plantation. On July 31, 1622, he and his wife, Mary, 12-year-old John Chaplin, and four servants set out on the *James*. On February 16, 1624, Isaac and his household were living at his plantation, Chaplin's Choice (56), and in March 1624 he represented that community and nearby Jordan's Journey (46) as a burgess. On December 27, 1624, he testified in court in litigation that involved Sir George Yeardley and Captain John Martin. When a muster was taken on January 21, 1625, Ensign Isaac Chaplin, Mary Chaplin, and Isaac's young kinsman, John, were living at Chaplin's Choice. Isaac was then credited with two dwellings, a boat, and some livestock, and he was amply supplied with stored food and defensive weaponry. On January 17, 1625, Ensign Isaac Chaplin was ordered to provide a house and ground to two men and their servant, people who were associated with Truelove's Company **(58)**. In February he was called on to testify again in the Yeardley-Martin suit. On May 1625, when a list of patented land was sent back to England, Isaac Chaplin was credited with 200 acres in the territory of Great Weyanoke, land that had been planted (seated). He also had 50 additional acres in the corporation of Charles City, which were listed as "unplanted." On May 9, 1625, the General Court's justices learned that Ensign Isaac Chaplin had been convicted of perjury earlier in his life and had never been pardoned; therefore, his earlier testimony in the Yeardley-Martin suit was disqualified. Despite this legal problem, in August 1626 Isaac Chaplin was made a justice of the monthly court that served the communities near the head of the James River. On December 8, 1628, the General Court learned that Ensign Isaac Chaplin had been lost at sea and gave his kinsman, John Chaplin, letters of administration. This raises the possibility that Isaac's wife, Mary, was dead (CBE 37, 69; SH 4; FER 138, 400; SR 3112; MCGC 37, 43, 58, 106, 178; HEN 1:128-129; VCR 4:553-554; DOR 1:20, 515-516).

MARY CHAPLIN (CHAPLINE, CHAPLAIN, CHAPLAINE, CHAPLYN) (MRS. ISAAC [ISAAK] CHAPLIN [CHAPLINE, CHAPLAIN, CHAPLAINE, CHAPLYN])

Mary, the wife of Isaac (Isaak) Chaplin (Chapline, Chaplain, Chaplaine, Chaplyn), came to Virginia in 1622 aboard the *James*. She was accompanied by 12-year-old John Chaplin and four servants. On February 16, 1624, Mary Chaplin was living at Chaplin's Choice **(56)** in a household her husband headed. On January 21, 1625, she was still there with her husband, young John Chaplin, and the family's servants. Mary probably predeceased her husband, who died prior to December 1628 (CBE 37, 51; DOR 1:20, 515-516).

JOHN CHAPLIN (CHAPLINE, CHAPLAIN, CHAPLAINE, CHAPLYN)

In 1622 John Chaplin (Chapline, Chaplain, Chaplaine, Chaplyn) came to Virginia on the *James* with Mary, Isaac Chaplin's wife,

and four servants. On February 16, 1624, John and the other members of the Chaplin household were living at Chaplin's Choice **(56)**, and they were still there on January 21, 1625. John Chaplin was then 15 years old. On December 8, 1628, John Chaplin of Chaplin's Choice was given letters of administration so that he could settle the estate of the late Ensign Isaac Chaplin. He probably was the decedent's son or a close kinsman (FER 400; CBE 37, 51; MCGC 178; DOR 1:20, 515-516).

***

ANTHONY CHAPMAN

On August 8, 1628, Anthony Chapman, who was being detained at Bridewell, indicated that he was willing to go to Virginia (CBE 83).

FRANCIS CHAPMAN

Ancient planter Francis Chapman, who came to Virginia on the *Starr* in 1608, was residing in urban Jamestown **(1)** on February 16, 1624. By February 4, 1625, he had moved to the lower side of the James River, where he headed a household in Paces Paines **(9)**. On December 5, 1620, Francis received a patent for a 100-acre parcel adjacent to Richard Pace's property and in May 1625, when a list of patented land was sent back to England, he was credited with that acreage. On January 21, 1628, Richard Richards and Richard Dolphenby, who had come into legal possession of Chapman's land, jointly conveyed it to Isabell Smythe Pace Perry, Richard Pace's remarried widow, who owned an adjacent piece of property. The two men's land became part of Paces Paines (CBE 38, 59; VCR 4:555; MCGC 63, 65, 159; PB 1 Pt. 1:62; DOR 1:39).

LUKE CHAPMAN (CHAPMANN)

Luke Chapman (Chapmann) came to Virginia in 1622 on the *John and Francis*. On February 7, 1625, he was living in Warresqueak **(26)** at Edward Bennett's plantation, where he was a servant (CBE 62).

NICHOLAS CHAPMAN

In 1619 Nicholas Chapman came to Virginia on the *Jonathan*, a vessel that brought a large number of Virginia Company servants and tenants. On February 16, 1624, he was living in Henrico at the College (66). On January 23, 1625, when a muster was made of the colony's inhabitants, Nicholas was living on the lower side of the James River and was a servant at Captain Samuel Mathews' plantation (15) (CBE 35, 60).

PHILLIP CHAPMAN

Phillip Chapman came to Virginia in 1621 on the *Flying Hart* and on February 16, 1624, was living in Elizabeth City (18). He was still there in early 1625 and was identified as a member of Sergeant John Wayne's household. Phillip was then age 23 (CBE 44, 65).

***

THOMAS CHAPMAN I

Thomas Chapman I, an ancient planter, came to Virginia in 1610 on the *Trial*. On December 19, 1617, when Captain Robert Smalley of Bermuda Hundred (39) made his will, he bequeathed some tobacco to Thomas Chapman, whom he identified as one of his servants in the corporation of Henrico. As Chapman was indebted to Smalley, he may have left him the sum he owed. On February 16, 1624, Thomas Chapman, his wife, Ann, and baby son, Thomas, were living at Jordan's Journey (46). They were still there on January 21, 1625, and occupied a dwelling of their own. They were relatively well supplied with stored food and defensive weaponry and had some livestock. In January 1625 the Chapman household included a 6-week-old infant, Ann Chapman. On May 1625, when a list of patented land was sent back to England, Thomas Chapman was credited with 100 acres on the south side of the James River in Elizabeth City (20 a, b, c), acreage that was unplanted. He also may have had some acreage near William Bikar's plantation (57) (CBE 37, 52; SR 3112; SH 4; WITH 78; VCR 4:558; PB 1 Pt. 2:475; DOR 1:18).

ANN CHAPMAN I
(MRS. THOMAS CHAPMAN I)

Ann I, Thomas Chapman I's wife, came to Virginia on the *George* in 1617 and on February 16, 1624, was living at Jordan's Journey (46) with her husband and young son, Thomas. The Chapmans were still there on

January 21, 1625. The household then included Thomas, wife Ann, son Thomas (age 2), and daughter Ann (age 6 weeks) (CBE 37, 52; DOR 1:18).

ANN CHAPMAN II

On January 21, 1625, Ann Chapman II, who was only 6 weeks old, was living with her parents, Ann and Thomas Chapman I, at Jordan's Journey (46). Also part of the household was little Ann's brother, Thomas II, who was age 2 (CBE 52; DOR 1:18).

THOMAS CHAPMAN II

On February 16, 1624, Thomas Chapman II was living at Jordan's Journey (46) with his parents, Ann and Thomas Chapman I. On January 21, 1625, when a muster was taken of the colony's inhabitants, Thomas Chapman II, who was Virginia-born, was described as age 2 (CBE 52).

***

JOSEPH CHARD

Sometime prior to the March 22, 1622, Indian attack, Joseph Chard sold 6 acres and two houses at Bermuda Hundred (39) to Francis Michell (Mitchell) (MCGC 79-80).

***

JOSHUA CHARD

Joshua Chard, an ancient planter, came to Virginia on the *Seaventure*, the ship that was transporting Sir Thomas Gates and was wrecked in Bermuda. Although the 1625 muster states that Joshua arrived in May 1607, Gates and his men actually left England in 1609 and reached Jamestown (1) in May 1610, aboard two vessels they built in Bermuda. On February 16, 1624, Joshua Chard was living at Bermuda Hundred (39). On January 24, 1625, when a muster was taken of that community's inhabitants, he was described as a 36-year-old household head. He and his wife, Ann, shared a dwelling and had an ample supply of stored food and defensive weaponry and some livestock. On May 1625, when a list of patented land was sent back to England, Joshua Chard was credited with 100 acres in the corporation of Charles City (CBE 36, 53; VCR 4:553; DOR 1:9).

ANN CHARD
(MRS. JOSHUA CHARD)

Ann, who became Joshua Chard's wife, went to Virginia on the *Bonny Bess* in 1623. On January 24, 1625, she was residing at Bermuda Hundred (**39**), where her husband was a household head. In 1625 Ann Chard was 33 years old (CBE 53).

***

CHARLES

On January 22, 1625, Charles, a 19-year-old servant who came to Virginia on the *Jacob* in 1624, was living at West and Shirley Hundred (**41**), where he was a servant in Henry Bagwell's household (CBE 53).

HENRY (HENRIE) CHARLTON

In 1623 Henry (Henrie) Charlton came to Virginia on the *George*. In early 1625 Henry, who was 19 years old, was living on the Eastern Shore where he was a member of Captain John Wilcocks' household, which was seated on the Company Land (**76**). Around 1634 Henry Charlton ran afoul of the law when he made threats against the Rev. William Cotton and called him a black-coated rascal. Henry died sometime prior to January 2, 1638, at which time Stephen Charlton and another man were ordered to inventory his estate (CBE 68; AMES 1:28, 96).

WILLIAM CHARTE

On March 22, 1622, when the Indians attacked Abraham Peircy's plantation on the Appomattox River (**39**), William Charte was killed (VCR 3:571).

WILLIAM CHARTER

On November 21, 1618, the authorities at Bridewell Prison decided that William Charter, a vagrant and young rogue, would be transported to Virginia (CBE 11).

NICHOLAS CHAUSTER

On September 26, 1618, officials at Bridewell decided that Nicholas Chauster, a boy brought in from the outskirts of Cripplegate, would be detained until he could be sent to Virginia (HUME 5).

RICHARD CHAUSTER

On September 26, 1618, the officials at Bridewell decided that Richard Chauster, a vagrant from Cripplegate Without, who was being detained, would be sent to Virginia (CBE 10).

JOHN CHAWKE

On December 8, 1635, when the Rev. Willis Hely (Heeley, Heyley, Heley), the rector of Mulberry Island Parish, patented some land, he used John Chawke as a headright (PB 1 Pt. 1:325).

***

EDWARD (EDMOND) CHEESMAN
(CHISMAN, CHEASEMAN, CHEASMAN)

In 1623 Edward (Edmond) Cheesman (Chisman, Cheaseman, Cheasman) came to Virginia on the *Providence* and on February 16, 1624, was living in Elizabeth City (**18**). He was still there in early 1625 and was a member of the household headed by his brother, John Cheesman. Edward was then age 22. He patented 300 acres in York County before 1637, and by 1650 he had come into possession of some acreage on the north side of the York River, in what eventually became Mathews County (CBE 44, 65; DOR 1:568-570).

JOHN CHEESMAN (CHISMAN, CHEASEMAN, CHEASMAN)

John Cheesman (Chisman, Cheaseman, Cheasman) came to Virginia in 1621 on the *Flying Hart* and on February 16, 1624, was living in Elizabeth City (**18**). On September 2, 1624, he was identified as a Kecoughtan gentleman when he patented 200 acres of land, using the headrights of four servants he had brought to the colony on the *Southampton* in 1622. In early 1625, when a muster was made of the colony's inhabitants, John was listed as a 27-year-old household head who shared a dwelling with his brother, Edward Cheesman. The two men were adequately supplied with stored food and defensive weaponry. On April 25, 1625, the General Court noted that Lieutenant John Cheesman was indebted to Thomas Spillman. In May 1625, when a list of patented land was sent back to England, John

Cheesman was credited with 200 acres on the south side of the James River, in Elizabeth City (**20 a, b, c**), land that had been claimed but not seated. In 1629 John's home in Kecoughtan was mentioned in a slander suit that involved Mrs. William Carter and Goodwife Gray. On January 23, 1629, John Cheesman and Rowland Powell, who were identified as merchants, were authorized to act as attorneys for John Jeffreys, Nathaniel Jeffreys' executor. John continued to acquire land and on November 21, 1635, patented 600 acres on the New Poquoson River (**19**), in what became York County. As time went on, he continued to acquire land. He also rose in prominence, becoming a lieutenant, captain, and lieutenant colonel of the militia. He also became a county justice, a burgess, and finally a member of the Council of State. John Cheesman went to England in 1661 and eventually died there. At that time, his son, John, a resident of Bermondsey, Surrey, England, served as his administrator (CBE 44, 65; PB 1 Pt. 1:46-47, 319; MCGC 56, 182, 197; EEAC 13; VCR 4:558; DOR 1:58, 568-569).

***

THOMAS CHEESMAN (CHISMAN, CHEASMAN)

On February 16, 1624, Thomas Cheesman (Chisman, Cheasman) was living in Elizabeth City (**18**). He was mentioned again in shipping records, which associated him with Newportes News (**24**) (CBE 44; SR 7076; DOR 1:568).

WILLIAM CHELMEDGE

In 1621 William Chelmedge came to Virginia on the *Temperance* at the expense of Sir George Yeardley. In 1628 Chelmedge's headright was assigned to Thomas Flint, who used it when patenting some land (MCGC 166; PB 1 Pt. 1:59).

RICHARD CHELSEY

On May 16, 1621, Richard Chelsey, one of Sir Lawrence Hyde's servants, was living with Thomas Cumber at Martin's Hundred (**7**) (VCR 3:451).

THOMAS CHERMANT

Thomas Chermant came to Virginia with Edward Grindon of Jamestown Island (**1**)

aboard the *James*. They set sail from England on July 31, 1622 (FER 400).

ANTHONY CHESTER

Anthony Chester, captain of the ship *Margaret and John*, left England in mid-December 1620. Aboard was Dr. Lawrence Bohun. The ship was attacked by the Spanish in the West Indies, and on March 19, 1621, Dr. Bohun was killed. Later, one of Captain Chester's passengers produced a narrative of his adventures, which was published in Dutch in 1707. Included was a description of the March 22, 1622, Indian attack. Although the writer's accuracy has been questioned, his presence in the colony around the time of the Native assault is documented (CHE 203-214; WITH 317).

WILLIAM CHESTER

On April 10, 1619, William Chester was identified as one of Sir William Throgmorton's and Richard Berkeley's cousins. On September 4, 1619, Virginia Company officials noted that William Chester planned to take 30 men to Berkeley Hundred (**55**) within the year (VCR 3:138-139, 205).

RICHARD CHESWRIGHT

In 1621 Richard Cheswright, a former servant of the Drapers Company in London, asked to be sent to Virginia. He indicated that he had been freed under the terms of Richard Osborne's will (SH 4).

***

JOHN CHEW

John Chew came to Virginia on the *Charity*, which left England in April 1622. He was the Bennett family's business representative in Virginia and settled the estate Warresqueak (**26**) merchant Robert Bennett after his death in 1623. In that capacity, he successfully brought suit against Captain William Douglas's estate and obtained some household goods from Mr. Calcar for the Rev. William Bennett's use. He also was obliged to pay the minister's salary. On February 20, 1624, while John Chew was a burgess for Warresqueak, he signed a statement rebutting certain Virginia Company officials' claims about conditions in the colony prior to 1619. On February 16,

1624, he was living on Hog Island (16). However, several months later he patented a small waterfront lot in urban Jamestown (1), land that abutted lots belonging to two other merchants. By late December 1624, Chew's lot contained a store that he rented to John Lamoyne.

Although John Chew took an active role Jamestown's affairs, he served as a burgess for Hog Island in 1625, 1628, and 1629. On February 4, 1625, he and his wife, Sarah, were living at Hog Island when a muster was made and had an ample supply of stored food and defensive weaponry. He also owned a boat, which would have been very useful in his mercantile business. John Chew was made commander of Hog Island in 1629, and in 1636 Governor John Harvey described him as one of the "ablest merchants in Virginia." Throughout the 1620s he made numerous appearances before the General Court. He sold imported fish on behalf of Treasurer George Sandys and procured corn from the Eastern Shore in 1625. He also hired Richard Bartlett of Warresqueak to build a house, probably for his use there while conducting business on behalf of the Bennetts. During 1625, John Chew made frequent visits to Warresqueak, where he collected debts owed to the Bennett estate. He was identified as a merchant when he served on the jury that investigated the death of George Pope, a child who tumbled into a well in Jamestown. Chew also took part in other inquests, and he was among those who ascertained that some of the tobacco Sir George Yeardley had tried to export was of poor quality. Like most merchants, John Chew occasionally was summoned to court on account of debts. In July 1625 he was arrested by Jamestown physician Dr. John Pott, who took legal action in order to make him pay what he owed. In 1630 John Chew was among those who established plantations at Chiskiack (30-38), on the York River. He eventually acquired several hundred acres in York County and by the late 1630s had moved there (33). In 1640 he was appointed one of York's tobacco viewers and in 1643 commenced representing York as a burgess. He donated part of his York County acreage on Chisman Creek as a parish glebe. John Chew probably died around 1652, shortly after his marriage to Rachel Constable, a York County widow. His son, Samuel, born around 1626, was his principal heir (VCR 4:402; MCGC 10, 13, 29-30, 37-38, 44, 47, 51, 53, 60-61, 66, 86, 98, 143, 192; HAI 915; HEN 1:128-129, 138; PB 1 Pt. 1:5, 7-8, 369, 445, 447; Pt. 2:616; 4:401; 7:701; CBE 61; York County Deeds, Orders, Wills 1633-1646:43; STAN 53-54, 63; MCGH 497, 507; DOR 44, 517-519).

SARAH CHEW
(MRS. JOHN CHEW)

Sarah, who became Jamestown (1) merchant John Chew's wife, came to Virginia on the *Seaflower* in 1621. On January 24, 1625, Sarah and John Chew were sharing a home on Hog Island (16). She died sometime prior to April 3, 1651 (CBE 61; DOR 1:518).

RACHEL (RACHAEL) CONSTABLE CHEW
(MRS. JOHN CHEW)

On April 3, 1651, John Chew of York County signed a marriage contract with the widowed Mrs. Rachel (Rachael) Constable, whom he intended to make his wife. John apparently died within a year of their marriage (DOR 1:518).

SAMUEL CHEW

Samuel, the son of John and Sarah Chew, was born around 1626. When John died around 1652, Samuel became his principal heir. By 1659 he had moved to Maryland, which he made his permanent home (DOR 1:519-520).

***

ROBERT CHEW

Sometime prior to March 12, 1624, Robert Chew, an indentured servant on his way to Virginia, asked to go ashore in the West Indies, but his request was denied (MCGC 13).

HENRY CHEYNEY

Henry Cheyney, a merchant from York, England, arrived in Jamestown (1) on September 12, 1623, on the *Bonny Bess* and took the oath of supremacy (MCGC 6).

HERCULES CHEYNEY

On July 18, 1634, Hercules Cheyney shipped goods from London to Virginia on the *Primrose* (CBE 117).

RICHARD CHIDLEY

On September 26, 1618, Richard Chidley, a vagrant from Newgate Market, was selected as one of the men to be sent to Virginia (CBE 10).

RICHARD CHIDLEY

Richard Chidley, a boy, was one of the children rounded up from the streets of London so that they could be sent to Virginia. On February 27, 1619, he was being detained at Bridewell (CBE 12).

THOMAS CHISELWOOD

On February 27, 1619, Thomas Chiselwood, a boy brought in from the streets of London, was detained at Bridewell so that he could be sent to Virginia (CBE 13).

ROBERT CHOLME

Robert Cholme came to Virginia on the *Charity*. On January 30, 1625, he was living on the Governor's Land (3) with James Standish, his partner. Both men came to Virginia together and had some stored food and powder. It is uncertain when they arrived. It is probable that both men were tenants on the Governor's Land (CBE 58; DOR 1:28).

RICHARD CHOLSER

On March 22, 1622, when the Indians attacked Martin's Hundred (7), Richard Cholser was slain (VCR 3:570).

CHOUPONKE

On February 16, 1624, an Indian known as Chouponke was living in Elizabeth City (18) in Captain William Tucker's household (CBE 43).

THOMAS CHRISTERLES (XERLES, CHIERLES?)

On March 22, 1622, when the Indians attacked the settlers living at the College (66) in Henrico, Thomas Christerles (Xerles, Chierles?) was slain (VCR 3:570).

***

DICTORIS (DICTRAS) CHRISTMAS (CHRISMAS)

Dictoris (Dictras) Christmas (Chrismas) came to Virginia sometime prior to February 16, 1624, at which time he and his wife were living in Elizabeth City (17), on the east side of the Hampton River. On November 28, 1625, he was identified as a former Southampton Hundred (44) servant who had been freed. This raises the possibility that he came to Virginia in 1618 on the *William and Thomas*, which brought 150 of the Society's people, or in April 1619, when Sir George Yeardley and his associates brought along another 35. After the March 1622 Indian attack, Southampton Hundred's surviving settlers were moved to Hog Island (16), considered a position of greater safety. It may have been shortly thereafter that Dictoris Christmas moved to Elizabeth City. On October 10, 1624, he testified that he had heard Captain John Martin make threatening statements, and in November 1624 he was identified among those who had provided corn to the surviving Southampton Hundred settlers. On September 12, 1625, he admitted that he was indebted to the Rev. Jonas Stogden, and he accepted a receipt from Thomas Edwards. On August 24, 1627, Dictoris was identified as a planter when he obtained a lease for 50 acres of land at the Strawberry Banks, located on the east side of the Hampton River. He stayed there until September 1628, when he assigned his lease to Lionel Roulston. Four years later, he conveyed the leasehold to John Neal, a merchant. In September 1628 Dictoris Christmas patented some land near the Fort Henry fields. He continued to acquire acreage and by November 1635 had accumulated 300 acres, using himself and his wife, Isabell as headrights. His last acquisition was land on the Old Poquoson River, near the mouth of the York River (19) (CBE 441 MCGC 21, 69, 70, 77; PB 1 Pt. 1:78, 89, 101, 134-135, 317).

ELIZABETH CHRISTMAS (CHRISMAS) (MRS. DICTORIS [DICTRAS] CHRISTMAS [CHRISMAS])

On February 16, 1624, Elizabeth, the wife of Dictoris (Dictras) Christmas (Chrismas), was sharing her husband's home in Elizabeth City (17) (CBE 44).

ISABELL CHRISTMAS (CHRISMAS) (MRS. DICTORIS [DICTRAS] CHRISTMAS [CHRISMAS])

On November 21, 1635, when Dictoris (Dictras) Christmas (Chrismas) patented some land on the Old Poquoson River, near the mouth of the York (**19**), he used his own headright and that of his wife, Isabell, noting that it represented their own personal adventures. As headrights could be retained until they were used, it is unclear whether Isabell was married to Dictoris before or after he had wed wife Elizabeth (PB 1 Pt. 1:317).

***

CHRISTOPHER

Christopher, a Welchman, died in Elizabeth City (**18**) sometime after April 1623 but before February 16, 1624 (CBE 45).

THOMAS CHRISTY

In 1621 Thomas Christy sent to Virginia a mill, stones, a bellows, skins, and other items that were needed by the Virginia Company's colonists (FER 322).

JAMES CINDUARE

James Cinduare died at Flowerdew Hundred (**53**) sometime after April 1623 but before February 16, 1624 (CBE 42).

CISLEY

Cisley, a maidservant, died in Elizabeth City (**17, 18**) sometime after April 1623 but before February 16, 1624 (CBE 45).

JOHN CLACKSON (CLAXON)

In 1619 John Clackson (Claxon) came to Virginia on the *Bona Nova* and on February 16, 1624, was residing in Elizabeth City (**18**). By February 4, 1625, he had moved to the Treasurer's Plantation (**11**), where he was one of Treasurer George Sandys' hired servants (CBE 44, 60).

***

WILLIAM CLAIBORNE (CLAIBORN, CLAYBORNE, CLEYBORN)

William Claiborne (Claiborn, Clayborne, Cleyborn), the Virginia Company's official surveyor, arrived in Virginia with incoming Governor Francis Wyatt in October 1621. He had some previous experience in colonization ventures, for in 1622 he was identified as an ancient planter and adventurer in New England. Claiborne was supposed to live in urban Jamestown (**1**) with the governor and perform surveys for three years. He was obliged to lay out all tracts of public land and those of particular (privately sponsored) plantations before performing surveys for others. Claiborne was to receive a housing allowance, a salary of 30 pounds a year, and 200 acres of land, and he was to be provided with books and instruments. His clients were to furnish room and board for him, a servant, and one other individual. At first, William Claiborne received a salary of 200 pounds of tobacco a year instead of currency. By 1623 he had been named to Virginia's Council of State, where he succeeded in getting his salary raised to 400 pounds of tobacco a year. He laid out the boundaries of several lots in urban Jamestown, in an area called the New Town, and some 12-acre homesteads in the eastern end of the island, which was rural. By June 1624 he had patented two parcels of land in Elizabeth City (**18**). In 1625 Claiborne became secretary of state, a position he held for a decade. In May 1625 he was credited with owning 250 acres in Archer's Hope (**6**), which he received via a court order and had 7 years to seat; 500 acres at Blunt Point (**22**); and 150 acres in Elizabeth City, a tract that already was planted. In May 1625 he compiled and sent a list of patented land home to England. During the summer months Claiborne witnessed a contract between George Harrison and Roger Smith, and Treasurer George Sandys' agreement to free Martin Turner. By the mid-1620s William Claiborne's interest in Indian trade and exploration had become evident. He paid boat-builder John Wilcox to construct a shallop, and he attempted to patent a method he had devised for keeping Indians as guides. Governor George Yeardley and Deputy-Governor John Pott successively authorized Claiborne to explore the Chesapeake Bay and trade with the Indians, and in

1629 he received permission to trade with the Dutch and with other English colonies. After William Claiborne became secretary of state, he demanded cattle, office land, and a servant as part of his stipend, and later he was given the right to take up 600 acres near Jamestown as the Secretary's Land. He witnessed Sir George Yeardley's 1627 will and transcribed the codicil added shortly thereafter. In 1629 William Claiborne commanded the forces combatting the Indians. Because he was in control of Kent Island, which formed the base of his Indian trading operations, he vehemently opposed Lord Baltimore's colonization of Maryland. Later, Claiborne forcibly seized Kent Island from the Calverts. As a result of their complaints, he was placed under arrest in Jamestown. During the 1630s William Claiborne clashed openly with Governor John Harvey, whose loyalty to the king impelled him to support the Calverts. Lord Baltimore, in turn, accused Claiborne of having the Indians attack his colony. Around 1635 William Claiborne married Elizabeth Boteler (Butler), the sister of an associate in the Kent Island trading operations. In 1647 Elizabeth patented 700 acres of land in Elizabeth City, noting that the land had been made over to her "in nature of and lieu of a jointure." William and Elizabeth Claiborne produced several children, including William II, Jane, Thomas, Leonard, and John.

In 1642, after Sir John Harvey had left office, William Claiborne became treasurer of Virginia, holding that position until 1660. In 1644 he led an army that landed in Pamunkey Neck, a retaliatory maneuver undertaken in the wake of an April 18, 1644, Indian attack. In 1652, when Governor Berkeley was obliged to surrender the colony to a Parliamentary fleet, Claiborne was one of the Commonwealth government's representatives. Afterward, he served as secretary of state from 1652–1660. Claiborne was said to be especially intolerant of religious dissenters. During the 1650s he patented vast tracts of land on the colony's frontier, in the Northern Neck, Middle Peninsula, and Pamunkey Neck, in time amassing more than 16,000 acres. He continued to play an active role in Indian trade and in 1653 went on an exploratory expedition to the south and west of the colonized area. After he was replaced as secretary, he was elected a burgess for New Kent County. In 1677 he dispatched a docu-

ment to England, asserting his trading rights. During Bacon's Rebellion he reportedly sided with Governor Berkeley and, afterward, plundered the goods of presumed Bacon supporters. William Claiborne died in Virginia in 1677, by which time he had established a family seat in Pamunkey Neck (CJS 2:286; 3:215; STAN 21, 24, 26, 31; VCR 1:483-484, 494; 3:477, 486, 580; 4:58, 250-251, 501, 551, 556-557; CBE 29, 71, 95, 104, 119; PB 1 Pt. 1:4-8, 40-41, 134; 3:34; 4:213, 456; MCGC 20, 34, 45, 64-65, 72-73, 76, 79, 103, 111, 118, 124, 133, 136, 147, 161, 167, 185, 473, 480-481, 492, 500, 562-563; CO 1/8 f 174; 1/39 ff 113, 118; HEN 1:137, 153, 170, 178, 187, 202, 377, 503; 2:39, 196-197, 249-250; SAIN 10:28, 176, 208; SH 9; AMES 1:18; FOR 2:7:6, 29; 2:9:14, 19, 21; 3:14:23; LNC B:140, 162; DOR 1:593-595).

ELIZABETH BOTELER (BUTLER) CLAIBORNE (CLAIBORN, CLAYBORNE, CLEYBORN) (MRS. WILLIAM CLAIBORNE [CLAIBORN, CLAYBORNE, CLEYBORN])

Elizabeth Boteler (Butler), who was born sometime prior to 1612, married William Claiborne (Claiborn, Clayborne, Cleyborn) around 1635. She was the sister of his Kent Island trading partner, John Boteler. In November 1647 Elizabeth patented 700 acres of land in Elizabeth City County, noting that it had been transferred to her by her husband three years earlier. Elizabeth and William Claiborne produced several children, including William II, Jane, Thomas, Leonard, and John. Elizabeth was still alive in 1669, at which time she transferred some land to her eldest son, William Claiborne II of New Kent County, born in 1636 (PB 2:82; DOR 595).

***

WILLIAM CLAPHAM

In 1619 officials at Newgate Prison decided that William Clapham, a burglar from Middlesex who had been found guilty of breaking into Lord Paggett's house and was being detained, would be sent to the colony. However, his transportation was delayed until November 20, 1622, when, on account of an outbreak of jail fever, Clapham was pardoned so that he could be sent abroad. Sometime prior to November 16, 1635, a

William Clapham (perhaps the same man) reached Virginia and succeeded in patenting 300 acres of land in Warresqueak (**26**). On November 11, 1636, he witnessed the will of Edward Dewell, an indentured servant, who lived in the same community (CBE 12, 29; PB 1 Pt. 1:308; SH 27).

[NO FIRST NAME] CLARE

Mr. Clare, master of the *Gift of God*, died in Jamestown (**1**) sometime after April 1623 but before February 16, 1624 (HOT 196).

ESTER CLARIETT

On December 9, 1628, Ester Clariett presented an inventory of the late Henry Bradford's goods. Ester, like Henry, may have resided in Jamestown (**1**) (MCGC 179).

BRIDGETT CLARK (CLARKE)

On February 16, 1624, Bridgett Clark (Clarke) was a servant in the Ascombe home in urban Jamestown (**1**) (CBE 38).

CHARLES CLARK (CLARKE)

On May 20, 1607, Charles Clark (Clarke), a sailor, accompanied Captain Christopher Newport on an exploratory trip up the James River (HAI 102).

***

EDWARD CLARK (CLARKE)

On February 16, 1624, Edward Clark (Clarke) was living at Jordan's Journey (**46**) with his wife and infant (CBE 37).

MRS. EDWARD CLARK (CLARKE)

Mrs. Edward Clark (Clarke) was living at Jordan's Journey (**46**) with her husband and infant on February 16, 1624, (CBE 37).

[NO FIRST NAME] CLARK (CLARKE)

On February 16, 1624, Edward Clark's (Clarke's) infant, whose name and gender are unknown, was living at Jordan's Journey (**46**) with his parents (CBE 37).

***

EDWARD CLARK (CLARKE)

On July 19, 1627, Edward Clark (Clarke) shipped goods from London to Virginia on the *James* (CBE 79). He may have been the same individual who was living at Jordan's Journey (**46**) three years earlier.

***

EDMUND CLARK (CLARKE)

Edmund Clark (Clarke) and his wife, who lived in Virginia, died sometime prior to June 5, 1632. Their orphaned child was returned to England and entrusted to the care of guardians who lived in Southwark (MCGC 201).

MRS. EDMUND CLARK (CLARKE)

Mrs. Edmund Clark (Clarke) and her husband, who lived in Virginia, died sometime prior to June 5, 1632. Their orphaned child was returned to England and entrusted to the care of guardians in Southwark. On March 15, 1634, Virginia officials reported on the status of settling Mrs. Clark's estate in the colony (MCGC 201; CBE 113).

[NO FIRST NAME] CLARK (CLARKE)

Sometime prior to June 5, 1632, the orphaned child of Edmund Clark (Clarke) and his wife, who had been sent to England, was mistreated by those entrusted with his care. William Emerson of Jordan's Journey (**46**) and Anthony Wills informed the General Court that when they were in England, at Southwark, they heard rumors that the Clark orphan was malnourished and inadequately clothed and frequently fled from his guardians, seeking refuge in the streets (MCGC 201).

***

FRANCIS CLARK (CLARKE)

On January 29, 1633, Francis Clark (Clarke) and Thomas Faucsett (Fossett) were identified as the masters of John Creed of Martin's Hundred (**7**) (SH 15).

GEORGE CLARK (CLARKE)

George Clark (Clarke), a Jamestown Island (**1**) gunsmith, lived in a house near Sandy

Hill, not far from the workshop of fellow gunsmith John Jackson. In July 1623 George Clark and Daniel Franck (an indentured servant) killed and butchered one of Sir George Yeardley's calves and stashed the meat in Clark's loft. Although both men were convicted of the crime, Clark, unlike Franck, was reprieved, probably because of his specialized skills. On February 16, 1624, George Clark was living at Warresqueak (**26**), the Bennett plantation, but by late November had returned to Jamestown. Thomas Gates testified that when he went to John Jackson's to collect a debt, he learned that Jackson had gone to Clark and asked him to pay Gates. Jackson said that if he did so, Jackson would consider Clark's own debt satisfied. George Clark died in Jamestown sometime prior to January 24, 1625 (MCGC 4-5, 33; CBE 42, 56; PB 1 Pt. 1:170).

JOHN CLARK (CLARKE)

John Clark (Clarke), an English pilot, set sail from London with Sir Thomas Dale and 300 men on March 17, 1611, and arrived in Virginia in early May. In June, when he boarded a Spanish ship at Old Point Comfort (**17**), he was seized and taken to Havana, Cuba, where he was interrogated. On July 23, 1611, Clark, who stated that he was age 35, described Jamestown (**1**) and the forts at Old Point Comfort. He said that there were approximately 1,000 people in Virginia, 600 of whom were physically fit. He also indicated that the settlement in Jamestown, which was defended by cannons, was surrounded by palisades and that the colonists' houses were built of wood. According to Clark's testimony, Sir Thomas Gates was expected to arrive in August 1611 with additional people and cattle. He said that the colonists exported timber and sassafras but relied on imported food and other commodities. He told the Spanish that Sir Thomas Gates and Sir George Somers had been shipwrecked in Bermuda but had managed to reach Virginia. He also said that the colonists alternately were at war and at peace with the Indians. In January 1612 John Clark was taken to Madrid, Spain, where he was interrogated in February 1616. This time, he estimated that there were approximately 100 wooden houses in Jamestown and that the colony's population consisted of 1,000 men and 30 women. Thanks to a prisoner exchange agreement

between the Spanish and English governments, John Clark was released and allowed to return to England. In 1620 he came to the New World as pilot of the *Mayflower*. He reportedly made many trips to Virginia on behalf of the Virginia Company and on one occasion transported cattle to the colony from Ireland for Daniel Gookin, who established a plantation called Marie's Mount or Newportes News (**24**). John Clark immigrated to Virginia in 1623 and reportedly died shortly thereafter, leaving a widow and children (AHR 25:455-456, 470, 476; VCR 1:599; 2:90; 4:456-457; HAI 533-548, 690-694).

JOHN CLARK (CLARKE)

On May 18, 1622, John Clark (Clarke) was described as a sawyer who worked at half-shares for the Company of Shipwrights, under the supervision of Thomas Nunn. On May 2, 1625, John was arrested and brought up to Jamestown (**1**), where he was placed in the custody of the provost marshal. The nature of his offense is uncertain (FER 378; MCGC 57).

JOHN CLARK (CLARKE)

John Clark (Clarke), a 33-year-old butcher from Oxfordshire, came to Virginia in 1619 aboard the *Bona Nova*, which arrived in Jamestown (**1**) in mid-November 1619. He probably was a Virginia Company servant or tenant (FER 295).

JOHN CLARK (CLARKE)

John Clark (Clarke), a tradesman, came to Virginia in 1608 in the 2nd Supply of new settlers. Therefore, he would have lived in Jamestown (**1**) (CJS 1:241; 2:191).

LAWRENCE CLARK (CLARKE)

On May 16, 1621, Virginia Company officials learned that Lawrence Clark (Clarke), one of Nicholas Hyde's servants at Martin's Hundred (**7**), was dead (VCR 3:451).

LAWRENCE CLARK (CLARKE)

Lawrence Clark (Clarke) was one of the people who came to Virginia on the *James* with Captain Isaac Chaplain and left England on July 31, 1622 (FER 400).

SUPRE (SUPRA) CLARK (CLARKE)

In January 1624 Supre (Supra) Clark and Thomas Luscam were identified as the former captains of the *Furtherance*, a vessel that made many trips to Virginia (MCGC 9).

THOMAS CLARK (CLARKE)

On February 16, 1624, Thomas Clark (Clarke) was listed among Vice Admiral John Pountis's servants in urban Jamestown (1). He died at sea on May 9, 1625, while aboard the *Elizabeth* of London, which was bound for Virginia. Thomas Clark's inventory was presented to the General Court on November 28, 1625, at which time its accuracy was verified by John Snade. Court records dating to 1629 indicate that Clark's inventory and appraisal were compiled by Farrar (Pharoah) Flinton and Joseph Cobb. Thomas Clark died indebted to William Webster (purser of the *Elizabeth*), Richard Wake (a shipboard surgeon), and Thomas Weekes (CBE 38; MCGC 77, 198-199).

THOMAS CLARK (CLARKE)

Thomas Clark (Clarke) was listed among those who died in Jamestown (1) sometime after April 1623 but before February 16, 1624 (CBE 39).

WILLIAM CLARK (CLARKE)

William Clark (Clarke) came to Virginia on the *Ambrose* in 1623 and on February 16, 1624, was living in Elizabeth City (18). He was still there in early 1625 and was identified as a 20-year-old servant in William Ganey's household. On November 18, 1635, William Clark patented 100 acres of land in Elizabeth City on the New Poquoson River (19), using two men as headrights (CBE 44, 66; PB 1 Pt. 1:310).

WILLIAM CLARK (CLARKE)

William Clark (Clarke) came to Virginia on the *Providence* in 1623 and on February 16, 1624, was living in Elizabeth City (18). On February 7, 1625, he was identified as a 25-year-old servant in Daniel Gookin's household in Newportes News (24). On July 1, 1635, William Clark patented 250 acres on the Nansemond River (20 c) in Warres-queak (Isle of Wight) County. His acreage was near that of John Parrett, a fellow servant in the Gookin household in 1625 (CBE 44, 63; PB 1 Pt. 1:195).

JOHN CLARKSON

On December 13, 1624, John Clarkson testified before the General Court in a suit involving the loss of Richard Tree's boat at Martin's Hundred (7). John stated that the vessel had been borrowed by Thomas Hethersoll and William Cooke, who failed to bring it ashore in advance of an approaching storm (MCGC 35-36).

RICHARD CLARKSON

On January 29, 1620, it was decided that Richard Clarkson, who was being detained at Bridewell Prison, would be sent to Virginia (CBE 18).

JOHN CLAUS

On February 5, 1628, John Claus was identified as an indentured servant of Edward Sharples of Jamestown (1) (MCGC 160-161).

***

JOHN CLAY (CLAYE)

John Clay (Claye), an ancient planter, came to Virginia on the *Treasurer* in February 1613. On January 21, 1625, he and his wife, Ann, were living at Jordan's Journey (46), where John was a household head. He was in possession of a dwelling, an ample supply of stored food, defensive weaponry, and some livestock, and shared his home with his wife, Ann, and a male servant. On July 13, 1635, John Clay received a patent for 1,200 acres of land within Charles City County, on the lower side of the James River near Ward's Creek (61). He and John Freme also purchased an adjacent 1,000-acre tract that became known as Clay's Clossett. In addition, John owned some acreage near Richard Milton's land in the vicinity of Westover (54), on the upper side of the James. John Clay, after being widowed sometime prior to 1645, married a woman named Elizabeth (CBE 51; PB 1 Pt. 1:230, 404, 432; 3:334; DOR 1:17, 643-644).

ANN CLAY (CLAYE)
(MRS. JOHN CLAY [CLAYE])

Ann, who became the wife of ancient planter John Clay (Claye), came to Virginia on the ship *Ann* in August 1623. On January 21, 1625, she was living at Jordan's Journey (**46**) in a household her husband headed (CBE 51).

***

RICHARD CLAYSON

Richard Clayson, a boy, was brought to Bridewell and detained. On February 29, 1619, officials decided that he would be kept until he could be sent to Virginia (HUME 24).

JOHN CLEMENT

John Clement, a 33-year-old sailor from Somersetshire, England, came to Virginia in 1619 aboard the *Bona Nova* (FER 295).

THOMAS CLEMENT

On August 23, 1633, officials at Bridewell decided that Thomas Clement, a boy brought in from Langborne, would be sent to Virginia (HUME 36).

***

JEREMIAH (JEFFREY, JEREMY, JEREMIE, JOREME, JEREME) CLEMENTS I

Jeremiah (Jeffrey, Jeremy, Jeremie, Joreme, Jereme) Clements I's wife, Elizabeth, and their children, Elizabeth, Jeremiah II, Ezekiell, and Nicholas, came to Virginia on the *George* in 1617. Jeremiah Clements I may have died in England or in Virginia before his family members set out for the colony (CBE 55).

ELIZABETH FULLER CLEMENTS (MRS. JEREMIAH CLEMENTS I, MRS. RALPH HAMOR [HAMER], MRS. TOBIAS FELGATE [FELLGATE]) (SEE MRS. RALPH HAMOR [HAMER], MRS. TOBIAS FELGATE [FELLGATE])

Elizabeth Fuller Clements, the daughter of Cuthbert Fuller and granddaughter of Nicholas Fuller, a London merchant and

Virginia Company member, came to Virginia on the *George* in 1617. She was accompanied by her children Elizabeth, Jeremiah (Jeremy, Jeremie, Joreme, Jereme) II, Ezekiell, and Nicholas Clements, and two servants. Elizabeth's husband, Jeremiah Clements I, most likely died prior to her departure for Virginia. Sometime before February 16, 1624, the widowed Elizabeth married Captain Ralph Hamor (Hamer) and was living in Jamestown (**1**). Sharing the Hamor home were two of Elizabeth and Jeremiah Clements' children, Elizabeth and Jeremiah II. By October 1626 Elizabeth had been widowed again. She was named Ralph Hamor's administrator and inherited his 200 acres on Hog Island (**16**). Sometime prior to February 8, 1628, she had wed Captain Tobias Felgate of the *Defiance* and made plans to go to England. She died before March 30, 1630 (CBE 38, 55; PB 1 Pt. 1:124, 419; DOR 1:699–700; MCGC 117, 122, 165).

ELIZABETH CLEMENTS

Elizabeth Clements, daughter of Jeremiah Clements I and his wife, Elizabeth, was baptized on November 9, 1609, and came to Virginia with her widowed mother on the *George* in 1617. On February 16, 1624, Elizabeth was living in urban Jamestown (**1**) with her mother, Elizabeth, her stepfather, Captain Ralph Hamor, and her brother Jeremiah II (CBE 38, 55; PB 1 Pt. 1:124; DOR 1:699–701).

EZECHIELL CLEMENTS

Ezechiell Clements, the son of Jeremiah Clements I and his wife, Elizabeth, was born in England and came to Virginia with his widowed mother and siblings on the *George* in 1617. He apparently died prior to February 16, 1624, for his name was not included in the colony's census records (PB 1 Pt. 1:124; DOR 1:700).

NICHOLAS CLEMENTS

Nicholas Clements, the son of Jeremiah Clements I and his wife, Elizabeth, was born in England and came to Virginia with his widowed mother and siblings on the *George* in 1617. He inherited some Virginia Company stock from his great-uncle Nicholas Fuller in 1620. He had some business dealings with Edward Mayhew and in January 1629 was to receive payment on Mayhew's behalf from Lieutenant Edward Waters, who was to pay him out of Captain Wilcocks' estate (PB 1 Pt. 1:124; MCGC 183;· DOR 1:700).

JEREMIAH (JEFFREY, JEREMY, JEREMIE, JOREME, JEREME) CLEMENTS II

Jeremiah (Jeffrey, Jeremy, Jeremie, Joreme, Jereme) Clements II, the son of Jeremiah Clements I and his wife, Elizabeth, was born in England and baptized on November 8, 1607. He came to Virginia with his widowed mother on the *George* in 1617 and on February 16, 1624, was living in urban Jamestown (1) with his mother, stepfather Captain Ralph Hamor, and sister, Elizabeth. On August 26, 1633, Jeremiah Clements II patented 350 acres on Upper Chippokes Creek within the corporation of James City. Sometime prior to June 11, 1635, he married his wife, Edye. In 1641 Jeremiah Clements II was a James City County burgess. By March 17, 1658, he was deceased (CBE 38, 55; PB 1 Pt. 1:124, 248; DOR 1:699-701; STAN 61).

EDYE CLEMENTS (MRS. JEREMIAH [JEFFREY, JEREMY, JEREMIE, JOREME, JEREME] CLEMENTS II)

On June 11, 1635, when Jeremiah (Jeffrey, Jeremy, Jeremie, Joreme, Jereme) Clements patented some land on Upper Chippokes Creek, within James City County, he used the personal adventure of his wife, Edye. The Clements couple had a daughter, whom they named Elizabeth (PB 1 Pt. 1:248; DOR 1:701).

***

JOHN CLEMENTS

On March 22, 1622, when the Indians attacked the settlers living at the College (66) in Henrico, John Clements was killed (VCR 3:566).

***

WILLIAM CLEMENTS (CLEMENT)

William Clements (Clement), a cook and gardener, and his wife were sent to Virginia on the *Margaret* of Bristol on September 1619 by the Society of Berkeley Hundred's investors. William was given a cash advance and placed under Captain John Woodlief's supervision at Berkeley Hundred (55). He was to receive 20 acres of land in exchange for serving six years. William Clements was present when a census was taken of the plantation's inhabitants on February 16, 1624, but his wife, who had accompanied him to Virginia, was not. Sometime prior to January 3, 1625, William and 15 other men were moved to Shirley Hundred (41), where they were employed on behalf of Berkeley Hundred (CBE 13-14, 35; VCR 3:187, 197, 199, 213; MCGC 42).

MRS. WILLIAM CLEMENTS (CLEMENT)

Mrs. William Clements (Clement) and her husband, a cook and gardener, were among those sent to Virginia by the Society of Berkeley Hundred's investors. They left England in September 1619 and were bound for Berkeley Hundred (55). Mrs. Clements probably died sometime prior to February 16, 1624, for her name was not included in a census of the colony's inhabitants (VCR 3:187; CBE 35).

***

WILLIAM CLEMENTS

William Clements died at Bermuda Hundred (39) sometime after April 1623 but before February 16, 1624 (CBE 36).

JOHN CLEVER

Captain John Clever, a mariner, died at the Treasurer's Plantation (11) in late August 1622 and was prepared for burial by Mrs. Peryue Taberlen, who resided there. On May 23, 1625, she and Mrs. Vencentia Castine testified that Mrs. Taberlin had laid him out properly (MCGC 60).

JAMES CLEY (CLAY?)

James Cley (Clay?), a joiner, went to Virginia in September 1619 on the *Margaret* of Bristol with Captain John Woodlief. He went at the expense of the Society of Berkeley Hundred's investors and was headed for Berkeley Hundred (55), where he was supposed to serve for three years. James Cley seems to have died within a short time of his arrival (VCR 3:198, 213; CBE 14).

THOMAS CLEYBOURNE (CLEBURN)

On July 6, 1627, Thomas Cleybourne (Cleburn), a merchant, shipped goods from London to Virginia on the *Golden Lion* of Dundee. Then, on July 31st, he sent another shipment from London to Virginia on the *Hopewell* (CBE 78-79).

RICHARD CLIFTON

On September 5, 1626, Richard Clifton witnessed the will of James Carter, who lived in the vicinity of Shirley Hundred (**41**) (WAT 1016-1017).

PETER CLIMGEON

On February 7, 1628, when Peter Climgeon testified before the General Court, he gave his age as 26 and said that he was born in St. Olive's Parish in Southwark, near London. He said that he had been at Edward Grindon's house at the Treasurer's Plantation (**11**) when William Mills admitted to stealing from Grindon and taking the stolen goods to John Tios's house (MCGC 163).

FRANCOIS CLITDEU

Laborer Francois Clitdeu, his wife, and five children were among the Walloons and French who indicated their willingness to go to Virginia. In August 1621 the Virginia Company agreed that they could immigrate (CBE 24).

EDMOND CLOAKE

On February 16, 1624, Edmond Cloake was living on the Eastern Shore at Captain William Eppes's plantation (**74**) (CBE 46).

WILLIAM CLOBERY (CLOBERRY)

On September 20, 1627, William Clobery (Cloberry), a merchant, shipped goods from London to Virginia on the *Parramore*. He sent another shipment from London to Virginia on the *Defense* on July 26, 1634 (CBE 80, 118).

PHETTIPLACE (PETIPLACE, PETTIPLACE, PHETIPLACE) CLOSE

Phettiplace (Petiplace, Pettiplace, Phetiplace) Close, an ancient planter, came to Virginia in 1608 on the *Starr*. Although very little is known about his first years in the colony, sometime prior to November 20, 1623, he advised Thomas Bilby, who was ill, to make a will. On February 16, 1624, Phettiplace was living on the lower side of the James River within the corporation of James City, at Paces Paines (**9**), to the west of Gray's Creek. On March 9, 1624, when he testified before the General Court in a dispute between Henry Horne and John Proctor, he said that he was 30 years old. Phettiplace returned to court on October 10, 1624, to testify about the death of Elizabeth Abbott, one of John Proctor's maidservants, who had been brutally beaten. He said that Elizabeth had been punished numerous times by the Proctors.

On February 4, 1625, Phettiplace Close was living at Paces Paines where he and Daniel Watkins headed a household that included two male servants. They were in possession of a dwelling and had an ample supply of stored food, defensive weaponry, and some livestock. On January 31, 1625, Phettiplace was ordered to send Thomas Parker's tobacco to his mother, who was in England. When a list of patented land was compiled in May 1625, Phettiplace Close was credited with 100 acres in the corporation of Henrico, on the south side of the James River near the falls (**67**), land that had not been seated. On October 12, 1626, when he was summoned before the General Court and questioned about how Mr. Proctor treated his servants, Thomas and Enica Fitch, he said that they received adequate care and were supplied with food, shelter, and clothing. On January 10, 1627, Phettiplace was authorized to move from Paces Paines to Blunt Point (**22**). In early December 1628 he was given a patent for 100 acres near the mouth of the Warresqueak (Pagan) River in exchange for the 100 acres in Henrico that he had received on May 2, 1619. The exchange was made on account of the "danger of planting" the original tract. In January 1629 Phettiplace Close began serving as a burgess for Mulberry Island (**21**), and in September 1632 he represented the area from Denbigh (**23**) to Water's Creek. He was still alive in 1635 and was in possession of some land in Elizabeth City County (18) (MCGC 8, 12, 23, 46, 119, 131; CBE 40, 59; VCR 4:552; PB 1 Pt. 1:67-68, 309; HEN 1:139, 179; DOR 1:39).

HUMPHREY CLOUGH

Sometime after April 1623 but before February 16, 1624, Humphrey Clough died at one of the settlements on the lower side of the James River, within the corporation of James City (8-15) (CBE 41).

EUSTACE CLOVELL

On May 31, 1607, Eustace Clovell, a gentleman and one of the first Jamestown (1) colonists, was shot by Indians while he was outside of the fort. Eustace died on June 8, 1607 (HAI 116).

WILLIAM CLUCH

On December 13, 1624, William Cluch agreed to swap a "peece" (firearm) for a hog. John Haule witnessed the bargain at Cluch's house on Jamestown Island (1) (MCGC 35).

JOHN COATES

In 1619 John Coates, a 32-year-old embroiderer from London, went to Virginia on the *Bona Nova* at the expense of the Virginia Company. Therefore, he probably was a Company servant or tenant (FER 295).

***

JOSEPH COBB

Joseph Cobb, an ancient planter, came to Virginia on the *Treasurer* in 1613. By early 1625 he was residing in Elizabeth City (18), where he was a household head. Joseph, who was said to be 25 years old, shared a home with his wife, Elizabeth, and John Snowood. The Cobb household was relatively well supplied with stored food and defensive weaponry. In 1625 Joseph Cobb testified that he and Pharoah Flinton had inventoried the goods of the late Thomas Clark, who had died at sea in May while aboard the *Elizabeth* of London. On August 4, 1637, Joseph Cobb patented 400 acres in Warresqueak (Isle of Wight) County, using as headrights himself, wife Elizabeth, and their sons Joseph and Benjamin. On March

1, 1654, when Joseph made his will, he indicated that he was age 60 and bequeathed land to his wife, Elizabeth, and livestock to sons Benjamin and Pharoah and daughter, Elizabeth. His son Joseph appears to have died (CBE 64; MCGC 198-199; PB 1 Pt.2:506, 901; Isle of Wight Deeds and Wills A:44; DOR 1:53, 702).

ELIZABETH COBB (MRS. JOSEPH COBB)

Elizabeth, the wife of Joseph Cobb, came to Virginia in 1623 on the *Bonny Bess* and in early 1625 was sharing her husband's home in Elizabeth City (18). She was age 25. When Joseph Cobb patented 400 acres in Warresqueak or Isle of Wight County on August 4, 1637, he used Elizabeth, himself, and sons Joseph and Benjamin as headrights, thereby suggesting that the family had made a round trip to England. On March 1, 1654, when Joseph Cobb made his will, he bequeathed land to his wife, Elizabeth, and livestock to sons Benjamin and Pharoah and daughter, Elizabeth (son Joseph appears to have died). On March 7, 1657, Elizabeth and her son, Pharoah sold some land that was adjacent to their plantation. She died sometime prior to April 10, 1671 (CBE 64; MCGC 198-199; PB 1 Pt. 2:506, 901; Isle of Wight Deeds and Wills A:44, 53; DOR 1:702-703).

***

WILLIAM COBB

William Cobb married Elizabeth Dagg (Dag), one of the young maids the Virginia Company sent to the colony in September 1621. On May 9, 1625, William Mutch (Moch) of Jamestown (1) testified that when William Cobb was preparing to go on a trading voyage, he made his will and gave Mutch three debtors' promissory notes. Mutch stated that shortly after Cobb's death, John Pountis had asked for the notes, for the decedent had failed to pay the cost of his wife's passage. Mutch said that he had given the notes to Richard Peirce to pass along to Pountis (MCGC 59; FER 309).

ELIZABETH DAGG (DAG) COBB (MRS. WILLIAM COBB)

Elizabeth Dagg (Dag) a young maid who came to Virginia in September 1621 on the *Warwick*, was 19 years old and was born in

Lynchowse, England. Prior to her departure, Christopher Marten and Sir Nicholas Couch had vouched for her character. Sometime after Elizabeth Dagg arrived in the colony, she married William Cobb, who died before he had paid mariner John Pountis for her transportation to Virginia (FER 309; MCGC 59).

***

***

RICHARD COCKE

On December 24, 1627, Richard Cocke, purser of the *Thomas and John*, was in Jamestown (1) where he testified that four of Mr. Sharples' men had run away while being transported to Virginia. He added that Mr. Moore, who was on the same voyage, had offered to supply five servants. On February 10, 1629, Richard, who was back in Virginia and serving as Patrick Canada's attorney, was ordered to take custody of Thomas Hunter's estate on Canada's behalf. On June 5, 1632, the justices of the General Court learned that Richard Cocke had married John Brown's widow and settled her late husband's estate. Because he was serving as conservator of the decedent's estate on behalf of his orphans, Cocke was awarded a modest commission (MCGC 158, 186, 201).

MRS. RICHARD COCKE (SEE MRS. JOHN BROWN [BROWNE])

***

SAMUEL COCKE

On September 26, 1627, Samuel Cocke, master of the *Samuell* of Newcastle, left London and set sail for Virginia (CBE 80).

RICHARD COCKWELL

On March 22, 1622, when the Indians attacked Edward Bennett's plantation in Warresqueak (26), Richard Cockwell was killed (VCR 3:571).

JOHN CODRINGTON (CUDDERINGTON, CODRINTON)

John Codrington (Cudderington, Codrinton), a gentleman, arrived in Virginia in 1608 as part of the 1st Supply of new settlers in Jamestown (1). On December 29, 1608, he was among those accompanying Captain John Smith on a journey to Pamunkey to search for some Germans who had fled from the colony. Smith included in his writings a verse by Codrington, who identified himself as a sometime-soldier turned templar (CJS 1:267, 313; 2:190, 216, 228).

THOMAS COE (COO)

Thomas Coe (Coo), a gentleman, reached Jamestown (1) in 1608 as part of the 1st Supply of new settlers. Later, he accompanied Captain John Smith on a trading voyage into the Pamunkey River. Smith later claimed that Coe spoke against him (CJS 1:216, 222, 274; 2:161, 193, 206).

DANIEL COGLEY (SEE DANIEL CUGLEY) JOHN COKER (COOKER)

On February 16, 1624, John Coker (Cooker) was living in Elizabeth City (18), where he was still residing in early 1625. He was a member of the household headed by William Gayne and Robert Newman, which included several people. John, who was age 25, appears to have been free (CBE 65).

[NO FIRST NAME] COLE

According to Ralph Hamor's 1614 narrative, in 1611 Mr. Cole, a man named Kitchens, and three others planned to head to Ocanahowan (now North Carolina), where it was reported that some Spanish people were living. Captain John Smith said that all five men were caught by the Indians who had been hired to bring them home. Smith claimed that Cole and Kitchens were ringleaders of the plan to abandon Jamestown (1) (CJS 2:240; HAI 822).

FRANCIS COLE

Francis Cole, an ancient planter, came to Virginia on the *Susan* in 1616. In early 1625 he was living in Elizabeth City (18) in the household headed by William Cole. Francis was then age 27 (CBE 73).

GEORGE COLE

On March 22, 1622, when the Indians attacked Edward Bennett's plantation in

Warresqueak (**26**), George Cole was killed (VCR 3:571).

JOHN COLE

John Cole set sail for Virginia in September 1619 on the *Margaret* of Bristol. He accompanied Captain John Woodlief and went to the colony at the expense of the Society of Berkeley Hundred's investors. Cole was headed for Berkeley Hundred (**55**), where he was supposed to serve for seven years in exchange for 40 acres. His rate of pay was to be set annually and his wife (who remained behind in England) was supposed to receive support from Berkeley Hundred's investors. John Cole seems to have died within a short time of his arrival in Virginia (VCR 3:187, 197, 199, 213-215; CBE 13-14).

SOLOMON COLE

On August 20, 1630, Solomon Cole witnessed Edward Waters' will, which was made in Elizabeth City (**18**) (SH 13).

WILLIAM COLE

William Cole went to Virginia in September 1619 on the *Margaret* of Bristol with Captain John Woodlief. He went at the expense of the Society of Berkeley Hundred's investors and was headed for Berkeley Hundred (**55**), where he was supposed to serve for seven years in exchange for 30 acres. William seems to have died within a short time of his arrival (VCR 3:198, 213; CBE 14).

WILLIAM COLE (COALE)

William Cole (Coale) came to Virginia in 1618 on the *Neptune* and on February 16, 1624, was living in Elizabeth City (**18**). On September 20, 1624, his land in Elizabeth City was in the hands of Captain Thomas Davis, who appears to have been a tenant. In early 1625, when a muster was taken of Elizabeth City's inhabitants, William was described as the head of a household that included 27-year-old Francis Cole and 26-year-old Roger Farbrase. They shared a dwelling and were relatively well supplied with stored food and defensive weaponry. In May 1625, when a list of patented land was sent back to England, William Cole was credited with 50 acres in Elizabeth City, land that had been planted (seated).

On October 16, 1629, William served as a burgess for the settlers in Nutmeg Quarter (**24**) (CBE 44, 63; PB 1 Pt. 1:37; VCR 4:558; HEN 1:139; DOR 1:52, 713).

[NO FIRST NAME] COLEMAN

Sergeant Coleman was ordered to arrest Elias LaGuard, one of merchant Richard Stephens' debtors, and bring him to court in Jamestown (**1**). Since Coleman failed to do so, on March 7, 1629, he was obliged to post a bond guaranteeing that he would comply (MCGC 193).

HENRY COLEMAN

Henry Coleman may have come to Virginia in 1622. On February 26, 1627, he testified that he had been aboard the *Furtherance* when Margaret Biard (Byard) died around August 3, 1622, while enroute to the colony. He said that Nathaniel Basse took custody of her belongings, which were inventoried accurately by William Newman. On January 3, 1633, Henry Coleman received Christopher Windmill's 60-acre leasehold in Elizabeth City (**17**), subletting it from Francis Hough, who had wed Windmill's widow. On May 30, 1634, Henry Coleman was identified as an Elizabeth City planter whose 60 acres abutted south on the Indian House Thicket. Later in the year, he was excommunicated from his local parish for wearing his hat in church and speaking scornfully, thereby raising the possibility that he was a religious dissenter. On June 6, 1635, he patented 150 acres in Elizabeth City on the basis of three headrights (MCGC 141, 481; PB 1 Pt. 1:147-148, 241).

[NO FIRST NAME] COLFER

Sometime prior to March 22, 1622, Mr. Colfer, an overseer of Lady Elizabeth Dale's Virginia property, loaned corn to Captain George Thorpe of Berkeley Hundred (**55**), a man who was killed in the Indian attack. On March 7, 1625, the General Court decided that Lady Dale's current overseer, Charles Harmer, would be compensated from Thorpe's estate. Lady Dale owned land on Jamestown Island (**1**), on the Eastern Shore (**72**), at Coxendale (**64**), and in Charles City near Shirley Hundred (**41**) (MCGC 48).

EDWARD COLLETT

Edward Collett came to Virginia with Edward Grindon on the *James* and set sail from England on July 31, 1622 (FER 400).

SAMUEL COLLIER

Samuel Collier, a youth, was one of the first Jamestown (1) colonists. In December 1608 he accompanied Captain John Smith on an overland journey to Werowocomoco, on the York River, and stayed behind with Powhatan so that he could learn the Indian language. In 1623 Smith described Samuel Collier as one of the "most ancientest Planters" and said that he was knowledgeable about the Indians' language, habitat, and living conditions. He also indicated that Samuel was accidentally slain by an English sentinel (CJS 1:209, 235, 245; 2:182, 193, 315).

HENRY COLLINGS

Henry Collings, a gentleman and Virginia Company investor, came to Virginia in the 1st Supply of new settlers and would have lived in Jamestown (1) (CJS 1:241; 2:190, 275).

EDWARD COLLINGWOOD

In June 1619 Edward Collingwood, a gentleman and citizen of London, claimed that Virginia Company adventurers were allowed to pay £12.10 for 100 acres of land (EAE 8).

[NO FIRST NAME] COLLINS

According to George Percy's narrative, during the winter of 1609–1610, the infamous "Starving Time," a Jamestown (1) resident named Collins murdered his wife and salted her flesh, preserving it as food. Percy said that Collins confessed to the crime under torture and was executed by being hung by the thumbs with weights on his feet (HAI 505).

[NO FIRST NAME] COLLINS

On March 22, 1622, when the Indians attacked Captain John Berkeley's plantation at Falling Creek (68), Thomas Wood's manservant, Collins, was killed (VCR 3:565).

***

MR. COLLINS

Mr. Collins died in Jamestown (1) after April 1623 but before February 16, 1624 (CBE 39).

MRS. COLLINS

Mrs. Collins died in Jamestown (1) after April 1623 but before February 16, 1624 (CBE 39).

***

DAVID COLLINS

Sometime after April 1623 but before February 16, 1624, David Collins died at one of the settlements on the lower side of the James River, within the corporation of James City (8-15) (CBE 41).

HENRY COLLINS

On December 4, 1634, when Hugh Cox received a court order entitling him to a patent, he listed Henry Collins as a headright (PB 1 Pt. 1:282).

JOAN (JONE) COLLINS

Joan (Jone) Collins came to Virginia with William Craddock on the *James* and left England on July 31, 1622 (FER 400).

***

JOHN COLLINS

John Collins came to Virginia on the *Supply* in 1620. By January 22, 1625, he and his wife, Susan, were living in West and Shirley Hundred (41) where he was a 30-year-old household head. The Collins family shared their home with 8-year-old Ann Usher. In 1625 John Collins' household was amply supplied with stored food and defensive weaponry and had some cattle and poultry. Court records suggest that John Collins was alive in June 1627 when his wife testified about events that took place at West and Shirley Hundred (CBE 52; MCGC 149; DOR 1:13).

SUSAN COLLINS (MRS. JOHN COLLINS)

Susan, John Collins' wife, was an ancient planter who came to Virginia in 1613 on the

Treasurer. By January 22, 1625, she was living with her husband at West and Shirley Hundred (41). Sharing the Collins home was 8-year-old Ann Usher, who was Virginia-born. In early 1625 Susan Collins was age 40 and was 10 years older than her husband. On June 4, 1627, Mrs. John Collins, her maidservant, and several other women were interviewed by William Farrer, a local official, about a young male servant's sexual activities with some girls at West and Shirley Hundred, one of whom was Ann Usher (CBE 52; MCGC 149).

***

JOSIAH (JOSIAS) COLLINS

Josiah (Josias) Collins died at Warresqueak (26) sometime after April 1623 but before February 16, 1624 (CBE 42).

PETER COLLINS

Peter Collins came to Virginia on the *Adam* in 1621 and on February 16, 1624, was living at Warresqueak (26). On February 7, 1625, when a muster was made of the plantation's inhabitants, Peter was identified as a servant in Edward Bennett's household. On March 13, 1626, the General Court determined that Peter Collins was supposed to serve Mr. Bennett for four years (CBE 42; HOT 241; MCGC 97).

ROBERT COLLINS

Robert Collins, a London haberdasher, arrived in Jamestown (1) on September 12, 1623, on the *Bonny Bess* and took the oath of supremacy. He may have been the Mr. Collins who died in Jamestown sometime prior to February 16, 1624 (MCGC 6; CBE 39).

STEPHEN COLLINS

On May 16, 1621, Stephen Collins was identified as one of the servants sent to Virginia by Nicholas Hyde. He was placed in John Boyse's household at Martin's Hundred (7) (VCR 3:451).

THOMAS COLLINS

On February 27, 1619, a boy named Thomas Collins, who was being detained at Bridewell and was one of the children rounded up from the streets of London, was among those to be sent to Virginia. A delay apparently occurred, for on May 13, 1620, he again was selected for transportation to the colony. On February 16, 1624, Thomas Collins was living at Warresqueak (26), Edward Bennett's plantation (CBE 13, 20, 42).

THOMAS COLLINS

On July 19, 1627, Thomas Collins shipped goods from London to Virginia on the *James* (CBE 79).

JAMES COLLIS

James Collis died in Elizabeth City (17, 18) sometime after April 1623 but before February 16, 1624 (CBE 45).

JOHN COLLISON (COLLSON?)

On July 31, 1627, John Collison (Collson?) shipped goods from London to Virginia on the *Hopewell* (CBE 79).

STEPHEN COLLOWE (COLLOE)

Stephen Collowe (Colloe) came to Virginia on the *George* in 1623. On February 16, 1624, he was living in Elizabeth City (18) and was a member of Captain William Tucker's household. In early 1625 Stephen was identified as age 23 and was still a member of the Tucker household (CBE 43, 63).

THOMAS COLLY

On February 16, 1624, Thomas Colly was living at Hog Island (16) (CBE 41).

ABRAHAM COLMAN

Sometime after April 1623 but before February 16, 1624, Abraham Colman died at one of the settlements on the lower side of the James River, within the corporation of James City (8-15) (CBE 41).

JOHN COLLSON

On May 20, 1607, John Collson, a mariner, accompanied Captain Christopher Newport on an exploratory voyage of the James River. Therefore, Collson would have spent time on Jamestown Island (1) (HAI 102).

SUSAN COLSON

On June 24, 1635, when Adam Thorogood patented some land, he indicated that he had paid for Susan Colson's transportation to Virginia on the *Hopewell* in 1628 (PB 1 Pt. 1:179).

***

HENRY COLTMAN

Henry Coltman, an ancient planter, came to Virginia on the *Noah* in August 1610. On February 16, 1624, he and his wife were living at Bermuda Hundred (39). On January 24, 1625, when a muster was taken of Bermuda Hundred's inhabitants, Henry was identified as a 30-year-old household head. His wife, Ann, was four years his junior. The Coltman household was relatively well supplied with stored food and defensive weaponry. In February 1625 Henry Coltman was called on to testify in some litigation involving Sir George Yeardley and Captain John Martin (CBE 36, 54, 69; DOR 1:11).

ANN COLTMAN
(MRS. HENRY COLTMAN)

Ann, who became Henry Coltman's wife, came to Virginia in May 1620 on the *London Merchant*. In February 1624 the Coltman couple was living at Bermuda Hundred (39). They were still there on January 24, 1625, at which time Ann was described as age 26 (CBE 36, 54).

***

WILLIAM COLTMAN

On February 10, 1622, when Anna Coltman of Christ Church, Newgate, London, made her will, she indicated that her son, William Coltman, was then in Virginia. Mrs. Coltman's will was proved on August 25, 1623 (EEAC 14; WAT 141).

FRANCIS COLUMBELL

On September 6, 1634, Francis Columbell shipped goods from London to Virginia on the *Revenge* (CBE 119).

THOMAS COMBAR

On March 22, 1622, when the Indians attacked Martin's Hundred (7), Thomas Combar was slain (VCR 3:570).

COMAHUM

In April 1623 Comahum, an Indian great man, accompanied a youth named Chanco (Chauco) to Martin's Hundred (7) and told the survivors that the Pamunkeys were detaining some of the colonists they had captured during the March 1622 attack. The Indian messengers said that Opechancanough offered to release the prisoners if the Indians were allowed to plant their corn. Comahum, who was implicated in the killings at Martin's Hundred, was sent to the governor in Jamestown (1) in chains. Later, he and Chanco were allowed to return to Pamunkey, and the prisoners were released in exchange for some beads (VCR 4:98-101).

THOMAS COMBE

On September 29, 1632, Thomas Combe, who was then in Virginia, sent a letter to John Smyth of Nibley discussing the cattle that belonged to Berkeley Hundred (55). He made reference to John Gibbs, Richard Milton, and the governor, and asked Smyth to consider reviving the plantation (S of N 41).

AUSTEN COMBES

Austen Combes, a servant in Sir George Yeardley's household, was living in urban Jamestown (1) on February 16, 1624 (CBE 38).

JAMES COMER

On November 4, 1631, James Comer shipped goods on the *Gift* from Barnstable to Virginia. He was the *Gift's* master (CBE 97).

JOHN COMES (COOMES)

John Comes (Coomes) came to Virginia on the *Marigold* and arrived on May 12, 1619. He was one of the Virginia Company servants whom Captain Christopher Lawne brought to the colony. John reportedly was given to incumbent Governor George Yeardley so that he could be put to the Company's use, and on February 16, 1624, he was living on the Eastern Shore, perhaps on the Company Land (76). By February 4, 1625, he had moved to the Treasurer's Plantation (11), across the James River from Jamestown Island (CBE 46, 60; MCGC 90).

WILLIAM COMES (COOMES)

On February 16, 1624, William Comes (Coomes) was living on Virginia's Eastern Shore (**72-78**). Later, he relocated to a plantation on the lower side of the James River, west of Gray's Creek (**8, 9**). He died there sometime prior to February 4, 1625 (CBE 46, 61).

NICHOLAS COMIN (COMON, CUMMINGS, COMMYN)

Nicholas Comin (Comon, Cummings, Commyn) came to Virginia on the *Gift* in 1622 and on February 16, 1624, was living on the lower side of the James River, within the corporation of James City, east of Gray's Creek (**10-15**). On February 4, 1625, Nicholas was living at the Treasurer's Plantation (**11**) and was identified as one of Treasurer George Sandys' servants. On May 5, 1626, he testified before the General Court about Thomas Hitchcock's securing his own freedom by paying Sandys' agent, Thomas Swift, for the time left on his contract (CBE 41, 60; MCGC 101-102).

FRANCES COMPTON

On February 16, 1624, Frances Compton was living in the Neck O' Land (**5**) within the corporation of James City (CBE 35).

JOHN COMPTON

On August 16, 1627, John Compton shipped goods from London to Virginia on the *Truelove* (CBE 79).

[NO FIRST NAME] CONDALL

Condall, a porter, set out for Virginia on April 17, 1619 (FER 107).

HENRY CONEY

On July 24, 1632, Henry Coney, a gentleman, received a 21-year lease for land in Archer's Hope (**6**), near the head of Archer's Hope (now College) Creek. Prior to the time his lease was confirmed, Coney cleared his acreage, constructed some buildings, and named the property "Coney Burrough" (PB 1 Pt. 1:130).

THOMAS CONLY

On March 22, 1622, when the Indians attacked Edward Bennett's plantation in Warresqueak (**26**), Thomas Conly was killed (VCR 3:571).

WILLIAM CONNER

On August 13, 1634, William Connor, an Elizabeth City planter, received a 21-year lease for some acreage on the Back River in Elizabeth City (**19**) (PB 1 Pt. 1:152).

***

EDWARD CONSTABLE

In 1624 Edward Constable of St. Clement Danes, Westminster, a 47-year-old scissors-maker, testified in litigation involving the Virginia-bound ships *Treasurer* and *Neptune* in 1618–1619. He said that he and his wife, Sibell, were passengers on the *Treasurer*, which the Earl of Warwick had declared he was assigning to his cousin Captain Samuel Argall (EAE 14).

SIBELL CONSTABLE (MRS. EDWARD CONSTABLE)

In 1624, Sibell, the 36-year-old wife of scissors-maker Edward Constable of St. Clement Danes, Westminster, testified that she and her husband were passengers on the *Treasurer*. Sibell's testimony was given in litigation concerning the ships *Treasurer* and *Neptune* which were in Virginia in 1618–1619 (EAE 14).

***

JOHN CONSTABLE (CUNSTABLE)

On February 8, 1634, John Constable (Cunstable) and some other Virginia colonists were accused of attempting to defraud customs officers with regard to a shipment of tobacco (CBE 111).

ROBERT CONSTABLE (CUNSTABLE)

On September 12, 1623, Robert Constable (Cunstable), a gentleman from North Allerton in Yorkshire, arrived in Jamestown (**1**) on the *Bonny Bess* and took the oath of supremacy. Earlier in the year he had been described as the brother of Philip Constable and Mrs. Place of Dinsdale. On February

16, 1624, Robert Constable was residing in the Jamestown Island household of John Osbourn. In November he inherited a sow from John Phillimore of Jamestown (CBE 40; MCGC 6, 27; VCR 4:164).

THOMAS CONSTABLE (CUNSTABLE)

According to records maintained by the Drapers Company in London, Thomas Constable (Cunstable), a poor man, settled in Virginia in 1618 (SR 879).

WILLIAM CONSTABLE (CUNSTABLE)

On August 31, 1625, William Constable (Cunstable) sent word to the Ferrars that he was dispatching a ship to Virginia with William Reynolds as master. Official records reveal that Constable and Arthur Swaine had sent out the *Flying Hart* of Flushing, a poorly provisioned ship that arrived in Virginia in December 1625. Both men seem to have had a working relationship with the Virginia Company. On March 13, 1626, the General Court acknowledged that William Constable was to receive some tobacco, a bequest from Robert Wright of Jamestown Island (1). Simultaneously, he was ordered to collect a debt from Captain Crowshaw's estate (MCGC 90, 97; CBE 71).

AARON (ARON) CONWAY (CONAWAY)

In 1622 Aaron (Aron) Conway (Conaway) came to Virginia on the *Southampton* and on February 16, 1624, was living on the lower side of the James River at Captain Samuel Mathews' plantation (15). On February 4, 1625, Aaron, who was age 20, was identified as one of Mathews' servants. On June 17, 1625, when Aaron Conway testified before the General Court, he gave his age as 22, identified himself as one of Captain Mathews' servants, and said that he had been involved in clearing some ground near Captain Powell's houses (14) (CBE 40, 60; MCGC 66).

[NO FIRST NAME] CONWELL

On July 4, 1623, Virginia Company officials were informed that Mr. Conwell would send his surplus goods to Martin's Hundred (7) (VCR 4:245-246).

MOSES CONYERS

Moses Conyers died at Bermuda Hundred (39) sometime after April 1623 but before February 16, 1624 (CBE 36).

PHILLIP COOCKE (COOKE?, COCKE?)

Phillip Coocke (Cooke?, Cocke?) died in Elizabeth City (17, 18) on July 8, 1624 (CBE 67).

ANN COOKE

On February 16, 1624, Ann Cooke was living in Elizabeth City (17, 18) (CBE 44).

ARTHUR COOKE

Arthur Cooke came to Virginia on the *Furtherance*. He died in Jamestown (1) sometime after April 1623 but before February 16, 1624 (CBE 39).

CHRISTOPHER COOKE

In 1621 Christopher Cooke, one of Sir Francis Wyatt's servants, accompanied him to Virginia, arriving on the *George*. On January 24, 1625, Christopher, who was 25-years-old, was residing in urban Jamestown (1) in the Wyatt household (CBR 54).

***

CISBY COOKE

On March 22, 1622, when the Indians attacked Martin's Hundred (7), Cisby Cooke was killed (VCR 3:570).

MRS. CISBY COOKE

Mrs. Cisby Cooke was slain on March 22, 1622, when the Indians attacked Martin's Hundred (7) (VCR 3:570).

***

EDWARD COOKE

On February 16, 1624, Edward Cooke was a servant in Sir Francis Wyatt's household in urban Jamestown (1) (CBE 38).

ELLIN COOKE

Ellin Cooke went to Virginia in June 1620 on the *London Merchant*. On January 22,

1625, she was living at West and Shirley Hundred (**41**), where she was a 25-year-old servant in Robert Partin's household (CBE 52).

GEORGE COOKE

George Cooke died in Elizabeth City (**17, 18**) sometime after April 1623 but before February 16, 1624 (CBE 45).

JAMES COOKE

On January 30, 1625, James Cooke, who was in Virginia, was identified as Edward Kingswell's "old servant" (WAT 1316).

JOHN COOKE

In 1619, it was decided that John Cooke of London, who had been convicted of stealing and was being detained in Newgate Prison, would be reprieved and sent to the colony (CBE 12).

***

JOHN COOKE

On June 20, 1620, John Cooke received a certificate from Governor George Yeardley, who acknowledged that he had fulfilled his obligation to the Virginia Company. It is unclear whether he was a Company tenant, employee, or servant. On January 3, 1625, John Cooke sued Peter Langman of Jamestown (**1**), who owed him funds. On the other hand, John was sued by Lewis Baily in 1628 and was jailed temporarily. By June 22, 1635, John Cooke was dead and his widow, Jane, had married Alexander Stoner, a brick-maker. When the Stoners patented some land, they used Jane's headright and that of her late husband, John Cooke (MCGC 41, 159; PB 1 Pt. 1:254).

JANE COOKE
(MRS. JOHN COOKE,
MRS. ALEXANDER STONER)
(SEE JANE COOKE STONER)

By June 22, 1635, Jane, the late John Cooke's widow, had married Alexander Stoner, a brick maker, who owned land on Jamestown Island (**1**) and in the Neck O'Land (**5**). When the Stoners patented some land, they used Jane's headright and

that of her late husband, John Cooke, who had fulfilled his obligation to the Virginia Company by June 20, 1620 (PB 1 Pt. 1:254).

***

JOHN COOKE

On February 16, 1624, John Cooke was living on Jamestown Island in the household of John Burrows. He was still there on January 24, 1625, and was identified as a 27-year-old servant in the Burrows household (CBE 38, 56).

RICHARD COOKE

On February 9, 1633, the justices of the General Court decided that Richard Cooke was entitled to compensation from Captain John Preene's estate for rental of warehouse space, cooperage, court appearances he had made on Preene's behalf, and for bringing a boat up to Jamestown (**1**). It is unclear where Richard Cooke's warehouse was located (MCGC 201-202).

ROBERT COOKE

On March 12, 1627, the justices of the General Court heard testimony about a violent fight between Robert Cooke and Thomas Lawley, which occurred while they were at sea aboard the ship *Plantation*. Lawley later died of the injuries he received (MCGC 144).

ROGER COOKE

According to Captain John Smith, Roger Cooke, a gentleman, was one of the first Jamestown (**1**) colonists, having arrived in 1607 (CJS 2:141).

THOMAS COOKE

On February 27, 1619, Thomas Cooke, a youth, was identified as one of the children rounded up from the streets of London so that they could be sent to Virginia. He may have been the individual killed in the Indian attack on the College (**66**), home to many of the Virginia Company servants who arrived in the colony in November 1619 (CBE 13).

THOMAS COOKE

On March 22, 1622, when the Indians attacked Edward Bennett's plantation in

Warresqueak **(26)**, Thomas Cooke was killed (VCR 3:571).

THOMAS COOKE

Thomas Cooke was slain on March 22, 1622, when the Indians attacked the settlers living at the College **(66)** (VCR 3:566).

WILLIAM COOKE

On February 16, 1624, William Cooke was living in Elizabeth City **(17, 18)**. Sometime prior to December 13, 1624, he and Mr. Thomas Hethersoll borrowed a boat from Jamestown Island **(1)** carpenter Richard Tree so that they could take their goods to Blunt Point **(22)**. The two men reportedly lost the boat when they carelessly abandoned it and went ashore at Martin's Hundred **(7)** (CBE 44; MCGC 35-36, 40).

WILLIAM COOKSEY

On February 16, 1624, William Cooksey was living at the College **(66)** in Henrico (CBE 35).

***

WILLIAM COOKSEY

On February 16, 1624, William Cooksey was living with his wife and infant in the Jamestown Island **(1)** household of John Haul (Hall). On January 24, 1625, when a muster was made of Jamestown's inhabitants, William was still there but his wife and child were not (CBE 40, 56).

MRS. WILLIAM COOKSEY

On February 16, 1624, Mrs. William Cooksey was living with her husband and infant in the Jamestown Island **(1)** household of John Haul (Hall) (CBE 40).

[NO FIRST NAME] COOKSEY

Mr. and Mrs. William Cooksey's child, an infant, was living with his parents in the Jamestown Island **(1)** household of John Haul (Hall) on February 16, 1624 (CBE 40).

***

WILLIAM COOKSEY

By December 2, 1628, William Cooksey, who was identified as a Warwick River

planter, had obtained a 150-acre leasehold on Blunt Point Creek **(22)**, adjacent to that of ancient planter John Laydon. Cooksey may have been the man living at the College **(66)** in 1624 (PB 1 Pt. 1:69, 95).

TOBIAS COOP

On July 24, 1621, Virginia Company officials noted that Tobias Coop, a clothier, had obtained two shares of Virginia land from Mr. Carter (VCR 1:523).

[NO FIRST NAME] COOPER

A man identified only as Cooper, who had been with Captain John Smith in Virginia, signed his narrative, *True Travels*, in 1629. He may have been Thomas Cooper (Couper, Cowper), one of the first Jamestown **(1)** colonists (CJS 3:219).

JOHN COOPER

In 1617 John Cooper, one of William Ganey's servants, accompanied him to Virginia on the *Treasurer*. On February 16, 1624, John was living in the Rev. George Keith's household in Elizabeth City **(18)**. On January 12, 1624, when William Ganey patented some land, he used John as a headright (PB 1 Pt. 1:39; CBE 44).

***

JUSTINIAN COOPER (COWPER, COUPER)

Justinian Cooper (Cowper, Couper) came to Virginia sometime prior to November 1624. By that time he had married Anne (Anna) Oliffe (Olife), the stepdaughter of Captain Christopher Lawne, whose plantation **(25)** in Warresqueak was established in 1619. On February 9, 1628, Justinian presented the inventory of Thomas Green of Warresqueak to the General Court and received letters of administration. On September 13, 1636, he patented 1,050 acres at the head of Lawnes Creek, citing his own personal adventure. When Cooper repatented that acreage on August 16, 1637, reference was made to his dwelling. By October 24, 1639, he had succeeded in acquiring an additional 850 acres adjacent to his own land. Justinian Cooper was described as a gentleman on March 16, 1642, when he patented 2,400 acres in Isle of Wight County, acquiring part of his land on behalf of his wife's £50 investment and personal adventure. He repatented that acreage in September 1645. When Justinian made his will on March 26, 1650, he named his wife, Anne, as his executrix (MCGC 35, 166; EEAC 15; PB 1 Pt. 1:380, 454; Pt. 2:681, 874; 2:32; BOD 531-532; Isle of Wight County Book A:101-103, 114).

ANNE (ANNA) OLIFFE (OLIFE) HARRISON COOPER (COWPER, COUPER) (MRS. JUSTINIAN COOPER [COWPER, COUPER], MRS. JAMES HARRISON)

Anne (Anna) Oliffe (Olife), Captain Christopher Lawne's stepdaughter, accompanied him and her mother to Virginia in spring 1619 and most likely went to his plantation (25). During the summer months, Captain Lawne and many of the inhabitants of his plantation became mortally ill. By November 1619 the survivors withdrew to Bermuda Hundred (39), where Lawne himself died. Anne Oliffe, meanwhile, married Ensign James Harrison, who was killed at Bennett's Welcome or Warresqueak (26) on March 22, 1622, and Anne too was reported dead. However, she survived and by November 8, 1624, had wed Justinian Cooper. As James Harrison's widow, Anne was ordered to satisfy the decedent's debt to Captain Hamor and one he incurred when purchasing the services of three indentured servants. When Justinian Cooper patented 2,400 acres of land in March 1642, he claimed 500 acres on the basis of wife Anne's £50 personal adventure and another 500 acres to which she was entitled as surviving heir of her brother, Robert Oliffe. On March 26, 1650, when Justinian Cooper made his will, he named wife Anne as his executrix. The Coopers do not appear to have produced heirs (MCGC 30-31, 35; PB 1 Pt. 2:874; BOD 531-532; Isle of Wight County Book A:101-103, 114).

***

THOMAS COOPER (COWPER, COUPER)

Thomas Cooper (Cowper, Couper), who came to Virginia in 1607 and was one of the first Jamestown (1) colonists, was a barber (CJS 1:209; 2:142).

THOMAS COOPER (COWPER, COUPER)

Thomas Cooper (Cowper, Couper) came to Virginia on the *Returne*. On February 4, 1625, he was living on Hog Island (16), where he was a servant in Ralph Hamor's household (CBE 61).

WALTER COOPER (COOP, COWPER, COUPER)

Walter Cooper (Cowper, Couper) came to Virginia on the *Jonathan* in 1619. On February 16, 1624, he was living at the College (66) in the corporation of Henrico. However, by February 4, 1625, he had moved to Captain Samuel Mathews' plantation (15) and was described as a 33-year-old servant in Mathews' household. The will made by London merchant John Westhope in 1656 reveals that a Walter Cooper (Cowper, Couper) was then living on the Maine (3), just west of Jamestown Island, and had a son named Thomas (CBE 35, 60; WITH 186).

WILLIAM COOPER (COUPER)

William Cooper (Couper) came to Virginia in 1618 on the *Neptune*, the ship that brought Lord Delaware and his men to Virginia. In early 1625 William was living in Elizabeth City (17) on the Virginia Company's land. Cooper was then a 22-year-old servant in the household of Captain Francis West, Lord Delaware's brother (CBE 67).

ROBERT COOPY

On September 7, 1619, Robert Coopy was identified as a husbandman from North Nibley in Gloucester County, England. He signed a contract with the Society of Berkeley Hundred's investors, agreeing to work for three years in exchange for all the privileges of a free man and 30 acres of land in Berkeley Hundred (55). Robert was to retain possession of his land for three lifetimes, that is, for three generations (VCR 3:210-211).

SAMUEL COOPY

Samuel Coopy went to Virginia in September 1619 on the *Margaret* of Bristol and accompanied Captain John Woodlief. He went at the expense of the Society of Berkeley Hundred's investors and was headed for

Berkeley Hundred (**55**), where he was supposed to serve for three years in exchange for 15 acres of land. Samuel Coopy seems to have died within a short time of his arrival (VCR 3:198, 213; CBE 14).

***

THOMAS COOPY

Thomas Coopy, a multi-talented worker, reportedly was a carpenter, smith, fowler, and turner. He went to Virginia in September 1619 on the *Margaret* of Bristol with Captain John Woodlief, at the expense of the Society of Berkeley Hundred's investors. Thomas was headed for Berkeley Hundred (**55**), where he was supposed to serve for three years in exchange for 30 acres of land. According to the agreement he made at Stoke, a third of his earnings were to be his own and during his absence, his wife, Joan, was supposed to receive annual support from the Society of Berkeley Hundred. Thomas Coopy, who later was identified as Berkeley Hundred's carpenter, apparently was satisfied with life in the colony, for he asked the Society of Berkeley Hundred to send his wife Joan, son Anthony, and daughter Elizabeth to Virginia. The Society's investors declined and said that he should pay for their passage. By September 10, 1620, a mutually acceptable solution had been found (VCR 3:187, 197, 199, 213-215, 397-400; CBE 13, 28).

JOAN (JOANE) COOPY (MRS. THOMAS COOPY)

On September 10, 1620, Joan (Joane) Coopy, Thomas Coopy's wife, set sail from Bristol on the *Supply*. She was accompanied by their son, Anthony, and daughter, Elizabeth. They were among the new colonists brought by William Tracy and were heading for Berkeley Hundred (**55**) to join Thomas Coopy. Joan was supposed to serve the Society of Berkeley Hundred for a certain number of years in exchange for some land. Joan Coopy and her children arrived at Berkeley Hundred on January 29, 1621, but all of them reportedly died shortly thereafter (CBE 21; VCR 3:396-397, 426).

ANTHONY COOPY

Anthony, the son of Thomas and Joan (Joane) Coopy, set sail for Virginia with William Tracy on September 10, 1620, on the *Supply* of Bristol. He was accompanied by his mother and his sister, Elizabeth, and was one of the new settlers bound for Berkeley Hundred (**55**). Anthony was supposed to serve the Society of Berkeley Hundred for a given amount of time in exchange for some acreage. He arrived at Berkeley Hundred on January 29, 1621, but died shortly thereafter (CBE 21; VCR 3:396, 426).

ELIZABETH COOPY

On September 10, 1620, Elizabeth Coopy, Thomas and Joan Coopy's daughter, set sail from Bristol on the *Supply* with her mother and brother, Anthony. They were among the new colonists being brought by William Tracy to Berkeley Hundred (**55**), where they were to join Thomas Coopy. Elizabeth was supposed to serve the Society of Berkeley Hundred for a certain number of years and, in exchange, was to receive some land. Elizabeth arrived at Berkeley Hundred on January 29, 1621. She survived the March 22, 1622, Indian attack on Berkeley Hundred and on August 1, 1622, Virginia Company officials noted that she was alive (CBE 21, 28; VCR 3:396-397, 426, 674).

***

WALTER COOPY

During mid-to-late summer 1619 the Society of Berkeley Hundred paid Walter Coopy for four squaring axes that he had brought in from Wooten. It is uncertain whether he was a supplier or a colonist being sent to Berkeley Hundred (**55**) (VCR 3:187).

PATRICK COPELAND

In late 1621 the Rev. Patrick Copeland, a clergyman, with financial support from mariners from the *Royal James*, proposed to build a free school in Virginia, in the corporation of Charles City. Virginia Company officials were enthusiastic about his proposal and in November 1621 gave him three shares of land, redeemable for a 300-acre private plantation. Afterward, his patent and compensation (three tenants) were confirmed by the Company. In February 1622 he informed the Company that he had found a suitable usher for the East India School, a man who was a good scholar. The Rev. Copeland was to be rector of the East India School and of the College (**66**), the location in which his parsonage was to be built, and he was named a member of the Council of State. In 1622 Copeland sent his servant, Elias Gale, to Virginia where he was to serve for ten years as an apprentice for the East India School. However, the Indian attack in March 1622 disrupted the plan to build the East India School and the area in which it was to be erected was considered unsafe. In January 1623 Virginia Company officials decided that when the men of the East India School reached Virginia, they should be placed with the surviving College tenants, who had been evacuated to safety and were then living on the lower side of the James River in the vicinity of William Ewen's plantation (13). Later, plans were made for the East India School's men to be sent to Martin's Hundred (7). However, several of those who came to establish the school died before the project actually got underway and officials decided not to build the school at Martin's Hundred. Although there was talk of reviving the project, eventually it was abandoned. In April 1624 the Rev. Patrick Copeland, who had returned to England, was given custody of an Indian boy whom colonist William Perry had sent to England. In 1626 Copeland went to Bermuda, where he became a clerical councilor and preacher. As time went on, he began to support Puritan views and in 1647 was punished with imprisonment. He died around 1651, perhaps in Bermuda (FER 339; VCR 1:531, 539-540, 550, 558-559, 580, 591, 600, 606-608; 2:49, 73, 75-76, 91, 496, 538; 3:531, 533, 537; 4:15, 245-246, 506; MCGC 52; LEF 1:697).

THOMAS CORDER

On February 16, 1624, Thomas Corder was living in Archer's Hope (6) (CBE 41).

JOHN CORDEROY

On March 22, 1622, when the Indians attacked Edward Bennett's plantation in Warresqueak (26), John Corderoy was killed (VCR 3:571).

MRS. CORKER

On December 8, 1624, Peaceable Sherwood, then a resident of Jamestown (1), informed the General Court that he knew that a trunk containing some documents had been broken open and that he had seen papers floating down the river. He said that Mrs. Corker indicated that they were articles of agreement. She may have been the wife of John Corker (MCGC 29).

***

JOHN CORKER

John Corker, Ensign James Harrison's servant, came to Virginia sometime prior to the March 22, 1622, Indian attack, at which time Harrison was killed. On November 21, 1624, Corker testified before local commander Captain William Tucker of Elizabeth City (17, 18) about a dispute being aired before the General Court. He stated that John Costard and David Barry were not partners and that he was not their servant. He also testified in a suit involving plaintiff Captain Ralph Hamor and defendants Justinian Cooper and his wife, Anne, the widow of James Harrison of Warresqueak (26). Sometime prior to September 1632 John Corker commenced serving as a burgess for Pasbehay (3), the mainland west of Jamestown Island, and he also was paid for some duties he performed on behalf of the public. In February 1633 Corker represented Pasbehay, Jamestown (1), and the settlements along the Chickahominy River, and in August 1633 he was ordered to keep an accurate account of the tobacco being collected to fund construction of a fort at Old Point Comfort. In February 1637 he patented 6 acres of land near Goose Hill in the eastern end of Jamestown Island, and in August 1640 he acquired a tiny lot in urban Jamestown. In 1645 he served simultaneously as burgess for Jamestown and as clerk of the assembly. He held office until the close of 1653, by which time he had begun representing newly formed Surry County. He also became clerk of Surry's monthly court and, in 1656, a justice of the peace. He increased his landholdings in Surry County and in 1657 patented 1,150 acres near Gray's Creek, across from Jamestown Island. In 1670 John Corker and William Thompson (Thomson), who rented Colonel Thomas Swann's ordinary in Jamestown, proved the will of Thomas Warren of Gray's Creek and Jamestown. Corker's wife in 1656 was named Dorothy. John Corker's political career and business dealings suggest that he was associated with the Jamestown area during the 1630s but moved to Surry during the 1640s or early 1650s (MCGC 35, 213; HEN 1:178, 196, 203, 222, 289, 370, 377; STAN 57-58; PB 1 Pt. 2:521, 730; 4:206; LEO 23-27, 29-31; Surry County Deeds, Wills 1652-1672:6, 13, 31, 76, 98).

DOROTHY CORKER (MRS. JOHN CORKER)

On January 1, 1656, Dorothy Corker was identified as the wife of John Corker of Surry County (Surry County Deeds, Wills 1652–1672:76).

***

JOHN CORNELIUS

John Cornelius, a Virginia Company investor, sent goods to Virginia with Captain Samuel Argall and Thomas Sedan, who were supposed to trade in the colony and then head north to fish for sturgeon (CJS 2:216, 275, 325).

WILLIAM CORNIE (CORME)

On February 16, 1624, William Cornie (Corme) was living in Elizabeth City (**17, 18**) (CBE 43).

PIERRE CORNILLE

In 1621 vine dresser Pierre Cornille, a young man, was among the Walloons and French who indicated their willingness to go to Virginia. In August 1621 the Virginia Company agreed that they could immigrate (CBE 24).

ELLIS CORNISH

On February 4, 1625, Ellis Cornish was authorized by Sir Fernando Gorges to salvage the goods aboard the ship that Captain Edward Stallings had allowed to run aground at Newportes News (**24**) (VCR 4:511-512).

***

JEFFREY CORNISH

Jeffrey Cornish was the brother of Richard Cornish alias Williams, master of the *Ambrose*, who was found guilty of raping a cabin boy. In December 1625 Jeffrey was quoted as insisting that his brother had been wrongfully executed. He also allegedly made threatening remarks about the governor (MCGC 78, 83).

RICHARD CORNISH ALIAS WILLIAMS

On November 30, 1624, Richard Cornish alias Williams was identified as master of the ship *Ambrose* when William Cowse (Couse), a cabin boy, appeared before the General Court. Cowse accused Cornish of sexually assaulting him while the *Ambrose* was anchored in the James River. He testified that afterward, Cornish continued to make advances toward him and threatened to punish him, if he resisted. On January 3, 1625, the ship's boatswain, Walter Mathew, testified in the case, verifying some of Cowse's allegations. Sometime prior to February 8, 1625, Richard Cornish was hanged and William Cowse was ordered to choose another master. Cornish's debts were to be paid from sale of his goods or earnings derived from the hire of Cowse, an indentured servant. The execution of Richard Cornish sparked controversy as far away as Canada and his brother, Jeffrey, threatened revenge (MCGC 34, 42, 47, 81, 85).

***

JOHN CORNISH

On July 31, 1622, John Cornish set sail for Virginia on the *James* and brought three men to the colony (FER 400).

THOMAS CORNISH

On December 31, 1619, officials at Bridewell Prison decided that Thomas Cornish, who was being detained, would be sent to Virginia. He came to the colony on the *Duty* in 1620 and on February 16, 1624, was living on the Eastern Shore. In early 1625 he was identified as a 25-year-old servant at Captain William Eppes's plantation (**74**). On January 1, 1637, Thomas Cornish was mentioned in connection with some timber-cutting on Eppes's plantation (CBE 15, 46, 68; AMES 1:67).

SIMON CORNOCKE (CURNOCKE)

On November 11, 1636, Simon Cornocke (Curnocke) was identified as the late Edward Dewell's master, when serving as

Dewell's executor. Both men lived in Warresqueak (**26**) (SH 27).

COSS (COOS)

In November 1624 Edward Grindon said that during Sir Thomas Dale's government (1611–1616), Captain Webb, then in command at Kecoughtan (**17, 18**), taught an Indian named Coss (Coos) how to shoot. Interpreter Robert Poole added that it was Webb's servant, John Powell, who actually had taught Coss to use a gun, doing so with Webb's permission (MCGC 28).

JOHN COSTARD

On March 22, 1622, when the Indians attacked Edward Bennett's plantation in Warresqueak (**26**), John Costard was slain. On November 30, 1624, when Captain Hamor sued his estate in order to recover a debt, John was identified as the business partner of James Harrison and David Barry, also residents of Warresqueak (VCR 3:571; MCGC 35).

JOHN COTSON

On June 13, 1607, Indians shot at John Cotson, a mariner, near the site of the fort built in Jamestown (**1**) (HAI 117).

THOMAS COTTLE

On May 29, 1635, Thomas Cottle's headright was used by John Parrott when patenting some land on the Nansemond River (**20 c**) (PB 1 Pt. 1:170).

ROBERT COTTON

Robert Cotton, a tobacco pipe maker, came to Virginia in 1608 in the 1st Supply of new colonists. Therefore, he would have resided in Jamestown (**1**) (CJS 1:223; 2:162).

WILLIAM COTTON

The Rev. William Cotton, a clergyman, came to Virginia sometime prior to February 19, 1634, at which time he complained that the churchwardens of Accomack had not gathered the tobacco and corn (church dues) that were to be his salary. His problems in collecting his pay were ongoing. He clashed with Henry Charleton, who allegedly said that if he had encountered Mr. Cotton outside of the churchyard, he would have "kickt him over the Pallyzados." He also called the minister a "black cotted [coated] raskoll." In November 1638 the Rev. William Cotton received a land certificate that would enable him to claim some acreage on Hungars Creek (**78**), using himself, his wife, Ann Graves, and five of his servants as headrights. He had secured a patent for that acreage in July 1637, several months before procuring a land certificate. Cotton was still living on the Eastern Shore in 1644 (PB 1 Pt. 1:434; AMES 1:10-11, 28, 64, 127; 2:330).

REBECCA COUBBER

On February 16, 1624, Rebecca Coubber was living in Elizabeth City (**17, 18**) (CBE 44).

HUGH COULD

On February 27, 1618, officials at Bridewell decided that Hugh Could, a boy, would be detained so that he could be sent to Virginia (HUME 10).

JOHN COUNTWAYNE (COUNTRIVANE, COUNTWAY)

John Countwayne (Countrivane, Countway) died in Jamestown (**1**) between April 1623 and February 16, 1624 (CBE 39).

PETER COURTNEY

On April 25, 1626, the General Court determined that Luke Eden (Aden) owed funds to Peter Courtney, who produced a bill, documenting the debt (MCGC 102).

THOMAS COWELL

On July 31, 1627, Thomas Cowell shipped goods from London to Virginia on the *Hopewell*. On September 26, 1627, he sent another shipment to the colony on the *Samuell* (CBE 79-80).

JOHN COWES

Adam Thorogood paid for John Cowes's transportation to Virginia on the *Bonaventure* in 1634 and on June 24, 1635, used his headright when patenting some land (PB 1 Pt. 1:179).

WALTER COWMAN

On October 14, 1622, Walter Cowman testified against William Wye of the *Garland*, on behalf of Nicholas Young (VCR 3:692-695).

GEORGE COWNDEN

On August 12, 1620, officials at Bridewell decided that George Cownden, a vagrant who was being detained, would be sent to Virginia (CBE 20).

[NO FIRST NAME] COWNES

On April 25, 1625, the General Court learned that Captain Cownes, a mariner who had obtained a supply of corn from Henry Spillman (Spellman) and promised to pay for it, had died before settling his debt (MCGC 56).

JOANNA COWPER

On November 20, 1622, Joanna Cowper, who was being detained in Newgate Prison, was pardoned on account of an outbreak of jail fever and selected to be sent to Virginia (CBE 29).

WILLIAM COWSE (COUSE)

On November 30, 1624, William Cowse, a 29-year-old cabin boy, appeared before the General Court. He alleged that on August 26th he had been sexually assaulted by Captain Richard Cornish alias Williams, master of the *Ambrose*, while the ship was anchored in the James River. Cornish was found guilty and executed. On February 8, 1625, William Cowse was ordered to decide whether he preferred to serve Captain Ralph Hamor (**16**) or Captain John West (**54**). He chose to serve Hamor, with whom he had been staying on Hog Island (MCGC 34, 42, 47).

HUGH COX

On December 6, 1634, Hugh Cox obtained a patent for 500 acres in Charles City near Shirley Hundred (**41**). On August 27, 1635, his land was described as adjacent to that of Walter Aston (PB 1 Pt. 1:282).

PHILIP COX (COXE)

Philip Cox (Coxe) came to Virginia with William Cradock on the *James* and left England on July 31, 1622 (FER 400).

RICHARD COXE

On April 9, 1628, the General Court learned that Richard Coxe, a servant being sent to Richard Bennett's plantation in Warresqueak (**26**), was found to be diseased and unfit to go to Virginia. He was allowed to leave Captain Preen's ship while it was in the Downes (MCGC 171).

RICHARD COXE

On September 4, 1632, when the assembly convened, Richard Coxe served as a burgess for Weyanoke (**52**) (HEN 1:178).

WILLIAM COXE

In 1610 William Coxe, an ancient planter, came to Virginia on the *Godspeed* and in early 1625 was living in Elizabeth City (**18**) in Thomas Boulding's household. He was then 26 years old and a free man. On September 9, 1628, Coxe received a patent for 100 acres of land in Elizabeth City (**17**) near the landholdings of Dictoris Christmas and Christopher Calthrop. In November 1636 William Cox patented 150 acres in what was then Henrico County, at a site above Arrohattock (**66**). He acquired some additional acreage a year later (CBE 66; PB 1 Pt. 1:89, 403, 435; DOR 1:727).

WILLIAM COXEN

On December 24, 1619, the justices of Bridewell Court decided that William Coxen, a prisoner, would be transported to Virginia (CBE 14).

JAMES COYNE

Sometime prior to January 1625 James Coyne came to Virginia on the *Mary Providence* and was Sergeant William Barry's servant. Coyne died after he reached the colony (MCGC 42).

CHARLES COYSE

Charles Coyse, Mr. Langley's man, set sail for Virginia in mid-September 1619 on the *Margaret* of Bristol. He accompanied Captain John Woodlief and went to the colony at the expense of the Society of Berkeley Hundred's investors. Coyse, a multi-skilled worker, was bound for Berkeley Hundred (**55**), where he was to serve for three years in exchange for 40 acres. He was a gun-maker and smith but also knew how to produce pitch and tar, and to fish. The Society of Berkeley Hundred paid for his fishing equipment and in return, he was supposed to keep their settlement supplied with seafood. Charles Coyse apparently died within a short time of reaching Virginia (VCR 3:198, 213; CBE 14).

JOHN CRADDOCK (CRADOUKE, CROODECKE, CROODICKE)

On January 10, 1627, John Craddock (Cradouke, Croodecke, Croodicke), a mariner, testified that two years earlier, Luke Boyse of Bermuda Hundred (**39**) had sent him to Accomack to retrieve a shipment of tobacco from Captain William Eppes's plantation (**74**). He did so, but on the return trip the tobacco got wet. On February 19, 1627, John Craddock made another appearance before the General Court. This time he testified that when he was at Martin's Brandon (**59**), he had seen Luke Boyse's widow, Alice, in bed with Captain William Eppes, behaving inappropriately. In May 1627, John Craddock was lost at sea near Newportes News (**24**), when the bark he was aboard sank in the James River. His death was reported to the General Court on August 27, 1627. As he died intestate, provost marshal Randall Smallwood was named his administrator. The General Court's justices noted that when John Craddock died, he had many debtors (MCGC 131, 140, 152).

***

WILLIAM CRADDOCK (CRADOUKE, CROODECKE, CROODICKE)

On February 20, 1618, William Craddock (Cradouke, Croodecke, Croodicke) was named provost marshal of Bermuda Hundred (**39**) and Bermuda City (**40**). He returned to England but on July 31, 1622, set sail for Virginia aboard the *James*, accompanied by his wife, Frances. Lieutenant Craddock died sometime prior to January 21, 1623. In May 1625 he was credited with 100 acres of land in the corporation of Charles City, the area in which both Bermuda settlements were located (VCR 3:75-76, 91; 4:553; SAIN 1:36; FER 400).

FRANCES CRADDOCK (CRADOUKE, CROODECKE, CROODICKE) (MRS. WILLIAM CRADDOCK [CRADOUKE, CROODECKE, CROODICKE])

Frances Craddock (Cradouke, Croodecke, Croodicke) and her husband, William, came to Virginia on the *James* and left England on July 31, 1622 (FER 400).

***

RICHARD CRAGG (CRAIG?)

In May 1625 Lieutenant Richard Cragg (Craig?) was credited with 250 acres of land in the corporation of Charles City (VCR 4:553).

THOMAS CRAGGE

On February 22, 1620, officials at Bridewell decided that Thomas Cragge, who was being detained, would be sent to Virginia (CBE 17).

THOMAS CRAGGE

On November 20, 1622, Thomas Cragge, who was then in Newgate Prison, was pardoned during an outbreak of jail fever so that he could be transported to Virginia. This may be the same individual who was being detained at Bridewell in 1620 (CBE 29).

JOHN CRAMPTON (CROMPTON)

On September 5, 1623, John Crampton (Crompton), a chandler from Bolton in the Moore in Lancashire, arrived in Jamestown (**1**) on the *Ann* and took the oath of supremacy (MCGC 6).

SAMUEL CRAMPTON

In July 1631 Samuel Crampton, a mariner, was identified as captain of the *Gift of God* when it made a trip from Virginia to London in 1629 (CBE 96).

THOMAS CRAMPTON (CROMPTON)

Thomas Crampton (Crompton) of Bolton in the Moore in Lancashire, arrived in Jamestown (**1**) on September 5, 1623, on the *Ann* and took the oath of supremacy (MCGC 6).

JOHN CRANICH (CRANAGE)

John Cranich (Cranage) came to Virginia on the *Marigold*. On March 7, 1624, the General Court acknowledged that he was a free man who agreed to serve Treasurer George Sandys, owner of the Treasurer's Plantation (11), until Christmastime, that is, early January 1625. In exchange for his service, Cranich was to receive 100 pounds of tobacco and three barrels of corn. On January 25, 1625, when a muster was made of Mulberry Island's (21) inhabitants, John Cranich was identified as a household head who was in possession of a dwelling, an ample supply of stored food, and some defensive weaponry (CBE 57; MCGC 11; DOR 1:47).

THOMAS CRANGE (CRANAGE?)

On January 22, 1619, Thomas Crange (Cranage?) was detained at Bridewell so that he could be sent to Virginia (HUME 19).

HUMPHREY (HUMFREY) CRAPEN (CROPEN)

On March 22, 1622, when the Indians attacked Edward Bennett's plantation in Warresqueak (26), Humphrey (Humfrey) Crapen (Cropen) was killed (VCR 3:571).

WILLIAM CRAPPLACE (CRAKEPLACE)

William Crapplace (Crakeplace) and his five servants came to Virginia in 1622 on the *Margaret and John*, with John Langley as master. In September or October 1623, when he presented a petition to Governor Francis Wyatt, Mr. Crapplace was identified as groom of the king's chamber and keeper of his house at Roiston. Crapplace asked for his goods, which the late John Langley's successor, Mr. William Douglas, was detaining; Douglas complied with the request. On December 11, 1623, Sir George Yeardley, who gave John Southern some tobacco to cover a debt to William Crapplace, asked to be released from the bond he had posted. Mr. Crapplace died in Jamestown (1) sometime prior to February 16, 1624 (VCR 4:274; MCGC 8; CBE 39).

WILIAM CRAUPLEY

William Craupley, a boy born in St. Andrew's Parish, was detained at Bridewell so that he could be sent to Virginia (CBE 12).

***

RICHARD CRAVEN

On February 4, 1623, Richard Craven and Nicholas Root (Roote) and his wife, Bridget, were among those involved in an altercation that was aired before the General Court. The case involved William Killdale's threatening to shoot Thomas Hethersall's dog. Craven and Root attacked Killdale with a stick, and then Bridget Root and Richard Craven seized his gun. The justices ordered Richard Craven to pay for William Killdale's medical treatment, and he and Nicholas Root were required to post a bond, guaranteeing their good behavior. On February 16, 1624, Richard Craven and his wife were residing in the mainland (3) just west of Jamestown Island. As Nicholas and Bridget Root and Thomas Hethersall resided there too, it is likely that the episode occurred there. In May 1625, when a list of patented land was sent back to England, Richard Craven was credited with 150 acres at Blunt Point (22). On February 9, 1628, Richard, who was termed a gentleman, testified that when he was in Archer's Hope (6), he had witnessed a fight between Amy Hall and William Harman and saw Theodore Moyses separate them (MCGC 3, 166; CBE 39; VCR 4:557).

MRS. RICHARD CRAVEN

On February 16, 1624, Mrs. Richard Craven and her husband were living on the Maine (3) or mainland just west of Jamestown Island (CBE 39).

***

***

RALEIGH (RAUGLEY, RAWLEIGH) CRAWSHAWE (CROSHAW, CROSHAIR, CROWSHAW)

Raleigh (Raugley, Rawleigh) Crawshawe (Croshaw, Croshair, Crowshaw), a gentleman and Virginia Company investor, came to Virginia in 1608 in the 2nd Supply of new colonists. On December 29, 1608, he and Captain John Smith went from Jamestown (1) to Werowocomoco, the York River village of the paramount Indian chief, Powhatan. Later, Smith sent Crawshawe back to Jamestown. Enroute, he encountered some of the men who had helped a group of Dutchmen flee from the settlement. In 1609 Smith and Crawshawe went to Pamunkey on a trading mission. Later, he said that Crawshawe had protected him from an assault. After the 1622 Indian attack, Raleigh Crawshawe went on a trading voyage to the Potomac River. He was supposed to meet with an Indian king who was not under the sway of Opechancanough, the known perpetrator. According to Smith, Crawshawe stayed at Potomac even though Opechancanough tried to have him killed, and he learned that some people taken captive during the 1622 attack were being detained at Pamunkey. Crashawe proposed sending some Indians to Opechancanough to bargain for the English prisoners' release, but the governor disregarded the plan. Captain John Smith said that he believed that Captains Crawshawe, Hamor, and Madison, with small parties of men, could have surprised and overwhelmed the Indians and expressed regret that 100 men were not available to accompany them. Later, Raleigh Crawshawe wrote a verse honoring Smith. On February 23, 1623, Lieutenant John Shipwarde, Daniel Gookin's agent, signed an agreement whereby Gookin of Newportes News (24) secured a debt to Raleigh Crawshawe by posting as collateral a substantial quantity of corn and some milk cows. Sometime prior to 1624 Crawshawe, who was identified as a gentleman of Kecoughtan, received a patent for 500 acres of land in Elizabeth City at Fox Hill (19) near Old Point Comfort. He was then said to have been in Virginia for 15 years. He used as headrights his wife and one or more servants, who came to Virginia on the *Bona Nova* in 1620.

On February 16, 1624, Captain Raleigh Crawshawe was living in Elizabeth City. As a burgess, he signed the General Assembly's rebuttal to Captain Nathaniel Butler's and Alderman Johnson's claims about the colony. On March 16, 1624, Crawshawe was authorized to trade for corn within the Chesapeake Bay, using the ship *Elizabeth*, a vessel in the possession of Treasurer George Sandys. Court testimony dating to November 1624 suggests that Crawshawe traded some powder and shot from the ship for a substantial quantity of furs. Captain Raleigh Crawshawe died sometime prior to December 27, 1624, when Captain Francis West, his administrator, was ordered to take an inventory of his goods. A substantial number of people were indebted to Crawshawe, but he also was a debtor. He reportedly had received some cattle from Lieutenant Sheppard and some corn from Thomas Spillman and was supposed to take Hugh Brett to England in 1625. In May 1625, when a list of patented land was sent back to England, Raleigh Crawshawe was credited with his 500 acres at Fox Hill. On March 13, 1626, Captain Francis West, as Crawshawe's administrator, was ordered to pay his debtors (CJS 1:228-229, 241, 243, 251, 253; 2:14, 56, 190, 200, 203-204, 275, 304-305, 308-310, 314, 316-317; MCGC 29-30, 37, 47-49, 52, 56, 97; PB 1 Pt. 1:2; CBE 43, 46; HAI 915; HEN 1:128-129; VCR 4:470, 558; DOR 1:768-769).

MRS. RALEIGH (RAUGLEY, RAWLEIGH) CRAWSHAWE (CROSHAW, CROSHAIR, CROWSHAW)

The wife of Raleigh (Raugley, Rawleigh) Crawshawe (Croshaw, Croshair, Crowshaw) came to Virginia on the *Bona Nova* in 1620 and was accompanied by one of his servants. Sometime prior to 1624, when Raleigh patented 500 acres at Fox Hill (19) near Old Point Comfort, he used his wife as a headright but failed to mention her given name (PB 1 Pt. 1:2; DOR 1:768-769).

***

WILLIAM CRAWSHAWE (CROSHAW, CROSHAIR, CROWSHAW)

In early 1625, when a muster was compiled, William Crawshawe (Croshaw, Croshair, Crowshaw) was living in Elizabeth City (18) in Captain William Tucker's household and was identified as an Indian who had been baptized. William, three baptized Africans, and several white people appear to have been servants. William Crawshawe may have been one of the Christianized Indians living in Elizabeth City who in March 1622 warned the settlers about an impending attack. Presumably he was named after the well-known English clergyman whose name he shared (CBE 63).

GILES CRAXTON

Giles Craxton left England on July 31, 1622, with William Felgate and went to Virginia on the *James* (FER 400).

RICHARD CREAMER

On February 5, 1620, officials at Bridewell decided that Richard Creamer would be sent to Virginia (CBE 18).

ELIZABETH CREASER

On June 24, 1635, when Adam Thorogood patented some land, he used Elizabeth Creaser's headright and claimed that he had paid for her transportation to Virginia (PB 1 Pt. 1:179).

THOMAS CREASER

On June 24, 1635, when Adam Thorogood patented some land, he used Thomas Creaser's headright and claimed that he had paid for his transportation to Virginia on the *John and Dorothy* in 1634 (PB 1 Pt. 1:179).

[NO FIRST NAME] CREMER (CRAMER?, CREAMER?)

On December 22, 1628, Mr. Cremer (Cramer?, Creamer?) asked the General Court to detain the tobacco in Mr. Stafferton's custody until his case was heard (MCGC 180).

JOHN CREED

On January 29, 1633, when John Creed of Martin's Hundred (7) prepared his will, he made bequests to his sister, Joane Perryer, and to his masters, Francis Clarke and Thomas Fausett. He also mentioned his brother, Cuthbert Creed, who was in England. John Creed named Thomas Fausett as his executor. His will was witnessed by Thomas Ward and Christopher Edwards. In April 1635 Thomas Fausett's wife, Ann, was named John Creed's administrator as Thomas was absent from Virginia (SR 3971; SH 15; WITH 80; EEAC 16).

JOSEPH CREW

Joseph Crew came to Virginia on the *London Merchant* and on January 30, 1625, was living in Pasbehay (3), the mainland just west of Jamestown Island. Joseph was a household head and had a modest supply of stored food and defensive weaponry. He may have been the man identified as Joshua Crew who had been living in the same area in 1624 (CBE 57; DOR 1:25).

JOSHUA CREW

On February 16, 1624, Joshua Crew was living on the Maine (3) or mainland just west of Jamestown Island (CBE 39).

***

RANDALL CREW

Randall Crew came to Virginia in 1621 on the *Charles*. On January 22, 1625, he was living at Shirley Hundred (41), where he was a 20-year-old servant in the household of the Rev. William Bennett's widow, Katherine. By January 11, 1627, Randall had obtained his freedom and had married Elizabeth, Captain Robert Smalley's widow. He testified on Elizabeth's behalf when she accused Deputy Governor Samuel Argall of seizing her late husband's oxen. Elizabeth died sometime prior to July 1638, by which time Randall had married Dorothy Beheathland. He appears to have been living in Warwick River County in 1647 but died two years later (CBE 53; MCGC 132; DUNN 26; PB 1 Pt. 2:584; DOR 1:766).

ELIZABETH SMALLEY CREW (MRS. RANDALL CREW, MRS. ROBERT SMALLEY) (SEE ELIZABETH SMALLEY)

On January 11, 1627, Elizabeth, the widow of Captain Robert Smalley, was identified as the wife of Randall Crew. She died sometime prior to July 1638 (MCGC 132; PB 1 Pt. 2:584).

DOROTHY BEHEATHLAND (BEHETHLEM) CREW (MRS. RANDALL CREW) (SEE DOROTHY BEHEATHLAND [BEHETHLEM])

The widowed Randall Crew married Dorothy Beheathland (Behethlem) sometime prior to July 1638, when he used her as a headright, identifying her as his wife (PB 1 Pt. 2:584; DOR 1:766).

***

ROBERT CREW

Robert Crew came to Virginia on the *Marmaduke* in 1623. On February 4, 1625, he was living in Archer's Hope (6) where he was a 23-year-old servant in Thomas Bradsby's household. On August 29, 1625, Robert and one of his fellow servants testified about seeing Joseph Johnson beat his wife. Both acknowledged that Mr. Bransbye (that is, Thomas Bradsby) was their master (CBE 58; MCGC 70).

THOMAS CRISPE

Thomas Crispe, a gentleman from Kent County, England, arrived in Virginia in December 1621. He was accompanied by three servants: Richard Peck (Packe), Margaret Riche, and Thomas Gynner. In January 1622 he brought in two more servants, Thomas Meare and John Whittaker. On February 16, 1624, Thomas Crispe was living in Elizabeth City (18). On November 21, 1625, his dispute with Edward Nevell was aired before the General Court. At issue were goods that Crispe had brought to Virginia and sold to Nevell, who had failed to pay him. Robert Newman also testified against Nevell. On December 5, 1625, Thomas Crispe and several others were ordered to appear before the General Court if they wished to pursue their suits against Mr. Thomas Weston, a merchant. Thomas Crispe testified before the General Court on December 19, 1625, about Arthur Avelinge's failure to obey a summons to court. He also recounted the statements Jeffrey Cornish had made against Virginia's governor and testified on behalf of Robert Newman in his suit against Thomas Weston. On February 20, 1626, Weston was ordered to compensate Crispe at his house in Kecoughtan (MCGC 50, 75-76, 78, 81, 82-83, 95; CBE 46).

ZACHARY (ZACHARIA) CRISPE (CRIPPS)

Zachary (Zacharia) Crispe (Cripps) came to Virginia in 1621 on the *Margaret and John* and on February 16, 1624, was residing on the lower side of the James River, on the Treasurer's Plantation (11). He was still there on February 4, 1625 and was part of a group of five men, who appear to have been Treasurer George Sandys' tenants. On May 30, 1625, he testified before the General Court, confirming Hugh Crowder's sworn statements about Captain William Powell's land. In June 1625 Zachary Crispe and Edmund White loaned some tobacco to Treasurer George Sandys. On December 12, 1625, Crispe and White were involved in a dispute over how large a share of the year's tobacco crop Phillip Kithly, a housemate, was entitled to. Court testimony reveals that Crispe and White had a short-term lease for a house and some ground, and that several men were sharing the dwelling. In early December 1625, when Thomas Swifte made a nuncupative will, it was witnessed by Zachary Crispe. Swifte asked Crispe and Edmund White to take custody of his estate; afterward, they were appointed the decedent's administrators. At the end of December 1625 Zachary Crispe and Edmund White acknowledged that they were indebted to the late Luke Eden.

On January 22, 1629, Crispe brought to the General Court an inventory of Edmund White's personal possessions, and on March 4, 1629, he proved Gilbert Peppet's will. The next day, Zachary Crispe, who was identified as a resident of the Warwick River area, received a patent for 100 acres at the mouth of the Warwick River (23). He claimed the land on the basis of two headrights he acquired from Samuel Mathews, from whom he also had purchased the acreage. On October 16, 1629, Zachary Crispe served as a burgess for the settlements along the Warwick River, and in February 1633 he represented Stanley Hundred (22). In September 1632 he was named a commissioner of the Warwick River area's monthly court. On February 9, 1633, Crispe, who was in possession of the late Theophilus Beristone's tobacco, was ordered to give it to Theophilus Stone, an orphan. During the 1640s he served as Mary Griffin's attorney, and in 1647, as a justice of the Warwick River County monthly court, he heard several cases (CBE 40, 60; MCGC 63, 80-81, 90, 94, 182, 189-190, 202; PB 1 Pt. 1:74; HEN 1:139, 187, 203; DUNN 21-22, 24-26, 182).

HENRY CROCKER

Henry Crocker came to Virginia on the *Abigail* in 1620 and on February 4, 1625, was living on the Maine (3), where he was one of Dr. John Pott's servants. Henry Crocker was then age 34 (CBE 58).

***

HENRY CROCKER

Henry Crocker came to Virginia on the *Marigold* and on February 4, 1625, was living on Hog Island (16) with his wife, Joan (Jone) (CBE 61).

JOAN (JONE) CROCKER (MRS. HENRY CROCKER)

Joan (Jone), who became Henry Crocker's wife, came to Virginia on the *Swann*. On February 4, 1625, she was living on Hog Island (16) with her husband (CBE 61).

***

RICHARD CROCKER (CROKER)

On August 16, 1624, Richard Crocker (Croker) informed the General Court that William Tyler had said that even if he were a man of means, he (William) would not be a member of the Council of State because the Council members ignored their consciences. A document that Richard had signed with an "x" in November 1624 was presented to the General Court on July 21, 1625, thereby revealing that he was illiterate. On January 1, 1627, Richard, who was living at Martin's Hundred (7), was accused of slandering Captain Ralph Hamor and cape merchant Abraham Peirsey. Two men who overheard him when he was in the woods near Mr. Harwood's house testified before the General Court. On January 13, 1627, Richard Crocker was sentenced to a month of imprisonment for his indiscretion. Afterward he was to be pilloried and have his ears nailed to the post (MCGC 20, 69, 132, 135-136).

RICHARD CROFTS

Richard Crofts, a gentleman, who came to Virginia in 1607 and was one of the first Jamestown (1) settlers, was from Ratcliff, England. According to Captain John Smith, Crofts kept Edward Maria Wingfield's trunk for him and was suspected of taking some items. The question arose because on September 17, 1607, he was in possession of Wingfield's copper kettle (CJS 2:141; HAI 193, 198).

WILLIAM CRONY

William Crony came to Virginia in 1623 on the *Providence* and on February 7, 1625,

was living at Newportes News (24), where he was a 24-year-old servant in Daniel Gookin's household (CBE 63).

THOMAS CROOKE

On October 3, 1618, Thomas Crooke, who was brought in from St. Andrews in Holborne, was detained at Bridewell until he could be sent to Virginia (CBE 10).

HENRY CROSBYE

On December 4, 1634, when Hugh Cox received a court order entitling him to a patent, he listed Henry Crosbye as a headright (PB 1 Pt. 1:282).

[NO FIRST NAME] CROSER

On January 3, 1625, the General Court noted that a man named Croser was among those living at Shirley Hundred (41), where he was employed on behalf of the Society of Berkeley Hundred (55) (MCGC 42).

BRIDGET (BRIDGETT) CROSS (CROSSE)

Bridget (Bridgett) Cross (Crosse), a young, marriageable maid who came to Virginia in 1621 aboard the *Warwick,* was born at Burford in Wiltshire. Her father, John Cross, died sometime prior to her departure. Bridget, who was 18 years old, was recommended by a man identified only as Robert-the-Porter (FER 309).

***

EDWARD CROSS (CROSSE)

On July 12, 1620, Edward Cross (Crosse) was accused of trying to entice Thomas Kiddar's son, Thomas, to go to Virginia. On August 4, 1623, Cross served on a jury in Jamestown (1) when two suspected cattle thieves were put on trial. In a January 7, 1624, court case, it was reported that Edward Cross and his son, Richard, had earned wages during a voyage of the *Furtherance* (VCR 1:401; MCGC 4-5, 9).

RICHARD CROSS (CROSSE)

On January 7, 1624, the General Court's justices learned that Richard, the son of Edward Cross (Crosse), had been hired for wages in a voyage of the *Furtherance*, which went to Virginia (MCGC 9).

***

JOHN CROSS (CROSSE)

On December 8, 1628, the justices of the General Court heard testimony about the late John Cross (Crosse), merchant of the ship *Truelove*. The decedent reportedly accepted some money from William Hosier and passed it along to Mrs. Hurte, the *Truelove's* owner. Hosier sued John Cross's estate in an attempt to recover his funds. On December 22nd, it was reported that John Cross, Henry Bagwell, and a merchant named Henry Moore owed money to Hugh Hawkridge (MCGC 178, 180).

SARA CROSS (CROSSE)

Sara Cross (Crosse), a young maid, came to Virginia in 1621 aboard the *Warwick*. She was the 21-year-old daughter of Peter Crosse, a baker at Lotheburie (FER 309).

THOMAS CROSS (CROSSE)

In 1620 Thomas Cross (Crosse) came to Virginia on the *Abigail*. On February 16, 1624, he was living on the Governor's Land (3), where he was an indentured servant in the household headed by Thomas Swinhow. In October 1624 Cross was summoned before the justices of the General Court to testify about John and Alice Proctor's cruel treatment of their servants, two of whom died. On January 24, 1625, Thomas Cross, who was identified as a 22-year-old servant, was living on Dr. John Pott's leasehold on the Governor's Land. On May 9, 1625, he testified in court that a sow killed at Dr. Pott's house actually belonged to another man (CBE 39, 58; MCGC 23, 59).

[NO FIRST NAME] CROTIAS

On February 9, 1629, Lieutenant Edward Waters presented Captain Crotias's inventory to the General Court. It had been compiled by Waters and the late John Bainham (MCGC 186).

HUGH CROUCH

On July 3, 1622, Hugh Crouch and his sister, Mary Young Tue, assigned 150 acres of land at Newportes News (24) to Daniel Gookin. Hugh and Mary were the heirs of their father, Hugh Crouch, a Virginia Company investor (VCR 2:74).

RICHARD CROUCH

Richard Crouch, a carpenter from Howton in Bedfordshire, England, arrived in Jamestown (1) on September 12, 1623, aboard the *Bonny Bess* and took the oath of supremacy. On February 16, 1624, he was living on the Maine (3) just west of Jamestown Island (MCGC 6; CBE 39).

THOMAS CROUCH (CROUTH)

Thomas Crouch (Crouth) came to Virginia on the *Bona Nova* and on February 16, 1624, reportedly was living in urban Jamestown (1) in Edward Blaney's household. Simultaneously he was attributed to the Blaney plantation (actually, Captain William Powell's land) (14) on the lower side of the James. He probably was being shifted from one location to the other, as his skills were needed. On February 4, 1625, Thomas Crouch was residing on the Blaney property on the lower side of the river. He was then described as a 40-year-old servant (CBE 38, 40, 59).

THOMAS CROUCHLEY

On July 13, 1618, it was decided that Thomas Crouchley, who was being detained in the Oxford Jail, would be sent to Virginia. He was to be turned over to Sir Thomas Smith of the Virginia Company (CBE 9).

HUGH CROWDER (CRUDER)

On June 25, 1623, Virginia Company officials were informed that Hugh Crowder (Cruder), a man of wealth, had died in Virginia. John Proctor, a resident of Paces Paines (9), was serving as the attorney of two London merchants to whom the decedent was in debt. This Hugh Crowder may have been the father of the Hugh Crowder who came to Virginia on the *Bona Nova* in 1619 (VCR 2:457).

HUGH CROWDER (CRUDER)

Hugh Crowder (Cruder) came to Virginia in 1619 on the *Bona Nova*. According to court testimony, in April 1622 he and several other members of his household cleared some land that Captain John Huddleson (Hurleston) had obtained from Captain William Powell (14). At issue was whether the workers were entitled to a share of the tobacco crop. On February 16, 1624, Hugh Crowder was living on the lower side of the James River, within the corporation of James City and east of Gray's Creek. On February 4, 1625, he was still there. He was a household head and was in possession of a plantation (12) that had two dwellings and a palisade. On April 11, 1625, Crowder testified before the General Court about the death of John Verone, a young servant who apparently committed suicide. On May 30, 1625, Hugh Crowder informed the General Court that Captain Samuel Mathews was claiming the land that he had been instrumental in clearing in 1622. He was eager to relocate, for Captain Huddleston's land was barren. Hugh was offered land at Martin's Hundred (7) and at the College (66) but declined it. In November 1626 he was given permission to relocate to Captain Francis West's land on the west side of Lower Chippokes Creek. Hugh Crowder died intestate sometime prior to April 21, 1628, at which time Rice Watkins of Hog Island (16) was named his administrator (CBE 40, 60; MCGC 53, 60, 63, 65, 123,171; DOR 1:41).

JAMES CROWDER (CRUDER)

James Crowder (Cruder) came to Virginia on the *Return* in 1623. He died at West and Shirley Hundred (41) sometime after February 16, 1624, but before January 22, 1625 (CBE 53).

JOHN CROWDECK (CROOKDEACK, CROWDICK)

On May 20, 1607, John Crowdeck (Crookdeack, Crowdick), a sailor, accompanied Captain John Smith on an exploratory journey up the James River and therefore would have spent time in Jamestown (1). On October 15, 1624, a John Crowdeck (probably the same man) testified before the General Court about the dealings between Captain John Martin and mariner Humphrey Rastell. On January 24, 1625, Thomas Nunn testified that Crowdeck took a passenger aboard at Salford's Creek, in Elizabeth City (18), and transported him to Warresqueak (26). Enroute, some tobacco was damaged due to rough seas. At issue was whether John

Crowdick was liable. On September 18, 1626, he testified before the General Court about statements he had heard two men make while at Mr. Farrar's house at Jordan's Journey (46) (HAI 102; MCGC 25, 45, 113-114).

JOHN CROWE

On November 21, 1621, John Crowe and his associates, who planned to take 100 new colonists to Virginia, received a patent for some land. On June 10, 1622, Crowe was identified as the holder of a patent for a particular (or private) plantation (VCR 1:553-554, 561-562; 3:643).

***

THOMAS CRUMP (CROMPE, CRUMPE, CRAMPE, CRUMFORT)

On February 16, 1624, Thomas Crump (Crompe, Crumpe, Crampe, Crumfort) was living on the Eastern Shore (72-78). By January 24, 1625, he had moved to Jamestown Island (1), where he shared a dwelling with John West. It was around that time that Crump began taking an active role in public life. Around 1625 he married the late Rev. Richard Buck's daughter, Elizabeth. As Thomas and Elizabeth Crump were residents of Jamestown Island from the mid-1620s until early 1632 and apparently did not own land there, they probably occupied the Rev. Richard Buck's property in the eastern end of Jamestown Island, acreage in which Elizabeth had a legal interest. During the mid- to late 1620s Thomas served on juries, and the General Court called on him to arbitrate disputes. He also presented two men's wills and in March 1629 brought suit against William Barnes, a debtor. In March 1629 Thomas Crump represented Jamestown in the assembly's February 1632 session, but in September he commenced serving as the Neck O'Land's (5) delegate. On September 28, 1633, he secured a patent there, acreage that abutted the Buck estate. Thomas died sometime prior to 1652. He was survived by his widow, Elizabeth, and their son, John, the Rev. Richard Buck's grandson and surviving male heir (CBE 46, 56; MCGC 44, 144, 153, 184, 187, 189-190, 201; HEN 1:154 178, 203, 405; STAN 56-58; PB 1 Pt. 1:287; DOR 1:428-429, 784).

ELIZABETH BUCK CRUMP (CROMPE, CRUMPE, CRAMPE, CRUMFORT) (MRS. THOMAS CRUMP [CROMPE, CRUMPE, CRAMPE, CRUMFORT])

The Rev. Richard Buck's daughter, Elizabeth, who may have immigrated to Virginia a year or two after her parents' deaths, married Sergeant Thomas Crump around 1625. As Thomas and Elizabeth were residents of Jamestown Island (1) from the mid-1620s until early 1632 and seemingly did not own land there until 1633, they probably occupied part of the Rev. Buck's homestead. Together they produced a son, John. In 1655, Elizabeth Buck Crump, then a widow, was sued by John Bromfield, the widower of Bridget Burrows, who sought to recover his late wife's legal interest in the Buck land-holdings in Archer's Hope (6). It was determined that Bridget, whose late husband, John Burrows, had been a guardian of the Buck heirs, was entitled to a life interest in the property, but not fee simple ownership, which ultimately descended to the Rev. Richard Buck's male heirs. Elizabeth Buck Crump married Mathew Page sometime prior to December 2, 1657, having conveyed to him the Archer's Hope acreage that she owned outright (HEN 1:405; DOR 1:428-429, 784; PB 6:298).

***

THOMAS CRUST

Thomas Crust came to Virginia in 1620 on the *George* and on January 24, 1625, was an indentured servant living in the urban Jamestown (1) household of John Southern (CBE 55).

JOHN CUFFE (CUFF)

Sometime after October 1620, John Cuffe (Cuff), a 39-year-old London merchant, testified before the High Court of the Admiralty. He stated that in June 1619 he had set sail for Virginia on the *Warwick,* serving as cape merchant, and that he had returned home on the *Garland.* Cuffe said that when he was at Gravesend, paying for some people's transportation to Virginia, there were 200 men, women, and children aboard the *Garland.* He indicated that 40 of those aboard were bound for Virginia. On June 5, 1623, Virginia Company officials noted that John Cuffe and William Webb were authorized to sell sassafras to recover the funds they were owed. On July 4, 1623, Cuffe was identified as a subscriber for the relief of the colony (EAE 7; VCR 2:455; 4:245-246).

MARTIN CUFFE (CUFF, CUSSE)

Sometime after April 1623 but before February 16, 1624, Martin Cuffe (Cuff, Cusse) died in Elizabeth City (17, 18) (CBE 45).

ROBERT CUFFE (CUFF)

Robert Cuffe (Cuff), a 26-year-old cook from Sommersetshire, went to Virginia in 1619 on the *Bona Nova,* which carried a large number of Virginia Company servants and tenants. The cost of Robert's transportation was paid by the Ferrars, who were major investors in the Virginia Company (FER 295).

***

DANIEL CUGLEY (COGLEY)

In 1620 Daniel Cugley (Cogley) came to Virginia on the *London Merchant* and on February 16, 1624, was residing on the Eastern Shore. When a muster of that area was taken in early 1625, Daniel, who was age 28 and appears to have been free, was living in the household of Thomas Gascon (Gascoyne) on Old Plantation Creek (73). In February 1629, Daniel Cugley testified that Richard Wheeler came to his house with a bundle of stockings he had gotten from Captain John Stone. He ran afoul of the law by criticizing the governor and his council. On September 14, 1630, he was sentenced to be pilloried, but ultimately was pardoned and released. In June 1635 he received a patent for 400 acres of land in Accomack, an indication that he was a successful planter. Accomack County court records reveal that Daniel Cugley died in late 1640 or early 1641 and that he was a widower. His estate inventory sheds a great deal of light on his household's material culture (CBE 465, 69; MCGC 185-186, 479; PB 1 Pt. 1:183, 188; AMES 1:passim; 2:66, 78-80).

HANNAH (ANN) SAVAGE [SAVADGE, SALVADGE] CUGLEY (MRS. THOMAS SAVAGE [SAVADGE, SALVADGE], MRS. DANIEL CUGLEY) (SEE HANNAH (ANN) SAVAGE [SAVADGE, SALVADGE])

Hannah (Ann), who by early 1625 had become the wife of Thomas Savage (Savadge, Salvadge) and was living in her husband's household on the Eastern Shore (77), was widowed by 1633. Afterward, she married her neighbor, Daniel Cugley, with whom she had a daughter, Margery (CBE 68; MEY 534; AMES 1:5, 29, 37-38, 107-108, 127, 158).

MARGERY CUGLEY

Sometime after 1638 Daniel Cugley and his wife, Hannah (Ann), the widow of Thomas Savage (Savadge, Salvadge), produced a daughter, Margery. When Margery was orphaned in 1647, her half-brother John Savage was named her guardian (MEY 534).

***

SAMWELL (SAMUEL) CULLY (CULTEY)

On February 16, 1624, Samwell (Samuel) Cully (Cultey) was living at Martin's Hundred (7). He was still there on February 4, 1625, and was residing in a home he shared with his partner, Samuel March, and March's wife, Collice. The household was relatively well supplied with stored food and defensive weaponry (CBE 42, 62; DOR 1:46).

THOMAS CULSTON

On January 22, 1619, officials at Bridewell decided that Thomas Culston, a boy, would be detained until he could be sent to Virginia (HUME 19).

JOHN CUMBER

On January 5, 1633, John Cumber testified that on January 25, 1632, when he and John May went to Thomas Farley's house in Archer's Hope (6) to collect eight tons of tobacco, Thomas Crump said that it had been sent aboard the *Defense* with Tobias Felgate (MCGC 201).

THOMAS CUMBER

On May 16, 1621, Virginia Company officials noted that Richard Chelsea, Sir Lawrence Hyde's servant, was living with Thomas Cumber at Martin's Hundred (7). Cumber, most likely a skilled worker, was supposed to receive wages and be provided with a house that measured 12 feet by 14 feet (VCR 3:451).

ELIZABETH CURTISSE

On June 24, 1635, when Adam Thorogood patented some land, he used Elizabeth Curtisse as a headright and indicated that he had paid for her transportation to the colony (PB 1 Pt. 1:179).

JOHN CURTIS (CURTISE, CUSTIS)

John Curtis (Curtise, Custis) came to Virginia in 1621 on the *Flying Hart* and on February 16, 1624, was living in Elizabeth City (17, 18). In November 1624 John Coker testified that the late Ensign James Harrison of Warresqueak (26) had purchased the contract of Curtis and two other servants from John Cheseman and that Harrison's wife, Anne (Anna), had paid Cheseman. Curtis signed an affidavit verifying the sale, endorsing it with an "x," an indication that he was illiterate. In early 1625 John Curtis, who was age 22 and free, was living in Elizabeth City (18), where he was a member of Thomas Godby's household. On November 14, 1625, when he was authorized to return to England, he was identified as one of Daniel Gookin's former servants (CBE 44, 66; MCGC 35, 75; DOR 1:786).

RICHARD CURTIS

On February 5, 1623, the Virginia Company authorized Richard Curtis of the *Mary Margaret* of Topsom to take some passengers to Virginia and then go on a fishing voyage (VCR 2:262).

THOMAS CURTIS

Thomas Curtis came to Virginia on the *Flying Hart* in 1621 and on February 16, 1624, was living in Newportes News (24). He was still there on February 7, 1625, and was a member of Daniel Gookin's household.

Thomas was then age 24 and free. On February 23, 1636, Anthony Younge made a bequest to Thomas Curtis, who was then residing in New Poquoson (**19**). He apparently was living there, for in 1640 he was named a tobacco viewer for the south side of the New Poquoson River. In 1642 he secured two patents for land in what is now Mathews County. He continued to acquire land in that area and rose in the ranks of society, in time becoming a major and local court justice. Prior to August 1657 he married a woman named Avarilla (CBE 44, 66; WITH 195; DOR 1:786; PB 1 Pt. 2:525, 794, 804).

CHRISTOPHER CUTLER

On March 16, 1627, Christopher Cutler confirmed the testimony of John Wayne (Waine), who had witnessed a fight between Thomas Lawley and Thomas Hittall while aboard the *Plantation*. Both men said that Robert Cooke separated the combatants (MCGC 145).

ROBERT CUTLER

Robert Cutler, a gentleman, arrived in Jamestown (**1**) in 1608 in the 1st Supply of new settlers (CJS 1:222; 2:161).

D

JOHN DADE

On May 4, 1622, Virginia Company officials learned that John Dade, who had a commission from Lady Delaware, tried to deliver it to Captain Edward Brewster, who already had left Virginia. In May 1625 Dade was listed as the patentee of 100 acres of land in the corporation of Charles City, acreage that had not been seated. Dade's patent may have been part of the land that Lady Delaware inherited in West and Shirley Hundred (**41**) and gradually sold off (C 24/490; VCR 4:553).

ELIZABETH DAG (DAGG) (MRS. WILLIAM COBB)

Elizabeth Dag (Dagg), one of the young maids who came to Virginia on the *Warwick*

in September 1621, was 19 years old when she left England. Her passage was paid by vice admiral John Pountis. Virginia Company records indicate that Elizabeth was born in Lynchowse and had been recommended by Christopher Marten and Sir Nicholas Couch. Sometime prior to May 9, 1625, Elizabeth Dag married William Cobb, who died before paying for her passage to the colony (FER 309; MCGC 59).

WILLIAM DALBY (DALBIE, DALBEE)

William Dalby (Dalbie, Dalbee), who was associated with the East India School and came to Virginia on the *Furtherance*, arrived shortly after the March 22, 1622, Indian attack. By February 16, 1624, Dalby had been sent to the College (**66**) in Henrico. However, on February 4, 1625, he was living on Captain Samuel Mathews' plantation (**15**) in Tappahannah. Within a year he returned to the College, where he was living on June 1, 1625. He was then identified as one of the College men (FER 272; CBE 35, 60; MCGC 60, 64).

NICHOLAS DALE

Nicholas Dale came to Virginia on the *Jacob* in 1624. In early 1625 he was living in Elizabeth City (**19**) in the household of Thomas Boulding, who owned land near the Old Poquoson. In 1625 Nicholas was described as a 24-year-old servant (CBE 66).

PETER DALE

Virginia Company records dating to July 31, 1622, indicate that Peter Dale came to Virginia on the *James* with John Cornish (FER 400).

***

SIR THOMAS DALE

In 1603 Sir Thomas Dale was captain of an infantry company in service to the Dutch. In 1606 his garrison was based in Oudewater in the Netherlands, where he served with Sir Thomas Gates, who set out for Virginia in 1609. In January 1611 the Dutch granted Dale a three-year leave of absence, which enabled him to go to Virginia. He married Elizabeth Throgmorten in February 1611 and, within a month, set sail for Virginia with three ships that transported 300 men (including artisans and tradesmen), provisions, and a substantial quantity of livestock. Shortly after Sir Thomas Dale arrived in Virginia, he added onto the code of military justice that Sir Thomas Gates had begun writing. Dale implemented Virginia Company policies that included planting settlements toward the head of the James River, away from the lower tidewater area's salt marshes. He also established a settlement on the Eastern Shore (72). Dale resided at Bermuda Hundred (39) much of the time he was in Virginia, although he had a farmstead in the eastern end of Jamestown Island (1) at Goose Hill. After the expiration of Dale's original leave of absence, he sought a two-year extension and compensation for the years he was in Virginia. He contended that during his stay in the colony he had strengthened the Dutch economy through trade and had been instrumental in converting the Indians to Christianity. In May 1611 Sir Thomas Dale informed his superiors that he had visited the Pasbehay Indians' village at the mouth of the Chickahominy River, which he found deserted, and he sent ships to Nova Scotia to combat foreign traders he heard were moving into that region. In August 1611, when Sir Thomas Gates returned to Virginia, Dale mistook the approaching ships for Spanish vessels and prepared to defend the colony. According to George Percy, Dale ordered his men aboard ship, for he feared that they would abandon the fort if it came under attack. In mid-August 1611 Dale told Sir Ralph Winwood that if he had 2,000 men he could assure the colony's success. He recommended that the James-York peninsula be secured just below the fall line and that towns be built in Jamestown, Kecoughtan, Chiskiack, and several other sites. He said that a Spanish vessel had arrived during the summer, and after three men had been put ashore, the ship's crew took off with his pilot. Dale was referring to John Clark, whom the Spanish took to Cuba and Spain for interrogation.

While Sir Thomas Dale and Sir Thomas Gates were in the colony, Dale had a second blockhouse built and saw that a stable, a munitions house, a sturgeon house, and a barn were erected in Jamestown. The church and storehouses also were repaired. Dale and Gates also had a forge built, as well as a bridge or wharf to serve shipping. Dale set up a salt works on the Eastern Shore, and in Jamestown he established a common garden where Virginia Company servants were employed growing food crops for the colony. He also was credited with subduing the Chickahominy Indians. In June 1613 Dale reported that he had divided his men into three groups and established a fortified settlement he called Henrico (63). He also seated groups of colonists at Coxendale (64), Digges Hundred (43), West and Shirley Hundred (41), Bermuda Hundred (39), and Bermuda City (40). He spoke of requiring his men to plant crops, retaining seed for the following year. Despite Sir Thomas Dale's efforts to plant sustainable settlements toward the head of the James River, by 1616 most of those communities had begun to falter and eventually failed. When Sir Thomas Gates left Virginia in 1614, Dale became marshal or deputy-governor, a title he held until May 1616 when he returned to England. By instituting martial law, enforceable by harsh penalties, Dale compelled the Virginia colonists to work toward their own support, repair their houses, and produce their own food supply. When Sir Thomas Dale returned to England in May 1616, he was accompanied by John Rolfe and his wife, Pocahontas, and a dozen or more other Indians. He also brought back samples of tobacco, sassafras, pitch and tar, potash, sturgeon, and caviar in an attempt to showcase the colony's economic potential. Dale's livestock in Virginia included cattle (which bore his mark on their horns) and goats. According to some estimates, when he returned home to England there were 351 colonists in Virginia, including 65 women. In 1619 Sir Thomas Dale became ill, and he died on August 9th, in the East Indies at Masulipatam. His widow, Lady Elizabeth, was sole heir to his Virginia property. Although Dale's administrative policies were harsh and attracted strong criticism, he usually is credited with saving the Virginia colony from extinction. He was accused posthumously of teaching Natives how to use firearms, an issue that surfaced after the 1622 Indian attack (OCAL 1:1-3, 9, 16-20; CJS 2:13, 218, 239-242, 244-250, 256; HAI 514-517, 521-532, 777-783, 801, 814-816, 822-826, 833-834, 845-846, 871-874, 878-879, 899, 902-903, 907-908; FOR 2:7:18; 3:2:7; CO 1/1 ff 94-95, 113-114; SP 14/87 f 67; C 24/489; SAIN 1:12; FER 40; VCR 1:265, 316, 338, 584, 588; 2:40-42, 396; 3:68-69, 122, 126; 4:116-117; MCGC 28, 73, 192; SR 3112; PB 1 Pt. 1:10).

LADY ELIZABETH THROGMORTEN DALE (MRS. THOMAS DALE)

Elizabeth Throgmorten, who was related to the Berkeleys, married Sir Thomas Dale in February 1611, a month before he set sail for Virginia. He was absent throughout much of their marriage and the couple failed to produce heirs. After Sir Thomas's death in 1619, Lady Elizabeth began taking an active role in managing the property she had inherited. She had a legal interest in a plantation called Coxendale (**64**) in the corporation of Henrico, in some land in Bermuda Hundred (**39**), in Shirley Hundred (now Eppes) Island (**41**), and in a massive tract on the Eastern Shore (**72**) at Magothy Bay. She also had a 12-acre parcel on Jamestown Island at Goose Hill (**1**), a small component of a vast estate. In March 1622 when the Indians attacked, Lady Dale reportedly had around 20–22 people at Coxendale, who sought refuge in a palisaded house. During the early 1620s Lady Elizabeth Dale sought Virginia Company officials' help in seeing that her tenants paid their rent and that her servants received the shipments of goods and equipment she sent to the colony. She complained about the unauthorized killing of her cattle and asked to be assigned land for a particular plantation. Over the years, Lady Elizabeth employed overseers to manage her Virginia property, notably William Hambey, Charles Harmer (who married Henry and Elizabeth Soothey's daughter and ultimate heir to their property on Jamestown Island), and Henry Watkins. Sometimes Lady Dale's overseers loaned livestock and supplies to the neighboring plantations. On July 25, 1638, when James Knott of Nansemond was asked to identify Sir Thomas Dale's holdings in Virginia, he listed them and added that after Sir Thomas's death, Lady Elizabeth preserved and maintained them. On July 4, 1640, when Lady Elizabeth Dale made her will, she enumerated her Virginia properties and bequeathed almost all of them to her Throgmorten and Hanby kin. The exception was her land at Goose Hill, which she instructed her executors to sell. Lady Elizabeth's will was presented for probate on December 2, 1640, and shortly thereafter her agents began distributing her estate in accordance with her instructions (VCR 1:483, 491-492; 2:14; 3:126, 168, 291, 293; 4:8-9; FER 322; MCGC 11, 48, 179, 192, 499; MCGH 252; EEAC 17; WAT 748-749; PB 1 Pt. 1:97-98; 3:391; AMES 2:74-75; GEN 2:51).

***

MARGARET DALTON

Margaret Dalton, Mrs. Wingate's maid, went to Virginia on the *Mayflower* in 1633–1635 (CBE 119).

ALLYN DAME

On November 8, 1624, Allyn Dame testified that William Gayne removed some copper furnaces and other goods from the ship *Treasurer*. Gayne was a resident of Elizabeth City (**18**) (MCGC 30).

WILLIAM DAME

On October 16, 1625, William Dame was ordered to pay Morris (Maurice) Thompson's assignees (MCGC 73).

BRIDGET DAMERON

Bridget Dameron died in Elizabeth City (**17, 18**) sometime after April 1623 but before February 16, 1624 (CBE 45).

JOHN DAMERON (DAMYRON, DAMIRON, DAMERIN)

On December 23, 1619, it was decided that John Dameron (Damyron, Damiron, Damerin), master of the *Duty*, would take 50 men from Bridewell to Virginia on behalf of the Virginia Company. The ship was then ready to depart. On July 16, 1621, Virginia Company officials noted that Dameron had the late Benjamin Gunston's estate in his custody. On February 4, 1625, Sir George Yeardley authorized John Dameron to take Captain Edward Stallings' ship and men to Kecoughtan (**17**) so that Captain William Tucker could make an inventory of the goods on board (VCR 1:288-289, 520; 4:511-512).

JAN DAMONT

Laborer Jan Damont and his wife were among the Walloons and French who indicated their willingness to go to Virginia. In August 1621 the Virginia Company agreed that they could immigrate (CBE 24).

LANCELOTT (LANSELOTT, LAWLEY) DAMPORT (DANSPORT)

Lancelott (Lanselott, Lawley) Damport (Dansport) went to Virginia on the *Duty* and on February 16, 1624, was an indentured servant in Edward Blaney's household (14) on the lower side of the James River. His name also was listed among the Blaney servants in Jamestown (1). On February 4, 1625, Lancelott, who was 29 years old, was living on the Blaney plantation on the lower side of the James River (CBE 38, 40, 59) .

***

LEONARD DANBY (DANSBY)

Leonard Danby (Dansby) died in Virginia sometime prior to April 30, 1621. He had already sent his sons, John Whitton and William Danby (Dansby), to the colony, where he was in possession of some land. After Leonard Danby's death, his widow married Thomas Harteasle (VCR 1:461-462).

MRS. LEONARD DANBY (DANSBY) (MRS. THOMAS HARTEASLE)

On April 30, 1621, Virginia Company officials noted that the widow of Leonard Danby (Dansby) had married Thomas Harteasle. The decedent already had sent his sons, John Whitton and William Danby (Dansby), to Virginia, where he had some land (VCR 1:461-462).

WILLIAM DANBY (DANSBY)

Sometime prior to April 30, 1621, William Danby (Dansby) and his brother, John Whitton, went to Virginia where William's father, Leonard Danby, had some land. After Leonard's death, his widow married Thomas Harteasle (VCR 1:461-462).

***

***

JOHN DANCY (DANSEY, DENCY, DAUNSEY, DANSYE)

John Dancy (Dansey, Dency, Daunsey, Dansye) came to Virginia on the *George* in 1621 and on February 16, 1624, was living on the lower side of the James River, to the east of Gray's Creek. On February 4, 1625, he was identified as a resident of the Treasurer's Plantation (11). On January 3, 1625, the justices of the General Court noted that John Dancy and his father, Thomas, had been brought to Virginia by Treasurer George Sandys. On February 6, 1628, John Dancy, who said that he was 25 years old and had been born in the city of Worcester, testified that while he was in bed at Grindall Hill (part of the Treasurer's Plantation), he was awakened during the night by Richard Littlefrere and had seen William Mills, an accused thief, leaving the storehouse that had been burglarized. In 1629 John Dancy presented Roger Pritchard's estate inventory to the General Court (CBE 40, 60; MCGC 39, 162, 200).

THOMAS DANCY (DANSEY, DENCY, DAUNSEY, DANSYE)

On December 1, 1624, when John Bainham patented some land, he used the headright of John Dancy (Dansey, Dency, Daunsey, Dansye), identified as the son of the late John Dancy. It is more likely that John's deceased father was *Thomas* Dancy, not *John*, for on January 3, 1625, the General Court noted that Thomas Dancy and his son, John, had been transported to Virginia by George Sandys. Bainham's patent states that George Sandys had brought Dancy to Virginia on the *George* in 1621 and had transferred Dancy's headright to Bainham. (PB 1 Pt. 1:17; MCGC 39).

***

WILLIAM DANCY (DANSEY, DENCY, DAUNSEY, DANSYE)

On April 26, 1624, Virginia Company officials identified William Dancy (Dansey, Dency, Daunsey, Dansye) as a servant who had been transported to Virginia by Garrett Weston and accompanied Weston's brother, Francis (VCR 2:532).

ROGER DANE

On January 15, 1620, the justices of Bridewell decided that Roger Dane, a boy brought in from Aldgate, would be detained until he could be sent to Virginia (HUME 18).

JOHN DANES

Court testimony taken on November 30, 1624, reveals that John Danes sometimes transported timber for Thomas Barwick of Jamestown Island (1), who oversaw the Company of Shipwrights' men in Virginia (MCGC 33).

DANIEL

On March 22, 1622, when the Indians attacked Lieutenant John Gibbs's household at Westover (54), Mr. Domelow's servant, Daniel, was killed (VCR 3:567).

DANIEL (DANYELL)

According to Captain John Smith, on May 20, 1607, Daniel (Danyell), a sailor, accompanied Captain Christopher Newport on an exploratory voyage up the James River. Therefore, Daniel would have been at the site of Jamestown (1) when the island was first seated (HAI 103).

ALWIN DANIEL

In September 1623 the General Council's justices noted that Alwin Daniel, a former sailor on the *Everett*, had hired himself out after reaching Virginia (MCGC 7).

CHRISTOPHER DANIEL (DANIELL)

In May 1625 Christopher Daniel (Daniell) was identified as the patentee of 100 acres of land in Warresqueak (26) (VCR 4:556).

***

HENRY DANIEL

On November 13, 1635, Henry Daniel patented 200 acres of land in James City County, adjacent to Alexander Stoner. He used as headrights his own personal adventure, that of his wife, Elizabeth, and those of two maidservants whose transportation he had paid (PB 1 Pt. 1:306).

ELIZABETH DANIEL (MRS. HENRY DANIEL)

When Henry Daniel patented 200 acres of land in James City County on November 13, 1635, he used his wife, Elizabeth, as a headright (PB 1 Pt. 1:306).

***

RICHARD DANIEL (DANYELL)

On May 16, 1622, Richard Daniel (Danyell) was identified as owner of the *Furtherance*. On August 4, 1623, he was in Jamestown (1) and served on a jury (FER 373; MCGC 4-5).

LANCELLOTT DANUP

On December 31, 1619, Lancellott Danup, a boy brought in from London, was detained by the justices of Bridewell so that he could be sent to Virginia or Bermuda (HUME 16).

JAMES DARIES (DAVIES?)

On February 16, 1624, James Daries (or perhaps Davies) was living on the lower side of the James River, within the corporation of James City, in one of the settlements east of Gray's Creek (10-16) (CBE 40).

JOHN DARKER

On October 12, 1626, John Darker appeared before the General Court, where he claimed that Captain Ward owed him wages in tobacco and had only paid him in part. Court testimony reveals that Ward gave Darker the tobacco bill of Captain Eppes, which Darker misplaced while he was at Gravesend, England. As another man had seen the tobacco bill in Darker's possession before he lost it, Captain Eppes was ordered to replace it unless he could prove that the debt was invalid (MCGC 119).

ELIZABETH DARKINS

On February 27, 1619, the justices of Bridewell decided that Elizabeth Darkins, a girl, would be detained so that she could be sent to Virginia (HUME 12).

***

JOSHUA DARY

Joshua Dary and his wife, who were living at Martin's Hundred (7), were killed during the March 22, 1622, Indian attack (VCR 3:570).

MRS. JOSHUA DARY

On March 22, 1622, when the Indians attacked Martin's Hundred (**7**), Joshua Dary and his wife were killed (VCR 3:570).

***

WILLIAM DARY (DARRY)

In 1619 William Dary (Darry) was sent to Virginia at the expense of the Ferrars, who were major Virginia Company investors. He may have been sent to Martin's Hundred (**7**) or Southampton Hundred (**44**), plantations in which the Ferrars had made a significant financial investment (FER 296).

RICHARD DASH

On March 22, 1622, when the Indians attacked Captain Francis West's plantation at Westover (**54**), Richard Dash was killed (VCR 3:567).

MARIE (MARY) DAUCKS (DAWKS, DAWK)

Marie (Mary) Daucks (Dawks, Dawk), a young maid, came to Virginia in September 1621 on the *Warwick*. Virginia Company records indicate that she was a 25-year-old widow and was a kinswoman of Mr. Slocum, a resident of Mayden Lane. On March 22, 1622, when the Indians attacked Edward Bennett's plantation in Warresqueak (**26**), Marie (Mary) was killed (FER 309; VCR 571).

ALSE DAUSON

Alse Dauson, a young maid, came to Virginia in September 1621 on the *Warwick*. She was age 18 and had been born in London and reared by her mother, who reportedly was an honest woman and known to Mrs. Ferrar (FER 309).

MARGARET DAUSON

Margaret Dauson, a young maid, came to Virginia in September 1621 on the *Warwick*. Virginia Company records indicate that she was 25 years old and was born at Woodham Market in Suffolk. Margaret was reared by Elizabeth Stevenson of Southwark, with whom she had been in service (FER 309).

JOHN DAUXE

John Dauxe, a gentleman, came to Virginia in 1608 in the 2nd Supply of new settlers. He would have lived in Jamestown (**1**) (CJS 1:241; 2:190).

ROGER DAVID

Roger David was killed at Captain Berkeley's plantation on Falling Creek (**68**) when the Indians attacked on March 22, 1622. He probably was associated with the ironworks whose construction was overseen by John Berkeley (VCR 3:565).

AP HUGH DAVID

Ap Hugh David, a tradesman, came to Virginia in 1608 in the 2nd Supply of new colonists to reach Jamestown (**1**) (CJS 1:241; 2:190).

[NO FIRST NAME] DAVIS

On March 7, 1629, Captain Davis was named a commissioner of the monthly court that handled matters in the "upper parts," that is, at the head of the James River (MCGC 193).

[NO FIRST NAME] DAVIS (DAVIES)

On March 22, 1622, when the Indians attacked Martin's Hundred (**7**), the brother of Walter Davis (Davies) was killed. He may have been the father of James and John Davis (Davies), who also were present (VCR 3:570).

AGNES DAVIS (DAVES)

On August 8, 1618, officials at Bridewell decided that Agnes Davis (Daves), a vagrant from Lombard Street, would be sent to Virginia (CBE 9).

ARTHUR DAVIS (DAVIES)

On February 16, 1624, Arthur Davis (Davies) was living in Elizabeth City (**17, 18**) (CBE 44).

DENNIS DAVIS (DAVIES, DAVYS)

On June 19, 1623, Dennis Davis (Davies, Davys) of St. Giles by Cripplegate in London, identified himself as a 25-year-old barber surgeon when he testified about the death of Thomas Hamor, which occurred in the first half of 1623. Davis, who had been in Virginia at the time, said that Hamor had succumbed to a burning fever while living in Jamestown (**1**) (EAE 14; HCA 13/44 f 147vo).

EDWARD DAVIS (DAVIES)

Edward Davis (Davies) died at Martin's Hundred (**7**) sometime after April 1623 but before February 16, 1624. On April 9, 1629, his will was proved before the General Court (CBE 42; MCGC 196).

ELIZABETH DAVIS (DAVIES)

Elizabeth Davis (Davies) was living in Elizabeth City (**17, 18**) on February 16, 1624 (CBE 44).

ELIZABETH DAVIS (DAVIES)

Between April 1623 and February 16, 1624, Elizabeth Davis (Davies), a resident of Elizabeth City (**17, 18**), died. She may have been the same woman who simultaneously was listed among the living (CBE 45).

GEORGE DAVIS (DAVIES)

On February 16, 1624, George Davis (Davies) was living in Elizabeth City (**17, 18**) (CBE 44).

HENRY DAVIS (DAVIES)

Virginia Company records indicate that Henry Davis (Davies) went to Virginia with Lord Delaware, who reached the colony in June 1610 and attempted a return visit in 1617. On March 29, 1620, Agnes Nicholls, Henry's mother, asked Company officials to transfer his land rights to his sister, Susan Hammond (VCR 1:331).

HENRY DAVIS

On November 1624 the justices of the General Court noted that James Harrison had bought the contract of Henry Davis, an indentured servant, from John Cheesman, then a resident of Kecoughtan (**17**) (MCGC 35).

HUGH DAVIS

On September 7, 1630, the General Court's justices decided to have Hugh Davis whipped for having sexual relations with a black woman (HEN 1:146; MCGC 479).

***

JAMES DAVIS

In 1607 Captain James Davis was captain of St. George's Fort in Sagadahoc, in what is now Maine. He returned to England, and in 1609 he set sail for Virginia in Sir Thomas Gates's fleet, which brought the 3rd Supply of new colonists. Davis arrived in Virginia in October 1609 in a small pinnace, the *Virginia*, in which he and his brother, Robert, had set sail. During 1609 George Percy, then president of the colony, sent Captain James Davis to the mouth of the James River to take command of Algernon Fort, which was located at Old Point Comfort in Kecoughtan (**17**). After the fort burned, Davis quickly had it rebuilt. When Sir Thomas Dale's fleet arrived in May 1611, Captain Davis was still there. Later, Dale placed Davis in charge of Coxendale (**64**) and its five small forts. James Davis died between April 1623 and February 16, 1624, at one of the communities on the lower side of the James River, east of Gray's Creek (**10-16**), an area to which many Henrico evacuees moved after the March 1622 Indian attack. On March 6, 1633, the late James Davis, formerly of Henrico, was described as a gentleman, an ancient planter, and the husband of Rachell Davis, also an ancient planter. The 100 acres apiece to which James and Rachell Davis were entitled descended to their son, Thomas, who decided to take up land in Warresqueak (**26**) (CJS 1:231; 2:219, 254; HAI 418, 440, 504, 506, 516, 518, 520, 825; CBE 60; PB 1 Pt. 1:128; DOR 1:804-805).

RACHELL DAVIS
(MRS. JAMES DAVIS)

Rachell Davis, the widow of James Davis of Henrico, died sometime prior to March 6, 1633. Rachell's and James's entitlement to 100 acres apiece, as ancient planters, descended to their son, Thomas, who selected land in Warresqueak (**26**). As Thomas Davis was age 26 in 1639, James and

Rachell Davis would have wed sometime prior to 1613 (PB 1 Pt. 1:128; EAE 85).

THOMAS DAVIS

On March 6, 1633, Thomas Davis, the son of ancient planters James and Rachell Davis of Henrico, patented 300 acres in Warresqueak (**26**). He acquired his land on the basis of his parents' headrights and the headrights he received for transporting two people to the colony. In 1639, when Thomas Davis made a sworn statement before the Admiralty Court, he identified himself as a 26-year-old merchant from Chuckatuck in Virginia (PB 1 Pt. 1:128; DOR 1:805; EAE 85).

***

JAMES DAVIS

On April 30, 1623, James Davis, the nephew and an heir of the late Walter Davis of Martin's Hundred (**7**), asked Virginia Company officials to give him the decedent's estate in Virginia. Davis appears to have been one of the Society of Martin's Hundred's servants, for sometime prior to November 8, 1624, he asked to be freed from his obligation to Mr. Emmerson. The General Court agreed but required James Davis to give Mr. Emmerson (probably Ellis Emmerson of Martin's Hundred) a cow and a servant boy (VCR 2:389; MCGC 30).

JANE DAVIS

Jane Davis came to Virginia in 1622 on the *Abigail*. On January 24, 1625, she was identified as a 24-year-old servant in Sir Francis Wyatt's household in urban Jamestown (**1**) (CBE 54).

JOAN (JONE) DAVIS (DAVIES)

On February 16, 1624, Joan (Jone) Davis (Davies) was a maidservant in Christopher Davison's household in urban Jamestown (**1**). However, on February 4, 1625, she was residing on Hog Island (**16**) and appears to have been free. By that date Davison was dead (CBE 38, 61).

JOAN (JONE) DAVIS (DAVIES)

On February 16, 1624, Joan (Jone) Davis (Davies) was living in Elizabeth City (**17, 18**) (CBE 44).

JOHN DAVIS (DAVIES)

On December 31, 1619, it was decided that John Davis (Davies), who had been brought in by the marshal of Middlesex, would be sent to Virginia (CBE 14; HUME 14).

JOHN DAVIS (DAVYS, DAVIES)

John Davis (Davys, Davies), a 30-year-old husbandman from Devonshire, came to Virginia in 1619 on the *Bona Nova*. His transportation costs were paid by the Ferrars, who were major Virginia Company investors. On March 22, 1622, when the Indians attacked Southampton Hundred (**44**), a settlement supported by the Ferrars and others, John Davis was killed (FER 295, 296; VCR 3:569).

JOHN DAVIS (DAVIES)

John Davis (Davies) came to Virginia on the *George* in 1617 and sometime prior to December 10, 1620, became a servant of Samuel Jordan, who resided at Bermuda or Charles Hundred (**39**) before patenting land at what became known as Jordan's Journey (**46**). On February 16, 1624, John was living at Jordan's Journey, the Jordan plantation. On January 21, 1625, when a muster was taken of the colony's inhabitants, John Davis was in residence at Jordan's Journey where he and his partner, William Emmerson, headed a household that included two servants. In 1628–1629 John Davis and William Emmerson were among the men who encountered Captain John Smith in England and told him about current living conditions in the colony (PB 8:125; CBE 37, 52; CJS 2:217, 219; DOR 1:19).

JOHN DAVIS (DAVIES)

In 1623 John Davis (Davies) came to Virginia on the *Southampton* and on February 16, 1624, was living at Flowerdew Hundred (**53**). On January 20, 1625, when a muster was made of the colony's inhabitants, he was still at Flowerdew and was identified as a 45-year-old servant in the household of Abraham Peirsey (CBE 37, 50).

JOHN DAVIS (DAVIES)

John Davies (Davis) came to Virginia on the *John and Francis* in 1623 and on February 16, 1624, was living in Elizabeth City

(18). In early 1625 he was identified as a 24-year-old servant in Percivall Ibbotson's household, east of Blunt Point **(22)** (CBE 44, 66).

JOHN DAVIS (DAVIES, DAVYS)

John Davis (Davies, Davys) came to Virginia on the *Gift* sometime prior to February 16, 1624, and was one of Ralph Hamor's servants. He was then living on the lower side of the James River on Hog Island **(16)**. He was still there on February 4, 1625, and was identified as a servant in Hamor's household. On January 3, 1625, when John, who was underage, received some money from the estate of his deceased brother, Walter Davis, it was noted that Ralph Hamor was his legal guardian. Later in the month John Davis became involved in a legal dispute between Hamor and William Harwood, Martin's Hundred's leader **(7)**. On January 10, 1627, after John Davis had come of age, he tried to recover the value of the corn that had belonged to his brother, Walter, barrels that William Peirce and others had brought up to Jamestown **(1)** after the March 1622 Indian attack. Davis also tried to collect a debt owed by Thomas Boyse of Martin's Hundred, a sum seemingly accruable to the estate of Walter Davis. John Davis apparently had his own financial troubles, for in January 1628 John Bottom had him arrested for indebtedness. On February 9, 1628, the General Court decided that John Davis was to be compensated by William Harwood for clearing the land at Martin's Hundred that had belonged to Walter Davis and Richard Staples. On July 9, 1635, Benjamin Harrison purchased 100 acres of land in Warresqueak **(26)** from John Davis of Chiskiack **(31-38)**. Harrison's patent notes that John Davies, as Walter Davies' heir, had received the 100 acres by means of a June 5, 1633, court order (CBE 40, 61; MCGC 39, 44, 131, 133, 160, 166; PB 1 Pt. 1:207).

JOHN DAVIS (DAVIES)

On July 4, 1635, John Davis (Davies) received a patent for 100 acres of James City County land called the Barren Neck. Half of the acreage he received was from his late master, Richard Perry, a London merchant, and half for transportation of Davis' servant, Richard Thomas. On May 27, 1673, John Davis' son and heir, Thomas, brought

suit against Robert Weekes in the General Court in an attempt to overturn a decision that had been made by the justices of James City County's monthly court. The case was transferred to York County, whose justices were instructed to see that the plaintiff received what he was due under the terms of his father's will (PB 1 Pt. 1:204; MCGC 341).

KATHERIN DAVIS (DAVIES)

Katherin Davis (Davies) came to Virginia on the *Southampton* and on February 4, 1625, was living at Hog Island **(16)**, where she was a servant in Edward Barkley's household (CBE 61).

LANCELOTT DAVIS (DAVYS, DAVIES)

On December 31, 1619, Bridewell's officials decided that Lancelott Davis (Davys, Davies) would be detained so that he could be sent to Virginia (CBE 15).

MARGARET DAVIS (DAVIES)

On March 22, 1622, when the Indians attacked Martin's Hundred **(7)**, Margaret Davis (Davies) was slain (VCR 3:570).

MATHEW DAVIS (DAVIES)

On January 22, 1619, the justices of Bridewell decided that Mathew Davis (Davies), a boy who had been brought in, would be detained until he could be sent to Virginia (HUME 16).

NICHOLAS DAVIS (DAVIES)

In 1618–1619 Nicholas Davis (Davies) came to Virginia on the *Marigold* and on February 16, 1624, was living in Elizabeth City **(18)**. When a muster was made of the colony's inhabitants in early 1625, Nicholas was identified as a 13-year-old servant in the household of Thomas Willoughby (CBE 44, 64).

RICHARD DAVIS (DAVIES)

Richard Davis (Davies) came to Virginia on the *Bona Nova* in 1620 and on February 16, 1624, was living in Elizabeth City **(17)**. At the beginning of 1625, when a muster was made of Elizabeth City's inhabitants, Richard was identified as a 22-year-old servant in the household of the Rev. Jonas Stockden, who was in possession of land on the east side of the Hampton River (CBE 44, 66).

RICHARD DAVIS (DAVIES)

Richard Davis (Davies) came to Virginia on the *Jonathan* in 1620. On January 23, 1625, he was living at the College (**66**), where he was a servant in Thomas Osborne's household (CBE 53).

ROBERT DAVIS

In 1607 Captain Robert Davis was sergeant major of St. George's Fort in what is now Maine. In 1609 he set sail for Virginia in Sir Thomas Gates's fleet, which brought the 3rd Supply. Robert was the brother of Captain James Davis, who also was at St. George's Fort and came to Virginia in 1609 (CJS 2:231; DOR 1:804-805).

ROBERT DAVIS

On March 22, 1622, Robert Davis was killed when the Indians attacked the settlement on the College Land (**66**) (VCR 3:566).

ROBERT DAVIS

On February 16, 1624, Robert Davis was living on the Maine (**3**) just west of Jamestown Island (CBE 39).

ROBERT DAVIS (DAVIES, DAVYS)

Robert Davis (Davies, Davys), one of John Rolfe's servants, witnessed his March 10, 1622 will, which was made at Jamestown (**1**). On July 17, 1622, Mr. Horwood (Harwood), a member of the Virginia Company, asked for Robert Davis's release. He said that Davis had outfitted himself to come to Virginia, had served John Rolfe for three years, and was eager to have his own land. On February 16, 1624, Robert Davis was living on the mainland in the Governor's Land (**3**), where he was a member of Richard Atkins' household. On March 29, 1626, Davis was identified as John Rolfe's former servant. Around January 1637 Robert Davis, then a 36-year-old planter and resident of Warresqueak (**26**), said that he had lived in Virginia more than 20 years and had been present three or four years earlier when William Hutchinson

(also of Warresqueak) chose his executors (SH 5; MCGH 861; VCR 2:97; MCGC 98; CBE 39; EAE 75).

SAMUEL (SAMUELL) DAVIS (DAVIES)

Samuel (Samuell) Davis (Davies) came to Virginia on the *Southampton* in 1622. On February 16, 1624, he was living within the corporation of James City, on the lower side of the James River, in one of the settlements east of Gray's Creek. He probably was residing on Captain Samuel Mathews' plantation (**15**), where he was living on February 4, 1625, and was described as an 18-year-old servant (CBE 40, 59).

THOMAS DAVIS (DAVIES)

Thomas Davis (Davies), a cooper and shingler, came to Virginia with Captain John Woodlief on the *Margaret* of Bristol in 1619 and was one of the settlers sent to establish Berkeley Hundred (**55**). Davis was supposed to serve the Society of Berkeley Hundred's investors for three years and in exchange, was to get 30 acres of land. He received 3 years' worth of compensation in advance of his voyage. Thomas Davis reportedly died within a relatively short time of reaching Virginia (VCR 3:187, 197, 199, 213; CBE 13-14).

THOMAS DAVIS (DAVIES)

When the assembly convened in its first session in July–August 1619, Thomas Davis (Davies), who represented Martin's Brandon (**59**), admitted that Captain John Martin's men took some of the Indians' corn by force (VCR 3:154, 157).

THOMAS DAVIS (DAVIES)

Thomas Davis (Davies) came to Virginia on the *John and Francis* in 1623 and on February 16, 1624, was residing in Elizabeth City (**18**). On September 20, 1624, Davis, who was identified as a captain, was renting William Cole's land in Kecoughtan, acreage that was adjacent to Alexander Mountney's. In early 1625, when a muster was made of the colony's inhabitants, Captain Thomas Davies, who was age 40, headed a household that he shared with his partner, Thomas Hewes. They were relatively well provisioned and supplied with defensive weaponry (CBE 44, 66; PB 1 Pt. 1:37; DOR 1:60).

THOMAS DAVIS (DAVIES)

Sometime after February 16, 1624, but before early 1625, Thomas Davis (Davies) died in Elizabeth City (**17, 18**) (CBE 67).

WALTER DAVIS (DAVIES)

Walter Davis (Davies) died at Martin's Hundred (**7**) during the March 22, 1622, Indian attack. Court testimony taken on January 10, 1627, indicates that shortly after the assault, William Peirce and some others from Jamestown (**1**) went to Martin's Hundred and retrieved barrels of stored corn that had belonged to Walter Davis. A reference to Walter's estate on January 3, 1625, mentions John, whom officials identified as the decedent's younger brother. On June 5, 1633, John Davis, as Walter Davis's surviving heir, patented some land in Warresqueak (**26**) that he acquired on the basis of his late brother's entitlement. He quickly sold that acreage to Benjamin Harrison (VCR 2:389; 3:570; MCGC 39, 131; PB 1 Pt. 1:207).

WILLIAM DAVIS (DAVIES)

William Davis (Davies) came to Virginia in 1622 on the *Margaret and John* and on February 16, 1624, was living on the Eastern Shore. In early 1625 he was still residing there and was a household head in the community of settlers on Old Plantation Creek (**73**). On February 9, 1625, Davis brought suit against Charles Harmer, a debtor. On September 7, 1632, when John Robins Sr. patented some land, he indicated that he had paid for William Davis's transportation to the colony and therefore was entitled to his headright (CBE 46, 69; MCGC 48; PB 1 Pt. 1:116; DOR 1:71).

WILLIAM DAVIS (DAVIES)

William Davis (Davies) died in Elizabeth City (**17, 18**) sometime after April 1623 but before February 16, 1624 (CBE 45).

***

CHRISTOPHER DAVISON

Christopher Davison came to Virginia around October 1621, perhaps with incoming Governor Francis Wyatt. He was added to the Council of State and became Secretary of State, holding that position until 1623. He also functioned as clerk of the Council. Christopher Davison lived in urban Jamestown (**1**), where his widow was residing in February 1624. The Virginia Company furnished Davison with some provisions and personal items, along with a barrel of seeds. In January 1622 he informed Company officials that most of the tenants on the Secretary's Land (**75**) in Accomack were deceased and later in the year, he reported that 13 of his own 20 servants were dead. He asked for more servants, some cattle, and reimbursement for his wife's transportation to Virginia. Christopher Davison most likely compiled the list of those killed during the March 1622 Indian attack and the information summarized in the February 1624 census. In April 1623 he told Company officials that contrary to agreement, Edward Blaney had brought his own brother, Thomas Finch, to the colony instead of Davison's little daughter. He also said that his tenants had produced so little tobacco that he was unable to pay Blaney what he owed the magazine. Davison then had 30 tenants and 4 cattle, part of his stipend as secretary. On September 3, 1623, Christopher Davison witnessed John Atkins' will and received a bequest from him. He also testified about Captain John Martin's tendency to be boastful. Sometime prior to February 16, 1624, Christopher Davison died. His widow, Alice, was then residing in urban Jamestown where she was a household head (CJS 2:286; STAN 21, 31; FER 308, 322, 571; VCR 1:478, 482, 488-489; 2:481; 3:585, 588, 609; 2:109-110; 3:482, 690; 4:115-116, 129-130, 185; CO 1/2 f 149; CBE 32; SAIN 1:43; WITH 35-36; MCGC 118).

ALICE DAVISON
(MRS. CHRISTOPHER DAVISON)

Alice Davison, the widow of Secretary of State Christopher Davison, was living in urban Jamestown (**1**) on February 16, 1624, where she was a household head. On January 3, 1625, she testified about Sir George Yeardley's indebtedness to George Thorpe's estate, in which she appears to have had a legal interest. Later in the year, she indicated that although Captain John Martin had boasted about his fine dwelling at Martin's Brandon (**59**), he merely occupied a windowless 14-foot-square blockhouse (CBE 38; MCGC 40; FER 571).

***

ELLEN DAVY

Ellen Davy, a young maid, came to Virginia in 1621 on the *Warwick* (FER 309).

***

HENRY DAWKES

On July 14, 1608, Henry Dawkes, an ancient planter, obtained a bill of adventure from the Virginia Company, a document which indicated that he was preparing to set out for the colony. It is uncertain how long Dawkes lived after he came to Virginia. However, on June 20, 1632, when his son, William Dawkes, secured a patent for 200 acres in the upper reaches of the James River, in the corporation of Henrico, he utilized his late father's bill of adventure, which entitled him to 100 acres, plus the 100 acres the elder man was due as an ancient planter. William also received an additional 50 acres as heir of his deceased uncle, William Leigh. On September 7, 1632, when William Dawkes's land was confirmed, reference was again made to Henry Dawkes's right to 100 acres as an ancient planter and his 1608 bill of adventure (PB 1 Pt. 1:107, 114).

WILLIAM DAWKES

William Dawkes was the son of ancient planter Henry Dawkes, who obtained a bill of adventure from the Virginia Company on July 14, 1608. On June 20, 1632, when William secured a patent for 250 acres in the corporation of Henrico, he cited his late father's land entitlement as an ancient planter and the acreage he was due as a Virginia Company investor. On September 7, 1632, a transcription of Henry Dawkes's bill of adventure was entered into the General Court's records. In March 1633 William Dawkes acquired a leasehold that gave him an additional 50 acres (PB 1 Pt. 1:107, 114, 138, 143).

***

JOAN DAWKES

On July 18, 1620, Joan Dawkes, who identified herself as a widow, transferred to Doctor Anthony the bill of adventure to which she was entitled (VCR 1:407).

HENRY DAWLEN

On February 16, 1624, Henry Dawlen was living on the Maine (3), just west of Jamestown Island (CBE 39).

MATHEWE DAWSE ALIAS SHELLA (SEE MATHEWE SHELLA)

MARGERY DAWSE (DAWES)

On February 16, 1624, Margery Dawse (Dawes) was living in Captain William Holmes's household in urban Jamestown (1) and probably was a servant (CBE 38).

ANN DAWSON

On January 29, 1620, Bridewell officials decided that Ann Dawson would be sent to Virginia (CBE 18).

CHARLES DAWSON

Sometime prior to December 1635 Charles Dawson of Flushing, Zeeland, who was age 42, decided to send his servant, Henry Morrell, and Mr. Harwood's servant, John Saddocke, to Virginia. A short time later, English officials noted that Captain Charles Dawson was among those going to Virginia on the *Constance* and sending servants there (EAE 57, 59).

ELIZABETH DAWSON

Elizabeth Dawson was one of the Newgate prisoners pardoned on November 20, 1622, on account of an epidemic of jail fever. She and many of her fellow inmates were to be put to work or transported overseas, perhaps to Virginia (CBE 29).

GEORGE DAWSON

George Dawson came to Virginia on the *Southampton* in 1623. On January 20, 1625, he was living at Flowerdew Hundred (53) where he was a 24-year-old servant in Abraham Peirsey's household (CBE 50).

JOHN DAWSON (DAWSONE)

On August 16, 1624, John Dawson (Dawsone) testified against William Tyler in a matter aired before the General Court. According to Dawson, Tyler said that because of Council members' lack of integrity, he would not serve as a councilor even if he were asked (MCGC 20).

OWEN DAWSON

Owen Dawson, a joiner from St. Martins in the Fields, arrived in Jamestown (1) on September 5, 1623, on the *Ann* and took the oath of supremacy. On May 30, 1634, Dawson's land in Elizabeth City (17) was mentioned as lying adjacent to Thomas Watts's leasehold (MCGC 6; PB 1 Pt. 1:149).

THOMAS DAWSON

An October 20, 1621, memorandum included in records associated with the Society of Berkeley Hundred (55) indicates that Thomas Dawson's tobacco was sold in England (S of N 39).

WILLIAM DAWSON

William Dawson, a refiner, came to Virginia in 1608 as part of the 2nd Supply of new colonists. He would have lived in Jamestown (1) (CJS 1:222; 2:162).

WILLIAM DAWSON

William Dawson came to Virginia in the *Discovery* in 1621 and on February 16, 1624, was living at Jordan's Journey (46). On January 21, 1625, Dawson was identified as a 25-year-old servant in the household headed by William Farrar and Sisley Jordan. In June 1637 when William Farrar's son and heir, William II, patented some land in Henrico County, he used William Dawson as a headright and indicated that he was one of his late father's servants. This occurred two years after Dawson himself patented 150 acres in Warresqueak (26) (CBE 36, 51; PB 1 Pt. 1:316, 436; DOR 1:814).

JOHN DAY

On May 30, 1635, John Day was identified as one of John Slaughter's servants. Slaughter used his headright when patenting some land (PB 1 Pt.1:169).

***

JOHN DAY

John Day came to Virginia on the *London Merchant* in 1620 and on February 16, 1624, was living at the College (66). However, by February 4, 1625, he had relocated to Hog Island (16), where he was identified as one of Sir George Yeardley's servants. Day, who was age 24, was married to a woman who had come to Virginia on the same ship that had brought him to the colony. Sometime during 1626, John Day, who was still residing on Hog Island, sold nails to Henry Ellyott of Martin's Hundred (7). He apparently was considered a respectable member of the community, for on May 7, 1627, he was called on to verify John Uty's claim that Richard Bickley refused to perform military duty. In October 1628 John Day again appeared before the General Court where he testified that Richard Tree, who was supposed to build a church on Hog Island, had said that he would delay construction until after planting season (CBE 35, 61; MCGC 135, 148, 175).

MRS. JOHN DAY

The woman who married John Day, one of Sir George Yeardley's servants, came to Virginia in 1620 on the *London Merchant*. Although John Day was not identified as a married man when census records were compiled in February 1624, he had wed by February 4, 1625, and was living at Hog Island (16) with his wife. Mrs. John Day, like her husband, appears to have been a servant in Sir George Yeardley's household (CBE 61).

***

THOMAS DAY

Thomas Day, a sea captain who was brought to Virginia at the expense of William Capps, was supposed to earn his passage by working for Captain Bullock during the crossing. Court testimony taken in Jamestown (1) on March 29, 1629, indicates that Captains Stone and Preene refused to allow Day to work and detained him at St. Christopher's in the Caribbean (MCGC 169).

THOMAS DAYHURST

On February 16, 1624, Thomas Dayhurst was living on the lower side of the James River, within the corporation of James City, at one of the settlements east of Gray's Creek (10-16) (CBE 40).

JEREMY DEALE

On May 20, 1607, Jeremy Deale, a sailor who came to Virginia with the first group of colonists, accompanied Captain Christopher Newport on an exploratory voyage up the James River. He would have spent time in Jamestown (1) (HAI 103).

JOSEPH DEANE

Joseph Deane came to Virginia on the *George* in 1621. In 1629 William Spencer of Jamestown Island (1) used him as a headright and informed the General Court that he had paid for Deane's transportation. However, on September 9, 1632, when Spencer patented some land on Lawnes Creek in Warresqueak (26), he indicated that Joseph Deane had come to Virginia on the *Abigail* in 1622 and that he had paid Captain John Tooke (Tuke), a mariner, for Dean's passage (MCGC 200; PB 1 Pt. 1:120).

RICHARD DEANE

On June 24, 1635, when John Russell patented some land, he listed Richard Deane as a headright (PB 1 Pt. 1:177).

JAN DE CARPENTRY

Laborer Jan De Carpentry, his wife, and two children were among the Walloons and French who indicated their willingness to go to Virginia. In August 1621 the Virginia Company agreed that they could immigrate (CBE 24).

MARTIN DE CARPENTIER

Brass founder Martin De Carpentier, a young man, was among the Walloons and French who indicated their willingness to go to Virginia. In August 1621 the Virginia Company agreed that he could immigrate (CBE 24).

JAN DE CRENNE

Glass maker Jan De Crenne and his wife and child were among the Walloons and French who indicated their willingness to go to Virginia. In August 1621 the Virginia Company agreed that they could immigrate (CBE 25).

ABEL DE CREPY

Shuttle worker Abel De Crepy, his wife, and four children were among the Walloons and French who indicated their willingness to go to Virginia. In August 1621 the Virginia Company agreed that they could immigrate (CBE 25).

JAN DE CROY

Sawyer Jan De Croy, his wife, and five children were among the Walloons and French who indicated their willingness to go to Virginia. In August 1621 the Virginia Company agreed that they could immigrate (CBE 24).

AEHM (JOACHIM?) DEFORE

On February 27, 1618, Bridewell's justices decided that Aehm (probably Joachim) Defore would be detained until he could be sent to Virginia (HUME 8).

JESSE DE FOREST

Dyer Jesse De Forest, his wife, and five children were among the Walloons and French who indicated their willingness to go to Virginia. In August 1621 the Virginia Company agreed that they could immigrate (CBE 24).

JOHN DE FRIZES

On February 5, 1628, John de Frizes was identified as a servant to Edward Sharples of Jamestown (1) (MCGC:160-161).

THOMAS DELAMAJOR (DELEMAJOR, DILLIMAGER)

On February 16, 1624, Thomas Delamajor (Delemajor, Dillimager), a joiner, was living at Flowerdew Hundred (53) where he was listed among Sir George Yeardley's servants. By June 24, 1624, Delamajor moved to Jamestown (1), where he was still a member of the Yeardley household. It was then that he and another man reportedly were seen near the "country house" (a public building) on the night someone broke into cape merchant Abraham Peirsey's store. On January 24, 1625, when a muster was made of Jamestown Island's inhabitants, Thomas Delamajor was residing in the eastern end of the island. During 1626 he made several appearances before the General Court to settle or collect debts. On one occasion he testified about two drunken people he and Roger Delke had seen while walking to Mrs. Soothey's house. All four individuals involved in the court testimony (inebriants and witnesses) lived in the eastern end of Jamestown Island. In February 1628 Thomas Delamajor was ordered to pay James Parker for a deceased servant. On March 14, 1629, he was granted a 10-year lease for 3 acres at Goose Hill, in the eastern end of Jamestown Island, the same parcel the General Court had awarded him in 1626 (CBE 37, 56; MCGC 15, 94, 115, 167, 192; PB 1 Pt. 1:97-98).

NICHOLAS DE LA MARLIER

Dyer Nicholas De La Marlier, his wife, and two children were among the Walloons and French who indicated their willingness to go to Virginia. In August 1621 the Virginia Company agreed that they could immigrate (CBE 24).

PHILIPPE DE LA MER

Carpenter Philippe De La Mer, a young man, was among the Walloons and French who indicated their willingness to go to Virginia. In August 1621 the Virginia Company agreed that he could immigrate (CBE 24).

JAN DE LA MET

Laborer Jan De La Met, a young man, was among the Walloons and French who indicated their willingness to go to Virginia. In August 1621 the Virginia Company agreed that he could immigrate (CBE 25-26).

[NO FIRST NAME] DE LA MONTAGNE

Monsieur De La Montagne, an unmarried medical student, was among the Walloons and French who indicated their willingness to go to Virginia. In August 1621 the Virginia Company agreed that he could immigrate (CBE 25-26).

ESAW (ISAYE) DELAWARE (DELYWARR)

Esaw (Isaye) Delaware (Delywarr) came to Virginia on the *Providence* in 1623 and on February 16, 1624, was a resident of Eliza-beth City (18). When a muster was taken of the people living at Newportes News (24) on February 7, 1625, Delaware was described as a 22-year-old servant in Daniel Gookin's household (CBE 43, 63).

***

LORD DELAWARE (DE LA WARR) (SEE THOMAS WEST)

LADY DELAWARE (DE LA WARR) (SEE CECILY (CECILEY, CECELIA, CISLEY) SHERLEY WEST)

***

JOHN DELBRIDGE

On August 20, 1628, John Delbridge of Barnstable, shipped goods to Virginia on the *John*. On January 13, 1632, he requested permission to offload his Virginia tobacco at Barnstable instead of London (CBE 84, 98).

RICHARD DELBRIDGE

In 1619 the Virginia Company of London granted a patent to Richard Delbridge, who was planning to transport people to Virginia that year. On December 19, 1621, he received a share of Virginia land from Francis Carter, acreage that appears to have been part of the West and Shirley Hundred (41) patent that Lady Cisley Delaware had inherited from her late husband. On February 27, 1622, Company officials noted that Delbridge then had a ship in Virginia that was to continue on to Bermuda (VCR 1:571, 605-606; 3:118).

JACQUES DE LECHEILLES

Brewer Jacques De Lecheilles, who was unmarried, was among the Walloons and French who indicated their willingness to go to Virginia. In August 1621 the Virginia Company agreed that he could immigrate (CBE 24).

ANTHOINE DE LIELATE

Vine dresser Anthoine De Lielate, his wife, and four children were among the Walloons and French who indicated their willingness to go to Virginia. In August 1621 the Virginia Company agreed that they could immigrate (CBE 25).

[NO FIRST NAME]
DELKE (DILKE)

On March 13, 1622, the Virginia Company decided to give Mr. Delke (Dilke) free passage to Virginia and 100 acres of land if he would serve the Company for 8 years. Delke, who was to be named master of the East India School if Virginia's governor agreed, was to be given books and was asked to find someone expert in teaching arithmetic. Mr. Delke probably did not immigrate to Virginia, for Company records dating to April 3, 1622, indicate that he resigned because he had found a job in England (VCR 1:616, 629).

***

CLEMENT DELKE (DILKE)

On June 25, 1623, Clement Delke (Dilke) and his associates received a patent from the Virginia Company, for they were planning to take 100 people to Virginia. He served as one of Jamestown's (1) burgesses in the assembly session of 1623–1624 and on February 16, 1624, when a census was taken, he and his wife were residing in the capital city. In 1624 Clement Delke signed a document called "A Tragical Relation," which described conditions in the colony. When he testified in court on November 25, 1624, about Mr. Whitaker's tobacco, he gave his age as 26. On December 13, 1624, Dr. John Pott of urban Jamestown testified that Mr. Delke informed him that he would soon be his neighbor, for he had made an agreement to purchase John Lightfoot's house and land. In April 1625, when Council secretary Edward Sharples was punished for surreptitiously sending documents back to England, he was ordered to serve Clement Delke for 7 years. On January 3, 1626, Delke testified that when he examined Lady Temperance Yeardley's tobacco from Hog Island (16), he found a mixture of good and bad quality leaves. He said that one of Lady Yeardley's employees, Maximillian Stone, asked not to be reported for negligence, and requested that Delke soften his criticism if he felt compelled to report Stone. On February 6, 1627, Clement Delke commenced leasing some land on the Eastern Shore, part of the acreage owned by the defunct Virginia Company (76). Several months later he patented 100 acres in Accomack, using the headrights of his wife, Elizabeth, and himself. Clement and Elizabeth Delk

died prior to June 1629. Captain Clement Delke's acreage was used as a reference point by several other Accomack landholders, and in September 1634 he was mentioned in a court case (VCR 2:438, 457; HEN 1:128-129; CBE 38; HAI 915; PB 1 Pt. 1:56, 76, 81, 86; MCGC 31-32, 36, 52, 83; STAN 53; AMES 1:21; 2:14).

ELIZABETH KENYTHORPE
DELKE (DILKE)
(MRS. CLEMENT DELKE [DILKE])

Elizabeth, who married Clement Delke (Dilke), came to Virginia on the *George* in 1622. On February 16, 1624, she and her husband, Clement, were living in urban Jamestown (1). On December 12, 1627, when Captain Clement Delke patented 100 acres of land on the Eastern Shore in Accomack, he used Elizabeth and himself as headrights. Elizabeth Kenythorpe Delke died in Virginia sometime prior to June 1629, at which time she was identified as a widow. Administration of her estate was granted to her sister, Catherine Kenythorpe (CBE 38; PB 1 Pt.1:56; EEAC 18; MOR 32).

***

***

ROGER DELKE (DILKE) I

Roger Delke (Dilke) I came to Virginia on the *Southampton*, Captain John Harvey's ship. On January 24, 1625, he was living at Hog Island (16), where he was one of Jamestown merchant John Chew's servants. By September 18, 1626, Roger Delke had relocated to Jamestown Island (1) and was lodging at Mrs. Soothey's house. It was then that he testified that he had seen Mrs. Fisher and John Southern staggering drunkenly, while he and Thomas Delamajor were heading home. On May 7, 1627, Roger Delke was fined for leaving his plantation for several days without permission of its commander. Although he served as a Stanley Hundred (Warwick) burgess in the February 1633 session of the assembly, a year later he was declared a chronic debtor. He died sometime prior to June 22, 1635, and was survived by his widow, Alice, and son, Roger II (CBE 61; MCGC 36, 52, 115, 148, 481; HEN 1:203; PB 1 Pt. 1:255; Pt. 2:472; 5:320; DOR 1:815).

ALICE DELKE (DILKE)
(MRS. ROGER DELKE [DILKE] I)

On June 22, 1635, Mrs. Alice Delke (Dilke), Roger Delke I's widow, owned land near Lawnes Creek, adjacent to that of Captain William Peirce. Alice and Roger I produced a son, Roger II. Sometime prior to August 28, 1637, Alice married Nicholas Reynolds, with whom she had two sons (PB 1 Pt. 1:255; Pt. 2:474; DOR 1:815).

ROGER DELKE (DILKE) II

Roger Delke (Dilke) II, the son of Alice and Roger Delke I, probably was born in 1634, for he was 40 years old when he testified in court on July 7, 1674. However, when he testified again on July 7, 1677, he gave his age as 48. In February 1664 Roger II obtained a patent for land that once belonged to his father (Surry County Deeds, Wills &c 1 [1652-1672]:346-348; 2 [1671-1684]:56, 144; PB 5:320; DOR 1:815-816).

***

WILLIAM DELKE (DILKE)

On November 20, 1622, William Delke (Dilke) of Clement Inn in Middlesex County, England, asked Virginia Company officials for a patent, stating that he intended to take 100 people to Virginia (VCR 2:132).

PETER (PETTER) DE MAIN

Peter (Petter) De Main died in Jamestown (1) sometime after April 1623 but before February 16, 1624 (CBE 39).

MARTIN (MARTINE) DEMOONE (DEMON)

Martin (Martine) Demoone (Demon) came to Virginia on the *George* in 1617 and on February 16, 1624, was living on the lower side of the James River, west of Gray's Creek. On February 4, 1625, when a muster was made of the colony's inhabitants, Demoone was identified as a 15-year-old servant in the household of Pettiplace Close, at Paces Paines (7) (CBE 40, 59).

WILLIAM DENHAM (DENUM)

William Denham (Denum) came to Virginia on the *Gift* in 1623 and on February 16,
1624, was living at Warresqueak (26), Edward Bennett's plantation. On February 7, 1625, when a muster was made of Warresqueak's inhabitants, Denham was identified as one of Bennett's servants. On August 20, 1635, William Denham patented 300 acres of land in what was then Warresqueak or Isle of Wight County (CBE 42, 62).

JOHN DENNETT

On July 7, 1635, John Dennett was used as a headright by Thomas Harwood, whose land was on Skiff's Creek. On July 10, 1635, Dennett was identified as the owner of 200 acres in James City County, within Martin's Hundred (7). Two weeks later he was described as the administrator of Thomas Harvey of Martin's Hundred when he conveyed Harvey's land to another man (PB 1 Pt. 1:208, 271, 276).

THOMAS DENINGTON

On April 24, 1623, Thomas Denington, a passenger on the *Margaret and John*, submitted a petition to Virginia's governor (VCR 4:127-128).

EDWARD DENISON

Edward Denison came to Virginia in 1623 on the *Truelove*. On January 21, 1625, he was living at Jordan's Journey (46), where he was a 22-year-old indentured servant in Nathaniel Causey's household (CBE 52).

JOHN DENMARKE

On February 16, 1624, John Denmarke was living on the lower side of the James River, within the corporation of James City, at one of the plantations east of Gray's Creek (10-16) (CBE 41).

JOHN DENNIS

On March 20, 1622, Virginia Company officials noted that Virginia's governor had released John Dennis, master of the *Marmaduke*, because he had exercised such great care in transporting passengers to the colony. Company officials asked Dennis to refund the money he had received for bringing three people to the colony who had decided not to stay. On April 30, 1623, John Dennis was among those who wrote a rebuttal to Captain Nathaniel Butler's derogatory statements about Virginia. He was still master of the *Marmaduke* in March 1624, when he testified that he had come to Virginia by way of the West Indies. In 1627 John Dennis was identified as part-owner of a new ship called the *Marmaduke* that had set sail for Virginia in August 1626. Edmund Pritchard was then serving as purser and Edmond Morgan was a co-owner (VCR 1:620; 2:386; 4:469; MCGC 13; EAE 18).

JOHN DENNIS

On February 20, 1626, George Medcalf of Elizabeth City (**17**) purchased John Dennis, an indentured servant, from John Hayes (MCGC 95).

ROBERT DENNIS

Sometime prior to April 25, 1625, Robert Dennis, a mariner then in Virginia, witnessed Robert Mansteed's will. The following month he served as attorney for John Dennis, master of the *Marmaduke*. On November 11, 1627, Robert Dennis appeared before the General Court where he proved the will of Edmund Pritchard, late purser of the *Marmaduke*. In January 1630, when he shipped some goods to the Caribbean, Robert identified himself as a mariner, a resident of Limehouse in Middlesex, and as master of the *Carlile*. He probably was a kinsman of mariner John Dennis (MCGC 56, 63, 133; EAE 21).

THOMAS DENTON (DEINTON)

Thomas Denton (Deinton) set out for Virginia on September 15, 1619, on the *Margaret* of Bristol and was one of the men being sent to Berkeley Hundred (**55**) by its investors. Denton, who may have been a skilled worker, was supposed to serve for 8 years under Captain John Woodlief's supervision in exchange for 20 acres of land. Virginia Company records indicate that Thomas Denton died shortly after he reached Virginia (CBE 14; VCR 3:198, 213).

PAUL DE PASAR

Weaver Paul De Pasar, his wife, and two children were among the Walloons and French who indicated their willingness to go to Virginia. In August 1621 the Virginia Company agreed that they could immigrate (CBE 24).

ANTOINE DE RIDOUET

On June 6, 1629, Antoine de Ridouet reported that the Baron de Sance wanted to settle French Protestants in Virginia, where they could plant vines, grow olives, and make silk and salt. De Ridouet requested and received letters of denizenation (naturalization) for himself and his son, George (CO 1/5 f 50; SAIN 1:98).

THOMAS DERMER (DIRMER)

In 1615 Thomas Dermer (Dirmer), a gentleman, accompanied Captain John Smith on his second voyage to New England. In 1618 he returned to New England and stated that he intended to live there. Sometime after November 4, 1619, Captain Thomas Dermer arrived in Jamestown (**1**) in a 5-ton bark. He left but returned the following spring, probably with some settlers. On July 10, 1621, Captain Dermer gave the Virginia Company a report on his discoveries at the head of the Chesapeake Bay (CJS 1:351, 427, 435; 2:268; VCR 1:504).

DERRICK

On July 3, 1627, Alice Proctor's legal representative, Captain Samuel Mathews, testified that a man named Garrett and a Dutch carpenter named Derrick had borrowed the late John Proctor's wherry (a small boat) and lost it. Mathews said that Derrick had offered to pay for half of the cost of the lost boat. Alice and John Proctor were then residing at Paces Paines (**9**) (MCGC 150).

ANTHOIN DESENDRE

Laborer Anthoin Desendre and his wife and child were among the Walloons and French who indicated their willingness to go to Virginia. In August 1621 the Virginia Company agreed that they could immigrate (CBE 25).

TOBIAS DESTINE (DISTINS)

On February 29, 1619, the justices of Bridewell decided that Tobias Destine (Distins), a boy from Ludgate Hill, would be sent to Virginia. On January 29, 1620, they again noted that they intended to send Tobias to the colony (CBE 15, 17).

JAN DE TROU

Wool carder Jan De Trou, his wife, and three children were among the Walloons and French who indicated their willingness to go to Virginia. In August 1621 the Virginia Company agreed that they could immigrate (CBE 25).

[NO FIRST NAME] DEVERELL

On April 3, 1620, Mr. Deverell offered to replace Bartholomew Lawton, a Virginia Company tenant and London goldsmith, who was then in Virginia. Company officials authorized Deverell to do so, if he could find one or two able men to replace him (VCR 1:334; FER 295).

GEORGE DEVERELL (DEVERILL, DEURILL)

George Deverell (Deverill, Deurill), who came to Virginia on the *Temperance* in 1620, was living in Flowerdew Hundred (**53**) on February 16, 1624, and was a servant in Sir George Yeardley's household. By January 24, 1625, Deverill had relocated to Yeardley's property in urban Jamestown (**1**) and was identified as an 18-year-old servant. On February 9, 1628, the General Court noted that Sir George Yeardley had brought George Deverell to Virginia in 1621 on the *Temperance*, an arrival date that contradicts his listing in the 1625 muster. By September 20, 1628, George's headright had been assigned to Thomas Flint of Elizabeth City (**17**) (CBE 37, 54; MCGC 166; PB 1 Pt. 1:59).

[NO FIRST NAME] DEVERN

On April 14, 1634, Mr. Devern, master of the *William*, was accused of illegal trading (CBE 113).

DAVID DEVRIES

David Devries, a Dutch mariner, came to Virginia in March 1633. On the way to Jamestown (**1**), he visited Samuel Mathews' plantation, Denbigh (**23**), and George Menefie's home, Littletown, on Archer's Hope (College) Creek. On March 11, 1633, when Devries arrived in Jamestown, he became Governor John Harvey's houseguest. In May 1635, when Devries returned to Virginia, he sailed up and down the James

River, collecting debts. He made another visit to the colony during autumn 1643 and sold wine to his factor. He also became Governor William Berkeley's houseguest in Jamestown. Devries commented on the fine wheat and flax then being grown in Virginia and noted that numerous Dutch and English ships were trading in the colony. He also said that the conflict between the monarchists and Parliament was very much in evidence. Devries' accounts of his adventures in Virginia provide many useful and otherwise unavailable insights into life in the colony during the 1630s and 40s. In 1642 he sued the estate of Richard Stephens of Jamestown (NEI 52, 94, 152).

HUGH DICKEN

On February 16, 1624, Hugh Dicken was living in Elizabeth City (**17, 18**) (CBE 44).

FRANCIS DICKENSON (DICKINSON)

In September 1630 Francis Dickenson (Dickinson)—a mariner from Norham in Devon who was bound for Virginia—made his will. He named Lawrence and Philip Dickenson as his heirs (CBE 91; EEAC 18).

***

JEREMY (JEREMIAH) DICKENSON (DICKINSON)

Jeremy (Jeremiah) Dickenson (Dickinson) came to Virginia in 1620 on the *Margaret and John* and on February 16, 1624, was living in Elizabeth City (**18**). In early 1625 Jeremy, who was then a married man, was still living in Elizabeth City and was described as a 26-year-old household head. The 1625 muster indicates that Jeremy Dickenson's wife, Elizabeth, was 12 years his senior (CBE 44; DOR 1:55).

ELIZABETH DICKENSON (DICKINSON) (MRS. JEREMY [JEREMIAH] DICKENSON [DICKINSON])

Elizabeth, who by early 1625 had married Jeremy Dickenson (Dickinson), came to Virginia in 1623 on the *Margaret and John*. In early 1625 the Dickensons were residing in Elizabeth City (**18**), where Jeremy was a household head. Elizabeth was then age 38 (CBE 64).

***

PETER DICKENSON (DICKINSON, DICKESON)

Peter Dickenson (Dickinson, Dickeson) came to Virginia on the *Southampton* in 1622. Sometime after April 1623 but before February 16, 1624, he died in Elizabeth City (17, 18). On September 2, 1624, when John Cheesman of Elizabeth City patented some land, he used Peter as a headright (CBE 67; PB 1 Pt. 1:47).

***

RALPH DICKENSON (DICKENS, DICKINSON, DIGGINSON)

Ralph Dickenson (Dickens, Dickinson, Digginson) came to Virginia in 1620. He was an indentured servant employed by one of the Society of Martin's Hundred's principal investors, Nicholas Hyde, whom he had agreed to serve for seven years. On May 16, 1621, Dickenson and his wife, Jane, were living at Martin's Hundred (7), where they were members of Thomas Boyce's (Boys's, Boise's, Boice's) household. Ralph Dickenson was slain at Martin's Hundred during the March 22, 1622, Indian attack. His wife Jane, though presumed dead, was captured and detained by the Pamunkey Indians (VCR 3:451, 570; 4:473).

JANE DICKENSON (DICKENS, DICKINSON, DIGGINSON) (MRS. RALPH DICKENSON [DICKENS, DICKINSON, DIGGINSON])

Jane Dickenson (Dickens, Dickinson, Digginson) came to Virginia in 1620 with her husband, Ralph, one of Nicholas Hyde's indentured servants. On May 16, 1621, the Dickensons were living at the Martin's Hundred plantation (7), where they were members of Thomas Boyce's (Boys's, Boise's, Boice's) household. On March 22, 1622, when the Indians attacked Martin's Hundred, Ralph Dickenson was killed. However, Jane and several other Martin's Hundred women, who were presumed dead, were captured by the Pamunkey Indians and detained for nearly a year. In 1623 the widowed Jane Dickenson was ransomed by Dr. John Pott, who purchased her from the Indians for 2 pounds of beads. Afterward she became a servant in the Pott home in urban Jamestown (1). On February 16, 1624, when a census was made of the colony's inhabitants, Mrs. Jane Dickenson was listed among Pott's servants in Jamestown. On March 30, 1624, when she asked the governor to set her free, she claimed that the ill treatment she had received as a servant in Dr. Pott's home was far worse than the time she had spent as a captive of the Indians (VCR 3:451, 570; 4:473; CBE 38).

***

WILLIAM DICKENSON

On May 30, 1635, when John Slaughter patented some land, he used William Dickenson as a headright (PB 1 Pt. 1:169).

LAWRENCE DICKSON

Lawrence Dickson, a 20-year-old husbandman from Cheshire, England, set sail for Virginia in 1619 on the *Bona Nova*. He probably was one of the Virginia Company's servants or tenants (FER 295).

JANE DIER (DYER)

Jane Dier (Dyer), one of the young, marriageable women sent to Virginia as prospective wives for the colonists, left England with the permission of her widowed mother, Ellen Dier of St. Catherine's. Jane's deceased father reportedly had been a waterman. When Jane Dier set out for Virginia in 1621 on the *Marmaduke*, she was only 15 years old. In August 1621 someone sent her a box of linen (FER 306, 308, 309).

JOHN DIER (DYER)

John Dyer (Dier), a carpenter from London, arrived in Jamestown (1) on September 12, 1623, on the *Bonny Bess* and took the oath of supremacy (MCGC 6).

JOHN DIER (DYER)

On June 24, 1635, when Adam Thorogood patented some land, he listed John Dier (Dyer) as a headright and stated that he had come to Virginia in a French ship in 1629 (PB 1 Pt. 1:179).

MARY DIER (DYER)

Mary Dier died in Jamestown (1) sometime after April 1623 but before February 16, 1624 (CBE 39).

WILLIAM DIER (DYER)

William Dier (Dyer), a gentleman, came to Virginia in 1608 in the 1st or 2nd Supply of new settlers. In December 1608 he accompanied Captain John Smith on a voyage to Werowocomoco. According to Smith, Dier was treacherous and a troublemaker who tried to escape from Virginia. A William Dier (perhaps the same man) died in Jamestown (1) sometime after April 1623 but before February 16, 1624 (CBE 39; CJS 1:216, 274; 2:213,392, 447, 458).

WILLIAM DIER (DYER)

Sometime during the latter part of 1625, William Dier (Dyer) of Accomack testified that he had been present when Captain Ward reduced indentured servant James Blackbourne's term of service by one year (MCGC 91).

BARTHELEMY DIGAUD

Sawyer Barthelemy Digaud, his wife, and eight children were among the Walloons and French who indicated their willingness to go to Virginia. In August 1621 the Virginia Company agreed that they could immigrate (CBE 24).

SIR DUDLEY DIGGES (DIGGS)

On June 13, 1621, the Virginia Company of London gave Sir Dudley Digges (Diggs) a patent. On June 10, 1622, he was identified as the holder of a patent for a particular (private) plantation in Virginia. His son, Edward, came to Virginia approximately two decades later (VCR 1:491-492; 3:643; DOR 1:823).

RICHARD DIGGES

On January 30, 1629, Richard Digges testified that he had taken custody of William Greene's tobacco notes and had given them to Greene's creditor, William Barker. Greene was a resident of Elizabeth City (17, 18) (MCGC 184).

JOHN DIMMOCKE

In November 1628 the General Court decided that John Dimmocke should serve one more year on Thomas Farley's plantation in Archer's Hope (6). However, Farley's brother, Humphrey Farley of London, was ordered to prove that Dimmocke was his servant (MCGC 178).

JOHN DIMSDALE

In early 1625 John Dimsdale was listed among those who died sometime after February 16, 1624, in one of the communities on the lower side of the James River, within the corporation of James City and east of Gray's Creek (10-16) (CBE 60).

WILLIAM DINGFIELD

In December 1619 the justices of Bridewell decided that William Dingfield would be detained until he could be sent to Virginia (CBE 15).

JOHN DINSE (DINSIE)

John Dinse (Dinsie) died in Jamestown (1) sometime after April 1623 but before February 16, 1624 (CBE 39).

ROBERT DITCHFIELD
ALIAS LAMBERT
(SEE ROBERT LAMBERT)

***

ADAM DIXON (DIXSON)

Adam Dixon (Dixson), a master caulker of ships, came to Virginia as a Virginia Company servant in 1611 with Sir Thomas Dale. On May 22, 1622, he presented a list of grievances to the governor and council, so that they could be forwarded to the king. He went to England, but later in the year returned to Virginia on the *Margaret and John* with his wife, Ann (Agnes), and daughter, Elizabeth. On April 24, 1623, Adam Dixon filed a petition in which he claimed that he had been detained for seven years rather than the two or three to which he had agreed. He said that Sir Samuel Argall had forced him to relinquish his pay and had arbitrarily extended his term. He also alleged that Argall had sold the Virginia Company's cattle and pocketed the money. Adam Dixon pressed his claim in England and on January 21, 1624, when testifying before Virginia Company officials, he indicated that he was age 42. While he was away, his wife, Ann (Agnes), who was residing on Jamestown Island (1), died.

By January 30, 1625, Adam Dixon had returned to Virginia and was living in Pasbehay (3). In 1625 he made several appearances before the General Court, where he testified against Sir Samuel Argall and provided information about William Hening's bequest. Dixon also was paid for a poor crop yield because he had been assigned to infertile land, and he was compensated by a Mr. Greene for some damage done by Reynolds' sow. When a list of patented land was sent back to England in May 1625, Adam Dixon was credited with 100 acres in Warresqueak (26). However, on May 8, 1626, he claimed another 200 acres via a court order, using the headrights of his wife, Agnes, daughter Elizabeth, servant John Martin, and himself, all of whom had come to Virginia on the *Margaret and John* in 1622. Adam Dixon was obliged to plant his land within seven years in order to substantiate his claim. He apparently did so, for on September 8, 1627, he secured his 200-acre patent for a tract that lay below Upper Chippokes Creek, in what later became Surry County. This time, Adam Dixon's patent listed his wife's name as Ann, not Agnes (VCR 1:631; 2:43-44, 127-128, 185; FER 522, 524; CBE 57; MCGC 40, 44, 46, 64, 103; PB 1 Pt. 1:53; DOR 1:25).

ANN (AGNES) DIXON (DIXSON) (MRS. ADAM DIXON [DIXSON])

On September 28, 1627, when Adam Dixon (Dixson) patented some land, he used as a headright his wife, Ann or Agnes, who had come to Virginia in 1622 on the *Margaret and John*. Ann (Agnes) Dixon (Dixson) died in Jamestown after April 1623 but before February 16, 1624 (CBE 39; MCGC 103; PB 1 Pt. 1:53).

ELIZABETH DIXON

Elizabeth Dixon (Dixson) came to Virginia on the *Margaret and John* in 1622 and was the daughter of Adam Dixon, an ancient planter, who used her headright when patenting some land on September 28, 1627. It

is unclear whether Elizabeth's mother was Adam's wife, Ann (Agnes) or whether she was the child of an earlier union (PB 1 Pt. 1:53; MCGC 103).

***

DAVID DIXON

On March 2, 1629, George Blight appeared before the General Court, where he released David Dixon from all debts whatsoever (MCGC 187).

RICHARD DIXON

Richard Dixon, a gentleman, came to Virginia in 1607 and was one of the first colonists. Therefore, he would have resided in Jamestown (1) (CJS 2:141).

STEPHEN (STEVEN) DIXON (DIXSON, DICKSON)

Stephen (Steven) Dixon (Dixson, Dickson) came to Virginia in 1619 on the *Bona Nova* and was an 18-year-old husbandman from Cheshire. On February 16, 1624, Stephen was living in Elizabeth City at Buckroe (17). In early January 1625 he was identified as a 25-year-old servant in Lieutenant William Barry's household, which lived on the Virginia Company's land in Elizabeth City, an area that included Buckroe. On October 14 1626, Stephen Dixon testified in court that in July 1626, after Thomas Savage's drowning death near Mr. English's house, he had removed the decedent's body from the mud and brought him ashore. William English lived on the west side of the Hampton River, in Elizabeth City (18) (CBE 45, 68; FER 295; MCGC 122).

GODFREY DIXSIE (DIXIE?)

On May 23, 1625, Lieutenant Thomas Osborne testified that in February 1623 he transported Godfrey Dixsie (Dixie?) and two other men back to the College or Arrohattock (66). He indicated that in the wake of the March 22, 1622, Indian attack, they had been evacuated to safety and had been living at William Ewen's plantation (13) across from Jamestown Island. On June 1, 1625, it was reported that Godfrey Dixsie had died at Arrohattock before the end of May 1623 (MCGC 60-61, 64).

JOHN DOCKER

On February 16, 1624, John Docker was living on the lower side of the James River, on one of the plantations within the corporation of James City, east of Gray's Creek (**10-16**). In early 1625 Docker was listed among those who had recently died in that area (CBE 40, 60).

***

JOHN DODD (DODDS, DODS)

John Dodd (Dodds, Dods), a laborer, came to Virginia in 1607 on the *Susan Constant* and was one of the first colonists. In 1608 John Dodd accompanied Captain John Smith on a voyage into the Pamunkey River, and on December 29, 1608, he was among the men who accompanied Smith to Werowocomoco, Powhatan's village on the York River. On February 16, 1624, John Dodd and his wife, Jane, were living at Bermuda Hundred (**39**). They were still there on January 24, 1625, at which time he was described as a 36-year-old household head who was very well supplied with stored food and defensive weaponry. In May 1625, when a list of patented land was sent back to England, John Dodd was credited with 50 acres in Charles City and 150 acres in Tappahannah, land to which he was entitled as an ancient planter. On January 11, 1627, Dodd appeared before the General Court where he testified that even though the late Luke Boise (also of Bermuda Hundred) had failed to make a will, he had said that he wanted his wife, Alice, and their child to have his estate. On February 9, 1628, John Dodd returned to court. This time the justices settled a land dispute he was having with William Vincent. The justices decided that each of them would have half of Joshua Chard's land and half of his house (CJS 1:244; 2:142, 193; CBE 35, 53; VCR 4:555; MCGC 132, 166; DOR 1:9).

JANE DODD (DODDS, DODS) (MRS. JOHN DODD [DODDS, DODS])

On February 16, 1624, Jane Dodd (Dodds, Dods) was living at Bermuda Hundred (**39**) with her husband, John, an ancient planter. The Dodds were still residing there on January 24, 1625 (CBE 35, 53).

***

JOHN DODSON

On April 19, 1625, John Dodson, who had arrived in Virginia, complained to the General Court about the severe shortage of food and drink aboard the ship in which he had secured passage. Maurice Thompson corroborated his testimony (MCGC 54).

ROBERT DODSON

Robert Dodson Jr. who came to Virginia at the expense of Robert Dodson Sr., left England aboard the *James* on July 31, 1622. On April 30, 1623, when he and others rebutted the allegations Captain Nathaniel Butler made about conditions in Virginia, Robert Dodson Jr. said that he had firsthand knowledge of the plantations east of Jamestown (**1**) (FER 400; VCR 2:386).

***

THOMAS DOE

On February 16, 1624, Thomas Doe and his wife were living in Pasbehay (**3**), just west of Jamestown Island. Sometime prior to January 11, 1627, Doe, who was a planter, received permission to move from Kecoughtan (**17**) to Hog Island (**16**). On October 16, 1629, when the assembly convened, Thomas Doe was the burgess for Archer's Hope (**6**), an indication that he probably owned land there (CBE 40; MCGC 132; HEN 1:138; STAN 54).

MRS. THOMAS DOE

On February 16, 1624, Mrs. Thomas Doe and her husband were living in Pasbehay (**3**), just west of Jamestown Island (CBE 40).

***

RICHARD DOLE

In 1608 Richard Dole, a blacksmith, came to Virginia in the 2nd Supply of new settlers. Therefore, he would have lived in Jamestown (**1**) (CJS 1:222; 2:162).

THOMAS DOLEMAN

On February 4, 1625, Thomas Doleman, who came to Virginia on the *Return*, was living on Hog Island (**16**) and was one of Ralph Hamor's servants (CBE 61).

ALSE (ALICE) DOLLINGS (DOLLINGES)

Alse (Alice) Dollings (Dollinges), a young maid, went to Virginia in September 1621 on the *Warwick* at age 22. Alse, whose parents were deceased, was from Mounton in Dorcestershire. Prior to coming to Virginia, she had been in service. Goodwife Bennett, in Warwickshire, vouched for Alse Dollings' good character (FER 309).

RICHARD DOLPHINBE (DOLSEMB, DOLPHENBY)

Richard Dolphinbe (Dolsemb, Dolphenby) came to Virginia on the *Gift* in 1618 and became one of Walter Davis's servants at Martin's Hundred (**7**). Sometime after December 5, 1620, but before January 21, 1621 or 1622, Dolphinbe and his partner, Richard Richards, acquired 100 acres at Paces Paines (**8**) from Francis Chapman and quickly sold the acreage to Izabella Pace, Richard Pace's wife. On February 16, 1624, Richard Dolphinbe was living on the lower side of the James River within the corporation of James City, on a plantation west of Gray's Creek. He probably was residing at Burrows Hill (**9**), where on February 4, 1625, he and Richard Richards jointly headed a household. They were in possession of a dwelling and a tobacco house and were relatively well supplied with defensive weaponry and stored food. On January 10, 1627 Richard Dolphinbe testified in court about some corn that was stored in a house at Martin's Hundred at the time of the March 22, 1622, Indian attack. He also discussed a signed document he had seen three days before the attack that bore the signature of Thomas Boyce, a man slain by the Indians during their assault on Martin's Hundred. This raises the possibility that Dolphinbe was still living at the plantation at the time the Indian attack occurred. On April 8, 1629, Richard Dophinbe made another appearance before the General Court. This time he was obliged to account for a gun that John Johnson had asked him to deliver to Edward Waller, but that Waller claimed never to have received (CBE 40, 59; PB 1 Pt.1:62; MCGC 131, 133, 195).

RICHARD DOMELOW (DOMELAWE)

Richard Domelow (Domelawe) came to Virginia sometime prior to July 15, 1620, when he was identified in Alexander Wincheley's will as someone to whom Robert Partin owed tobacco. On February 16, 1624, Richard was living on West and Shirley Hundred (Eppes) Island (**41**). He apparently died in Virginia shortly thereafter, for his will, which was witnessed by Francis West, William Holmes, and Thomas Bunn (a surgeon), was presented to English probate officials on September 9, 1624. Richard Domelow, as a testator, identified himself as a bachelor and resident of London. He nominated William Farrar and Captain Samuel Mathews as his executors and left Mathews money for a ring. He instructed his executors to take custody of his goods and property in Virginia and to divide the proceeds of his estate among family members in England. Later, Richard's brother, John Domelow, was named administrator. In May 1625, when a list of patented land was sent back to England, Richard Domelow was credited with 150 acres of land at Blunt Point (**22**) (CBE 38, 48; WITH 69-70; SH 6; VCR 4:557; EEAC 18).

WILLIAM DOMUS

On January 29, 1620, the justices of Bridewell decided that William Domus was to be sent to Virginia (CBE 18).

[NO FIRST NAME] DONNE

In August 1631, Sergeant Major Donne returned to Virginia, where he was the muster-master general (CBE 96).

JOHN DONSTON

On February 16, 1624, John Donston was living on Hog Island (**16**) (CBE 41).

JAMES DORE

James Dore came to Virginia in 1621 on the *Bona Nova*. On January 21, 1625, he was living at Jordan's Journey (**46**), where he was a 19-year-old servant in Nathaniel Causey's household (CBE 52).

NICHOLAS DORINGTON

Sometime after April 1623 but before February 16, 1624, Nicholas Dorington died at Martin's Hundred (**7**) (CBE 42).

HENRY DORMER

On September 6, 1628, Henry Dormer sent Hugh Kiddermaster, a longtime inmate in Bridewell Prison, to Virginia (CBE 84).

WILLIAM DORRELL

William Dorrell came to Virginia on the *Truelove* and on January 30, 1625, was living in Pasbehay (3). He was identified as one of the Governor's men and was 18 years old (CBE 57).

***

GREGORY DORY (DOREY, DORIE)

Gregory Dory (Dorey, Dorie), a 24-year-old carpenter from Somerset, England, came to Virginia in 1619 or 1620 on the *Bona Nova*. On August 8, 1623, Virginia Company officials learned that Dory had been at Gravesend when he was involuntarily taken aboard a ship bound for Virginia. Therefore they forwarded his petition to the colony's governor. On February 16, 1624, Gregory Dory was living in Elizabeth City at the Indian Thicket (17). In early 1625 he and his wife and their infant were living in the same area, part of the Virginia Company's land in Elizabeth City. Gregory was then described as a 36-year-old household head, who was in possession of a dwelling, a palisade, a supply of stored food, and some defensive weaponry. On January 3, 1626, Gregory Dory paid a quantity of tobacco to the Rev. Jonas Stockden, Elizabeth City's minister. By January 9, 1627, Gregory, then described as a yeoman, had acquired 100 acres from Robert Greenleafe, land at the head of the Blunt Point (Warwick) River (22) (CBE 43, 67; FER 295; VCR 2:465; MCGC 87, 129; DOR 1:66).

MRS. GERGORY DORY (DOREY, DORIE)

In early 1625 the wife of Gregory Dory (Dorey, Dorie), whose first name is unknown, was living in Elizabeth City, on the east side of the Hampton River on Virginia Company land (17). She shared the family home with her husband and infant (CBE 67).

[NO FIRST NAME] DORY (DOREY, DORIE)

In early 1625 the infant of Gregory Dory (Dorey, Dorie) and his wife was living in his/her parents' Elizabeth City home on the east side of the Hampton River, on land that belonged to the Virginia Company (17). The Dory child, whose gender is unknown, was born in Virginia (CBE 67).

***

THOMAS DOUGHTIE (DOUGHTY)

Thomas Doughtie came to Virginia on the *Abigail* and on February 16, 1624, was living at Martin's Hundred (7). On February 4, 1625, he was still there and was identified as a 26-year-old servant in the household of the settlement's leader, William Harwood (CBE 42, 61).

***

THOMAS DOUGHTIE (DOUGHTY)

Thomas Doughtie (Doughty) came to Virginia on the *Marigold* in 1619. On February 16, 1624, he and his wife, Ann, were living at Flowerdew Hundred (53), and on January 20, 1625, they were still there. Thomas headed a household that was relatively well provisioned and equipped with defensive weaponry (CBE 37, 50; DOR 1:22).

ANN DOUGHTIE (DOUGHTY) (MRS. THOMAS DOUGHTIE [DOUGHTY])

Ann, the wife of Thomas Doughtie (Doughty), came to Virginia in 1621 on the *Marmaduke*. On February 16, 1624, she was living at Flowerdew Hundred (53) with her husband, Thomas, a household head. She was still there on January 20, 1625 (CBE 37, 50).

***

JOHN DOUGLAS

John Douglas, master of the *Primrose*, sailed from London to Virginia on July 18, 1634 (CBE 117).

WILLIAM DOUGLAS (DOUGLASS, DUGLAS)

In 1621, Captain William Douglas (Douglass, Duglas), master of the *Margaret and John*, brought some passengers to Virginia, taking over for master John Langley, who died at sea. Afterward, Douglas was sued by John Robinson and Jamestown **(1)** merchant John Chew, whose goods he retained. In April 1623 Douglas was summoned to court where he was accused of refusing to pay his crew and failing to give his passengers their goods without security (a bond). Despite these allegations, he was named administrator of the estate of Mathew Brocbanke, a passenger who died at sea. In May 1625 William Douglas was identified as the patentee of 250 acres of land on the Appomattox River in Charles City, acreage that had not been seated. He appeared before the General Court on June 7, 1625, and twice during 1626, on all three occasions giving testimony about the ships *Tiger* and *Deal*. On March 12, 1627, William Douglas and Thomas Gregory brought in the inventory of the late Captain William Holmes, a merchant and mariner. Captain Douglas was identified as master of the *Saker* when he testified about an incident that occurred in the West Indies. On March 24, 1628, he was described as master of the *Catt* when testifying about the use of some of Sir George Yeardley's sack (a wine) at sea for the benefit of sick passengers. In June and July 1632, Captain William Douglas was described as owner of the *Falcon*, which left Tilbury for Virginia on August 12, 1631. As his ship's rigging and equipment were old, the vessel was refitted in Virginia. However, while the *Falcon* was anchored between Hog Island **(16)** and Mulberry Island **(21)**, it broke loose and was driven ashore. Some tobacco aboard the *Falcon* was ruined on the way to England, probably because the ship was leaky. In 1656, when William Sarsen patented some land on Jamestown Island that formerly had belonged to Lady Elizabeth Dale, William Douglas served as her attorney (VCR 4:5-6, 95-97, 127-128, 554; MCGC 10, 65, 87, 95, 143-144, 168; EAE 30-31; PB 3:391).

WILLIAM DOUGLAS (DOUGLASS, DUGLAS)

William Douglas (Douglass, Duglas) came to Virginia on the *Margaret and John* in 1621 and may have been a kinsman of Captain William Douglas, the ship's master. On February 16, 1624, William was living in Elizabeth City **(17)** on the east side of the Hampton River. When a muster was taken in early 1625, he was identified as a 16-year-old indentured servant in the household of the Rev. Jonas Stockden (CBE 44, 66).

RICHARD DOWESS

In 1619 Richard Dowess went to Virginia at the expense of the Ferrars, who were major investors in the Virginia Company (FER 296).

JOHN DOWLER

On March 22, 1622, when the Indians attacked the ironworks at Falling Creek **(68)**, John Dowler was killed at Captain John Berkeley's plantation (VCR 3:565).

LAWRENCE DOWLER

On March 22, 1622, when the Indians attacked Captain John Berkeley's plantation, where the Falling Creek **(68)** ironworks was located, Lawrence Dowler was killed (VCR 3:565).

WILLIAM DOWMAN

William Dowman, a gentleman, came to Virginia in 1608 in the 2nd Supply of new settlers and was one of the first Jamestown **(1)** colonists (CJS 1:241; 2:190).

***

JOHN DOWNMAN (DOWNEMAN)

John Downman (Downeman), an ancient planter, came to Virginia in 1611 on the *John and Francis*, one of the ships in Sir Thomas Dale's fleet. On December 19, 1617, he was residing in Dale's home community, Bermuda Hundred **(39)**, where he witnessed Captain Robert Smalley's (Smallay's) will. By February 16, 1624, John Downman had married and moved to Elizabeth City **(18)**, where he was a household head. On September 1, 1624, Albiano Lupo (also of Elizabeth City) transferred Daniel Palmer's headright to John Downman, which enabled him to patent 50 acres of land in addition to what he already owned. On January 17, 1625, John Downman was brought before the General Court, where he was fined and made to publicly apologize to Nicholas Martiau, whom he had slandered at Kecoughtan **(17)**. In early 1625 John and Elizabeth Downman and a servant were living in Elizabeth City in a fortified dwelling. The household John headed was relatively well supplied with provisions and defensive weaponry. The couple's young daughter, Mary, had died during the year. In May 1625, when a list of patented land was sent back to England, John Downman was credited with 100 acres of land on the south side of the James River, acreage that had not been planted. In March 1629 Downman was named a commissioner of Elizabeth City's monthly court, and in October 1629 he served as a burgess for Elizabeth City (CBE 44, 63; PB 1 Pt. 1:33; MCGC 43, 193; SH 4; SR 3112; VCR 4:558; HEN 1:132, 139; DOR 1:52).

ELIZABETH DOWNMAN (DOWNEMAN) (MRS. JOHN DOWNMAN [(DOWNEMAN)])

Elizabeth, the wife of ancient planter John Downman (Downeman), came to Virginia on the *Warwick* in 1621 and may have been one of the young marriageable women who came to Virginia as wives for the colonists. On February 16, 1624, Elizabeth Downman and her husband were living in Elizabeth City (18). In early 1625, when a muster was made, Elizabeth and John Downman were still residing there in a household he headed. Elizabeth, who was 22 years old, had just lost her young daughter, Mary Downman (CBE 44, 63).

MARY DOWNMAN (DOWNEMAN)

Mary, the daughter of John and Elizabeth Downeman of Elizabeth City (18), died sometime during 1625. She was described as a child (CBE 63).

***

EUSTIS DOWNES

Eustis Downes came to Virginia on the *Abigail* in 1622. On January 21, 1625, he was among those living at Jordan's Journey (46). Eustis Downes was then described as a 25-year-old servant in John Davis's household (CBE 52).

GEORGE DOWNES

In October 1628 the General Court ordered John Morris's attorney to pay Morris's debt to George Downes, a merchant. He was to give the funds to Captain William Tucker of Elizabeth City, who was to pay Downes. On February 12, 1632, George Downes was identified as the owner of some land at Strawberry Banks, in Elizabeth City (17). He was a commissioner of Elizabeth City's monthly court and a burgess for the lower (eastern) parish of Elizabeth City. On November 20, 1635, George Downes patented some land on the lower side of the James River, near Lynnhaven (20 b) (MCGC 175; HEN 1:154, 170, 179, 187; PB 1 Pt.1:135, 315).

JOHN DOWNES

On March 22, 1622, when the Indians attacked Maycock's plantation (48), John Downes was killed (VCR 3:565).

JOHN DOWNES

John Downes, a grocer from London, arrived in Jamestown (1) aboard the *Bonny Bess* on September 12, 1623, and took the oath of supremacy (MCGC 6).

RICHARD DOWNES

Richard Downes, a scholar, came to Virginia on the Jonathan around 1619. On June 18, 1623, his father, Edward Downes, asked Virginia Company officials to free him and give him some land. He said that Richard had been in Virginia for four years and was supposed to have been assigned to a position at the College (66) in Henrico. On February 16, 1624, Richard Downes was living on the Maine (3), just west of Jamestown Island. By January 25, 1625, he had been freed and was living at Mulberry Island (21). Richard Downes headed a household that was relatively well supplied with provisions and defensive weaponry (VCR 2:442; CBE 39, 57; DOR 1:47).

WILLIAM DOWNES

William Downes died in Elizabeth City (17, 18) sometime after April 1623 but before February 16, 1624 (CBE 45).

ABIGAIL DOWNING

In July 1623, when John Downing of St. Clement Danes in Middlesex made his will, he named his daughter, Abigail, as one of his heirs, stipulating that she would receive money if she went to Virginia (CBE 33; EEAC 18; WAT 204).

FRANCIS DOWNING

Francis Downing arrived in Virginia in March 1624 on the ship *Returne*. On January 22, 1625, he was living at Shirley Hundred **(41)**, where he was a 24-year-old servant in John Throgmorton's household (CBE 53).

BARBARA DOWSE

On September 19, 1618, the justices of Bridewell Court identified Barbara Dowse as a vagrant from Cornhill who had been imprisoned for a long period of time. On February 27, 1619, they decided that Barbara, whom they described as a wench, would be sent to Virginia (CBE 9, 13).

***

THOMAS DOWSE (DOUSE)

Thomas Dowse (Douse), a laborer, came to Virginia in 1608 in the 2nd Supply of new settlers. Therefore, he would have lived in Jamestown **(1)**. Captain John Smith claimed that in 1609 Dowse and Thomas Mallard began conspiring with the paramount Indian chief Powhatan, but then thought better of it. He added that he had sent them to bring in the Dutchmen who had fled to the Indians. In 1610 Smith identified Thomas Dowse as a taborer (drummer) and said that he was among those who survived the attack on the Appomattock Indian Town. In July 1619, when the Virginia assembly convened, Thomas Dowse served as a burgess for the city of Henricus **(63)**. On March 6, 1620, he was credited with seating and clearing some fertile acreage at Arrohattock **(66)**, part of the College Land, where Deputy Governor Samuel Argall (1617–1618) had given him a patent. Because William Weldon claimed that acreage on behalf of the College, Dowse was forced to leave. A document dated June 26, 1621, suggests that he moved briefly to Shirley Hundred **(41)** but by February 16, 1624, had relocated to Elizabeth City **(17, 18)**, where he was living with his wife. The Dowses may have stayed on in that location, for the Rev. Jonas Stockden of Elizabeth City was ordered to pay him. In May 1625 when a list of patented land was sent back to England, Thomas Dowse was credited with 400 acres in the corporation of Charles City, land that was unseated and may have been at Shirley Hundred. Court testimony taken on September 12, 1626, reveals that Captain

Thomas Dowse and his wife, Ann, returned to England for a time and were living at Kinsalle when he became involved with Charity, the wife of Troylus Lovell. According to several witnesses, Captain Dowse abandoned his wife, to whom he had given his power of attorney and possession of his Virginia property, and fled to Ireland with Mrs. Lovell. Some Kinsalle merchants took pity on Ann Dowse and paid for her transportation to Virginia, where the General Court gave her custody of her husband's goods, servants, and real estate. Captain William Tucker of Elizabeth City was ordered to prepare an inventory of Captain Dowse's real and personal estate, after which time his wife, Ann, was to be given custody of his property. On January 10, 1627, two witnesses from Elizabeth City informed the General Court that Robert Todd was supposed to serve for seven years, but at Easter 1624 Captain Dowse had given him two years of his time. The men said that they had witnessed the agreement between Dowse and Todd (CJS 1:242; 2:191, 216; HAI 511-512; VCR 3:154, 262-265; 4:553; FER 268; CBE 43; MCGC 70, 113, 131).

ANN DOWSE (DOUSE) (MRS. THOMAS DOWSE [DOUSE])

On February 16, 1624, Mrs. Thomas Dowse (Douse) and her husband were living in Elizabeth City **(17, 18)**. Sometime prior to September 12, 1626, she and her husband returned to England and took up residence in Kinsalle, where he became involved with Charity Lovell, a married woman, with whom he fled to Ireland. Although Ann Dowse had her husband's power of attorney and had been given the right to his property in Virginia, she was destitute when he abandoned her in Kinsalle and had to depend on the generosity of local merchants. They paid her way to Virginia, where she sought the aid of the General Court in recovering her husband's real and personal estate. She was given the right to use it as she pleased toward her own maintenance (CBE 43; MCGC 113).

***

HENRY DOWTIE (DOUGHTY?)

Henry Dowtie (Doughty?) came to Virginia on the *Jonathan* and on January 3, 1625, was living at Pasbehay **(3)** where he was one of the Governor's servants. He was then age 19 (CBE 57).

HENRY DOWTON

On January 22, 1620, the justices of Bridewell court decided to send Henry Dowton, who was from Ludgate Ward, to Virginia (CBE 17).

HENRY DRAPER

Henry Draper came to Virginia on the *George* in 1621 and on February 16, 1624, was living in Elizabeth City **(17)**. In early 1625, when a muster was taken of the colony's inhabitants, Henry was identified as a 14-year-old servant in the household of Albiano Lupo of Elizabeth City (CBE 43, 63).

ROBERT DRAPER

Robert Draper came to Virginia on the ship *Jacob* in 1624 and on December 1st· when John Bainham patented some land, he used Robert as a headright. In early 1625, when a muster was made of the colony's inhabitants, Robert Draper was described as a 16-year-old indentured servant who lived in the Elizabeth City **(18)** household headed by ancient planters John Bainham and Robert Sweete (CBE 64; PB 1 Pt. 1:17).

JOHN DRASON (DRAYSON)

On April 29, 1623, John Drason (Drayson), a sailor from Greenwich in Kent, testified against Edward Brewster in the lawsuit brought by Robert Rich, the Earl of Warwick, concerning events in Jamestown **(1)** in 1618. Drason was then age 43 (HCA 12/44 ff 118vo-120vo; EAE 13).

EDWARD DREW (DREWE)

Edward Drew (Drewe) came to Virginia in 1618 on the *Sampson* and on February 16, 1624, was living on the Eastern Shore. When a muster was taken of the colony's inhabitants in early 1625, he was still residing there and was identified as a 22-year-old household head who was in possession of a dwelling and a storehouse and was relatively well supplied with provisions and defensive weaponry. Edward and three other men who also came on the *Sampson* in 1618 were living in the vicinity of Old Plantation Creek **(73)**. Edward Drew was

still living on the Eastern Shore in November 1638. He was a respected citizen who served on vestries, was chosen to arbitrate disputes, and was nominated as sheriff. He was still alive in 1645 (CBE 46, 69; AMES 1:39, 58, 96, 127; 2:38, 44, 63, 267, 288, 317, 453, 456-457; DOR 1:69).

ANNE (ANN) DREW (DREWE)

On November 20, 1622, Anne (Ann) Drew (Drewe), an inmate at Newgate Prison, was among those pardoned so that they could be put to work or sent to the colonies, probably Virginia. This decision was made because jail fever was rampant (CBE 29).

JOHN DRINKARD

John Drinkard, a carpenter for the Company of Shipwrights, worked under the supervision of Thomas Nunn. Nunn and his men came to Virginia in 1621 and became established on Jamestown Island **(1)**, where most of them died (FER 378).

BENJAMIN DRURY

On January 11, 1627, Benjamin Drury testified that in June 1626, Samuel Acton, one of Henry Woodward's servants, showed him a note from Captain William Tucker. It stated that Drury and Samuel Talbott were to go to Warresqueak **(26)** with Henry Woodward and stay there until further word was received from Drury's and Talbott's master, Captain John Stone. This suggests that Drury and Talbott were assigned to Stone on account of Woodward's indebtedness (MCGC 134).

ELLEN DRURY

Ellen Drury went to Virginia on the *Warwick* in September 1621, when she was 22 years old. She was born in Northampton, England, and until she went to Virginia was in the employ of Goodwife Smith, who gave her a good recommendation. Ellen was one of the marriageable young women sent to the colony as prospective wives for the settlers (FER 309).

WILLIAM DRY

On February 16, 1624, William Dry was living on Virginia's Eastern Shore **(72-78)** (CBE 46).

THOMAS DRYHURST

In 1618 Thomas Dryhurst went to Virginia on the *Neptune* at the expense of Samuel Mathews. On March 5, 1628, when Zachariah Cripps patented some land, he used Thomas's headright, indicating that it had been transferred to him by Mathews (MCGC 190; PB 1 Pt. 1:74).

STEPHEN DUBO

On March 22, 1622, when the Indians attacked Richard Owen's house near Westover (**54**), Stephen Dubo was slain (VCR 3:567).

ANDREW DUDLEY

Andrew Dudley went to Virginia on the *Truelove*, which arrived shortly after the March 22, 1622, Indian attack. On February 16, 1624, he was living at West and Shirley Hundred (**41**). When the Indians made another assault on the settlement on March 18, 1624, Andrew Dudley was slain. When a muster of the community was taken on January 22, 1625, he was listed among the dead. On April 7, 1625, three inhabitants of West and Shirley Hundred informed the General Court that Andrew Dudley had died at the hands of the Natives and that they had viewed his corpse. They identified him as one of Richard Biggs's servants at Shirley Hundred (CBE 36, 53; MCGC 51).

JOHN DUFFIELD (DUFFY, DIFFILL)

On July 31, 1622, John Duffield (Duffy, Duffill) set out for Virginia on the *James* and accompanied William Felgate. On February 16, 1624, John was living at Chaplin's Choice (**56**). When a muster was taken of the settlement's inhabitants on January 21, 1625, John was identified as a 14-year-old servant in Isaac Chaplin's home (FER 400; CBE 37, 51).

WILLIAM DUFFIELD

William Duffield set out for Virginia with Richard Tatem on the *James* and left England on July 31, 1622 (FER 400).

THEODORE DU FOUR

Draper Theodore du Four, his wife, and two children were among the Walloons and French who indicated their willingness to go to Virginia. In August 1621 the Virginia Company agreed that they could immigrate (CBE 24).

WILLIAM DUM

In 1621 William Dum, carpenter of the ship *George*, paid for James Tooke's transportation to Virginia. Later, he sold Tooke's headright to William Spencer of Jamestown Island (**1**), who used it when patenting some land on September 9, 1631 (PB 1 Pt.1:120).

MICHEL DU PON

Hatter Michel du Pon, his wife, and two children were among the Walloons and French who indicated their willingness to go to Virginia. In August 1621 the Virginia Company agreed that they could immigrate (CBE 24).

JOHN DUMPORT

John Dumport died in Jamestown (**1**) sometime after April 1623 but before February 16, 1624 (CBE 39).

JOHN DUNDAS

On May 27, 1631, John Dundas, master of the *Warwick*, went to Virginia with a supply of shot (CBE 95).

THOMAS DUNFFORD

Thomas Dunfford, a 33-year-old gentleman from Devonshire, immigrated to Virginia in 1619 aboard the *Bona Nova*, which transported a large number of Virginia Company servants and tenants to the colony (FER 295).

WILLIAM DUNGFIELD

On December 31, 1619, the justices of Bridewell decided that William Dungfield, a boy brought in from London, would be detained so that he could be sent to Virginia or Bermuda (HUME 15).

PETER DUNN (DUN)

Sometime after April 1623 but before February 16, 1624, Peter Dunn (Dun) died at Hog Island (**16**) (CBE 42).

ROGER DUNN (DUNNE)

On November 20, 1622, Roger Dunn (Dunne), a prisoner at Newgate, was selected for transportation overseas (CBE 29).

THOMAS DUNN (DUNNE)

Thomas Dunn (Dunne) came to Virginia in 1620 on the *Temperance* and on February 16, 1624, was residing at Flowerdew Hundred (**53**), Sir George Yeardley's plantation. On January 24, 1625, Thomas, who was 14 years old, was a servant in the Yeardley home in Jamestown (**1**) (CBE 37, 54).

WILLIAM DUNN

On May 6, 1629, William Dunn, a 29-year-old sailor from Limehouse in Middlesex, testified that when the ship *Saker* arrived in Virginia in 1627, it delivered one passenger, an African, to William Ewen's plantation (**13**) (EAE 19).

FRANCIS DUNNING

On June 24, 1625, Francis Dunning, one of Captain Samuel Mathews' servants, told Eleanor Sprade, one of Thomas Alnutt's servants in Jamestown (**1**), that the Rev. David Sandys was trying to lure Mara Buck (a young, slow-witted heiress) into marriage. It is likely that Dunning was a resident of Hog Island (**16**), where Mathews owned property and Sandys lived. (MCGC 16).

SAMUEL DUNTHORNE (DONTHORNE)

Samuel Dunthorne (Donthorne) was living in Elizabeth City (**17, 18**) on February 16, 1624. He may have been related to Thomas Dunthorne, who also lived in that area (CBE 44).

***

THOMAS DUNTHORNE (DONTHORNE)

Thomas Dunthorne (Donthorne) came to Virginia on the *Margaret and John* in 1620 and was a Virginia Company tenant. Sometime prior to February 16, 1624, he married Elizabeth, an ancient planter. The couple then made their home in Elizabeth City (**17, 18**). On September 20, 1624, when Eliza-beth Dunthorne patented the 100 acres she received as an ancient planter, Thomas was identified as a yeoman of Kecoughtan. By early 1625 the Dunthornes were residing on Elizabeth's land, which was located on the west side of the Hampton River's mouth. Thomas was then 27 years old, whereas Elizabeth was 38. The Dunthorne household included six servants, one of whom was an Indian boy. The Dunthornes had two dwellings, a fortification, a boat, and an ample supply of stored food and defensive weaponry. A May 23, 1625, court document makes reference to Thomas Dunthorne's house in Elizabeth City. On October 3, 1625, the justices of the General Court agreed that Thomas Dunthorne, a Virginia Company tenant, should be freed as soon as possible; however he was ordered to pay the Company, by then defunct, for the time remaining on his contact. A document dating to January 12, 1627, indicates that Thomas was one of the Virginia Company tenants who had been assigned to Captain William Tucker. In early December 1625 Thomas Dunthorne was instructed to pay Sergeant John Harris the funds that were owed by the late William Gauntlett. On February 27, 1626, Thomas was summoned to court, where he was accused of concealing the illness of George Allen, one of his servants. He returned to court on October 31, 1626, and presented the will of his wife, Elizabeth. He died sometime prior to April 3, 1627, at which time the Rev. Jonas Stockden of Elizabeth City brought his will to the General Court. Archaeological excavations undertaken during the 1940s on the Dunthorne property in the city of Hampton yielded a large cache of early seventeenth-century trade beads and fragments of military equipment (CBE 44, 66; PB 1 Pt. 1:38; MCGC 62, 72, 78, 96, 123, 137, 146; DOR 1:62).

ELIZABETH DUNTHORNE (DONTHORNE) (MRS. THOMAS DUNTHORNE [DONTHORNE])

Elizabeth, an ancient planter, came to Virginia on the *Tryall* (*Trial*) in 1610 and on February 16, 1624, was living in Elizabeth City with her husband, Thomas Dunthorne (Donthorne). On September 20, 1624, when Elizabeth received 100 acres as her first dividend of land, acreage on the west side of the Hampton River's mouth, she was identified as an ancient planter and Thomas's wife. In early 1625 Elizabeth Dunthorne and her husband were living in Elizabeth City (**18**), probably on the property she had patented. She was then age 38. In May 1625 when a list of patented land was sent back to England, Elizabeth was credited with 100 acres in Elizabeth City, property that had been seated. She died sometime prior to October 31, 1626, at which time her husband, Thomas Dunthorne, presented her will to the General Court. It was proved by Elizabeth City's clergyman, the Rev. Jonas Stockden (CBE 44, 66; PB 1 Pt. 1:38; VCR 4:558; MCGC 123).

***

EDWARD DUPPER

Edward Dupper died in Elizabeth City (**17, 18**) sometime after April 1623 but before February 16, 1624 (CBE 45).

DAVID DUTTON

David Dutton died at Hog Island (**16**) on Sir George Yeardley's property sometime after February 16, 1624, but before February 4, 1625. It is likely that he was one of Yeardley's servants (CBE 61).

RICHARD DUTTON

Richard Dutton set out from Bristol, England, on the ship *Supply* and accompanied William Tracy. He was bound for Berkeley Hundred (**55**), where he was supposed to work for a certain number of years in exchange for some acreage of his own. Richard Dutton died shortly after his January 29, 1621, arrival at Berkeley Hundred (CBE 21; VCR 3:397, 426).

JOHN DYUS (DYAS)

On May 8, 1626, the General Court was informed that the late John Dyus (Dyas) had not been paid for providing medical treatment to the cattle belonging to the Rev. Richard Buck's orphans. Dyus, who was unable to write, reportedly had John Southern prepare a bill, which he took to the Buck home on Jamestown Island (**1**) for acknowledgment. As no one was home, Dyus returned the bill to Southern. John Dyus died before being compensated (MCGC 102-103).

E

SAMUEL EACH

On March 13, 1622, Virginia Company officials noted that Captain Samuel Each of the *Abigail* had offered to transport five people to Virginia. He also proposed building a blockhouse on an oyster bank near Blunt Point (**22**) within a year's time, and asked for carpenters, materials, and tools. Company officials found Each's plan appealing and hired him. They also awarded him 500 acres of land, acreage that he asked to be confirmed. The Company agreed to provide Each with 12 carpenters and 40 men to build the blockhouse, plus the necessary tools and a lighter (small watercraft). Samuel Each set sail for Virginia on the *Abigail* on October 12, 1622, after a delay of $2^{1}/_{2}$ months. Aboard were Lady Margaret Wyatt, Secretary of the Colony Christopher Davison, and others. Captain Samuel Each died shortly after his arrival in Virginia. On April 4, 1623, Governor Francis Wyatt reported that Each expired before he had seen the site on which he had proposed building a fort and that it was a poor and impractical choice. In May 1625, when a list of patented land was sent back to England, Each was credited with 500 acres of land on the east side of Upper Chippokes Creek, acreage that had not been planted. Thus, his property, which was on the lower side of the James River and in Charles City, probably was in the vicinity of Martin's Brandon (**59**), or perhaps near the plantations that belonged to Captain John Bargrave (**60**) and Captain John Ward (**61**) (VCR 1:619; 2:10-11, 23; 3:617-618, 647, 683-690, 690-692; 4:9, 100, 228-229, 236-238, 555).

EDWARD EADE

On May 8, 1626, the General Court determined that Edward Eade had agreed to serve Mr. Robert Gyer, a mariner, for five years and that Gyer had given Eade some money to seal their contract (MCGC 103).

HENRY EAGEL (EGLE)

On August 30, 1628, Henry Eagel (Egle) was described as a vagrant boy from St. Sepulchers and an "old prisoner," someone who had been incarcerated for a long time. The justices of Bridewell Court decided to send him to Virginia, but he was rejected and returned to jail. On September 6, 1628, when the matter was reconsidered, Eagel was warned about his behavior, given a shirt, and sent to Virginia (HUME 34; CBE 84).

JOHN EARDNIN

On February 27, 1618, John Eardnin, a boy, was among those whom Bridewell officials chose to be sent to Virginia. He probably was one of the children rounded up from the streets of London so that they could be sent to the colony (HUME 8).

[NO FIRST NAME] EARELY

In 1610, when Sir Thomas Gates placed some men at Kecoughtan (**17**), he put Lieutenant Earely in charge of them (HAI 508).

NATHANIEL EARLE

On March 22, 1622, Nathaniel Earle was slain at Lieutenant Gibbs's plantation when the Indians attacked Westover (**54**) (VCR 3:567).

EDWARD EASON

Edward Eason and his pregnant wife were in the 3rd Supply of new colonists and were aboard the *Seaventure* when it ran aground in Bermuda in 1609. While the Easons were there, Edward's wife gave birth to a boy, whom they named Bermuda. On March 25, 1610, when Bermuda Eason was baptized, Captain Christopher Newport, William Strachey, and Mr. James Swift served as his godfathers. It is uncertain whether any of the Easons continued on to Virginia (HAI 413).

RICHARD EAST (EASTE)

On February 16, 1624, Richard East (Easte) was listed among those living in Elizabeth City (**18**), on the west side of the Hampton River (CBE 44).

EDWARD EASTWOOD

In 1621 Edward Eastwood was transported from Bermuda to Virginia on the *George* at the expense of the colony's treasurer, George Sandys. On December 4, 1624,

when Sandys used Eastwood as a headright, he identified him as a servant and indicated that they had come to Virginia together (PB 1 Pt. 1:16).

THOMAS EATON

On March 11, 1634, Mr. Thomas Eaton patented 250 acres on the Back River within the shire or county of Elizabeth City (**19**). In 1638 he added to his acreage. When Eaton made his September 19, 1659 will, he identified himself as a resident of that area and bequeathed his 600-acre plantation, livestock, and personal effects toward the support of a free school that would serve poor children born in Elizabeth City County (PB 1 Pt. 1:159; NEAL 298).

NATHANIEL EAVES

On September 2, 1631, the justices of Bridewell Court decided that Nathaniel Eaves, a boy, would be sent to Virginia (HUME 37).

THOMAS EBES

Thomas Ebes died in Elizabeth City (**17, 18**) and was buried on July 12, 1624 (CBE 67; DOR 1:63).

ANTHONY EBSWORTH

Anthony Ebsworth came to Virginia in 1621 on the *Flying Harte* and on February 16, 1624, was living in Elizabeth City (**18**). The census-taker listed him with Agnes Ebsworth, probably a kinswoman. On February 7, 1625, Anthony Ebsworth was living at Newport News (**24**) and was a 26-year-old servant in Daniel Gookin's household. Listed with Anthony was Anne Ebsworth, who was age 44 and also a Gookin servant (CBE 43, 63).

AGNES EBSWORTH

On February 16, 1624, Agnes Ebsworth was living in Elizabeth City (**18**). She was listed with Anthony Ebsworth, who may have been a kinsman (CBE 43).

ANNE EBSWORTH

Anne Ebsworth came to Virginia on the *Providence* in 1623. On February 7, 1625, she was living at Newportes News (**24**) where she was a 44-year-old servant in

Daniel Gookin's household. Also in the Gookin household was Anthony Ebsworth, age 26, who may have been Anne's kinsman (CBE 63).

PETER ECCALLOWE (ECALL)

In early 1625 Peter Eccallowe (Ecall), who came to Virginia on the *Southampton*, was living in Captain Nicholas Martiau's household in Elizabeth City (**18**). Eccallowe was described as 30 years old and free. On January 17, 1625, he was summoned before the General Court, where he testified about John Downman's alleged slandering of Nicholas Martiau (CBE 64; MCGC 43; DOR 1:56).

THOMAS ECKSEY

On February 27, 1619, the Bridewell Court decided that Thomas Ecksey, a boy, would be sent to Virginia. He was part of a large group of children rounded up from the streets of London and transported to the colony (CBE 12).

GEORGE EDEN (EADEN, ADEN)

Virginia Company records for January 14, 1620, indicate that George Eden (Eaden, Aden) had been assigned to the Society of Smith's (Southampton) Hundred so that he could be sent to Southampton Hundred (**44**). In exchange, Mr. Hansbie's man was given to William Weldon, who was responsible for the Virginia Company tenants being placed on the College Land (**66**). On March 3, 1630, George Eden's widow, Elizabeth, received letters of administration from the Prerogative Court of Canterbury because George had died in Virginia (VCR 3:254; MOR 35).

LUKE EDEN (ADEN, EADEN)

On February 16, 1624, Luke Eden (Aden, Eaden) was living in Elizabeth City (**17, 18**). Sometime prior to September 27, 1624, he undertook a voyage to Canada where he purchased some goods for Michael Marshott (Marshall), who paid him in tobacco. Afterward, Eden brought suit against Marshott in the General Court, alleging that the tobacco with which he had been paid was of such poor quality that he was unable to use it to purchase a shipment of fish in Canada. Marshott was ordered to pay Eden and to allow him to purchase goods at the rate then current in Virginia. In May 1625 Luke Eden ran afoul of the law when he behaved disrespectfully toward Secretary George Sandys, one of his debtors, when addressing him in the council chamber. Eden was fined for his affront, put on display "neck and heels" in the marketplace, and ordered to post a peace bond. By late December 1625 Luke Eden was ill. Captain William Eppes testified that on December 27th Eden, who was very sick and weak, expressed his desire to make a will and began enumerating his assets. He listed William Ganey, Edmund White, and Zachariah Cripps among his debtors and said that others also were in his debt. He told Eppes that he had left a young male servant in Thomas Spillman's custody at Chaplin's Choice (**56**), and that the chest he had at Henry Geney's place in Elizabeth City (**18**) contained papers, powder, spices, and other items. John How (Howe), who was present when Luke Eden began expressing his last wishes, asked him to remember his servant, Alexander. Captain Eppes agreed to make Eden's will the following day, but Eden died during the night. On January 13, 1627, Captain Eppes and John How testified that when they went to Henry Geney's, they discovered that someone had broken into Luke Eden's chest, which was empty. Among the decedent's debtors were Sir Francis Wyatt, Peter Courtney, William Eppes, Vincent Barber, George Menefie, and Richard Stephens. The General Court decided that the two indentured servants belonging to Luke Eden's estate should be allowed to choose new masters. On April 4, 1627, John How presented the General Court with an account of the decedent's estate (MCGC 20-21, 24, 36, 57, 94, 101, 117-118, 137, 148).

WILLIAM EDEN ALIAS SAMPSON (SEE WILLIAM SAMPSON)

ESTER EDERIFE (EVERE)

Ester Ederife (Evere), one of William Peirce's maidservants, came to Virginia on the *Jonathan*. On February 16, 1624, she was residing in the Peirce household in urban Jamestown (**1**). She was still there on January 24, 1625 (CBE 38, 55).

WILLIAM EDES

On June 23, 1627, when John Throgmorton of Shirley Hundred (**41**) made a nuncupative will, he bequeathed his servant, William Edes, two years of his time (MCGC 153).

WILLIAM EDGER

William Edger died at Flowerdew Hundred (**53**) sometime after April 1623 but before February 16, 1624 (CBE 37).

***

MATHEW EDLOE (EDLOWE) I

Mathew Edloe (Edlowe) I came to Virginia in 1618 aboard the *Neptune*, Lord Delaware's ship, and on February 16, 1624, was living at the College (**66**), probably at Arrohattock, the site of an abandoned Indian village. On January 23, 1625, Mathew was still in residence on the College property and was a solitary household head who was relatively well equipped with defensive weaponry and had a modest supply of provisions. He probably was a tenant farmer. In March 1626 witnesses who appeared before the General Court agreed that in 1625 John Watson had purchased some cloth from cape merchant Edward Blaney and delivered it to Mathew Edloe at Arrohattock. Sometime after April 4, 1627, but before October 1628, Mathew Edloe married Alice, the widow of Luke Boyse of Bermuda Hundred (**39**). The Edloes were summoned to court to testify in a suit William Besse brought against Alice. On March 7, 1629, Mathew and Alice Edloe presented the General Court with an account of her late husband's estate. On October 16, 1629, Mathew Edloe served as a burgess for the College, in the corporation of Henrico. He died sometime prior to November 1635, at which time Alice was identified as a widow. On July 12, 1637, Mathew Edloe's son and heir patented 1,200 acres in Charles City, using as headrights the servants his late father had transported at his own expense (CBE 35, 53; MCGC 97, 173, 193; HEN 1:138; PB 1 Pt. 1:351, 435; DOR 1:18).

MRS. ALICE BOYSE (BOISE, BOYCE) EDLOE (EDLOWE) (MRS. MATHEW EDLOE [EDLOWE] I) (SEE MRS. ALICE BOYSE [BOISE, BOYCE])

Sometime after April 4, 1627, but before March 7, 1629, Alice Boyse (Boice Boyce), the widow of Luke Boyse of Bermuda Hundred (**39**), wed Mathew Edloe (Edlow) of the College or Arrohattock (**66**). On March

7, 1629, Alice and her new husband, Mathew, who was a burgess, presented the General Court with an account of the estate of her late husband, Luke Boyse. Alice was widowed again sometime prior to November 1635, for her marital status was mentioned when she patented some land (MCGC 173, 193; HEN 1:138; PB 1 Pt. 1:351).

MATHEW EDLOE (EDLOWE) II

On July 12, 1637, Mathew Edloe (Edlowe) II, the son and heir of Mathew Edloe I, patented 1,200 acres in Charles City, using as headrights the servants transported at his late father's expense. As Mathew II would have been age 21 or older when he secured his patent, he was the son of Mathew Edloe I and a former wife. It is uncertain when Mathew II came to the colony or where he was born (PB 1 Pt. 1:435).

***

[NO FIRST NAME] EDMONDS

On February 16, 1620, the Virginia Company authorized Mr. Edmonds, master of the *Trial*, to set sail for Virginia at the first fair wind (VCR 1:312).

JOHN EDMONDS

On January 29, 1620, John Edmonds, a vagrant brought in from the Cordwainer Ward, was among those the Bridewell Court decided should be sent to Virginia. Edmonds came to the colony in 1622 aboard the *Southampton* and died at West and Shirley Hundred (**41**) sometime after April 1623 but before February 16, 1624. On September 2, 1624, when John Sibsey or Sipsey patented some land in Elizabeth City (**18**), he used John Edmonds as a headright and indicated that he had paid for his transportation to Virginia (CBE 18, 36; PB 1 Pt. 1:46).

ROBERT EDMONDS (EDMUNDS)

Robert Edmonds (Edmunds) came to Virginia on the *Marigold* in 1619, the ship that Captain Christopher Lawne brought to the colony. On February 16, 1624, Edmonds was living on the Eastern Shore. However, by February 4, 1625, he had moved to George Sandys' property, the Treasurer's Plantation (**11**), on the lower side of the James River, across from Jamestown, where he was living with several others who had arrived on *Marigold* in 1619. On April 11, 1625, Robert Edmonds testified at an inquest held to investigate the cause of John Verone's death. Then, on January 3, 1626, he made another court appearance in which he testified about some corn that belonged to John Evins and was stored in a loft belonging to Treasurer George Sandys. By January 11, 1627, Robert Edmonds had moved to the corporation of Warresqueak **(26)**. It was then that he sought the Council of State's permission to plant in the corporation of Elizabeth City **(17-20 c)** (CBE 46, 60; MCGC 53, 86, 133).

RICHARD EDMONDS (EDMUNDS)

Richard Edmonds (Edmunds) died on the lower side of the James River, within the corporation of James City **(8-15)** sometime after April 1623, but before February 16, 1624 (CBE 39).

EDWARD

According to Captain John Smith, one of the first Jamestown **(1)** colonists who arrived in 1607 was a laborer known as Old Edward (CJS 2:142).

EDWARD

On March 22, 1622, when the Indians attacked Edward Bennett's plantation at Warresqueak **(26)**, Edward was killed (VCR 3:571).

EDWARD

Edward, a servant, died at Bermuda Hundred **(39)** sometime after April 1623 but before February 16, 1624 (CBE 36).

EDWARD

On February 16, 1624, Edward, an African, was a servant in Richard Kingmill's household in the Neck O'Land **(5)**. He was still there on February 4, 1625 (CBE 35, 58).

ANTHONY EDWARDS

On October 20, 1617, Anthony Edwards, who was found guilty of stealing a prisoner woman, was pardoned by Deputy-Governor Samuel Argall. In May 1625 Anthony was identified as the patentee of 100 acres on the south side of the James River, below

The Falls **(67)** and within the corporation of Henrico (VCR 3:74; 4:552).

ARTHUR EDWARDS

Arthur Edwards died in Jamestown **(1)** sometime after April 1623, but before February 16, 1624 (CBE 39).

JOHN EDWARDS

On April 8, 1620, John Edwards sent a petition to the Virginia Company, whose officials forwarded it to Virginia's governor John may have been one of the two men named John Edwards whose estates were presented to the Prerogative Court of Canterbury for probate between 1623 and 1625 (VCR 1:337; MOR 35).

JOHN EDWARDS

John Edwards came to Virginia in 1621 on the *George* and on February 16, 1624, was living on the lower side of the James River on one of the plantations east of Grays Creek **(10-16)**. On February 4, 1625, John Edwards was a servant living on the Treasurer's Plantation **(11)**, which belonged to Treasurer George Sandys. On February 7, 1628, John Edwards, then listed among Edward Grindon's servants at the Treasurer's Plantation, testified about an event that occurred at the home of John Tios (Tyos), a local man (CBE 41, 60; MCGC163).

RICHARD EDWARDS

On February 26, 1620, the justices of Bridewell Court decided that Richard Edwards, a prisoner at Newgate, would be sent to Virginia. He came to the colony in 1624 on the *Jacob*. In early 1625 Richard was living in Elizabeth City where he was a 23-year-old servant in Thomas Boulding's household on the west side of the Hampton River **(18)** (CBE 19, 66).

ROBERT EDWARDS

On July 4, 1623, Robert Edwards, an English merchant, informed Virginia Company officials that he would send his surplus commodities to Virginia (VCR 4:245-246).

THOMAS EDWARDS

On March 12, 1625, Thomas Edwards, a merchant, served on the jury impaneled to investigate the cause of John Verdone's possible suicide. On April 19, 1625, Edwards testified that he was satisfied with the accommodations provided to the passengers who had come to Virginia on the *Ann*. On May 30, 1625, he was ordered to pay Robert Bennett for a hogshead of beer that he was supposed to deliver to Captain Peirce. One witness who testified in Edwards' defense said that he had brought a pipe of sack (a wine) from the *Abigail* to Robert Bennett but had not been paid. On September 12, 1625, Edwards informed the General Court that the Rev. Jonas Stockton (Stogden) had paid him and that he gave the clergyman's receipt to Dictoris Christmas. He added that later the receipt had been destroyed by fire. On October 2, 1626, Thomas Edwards asked the Rev. Francis Bolton, rector of James City Parish, to post the marriage bands of his maidservant, Mary, who wanted to marry Thomas Harvie. Edwards said that he had transported Mary to Virginia and had freely given her to Harvie to be his wife. Most of the people involved in business dealings with Thomas Edwards were planters whose property was located on the lower James River (MCGC 53-54, 63-64, 70, 115).

WILLIAM EDWARDS

Mr. William Edwards died in the corporation of James City sometime after April 1623 but before February 16, 1624, at a plantation on the lower side of the James River, west of Grays Creek **(8, 9)**. Court testimony taken on October 25, 1624, reveals that Edwards had been the mate on the ship *Unity* (MCGC 26; CBE 41).

WILLIAM EDWARDS

William Edwards came to Virginia in 1628 on the *Hopewell* at the expense of Adam Thorogood, who on June 24, 1635, used his headright when securing a patent (PB 1 Pt. 1:179).

ROBERT EEDES

On January 28, 1628, Henry Catelyne, a merchant, sued Robert Eedes so that he could recover the cost of transporting a woman to Virginia whom Eedes married after her arrival. Court testimony reveals that Robert Eedes was the *Hopewell's* surgeon (MCGC 160).

THOMASIN EESTER (EASTER)

In 1617 Thomasin Eester (Easter) came to Virginia on the *Falcon* and in early 1625 was living in Elizabeth City, where she was a 26-year-old servant in William Ganey's household, on the west side of the Hampton River **(18)** (CBE 66).

ARTHUR EGGLESTON

Arthur Eggleston came to Virginia in 1634 on the *John and Dorothy* at the expense of Adam Thorogood, who on June 24, 1635, used his headright when patenting some land (PB 1 Pt. 1:179).

WILLIAM ELBERRY

William Elberry came to Virginia on the *Eleanor* in 1622. On June 1, 1633, Captain William Tucker used him as a headright when patenting some land (PB 1 Pt. 1:122).

WILLIAM ELBRIDG (ELGRIDG)

William Elbridg (Elgridg) died in Elizabeth City **(17, 18)** sometime after April 1623 but before February 16, 1624 (CBE 45).

JOHN ELFORD

On February 27, 1619, John Elford, a boy, was among those the justices of Bridewell Court decided to send to Virginia (CBE 12).

NICHOLAS ELFORD

Virginia Company records dating to October 18, 1622, indicate that the orders given to Captain Nicholas Elford of the *Tiger* were the object of a bet between Virginia colonist Thomas Hamor and Captain Sampson. The wager involved whether or not Elford, who was then in Virginia, had received orders to sail. Nicholas Elford died and on January 7, 1624, William Peirce, as his administrator, was ordered to pay for the goods the decedent had bought from the *Furtherance's* merchant as soon as he was presented with the bill (VCR 3:695; MCGC 9).

NATHANIEL ELIE

On March 22, 1622, when the Indians attacked Weyanoke **(52)**, Nathaniel Elie, one of Sir George Yeardley's servants, was killed (VCR 3:569).

ELINOR

On February 16, 1624, a woman named Elinor was living in Jamestown (1) in the household of merchant Edward Blaney (CBE 38).

ELIZABETH

A woman named Elizabeth died in Elizabeth City (17, 18) sometime after April 1623 but before February 16, 1624 (CBE 45).

ELIZABETH

On March 22, 1622, when the Indians attacked William Farrar's plantation on the east side of the Appomattox River, somewhat inland from Bermuda City (40), Elizabeth, one of Hendricke Peterson's maidservants, was killed (VCR 3:566).

ELIZABETH

On January 24, 1625, a maidservant named Elizabeth was living at Bermuda Hundred (39) where she was a member of Thomas Harris's household (CBE 54).

RICHARD ELKINGTON

Richard Elkington, a 36-year-old cloth worker from Wiltshire, went to Virginia in 1619 on the *Bona Nova*. His transportation costs were paid by the Ferrars, who were major Virginia Company investors (FER 295).

JOHN ELLEN

John Ellen—who was living at Thomas Sheffield's house (69), three miles from Falling Creek on the lower side of the James River—was killed in the March 22, 1622, Indian attack (VCR 3:565).

WILLIAM ELLESTON

On July 31, 1622, William Elleston set sail for Virginia on the *James*. He accompanied John Harrison (Harryson), who brought three men to the colony after acquiring three shares of land a few months earlier (FER 400).

WILLIAM ELLETT (ELLET)

On March 31, 1628, the justices of the General Court ordered the Rev. Jonas Stockdon of Elizabeth City (17) to free his servant, William Ellett (Ellet), who was being wrongfully detained after the expiration of his indenture. On March 24, 1629, William Ellett's widow, Mary, received letters of administration from the Prerogative Court of Canterbury, which noted that William had died abroad (MCGC 171; MOR 35).

HENRY ELLIOTT (ELLYOTT)

On January 12, 1627, Thomas Ward of Martin's Hundred (7) informed the justices of the General Court that on March 30, 1626, when he and some other men were in the woods, he had overheard Henry Elliott (Ellyott) and another man talking about the high price of nails. Elliott allegedly commented that John Day, who sold nails at Hog Island (16), had raised his prices because Captain Ralph Hamor had been charging more (MCGC 135).

JOHN ELLIOTT (ELLIATT)

John Elliott (Elliatt) came to Virginia on the *Margaret and John* in 1621 and on February 16, 1624, was living on the lower side of the James River, within the corporation of James City, west of Grays Creek. On February 4, 1625, when a muster was made of the colony's inhabitants, John Elliott was identified as a 15-year-old servant in the household of John Smith, who resided at Burrows Hill (8) (CBE 40, 59).

MARY ELLIOTT (ELLYOTT)

Mary Ellyott, a young maid, came to Virginia in 1621 on the *Warwick*. Virginia Company officials noted that she was the granddaughter-in-law of Maximillian Russell, who had reared her, and that she was accompanying him to Martin's Hundred (7) (FER 309).

DAVID ELLIS

David Ellis, who came to Virginia in 1608 in the 2nd Supply of Jamestown (1) colonists, accompanied Captain John Smith to Powhatan's village, Werowocomoco, in December 1608. Smith identified him variously as an artisan, a soldier, and a sailor (CJS 1:241, 244 ; 2:191, 193, 244).

DAVID ELLIS

On February 16, 1624, David Ellis was living at Chaplain's Choice (56), within the corporation of Charles City (CBE 37).

***

DAVID ELLIS

David Ellis came to Virginia on the *Mary Margaret*. On February 16, 1624, he and his wife were living on the Governor's Land (3), probably in a household headed by John Carter. David and his wife, Margaret, were still there on January 30, 1625. Their names were listed right after John Carter's, suggesting that their homes were in close proximity. David Ellis, a household head, appears to have been a tenant farmer, whose family was relatively well provisioned and supplied with defensive weaponry. Sometime prior to January 1625 David Ellis purchased Lt. Batters' land at Black Point, in the eastern end of Jamestown Island (1). On January 24, 1625, he received a patent for the Batters property, which he promptly sold to John Radish. By March 18, 1626, David and Margaret Ellis had a child. David was then described as John Carter's brother (probably brother-in-law) and an heir of Thomas Swinehow, from whom he inherited a ring (CBE 39, 58; MCGC 44, 98-99; DOR 1:27).

MARGARET ELLIS (MRS. DAVID ELLIS)

Margaret Ellis came to Virginia on the *Mary Margaret*. On February 16, 1624, she and her husband, David, were living on the Governor's Land (3), probably in a household headed by John Carter, who may have been her brother. The Ellises were still residing on the Governor's Land on January 30, 1625, at which time David was identified a household head. The Ellises occupied their own home. Sometime prior to January 24, 1625, David Ellis purchased Lt. Batters' land on Jamestown Island (1) at Black Point, but quickly sold it to John Radish. On March 18, 1626, Margaret Ellis was sharing her household with husband David and a child. As the late Thomas Swinhowe's designated heirs, she and her child were to receive rings (MCGC 98-99; CBE 39, 58).

[NO FIRST NAME] ELLIS

On March 18, 1626, David and Margaret Ellis's child, whose name, age, and gender are unknown, was identified as one of the late Thomas Swinhowe's heirs and stood to

receive a ring. The child lived with his/her parents, probably on the Governor's Land (3), but was not listed when the muster was taken on January 30, 1625 (MCGC 98-99).

***

JOHN ELLIS (ELLIES)

On February 26, 1620, the justices of Bridewell Court decided that John Ellis (Ellies), an inmate at Newgate Prison, would be sent to Virginia (CBE 19).

***

JOHN ELLISON (ELISON, ELISONE)

John Ellison (Elison, Elisone) came to Virginia on the *Prosperous* and by February 16, 1624, was living in Archer's Hope (6), where he headed a household that he shared with his wife. Sometime prior to January 3, 1625, John advanced a small sum of money on behalf of Mr. Nicholas Hyde, a Virginia Company investor, who had one or more servants in Martin's Hundred (7). On February 4, 1625, John was still living in Archer's Hope with his wife, Ellin, and a servant. John Ellison and his household were well supplied with provisions and defensive weaponry. The Ellisons' son, George, was recently deceased. On May 23, 1625, it was noted in court that John Ellison had put the governor's mark on a free-ranging cow on Jamestown Island (1) and that Robert Partin had claimed it. On November 21, 1625, Ellison testified that he had witnessed an agreement Thomas Farley and the widow Susan Bush made for some land in Archer's Hope (CBE 41, 59; MCGC 40, 59-60, 76; DOR 1:37).

ELLIN ELLISON (ELISON, ELISONE) (MRS. JOHN ELLISON [ELISON, ELISONE])

Ellin Ellison (Elison, Elisone) came to Virginia on the *Charitie*, and on February 16, 1624, she and her husband, John, were living in Archer's Hope (6). The Ellison couple was still residing in Archer's Hope on February 4, 1625. Their child, George, was recently deceased (CBE 41, 59).

GEORGE ELLISON (ELISON, ELISONE)

George Ellison (Elison, Elisone), the child of John and Ellin Ellison, died in Archer's Hope (6) sometime after February 16, 1624, but before February 4, 1625 (CBE 58).

***

WILLIAM ELLISON (ELLYSON)

William Ellison (Ellyson) came to Virginia on the *Swan* in 1624. In early 1625 he was living in the Elizabeth City (18) household of ancient planter Robert Salford and his son, John. Ellison, who was a servant, was age 44 (CBE 65).

WILLIAM ELLISON (ELLYSON)

On August 20, 1628, William Ellison (Ellyson) was identified as the master of the *John*, which had made a voyage from Barnstaple to Virginia. Then, on December 19, 1631, Ellyson was identified as the master of the *Pleasure*, a Barnstaple ship that was authorized to go to Virginia or New England (CBE 84, 98).

HENRY (HENER) ELWOOD (ELSWOOD)

Henry (Hener) Elwood (Elswood) came to Virginia on the *Francis Bonaventure* and on February 16, 1624, was living at Hog Island (16). He was still there on February 4, 1625, and appears to have been a free man. On August 28, 1626, Elwood informed the General Court that when he was at John Stone's house on Hog Island, he saw Henry Woodward leave a cornfield from which some corn had been stolen (CBE 41, 61; MCGC 110).

***

WALTER ELY

On February 16, 1624, Walter Ely and his wife and child were living in Elizabeth City on the east side of the Hampton River, on land owned by the Virginia Company (17). In early 1625, when a muster was made of the colony's inhabitants, the Elys were still there, sharing their home with their infant daughter, Ann. Although Walter Ely and his wife, Elizabeth, lacked servants, they were well supplied with provisions and Walter was credited with a piece of ordnance. He was a free man and perhaps was a Virginia Company tenant (CBE 43, 67; DOR 1:65).

ELIZABETH ELY (MRS. WALTER ELY)

Elizabeth Ely came to Virginia on the *Warwick* in 1622. On February 16, 1624, she and her husband, Walter, and their infant were living in Elizabeth City on the Virginia Company's land (17) on the east side of the Hampton River. In early 1625 Elizabeth and Walter Ely and their daughter, Ann, were living in the same area, and Walter was a household head (CBE 43, 67; DOR 1:65).

ANN ELY

Included in the February 16, 1624, census was Ann Ely, the Virginia-born infant of Walter and Elizabeth Ely, who were living on the east side of the Hampton River in Elizabeth City (17). When a muster was made of the colony's inhabitants early in 1625, Ann's name was included, and she was still sharing her parents' home in Elizabeth City (CBE 43, 67).

***

JOHN EMAN (ENIMS)

John Eman or Enims, a goldsmith from London, arrived in Jamestown (1) on September 12, 1623, aboard the *Bonny Bess* and took the oath of supremacy. He died in Jamestown sometime prior to February 16, 1624 (MCGC 6; CBE 39).

EDWARD EMBER

On March 22, 1622, when the Indians attacked the settlers living at the College (66), Edward Ember was killed (VCR 3:566).

ALICE (ALLICE) EMERSON

Alice (Allice) Emerson, a girl who lived at Martin's Hundred (7), died sometime after February 16, 1624, but before February 4, 1625. She may have been the daughter of Ellis Emerson, a household head at Martin's Hundred (CBE 62).

***

ELLIS EMERSON

Ellis Emerson and his family came to Virginia on the *George* in 1623 and immediately seated at Martin's Hundred (**7**). He reportedly was instrumental in persuading Robert Adams to stay on at the plantation, despite difficult living conditions. On February 4, 1625, Ellis Emerson was living at Martin's Hundred with his wife, Ann, and 11-year-old son, Thomas. Ellis was a household head and was relatively well supplied with provisions and defensive weaponry. The Emersons had two servants, one of whom (Thomas Goulding) came with them on the *George* in 1623. On April 11, 1625, Ellis Emerson testified that he had put Elias Gail (a young male servant and one of the East India School's apprentices) to work on the Rev. Patrick Copeland's behalf. On June 15, 1625, Mr. Emerson and Martin's Hundred's leader, William Harwood, offered accommodations to the people who came to Virginia to establish the East India School. Ellis Emerson died sometime prior to October 31, 1626, at which time Robert Scotchmore of Martin's Hundred presented his will to the justices of the General Court. He may have been the father of Alice Emerson who died in 1624–1625 (CBE 61; VCR 4:562-567; MCGC 52, 123; FER 572; DOR 1:45).

ANN EMERSON
(MRS. ELLIS EMERSON)

Ann, the wife of Ellis Emerson, came to Virginia on the *George* in 1623. She was accompanied by Ellis, his son Thomas, and perhaps a daughter named Alice. The Emerson family seated land at Martin's Hundred (**7**), where Ellis was a household head. On January 3, 1626, Mrs. Emerson was ordered to pay two of the debts incurred by the late Matthias Fenton, taking the funds from his estate. She was widowed prior to October 31, 1626 (CBE 61; MCGC 84, 123; DOR 1:45).

THOMAS EMERSON

In 1623 Thomas Emerson and his father, Ellis, came to Virginia on the *George* and by February 4, 1625, had seated some land at Martin's Hundred (**7**). Thomas was then age 11. He may have been the son of Ellis

Emmerson's wife, Ann, and the brother of Alice Emerson, a girl who died at Martin's Hundred (CBE 61).

***

WILLIAM EMERSON
(EMMERSON)

William Emerson (Emmerson) came to Virginia on the *Sampson* in 1618 and on February 16, 1624, was residing at Jordan's Journey (**46**). Sometime prior to November 8, 1624, he agreed to free his servant, James Davis, and to pay Lieutenant John Gibbs for two years' use of his servant, William Popleton. The issue surfaced again in December 1624 when William Emerson and his partner, John Davis, testified that they had paid Gibbs for the right to use Popleton for two years. On January 21, 1625, William Emerson and partner John Davis were living at Jordan's Journey with two male servants, one of whom was William Popleton. Emerson and Davis and their servants shared a home and were well supplied with provisions and defensive weaponry. Around 1629, William Emerson made a trip to England, where he was interviewed by Captain John Smith about conditions in the colony. Later, Smith included portions of his narrative in his text. On June 5, 1632, when William Emerson, who by then had returned to Virginia, was summoned to testify before the General Court, he gave his age as 32. He stated that people in Southwark, England, where Edmund Clarke's child was boarded, claimed that the youngster was mistreated and malnourished and had run away. In July 1632 William Emerson was named one of the late William Popleton's administrators. Popleton, who was from St. Giles, Cripplegate, London, divided his Virginia land among Emerson and two others. On February 1, 1633, William Emerson commenced serving as a burgess for Weyanoke (**52**) (CBE 37, 52; MCGC 30, 34, 201; CJS 3:215-218; HEN 1:202; DOR 1:19).

THOMAS EMMERY (EMRY)

On December 10, 1607, Mr. Thomas Emmery (Emry) and John Robinson left Jamestown (**1**) and joined Captain John Smith in exploring the Chickahominy River. According to Smith's account, both men were slain by the Indians (HAI 195).

WILLIAM ENRY (ENDRYE)

On July 11, 1625, William Enry (Endry), who was from Feverfam in Kent, England, informed the General Court that he had come to Virginia on the *Black Bess,* a Flushing man-of-war under the command of Captains Jonnes and Powell. He said that the ship took on victuals at Isle of Wight and then paused in the West Indies before continuing on to Virginia. Enry was among several people testifying about the privateering activities of the *Black Bess* and the actions of Captain Powell's men who were aboard. William Enry stayed on in Virginia but by May 1628 had become ill. Later in the year, Thomas Marlott, a planter who lived on the Maine (**3**), testified that Enry had asked for his help in making a will. Because Marlott indicated that he was incapable of doing so, Emry made known his last wishes via a nuncupative will. He named William Bedford of Paces Paines (**9**) as his administrator and sole heir. Bedford stood to receive all of the testator's goods, houses, and land, and the residue of his estate in Virginia after his just debts were paid. William Enry's close contacts resided at the Maine and Paces Paines, suggesting that he may have lived within the corporation of James City (MCGC 66-68, 174).

FRANCIS ENGLAND

On March 25, 1629, Francis England, who was age 20, testified before the General Court whose justices were trying to decide whether Thomas alias Thomasina Hall, a hermaphrodite, should be classified as a man or a woman. England and another man forcibly examined Hall so that they could determine his physical characteristics. All of those involved resided on the lower side of the James River, within what is now Surry County (MCGC 194).

JOHN ENGLAND

John England was slain during the March 22, 1622, Indian attack on William Farrar's plantation in the corporation of Charles City, somewhat inland from Bermuda Hundred (**39**), and on the east side of the Appomattox River (VCR 3:554, 566).

ANNIE ENGLISH

On March 22, 1622, Annie English was killed when the Indians attacked Warresqueak

(**26**), Edward Bennett's plantation (VCR 3:571).

JAMES ENGLISH

James English was killed at Captain Francis West's plantation at Westover (**54**) during the March 22, 1622, Indian attack (VCR 3:566).

JOHN ENGLISH
(ENGLES, ENGLESH)

On November 20, 1622, John English (Engles, Englesh), an inmate at Newgate Prison, was pardoned on account of an epidemic of jail fever. He was to be put to work or transported overseas (CBE 29).

JOHN ENGLISH

John English died at Flowerdew Hundred (**53**) sometime after February 16, 1624, but before January 20, 1625. He may have been the former Newgate prisoner of that name (CBE 51).

***

RICHARD ENGLISH I

Richard English I left England on July 31, 1622, and came to Virginia aboard the *James* with his son, Richard II, and a male servant (FER 400).

RICHARD ENGLISH II

On July 31, 1622, Richard English II left England on the *James* with his father, Richard I, and a male servant. All three of them were bound for Virginia. On February 16, 1624, Richard English II was living at Jordan's Journey (**46**). When a muster was made of the settlement's inhabitants on January 21, 1625, Richard English II was identified as an 11-year-old servant in Thomas Palmer's household. The muster-taker's records also corroborate the fact that he came to Virginia in 1622 aboard the *James*. Richard English II probably was an orphan, for his father's name was not included in the demographic records compiled in 1624 and 1625 or in contemporary legal records (FER 400; CBE 51).

***

WILLIAM ENGLISH

On January 31, 1625, William English, a gentleman who resided on the west side of the Hampton River in Elizabeth City (**18**), testified before the General Court in a suit Captain John Wilcox brought against John Crowdick. At issue was some tobacco that was ruined while Crowdick was transporting it to Jamestown (**1**). English appeared in court again on January 3, 1626, and testified in a case involving the expenditures he and William Ganey had made when providing clothes for Mr. Humphrey Rastell's servants. On October 13, 1626, William English and William Ganey received passes authorizing them to return to England. The next day, English's house was mentioned in court testimony concerning the accidental drowning of William Ganey's servant, Thomas Savage. One of English's servants reportedly had helped bury the deceased servant. By October 16, 1629, William English had been elected a burgess for Elizabeth City and in 1632 and 1633 he represented Elizabeth City's lower parish. During 1632 he also served as a commissioner (or justice) for Elizabeth City's court (MCGC 45-46, 86, 121-122; HEN 1:139-140, 170, 179, 187, 203).

JOHN ENIES

John Enies came to Virginia in 1633 on the *Hopewell* at the expense of Adam Thorogood, who on June 24, 1635, used him as a headright (PB 1 Pt. 1:179).

JOHN ENINES

Sometime after April 1623 but before February 16, 1624, John Enines died at one of the plantations on the lower side of the James River, within the corporation of James City (**8-15**) (CBE 41).

***

FRANCIS EPPES (EPES) I

Francis Eppes (Epes) I, who was baptized on May 14, 1597, was the son of John and Thomazine Fisher Eppes of Ashford, Kent, England. He came to Virginia sometime prior to April 1625, at which time he was elected to the assembly, representing the settlers living at Shirley Hundred (**41**). Eppes, who by January 9, 1626, had at-

tained the rank of ensign, testified before the General Court in a slander suit involving the Rev. Grivel Pooley and Mr. Thomas Pawlett. On August 8, 1626, Francis Eppes was appointed a commissioner of the monthly court for the "Upper Parts," the area near the head of the James River. He also was identified as the master of John Joyce, a runaway servant who had stolen a weapon and a boat. On July 4, 1627, Eppes and Pawlett were placed in command of the men who were to attack the Weyanoke and Appomattox Indians. Francis Eppes apparently returned to England, for his wife, Marie or Mary, gave birth to their son Thomas in London on September 8, 1630. By 1632 Francis Eppes had returned to Virginia where he was elected a burgess for Shirley Hundred, Chaplin's Choice (**56**), and Mr. Farrar's plantation, probably Jordan's Journey (**46**). On August 26, 1635, he was granted 1,700 acres of land on the east side of the Appomattox River's mouth, within Charles City (now Prince George) County. He also had land on West and Shirley (now Eppes) Island. Captain Francis Eppes served in the assembly, representing Charles City in 1640 and 1646. In 1652 he was named to the Council of State. Eppes consolidated his landholdings in a 1668 patent, but by September 30, 1674, was dead (MCGC 88-89, 105-106, 151; PB 1 Pt. 1:280; Pt. 2:787; 2:12; 6:203; HEN 1:154, 168; DOR 1:854-856).

MARIE (MARY) EPPES (EPES)
(MRS. FRANCIS EPPES [EPES] I)

Very little is known about Marie or Mary, the wife of Francis Eppes (Epes) I, except that she gave birth to her husband's youngest son, Thomas, on September 8, 1630, in London. On January 12, 1644, when Thomas Pawlett of Shirley Hundred (**41**) made his will, he left Mary Eppes his Bible and enough money to purchase a ring (DOR 1:856).

FRANCIS EPPES (EPES) II

Francis Eppes (Epes) II, the son of Francis Eppes I, was born around 1627 or 1628, probably in Virginia. On August 26, 1635, when the elder man patented 1,700 acres of land on the Appomattox River, he listed son Francis II as a headright and indicated that he had paid for his transportation to Virginia. Prior to April 20, 1658, Francis

Eppes II became a justice of Charles City County's monthly court, and in June 1660 he was a militia captain. A year later he was placed in command of a militia unit charged with keeping watch over the territory around Fort Henry, a military post near the falls of the Appomattox River. Francis Eppes II moved to Henrico County and by February 1665 had become a county justice. Later he served as a burgess. He died between August 20 and August 28, 1678 (PB 1:Pt. 1:280; Charles City County Order Book 1655-1665:137, 233; 1676-1679:200; HEN 2:330; DOR 1:857-858).

JOHN EPPES (EPES)

John, the eldest son of Francis Eppes (Epes) I, was born in 1626, probably in Virginia. On August 26, 1635, when Francis acquired a patent for some land on the Appomattox River, he used his son John as a headright and said that he had transported him to the colony. John Eppes married Mary Kent around 1645, and by 1657 he had made Shirley Hundred (Eppes) Island his home. In 1661 John became a captain of the Charles City County militia, and in 1673 he attained the rank of lieutenant colonel. John Eppes became the sheriff of Charles City County in February 1676, an indication that he also was a county justice. He was alive on August 4, 1679, but died sometime prior to October 16, 1679 (PB 1 Pt. 1:280; Charles City County Order Book 1655-1665:174; 1672-1674:527; 1676-1679:210, 228, 395, 410; 1687-1695:209; DOR 1:857).

THOMAS EPPES (EPES)

Thomas, the son of Francis Eppes (Epes) I and his wife, Marie or Mary, was born in London on September 8, 1630. On August 26, 1635, when Captain Francis Eppes patented some land on the Appomattox River in Charles City (Prince George) County, he used his son Thomas as a headright, noting that he had paid for his transportation to Virginia. Thomas Eppes made his home in Charles City County, and when he was deposed in February 1665, he stated that he was age 35. Like his brother John, he became a county justice. Thomas died sometime between 1673 and 1679 in Charles City County (PB 1 Pt. 1:280; Charles City County Order Book 1655-1665:71, 633; 1672-1674:533; 1676-1679:391, 406; DOR 1:856, 859).

PETER EPPES (EPPS, EPES)

Peter Eppes (Epps, Epes), the son of John and Thomazine Fisher Eppes of Ashford, Kent, England, and the brother of Captains William and Francis Eppes I, was living on the Eastern Shore on February 16, 1624. On January 3, 1625, Peter Eppes, who had been sued by Simon Tuchin, was found to owe him money. On February 5, 1627, when the General Court discussed the events that occurred at Captain John Ward's plantation (61) in the wake of the March 22, 1622, Indian attack, the justices noted that Peter Eppes had evacuated Ward's servants to safety (CBE 46; MCGC 40, 139; DOR 1:854).

WILLIAM EPPES (EPPS, EPES)

William Eppes (Epps, Epes), who was baptized on March 7, 1595, was the son of John and Thomazine Fisher Eppes of Ashford, Kent, England, and the brother of Peter and Francis Eppes I. He served in France and in the Low Countries in 1616 and in 1618 came to Virginia on the *William and Thomas*, arriving on August 29th. The Virginia Company furnished him with books and other supplies. In 1618 William Eppes, as Sir Nicholas Tufton's agent, was given command of the settlers in Smyth's (Southampton) Hundred (44) and was there when Governor George Yeardley arrived in April 1619. Sometime prior to November 17, 1619, while William Eppes was responsible for Smyth's Hundred, he got into a fight with Captain Edward Roecroft alias Stallings and struck him with a sheathed sword. The forceful blow fractured Roecroft's skull and he died. Eppes was tried by the General Court and found guilty of manslaughter. However, within a short time, his command was restored and he was given the rank of captain. At the time of the March 22, 1622, Indian attack, William Eppes was renting Captain John Ward's plantation (61) in Charles City. Afterward, he and his brother Peter returned to evacuate the survivors, servants they took to the Eastern Shore. In 1623 William Eppes was placed in command of the Eastern Shore. One of his duties was to report anyone who traded with the area's Indians without a license. On February 16, 1624, William Eppes and his wife were living on the Eastern Shore. Later in the year, he got into a dispute with Ensign Thomas Savage, whom he accused of slander; exercising his authority, he had Savage laid "neck and heels." A contemporary account referred to Eppes as a "mad, ranting fellow." In early 1625, when a muster was made of the Eastern Shore's inhabitants, William Eppes and his wife, Margaret, and their 13 servants were living on his plantation (74), which had two dwellings, three storehouses, and a palisade. On February 3, 1626, William Eppes patented 450 acres of land on the Eastern Shore, using as headrights nine men he had transported to the colony. During 1625, 1626, and 1627 Eppes made several appearances before the General Court, sometimes in an official capacity and sometimes as a litigant. He served as Mrs. Katherine Bennett's attorney, and he also testified that he had seen Luke Eden shortly before his death and that Eden's trunk had been broken open and emptied of its contents. Eppes bought a shallop from shipwright Thomas Nunn but failed to pay for it, and he also was identified as one of Luke Boyse's debtors. He was ordered to give John Darker a replacement tobacco bill. In July 1626 William Eppes testified that the Indians on the Eastern Shore were friendly to the colonists, and three months later Eppes was authorized to talk with the Natives about some hogs they allegedly killed. He was given permission to take a captured Weyanoke Indian to the Eastern Shore and then to England.

During the latter part of 1626, Captain William Eppes's scandalous social behavior resulted in his being brought before the General Court. Sometime after late June 1626 but before February 19, 1627, Eppes, who was visiting James Slight at Martin's Brandon (59), became quite drunk and had sex with the widowed Alice Boyse, who crept into his bed. Several people who were present at the time testified about this affront to public morality, but ultimately the charges against Eppes, a married man, were dismissed. Despite this lapse in decorum, in March 1629 he was made a commissioner of the monthly court for the "Upper Parts." His landholdings on the Eastern Shore were mentioned in patents secured in 1628 and 1629. William Eppes left Virginia and by May 3, 1630, was living in St. Christopher's, where he was a member of the Council. By the late 1630s he had returned to his home in England. When he made his will during the early 1640s, he named as heirs his wife, Margaret, son William II, and daughter Frances (VCR 1:274; 3:121, 242; CBE 46, 68; MCGC 15, 48, 50, 91, 93-94, 99-100, 104, 116, 119, 131, 139-140, 148, 151, 188, 193; PB 1 Pt. 1:49, 71; FER 141; DOR 1:67, 854-855).

MARGARET EPPES (EPPS, EPES) (MRS. WILLIAM EPPES [EPPS, EPES])

Margaret, who married William Eppes (Epps, Epes), came to Virginia on the *George* in 1621. It is uncertain whether she was married when she arrived. On February 16, 1624, Mrs. Margaret Eppes was living on the Eastern Shore with her husband, William. When a muster was taken of the Eastern Shore's inhabitants in early 1625, the Eppes were still residents of his plantation (74) on the Eastern Shore. By May 1630 William Eppes had been named a member of the Council for St. Christopher's, in the West Indies. On July 18, 1633, he gave a power-of-attorney to William Stone and authorized him to dispose of his Virginia land. During the late 1630s the Margaret and William returned to England, settling in Ashford, Kent. Margaret Eppes was still alive in January 1641, when William Eppes made his will and named her as an heir. Also named were their son William and daughter Frances. Margaret Eppes remarried, taking as her husband the Rev. Dr. Henry Bradshaw, rector of Chawton, Hampshire, and Prebendary of Winchester Cathedral. She was buried on January 19, 1674 (CBE 43, 68; SAIN 1:115; Northampton Orders, Deeds, Wills 1632-1640:212; DOR 1:855).

***

PETER EPPES (EPPS, EPES)

On September 2, 1631, officials at Bridewell noted that Peter Epes, a boy who was being detained, was to be sent to Virginia by a merchant (CBE 96).

JOHN ERWINS

On April 11, 1625, John Erwins testified at the inquest held in the wake of John Verone's death. As Verone lived on the lower side of the James River on Hugh Crowder's plantation (12), east of Gray's Creek, Erwins probably was associated with the same vicinity. He may have been the man called John Evans (Evens) who on

February 4, 1625, was living at the Treasurer's Plantation (11), close to the scene of John Verone's death (MCGC 53).

CUTHBERT ESSINGTON

On July 10, 1621, Cuthbert Essington, a tenant assigned to the incumbent Physician General's office land, sent a letter to the Virginia Company, asking to be released from his contract with the late Dr. Lawrence Bohunne (Bohunn, Bohune). He said that he had been in the West Indies with Dr. Bohunne when two Spanish ships attacked their vessel and the physician was killed. Essington said that he had continued on to Virginia, where his master had a patent as well as some office land. He also stated that he had made a private contract with Dr. Bohunne, who had modified the agreement without his consent. After due consideration, Virginia Company officials decided that Cuthbert Essington should be freed from his obligation to Dr. Bohunne's estate and given passage back to England (VCR 1:508-509).

NATHANIEL ETHERINGTON

On April 3, 1622, Nathaniel Etherington received some shares of Virginia land from Ambrose Wood (VCR 1:630).

CHRISTOPHER EVANS

Christopher Evans died at Flowerdew Hundred (54) sometime after April 1623 but before February 16, 1624 (CBE 37).

CLEMENT EVANS (EVAND, EVANDS)

Clement Evans (Evand, Evands), an ancient planter, came to Virginia in 1616 on the *Edwin* and on February 16, 1624, was living in Elizabeth City (18). In early 1625, he was still there and was a 30-year-old servant in the home of Susan Bush, a widow (CBE 45, 64).

GEORGE EVANS

On February 16, 1624, George Evans was living in Elizabeth City (18) (CBE 44).

JOHN EVANS (EVENS, EVINS)

John Evans (Evens, Evins) came to Virginia in 1619 on the *Marigold*. According to Cap-

tain John Smith, in 1619 he intended to settle on Captain Christopher Lawne's plantation (25) in Warresqueak. On February 16, 1624, John Evans was living in Elizabeth City (18). However, by early 1625 he had relocated to the Treasurer's Plantation (11) on the lower side of the James River. On January 3, 1626, he testified that he had stored some corn in Treasurer George Sandys' loft (CBE 44, 60; MCGC 86; CJS 2:266).

JOHN EVANS

On December 31, 1619, John Evans, an inmate at Bridewell, was among those chosen to be sent to Virginia. Virginia Company records indicate that in 1619 the Ferrars, who were major Company investors, planned to pay for John Evans' transportation to Virginia. On February 16, 1624, he was living on the Eastern Shore (72-78) (CBE 15, 46; FER 295, 296).

LAWRENCE EVANS

Lawrence Evans came to Virginia on the *James* in 1622 and on February 16, 1624, was living at Jordan's Journey (46). When a muster was taken of Jordan's Journey's inhabitants on January 21, 1625, Lawrence was identified as a 16-year-old servant in the household of Nathaniel Causey (CBE 37, 52).

MARK (MARKE) EVANS

On February 16, 1624, Mark (Marke) Evans was living in Elizabeth City (18) (CBE 44).

RICHARD EVANS (EVANDS)

Richard Evans (Evands) came to Virginia on the *Neptune* in 1618 and on February 16, 1624, was living at Basses Choice (27), within the corporation of Warresqueak. When a muster was made of Basses Choice's inhabitants on February 7, 1625, Richard Evans was identified as a 35-year-old household head, who was in possession of some stored food and defensive weaponry. In mid-December 1625 he appeared before the General Court, where he was described as Captain William Tucker's sergeant. Richard Evans forbade his servant, Arthur Avelinge, to obey a General Court summons to go to Jamestown (1). Evans indicated that he was willing to send Avelinge if Mr. Weston were to post a bond, guaranteeing his safe return. Because he prevented Avelinge from appearing in court, Richard Evans was fined and both men were summoned to Jamestown. In another matter, Evans testified that he had encouraged William Ganey, Robert Newman's partner and a resident of Elizabeth City, to pay his debt to Humphrey Rastell, a merchant (CBE 46, 62; MCGC 81-85; DOR 1:49).

RICHARD EVANS

On June 25, 1635, Richard Evans was listed as a headright by William Andrews of Accomack. He may have been the same individual who had been living in Elizabeth City a decade earlier (PB 1 Pt. 1:181).

ROBERT EVANS

On February 27, 1618, Robert Evans was identified as a boy who was being detained at Bridewell so that he could be sent to Virginia. On September 19, 1618, he was described as a vagrant who was born at St. Sepulcher's and had been taken into custody on Tower Street. On August 18, 1627, when Gilbert Peppett patented some land, he used Robert Evans as a headright, and indicated that he had paid for Evans' transportation from Newfoundland to Virginia on the *Temperance,* a vessel that reached the colony in 1620 (CBE 9, 13; HUME 3, 10; PB 1 Pt. 1:50).

SAMUEL EVANS

On September 30, 1627, the justices of Bridewell Court decided that Samuel Evans, a vagrant brought in from Bishopsgate, would be sent to Virginia (CBE 80).

THOMAS EVANS

On January 29, 1620, Thomas Evans was among those selected by the justices of Bridewell Court to be sent to Virginia. On March 22, 1622, Thomas Evans, who was identified as one of Sir George Yeardley's servants, was killed when the Indians attacked Weyanoke (52) (CBE 18; VCR 3:569).

THOMAS EVANS (EVANDS)

Thomas Evans (Evands) came to Virginia on the *George* in 1623 and on February 16, 1624, was living in Elizabeth City (18).

When a muster list of the colony's inhabitants was compiled in early 1625, Thomas Evans was identified as a 23-year-old servant in Captain William Tucker's household, on the upper side of the Hampton River in Elizabeth City (CBE 43, 63).

WILLIAM EVANS (EVANDS, EWINS)

William Evans (Evands, Ewins) came to Virginia in 1619 on the *Bona Nova,* a ship that carried a large number of Virginia Company servants and tenants. On February 16, 1624, he was living in Elizabeth City (17). When a muster of the colony's inhabitants was taken early in 1625, William Evans was living on the Virginia Company's land on the east side of the Hampton River and was a servant in Lieutenant William Barry's household. On January 12, 1627, when the defunct Virginia Company's servants and tenants were parceled out among the colony's highest-ranking officials, William Evans was assigned to Sir George Yeardley (CBE 43, 68; MCGC 136).

ROBERT EVERS (EVARS, EVANS, EPERS)

In 1619 Robert Evers (Evars, Evans, Epers) reportedly witnessed Governor George Yeardley's consummation of a treaty with the Chickahominy Indians. William Fairfax's February 20, 1619, patent for a tract of land in the eastern end of Jamestown Island (1) reveals that Evers was then in residence on Mary Bayly's property. On May 30, 1624, Virginia Company officials reviewed a petition sent to them by Ralph Hamor, who claimed that Mr. Robert Evers had obtained from former Governor George Yeardley a patent for 490 acres on Hog Island (16). Although Evers purportedly neglected to seat his patent, later he tried to claim Hog Island in its entirety. This prompted Ralph Hamor to make an official complaint. On June 28, 1624, Robert Evers was summoned before the General Court and told to present his patent for Hog Island. He was identified as Mary Bayly's guardian when she expressed an interest in purchasing the rest of Hog Island. Sometime after February 16, 1624, but before February 4, 1625, Robert Evars died on the lower side of the James River, within the corporation of James City and east of Grays

Creek (**10-16**). In May 1625 he was identified as the patentee of 100 acres of land in Tappahannah, the name by which that area was known (FER 113; VCR 4:482-483, 555; MCGC 15-17; CBE 61-62; PB 1 Pt. 2:648, 880).

JOHN EWEN (EWENS, EWYNE, EWINS)

John Ewen (Ewens, Ewyne, Ewins) arrived in Virginia on the *Marigold* with Captain Christopher Lawne, who transported a few Virginia Company servants to the colony. On May 20, 1619, Ewen was assigned to Governor George Yeardley for the Company's benefit. Two men named John Ewen who resided on the lower side of the James River, within the corporation of James City (**8-15**), died between April 1623 and February 16, 1624. It is unclear whether the same man was listed twice or whether there were two individuals with the same name (MCGC 90; CBE 41).

JOHN EWEN (EWENS, EWINS)

On February 19, 1627, the justices of the General Court summoned John Ewen (Ewens, Ewins) and Jane Hill, both of whom resided at West and Shirley Hundred (**41**) and were accused of lewd behavior. When the couple appeared in court on March 5, 1627, Ewen said that they had had a consensual sexual relationship, which began in August 1626, and they had planned to marry. Hill, the daughter of the widowed Goodwife Rebecca Rose, agreed but said that she no longer loved Ewen and did not want to marry him. Both were punished for their infraction of moral law. Ewen was publicly whipped in Jamestown (**1**) and was sent back to Shirley Hundred, where he was whipped a second time. Hill was publicly shamed by being made to stand up in the church in Jamestown, wrapped in a white sheet, and she was ordered to do the same at Shirley Hundred (MCGC 139, 142).

***

WILLIAM EWEN (EWENS, EWINS, EVANS)

In late August 1619 William Ewen (Ewens, Ewins, Evans), a sea captain, went to Old Point Comfort (**17**) with Lieutenant William Peirce and John Rolfe to meet the ship *Treasurer*, which had brought some Afri-

cans to Virginia. In July 1621 Ewen was identified as captain of the *George*, when the Virginia Company hired him to take 80 people from Isle of Wight to Virginia. One of his passengers was incoming governor, Sir Francis Wyatt. William Ewen owned the ship *Charles*, which he leased to the Virginia Company. In July 1622 he brought three men to Virginia on the *James*. On April 20, 1623, when William Ewen refuted the claims that Captain Nathaniel Butler had made about conditions in the colony, he said that he had made four trips to Virginia as the master of ships and had lived there for a year. In July 1623 he promised Virginia Company officials that he would send surplus supplies to Virginia. In May 1625 William Ewen was credited with a 100-acre plantation (**13**) on the lower side of the James River, opposite Jamestown, property that already had been seated. On May 23, 1625, the General Court's justices noted that when the men from the College (**66**) in Henrico were evacuated to safety after the March 22, 1622, Indian attack, they had been placed on Mr. Ewen's plantation. He also took custody of the supplies sent to the people who intended to establish the East India School. On May 26, 1634, William Ewen, who was then in England, was among those claiming that they had had families in Virginia for several years and feared for their well-being if Morris Thompson became the colony's sole supplier. In March 1640 Ewen was described as a merchant by colonist George Read. On April 2, 1649, when William Ewen made his will, which was proved in August 1650, he indicated that he was a mariner and native of Greenwich, in Kent, England. He named as heirs his wife and his daughter, both of whom were named Mary, and indicated that he still owned some land in Virginia, the property he had acquired during the 1620s (VCR 1:454-455, 466, 497, 506; 2:385; 3:243, 465-466; 4:245-246, 555; FER 400; MCGC 60; CBE 20, 115-116; C.O. 1/10 f 176; EEAC 20; WITH 283).

MARY EWEN (EWENS, EWINS, EVANS) I (MRS. WILLIAM EWEN [EWENS, EWINS, EVANS])

On April 2, 1649, when William Ewen (Ewens, Ewins, Evans) made his will, he named his wife, Mary I, as his executrix. She and their daughter, Mary, were his principal beneficiaries. The testator, a mariner and merchant, owned a Virginia plantation (13) at the time of his death, which occurred sometime prior to August 1650. The widowed Mary Ewen disposed of her late husband's Virginia property (EEAC 20; WITH 283).

MARY EWEN (EWENS, EWINS, EVANS) II

On April 2, 1649, when William Ewen (Ewens, Ewins, Evans) made his will, he named his daughter, Mary (II), and his wife, Mary (I), as his principal beneficiaries. The testator owned a Virginia plantation (13) at the time of his death, which occurred sometime prior to August 1650 (EEAC 20; WITH 283).

***

WILLIAM EXETER

On December 31, 1619, the justices of Bridewell Court decided that William Exeter, who was brought in by the Marshal of London, would be detained so that he could be sent to Virginia or Bermuda (CBE 15).

WILLIAM EXTON

On June 25, 1635, when John Russell, one of Edward Blaney's former servants, patented some land on the lower side of the James River, he used William Exton as a headright (PB 1 Pt. 1:177).

ROBERT EYRE

On July 19, 1627, Robert Eyre shipped some goods from London to Virginia on the *James*. On February 28, 1628, while Eyre was in Virginia, he proved the nuncupative will of Marmion Leake, who died aboard the *Samuel*, and he confirmed the court testimony of William Southey, a witness to Leake's will. On March 25, 1629, Robert Eyre was identified as the master of Thomas Hall, an indentured servant and hermaphrodite who lived at Edward Grindon's settlement on the Treasurer's Plantation (11) (CBE 79; MCGC 168, 195).

NICHOLAS EYRES (EYROS)

Nicholas Eyres (Eyros) came to Virginia in 1622 on the *Gift*. On February 4, 1625, when a muster list was compiled of the people living on the Treasurer's Plantation (11) on the lower side of the James River, Nicholas was identified as a boy and was one of Treasurer George Sandys' servants. On March 25, 1629, when there was court testimony about the indeterminate gender of Thomas Hall, reference was made to an event that occurred at Nicholas Eyre's house, probably on the Treasurer's Plantation (CBE 60; MCGC 195).

F

JOAN (JONE) FAIRCHILD

On August 8, 1618, the Bridewell Court decided that Joan (Jone) Fairchild, a vagrant brought in from London's Lombard Street, would be sent to Virginia. Later in the year, she came to the colony on the *George*. In early 1625 Joan, a 20-year-old servant in the household of Francis West, was residing on the east side of the Hampton River on the Virginia Company's land in Elizabeth City (17) (CBE 9, 67).

***

WILLIAM (WINSTER) FAIRFAX (FIERFAX, FAIREFAX, FFAX)

Ancient planter William Fairfax (Fierfax, Fairefax, Ffax), who immigrated to Virginia in 1611, was a yeoman farmer. He built a house on a 12-acre parcel in the eastern part of Jamestown Island (1) and received a patent for his acreage on February 20, 1619. William and his wife, Margery, as ancient planters, together were entitled to 200 acres of land as their first dividend. William's 1619 patent reveals that he and Margery came to Virginia as a married couple. According to Captain John Smith, one Sunday in 1617, while William Fairfax was at church, some Indians went to his house, where they killed three children and a youth. As Mrs. Fairfax had left home and gone to meet her husband, her life was spared. Smith indicated that the Fairfax dwelling was a mile from Jamestown. As the Fairfax acreage on Jamestown Island is approximately a mile from the church and is the only parcel attributable to the Fairfaxes during the 16-teens, the Indians probably ventured onto Jamestown Island to make their attack. On December 18, 1620, William Fairfax sold his Jamestown Island homestead to the Rev. Richard Buck, rector of the church in Jamestown, noting that the land contained his dwelling and a smaller house. Fairfax, who was visiting Kecoughtan (**17, 18**) when he made the sale, promised to send his original patent to Buck. On March 22, 1622, when the Indians of the Powhatan Chiefdom made a concerted effort to drive the colonists from their territory, William Fairfax was killed. As his death occurred at Ensign William Spence's house in Archer's Hope (**6**), a region in which Fairfax had patents of 100 acres and 200 acres, he may have moved there after selling his Jamestown Island property to the Rev. Richard Buck (CJS 2:265; PB 1 Pt. 2:648, 650; VCR 3:570; 4:551, 556).

MARGERY FAIRFAX (FIERFAX, FAIREFAX, FFAX) (MRS. WILLIAM (WINSTER) FAIRFAX [FIERFAX, FAIREFAX, FFAX])

Margery Fairfax (Fierfax, Fairefax, Ffax) and her husband, William, who were ancient planters, came to Virginia as a married couple. Together, they were entitled to 200 acres of land as their first dividend. On February 20, 1619, William received a patent for a 12-acre parcel in the eastern end of Jamestown Island (**1**). According to Captain John Smith, one Sunday in 1617, while William Fairfax was at church, some Indians went to the family home and killed three children and a youth. Mrs. Fairfax, who had gone to meet her husband, escaped with her life. Smith indicated that the Fairfax dwelling was a mile from the church in Jamestown (PB 1 Pt. 2:648, 650; CJS 2:265).

***

ALEXANDER FALCON

On January 8, 1620, Alexander Falcon, who had been brought to Bridewell by the marshal of Middlesex, was among several men to be sent to Virginia (CBE 16).

JAMES FALKNER

James Falkner, a 20-year-old sailor from Yorkshire, England, came to Virginia in 1619 on the *Bona Nova*. He may have been a Virginia Company servant or tenant (FER 295).

EDWARD FALLOWES

Edward Fallowes came to Virginia on the *Hopewell* in 1623. On January 21, 1625, he was living in Chaplin's Choice (**56**) where he was a 30-year-old servant in the household of Walter Price and Henry Turner (CBE 51).

ROGER FARBRACKE (FARBRASE)

Roger Farbracke (Farbrase) came to Virginia on the *Elizabeth* in 1621 and on February 16, 1624, was living in Elizabeth City. In early 1625 he was still there and was identified as a 26-year-old servant in the household of William and Francis Cole, on the west side of the Hampton River (**18**) (CBE 44, 63).

HUMPHREY FARLEY (FAIRLEY)

Humphrey Farley (Fairley), who was born in Worcestershire, was a grocer in the St. Stephen Walbrook area of London. He became a Virginia trader and in August 1626 shipped marketable goods to Virginia on the *Marmaduke*. A year later he dispatched another shipment from London to Virginia, this time on the *Samuell*. In November 1628 the justices of the General Court ordered Humphrey Farley of London to prove that he owned John Dimmocke, one of the servants being used by Thomas Farley at his Archer's Hope plantation (**6**). On May 26, 1633, Humphrey Farley was part of a group that sent a petition to the Privy Council, alleging that Governor John Harvey and his council were trying to make Maurice (Morris) Thompson and his associates the sole shippers of the tobacco exported from Virginia. The following year he and some Virginia planters, who said that they had had families in the colony for several years, stated that they feared significant financial losses if Thompson was given a shipping monopoly. In October 1635 Humphrey Farley was identified as a 41-year-old trader in Virginia tobacco. As Humphrey and Thomas Farley were from Worcestershire and did business together, they probably were kinsmen, perhaps brothers. It is unclear whether Humphrey Farley ever settled in Virginia (CBE 73, 80, 115-116; MCGC 178; G&M 187-188; EAE 55-56).

***
THOMAS FARLEY (FAIRLEY)

Thomas Farley or Fairley arrived in Jamestown (1) on the *Ann* on September 5, 1623, and was described as a gentleman from Worcestershire. On February 16, 1624, Thomas, his wife, Jane, and their daughter, Ann, were living in Archer's Hope (6). The Farleys were still there on February 4, 1625. Thomas, a household head, had a dwelling of his own and was relatively well supplied with stored food and defensive weaponry. He also had some livestock. In January 1625 Thomas Farley sought the General Court's assistance in recovering funds from Rowland Loftis so that he could pay his own debt to Stephen Webb. In November 1625 he made arrangements to sign a 6-year lease for some land in Archer's Hope, property that had descended to Ensign William Spence's young orphaned daughter, Sara. Farley indicated that he had cleared part of the Spence land and built a house prior to securing a lease from Mrs. Susan Bush, Sara Spence's guardian. In August 1626 Thomas Farley was summoned to court and fined for failing to attend church and for hunting hogs on Jamestown Island on Sundays. He also was reprimanded for making a resentful remark about being fined. Later in the year, Thomas Farley's Archer's Hope neighbor, Joseph Johnson, threatened him with bodily harm because Farley's hogs had damaged his corn crop. Court testimony in November 1628 reveals that Thomas Farley was associated with Humphrey Farley of London, who had provided him with servants. Both men were from Worcestershire and probably were kinsmen. In 1630 Thomas Farley served as a burgess for territory that stretched from Archer's Hope to Martin's Hundred (7) and included the settlers in Harrop. His dwelling in Archer's Hope was mentioned in January 1632, when two men went there by boat to collect the tobacco he owed as taxes. The following month he served as Archer's Hope's burgess. On May 26, 1634, Thomas Farley and some other planters sent a petition to the Privy Council, expressing their concern about what would happen if Maurice Thompson and his associates were made the sole shippers of Virginia tobacco (MCGC 6, 38-40, 76, 107-108, 123, 178, 201; CBE 41, 58, 115-116; HEN 1:148, 154; G&M 187-188; DOR 1:37).

JANE FARLEY (FAIRLEY) (MRS. THOMAS FARLEY [FAIRLEY])

In 1623, Jane, the wife of Thomas Farley (Fairley), came to Virginia on the *Ann* with her husband and daughter, Ann. On February 16, 1624, the Farleys were living in Archer's Hope (6). A muster taken on February 4, 1625, indicates that Mrs. Jane Farley was still there with her husband and daughter (CBE 41, 58).

ANN FARLEY

In 1623 Ann, the daughter of Thomas and Jane Farley (Fairley), came to Virginia on the *Ann*. On February 16, 1624, she and her parents were living in Archer's Hope (6). A muster taken on February 4, 1625, indicates that Ann and her parents were still residing there (CBE 41, 58).

***

HENRY FARMAN ALIAS GURNER

On February 5, 1620, the justices of Bridewell Court decided that Henry Farman alias Gurner, a vagrant, would be sent to Virginia (CBE 18).

CHARLES FARMER (HARMER?)

On February 16, 1624, Charles Farmer was living on the Eastern Shore. It is likely that this individual was Lady Elizabeth Dale's overseer, Charles Harmer, who was then living on the Eastern Shore but whose name was omitted from the 1624 census (CBE 46).

HENRY FARMER (FARMOR)

On February 16, 1624, Henry Farmer (Farmor) was a servant in William Peirce's household in urban Jamestown (1) (CBE 38).

THOMAS FARMER

Thomas Farmer, an ancient planter, came to Virginia on the *Trial* in 1616 and on February 16, 1624, was living in Bermuda Hundred (39). On January 24, 1625, when a muster was compiled of the community's inhabitants, Farmer was still there and was described as a 30-year-old household head. Although he lived alone, he was relatively well supplied with stored food and defensive weaponry. Thomas Farmer served as a burgess in the March 1630 session of the colony's assembly, representing the community of settlers then residing on the College Land (66) in Henrico and in Bermuda Hundred (CBE 35, 54; HEN 1:147).

THOMAS FARNARCQUE

Locksmith Thomas Farnarcque, his wife, and seven children were among the Walloons and French who indicated their willingness to go to Virginia. In August 1621 the Virginia Company agreed that they could immigrate (CBE 25-26).

CHARLES FARNBY

On October 3, 1618, Bridewell's justices decided that a boy named Charles Farnby would be detained until he could be sent to Virginia (HUME 7).

THOMAS FARNBY

On October 3, 1618, Bridewell's justices decided to send Thomas Farnby, a vagrant who was being detained, to Virginia (CBE 10).

ROBERT FARNELL

Robert Farnell was living at the College (66) on February 16, 1624, when a census was compiled (CBE 35).

JOHN FARRAR (FERRAR)

On February 16, 1624, John Farrar was listed among those who had died in Elizabeth City (17, 18) since April 1623 (CBE 45).

THOMAS FARRAR (FERRAR)

On May 13, 1620, the justices of Bridewell court decided that Thomas Farrar (Ferrar) was to be sent to Virginia (CBE 20).

***

WILLIAM FARRAR (FERRAR, FERRER) I

William Farrar (Ferrar, Ferrer) I came to Virginia on the *Neptune* in 1618, the vessel that brought Lord Delaware to the colony. He was a kinsman of Nicholas Ferrar Sr., a merchant and prominent Virginia Company

investor. On June 17, 1619, Company officials authorized Captain William Wye to take the *Garland* of London to Bermuda, where it was to leave 130 passengers and then continue on to Virginia to deliver 40 people. The *Garland's* captain was to take the prospective Virginia colonists to William Farrar, a Virginia Company shareholder, if he was in Virginia at that time. Farrar established a particular (or private) plantation on the Appomattox River somewhat inland from Bermuda Hundred (39), sometime prior to the March 22, 1622, Indian attack, which claimed 10 of his settlers' lives. Afterward, he relocated to Jordan's Journey (46), one of the positions strengthened and held after the Indian assault, and moved into the home of Cisley Jordan, a young widow whose late husband's estate he was settling. Controversy surrounding the unwed couple's living arrangements, termed "scandalous," was fueled by a breach-of-promise suit filed by the Rev. Grivel Pooley, who claimed that Mrs. Jordan had promised to marry him. As it was the General Court's first case of that kind, Virginia's governing officials took witnesses' testimony and then sought advice from England.

On February 16, 1624, William Farrar and Cisley Jordan were sharing a home, and when a muster was taken of Jordan's Journey's inhabitants on January 21, 1625, they were still there. William Farrar was described as age 31 and Mrs. Jordan was 24. Together they had 10 servants and were well supplied with stored food and defensive weaponry. After Grivel Pooley withdrew his lawsuit and promised that he would make no further claim, William Farrar and Cisley Jordan were wed. In May 1625, when a list of patented land was sent back to England, Farrar was credited with 100 acres on the Appomattox River, the acreage he had been occupying in March 1622. In March 1626 William Farrar was named to the Council of State, and later in the year he was designated a commissioner of the monthly courts for the "Upper Parts," held at Jordan's Journey and Shirley Hundred (41), to settle petty disputes in the communities west of Flowerdew Hundred (53). He served as a commissioner for several years and on occasion interviewed local citizens whose litigation was pending before the General Court. William Farrar continued to live at Jordan's Journey with his wife, Cisley. In January 1627 he was ordered to make an accounting of the Society of Berkeley Hundred's cattle and interviewed those who had custody of them. In March 1629 he patented 100 acres of land on the Eastern Shore, obtaining it on the basis of two headrights, and quickly transferred his acreage to William Andrews. One of William Farrar's duties as a councilor was to find men to plant at Chiskiack (**30-38**), on the York River frontier. In July 1631 he was among the planters who sent a petition to England, asking for relief from customs duties. Toward the end of the year he went to England and sold his interest in some inherited property, a transaction that makes reference to his wife, Cisley, and children Cisley II and William II. William Farrar returned to Virginia and died before June 11, 1637, when his son and heir, William II, received a patent for land adjoining what became known as Farrar Island, the site of Henricus (**63**), a settlement established by Sir Thomas Dale. The Farrar couple also had a son named John (VCR 3:145, 324, 566; 4:218-220, 554; CJS 2:301; CBE 36, 51; MCGC 41, 57, 106, 113-114, 134, 149, 188, 193; HEN 1:137, 140, 147, 153, 168, 178, 202; G&M 165; PB 1 Pt. 1:436; DOR 1:16, 926-928).

CISLEY (CICELEY, CECILY, SYSELY, SISLEY) JORDAN (JORDAIN, JORDEN, JERDEN) FARRAR (FERRAR, FERRER) (MRS. SAMUEL JORDAN [JORDAIN, JORDEN, JERDEN], MRS. WILLIAM FARRAR [FERRAR, FERRER]) (SEE CISLEY [CICELEY, CECILY, SYSELY, SISLEY] JORDAN [JORDAIN, JORDEN, JERDEN]) CISLEY (CICELEY, CECILY, SYSELY, SISLEY) FARRAR (FERRAR, FERRER) II

On September 6, 1631, when William Farrar (Ferrar, Ferrer) sold some property in England to his brother Henry, he made reference to his wife Cisley, daughter Cisley II, and son William II (DOR 1:927).

JOHN FARRAR (FERRAR, FERRER)

On October 1, 1649, William Farrar (Ferrar, Ferrer) II, his late father's heir, gave part of his land to his own brother, John, who sur-

vived until at least February 1, 1678 (DOR 1:929-930).

WILLIAM FARRAR (FERRAR, FERRER) II

On June 27, 1637, William Farrar (Ferrar, Ferrer) II, as his late father's heir, received a patent for 2,000 acres in Henrico County, adjoining what became known as Farrar (formerly Henricus [**63**]) Island. As he was an adult when he gave part of his land to his brother, John, on October 1, 1649, he probably was born around 1627–1628 (PB 1 Pt. 1:436; DOR 1:929).

***

GARRET FARREL

On March 22, 1622, Garret Farrel was killed at Westover (**54**), when the Indians attacked Owen Macar's house (VCR 3:568).

INGRAM FARRES

On January 24, 1629, Ingram Farres served on the jury that convened in Jamestown (**1**) and tried William Reade for mortally wounding John Burrows (MCGC 184).

EDWARD FARRIER

On February 29, 1619, it was decided that Edward Farrier, a boy brought into Bridewell Court, would be detained until he could be sent to Virginia (HUME 22).

NICHOLAS FATRICE

Nicholas Fatrice died sometime after April 1623 but before February 16, 1624, at one of the plantations on the lower side of the James River (**8-15**) within the corporation of James City (CBE 41).

EDWARD FAUCET

On February 27, 1622, Virginia Company officials noted that Edward Faucet had assigned three shares of Virginia land to Nicholas Ferrar (VCR 1:608).

THOMAS FAULKNER

Thomas Faulkner came to Virginia on the *Mary Providence* in 1622 and on February 16, 1624, was living in Elizabeth City.

When a muster was taken in early 1625, Thomas was identified as a 28-year-old servant in the household of Robert and John Salford, who resided within the territory on the west side of the Hampton River (**18**), between Blunt Point (**22**) and Newportes News (**24**) (CBE 43, 65).

JAMES FAULKONER

On March 22, 1622, when the Indians attacked the settlers living at the College (Arrohattock) (**66**), James Faulkoner was killed (VCR 3:566).

GEORGE FAWDON (FADOM, SHEDAM)

On November 1, 1624, George Fawdon (Fadom, Shedam) informed the General Court that on July 4, 1624, he had assisted John Phillimore by writing his will and that the testator had bequeathed him a pig. All who testified about Phillimore's will were residents of Jamestown Island (**1**) or the Neck O'Land (**5**), raising the possibility that George Fawdon lived in one of those two areas. On February 8, 1628, George and two other men received permission to move to Warresqueak (**26**). On June 26, 1635, he patented some land on the Nansemond River (**29**) adjacent to Richard Bennett's property. When James Rocke, a Warresqueak planter, made his will, he indicated that when he set sail for Virginia in January 1649, he designated Captain George Fawdon as his attorney. Fawdon witnessed deeds and other legal documents and conveyed some Isle of Wight (formerly Warresqueak) County land to others during the 1640s. He died sometime prior to July 9, 1655 (MCGC 27, 165; PB 1 Pt. 1:186; EEAC 48; SR 4107; Isle of Wight Record Book A).

WILLIAM FAWNE

William Fawne came to Virginia on the *Hopewell* in 1633 at the expense of Adam Thorogood, who used his headright when patenting some land on June 24, 1635 (PB 1 Pt. 1:179).

HENRY FEARNE

On February 16, 1624, Henry Fearne was listed among those who had died in Elizabeth City (**17, 18**) sometime after April 1623 (CBE 45).

JAMES FEATS (FEATH)

On January 29, 1620, the justices of Bridewell Court decided that James Feats (Feath) would be detained until he could be sent to Virginia (CBE 18).

GEORGE FEDAM

George Fedam reportedly died at the Neck O'Land (**5**) sometime after April 1623 but before February 16, 1624. The possibility exists that George was erroneously reported dead and that he actually was the George Fawdon who was associated with Jamestown Island (**1**) and the Neck O'Land later in the year and who moved to Warresqueak (**26**) in 1628 (CBE 35).

HENRY (HENRIE) FEELDES (SEE HENRY [HENRIE] FIELD [FIELDS, FEELDES])

[NO FIRST NAME] FELGATE (FELLGATE)

Sometime after March 1622 but before 1624, a Mr. Felgate (Fellgate) was present at Kecoughtan (**17, 18**) when Michael Fuller, whose small boat was blown across the James River in a storm, made his way back. Felgate accompanied Fuller when he rescued his companions. On September 11, 1626, Mr. Felgate, who was still associated with the Elizabeth City area, testified in court that Mrs. Joan Wright, an accused witch, had accurately predicted his wife's death (CJS 2:319; MCGC 159).

[NO FIRST NAME] FELGATE (FELLGATE)

On January 14, 1628, Captain Felgate (Fellgate) was fined for failing to appear before the General Court despite being summoned by the provost marshal. It is uncertain which Captain Felgate (Robert or Tobias) had ignored the summons (MCGC 159).

JOHN FELGATE (FELLGATE)

On November 13, 1633, John Felgate (Fellgate) and Thomas Rey witnessed the will made by William Parke, who died in Virginia. On December 23, 1635, Felgate received a patent for 1,200 acres in Chequers (Checkerhouse) Neck on the

Chickahominy River, within James City County (SH 15; PB 1 Pt.1:328).

***

ROBERT FELGATE (FELLGATE)

Sea captain Robert Felgate (Fellgate), the brother of Tobias and William Felgate, left England on the *Garland* and arrived in Bermuda in November 1619, having survived a hurricane. According to Captain John Smith, Robert Felgate was Bermuda governor Nathaniel Butler's lieutenant general. In 1620 he served on Bermuda's Council of State and held the rank of captain. He returned to England and on July 31, 1627, shipped goods from London to Virginia on the *Hopewell*. He also served as captain of the *Saker* in 1627 when it brought an African servant to William Ewin's plantation (**13**). Robert Felgate settled in Virginia and in 1629 was named administrator of Lieutenant Giles Allington's estate. In October 1629 when the Virginia assembly convened, Robert Felgate served as a burgess for the plantations on "other side of the water," what is now Surry County. He was returned to the assembly in March 1630 and was among those called on to inspect the site at Old Point Comfort where a fort was to be built. Captain Robert Felgate moved to Warresqueak (**26**) and served as a commissioner of the monthly court. On April 25, 1632, he received a patent for 350 acres at Chiskiack (**31**), adjacent to Captain John West's plantation (**32**), using as headrights his son, himself, and four servants. In time, the Felgate plantation became known as Ringfield. Robert Felgate married a woman named Isabella (Sibella), who after being widowed successively wed George Beach (Beech) and Nicholas Martiau (CJS 2:375, 389; CBE 79; DOR 2:504; MCGC 197; HEN 1:138, 148, 150, 187; PB 1 Pt.1:104; 2:301).

ISABELLA (SIBELLA) FELGATE (FELLGATE) (MRS. ROBERT FELGATE [FELLGATE]) (SEE ISABELLA [SIBELLA] FELGATE [FELLGATE] MARTIAU)

When John Perines (Perins) patented some land on April 3, 1651, he used the headrights of Captain Robert Felgate (Fellgate) and his wife, Isabella (Sibella), noting that after Robert Felgate died,

Isabella married George Beech (Beach) and then Nicholas Martiau (PB 2L301; DOR 2:504).

TOBIAS (TOBY) FELGATE (FELLGATE)

In July 1619 the Society of Berkeley Hundred's investors hired Tobias (Toby) Felgate (Fellgate), an experienced mariner from Ratcliffe, England, to take their settlers to Virginia to seat at Berkeley Hundred (**55**). He set sail on September 15, 1619, on the *Margaret* of Bristol. Captain Felgate, whose brothers were Robert and William Felgate, acquired some Virginia land from brother William in May 1622. Tobias Felgate set out for the colony on July 17, 1622, as master of the *James* of London, which was transporting a large group of passengers. On April 30, 1623, when he rebutted Bermuda Governor Nathaniel Butler's allegations about conditions in Virginia, he testified that he had been to the colony five times as the master of ships and could speak from firsthand experience. In November 1626 he brought a shipment of goods to the colony on the *James*, commodities London merchant Edward Bennett sent to Richard Bennett, who paid in Virginia tobacco. By February 8, 1628, Felgate had married Elizabeth, Jamestown (**1**) merchant Ralph Hamor's widow and the administrator of his estate. Tobias Felgate continued to ply the Atlantic and in January 1632 was identified as captain of the *Defense*, which took aboard Thomas Farley's tobacco. Tobias's wife, Elizabeth, died sometime prior to March 30, 1630, when he married Sarah Price in England. Felgate was identified as a mariner on April 25, 1632, when he patented 150 acres of land at Chiskiack (**32**), adjacent to the property of his brother Robert. Tobias Felgate's patent states that he had received his acreage by virtue of a December 7, 1630, court order. On July 26, 1634, Felgate was identified as master of the *Defense* (*Defiance*), which was then making a trip from London to Virginia. Later in the year, he became very ill while he was at Westover (**54**). When he made a nuncupative will on December 24, 1634, he named as heirs wife Sarah, their daughter, Sarah, and their son, William. Tobias Felgate lived only eight days after making his will. His widow, Sarah, who was in England, was named his administrator. Tobias Felgate's will was presented to probate officials in London on April 23, 1635 (VCR 2:17, 98; 3:178, 199, 231, 386; MCGC 124, 165, 201; CBE 79, 118; EAE 19; PB 1 Pt.1:105; SH 19; EEAC 21; SR 3972; DOR 1:700).

ELIZABETH FULLER CLEMENTS HAMOR FELGATE (FELLGATE) (MRS. JEFFREY CLEMENTS, MRS. RALPH HAMOR [HAMER], MRS. TOBIAS FELGATE [FELLGATE]) (SEE ELIZABETH FULLER CLEMENTS, ELIZABETH FULLER CLEMENTS HAMOR [HAMER])

Elizabeth Hamor was widowed twice prior to October 11, 1626, at which time she was named administratrix of the estate that had belonged to her late husband, Ralph Hamor, a merchant and resident of urban Jamestown (1). By February 8, 1628, Elizabeth had married Tobias Felgate (Fellgate). Because she intended to go to England, she was released from her bond as administratrix, and George Menefie agreed to finish settling the late Ralph Hamor's estate. Elizabeth died sometime prior to March 30, 1630, at which time Tobias Felgate remarried (MCGC 117, 165; SR 3972; DOR 1:700).

SARAH PRICE FELGATE (FELLGATE) I (MRS. TOBIAS FELGATE [FELLGATE])

On March 30, 1630, Sarah Price married mariner Tobias Felgate (Fellgate), who was in England. Together, they produced a son, William, and a daughter, Sarah II. On December 24, 1634, when Captain Tobias Felgate was at Westover (54), he made his will, naming wife Sarah as his executrix. He made bequests to her and to his son, William, and daughter, Sarah. Mrs. Sarah Felgate was named as her husband's reversionary heir (SR 3972; DOR 700).

SARAH FELGATE (FELLGATE) II

On December 24, 1634, when Tobias Felgate (Fellgate) of Westover (54) made his will, he named his daughter, Sarah II, as one of his beneficiaries and left her £250 on the day of her marriage. Sarah was the daughter of Tobias and Sarah Felgate I, who

wed in England on March 30, 1630. Thus, she was very young when her father died (SR 3972; SH 19; EEAC 21; DOR 1:700).

WILLIAM FELGATE (FELLGATE) II

On December 24, 1634, when Captain Tobias Felgate (Fellgate) was at Westover (54), he became ill, made his will, and died a short time later. One of the beneficiaries he named was his eldest son, William II (SR 3972; SH 19; EEAC 21; DOR 1:700).

WILLIAM FELGATE (FELLGATE)

William Felgate (Fellgate), the brother of mariners Robert and Tobias Felgate, was a London merchant and investor in the Virginia Company. In 1618 he received some shares of land in Bermuda, within the section known as Warwicks Tribe. On May 20, 1622, he assigned to his brother Tobias his interest in some Virginia land. William Felgate was then identified as a citizen of London and a skinner. Two months later, on May 20, 1622, William set out for Virginia on the *James*, bringing seven men. He apparently returned to England within a short time, for on July 4, 1623, he was identified as a subscriber for the relief of the colony. On July 19, 1627, William Felgate again shipped goods from London to Virginia, this time aboard the *James*. In September 1632 a ship in which he, Maurice Thompson, and some other merchants had an interest, was lost at sea while loaded with tobacco (CJS 2:276, 371; VCR 2:17; 4:245-246; FER 400; CBE 79; EAE 31).

***

HENRY FELL

Henry Fell, an Oxford University student, arrived in Jamestown (1) on September 12, 1623, on the *Bonny Bess* and took the oath of supremacy. He was from Christchurch in Oxford. Henry died in Jamestown sometime prior to February 16, 1624 (MCGC 6; CBE 39).

JOHN FELLS

On May 14, 1623, the Virginia Company of London gave John Fells a patent for some land in the colony (VCR 2:428).

RICHARD FENN

On February 16, 1624, Richard Fenn was living on the lower side of the James River, within the corporation of James City and west of Grays Creek. He resided at Paces Paines (9) or neighboring Burrows Hill (8) (CBE 40).

ROBERT FENNELL

On February 16, 1624, when a census was made of the colony's inhabitants, Robert Fennell was living on the Eastern Shore. In early 1625, when demographic records were compiled, it was noted that he had come to Virginia on the *Charles* in 1624 and was a 20-year-old servant in the household headed by Charles Harman (Harmar), whose acreage was on Old Plantation Creek (73). Harmer was the overseer of Lady Elizabeth Dale's plantation (CBE 46, 69).

JOHN FENNER

On February 15, 1619, Virginia Company officials noted that Captain John Fenner was taking Sir Edward Zouch's ship, the *Silver Falcon*, to Virginia (VCR 3:135).

***

WILLIAM FENNINGE

On January 17, 1620, William Fenninge of the *Abigail*, a mariner from East Smithfield, Middlesex, who was preparing to set sail for Virginia, made his will. He named wife, Margaret, as his executrix and principal heir. Fenninge died overseas and on July 7, 1623, his will was proved at St. Butolph Aldgate, London. His widow, Margaret, was then authorized to settle his estate in England and in Virginia (EEAC 21; WAT 441).

MARGARET FENNINGE (MRS. WILLIAM FENNINGE)

Mariner William Fenninge, who made his will on January 17, 1620, on the eve of his departure for Virginia on the *Abigail*, designated his wife, Margaret, his executrix and principal heir. She presented his will for probate on July 7, 1623, at St. Butolph Aldgate, London (EEAC 21; WAT 441).

***

[NO FIRST NAME] FENTON

The Reverend Mr. Fenton died in Elizabeth City (18, 19) sometime after February 16, 1624, but before the first part of 1625, when a muster was compiled (CBE 67).

FRANCIS FENTON

In November 1628 Francis Fenton and John Southern of Jamestown (1) appeared before the General Court and proved Thomas Gregory's will. Gregory was purser of the *Saker* (MCGC 178).

JAMES FENTON

James Fenton died in Elizabeth City (17, 18) sometime after April 1623 but before February 16, 1624 (CBE 45).

MATTHIAS (MATT, MATTATHIAS) FENTON

Matthias (Matt, Mattathias) Fenton died intestate sometime prior to January 3, 1626. When his goods were appraised, they were found to be worth 80 pounds of tobacco. Mrs. Emerson, perhaps Ann, the wife of Ellis Emerson of Martin's Hundred (7), was ordered to pay the decedent's debts to Mr. Stephens and Captain West. However, Fenton's other creditors were advised to collect their debts from his friends in England, not Mrs. Emerson. This raises the possibility that Mrs. Emerson was Fenton's kinswoman or his employer (MCGC 84).

ROBERT FENTON

Robert Fenton arrived on Jamestown Island (1) in 1607 and was one of the first colonists. He survived until at least 1608, when he co-authored a verse that Captain John Smith included in his *General History* (CJS 1:197; 2:141, 153).

JOHN FERBAS

On February 27, 1619, the justices of Bridewell Court decided that John Ferbas, a boy, would be sent to Virginia (HUME 8).

RICHARD FEREBY (FERRIBY)

In September 1620 Richard Fereby (Ferriby), a gentleman, set sail from Bristol on the *Supply* and was among those accompanying William Tracy to Berkeley Hundred (**55**). Fereby was supposed to serve a certain number of years in exchange for some acreage. He arrived in Berkeley Hundred on January 29, 1621, but when the Indians attacked the settlement on March 22, 1622, he was slain (CBE 20-21; VCR 3:396, 426, 567).

ROBERT FERNALL

Robert Fernall came to Virginia in 1619 aboard the *London Merchant*. On February 4, 1625, he was described as a 31-year-old indentured servant at Captain Samuel Mathews' plantation (**15**) in Tappahannah (CBE 60).

JOHN FERNE

On December 2, 1619, John Ferne of London, a yeoman, prepared a will in which he bequeathed to his sons John, James, and Daniel all of his land in Virginia. He also left Daniel some acreage he owned in the Somers Isles (Bermuda). John Ferne's will was presented for probate on January 7, 1620. Captain John Smith identified him as an adventurer in the Virginia Company (EEAC 21; WAT 623; CBE 16; CJS 2:276).

THOMAS FERNLEY

On February 27, 1619, the justices of Bridewell Court decided that Thomas Fernley, a boy, would be sent to Virginia. He was one of the children rounded up from the streets of London so that they could be sent to the colony. When a census of Virginia's inhabitants was made on February 16, 1624, Fernley was listed among those who had died at Bermuda Hundred (**39**) sometime after April 1623 (CBE 13, 36).

GEORGE FERRIS (FERRYS)

On March 4, 1628, George Ferris (Ferrys) shipped some goods from Barnstaple to Virginia on the *Pleasure* of Bideford. Then, on November 4, 1633, he sent another shipment from Barnstaple to Virginia on the *George* (CBE 82, 108).

THOMAS FERRIS

On March 22, 1622, when the Indians attacked Edward Bennett's plantation (**26**) in Warresqueak, Thomas Ferris was slain (VCR 3:571).

JOHN FETHERSTON

On February 16, 1624, John Fetherston was listed among those who had died at Flowerdew Hundred (**53**) since April 1623 (CBE 37).

RICHARD FETHERSTONE (FEATHERSTONE)

Richard Fetherstone (Featherstone), a gentleman, came to Virginia in January 1608 in the 1st Supply of Jamestown (**1**) colonists. He accompanied Captain John Smith on two exploratory journeys within the Chesapeake Bay. Fetherstone became fatally ill while on a trip to the Rappahannock River. He died there and was buried at a site Smith called Featherstone's Bay (CJS 1:223-224, 230, 232; 2:161, 163, 170, 174-175).

***

MICHAEL FETTIPLACE (PHETTIPLACE)

Michael Fettiplace (Phettiplace), a gentleman who arrived in Virginia in January 1608 in the 1st Supply of new settlers, accompanied Captain John Smith on an exploratory voyage into the Pamunkey River in late December 1608. Fettiplace also went with Smith to Powhatan's York River village, Werowocomoco, and returned overland to Jamestown (**1**). In 1620 Smith identified Michael Fettiplace as a Virginia Company investor and credited him and his brother, William, with co-authoring a verse that lauded Smith (CJS 1:222, 317-318, 432; 2:193, 206, 229-230, 244, 260, 276).

WILLIAM FETTIPLACE (PHETTIPLACE)

In January 1608 William Fettiplace (Phettiplace), a gentleman, arrived in Virginia in the 1st Supply of new colonists. On December 29, 1608, he left Jamestown (**1**) and accompanied Captain John Smith on a trading voyage to Pamunkey. Smith placed him in charge of the pinnace in which they traveled. Fettiplace also went with Captain Christopher Newport to see Powhatan at Werowocomoco on the York River. Smith mentioned Fettiplace when he wrote an account of New England in 1622. The two men's admiration apparently was mutual, for William Fettiplace and his brother,

Michael, produced a narrative that Smith found useful. On July 17, 1622, Virginia Company officials identified William Fettiplace as an ancient planter and awarded him a patent for 100 acres in exchange for the funds he had invested with Sir Thomas Smith (CJS 1:216, 243, 251, 432; 2:193, 200, 203, 207, 229-230; VCR 2:97).

***

ALEXANDER FFALERN

On December 31, 1619, the justices of Bridewell decided that Alexander Ffalern, a boy, would be detained until he could be sent to Virginia (HUME 16).

DAVID FFEND

On January 22, 1619, David Ffend, a boy, was brought before the justices of Bridewell, who decided that he would be detained until he could be sent to Virginia (HUME 19).

JOHN FFURTER

On July 26, 1628, the justices of Bridewell decided to send John Ffurter, a boy from Vintrey Ward or Bethlem, to Virginia (HUME 33).

HENRY (HENRIE) FIELD (FIELDS, FEELDES)

Henry (Henrie) Field (Fields, Feeldes) came to Virginia on the *Jacob* in 1624. In early 1625 he was living within the corporation of Elizabeth City (**18**) and was a 26-year-old servant in the home of Thomas Purfray (Purfoy), on the west side of the Hampton River (CBE 64).

JAMES FIELD

James Field came to Virginia in 1624 on the *Swan*. In early 1625 he was living in Elizabeth City (**18**), where he was a 20-year-old indentured servant in the household jointly headed by ancient planter Mihell (Michael) Wilcockes and John Slater (CBE 64).

THOMAS FIELD

Thomas Field, an apothecary, arrived in Virginia in 1608 in the 2nd Supply of new colonists. He would have lived in Jamestown (**1**) (CJS 2:162).

WILLIAM FIELD

William Field came to Virginia on the *Charles* in 1621 and on February 4, 1625, was living on the lower side of the James River, within the corporation of James City. Field was then identified as a 23-year-old servant on the plantation of Captain Samuel Mathews (**15**) (CBE 60).

THOMAS FILENST

On February 16, 1624, Thomas Filenst was living at Flowerdew Hundred (**53**), where he appears to have been an indentured servant (CBE 37).

JOHN FILMER

John Filmer was living in the Neck O'Land (**5**) behind Jamestown Island on February 16, 1624, and appears to have been an indentured servant in the household headed by Richard Kingsmill (CBE 35).

CATHERINE (KATHERINE) FINCH

Catherine (Katherine) Finch, a young maid who came to Virginia on the *Marmaduke* in 1621, was born in Mardens Parish in Herfordshire. As her parents were dead, she was reared by her brother Erasmus, who lived in the Strand and was a crossbow-maker in service to the King. Catherine's other brother, Edward Finch, was a locksmith in St. Clement's Parish. By January 1625 Catherine may have married ancient planter Robert Fisher (FER 306, 309).

HENRY FINCH

On October 29, 1630, Henry Finch, Sir John Finch's brother, was made a councilor and Secretary of the Colony. He retained both positions during 1632 and 1633, but around December 7, 1633, was turned out of office (G&M 157; HEN 1:153, 202; MCGC 480).

THOMAS FINCH

Thomas Finch, who by April 14, 1623, was dead, was described as the brother (probably a brother-in-law, stepbrother, or half-brother) of Mr. Bland and Christopher Davison, a resident of Jamestown (**1**) and secretary of the colony (VCR 4:115-116; SAIN 1:43).

WILLIAM FINCH (FINCHE)

In September 1620 William Finch (Finche), his wife, Margaret, and their daughter, Frances, set sail from Bristol on the *Supply*. They accompanied William Tracy to Berkeley Hundred (**55**), arriving there on January 29, 1621. William Finch had agreed to be a Berkeley Hundred tenant for three years in exchange for an allotment of land. He died sometime prior to August 1622 and his widow, Margaret, married John Flood (CBE 21; VCR 3:396-397, 426, 674).

MARGARET FINCH (FINCHE) (MRS. WILLIAM FINCH [FINCHE], MRS. JOHN FLOOD [FLUD, FLUDD, FLOYD])

Margaret Finch (Finche), her husband William, and their daughter, Frances, left Bristol on the *Supply* in September 1620 and were bound for Berkeley Hundred (**55**). The Finches arrived at their destination on January 29, 1621. William Finch, a Berkeley Hundred tenant, died sometime prior to August 1622, by which time the widowed Margaret Finch had married ancient planter John Flood (Flud, Fludd, Floyd). On January 21, 1625, John and Margaret Finch Flood were residing at Jordan's Journey (**46**), where he was a household head. The family included her young daughter, Frances Finch, and the couple's 3-week-old son, William Flood (CBE 21, 28, 52; VCR 3:396-397, 426; DOR 1:18).

FRANCES (FRANCIS) FINCH (FINCHE)

In September 1620 Frances (Francis) Finch (Finche) left Bristol, England, on the *Supply* with her parents, William and Margaret Finch. The Finches were headed for Berkeley Hundred (**55**) with William Tracy, the settlement's leader. Frances and her parents arrived at their destination on January 29, 1621. Her father died sometime prior to August 1622 and her mother, Margaret, married John Flood (Flud, Fludd, Floyd). On January 21, 1625, the Floods, Frances Finch, who was said to be age 3, and her infant half-brother, William Flood, were residing at Jordan's Journey (**46**). As Francis Finch came to Virginia in 1620, she would have been at least 5 years old in January

1625 (CBE 21, 28, 52; VCR 3:396-397, 426; DOR 1:18).

***

RICHARD FINE

On January 25, 1625, Richard Fine, who came to Virginia on the *Neptune*, was living at Mulberry Island (**21**). He was a household head and was equipped with defensive weaponry (CBE 57; DOR 1:47).

RICHARD FIRMLEY

On January 3, 1625, Richard Firmley was identified as one of the Society of Berkeley Hundred's men (**55**) who was temporarily living at Shirley Hundred (**41**) (MCGC 42).

RICHARD FIRTH

Richard Firth, at gentleman, arrived in Virginia in 1607 and was one of the first Jamestown (**1**) settlers. Captain John Smith identified Firth as an investor in the Virginia Company (CJS 2:142, 276).

EDWARD FISH

On December 5, 1625, the justices of the General Court ordered John Proctor of Pace's Paines (**9**) to pay Mr. Perry (William Perry, also of Paces Paines) for the loss of his shallop. Peter Busbey testified that while the shallop was headed downstream, loaded with passengers and a cargo of tobacco, Edward Fish asked his fellow passengers to help him catch a duck. As a result, the shallop became unbalanced and capsized or ran aground and was lost. Edward Fish probably was one of John Proctor's servants (MCGC 78).

[NO FIRST NAME] FISHER

On September 18, 1626, the justices of the General Court were informed that around August 26, 1625, Mrs. Fisher and John Southern were seen walking along, staggering drunkenly, near the widowed Mrs. Henry Southey's house on Jamestown Island (**1**). Mrs. Fisher reportedly was so inebriated that she tripped over a sheep or cow and fell down. She may have been the widow of Thomas Fisher, who died in Jamestown between April 1623 and February 16, 1624 (MCGC 115; CBE 39).

***

EDWARD FISHER

On February 16, 1624, Edward Fisher was living on the Maine or Pasbehay (3), just west of Jamestown Island. On January 30, 1625, when a muster was made of that area's inhabitants, he was identified as head of a household that included his wife, Sarah, her 6-year-old son, Edward Kidall, and 10-year-old Clare Ren. The family was relatively well supplied with provisions and defensive weaponry. On January 16, 1626, Christopher Barker testified before the General Court that sometime prior to Christmas 1624 (that is, January 1625), when he had been at Kecoughtan (18), he had overheard Richard Stephens (a Jamestown merchant) and Edward Fisher talking about how Stephens hired Fisher to go on a 30-day trading voyage in his pinnace. At issue was Fisher's compensation. At some point, Edward Fisher and his wife, Sarah, lived in Jamestown (1). He was among the planters who on July 15, 1631, sent a petition to England, requesting relief from the customs fees then being levied on tobacco. Fisher's hogsheads of tobacco bore the mark *EF* (CBE 39, 57; MCGC 89-90, 93; G&M 165; DOR 1:26).

SARAH FISHER
(MRS. EDWARD FISHER,
MRS. [NO FIRST NAME] KIDALL
[KILDALE?])
(SEE SARAH KIDALL
[KILDALE, KILLDALE?])

Sarah, who married Edward Fisher, reportedly came to Virginia on the *Warwick*. On January 30, 1625, she was living in Pasbehay (3) with her husband, Edward, and her 6-year-old-son, Edward Kidall. Thus, Sarah was a widow who had remarried. Also part of the Fisher household in 1625 was 10-year-old Clare Ren. On February 4, 1626, Sarah Fisher testified in court that Peter Marten, when visiting the home she and her husband, Edward, shared in Jamestown (1), said that Richard Cornish (alias Williams) had been wrongfully executed. Therefore, during the mid-1620s the Fishers moved from Pasbehay to urban Jamestown or vice-versa (CBE 57; MCGC 93).

***

***

HENRY FISHER

On February 16, 1624, Henry Fisher and his wife and child were living at Jordan's Journey (46) (CBE 37).

MRS. HENRY FISHER

Mrs. Henry Fisher was living at Jordan's Journey (46) with her husband and child on February 16, 1624 (CBE 37).

[NO FIRST NAME] FISHER

Mr. and Mrs. Henry Fisher's child, whose name is unknown, was sharing their home at Jordan's Journey (46) on February 16, 1624 (CBE 37).

***

JAMES FISHER

On February 16, 1624, James Fisher was listed among those who had died at Warresqueak (26) sometime after April 1623. He reportedly had been killed (CBE 42).

JOHN FISHER

On September 19, 1618, John Fisher, a vagrant, was detained by the justices of Bridewell Court so that he could be sent to Virginia (CBE 10).

JOHN FISHER

On February 16, 1624, John Fisher was living on the Maine (3), just west of Jamestown Island. He may have been the vagrant sent to Virginia by the justices of Bridewell Court (CBE 39).

JOHN FISHER (FISSHER)

On February 16, 1624, John Fisher (Fissher), one of Captain William Eppes's servants, was living on the Eppes plantation (74) on the Eastern Shore. On July 7, 1634, when Fisher testified before the monthly court in Accomack, he indicated that he was 30 years old and identified himself as one of Eppes's former servants. When he made his will on December 4, 1639, he made a bequest to his son, John; the testator died before March 23, 1640 (CBE 46; AMES 1:21, 161-162).

***

ROBERT FISHER

Robert Fisher, an ancient planter, arrived in Virginia in May 1611 on the *Elsabeth* (*Elizabeth*). In December 1624 Robert Fisher filed a compensatory claim against the estate of Captain George Thorpe of Berkeley Hundred, who had perished in the March 1622 Indian attack. He claimed that Thorpe owed him payment for 5 weeks' work, building a house for Opechancanough, a project for which Sir George Yeardley also was owed funds. On January 21, 1625, Robert Fisher was living at Jordan's Journey (46), where he headed a household. He shared his home with his wife, Katherine (Catherine), and their 1-year-old daughter, Sisley (CBE 51; MCGC 36; S of N 43; DOR 1:17).

KATHERINE (CATHERINE) FISHER (MRS. ROBERT FISHER) (SEE CATHERINE [KATHERINE] FINCH)

On January 21, 1625, Katherine (Catherine), the wife of ancient planter Robert Fisher, was living at Jordan's Journey (46). She shared the family home with her husband and 1-year-old daughter, Sisley. The muster-taker noted that Katherine had come to Virginia on the *Marmaduke*, which had arrived in October 1621. This raises the possibility that she was the former Catherine Finch, one of the young maids who arrived aboard the *Marmaduke* in 1621, for she was the only one in the group who was named Catherine (CBE 51; FER 306, 309).

SISLEY FISHER

On January 21, 1625, Sisley Fisher, the 1-year-old daughter of Robert and Katherine (Catherine) Fisher, was living at Jordan's Journey (46) in her parents' home (CBE 51).

***

SAMUEL (SAMWELL) FISHER

On July 31, 1622, Samuel (Samwell) Fisher set sail for Virginia aboard the *James* at the expense of John Jefferson, a gentleman who owned 250 acres in Archer's Hope (6). Samuel was listed among those who had died on the lower side of the James River, within the corporation of James City (8-15), sometime after April 1623 but before February 16, 1624 (FER 400; CBE 39).

THOMAS FISHER

Thomas Fisher died in Jamestown (1) sometime after April 1623 but before February 16, 1624 (CBE 39).

NICHOLAS FISKINS

On February 6, 1627, Nicholas Fiskins patented some land in Accomack that was adjacent to Clement Dilk's and had been part of the Virginia Company's tract of Company Land (76) (PB 1: Pt. 1:76).

JOSEPH FITCH

Joseph Fitch was sent to Virginia in 1621 by the Company of Mercers. He was an apothecary and accompanied Dr. John Pott, who resided in urban Jamestown (1). Fitch was killed at Falling Creek (68) during the March 22, 1622, Indian attack (FER 297; VCR 3:468, 565).

MATHEW FITCH (FYTCH)

Mathew Fitch (Fyth), a mariner, was one of one of the first Jamestown (1) colonists. On May 20, 1607, he accompanied Captain Christopher Newport on an exploratory voyage of the James River. According to Captain John Smith, on June 13, 1607, Fitch was mortally wounded in Jamestown when he was shot in the chest by Indians (CJS 1:19; HAI 102, 117).

***

THOMAS FITCH

Thomas Fitch, who lived on the lower side of the James River at Pace's Paines (9), died sometime after February 16, 1624 but before February 4, 1625. Erica (Enecha) Fitch, Thomas's wife or kinswoman, died during the same period. On October 12, 1626, when Phetiplace Close was called on to testify about how John Proctor of Pace's Paines took care of his servants, he said that Proctor provided the Fitches with food, clothing, and medical care comparable to what other Virginia servants received. Close said that he lived in the same house as the Fitches and saw firsthand how Proctor treated them (CBE 60; MCGC 119).

ERICA (ENECHA) FITCH (MRS. THOMAS FITCH?)

Erica (Enecha) Fitch, who resided at Pace's Paines (**9**), died sometime after February 16, 1624 but before February 4, 1625. She and Thomas Fitch (perhaps her husband or kinsman) were servants in the household of John Proctor. On October 12, 1626, Phetiplace Close testified that the Fitches had received the same amount of food, clothing, and medical care from Proctor as other indentured servants did. Close indicated that he shared a house with the Fitches and was aware of how they were treated by Proctor (CBE 60; MCGC 119).

***

ROBERT FITT (FITTS)

Robert Fitt (Fitts) came to Virginia on the *George*. He witnessed Thomas Harralde's will in November 1623 and on February 16, 1624, was living in the rural part of Jamestown Island (**1**) with his wife, Ann (Anne). On January 24, 1625, the muster-taker credited Robert and Ann Fitt, who were still residing on Jamestown Island, with a house and some livestock. In May 1625 Robert Fitt was fined for drunkenness, for he had imbibed so heavily at the home of John Radish (who lived in the eastern end of Jamestown Island) that he was unable to walk home. In the same court session, Fitt testified that he had heard Christopher Hall say that Dr. John Pott had killed a certain hog. On September 17, 1627, Robert Fitt and his wife, who had moved to Archer's Hope (**6**) and had been disturbing the peace by quarreling with their neighbors, were obliged to post a bond, guaranteeing their own good behavior. In January 1628 they were released from that obligation. On February 9, 1628, David Mansfield and Robert Fitt assumed William Harman's lease for 100 acres in Archer's Hope. In 1628 Robert Fitt and his wife, Ann, asked to be released from paying customs duties on tobacco and said that they had been in Virginia for 14 years. If so, they were ancient planters. On July 15, 1631, Robert Fitt identified himself as a Virginia planter

when he signed a petition asking to be released from customs; he indicated that his hogsheads of tobacco bore the mark *RF* (MCGC 33, 58, 153, 159, 166; CBE 33, 40, 56, 81; G&M 165).

ANN (ANNE) FITT (FITTS) (MRS. ROBERT FITT [FITTS])

Ann (Anne), who became the wife of Robert Fitt (Fitts), came to Virginia on the *Abigail*. On February 16, 1624, Robert and Ann were living in the eastern part of Jamestown Island (**1**). They were still residing there on January 24, 1625. Sometime prior to September 17, 1627, Ann and her husband, Robert, moved to Archer's Hope (**6**), where they apparently quarreled with some of their neighbors. Therefore, the Fitts and their adversaries, the Halls, were obliged to post a bond to guarantee their good behavior. In 1628 Ann Fitt and her husband, Robert, sent a petition to England, asking to be released from paying customs on tobacco. Both indicated that they had been living in Virginia for 14 years. If that statement was correct, they would have been ancient planters (MCGC 153; CBE 40, 56, 81).

***

***

THOMAS FITTS

Thomas Fitts, who was living on the lower side of the James River within the corporation of James City (**8-15**), died sometime after April 1623 but before February 16, 1624. His wife, Alice, perished around the same time (CBE 40).

ALICE FITTS (MRS. THOMAS FITTS)

Alice Fitts and her husband, Thomas, who lived on the lower side of the James River, within the corporation of James City (**8-15**), died sometime after April 1623 but before February 16, 1624 (CBE 40).

***

[NO FIRST NAME] FITZ-JAMES (PHITZ-JAMES)

Captain John Smith complimented Captain Fitz-James (Phitz-James), who was in Vir-

ginia when the colony was first established.
Fitz-James would have lived in Jamestown
(1) (CJS 1:270; 2:222).

GEORGE FITZ-JEFFRY (FITZ-JEFFERYS, FITZJEFFRIES, FITZJEFFREYS)

George Fitz-Jeffry (Fitz-Jefferys, Fitzjeffries,
Fitzjeffreys), a gentleman, arrived in
Jamestown **(1)** on September 12, 1623, on
the *Bonny Bess* and took the oath of supremacy. He was from Howton Conquest,
in Bedfordshire, England. George and a Mr.
Roper (probably Thomas Roper) obtained a
patent from the Virginia Company, as they
were taking 100 people to the colony and
were making the trip themselves. Thomas
Roper, who died in Jamestown sometime
prior to February 16, 1624, made a will in
which he asked George Fitz-Jeffry to take
custody of his Virginia tobacco on behalf of
John Roper, one of the heirs the testator
designated (MCGC 6; VCR 2:345, 428; CBE
39; WITH 487).

WILLIAM FITZ-JEFFRY (FITZ-JEFFERYS)

William Fitz-Jeffry (Fitz-Jeffreys), a gentle-
man from Staples Inn, arrived in James-
town **(1)** on September 12, 1623, on the
Bonny Bess and took the oath of supremacy.
He died in Jamestown sometime prior to
February 16, 1624 (MCGC 6; CBE 39).

HENRY FLEET (FLEETE)

Henry Fleet (Fleete) was the son of Virginia
Company member William Fleet of Chart-
ham (Chatham), County Kent, and Gray's
Inn, London. His mother, Deborah Scott,
was a first cousin of Virginia governor Sir
Francis Wyatt and a cousin to Sir Edward
Filmer and Robert Filmer. Henry Fleet
probably came to Virginia around 1621
with incoming Governor Wyatt. In 1623 he
was captured by the Indians while on a trading expedition to the Potomac River and
was detained for five years. During that period he learned the Natives' language and
gained an understanding of their way of
life. He was ransomed by friends and sometime prior to March 14, 1628, patented
some land on the Eastern Shore, abutting
the acreage of Thomas Graves and John
Blower, whose plantation was on Old Plan-

tation Creek **(73)**. Henry Fleet returned to
England where he formed a connection
with William Claiborne and his Kent Island
associates, who sent him back to Virginia as
master of one of their vessels. In 1634 when
Lord Baltimore's party entered the Chesapeake Bay, intent on planting a colony in
Maryland, they took aboard Henry Fleet,
known to be a skillful interpreter. He was
awarded a grant of 4,000 acres on St.
George's River, land that he seated and then
sold. After returning to Virginia, he served
the colony as an interpreter and in 1646 negotiated a treaty with the Indians. Fleet
went on to patent more than 13,000 acres in
Northern Neck, where he served as a burgess, county justice, and lieutenant colonel
of militia. He died between April 12, 1660,
and May 8, 1661, leaving a widow, the
former Sarah Burden (PB 1 Pt. 1:72, 98;
EEAC 22; DOR 1:970-972; AMES 1:5-6, 17, 33,
41-42, 90).

***

WILLIAM FLEET

On July 17, 1622, Virginia Company officials acknowledged that William Fleet had
transferred some Virginia land to his daughter, Katherine Fleet (VCR 2:93).

KATHERINE FLEET

On July 17, 1622, Virginia Company officials noted that Katherine Fleet had received some Virginia land from her father,
William Fleet. It is uncertain whether she
came to the colony or made use of her property (VCR 2:93).

***

[NO FIRST NAME] FLEETWOOD

Virginia Company records that date to May
1609 note that a Mr. Fleetwood, who was
going to Virginia with Sir Thomas Gates,
was to be a councilor. He may have been
Edward or William Fleetwood, both of
whom were prominent Virginia Company
investors (VCR 3:13, 83, 324).

ROBERT FLEMING (FLEMYNG)

On December 1, 1631, Robert Fleming
(Flemying) shipped goods from Barnstaple
to Virginia on the *Seraphim* (CBE 97).

EDWARD FLETCHER

Edward Fletcher, who resided on the lower side of the James River, within the corporation of James City (**8-15**), died sometime after April 1623 but before February 16, 1624 (CBE 41).

***

HANNIBALL FLETCHER

On June 24, 1635, Hanniball Fletcher patented 150 acres on Lower Chippokes Creek, adjacent to James Russell. As his land lay between Lower Chippokes and Lawnes Creeks, his acreage would have been west of Christopher Lawne's plantation (**25**), within what became Surry County. Hanniball Fletcher used as headrights his wife, Elizabeth, and his servants Thomas Owen and Francis Francklin. A year later he acquired some additional acreage with three more headrights (PB 1 Pt. 1:176, 190, 399).

ELIZABETH FLETCHER (MRS. HANNIBALL FLETCHER)

On June 24, 1635, when Hanniball Fletcher patented some acreage on the lower side of the James River between Lower Chippokes and Lawnes Creeks, he used his wife, Elizabeth, as a headright and noted that she had come to Virginia on the *Primrose* in 1634 (PB 1 Pt. 1:176).

***

JOAN EGERTON FLETCHER

Joan Fletcher, a widow and the daughter of John Egerton, was among the marriageable young women sent to Virginia as prospective wives for the colonists. She reportedly was the niece of Ralph Egerton of Morley House near Bridge Stafford in Cheshire, by Mr. Gibson's house near Three Nuns without Aldsgate. According to Virginia Company records, in August 1621 Joan set sail on the *Marmaduke*, but her trunk was loaded aboard the *Margaret*. When Joan Fletcher reached Isle of Wight (in England), she disembarked and decided not to continue her journey. Ann Buergen was sent in her place (FER 306, 308, 309).

ISACK FLETCHER

On August 30, 1628, Isack Fletcher, "an old customer" (longtime inmate) in the Bridewell prison, indicated that he was willing to go to Virginia with Mrs. Acourt's son (CBE 84).

RICHARD FLETCHER

On August 25, 1621, the justices of Bridewell Court decided that Richard Fletcher, a vagrant, would be detained so that he could be sent to Virginia (CBE 25).

WILLIAM FLETCHER

William Fletcher was among those brought to the colony by Adam Thorogood and used as a headright when he patented some land on June 24, 1635. Fletcher reportedly came to Virginia in 1634 in Mr. Middleton's ship (PB 1 Pt. 1:179).

PRICILLA FLINT

Priscilla Flint, one of the young maids sent to Virginia as wives for the colonists, set sail in 1621 on the *Bona Nova* (FER 309).

***

THOMAS FLINT (FLYNT)

Thomas Flint (Flynt) came to Virginia in 1618 on the *Diana* and on February 16, 1624, was living at Buckroe, on the east side of the Hampton River, in Elizabeth City (**17**). When a muster was compiled early in 1625, Flint was living on the Virginia Company's tract of Company-owned land, an area that included Buckroe. Thomas Flint headed an all-male household that included five other free men. Flint's household, which had a dwelling and a storehouse, was relatively well provisioned and outfitted with defensive weaponry. On January 9, 1626, he was summoned to appear before the General Court, whose justices noted that he owed money to Mr. Langley, a merchant. Lieutenant Thomas Flint purchased from Giles and Elizabeth Jones 50 acres located on the east side of the Hampton River; however, on February 5, 1627, he was ordered to take up other land, for the property he had bought lay within the boundaries of the defunct Virginia Company's 3,000 acres, whose legal claim was uncertain. Flint also was in possession of a lease for 50 acres known as the Indian Thicket, Company-owned land formerly taken up by Captain Jabez Whitaker, whose land was near the acreage occupied by the Rev. Jonas Stockden. During 1627 Thomas Flint was allowed to take possession of 50 acres at Fox Hill (**19**), as long as it was not part of the Virginia Company's land. In 1628 Thomas Flint's wife, Mary, an ancient planter, also was identified as the owner of land in Fox Hill. The couple apparently relinquished their leasehold in the Indian House Thicket, which by September 1628 was in the hands of another planter. On September 20, 1628, Thomas Flint received a patent for 1,000 acres on the south side of the Warwick River in Stanley Hundred (**22**), acquiring his land on the basis of 20 headrights. His property appears to have been near the lower end of Mulberry Island (**21**). Within a few months, Thomas and Mary Flint disposed of their interest in the 1,000 acres.

Thomas Flint may have been volatile and easily angered. In November 1628 he was detained at Robert Poole's house, stripped of his rank as lieutenant, and fined for contempt for becoming enraged and treating the governor disrespectfully. At issue was some meal that Flint had loaned the governor, who had failed to return it. Moreover, West had scolded Flint for openly having an affair with his daughter-in-law (stepdaughter), Dorothy Beheathland, despite his wife's objections. Thomas Flint also had a heated dispute with Peter Stafferton, which led to their being summoned to court. Despite his quarrelsome nature, Flint became increasingly prominent and by October 1629 was serving as a burgess for the Warwick River area. He was among those given the responsibility of finding men to plant at Chiskiack (**30-38**), on the York River. In 1632 Thomas Flint became burgess for the territory between Skiff's Creek and Saxon's Gaol, below Mulberry Island. He also served as the burgess for Denbigh and for Stanley Hundred and was named a commissioner of the Warwick River monthly court. Captain Thomas Flint survived until at least November 20, 1636, at which time he witnessed the Rev. Thomas Butler's will and received a bequest (CBE 45, 67; MCGC 87, 138, 176-177, 180; PB 1 Pt. 1:59, 73, 77, 79, 90, 147, 271; HEN 1:139-140, 148, 154, 179, 187, 203; WITH 49; DOR 1:66).

MARY BEHEATHLAND
FLINT [FLYNT])
(MRS. ROBERT BEHEATHLAND,
MRS. THOMAS FLINT [FLYNT])

Mary, Robert Beheathland's widow and an ancient planter, married Thomas Flint (Flynt) sometime prior to 1628, when she patented 100 acres in Elizabeth City called Fox Hill (**19**). In November 1628 she spoke to Governor West about her husband's inappropriate behavior with Dorothy Beheathland, his daughter-in-law (stepdaughter), and threatened to discuss it with Dorothy's grandmother when she arrived from England. Despite the Flint couple's tumultuous relationship, Mary Flint asked the governor to release her husband, who had been arrested and detained. Afterward, he refused to accompany her home. On January 20, 1629, Mary Flint demanded some barrels of corn from Captain William Pierce, who claimed that he owed her considerably less than she alleged. That same day she and her husband, Thomas, conveyed their interest in 1,000 acres at Stanley Hundred (**22**) to another individual. On November 20, 1636, Mary received a bequest from the Rev. Thomas Butler, a friend. A Warwick County court record dating to February 7, 1650, suggests that Mary Flint was still alive, for she was said to have borrowed Captain William Bullock's boat, grindstone, and some equipment (PB 1 Pt. 1:73; MCGC 177, 180; WITH 49; DUNN 171).

***

ELIZABETH FLINTON (FINTON)

On February 16, 1624, Elizabeth Flinton was living in Elizabeth City (**18**). She probably was a kinswoman of Pharoah Flinton and his wife, Joan, with whom she was listed in the census (CBE 44).

***

PHAROAH (FARROW, FARRAR)
FLINTON (FINTON)

Pharoah (Farrow, Farrar) Flinton (Finton), who came to Virginia on the *Elizabeth* in 1612, was an ancient planter. On May 20, 1622, he asked the Virginia Company to give him the land Governor George Yeardley assigned to him, which later was claimed by Captain Roger Smith for the Company's use. This suggests that Flinton may have seated some land near the mouth of the James River, for he seems to have been almost continuously associated with Elizabeth City. On February 16, 1624, Pharoah Flinton and his wife, Margaret, were residing in Elizabeth City (**18**). By

December 1, 1624, he had acquired 150 acres between Newportes News (**24**) and Blunt Point (**22**), laying claim to 100 acres as his own personal adventure and 50 acres for the headright of his servant, Hugh Hall. Flinton's land, which adjoined that of John Salford and Giles Allington, lay within what in 1634 became Warwick River (later, Warwick) County. In early 1625, when a muster was taken of the colony's inhabitants, Pharoah and Margaret Flinton were identified as residents of Elizabeth City, where he headed a household that included four servants. He was then age 36. In May 1625, when a list was made of Virginia land that had been patented, Pharoah Flinton's 150 acres below Blunt Point were described as planted (seated). In 1625 he testified in court that he and John Cobb had inventoried the belongings of Thomas Clarke, who had died at sea in May aboard the *Elizabeth* of London. This suggests that Pharoah Flinton made a trip to England and then returned home to Virginia. Sometime prior to March 12, 1627, he left again. In his absence, he was sued by Arthúr Smythe, John Bainham, and John Snoade, who claimed that Pharoah was supposed to bring them servants. Since Pharoah Flinton had failed to appoint an attorney to manage his business affairs while he was away, Captain William Tucker was ordered to pay the plaintiffs by liquidating some of Flinton's personal property. Pharoah Flinton survived until at least July 15, 1631, at which time he was among the Virginia planters who asked for relief from the customs duties on tobacco (VCR 2:16; 4:557; CBE 44, 65; PB 1 Pt. 1:21-23; MCGC 81, 145, 198-199; G&M 165-166; DOR 1:58).

JOAN FLINTON (FINTON) (MRS. PHAROAH [FARROW FARRAR] FLINTON [FINTON])

Joan, who became the wife of Pharoah (Farrow, Farrar) Flinton (Finton), went to Virginia in 1612 on the *Elizabeth* and was an ancient planter. On February 16, 1624, she and her husband were living in Elizabeth City (**18**). In early 1625, she was 38 years old and Pharoah, who was a household head, was two years her junior (CBE 44, 65; DOR 1:58).

***

[NO FIRST NAME] FLIT

A miller known as Monsieur (Mr.) Flit, his wife, Marie, and two children were among the Walloons and French who indicated their willingness to go to Virginia. In August 1621 the Virginia Company agreed that they could immigrate (CBE 25-26).

MARIE FLIT (MRS. [NO FIRST NAME] FLIT)

Marie Flit, whose husband was a miller known only as Monsieur Flit, and their two children were among the Walloons and French who indicated their willingness to go to Virginia. In August 1621 the Virginia Company agreed that they could immigrate (CBE 25-26).

***

[NO FIRST NAME] FLOOD (FLOUD)

A male laborer whose surname was Flood (Floud) came to Virginia in 1608 as part of the 2nd Supply of new colonists to Jamestown (**1**) (CJS 2:191).

GEORGE FLOOD (FLUDD)

On February 27, 1619, George Flood (Fludd), a boy, was among those selected to be sent to Virginia (CBE 12).

***

JOHN FLOOD (FLUD, FLUDD, FLOYD)

John Flood (Flud, Fludd, Floyd), an ancient planter, came to Virginia in 1610 on the *Swann*. On January 24, 1625 he and his wife, Margaret, were living with their son William and John's stepdaughter, Frances Finch, at Jordan's Journey (**46**), in what became Prince George County. John headed a household that was abundantly supplied with defensive weaponry, had an ample supply of stored food, and some livestock. On February 4, 1625, John Flood was described as a former servant to "Captain Whittakers," probably Isaac or Jabez Whittaker, both of whom were Virginia Company employees. It was in 1625 that

Sir George Yeardley accused John Flood and another Whitaker servant of using his seed corn as food. That same month Flood testified in the suit involving Captain John Martin and Sir George Yeardley. In 1628 John Flood, who was then in England, was one of the men Captain John Smith interviewed about current conditions in Virginia. In March 1630 Flood was Flowerdew Hundred's (**53**) burgess, and in 1632 he represented Flowerdew, Westover (**54**), and Weyanoke (**52**). In May 1638 John Flood patented 2,100 acres of land on the lower side of the James River, in the mouth of Pipsico Bay, within the area that later became Surry County. He used his headright, the headrights of wife, Margaret, and stepdaughter Frances Finch, and those of some servants he had transported. In 1639 English officials noted that John Flood, who was then living at Westover, had received 100 acres from Richard Elle, land to which he (John) was entitled as an ancient planter; he also purchased some acreage from John Bradston. He continued to acquire land on both sides of the James and in 1640 served as a justice of the peace for Charles City County. Although John and Margaret Flood's son, William, seemingly did not survive to adulthood, the couple had two other children: Thomas and Jane. In March 1643 Captain John Flood served as a burgess for James City, which then included the area that became Surry County in 1652. He was returned to office in 1645, 1652, and 1655–1656. Captain-later-Colonel John Flood seems to have been involved in Indian trade, for in 1646, when a treaty was negotiated, he was designated one of the colony's official interpreters. Indians needing to make an official visit to the governor were to go to Fort Henry (on the Appomattox River) or to Colonel John Flood's house on the lower side of the James. After the death of his wife, Margaret, John Flood married Fortune Jordan. Together they produced a son, Walter, who was born around 1656. John Flood died between June and November 1658. The will he made seemingly does not exist (CBE 52, 69; VCR 4:504, 511; CO 1/10 ff 18-19; HEN 1:148, 154, 178, 239, 325, 328; CJS 3:217, 219; PB 1 Pt. 2:548, 629, 929; 2:227; 3:3; 4:18; STAN 63-64, 68, 72; DOR 1:18, 994-997; SR 4545).

MARGARET FINCH (FINCHE) FLOOD (FLUD, FLUDD, FLOYD) (MRS. WILLIAM FINCH, MRS. JOHN FLOOD [FLUD, FLUDD, FLOYD])

Margaret and William Finch came to Virginia on the *Supply* in 1620 and went to Berkeley Hundred (**55**). After William's death sometime prior to August 1622, Margaret married ancient planter John Flood (Flud, Fludd, Floyd). On February 4, 1625, the Floods were living at Jordan's Journey (**46**) in a household John headed. With them was the couple's infant son, William, and Margaret's young daughter, Frances Finch (CBE 52).

WILLIAM FLOOD (FLUD, FLUDD, FLOYD)

On February 4, 1625, William Flood (Flud, Fludd, Floyd), who was 3 weeks old, was living in the household of his parents, John and Margaret Flood, in Jordan's Journey (**46**). William also shared the family home with his half-sister, Frances Finch (CBE 52).

***

DANIEL FLOYD

On November 15, 1620, Virginia Company officials were informed that Henry Rowland, a goldsmith, wanted the share of Company stock to which his late brother, Daniel Floyd, had been entitled. It was noted that Daniel Floyd had died in Virginia 10 years earlier, an event verified by Captain William Tucker of Kecoughtan (**17**) (VCR 1:426).

NATHANIEL FLOYD (FLOID)

Nathaniel Floyd (Floid) came to Virginia on the *Bona Nova*. On February 4, 1625, he was identified as a 24-year-old servant in Edward Blaney's household, which occupied the late William Powell's plantation (**14**). Sometime prior to August 18, 1627, Floyd obtained his freedom and acquired some land on the Warwick River, adjacent to Lieutenant Gilbert Peppett. Nathaniel Floyd and John Shelley ran afoul of the law when they stole a maidservant from Captain Francis West. For that offense, Floyd was ordered to return her and was made to sit in the stocks (CBE 59; PB 1 Pt. 1:50; MCGC 149).

THOMAS FLOYD

On February 16, 1624, Thomas Floyd was living at West and Shirley Hundred (**41**), where he appears to have been a servant (CBE 36).

WALTER FLOYD

On April 24, 1632, Walter Floyd, Roger Race, Thomas Smith, and Silvester Tatnam (a carpenter) obtained a 21-year-lease for 400 acres in Martin's Hundred (**7**), near Skiff's Creek (PB 1 Pt. 1:130).

AGNES FLOWER

On October 31, 1618, Agnes Flower, who was brought into court from the Middlesex House of Correction, was detained so that she could be sent to Virginia (CBE 11).

ANNE FLOWER

On February 27, 1619, the justices of Bridewell decided that Anne Flower, a girl, was to be detained so that she could be sent to Virginia (HUME 12).

GEORGE FLOWER

George Flower, a gentleman, came to Virginia in 1607 and was one of the first Jamestown (**1**) settlers. He reportedly died of a "swelling" (CJS 1:19; 2:141; HAI 99).

JOHN FLOWER (FLORES)

On March 22, 1622, when the Indians attacked Weyanoke (**52**), John Flower (Flores) was slain. Afterward, he was identified as one of Sir George Yeardley's servants (VCR 3:569).

JOHN FLOWER (FLOURES)

In March or April 1623 Richard Frethorne of Martin's Hundred (**7**) sent word to England that John Flower (Floures), who had come to the settlement at Christmas (that is, January 1623), had died while living at the house of William Harwood. In September 1623 the General Court noted that Flower, formerly a sailor on the *Everett*, had hired himself out in Virginia (VCR 4:60; MCGC 7).

THOMAS FLOWER

Thomas Flower came to Virginia on the *George* in 1623 and on February 16, 1624, was living on the lower side of the James River, at Paces Paines (**9**) where he was a servant in John Proctor's household. On March 9, 1624, the justices of the General Court noted that Proctor had offered Thomas Flower to Henry Horner instead of Richard Grove, another servant. A bargain may have been struck, for by early 1625 22-year-old Thomas Flower was living in Elizabeth City (**17**) and was a servant in the household of William Julian, who lived on the Virginia Company's land (CBE 40, 64; VCR 4:466-467; MCGC 13).

THOMAS FLUELLING (LLEWELYN)

On August 31, 1636, when John Ring, a London yeoman, set sail for Virginia on the *Great Hopewell,* he made a bequest to his friend, Thomas Fluelling (Llewelyn), who already was living in the colony at Potash Quarter, near Samuel Mathews' plantation (**23**). Ring also left part of his personal estate to Richard and Abigail Atkins, residents of Mulberry Island (**21**) and to Robert Burnett's wife, Margaret. John Ring, a bachelor, died abroad and his will was proved on April 19, 1637 (EEAC 48; SR 3977; WITH 152).

RALPH FOGG

On November 13, 1620, the Virginia Company noted that Ralph Fogg had received a bill of adventure from Edward Harrison, an investor (VCR 1:418-419).

STEPHEN FONT

On February 27, 1619, officials at Bridewell decided that Stephen Font, a youth, would be sent to Virginia with a group of boys and girls (CBE 12).

JOSHUA FOOTE

In 1629 Joshua Foote, an English ironmonger, joined Richard Nicholas in supplying ironware to Governor John Harvey for sale in the colony. In 1635 and 1636 Foote indicated that Harvey, a resident of Jamestown (**1**), had never paid for the goods he supplied. He claimed that Harvey owed him £45 for ironware (SAIN 1:225; CO 1/9 f 11).

ROBERT FORD

Robert Ford, a gentleman, came to Virginia in 1607 and was one of the first Jamestown (1) settlers. In late December 1608 he accompanied Captain John Smith to Werowocomoco on the York River, at which time he was identified as the clerk of the council. Earlier in the year, Ford went to the Pamunkey Indians' territory in the *Discovery* with Smith, who intended to trade with Powhatan's brother, Opechancanough (CJS 1:208, 251; 2:141, 193, 200, 204, 208).

WILLIAM FORD (FOORD)

On February 27, 1619, a decision was made to send William Ford (Foord), a boy, to Virginia. He was among a large group of boys and girls rounded up from the streets of London so that they could be sent to the colony (CBE 12).

SAMWELL (SAMUEL) FOREMAN

Samwell (Samuel) Foreman died at West and Shirley Hundred (41) sometime after April 1623 but before February 16, 1624 (CBE 36).

GEORGE FOREST

George Forest, a gentleman, arrived in Virginia in January 1608 in the 1st Supply of new Jamestown (1) colonists. He was shot at by the Indians and received wounds from 17 arrows. According to Captain John Smith, he was very courageous and lived six or seven days. Ultimately, he died from lack of medical treatment (CJS 2:161, 221).

***

THOMAS FOREST

Thomas Forest, a gentleman, arrived in Jamestown (1) in 1608 in the 2nd Supply of new colonists. He was accompanied by his wife and her maid, Anne Burras, who were Virginia's first female settlers. In 1620 Captain John Smith identified Thomas Forest as an investor in the Virginia Company (CJS 190, 276).

MRS. THOMAS FOREST

In 1608 Mrs. Thomas Forest accompanied her husband to Virginia and was part of the 2nd Supply of Jamestown (1) colonists. Mrs. Forest and her maid, Ann Burras, were the first female colonists to arrive (CJS 1:238, 242; 2:184, 191).

***

[NO FIRST NAME] FORTESQUE

In 1624 Virginia officials noted that Sergeant Fortesque, who had been responsible for Sir George Yeardley's servants at Flowerdew Hundred (53), had mistakenly tied up some damp tobacco, which led to its deterioration and loss (MCGC 27).

SYMON (SIMON, SYMOND) FORTESQUE

On October 31, 1621, Virginia Company officials noted that Simon (Symon, Symond) Fortesque had died on his way from Virginia to England. His uncle and executor, Captain Henry Fortesque, indicated that he would be settling the decedent's estate. In May 1625, when a list of patented land was sent back to England, Simon Fortesque was credited with 100 acres in Charles City. He may have been the Sergeant Fortesque who had been associated with Flowerdew Hundred (53), situated in the same corporation in which Simon Fortesque's patent was located (VCR 1:543; VCR4:553).

JOHN FORTH

In 1622 John Forth came to Virginia on the *Bona Nova*. On February 16, 1624, he was living in Elizabeth City, where he was a servant in the household of Francis Chamberlin, whose home was on the east side of the Hampton River (17). In early 1625 John Forth was identified as Chamberlin's servant. He was then age 16 (CBE 44, 60).

THOMAS FOSKEW

On February 16, 1624, Thomas Foskew, a deceased resident of Hog Island (16), was described as "lost" (killed) (CBE 41).

THOMAS FOSSETT (FAWCETT, FAUSETT)

Thomas Fossett (Fawcett, Fausett) may have been one of Captain John Berkeley's men at the Virginia Company's ironworks, for he became ill with dropsy while living at Falling Creek **(68)** and received medical treatment from Edward Giften. Afterward, Fossett moved to Weyanoke **(52)**. On February 16, 1624, Thomas Fossett and his wife, Ann, were living on West and Shirley Hundred (Eppes) Island **(41)**. By October 1629 Thomas had become a burgess for Martin's Hundred **(7)**. He also served on the community's behalf the following year. On January 29, 1633, when John Creed of Martin's Hundred made his will, he identified Thomas Fossett and Francis Clarke as his masters. He designated Thomas as his executor and Ann Fossett as his administrator, noting that she was then in Virginia, simultaneously implying that Thomas was not (MCGC 11; CBE 36; HEN 1:139, 148; SH 15; EEAC 16; WITH 80).

ANN FOSSETT (FAWCETT, FAUSETT) (MRS. THOMAS FOSSETT (FAWCETT, FAUSETT)

On February 16, 1624, Ann Fossett (Fawcett, Fausett) was living on West and Shirley Hundred (Eppes) Island **(41)** with her husband, Thomas. She accompanied him to Martin's Hundred **(7)**, where both of them were living in 1633 when John Creed named Ann as his administrator and Thomas as his executor, noting that Ann was then in Virginia. In April 1635 Ann Fossett served as John Creed's administrator (CBE 36; SH 15; EEAC 16).

***

JOHN FOSTER

On February 16, 1624, John Foster was an indentured servant living in the Jamestown **(1)** household of Sir George Yeardley (CBE 38).

JOHN FOSTER

On February 16, 1624, John Foster was living on the east side of the Hampton River in Elizabeth City, in a settlement known as the Indian Thicket **(17)**. On January 30, 1626, the General Court heard testimony about John and another man who drowned during some New Year's Eve revelry that probably occurred in March 1625. According to the men on the ship *Grace*, Adam Thorogood and some others came aboard, took the ship's boat, and cast off. Later, when John Foster and Thomas Lum fell overboard and drowned, the men on the *Grace* heard cries for help. The incident appears to have occurred in Elizabeth City **(17, 18)** at the mouth of the James River (CBE 43; MCGC 91-92).

WILLIAM FOSTER

On December 12, 1625, William Foster informed the General Court that when he was in Canada, he had asked Mr. Edward Nevell why Richard Cornish alias Williams had been hanged. Less than two months later, Foster and two other men were brought before the court and ordered to pay for the wine and goods they had taken from Nevell's cabin. William Foster of Elizabeth City **(17, 18)** died on December 10, 1626. Richard Popeley presented his will to the General Court's justices on December 18, 1626, and was appointed the decedent's administrator. Popeley was ordered to bring in an inventory of Foster's estate. William Foster's will was proved by John Howe on February 5, 1627 (MCGC 81, 95, 128, 138).

WILLIAM FOUKS (FOOCKES, FOULKE)

William Fouks (Foockes, Foulke) came to Virginia in 1621 on the *Flying Hart* and on February 16, 1624, was living in Elizabeth City **(18)**. On February 7, 1625, Fouks was residing in Newportes News **(24)**, where he was a 24-year-old servant in Daniel Gookin's household; simultaneously he was listed among Gookin's men in Elizabeth City (CBE 44, 63).

THOMAS FOULKE

Thomas Foulke died sometime after April 1623 but before February 16, 1624, within the corporation of James City and on the lower side of the James River **(8-15)** (CBE 41).

FRANCOIS FOURDRIN

Leather dresser Francois Fourdrin, a young man, was among the Walloons and French who indicated their willingness to go to Virginia. In August 1621 the Virginia Company agreed that they could immigrate (CBE 25-26).

[NO FIRST NAME] FOWLER

On February 16, 1624, a Mrs. Fowler, who was identified only as a widow, was living in Elizabeth City (18) (CBE 43).

EDWARD FOWLER (FOULER, FOULLER)

Edward Fowler (Fouler, Fouller), a tenant of the defunct Virginia Company, was assigned to the governor on January 12, 1627. Therefore, he probably became a resident of the Governor's Land (3) (MCGC 136).

FRANCIS FOWLER (FOULER, FOULLER)

On February 16, 1624, Francis Fowler (Fouler, Fouller) was a servant in Captain Roger Smith's household in urban Jamestown (1). By February 4, 1625, he was living on Smith's plantation (10) on the lower side of the James River. Fowler was then 23 years old. By August 1626 Fowler was a free man with two servants of his own. However, in January 1627 he was identified as a Virginia Company tenant who had been assigned to Captain Roger Smith. In March 1629 Francis Fowler sued ancient planter Robert Wright, a resident of the eastern end of Jamestown Island, and had him jailed. Fowler also served on a jury. In April 1629 he agreed to build a house with a chimney for his business partner, Bridges Freeman, with whom he shared ownership of some land near the mouth of the Chickahominy River. In 1640 the General Court ordered Francis Fowler to see that Ann Belson, Theodore Moses' former maidservant, received adequate freedom dues. In January 1641 Francis Fowler was one of James City's burgesses (CBE 38, 59; MCGC 107-108, 136, 188, 199, 197, 465; STAN 61; PB 1 Pt. 1:302).

JAMES FOWLER

On December 4, 1634, when Hugh Cox received a court order entitling him to a patent, he listed James Fowler as a headright (PB 1 Pt. 1:282).

JOHN FOWLER

John Fowler reportedly was killed at Ensign William Spence's house in Archer's Hope (6) during the March 22, 1622, Indian attack. In May 1625 Fowler and Spence together were credited with a 300-acre patent in Archer's Hope (VCR 3:570; 4:556).

***

WILLIAM FOWLER (FOULLER)

William Fowler (Fouller) arrived in Virginia in 1621 aboard the *Abigail*, and on February 16, 1624, he and his wife were living in Elizabeth City (17). A year later William was described as a 30-year-old household head who resided on the Virginia Company's land on the east side of the Hampton River. William Fowler and his wife, Margaret, were relatively well provisioned and supplied with defensive weaponry. In January 1627 William was identified as a Virginia Company tenant when he was assigned to the governor. By December 12, 1627, he had come into possession of William Hampton's acreage in Buckroe, land that was adjacent to that of John Henry and opposite Old Point Comfort Island (CBE 43, 67; MCGC 136; PB 1 Pt. 1:83; DOR 1:39).

MARGARET FOWLER (FOULLER) (MRS. WILLIAM FOWLER [FOULLER])

Margaret, the wife of William Fowler (Fouller), came to Virginia on the *Abigail* in 1621. It is uncertain whether they were married at the time they left England. On February 16, 1624, the Fowlers were sharing a home in Elizabeth City (17). A year later they were still there, residing on property on the east side of the Hampton River that belonged to the then-defunct Virginia Company. Margaret Fowler and her husband, William, were age 30, and he was a household head. In January 1627 he was identified as a Virginia Company tenant who was being assigned to the governor (CBE 43, 67; MCGC 136).

***

***

JOHN FOX

John Fox died aboard the *Elizabeth* while it was enroute to Virginia. On October 16,

1625, after the ship arrived, the provost marshal was ordered to take custody of the decedent's goods. On November 28, 1625, the justices of the General Court told the provost marshal to sell John Fox's goods and to send the equivalent in tobacco to his widow, Elizabeth, and his other heirs in England (MCGC 73, 76).

ELIZABETH FOX
(MRS. JOHN FOX)

Elizabeth Fox was the widow of John Fox, who died aboard the *Elizabeth* while it was on the way to Virginia. In October and November 1625 the General Court's justices ordered the provost marshal to take custody of the decedent's goods, sell them, and send the proceeds to Elizabeth and his other heirs in England (CBE 40, 600; MCGC 73, 76).

***

THOMAS FOX

In 1608 Thomas Fox, a laborer, arrived in Virginia in the 2nd Supply of Jamestown (1) colonists (CJS 242; 2:191).

RICHARD FOXCROFTE

On September 18, 1626, Richard Foxcrofte was identified as purser of the *Ann,* which had made a voyage to Virginia (MCGC 114).

JOHN FOXEN

On February 16, 1624, John Foxen was living on the lower side of the James River, at a plantation east of Gray's Creek and within the corporation of James City (10-16). By January 24, 1625, he was dead (CBE 40, 60).

VICTOR FRAFORD

On June 24, 1635, when Adam Thorogood patented some land, he used Victor Fraford as a headright and indicated that he had paid for his transportation on the *Africa* (PB 1 Pt. 1:179).

MARTIN FRAMERIE

Musician Martin Framerie and his wife and child were among the Walloons and French who indicated their willingness to go to Virginia. In August 1621 the Virginia Company agreed that they could immigrate (CBE 25-26).

FRANCES

On February 16, 1624, an African named Frances was living at Warresqueak (26) (CBE 42).

RALPH FRANCES

On February 27, 1619, Ralph Frances, a boy, was part of a large group of young people rounded up from the streets of London so that they could be sent to Virginia (CBE 13).

FRANCIS

According to Captain John Smith, a German named Francis—who was among those who sought refuge with the Indians and was at Pamunkey in 1608—was sent to Jamestown (1) by Opechancanough. On one occasion, Powhatan purportedly sent Francis to the Glasshouse (2) disguised as an Indian, so that he could ambush Smith. In 1610, when Lord Delaware arrived, Francis fled to Powhatan, who reportedly executed him (CJS 1:250, 259-260; 2:199, 209, 226).

FRANCIS

Francis, an Irishman, was killed at Richard Owen's plantation near Westover (54) during the March 22, 1622, Indian attack (VCR 3:567).

JOHN FRANCIS

In 1628 John Francis's inventory was presented to the General Court by Richard Bennett. This raises the possibility that the decedent lived in Warresqueak (26), where the Bennett plantation was located (MCGC 173).

***

RICHARD FRANCIS

On February 22, 1620, Richard Francis was awarded 200 acres of land by the Virginia Company because he had sent four servants to the colony. Company records note that Richard's sons, William and Arthur, already were in Virginia (VCR 1:315).

ARTHUR FRANCIS

Arthur, the son of Richard Francis, went to Virginia with his brother, William, sometime prior to February 22, 1620, when he was mentioned in Virginia Company records (VCR 1:315).

WILLIAM FRANCIS

William Francis and his brother, Arthur, the sons of Richard Francis, went to Virginia sometime prior to February 22, 1620, at which time he was mentioned in Virginia Company records (VCR 1:315).

***

MATHIAS FRANCISCO

Mathias Francisco came to Virginia in 1624 on the *Jacob* and in early 1625 was living in Elizabeth City **(18)**. He was then an 18-year-old servant in Edward Waters' household (CBE 66).

[NO FIRST NAME] FRANCK

On June 11, 1621, Mr. Franck informed Virginia Company officials that his sons were in Virginia and that he had sent four men and some supplies to the colony, which Captain Peirce had seized illegally (VCR 1:485).

DANIEL FRANCK (FRANK)

On May 2, 1622, the Bridewell Court decided that Daniel Franck (Frank), a prisoner in White Lion, Southwark, would be sent to Virginia. On September 5, 1622, Virginia Company officials noted that Franck, a reprieved criminal, was never to return, and that he was to serve Eleanor Phillips, who had agreed to pay for his passage. In August 1623 Franck, who was residing on Jamestown Island **(1)** and was described as a laborer, ran afoul of the law by killing one of Sir George Yeardley's calves. He also stole some personal items from Randall Smallwood, the provost marshal. Franck was tried, convicted, and sentenced to death for thievery. On February 16, 1624, he was listed among those who had died at West and Shirley Hundred **(41)** sometime after April 1623. On June 5, 1633, Elmer Phillips used Daniel Franck as a headright and indicated that both of them had come to Virginia on the *Southampton* in 1622. There probably was a familial relationship between Eleanor and Elmer Phillips (CBE 27, 36; VCR 2:102; MCGC 4-5; PB 1 Pt. 1:123).

FRANCIS FRANCKLIN (FRANKLIN)

Francis Francklin (Franklin) came to Virginia on the *Revenge* in 1634. He was identified as Hanniball Fletcher's servant when Fletcher patented some land on June 24, 1635, using Francklin's headright (PB 1 Pt.1:176).

HENRY FRANCKLIN (FRANKLIN)

On June 24, 1635, when Adam Thorogood patented some land, he used Henry Francklin (Franklin) as a headright, indicating that he had brought him to Virginia on the *John and Dorothy* in 1634 (PB 1 Pt. 1:179).

JOYCE FREAKE

On July 10, 1621, the Virginia Company identified Joyce Freake as a poor widow who was entitled to two shares of land for her personal adventure and the goods she had left in the colony in the Company's store. This raises the possibility that Mrs. Freake had gone to Virginia at her own expense but had returned to England (VCR 1:509).

JOHN FREAM (FREME, FRAME)

John Fream (Freme, Frame) went to Virginia in 1622 on the *Southampton* and on February 16, 1624, was living at Jordan's Journey **(46)**. When a muster of the colony's inhabitants was taken on January 21, 1625, Fream was identified as a 16-year-old servant in the household of William Farrar and Mrs. Cicely Jordan. In June 1637, when Farrar's son patented some land in Henrico County, he listed John Fream as a headright, noting that his father had paid for Fream's transportation to the colony. Later that year, Fream and John Clay, who also had resided at Jordan's Journey in 1625, acquired some land of their own (CBE 36, 51; PB 1 Pt. 1:436; 3:334).

***

BENNETT FREEMAN

On December 1, 1635, when Bridges Freeman patented some land, he used the headright of his brother, Bennett. Bennett Freeman patented 400 acres of land on December

20, 1648. Half the acreage had been inherited from Mrs. Antonia Fowler and half had been given to him by his brother, Bridges (PB 1 Pt. 1:324; 2:171; DOR1:1008).

BRIDGES FREEMAN

Bridges Freeman, who was born in 1603, was the son of Thomas Freeman and his wife, Frances Bennett, of Preston Crowmarsh, Oxfordshire, England. On February 16, 1624, he was living in Elizabeth City (**17**) in the household of Jabez Whitaker, who occupied part of the Virginia Company's land. By 1626 Bridges Freeman and yeoman James Sleight were living at Martin's Brandon (**59**) on a leasehold that Freeman had secured from Captain John Martin. On May 21, 1627, the two men received permission to move to a more secure location, but two months later they leased some additional ground at Martin's Brandon and stayed on. While living at Martin's Brandon, they testified about the scandalous behavior of Captain William Eppes and the widowed Alice Boyse. Bridges Freeman, who in 1629 gave his age as 26, testified that he had heard Roger Peirce admit to being indebted to Captain William Peirce. In January 1629 David Mynton unsuccessfully sued Freeman in an attempt to recover the cost of the medical care he had required as a result of injuries he had received from Freeman. Two months later, Bridges Freeman was re-appointed commander of the magazine in Jamestown (**1**). Later in the year, he went to court to make a contract with Francis Fowler, who agreed to build house with a chimney for him. By that time Freeman was serving as a burgess for Pasbehay (**3**). He and Fowler, who became his partner and perhaps was related by marriage, had patented some land by 1630 on the east side of the Chickahominy River's mouth, within the 3,000-acre tract that in 1619 had been set aside as the corporation of James City's Company Land (**4**). In time, a promontory that extended into the river became known as Freeman's Point. In 1632 Bridges Freeman was a burgess representing the planters living along the Chickahominy River. He became that area's tobacco viewer in 1640 and later was collector of revenue. He also was called on to see whether a maidservant's freedom dues were adequate. By that date he had patented a large tract of land on the west side of the Chickahominy, using as

headrights the personal adventures of his wife, Bridgett, and brother, Bennett. In 1647 Captain Bridges Freeman served as one of James City County's burgesses, and in 1650 he was appointed to the Council of State. Bridges Freeman's second wife, Jane, was the eldest daughter of George Evelyn, an English gentleman involved in colonizing Maryland. Freeman became a captain and then a lieutenant colonel in the militia. He died between January 1658 and March 1663. His brother Thomas reportedly was a mining expert (CBE 43; MCGC 139-142, 149, 151, 182, 192, 199, 465; Hen 1:148, 178; PB 1 Pt. 1:137, 150, 302, 324, 331; STAN 66; HAR 28/2/27A; DOR 1:1007-1008).

BRIDGETT FREEMAN
(MRS. BRIDGES FREEMAN)

On December 1, 1635, when Bridges Freeman patented some land, he used his wife, Bridgett, as a headright (PB 1 Pt. 1:324; DOR 1:921-922, 924, 1008).

JANE FREEMAN
(MRS. BRIDGES FREEMAN)

After the death of Bridgett, Bridges Freeman's wife, he married Jane, the daughter of George Evelyn, who was involved in colonizing Maryland (DOR 1:1008).

***

RALPH FREEMAN

Ralph Freeman came to Virginia in 1622 on the *Margaret and John*. He was among those who died at West and Shirley Hundred (**41**) after February 16, 1624, but before January 22, 1625 (CBE 53).

THOMAS FREEMAN

On March 22, 1622, when the Indians attacked the settlers living on the College land (**66**), Thomas Freeman was killed (VCR 3:566).

URSULA FRENCH

Elias Longe came to Virginia in 1620. On May 8, 1622, Ursula French, who described herself as a poor widow, asked Virginia Company officials to give her an allowance from Longe's earnings, for he was her apprentice as well as a Company servant. On

February 16, 1624, Longe was living at West and Shirley Hundred (**41**). On April 26, 1624, Mrs. French asked Company officials to free Elias Longe, for he had served for four years. Company officials may have disagreed, for sometime prior to February 4, 1625, he was moved to the Treasurer's Plantation (**11**), which was owned by Virginia Treasurer George Sandys, manager of the Company's artisans. On June 15, 1625, Virginia Company officials noted that Elias Longe had procured his freedom from Ursula French by making a payment in tobacco (VCR 1:634; 2:529; 4:562-567; CBE 36, 60).

AMBROSE FRESEY

Sometime after April 1623 but before February 16, 1624, Ambrose Fresey died on Jamestown Island (**1**) (CBE 39).

RICHARD FRETHORNE (FRETHRAM)

In 1623 Richard Frethorne (Fretham) of Martin's Hundred (**7**), a young indentured servant, sent a letter to his parents, describing the miserable living conditions in his settlement. He said that the people there were starving and insufficiently clothed and asked his parents to help him. He indicated that he was living in the house of William Harwood, the settlement's leader. Frethorne spoke fondly of Mr. and Mrs. John Jackson of Jamestown (**1**), who had built a cabin for his use whenever he came to the capital city on business for his master. He said that otherwise he would have had to stay overnight in an open boat. Richard said that most of the servants who had accompanied him to Martin's Hundred were dead after the 1622 Indian attack and that the Natives continued to harass the settlers living there. In a March 5, 1623, letter to a Mr. Bateman, an English clergyman, he again spoke of the hardships he was enduring and asked to be brought home. Sometime after April 1623 but before February 16, 1624, Richard Frethorne died at Martin's Hundred (VCR 4:41-42, 53-62; CBE 42).

RICHARD FRISBIE (FRISHBY)

Richard Frisbie (Frishby) came to Virginia on the ship *Jonathan* in 1619 and on November 25, 1624, testified in some litigation involving John Gayne and Jabez Whitaker. He then gave his age as 34. In early 1625, when a muster was made of the colony's inhabitants, Richard Frisbie was identified as a 34-year-old servant in the household of William Barry, who lived on the east side of the Hampton River on the Virginia Company's land (**17**) (CBE 68; MCGC 31-32).

MARGERY FRISLE

Margery Frisle died in the corporation of Elizabeth City (**17, 18**) sometime after April 1623 but before February 16, 1624 (CBE 45).

JOHN FROGMORTON (THROGMORTON?)

On February 16, 1624, John Frogmorton was living on the Mainland (**3**) just west of Jamestown Island. This individual may have been John Throgmorton, who at the same time was attributed to a community on Virginia's Eastern Shore (CBE 39).

JOHN FROMAGE

In 1621 John Fromage, Mr. Jamison's servant, was sent to Virginia by the Company of Mercers (FER 297).

HENRY FRY

Sometime after April 1623 but before February 16, 1624, Henry Fry died on Jamestown Island (**1**) (CBE 39).

JOHN FRY

John Fry died at Flowerdew Hundred (**53**) sometime after April 1623 but before February 16, 1624 (CBE 37).

JOHN FRYE

On February 16, 1624, John Frye was living in Elizabeth City (**17, 18**) (CBE 37).

***

GEORGE FRYER (FRIER)

George Fryer (Frier) came to Virginia on the *William and Thomas*, and on February 16, 1624, he and his wife were living on the mainland (**3**) just west of Jamestown Island. On January 30, 1625, when a muster was made of the colony's inhabitants, George Fryer and his wife, Ursula, still were living there. He then headed a relatively well-supplied household. On January 3, 1625, he testified about a bequest that William Hening had made to Stephen Webb. At the end of the month George Fryer was paid for the loss of his crop yield. On March 14, 1625, while Fryer was living in Pasbehay, he sold some boards to William Harwood of Martin's Hundred (**7**). This raises the possibility that he was a sawyer. On April 25, 1626, George Fryer was jailed for failing to pay for the work done for him by Robert Wright (a Jamestown Island carpenter) and another man. Court records dating to December 8, 1628, indicate that the late Leonard Huett had bequeathed Goodman George Fryer his chest and its contents, in an attempt to repay him for his kindness (CBE 40, 57; MCGC 40-41, 46, 50, 101, 179; DOR 1:25).

URSULA FRYER (FRIER)
(MRS. GEORGE FRYER [FRIER])

Ursula, the wife of George Fryer (Frier), came to Virginia on the *London Merchant* and on February 16, 1624, was sharing his home on the mainland (**3**) just west of Jamestown Island. On January 30, 1625, Ursula Fryer and her husband were living in Pasbehay, where they had been residing the previous year. The couple was relatively well provisioned and appear to have been living in a home of their own (CBE 40, 57; DOR 1:25).

***

RICHARD FRUBBUSHER

In 1609 Richard Frubbusher, a skillful shipwright who was born at Gravesend and lived at Limehouse, accompanied Sir Thomas Gates on a voyage to Virginia and was shipwrecked in Bermuda. Using the native cedar wood, Frubbusher built the pinnace that transported Gates to Jamestown (**1**) (HAI 403).

JOHN FRUDE

Between March and May 1630 it was noted that John Frude, mate and carpenter of the *Sun*, a leaky vessel, died in Virginia (EAE 21-22).

AMBROSE FUE

Ambrose Fue, a miller, immigrated to Virginia in April 1619 (FER 107).

THOMAS FULHAM

Thomas Fulham died in Elizabeth City (**17, 18**) sometime after April 1623 but before February 16, 1624 (CBE 45).

JOHN FULLER

John Fuller, a 24-year-old chandler from Kent, England, came to Virginia in 1619 on the *Bona Nova* and probably was a Virginia Company tenant or servant (FER 295).

MICHAEL FULLER

According to Captain John Smith, sometime after March 1622 but before 1624, Michael Fuller, who was aboard a ship anchored at Kecoughtan (**17**), tried to go ashore to trade. However, his small boat was blown across the James River. Fuller managed to return to shore and saw that his companions were rescued. Smith indicated that Michael Fuller was associated with the men Captain Nathaniel Butler brought to Virginia (CJS 2:318-320).

THOMAS FULLER

On September 2, 1624, when John Cheesman patented some land, he listed Thomas Fuller as a headright and described him as a servant he had transported to Virginia on the *Southampton* in 1622 (PB 1 Pt. 1:47).

REV. THOMAS FULLER

Court testimony dating to April and May 1622 indicates that the Rev. Thomas Fuller, a 28-year-old clergyman, had lived in Virginia four or five years earlier, when Sir Samuel Argall was deputy governor. Fuller testified that he was in Jamestown (**1**) in 1618 when the *Neptune* arrived and that he also was present when Edward Brewster was sentenced to death in a court martial. Richard Brewster, who had brought suit against Argall, testified that the Rev. Fuller arrived on the *Neptune* and was in Jamestown very briefly. Brewster said that Fuller decided that he did not like Virginia and returned to England, having only preached once. On April 19, 1622, the Rev. Thomas Fuller indicated that he was then living at John Lee's house in Little Minories without Aldergate, in London (C 24/489 f 1, 24/490; SR 9947).

SAMUEL FULSHAW

Samuel Fulshaw, who lived on the lower side of the James River within the corporation of James City (8-15), died sometime after April 1623 but before February 16, 1624 (CBE 41).

JOHN FULWOOD

On February 16, 1624, John Fulwood was living on Hog Island (16). Sometime prior to October 15, 1629, he had obtained land in Accomac, in an area south of William Smith's 100-acre leasehold (CBE 41; PB 1 Pt.1:100).

[NO FIRST NAME] FURLOW

Sometime after April 1623 but before February 16, 1624, Mr. Furlow's child died on Jamestown Island (1). It is uncertain whether Mr. Furlow himself was in the colony (CBE 39).

GEORGE FURZMAN

On April 28, 1624, George Furzman was assigned part of John Bernard's land at Martin's Hundred (7). According to Virginia Company records, Furzman's acreage was identified on a map of the settlement (VCR 2:532-533).

JOHN FYERBRASSE

In 1619 John Fyerbrasse of London, who was found guilty of stabbing someone, was imprisoned in Newgate. Later he was reprieved and found fit for service in "foreign parts" (CBE 11).

NICHOLAS FYNLOE

On December 21, 1624, Nicholas Fynloe was named to the jury that was impaneled to investigate young George Pope II's drowning death on Jamestown Island (1) MCGC 38).

G

ROBERT GAGE

On April 8, 1629, the justices of the General Court discussed the fact that when George Ungwin's servant, Dorcas Howard, had a miscarriage on March 22nd, she admitted that Robert Gage was the baby's father. Ungwin, who lived within the corporation of James City, was ordered to see that Howard appeared in court to answer the justices' questions (MCGC 194).

ELIAS (ELLIAS) GAILE (GALE)

On February 16, 1624, Elias (Ellias) Gaile (Gale) was living in John Burrows' Jamestown Island (1) household. He was still sharing the Burrows family's home on January 24, 1625, and was a 14-year-old indentured servant. Elias was sent to Virginia in late 1622 by the Rev. Patrick Copeland as an apprentice for the East India School and was supposed to serve Copeland for 10 years. On February 19, 1626, when Elias Gaile was 15, he witnessed a dispute between Thomas Leister and Roger Stanley, which resulted in a sword fight. Afterward, he was called on to testify before the General Court (CBE 38, 56; MCGC 52, 94-95).

JOHN GAILE (GALE)

On February 16, 1624, John Gaile (Gale) was living at Flowerdew Hundred (53) and probably was one of Abraham Peirsey's servants (CBE 37).

ROBERT GAILE

On October 24, 1621, Virginia Company officials learned that Robert Gaile had filed suits against John Burrows of Jamestown Island (1) and the estate of William Tracy of Berkeley Hundred (55) (VCR 1:535-536).

ROBERT GAINNE

Robert Gainne came to Virginia in 1634 on the *John and Dorothy* at the expense of Adam Thorogood, who used his headright on June 24, 1635, when patenting some land (PB 1 Pt. 1:179).

JOHN GALEN

On July 26, 1628, officials decided that John Galen, a boy brought in from Fleet Street and being detained in Bridewell or Bethlem, would be sent to Virginia (HUME 33-34).

WILLIAM GALLAWAY

William Gallaway came to Virginia on the *Anne* in 1623 at the expense of Captain William Eppes, who used his headright when patenting some land on February 3, 1626 (PB 1 Pt. 1:49).

WILLIAM GALLOPIN

On June 14, 1632, William Gallopin and Percival Champion's wife, Jane, were sentenced to hanging after being found guilty of murdering their illegitimate child and concealing the death. In 1635 Percival Champion was living in the upper portion of Elizabeth City (**18**) that eventually became Warwick County (MCGC 480).

STEPHEN GALTHORPE (CALTHROP, HALTHROP)

According to George Percy's narrative, Stephen Galthorpe (Calthrop, Halthrop) died in Jamestown (**1**) on August 15, 1607. Captain John Smith later said that Edward Maria Winfield claimed that Stephen had led a mutiny (HAI 99; CJS 1:20; 2:139).

NATHANIEL GAMMON (GANNON)

On February 16, 1624, Nathaniel Gammon (Gannon) was living at Basses Choice (**27**) in the corporation of Warresqueak (CBE 46).

***

HENRY GANEY (GAINEY, GENY, GENEY, GANY, GAYNE)

Henry Ganey (Gainey, Geny, Geney, Gany, Gayne) came to Virginia on the *Duty* in 1619 and probably was one of the young male servants dubbed by their contemporaries as "the *Duty* boys." Prior to his departure from England, Ganey received a small sum from a Mr. Langley. On February 16, 1624, Henry Ganey was living in Elizabeth City. He was still there in early 1625, at which time he was identified as a 21-year-old servant in Francis Mason's home in Elizabeth City (**18**). In October 1625 Ganey was summoned to court and found guilty of illegal trading. A month later, he got into a dispute with Lieutenant William Barry. In December 1625 Henry Ganey was questioned about the late Luke Eden's chest, which had been broken open and emptied of its contents while in his custody. On November 6, 1626, he pled poverty and was released from the bond he had been required to post on account of illegally trading corn. However, within a week he was back in court and was fined for drunkenness. By February 12, 1628, Henry Ganey was dead. The General Court named Augustine Leake of Martin's Hundred (**7**) as his administrator. In September 1635 William Ganey, Henry's brother, listed him as a headright and claimed his personal adventure (VCR 3:183; CBE 44, 65; MCGC 73, 77, 86, 94, 123, 133, 167; PB 1 Pt.1:286).

WILLIAM GANEY I (GANY, GEYNY, GAINEY, GAINYE, GENY, GENEY, GAYNE) I

William Ganey (Gany, Geyny, Gainey, Gainye, Geny, Geney, Gayne) I, an ancient planter and mariner, came to Virginia on the *Treasurer* or the *George* in 1616. According to Captain John Smith, Ganey was a gunner and had piloted a ship for Edward Brawnd that was heading for Plymouth. Ganey arranged for Thomas Jones of the *Falcon* to take a shipment of sassafras to London in 1621. Virginia Company records that date to early 1623 note that William Ganey was related to John Robinson, who was then in Virginia. Captain John Smith said that Ganey was aligned with Captain Nathaniel Butler and others who favored a more forceful, martial approach to governing the colony. Smith called Ganey a brave man and said that when a trading vessel he was aboard was blown across the James River at Kecoughtan, he went for help and saw that his shipmates were rescued. On January 12, 1624, when William Ganey patented 200 acres of land in Elizabeth City (**18**) on the west side of the Hampton River, he used his own headright and that of his three servants. When a census was taken on February 16, 1624, Ganey was living in Elizabeth City with his wife and daughter, both of whom were named Anna. Later in the month, he filed a claim against Captain Thomas Nuce's estate in an attempt to recover compensation for the voyages he had undertaken to Newfoundland on Nuce's behalf and the trading voyages in which he had participated. Like many other colonists, William Ganey occasionally had problems with debt. He reportedly obtained a quantity of fish from Jamestown (1) merchant John Chew under false pretenses and then used it himself. He also sent a Dutchman aboard the *Treasurer*, in violation of the law, to retrieve some copper furnaces, presumably distillation equipment. On the other hand, Ganey curried the authorities' favor when he testified against Captain John Martin. When a muster was compiled in early 1625, William Ganey, who was age 33, was living in Elizabeth City, where he headed a household that included his 24-year-old wife, Anna (I), their daughter, Anna (II), and seven servants. The Ganey household was in possession of three dwellings, a palisade, an abundant supply of stored food and defensive weaponry, and some livestock. In May 1625 William Ganey was credited with 200 acres of land in Elizabeth City, acreage that was planted. He appeared in court twice during 1625 and testified about dealings that involved William Harwood, Luke Eden, and Humphrey Rastell. In early 1626 he was fined for disobeying a court order, for he had failed to bring a shallop-load of corn to John Chew in Jamestown. In October 1626 he received a pass to go to England. It was around that time that Thomas Savage, one of his young servants, drowned while assisting another man. When William Ganey went to England, he may have taken along his wife, Anna, and children, Anna and William, for all of them were listed as headrights when he claimed 1,250 acres of land in Accomack on September 17, 1635. He also used the headright of his deceased brother, Henry. William Ganey died sometime prior to January 1643, at which time his wife was identified as a widow (CJS 2:318-320; 3:320; EAE 11; VCR 4:5-6, 288, 455-456, 558; CBE 44, 66, 69-70; PB 1 Pt. 1:38-39, 286; MCGC 21, 30, 46-47, 57, 84, 86-87, 94, 121-122, 131; AMES 1:55, 98; DOR 1:62).

ANNA (ANN, ANNE) GANEY I (MRS. WILLIAM GANEY [GANY, GEYNY, GAINEY, GAINYE, GENY, GENEY, GAYNE] I)

Anna (Ann, Anne), who became the wife of ancient planter William Ganey (Gany, Gey-

ny, Gainey, Gainye, Geny, Geney, Gayne) I, came to Virginia in 1620 on the *Bona Nova*. On February 16, 1624, the Ganeys were residing in Elizabeth City (18) where William was a household head. On November 16, 1624, Mrs. Anna Ganey appeared before the General Court and asked the justices to prevent Captain Whittaker from departing before her husband came home. Witnesses claimed that Whitaker had demanded payment in tobacco from Mrs. Ganey, who had none that was cut and cured. Ultimately, Whitaker, who was ready to set sail for England, was permitted to leave. When a muster was taken in early 1625, 24-year-old Anna Ganey, her husband, and their daughter, Anna II, were living in Elizabeth City in a home they shared with 7 servants. On October 14, 1626, Mrs. Ganey appeared in court to testify about the accidental drowning of her husband's servant boy Thomas Savage. On September 17, 1635, William Ganey I used his wife's personal adventure as a headright when patenting some land on the Eastern Shore and also listed his son and daughter, William II and Ann II. Mrs. Anna Ganey outlived her husband and in January 1643 was described as a widow when she gave her power of attorney to Edward Hurd, a creditor (CBE 44, 66; MCGC 31-32, 122; PB 1 Pt. 1:286; EEAC 23).

ANNA GANEY (GANY, GEYNY, GAINEY, GAINYE, GENY, GENEY, GAYNE) II

Anna Ganey II (Gany, Geyny, Gainey, Gainye, Geny, Geney, Gayne), who was born in Virginia, was living with her parents, William and Anna Ganey I, in Elizabeth City (18) when a census was taken on February 16, 1624. When a muster was made of the colony's inhabitants in early 1625, Anna II was living in a household headed by her father. William Ganey I used the headright of his daughter, Anna II, when patenting some land in Accomack on September 17, 1635 (PB 1 Pt.1:286).

WILLIAM GANEY (GANY, GEYNY, GAINEY, GAINYE, GENY, GENEY, GAYNE) II

William Ganey (Gany, Geyny, Gainey, Gainye, Geny, Geney, Gayne) I of Elizabeth City (18) used the headright of his son, William Ganey II, when patenting some land on September 17, 1635. William Ganey II probably was born after a muster was taken in early 1625 (PB 1 Pt.1:286).

***

WILLIAM GANEY (GAYNE, GAINES)

William Ganey (Gayne, Gaines) came to Virginia in 1620 on the *Bona Nova* and on February 16, 1624, was residing in Elizabeth City on the west side of the Hampton River **(18)**. In early 1625 William Ganey, who was 26 years old, was still residing in Elizabeth City and was sharing a dwelling with his partner, Robert Newman. The two men shared their home with six others and had an ample supply of stored food and defensive weaponry. In January 1627 William was identified as one of the Virginia Company's tenants who had been assigned to Captain William Tucker (CBE 44, 65; MCGC 136; DOR 1:59).

ROBERT GANDE

On June 18, 1629, Robert Gande shipped some goods from Plymouth, England, to Virginia (CBE 46).

P. GANTOIS

P. Gantois, a young male theology student, was among the Walloons and French who indicated their willingness to go to Virginia. In August 1621 the Virginia Company agreed that they could immigrate (CBE 24).

HENRY GAPE

On March 22, 1622, when the Indians attacked Weyanoke **(52)**, Henry Gape, one of Sir George Yeardley's men, was killed (VCR 3:569).

CLEMENT GARDNER

On February 27, 1619, Clement Gardner, a boy being detained at Bridewell Prison, was among those to be sent to Virginia. He was one of the children who had been rounded up from the streets of London so that they could be transported to the colony (CBE 12).

EDWARD GARDNER

On February 16, 1624, Edward Gardner was living at West and Shirley Hundred **(41)** (CBE 36).

JAMES GARDNER

On January 29, 1620, James Gardner, a vagrant brought in from St. Dunstan's, appeared before the Bridewell Court, where the justices decided that he should be sent to Virginia (CBE 17).

JOHN GARDNER

On February 27, 1619, John Gardner, a boy being detained at Bridewell, was among those chosen to be sent to Virginia. He was one of the children who had been rounded up from the streets of London so that they could be transported to the colony (CBE 12).

JOHN GARDNER

On August 30, 1628, the justices of Bridewell Court decided to send John Gardner, a runaway apprentice brought in from London's Cheap Ward, to Virginia. Because he had run away nine times, his master released him from his contract so that he could be sent to the colony (CBE 84).

EDWARD GAREN

On March 16, 1627, Edward Garen, who was age 38, testified before the General Court. He said that approximately a month earlier, when he and Thomas Lawley stopped overnight at Martin's Brandon **(59)**, Lawley complained of being ill. He said that Lawley died the very next day, shortly after arriving at his home in Shirley Hundred **(41)**. Garen said that Lawley had fought with Robert Cooke while aboard the *Plantation* and had sustained a chest injury. Other witnesses' accounts varied slightly (MCGC 144-146).

PATRICK GARLAND

On February 10, 1632, Patrick Garland, master of the *Merlyn*, left Barnstaple, England, bound for Virginia (CBE 100).

WALTER GARLAND

On December 24, 1619, Walter Garland was among the men and boys brought in from the streets of London so that they could be sent to Virginia. He escaped from prison during the night, and it is uncertain whether he was captured (CBE 14).

THOMAS GARNETT

Ancient planter Thomas Garnett came to Virginia in 1610 on the *Swan*, a ship in the fleet that brought Lord Delaware to the colony. On August 3, 1619, when the assembly convened for its first session, Captain William Powell Jamestown (**1**), a burgess, made allegations against Garnett, who was one of his servants. He claimed that Garnett was lewd and treacherous and said that he had behaved wantonly with a widowed female servant. He also said that when confronted in the presence of the governor, Garnett called Powell a thief and a drunkard. Powell claimed that Garnett had caused him financial losses and had sought to have him deposed from office, even killed. Several other servants testified against Garnett in support of Powell's allegations. Afterward, the assembly, acting as a judicial body, found Thomas Garnett guilty as charged and sentenced him to a daily public whipping for four consecutive days and to stand with his ears nailed to the pillory for the same length of time. By February 16, 1624, Thomas Garnett was a free man and household head, and was living in Elizabeth City (**18**) with his wife, Elizabeth, and daughter, Susan. In early 1625 Thomas was age 40 and his wife, Elizabeth, was 26. The Garnetts, who had a 3-year-old, Virginia-born daughter named Susan, occupied a dwelling of their own and had a good supply of stored food and defensive weaponry. Sharing the Garnett home was another couple, Virginia Company tenant and carpenter/sawyer Ambrose Griffin and his wife, Joyce. On July 3, 1635, Thomas Garnett patented 200 acres of land in Elizabeth City (**19**) near the Little Poquoson River, acquiring his acreage by means of the headright system (VCR 3:169; CBE 13, 44, 66; PB 1 Pt. 1:202; DOR 1:61).

ELIZABETH GARNETT (MRS. THOMAS GARNETT)

Elizabeth, who married ancient planter Thomas Garnett, came to Virginia in 1619 on the *Neptune*. On February 16, 1624, she was living in Elizabeth City (**18**) with her husband, Thomas, and daughter, Susan. At the beginning of 1625 the Garnetts were still living in Elizabeth City and occupied a dwelling of their own. Thomas Garnett, who was age 40, was a household head.

Elizabeth was then 26 years old and daughter, Susan, was age 3. Another couple, the Griffins, shared their home (CBE 44, 66).

SUSAN GARNETT

On February 16, 1624, Susan Garnett was living with her parents, Thomas and Elizabeth Garnett, in Elizabeth City (**18**). In early 1625 Susan and her parents were still residing in Elizabeth City. She was then age 3 and was described as Virginia-born (CBE 44, 66).

***

[NO FIRST NAME] GARRETT

On July 3, 1627, Alice Proctor's legal representative, Captain Samuel Mathews, testified that a man named Garrett and a Dutch carpenter named Derrick had borrowed the late John Proctor's wherry (a small boat) and lost it. Mathews said that Derrick had offered to pay for half of the cost of the missing boat. Alice and John Proctor were then residing at Paces Paines (**9**) (MCGC 150).

SAMUEL GARRETT

On December 17, 1631, Samuel Garrett and Richard Bennett, a London merchant, shipped goods from Barnstaple, England, to Virginia on the *Eagle* of Northam (CBE 97).

WILLIAM GARRETT (GARRET)

Captain John Smith reported that William Garrett (Garret), a bricklayer, was one of the first planters and arrived in Virginia during spring 1607. He was one of the first Jamestown (**1**) colonists (CJS 1:209; 2:142).

WILLIAM GARRETT (GARRET)

William Garrett came to Virginia in 1619 aboard the *George*. By January 20, 1625, he was residing at Flowerdew Hundred (**53**), where he was a 22-year-old servant in Abraham Peirsey's household. On October 10, 1627, William Garrett, who was still a Peirsey servant, was brought before the General Court, where he was accused of having behaved lewdly with fellow servant Katherine Lemon. The justices found insufficient proof that Garrett needed to be disciplined beyond the punishment he already had received from Peirsey (CBE 50; MCGC 154).

THOMAS GARSES

Court testimony taken on May 30, 1625, indicates that in April 1622 Thomas Garses was among those who cleared ground on Hog Island (16) and therefore was entitled to two shares of that cleared acreage (MCGC 163).

JOHN GARYE

On February 13, 1635, John Garye received a patent for 300 acres of land on the southeast side of the Nansemond River (20 c) (PB 1 Pt. 1:332).

GEORGE GASCOIGNE

In 1619 George Gascoigne, a London burglar or housebreaker, who was being detained in Newgate Prison, was reprieved and sentenced to transportation to "foreign parts," probably Virginia (CBE 11).

JOHN GASCOIGNE

On September 17, 1630, John Gascoigne, a vagrant boy brought in from St. Sepulcher's in London, indicated that he was willing to go to Virginia (CBE 92).

THOMAS GASKON (GASKOYNE, GASCOIGNE, GASKINE, GASKINS, GASKO)

Thomas Gaskon (Gaskoyne, Gascoigne, Gaskine, Gaskins, Gasko) came to Virginia on the *Bona Nova* in 1619 and probably was a Virginia Company servant or tenant. On February 16, 1624, he was living at Flowerdew Hundred (53), but by early 1625 had moved to the Eastern Shore where he was a household head, probably on Old Plantation Creek (73). Gaskon was then age 34 and shared his home with two other men. The household had an ample supply of stored food and defensive weaponry. In May 1635 Thomas Gaskon appeared before Accomack's monthly court, where he verified his eligibility to patent land on the basis of 6 headrights of people he had transported from the Bermuda Islands. When he received a patent for 300 acres in September 1636, the names of family members

Josias, Elizabeth, Alice, and Mary Gaskon were listed. On January 10, 1645, Thomas affixed his mark to an inventory, verifying its accuracy. In 1649 he patented some land in Northumberland County and began making the Northern Neck his home. He purchased some land in Lancaster County, quickly reselling it. In 1658, when testifying in court, he said that he was age 60. When he made his will in June 1663, he named his sons Josias, Thomas, and Henry, son-in-law Henry Mayes, and daughters Elizabeth, Elitia, Alice, and Mary. Thomas Gaskon died prior to November 20, 1665 (CBE 37, 69; AMES 1:35; 2: 51-52, 183, 198, 226, 401; DOR 1:70; 2:54-55; PB 1 Pt. 1:377; 2:180).

PIERRE GASPAR

Pierre Gaspar was among the Walloons and French who indicated their willingness to go to Virginia. In August 1621 the Virginia Company agreed that they could immigrate (CBE 25-26).

EBEDMELECK GASTRELL

On February 16, 1624, Ebedmeleck Gastrell was living at the College (66) (CBE 35).

WILLIAM GASTROCK

William Gastrock came to Virginia in 1633 on the *Hopewell* at the expense of Adam Thorogood, who used his headright when patenting some land on June 24, 1635 (PB 1 Pt. 1:179).

[NO FIRST NAME] GATES

In November 1622 a man named Gates, who was heading to Virginia on the *Seaflower*, was supposed to take aboard his own tobacco and Maurice Thompson's. As Thompson owned 150 acres of land between Newportes News (24) and Blunt Point (22), Gates may have been associated with the westernmost part of the corporation of Elizabeth City (EAE 12).

DANIEL GATES

On November 21, 1621, Virginia Company officials authorized Daniel Gates, master of the *Darling,* to trade and fish (VCR 1:554, 562; 3:514-515).

HENRY GATES

On October 7, 1622, Virginia Company officials noted that Henry Gates and Captain William Tucker had failed to account for Company goods that were in their possession in Virginia. Tucker was then the commander of the people in Kecoughtan (**18**) on the west side of the Hampton River (VCR 2:104).

JOHN GATES

On September 28, 1628, it was decided that John Gates, who had been delivered to the Rev. Lewis Hughes, would be sent to Virginia (CBE 84).

SIR THOMAS GATES

Sir Thomas Gates was born at Colyford in Colyton Parish, Devonshire, England. He came to America in 1585-1586 with Sir Francis Drake and later distinguished himself in the fight to take Cadiz. Gates was knighted in June 1597, and early in King James I's reign he enlisted in the army and served in the Netherlands, where he was captain of a company of soldiers. It was there in Oudewater that he became acquainted with Sir Thomas Dale. On April 24, 1608, the Dutch granted Gates a leave of absence to go to Virginia for a year. On July 5, 1609, he left England in a fleet of eight ships and a pinnace, vessels that transported 500 men and women to Virginia. Among those in Gates's party (the 3rd Supply of new colonists) were 100 landsmen. Gates brought along provisions and various types of equipment. The detailed instructions he received from the Virginia Company required him to build towns, see that the colony was adequately defended, and produce commodities that could be exported. He also was authorized to establish a new capital city at an inland site that was considered safe, and he was allowed to exact tribute from the Indians. Enroute to Virginia, Gates's fleet encountered a hurricane. The *Seaventure*, the ship carrying Gates and the colony's other leaders, wrecked in Bermuda on July 28, 1609, although most of the other vessels in the fleet reached Virginia. Finally, on May 10, 1610, Gates and approximately 100 other survivors left Bermuda in two vessels they built from the native cedar wood. When Gates arrived in Jamestown (**1**) on May 21st, he found the 60 surviving colonists starving and in dire straits. Because the provisions he had brought from Bermuda were insubstantial and could not meet the Jamestown colonists' needs, he decided to evacuate them to Newfoundland, where they could secure passage to England. Only the timely arrival of Lord Delaware's fleet in June 1610, which encountered the departing settlers, averted abandonment of the colony. On June 10, 1610, the colonists returned to Jamestown, and two days later Lord Delaware named Gates second in command. Within weeks, he had his men attack the Kecoughtan Indians' town, forever claiming for the colonists the area around Old Point Comfort (**17**). In late July 1610 Delaware dispatched Gates to England to bring back additional colonists, supplies, and livestock. Delaware became ill and by March 1611 left the colony so that he could recover his health. Sir Thomas Dale arrived in Virginia on May 10, 1611, and served as the colony's principal leader until Sir Thomas Gates returned on August 1, 1611, to take over as acting governor. When Gates's fleet of six ships approached Jamestown, Dale mistook it for a Spanish invasion and prepared the colonists to defend themselves. Gates brought to the colony 280 men, 20 women, 200 kine, and 200 swine, along with supplies and equipment. In an attempt to make the settlers work toward their own support, Gates enacted a strict military code of justice, which Dale later enhanced and enforced. During the time Gates held office, he undertook construction of three forts at the mouth of the James River.

Although Sir Thomas Dale set out to establish new settlements toward the head of the James River and resided at Bermuda Hundred (**39**), Sir Thomas Gates erected many improvements in Jamestown, where he lived. Under Gates's government, a new wharf, an additional blockhouse, a governor's house, and several other new buildings were constructed in Jamestown. According to Ralph Hamor, Gates had a garden in Jamestown that contained small but vigorously growing fruit trees. Sir Thomas Gates returned to England in March 1614, leaving Sir Thomas Dale in command as deputy governor. Although the Gates and Dale regimes were harshly criticized because of the forceful means used to compel the colonists to work, both leaders were credited with saving the colony from extinction. In 1618 Sir Thomas Gates received compensation from the Dutch for the period he was absent from the Netherlands. Like Dale, he was credited with developing the Virginia colony into a base of trading operations, thereby enhancing commerce with the Dutch. In 1620 Virginia Company officials asked Gates's advice about building a fort in Virginia. He told them that he could recommend a Frenchman with the necessary skills, who might be persuaded to move to Virginia. Gates, a hardliner who favored a military style of government for the colony, petitioned for Governor George Yeardley's removal. Sir Thomas Gates never returned to Virginia. He died in the Netherlands in September 1622 and on June 13, 1623, his son, Thomas, was given administration of his estate. At the time of his death, Sir Thomas Gates was a resident of Halden, in Kent, England (OCAL 1:2, 16; CJS 1:127; 2:218, 233-234, 236-239, 241, 277, 327, 347, 390; VCR 1:313, 316-317; 3:12-24, 231-232; 4:78; FOR 1:7:9, 11, 13; 2:7; 3:1:9-11, 14, 18; HAI 28, 415, 419-420, 423, 427, 433, 435, 438, 442-443, 459, 508-509, 517, 823, 825-826, 895-896, 899, 901-902, 907; BRO 320, 324, 345, 402, 404-405, 449, 473, 741, 749; AP 70-71, 73, 75-76; HAR 206-208; PB 1 Pt.1:12; MOR 42).

***

THOMAS GATES

Ancient planter Thomas Gates came to Virginia on the *Starr* in 1609. He identified himself as age 37 and a former Virginia Company servant on January 21, 1624, when he filed a petition with Virginia's governor and council, a copy of which was forwarded to England. He said that he had been hired by Sir Thomas Smith to make pitch and tar for three years, but that Deputy-Governor Samuel Argall had detained him for eight, forcing him to work without pay from dawn to dusk. He said that Argall had mistreated four of the six Polanders the Virginia Company had sent to Virginia and had sold the Company's cattle, pocketing the money. On February 16, 1624, Thomas Gates and his wife were living on the lower side of the James River, west of Grays Creek. On February 4, 1625, Gates and wife, Elizabeth, were identified as residents of Paces Paines (**9**), where they were in possession of a dwelling and had an ample supply of stored food and defensive weaponry. The Gates couple shared their home with William Bedford, who may have been Thomas's partner. On October 10, 1624, Thomas Gates testified before the General Court, which inves-

tigated the beating death of John and Alice Proctor's maidservant, Elizabeth Abbott, also of Paces Paines. On November 20, 1624, Thomas, who was seeking to recover a debt from John Jackson of Jamestown (**1**), was described as a man capable of making a house "tight." Thus, Thomas appears to have earned some income by caulking buildings, perhaps utilizing the pitch or tar that he knew how to make. In May 1625 Thomas Gates was credited with 100 acres of land on the lower side of the James, acreage to which he was entitled as an ancient planter. On December 18, 1626, he appeared in court, where he acknowledged that he owed some tobacco to George Riddle. He returned to court on June 4, 1627, and sued Captain John Martin for a tobacco bond dated April 20, 1626 (FER 523, 524; CBE 40, 59; VCR 4:558; MCGC 22, 33, 128, 150; DOR 1:39).

ELIZABETH GATES (MRS. THOMAS GATES)

Elizabeth, who married ancient planter Thomas Gates, came to Virginia in 1620 on the *Warwick* and may have been one of the young maids sent to the colony as prospective wives. On February 16, 1624, Elizabeth Gates and her husband were living on the lower side of the James River, west of Grays Creek. They most likely were residing at Paces Paines (**9**), where they were living on February 4, 1625, in a home they shared with William Bedford. Court testimony taken on September 11, 1626, in connection with allegations against Joan Wright, an accused witch, referred to Mrs. Wright's claim that Goodwife Gates's maidservant had stolen some firewood. On September 18th, when Elizabeth Gates appeared in court, she said that Mrs. Wright had threatened her maidservant and that when living in Kecoughtan, Mrs. Wright had placed a curse on a man's chickens, which died (CBE 40, 59; MCGC 111-112, 114).

***

JOHN GATHER (GATTER, GAITHER)

John Gather (Gatter, Gaiter) came to Virginia on the *George* in 1620 and on February 16, 1624, was an indentured servant in the household of Sir Francis Wyatt, who resided in urban Jamestown (**1**). By January 25, 1625, when a muster was taken of the colony's inhabitants, John Gather was living on Mulberry Island (21), where he was a servant in Captain William Peirce's household. He returned to England but by 1636 was back in the colony with his wife, Joan. When he left England, John indicated that he was age 36; his wife, Joan, was 23 years old. In 1636 John Gather secured three patents for land on the Elizabeth River (20 a), in what was then Elizabeth City County, and moved there. In 1640 he was designated a tobacco viewer for the area in which he lived. By February 1646 he had married a woman named Mary, with whom he moved to Maryland in 1649–1650. He died there sometime prior to November 24, 1652 (CBE 38, 57; DOR 1:47; 2:1-2; PB 1 Pt. 1:389; Pt. 2:578).

GEORGE GAUNTLETT

On January 3, 1626, the General Court's justices ordered merchant Humphrey Rastell to obtain a receipt from George Gauntlett and submit it to them before January 17th. Confirmation was required because Rastell was supposed to have satisfied his debt to Gauntlett in accord with a January 17, 1624, court order (MCGC 87).

WILLIAM GAUNTLETT (GAWNTLETT)

In 1621 William Gauntlett (Gawntlett) of Elizabeth City (18) made an agreement with Thomas Jones, captain of the ship *Falcon*, who agreed to take some sassafras to London. However, Gauntlett died in Elizabeth City sometime after April 1623 but before February 16, 1624. On October 10, 1624, the General Court ordered his executor to bring in an account of his estate, as the decedent, a churchwarden, had in his possession some funds collected as payment to some workmen building a new church. On April 8, 1625, the attorney of ship captain Thomas Jones reported that the sassafras shipped by William Gauntlett and other Kecoughtan residents had been sold on July 18, 1624. On December 5, 1625, Thomas Dunthorne, then functioning as Gauntlett's executor, was ordered to pay the decedent's debt to Sergeant John Harris (EAE 11; CBE 69-70; MCGC 22, 79).

JOHN GAVETT

John Gavett died in the corporation of Elizabeth City (17, 18) sometime after April 1623 but before February 16, 1624 (CBE 45).

JAMES GAY

On November 13, 1620, Virginia Company officials noted that James Gay, one of the late Captain Christopher Lawne's apprentices, had been assigned to Captain Ralph Hamor. Lawne, whose plantation (25), like Hamor's, was in the corporation of Warresqueak (26), had transferred the young man to Hamor. The Company decided to inform William Gay, James's father, that he could return to England if his transportation costs were paid. James Gay may have never returned home, for on February 16, 1624, he was living at West and Shirley Hundred (41) (VCR 1:419; CBE 36).

JOHN GAY

On January 24, 1629, John Gay, who indicated that he was 22 years old, identified himself as Benjamin Jackson's servant. He said that on New Year's day (that is, March 25, 1628), he had been mending a pint pot at his master's house at Blunt Point (22) when William Reade and John Burrows got into an argument and Reade gave Burrows a fatal stab wound (MCGC 183).

THOMAS GAY

On March 22, 1622, when the Indians attacked Lieutenant John Gibbs's plantation at Westover (54), Thomas Gay was killed (VCR 3:567).

WILLIAM GEALES

William Geales died in Elizabeth City (17, 18) sometime after April 1623 but before February 16, 1624 (CBE 45).

GUILBERT GEALIE

On January 29, 1620, Guilbert Gealie was among those sentenced by the justices of Bridewell Court to transportation to Virginia (CBE 18).

JOHN GEE

Between February 14, 1624, and January 25, 1625, John Gee died in Jamestown (1). On December 22, 1626, Jane Roode, who was identified as the daughter of John Gee of Burneham in Somerset, was granted administration of his estate (CBE 56; MOR 43).

GEORGE GEFFREY

On September 12, 1618, George Geffrey, a vagrant boy brought in from St. Sepulcher's, was among those chosen to be sent to Virginia (CBE 9).

ALEXANDER GEORGE

On March 12, 1627, Alexander George brought suit against the company of the *Peter and John*, whom he accused of stealing some of his wine on the voyage to Virginia. George died in Virginia sometime prior to August 13, 1627. When he made his will, he designated Thomas Harwood and William Perry as overseers and asked them to take custody of his estate. The General Court appointed them the decedent's administrators (MCGC 151-152).

RICHARD GENOWAY

On May 20, 1607, Richard Genoway, a sailor who was in Jamestown (1), accompanied Captain Christopher Newport on an exploratory voyage of the James River (HAI 102).

VALLENTYNE GENTLER

Vallentyne Gentler died in Jamestown (1) sometime after April 1623 but before February 16, 1624 (CBE 39).

RICHARD GERRARD

On July 10, 1634, George Calvert named Richard Gerrard as custodian of his goods in Maryland and Virginia, if he were to die overseas (SH 19).

CLAUDE GHISELIN

Tailor Claude Ghiselin, a young man, was among the Walloons and French who indicated their willingness to go to Virginia. In August 1621 the Virginia Company agreed that they could immigrate (CBE 25).

HENRY GIBBINS ALIAS TIREMAKER

On November 20, 1622, Henry Gibbins alias Tiremaker, an inmate of Newgate Prison, was pardoned due to an epidemic of jail fever and was among those chosen for transportation to Virginia (CBE 29).

JOHN GIBBONS

On February 27, 1619, John Gibbons, a boy from the streets of London, was among the youngsters rounded up so that they could be sent to Virginia (CBE 12).

WILLIAM GIBBINS

On September 26, 1618, William Gibbins, who was brought in from St. Bartholomew's Hospital, was among those designated for transportation to Virginia (CBE 10).

FRANCIS GIBBS (GIBSON)

Francis Gibbs (Gibson) came to Virginia aboard the *Seaflower* and on February 16, 1624, was living in Ralph Hamor's household in urban Jamestown (1). On January 24, 1625, Francis, who was a young male servant, was still residing there (CBE 55).

JOHN GIBBS

In July and August 1619 Lieutenant John Gibbs served as a burgess for Captain John Ward's plantation (61). Afterward, he moved to Westover (54) and took up his own dividend of land. On March 22, 1622, when the Indians attacked Westover, Lieutenant John Gibbs and a dozen others were slain at his plantation (VCR 3:154, 567; CJC 2:301).

JOHN GIBBS (GIBBES)

John Gibbs (Gibbes) left Bristol, England, on September 10, 1620, on the *Supply*, with a group of settlers bound for Berkeley Hundred (55). Aboard was Arnold Oldisworth, Gibbs's master, who employed by John Smyth of Nibley. John Gibbs arrived at Berkeley Hundred on January 29, 1621. He was supposed to receive a certain number of acres of land in exchange for his years of service. Gibbs survived the March 22, 1622, Indian attack and afterward moved to Jordan's Journey (46), a fortified position of greater safety. He was still living there on February 16, 1624. On January 21, 1625, John Gibbs and his partner, Christopher Safford, jointly headed a Jordan's Journey household that included one male servant. Gibbs apparently maintained some ties to the Society of Berkeley Hundred's investors, for on June 28, 1624, he testified about the late George Thorpe's indebtedness to Mr. Dade. In 1632 John Gibbs asked those who had been members of the Society of Berkeley Hundred to consider reviving their plantation and requested some servants (CBE 21, 37, 51; S of N 41; VCR 3:397, 405-406, 426, 674; MCGC 17-18).

JOHN GIBBS (GIBBES, GYBS)

On August 1, 1622, Virginia Company officials noted that John Gibbs (Gibbes, Gybs), who came to Virginia in 1621 on the *Abigail*, had been sent to the colony as a Company servant. In early 1625 he was living on the south side of the Elizabeth River, on the Virginia Company's land (17) and was a 24-year-old servant in Sergeant William Barry's household. On January 12, 1627, when the defunct Virginia Company's servants and tenants were being assigned to high-ranking officials, John Gibbs was given to Governor George Yeardley (CBE 28, 68; VCR 3:674; MCGC 136).

MARY GIBBS (GHIBBS)

Mary Gibbs (Ghibbs), a young maid born in Cambridgeshire, came to Virginia in 1621 on the *Marmaduke*. Virginia Company records indicate that her late father was a blacksmith and that her mother was still living at Deptford. Before coming to the colony, Mary lived with Robert Peere (probably Perry), an uncle on her mother's side. Gabriel Barber, a Virginia Company investor, said that she was capable of making bone lace (FER 306, 309).

THOMAS GIBBS (GIBBES)

Court documents filed in March 1630 reveal that Lieutenant Thomas Gibbs (Gibbes) was in Virginia between 1619 and 1621, while Sir George Yeardley was governor and Receiver General of the Society of Southampton Hundred (44). Gibbs returned to England but on July 31, 1622, he and three servants set sail for Virginia on the *James*. Official records reveal that while Lieutenant Thomas Gibbs was living at Flowerdew Hundred (53), he agreed to sell some cattle to Thomas Hamor, but failed to uphold his end of the bargain. When the suit was settled on June 28, 1624, Gibbs was ordered to compensate Hamor's heirs no later than November 20th. On August 16, 1627, Thomas Gibbs was identified as master of the *Truelove*. On March 14, 1630, when he testified before the justices of Canterbury's Chancery Court, he identified himself as a resident of St. Butolph without Bishopsgate, London, and said that he was age 64. He was then a participant in the law suit Edmund Rossingham brought against Ralph Yeardley, the late Sir George Yeardley's administrator, and recounted events that took place during Sir George's first term as governor (FER 400; MCGC 9-11, 17; CBE 79; C 24/560 Pt. 2 f 84).

THOMAS GIBLIN

Thomas Giblin arrived at Martin's Hundred (7) around mid-January 1623, in a group of the Society of Martin's Hundred's servants. According to fellow servant, Richard Frethorne, Giblin died shortly thereafter at the home of Mr. William Harwood, the settlement's principal leader (VCR 4:60).

ANN GIBSON

Ann Gibson, a young maid, came to Virginia in 1621 on the *Tiger*. According to Virginia Company records, she was 21 years old and had been recommended by Mr. Switzer of the Blackfriars (FER 309).

FRANCIS GIBSON
(SEE FRANCIS GIBBS)

THOMAS GIBSON

Thomas Gibson, a tradesman, came to Virginia in early 1608, in the 1st Supply of new colonists arriving in Jamestown (1). During the year, he accompanied Captain John Smith on a visit to Werowocomoco. In 1608 Gibson was one of the men sent overland to build a house for Powhatan (CJS 1:241, 244; 2:191, 193).

ACHILLIS GIFFORD

Achilles Gifford, a 27-year-old gentleman from Devonshire, came to Virginia in 1619 on the *Bona Nova* and probably was a Virginia Company servant or tenant. His transportation cost was borne by the Ferrars, who were major Company investors (FER 295, 296).

FRANCIS GIFFORD

When a census was taken of the colony's inhabitants in March 1620, Francis Gifford was on a trading voyage to Accomack and Acohanock. He returned briefly, but left again. In May 1625, when a list of patented land was sent back to England, Francis Gifford was credited with 50 acres at Blunt Point (22), property that already had been seated (FER 159; VCR 4:557).

ISABELL GIFFORD
(SEE ISABELL GIFFORD RAYNER, MRS. ADAM RAYNER)

J. GIFFORD

On December 26, 1626, mariner and merchant Maurice Thompson informed Virginia Company officials that J. Gifford, who was supposed to transport an Indian to England, was still in Virginia. Gifford's first name is unknown (FER 606).

EDWARD GIFTEN (GIBSON)

On March 7, 1624, it was reported to the General Court that Edward Giften or Gibson had administered physic to the sick at Falling Creek (68). He also had treated the sick at Weyanoke (52). Thus, he probably was a surgeon or an apothecary (MCGC 11).

GILBERT

Someone named Gilbert was killed in Elizabeth City (17, 18) sometime after April 1623 but before February 16, 1624 (CBE 45).

THOMAS GILBERT

In 1621 Nicholas Ferrer sent a packet to Thomas Gilbert, who was in Virginia (FER 322).

ELIZABETH GILDING (GILDINGE)

Elizabeth Gilding (Gildinge) was among the Newgate prisoners pardoned on November 20, 1622, on account of an epidemic of jail fever. She was to be put to work or sent to Virginia (CBE 29).

JONATHAN (JONATHIN, JOHN) GILES

Jonathan (Jonathin, John) Giles came to Virginia in 1619 on the *Trial*. On February 16, 1624, he was living on the Governor's Land (3) and was one of Sir Francis Wyatt's men. By January 24, 1625, he had become part of Wyatt's household in urban Jamestown (1) and was identified as a 21-year-old indentured servant. In July 1627 Jonathan Giles, whose contract apparently had been sold, sued for his freedom in Elizabeth City's court, claiming that his time of service with Nicholas Roe (17) had expired. Merchant Thomas Weston successfully disputed Giles's assertion, and he was required to serve an additional six months, two of which were to cover court costs. On December 5, 1628, Jonathan testified about a conversation he had had with Jeffrey Cornish, whose brother had been executed (CBE 39, 54; MCGC 78, 165).

MARGARET GILES

On February 16, 1624, Margaret Giles was living at Basses Choice (27) (CBE 46).

WILLIAM GILES

On January 3, 1625, the justices of the General Court determined that William Giles owed funds to Simon Tuchin but had given a bill of exchange to Edward Tuchin, his brother (MCGC 40).

ALEXANDER GILL

Alexander Gill, who was from Maldon in Bedfordshire, England, arrived in Jamestown on September 12, 1623, on the *Bonny Bess* and took the oath of supremacy. On February 16, 1624, Gill was a servant in the household of Captain William Perse (Peirce) in urban Jamestown (1). By January 24, 1625, he had moved to Mulberry Island (21), where he was listed among Captain Peirce's servants. He was then age 20. Sometime prior to February 5, 1627, Peirce was ordered to free Alexander Gill or compensate him. He was then identified as Thomas Roper's servant, who had been hired out to Peirce (MCGC 6; CBE 38, 57; WITH 487).

JOHN GILL

On March 12, 1624, the General Court noted that John Gill was indebted to Mr.

Bennett. Two years later he received some tobacco from Robert Wright of Elizabeth City (17) on behalf of William Constable. On January 3, 1625, Gill, who was a merchant and gentleman, testified that he gave "Toby" (probably Toby Fellgate) one of Captain Hamor's tobacco notes. On April 3, 1626, Gill brought suit against Michael Marshott, one of his debtors. If he failed to pay, Gill was to be assigned his goods and servants. On April 3, 1626, Mr. John Gill was released from his contract with the Virginia Company. The General Court acknowledged that he had made many trips to Virginia. On March 28, 1627, Gill was described as a merchant when he sued Jamestown (1) gunsmith John Jackson, to whom he had brought an indentured servant with gunsmithing skills. On October 11, 1627, John Gill hired Benjamin Sims's servant, Joan Meatherst, for two years and agreed to pay him for her services. Gill returned to the General Court on January 21, 1628, to bring suit against Richard Alford, a debtor (MCGC 13, 40, 55, 97, 99-100, 154-155, 159, 169).

JAN GILLE

Laborer Jan Gille, his wife, and his three children were among the Walloons and French who indicated their willingness to go to Virginia. In August 1621 the Virginia Company agreed that they could immigrate (CBE 25).

RICHARD GILLETT

Richard Gillett died in Elizabeth City (17, 18) sometime after April 1623 but before February 16, 1624 (CBE 45).

WILLIAM GILLIAM

Sometime prior to December 1635 William Gilliam was sent to Virginia on the *Constance*. He was a servant to Christopher Boyse (Boyce, Boise), a Virginia colonist whose plantation was at Blunt Point (22) (EAE 58).

NICHOLAS GILLMAN

Nicholas Gillman, a carpenter, was sent to Virginia by the Company of Shipwrights in 1622 and was to work under the supervision of master boat-builder Thomas Nunn. The agreement Company of Shipwrights made with Gillman on May 18, 1622, specified that he would be compensated from the proceeds of his work. After five years of service, he was entitled to five acres of land. Several days after Nicholas Gillman signed the contract, he was given some money because he had agreed to go to Virginia. The Company of Shipwrights' workmen settled on Jamestown Island (1), where most of them died. In 1623 some of the survivors were sent to Elizabeth City (17, 18) (FER 378, 386; MCGC 99-100; VCR 4:108).

WILLIAM GILMAN

On December 31, 1619, William Gilman, an inmate at Newgate Prison, was selected to be sent to Virginia. On January 3, 1625, he was identified as one of the Society of Berkeley Hundred's (55) men who were planted at Shirley Hundred (41) (CBE 15; MCGC 42).

SAMUEL GILPHIN

Sometime prior to February 27, 1628, Samuel Gilphin, who was headed for Virginia, died aboard the *Samuel*. His will was witnessed by Thomas Gregory and surgeon William Southey (MCGC 168).

POST GINNAT

Post Ginnat, a surgeon, arrived in Virginia in 1608 in the 1st Supply of new colonists (CJS 1:223; 2:162).

[NO FIRST NAME] GIVE

In September 1632 the Virginia assembly voted to see that Captain Give was paid from public funds (HEN 1:196).

NICHOLAS GLEADSTON

Nicholas Gleadston died at Martin's Hundred (7) sometime after April 1623 but before February 16, 1624 (CBE 42).

MATHEW GLOSTER (GLOUCESTER)

Mathew Gloster (Gloucester) came to Virginia on the *Warwick* in 1621 and on February 16, 1624, was living at West and Shirley Hundred (41). When a muster was taken there on January 22, 1625, Mathew was identified as a 20-year-old servant in Christopher Woodward's household (CBE 36, 52).

HENRY GLOVER

On February 16, 1624, Henry Glover was living in the Jamestown Island (1) household of John Grevett (CBE 40).

JOHN GLOVER ALIAS JARVICE (SEE JOHN JARVICE)

NICHOLAS GLOVER

In August 1612 English probate officials noted that Nicholas Glover, a bachelor, had died in Virginia. Administration of his estate was given to his nephew, John Carter (EEAC 24).

***

THOMAS GODBY (GOODBY, GODBIE)

Thomas Godby (Goodby, Godbie), an ancient planter, arrived in Virginia in 1610 on the *Deliverance*, one of the vessels built by Sir Thomas Gates's men after they were marooned in Bermuda. On February 16, 1624, when a census was made of the colony's inhabitants, Thomas Godby and his wife were living in Elizabeth City (18). On December 1, 1624, Thomas, a yeoman farmer, patented 100 acres of land between Blunt Point (22) and Newportes News (24), his first dividend as an ancient planter. When a muster of Elizabeth City's inhabitants was compiled in early 1625, Thomas Godby was identified as a 38-year-old household head who shared his home with his wife, Joan, and two men who appear to have been free. The Godby household was well supplied with stored food and defensive weaponry. In May 1625, when a list of patent land was sent to England, Thomas Godby's 100 acres in Elizabeth City below Blunt Point were included. On December 5, 1625, he and several others were summoned to appear in the General Court on December 12th, at which time they were to present their claims against merchant Thomas Weston. On February 8, 1629, Thomas Godby, who was described as an Elizabeth City planter, went to William Parker's house at Merry Point, where he and several other men consumed a large quantity of wine. During the evening, William Bentley, who was descending the

James River in a borrowed boat, ran aground but nobody responded to his calls for help. Bentley became very angry and when he reached William Parker's house, he and Godby exchanged insults, then blows that culminated in Thomas Godby's death. On March 3, 1629, Bartholomew Weathersby was given letters of administration so that he could settle the late Thomas Godby's estate and a few days later, William Bentley was tried and found guilty of manslaughter (CBE 44, 65; PB 1 Pt. 1:25; VCR 4:557; MCGC 78, 188, 190-191; DOR 1:59).

JOAN GODBY (GOODBY, GODBIE) (MRS. THOMAS GODBY, GODBIE)

Joan, who married ancient planter Thomas Godby (Goodby, Godbie), came to Virginia in 1621 on the *Flying Hart*. On February 16, 1624, Thomas and Joan Godby were living in Elizabeth City (18). A year later, when a muster was compiled, Joan was described as age 42. Thus, she was four years older than her husband, who was a household head. In March 1629 Bartholomew Weathersby was named administrator of the late Thomas Godby's estate, thereby raising the possibility that Joan also was dead (CBE 44, 65).

***

THOMAS GODBY

Thomas Godby, a 25-year-old husbandman from Leicestershire, came to Virginia in 1619 on the *Bona Nova*, a vessel that arrived in mid-November and brought many Virginia Company tenants and servants to the colony (FER 295).

RICHARD GODFREY (GODFREE)

Richard Godfrey (Godfree), a joiner, set sail for Virginia on the *Margaret* of Bristol in September 1619 with Captain John Woodlief, one of the principal leaders of Berkeley Hundred (55). Godfrey's contract with the Society of Berkeley Hundred's investors permitted him to retain a tenth of his earnings and a tenth of his work product. The Society also agreed to furnish him with woodworking tools. While Richard Godfrey was in Virginia, the Society of Berkeley Hundred was supposed to provide his wife with some financial support. Godfrey sent some tobacco back to England with ship captain Tobias Felgate, who had orders to leave Virginia before March 24, 1620. In June 1620 Virginia Company officials noted that Richard Godfrey had not communicated with his wife or with John Smyth of Nibley, one of Berkeley Hundred's principal investors. A notation by the list of people who went to Berkeley Hundred with John Woodlief indicates that Richard Godfrey drowned. When or where he perished is not known (CBE 13-14; VCR 3:178, 187, 197, 199, 213-215, 293, 435-436).

WILLIAM GODFREY

On July 6, 1627, William Godfrey shipped goods from London to Virginia on the *Golden Lion* of Dundee (CBE 78).

JOHN GODSON

On July 4, 1623, John Godson was listed among those who agreed to provide relief to the colony by sending supplies (VCR 4:245-246).

ROBERT GODWIN (GODWYN)

Robert Godwin (Godwyn) came to Virginia on the *Swan* in 1624 and in early 1625 was living on the east side of the Hampton River on land that was owned by the Virginia Company (17). Robert was then described as a 19-year-old servant in the household headed by Anthony Bonall, one of the Frenchmen sent to the colony to produce wine and silk. On February 9, 1633, Robert Godwin was identified as the father-in-law (actually, stepfather) of Theophilus Stone, an orphan, who had been left a bequest by the late Thomas Beristone (CBE 68; MCGC 202).

REIGN GODWINE

On January 13, 1627, Reign Godwin, one of the defunct Virginia Company's tenants, was assigned to provost marshal Randall Smallwood, who lived in urban Jamestown (1) (MCGC 137).

THOMAS GODWORD

On May 20, 1607, Thomas Godword, a sailor, went with Captain Christopher Newport on a discovery of the James River (HAI 102).

JOHN GOFFE

John Goffe, a 40-year-old husbandman from Sommersetshire, came to Virginia in 1619 on the *Bona Nova*, a ship that brought a large number of Virginia Company servants and tenants to the colony (FER 295).

JOHN GOFFE

On July 29, 1626, the justices of Bridewell Court decided that John Goffe, a boy, would sent to Virginia (HUME 31).

HENRY GOLD (GOULD)

On October 10, 1618, the justices of Bridewell Court decided that Henry Gold (Gould), a vagrant brought in from Wood Street by the churchwardens, would be transported to Virginia (CBE 10).

HUGH GOLD (GOULD)

On February 27, 1619, the Bridewell Court decided that Hugh Gold (Gould), a boy rounded up from the streets of London, would be sent to Virginia (CBE 13).

JOHN GOLD (GOULD)

On June 15, 1629, when a list of defaulters was compiled at Dorchester, John Gold (Gould) was identified as a man who had gone to Virginia (CBE 87).

NATHANIEL GOLD (GOULD)

On February 26, 1620, it was decided that Nathaniel Gold (Gould), a prisoner at Newgate, would be sent to Virginia (CBE 19).

PETER (PEETER) GOLD (GOULD)

Peter (Peeter) Gold (Gould) died in Jamestown (1) sometime after April 1623 but before February 16, 1624 (CBE 39).

PHILIP GOLD (GOULD)

In February 1621 Philip Gold (Gould), a prisoner at Norwich, was among those chosen by Sir Thomas Smith of the Virginia Company to be sent to Virginia (CBE 23).

***
ARTHUR GOLDSMITH (GOULDSMITH)

Arthur Goldsmith (Gouldsmith) went to Virginia in 1618 on the *Diana*. On October 7, 1622, his father, Thomas Goldsmith, sent a petition to Virginia Company officials, demanding that Arthur be freed. He claimed that Governor George Yeardley was detaining Arthur as a tenant or farmer beyond the three years he had agreed to serve. He added that any contract Arthur himself might have signed when he left England was invalid, for he was a minor at the time. Thomas Goldsmith's petition was forwarded to a committee, but Company officials recommended that the youth be freed. It does not appear that he was, for on February 16, 1624, Arthur Goldsmith was living on the lower side of the James River, east of Grays Creek, within the corporation of James City. When a muster was compiled on February 4, 1625, Arthur was living at Captain Samuel Mathews' plantation (**15**), probably where he had been residing in February 1624, and was identified as a 26-year-old servant (CBE 40, 60; VCR 2:50, 113, 119).

THOMAS GOLDSMITH (GOULDSMITH)

Thomas Goldsmith (Gouldsmith) was the father of Arthur Gouldsmith (Gouldsmith), a young man sent to Virginia when he was a minor. On June 19, 1622, Thomas asked Virginia Company officials to free his son, who was being detained by Governor George Yeardley. He contended that Arthur's contract required him to serve as a tenant for only three years and that Yeardley had detained him for a longer period. He added that his son, Arthur, was a minor when he left England and, therefore, any contract he might have signed was invalid (VCR 2:50, 113, 119).

***
JOHN GOLDSMITH (GOULDSMITH)

On February 5, 1620, the justices of Bridewell Court decided to send John Goldsmith (Gouldsmith), a vagrant, to Virginia (CBE 18).

NICHOLAS GOLDSMITH (GOULDSMITH, GOULDFINCH)

On February 16, 1624, Nicholas Goldsmith (Gouldsmith, Gouldfinch), an indentured servant, was a member of John Burrows' Jamestown Island (**1**) household. On January 24, 1625, he was still living in the Burrows home and was described as a 19-year-old servant. When an inquest was held after the death of Elizabeth Abbott (one of John Proctor's maidservants), Nicholas testified about the extent of her injuries. He said that he had seen Elizabeth's wounds when he and his master, John Burrows, had gone to Burrows Hill (**8**), which was next door to the plantation on which the Proctors lived (**9**). On February 6, 1626, John Burrows identified Nicholas as one of his servants when using him as a headright (CBE 38, 56; MCGC 22, 93).

PETER GOODALE

On March 22, 1622, when the Indians attacked Powel-Brooke (**50**), Peter Goodale was killed (VCR 3:569).

***
RICHARD GOODCHILD

Sometime after April 1623 but before February 16, 1624, Richard Goodchild and his young son, Christenus (Christmas), died in the corporation of Elizabeth City (**17, 18**) (CBE 45).

CHRISTENUS (CHRISTMUS) GOODCHILD

Christenus (Christmas) Goodchild (a boy) and his father, Richard, died in the corporation of Elizabeth City (**17, 18**) sometime after April 1623 but before February 16, 1624 (CBE 45).

***
RAYMOND GOODISON

In 1608 Raymond Goodison, a laborer, arrived in Virginia in the 1st Supply of new settlers and would have lived in Jamestown (**1**) (CJS 1:223; 2:161).

ROBERT GOODMAN

In 1619 Robert Goodman came to Virginia on the *Bona Nova* and on February 16,

1624, was living in Elizabeth City on the east side of the Hampton River. A year later, he was still there. Goodman, who was age 24 in early 1625, was identified as a servant in John Ward's household, which resided on part of the Virginia Company's land in Elizabeth City (**17**). On January 12, 1627, Robert Goodman was one of the Virginia Company tenants assigned to Sir George Yeardley (CBE 43, 67; MCGC 136).

JOANE GOODWAY

On January 22, 1619, Joane Goodway was brought before the Bridewell Court whose justices decided that she would be sent to Virginia (HUME 20).

SIR FRANCIS GOODWIN

On February 13, 1622, three shares of the late Lord Delaware's land were transferred to Sir Francis Goodwin, who had acquired the acreage from Francis Carter (VCR 1:604).

JANE GOODWIN

In May 1620 it was decided that Jane Goodwin, who had stolen some clothes, would be transported to Virginia (CBE 20).

JOANE GOODWIN (GOODWYN)

On January 22, 1620, when Joane Goodwin (Goodwyn) was brought into Bridewell Court, it was decided that she would be sent to Virginia (CBE 17).

REINOLD (REINOULD) GOODWIN (GOODWYN, GODWIN)

Reinold (Reinould) Goodwin (Goodwyn, Godwin) came to Virginia in 1620 on the *Abigail* and on February 16, 1624, was living on the east side of the Hampton River, in Elizabeth City (**17**). A year later, he was still there. Reinold, who in early 1625 was age 30, was a servant in Francis West's household on part of the Virginia Company's land. On January 12, 1627, Reinold Goodwin was identified as a Virginia Company tenant who had been assigned to provost marshal Randall Smallwood, a resident of Jamestown Island (**1**) (CBE 43, 67; MCGC 137).

SAMUEL GOODWIN (GOODWINE)

On March 22, 1622, Samuel Goodwin (Goodwine), one of Sir George Yeardley's people, was killed when the Indians attacked Weyanoke (**52**) (VCR 3:569).

***

DANIEL GOOKIN (GOOKINS, COOKINS, GOEGEN) I

In 1620 Daniel Gookin (Gookins, Cookins, Goegen) I presented a proposal to the Virginia Company in which he offered to transport cattle from Ireland to the Virginia colony. In return, he asked for as much land as Captain William Nuce had received, acreage that Gookin and his associates could develop into a particular plantation. Gookin already held the rights for the Virginia land that formerly had been assigned to Mary Tue. He also had an estate in County Longford, Ireland, and a leasehold for land and a castle at Carygoline in County Cork. Gookin brought 50 men to Virginia on the *Flying Hart*, which arrived on November 22, 1621, and planted a settlement at the promontory called Newportes News (**24**), where they built houses and fortifications. The fledgling community, variously known as Marie's Mount and as "the Irish plantation," withstood the March 22, 1622, Indian attack. Gookin's settlers stayed on, but he set sail for England in late April or early May 1622, intent on securing his patent and some provisions for his colonists. Lieutenant John Richards alias Shephard served as Gookin's agent during his absence. Gookin dispatched 40 new immigrants and supplies for his plantation on the *Providence*, which had a long and difficult passage. When the ship reached Virginia, the newcomers found that only 7 or 8 of Gookin's men were still alive and the plantation was vulnerable to harassment by the Indians. During 1623 Daniel Gookin I incurred a substantial amount of debt. On February 7, 1625, when a muster was taken of the people at Gookin's plantation in Newportes News, there were 8 men who had come on the *Flying Hart* in 1621 and 10 men and 2 women who had arrived on the *Providence* in 1623. Although Daniel Gookin I never returned to Virginia, he continued to pursue his interest in colonization. When he died in 1633, he had little to leave his heirs except his land rights in Virginia

(VCR 1:501-502, 535, 553-554, 561-562, 618; 2:74; 3:497, 587, 643; 4:105, 116, 229, 456-457, 557; CJS 2:287, 302-303; CBE 32, 63; MCGC 10, 30, 46-47, 56, 75; DOR 1:50; 2:99-101).

DANIEL GOOKIN (GOOKINS, COOKINS, GOEGEN) II

Daniel Gookin (Gookins, Cookins, Goegin) II, the son of Daniel Gookin I, arrived in Virginia sometime prior to February 1, 1631, at which time he conveyed 50 acres to Thomas Addison, one of his father's former servants. Dutch mariner Peter DeVries visited the Gookin plantation in Newportes News (**24**) in 1634. On February 25, 1635, Daniel Gookin II obtained a patent for 2,500 acres on the lower side of the James River, between the Nansemond River (**20 c**) and Chuckatuck Creek, using as headrights the servants that his late father had sent to Virginia on the *Flying Hart* and the *Providence*. Daniel Gookin II stayed in what became Nansemond County for nearly a decade and served as a county justice and militia commander. In 1643, however, he moved to Maryland, where he stayed briefly, and then continued on to Massachusetts, where he became permanently established as part of the Puritan community (MCGC 498; PB 1:511; DOR 1:50; 2:101-102; CBE 50).

***

RICHARD GORE

On February 27, 1619, Richard Gore, a boy brought in from London's Silver Street, was one of the poor children rounded up from the streets of London so that they could be sent to Virginia (CBE 13).

ELIZABETH GOSMORE

On June 24, 1635, when Adam Thorogood patented some land, he used Elizabeth Gosmore as a headright and indicated that he had brought her to Virginia on the *Christopher and Mary* (PB 1 Pt. 1:179).

***

ANTHONY GOSNOLD I

Anthony Gosnold I, a gentleman and the elder colonist of that name, came to Virginia in 1607 as one of the first Jamestown (**1**) settlers. Captain John Smith indicated that

in late 1607, Gosnold was present when there was talk of abandoning the colony. In 1609 he was among those who went to Hog Island (**16**) with Mr. Scrivener. Anthony Gosnold I apparently died in Virginia (CJS 1:214; 2:141, 153, 203).

ANTHONY GOSNOLD II

Anthony Gosnold II accompanied his father, Anthony I, to Virginia in 1607 and was one of the first colonists to become established in Jamestown (**1**). Captain John Smith said that only five of the people who accompanied the younger Anthony Gosnold to Virginia managed to survive. Smith scholar Philip Barbour surmised that Anthony Gosnold II, a cousin of Bartholomew Gosnold, returned to England and was living there in 1623 (CJS 1:208; 2:141; 3:285).

ANTHONY GOSNOLD III

In November 1615 Anthony Gosnold III, the son of Anthony Gosnold II, purportedly was in Virginia. On October 31, 1621, he was awarded two shares of land: one for the money he had invested and the other for his personal adventure 6 years earlier. Anthony Gosnold III claimed that he had inherited two kinsmen's rights to Virginia land and cited his long service to the Virginia Company. He also asserted that he had been detained as a servant long after he should have been freed and that he wanted to pass his shares of land along to his brother, Robert, and to Roger Castle. Virginia Company officials gave Anthony Gosnold III and his associates a patent for a particular plantation in Virginia, but told him that that before he could have the land he purportedly inherited, he had to prove his claim to Governor George Yeardley's satisfaction. Anthony III may have come to Virginia to present his case in person (CBE 7; EEAC 24; WITH 158; VCR 1:541-542).

BARTHOLOMEW GOSNOLD

Bartholomew Gosnold, a cousin of Anthony Gosnold II who studied at Cambridge University and the Inns of Court, crossed the Atlantic in 1602 and, as Captain Christopher Newport's lieutenant, explored what became Massachusetts. He tried in vain to establish a settlement on one of the Elizabeth Islands. His navigation experience and family and political connections enabled him to enlist support for colonizing Virginia. Gosnold was described by Captain John Smith as the prime mover in organizing the Virginia Company, and he served as vice-admiral of the small fleet that brought the first colonists to Virginia in 1607. When the fleet arrived on the Virginia coast, at what became Cape Henry, it was attacked by Indians. Smith said that Gosnold was a council member and was held in high esteem by Edward Maria Wingfield, the first president of the Virginia colony. On June 22, 1607, Gosnold was among those who sent a letter to England describing the status of the colony. He died in Jamestown (1) on August 22, 1607, only 13 weeks after his arrival. His burial ceremony was marked by a volley of small shot (CJS 1:7, 20, 33, 203, 205, 207, 210; 2:138, 140; HAI 124-126, 99, 184-185, 199-200; DOR 2:115-117).

ROBERT GOSNOLD

On October 31, 1621, Robert Gosnold, the brother of Anthony Gosnold III, informed Virginia Company officials that he wanted a share of the land to which Anthony III was entitled (VCR 1:541-542).

***

[NO FIRST NAME] GOSNULT (GOSNOLD?)

Mr. Gosnult (Gosnold?) arrived in Jamestown (1) on July 31, 1622, and took the oath of allegiance. He came to Virginia on the *James* and brought along two men. This individual may have been Anthony Gosnold III, who was attempting to claim some Virginia land (FER 400).

***

ROBERT GOSSE

On March 22, 1622, when the Indians attacked Southampton Hundred (44), Robert Gosse and his wife were killed (VCR 3:569).

MRS. ROBERT GOSSE

Mrs. Robert Gosse and her husband were killed at Southampton Hundred (44) when the Indians attacked on March 22, 1622 (VCR 3:569).

***

ALICE GOUGHE

Alice Goughe, a young maid, came to Virginia in 1621 on the *Tiger*. Her parents were described as gentlefolk (FER 309).

GEORGE GOULDING

In 1607 George Goulding, a laborer, arrived in Virginia in the first group of colonists that settled on Jamestown Island (1) (CJS 2:142).

GEORGE GOULDING

George Goulding arrived at Martin's Hundred (7) around mid-January 1623 and was one of the Society of Martin's Hundred's servants. According to fellow servant, Richard Frethorne, Goulding died shortly thereafter in the home of Mr. William Harwood, the settlement's principal leader (VCR 4:60).

SARA GOULDINGE (GOULDOCKE)

Sara Gouldinge (Gouldocke) came to Virginia on the *Ann* in 1623. In early 1625 she was living within the corporation of Elizabeth City, where she was a 20-year-old servant in the household headed by John Banum and Robert Sweete (18) (CBE 64).

THOMAS GOULDING

Thomas Goulding came to Virginia on the *George* in 1623 and on February 4, 1625, was living at Martin's Hundred (7), where he was a 26-year-old servant in Ellis Emmerson's house. In August 1638 Thomas Goulding secured a patent for a lot in urban Jamestown (1) (CBE 61; PB 1 Pt. 2:595).

HENRY GOULDWELL

On February 16, 1624, Henry Gouldwell was living in Elizabeth City (17, 18) (CBE 44).

JEAN GOURDEMAN

Laborer Jean Gourdeman, his wife, and his five children were among the Walloons and French who indicated their willingness to go to Virginia. In August 1621 the Virginia Company agreed that they could immigrate (CBE 24).

[NO FIRST NAME] GOURGAING (GOUYNGE)

In the July 1619 session of the assembly Mr. Gourgaing (Gouynge), a burgess, represented the community called Argalls Gift, which Deputy Governor Samuel Argall inappropriately seated on what became the Governor's Land (**3**). In September 1619 the Virginia Company approved payment to Mr. Gourgaing for sending large quantities of vinegar and oil to Berkeley Hundred (**55**) (VCR 3:154, 187).

THOMAS GOWER

According to George Percy, Thomas Gower, a gentleman who came to Virginia in the first group of colonists, died in Jamestown (**1**) on August 16, 1607 (CJS 1:20; HAI 99).

RICHARD GOWRY

On February 5 1619, the Bridewell Court decided that Richard Gowry, a boy, would be sent to Virginia (HUME 26).

FRANCIS GOWSCH (GOWSE)

On March 22, 1622, Francis Gowsch (Gowse) was killed at Falling Creek (**68**) when the Indians attacked Captain John Berkeley's plantation. Thus, he probably was among the men sent to the colony to build an ironworks (VCR 3:565).

JOHN GOWTON

John Gowton, a gentleman from Hatfield in Surrey, England, arrived in Jamestown on September 5, 1623, aboard the *Ann*, and took the oath of supremacy (MCGC 6).

***

ROWLAND (ROULAND) GRAINE (GRAYNE)

The Rev. Rowland (Rouland) Graine (Grayne) came to Virginia sometime prior to April 21, 1628, when he was summoned before the General Court. He and his wife and a young male servant lived in Elizabeth City (**17, 18**), where he was the parish rector. The Rev. Graine was called to account for refusing to loan his boat to Sergeant John Wayne, who wanted to use it in public

service. Although Wayne displayed a warrant from Captain William Tucker, Kecoughtan's commander, Graine refused to allow the boat to be moved from the landing near his house, insisting that it was more important for him to administer communion than to assist secular authorities. To underscore the point, the Rev. Graine called for his gun and ordered Sergeant Wayne to leave. This resulted in Graine's being summoned to court. Later in the year, the Rev. Rowland Graine was obliged to post a bond as security for the late Albiano Lupo's goods, of which he had custody. On February 9, 1629, Graine appeared before the General Court, where he and another witness proved the will of John Bainham of Elizabeth City. Later in the year, the Graine presented parish statistics for "the Upper Parts," a term usually applied to the territory in the upper reaches of the James River. This raises the possibility that Graine moved to another parish toward the end of 1629. In 1633 he brought suit against George Travellor, a resident of the Eastern Shore (MCGC 171-173, 185, 200; AMES 1:4).

MRS. ROWLAND GRAINE

Court testimony taken on April 25, 1628, made reference to a warning by Mrs. Rowland Graine to her husband, cautioning him that Sergeant John Wayne was going to take his boat despite his refusal to loan it. The Graines lived in Elizabeth City (**17, 18**) until at least early 1629 (MCGC 172).

***

AMY GRAMSBY

On May 18, 1622, Amy Gramsby was identified as a maidservant assigned to boat-builder Thomas Nunn, who was employed by the Company of Shipwrights. She came to Virginia with Nunn and his wife and was to receive a moiety (share of their profits) in exchange for her work as a domestic (FER 378).

***

NICHOLAS GRANGE (GRAUNGER, GRAINGER, GRINDGER, GRINGER)

On February 27, 1619, Nicholas Grange (Graunger, Grainger, Grindger, Gringer), a youth, was identified as one of the children rounded up from the streets of London so that they could be sent to Virginia. He arrived in the colony on the *George* in 1619. On February 16, 1624, Nicholas was living on the Eastern Shore. When a muster was compiled in early 1625, he was identified as a 15-year-old servant on the plantation of Captain William Eppes (**74**). On August 13, 1638, Alice Robins was quoted as saying that if Nicholas Grange had not been sent to Virginia, he would have been hanged. In April 1639, when Nicholas Harwood made his will, he made a bequest to Goodman Grange, an indication of the heir's social status. Nicholas Grange acquired 200 acres in 1640, using his wife, Elizabeth, as a headright. He patented 350 acres of land in Northampton County on September 20, 1647, and deeded a heifer to his daughter, Christian, in anticipation of her marriage. He also patented 350 acres on Pungoteague River. Nicholas Grange or Graunger died sometime after March 11, 1652, at which time he signed a document concerning the Commonwealth government's takeover of England (CBE 12, 46, 68; Northampton County Orders, Wills, Deeds 1632-1640:46, 146, 182; Deeds, Wills &c. 1645-1651:94; 1651-1654:188; PB 2:110; 3:333; DOR 2:119-120).

ELIZABETH GRANGE (GRAUNGER, GRAINGER, GRINDGER, GRINGER) (MRS. NICHOLAS GRANGE [GRAUNGER, GRAINGER, GRINDGER, GRINGER])

On August 3, 1640, when Nicholas Grange (Graunger, Grainger, Grindger, Gringer) received a certificate from the Northampton County Court, one of the headrights he used was that of his wife, Elizabeth. They probably wed sometime prior to 1635, when 33-year-old Elizabeth Grange made a deposition in the local court (DOR 2:119-120; AMES 2:27).

***

WILLIAM GRANGE

William Grange, a boy, was identified on February 27, 1619, as one of the children rounded up from the streets of London so that they could be sent to Virginia (CBE 12).

***

GEORGE GRAVES (GRAVE)

George Graves (Grave) came to Virginia on the *Seaventure*. On February 16, 1624, he and his wife were living in urban Jamestown (**1**), where he was a household head. On January 24, 1625, George was still there with his wife, Eleanor, a former widow. The Graves couple, George's son, John, and Eleanor's daughters, Sara and Rebecca Snowe, shared a house and had some livestock. In April 1625 George Graves claimed that his hog had been wrongfully killed 2½ years earlier. Because the accused perpetrators were prominent citizens and the man who witnessed the event was deemed unreliable, the case was dismissed. A few months later, George Graves was given the responsibility of seeing that Robert Wright, a resident of the eastern end of Jamestown Island, appeared in court. On January 8, 1627, Graves presented the General Court with an inventory of the late Robert Lindsey's estate. Then, on October 9, 1627, he asked for some land in the Governor's Garden, which was in the rural part of Jamestown Island, near the governor's house. On January 24, 1629, George Graves served on a jury that tried a capital case. He appears to have been a respected member of the community (CBE 38, 55; MCGC 54, 79, 81, 128, 154, 184).

ELEANOR (ELINOR, ELLENOR) SNOW (SNOWE) GRAVES (GRAVE) (MRS. [NO FIRST NAME] SNOW [SNOWE], MRS. GEORGE GRAVES [GRAVE]) (SEE ELEANOR (ELINOR, ELLENOR) SNOW [SNOWE])

On February 16, 1624, Mrs. George Graves (Grave) and her husband were living in urban Jamestown (**1**), where he headed a household. On January 24, 1625, she was identified as Eleanor Graves, who had come to Virginia aboard the *Susan*. The Graves couple shared their home with George's son, John, and Eleanor's daughters, Rebecca and Sara Snowe. On January 8, 1627, Mrs. Eleanor Graves was identified as the mother of Sara Snowe, who stood to receive a bequest from Robert Lindsey (CBE 38, 55; MCGC 128).

JOHN GRAVES (GRAVE)

On January 24, 1625, John Graves (Grave) was identified as the 10-year-old son of George Graves. The Graves family, which included Eleanor, and her daughters, Sara and Rebecca Snowe, was living in urban Jamestown (1) in a dwelling of their own (CBE 38, 55).

***

NATHANIEL GRAVES

Nathaniel Graves, a gentleman who lived in Jamestown (1), accompanied Captain John Smith on a December 29, 1608, voyage to Pamunkey on the barge *Discovery* (CJS 2:192).

ROBERT GRAVES

Robert Graves came to Virginia on the *Southampton* in 1623 and on January 20, 1625, was living at Flowerdew Hundred (53), where he was a 30-year-old servant in Abraham Peirsey's household (CBE 50).

***

THOMAS GRAVES (GRANES, GRAYES) I

According to Captain John Smith, Thomas Graves (Granes, Grayes) I, a gentleman and Virginia Company investor, came to Virginia in 1608 in the 2nd Supply of new settlers. The 1625 muster indicates that Graves arrived in 1607 (Old Style) aboard the *Mary and Margaret*. Smith noted that Graves had been captured by the Indians during a journey of exploration and was rescued from the town of the Native leader Opechancanough. On May 30, 1618, after Captain William Eppes killed Captain Edward Stallings in a fight, Captain Thomas Graves was named commander of Smyth's or Southampton Hundred (44). In July and August 1619 he served as the community's burgess. Graves went to Ireland and on November 20, 1622, was in Dublin when he asked Virginia Company officials for a patent, stating that he was taking 100 people to Virginia. By February 16, 1624, Captain Thomas Graves had taken up residence on Old Plantation Creek (73) on the Eastern Shore. He was a solitary household head in early 1625 when a muster was compiled, and was relatively well supplied with

stored food and defensive weaponry. During the 1620s Graves made several appearances before the General Court. In February 1625 he was mentioned in connection with some inferior tobacco that had been collected as taxes. On January 11, 1627, Captain John Martin testified that he told Elizabeth Smalley that Thomas Graves knew what had happened to her late husband's oxen. Martin's insinuation apparently failed to damage Graves's reputation, for on February 8, 1628, he was made commander of the plantation of Accomack. On March 14, 1628, Thomas Graves, as an ancient planter, received 200 acres on Old Plantation Creek, acquiring the land on account of his own personal adventure and the £25 he had invested in the Virginia Company. In March 1630, while Graves was serving as a burgess for Accomack, he was ordered to inspect the site of the fort built at Old Point Comfort (17). In 1632 Captain Thomas Graves served as a burgess for Accomack, commissioner of the Accomack monthly court, and as a parish vestryman. He died between November 1635 and January 5, 1636. A patent issued to his son, John, on August 9, 1637, reveals that Thomas Graves paid for the transportation of his wife, Katherine, and sons John and Thomas II. He died sometime prior to November 1642 (CBE 46, 68; CJS 1:242; 2:190, 277, 290; VCR 2:132; 3:12, 154; MCGC 46, 132, 165; PB 1 Pt. 1:72, 443; HEN 1:149-150, 170, 179, 187; Northampton County Orders, Wills, Deeds 1632-1640:58, 66; DOR 1:69; 2:131-132; AMES 2:223).

KATHERINE GRAVES (GRANES, GRAYES) (MRS. THOMAS GRAVES [GRANES, GRAYES])

On August 9, 1637, John, the son of Thomas Graves (Granes, Grayes) I, patented some land in Elizabeth City (19) near the Back River. He used the headrights to which his late father was entitled on account of paying for his own transportation to Virginia and that of his wife, Katherine, sons John (the patentee) and Thomas II, and 8 servants (PB 1 Pt.1:443; DOR 2:132).

ANN GRAVES (GRANES, GRAYES)

Ann, the daughter of Thomas Graves (Granes, Grayes) I, was born around 1620 and in November 1662 identified herself as

42 years old. She married three clergymen in succession, the first of whom was the controversial minister, the Rev. William Cotton (DOR 2:133-134; PB 1 Pt. 1:434; Pt. 2:823).

FRANCIS GRAVES (GRANES, GRAYES)

Francis, the son of Thomas Graves (Granes, Grayes) I, was born around 1630 and by 1642 was identified as an orphan. He settled in Old Rappahannock (now Caroline) County (DOR 2:136-137; AMES 2:223).

JOHN GRAVES (GRANES, GRAYES)

John, the son of Thomas Graves (Granes, Grayes) I, was born in England around 1605 and by February 1635 was living in Accomack County. In August 1637 he patented some land in Elizabeth City, using his parents, his brother Thomas, and himself as headrights. However, by February 1644 John was dead (AMES 1:27; 2:330; PB 1 Pt. 1:443).

KATHERINE GRAVES (GRANES, GRAYES)

Katherine, the daughter of Thomas Graves (Granes, Grayes) I, married William Roper of Accomack County, a military leader, county justice, and burgess. After being widowed in 1650, Katherine wed Thomas Sprigg (DOR 2:136).

THOMAS GRAVES (GRANES, GRAYES) II

Thomas Graves II, the son of Thomas Graves (Granes, Grayes) I, settled in Abingdon Parish of Gloucester County and patented land there in March 1658 (PB 4:523, 530).

VERLINDA GRAVES (GRANES, GRAYES)

Verlinda, the daughter of Thomas Graves (Granes, Grayes) I, married Captain William Stone sometime prior to 1640 (DOR 2:135).

***

[NO FIRST NAME] GRAY

In 1629 the justices of the General Court ordered Mrs. William Carter of Jamestown Island (1) to apologize to Goodwife Gray in open court. Mrs. Carter reportedly had referred to Goodwife Gray as a whore when both women were at Mr. Cheeseman's house in Elizabeth City (18). Mrs. Carter denied that Goodwife Gray was one of her cousins (MCGC 197-198).

JOHN GRAY

John Gray, one of Sir George Yeardley's men, was killed at Weyanoke (52) during the March 22, 1622, Indian attack (VCR 3:569).

ROBERT GRAY

On March 22, 1622, when the Indians attacked Edward Bennett's plantation (26) in Warresqueak, Robert Gray was killed (VCR 3:571).

***

THOMAS GRAY (GRAYE) I

Thomas Gray (Graye) I, an ancient planter, came to Virginia sometime prior to May 1616. On February 16, 1624, when a census was taken, Gray and his wife were living in the eastern end of Jamestown Island (1) in a household that included his son, William, and daughter, Jone. On January 24, 1625, Thomas Gray and his second wife, Margaret, were residing on Jamestown Island, where he headed a household that included his 3-year-old son, William, and 6-year-old daughter, Jone. The Grays were amply supplied with stored food and defensive weaponry and were in possession of some livestock. Thomas Gray was widowed but by September 11, 1626, had married his third wife, Rebecca, who made a court appearance in Jamestown. On October 12, 1626, Thomas Gray testified that he had seen Margaret Jones fight with her neighbor, John Butterfield, on the Maine (3), just west of Jamestown Island. On February 29, 1631, Captain Thomas Gray, claiming his entitlement as an ancient planter, patented 100 acres in the corporation of Elizabeth City (18). Four years later, shortly after he acquired 550 acres in what later became Surry County, he assigned his Elizabeth

City acreage to Captain Thomas Purfoy. Gray's November 28, 1635, patent reveals that he already owned some contiguous property and that his land on the lower side of the James River bordered William Perry's (**9**), on what became known as Grays Creek. Thomas Gray's patent also indicates that his first wife was named Anis (Annis). On July 20, 1639, Gray added 400 acres to his landholdings on Grays Creek, and on June 7, 1642, he enhanced his property through the addition of another 400 acres. On March 14, 1653, he consolidated his holdings. When he testified in court in March 1654, he indicated that he was 60 years old. Thomas Gray appears to have died before November 2, 1658. He had outlived his third wife, with whom he had four children, and had wed a fourth time (CBE 38, 56; MCGC 119; PB 1 Pt. 1:283, 323, 631, 669, 787, 950; 3:158; Surry County Deeds, Wills &c. 1652-1672:41, 121; DOR 1:35; 2:198-199).

ANISE (ANNIS) GRAY (GRAYE) (MRS. THOMAS GRAY I)

On August 27, 1635, when ancient planter Thomas Gray (Graye) I patented some land within what is now Surry County, he used the headright of Anise (Annis) Gray, identifying her as his first wife. She is thought to be the mother of Thomas's children, William and Jone, whose names were included in the 1624 census (PB 1 Pt. 1:283; CBE 38; DOR 2:198-199).

MARGARET GRAY (GRAYE) (MRS. THOMAS GRAY I)

On January 24, 1625, Margaret, Thomas Gray (Graye) I's second wife, was sharing a rural Jamestown Island (**1**) home with him and his two children, 6-year-old Jone and 3-year-old William. Margaret Gray died sometime prior to September 11, 1626, by which date Thomas had remarried (CBE 56; DOR 2:198-199; MCGC 111).

REBECCA GRAY (GRAYE) (MRS. THOMAS GRAY I)

On September 11, 1626, Rebecca, Thomas Gray (Graye) I's third wife, testified before the General Court in a case involving Joan Wright, who was accused of practicing witchcraft. Rebecca Gray said that Mrs. Wright, a midwife, had expected to deliver the child of Mrs. Giles Allington, a resident of Elizabeth City (**18**). However, because Mrs. Allington preferred to have Rebecca (who also was a midwife) deliver the child, Mrs. Wright became angry and predicted that the pregnant woman's husband would die. On August 27, 1635, when Thomas Gray patented some land within what is now Surry County, he used his "now wife" Rebecca as a headright. Together, Rebecca and Thomas Gray produced four children (PB 1 Pt. 1:283; MCGC 111-112; DOR 2:198-200).

FRANCIS GRAY (GRAYE)

Francis Gray (Graye), the son of Thomas Gray (Graye) I, was born around 1630–1635 and died sometime prior to May 1679, at which time his widow was named his administrator (DOR 2:200).

JONE GRAY (GRAYE)

Jone Gray, the daughter of Thomas Gray (Graye) I, was living in her father's rural Jamestown Island (**1**) home on February 16, 1624. She was still there on January 24, 1625, at which time she was said to be age 6. With Jone was her 3-year-old brother, William. Her mother probably was Thomas Gray's first wife, Anise (Annis) (CBE 38, 56).

THOMAS GRAY (GRAYE) II

On August 27, 1635, when Thomas Gray (Graye) I patented some land within what is now Surry County, he used the headright of his son, Thomas Gray II (PB 1 Pt. 1:283).

WILLIAM GRAY (GRAYE)

William Gray (Graye), the son of Thomas Gray (Graye) I, was living in their rural Jamestown Island (**1**) home on February 16, 1624. He was still there on January 24, 1625, at which time he was 3 years old. William's sister, Jone, was age 6. On August 27, 1635, when Thomas Gray patented some land on the lower side of the James River, in what became Surry County, he used his son, William, as a headright. William's mother probably was Thomas Gray's first wife, Anise (Annis) (CBE 38, 56; PB 1 Pt. 1:283).

***

[NO FIRST NAME] GREEN (GREENE)

On May 30, 1625, the justices of the General Court ordered Mr. Green (Greene) to pay Adam Dixon for the damage that Mr. Reynolds' sow did to his corn. As Dixon then lived in Pasbehay **(3)**, the destruction probably occurred there (MCGC 64).

[NO FIRST NAME] GREEN (GREENE)

On December 24, 1634, Mr. Green (Greene) was identified as overseer of the will of Tobias (Toby) Felgate, a resident of Westover **(54)** (SH 19).

ANDERTON (ADERTON) GREEN (GREENE)

On July 31, 1622, Anderton (Aderton) Green (Greene) arrived in Virginia on the *James*, accompanying William Rowley. Sometime after April 1623 but before February 16, 1624, Green died at one of the plantations on the lower side of the James River within the corporation of James City **(8-15)** (FER 400; CBE 41).

ANN GREEN (GREENE)

Ann Green (Greene) was killed on March 22, 1622, when the Indians attacked one of the communities across the James River from Flowerdew Hundred **(53)** (VCR 3:568).

DOROTHY GREEN (GREENE)

Dorothy Green (Greene), one of Mrs. Elizabeth Clements' servants, came to Virginia on the *George* in 1617 and may have lived with the Clements in urban Jamestown **(1)**. On August 26, 1633, when Mrs. Clements' son, Jeremiah, patented some land, he listed several family members and Mrs. Clements' servants as headrights (PB 1 Pt. 1:124).

FRANCIS GREEN (GREENE)

On February 27, 1619, the justices of Bridewell Court decided that Francis Green (Greene), a child, would be detained and sent to Virginia. This occurred at a time when children were rounded up from the streets of London and sent to the colony (HUME 8).

JAMES GREEN (GREENE)

On February 27, 1619, James Green (Greene), a boy brought in from the streets of London, was among those chosen to be sent to Virginia (CBE 12).

JOANE (JOAN) GREEN (GREENE)

On September 10, 1620, Joane (Joan) Green (Greene), who was from Bristol, England, was supposed to go to Virginia on the *Supply* with William Tracy and settle at Berkeley Hundred **(55)**. Virginia Company records suggest that Joane chose not to go to the colony (CBE 21; VCR 3:396).

JOHN GREEN (GREENE)

On January 15, 1620, the justices of Bridewell Court decided that John Green (Greene), a vagrant brought in from Fenchurch Street in London, would be sent to Virginia (CBE 17).

JOHN GREEN (GREENE)

Sometime after April 1623 but before February 16, 1624, John Green (Greene) died in Warresqueak **(26)** (CBE 42).

JOHN GREEN (GREENE)

On February 16, 1624, John Green (Greene) was living in Elizabeth City on the east side of the Hampton River **(17)** in an area known as the Indian Thicket, part of the Virginia Company's land. He may have been a Company servant or tenant and former inmate of Bridewell Prison (CBE 43).

JOHN GREEN (GREENE)

On February 16, 1624, John Green (Greene) was a servant in the Jamestown household **(1)** headed by provost marshal Randall Smallwood (CBE 38).

JOHN GREEN (GREENE)

Sometime prior to February 20, 1626, John Green (Greene) and two other men stole some wine and other items from Edward Nevell's cabin. All of them were obliged to pay for the stolen goods (MCGC 95).

NATHANIEL GREEN (GREENE)

Nathaniel Green (Greene) embarked for Virginia on April 17, 1619, at the expense of the Virginia Company. He probably was one of the Company's servants or tenants (FER 107).

RICHARD GREEN (GREENE)

On December 31, 1619, it was decided that Richard Green (Greene), a Bridewell prisoner, would be detained so that he could be sent to Virginia (CBE 15).

RICHARD GREEN (GREENE)

On July 31, 1622, Richard Green (Greene) set sail for Virginia with William Rowley on the *James*. By February 16, 1624, he was living on the lower side of the James River, opposite Jamestown and west of Grays Creek (**8, 9**). In January 1625 he was listed among that area's dead (FER 400; CBE 40, 60).

***

ROBERT GREEN (GREENE, GREENLEAF?) (SEE ROBERT GREENLEAF [GREENLEAFE])

On February 16, 1624, Robert Green (Greene, Greenleaf?) was living at Bermuda Hundred (**39**) with his wife and child. His family may have been the household identified as the Greenleafs in the 1625 muster, for they too were residents of Bermuda Hundred (CBE 36).

MRS. ROBERT GREEN (GREENE, GREENLEAF?)

Mrs. Robert Green (Greene, Greenleaf?) was living at Bermuda Hundred (**39**) with her husband and child on February 16, 1624 (CBE 36).

[NO FIRST NAME] GREEN (GREENE, GREENLEAF?)

The child of Robert Green (Greene, Greenleaf?) and his wife was living at Bermuda Hundred (**39**) on February 16, 1624 (CBE 36).

***

SOLOMON (SALAMON) GREEN (GREENE)

Solomon (Salamon) Green (Greene) came to Virginia in 1618 on the *Diana* and on February 16, 1624, was living on the Eastern Shore. On March 7, 1624, Solomon, who was 26 years old, testified before the General Court about John Vaughan, a Virginia Company servant loaned to Ensign Thomas Savage of Accomack. When a muster was made early in 1625, Solomon Green was still living on the Eastern Shore. He was described as a 27-year-old household head who was in possession of a dwelling and a storehouse, probably on the banks of Old Plantation Creek (**73**). Solomon Green's name appeared in Accomack court records as late as January 1634 (CBE 46, 69; MCGC 10; AMES 1:10; DOR 1:70).

SISLEY (CISLEY) GREEN (GREENE)

Sisley Green (Greene) was living in Ralph Hamor's household in urban Jamestown (**1**) on February 16, 1624 (CBE 38).

THOMAS GREEN (GREENE)

Thomas Green (Greene) of Warresqueak (**26**) died sometime prior to February 9, 1628, when Justinian Cooper (Cowper) bought in an inventory of his estate (MCGC 166).

WILLIAM GREEN (GREENE)

On January 29, 1620, the Bridewell Court decided that William Green (Greene), who was brought in from the Poultry, in London, would be sent to Virginia (CBE 18).

WILLIAM GREEN (GREENE)

On April 30, 1623, William Green (Greene), a surgeon, who came to Virginia on the *Temperance*, stated that he had been in the colony for 17 months. Court testimony dating to June 13, 1625, indicates that he had provided medical treatment to John Stephens and his servants while at sea and had witnessed the wills made by Stephens and by Robert Mansteed (Monstidge). Because William Green was planning to leave Virginia, he asked the General Court to see that he was paid for the medical care he had rendered to the late John Stephens. The justices agreed and ordered John Southern to pay Green on Stephens' behalf. He may have been a kinsman of merchant Richard Stephens of Jamestown (1), who authorized John Southern and William Harwood to inventory the goods the decedent had brought to Virginia on the *James*. On January 30, 1629, the General Court determined that William Green was indebted to mariner William Barker and ordered John Southern to give Barker some tobacco notes that Green had recovered from Richard Digges (VCR 2:386; MCGC 56, 65, 184).

WILLIAM GREEN (GREENE)

William Green (Greene) came to Virginia on the *Hopewell* in 1623 and in early 1625 was living in Elizabeth City. He was then identified as a 28-year-old servant in Percivall Ibbotson's household, which probably resided at Blunt Point (22) (CBE 66).

NICHOLAS GREENHILL

Nicholas Greenhill came to Virginia in 1623 on the *Marmaduke*. When he testified before the General Court on March 12, 1624, he gave his age as 25 and said that the ship on which he had come to the colony had stopped at St. Christopher's in the West Indies. Nicholas said that William Royly, a servant being sent to Lieutenant George Harrison, had absconded at that time. On January 3, 1625, Nicholas Greenhill returned to court, where he testified about a written agreement between Rowland Loftis and George Harrison that he had entered into a book. On February 4, 1625, when a muster was taken of the settlers living in Archer's Hope (6), Nicholas Greenhill was identified as a 24-year-old servant in Thomas Bradby's household (CBE 58; MCGC 12, 39).

***

ROBERT GREENLEAF (GREENLEAFE)

Robert Greenleaf (Greenleafe), an ancient planter, came to the colony on the ship *Tryall*, which arrived in August 1610. Although he and his household were not included in the February 16, 1624, census, he may have been misidentified as Robert Green. On January 24, 1625, 43-year-old

Robert Greenleaf was residing at Bermuda Hundred (39), where he headed a household that included his 23-year-old wife, Susan, and children Thomas (age 3) and Ann (age 22 weeks). Greenleaf and his family were relatively well supplied with stored food and defensive weaponry and had some livestock. Robert Greenleaf's name was not included in the May 1625 land list. However, on January 9, 1627, he testified that he had executed a deed of gift, transferring to yeoman Gregory Dory his right to the 100 acres to which he (Greenleaf) was entitled as a personal dividend. Dory then indicated that he wanted to take up land at the head of the Blunt Point (Warwick) River. Robert Greenleaf died prior to November 20, 1635, by which time his widow, Susan, had married Thomas Warren of what became Surry County (CBE 54; MCGC 129; PB 1 Pt. 1:314; DOR 1:11).

SUSAN GREENLEAF (GREENLEAFE) (MRS. ROBERT GREENLEAF [GREENLEAFE], MRS. THOMAS WARREN) (SEE SUSAN GREENLEAF WARREN)

Susan Greenleaf (Greenleafe) came to Virginia on the *Jonathan* in May 1620 and on January 24, 1625, was identified as the wife of ancient planter Robert Greenleaf of Bermuda Hundred (39). She was then age 23 and the mother of 3-year-old Thomas Greenleaf and his sister, Ann, who was 22 weeks old. By November 20, 1635, the widowed Susan Greenleaf had married Thomas Warren. Susan Greenleaf and her husband may have been misidentified in the 1624 census as Mr. and Mrs. Robert Green, also residents of Bermuda Hundred (CBE 54; PB 1 Pt. 1:314).

THOMAS GREENLEAF (GREENLEAFE)

On January 24, 1625, Thomas Greenleaf (Greenleafe) was identified as the 3-year-old son of ancient planter Robert Greenleaf and his wife, Susan, who were residents of Bermuda Hundred (39). Thomas Greenleaf had a baby sister, Ann, who was 22 weeks old. Thomas Greenleaf may have been misidentified in the 1624 census as the nameless child of Robert Green and his wife, whose household was then residing at Bermuda Hundred (CBE 54).

ANN GREENLEAF (GREENLEAFE)

On January 24, 1625, Ann Greenleaf (Greenleafe) was identified as the 22-week-old daughter of ancient planter Robert Greenleaf and his wife, Susan. The Greenleaf family was then residing in Bermuda Hundred (**39**) (CBE 54).

***

MARY GREENSMITH

On January 15, 1620, the justices of Bridewell Court decided that Mary Greensmith would be detained and sent to Virginia (CBE 17).

JOHN GREFRIHE (GRIFFITH?)

On July 31, 1622, John Grefrihe (Griffith?) set sail for Virginia on the *James*, accompanying John Hitch (FER 400).

RICHARD GREGORY

Richard Gregory came to Virginia in 1620 or 1621 on the *Temperance* and on February 16, 1624, was living at Flowerdew Hundred (**53**), where he was one of Sir George Yeardley's servants. By January 25, 1625, he had moved to urban Jamestown (**1**), where he was a 40-year-old servant in the Yeardley household. On February 9, 1628, Sir George Yeardley's widow and executrix, Lady Temperance, testified in court that Richard Gregory was one of the servants her late husband had brought to Virginia on the *Temperance* in 1621 and used as a headright when acquiring the Elizabeth City plantation known as Stanley Hundred (**18**). She said that Gregory's headright had been transferred to Thomas Flint, who purchased the plantation. On September 20, 1628, when Flint received a patent for the Yeardley acreage, he noted that the land and Gregory's headright had been assigned to him (CBE 37, 54; MCGC 166; PB 1 Pt. 1:59).

THOMAS GREGORY

On March 12, 1627, Thomas Gregory, purser of the ship *Saker*, testified that he had inventoried Captain Holmes's estate, and he recounted an incident that involved the ship while it was in the West Indies. In December 1627 Thomas Gregory was identified as one of the late William Saker's servants, who had been brought to Virginia by Captain Preen of the *Samuel*, to whom Saker was indebted for his passage. On February 27, 1628, Thomas Gregory witnessed Samuel Gilphin's will while both men were aboard the *Samuel*. Thomas died prior to November 1628, at which time his will was proved by John Southern and Francis Fenton. He was then identified as a merchant. As administrators, Southern and Fenton were obliged to see that some of the late Captain Saker's debts were paid out of funds that were in Gregory's hands at the time of his death (CBE 80; MCGC 143-144, 168, 174, 178, 180; EEAC 50; WITH 194).

***

EDWARD GRENDON (GRINDON, GRINDALL) I

Edward Grendon (Grindon, Grindall) I, an ancient planter, immigrated to Virginia between 1611 and 1616, while Sir Thomas Dale was deputy-governor. He took an active role in public life and seems to have been widely respected. Court testimony suggests that he had offered employment to the late Lord Delaware's skilled workers who arrived in Jamestown (**1**) in August 1618. He was present in 1619 when Governor George Yeardley made a treaty with the Chickahominy Indians. Grendon returned to England and informed Virginia Company officials that Captain John Martin's plantation (**59**) provided refuge to debtors. In 1622 he was awarded 150 acres on the south side of the James River for services he performed on behalf of the colony. A surveyor was to lay out his land, which he was eager to place under cultivation. This probably was the plantation he called Grendon Hill, which eventually became part of the Treasurer's Plantation (**11**). Edward Grendon set sail for Virginia on the *James* on July 31, 1622, accompanied by his wife and two of his three children. Sometime prior to August 14, 1624, he came into possession of a ridge of land in the eastern part of Jamestown Island (**1**), and in late 1624 he acquired some acreage in Archer's Hope (**6**), near the James City Parish glebe and the patent of Ensign William Spence. He also purchased 400 acres of land on the east side of Archer's Hope (College) Creek, in what eventually became Kingsmill Plantation. Grendon made several appearances before the General Court to testify about various events that occurred during the Dale administration. He claimed that several high-ranking officials had taught Indians how to use firearms and that one official had an Indian living in his home. Grendon also served as a witness from time to time. On one occasion, he accused one of his servants of breaking into his store at Grendon Hill, where his house also was located. In October 1626 he received permission to use the late John Bayly's land (which had descended to his underage daughter, Mary) or to place it in the hands of tenants. At that juncture, Grendon executed a 3-year lease with Sir George Yeardley for the Bayly land, which probably was on Hog Island (**16**). On February 16, 1624, Edward Grendon was residing at Grendon Hill, his 150-acre plantation on the lower side of the James River. By early 1625 his land had become part of the Treasurer's Plantation, the central portion of which was then owned by Treasurer George Sandys. Grendon Hill lay directly across the James River from Edward Grendon's acreage on Jamestown Island. In 1627 Grendon was second in command in an expedition against the Tappahannah Indians. In October 1628 when he was asked to serve as John Moseley's attorney, he declined. He died shortly thereafter and on December 9, 1628, his will was presented to the General Court. Edward Grendon was survived by his wife, Elizabeth, who was then living in Virginia, and his adult son, Thomas, his principal heir and a resident of England. In 1649, when Thomas Grendon disposed of his late father's property on the lower side of the James, no mention was made of his Jamestown Island acreage (VCR 2:43, 93, 95; 4:551, 555; PB 1 Pt. 1:12, 19, 54; Pt. 2:630; 2:100; 4:316; FER 113, 400; CBE 40; C 24/490; MCGC 27-28, 44, 122, 151, 159, 162-164,176-177, 179; DOR 2:225).

ELIZABETH GRENDON (GRINDON, GRINDALL) (MRS. EDWARD GRENDON [GRINDON, GRINDALL] I)

Mrs. Elizabeth Grendon (Grindon, Grindall), Edward's wife, came to Virginia aboard the *James*, which departed from England on July 31, 1622. On February 6, 1628, Edward Grendon quoted a statement Elizabeth had made on January 14th about something one of his servants had done (FER 400; MCGC 162).

EDWARD GRENDON (GRINDON, GRINDALL) II

Edward Grendon, a baby, came to Virginia on the *James* with his parents and sister, Temperance, and left England on July 31, 1622 (FER 400).

TEMPERANCE GRENDON (GRINDON, GRINDALL)

Temperance, Edward Grendon's daughter, came to Virginia with her parents and baby brother, Edward, on the *James*. She departed from England on July 31, 1622 (FER 400).

THOMAS GRENDON (GRINDON, GRINDALL)

Thomas Grindon, who on December 9, 1628, was described as Edward Grindon's son and principal heir, remained in England after his parents moved to Virginia. On August 16, 1627, he sent a shipment of goods from London to Virginia on the *Truelove*. He reportedly invested £1,400 in outfitting and sending people to Virginia and also paid for the transportation of skilled workers capable of constructing various types of mills and in making rape oil and pot ashes. The Privy Council praised Thomas Grendon's efforts to strengthen and sustain the colony. By July 15, 1631, he had moved to Virginia and was among a group of planters who sent tobacco to England and petitioned for relief from customs. In the February 1633 session of the Virginia assembly, Thomas Grendon served as a burgess for the communities on the lower side of the James River, within the corporation of James City. On April 12, 1638, when Thomas patented some land, he was identified as a London merchant. His will, dated December 15, 1678, stated that he was a resident of Dukes Place and was a citizen and draper of London (CBE 79, 92; HEN 1:203; G&M 157, 165; DOR 2:225).

***

THOMAS GRENDON (GRINDAL)

On March 22, 1622, Thomas Grinden (Grindal) was killed when the Indians attacked Thomas Swinhowe's plantation (**47**) in Charles City (VCR 3:568).

ANTOINE GRENIER

Gardener Antoine Grenier and his wife were among the Walloons and French who indicated their willingness to go to Virginia. In August 1621 the Virginia Company agreed that they could immigrate (CBE 24).

FRANCES GRENVILLE (GREVILL, GREVELL) (MRS. NATHANIEL WEST, MRS. ABRAHAM PEIRSEY, MRS. SAMUEL MATHEWS I) (SEE MRS. NATHANIEL WEST, MRS. ABRAHAM PEIRSEY, MRS. SAMUEL MATHEWS I)

Frances Grenville (Grevill, Grevell) left Bristol, England, in September 1620 on the *Supply,* which transported William Tracy and his wife to Virginia and arrived at Berkeley Hundred (**55**) on January 29, 1621. She married Nathaniel West in 1621 and outlived him. By February 16, 1624, Frances and her little son, Nathaniel West II, were living in the household of her brother-in-law, John West, on the lower side of the James River, to the east of Grays Creek within the corporation of James City (**10-15**). By early 1625 Frances and her child had moved to the home of another brother-in-law, Francis West, who then lived on the east side of the Hampton River (**17**) in Elizabeth City. In late 1625 or early 1626 Frances Grenville West wed cape merchant Abraham Peirsey of Flowerdew Hundred (**53**), a widower with two children. She outlived Peirsey and sometime after March 24, 1628, married Samuel Mathews I, who then resided at the plantation known as Mathews Manor or Denbigh (**23**). Frances Grenville West Peirsey Mathews died prior to 1633 (CBE 21, 40, 67; VCR 3:396, 426; DOR 2:638, 803, 805).

***

***

JOHN GREVETT (GREEVETT, GRUETT)

John Grevett (Greevett, Gruett), a Virginia Company tenant, was a carpenter and sawyer assigned to Governor Francis Wyatt. On April 7, 1623, it was reported that prior to the March 1622 Indian attack, Grevett and Ambrose Griffin (another carpenter/sawyer and Virginia Company tenant) had been in the process of constructing a guesthouse or inn in Jamestown (**1**) for the reception of newly arrived immigrants. Both men also had been involved in building a palisade and court of guard there. On February 16, 1624, John Grevett and his wife were living on Jamestown Island. John and Ellin (Ellen) Grevett were still residing there on January 24, 1625, probably in the eastern part of the island, a rural area. The Grevetts were in possession of a dwelling, defensive weaponry, and some swine (VCR 4:104-106; CBE 40, 56; CO 1/2 f 145; DOR 1:34).

ELLIN (ELLEN) GREVETT (GREEVETT, GRUETT) (MRS. JOHN GREVETT [GREEVETT, GRUETT])

On February 16, 1624, Mr. and Mrs. John Grevett (Greevett, Gruett) were living on Jamestown Island (**1**), where he was a household head. On January 24, 1625, Mrs. Ellin (Ellen) Grevett and her husband were still living there. John was a Virginia Company servant as well as a carpenter and sawyer. On February 13, 1629, Thomas Warnett, a Jamestown merchant, made a bequest to Ellin Grevett (CBE 40, 56; VCR 4:104-106; SH 11-12).

***

***

AMBROSE GRIFFIN (GYFFITH, GRIFFITH)

Ambrose Griffin (Gyffith, Griffith), a 30-year-old sawyer/carpenter from Gloucestershire, England, came to Virginia on the *Bona Nova* in 1619. Court records dating to April 7, 1623, indicate that prior to the March 1622 Indian attack, Ambrose and fellow sawyer/carpenter John Greevett had worked on constructing a guesthouse or inn in Jamestown (**1**), a building intended to provide accommodations to newcomers. Griffin also had been involved in building the palisade and court of guard in Jamestown. On December 8, 1623, Elizabeth City's commander, Captain William Tucker, was ordered to send Ambrose Griffin to Warresqueak (**26**) to assist Captain

Roger Smith in building a fort there. On February 16, 1624, when census records were compiled, Ambrose Griffin was living at Buckroe (17) on land that belonged to the Virginia Company. In early 1625, he was described as a resident of Elizabeth City (18), where he and his wife, Joyce, lived in the home of Thomas Garnett, an ancient planter. Ambrose was then age 33 and his wife was 20. Both were free and Ambrose probably was a Virginia Company tenant. Ambrose Griffin and his wife may have moved to the lower side of the James River by 1629, when she testified in a court case involving a person who lived at the Treasurer's Plantation (11) (CBE 45, 66; FER 295; VCR 4:104-106, 441-442; CO 1/2 f 145; MCGC 195).

JOYCE GRIFFIN (GYFFITH, GRIFFITH) (MRS. AMBROSE GRIFFIN [GYFFITH, GRIFFITH])

Joyce Griffin (Gyffith, Griffith) came to Virginia on the *Jacob* in 1624. By early 1625 she and her husband, Ambrose, a carpenter/sawyer, were living in Elizabeth City (18) with Thomas Garnett and his wife. Joyce and Ambrose Griffin appear to have been free, although he was a Virginia Company tenant until at least 1624. On March 25, 1629, Mrs. Ambrose Griffin (probably Joyce) was identified as one of the women who had examined Thomas Hall, a hermaphrodite, in order to determine his gender. Because Hall, one of Edward Grendon's servants, lived on the lower side of the James River at the Treasurer's Plantation (11), Mrs. Griffin may have been residing there too (CBE 66; MCGC 195).

***

GEORGE GRIFFIN

In 1631 George Griffin and Company, owners of the *Warwick* of London, sent the ship to Virginia and New England to trade. On July 10, 1634, English officials noted that Governor John Harvey had detained the vessel in Virginia (CBE 117).

JOHN GRIFFIN (GRIFFEN)

John Griffin (Griffen) came to Virginia on the *William and John* in 1624 and on January 24, 1625, was identified as a 26-year-

old servant in the household of George Menefie in urban Jamestown (1) (CBE 56).

JOHN GRIFFIN

In May 1625 John Griffin was identified as the patentee of 50 acres in Coxendale (64), within the corporation of Henrico. Griffin's land was described in an October 20, 1634, patent as lying north of Thomas Sheffield's acreage (69) but south of Christopher Branch's land (VCR 4:552; PB 1 Pt. 1:155).

JOHN GRIFFIN (GRUFFIN)

John Griffin (Gruffin) reportedly was killed at Warresqueak (26) during the March 22, 1622, Indian attack (VCR 3:571).

JOHN GRIFFIN (GRUFFIN)

John Griffin or Gruffin who resided on the lower side of the James River, within the corporation of James City (8-15), died between April 1623 and February 16, 1624 (CBE 41).

LEONARD GRIFFIN

In 1621 Leonard Griffin was identified as one of the men associated with the East India School (FER 272).

MATHEW GRIFFIN (GRIFFINE)

Mathew Griffin (Griffine) died sometime after April 1623 but before February 16, 1624. He had been living on the lower side of the James River, within the corporation of James City (8-15) (CBE 41).

RALPH (RAFE) GRIFFIN (GRIPHIN)

On February 16, 1624, Ralph (Rafe) Griffin (Griphin) was living in the Neck O'Land (5) in James City, the area in which the late Rev. Richard Buck's orphans owned property. On June 24, 1624, Griffin testified in court that when he was with his mistress, Mrs. Jane Kingsmill, at the Buck family's home, he overheard Eleanor Spradd and Robert Marshall discuss their plans to marry. Richard Kingsmill, as an overseer of Rev. Buck's will and guardian of his orphans, had temporary possession of his property in the Neck O'Land (CBE 35; MCGC 17).

RICE (RISE) GRIFFIN

Rice (Rise) Griffin came to Virginia on the *Flying Hart* in 1621 and on February 16, 1624, was living in Elizabeth City **(18)**. On February 7, 1625, when a muster was compiled, he was identified as a 24-year-old servant at Daniel Gookin's plantation, Newportes News **(24)** (CBE 44, 63).

RICHARD GRIFFIN

Sometime after April 1623 but before February 16, 1624, Richard Griffin died in Elizabeth City **(17, 18)** (CBE 45).

RICHARD GRIFFIN

Richard Griffin died at Flowerdew Hundred **(53)** sometime after April 1623 but before February 16, 1624 (CBE 37).

ROWLAND GRIFFIN

On October 9, 1624, the Bridewell Court decided that Rowland Griffin, a vagrant from Farrington Without, would be sent to Virginia (CBE 48).

THOMAS GRIFFIN

Thomas Griffin set sail for Virginia on July 31, 1622, on the *James*, accompanying his master, Alexander Lake. Thomas died at Warresqueak **(26)** sometime after April 1623 but before February 16, 1624 (FER 400; CBE 42).

JOHN GRIGGS

John Griggs left England on July 31, 1622, on the *James* and came to Virginia as Robert Dodson's servant and (FER 400).

SAMUEL GRIGGS

On August 4, 1635, Samuel Griggs's plantation was described as being adjacent to Samuel Snead's, which was located at the head of Skiff's Creek in James City County. Both men's acreage probably was situated within what had been Martin's Hundred **(7)** (PB 1 Pt. 1:268).

ANN GRIMES

On February 16, 1624, Ann Grimes was a servant in the Yeardley household in urban Jamestown **(1)** (CBE 38).

EDWARD GRIMES (GRYMES)

On December 16, 1631, the justices of the General Court ordered Edward Grimes (Grymes), who had had a sexual liaison with Alice West, to post a bond guaranteeing that he would not marry another woman until the court had made a final decision. On November 12, 1635, Edward Grimes's land was described as lying opposite William Stafford's patent, which was on the east side of Skiff's Creek in Warwick County (MCGC 480; PB 1 Pt.1:305).

GEORGE GRIMES (GRYMES)

George Grimes (Grymes) came to Virginia sometime prior to January 11, 1622, at which time he made an agreement to clear part of Richard Tailor's land in Bermuda Hundred **(39)** in exchange for a 5-acre plot. Grimes died at Bermuda Hundred sometime after April 1623 but before February 16, 1624, leaving behind some debt. On December 11, 1623, the General Court noted that he had bought some of the Virginia Company's oatmeal from Captain Barwick. Then, on January 3, 1625, the court assigned part of Grimes's land to Captain Nathaniel Basse, one of his creditors. In May 1625 when a list of patented land was sent back to England, George Grimes was credited with 30 acres in Charles City, land that had been planted. On January 9, 1627, Richard Tailor asserted that George Grimes and others had illegally seated his land. Witnesses then proved that Tailor had offered 5 acres to each of the several men he had hired to clear his property (CBE 36; MCGC 8, 40, 129; VCR 4:553).

ELIZABETH GRIMLEY

Elizabeth Grimley, a young marriageable maid who was 26 years old, came to Virginia in September 1621 on the *Warwick*. She was brought to the colony as a replacement for Allice Lillowe (FER 309).

THOMAS GRINDER

On February 16, 1624, Thomas Grinder was living at Flowerdew Hundred **(53)** (CBE 37).

PETER GRINLINE

On July 31, 1622, Peter Grinline set sail for Virginia on the *James* with Robert Parker (FER 400).

***
JOHN GRINETT

On November 14, 1635, when John Grinett patented 150 acres of land on Deep Creek in Harwoods Neck, within Warwick River County, he used the headrights of his first wife, Alice, his second wife, Elizabeth, and Alice's son, Peter Hooper (PB 1 Pt. 1:306).

ALICE HOOPER GRINETT (MRS. [NO FIRST NAME] HOOPER, MRS. JOHN GRINETT)

Alice Grinett was identified as the first wife of John Grinett when he patented some Warwick County land on November 14, 1635, and used her as a headright. By that date, Alice was dead and John Grinett had remarried. John's patent reveals that Alice had a son named Peter Hooper, whose headright he also used (PB 1 Pt. 1:306).

ELIZABETH GRINETT (MRS. JOHN GRINETT)

On November 14, 1635, when John Grinett patented 150 acres of Warwick County land, he used the headright of his second wife, Elizabeth, as well as those of his first wife, Alice, and Alice's son, Peter Hooper (PB 1 Pt. 1:306).

***

WILLIAM GRIVELL

William Grivell, a gentleman, came to Virginia in 1608 in the 1st Supply of new settlers to Jamestown (**1**) (CJS 1:222; 2:161).

JOHN GROCER

On July 18, 1620, John Grocer's parents, John and Susan Grocer, asked Virginia Company officials to send their son home from the colony (VCR 1:408).

MATHEW (MATHEWE) GROSE (GROSSE)

On January 15, 1620, the justices of Bridewell Court decided that Mathew (Mathewe) Grose (Grosse), a vagrant from Billingsgate who was born in Colchester, would be sent to Virginia (CBE 17).

ELIZABETH GROSSE

On January 29, 1620, it was decided that Elizabeth Grosse would be sent from Bridewell Prison to Virginia. She appears to have been one of the poor children rounded up from the streets of London so that they could be shipped to the colony (CBE 17).

ELIZAETH GROTTE

On February 29, 1619, the justices of Bridewell Court had a girl named Elizabeth Grotte detained until she could be sent to Virginia (HUME 22).

ALICE GROVE

Alice Grove, a young maid, came to Virginia in 1621 on the *Bona Nova* and was 26 years old (FER 309).

RICHARD GROVE

Richard Grove came to Virginia on the *George* in 1623. Virginia Company records reveal that he was outfitted by Henry Horner, who had paid for his transportation from London to Portsmouth. Grove set sail, believing that he was one of John Proctor's servants. After they were at sea, however, Proctor transferred Grove's indenture to Horner. On March 9, 1624, Richard Grove, who was 28 years old, testified before the justices of the General Court that after he arrived in Jamestown (**1**), Proctor told him that Horner would be his master if he (Grove) agreed. Thomas Flower, who like Proctor and Grove came to the colony on the *George*, testified that the servant Henry Horner had planned to bring to Virginia had become ill and that Proctor had offered Horne one of his own servants, if he was willing to pay the price. Ultimately, it was agreed that Richard Grove would serve John Proctor for 3 years and Thomas Flower would serve Henry Horner for a like amount of time. If Horner decided not to keep Flower, he was to be offered to Proctor. In October 1624 Richard Grove testified about Elias Hinton, a deceased Proctor servant, who had been beaten by his master. He also talked about the beating inflicted on Elizabeth Abbott, one of John Proctor's maidservants. On February 4, 1625, when a muster was made of Paces Paines' (**9**) inhabitants, Richard Grove was listed as a 30-year-old servant in John Proctor's household. Grove apparently was a capable mariner, for in late 1633 or early 1634 he was hired by George and Maurice Thompson to take passengers to Virginia on the *Expedition*, which was detained at Gravesend, England (VCR 4:466-467; MCGC 12, 23; CBE 59; EAE 42).

WILLIAM GROWLE

On September 26, 1626, it was reported that William Growle sent goods to the colony on the *Plantation* (CBE 74).

JOHN GRUBB

On February 20, 1619, John Grubb and Joachim Andrews were in possession of land in the eastern end of Jamestown Island (1), to the south of William Fairfax's patent. In May 1625, when a list of patented land was sent back to England, Grubb was credited with 100 acres in Archer's Hope (6) (PB 1 Pt.12:648; VCR 4:556).

THOMAS GRUBB

On October 31, 1622, Thomas Grubb, a joiner who had come to Virginia on the *George*, agreed to serve Treasurer George Sandys for four months. He was summoned to court on November 1, 1624, at which time Sandys convinced his fellow justices that Grubb should serve him another four months. On January 24, 1625, Grubb was living in the eastern end of Jamestown Island (1) and was credited with a house and a modest supply of stored food. On April 25, 1625, the General Court decided that the newly fenced leasehold occupied by Thomas Grubb and his partner, Robert Marshall, should be divided into equal shares. The men may have been sharing the property when the muster was taken in January 1625, as Grubb's name was listed immediately after that of Marshall. When Thomas Grubb made his will, which was proved on May 21, 1627, he bequeathed his leasehold to Robert Wright and Andrew Rawleigh. On October 10, 1628, the General Court transferred Grubb's property rights to Wright and Rawleigh for a period of 10 years (MCGC 28, 56, 148, 154; CBE 56; DOR 1:35).

JEANE GRUNDYE (GRUNDIE)

Jeane Grundye (Grundie), a young marriageable maid, went to Virginia in 1621 on the *Warwick*, with her mother's consent. She was the daughter of William Grundye's brother in Newgate Market and had been recommended to Virginia Company officials by Joseph Stone, a yeoman in the king's guard. Stone's wife also gave Jeane a good endorsement (FER 309).

JOHN GUDDERINGTON

John Gudderington, a gentleman, came to Virginia in 1608 as part of the 2nd Supply of new settlers and would have resided in Jamestown (1) (CJS 1:241).

NATHANIEL GUILD

On February 25, 1620, it was decided that Nathaniel Guild, a boy brought in from Newgate Prison, would be detained until he could be sent to Virginia (CBE 29).

GRIFFIN GUINE (GWIN?)

On February 16, 1624, Griffine Guine (Gwin?) was living on the Maine (3), just west of Jamestown Island (CBE 39).

THOMAS GUINE (GUNIE, GWIN?)

Thomas Guine (Gunie, Gwin?) died in Jamestown (1) sometime after April 1623 but before February 16, 1624 (CBE 39).

CHRISTOPHER GUILLIAM

On March 22, 1622, Christopher Guilliam was killed in the Indian attack on Martin's Hundred (7) (VCR 3:570).

THOMAS GUISCE

On December 15, 1631, Thomas Guisce was identified as master of the *Delight*, which was setting sail for Virginia (CBE 97).

***

CHAD GULSTON

Chad Gulston and his wife and child reportedly died in Elizabeth City (17, 18) sometime after April 1623 but before February 16, 1624. If he was erroneously reported dead, he may have been the man identified as Chad Gunston, who was then living on the Eastern Shore (CBE 45).

MRS. CHAD GULSTON

Sometime after April 1623 but before February 16, 1624, Mrs. Chad Gulston died in Elizabeth City (**17, 18**), as did her husband and son (CBE 45).

[NO FIRST NAME] GULSTON

Mr. and Mrs. Chad Gulston's child died in Elizabeth City (**17, 18**) sometime after April 1623 but before February 16, 1624 (CBE 45).

***

THOMAS GULSTON

On January 22, 1620, the justices of Bridewell Court decided that Thomas Gulston, a vagrant, would be sent to Virginia (CBE 17).

***

JOHN GUNDRIE (GUNDY, GRINDY, GUNNERY) I

John Gundrie (Gundy, Grindy, Gunnery) I, an ancient planter, came to Virginia on the *Starr* in 1610. In 1617–1618, while Sir Samuel Argall was deputy governor, he gave Gundrie some land on the east side of the Hampton River in Elizabeth City (**17**). However, when Sir George Yeardley arrived in mid-April 1619, he claimed 3,000 acres of land there for the Virginia Company's exclusive use. As a result, John Gundrie, his wife, and his child were evicted from the house he had built prior to Yeardley's arrival. On June 19, 1622, Gundrie was among those who sent a petition to the Virginia Company protesting their ill treatment. Adam Dixon, the petition's author, said that all of the displaced men were ancient planters and the colony's best mechanics. By June 3, 1624, John Gundrie had been awarded some land on the west side of the Hampton River (**18**), adjacent to the acreage of William Claiborne. In early 1625 Gundrie, a 33-year-old household head, was living there with his 20-year-old wife, Mary, and 2-year-old son, John II. The Gundries occupied a dwelling of their own and were well supplied with stored food and defensive weaponry. In May 1625, when a list of patented land was sent back to England, John Gundrie was credited with 150 acres of land in Elizabeth City, acreage that was planted. On February 5, 1628, he sued

John Jackson and Richard Kingsmill, claiming that they had accepted his tobacco and, in exchange, were supposed to pay Humphrey Barret, a mariner. On February 13, 1629, when Jamestown merchant Thomas Warnett made his will, he named John Gundrie as one of his beneficiaries (VCR 2:45, 4:558; PB 1 Pt.1:41; CBE 65; MCGC 161; SH 11-12; DOR 1:57).

MARY (MARIE) GUNDRIE (GUNDY, GRINDY, GUNNERY) (MRS. JOHN GUNDRIE [GUNDY, GRINDY, GUNNERY] I)

Mary (Marie), who married John Gundrie (Gundy, Grindy, Gunnery) I, came to Virginia in 1618 on the *George*. If they were wed prior to Governor George Yeardley's April 1619 arrival in the colony, they resided on the east side of the Hampton River in Elizabeth City (**17**), on acreage that Yeardley later claimed on behalf of the Virginia Company. Afterward, Mary Gundrie, husband John, and their 2-year-old son, John II, moved to the west side of the Hampton River (**18**), where they established a home on land for which John held a patent. In early 1625 Mary was 20 years old and her husband was 33 (VCR 2:45, 4:558; PB 1 Pt. 1:41; CBE 65).

JOHN GUNDRIE (GUNDY, GRINDY, GUNNERY) II

In early 1625, 2-year-old John Gundrie (Gundy, Grindy, Gunnery) II was living with his parents, John and Mary (Marie) Gundrie, on the west side of the Hampton River (**18**) in Elizabeth City (CBE 65).

***

BENJAMIN GUNSTON

On July 16, 1621, Benjamin Gunston's widow asked Virginia Company officials for her late husband's estate, which was in Mr. Damiron's hands (VCR 1:520).

CHAD GUNSTON

On February 16, 1624, Chad Gunston was living on the Eastern Shore (**72-78**). He may have been the same man identified as Chad Gulston, who reportedly died in Elizabeth City (CBE 46).

***

EDWARD GURGANAY (GURGANEY, GURGANA)

Edward Gurganay (Gurganey, Gurgana), a gentleman who came to Virginia in 1608 in the 2nd Supply of new settlers, resided in Jamestown (1). In his *General History*, Captain John Smith included an account that Gurganey and others wrote in 1616. On October 1, 1617, Edward Gurganay acquired 400 acres called Longfield or Curles (42) by means of a court order he had received from the Virginia Company. Gurganay died sometime prior to February 11, 1620, at which time his widow, Ann, bequeathed his land to Thomas Harris. On April 16, 1622, Edward Brewster, who brought suit against Sir Samuel Argall, alleged that Gurganay had sold him a boat and that Argall had seized it, claiming that it was for the colony's use. He said that Argall had used it instead for the *Treasurer's* voyage to the West Indies (CJS 1:222; 2:258; PB 1 Pt. 1:438; C 24/460).

ANN GURGANAY (GURGANEY, GURGANA) (MRS. EDWARD GURGANEY [GURGANEY, GURGANA])

On February 11, 1620, Ann Gurganay (Gurganey, Gurgana) bequeathed to Thomas Harris 400 acres called Longfield or Curles, in the corporation of Henrico and east of Henricus Island (63). Harris's patent indicates that Ann's late husband, Edward Gurganay, had acquired the acreage on October 1, 1617, by means of a court order, and that the land had descended to her (PB 1 Pt. 1:438).

***

HENRY GURNER ALIAS FARMAN

On February 5, 1620, the justices of Bridewell Court decided that Henry Gurner alias Farman, a vagrant, would be sent to Virginia (CBE 18).

WILLIAM GURNEY

On February 27, 1619, William Gurney, a boy, was identified as one of the children rounded up from the streets of London so that they could be sent to Virginia (CBE 13).

GEORGE GURR

George Gurr, one of George Sandys' servants, came to Virginia on the *Tiger* in 1621, having formerly lived in Bermuda. On February 16, 1624, George Gurr was living on the lower side of the James River, within the corporation of James City and east of Grays Creek, probably residing on the Treasurer's Plantation (11). When a muster was compiled of the Treasurer's Plantation's inhabitants on February 4, 1625, George Gurr was said to have been killed by the Indians. On December 4, 1624, when Treasurer George Sandys patented some land, he identified Gurr as one of his servants and said that he had paid for his transportation to the colony (CBE 40, 61; PB 1 Pt. 1:12).

BARNARD GURRIER

Barnard Gurrier, a millwright, set sail for Virginia on April 17, 1619, and probably was a Virginia Company tenant or servant (FER 107).

ARTHUR GUY

On August 24, 1621, Arthur Guy, captain of the *Warwick*, was given a commission to take 100 passengers to Virginia, including some of the young women who went to be wives. On November 19, 1627, Guy was identified as captain of a ship that figured in a court case (VCR 3:498-499; MCGC 158).

JAMES GUY

James Guy came to Virginia in 1622 on the *Marigold*. On January 21, 1625, he was living at West and Shirley Hundred (41), where he was a 20-year-old servant in the home of Richard Biggs (CBE 52).

ROBERT GUY

Robert Guy came to Virginia on the *Swann* in 1619 and on February 16, 1624, was living at Flowerdew Hundred (53). By February 4, 1625, he had moved to Hog Island (16). Guy was then 20 years old and was one of Sir George Yeardley's servants (CBE 37, 61).

WHITNEY GUY

Whitney Guy died in Elizabeth City (17, 18) sometime after April 1623 but before February 16, 1624 (CBE 45).

GILBERT GYE

Adam Thorogood paid for the transportation of Gilbert Guy, who came to Virginia on the *Hopewell* in 1633. On June 24, 1635, Thorogood used Guy's headright when patenting some land (PB 1 Pt.1:179).

ROBERT GUYAR (GEYER, GIER, GIRE, GYER)

Robert Guyar (Geyer, Gier, Gire, Gyer) reportedly paid for Robert Browne's transportation to Virginia on the *Marigold* in 1618. Later, William Ganey defrayed the cost of Browne's passage and used his headright when patenting some land. In a lawsuit aired before the General Court in March 1624, Robert Guyar was identified as master of the ship *Southampton*, which was owned by John Harvey, a former sea captain who became Virginia's governor and a titled nobleman. Harvey accused Guyar of mutiny because he had objected to Harvey's attempt to detain the *Southampton* in Virginia instead of allowing Guyar to take it on an agreed-upon fishing voyage. On May 8, 1626, Edward Dade was identified as one of Robert Guyar's servants. On October 15, 1627, Captain Guyar asked the justices of the General Court to see that Captain William Peirce's personal estate was inventoried so that he could recover a debt (PB 1 Pt. 1:39; VCR 4:459-461; MCGC 13-14, 103, 156-157).

THOMAS GYNNER

Thomas Crispe of Kecoughtan (17) paid for the transportation of several servants to Virginia in December 1621. One was Thomas Gynner (MCGC 50).

H

JAMES HABERLY

On February 5, 1623, James Haberly and his father, Mr. Haberly, received a patent for some Virginia land (VCR 2:262).

THOMAS HACK (HAKES?)

On February 16, 1624, Thomas Hack (Hakes?) was living at Flowerdew Hundred (53) (CBE 39).

JOHN HACKER

John Hacker came to Virginia on the *Hopewell* and was from Limehouse, Stepney, in Middlesex. On February 4, 1625, he was identified as a 17-year-old servant living at Edward Blaney's plantation (14) on the lower side of the James River. On May 3, 1636, John Hacker obtained a patent for 150 acres on Upper Chippokes Creek in Charles City County. When he made his will on January 7, 1653, he described himself as a Virginia planter and left his plantation, household furnishings, cattle, servants, and crops to his wife, Elizabeth, and son, John Hacker. He bequeathed cattle to his friend, William Rookinge, and to his manservant, James. John Hacker's will was proved on June 8, 1654. Elizabeth Hacker may have been living in England, for she inherited a cottage in Frethorne, Gloucestershire, but the decedent's son, John, moved to Virginia (CBE 59; PB 1 Pt. 1:339; EEAC 26; WAT 878; DOR 1:40).

EDMUND HACKET

On July 4, 1623, Virginia Company officials identified Edmund Hacket as a subscriber for the relief of the colony (VCR 4:245-246).

MARY HACKETT

On February 27, 1619, Mary Hackett, a "young wench," was one of the youngsters rounded up from the streets of London so that they could be sent to Virginia (CBE 13; HUME 11).

THOMAS HACKTHORPE

On November 28, 1625, the General Court decided that Thomas Hackthorpe, ship captain Richard Page's servant, would be delivered to Abraham Peirsey in exchange for the two male servants that Page was supposed to deliver to Peirsey but lost. Hackthorpe may have been taken to Peirsey's plantation, Flowerdew Hundred (53), or stayed in Jamestown (1) (MCGC 77).

THOMAS HADDOCK

On February 15, 1620, Thomas Haddock, a boy, was brought to Bridewell Prison by Mr. Ferrar of the Virginia Company, so that he could be detained and sent to Virginia (CBE 18; HUME 27).

MOSES HADLEY

On July 31, 1622, Moses Hadley set sail for Virginia on the *James*. He accompanied Isaac Chaplain, who intended to establish the plantation known as Chaplin's Choice (**56**) (FER 400).

JOHN HAIGHES (HAYES?)

In January 1628 probate officials designated Edward Haighes as administrator for John Haighes (Hayes?), a bachelor who died in Virginia (CBE 81; MOR 48).

THOMAS HAKES

Thomas Hakes died on Jamestown Island (**1**) sometime after April 1623 but before February 16, 1624. He may have been the man identified as Thomas Hack, who was living at Flowerdew Hundred (**53**) on February 16, 1624 (CBE 39).

***

ROBERT HALAM (HOLLAM, HALLAM) I

Robert Halam (Hollam, Hallam) I came to Virginia on the *Bonaventure* in August 1620 and on February 16, 1624, was living in Bermuda Hundred (**39**). He was still residing there on January 24, 1625, at which time he was identified as a 23-year-old servant in the household headed by Luke Boyse, who later used his headright. He married Ann, John Price's widow, around 1630 and died sometime prior to May 6, 1638 (CBE 35, 53; DOR 1:8; 2:231-232; PB 1 Pt. 1:351; Pt. 2:547).

ANN PRICE HALAM (HOLLAM, HALLAM) (MRS. JOHN PRICE I, MRS. ROBERT HALAM [HOLLAM, HALLAM] I, MRS. DANIEL LLEWELYN)

(SEE ANN PRICE)

Ann I, the widow of John Price, married Robert Halam (Hollam, Hallam) I around 1630. Together, they had three children: Ann II, Robert II, and Sarah (DOR 2:232).

ANN HALAM (HOLLAM, HALLAM) II

Ann II, the eldest child of Robert Halam (Hollam, Hallam) I and his wife, Ann I, survived to adulthood and married John Gundrie (Gundry) of Elizabeth City (**17, 18**) (DOR 2:232).

ROBERT HALAM (HOLLAM, HALLAM) II

Robert II, the son of Robert Halam (Hollam, Hallam) I and his wife, Ann I, was sent to England after his father's death. He died without producing living heirs (DOR 2:232).

SARAH HALAM (HOLLAM, HALLAM)

Sarah, the daughter of Robert Halam (Hollam, Hallam) I and his wife, Ann I, was born around 1632. She married Samuel Woodward prior to August 1654 (DOR 2:232).

***

EDWARD HALE

On July 21, 1635, Edward Hayle was in possession of a plantation in Martin's Hundred (**7**) that was located north of Thomas Smith's (PB 1 Pt. 1:258).

GEORGE HALE (HAYLE, HEALE)

George Hale (Hayle, Heale), a drummer, left Bristol, England, on the *Supply* in September 1620 and was among those who accompanied William Tracy to Berkeley Hundred (**55**). Hale, a Virginia Company servant or tenant, was supposed to work for a certain number of years in exchange for a given amount of acreage (CBE 21, 28; VCR 3:187, 396-397, 674).

RICHARD HALE (HEALE)

Richard Hale (Heale) came to Virginia on the *Eleanor* in 1622 at the expense of Captain William Tucker, who used him as a headright when patenting some land on June 1, 1633 (PB 1 Pt. 1:122).

THOMAS HALE (HAILE, HAYLE)

Thomas Hale (Haile, Hayle), the son of Symon Hayle of St. Mary Summerset Parish in London, a porter, came to Virginia on the *George* in October 1623. On February 16, 1624, he was living at West and Shirley Hundred (41), and he was still there on January 22, 1625, at which time he was identified as a 20-year-old servant in Robert Partin's household. On June 4, 1627, the justices of the General Court decided that Thomas Hale (then described as age 19) would be executed in Jamestown (1) after being found guilty of raping four young girls in Shirley Hundred (CBE 36, 52; MCGC 149).

WILLIAM HALILA

William Halila came to Virginia in 1617 at the expense of ancient planter Richard Kingsmill of Jamestown (1). On January 24, 1625, Kingsmill acknowledged to the General Court that he had brought Halila to the colony. He was not listed in the 1624 census or 1625 muster (MCGC 44).

[NO FIRST NAME] HALL

Mr. Hall, who seems to have been associated with the Virginia Company and went to Virginia, died sometime prior to incoming Governor George Yeardley's arrival in Jamestown (1) on April 19, 1619 (VCR 3:121).

BARBARA HALL

On March 25, 1629, when several people testified about the indeterminate gender of Thomas or Thomasina Hall, Barbara Hall was identified as one of the women present at Nicholas Eyros's house at the Treasurer's Plantation (11) when the hermaphrodite was subjected to a physical examination (MCGC 195).

***

CHRISTOPHER HALL (HAULE, HAUL)

Christopher Hall (Haule, Haul) came to Virginia sometime prior to February 16, 1624, at which time he was living on the Governor's Land (3) in a household headed by John Carter. Hall apparently was a planter, for later in the year he gave a tobacco note to Captain William Holmes, who passed it on to two other men. By January 24, 1625, Christopher Hall had moved to the rural part of Jamestown Island (1), where he was a household head. He probably lived on the periphery of the urbanized area, near Dr.

John Pott's lot, for he was aware that Pott's tobacco and corn had been damaged by free-roaming swine and cattle. On May 9, 1625, Christopher Hall came into court, where he testified that Dr. Pott had urged him to shoot one of Captain Powell's hogs. He also said that at least four swine had been killed and dressed at Pott's orders. Christopher Hall and his wife, Amy, apparently were bad-tempered. In August 1625 Christopher argued with his Jamestown Island neighbor, Thomas Passmore, over the division of a tobacco crop and a land agreement the two men had made. By September 1627 the Halls had moved to Archer's Hope (6), where Christopher and a partner, William Harman, shared a 100-acre leasehold. On at least one occasion, Amy Hall and Harman came to blows. Afterward, Christopher and Amy Hall were obliged to post bonds guaranteeing her good behavior. By February 9, 1628, Christopher Hall was dead (CBE 39, 56; EAE 89; MCGC 59, 69, 153, 166; DOR 1:34).

AMY HALL (HAULE, HAUL) (MRS. CHRISTOPHER HALL [HAULE, HAUL])

Amy, the wife of Christopher Hall (Haule, Haul), apparently had a volatile disposition, for she was known as a scold and on at least one occasion came to blows with her husband's partner, William Harman. Harman and the Halls lived in Archer's Hope (6) where they shared a 100-acre leasehold. On September 17, 1629, Christopher Hall was obliged to post a bond guaranteeing his wife's good behavior, and she was sentenced to a ducking in the river and to being towed behind a ship. In January 1628 the Halls's peace bonds were canceled. In February 1628, when Amy Hall again was brought into court for physically fighting with William Harman, she was described as a widow (MCGC 153, 159, 166).

***

EDWARD HALL

On November 12, 1635, Edward Hall's land in Elizabeth City on Skiff's Creek was mentioned in William Stafford's patent for some adjoining acreage. Hall's land would have been in what became Warwick County (PB 1 Pt. 1:305).

GEORGE (GEORG) HALL

George (Georg) Hall came to Virginia in 1620 on the *Supply*, the ship that transported the Society of Berkeley Hundred's settlers to Berkeley Hundred (**55**). By February 24, 1624, he had moved to urban Jamestown (**1**) where he was an indentured servant in Governor Francis Wyatt's household. On January 24, 1625, George Hall still was a member of the Wyatt household in Jamestown and was described as a 13-year-old servant (CBE 38, 55; VCR 3:426).

HENRY HALL

On September 30, 1617, Henry Hall, a convicted felon, was reprieved from the Cambridge jail and delivered to Sir Thomas Smith so that he could be sent to Virginia (PC 2/29; SR 4525).

HUGH HALL

Hugh Hall came to Virginia in 1622 or 1623 on the *Margaret and John* and on February 16, 1624, was living in Elizabeth City (**18**) in Pharaoh Flinton's household. Flinton used Hall's headright when patenting some land on December 1, 1624, and indicated that he had paid for his passage from England. Hugh Hall was still living in the Flinton household in early 1625 and was identified as a 13-year-old servant. In October 1628 Hugh Hall was granted a certificate of freedom, as he had posted a bond guaranteeing that he was entitled to be released from servitude. This raises the possibility that Hugh's age was listed inaccurately in the 1625 muster, for in 1628 he would have still been a minor (CBE 44, 65; PB 1 Pt. 1:22; MCGC 175).

JEFFREY HALL

On February 16, 1624, Jeffrey Hall was living in Elizabeth City (**17, 18**) (CBE 43).

JOHN HALL (HAUL)

On February 5, 1620, John Hall (Haul), a boy from Langborne Ward, was brought to Bridewell by Mr. Ferrar of the Virginia Company. He was detained until he could be sent to Virginia (CBE 18; HUME 26).

***

JOHN HALL (HAULE)

John Hall (Haule) came to Virginia on the *John and Francis* and by February 16, 1624, was living with his wife in the eastern end of Jamestown Island (**1**). In April 1624 John Hall sued his neighbor, John Johnson I, who had failed to pay the £10 he promised him for serving as Johnson's substitute in a March 1623 offensive against the Indians. Johnson also owed a debt to Hall for the clothing Hall's servant had made for him. Later in the year, Johnson broke the law by selling Hall a young, unmarked hog. On January 24, 1625, John Hall and his wife, Susan, were still living on Jamestown Island. On August 22, 1625, the General Court granted John the 4 acres of land and house he then occupied. The property, which abutted Thomas Passmore's patent on Back Creek, was in the east end of Jamestown Island. Court testimony taken on January 30, 1626, reveals that a year or more prior to the time John Hall received a legal title to his property, he used it as collateral when securing a debt to Thomas Passmore. Since Hall died before he repaid the debt, on February 6, 1626, his widowed new wife, Bridgett, was obliged to assign her late husband's land and house to Passmore (CBE 40, 56; VCR 4:474; MCGC 35, 69, 92-93; DOR 1:35).

SUSAN HALL (HAULE)
(MRS. JOHN HALL [HAULE])

Susan, who became the wife of John Hall (Haule), came to Virginia on the *London Merchant*. On February 16, 1624, she was living on Jamestown Island (**1**) in her husband's household. She was still there on January 24, 1625, when a muster was made of that area's inhabitants. However, she died sometime prior to February 6, 1626, by which time John Hall had remarried but also had died (CBE 40, 56; MCGC 93).

BRIDGETT HALL (HAULE)
(MRS. JOHN HALL [HAULE])

John Hall (Haule) of Jamestown Island (**1**) married Bridgett shortly after his late wife Susan's decease. On February 6, 1626, Bridgett Hall appeared before the General Court, where she acknowledged a debt against her late husband's estate and agreed to surrender his house and land to Thomas Passmore (MCGC 93).

***

JOSEPH HALL

According to Virginia Company records, Joseph Hall set sail for Virginia on April 17, 1619. He probably was a Company servant or tenant (FER 107).

RICHARD HALL

Richard Hall came to Virginia on the *George* in 1617 and on February 4, 1625, was a servant at Hugh Crowder's plantation (**12**) (CBE 60).

RICHARD HALL

On June 2, 1634, Richard Hall exported a large shipment of tobacco from Virginia on the ship *Expedition*, which was bound for London. In January 1668, when the will of Richard Hall, a widower who died in Virginia, was presented for probate, his son Richard was named administrator. The decedent may have been the same individual who was in Virginia during the 1620s and 30s (EEAC 27; SR 3490).

ROBERT HALL

On December 19, 1621, Virginia Company officials noted that Robert Hall had received two shares of Virginia land from Francis Carter, who had obtained them from Lady Cicely Delaware (VCR 1:571).

SUSAN (SUSANNA) HALL

Susan (Susanna) Hall went to Virginia on the *William and Thomas* in 1618 and on February 16, 1624, was living in urban Jamestown (**1**) where she was a servant in Sir George Yeardley's household. She was still there on January 24, 1625. On October 12, 1627, Susan was among those who witnessed Sir George's will and on February 5, 1628, she appeared before the General Court to attest to its authenticity. By May 21, 1630, Mrs. Susan Hall had returned to England. She then testified before the Chancery Court about Sir George Yeardley's activities during the years she was in Virginia and identified others who had been members of the Yeardley household. In May 1630 Susan Hall gave her age as 22 and said that she had been a Yeardley servant since 1619 or 1620 (CBE 38, 54; SH 9; MCGC 161; SR 9963; C 24/561 Pt. 2 f 4).

THOMAS OR THOMASINE HALL

Thomas or Thomasine Hall, a hermaphrodite, came to Virginia sometime prior to March 1629. Thomas, who was then living in Warresqueak (**26**), told the General Court that he was born in Newcastle Upon Tyne, had been christened with the name Thomasine, and had dressed as a female until age 12. He was then sent to London, where he lived with his aunt for ten years. Hall said that after his brother was drafted into the army, he decided to join too. Thomas/Thomasine Hall cut his hair, dressed as a man, enlisted, and saw military service in the Isle of Ree. Afterward, he returned to Plymouth, began dressing as a woman, and worked as a lace-maker. Hall also admitted that he sometimes wore women's clothing when begging for food to feed his cat. On one occasion Hall was forcibly examined by some men, intent on determining his gender. When accused of having sexual relations with "Great Bess," one of Richard Bennett's servants, he denied it. On April 8, 1629, the General Court decided that it should be proclaimed throughout the community in which Thomas Hall lived that he was both male and female. As an outward sign of his medical condition, he was ordered to wear men's clothing but also to wear a woman's cap, cross-cloth, and apron. Thomas Hall, who by early 1629 was John Atkins' servant, died sometime prior to February 9, 1633, when Francis Poythress was given letters of administration (MCGC 159, 162-164, 194-195, 202).

THOMAS HALL

Thomas Hall, a 17-year-old husbandman from Cambridgeshire, came to Virginia in 1619 aboard the *Bona Nova*, a vessel that brought a substantial number of Virginia Company servants and tenants. On February 16, 1624, he was living on the Eastern Shore, probably on the Company Land (**76**). By February 4, 1625, he had been moved to the Treasurer's Plantation (**11**), where he was one of Edward Grindon's servants. On

March 2, 1626, Hall informed the General Court that he had been given two barrels of William Banks's corn by Mr. Thomas Swifte, who also lived at the Treasurer's Plantation, and that Swifte had indicated he would compensate Banks. In January 1628, when Thomas Hall was summoned to appear before the General Court, he identified himself as one of Edward Grindon's servants at the Treasurer's Plantation and said that he resided in the home of John and Jane Tyos. In early February 1628 Hall and the Tyos couple returned to court where they were accused of possessing goods stolen by William Mills, a known thief. Thomas Hall then stated that he was 26 years old and from Wisbige in Cambridgeshire. He admitted that he had purchased some shoes from Mills and had been present when Mills brought poultry to the Tyos's house. Thomas Hall and John Tyos were sentenced to a whipping, as they were considered accessories to William Mills's crime (FER 295; CBE 46, 60; MCGC 96, 159, 162-164).

THOMAS HALL

On February 15, 1620, Thomas Hall, a boy, was brought to Bridewell Prison by Mr. Ferrar of the Virginia Company so that he could be detained until he could be sent to Virginia (CBE 18; HUME 27).

THOMAS HALL

Thomas Hall died in Elizabeth City (**17, 18**) sometime after April 1623 but before February 16, 1624 (CBE 45).

WILLIAM HALL

On February 27, 1619, William Hall, a boy, was one of the youngsters rounded up from the streets of London so that they could be transported to Virginia. On November 20, 1623, Hall, who was in the colony, told the General Court that when Thomas Bilby lay dying, he said that he wanted Lewis Bayly to have his worldly goods. William Hall died at one of the settlements on the lower side of the James River (**11-16**) in James City sometime after February 16, 1624, but before early 1625 (CBE 13, 68; MCGC 8).

JULIAN HALLERS (HOLLIER)

Julian Hallers (Hollier) came to Virginia on the *Truelove* in 1623 and on January 30,

1625, was living in Pasbehay (**3**), where he was a 19-year-old servant in the household headed by John Moone. On March 6, 1633, when Moone patented some land, he used Julian's headright and indicated that he had paid for his transportation to the colony in 1623 on the *Returne* of London (CBE 57; PB 1 Pt. 1:127).

IDYE (EDITH) HALLIERS (HOLLIS)

In 1619 Idye (Edith) Halliers (Hollis) came to Virginia on the *Jonathan* and on February 16, 1624, was living at Jordan's Journey (**46**). When a muster of the community's inhabitants was taken on January 21, 1625, Idye was described as a 30-year-old servant in Robert Fisher's household (CBE 37, 51).

MERCIFUL HALLEY

Merciful Halley came to Virginia on the *Africa* at the expense of Adam Thorogood, who used her as a headright when patenting some land on June 24, 1635 (PB 1 Pt. 1:179).

STEPHEN HALTHORP

Stephen Halthorp, a gentleman, arrived in Virginia in 1607 and was one of the first Jamestown (**1**) planters (CJS 2:141).

JOSEPH HAM (HAMAN)

Joseph Ham (Haman) came to Virginia on the *Warwick* in 1621 and on February 16, 1624, was living in Elizabeth City (**18**) in Albiano Lupo's household. In early 1625 he was still there and was identified as a 16-year-old servant (CBE 43, 64).

JOHN HAMAN (HAMUN)

John Haman (Hamun) died in Jamestown (**1**) sometime after April 1623 but before February 16, 1624. His name was listed twice among those who died in Jamestown (CBE 39).

MATHEW HAMAN (HAMON)

Mathew Haman (Hamon) came to Virginia on the *Southampton* in 1622 and on February 16, 1624, was living across from Jamestown at the Treasurer's Plantation (**11**). On February 4, 1625, he was still there. He appears to have been free and may have been one of Treasurer George Sandys' tenants (CBE 40, 60).

WILLIAM HAMBEY

On April 3, 1627, Charles Harmar, Lady Elizabeth Dale's former overseer, appeared before the General Court and under oath delivered an account of her personal estate to William Hambey. Included were the cattle, tobacco, corn, and other goods that had been in Harmar's custody since he had received them from Henry Watkins, his predecessor. William Hambey appears to have been Charles Harmar's successor (MCGC 146).

[NO FIRST NAME] HAMDEN

On January 3, 1625, Mr. Hamden was identified as one of the Berkeley Hundred (55) men then seated at Shirley Hundred (41) and employed on behalf of the Society of Berkeley Hundred (MCGC 42).

WILLIAM HAMES

On February 16, 1624, William Hames was living at one of the plantations on the lower side of the James River, across from Jamestown Island (10-16) (CBE 40).

ROBERT HAMMERTON

According to Virginia Company records, Robert Hammerton, a waterman from London, set sail for Virginia in 1619. He probably was a Company servant or tenant (FER 295).

***

RALPH HAMOR (HAMER)

Ralph Hamor (Hamer), an ancient planter, came to Virginia in 1609 and began a lengthy period of public service to the colony. On June 12, 1610, Lord Delaware designated him clerk of his Council, and he served as Secretary of State from 1611 to 1614. In 1611 Hamor, accompanied by interpreter Thomas Savage, visited Powhatan at his village, Matchcot, and brought him gifts. Although Hamor failed to wear the special chain of pearls signifying that he was a government emissary, he told

Powhatan that Sir Thomas Dale would like to marry one of his daughters. In 1614 Ralph Hamor wrote a treatise in which he described the status of the fledgling colony. As vice-admiral he left Virginia but returned in May 1617. He received a land grant from the Virginia Company in June 1621 and reportedly intended to establish a particular (private) plantation of his own. One of his official duties was making sure that Lady Cecily Delaware, as her husband's heir, was satisfied with the Virginia land she had been assigned. At the time of the March 22, 1622, Indian attack, Captain Ralph Hamor and his brother, Thomas, were building homes in Warresqueak (26), where the Bennett family also had seated land. According to Captain John Smith, the Hamor brothers and their men fended off the attacking Natives with tools, brickbats, and whatever came to hand. Afterward, Ralph Hamor was ordered to evacuate the surviving Warresqueak settlers to the safety of Jamestown Island (1), and he was placed in command of the Martin's Hundred (7) settlers, who also were brought up to Jamestown. Within a relatively short time, Ralph Hamor found himself in a dispute with Edward Bennett of Bennett's Welcome in Warresqueak, seemingly over land ownership. During the next few months Hamor embarked on a number of trading expeditions and retaliatory raids against the Indians. In October 1623 he updated Virginia Company officials on conditions in the colony. Later, when he was authorized to go on a trading expedition in the Chesapeake Bay, he was given a substantial quantity of blue beads to use as a medium of exchange.

On February 16, 1624, Ralph Hamor and his wife, Elizabeth, were residing in urban Jamestown in a household that included her children, Jeremiah (Jeffrey, Jeremy, Jeremie, Joreme, Jereme) II and Elizabeth Clements, and 6 servants. They probably occupied a house on the half-acre lot that Hamor patented on August 14, 1624, which already contained a dwelling. During spring 1624 Ralph Hamor became involved in a legal dispute with the orphaned Mary Bayly's guardian, Ralph Evers. At issue was some acreage on Hog Island (16) that Hamor had cleared and seated. He then identified himself as a Virginia Company investor who had transported servants to the colony and lived there for 15 years. He insisted that he had not impinged on the Bayly patent. Years later, when the suit was settled, Hamor was compensated for the buildings he had erected on the Bayly property, and he was awarded a 200-acre patent for some land on Hog Island. When Ralph Hamor's brother, Thomas, died in 1623, Ralph was his heir. On January 24, 1625, Ralph and Elizabeth Hamor and the Clements children still were living in urban Jamestown with 3 servants. However, his other servants were attributed to his acreage on Hog Island. In January 1625 Ralph Hamor transferred his 100 acres in Archer's Hope (6) to Richard Kingsmill. The Hamors were actively involved in the Jamestown community's goings-on and appeared in court from time to time. In May 1625, when a list of patented land was sent back to England, Ralph Hamor was credited with 250 acres on Hog Island (acreage that already had been seated) and 500 acres at Blunt Point (22). The Hamor couple testified before the General Court about some boastful (perhaps illegal) comments they had overheard Captain John Martin make, and early in 1625 Ralph, as guardian of Walter Davis's orphaned son, John, sought to claim funds owed to the decedent's estate. Hamor also served as security for Mrs. Susan Bush, guardian of the orphaned Sara Spence. However, some of Ralph and Elizabeth Hamor's actions were of a questionable nature. For example, he was accused of price-gouging, and she was said to have been selling alcoholic beverages, contrary to law. In 1625 Ralph Hamor was authorized to arrest Jamestown Island gunsmith John Jefferson, who had eloped with his maidservant. Hamor died sometime prior to October 1626, at which time his estate was valued at 4,000 pounds of tobacco. His widow, Elizabeth, served as his administrator. Merchants George Menefie and Edward Bennett later brought suit against the decedent's estate (HAI 433, 795-856, 915; STAN 21, 28; CJS 2:239-250, 262, 296, 309, 314-317; VCR 1:491-492, 509, 605-606, 619; 2:103, 481; 3:482, 550, 610, 622, 643, 696-697; 4:9, 110, 447-448, 482-483, 556-557; PB 1 Pt.1:1, 5, 7; MCGC 10-11, 16-17, 19-21, 28, 30-32, 35-37, 39-40, 42, 44, 47, 51-52, 56-57, 79, 102, 117, 122, 128-129, 132, 134, 170; CBE 38, 55, 71; HEN 1:128-129; FER 571; MEY 30; DOR 1:30, 43, 700).

ELIZABETH FULLER CLEMENTS HAMOR (HAMER) (MRS. JEREMIAH CLEMENTS I, MRS. RALPH HAMOR [HAMER], MRS. TOBIAS FELGATE) (SEE ELIZABETH FULLER CLEMENTS, ELIZABETH FELGATE [FELLGATE])

On February 16, 1624, the former Elizabeth Fuller, widow of Jeremiah Clements I, was residing in urban Jamestown (1) with her husband, ancient planter Ralph Hamor (Hamer) and two children from her former marriage, Jeremiah (Jeffrey, Jeremy, Jeremie, Joreme, Jerene) II and Elizabeth Clements. The Hamor household was still there on January 24, 1625. In October 1624 Elizabeth Hamor testified before the General Court about the late Sybill Royall's will, and in May 1625 she described a conversation she had had with Mrs. Edward Blaney. The Hamors, as a couple, appeared as witnesses against Captain John Martin. In December 1624 it was alleged that Elizabeth Hamor had sold bottles of alcoholic beverages, contrary to law. Ralph Hamor died sometime prior to October 11, 1626, leaving his widow and executrix, Elizabeth, as his sole heir. She inherited not only his Jamestown property but also his 200-acre Hog Island (16) patent. By February 8, 1628, the twice-widowed Elizabeth Hamor had married Tobias Felgate (Fellgate). Because she intended to go to England, she was released from her bond as Ralph Hamor's administrator, and George Menefie agreed to become responsible for the decedent's estate, which included settling some outstanding debts. Elizabeth died sometime prior to March 30, 1630, having bequeathed virtually all of her Virginia property to Jeremiah Clements, a son by her first marriage (CBE 38, 55; MCGC 21, 37, 58, 61-62, 117, 122, 165; MEY 30, 199; PB 1 Pt.1:1, 5, 7; 2:4; SR 3972; DOR 1:699-700).

THOMAS HAMOR (HAMER)

Sometime prior to the March 22, 1622, Indian attack, Thomas Hamor and his brother, Captain Ralph Hamor, seated some land in Warresqueak (26) where they built houses. When the Indians attacked, Thomas Hamor was at Master Harrison's house with six men and a large group of women and children. The Indians set a tobacco house ablaze and then fired on those who ventured out to quench the fire. Hamor fled back to Harrison's house, which the Indians set on fire, and finally managed to reach his own dwelling, despite an arrow that pierced his back. In the wake of the Indian attack, Thomas Hamor and his household (like other residents of Warresqueak) were evacuated to Jamestown Island (1), considered a more secure position. On October 18, 1622, Hamor admitted to governing officials that he had made—and lost—a wager about the date of a certain ship's departure. By January 21, 1623, Thomas Hamor and his wife and daughter, who were still living on Jamestown Island, had become seriously ill. He died shortly thereafter. On June 11, 1623, Samuel Mole (Moll), a surgeon, said that Thomas Hamor had died of a burning fever and that his coffin was made by Nathaniel Jeffreys, a Jamestown Island joiner. When Hamor's estate was settled, his executor recovered funds from his creditors. Thomas Hamor's brother, Ralph, was his primary heir (CJS 2:296; SR 5860; HCA 13/44 ff 147ro-147vo; VCR 3:695; SAIN 1:36; CBE 31; MCGC 9-10, 17; PB 1 Pt. 1:18).

MRS. THOMAS HAMOR (HAMER)

Thomas Hamor's wife, whose first name is unknown, was severely wounded in the March 22, 1622, Indian attack. She survived and was among those who moved from Warresqueak (26) to the safety of Jamestown Island (1). According to a letter written on January 24, 1623, by George Harrison, who also lived in Jamestown, Mrs. Thomas Hamor, her husband, and her daughter were then quite ill. She was widowed prior to June 11, 1623, and may have died shortly thereafter (SAIN 1:36; CBE 31; SR 5860).

[NO FIRST NAME] HAMOR (HAMER)

On January 24, 1623, George Harrison sent word to England that Thomas Hamor, his wife, and his daughter were ill. The Hamors, who formerly resided at Warresqueak (26), were among those evacuated to Jamestown Island (1) after the March 22, 1622, Indian attack (SAIN 1:36; CBE 31).

***

THOMAS HAMPTON

In 1620 Captain John Smith identified Thomas Hampton as a Virginia Company investor (CJS 2:278).

WALTER HAMPTON

Walter Hampton set sail for Virginia on September 15, 1619, on the *Margaret* of Bristol and went to Berkeley Hundred (55) to work under Captain John Woodlief's supervision. Hampton's contract with the Society of Berkeley Hundred's investors specified that he was to serve for three years in exchange for 30 acres of land. Walter Hampton died within a relatively short time after reaching the colony (CBE 14; VCR 3:183, 187, 198, 213).

***

WILLIAM HAMPTON

William Hampton came to Virginia in 1621 on the *Bona Nova*. On February 16, 1624, he and his wife were living on the east side of the Hampton River in Elizabeth City (17), in Buckroe. In early 1625 William Hampton, who was age 34, was still living there on the Virginia Company's land, and headed a well-supplied household that included his wife, Joan (Joane), and John Arndell (Arundell), who was age 22. On January 12, 1627, William Hampton was identified as a Virginia Company tenant when he was assigned to Captain Francis West, who lived nearby. By December 10, 1627, William had obtained a 10-year lease for 50 acres at Buckroe, across from Old Point Comfort Island. In 1634 he commenced leasing 100 acres on the east side of Harris Creek (19), near the mouth of the York River. Later in the year, he purchased some of the late Thomas Lee's goods, which were sold by Bartholomew Hopkins, and in 1639 he testified in a lawsuit involving Lee's estate. Finally, in 1640 he acquired a patent for 550 acres in Elizabeth City, using the personal adventures of himself and his wife, Joan, and the headrights of several others. It should be noted that in early 1625 Elizabeth City's muster-takers might have mistakenly listed William Hampton and his wife twice, simultaneously attributing them to two localities (CBE 45, 68, 208; MCGC 136; PB 1 Pt. 1:84, 153; Pt. 2:752; DOR 1:67; 2:247-248).

JOAN (JOANE) HAMPTON (MRS. WILLIAM HAMPTON)

On February 16, 1624, Virginia Company tenant William Hampton and his wife, Joan (Joane), were sharing a home in the Buckroe area of Elizabeth City (**17**). In early 1625 the Hamptons were still living in the same area, which was part of the Virginia Company's land, and William was a household head (CBE 45, 68; MCGC 136; DOR 1:67).

***

***

WILLIAM HAMPTON

William Hampton came to Virginia in 1620 on the *Bona Nova*. In early 1625 he and his wife, Joan, were living in Elizabeth City (**18**) in a household headed by Edward Waters. William, who appears to have been free, was 40 years old. It is unclear whether Elizabeth City's muster-takers mistakenly listed William Hampton and his wife twice, attributing them to two localities and two households, or whether there was another couple bearing the same names (CBE 65; DOR 2:247-248).

JOAN HAMPTON (MRS. WILLIAM HAMPTON)

Joan, William Hampton's wife, came to Virginia in 1621 on the *Abigail*. In early 1625 the Hamptons, who appear to have been free, were living in Elizabeth City (**18**) in a household headed by Edward Waters. Joan was then age 25. Elizabeth City's muster-takers may have mistakenly listed Joan and William Hampton twice, simultaneously attributing them to two localities and two households (CBE 65; DOR 2:247-248).

***

GEORGE HAMS

On December 31, 1619, George Hams, a boy brought in from Newgate, was detained so that he could be sent to Virginia. He may have been the same individual later identified as George Hans (HUME 17).

GEORGE HANCKLE (HANKLE)

On October 3, 1618, officials at Bridewell decided that George Hanckle (Hankle), a vagrant from Cripplegate, would be detained until he could be sent to Virginia (CBE 10; HUME 7).

THOMAS HAND

Thomas Hand came to Virginia on the *Charles* in 1621 at the expense of John Bush, who used him as a headright on December 1, 1624, when patenting some land (PB 1 Pt. 1:31).

BENJAMIN HANDCLEARE

On February 16, 1624, Benjamin Handcleare was living in Basses Choice (**27**). He died sometime prior to February 7, 1625 (CBE 46, 62).

ELIZABETH HANDSLEY

In April 1620 the officials at Middlesex decided that Elizabeth Handsley, a thief, would be transported to Virginia (CBE 19).

***

JOHN HANEY (HAYNEY, HEINY, HAINE, HEMY, HENRY)

John Haney (Hayney, Heiny, Haine, Hemy, Henry) came to Virginia in 1621 on the *Margaret and John*. On February 16, 1624, he and his wife were living on the lower side of the Hampton River in Elizabeth City (**17**), in Buckroe. In early 1625 John, who was age 27, was still living there on the Virginia Company's land. He and his partner, Nicholas Rowe, headed a well-supplied household whose members included John's wife, Elizabeth, two servants, and another married couple. The Haney-Rowe household had use of a dwelling, three storehouses, and a protective palisade. On January 3, 1626, John Haney was censured by the General Court for going aboard a ship without official permission and for saying that Captain William Tucker was responsible for Robert Leister's death and would be the death of him. For these affronts to authority, Haney was sentenced to imprisonment in Jamestown (**1**) and publicly whipped. On January 12, 1627, John Haney was identified as a Virginia Company tenant when he was assigned to Mr. Farrar, probably Council member William Farrar of Jordan's Journey (**46**). On December 12, 1627, John Haney was identified as a planter when he acquired 150 acres at

Buckroe, near Old Point Comfort Island and adjacent to William Hampton's leasehold (CBE 45, 68; MCGC 85, 108, 136; PB 1 Pt. 1:83, 136; DOR 1:68).

ELIZABETH HANEY (HAYNEY, HEINY, HAINE, HEMY, HENRY) (MRS. JOHN HANEY [HAYNEY, HEINY, HAINE, HEMY, HENRY])

Elizabeth, who became the wife of Virginia Company tenant John Haney (Hayney, Heiny, Haine, Hemy, Henry), came to Virginia on the *Abigail* in 1622. On February 16, 1624, she was sharing a home with him in the Buckroe area of Elizabeth City (17). In early 1625 Elizabeth and John Haney and John's partner, Nicholas Rowe, were members of a household that included four other people. They were still living in the same area, which was part of the Virginia Company's land (CBE 45, 68; MCGC 136).

***

NATHANIEL (NATHAINIELL) HACKWORTH (HAUKWORTH)

Nathaniel (Nathianiell) Hackworth (Haukworth) died at Warresqueak (26) sometime after February 16, 1624, but before February 7, 1625 (CBE 62).

GEORGE HANS

On January 8, 1620, George Hans, who was moved from Newgate to Bridewell Prison, was reprieved so that he could be sent to Virginia. He may have been the youth described as George Hams (CBE 16).

GEORGE HANSON

On February 27, 1619, George Hanson, a boy from St. Giles, Cripplegate, was among the youngsters brought in from the streets of London so that they could be sent to Virginia (CBE 13).

HELEN HANSON

On November 20, 1622, officials at Bridewell decided that Helen Hanson, who was being detained at Newgate, would be transported overseas (CBE 29).

ELIZABETH HANSTYE

On November 20, 1622, it was decided that Elizabeth Hanstye, who was being detained at Newgate, would be transported overseas (CBE 29).

[NO FIRST NAME] HARDCASTLE

In 1633 someone named Hardcastle exported tobacco from Virginia on the *Christopher and Mary*. The crop was consigned to John Punchard of Limehouse, Middlesex, a mariner (EAE 41).

MATHEW HARDCASTLE (HARDCASTELL)

Mathew Hardcastle (Hardcastell) came to Virginia on the *Jacob* in 1623. In early 1625 he was living in Elizabeth City (18), where he was a 20-year-old servant in Pharaoh Flinton's household (CBE 65).

JOHN HARDEN

On February 27, 1619, John Harden, a boy, was one of the youngsters brought in from the streets of London so that they could be sent to the colony (HUME 11).

CHRISTOPHER HARDING (HARDYN)

Christopher Harding (Hardyn) came to Virginia sometime prior to December 19, 1617, at which time he was identified as one of Captain Robert Smalley's (Smallay's) men at Bermuda Hundred (39). Harding was killed at West and Shirley Hundred (41) sometime after April 1623 but before February 16, 1624. When a list of patented land was sent back to England in May 1625, Christopher Harding, though deceased, was credited with 100 acres in the Great Weyanoke (52) (CBE 36; SH 4; VCR 4:554).

RICHARD HARDING

On November 15, 1617, officials at Bridewell decided that Richard Harding, a prisoner in the White Lyon in Suffolk, who had been condemned for a felony, would be delivered to Sir Thomas Smith of the Virginia Company so that he could be sent to Virginia (SR 4525; PC 2/29 f 167).

THOMAS HARDING

On February 16, 1624, Thomas Harding was living in Elizabeth City (**17**). On January 12, 1627, he was identified as one of the Virginia Company tenants being assigned to Governor George Yeardley (CBE 43; MCGC 136).

[NO FIRST NAME] HARDWIN

In 1608 a laborer whose surname was Hardwyn was among those who came to Virginia in the 2nd Supply of new colonists. He would have resided in Jamestown (**1**) (CJS 1:242; 2:191).

NICHOLAS HARECOURT

On July 21, 1627, it was determined that Nicholas Harecourt, Mr. Vassall's servant, would be sent to Virginia (CBE 79).

JOHN HARFORD

John Harford, an apothecary, came to Virginia in 1608 in the 1st Supply of new settlers and therefore would have lived in Jamestown (**1**) (CJS 1:223; 2:162).

WILLIAM HARGETTS

On September 8, 1626, officials at Bridewell decided that William Hargetts, who was being detained, would be sent to Virginia (CBE 73).

THOMAS HARLEY

On August 28, 1628, Thomas Harley was identified as master of the *London Merchant,* which was making a voyage from London to Virginia (CBE 84).

ANTHONY HARLOW

On February 16, 1624, Anthony Harlow was a member of Ensign William Spence's household, which resided in the eastern end of Jamestown Island (**1**) (CBE 40).

JOHN HARLOW

John Harlow came to Virginia on the *Sampson* in 1619 and on February 16, 1624, was living in Elizabeth City (**18**). In early 1625 he was still there and was identified as a member of John Waine's (Wayne's) household. John Harlow was age 28 and was a free man (CBE 46, 65).

JOHN HARMAN

On December 31, 1619, it was determined that John Harman, who was being detained at Bridewell, would be sent to Virginia (CBE 15).

WILLIAM HARMAN

William Harman, who by mid-September 1627 shared a 100-acre leasehold in Archer's Hope (**6**) with Christopher Hall, frequently clashed with his partner's wife, Amy. Because they had come to blows on more than one occasion, William Harman and Amy Hall were required to post bonds, guaranteeing their good behavior (MCGC 153, 159, 166).

***

AMBROSE HARMAR (HARMER)

Ambrose Harmer married Jane, Richard Kingsmill's widow, sometime after July 7, 1630, but before May 1637. The Harmers resided on Jamestown Island (**1**) and occupied a home located on Jane's dower share of her late husband's property. Ambrose Harmer represented Jamestown in the colony's assembly in 1645 and 1646 but never personally owned land on the island; however, Jane's acreage would have made him eligible to hold office. Ambrose Harmer was speaker of the assembly in 1646 and a member of the Council of State in 1639 and 1640. In November 1638, when Ambrose and Jane Harmer patented some land on the Chickahominy River, reference was made to Jane's late husband, Richard Kingsmill, and his daughter, Elizabeth. Ambrose Harmer may have been involved in trapping or in Indian trade, for in August 1635 he sent a substantial number of beaver skins and coats home to England.

On May 6, 1637, Ambrose Harmer asked officials in England to appoint him guardian (or custodian) of Benomi Buck, the Rev. Richard Buck's retarded son, who had just turned 21. He said that the colony's laws made no provision for incompetent heirs and claimed that he had looked after Benomi and one of his brothers for the past 13 years. He added that although Benomi had inherited very little, he was unable to manage even that. England's Court of Wards and Leveries responded by ordering Harmer and two people of his choice to assess Benomi Buck's competency. Afterward, a written report was to be sent to the Court so that provisions could be made for custodial care, if it were needed. On July 25, 1638, when Governor John Harvey received an official copy of the Court order, he refused to implement it, for he believed that as governor, he had the right to appoint custodians for the mentally impaired. When he learned of Harvey's actions, Ambrose Harmer returned to England and filed another petition with the Court of Wards and Leveries, whose justices asked Governor Harvey to explain himself. On May 20, 1639, Governor Harvey replied that because Ambrose Harmer had complained about the cost of caring for Benomi Buck and his estate, he had assigned that task to another man, someone of great integrity. He claimed that Harmer and his wife, Jane, Richard Kingsmill's widow, had long coveted the Buck orphans' inheritance and that the Kingsmills had gotten rich from the estate. Meanwhile, Ambrose Harmer returned from England with a commission giving him guardianship. By that time, Benomi Buck was dead. Ambrose Harmer himself seems to have died sometime prior to 1652 (SAIN 1:251, 294; HCA 13/52; EAE 54; CO 1/9 f 129ro, 131; 1/10 ff 65-68; PC 2/49:344; G&M 234; STAN 34, 64; MCGC 495; HEN 1:289, 298, 322; LNC Book A:59; PB 3:184).

JANE KINGSMILL HARMAR (HARMER)
(MRS. RICHARD KINGSMILL, MRS. AMBROSE HARMAR [HARMER])
(SEE JANE KINGSMILL)

Sometime after July 7, 1630, but before July 1638, Jane, the widow of Richard Kingsmill, married burgess and councilor Ambrose Harmar (Harmer), who immediately sought custody of the Rev. Richard Buck's estate. The Harmers resided on Jamestown Island and probably occupied a home located on Jane's dower share of her late husband's estate. Jane Kingsmill Harmar and husband Ambrose provided care to the orphaned Benomi Buck, who was mentally impaired and died while he was living with them. Governor John

Harvey claimed that she was greedy and that she and her former husband had profited handsomely from the Buck estate. In 1652 Mrs. Jane Kingsmill Harmar patented 2,000 acres of land in Northumberland County. She died or sold her Jamestown Island land sometime prior to June 5, 1657. However, "Mrs. Harmer's cart path" was identified in a patent and on a plat during the early 1660s (PB 3:184; CO 1/10 ff 65-68; AMB 11, 135-136).

***

ANN HARMAR (HARMER)

In 1621, Ann Harmar (Harmer), a marriageable young maid who was born in Baldock in Hartfordshire, set sail for Virginia on the *Marmaduke*. She was 21 years old and left behind five brothers and two sisters. Virginia Company records indicate that Ann's father was a gentleman of good reputation and that her mother was a Kempton. Two of Ann Harmer's cousins, a Mr. Underhill and a Mr. Farblow, were grocers (FER 306, 309).

***

CHARLES HARMAR (HARMOR, HARMER, HARMAN)

Charles Harmar (Harmor, Harmer, Harman) came to the colony on the *Furtherance* in 1622. As Lady Elizabeth Dale's overseer and successor to Henry Watkins, he managed her property at West and Shirley Hundred Island (**41**) on the Eastern Shore (**72**), and perhaps on Jamestown Island (**1**). In January 1623 Harmar informed the General Court that John Raimond had killed one of Lady Dale's cattle near the Chickahominy River. In August he returned to court to serve on a jury. On June 21, 1624, Charles Harmar, who gave his age as 24, testified in a slander suit that involved Captain William Eppes and Ensign Thomas Savage and concerned an incident that had occurred on the Eastern Shore. By early 1625 Harmar was living there and shared a home with three other men. On February 9, 1625, he was still identified as Lady Dale's overseer when plans were made to settle certain debts attributable to the late George Thorpe. Harmar was indebted to surgeon Thomas Bunn and his neighbor, William Davis, whom he was ordered to pay. On April 3, 1627, Charles Harmar, described as Lady

Elizabeth Dale's former overseer, appeared before the General Court and under oath delivered to William Hambey an account of her personal estate. Included were the cattle, tobacco, corn, and other goods that had been in Harmar's possession since he had taken custody of them from Henry Watkins, his predecessor. On December 9, 1628, Charles Harmar was given permission to plant a neck of land on the south side of Old Plantation Creek **(73)**, property rumored to belong to Lady Elizabeth Dale. By 1632 Harmar had become a burgess and a commissioner of Accomack's local court. In June 1635 he patented a large tract of land on the Eastern Shore, using as headrights himself and his wife, Ann, the daughter and final heir of the late Henry Soothey of Jamestown Island. Among those with whom Charles Harmer had business dealings was cape merchant Abraham Peirsey. Harmer made his will in July 1639 and died sometime prior to 1644. Although his widow, Ann, received her dower share of his estate, his principal heir was Dr. John Harmar of Oxford, England. Charles and Ann Soothey Harmar's daughter, Elizabeth, inherited her parents' land on the Eastern Shore (VCR 4:8; MCGC 4-5, 15, 48, 73-74, 146, 179; CBE 69; HEN 1:170, 179, 187; PB 1 Pt.1:106, 245; EAE 89; EEAC 27; WITH 573; DOR 1:70).

ANN SOOTHEY HARMAR (HARMOR, HARMER, HARMAN) (MRS. CHARLES HARMAR [HARMOR, HARMER, HARMAN], MRS. NATHANIEL LITTLETON) (SEE ANN SOOTHEY [SOUTHEY, SOTHEY])

Ann, the daughter of Henry and Elizabeth Soothey, went to Virginia in 1622 on the *Southampton*. During 1624 and 1625 she and the surviving members of her family lived on Jamestown Island **(1)**. Ann married Charles Harmar (Harmor, Harmer, Harman), who during the first quarter of the seventeenth century was employed as overseer of Lady Elizabeth Dale's property in the corporation of Charles City **(41)** and on the Eastern Shore **(72)**. In June 1635, when Charles Harmar patented some land on the south side of Old Plantation Creek, **(73)**, he used Ann as a headright. The couple resided on the Eastern Shore, where he became politically prominent. At Charles Harmar's

death around 1644, Ann inherited a dower share of his estate. Ann Soothey Harmar, as her parents' sole surviving heir, seems to have inherited a parcel of land in the eastern part of Jamestown Island, abutting what briefly was known as Harmer Creek. Sometime after June 1635 but before November 23, 1640, the widowed Ann Soothey Harmar married Nathaniel Littleton (MCGC 152; WITH 573; CBE 27, 38, 56; PB 1 Pt. 1:245; PB 7:228-229; AMES1:42).

ELIZABETH HARMER (HARMOR, HARMER, HARMAN)

On September 17, 1644, Elizabeth Harmar (Harmor, Harmer, Harman), the daughter of Charles and Ann Soothey Harmar, renewed her father's patent for some acreage on the Eastern Shore, on the south side of Old Plantation Creek **(73)** (PB 1 Pt. 1:245; AMES 2: 301).

***

SUSAN HARMOND

On March 29, 1620, Virginia Company officials noted that Susan Harmond, the sister of Henry Davies, was entitled to his Virginia land (VCR 1:331).

FRANCIS HARPER

On December 4, 1634, when Hugh Cox received a court order entitling him to a patent, he listed Francis Harper as a headright (PB 1 Pt. 1:282).

JOHN HARPER

John Harper, a gentleman and Virginia Company investor, came to Virginia in 1608 in the 1st Supply of new settlers. Therefore, he would have lived in Jamestown **(1)** (CJS 2:161, 277).

JOSYAS (JOSIAS) HARR (HARTT)

On September 12, 1623, Josyas (Josias) Harr (Hartt), a London haberdasher, arrived in Jamestown **(1)** on the *Bonny Bess* and took the oath of supremacy (MCGC 6).

THOMAS HARRALDE

On November 30, 1624, Hugh Hayward of the Governor's Land **(3)** and Thomas Fitt of

Jamestown Island (1), testified that they were present when Thomas Harralde made his will and served as witnesses. They verified the authenticity of Harralde's will, which Richard Kingsmill brought to the justices of the General Court, and they indicated that the testator lived approximately a month after preparing it (MCGC 33).

EDWARD HARRINGTON (HARINGTON)

Edward Harrington (Harington) came to Virginia in 1607 and was one of the first Jamestown (1) colonists. According to Captain John Smith, he coauthored a verse that was published in Smith's writings about Virginia. George Percy indicated that Edward Harrington died on August 24, 1607, and was buried the same day (CJS 1:197; 2:141, 153; HAI 99).

[NO FIRST NAME] HARRIS

On February 16, 1624, Lieutenant Harris, whose given name is unknown, was living in Archer's Hope (6). This individual should not be confused with Lieutenant John Harris, a married man with children then living at West and Shirley Hundred (41) (CBE 41).

ALEXANDER HARRIS

On August 19, 1628, it was noted that Alexander Harris had shipped goods from London to Virginia on the *Friendship* (CBE 88).

ALICE HARRIS

On February 16, 1624, Alice Harris was living in Elizabeth City (18) (CBE 44).

ALICE HARRIS

In 1628, Alice Harris, who identified herself as a widow who had been living in Virginia for 14 years, asked to be relieved of taxes on the tobacco she exported. She may have been the same individual who in 1624 was living in Elizabeth City (CBE 80).

EDWARD HARRIS

On September 26, 1627, Edward Harris, an English merchant, shipped goods from

London to Virginia on the *Samuell*. In 1639–1640 he dispatched a shipment of shoes, clothing, soap, and strong waters (CBE 80; SR 3506; E 190/44/1).

ELEANOR (ELINOR, ELLINOR) HARRIS

Eleanor (Elinor, Ellinor) Harris came to Virginia in 1623 on the *Providence* and on February 16, 1624, was living in Elizabeth City. She was still there on February 7, 1625, and was a 21-year-old servant in Daniel Gookin's household in Newportes News (24) (CBE 43, 63).

ELIZABETH HARRIS

On January 22, 1620, officials at Bridewell decided that Elizabeth Harris, a vagrant who was being detained, would be sent to Virginia (CBE 17).

JOHN HARRIS

On December 31, 1619, it was decided that John Harris, who was being detained at Bridewell, would be kept until he could be sent to Virginia (CBE 15).

JOHN HARRIS

John Harris came to Virginia in 1624 on the *Jacob*. In early 1625 he was living in Elizabeth City (18), where he was a servant in Thomas Spellman's household. John was then 21 years old (CBE 65).

JOHN HARRIS

John Harris came to Virginia on the *Truelove* in 1628 at the expense of Adam Thorogood, who used him as a headright when patenting some land on June 24, 1635 (PB 1 Pt. 1:179).

***

JOHN HARRIS I

On June 4 and November 17, 1623, Lieutenant John Harris I provided testimony about the marriage contract made by the Rev. Grivel Pooley and the widowed Sisley Jordan of nearby Jordan's Journey (46). On February 16, 1624, John and his wife, Dorothy (Dorithe) I, and their two children were among those living in West and

Shirley Hundred (**41**). One would have been their daughter, Dorothy II, who was born around 1620. The Harrises went to England, where on May 1, 1624, Dorothy gave birth to John Harris II, who was baptized at St. Dunstan's in Stepney. In May 1625 when a list of patented land was sent back to England, John Harris was credited with 200 acres of land in the corporation of Charles City, acreage that had been seated. On April 7, 1625, John, who was then a sergeant, was identified as one of the planters who had asked the king to raise the price of tobacco. On March 5, 1627, he appeared before the General Court where he testified about a sexual encounter between Captain William Eppes and Mrs. Alice Boyse at Martin's Brandon (**59**). On January 28, 1629, Sergeant John Harris was summoned to court by Thomas Ironmonger, to whom he was in debt, and was identified as a resident of Shirley Hundred. In 1629 and 1630 John served as a burgess for the Shirley Hundred Maine (mainland), and in March 1629 he was a juryman (VCR 4:218-220, 553; CBE 36; MCGC 51, 141-142, 160, 190; HEN 1:138, 147; DOR 2:262-263).

DOROTHY (DORITHE) HARRIS I (MRS. JOHN HARRIS I)

On February 16, 1624, Dorothy (Dorithe) I, Lieutenant John Harris I's wife, was living in West and Shirley Hundred (**41**) with her husband and two young children. One would have been their daughter, Dorothy II. The Harrises went to England, where on May 1, 1624, Dorothy gave birth to John Harris II, who was baptized at St. Dunstan's in Stepney. In 1627 the General Court ordered Mrs. Harris to punish her 7-year-old daughter, Dorothy, who had been molested by Charles Maxey, a young indentured servant (CBE 36; MCGC 149; DOR 2:262-263).

[NO FIRST NAME] HARRIS

On February 16, 1624, Lieutenant John Harris I and his wife, Dorothy I, and their two children were living in West and Shirley Hundred (**41**) (CBE 36).

DOROTHY HARRIS II

On February 16, 1624, Dorothy Harris II, the daughter of Lieutenant John Harris I and his wife, Dorothy I, was living in West and Shirley Hundred (**41**) with her parents

and another sibling. On May 1, 1624, while the Harrises were in England, John Harris II was born and baptized. In early 1627, Dorothy II, who was around 7 years old, was molested by Charles Maxey, a young male servant. The General Court ordered Dorothy's mother to punish her twice for her involvement in what was considered a sex offense, whereas Maxey received two public whippings. Sometime prior to November 20, 1637, Dorothy Harris II married John Baker (CBE 36; MCGC 149; DOR 2:262-263; PB 1 Pt. 2:668).

JOHN HARRIS II

On May 1, 1624, Dorothy Harris I, the wife of John Harris I, was in England, where she gave birth to her son, John Harris II, who was baptized at St. Dunstan's in Stepney (DOR 2:262-263).

***

SARAH HARRIS

On November 20, 1622, officials at Bridewell decided that Sarah Harris, who was being detained at Newgate, would be sent to Virginia (CBE 29).

***

THOMAS HARRIS

Thomas Harris, an ancient planter, arrived in Virginia on the *Prosperous* in the month of May; surviving records fail to disclose the year in which he reached the colony. As Harris was associated with Bermuda Hundred (**39**), a settlement established by Sir Thomas Dale, he may have been among those arriving with Dale in May 1611. On February 11, 1620, Ann Gurganay (Gurganey, Gurgana) bequeathed to Thomas Harris 400 acres called Longfield or Curles (**42**), in the corporation of Henrico and east of Henricus Island (**63**). Harris's patent indicates that Ann's late husband, Edward Gurganay, had acquired the acreage on October 1, 1617, by means of a court order, and the land had descended to her. The relationship between Ann and Thomas is uncertain. Sometime prior to January 9, 1624, Thomas Harris loaned some corn to Captain Nathaniel West of nearby Westover (**54**). On February 16, 1624, Thomas Harris and his wife, Adria, were residents of Bermuda Hundred, the community for which he served as a burgess. On January 24, 1625, when a muster was made of Bermuda Hundred's inhabitants, Thomas, wife Adria, Ann Woodlace (the couple's kinswoman), and a young female servant were sharing a home. Thomas was then age 38. On January 9, 1625, Thomas Harris was listed among those to whom the late George Thorpe of Berkeley Hundred (**55**) was in debt. A year later, Thomas was summoned to court to testify on behalf of Henry Williams. Thomas Harris reputedly was a womanizer. One of his neighbors, Joan Vincent, a known gossip, claimed that he had had sex with at least seven women in the community, sometimes forcibly. On the other hand, Joan's husband, William Vincent, was then suing Thomas in an attempt to recover a debt and perhaps was eager to see him discredited. Despite Thomas Harris's somewhat blemished reputation, he was made a commissioner of the area's monthly court, and in September 1626 he testified before the General Court, speaking against a woman accused of witchcraft. By January 1627, Harris, too, had run afoul of the law, for he allegedly had encroached on Richard Taylor's land in Bermuda Hundred. As Taylor and Harris were known to have made an agreement on January 11, 1622, Harris was awarded 5 acres in payment for having cleared part of Taylor's land. On January 9, 1627, Harris testified about a cow that was in the possession of his neighbor, Luke Boyse, and six months later, he was made second in command of an expedition against the Indians. On November 11, 1635, he received a patent for 750 acres in Henrico at Digges Hundred (**43**), land abutting that of his current wife, Joan (Joane), and the land he had inherited from Ann Gurganay. He acquired 100 acres of the tract on the basis of being an ancient planter and the remainder on account of headrights. In 1638 when he repatented his landholdings, expanding them to 820 acres, he claimed that his first wife, Adria, was an ancient planter. In January 1639 Captain Thomas Harris served as a burgess for Henrico. He died around 1649 (HEN 1:128-129; STAN 53, 61; MCGC 11, 36, 47, 86, 96-97, 106, 111-112, 129, 151; CBE 35, 54; PB 1 Pt. 1:304, 438; Pt. 2:615; MEY 356; DOR 1:9; 2:264-265).

ADRIA (ADRY) HARRIS (MRS. THOMAS HARRIS)

Adria (Adry), the first wife of ancient planter Thomas Harris, came to Virginia on the *Marmaduke* in November 1621. On February 16, 1624, she and her husband, a burgess, were living in Bermuda Hundred (**39**). On January 24, 1625, Adria and Thomas Harris were still residing at Bermuda Hundred, where he was a household head. She was then age 23. The Harrises shared their home with Ann Woodlace, who was 7 years old. Court testimony that dates to September 11, 1626, indicates that Thomas Harris's first wife was deceased. Adria or Adry Harris may have been the former Audry (Audrey) Hoare, who came to Virginia on the *Marmaduke* in 1621. Interestingly, in 1638, when Captain Thomas Harris repatented the acreage called Longfield that he had inherited from Ann Gurganay, he claimed some additional acreage and alleged that his first wife, Adria, was an ancient planter (CBE 35, 54; MCGC 111-112; DOR 1:9; 2:264-265; PB 1 Pt. 2:615).

JOAN (JOANE) HARRIS (MRS. THOMAS HARRIS)

Joan (Joane), who married the widowed ancient planter Thomas Harris, came into possession of some land in Henrico sometime prior to November 11, 1635 (PB 1 Pt. 1:302).

***

THOMAS HARRIS

Thomas Harris came to Virginia on the *Temperance* in 1621 at the expense of Sir George Yeardley. Later, Harris's headright was transferred to Thomas Flint who used it when patenting some land on September 20, 1628 (MCGC 166; PB 1 Pt. 1:59).

WILLIAM HARRIS

On December 31, 1619, it was decided that William Harris, who had been brought in by the marshal of Middlesex, would be sent to Virginia (CBE 14).

WILLIAM HARRIS

William Harris died at Martin's Hundred (**7**) sometime after April 1623 but before February 16, 1624 (CBE 42).

WILLIAM HARRIS

On February 16, 1624, William Harris was living in Elizabeth City (**17, 18**) (CBE 44).

WILLIAM HARRIS

William Harris came to Virginia in 1621 on the *George* at the expense of William Claiborne. On September 20, 1628, William, who was described as a Warwick River planter, received a leasehold entitling him to 100 acres below Blunt Point (**22**). Two months later, he was assigned a patent for an additional 50 acres that adjoined the same property and abutted that of Richard Tree, Anthony Burrows, and John Laydon. On July 15, 1631, William Harris was among the Virginia planters who asked the king for relief from customs duties. His hogsheads of tobacco bore the marks *WH* and *WB*. In July 1637 William Harris's goods allegedly were pilfered while aboard a ship anchored at Jamestown (**1**). William Harris may have been the same individual who on February 16, 1624, was living in Elizabeth City (**17, 18**), a corporation then encompassing Blunt Point (PB 1 Pt. 1:41, 69, 88, 94; G&M 166; HCA 13/53 f 249; EEAC 75-76).

BENJAMIN HARRISON

In 1634 Benjamin Harrison certified that he had transcribed the inventory made after George Thorpe's death at Berkeley Hundred (**55**) on March 22, 1622. On July 7, 1635, Harrison patented 200 acres in Warresqueak (**26**), land that he had purchased from John Davis, Walter Davis's heir. The Davises had been associated with Martin's Hundred (**7**), where Walter Davis was killed in the March 1622 Indian attack (S of N 43; PB 1 Pt. 1:207).

EDWARD HARRISON

Virginia Company records dating to November 13, 1620, note that Edward Harrison gave Ralph Fogg his bill of adventure for some Virginia land (VCR 1:418-419).

GEORGE HARRISON

On August 31, 1617, George Harrison, who had been condemned for stealing a horse, was reprieved from the Hertford jail and was delivered to Sir Thomas Smith of the Virginia Company so that he could be sent to the colony. On August 24, 1618, a warrant was issued for George's transportation to Virginia (SR 4525; PC 2/29; CBE 9).

***

GEORGE HARRISON

In March 6, 1621, the Virginia Company awarded Lieutenant George Harrison, a gentleman, 200 acres in the corporation of Charles City, on the lower side of the James River, across from Upper Chippokes Creek. Harrison was entitled to his land on the basis of four headrights, one of which was his own. In a May 12, 1622, letter he sent from Jamestown (**1**) to his brother, John, then in London, George said that many people had died in Virginia since the March 1622 Indian attack. He also spoke of his business dealings with the Bennetts of Warresqueak (**26**) and said that he was anticipating a good tobacco crop. He asked that certain goods be sent to him at Jamestown and indicated that one of the four servants his brother had sent him was dead. On March 17, 1624, when the ailing George Harrison prepared his will, he asked to be buried in the church yard in Jamestown and bequeathed his land and house in Archer's Hope (**6**) to his brother, John. However, he left his furniture and clothing to Rowland Loftis's wife, Elizabeth, who had taken care of him during his final illness. A letter sent to England sometime prior to April 28, 1624, reveals that George Harrison succumbed to a wound he received in a duel with merchant Richard Stephens of Jamestown. George, who received a severe cut on his knee, obtained medical treatment from surgeon Christopher Best, who also resided in the capital city, in John Pountis's household. George Harrison died shortly after being wounded, probably as a result of infection, but afterward his death was the subject of an inquest. James Carter disposed of the decedent's seven servants and settled his estate. It was determined that Rowland Loftis owed the late George Harrison some funds and that John Dennis was supposed to provide him with another servant. Court records reveal that George Harrison had borrowed a boat from James Harrison of Warresqueak, perhaps a kinsman, and had failed to return it. In May 1625, when a list of patented land was sent back to England, Lieutenant George Harrison was credited with 200 acres in Charles City (CBE 19, 27, 31, 47; VCR 3:432-433; 4:469, 555; SAIN 1:25, 29, 36, 61; MCGC 13, 30-31, 38-39, 44, 63).

JOHN HARRISON

On February 13, 1622, John Harrison of London obtained three shares of Virginia land from Sir John Wolstenholme, who had acquired them in October 1621. In September 1623 John Harrison sent some goods to his brother, Lieutenant George Harrison, who already was in the colony. In August 1624, after George's death, John utilized a power-of-attorney to dispose of his late brother's servants. On January 11, 1627, John Harrison was identified as someone who was doing business with Jamestown (1) merchant George Menefie and Thomas Bransby of Archer's Hope (6) (VCR 1:597; CBE 34, 47; MCGC 133).

***

HARMON HARRISON

Harmon Harrison, a gentleman and Virginia Company investor, came to the colony in 1608 in the 2nd Supply and therefore would have resided in Jamestown (1) (CJS 1:241; 2:190, 278).

***

JAMES HARRISON

Sometime prior to July 1619, Ensign James Harrison took Captain John Martin's shallop into the Chesapeake Bay and forcibly took corn from the Indians. Ensign Harrison was slain on March 22, 1622, when the Indians attacked Warresqueak (26), Edward Bennett's plantation. Although Mrs. Anne (Anna) Harrison reportedly was killed, she did in fact survive and by November 1624 had wed Justinian Cooper. It was then acknowledged that James Harrison and his partners, David Barry and John Costarde, were indebted to Captain Ralph Hamor (VCR 3:157, 571; PB 1 Pt. 2:874; MCGC 35).

ANNE (ANNA) OLIFFE HARRISON (MRS. JAMES HARRISON, MRS. JUSTINIAN COOPER) (SEE ANNE [ANNA] OLIFFE HARRISON COOPER [COWPER, COUPER])

On March 22, 1622, when the Indians attacked Warresqueak (26), Edward Bennett's plantation, Ensign James Harrison was

killed. Although Mrs. Anne (Anna) Harrison also was reported dead, she survived and by November 1624 had married Justinian Cooper. When Cooper patented some land, he identified his wife as the former Anna Oliffe. She was still alive in 1650 and became Justinian Cooper's executrix (VCR 3:571; MCGC 35; PB 1 Pt. 2:874; Isle of Wight Book A:101-103, 114).

***

JOHN HARRISON

On February 12, 1620, officials at Bridewell decided that John Harrison, who was being detained, would be sent to Virginia (CBE 18).

JOHN HARRISON (HARRYSON)

On July 31, 1622, John Harrison (Harryson) set out for Virginia on the *James*, accompanied by three men he was bringing to the colony (FER 400).

***

RALPH HARRISON

Ralph Harrison died in Elizabeth City (17, 18) sometime after April 1623 but before February 16, 1624 (CBE 45).

ANN HARRISON (MRS. RALPH HARRISON)

On February 16, 1624, Ann Harrison was living in Elizabeth City (17, 18). Her husband, Ralph, was deceased (CBE 44).

***

GYLES (GILES) HARROD

In 1629, when Gyles (Giles) Harrod and Thomas Stroud were brought before the General Court, they admitted that they had stolen two hens from William White. Robert Martin, a sometime resident of Hog Island (16), testified that in January, when he and Stroud were leaving John Mills's house, Stroud had admitted to stealing poultry from White. Thomas Stroud received a whipping at Jamestown's (1) gallows but Gyles Harrod was released because the court's justices felt that he had been led astray (MCGC 200).

[NO FIRST NAME] HART (HARTT)

On February 16, 1624, Captain Hart (Hartt) was residing in Mr. Cann's household in urban Jamestown (1) (CBE 38).

HENRY HART

Sometime prior to April 3, 1627, Caleb Page bequeathed his servant Henry Hart two years of his time (MCGC 147).

JOHN HART

On May 3, 1623, John Hart was identified as the master of Anthony Hinton, who was setting sail for Virginia on the *Bonny Bess.* Also aboard were 45 gentlemen, some of whom brought their wives and children. John Hart and Anthony Hinton had been outfitted by Gabriel Barber, who intended to leave some supplies at Martin's Hundred (7). On August 6, 1623, Company officials noted that John Hart and Richard Stephens were supposed to decide where a bloomery would be built at Martin's Hundred. John Hart posted a bond guaranteeing that he would have a servant sent from Ireland to John Bainham of Elizabeth City. If he failed to do so by December 25, 1626, he would forfeit the money he had posted (VCR 4:164, 262-263; MCGC 118).

MRS. THOMAS HARTEASLE (SEE MRS. LEONARD DANBY [DANSBY])

WILLIAM HARTLEY

William Hartley came to Virginia on the *Charles* and on February 16, 1624, was living in Edward Blaney's household in urban Jamestown (1). He also was listed among Blaney's servants who lived at his plantation, the Powell orphans' property (14) on the lower side of the James River. On February 4, 1625, William Hartley was identified as a 23-year-old servant who was residing on the Blaney/Powell plantation (CBE 38, 40, 59).

HENRY HARTWELL

On July 15, 1631, Henry Hartwell was among the Virginia planters who asked the king's agents to give them relief from customs duties. His initials, *HH*, were affixed to his hogsheads of tobacco. This individual may have been a forebear of attorney Henry Hartwell, who came to Virginia sometime prior to November 1671 and lived until 1699 (G&M 166).

***

JOHN HARVEY

In November 1620 Captain John Harvey, who had just spent three years in Guiana, received from William Litton three shares of Virginia Company stock that entitled him to land in the colony. In April 1623 Harvey informed Company officials that he was planning to undertake a fishing voyage in his ship, the *Southampton,* and was willing to compile information on the status of the Virginia colony, if the king so desired. He received authorization to take passengers and goods to Virginia and set sail sometime after October 24, 1623, bringing along a lengthy list of queries to which the Privy Council wanted answers. On January 12, 1624, Captain John Harvey obtained a patent for a waterfront lot in urban Jamestown (1), a large parcel that already contained some houses. Shortly after the *Southampton* reached Virginia, Harvey became embroiled in a legal dispute with the ship's master, mate, and crew. At issue was Harvey's insistence on the ship's staying in Virginia instead of going to New England, where a cargo of fish could be procured for sale in Europe. Harvey insisted that, as the *Southampton's* owner, he had a right to overrule the ship's officers and crew. They, in turn, claimed that he had signed on as a passenger, not as captain. Ultimately, the *Southampton* went to Canada for fish but Harvey stayed behind in Virginia. His personal correspondence reveals that he was closely aligned with the Virginia Company's "hard-liners," who favored a return to martial law and a military-style government. Harvey's loyalties and autocratic attitude earned him the animosity of those who preferred a more flexible style of government. However, Harvey's eagerness to assist the king and Privy Council paid off handsomely, for he was knighted and in August 1624 was named to the Council of State.

General Court records dating to January 31, 1625, reveal that John Harvey was volatile and had an explosive temper. When William Mutch, one of his indentured servants, demanded his freedom dues, Harvey threatened and insulted him, and then struck him over the head with his truncheon. Harvey left Virginia to take command of a ship that was part of a naval expedition to Cadiz. While he was away, a London merchant's representative demanded immediate payment of a ?20 bond. In January 1627 the General Court responded by awarding him use of Harvey's house and land in Jamestown, so that the property could be rented and the proceeds used to retire the debt. In March 1628 Sir John Harvey was designated Governor George Yeardley's successor. He reached Virginia in August and purchased the Jamestown estate formerly occupied by Sir Francis Wyatt. Shortly thereafter, he acquired a neighboring lot that formerly belonged to Sir George Yeardley. Governor Harvey immediately began implementing the instructions he had received from the king, which included producing marketable commodities that could be sold profitably in England. Harvey himself capitalized on the colony's shortage of goods by purchasing ironware that he could sell in Virginia and investing in the production of soap ashes and pot ashes. Harvey, as governor, was supposed to receive all Quarter (or General) Court fines as compensation for his official duties. This, in essence, made him dependent on the members of his Council, who were the General Court's justices and therefore imposed the fines that funded his office.

Governor John Harvey asked for munitions from England and updated the Privy Council on conditions in the colony. In May 1630 he also sent samples of several locally produced commodities to England as proof that he was carrying out the Privy Council's instructions. He said that people were planting marketable agricultural crops, and he indicated that he intended to see that Chiskiack (37) was planted the following spring and that he would like to build a fort at Old Point Comfort (17). Harvey told his superiors that he had placed the former deputy-governor, Dr. John Pott, under house arrest and had removed him from the Council because he had freed a convicted murderer; however, a few months later, Harvey sought Pott's pardon when his skills as a physician were needed. During the early 1630s Governor John Harvey tried diligently to strengthen Virginia's economy. He informed the Privy Council that the colony was in great need of skilled workers and that shipbuilding had gotten underway. It was while Governor Harvey was in office

that a law was passed requiring all incoming vessels to open their cargoes in Jamestown. By 1631 Governor John Harvey and his Council had begun having serious disagreements. In May 1632 he informed his superiors that he lived very poorly and had not been paid in a long time. He claimed that his home in Jamestown was serving as the colony's statehouse and that he had been Virginia's official host for three years. David Devries, who in mid-March 1633 was a houseguest of Harvey's, wrote about the governor's welcoming him "with a Venice glass of sack" and said that he and several other visitors had shared a meal at his home. At the site of Governor Harvey's Jamestown mansion, National Park Service archaeologists have found pieces of Venetian glass and fragments of plaster molding embellished with portions of Harvey's armorial crest.

In late August 1633 Governor John Harvey traded a 500-acre parcel in Archer's Hope (6) for 500 acres at Powhatan Swamp, near Powhatan's Tree, in the immediate vicinity of the Governor's Land (3). In time, the differences between Governor John Harvey and his Council became so pronounced that they ousted him from office. They were highly critical of Harvey's willingness to assist Lord Baltimore (a Catholic) in colonizing Maryland, territory many Virginians considered theirs. In 1634 one visitor said that only two of Harvey's councilors supported him and that they were relatively weak. Captain Samuel Mathews led the faction opposing Harvey, and Mathews' brother-in-law (the son of councilor Sir Thomas Hinton) aspired to replace Harvey as governor. Despite these problems, Governor Harvey persisted in his attempts to strengthen the colony. He had a palisade built across the James-York peninsula and fortified Old Point Comfort. In February 1634 he sent word to the Privy Council that a customs house was needed badly in Virginia and that the colony lacked the arms and ammunition critical to its defense. In mid-July Harvey reminded his superiors of his accomplishments, which included improving agricultural productivity to the point that Virginia had become the granary of the English colonies. He mentioned that he was having great problems with his Council members, who opposed his support of Lord Baltimore in the controversy over Kent Island, and that at times he feared for his own life. Matters came to a head on April 28, 1635, when Governor Harvey was thrust from office and Captain John West (a councilor) was made acting governor. The Council outlined the charges against Harvey and placed him under house arrest until he could be sent home. As soon as Sir John Harvey reached England, he had two of his opponents arrested and then set about strategizing his own defense. Despite the seriousness of the charges, the Privy Council reinstated Harvey as governor, thereby upholding the king's authority instead of yielding to popular pressure.

Governor John Harvey spent the next few months preparing for his return to the colony. After his formal reinstatement on April 2, 1636, he was given an old leaky vessel in which to return to Virginia. After the ship set sail, it was obliged to return to port because it was unseaworthy. Harvey finally reached Virginia on January 18, 1637, and had his new commission read in Elizabeth City. Within days of his arrival, Governor John Harvey thoroughly alienated his Council by giving Henry Lord Maltravers (the Duke of Norfolk's son and a favorite of the king) a patent for a vast expanse of land that included Nansemond and Norfolk Counties and parts of Isle of Wight County and Carolina. They did not take into account the fact that he was implementing explicit instructions he had received from the king. Harvey lost no time in taking revenge on those who had put him out of office. He had five councilors arrested and sent to England, alleging that they had usurped the king's authority when ousting him. He seized the stipendiary tobacco paid to one of his most vocal critics, the Rev. Anthony Panton of York County, and had him expelled from his pulpit and the colony. In 1638 Governor John Harvey married the widowed Elizabeth Peirsey Stephens, whose husband's teeth he had dislodged during an angry outburst at a 1635 Council meeting. Harvey and his Council convened in late January 1637, and on February 20th the assembly passed an act intended to strengthen Jamestown as the capital city. Governor John Harvey told his superiors that many colonists disliked the idea of limiting trade to Jamestown, which he considered a necessity if the capital was to be urbanized. On December 8, 1638, Sir Francis Wyatt was appointed Governor Harvey's successor, and by August 1639 Harvey had entered a period of decline. His problems were manifold, for he was physi-

cally ill, deeply in debt, and almost devoid of political power. On April 17, 1640, after Sir Francis Wyatt arrived and took over as governor, the General Court ordered Sir John Harvey to appoint an agent to dispose of his real and personal property so that his creditors could be paid. He lost his townstead in urban Jamestown, his plantation in York County, and the Glasshouse tract (2) on the mainland near Jamestown Island. However, he was allowed to keep some of his cattle and the furniture in his dwelling until he left for England. By late 1641 Sir John Harvey had returned to England and on September 15, 1646, when he made his will, he indicated that he was preparing to go to sea. He stated that people in Virginia owed him £2,000 and that he was due £5,500 in back pay as governor. Harvey left the bulk of his estate to daughters Ursula and Ann. His will was presented for probate on July 16, 1650 (SAIN 1:18, 53-54, 58, 69, 77, 88, 92, 94-95, 100, 113, 116-118, 129, 133, 138, 151, 160, 175-176, 183-184, 189-190, 193, 201, 207-208, 212, 216-217, 221, 224-225, 231-233, 236-242, 245, 250, 252, 260, 262-264, 266, 276, 281-282, 287-289, 294, 302, 310-311, 314; VCR 1:418-419; 2:74, 388, 463; 3:62; 4:87-88, 210, 294-295, 459-464, 471-472, 476-477, 501, 504, 562; CJS 3:218; CO 1/4 f 84; 1/5 ff 65-66, 71-73, 176-177, 180, 195, 203, 207, 210-212; 1/6 ff 135-136, 195; 1/8 ff 166-170, 193-194, 202; 1/9 ff 11, 15, 40, 64-77, 97, 188, 198, 202, 209; 1/10 ff 8, 14, 65-68, 160, 176, 190, 300; 1/32 f 7; 5/1354 ff 199-200, 248; 5/1359 f 383; PRO 30/ 15/2 f 400; STAN 14-15, 31; PB 1 Pt. 1:7; 3:367; MHS 9:60-73, 107-108, 111-112, 131, 150; MCGC 13-14, 46, 130-131, 176-177, 480-482, 484, 492, 495-497; CBE 71, 82-83, 87, 90-91, 95, 102-103, 106, 117-120; WITH 159, 588; SR 626, 4000; HEN 1:147, 153, 166, 178, 223; JHB 124; DEV 34-36, 74; NEI 118, 125, 133, 135, 152; PB 1 Pt. 1:308; LNC B:79, 86; YORK 1633-1646:44; AMB 78; SH 43; MCGH 206; EEAC 28).

ELIZABETH PEIRSEY STEPHENS HARVEY
(MRS. RICHARD STEPHENS, MRS. JOHN HARVEY)
(SEE ELIZABETH PEIRSEY STEPHENS)

Elizabeth, Richard Stephens' widow, married Sir John Harvey in 1638. She was the daughter of cape merchant Abraham Peirsey and had come to Virginia in 1623 on the *Southampton*, Captain John Harvey's ship. Around 1628 Elizabeth married Jamestown (**1**) merchant Richard Stephens, with whom she produced a son, Samuel. After Stephens' death in 1636, Elizabeth married Governor John Harvey, who was many years her senior and one of her late husband's enemies. The Harveys lived in urban Jamestown. In September 1642 Dutch mariner David Devries sued Lady Elizabeth Harvey to recover funds from the late Richard Stephens' estate, claiming that she had sold his goods. After Sir John Harvey fell on hard times and was replaced as governor, Elizabeth returned with him to England. She died there sometime prior to September 15, 1646, when Sir John made his will (MEY 481-482; NEI 152).

***

MARY HARVEY (HARVIE, HARVAY)

On July 15, 1631, Mary Harvey (Harvie, Harvay) was among the Virginia planters who asked the royal government for relief from customs duties. She may have been the wife of former Virginia Company tenant Thomas Harvey (G&M 166).

SAMUEL (SAMWELL) HARVEY (HARVIE)

Samuel (Samwell) Harvey (Harvie) died in Elizabeth City (**17, 18**) sometime after April 1623 but before February 16, 1624 (CBE 45).

***

THOMAS HARVEY (HARVIE, HARVAY)

Thomas Harvey (Harvie, Harvay), a Virginia Company tenant, came to Virginia sometime prior to the demise of the Company in 1624. On February 4, 1625, he was living at Captain Roger Smith's plantation (**10**) across from Jamestown Island and was a 24-year-old household head. He was adequately supplied with stored food and defensive weaponry. By October 2, 1626, Thomas had wed Mary, one of Thomas Edwards' servants, with Edwards' consent. On January 12, 1627, Thomas Harvey was identified as a Virginia Company tenant who had been assigned to Sir George Yeardley. On April 12, 1633, when Harvey

acquired a 50-acre leasehold on Swan House Creek in the vicinity of Martin's Hundred (**7**), he was identified as a tailor. He died there sometime prior to August 24, 1635, when John Dennett was appointed his administrator (CBE 59; MCGC 115, 136; PB 1 Pt. 1:142, 276; DOR 1:39).

MARY HARVEY (HARVIE, HARVAY) (MRS. THOMAS HARVEY [HARVIE, HARVAY])

Mary, who sometime prior to October 2, 1626, married Thomas Harvey (Harvie, Harvay), a Virginia Company tenant, was brought to Virginia by Thomas Edwards, who covered the cost of her transportation but permitted her to wed. Thomas Harvey was residing at Captain Roger Smith's plantation (**10**) in early 1625, and in 1627 he was assigned to Sir George Yeardley. Around 1633 Thomas Harvey patented land near Martin's Hundred (**7**). He died sometime after April 12, 1633, but before August 24, 1635 (MCGC 115; PB 1 Pt. 1:142, 276).

***

FRANCIS HARWELL

On February 13, 1622, Virginia Company officials noted that Francis Harwell, the brother and heir of Sir Edmund Harwell, had inherited his three shares of Virginia land. On June 10, 1622, Francis Harwell was identified as the holder of a patent for a particular plantation. Then, on May 14, 1623, Company officials noted that his patent had been confirmed (VCR 1:597; 2:428; 3:643).

NICHOLAS HARWOOD

On October 20, 1634, Nicholas Harwood, a cooper, received a 21-year lease for 50 acres in Accomack County, land that formerly had belonged to Roger Saunders. The acreage was on the upper side of Old Plantation Creek (**73**) (PB 1 Pt. 1:157).

PAUL (PAULE) HARWOOD

Paul (Paule) Harwood came to Virginia on the *Bona Nova* in 1622 and on February 16, 1624, was living in Elizabeth City (**18**). He was still there in early 1625 and was identified as a 20-year-old servant in Edward Waters' household. On January 30, 1626,

Harwood and several companions were brought before the General Court, where they were implicated in two men's deaths on New Year's Eve. He was among those who went aboard Edward Waters' ship, the *Grace*, which was anchored offshore. Two men in a small craft reportedly attempted to go out to the *Grace* and drowned. Witnesses were queried about whether any of the men were inebriated. Paul Harwood and his companions were fined and made to post a bond guaranteeing their good behavior (CBE 44, 66; MCGC 91-92).

***

THOMAS HARWOOD

Thomas Harwood came to Virginia sometime prior to December 31, 1619, when his land was mentioned in a Mulberry Island (21) patent issued to William Peirce, with whom he seems to have been associated. Harwood went back to England but returned to the colony in 1622 on the *Margaret and John*, which had a long, difficult crossing that included a lengthy stay in the West Indies. In April 1623 he was among the ship's passengers who complained about the vessel's voyage and the vessel's captain, the late John Langley. They also grumbled about Langley's successor, William Douglas, who refused to release the passengers' goods. On February 16, 1624, Thomas Harwood was living in the Neck O'Land (5), but by January 25, 1625, he had moved to Mulberry Island where he headed a household that included his wife, Grace, and one servant. On May 8, 1626, Thomas Harwood was awarded 100 acres of land at the mouth of Blunt Point (22) Creek, on the basis of the headright system. In November he brought suit in the General Court, in an attempt to recover the funds he had paid William Claiborne for a shallop that John Wilcox was supposed to build.

In February 1627 Thomas Harwood was identified as a resident of the Maine (3) when Thomas Bagwell unsuccessfully brought suit against him on behalf of Bagwell's wife, a former resident of the Neck O'Land. Then, on July 4, 1627, Harwood was named second in command to William Peirce, who was to lead an expedition against the Chickahominy Indians. Shortly thereafter, Thomas Harwood and William Perry presented Alexander George's will to the General Court, noting that the de-

cedent had chosen them as overseers. Later in the month Harwood was listed among those who had sent goods from London to Virginia on the *Truelove*. On January 14, 1628, he proved to the General Court's satisfaction that he needed more acreage in the Neck O'Land than he had been assigned by the Rev. Richard Buck's representatives and was given the right to select some additional property elsewhere.

On March 31, 1628, Thomas Harwood brought suit against merchant Edward Hurd, claiming that Hurd had detained some of his meal in the West Indies. Harwood, a respected member of the community, served as a juror in March 1629. Later in the year he was elected a burgess for Mulberry Island and was among those ordered to find men to seat land at Chiskiack (30-38), on the York River. In September 1632 he was identified as a Skiff's Creek gentleman when he patented two tracts of land that he had acquired from Hugh Heyward. In 1632 and 1633 Thomas Harwood represented the territory from Skiff's Creek to Saxon's Gaol, an area that encompassed Mulberry Island. In September 1632 he received a patent for 100 acres of land bordering the Mulberry Island acreage he had claimed in 1619. In 1633 Harwood informed the General Court that he would pay Thomas Sparkes's freedom dues on Edward Hurd's behalf. In July 1635 Harwood patented 1,500 acres of land at the head of Skiff's Creek, adjacent to the acreage he already owned, and he acquired 1,850 acres in James City County, on the east side of Skiff's Creek. In August 1635 he went to England to give the king letters that were critical of deposed Governor John Harvey. Harvey retaliated by having him arrested. Thomas Harwood returned to Virginia and in June 1636 conveyed his plantation, Queen Hive or Hith, to Edward Hurd, to whom he had mortgaged it. Later, Harwood became a tobacco viewer for Mulberry Island Parish and the Skiff's Creek area. In April 1652 he was named to the Council of State but by November was dead, at which time his son, Humphrey, became his heir. Captain Thomas Harwood was survived by his widow, Anne (PB 1 Pt. 1:110-111, 208, 271 534; Pt.2:927; 3:102; VCR 4:127-128; CBE 35, 57, 79; MCGC 103, 124, 137, 151-152, 159, 170-171, 192, 202; HEN 1:139-140, 148, 154, 179, 203, 250, 371-372; SAIN 1:214; MEY 363; SR 4540; DOR 1:48; 2:299-301; DUNN 161-163).

GRACE HARWOOD
(MRS. THOMAS HARWOOD)

Grace, who became the wife of Thomas Harwood, came to Virginia on the *George* and on January 25, 1625, was living at Mulberry Island (21) in a household headed by her husband. She may have died within a relatively short time, for he remarried, taking as his bride the woman who became the mother of his surviving children (CBE 57; DOR 2:299-301).

ANNE (ANN) HARWOOD
(MRS. THOMAS HARWOOD)

Anne (Ann), who married Thomas Harwood, was the mother of Humphrey Harwood, Thomas's only son and primary heir. In November 1652 he repatented his late father's land. An official document that dates to 1653 identifies Humphrey, Grace, and Margaret Harwood as Thomas and Anne Harwood's children (DOR 2:301; DUNN 28-29, 588).

***

WILLIAM HARWOOD

William Harwood came to Virginia on the *Francis Bonaventure* and arrived in August 1620. In June 1621 Virginia Company officials identified Harwood as the leader or "governor" of Martin's Hundred (7) when they named him to the Council of State. He probably was appointed on account of his ties to the Ferrars and Sir John Wolstenholm, influential Virginia Company officials who had invested heavily in Martin's Hundred. Harwood, as the settlement's headman, received substantial shipments of weapons, tools, clothing, and food stuffs from the Society of Martin's Hundred's sponsors. He also was provided with a rundlet of beads that could be used in trading with the Indians. In time, the arbitrary manner in which William Harwood carried out his administrative duties earned him the resentment of fellow settlers. A number of skilled workers were sent to Martin's Hundred as were others who were supposed to assist Harwood. On March 22, 1622, when the Indians attacked Martin's Hundred, a substantial number of colonists were killed. Afterward, the survivors were evacuated to Jamestown Island (1). By January 1623 the plantation had been reoccupied and a new

group of immigrants had arrived. Living conditions were harsh, and some of the settlement's inhabitants blamed William Harwood. They claimed that he was greedy and selfish and curried favor by giving the Society of Martin's Hundred's provisions to influential people. Moreover, in 1623 when the Indians returned to attack Martin's Hundred, Harwood reportedly fled into his house and locked the door, leaving those outside to fend for themselves.

On February 16, 1624, William Harwood was living at Martin's Hundred. On February 4, 1625, he was identified as a household head who had three houses and was well supplied with stored food and defensive weaponry. During 1625 Harwood made several appearances before the General Court. In January he was ordered to provide Captain Ralph Hamor with several barrels of corn and some tobacco, compensation for a debt he owed to the orphaned John Davis. In March he purchased some sawn boards from George Fryer, a resident of the Governor's Land (3). He also was asked to account for some of Sir Samuel Argall's cattle and to take custody of the late John Stephens' goods. In June 1625 William Harwood was ordered to offer accommodations at Martin's Hundred to the people sent to Virginia to establish the East India School. He provided some supplies to Captain Nuce of Elizabeth City (17, 18) and to John Uty for the use of Southampton Hundred's (44) surviving settlers. In September 1626 he was ordered to reimburse Captain John Stone for the house he had built at Martin's Hundred, and he was ordered to relinquish some of the public livestock being kept at the settlement. In January 1629 he was instructed to see that Anne Jackson, a young woman who survived captivity with the Indians, was kept safe until she could be sent to England. During 1628 and 1629 he made several other appearances before the General Court. On April 9, 1629, William Harwood was ordered to pay half of the Rev. John Lyford's salary because he had made too generous an agreement with the clergyman. In November 1635 he was summoned to England by the Privy Council and seemingly never returned to Virginia (VCR 1:382-383, 479; 3:482, 651; 4:562-567; MCGC 44, 50, 55-56, 77-78, 108, 114, 132, 136, 166, 180-181, 184, 196; FER 113, 322, 339, 391, 569, 572; CBE 42, 61; SR 4540; PC 2/45 f 236; DOR 1:14-15, 45).

WALTER HASELWOOD

Walter Haselwood came to Virginia on the *Due Return*. On February 4, 1625, he was living on Hog Island **(16)** where he was a servant in John Chew's household (CBE 61).

JOHN HASLEY

John Hasley came to Virginia on the *Abigail* and on February 16, 1624, was living in Martin's Hundred **(7)**. On February 4, 1625, he was still there and was identified as a 22-year-old servant in William Harwood's household (CBE 42, 61).

THOMAS HASTLES

In 1621 Thomas Hasteles was identified as part of the *Falcon's* crew, which was going to Jamestown **(1)** (EAE 11).

BARNERD (BARNARD, BERNARD) HATCH

Barnerd (Barnard, Bernard) Hatch, a 30-year-old carpenter from Essex, England, came to Virginia in 1619 aboard the *Bona Nova* and probably was a Virginia Company tenant or servant (FER 295).

MARGARET HATCH

On June 24, 1633, Margaret Hatch was indicted for murdering her child. A jury found her guilty of manslaughter and sentenced her to hang. She pleaded pregnancy but a jury of matrons examined her and determined that she was not pregnant (MCGC 480; HEN 1:209).

REBECCA HATCH

On February 16, 1624, Rebecca Hatch was living in Elizabeth City **(17, 18)** (CBE 44).

THOMAS HATCH

Thomas Hatch came to Virginia in 1619 on the *Duty* and became one of Sir George Yeardley's servants in Jamestown **(1)**. On June 24, 1624, witnesses reported that Hatch had been seen in the vicinity of the fort, country house, and store on the night a break-in occurred. On January 24, 1625, Thomas Hatch was described as being a 17-year-old servant in Governor George Yeardley's household. Later, he was heard to say that a man had been wrongfully executed for an alleged homosexual relationship. For criticizing a government decision, Thomas Hatch, who was identified as a *Duty* boy, was arrested, whipped, pilloried, and required to serve Yeardley an extra seven years. He also had an ear severed as part of his punishment (MCGC 15, 93; CBE 54).

HENRY HATE

On February 27, 1619, Henry Hate, a boy, was one of the youngsters brought in from the streets of London so that they could be transported to Virginia (CBE 13).

JOSEPH HATFIELD (HATTFIELD)

Joseph Hatfield (Hattfield), a 19-year-old husbandman from Leicestershire, England, came to Virginia on the *Bona Nova* in 1619 at the expense of the Ferrars, important Virginia Company investors. On February 16, 1624, he was living in Buckroe, part of the Virginia Company's land in Elizabeth City **(17)**. In early 1625 he was still there and was identified as a 24-year-old servant in William Barry's household. On January 9, 1627, Joseph Hatfield was authorized to plant some land on the Eastern Shore, in Accomack. However, on October 31, 1633, he obtained a 21-year lease for 50 acres on the east side of the Hampton River, acreage that formerly had been owned by the Virginia Company (FER 295, 296; CBE 45, 68; MCGC 130; PB 1 Pt. 1:145).

WILLIAM HATFIELD (HATFEILD)

William Hatfield (Hatfeild) came to Virginia on the *Southampton* in 1622 and on February 16, 1624, was living on West and Shirley Hundred Island **(41)**. By January 21, 1625, he had moved to Jordan's Journey **(46)**, where he was a servant in the household headed by William Farrar and Mrs. Cicely Jordan. In August 1638 William Hatfield patented three tracts of land on the Nansemond River **(20 c)** (CBE 36, 51; PB 1 Pt. 2:592).

***

JOHN HATTON (HATTONE)

John Hatton (Hattone), an ancient planter, came to Virginia in 1613 on the *Treasurer*. In early 1625 he and his wife, Olive, were living in Elizabeth City **(18)**. John, who was

26 years old, headed a household that was relatively well supplied with stored food and defensive weaponry. On February 13, 1629, he was designated one of Jamestown (1) merchant and mariner Thomas Warnett's beneficiaries. He stood to receive some of Warnett's personal effects along with some lead and powder (CBE 64; WAT 39; DOR 1:55).

OLIVE HATTON (HATTONE) (MRS. JOHN HATTON [(HATTONE])

Olive, who became the wife of ancient planter John Hatton (Hattone), came to Virginia on the *Abigail* in 1620. In early 1625 the Hattons were living in Elizabeth City (18) where John was a household head. Olive Hatton was then age 32 (CBE 64).

***

LAZARUS HAVERD (HAUERD)

On November 13, 1620, Lazarus Haverd (Hauerd), a Virginia Company employee, asked Company officials for compensation. He said that Governor George Yeardley had sent him out on a shallop to obtain fish and that he had undertaken three dangerous voyages on behalf of the colony (VCR 1:419-420).

THOMAS HAVERD (HAUERD)

Thomas Haverd (Hauerd), a 23-year-old husbandman from Brecknockshire, came to Virginia in 1619 aboard the *Bona Nova* and probably was a Virginia Company servant or tenant (FER 295).

***

HUGH HAWARD (SEE HUGH HAYWARD [HAWARD, HEYWARD) SUSAN HAWARD (MRS. HUGH HAWARD) (SEE SUSAN HAYWARD [HAWARD, HEYWARD])

***

NICHOLAS HAWES

On May 16, 1622, a 40-year-old gentleman named Nicholas Hawes, who stated that he was a resident of St. Alphage near Cripplegate, London, informed Chancery officials that Lady Cicely Delaware had Sir Samuel Argall arrested four times and that he and various others had posted Argall's bail each time. Hawes, who seemed to be speaking from firsthand knowledge, said that when Edward Brewster was in Virginia he had challenged Argall, who refused to fight, and that Brewster had vowed to seek revenge (C 24/489; SR 9947).

AUSLE HAWKINS

Ausle Hawkins, a marriageable young maid, came to Virginia on the *Warwick* in 1621. Her mother reportedly brought her to the ship. Ausle's father was described as a draper at "Shashire," perhaps a reference to Cheshire or Shropshire (FER 309).

THOMAS HAWKINS

Thomas Hawkins came to Virginia aboard the *James* and left England on July 31, 1622. On February 16, 1624, he was living on the lower side of the James River, at Hugh Crowder's plantation (12), and on February 4, 1625, was identified as one of Crowder's servants. On April 11, 1625, Thomas Hawkins testified at John Verone's inquest. By February 1, 1633, he had begun serving as burgess for the settlers in the Denbigh area, where Samuel Mathews' plantation (23) was located (FER 400; CBE 40, 60; MCGC 53; HEN 1:203).

HUGH HAWKERIDGE (HAWKRIDGE)

On December 22, 1628, the General Court ordered Henry Bagwell to pay his debt to Hugh Hawkeridge (Hawkridge). On March 1, 1629, Hugh was identified as master of the *Truelove* (MCGC 180; CBE 82).

***

MATHEW HAWTHORNE

On March 22, 1622, when the Indians attacked William Bikar's house (57), Mathew Hawthorne and his wife were slain (VCR 3:568).

MRS. MATHEW HAWTHORNE

On March 22, 1622, when the Indians attacked William Bikar's house (57), Mrs.

Mathew Hawthorne and her husband were killed (VCR 3:568).

***

THOMAS HAWAY

On February 16, 1624, Thomas Haway was living at Flowerdew Hundred (**53**) (CBE 37).

JOHN HAYCOCK

On July 29, 1626, officials at Bridewell decided that John Haycock would be sent to Virginia (CBE 72).

ELIZABETH HADEN

Elizabeth Haden, an indentured servant, came to Virginia on the *London Merchant* in 1620 at the expense of Albiano Lupo, who used her as a headright when patenting some land on September 1, 1624 (PB 1 Pt. 1:33).

ROBERT HAYE

On July 19, 1627, Robert Haye shipped goods from London to Virginia on the *James* (CBE 79).

JOHN HAYES

John Hayes, an indentured servant, came to Virginia on the *George* in 1617 at the expense of Albiano Lupo, who used him as a headright when patenting some land on September 1, 1624 (PB 1 Pt. 1:33).

JOHN HAYES

On February 20, 1626, the General Court heard testimony about a dispute between John Hayes, a merchant, and George Medcalfe. According to witnesses, Hayes brought a manservant to Medcalfe but refused to let him disembark from the ship until Medcalfe had paid for him. When George Medcalfe sent one of his servants with the payment in tobacco, John Hayes reportedly said that it had come too late. Ultimately, George Medcalfe was given his servant, John Dennis, but was ordered to pay John Hayes within a week. In September 1626 Hayes was among the men who sent goods from London to Virginia on the ship *Plantation*. He died intestate in May

1627, and Captain Francis West of Elizabeth City (**17**), with whom he seemed to have had a working agreement, was named his administrator and ordered to collect any debts against his estate (MCGC 95, 152, 186-187; CBE 74).

MATHEW HAYMAN

On December 12, 1625, the General Court learned that Philip Kyteley, who shared a house with Mathew Hayman, Zachariah Cripps, and Edmund White at the Treasurer's Plantation (**11**), was supposed to have a portion of the tobacco crop produced there. After Hayman's death, Kyteley said he wished there were more workers (MCGC 80).

HENRY HAYNES

On March 22, 1622, when the Indians attacked Weyanoke (**52**), Henry Haynes was slain. He was one of Sir George Yeardley's men (VCR 3:569).

JOAN HAYNES

Joan Haynes, a young maid, came to Virginia on the *Charles* in 1621. She was Mintrene Joyner's sister (FER 309).

WILLIAM HAYNES

On December 17, 1622, Virginia Company officials noted that William Haynes, one of the Society of Martin's Hundred's (**7**) servants, was supposed to serve for seven years (FER 309).

WILLIAM HAYNES (HEYNES) JR.

William Haynes Jr., an indentured servant, went from Bermuda to Virginia on the *Tiger* in 1621 at the expense of his master, George Sandys, who used him as a headright when patenting some land on December 4, 1624 (PB 1 Pt. 1:12).

THOMAS HAYRICK (HEYRICK)

On March 24, 1630, Thomas Hayrick (Heyrick) was serving as a burgess for the western part of Elizabeth City (**18**). In that capacity, he was ordered to inspect the site of the fort built at Old Point Comfort (HEN 1:149-150).

***

HUGH HAYWARD
(HAWARD, HEYWARD)

Hugh Hayward (Haward, Heyward) came to Virginia on the *Starr*. On November 30, 1624, he and Robert Fitt informed the General Court that they had witnessed Thomas Harralde's will. On January 30, 1625, Hugh and his wife, Susan, were living on the Governor's Land (**3**), in Pasbehay, where he was a household head. On June 29, 1631, Sergeant Hugh Hayward received a patent for 140 acres by means of a court order, and on September 1, 1632, he transferred it to Thomas Harwood (CBE 57; MCGC 33; PB 1 Pt. 1:110-111; DOR 1:25).

SUSAN HAYWARD (HAWARD, HEYWARD)
(MRS. HUGH HAYWARD [HAWARD, HEYWARD])

Susan, who became the wife of Hugh Hayward (Haward, Heyward), came to Virginia on the *George*. On January 30, 1625, she and her husband were living on the Governor's Land (**3**), in Pasbehay (CBE 57).

***

HUMPHREY HAYWARD
(HEYWARD)

Humphrey Hayward (Heyward) came to Virginia on the *John and Dorothy* in 1634 at the expense of Adam Thorogood, who used him as a headright when patenting some land on June 24, 1635 (PB 1 Pt. 1:179).

THOMAS HAYWARD

Thomas Hayward came to Virginia in 1619 on the *Bona Nova* and probably was a Virginia Company servant or tenant (FER 295).

***

JOHN HAZARD (HASSARDE)

John Hazard (Hassarde) came to Virginia in 1618 on the *William and Thomas* and was a servant associated with Southampton Hundred (**44**), a settlement hard hit by the March 22, 1622, Indian attack. In early December 1623 Hazard, who had moved to Elizabeth City (**18**), provided some corn to Nathaniel Basse of Basses Choice (**27**). On February 16, 1624, John Hazard and his wife, Joan (Joane), were residents of Elizabeth City. In November 1624 he and Dictoris Christmas, who also was one of the Society of Southampton Hundred's servants and lived in Elizabeth City (**17**), furnished corn to John Pountis, the Treasurer of Southampton Hundred. John Hazard, who was 40 years old in early 1625, was still residing in Elizabeth City and shared his home with a servant, 14-year-old Abraham Pelteare. The household Hazard headed was adequately supplied with stored food and defensive weaponry. On September 12, 1625, the Rev. Jonas Stogden acknowledged that John Hazard and Dictoris Christmas had paid their debt to John Pountis. Court testimony taken on November 28, 1625, reveals that both men, former Southampton Hundred servants, had bought their own freedom. On August 28, 1626, Sir George Yeardley presented the General Court with a petition he had received from Abraham Pelteare's mother, Margaret, who was then in England. It disclosed that although young Pelteare had not gone to Virginia as Humphrey Rastall's apprentice, Rastall had sold him to John Hazard. As Hazard had conveyed the youth's indenture to Robert Thresher, he and Thresher were ordered to pay Pelteare for his service (CBE 44, 64; MCGV 69, 70-71, 77, 109; DOR 1:54).

JOAN (JOANE) HAZARD
(HASSARDE)
(MRS. JOHN HAZARD [HASSARDE])

On February 16, 1624, Joan (Joane) Hazard (Hassarde) was living in Elizabeth City (**18**) with her husband, John, and another male (CBE 44).

***

[NO FIRST NAME] HAZELL

On January 30, 1622, Captain Hazell presented a petition to the Virginia Company on behalf of Captain John Martin, the owner of Martin's Brandon (**59**). The petition was endorsed by Sir Thomas Smith, Sir Samuel Argall, Francis West (the late Lord Delaware's brother) and Robert Rich, Earl of Warwick (VCR 1:594).

WILLIAM HEAD

On March 22, 1622, when the Indians attacked Powle-Brooke or Merchants Hope (**50**), William Head was killed (VCR 3:569).

JOHN HEADLAND

On March 12, 1627, John Headland, a mariner and master of the *Peter and John*, testified that while his ship was at Gravesend, George Sandys had brought aboard seven servants but paid for the passage of only six. Although Sandys promised to pay for the additional man on reaching Virginia, he had failed to do so (MCGC 144).

ROBERT HEASELL

Robert Heasell came to Virginia on the *Hopewell* in 1628 at the expense of Adam Thorogood, who used him as a headright when patenting some land on June 24, 1635 (PB 1 Pt. 1:179).

ROGER HEARNE

On September 2, 1631, officials at Bridewell decided that Roger Hearne, a boy who was being detained, would be sent to Virginia at the expense of a merchant willing to pay his passage (CBE 96).

RICHARD HEATH

Richard Heath, age 57, a smith from Surrey, England, came to Virginia in 1619 aboard the *Bona Nova* and probably was a Virginia Company tenant or servant (FER 295).

ROBERT HEATH

On January 26, 1620, Robert Heath and William Tracy of Gloucestershire, a Virginia Company investor, asked Company officials for a patent, because they were planning to take 500 people to Virginia to establish a plantation. Tracy was then involved in Berkeley Hundred (**55**) (VCR 1:296-297).

THOMAS HEATH

On March 23, 1608, Thomas, the 4-year-old son of Jeremy Heath, a white baker, was admitted from St. Giles Cripplegate to Christ Church Hospital. On May 2, 1629,

he was placed with Lady Altome and then in September was sent to Virginia (CH 11).

THOMAS HEBBS (HEBB)

Thomas Hebbs or Hebb was living in Nathaniel Jeffreys' household in urban Jamestown (**1**) on February 16, 1624. He died sometime prior to March 31, 1628, at which time his administrator, Mr. Sweete, filed a claim against Captain Ralph Hamor's estate (CBE 38; MCGC 170).

ROBERT HEDGES

Robert Hedges, a servant, was living in William Peirce's household in urban Jamestown (**1**) on February 16, 1624. By January 25, 1625, Hedges had been moved to Mulberry Island (**21**), where he was listed among Captain William Peirce's servants. At that time Hedges was age 40 (CBE 38, 57).

***

[NO FIRST NAME] HEDDINGTON

Thomas Heddington and his brother, whose first name is unknown, left England on July 31, 1622, and came to Virginia with Mr. Gosnult on the *James* and (FER 400).

THOMAS HEDDINGTON

Thomas Heddington and his brother came to Virginia with Mr. Gosnult on the *James* and departed from England on July 31, 1622 (FER 400).

***

ROGER HEFORD

Robert Heford came to Virginia in 1623 on the *Return*. On February 7, 1625, he was living at Basses Choice (**27**) where he was a member of Thomas Bennett's household. Heford was then age 22 (CBE 62).

THOMAS HELCOTT

On March 4, 1620, officials decided that Thomas Helcott, who had been brought in from the Bridge and was being detained at Bridewell, would be sent to Virginia. On February 16, 1624, he was living on the

Maine or Governor's Land (3). However, by early 1625 he had been moved to the Eastern Shore, where he died (CBE 19, 69).

***

JOHN HELLINE (HELIN)

On February 16, 1624, John Helline (Helin), his wife, and their son and new baby were living in the household of merchant Delpheus Cann in urban Jamestown (1). Simultaneously, the Hellines were attributed to Martin's Hundred (7) (CBE 38, 42).

MRS. JOHN HELLINE (HELIN)

On February 16, 1624, Mrs. John Helline, her husband, and their son and new baby were living in the household of merchant Delpheus Cann in urban Jamestown (1). They also were listed as being at Martin's Hundred (7) (CBE 38, 42).

[NO FIRST NAME] HELLINE (HELIN)

Mr. and Mrs. John Helline's (Helin's) son and his sibling (an infant) were living in the household of merchant Delpheus Cann in urban Jamestown (1) on February 16, 1624. They also were listed as being at Martin's Hundred (7) (CBE 38, 42).

[NO FIRST NAME] HELLINE (HELIN)

Mr. and Mrs. John Helline's (Helin's) infant and his/her brother were living in the household of merchant Delpheus Cann in urban Jamestown (1) on February 16, 1624. They also were attributed to Martin's Hundred (7) (CBE 38, 42).

***

ROBERT HELLUE

Robert Hellue died on the lower side of the James River, within the corporation of James City (8-15), sometime after April 1623 but before February 16, 1624 (CBE 41).

GEORGE HELY (HEELE)

George Hely (Heele) was brought to Virginia by John Parrott, who used him as a

headright when patenting some land on May 29, 1635 (PB 1 Pt. 1:170).

JOHN HELY

John Hely came to Virginia on the *Charles* in November 1621 and on February 16, 1624, was living at Jordan's Journey (46). He was still there on January 21, 1625, at which time he was identified as a 24-year-old servant in the household jointly headed by William Farrar and Mrs. Cicely Jordan (CBE 36, 51).

***

ROBERT HELY (HEELEY, HEYLEY, HELEY)

When the Rev. Willis Hely (Heeley, Heyley, Heley), the rector of Mulberry Island Parish, obtained a patent for 250 acres in the vicinity of Mulberry Island (21) on December 8, 1635, he used the headright of his brother, Robert (PB 1 Pt. 1:271, 325).

WILLIS HELY (HEELEY, HEYLEY, HELEY)

On August 17, 1635, the Rev. Willis Hely (Heeley, Heyley, Heley), the rector of Mulberry Island Parish, obtained a patent for 250 acres in the vicinity of Mulberry Island (21). He received his patent by means of a court order, in recognition for his service as a minister. On December 8, 1635, Mr. Hely acquired a patent for 250 acres of adjacent land on the basis of five headrights, which included wife Eleanor and his brother, Robert (PB 1 Pt. 1:271, 325).

ELEANOR (ELIANOR) HELY (HEELEY, HEYLEY, HELEY) (MRS. WILLIS HELY [HEELEY, HEYLEY, HELEY])

On December 8, 1635, when the Rev. Willis Hely (Heeley, Heyley, Heley) patented some land in Mulberry Island Parish, he used the headright of his wife, Eleanor (Elianor) (PB 1 Pt. 1:325).

***

WALTER HELY (HEELEY, HEYLEY, HELEY)

On September 20, 1628, Walter Hely (Heeley, Heyley, Heley), an ancient planter, acquired a

50-acre leasehold in Elizabeth City (**17**) on the lower side of the Hampton River. Walter's land was mentioned in a November 30, 1628, patent for some neighboring land, and one that was issued to another individual on June 6, 1632 (PB 1 Pt. 1:91, 93, 101).

JOHN HEMPDEN

On December 24, 1624, the Bridewell Court decided that John Hempden, who was being detained, would be sent to Virginia (CBE 14).

CHRISTOPHER HENLEY

On March 22, 1622, when the Indians attacked the settlement at the College (**66**), Christopher Henley was slain (VCR 3:566).

WILLIAM HENING

William Hening died sometime prior to January 3, 1625. According to George Fryer, Hening, when on his deathbed, bequeathed a quantity of corn and tobacco to Stephen Webb, crops that he was due to receive from Thomas Farley in fulfillment of a debt. Fryer and Webb were then residents of the Governor's Land (**3**), whereas Farley lived in Archer's Hope (**6**) (MCGC 40).

HENRY HENNETT

In mid-May 1625 mariner Henry Hennett and several others were at Captain William Tucker's house in Elizabeth City (**18**) when Tucker offered to pay merchant Walter Williams for the labor of Mr. William Lucas on the homeward voyage of Captain Michael Marshatt's ship, the *Supply*. On March 5, 1629, Robert Poole verified that he had been present at the time the offer was made. Court testimony suggests that Lucas was a gentleman but also an indentured servant (MCGC 190).

HENRY

On February 16, 1624, a male known as Henry was living in Elizabeth City (**18**). He probably was associated with the household of John Hazard and his wife, with whom he appears to have been listed (CBE 44).

HENRY

On March 22, 1622, when the Indians attacked Martin's Hundred (**7**), a Welchman named Henry was killed (VCR 3:570).

JOHN HENRY (HEMY)

On December 12, 1627, John Henry (Hemy), a planter, obtained a lease for 150 acres at Buckroe in Elizabeth City (**17**). Two days earlier his land was mentioned in an adjacent parcel that was being patented (PB 1 Pt. 1:83-84).

JOHN HERD

John Herd came to Virginia in 1607 and was one of the first Jamestown (**1**) colonists (CJS 1:209).

PETER HEREFORD

On February 16, 1624, Peter Hereford was living in Elizabeth City (**17, 18**) (CBE 43).

OBLE HERO

Oble Hero came to Virginia on the *Abigail* in 1622 and was one of the Frenchmen from Languedoc sent to Virginia to cultivate mulberry trees and vines. In early 1625 Oble was living on the Virginia Company's land in Elizabeth City (**17**) with Verbitt Hero, probably a kinsman. Both men resided in a household headed by Anthony Bonall, who also was French and was the master of the king's silkworms (CBE 68; VCR 1:459).

VERBITT HERO

Verbitt Hero, a Frenchman from Languedoc, came to Virginia on the *Abigail* in 1622 and was one of the Frenchmen sent to Virginia on account of their expertise in growing mulberry trees and vines. In early 1625 Verbitt was living on the Virginia Company's land in Elizabeth City (**17**) with Oble Hero, probably a kinsman. Both men resided in a household headed by Anthony Bonall, master of the king's silkworms and also a Frenchman (CBE 68; VCR 1:459).

NICHOLAS HEROGHE

Nicholas Heroghe came to Virginia on the *James,* which left England on July 31, 1622. He accompanied Anthony Banham (FER 400).

ALICE HESKINS

On January 29, 1621, Virginia Company officials learned that Alice Heskins had arrived at Berkeley Hundred (**55**) (VCR 3:426).

ROBERT HESKINS (HELSYNS)

In 1619 officials at Newgate Prison decided that Robert Heskins (Helsyns) of London, who had been found guilty of stealing a mare, would be transported overseas (CBE 12).

***

THOMAS HETHERSALL (HETERSALL, HOTHERSALL, HITHERSALL)

On January 26, 1621, Thomas Hethersall (Hetersall, Hothersall, Hithersall), a gentleman living in Pasbehay (3), received a patent for 200 acres of land at Blunt Point (22). He acquired his acreage on the basis of four headrights: his own, wife Francis (Frances), daughter Mary, and son Richard. The Hethersalls may have stayed in Pasbehay a year or so after acquiring land of their own, for during an altercation that involved several people who lived there, Thomas's dog bit someone. In early February 1623, when the incident was first aired before the General Court, Thomas Hethersall was summoned. Because he failed to appear, he was apprehended and made to lay "neck and heels" all night. By February 16, 1624, Thomas Hethersall had moved to Elizabeth City (18). Sometime prior to December 13, 1624, he and William Cooke of Elizabeth City borrowed a boat from Richard Tree, a Jamestown Island (1) carpenter, so that they could carry their goods to Blunt Point. The vessel reportedly was lost near Martin's Hundred (7) due to the two men's carelessness. When a list of patented land was sent back to England in May 1625, Thomas Hethersall was credited with 200 acres at Blunt Point (PB 1 Pt. 1:1; MCGC 3, 35–36; CBE 44; VCR 4:557).

FRANCIS (FRANCES) HETHERSALL (HETERSALL, HOTHERSALL, HITHERSALL) (MRS. THOMAS HETHERSALL [HETERSALL, HOTHERSALL, HITHERSALL])

On January 26, 1621, when Thomas Hethersall (Hetersall, Hothersall, Hithersall) of Pasbehay (3), a gentleman, patented some land at Blunt Point (22), he used his wife, Francis (Frances), as a headright (PB 1 Pt. 1:1).

MARY HETHERSALL (HETERSALL, HOTHERSALL, HITHERSALL)

Thomas Hethersall (Hetersall, Hothersall, Hithersall) of Pasbehay (3), a gentleman, patented some land at Blunt Point (22) on January 26, 1621, and used his daughter, Mary, as a headright (PB 1 Pt. 1:1).

RICHARD HETHERSALL (HETERSALL, HOTHERSALL, HITHERSALL)

On January 26, 1621, when Thomas Hethersall (Hetersall, Hothersall, Hithersall) of Pasbehay (3), a gentleman, patented some land at Blunt Point (22), he used his son, Richard, as a headright (PB 1 Pt. 1:1).

***

HUMPHREY HEWES (HUGHS, HUGHES)

On February 26, 1620, it was decided that Humphrey Hewes (Hughs, Hughes), who was being detained at Newgate, would be sent to Virginia (CBE 19).

JOHN HEWES (HUGHS)

John Hewes (Hughs) came to Virginia on the *Neptune* in 1618 at the expense of Captain Samuel Mathews, who transferred Hewes's headright to Gilbert Peppett. Peppett used the headright when patenting some land on August 18, 1627 (PB 1 Pt. 1:50).

THOMAS HEWES (HUGHS, HUGHES)

Thomas Hewes (Hughs, Hughes) came to Virginia in 1623 on the *John and Francis*. On February 16, 1624, he was living in Elizabeth City (18) with his partner, Captain Thomas Davis, who came to the colony on the same ship. In early 1625 Thomas Hewes, who was then 40 years old, was still living in Elizabeth City. He and his partner shared a dwelling and were adequately supplied with stored food and had an abundance of defensive weaponry (CBE 44, 66; DOR 1:60).

RICHARD HEWES (HUGHES)

On January 12, 1627, Henry Bysant, boatswain of the *Marmaduke*, testified that before the ship left Cowes, in England, the ship's surgeon, Richard Hewes (Hughes), guaranteed that if a certain young male servant belonging to colonist William Capps went ashore, he would return to the ship. Bysant stated that the youth later made many trips ashore and always returned. Eventually, however, the boy fled and Patrick Kennedy, the ship's captain, was ordered to compensate Capps's representative, Edward Waters (MCGC 134).

HENRY HEWET (HUETT)

Sometime prior to December 13, 1624, Henry Hewet (Huett), who was then in Canada, advised Corbin, a merchant, not to sell a shipment of fish to Luke Aden, whose tobacco was of poor quality. On August 31, 1625, William Constable, who was in the Netherlands, asked Virginia Company officials to give Henry Hewet a commission to take some people to Virginia and to send a letter to the governor, asking him to treat them hospitably. Constable apparently was unaware that the Virginia Company's charter had been revoked (MCGC 36, 90).

SIR THOMAS HEWETT (HEWET)

In February 1624 the will of Sir Thomas Hewett (Hewet) was presented for probate. The decedent, a Virginia Company member and investor in Virginia, Ireland, and Bermuda, was from St. Martin's in the Fields, in Middlesex, and Old Jewry in London. Probate privileges were granted to Sir William Hewett, the decedent's brother (CBE 35; EEAC 29; WITH 75-76).

RICHARD HEWTYE

On October 14, 1623, Richard Hewtye testified against William Wye of the *Garland* on behalf of Nicholas Young (VCR 3:692-695).

EDWARD HEYDON

On March 22, 1622, when the Indians attacked Captain Roger Smith's plantation in the vicinity of Bermuda Hundred (39), Edward Heydon was slain (VCR 3:566).

HUGH HEYWARD
(SEE HUGH HAYWARD)

NATHANIAL HIATT
(HYATT, HUATT)

When a list of patented land was sent back to England in May 1625, Nathanial Hiatt (Hyatt, Huatt) was credited with 200 acres near Mulberry Island (21) (VCR 4:556).

[NO FIRST NAME] HICHCOCK (HICKCOCKE, HITCHCOCKE, HITCHCOK)

Captain Hichcock (Hickcocke, Hitchcocke, Hitchcok) died in Elizabeth City (17, 18) sometime after April 1623 but before February 16, 1624 (CBE 45).

KILIBETT (KELINET) HICHCOCK (HITCHCOCKE, HITCHCOK)

On February 16, 1624, when a census was taken of the colony's inhabitants, Kilibett (Kelinet) Hichcock (Hitchcocke, Hitchcok) was listed among those living in urban Jamestown (1) in Sir George Yeardley's household. On November 21, 1625, Hichcock was identified as a gentleman when he testified about witnessing an agreement between Thomas Farley and Mrs. Susan Bush, the orphaned Sara Spence's guardian, over rental of the Spence property in Archer's Hope (6). On January 13, 1627, Kilibett Hichcock was described as one of Lady Temperance Yeardley's employees when he negotiated a rental agreement with John Upton, who wanted to lease some Yeardley land in the eastern end of Jamestown Island at Black Point (CBE 38:173; MCGC 76, 137).

***

THOMAS HICHCOCK (HITCHCOCKE, HITCHCOK)

Thomas Hichcock (Hitchcocke, Hitchcok) came to Virginia on the *Marigold* and on February 16, 1624, was living on the Maine or Governor's Land (3), just west of Jamestown Island. By February 4, 1625, he had moved to Hog Island (16), where he shared a home with his wife, Alice. On May 5, 1626, Martin Turner and Nicholas Comins stated that they had been present when Thomas Hichcock gave a substantial quantity of tobacco to Thomas Swifte, Treasurer George Sandys' agent, in payment for his freedom. On August 28, 1626, Thomas Hichcock testified before the General Court in the case against Henry Woodward, an accused thief. He said that Woodward was known to Jamestown Island's inhabitants as a "pilfering fellow" and that he had discovered him at his own house one dark, rainy night. Henry Woodward explained his presence by claiming that he was looking for his dog. Other Hog Island residents spoke against the alleged burglar (CBE 38, 61; MCGC 101-102, 110; DOR 1:44).

ALICE HICHCOCK (HITCHCOCKE, HITCHCOK)
(MRS. THOMAS HICHCOCK [HITCHCOCKE, HITCHCOK])

On February 4, 1625, Alice, the wife of Thomas Hichcock (Hitchcocke, Hitchcok) was living on Hog Island **(16)** in a household her husband headed (CBE 61).

***

THOMAS HICHCOCK (HITCHCOCKE, HITCHCOK)

On February 16, 1624, Thomas Hichcock (Hitchcocke, Hitchcok) was living on the Eastern Shore **(72-78)** (CBE 46).

WILLIAM HICHCOCK (HITCHCOCKE, HITCHCOK)

William Hichcock (Hitchcocke, Hitchcok) died at Hog Island **(16)** sometime after April 1623 but before February 16, 1624. He was described as having been "lost" (CBE 41).

THOMAS HICKENS

On January 22, 1619, officials at Bridewell decided that Thomas Hickens, a boy, would be detained so that he could be sent to Virginia (HUME 19).

***

JAMES HICKMORE (HICKMOTE, HICKMOATE, HICMOTT, HICKMOTT)

On August 4, 1623, James Hickmore (Hickmote, Hickmoate, Hicmott, Hickmott), who came to Virginia on the *Bonaventure*, served on a jury, an indication that he was a free man. On February 16, 1624, Hickmore was residing in John Pountis's household in urban Jamestown **(1)**. On September 27, 1624, he was fined for being drunk and disorderly, an infraction of moral law, but on December 21, 1624, he participated in an official inquiry into a Jamestown youngster's drowning death. By January 24, 1625, James Hickmore had become head of a household he shared with his wife in urban Jamestown. The couple had a modest supply of stored food and some livestock. On March 12, 1625, Hickmore participated in an inquest held to determine whether John Verone's death was attributable to suicide. He returned to court on February 4, 1626, to give testimony about controversial statements Peter Martin and Thomas Hatch had made at Edward Fisher's house in the Governor's Land **(3)**. By August 21, 1626, James Hickmore had become the churchwarden of James City Parish. In that capacity, he reported a man for failing to attend church (CBE 38, 55; MCGC 4-5, 20, 38, 53, 93, 107-108; DOR 1:31).

MRS. JAMES HICKMORE (HICKMOTE, HICKMOATE, HICMOTT, HICKMOTT)

On February 16, 1624, Mrs. James Hickmote was living in urban Jamestown **(1)**. She was still there on January 24, 1625, and resided in a household headed by her husband (CBE 38, 55).

***

ELIZABETH HIGGINS

On February 16, 1624, Elizabeth Higgins was living in Elizabeth City **(18)** (CBE 43).

JOHN HIGGINS

John Higgins came to Virginia on the *George* in 1616. On January 22, 1625, he was living at West and Shirley Hundred **(41)** in a household with his partners, Christopher Woodward and Rice Howe, and two male servants. John Higgins was then age 21 (CBE 52).

JOHN HIGGLET

On March 22, 1622, when the Indians attacked Lieutenant John Gibbs's plantation at Westover **(54)**, John Higglet was slain (VCR 3:567).

EROL HIGHHAM (HIGHAM)

On March 4, 1620, it was decided that Erol Highham (Higham), a boy brought in from

Newgate, would be detained so that he could be sent to Virginia (HUME 30).

HENRY HIGISON

In 1619 Henry Higison, a 22-year-old husbandman from Cheshire, England, was sent to Virginia on the *Bona Nova* and probably was a Virginia Company tenant or servant (FER 295).

[NO FIRST NAME] HILL

On July 15, 1631, Mrs. Hill, whose given name is unknown, was identified as one of the Virginia planters who asked for relief from customs when sending tobacco to England (G&M 166).

***

EDWARD HILL

Edward Hill came to Virginia sometime prior to July 16, 1622. He was then living in Elizabeth City (**18**) in a house on the west side of the Hampton River, within an area under the command of Captain William Tucker. On April 14, 1623, Edward sent word to his brother, John Hill, a London mercer in Lumbar Street, that 400 people were killed in the March 22, 1622, Indian attack and that 20 people had been slain since then. He said that he intended to return to England after he recovered his losses. Edward Hill indicated that he had lost many cattle at his plantation in Elizabeth City, and he complained about the high prices being charged for food and equipment, adding that he expected his household to perish from famine. On February 16, 1624, Edward Hill was still living in Elizabeth City and was sharing his home with his wife, Hanna (Hannah), and daughter Elizabeth. A patent issued to a neighbor in September 1624 mentioned Edward's land, whereas a December 1, 1624, patent for a neighboring property noted that he was deceased. Edward Hill of Elizabeth City was buried on May 15, 1624. By early 1625 his widow had married the Hills's neighbor, Thomas Spellman (Spillman, Spelman, Spilman), who on January 10, 1627, served as the decedent's administrator. When a list of patented land was sent back to England in May 1625, the late Edward Hill was credited with 100 acres in Elizabeth City, acreage that had been planted (CBE 44; VCR 3:664; 4:234, 558; PB 1 Pt. 1:35, 37; MCGC 130).

HANNA (HANNAH) BOYLE HILL (MRS. EDWARD HILL, MRS. THOMAS SPELLMAN [SPILLMAN, SPELMAN, SPILMAN], MRS. ALEXANDER MOUNTNEY) (SEE MRS. THOMAS SPELLMAN [SPILLMAN, SPELMAN, SPILMAN], MRS. ALEXANDER MOUNTNEY)

Hanna (Hannah) Boyle, who married Edward Hill, came to Virginia on the *Bona Nova* in 1620 and on February 16, 1624, was living in Elizabeth City (**18**) in a house on the west side of the Hampton River. The household then included Hanna and Edward, and Elizabeth Hill, a child. Edward died later in the year and was buried on May 15, 1624. By early 1625 Hanna had married her neighbor, Thomas Spellman (Spillman, Spelman, Spilman). The couple shared their home with Virginia-born Elizabeth Hill, who may have been Hanna's daughter. In early 1625 Hanna Hill Spellman was 23 years old. On January 10, 1627, Thomas Spellman represented his stepdaughter, Elizabeth, when settling her late father's estate. Thomas Spellman went to England shortly thereafter and by March 1627 was dead. When he made a nuncupative will, he named his widow, Hanna, as heir to his real and personal property in Virginia and left to their daughter, Mary (Marie), his property in England. After being widowed a second time, Hanna Hill Spellman married Alexander Mountney. She was widowed again by February 1644 (CBE 44, 65; 130; DOR 1:357-358; SR 3115, 3118; AMES 2:326).

ELIZABETH HILL

On February 16, 1624, Elizabeth Hill was living in Elizabeth City (**18**) in a house on the west side of the Hampton River. She shared a home with her father, Edward Hill, and Hanna Hill, who probably was her mother. Elizabeth's father died prior to May 15, 1624, and Hanna married the family's neighbor, Thomas Spellman. In early 1625 Elizabeth, who was identified as Virginia-born, was living in the household Spellman headed. On January 10, 1627, Spellman, who was appointed administrator of Edward Hill's estate, represented Elizabeth Hill, her father's heir, in settling Edward's estate (CBE 44, 65; MCGC 130).

***

ELIAS (ELIS) HILL

According to Captain John Smith, Elias (Elis) Hill and Henry Spellman were in the Potomac River at Chicacoan, in a small bark, when they learned of the March 22, 1622, Indian attack. Smith said that the two men heard about the killings from an Indian, who blamed the paramount chief Opechancanough. He also said that Spellman left Elias Hill with the King of the Patawomek (an adversary of Opechancanough) while the rest of the men returned to Elizabeth City (**17, 18**) (CJS 2:304-305).

FRANCIS (FRANCES) HILL

Francis (Frances) Hill came to Virginia in 1619 on the *Bona Nova* and on February 16, 1624, was living in Elizabeth City (**17**) on the Virginia Company's land. He was still there in early 1625 and was described as a 22-year-old servant in Sergeant William Barry's household. On January 12, 1627, when the defunct Virginia Company's tenants and servants were distributed among the colony's high-ranking officials, Francis Hill was assigned to Governor George Yeardley. He was described as a Company tenant (CBE 44, 65; MCGC 136).

GEORGE HILL

George Hill, a gentleman, came to Virginia in 1608 as part of the 1st Supply of new settlers. Therefore, he would have resided in Jamestown (**1**) (CJS 1:222; 2:161).

HENRY HILL

On January 14, 1630, Henry Hill reportedly witnessed Lyonell Roulston's transfer of 50 acres in Elizabeth City (**17**) at Strawberry Banks to his friend John Neal (PB 1 Pt. 1:134).

HENRY HILL

Henry Hill came to Virginia on the *John and Dorothy* at the expense of Adam Thorogood, who used him as a headright when patenting some land on June 24, 1635 (PB 1 Pt. 1:179).

***

ISMAEL HILL

Ismael Hill, a Virginia Company tenant, came to the colony sometime prior to February 16, 1624, when he was living on the Eastern Shore, probably on the Company's land (**76**). By late July 1626 he married a woman named Barbara (Barbary), to whom John Parsons of the Treasurer's Plantation (**11**) (but formerly of the Eastern Shore) had bequeathed some of his goods. On August 8, 1626, Ismael Hill testified that he had been present when Martin Turner, a resident of the Treasurer's Plantation, made his nuncupative will. On January 12, 1627, Ismael was identified as a tenant of the defunct Virginia Company when he was assigned to Abraham Peirsey, a member of the Council of State (CBE 46; MCGC 123, 107, 137).

BARBARA (BARBARY) HILL (MRS. ISMAEL HILL)

In late July 1626, when John Parsons of the Treasurer's Plantation (**11**) made his nuncupative will, he bequeathed his bedding and a barrel of corn to Barbara (Barbary), the wife of Ismael Hill. Parsons and Ismael Hill, who were Virginia Company tenants, had been living on the Eastern Shore (**76**) in mid-February 1624 but afterward moved to the Treasurer's Plantation. Barbara may have been there too. On November 13, 1626, John Parsons' bequest to Barbara Hill was mentioned when his estate was being settled (MCGC 123; CBE 46).

***

REBECCA HILL (SEE REBECCA [REBECKA] HILL ROSE [ROSSE])

JANE HILL

Jane Hill came to Virginia on the *Marigold* in May 1619 and on January 22, 1625, was living in West and Shirley Hundred (**41**) in the household headed by her widowed mother, Mrs. Rebecca Rose. Jane was then 14 years old. Also living in the Rose household was 11-year-old Marmaduke Hill, who was Jane's brother. On February 19, 1627, the justices of the General Court issued a warrant for the arrest of Jane Hill and John Ewen, who were to be brought to Jamestown (**1**) and interrogated about their "lewd behavior" at West and Shirley Hundred. When the couple was interviewed on March 5, 1627, they admitted that they had begun having consensual sex in August 1626, shortly after John arrived at Shirley, and said that they had agreed to marry. Jane, however, told the General Court's justices that she had changed her mind, for she no longer loved John. Because John Ewen and Jane Hill were found guilty of fornication, a crime and offense against moral law, John was sentenced to a whipping at Jamestown and at Shirley Hundred. Jane, on the other hand, was subjected to public shaming. She was ordered to stand before the congregation at Jamestown's church wearing a white sheet, and to also do so at Sunday services at Shirley Hundred (CBE 52; MCGC 139, 142).

MARMADUKE HILL

Marmaduke Hill came to Virginia on the *Marigold* in May 1619. On January 22, 1625, he was living in West and Shirley Hundred (**41**) in the household headed by his mother, the widowed Mrs. Rebecca Rose. He was then age 11. Also living in the Rose household was 14-year-old Jane Hill, Marmaduke's sister (CBE 52).

***

JOHN HILL

On April 2, 1610, John Hill, the 4-year-old son of Otewell Hill, a cordwainer, was transferred from St. Bride's to Christ Church Hospital. On August 18, 1617, John, who was described as Otewell's "half-son," was apprenticed to the Virginia Company at a time when Company officials were trying to find children to send to the colony (CH 11).

JOHN HILL

John Hill came to Virginia on the *Bona Nova* in 1620 and on February 16, 1624, was living in Elizabeth City (**18**). In early 1625 he was still there and was identified as a 26-year-old servant in a household headed by John Banum and Robert Sweet. In 1628 John Hill and Robert Brittaine (another resident of Elizabeth City) were named administrators of Nicholas Thredder's estate. On April 21, 1635, John Hill patented 350 acres on the lower side of the James River, on the Elizabeth River in Elizabeth City (**20 a**) (CBE 44, 64; MCGC 174; PB 1 Pt. 1:166).

JOHN HILL

John Hill came to Virginia on the *John and Dorothy* in 1634 at the expense of Adam Thorogood, who used him as a headright when patenting some land on June 24, 1635 (PB 1 Pt. 1:179).

***

MARY HILL I

Mary Hill I, the mother of Mary Hill II, came to Virginia on the *John and Dorothy* in 1634 at the expense of Adam Thorogood, who used her as a headright when patenting some land on June 24, 1635. Thorogood's patent refers to the older Mary as "the elder" (PB 1 Pt. 1:179).

MARY HILL II

Mary Hill II, the daughter of Mary Hill I, came to Virginia on the *John and Dorothy* in 1634 at the expense of Adam Thorogood, who used her as a headright when patenting some land on June 24, 1635 (PB 1 Pt. 1:179).

***

***

THOMAS HILL

On February 16, 1624, Thomas Hill was living in Elizabeth City (**18**). On July 5, 1627, he paid wages to the men of the *Unity*, a vessel in which he had a legal interest. On November 17, 1629, he witnessed Captain Francis West's will while he was in England. Sometime prior to May 1633, Hill, who was living in Stanley Hundred (**22**), married Mary, the daughter of cape merchant Abraham Peirsey (Persey, Perseye, Pearsey). Thomas Hill was one of Governor John Harvey's supporters, and when Samuel Mathews was arrested in May 1637, Secretary Richard Kemp gave Mathews' goods to Hill. This prompted Mathews to seek redress in England, and Hill was ordered to return Mathews' belongings. On August 1, 1638, Thomas Hill secured a patent for a 3/10-acre lot in urban Jamestown (**1**), next door to the lot and brick house owned by Richard Kemp. In January 1641 he served a term as a James City burgess, probably representing Jamestown. In April 1643 Thomas Hill acquired a 600-acre subunit of Richard Kemp's 4,332-acre Rich Neck tract near Middle

Plantation (later, the site of Williamsburg). In April 1648 Hill, who was described as a gentleman and planter, assigned his 3,000-acre Upper Chippokes tract (on the lower side of the James River) to Edward Bland (CBE 44; C 24/531 Pt. 2:17; CO 1/9 f 289; 1/10 ff 73-74; PC 2/50 ff 428, 543; SR 9957; WITH 51; PB 1 Pt.2:587-588, 877; 2:46, 141; SAIN 1:281; STAN 61; DOR 2:805).

MARY PEIRSEY ((PERSEY, PERSEYE, PEARSEY) HILL (MRS. THOMAS HILL, MRS. THOMAS BUSHROD) (SEE MARY PEIRSEY [PERSEY, PERSEYE, PEARSEY])

Mary, the daughter of cape merchant Abraham Peirsey (Persey, Perseye, Pearsey) and his wife, Elizabeth, married Captain Thomas Hill of Stanley Hundred (**22**) prior to May 1633. She was widowed and in 1657 married Thomas Bushrod of York County (DOR 2:805).

***

WALTER HILL

On February 27, 1619, Walter Hill, a boy, was among the youngsters brought in from the streets of London so that they could be transported to Virginia (CBE 12).

WILLIAM HILL

In May 1620 officials at Bridewell decided that William Hill, whom Middlesex officials convicted of stealing a bull, would be sent to Virginia. On February 16, 1624, a William Hill (perhaps the same man) was living in Elizabeth City (**18**) (CBE 20, 44).

[NO FIRST NAME] HILLIARD (HELLYARD)

In 1608 a boy named Hilliard (Hellyard) came to Virginia in the 2nd Supply of new settlers to arrive in Jamestown (**1**) (CJS 1:242; 2:191).

GREGORY HILLIARD

Gregory Hilliard died in Elizabeth City (**17, 18**) sometime after April 1623 but before February 16, 1624 (CBE 45).

JOHN HILLIARD

John Hilliard died in Elizabeth City (**17, 18**) sometime after April 1623 but before February 16, 1624. When a list of patented land was sent back to England in May 1625, he was credited with 100 acres of land on the south side of the James River below the falls (**67**) (CBE 45; VCR 4:552).

HUGH HILTON

Hugh Hilton came to Virginia on the *Edwine* in May 1619 and on February 16, 1624, was living at Bermuda Hundred (**39**). He was still there on January 24, 1625, and was a 36-year-old household head, living alone. He had an ample supply of stored food, some defensive weaponry, and some poultry. Hugh Hilton died sometime prior to July 21, 1627, at which time John Passman presented his will to the General Court (CBE 35, 54; MCGC 151; DOR 1:10).

AGNES HINCHLEY

On September 19, 1618, officials at Bridewell decided to send Agnes Hinchley, a vagrant from Smithfield, to Virginia (CBE 10).

WILLIAM HINES

William Hines came to Virginia in a French ship in 1629 at the expense of Adam Thorogood, who used him as a headright when patenting some land on June 24, 1635 (PB 1 Pt. 1:179).

JOHN HINSLEY

On February 9, 1628, the will of John Hinsley, a mariner, was presented to the General Court by William Webster, a merchant (MCGC 166).

ANTHONY HINTON

On May 4, 1623, Virginia Company officials noted that Anthony Hinton, the son of Elizabeth Hinton of Harworth, John Ward's schoolmate, and Robert Ward's cousin, was setting sail for Virginia on the *Bonny Bess.* Also aboard were Hinton's master, John Hart, and 45 gentlemen, some of whom were accompanied by their wives and children. Hinton and Hart had been outfitted by

Gabriel Barber, who intended to leave some supplies at Martin's Hundred (7). Because John Hart and Richard Stephens were supposed to select a site at Martin's Hundred where a bloomery was to be built, it is likely that Hart and his servant, Anthony Hinton, went there too (VCR 4:164, 262-263).

ELIAS HINTON (HENTON)

On February 16, 1624, Elias Hinton (Henton) was living on the lower side of the James River at Paces Paines (9). On October 10, 1624, when the General Court investigated the beating death of Elizabeth Abbott, one of John Proctor's maidservants, fellow servants said that Proctor often struck Elias Hinton. Two men said that Elias died in July 1624 after receiving an especially severe beating with a rake. Another man described Elias Hinton as a stubborn and desperate man who sometimes threatened suicide. On February 4, 1625, Elias Hinton was listed among those who died on the lower side of the James River (CBE 40, 60; MCGC 23-24).

JOHN HINTON

On February 16, 1624, John Hinton was living in urban Jamestown (1) in the household of Clement Dilke, a burgess (CBE 38).

***

THOMAS HINTON

Samuel Mathews' father-in-law, Sir Thomas Hinton, retired to Virginia and in 1634 was a councilor. On December 11, 1635, Governor John Harvey removed Hinton from the Council of State, thereby alienating both Mathews and Hinton. Sir Thomas Hinton's son, a gentleman of the Privy Chamber, was considered a possible replacement for Harvey as governor (STAN 33; NEI 111; MHS 107; EEAC 23).

ANNE HINTON
(MRS. THOMAS HINTON)

In February 1635, Anne, the wife of Sir Thomas Hinton, a Virginia councilor, was identified as the granddaughter of Anne Garrard of Upper Lambourne, Berkshire, a widow (EEAC 23).

***

TILLMAN HINTON (HENTON)

On October 14, 1623, Tillman Hinton (Henton) testified against William Wye of the *Garland* on behalf of Nicholas Young (VCR 3:692-695).

HENRY HITCH

On April 30, 1623, Henry Hitch, surgeon on the *James*, rebutted the critical statements Captain Nathaniel Butler made about the Virginia colony. Hitch said that he had made two voyages to Virginia and had lived in the colony for five months (VCR 2:386).

JOHN HITCH

On July 17, 1622, Virginia Company officials noted that John Hitch of London had obtained some shares of Virginia land from Francis Carter, who had acquired a large number of them from Lord Delaware's widow. On July 31, 1622, Mr. John Hitch set sail on the *James*, bringing with him Edward Pope and John Grefrihe. John Hitch may have been John Hitchy, who on January 24, 1625, was living in the eastern end of Jamestown Island (VCR 2:93; FER 400).

JOHN HITCHY

On January 24, 1625, John Hitchy was living in the eastern end of Jamestown Island (1). He may have been John Hitch, who set sail on the *James* on July 31, 1622 (CBE 56).

THOMAS HITALL

On March 16, 1627, several men who had been aboard the ship *Plantation* testified that while they were at sea, Thomas Hitall and Thomas Lawley got into a fight and that Robert Cooke (one of Hitall's crewmates) separated them. Cooke and Lawley fought again, and Lawley died after the ship reached Virginia (MCGC 145).

AUDRY (AUDREY) HOARE

Audry (Audrey) Hoare, a marriageable young maid, came to Virginia in August 1621 on the *Marmaduke*. Virginia Company records indicate that Audry, who was 19 years old, was born at Alesburie in Buckinghamshire. Both of her parents were alive when she went to the colony. Her father was a shoemaker and her brother, Richard, was a fustian dresser's apprentice. Audry had two sisters, one of whom was Joane Childe of Blackfriars. Audry's cousin, Thomas Beling, was a merchant, and another cousin, George Blunder, was an upholsterer in Cornwall. Audry Hoare had some specialized sewing skills and was capable of doing plain work, black work, and making buttons (FER 309).

WILLIAM HOBART

On April 12, 1623, William Hobart, who came to Virginia on the *Abigail*, described his voyage and conditions in the colony. Shortly after his arrival he went to Daniel Gookin's plantation, Newportes News **(24)** (VCR 4:229).

JOHN HOBBS

On September 19, 1625, Walter Horsefoot testified before the General Court about a matter involving Mr. Peirsey, probably cape merchant Abraham Peirsey. Horsefoot said that while he was in England, John Hobbs, a servant being transported to Virginia by Captain Bickley, left the ship *Elizabeth* but was returned by Mr. Page. Horsefoot also stated that some of Mr. Peirsey's servants, who were present, offered to assist Page in bringing John Hobbs back to the ship (MCGC 71).

***

MR. HOBSON

On March 22, 1622, when the Indians attacked the settlers across from Flowerdew Hundred **(53)**, near Weyanoke **(52)**, Mr. Hobson and his wife were slain (VCR 3:568).

MRS. HOBSON

On March 22, 1622, when the Indians attacked the settlers across from Flowerdew Hundred **(53)**, near Weyanoke **(52)**, Mrs. Hobson and her husband were slain (VCR 3:568).

***

EDWARD HOBSON

Edward Hobson, a 19-year-old smith from Buckinghamshire, England, came to Virginia aboard the *Bona Nova* in 1619. On February 16, 1624, he was living on the College Land **(66)** in Henrico. When a muster was taken there on January 23, 1625, he was listed a household head who lived alone and had a very modest supply of stored food. Edward Hobson, who probably was a Virginia Company tenant or servant, would have been under the supervision of Lieutenant Thomas Osborne. He may have been a kinsman of Thomas Hobson, who also was a smith from Buckinghamshire and lived at the College (FER 295; CBE 35, 53; DOR 1:7).

JOHN HOBSON

On November 4, 1620, John Hobson, one of Captain Christopher Lawne's fellow adventurers, asked the Virginia Company to confirm his group's patent and said that they intended to establish a settlement called the Isle of Wight plantation. Even so, the settlement associated with Lawne continued to be known as Captain Lawne's plantation **(25)**. In 1637 a John Hobson, perhaps the same man, was a member of the Council of State (VCR 1:414; STAN 33).

THOMAS HOBSON

Thomas Hobson, a 13-year-old smith from Buckinghamshire, England, came to Virginia in 1619 on the *Bona Nova* and probably was a Virginia Company servant. Sometime prior to January 1620 he took a message from Governor George Yeardley to Opechancanough. Although Hobson was listed among those killed at the College **(66)** during the March 22, 1622, Indian attack, he did in fact survive and on February 16, 1624, was among those living at the College. On February 4, 1625, Hobson was described as a servant to Mr. Whitaker, who reportedly loved him like a son. After Whittaker's death, Thomas Hobson reportedly compiled an inventory of his estate. When a list of patented land was sent back to England in May 1625, Thomas Hobson was credited with 150 acres in the corporation of Charles City. He may have been a kinsman of Edward Hobson, who also was a smith from Buckinghamshire, arrived on the same ship, and lived at the College (FER 295; VCR 3:244-245, 566; 4:510-511, 553; CBE 35).

ELIZABETH HODGES

Elizabeth Hodges came to Virginia on the *Abigail* and on February 16, 1624, was living on the Governor's Land or Maine (3). On January 30, 1625, Elizabeth was identified as a servant in the household of Thomas Bunn, a surgeon (CBE 39, 57).

JOHN HODGES

John Hodges died sometime after April 1623 but before February 16, 1624. He lived at a plantation on the lower side of the James River, within the corporation of James City (8-15) (CBE 41).

NICHOLAS HODGES

On December 5, 1625, Nicholas Hodges testified before the General Court in Jamestown (1). He said that when he was in Canada, he heard Mr. Weston (a mariner) tell Nicholas Roe that unless he would sign a release, he would put his two servants ashore instead of transporting them to Virginia (MCGC 78).

ANTHONY HODGSKINS (HODGKINS, HOSKINS)

On April 29, 1622, Anthony Hodgkins (Hodgkins, Hoskins), a 39-year-old servant to Lady Delaware, testified before the Chancery Court in England. He stated that Francis West (the late Lord Delaware's brother) had told him that Sir Samuel Argall had been in possession of the decedent's goods in Jamestown (1) and had given a list of them to Lady Delaware. Hodgskins testified in detail about the disposal of Lord Delaware's goods in Virginia. In 1637 he purchased a shallop on behalf of Edward Walker and Company, and three years later he received a license to keep an ordinary on the Eastern Shore. He was still alive in July 1645 and made an appearance in the local court (C 24/486 Pt. 1:13; SR 9946; AMES 1:136, 153; 2:452).

JOHN HODGSKINS (HODGKINS, HOSKINS, HOGSKINS)

John Hodgskins (Hodgkins, Hoskins, Hogskins) came to Virginia on the *George* in 1621 at the expense of George Sandys, who transferred his headright to John Bainham, Sr. On December 1, 1624, Bainham used Hodgskins' headright when patenting some land. On January 3, 1625, Treasurer George Sandys verified that he had brought John Hodgskins to the colony (PB 1 Pt. 1:17; MCGC 39).

***

NICHOLAS HODGSKINS (HODGSKINES, HODGSINS, HOSKINS, HOPKINS)

Nicholas Hodgskins (Hodgskines, Hodgsins, Hoskins, Hopkins), an ancient planter, came to Virginia on the *Edwin* in 1616 and on February 16, 1624, was living on the Eastern Shore. In early 1625 he was identified as head of a household that lived on Old Plantation Creek (73) and included his wife, Temperance, and daughter, Margaret. Nicholas was then age 27. In February 1625 he testified in a suit Captain John Martin brought against Governor George Yeardley and others. On February 5, 1627, Nicholas Hodgskins of Accomack, a yeoman, obtained a 20-acre leasehold, part of the defunct Virginia Company's property (76) on the Eastern Shore (CBE 46, 69; PB 1 Pt. 1:85; DOR 1:70).

TEMPERANCE HODGSKINS (HODGSKINES, HODGSINS, HOSKINS, HOPKINS) (MRS. NICHOLAS HODGSKINS [HODGSKINES, HODGSINS, HOSKINS, HOPKINS])

Temperance, who became the wife of Nicholas Hodgskins (Hodgskines, Hodgsins, Hoskins, Hopkins), came to Virginia on the *Jonathan* in 1620. In early 1625 she was living on the Eastern Shore (73) in a household headed by her husband. Also present was Nicholas's daughter, Margaret, a child born in Virginia (CBE 69).

MARGARET HODGSKINS (HODGSKINES, HODGSINS, HOSKINS, HOPKINS)

Margaret, the daughter of Nicholas Hodgskins (Hodgskines, Hodgsins, Hoskins, Hopkins), was born in Virginia and on February 16, 1624, was living on the Eastern Shore with her father. She was still there in early 1625 and was sharing a home on Old Plantation Creek (73) with her father and his wife, Temperance, who probably was Margaret's mother or stepmother (CBE 46, 69).

***

RICE (RYCE) HOE (HOOE, HOW, HOWE)

Rice (Ryce) Hoe (Hooe, How, Howe) came to Virginia on the *Gift* in 1618. On March

18, 1624, he was living at West and Shirley Hundred (41) when he saw Andrew Dudley attacked and slain by Indians. Later, he testified in court about the circumstances under which Dudley died. On January 22, 1625, Hoe, who was 26 years old, was still residing at Shirley Hundred and shared a home with his partners, John Higgins and Christopher Woodward. On December 4, 1626, Rice Hoe was ordered to take custody of some documents that belonged to William Besse of Jordan's Journey (46), who had returned to England. He also was told to compile an account of Besse's tobacco crop. Rice Hoe served as a burgess for Shirley Hundred in 1633. He went to England briefly but on June 23, 1635, returned to Virginia on the *America*. He then gave his age as 36. On May 2, 1636, Rice Hoe patented 1,200 acres of land near Merchant's Hope (50), the community in which he made his home, and used himself and his wife as headrights. Later, he added to his holdings, patenting land in what later became Surry County. In 1640 Rice was designated the tobacco viewer for Merchant's Hope. In 1645 and 1646 he represented Charles City County in the assembly. Rice Hoe died sometime after September 1655 but before December 3, 1655, at which time his widow, Sarah, was named his administrator (CBE 52, 153; MCGC 51, 126; HEN 1:202; PB 1 Pt. 1:338; MEY 372; DOR 1:13; 2:337-338).

THOMAS HOLCROFT (HOWLDCROFT, HOLDCROFT, HOLECROFT)

Thomas Holcroft (Howldcroft, Holdcroft, Holecroft) arrived in Virginia in June 1610 with Lord Delaware, who on June 12, 1610, designated him captain of a company. Later in the year, Sir Thomas Gates ordered him to build a fort in the woods near Kecoughtan (17). In October 1610 Lord Delaware commanded Captain George Yeardley and Captain Thomas Holcroft, who were in charge of the forts at Kecoughtan, to bring their men to Jamestown (1) so that they could join him in an exploratory journey toward the mountains (CJS 2:234; HAI 433, 508-509, 898).

HELEN HOLDEN

On November 20, 1622, it was decided that Helen Holden, a woman being detained at Newgate, would be sent to Virginia (CBE 29).

NICHOLAS HOLGRAVE

Nicholas Holgrave came to Virginia in 1607 and was one of the first Jamestown (1) colonists (CJS 1:208; 2:141).

ELIZABETH HOLLAND

On September 28, 1628, Elizabeth Holland was among the several people released from detention and delivered to the Rev. Lewis Hughes so that they could be sent to Virginia (CBE 84).

FRANCIS (FRANCES) HOLLAND

On February 27, 1619, Francis (Frances) Holland, a boy from Bishopsgate, was one of the youngsters rounded up from the streets of London so that they could be transported to Virginia (HUME 10).

GABRIEL HOLLAND

Gabriel Holland left Bristol, England, on the *Supply* during September 1620 with William Tracy and arrived at Berkeley Hundred (55) on January 29, 1621. Holland was supposed to serve for a certain number of years in exchange for some acreage. However, he reportedly died shortly after he arrived at Berkeley. He may have been a kinsman of the Gabriel Holland who for a time oversaw the servants the Society of Berkeley Hundred sent to Shirley Hundred (41) (CBE 21; VCR 3:396, 426).

***

GABRIEL HOLLAND

Gabriel Holland, a yeoman, came to Virginia sometime prior to 1619. In 1623–1624, he served as a burgess and was among those signing a document describing the hardships of life in Virginia prior to Governor George Yeardley's April 1619 arrival. On February 16, 1624, Holland was residing at the College (66) in Henrico. However, on January 2, 1625, he testified that he formerly had lived at Shirley Hundred (41), where he held the rank of sergeant and had been responsible for 15 of Berkeley Hundred's male servants. By August 1624 Gabriel Holland had wed Mary, the widow of ancient planter William Pinke alias Jonas, who had patented and seated a 12-acre tract in the eastern end of Jamestown

Island (1). Mary died sometime after August 14, 1624, and Gabriel promptly remarried. On January 24, 1625, he and his new wife, Rebecca, were in residence in rural Jamestown Island, probably on his late wife's land. Gabriel was credited with a dwelling, some swine, and an ample supply of stored food and defensive weaponry. Gabriel Holland, a respected member of the Jamestown Island community, made several appearances in the General Court during 1627 and 1628, at which time he arbitrated disputes and collected debts attributable to merchant Humphrey Rastall's estate. In 1627 he helped in settling a dispute between Jamestown Island residents John Upton and Caleb Page, and he had Robert Marshall arrested. In late January 1627 Holland was described as a yeoman and resident of the island. When one of Gabriel Holland's indentured servants, Ann Behoute, died, he was named administrator of her estate. Holland died sometime after 1632 (STAN 53; HEN 1:128-129; CBE 35, 56; HAI 915; PB 1 Pt. 1:11; MCGC 42, 137, 144, 158, 173; Charles City County Order Book 1655-1695:1; DOR 1:35).

MARY PINKE ALIAS JONAS HOLLAND
(MRS. WILLIAM PINKE ALIAS JONAS, MRS. GABRIEL HOLLAND)
(SEE MARY PINKE ALIAS JONAS)

Mary, the widow of William Pinke alias Jonas, promptly repatented the 12-acre homestead she and her late husband had owned and occupied in the eastern end of Jamestown Island (1); however, she did not inherit the remainder of the 100 acres he was due as an ancient planter. On August 14, 1624, when she secured her title to Pinke's land, she indicated that she had already married Gabriel Holland, a yeoman. Mary Pink alias Jonas Holland died between August 14, 1624, and January 24, 1625. At that point, her 12 acres, which she owned outright, descended to her new husband, Gabriel. Mary's property was mentioned in neighboring patents (PB 1 Pt. 1:10-11, 55, 423).

REBECCA HOLLAND
(MRS. GABRIEL HOLLAND)

Rebecca, who sometime after August 14, 1624, but before January 24, 1625, married the recently widowed Gabriel Holland, came to Virginia aboard the *John and Francis*. The Hollands made their home in the eastern end of Jamestown Island (1), occupying a parcel Gabriel inherited from his former wife, Mary, the widow of ancient planter William Pinke alias Jonas (CBE 56; PB 1: Pt. 1:10; Pt. 2:423).

***

JAMES HOLLAND

On September 26, 1618, officials at Bridewell noted that James Holland, a youth who had been born in Bishopsgate Street and brought in from Rede Lane, would be detained until he could be sent to Virginia. On February 27, 1619, James, who was described as a boy, was listed among the children rounded up from the streets of London so that they could be sent to the colony (CBE 10, 13).

RICHARD HOLLAND

In September 1620 Richard Holland left Bristol, England, on the *Supply* and accompanied William Tracy, who intended to seat at Berkeley Hundred (55). Holland reportedly arrived at Berkeley on January 29, 1621. He was supposed to serve a certain number of years in exchange for some acreage, but died shortly after he arrived at Berkeley (CBE 21; VCR 3:396, 426).

RICHARD HOLLAND

Richard Holland came to Virginia with Edward Grindon on the *James*, which set sail from England on July 31, 1622. If he survived, he probably went to Grindon's property in the eastern end of Jamestown Island (1) or to his plantation on the lower side of the James River, which eventually became part of the Treasurer's Plantation (11) (FER 400).

THOMAS HOLLAND

On March 22, 1622, when the Indians attacked Captain Berkeley's plantation at Falling Creek (68), Thomas Holland was slain (VCR 3:565).

THOMAS HOLLAND

Thomas Holland perished on March 22, 1622, when the Indians attacked Edward

Bennett's plantation in Warresqueak **(26)** (VCR 3:571).

WILLIAM HOLLAND

On October 25, 1625, William Holland, a gentleman who was in Virginia, testified in a lawsuit between Captain John Martin and mariner Humphrey Rastall. Holland stated that Rastall's ship became leaky while they were at sea and that they were forced to go to New England to secure another vessel. In October 1628 William Holland again testified about some dealings that involved Humphrey Rastall. He said that Rastall had been transporting a shipment of tobacco to Newfoundland on the *Anne Fortune*, but was obliged to throw 200 pounds of it overboard. William Holland's ongoing involvement in Humphrey Rastall's business affairs raises the possibility that he was one of Rastell's employees (MCGC 25, 175).

ANTHONY HOLLIDAY

On August 26, 1626, officials at Bridewell decided that Anthony Holliday, a vagrant who was being detained at Bridewell, would be sent to Virginia (CBE 73).

SAMPSON HOLLYDAY (HOLLIDAY)

On January 15, 1620, officials decided that Sampson Hollyday (Holliday), a vagrant from Aldgate who was being detained at Bridewell Prison, would be sent to Virginia (CBE 48).

ROGER HOLLIOCK

On December 8, 1635, when the Rev. Willis Hely (Heeley, Heyley, Heley), the rector of Mulberry Island Parish, patented some land, he used Roger Holliock as a headright (PB 1 Pt. 1:325).

JARRETT HOLLOCK

On February 4, 1625, Jarrett Hollock was identified as one of Mr. Whitaker's servants who had used his seed corn for subsistence. Hollock was one of the men entrusted to the care of Jabez Whitaker, who was responsible for the people living on the College **(66)** tract, where food and clothing were in short supply (VCR 4:511).

PETER HOLLOWAY

On December 4, 1634, when Hugh Cox received a court order entitling him to a patent, he listed Peter Holloway as a headright (PB 1 Pt. 1:282).

THOMAS HOLMAN

On August 24, 1635, Thomas Holman received a patent for 100 acres in Martin's Hundred **(7)** (PB 1 Pt. 1:276).

JOHN HOLMEDEN

In September 1620 John Holmeden, a gentleman, left Bristol, England, on the *Supply* with William Tracy and reportedly arrived at Berkeley Hundred **(55)** on January 29, 1621. He was supposed to serve three years in exchange for 50 acres of land (CBE 20-21; VCR 3:396-397, 426).

ALICE HOLMES

On February 16, 1624, Alice Holmes was living on the lower side of the James River **(10-16)**, within the corporation of James City (CBE 40).

ANN HOLMES

Ann Holmes, a young maid who was born in Newcastle, came to Virginia on the *Warwick* in 1621. She was 20 years old and had been a servant in the household of Mr. Emmons, a scrivener near the Exchange (FER 309).

GEORGE HOLMES

Captain George Holmes, a mariner, died sometime prior to early March 1627. An inventory of his estate was presented by Captain William Douglas and Thomas Gregory, purser of the *Saker* (MCGC 144).

***

GEORGE HOLMES

In 1629 George Holmes posted a bond guaranteeing another man's good behavior. When he patented some land on August 4, 1635, he used his wife, Rebecca, as a headright (MCGC 200; PB 1 Pt. 1:269).

REBECCA HOLMES
(MRS. GEORGE HOLMES)

On August 4, 1635, when George Holmes patented some land, he used his wife, Rebecca, as a headright (PB 1 Pt. 1:269).

***

GEORGE HOLMES

In September 1635 Captain George Holmes, a mariner, came to Virginia with Dutch mariner David Devries. He may have been the same individual who secured a patent in August 1635 (DEV 77).

JAMES HOLMES

On December 31, 1619, James Holmes, a boy brought in from Newgate, was detained so that he could be sent to Virginia (HUME 16).

JOHN HOLMES

John Holmes came to Virginia in 1622 on the *Southampton*. The cost of his transportation was paid by William Farrar, who used his headright in 1628 when patenting 100 acres on the Eastern Shore near Captain William Eppes's plantation (74) (PB 1 Pt. 1:71; MCGC 188).

***

WILLIAM HOLMES

On February 16, 1624, Captain William Holmes, a mariner, was living in urban Jamestown (1), where he headed a household he shared with Mr. and Mrs. Calcker and their infant. In mid-March 1624 it was noted that Holmes had sold chests of physic (medical supplies that Holmes kept at his dwelling) to Dr. John Pott. On March 23, 1624, Captain Holmes testified about a bargain Jamestown merchant John Chew made with Mr. Calcker (Calker), and in August a reference was made to Holmes's house in the capital city. During the latter part of 1624, Holmes witnessed the will made by Richard Domelawe, a Shirley Hundred resident who probably died in Jamestown. Sometime prior to September 7, 1626, William Holmes returned to England and sent some goods to Virginia on the *Peter and John*. However, by March 1, 1627, he was dead, having failed to survive the voyage to the colony. On March 12, 1627, his widow presented the General Court with an inventory of his estate. At that time, Dr. John Pott was ordered to take charge of the decedent's goods, which included a trunk full of linen and apparel. Captain Samuel Mathews assisted in the settlement of Captain William Holmes's estate. He paid a debt the decedent owed to Abraham Piersey, and in 1638 he testified on behalf of Holmes's widow, Elizabeth, who had married Joshua Mullard. When Captain William Holmes made his will, he named as heirs his sons William and Robert and his Parkinson and Grabe sisters and nephews, who were in England. He also left money to the two children of his kinsman Mathye (Matthew?) Holmes, funds that would cover the cost of their passage to Virginia, and made a bequest that would enable his own children to come to the colony (SH 6; MCGC 12-13, 18-19, 143, 147; CBE 38, 73; EAE 89; EEAC 30; SR 3997).

ELIZABETH HOLMES
(MRS. WILLIAM HOLMES,
MRS. JOSHUA MULLARD)

In April 1627 Captain William Holmes's widow, Elizabeth, presented the General Court with an account of her late husband's estate. In January 1638 Captain Samuel Mathews testified on her behalf. By that date, Elizabeth had married Joshua Mullard (MCGC 147; EAE 89).

***

MAURICE HOLSTEN

Maurice Holsten died between October 1623 and February 1624. He was a skilled worker who had been sent to the colony by the Virginia Company (VCR 4:287).

JAMES HOLT

James Holt, a carpenter from London, arrived in Jamestown (1) on September 12, 1623, on the *Bonny Bess* and took the oath of supremacy (MCGC 6).

JOHN HOLT (HOULT)

John Holt (Hoult), a gentleman, came to Virginia in 1608 as part of the 2nd Supply of new settlers. He would have lived in Jamestown (1) (CJS 1:241; 2:190).

***

RANDALL HOLT (HOWLETT) I

Randall Holt (Howlett) I came on the *George* in 1620–1621, probably at Dr. John Pott's expense, and on February 16, 1624, was a servant in Pott's household in urban Jamestown (1). By January 30, 1625, he had moved to Pott's leasehold in the Governor's Land (3), where he was described as an 18-year-old servant. On March 20, 1626, the General Court noted that Randall Holt was obliged to serve Dr. Pott until Christmas (that is, early January 1627) and then was to be freed. Around 1629 Randall Holt married Mary Bailey (Baily, Bayly, Bayley, Bailie, Baile), the daughter and sole heir of John Bayly. In September 1636 he patented 400 acres at the head of Lower Chippokes Creek, and in July 1639 he acquired 490 acres of land on Hog Island (16), along with the 400 acres his late wife had inherited there. Sometime prior to March 9, 1640, Randall Holt I sold two Africans to merchant George Menefie, owner of a lot in urban Jamestown and a plantation in Charles City. Randall and Mary Bailey (Baily, Bayly, Bayley, Bailie, Baile) Holt produced a son and heir, Randall Holt II, around 1629. He was still alive in July 1639 and may have predeceased his wife, who died prior to August 1643 (CBE 38, 58; MCGC 98; G&M 165; PB 1 Pt. 1:113, 386; Pt. 2:656, 880, 704, 880; MEY 367; DOR 1:28; 2:311).

MARY BAILEY (BAILY, BAYLY, BAYLEY, BAILIE, BAILE) HOLT (HOWLETT) (MRS. RANDALL HOLT [HOWLETT]) I)

Mary Bailey (Baily, Bayly, Bayley, Bailie, Baile), John Bailey's underage daughter, inherited his acreage in the eastern end of Jamestown Island (1) sometime prior to February 20, 1620. She also inherited his 490 to 500 acres at Hog Island (16). Mary's guardians, Robert Evers and Richard Bailey (and Bailey's surrogate, Edward Grindon), generated income on her behalf by placing her real estate in the hands of tenants. At times Evers personally occupied one of Mary's tracts on Jamestown Island, and in September 1628 a tenant named Elmer Philips (Phillips) was living on her other parcel. In 1626 Sir George Yeardley commenced renting Mary's Hog Island prop-

erty. Mary Bailey married Randall Holt (Howlett) I around 1629 and gave birth to a son, Randall Holt II, shortly thereafter. The household resided on her property at Hog Island. Mary died sometime prior to August 1, 1643, at which time son Randall Holt II repatented her acreage (PB 1 Pt. 1:386; Pt. 2:656, 880; 2:240; MCGC 17, 122; DOR 1:215–216; 2:311).

RANDALL HOLT (HOWLETT) II

Randall Holt (Howlett) II, the son of Randall and Mary Bailey (Baily, Bayly, Bayley, Bailie, Baile) Holt, was born around 1629. On August 1, 1643, he was given a patent for his late mother's acreage in the eastern end of Jamestown Island (1) and on the lower side of the James River at Hog Island (16). By November 5, 1654, he had disposed of his acreage on Jamestown Island, but he resided on Hog Island for the rest of his life. In May 1654 Major Randall Holt II asked Surry County's justices to compensate him for the use of his boat and servants, which had been pressed into service. Two years later, he was censured for making disparaging remarks about some of the county's justices. Around 1663 Randall Holt II married the widowed Elizabeth Hansford Wilson, and in 1668 he became a Surry County justice of the peace. In April 1679, when Randall Holt II prepared his will, he left his personal property to his wife, Elizabeth, and all of his land to his eldest son, John. Sons William and Thomas were named as reversionary heirs if John failed to outlive his father. Randall Holt II's will was presented to the county court on September 2, 1679 (PB 1 Pt. 2:880; 2:240–241; Surry County Deeds, Wills &c. 1652–1672:35, 28, 84; 1671-1684:222; MEY 367-368; MCGH 200; DOR 2:311-312).

***

RANDOLPH HOLT

Randolph Holt came to Virginia at the expense of Dr. John Pott, who used him as a headright when patenting some land on September 1, 1632. He probably was the same individual identified as Randall Holt I, who was a Pott servant (PB 1 Pt. 1:113).

JOHN HOLTON

John Holton came to Virginia on the *John and Dorothy* in 1634 at the expense of

Adam Thorogood, who used him as a headright when patenting some land on June 24, 1635 (PB 1 Pt. 1:179).

WILLIAM HOLTON

William Holton came to Virginia on the *John and Dorothy* in 1634 at the expense of Adam Thorogood, who used him as a headright when patenting some land on June 24, 1635 (PB 1 Pt. 1:179).

FRANCES (FRANCIS) HOME

On December 31, 1619, Frances (Francis) Home, a young person brought in from the streets of London, was detained at Bridewell until he or she could be sent to Virginia (HUME 15).

HENRY HOME (HORNE)

On February 16, 1624, Henry Home (Horne) was living on the lower side of the James River, west of Gray's Creek (**8, 9**) (CBE 40).

JAMES HOME

On December 31, 1619, it was decided that James Home, who was brought in from the streets of London, would be detained at Bridewell until he could be sent to Virginia or Bermuda (CBE 15).

JOHN HOME
(SEE JOHN HOW [HOWE, HOME])

RICHARD HOME (HORNE)

On February 16, 1624, Richard Home (Horne) was living on the lower side of the James River and west of Gray's Creek (**8, 9**) (CBE 40).

RALPH HOODE

Ralph Hoode came to Virginia in 1621 on the *Abigail*. In early 1625 he was living in Elizabeth City (**17**) on the lower side of the Hampton River, on the Virginia Company's land. Ralph was a 19-year-old servant in the household jointly headed by Nicholas Rowe and John Haney (CBE 68).

ROBERT HOOKE

On July 31, 1627, Robert Hooke shipped goods from London to Virginia on the *Thomas and John* (CBE 79).

THOMAS HOOKER

On February 16, 1624, Thomas Hooker was a servant in the household of Governor Francis Wyatt in urban Jamestown (**1**) (CBE 38).

WILLIAM HOOKES

William Hookes came to Virginia in a French ship in 1629 at the expense of Adam Thorogood, who used him as a headright when patenting some land on June 24, 1635 (PB 1 Pt. 1:179).

JOHN HOOKS

John Hooks died sometime after April 1623 but before February 16, 1624, at a plantation on the lower side of the James River, within the corporation of James City (**8-15**) (CBE 41).

PETER HOOPER

On November 14, 1635, when John Grinett patented some land in Warwick County, he used the headrights of his first wife, Alice, and her son, Peter Hooper (PB 1 Pt. 1:306).

JOHN HOPE

On January 26, 1620, Virginia Company officials noted that John Hope, a mariner, had acquired Stephen Sparrow's Company stock (VCR 1:300).

THOMAS HOPE

Thomas Hope, a tailor, came to Virginia in 1608 in the 1st Supply of new settlers and would have lived in Jamestown (**1**). During 1608 he accompanied Captain Christopher Newport on a visit to Powhatan's village. Captain John Smith later identified Hope as a coauthor of his *Proceedings* (CJS 1:197, 216; 2:162).

WILLIAM HOPKICKE (HOPKIRKE)

William Hopkicke (Hopkirke) died in Elizabeth City (**17, 18**) sometime after April 1623 but before February 16, 1624 (CBE 45).

[NO FIRST NAME] HOPKINS

On July 3, 1622, Virginia Company officials learned that Mr. Hopkins, a clergyman, wanted to go to Virginia at his own expense (VCR 2:76).

***

BARTHOLOMEW HOPKINS (HOPSKINS, HOSKINS)

According to a 1624 patent, Bartholomew Hopkins (Hopskins, Hoskins) was an ancient planter. On February 16, 1624, he was living in Elizabeth City (17) on the east side of the Hampton River. On November 3, 1624, he patented 100 acres of land at Buckroe, his first dividend of land as an ancient planter. Hopkins was credited with the property in May 1625 when a list of patented land was sent back to England. On April 11, 1625, Bartholomew Hopkins testified before the General Court when an investigation was held concerning John Verone's possible suicide. During the early 1630s Bartholomew Hopkins' land at Buckroe was used as a reference point in neighboring patents, thereby suggesting that he retained his property. Hopkins went to England and returned with his wife on the *James* in 1634. In 1639 they went back to England to respond to a Chancery suit initiated by Joane Carter, Thomas Lee's remarried widow. The Hopkins couple then identified themselves as residents of Elizabeth City. Mrs. Carter accused Bartholomew Hopkins of refusing to relinquish the funds derived from selling her late husband's goods, which several Elizabeth City residents had purchased. In 1641 a London scrivener successfully brought suit against Bartholomew Hopkins in an attempt to settle a debt to John Pennell, also of London. James Neale of Elizabeth City was authorized to recover the plaintiff's funds (CBE 43, 208, 220; MCGC 53; PB 1 Pt. 1:44-45, 109, 116; VCR 4:558; SH 34; C 24/640:28, 47; SR 9988).

MRS. BARTHOLOMEW HOPKINS (HOPSKINS, HOSKINS)

Bartholomew Hopkins (Hopskins, Hoskins) and his wife, whose given name is unknown, went to Virginia on the *James* in 1634. In 1639 they returned to England and testified in Chancery case in which Bartholomew was being sued. At that time they were identified as residents of Elizabeth City (17) (SH 34; C 24/640: 28, 47; SR 9988).

***

JOHN HOPKINS

John Hopkins, a 21-year-old baker from Berkshire, England, came to Virginia in 1619 on the *Bona Nova* and probably was a Virginia Company servant or tenant. On March 22, 1622, when the Indians attacked the settlers living near Mulberry Island (21), John Hopkins was killed (FER 295; VCR 3:570).

NICHOLAS HOPKINS (HODGSKINS, HODGSKINES, HODGSINS, HOSKINS) (SEE NICHOLAS HODGSKINS [HODGSKINES, HODGSINS, HOSKINS, HOPKINS])

On February 5, 1627, Nicholas Hopkins (Hodgskins, Hodgskines, Hodgsins, Hoskins) of Accomack, a yeoman, obtained a leasehold—20 acres of the defunct Virginia Company's property (76) on the Eastern Shore (PB 1 Pt. 1:85).

PHOEBUS HOPKINS

Phoebus Hopkins came to Virginia on the *George* in 1621 at the expense of George Sandys, who used him as a headright when patenting some land on December 4, 1624. Sandys indicated that he had brought Phoebus Hopkins from Bermuda (PB 1 Pt. 1:16).

RICHARD HOPKINS

On September 10, 1620, Richard Hopkins left Bristol, England, on the *Supply* with Robert Bisaker (Bysaker) and his wife, Faith (Fayth), and William Tracy, who intended to seat at Berkeley Hundred (55). Hopkins and the Bisaker couple were transported to Virginia at the expense of the Society of Berkeley Hundred, whose investors agreed to provide them some support when they first arrived. After they became established, Hopkins and the Bisakers were expected to become sharecroppers (CBE 21; VCR 3:393-394).

THOMAS HOPKINS

In 1624 Thomas Hopkins, a 46-year-old sailor from Ratcliffe, in Surrey, England, testified in the lawsuit involving the ships *Neptune* and *Treasurer*, which had been in Virginia in 1618 and 1619. The litigation involved the late Lord Delaware's goods and the role that former Deputy Governor Samuel Argall had played in their depletion while they were stored at Jamestown (**1**) (EAE 14).

***

DANIEL (DANIELL) HOPKINSON

Daniel (Daniell) Hopkinson came to Virginia sometime prior to February 25, 1634, at which time Daniel Gookin was authorized to patent some land using Hopkinson's headright. On November 21, 1636, when Hopkinson made his will, which was witnessed by Thomas Nant, he asked to be buried in the graveyard of Kecoughtan Church in Elizabeth City (**17**). He made bequests to his wife, Sarah; his mother, Katherine; his sister, Barbara; his brother Abraham; and his in-laws, the Cliftons and the Soles. The testator also left his surgery chest and books to his brother Michael Markland. Daniel Hopkinson indicated that he owned the ship *Tristan and Jane*. He died in Virginia sometime prior to April 1637 (SH 28; WITH 151-152; SR 3976).

SARAH HOPKINSON (MRS. DANIEL [DANIELL] HOPKINSON)

On November 21, 1636, when Daniel (Daniell) Hopkinson, owner of the *Tristan and Jane*, made his will, he was in Virginia in Elizabeth City (**17**). He left his wife, Sarah, who may have remained behind in England, the value of the goods on his ship (SH 28; WITH 151-152; SR 3976).

***

THOMAS HOPSON

Thomas Hopson came to Virginia on the *Bona Nova* in 1618. On February 4, 1625, he was living on the lower side of the James River, where he was a 12-year-old servant on Captain Samuel Mathews' plantation (**15**) (CBE 60).

HENRY HORNER (HORNE)

On March 9, 1624, Henry Horner (Horne) presented a petition to Governor Francis Wyatt in which he complained about some business dealings with Virginia colonist John Proctor of Pace's Paines (**9**). He also sent a copy of his petition to Virginia Company officials. Horner, who was in England and described himself as a young and impoverished gentleman, stated that while he was making plans to come to Virginia, he encountered John Proctor, who was going to transport goods and some servants on the *George*. Proctor recommended that Horner put his goods aboard the ship under Proctor's name, to guarantee that they would be transported. He also sold Horner a male servant, Richard Grove. Horner said that he had paid for Grove's transportation from London to Portsmouth and for his passage from there to Virginia. However, once the *George* reached the colony, John Proctor refused to give Henry Horner his goods and also was reluctant to release his servant. Although Richard Grove supported Henry Horner's allegations, the General Court assigned an indentured servant named Thomas Flower to Horner, who was told to supply Proctor with another man (VCR 4:466-467; MCGC 12).

ROBERT HORNER

Robert Horner, a 26-year-old freemason from Shropshire, England, came to Virginia in 1619 on the *Bona Nova*. On March 22, 1622, when the Indians attacked Captain Berkeley's plantation at Falling Creek (**68**), Robert was killed. In the list of casualties, his name and trade were listed (FER 295; VCR 3:565).

THOMAS HORNER

Thomas Horner died at Martin's Hundred (**7**) sometime after April 1623 but before February 16, 1624 (CBE 42).

JOHN HORNHOLD

On February 12, 1620, officials at Bridewell decided that John Hornehold, who had been brought in from the Middlesex House of Correction, would be sent to Virginia (CBE 18).

JOHN HORRY

On May 12, 1623, John Horry, a barber surgeon from Waltham Row in Essex, testified in the lawsuit between the Earl of Warwick and

Edward Brewster. Horry stated that he had been in Jamestown (1) around the time of Lord Delaware's death and was familiar with Brewster's actions and subsequent court martial hearing (HCA 13/44 ff 134ro-135vo).

WALTER HORSEFOOT

On September 19, 1625, Walter Horsefoot, who was in Jamestown (1), testified before the General Court. He said that the ship *Elizabeth* had been seized at Dover for the King's Service but the vessel's purser had sought the assistance of the lieutenant at Dover Castle and gotten it released. On October 3, 1629, Walter Horsefoot was ordered to post a bond, guaranteeing that he would pay his debts to the purser and crew of the *Elizabeth* (MCGC 71-72).

[NO FIRST NAME] HORTON

On November 26, 1609, Mrs. Horton's maidservant, Elizabeth Persons, married Thomas Powell in Bermuda (HAI 413).

WILLIAM HORTON

In late 1634 William Horton and several others purchased some of the late Thomas Lee's goods, which were sold by Bartholomew Hopkins, probably in Elizabeth City (17) (CBE 208).

NICHOLAS HOSKINS (SEE NICHOLAS HODGSKINS [HODGSKINES, HODGSINS, HOSKINS, HOPKINS])

[NO FIRST NAME] HOSIER

A person named Hosier, who came to Virginia on the *Furtherance*, died in Jamestown (1) sometime after April 1623 but before February 16, 1624 (HOT 196).

EDWARD HOSIER (HOSYER)

Edward Hosier (Hosyer), a vintner from Ratcliffe, England , arrived in Jamestown (1) on September 12, 1623, on the *Bonny Bess* and took the oath of supremacy. Sometime after April 1623 but before February 16, 1624, he died on Jamestown Island (MCGC 6; CBE 39).

WILLIAM HOSIER (HOSYER)

On December 8, 1628, William Hosier (Hosyer) brought suit against the estate of the late John Cross, merchant of the *Truelove*. Hosier said that when the ship was in New England, he paid Cross. However, after Cross's death, Hosier's goods were given to Mrs. Hurte, the *Truelove's* owner (MCGC 178).

[NO FIRST NAME] HOTCHKINS (HODGSKINS?)

On July 15, 1631, Mr. Hotchkins (perhaps Hodgskins) identified himself as a Virginia planter when asking for relief from customs duties. The mark his hogsheads bore was not recorded (G&M 166).

***

EDWARD HOW

Edward How and his wife and child perished on March 22, 1622, when the Indians attacked Martin's Hundred (7) (VCR 3:570).

MRS. EDWARD HOW

On March 22, 1622, when the Indians attacked Martin's Hundred (7), Mrs. Edward How and her husband and child perished (VCR 3:570).

[NO FIRST NAME] HOW

On March 22, 1622, when the Indians attacked Martin's Hundred (7), the child of Edward How and his wife was killed (VCR 3:570).

***

JOHN HOW (HOWE, HOME)

John How (Howe, Home) came to Virginia on the *Margaret and John* in 1621 and on February 16, 1624, was living on the Eastern Shore. In early 1625 he was still there and was part of the community of settlers living on Old Plantation Creek (73). John, who was age 25, was a solitary household head and had an ample supply of stored food and defensive weaponry. On January 31, 1625, he testified before the General Court about the late Thomas Parke's estate. He said that before Parke left Accomack, he was asked whether he intended to make a will. Parke declined, saying that he had given all that he had to his partner, William Bibby, and that he had sent some tobacco to his mother in England. John How apparently was a planter, for on February 8, 1625, Gilbert Peppett testified about some tobacco Captain Thomas Graves had purchased from him and from John Wilkins, who also lived on the Eastern Shore. On February 13, 1626, John How, who was described as a gentleman, told the General Court that Luke Aden (Eden) had made a nuncupative will, disposing of his goods and mentioning a servant who had been left at Chaplin's Choice **(56)**. He said that he had asked the testator to remember his faithful servant, Alexander. The justices of the General Court designated John How as Luke Aden's administrator and authorized him to settle his estate. On May 1, 1626, How was ordered to post security, guaranteeing that he would pay a just debt. In early February 1627 he presented the will of William Foster, a resident of Elizabeth City **(17, 18)**, and two months later he produced an account of Luke Aden's estate. The fact that he was entrusted with these responsibilities suggests that he was considered a responsible and respectable citizen. On September 20, 1628, John How received a 30-acre leasehold in Accomack, adjacent to the defunct Virginia Company's land **(76)** and the Secretary's land **(75)**. He also held patents for several other tracts. In 1632 How was named a commissioner of the Accomack court, and he commenced serving as a burgess. He also served on his parish vestry. John How died sometime prior to February 12, 1638 (CBE 46, 69; MCGC 46, 94, 101, 117-118, 138, 148; PB 1 Pt. 1:85-86; HEN 1:154, 170, 179, 187, 203; AMES 1:39, 43, 101; 2:14; DOR 1:71).

DORCAS HOWARD

On April 8, 1629, the justices of the General Court noted that on March 22nd, Dorcas Howard, a maidservant and field hand employed by George Ungwin, a resident of rural Jamestown Island **(1)**, had a miscarriage. Howard admitted that Robert Gage was the baby's father. Ungwin was ordered to see that she appeared in court to answer the justices' questions. It is uncertain how long she continued in Ungwin's employ (MCGC 194).

JOHN HOWARD

John Howard perished on March 22, 1622, when the Indians attacked Edward Bennett's plantation in Warresqueak **(26)** (VCR 3:571).

JOHN HOWARD

John Howard came to Virginia on the *Swan* in 1624. In early 1625 he was living in Elizabeth City **(17)** on the Virginia Company's land. John, who was age 24, lived in Captain John Martin's household and appears to have been free (CBE 67).

JUDETH HOWARD

On March 22, 1622, when the Indians attacked Thomas Sheffield's plantation **(69)**, Judeth Howard was killed (VCR 3:565).

JOHN HOWBECK

On January 9, 1624, John Howbeck, who indicated that he was 35 years old, testified before the General Court. He said that Mr. Weston had purchased a servant named Becgam (Beckham?) and some goods from the ship *Sparrow* before it left Plymouth, England. He also said that a cargo of fish brought from Canada to Virginia belonged to Mr. Weston (MCGC 10).

ANDREW HOWELL

On February 16, 1624, Andrew Howell was a servant in John Burrows' Jamestown Island **(1)** household. He was still a member of the Burrows household on January 24, 1625, at which time he was described as a 13-year-old servant (CBE 38, 56).

COB. HOWELL

Cob. Howell came to Virginia on the *John and Dorothy* in 1634 at the expense of Adam Thorogood, who used him/her as a headright when patenting some land on June 24, 1635 (PB 1 Pt. 1:179).

JAMES HOWELL

James Howell died at the College **(66)** sometime after April 1623 but before February 16, 1624. Official records indicate that he was killed (CBE 35).

JOHN HOWELL

On February 16, 1624, John Howell was living on the Maine **(3)** just west of Jamestown Island (CBE 39).

THOMAS HOWES

According to a letter written by Richard Frethorne at Martin's Hundred (**7**) in March or April 1623, Thomas Howes arrived at the plantation at Christmastime (that is, early January 1623) and died while living in the home of William Harwood, the settlement's leader (VCR 4:60).

***

JOHN HOWLETT (HOWLET) I

John Howlett (Howlet) I left Bristol, England, on the *Supply* on September 10, 1620, with his sons, John II and William, who accompanied William Tracy to Berkeley Hundred (**55**). The Howletts reportedly arrived at Berkeley on January 29, 1621. John I was supposed to serve for three years in exchange for 50 acres of land. On March 22, 1622, when the Indians attacked Captain John Berkeley's settlement at Falling Creek (**68**), where an ironworks was being built, John Howlett I and his son, John II, were killed (CBE 21; VCR 3:397, 426, 565).

JOHN HOWLETT (HOWLET) II

John Howlett (Howlet) II, his father, John I, and his brother, William, departed from Bristol, England, on the *Supply* on September 10, 1620. They were among those accompanying William Tracy, who intended to seat at Berkeley Hundred (**55**). The Howletts reached Berkeley on January 29, 1621. They were supposed to serve for a certain number of years in exchange for some acreage. On March 22, 1622, when the Indians attacked Captain John Berkeley's settlement at Falling Creek (**68**), where an ironworks was being built, both John Howletts (I and II) were killed (CBE 21; VCR 3:397, 426, 565).

WILLIAM HOWLETT (HOWLET)

William Howlett with his father, John Howlett I, and brother, John Howlett II, set sail from Bristol, England, on the *Supply* on September 10, 1620 and went to Virginia. They were among those accompanying William Tracy, who intended to seat at Berkeley Hundred (**55**). They were supposed to serve a certain period of time in exchange for a given amount of acreage. The Howletts arrived at Berkeley on January 29,

1621. William's father and brother were killed on March 22, 1622, when the Indians attacked Captain John Berkeley's settlement at Falling Creek (**68**), where an ironworks was being built. It is uncertain whether William was there too and survived, or was elsewhere at the time of the assault. William Howlett died in Jamestown (**1**) sometime after April 1623 but before February 16, 1624. This raises the possibility that he was among those evacuated from outlying areas that were considered too dangerous (CBE 21, 39; VCR 3:397, 426, 565).

***

NICHOLAS HOWSDON

On March 22, 1622, when the Indians attacked William Bikar's house (**57**) in Charles City, Nicholas Howsdon was slain (VCR 3:568).

JOHN HUBBARD

John Hubbard set sail for Virginia on July 31, 1622, aboard the *James*. He was sent to the colony by Mr. Tuker, probably Captain William Tucker of Elizabeth City (**18**) (FER 400).

EDWARD HUBBERSTEAD

Edward Hubberstead came to Virginia in 1623 on the *Southampton*. On January 20, 1625, he was living at Flowerdew Hundred (**53**), where he was a 26-year-old servant in Abraham Peirsey's household (CBE 50).

JAMES HUDDLESTON

On June 23, 1620, the Virginia Company noted that James Huddleston, master of the *Bona Nova*, was a capable mariner. On November 21, 1621, he was authorized to take 45 people to Virginia on the *Bona Nova* and afterward to go on a fishing expedition (VCR 1:369; 3:516).

JOHN HUDDLESTON (HUDDLESTONE, HUDLESTON, HUDLESTONE)

In June 1619, 33-year-old John Huddleston (Huddlestone, Hudleston, Hudlestone), a mariner in Ratcliffe, Middlesex, was identified as former quartermaster of the *Starr* of London and master of the *Bona Nova*, which was going to Virginia. In November 1621 Huddleston was authorized to take the *Bona Nova* to Virginia where he could trade and fish. According to Captain John Smith, he was the first to reach England with word of the March 1622 Indian attack. By November 1626 Captain John Huddleston apparently had decided to make some money growing tobacco. However, because the land he was assigned was barren, he moved to Captain Francis West's plantation at Chippokes. In February 1627 Huddleston testified before the General Court about an incident that had occurred at Martin's Brandon **(59)**. He said that Captain William Eppes and the widowed Alice Boyce, while inebriated, had had a sexual encounter. At the close of 1627 Captain Huddleston informed the General Court that five of Mr. Sharples' servants were sent to Virginia, but none had been transported for Mr. Moore (EAE 8; CBE 25; VCR 1:554, 562; CJS 1:432; MCGC 123, 139-40, 158).

***

EDWARD HUDSON

On February 16, 1624, Edward Hudson and his wife, who appear to have been free, were living in urban Jamestown **(1)** in Edward Blaney's household. Simultaneously, they were attributed to the Blaney plantation **(14)** on the lower side of the James River. In May 1625 Edward Hudson held a patent for 100 acres on the south side of the James River, below the falls **(67)** (CBE 38, 40; VCR 4:552).

MRS. EDWARD HUDSON

On February 16, 1624, Mrs. Edward Hudson and her husband, who appear to have been free, were living in urban Jamestown **(1)** in Edward Blaney's household. Simultaneously, they were credited to the Blaney plantation **(14)** on the lower side of the James River (CBE 38, 40).

***

EDWARD HUDSON (HUSON, HAWSONE)

In 1621 Virginia Company officials noted that Edward Hudson (Huson, Hawsone) was among those going to Virginia on behalf of the East India School. He may have been a kinsman of Leonard Hudson, who was associated with the same educational institution. Because the group arrived right after the March 22, 1622, Indian attack, they did not go to the College land, Arrohattock **(66)**, where the school was to be built. Instead, most (if not all) were seated on the lower side of the James River at William Ewin's plantation **(13)** until it was safe to go to their intended destination. On June 1, 1625, officials noted that Edward Hudson died before it was safe for him to go to Arrohattock (FER 272; MCGC 64).

***

JOHN HUDSON

John Hudson, who served as provost marshal during Sir Thomas Dale's government (1611–1616), was tried at a court martial hearing in Jamestown **(1)** and sentenced to death. However, Dale intervened and saw that he was reprieved. By June 7, 1617, Hudson again had run afoul of the law. As a result, Deputy Governor Samuel Argall had him banished from Virginia, threatening him with death if he ever returned (VCR 3:69-70).

***

LEONARD HUDSON (HUSON, HUSONE)

In June 1622 master carpenter Leonard Hudson, his wife and children, and five apprentices set sail for Virginia. Hudson and the other men were supposed to commence construction of the East India School, an educational institution whose establishment was underwritten by some of the East India Company's investors. It was supposed to be erected at Arrohattock, on the property assigned to the College **(66)**, on the north side of the James River, within the corporation of Henrico. When Leonard Hudson and his group arrived in Virginia, they learned about the March 1622 Indian attack and found out that the survivors from the College tract had been evacuated to the safety of William Ewen's plantation **(13)**, which lay across the James River from Jamestown Island **(1)**. Virginia officials decided that the Hudson household would be seated at Ewen's plantation with the refugees from the College. Before the settlers from the College were able to return to their settlement, Leonard Hudson, his wife, and their children became ill and died (VCR 3:650; MCGC 60, 64).

MRS. LEONARD HUDSON (HUSON, HUSONE)

In 1622 Mrs. Leonard Hudson (Huson, Husone) and her husband and children set sail for Virginia, where he and his five apprentices were supposed to construct the East India School on the College (66) property. As Mrs. Hudson and her traveling companions arrived in the wake of the March 22, 1622, Indian attack, they were ordered to take up residence at William Ewen's plantation (13). Mrs. Leonard Hudson, her husband, and her children became ill and died before they were able to go up to the College (VCR 3:650; MCGC 60, 64).

[NO FIRST NAMES] HUDSON (HUSON, HUSONE)

In 1622 master carpenter Leonard Hudson (Huson, Husone) and his wife and children came to Virginia and were supposed to go to the College (66) on behalf of the East India School. However, because they arrived shortly after the March 1622 Indian attack, they were placed at William Ewen's plantation (13). All of the Hudsons died there before they were able to go up to the College property (VCR 3:650; MCGC 60, 64).

***

ROBERT HUDSON

Robert Hudson set sail for Virginia on the *James* on July 31, 1622, and accompanied William Felgate. On February 16, 1624, Hudson was living at Chaplin's Choice (56). He was still there on January 21, 1625, and was identified as a 30-year-old servant in Isaac Chaplin's household (FER 400; CBE 37, 51).

THOMAS HUDSON

Sometime prior to December 1635, Thomas Hudson and three other men went to Virginia on the *Constance* as servants of Christopher Boyse, a Virginia planter and resident of Blunt Point (22) (EAE 58, 60)

THOMAS HUDSON (HUSON, HUSONE)

Thomas Hudson (Huson, Husone) came to Virginia on the *Temperance* in 1621, at the expense of Governor George Yeardley (MCGC 166).

WILLIAM HUDSON

On February 12, 1620, officials at Bridewell decided that William Hudson, who was being detained, would be sent to Virginia (CBE 18).

LEONARD HUETT (HEWETT)

Leonard Huett (Hewett) died sometime prior to December 8, 1628. Before he expired he told Susan Balden that he wanted his chest and its contents to go to Goodman Fryer in repayment for his kindness. Goodman George Fryer (Frier) lived on the Governor's Land (3) (MCGC 179).

***

FRANCIS HUFF (HOUGH)

Francis Huff (Hough) came to Virginia on the *Swan* in 1624. In early 1625 he was living in Elizabeth City (18), where he and James Sleight jointly headed a household that was well supplied with stored food and defensive weaponry. Francis was then age 24. Sometime prior to October 20, 1632, Francis Huff married Christopher Windmill's widow. He then conveyed Windmill's leasehold at the Indian Thicket (17) to another individual. On February 1, 1633, Francis served as a burgess for Nutmeg Quarter. He apparently was a successful planter, for on November 12, 1635, he received a patent for 800 acres on the Nansemond River (20 c) (CBE 65; PB 1 Pt. 1:145, 147–148, 305; HEN 1:203; DOR 1:58).

MRS. FRANCIS HUFF (HOUGH) (MRS. CHRISTOPHER WINDMILL [WENDILE, WYNWILL, WENDMILL])

Sometime prior to October 20, 1632, Christopher Windmill's widow married Francis Huff (Hough). Both men were residents of Elizabeth City (17, 18) (PB 1 Pt. 1:145, 147).

***

HENRY HUFF

On February 25 or 26, 1620, it was decided that Henry Huff, a boy who was being detained at Newgate, would be sent to Virginia (CBE 19; HUME 28).

HUGH

On March 22, 1622, when the Indians attacked Edward Bennett's plantation at Warresqueak (**26**), a man named Hugh was killed (VCR 3:571).

EDWARD HUGHS (HUIES, HUGHES)

Edward Hughs (Huies, Hughes) died sometime after April 1623 but before February 16, 1624, at a plantation on the lower side of the James River, within the corporation of James City (**8-15**) (CBE 41).

***

HUGH HUGHS (HUGHES, HUES)

Hugh Hughs (Hughes, Hues), went to Virginia on the *Guift (Gift)* sometime prior to December 1621. He then informed Virginia Company officials that he was being wrongly kept by Peter Ascom (Ascam) as a servant instead of a tenant at half-shares. The Company saw that Hughs was freed immediately. On February 16, 1624, Hugh Hughs was living at Martin's Hundred (**7**). He was still there on February 4, 1625, and was living in the household of the settlement's leader, William Harwood. Despite the fact that Hugh Hughs was a Company tenant, he was listed as one of Harwood's servants. His wife, Ann, also was classified as a Harwood servant (FER 339; CBE 42, 61).

ANN HUGHS (HUGHES, HUES) (MRS. HUGH HUGHS [HUGHES, HUES])

Ann, the wife of Hugh Hughs (Hughes, Hues), came to Virginia on the *Abigail*. On February 4, 1625, she and her husband were living at Martin's Hundred (**7**) where they were listed as servants in the household of headman William Harwood. Other Harwood servants came to the colony in 1623 on the *Abigail*, raising the possibility that Ann came at that time (CBE 61).

***

LEWIS HUGHS

On September 28, 1628, the Privy Council decided that a few people would be deliv-

ered to the Rev. Lewis Hughs so that they could be sent to Virginia (CBE 84).

WILLIAM HUELETT (HULETT)

Sometime prior to December 1635, William Huelett (Hulett) and three other men went to Virginia on the *Constance* as servants of Christopher Boyse, a Virginia planter and resident of Blunt Point (**22**) (EAE 58, 60).

GEORGE HULL

Sometime prior to July 3, 1635, George Hull began occupying some land in Elizabeth City (**19**) near the New Poquoson River and Thomas Garnett's property. On October 12, 1635, he was credited with 450 acres in the same vicinity (PB 1 Pt. 1:101, 292).

JEFFREY (JEFFRIE) HULL

Jeffrey (Jeffrie) Hull came to Virginia on the *George* in 1617. On February 4, 1625, he was living at Hog Island (**16**) where he was identified as one of Ralph Hamor's servants. On August 26, 1633, Hull was identified as one of the late Elizabeth Clements' servants when her son and heir, Jeremiah II, patented some land (CBE 61; PB 1 Pt. 1:124).

PETER HULL

Sometime prior to February 10, 1635, Peter Hull of Blunt Point (**22**) acquired a tract of land at the head of Merchants Hope Creek and conveyed it to Richard Tisdall. On November 20, 1636, Hull received a bequest from the Rev. Thomas Butler (PB 1 Pt. 2:697; WITH 49).

JOHN HULLAWAY (SEE JOHN KULLAWAY)

ROBERT HUMESDON (HUMERDON)

Robert Humesdon (Humerdon), a butcher, embarked for Virginia on April 17, 1619, at the expense of the Virginia Company. He probably was a Company servant or tenant (FER 107).

JOAN (JONE) HUMFREY (HUMPHREY)

On February 27, 1619, Joan (Jone) Humfrey (Humphrey), a young wench, was identified as one of the youngsters brought in from the streets of London so that they could be sent to Virginia (CBE 13).

JOHN HUMFREY (HUMFREYS)

On March 16, 1627, 23-year-old John Humfrey (Humfreys) testified that while he was aboard the *Plantation*, he saw Robert Cooke and Thomas Lawley fight, and Lawley's chest was badly injured. In September 1656 John Humfrey's will was proved. He was from Honiton, in Devon, but died in Virginia. Administration of his estate was given to his brother, Henry Humfrey (MCGC 145-146; EEAC 31).

THOMAS HUMFREY

On July 31, 1622, Thomas Humfrey set sail for Virginia on the *James* and accompanied Richard Tatem (FER 400).

WILLIAM HUMFREY

In 1621 William Humfrey was identified as one of the men going to Jamestown (1) on the *Faulcon* (EAE 11).

GEORGE HUMFREYS (HUMPHREYS)

On July 26, 1628, officials at Bridewell decided that George Humfreys (Humphreys), a boy from Vintrey Ward who was being detained at Bridewell or Bethlem, would be sent to Virginia (HUME 33).

EDMUND HUN

On November 6, 1622, Edmund Hun received a share of Virginia land from Virginia Company investor John Ferrar (VCR 2:122).

JOHN HUNT

On March 22, 1622, when the Indians attacked Captain Berkeley's plantation at Falling Creek (68), John Hunt was slain (VCR 3:565).

NICHOLAS HUNT

Nicholas Hunt perished on March 22, 1622, when the Indians attacked Edward Bennett's plantation in Warresqueak (26) (VCR 3:571).

ROBERT HUNT

The Rev. Robert Hunt, who immigrated to Virginia in the first party of settlers, was the vicar of Heathfield Parish, in Sussex, England. When he prepared his will on November 20, 1606, he mentioned his wife, Elizabeth, and a son and daughter. Hunt apparently suspected that his wife was unfaithful, for he put numerous restrictions on her widowhood. For example, if she were to associate with her neighbor, John Taylor Jr., she stood to be disinherited. According to Captain John Smith, the Rev. Robert Hunt became quite ill before his ship left England. However, he survived the transatlantic crossing and administered to the needs of the first colonists by preaching and performing other religious duties. On January 1608, when the fort accidentally caught on fire, all of his books, clothing, and personal belongings were destroyed. Hunt apparently died within a few months, for his will was proved in England on July 14, 1608 (WITH 427; CJS 1:140, 204, 207, 214, 217; 2:137, 153, 157).

ROBERT HUNT

On February 27, 1619, Robert Hunt, a boy, was one of the youngsters brought in from the streets of London so that they could be transported to Virginia (CBE 12).

THOMAS HUNT (HUNTE)

In December 1619 Thomas Hunt (Hunte), who was brought in from the streets of London, was detained at Bridewell until he could be sent to Virginia or Bermuda (CBE 15).

THOMAS HUNT

On May 26, 1630, Thomas Hunt, who indicated that he was familiar with Sir George Yeardley's handwriting, was among those who proved his October 12, 1627, will, which was made at Jamestown (1). Hunt may have been a Yeardley servant (SR 9963; C 24/561 Pt. 2 f 6).

ROBERT HUNTER

On October 10, 1618, officials at Bridewell decided that Robert Hunter, a vagrant brought in from Wood Street, would be sent to Virginia (CBE 10).

ROBERT HUNTER

On February 27, 1619, Robert Hunter, a boy, was among the youngsters brought in from the streets of London so that they could be transported to the colony (CBE 12-13).

***

THOMAS HUNTER

Thomas Hunter died in Elizabeth City (18) sometime after February 16, 1624, but before early 1625. On January 10, 1627, John Arundell testified that Edward Waters had brought the decedent's will to court and said that Hunter was of sound mind at the time he made it. On February 10, 1629, the General Court ordered Waters, who had been given letters of administration, to deliver Thomas Hunter's estate to Richard Cocke, Patrick Canada's attorney. However, the General Court's justices reversed their order on March 2, 1629, and instructed Waters to retain custody of the estate, as Hunter's widow, Cecily, was presenting claims against it (CBE 67; MCGC 130, 186-187).

CECILY HUNTER
(MRS. THOMAS HUNTER)

On March 2, 1629, the General Court was informed that Cecily, Thomas Hunter's widow, wanted the proceeds of his estate, which Edward Waters (as Hunter's administrator) had in his custody (MCGC 187).

***

EDWARD HURD

In early May 1623 the Virginia Company granted a patent to Edward Hurd and his associates, who were planning to transport 100 people to Virginia on July 19, 1627. Hurd, a London ironmonger, shipped some goods to Virginia on the *James*. On March 31, 1628, he asked the General Court to see that the meal he had sent to Thomas Harwood of Mulberry Island (21) was released. He claimed that Captain William Stone had detained it unlawfully in the West Indies. On February 9, 1633, Thomas Harwood asked the General Court to note that he was giving Edward Hurd's servant, Thomas Sparkes, his freedom dues. In January 1643 Hurd was listed as a creditor

of Mrs. Anne Ganey, a widow who had died in Virginia (VCR 2:412, 428; CBE 79; MCGC 170-171, 202; EEAC 23).

JOHN HURD

John Hurd set sail for Virginia on September 15, 1619, on the *Margaret* of Bristol. He accompanied Captain John Woodlief, one of the principal leaders of Berkeley Hundred (55). John's contract with the Society of Berkeley Hundred's investors specified that he serve for six years under Captain Woodlief's supervision in exchange for 30 acres of land. Walter Hampton died within a relatively short time after he reached the colony (CBE 14; VCR 3:188, 198, 213).

JOHN HURDEN

On February 27, 1619, John Hurden, a boy, was one of the youngsters brought in from the streets of London so that they could be transported to Virginia (CBE 13).

JOHN HURLESTON (HURLSTONE, HARLESTON)

In May 1625 John Hurleston (Hurlstone), a mariner, was credited with 100 acres of land below Blunt Point (22), acreage that had not been planted (seated). He also was listed as patentee of some acreage in Tappahannah, property within the corporation of Charles City that had been planted; however, no amount of land was listed. On August 12, 1626, John was identified as master of the *Marmaduke*. Then on July 31, 1627, he was master of the *Thomas and John*. It is likely that John was one of the mariners who acquired substantial quantities of land by bringing indentured servants to the colony and availing himself of the headright system (VCR 4:555, 557; CBE 73, 79).

THOMAS HURLESTON
(HURLSTONE)

On July 17, 1627, Thomas Hurleston (Hurlstone) was identified as master of the *Robert and John*, which was taking a shipment of goods to Virginia (CBE 79).

TOBIAS (TOBY) HURST (HURT)

Tobias (Toby) Hurst (Hurt) came to Virginia on the *Treasurer* in 1618 and on February 16, 1624, was living in Elizabeth City (**18**). He was still there in early 1625 and was a 22-year-old household head who lived alone. He had on hand an ample supply of stored food and defensive weaponry (CBE 44, 66; DOR 1:62).

[NO FIRST NAME] HURT

On March 22, 1622, when the Indians attacked Weyanoke (**52**), a man named Hurt was slain. He was one of Sir George Yeardley's men (VCR 3:569).

[NO FIRST NAME] HURT

On December 8, 1628, Mrs. Hurt, whose first name is unknown, was identified by the General Court as owner of the ship *Truelove*, for which the late John Crosse (Cross) had served as merchant. Crosse reportedly accepted some money from William Hosier and passed it along to Mrs. Hurt. Hosier later sued John Crosse's estate in an attempt to recover his funds (MCGC 178, 180).

EDWARD HUSON (HAWSONE) (SEE EDWARD HUDSON)

***

LEONARD HUSON (HUSONE) (SEE LEONARD HUDSON)
MRS. LEONARD HUSON (HUSONE) (SEE MRS. LEONARD HUDSON)

***

THOMAS HUSON (HUSONE) (SEE THOMAS HUDSON)

[NO FIRST NAME] HUSSY

Mr. Hussy died in Elizabeth City (**17, 18**) sometime after April 1623 but before February 16, 1624 (CBE 45).

ROBERT HUSSYE

Robert Hussye died at Flowerdew Hundred (**53**) sometime after April 1623 but before February 16, 1624 (CBE 51).

ROBERT HUTCHINS

In May 1625 when a list of patented land was sent back to England, Robert Hutchins

was credited with 100 acres below Blunt Point (**22**), acreage that was undeveloped. On March 14, 1628, Robert was identified as a mariner when his land was mentioned in an Elizabeth City patent for acreage below Waters Creek, now dammed to form Lake Maury (VCR 4:557; PB 1 Pt. 1:70).

THOMAS HUTCHINS

On January 22, 1620, officials at Bridewell decided that Thomas Hutchens, a detainee from Aldermanbury, would be sent to Virginia (CBE 17).

[NO FIRST NAME] HUTCHINSON

On July 31, 1622, a Mr. Hutchinson, whose given name is unknown, brought Edward Thomas to Virginia on the *James* (FER 400).

***

HENRY HUTCHINSON

On March 13, 1622, Virginia Company officials noted that Henry Hutchinson of London had gotten some Virginia land from Captain Ralph Hamor. Henry's son, William, came to Virginia and settled in Warresqueak (**26**), where he died during the mid-1630s. Henry Hutchinson came to the colony to settle William's estate but died in Virginia (VCR 1:619; EAE 73; BOD 93-95).

WILLIAM HUTCHINSON

William Hutchinson came to Virginia on the *Diana* in 1618 and on February 16, 1624, was living in Elizabeth City (**18**). He was still there in early 1625 and was described as a 21-year-old a servant in Captain William Tucker's household. Meanwhile, in March 1622, William Hutchinson's father, Henry Hutchinson of London, had obtained some shares of Virginia land. Sometime prior to February 1632 William Hutchinson settled in Warresqueak (later Isle of Wight County) where he became a commissioner of the local court and, eventually, a burgess. He died there during the mid-1630s. His father, Henry, came to Virginia to settle his estate but died in the colony. Thomas Burbage was ordered to take an inventory of William Hutchinson's estate and to dispose of his goods. Hutchinson was relatively wealthy and was in possession of a plantation, livestock, and servants in Virginia (CBE 43, 63; HEN 1:169, 179, 187; EAE 73; BOD 93-95).

***

ROBERT HUTCHINSON

Robert Hutchinson, a mariner, came to Virginia sometime prior to February 16, 1624, at which time he was living in Pasbehay on the Governor's Land (3). He was a colorful character and during his first few years in the colony had many skirmishes with the law. In August 1626 he was censured for being drunk and disorderly, and a few months later he was fined for misbehaving in court. He also was found guilty of committing adultery with the wife of his neighbor, Thomas Jones, one of his favorite drinking companions. In January 1627 Hutchinson asked permission to leave Pasbehay in order to move elsewhere. At that time he was identified as a planter. During 1629 Hutchinson was jailed for indebtedness and on another occasion was fined for refusing to assist the provost marshal in carrying out his official duties. By 1639 Robert Hutchinson apparently had gained respectability. It was then that he and Thomas Harvey were appointed tobacco viewers (or inspectors) for a region that encompassed Jamestown Island (1), Pasbehay, and the Maine. Hutchinson's selection indicates that he resided within the territory he served. Robert Hutchinson's upward mobility seems to have continued, for by 1640 he had become the sheriff of James City County, an indication that he was a local justice of the peace. He apparently found favor with Governor John Harvey, for he was paid generously with some of the goods Harvey seized from the Rev. Anthony Panton of York County. A high point in Captain Robert Hutchinson's political career was his election to the assembly in 1641, a post he held until at least November 1647. In May 1642 Captain Robert Hutchinson obtained a lease for a 100-acre parcel in the Governor's Land, adjacent to Sir Francis Wyatt's acreage. On June 12, 1648, he doubled the size of his leasehold and obtained a 21-year rental agreement. The following day, he assigned his lease to Sir William Berkeley. The acreage Hutchinson leased appears to have been in the northeastern part of the Governor's Land, near Green Spring. On February 22, 1643, Captain Robert Hutchinson obtained a patent for a lot on Jamestown Island, acreage that originally belonged to Sir George Yeardley. Hutchinson was obliged to develop his lot within six months or face forfeiture. Robert Hutchinson apparently died sometime prior to July 1650, at which time his sister, Jane, was named his administrator (CBE 39; MCGC 107-108, 119, 129, 144, 199, 190, 197, 496-497; STAN 61, 63-64, 66; PB 1 Pt. 2:757, 772, 944; HEN 1:239, 289; EEAC 31; SR 9963; C 24/561 Pt. 1:8).

SUSAN HUTCHINSON

On February 27, 1619, Susan Hutchinson, a young wench, was one of the youngsters brought in from the streets of London so that they could be transported to the colony (CBE 13).

NATHANIEL HUTT

Sometime prior to August 14, 1624, ancient planter Nathaniel Hutt received a patent for 12 acres of land on Jamestown Island (1) at Black Point. He apparently relocated sometime prior to January 24, 1625, for by that date his acreage and tenement on Jamestown Island had come into the hands of Percival Wood and his wife. In May 1625, when a list of patented land was sent back to England, Nathaniel Hutt, who was identified as an ancient planter, was credited with 200 acres near Mulberry Island (21) (PB 1 Pt. 1:11; MCGC 45; VCR 4:556).

DANIEL HUTTON

Daniel Hutton came to Virginia on the *Hopewell* in 1633 at the expense of Adam Thorogood, who used him as a headright when patenting some land on June 24, 1635 (PB 1 Pt. 1:179).

***

JOHN HUTTON

On February 16, 1624, John Hutton and his wife, Elizabeth, were living in Elizabeth City (18) (CBE 44).

ELIZABETH HUTTON (MRS. JOHN HUTTON)

On February 16, 1624, Elizabeth Hutton and her husband, John, were living in Elizabeth City (18) (CBE 44).

***

LAWRENCE HYDE (HIDE)

On May 16, 1621, Virginia Company officials noted that Sir Lawrence Hyde (Hide) and his brother, Nicholas, had sent some servants to Virginia. They were placed at Martin's Hundred **(7)** where they were under the supervision of John Boyse (VCR 3:450-451).

NICHOLAS HYDE (HIDE)

Sometime prior to May 16, 1621, Nicholas Hyde (Hide) dispatched his servant, Stephen Collins, to Virginia. Collins was sent to Martin's Hundred **(7)** and placed in the household of John Boyce. On January 3, 1625, the General Court noted that Nicholas Hyde had borrowed some money from John Elyson. Jamestown **(1)** merchant John Southern acknowledged that he had posted a bond, guaranteeing that Hyde's debt would be repaid (VCR 3:451; MCGC 40).

THOMAS HYNDE

Thomas Hynde came to Virginia with William Rowley on the *James* and left England on July 31, 1622. Rowley and his household lived on Jamestown Island **(1)** (FER 400).

I

***

PERCIVAL IBOTSON (IBBOTTSON, IBBISON)

Percival Ibotson (Ibbottson, Ibbison) came to Virginia in 1618 on the *Neptune*, the ship on which Lord Delaware set sail for the colony. On February 16, 1624, he was living in Elizabeth City **(18)** with his wife, Elizabeth, and daughter or sister, Ann. On August 14, 1624, Percival Ibotson's land was mentioned in a patent for acreage east of Blunt Point **(22)**. In May 1625, when a list of patented land was set back to England, Ibotson was credited with a 50-acre tract at Blunt Point. When a muster was compiled in early 1625, Percival Ibotson was described as a 24-year-old household head who shared his home with his 23-year-old wife, Elizabeth, and two male servants. Also present was John Davis, who was free. Missing was the name of Ann Ibotson. Percival Ibotson was credited with two dwellings and was amply

supplied with stored food and defensive weaponry. On April 11, 1625, he and some other men were summoned before the General Court to testify about some cattle that Lieutenant Sheppard had assigned to Captain Crowshaw (CBE 44, 66; PB 1 Pt. 1:18; VCR 4:557; MCGC 52; DOR 1:60).

ELIZABETH IBOTSON (IBBOTTSON, IBBISON) (MRS. PERCIVAL IBOTSON [IBBOTTSON, IBBISON])

Elizabeth, who married Percival Ibotson (Ibbottson, Ibbison), came to Virginia in 1623 on the *Flying Hart*. On February 16, 1624, she was living in Elizabeth City **(18)** with her husband, Percival, and his daughter or sister, Ann. When a muster was taken in early 1625, Elizabeth Ibotson was described as age 23. Missing from the household was Ann Ibotson. The Ibotsons shared their home at Blunt Point **(22)** with two male indentured servants and a man who was free (CBE 44, 66).

ANN IBOTSON (IBBOTTSON, IBBISON)

On February 16, 1624, Ann Ibotson (Ibbottson, Ibbison) was living in Elizabeth City **(18)** with her 24-year-old father or brother, Percival Ibotson, and his wife, Elizabeth. When a muster was compiled in early 1625, Ann's name was missing, suggesting that she was deceased, had married, or was overlooked by the officials gathering demographic records (CBE 44).

***

JONADAB ILLETT

On February 16, 1624, Jonadab Illett was living in Elizabeth City on the west side of the Hampton River **(18)** (CBE 44).

GODFREY INGE

In 1621 Godfrey Inge was identified as one of the men associated with the East India School, which was to be built in Virginia (FER 272).

JOHN INGRAM

On November 30, 1622, John Ingram, an inmate of Newgate Prison, was among those pardoned on account of an epidemic of jail fever. He was to be put to work or transported overseas, possibly to Virginia (CBE 29).

JOHN INMAN (INIMAN, JINMAN)

John Inman (Iniman, Jinman) came to Virginia on the *Falcon* in 1619 and on February 16, 1624, was residing in Elizabeth City. When a muster list was compiled in early 1625, Inman, who was then 26 years old, was residing in Richard Mintrene's household in Elizabeth City (**18**). On March 3, 1629, John Inman, who identified himself as a surgeon, went to court in an attempt to gain his freedom. It was then noted that he and some other servants had been transported to Virginia by Edward Bennett. Inman was ordered to continue serving Bennett until he received word from England that he should be freed. As Bennett owned the Warresqueak plantation called Bennett's Welcome (**26**), John Inman may have been residing there in 1629 (CBE 44, 65; MCGC 188).

JOHN INNES

On February 26, 1620, John Innes, a prisoner in Newgate, was among those being sent to Virginia (CBE 19).

IOTAN
(SEE OPITCHAPAM)

JOHN IRELAND

On May 5, 1622, the Privy Council decided that John Ireland, a prisoner in the White Lion in Southwark, would be sent to Virginia (CBE 27).

JOHN IRELAND

On September 7, 1626, John Ireland was identified as master of the *Peter and John*. He was going to take a shipment of goods to Virginia (CBE 73).

RICHARD IRNEST (ERNEST?)

Richard Irnest (Ernest?) came to Virginia on the *Marmaduke* in 1621 and was one of Richard Pace's servants, probably at Paces Paines (**9**). On September 1, 1628, when Pace's son and heir, George Pace, patented some land, he used Richard Irnest's headright and indicated that his father had paid the cost of Irnest's transportation to the colony (PB 1 Pt. 1:64).

THOMAS IRONMONGER

On January 21, 1625, Thomas Ironmonger was living at Jordan's Journey (**46**), where he was a solitary household head who had an ample supply of stored food and defensive weaponry. On January 28, 1628, Ironmonger appeared before the General Court on account of some suits that were pending. He had had Sergeant John Harris of Shirley Hundred (**41**) arrested because of a debt, and Ironmonger himself was being sued by Bridget, the widow of surgeon Thomas Bunn. It is uncertain when Thomas Ironmonger arrived in the colony or how long he survived (CBE 52; MCGC 160).

[NO FIRST NAME] ISAAC
(ISAACK)

Mr. Isaac (Issack), a 26-year-old man who resided in Dr. John Pott's house in urban Jamestown (**1**), was among those implicated in killing and butchering a calf on February 24, 1622 or 1623. The case was discussed by the justices of the General Court on March 1, 1623 (MCGC 3-4).

ISABELLA (ISABELL)

On February 16, 1624, Isabella (Isabell), an African, was living in Elizabeth City (**18**) in Captain William Tucker's household. She was still there in early 1625, at which time she was identified as a servant. Listed with Isabella in 1624 was an African manservant named Anthony, her husband. By early 1625 Anthony and Isabella had a child, William, and all three had been baptized (CBE 43, 63).

GEORGE ISACKE

In March 1618 George Isacke was reprieved by the Middlesex Court and sentenced to transportation to Virginia (CBE 8).

JOHN ISGRAVE

On February 16, 1624, John Isgrave was living in George Graves I's household in urban Jamestown (**1**) (CBE 38).

FRANCIS ISLEY

Francis Isley, a bricklayer, was included in an April 17, 1619, list of people who immigrated to Virginia (FER 107).

ITOYATIN
(SEE OPITCHAPAM)

ANTON IVE

Anton Ive left England on July 31, 1622, on the *James*. He accompanied his master, William Rowley, who was heading to Jamestown (1) (FER 400).

J

SOLOMAN JACKMAN

Soloman Jackman came to Virginia on the *Southampton* in 1623. On January 20, 1625, he was living at Flowerdew Hundred (53), where he was a 30-year-old servant in Abraham Peirsey's household (CBE 50).

ANN (ANNE) JACKSON

In August 1621 Ann (Anne) Jackson, one of the young, marriageable maids sent to Virginia by the Virginia Company of London, set sail from Portsmouth, England, on the *Marmaduke*. Her father, William, described in Company records as an honest man, was a gardener in Tuttleside, near the Red Lion in the Westminster area of London. Ann, who was age 21, was bound for Martin's Hundred (7) to join her brother, John Jackson. When the Indians attacked Martin's Hundred on March 22, 1622, Ann was one of the 19 women they captured and spirited away to their stronghold on the Pamunkey River. At first, the missing women were presumed dead. However, some survived and were ransomed the following spring. Ann probably was the girl named Jackson who was living in John Jackson's Martin's Hundred household on February 16, 1624. Ann Jackson apparently never fully recovered from her ordeal and was eager to return to England. In January 1629, her brother, John, a bricklayer at Martin's Hundred, promised the justices of the General Court that he would "keep her safe" and see

that she was provided with transportation back to England (FER 306, 309; MCGC 181; VCR 3:570; 4:232; CBR 42).

BENJAMIN JACKSON

Benjamin Jackson, whose house was at Blunt Point (22), was the master of John Gay, a young servant who impetuously stabbed John Burrows (MCGC 183).

BERNARD (BARNARD) JACKSON

Bernard (Barnard) Jackson came to Virginia on the *Margaret and John* in 1623 and on February 16, 1624, was living on West and Shirley Hundred Island (41). He died there sometime prior to January 22, 1625 (CBE 36, 53).

EPHRIAM JACKSON

On February 16, 1624, Ephriam Jackson, who appears to have been an adult, was living in gunsmith John Jackson's household in urban Jamestown (1) (CBE 38).

***

JOHN JACKSON (JAXON) I

Sometime prior to 1623, gunsmith John Jackson (Jaxon) I patented a waterfront lot in urban Jamestown (1), next door to merchant Richard Stephens. Jackson and his wife befriended Richard Frethorne, a young servant in the household of William Harwood, the leader of Martin's Hundred (7). In April 1623 Frethorne told his parents that whenever Mr. Harwood sent him and his fellow servants to Jamestown, he stayed with the Jacksons, who were kind and generous and treated him like a son. He said that they provided him with food and had built a cabin in which he could take shelter whenever he came to town. Otherwise, he added, he would have been obliged to huddle overnight in an open boat, regardless of the weather. Frethorne said that the Jacksons gave him extra food to take back to Martin's Hundred, where living conditions were harsh, and he noted that Goodman John Jackson of Jamestown and John Jackson of Martin's Hundred were kinsmen. On February 16, 1624, when a census was made of Jamestown's inhabitants, John Jackson, his wife, and an adult male named Ephraim Jackson were sharing a home. William Jackson, who died between April 1623 and February 16, 1624, also had been living in Jamestown, perhaps in the same household, and John Jackson's neighbor, Richard Stephens, then had in his employ a Virginia Company tenant named John Jackson. On January 24, 1625, when a muster was made, John Jackson of Jamestown headed an all-male household that included himself, his 9-year-old son, John II, and 10-year-old Gercian Buck, one of the late Rev. Richard Buck's orphans. The Jackson household was in possession of an ample supply of stored food, a gun, ammunition, and some livestock.

Court records suggest that John Jackson, a gunsmith, was in partnership with George Clarke, who plied the same trade. A March 1623 court case made reference to a theft that occurred while "Jackson the smith was at work in the shop" with his partner, and after Clarke's death, Jackson was called on to testify about one of his debts. In 1624 Jackson informed the General Court about a rumor he had heard concerning the marriageable but slow-witted orphan Mara Buck. He also participated in a coroner's inquest, performed jury duty, and in 1626 certified the will of Jamestown neighbor Thomas Alnutt. In 1627–1628 John Jackson was sued by mariner-and-merchant John Gill, from whom he had bought an indentured servant who was a gunsmith. As Jackson failed to fully pay what he owed, Gill brought suit. In 1629 Jackson was named substitute administrator of Abraham Porter's estate, replacing his neighbor, Captain William Peirce. John Jackson's fiduciary appointment, done at Peirce's request, and his selection as one of the Buck children's guardians, suggests that he was a respected member of the community. As a guardian, Jackson testified about the medical treatment John Dyos (a resident of Jamestown Island) provided to the Buck orphans' cattle, and he took custody of the tobacco that John Gunnery of Elizabeth City **(17, 18)** owed to the Buck estate. In 1629, while John Jackson was serving as a James City Parish churchwarden and commander of the Neck O'Land **(5)** behind Jamestown Island, Edward Wigg stole his canoe. In 1632 and 1633 Jackson represented Jamestown in the assembly and continued as commander of the Neck O'Land community. In 1637 and 1638 he patented some acreage in Charles River (York) County and on the Chickahominy River. Afterward, his name disappeared from official records (PB 1:Pt. 1:1; MCGC 4-5, 15-16, 33, 53, 102-103, 107-108, 161, 169, 184, 187-188, 192, 197, 200; CBE 38, 55; VCR 4:41, 59-60; HEN 1:178, 203; NUG 1:65, 97; DOR 1:32).

MRS. JOHN JACKSON

Mrs. John Jackson of urban Jamestown **(1)**, whose first name is unknown, tended to Martin's Hundred servant Richard Frethorne with motherly kindness. On February 16, 1624, when a census was taken of the colony's inhabitants, Mrs. Jackson was living in the Jamestown household headed by her husband, John, a gunsmith. Also present was 8-year-old John Jackson II and Ephraim Jackson. On January 24, 1625, when a muster was made, Mrs. Jackson's name was absent from the demographic records that were compiled, perhaps because she was deceased (VCR 4:59-60; CBE 38).

JOHN JACKSON II

On January 24, 1625, 9-year-old John Jackson II, the son of gunsmith John Jackson, was living in urban Jamestown **(1)** in a household headed by his father and mother or stepmother. Also present was Ephraim Jackson. It is uncertain whether John Jackson II's name was omitted from the February 1624 census or whether he came to the colony after the census was compiled (CBE 55; DOR 1:32).

***

JOHN JACKSON (JAXON)

On February 16, 1624, John Jackson was living in merchant Richard Stephens' household in urban Jamestown **(1)**. Jackson was a Virginia Company tenant who on January 12, 1627, was assigned to Sir George Yeardley, also a resident of Jamestown Island. John may have been related to gunsmith John Jackson, who lived next door (CBE 38; MCGC 136).

***

JOHN JACKSON (JAXON) I

John Jackson (Jaxon) I came to Virginia in 1619 on the *Warwick* and was the son of William Jackson, a gardener who resided in Tuttleside, near the Red Lion in the Westminster area of London. In July and August 1619, when the colony's assembly first convened, John Jackson served as a burgess for Martin's Hundred (**7**). Like the other colonists who came to plant a settlement at Martin's Hundred, he would have spent 1619 and the early part of 1620 at Argall Town, a community that Deputy Governor Samuel Argall established on part of the acreage the Virginia Company had designated as the Governor's Land (**3**). In 1621 John Jackson's sister, Ann, joined the Jackson household at Martin's Hundred. On March 22, 1622, when the Indians raided the settlement, she was captured and one of the Jackson children was killed. When a census was taken on February 16, 1624, John Jackson headed a household that included his wife and a girl, perhaps his sister, Ann, who had been ransomed from the Indians. On February 4, 1625, when a muster was made of Martin's Hundred's inhabitants, John Jackson, his wife, Ann, and their 20-week-old son shared a home with two male servants, Thomas Ward and John Stephens. A letter John Jackson wrote on May 20, 1625, complaining about the dangerous living conditions at Martin's Hundred and workers' shortage of tools and clothing, reveals that he was a bricklayer and that Thomas Ward was a potter. During early 1625 Jackson was ordered to appear before the General Court, where he, on behalf of Martin's Hundred's residents, was asked to account for Sir Samuel Argall's cattle. During August 1626, John Jackson testified in court about an incident that took place at Warresqueak (**26**). He returned to court on January 8, 1627, where he talked about accompanying Robert Lindsey and some Indians to Pamunkey in April 1626. He said that the Indians had permitted him to leave but that Lindsey was detained. Jackson was back in court on January 20, 1629, and was ordered to send his sister, Ann, to England as soon as possible and to keep her safe until that time. William Harwood, Martin's Hundred's leader, was instructed to see that this was accomplished (VCR 3:154, 570; FER 309, 569; CBE 42, 62; MCGC 53, 55, 110, 128, 181; DOR 1:46).

ANN JACKSON (JAXON) (MRS. JOHN JACKSON)

Ann, the wife of John Jackson (Jaxon) of Martin's Hundred (**7**), came to Virginia on the *Warwick* and on February 16, 1624, she

and her husband were sharing a home. On February 4, 1625, she and her husband and their 20-week-old son, John II, were living at Martin's Hundred. She may have been the mother of the Jackson child killed at Martin's Hundred during the March 22, 1622, Indian attack (CBE 62).

[NO FIRST NAME] JACKSON (JAXON)

On March 22, 1622, when the Indians attacked Martin's Hundred (**7**), John Jackson's (Jaxon's) child was killed (VCR 3:570).

JOHN JACKSON (JAXON) II

On February 4, 1625, when a muster was made of Martin's Hundred's (**7**) inhabitants, 20-week-old John Jackson (Jaxon) II was living with his parents, Ann and John Jackson (CBE 42).

***

JOHN JACKSON

On February 16, 1624, John Jackson was living in Elizabeth City (**17, 18**). He died and was buried on May 12, 1624 (CBE 43, 67).

JOHN JACKSON

John Jackson came to Virginia on the *Abigail*. On February 4, 1625, he was living in the Neck O' Land (**5**) where he was an indentured servant in Richard Kingsmill's household (CBE 58).

JOHN JACKSON

On June 9, 1635, John Jackson patented 100 acres on Chisman Creek, in what became lower York County (**19**), using two servants as headrights (PB 1 Pt. 1:242).

MRS. JOHN JACKSON

In 1629 the churchwardens of Stanley Hundred (Newportes News) (**24**) informed the General Court that Mrs. John Jackson had committed adultery with Henry King while her husband was away. King was ordered to stay elsewhere, which suggests that he may have been sharing a dwelling with Mrs. Jackson (MCGC 200).

ROBERT JACKSON

On May 20, 1607, Robert Jackson, a sailor aboard one of the vessels that brought the first Jamestown (1) colonists to Virginia, accompanied Captain Christopher Newport on an exploratory voyage of the James River (HAI 102).

WALTER JACKSON

Walter Jackson came to Virginia in 1623 on the *Southampton*. On January 20, 1625, he was living at Flowerdew Hundred (53) and was a 24-year-old servant in Abraham Peirsey's household (CBE 50).

WILLIAM JACKSON

William Jackson came to Virginia on the *Furtherance*. He died on Jamestown Island (1) sometime after April 1623 but before February 16, 1624 (CBE 39).

THOMAS JACOB

Thomas Jacob, a gentleman and one of the first planters, resided in Jamestown (1). According to George Percy, he died on September 4, 1607, at which time he held the rank of sergeant (CJS 2:141; HAI 99).

WILLIAM JACOB

On July 19, 1633, William Jacob, a boy brought in from Fleet Street in London, indicated that he was willing to go to Virginia (HUME 38).

***

HENRY JACOBS

Court testimony taken on February 7, 1628, indicates that the Rev. Henry Jacobs died in 1622–1623. Afterward, merchant Richard Stephens, the Rev. Richard Buck, and Provost Marshal Randall Smallwood, all of whom lived in Jamestown (1), assisted in settling his estate. Stephens was named Jacobs' administrator, whereas Buck and Smallwood inventoried his personal possessions (MCGC 163-164).

SARA JACOBS
(MRS. HENRY JACOBS)

On February 7, 1628, the justices of the General Court discussed a request they had received from Sara, the widow of the Rev. Henry Jacobs. Mrs. Jacobs asked that administrator Richard Stephens be allowed to sell her late husband's goods and send the proceeds to her in England (MCGC 164).

***

***

JAMES JACOBSON

On May 20, 1622, the Virginia Company assigned Phillip Jacobson's shares of Virginia land to his brother, James. Both men were identified as English merchants (VCR 2:17).

PHILLIP JACOBSON

Officials of the Virginia Company assigned Phillip Jacobson's shares of Virginia land to his brother, James, on May 20, 1622. The Jacobson brothers were English merchants (VCR 2:17).

***

***

THOMAS JADWIN
(JADWYN, JUDWIN, JUDWYN) I

Captain John Smith identified Thomas Jadwin (Jadwyn, Judwin, Judwyn) I as a Virginia Company investor who in 1615 had shares of land in Bermuda. Company records dating to July 2, 1621, indicate that he attempted to recover some money owed to him by the late Thomas Woodlief. On November 4, 1626, when Thomas Jadwin made his will, he identified himself as a cutler and a resident of St. Michael, Paternoster Row, London. He named his widow, Elizabeth, as his executrix and bequeathed his Virginia land to his son, Thomas II. Thomas Jadwin I died sometime prior to March 5, 1628, at which time his will was presented for probate (CJS 2:370; VCR 1:501; EEAC 32; WAT 289; CBE 82).

THOMAS JADWIN (JADWYN, JUDWIN, JUDWYN) II

Thomas Jadwin (Jadwyn, Judwin, Judwyn) II, the son and principal heir of his father, Thomas Jadwin (Jadwyn, Judwin, Judwyn) I, a London cutler, inherited his Virginia land sometime prior to March 5, 1628. It is uncertain whether Thomas Jadwin II asserted his claim or came to Virginia (EEAC 32; WAT 289; CBE 82).

***

JAMES JAKINS

James Jakins died in Jamestown (1) sometime after April 1623 but before February 16, 1624 (CBE 39).

JAMES

An Irishman named James died in Elizabeth City (18) sometime after April 1623 but before February 16, 1624 (CBE 45).

JAMES

On February 16, 1624, a man known as James, "called piper," was living on the Eastern Shore (72-78) (CBE 46).

JAMES

James, a Frenchman, was living in Elizabeth City on the east side of the Hampton River at the Indian Thicket (17), part of the Virginia Company's land, on February 16, 1624 (CBE 43).

***

JOHN JAMES

John James, who was entitled to some land in Martin's Hundred (7), died sometime prior to April 28, 1624, leaving three shares of land he had procured from the Virginia Company. By that date, John's widow had remarried and her new husband, Captain John Bernard (Barnard), also had died. George Furzman, who had obtained part of John James's land at Martin's Hundred from Captain Bernard, noted that James's heirs retained a legal interest in the remainder (VCR 2:532-533).

MRS. JOHN JAMES
(MRS. JOHN BERNARD [BARNARD])

Mrs. John James outlived her husband, a Virginia Company investor who owned three shares of land in Martin's Hundred (7). The widowed Mrs. James married Captain John Bernard (Barnard), who conveyed part of John James's land to George Furzman. By

April 28, 1624, Captain Bernard and his wife were dead (VCR 2:532-533).

***

RICHARD JAMES

In October 1628 the Rev. Richard James informed the justices of the General Court that he had been at Mr. Robert Poole's house in Elizabeth City (18) when Lieutenant Thomas Flint complained about the incumbent governor and expressed his desire to see him replaced (MCGC 176).

[NO FIRST NAME] JANES

On July 15, 1631, Mrs. Janes, a Virginia planter who was among those asking for relief from customs duties, described herself as a very poor woman. Mrs. Janes's hogsheads of tobacco reportedly were unmarked (G&M 166).

THOMAS JANNY

Thomas Janny was sent to Virginia by the Company of Mercers sometime prior to 1622 (FER 297).

JAPAZOUS

In January 1620 Japazous, the brother of the King of the Potomac Indians, came to Jamestown (1) and invited the colonists to trade (VCR 3:244).

SAMUEL JARRETT (JARRET)

On March 22, 1622, when the Indians attacked Flowerdew Hundred (53), Samuel Jarrett (Jarret) was killed. In May 1625 when a list of patented land was sent to England, Jarrett was credited with 100 acres in Charles City. This raises the possibility that he was an ancient planter (VCR 3:568; 4:553).

WILLIAM JARRETT

On November 13, 1620, William Jarrett was identified as an ancient planter who had been in Virginia for 13 years. If so, he would have been one of the first Jamestown (1) colonists. Jarrett also was described as a skillful man and Virginia Company tenant. Jarrett was assigned to Captain Nuce in Elizabeth City (17), and his wife and children were to be sent to Virginia free of charge. When a list of patented land was sent back to England in May 1625, William Jarrett was credited with 200 acres at Great Weyanoke **(52)** in Charles City (VCR 1:419; 4:554).

JOHN JARVICE ALIAS GLOVER

On February 16, 1624, John Jarvice alias Glover was living on Hog Island **(16)** (CBE 41).

JOHN JEFFERSON

John Jefferson, a gunsmith, came to Virginia aboard the *Bona Nova* as a Virginia Company tenant and on February 16, 1624, was living in Elizabeth City **(18)**, on the west side of the Hampton River. By January 24, 1625, John Jefferson and Walgrave Marks, who jointly headed a household, were residing on Jamestown Island **(1)**, just east of the urbanized area. On May 2, 1625, a warrant was issued for Jefferson's arrest because he had eloped with Captain Ralph Hamor's maidservant. In early January 1626 John Jefferson was hauled into court, where he was censured for the deficiencies of his work as a gunsmith. As punishment he was ordered to pay Dr. John Pott for the medical treatment provided to Henry Booth, who had been injured on account of a gun barrel that he had mended improperly. He also was obliged to contribute toward Booth's maintenance during his convalescence from an eye injury. The justices noted that they had been lenient toward Jefferson because the gun barrel itself was defective and he was "a poore man and A Tenant to the Company." In mid-January 1627, when the Council of State decided what to do with the defunct Virginia Company's tenants and indentured servants whose contracts had not expired, John Jefferson was assigned to Captain Francis West, a councilor who resided in Elizabeth City. It is uncertain when Jefferson's contract with the Virginia Company expired. In 1664, when a plat was made of John Knowles's acreage abutting urban Jamestown's Back Street, the name "Jno Jefferson" was written at a site just east of Orchard Run. This raises the possibility that Jefferson-the-gunsmith acquired land there and perhaps set up shop after completing his term of tenancy. The Knowles plat, which is at the Library of Congress, is part of the Ambler Papers (CBE 43, 56; MCGC 57, 84, 16; AMB 135-136; DOR 1:33).

JOHN JEFFERSON

In 1619 John Jefferson, a gentleman and ancient planter, received a patent for 250 acres of land in Archer's Hope **(6)**, on the east side of Archer's Hope (now College) Creek. On November 12, 1619, he was appointed an official tobacco taster. Jefferson apparently experienced some significant financial losses, for in November 1620 he asked Virginia Company officials for special compensation. In May 1622 he was among those testifying against Captain John Martin, which suggests that he was one of Sir George Yeardley's supporters. During July 1622 Jefferson paid for Samuel Fisher's transportation to Virginia, and in October 1623 he was one of the men appointed on behalf of the king to gather information about conditions in the colony. Sometime after April 1623 but before February 16, 1624, Jefferson's servant, Samuel Fisher, died at one of the communities on the lower side of the James River **(10-16)**. Shortly thereafter, John Jefferson abandoned his 250 acres in Archer's Hope and left for the West Indies. After he had been gone for three years, his land escheated to the Crown; in October 1628 it was reassigned to John Uty. On December 26, 1645, when John Jefferson made his will, he identified himself as a citizen of St. Peter and Vincula Parish, near the Tower of London. He mentioned his sons John and Nathaniel and daughters Elizabeth and Dorothy, but made no reference to real or personal property in Virginia. Jefferson's will was presented for probate on October 30, 1647. He was identified as a boyer or member of the upper class (VCR 1:421, 424; 2:44; 3:154, 219, 228; 4:551, 556; MCGC 79, 173-174; WITH 412; FER 400).

JOHN JEFFERSON

On July 3, 1635, when George Burtcher patented some land, he used John Jefferson as a headright, noting that Jefferson was the son of his wife, Jane (PB 1 Pt.1:203).

EDWARD JEFFERY

On August 18, 1628, Edward Jeffery and Company shipped goods from Plymouth to Virginia aboard the *Prudence* of Stonehouse (CBE 83-84).

JOHN JEFFERYS (JEFFREYS)

John Jefferys (Jeffreys) died in Jamestown (1) sometime after April 1623 but before February 16, 1624 (CBE 39).

***

JOHN JEFFERYS (JEFFRIES, JEFFREY)

On January 23, 1629, the General Court noted that John Jefferys (Jeffries, Jeffrey), Nathaniel Jefferys' brother and executor, had given his power of attorney to John Cheeseman and Rowland Powell. After John Jefferys' letter of authorization was authenticated, Cheeseman and Powell were allowed to serve on behalf of the late Nathaniel Jefferys (MCGC 182).

NATHANIEL JEFFERYS (JEFFRIES, JEFFREYS)

Nathaniel Jefferys (Jeffries, Jeffreys), who came to Virginia on the *Gift*, was a resident of Martin's Hundred (7), where his wife was killed during the March 22, 1622, Indian attack. Jefferys, like other Martin's Hundred survivors, was evacuated to Jamestown Island (1) for safety's sake. Surgeon Samuel Mole (Moll), who eventually returned to England, testified in court that in January 1623 he had shared a dwelling with Nathaniel Jeffreys in Jamestown and that Jefferys, who was a joiner, had made a coffin for Thomas Hamor. On August 4, 1623, Nathaniel Jefferys served on a jury, and by February 16, 1624, he and his wife were residing in urban Jamestown. It is uncertain whether he had remarried or whether his wife was one of the Martin's Hundred women presumed dead but later found to have been captured by the Indians. In September 1624 Nathaniel Jefferys was fined for being drunk and boisterous. Three months later, he was back in court where he served on the jury that investigated little George Pope II's drowning death. On January 24, 1625, when a muster was taken of Jamestown Island's inhabitants, Nathaniel Jefferys and Edward Cage (Cadge) were sharing a home within the urbanized area. By that date, Mrs. Nathaniel Jefferys was dead. Court testimony taken on April 4, 1625, reveals that Nathaniel Jefferys had been the late Robert Whitehed's servant and that he could be freed of any legal obliga-

tion to the decedent's heirs if he paid them a sum of money. Nathaniel made two other appearances in court: once to serve on a jury and again on March 27, 1626, to testify about surgeon Thomas Bunn's patient, William Atkins. By November 1628 Nathaniel Jefferys was dead, at which time Richard Powell was identified as one of his assignees. In January 1629 the justices of the General Court learned that in 1626 Nathaniel Jefferys had agreed to deliver a servant to John Southern but had failed to do so. Because Jefferys died with servants in Virginia and Southern was willing to accept one of them, the court decided that James Budworth (who had four years left to serve) would live with Southern for two years. Because John Jefferys, Nathaniel's brother and executor, was not in the colony, Rowland Powell and John Cheesman (the decedent's creditors and holders of his executor's power of attorney) were authorized to act on his behalf (CBE 38, 55-56; MCGC 4-5, 20, 38, 51, 53, 98, 176, 178, 182; HCA 13/44 f 147ro; VCR 3:570; SR 5860; DOR 1:32).

MRS. NATHANIEL JEFFERYS (JEFFRIES, JEFFREYS)

On March 22, 1622, when the Indians attacked Martin's Hundred (7), Mrs. Nathaniel Jefferys (Jeffries, Jeffreys) reportedly was slain. As Nathaniel Jefferys and his wife were residing in Jamestown (1) on February 16, 1624, it is uncertain whether she was among the women the Indians captured at Martin's Hundred and later released or whether Nathaniel had remarried (VCR 3:570; CBE 38).

[NO FIRST NAME] JEFFERYS (JEFFRIES, JEFFREYS) (MRS. NATHANIEL JEFFERYS [JEFFRIES, JEFFERYS])

On February 16, 1624, Mrs. Nathaniel Jefferys (Jeffries, Jeffreys) was living in urban Jamestown (1) with her husband. By January 24, 1625, Mrs. Jefferys (then identified as Goodwife Jefferys) was dead (CBE 38, 56).

***

RICHARD JEGO

On June 24, 1635, when Adam Thorogood patented some land, he listed Richard Jego as a headright and claimed to have paid for his transportation on the *Hopewell* in 1628 (PB 1 Pt. 1:179).

***

JAMES JELFE

On September 10, 1620, James Jelfe and his wife, Jane, left Bristol, England, on the *Supply* with William Tracy. They were heading for Berkeley Hundred (**55**), where Jelfe was to serve for several years in exchange for some land of his own. On January 29, 1621, the *Supply* arrived at Berkeley. Shortly thereafter, James Jelfe and his wife reportedly died (CBE 21; VCR 3:397, 426).

JANE JELFE
(MRS. JAMES JELFE)

Jane Jelfe and her husband, James, left Bristol, England, on September 10, 1620, on the *Supply* and were bound for Berkeley Hundred (**55**). Jane's husband, who was to serve under the leadership of William Tracy for several years, was to get land of his own. On January 29, 1621, the group arrived at Berkeley, but shortly thereafter Jane and James Jelfe died (CBE 21; VCR 3:397, 426).

***

PETER JEMAINE

On July 31, 1622, Peter Jemaine left England on the *James* and accompanied William Rowley, a surgeon. It is likely that Jemaine, like Rowley, settled in Jamestown (**1**). On April 1, 1623, the Virginia Company learned that all ten of William Rowley's male servants were dead (FER 400; VCR 4:235).

GEORGE JEMISON

On October 8, 1623, George Jemison, master of the *Enerell*, sent a petition to Governor Francis Wyatt, seeking his help in recovering his wages. Jemison said that he was supposed to have been paid in Middleborough by Martin Tiffe and Alluin Daniel, but they had failed to do so (VCR 4:289-290).

RICHARD JENERIE

On June 24, 1635, when Adam Thorogood patented some land, he listed Richard

Jenerie as a headright and stated that he had paid for Jenerie's transportation to Virginia on the *Hopewell* in 1628 (PB 1 Pt. 1:179).

***

OLIVER JENKIN

In early 1625, Oliver Jenkin, his wife, Joane, and their infant, were living on the Virginia Company's land in Elizabeth City (**17**), in the household headed by John Ward. The Jenkins probably were free, for they were not identified as servants. Oliver Jenkin's presence on the Company land and free status suggest that he was one of the Virginia Company's tenants. He was then age 40 (CBE 67; DOR 1:66).

JOANE JENKIN
(MRS. OLIVER JENKIN)

In early 1625 Joane, the wife of Oliver Jenkin, was living on the Virginia Company's land, on the east side of the Hampton River, in Elizabeth City (**17**). Joane and Oliver Jenkin and their infant resided in a household headed by John Ward and probably were free (CBE 67).

[NO FIRST NAME] JENKIN

In early 1625 Oliver and Joane Jenkin's baby, whose gender is unknown, was living on the east side of the Hampton River, in Elizabeth City (**17**), on the Company land. The Jenkin infant's parents appear to have been free and resided in the home of John Ward (CBE 67).

***

***

OLIVER JENKINES (JENKINS, JINKINES, JENKINSON)

Oliver Jenkines (Jenkins, Jinkines, Jenkinson), an ancient planter, came to Virginia in 1610 or 1611 on the *Mary James*. On February 16, 1624, he and his wife, Joan, were living in Elizabeth City (**18**), and they were still there at the beginning of 1625. Oliver, who was then 30 years old, headed a household that included his wife, Joan, and their young son, Alexander, who was Virginia-born. The Jenkines family was relatively well supplied with stored food and had some defensive weaponry (CBE 44, 65; DOR 1:59).

JOAN JENKINES (JENKINS, JINKINES, JENKINSON) (MRS. OLIVER JENKINES [JENKINS, JINKINES, JENKINSON])

Joan, the wife of Oliver Jenkines (Jenkins, Jinkines, Jenkinson), came to Virginia in 1617 on the *George*. On February 16, 1624, she was living with her husband in Elizabeth City (**18**). When a muster of that area's inhabitants was compiled in early 1625, Oliver was identified as the head of a household that included 26-year-old Joan and their young son, Alexander, who was Virginia-born (CBE 44, 65).

ALEXANDER JENKINES (JENKINS, JINKINES, JENKINSON)

Alexander, the son of Oliver and Joan Jenkines (Jenkins, Jinkines, Jenkinson), was born in Virginia sometime after February 16, 1624 but before early 1625. He resided with his parents in Elizabeth City (**18**) (CBE 44, 65).

***

JOHN JENKINS

On February 16, 1624, John Jenkins was living in Warresqueak (**26**) (CBE 42).

MARY JENKINS

On February 16, 1624, Mary Jenkins was living in Elizabeth City (**17, 18**) (CBE 44).

THOMAS JENKINS

On August 21, 1624, the justices of Bridewell court decided that Thomas Jenkins, a vagrant brought in from Lime Street, would be transported to Virginia (CBE 47).

WALTER JENKINS

Sometime prior to December 1635, Walter Jenkins, who identified himself as a 35-year-old planter from St. Margaret, Westminster, in Middlesex, arranged for six servants to go to Virginia on the *Constance* (EAE 59).

ABRAHAM JENNINGS (JENNENS)

Abraham Jennings (Jennens), a London merchant, sent three shipments of goods to Virginia during 1626. On August 12, 1626, he dispatched a cargo from London on the *Marmaduke*. Then, on September 7, 1626, he sent some goods on the *Peter and John*. Finally, on September 26, 1626, he sent commodities from London to Virginia on the *Plantation*. Shipping records indicate that on February 25, 1629, Jennings again dispatched cargo to Virginia. This time he shipped goods from Plymouth on the *Goodwill* of Topsham (CBE 73-74, 86).

AGNES JENNINGS

In 1618 it was decided that Agnes Jennings, a vagrant from Cheapside, would be sent to Virginia (CBE 10).

ANNE JENNINGS

On February 27, 1619, officials at Bridewell decided that Anne Jennings, a wench, would be sent to Virginia. She was among the children rounded up from the streets of London so that they could be transported to the colony (CBE 13).

JANE JENNINGS

On November 20, 1622, Jane Jennings, who was being detained in Newgate Prison, was pardoned so that she could be transported overseas. This decision was made while jail fever was rampant (CBE 29).

MATHEW JENNINGS (JENINGS)

Sometime after April 1623 but before February 16, 1624, Mathew Jennings (Jenings) died on the lower side of the James River, within the corporation of James City (**8-15**) (CBE 41).

THOMAS JENNINGS (JENNINGES)

According to records maintained by the Drapers Company in London, Thomas Jennings (Jenninges), an upholsterer, settled in Virginia in 1620 (SR 879).

ARCHBOLL JENNISON

On September 10, 1627, Archboll Jennison was identified as master of a ship that was going from London to Virginia (CBE 79).

JOHN JERVAS

On February 27, 1619, the justices of Bridewell decided that John Jervas, a boy, would be sent to Virginia. He was one of the children rounded up from the streets of London so that they could be transported to the colony (CBE 12).

GEORGE JEWELL

On December 1, 1631, George Jewell, master of the *Seraphim*, set out for Virginia (CBE 97).

WILLIAM JEWELL

On January 22, 1619, the justices of Bridewell court decided that William Jewell, a boy who had been brought in, would be detained so that he could be sent to Virginia (HUME 20).

JIRO

Sometime after April 1623 but before February 16, 1624, an African man named Jiro died at one of the plantations on the lower side of the James River **(8-15)**, within the corporation of James City (CBE 40).

JOAN

In early 1625 a child named Joan was living in the household of George Medcalfe (Medcalf) and his wife on the east side of the Hampton River in Elizabeth City **(17)**. She may have been the Medcalfe couple's daughter (CBE 67).

JOHN

On March 22, 1622, when the Indians attacked Edward Bennett's plantation at Warresqueak **(26)**, a man named John was killed (VCR 3:571).

JOHN

John, William Ewins' African servant, left England on July 31, 1622 and came to Virginia on the *James* (FER 400).

JOHN

An Irishman named John died in Elizabeth City **(18)** sometime after April 1623 but before February 16, 1624 (CBE 45).

JOHN

Mr. Pearns's servant, John, died in Jamestown **(1)** sometime after April 1623 but before February 16, 1624 (CBE 39).

JOHN

On February 16, 1624, an African named John was living at Flowerdew Hundred **(53)** (CBE 37).

JOHN

In 1628 the General Court gave letters of administration to a man identified as John, enabling him to settle William Morton's estate. The court records describing this act are fragmentary and John's surname is missing (MCGC 174).

[NO FIRST NAME] JOHNSON

On February 16, 1624, a Mrs. Johnson, who was identified as a widow, was living in Elizabeth City **(17, 18)** (CBE 43).

ANDREW JOHNSON ALIAS ANDREWES

On November 20, 1622, it was decided that Andrew Johnson alias Andrewes, who was being detained in Newgate Prison, would be pardoned so that he could be sent to the colony and put to work (CBE 29).

ANNE JOHNSON

Anne Johnson, a prisoner in Newgate, was pardoned on November 20, 1622, so that she could be sent to the colony or put to work (CBE 29).

CORNELIUS JOHNSON

In January 1622 Cornelius Johnson, who was from Horne in the Netherlands, was identified as the master of Daniel Gookin's Irish ship, probably the *Flying Hart*, a vessel that brought colonists to Newportes News **(24)** and also transported cattle. Johnson reportedly expressed an interest in returning to Virginia with a master workman capable of building wind-propelled sawmills (VCR 3:558).

***
EDWARD JOHNSON

Edward Johnson, a Virginia Company tenant, came to Virginia on the *Abigail* in 1621 and on February 16, 1624, was living in Elizabeth City. When a muster was compiled in early 1625, Edward and his Virginia-born child shared their home with another person, probably Edward's wife, who came to Virginia on the *Bona Nova* in 1621. The Johnson household lived on the east side of the Hampton River, on the Virginia Company's land (**17**). Edward Johnson was then a 26-year-old household head who was in possession of a dwelling, two storehouses, and an ample supply of stored food and defensive weaponry, including two pieces of mounted ordnance. On January 12, 1627, Edward Johnson was identified as a tenant of the defunct Virginia Company when he was assigned to Governor George Yeardley. On November 24, 1627, Johnson, then described as a yeoman, obtained a lease for 50 acres of land on the Strawberry Banks, next to Edward Waters' acreage. On July 15, 1631, Edward Johnson was among the Virginia planters who asked for relief from customs duties. His hogsheads of tobacco bore the mark *ER* (CBE 43, 67; MCGC 136; PB 1 Pt. 1:77; G&M 164; DOR 1:65).

MRS. EDWARD JOHNSON (?)

When a muster was compiled of Elizabeth City's inhabitants in early 1625, the household headed by Virginia Company tenant Edward Johnson included an unnamed individual who had come to Virginia on the *Bona Nova* in 1621. As the *Bona Nova* passenger was listed directly below Edward Johnson's name, and just before the name of his child, the anonymous person probably was Edward's wife (DOR 1:65).

[NO FIRST NAME] JOHNSON

In early 1625 when a muster was made of those who lived on the east side of the Hampton River on the Virginia Company's land (**17**), Edward Johnson's child was living in the household his father headed. Also present was an unidentified individual, probably Edward Johnson's wife (CBE 67).

***

ELIZABETH JOHNSON

On July 15, 1631, Elizabeth Johnson, a Virginia planter, was among those who asked for relief from customs duties. According to shipping records, her hogsheads of tobacco were unmarked (G&M 166).

ELLEN JOHNSON

On September 19, 1618, the Bridewell court decided that Ellen Johnson, a vagrant brought in from Bishopsgate, would be sent to Virginia. When she was listed again on February 27, 1619, she was described as a wench and was among the large group of children from London who were being transported to the colony (CBE 10, 13).

FRANCIS JOHNSON

On February 27, 1618, the justices of Bridewell decided that Francis Johnson would be detained and sent to Virginia. The records fail to indicate Francis's gender (HUME 10).

HENRY JOHNSON

On September 25, 1618, Henry Johnson, a prisoner in Newgate, was reprieved and sent to Sir Thomas Smith so that he could be employed in Virginia (SR 0425; PC 2/29).

JAMES JOHNSON

On February 27, 1619, James Johnson, a boy, was detained so that he could be sent to Virginia. He was one of the children rounded up from the streets of London so that they could be transported to the colony (CBE 13).

JANE JOHNSON

On July 27, 1621, the Virginia Company decided that Jane Johnson, a Dutch woman, was to be paid £600. No reason was given for her compensation (VCR 1:524).

JOHN JOHNSON

On September 26, 1618, the justices of Bridewell decided that John Johnson, a vagrant from Billingsgate, would be transported to Virginia (CBE 10).

JOHN JOHNSON

In 1619 the Virginia Company paid for John Johnson, a 32-year-old husbandman from Nottinghamshire, to be transported to Virginia. He probably was a Virginia Company servant or tenant (FER 295).

JOHN JOHNSON

John Johnson, master of the *Bona Nova*, set sail for Virginia on May 26, 1619 (VCR 1:218).

JOHN JOHNSON

In June 1619 John Johnson, pilot of the ship *Garland*, testified in a lawsuit about a voyage he had undertaken (EAE 7).

JOHN JOHNSON

John Johnson, an indentured servant in the household of Martin's Hundred's (7) leader, William Harwood, arrived at the plantation around Christmas, that is, January 1623. Fellow servant Richard Frethorne indicated that Johnson died within a relatively short time and had lived in Harwood's house (VCR 4:60).

***

JOHN JOHNSON I

On January 12, 1624, John Johnson I, an ancient planter and yeoman, patented 15 acres abutting the Back River in the northeastern portion of Jamestown Island (1), a farmstead he made his home. He received the initial title to his acreage from Governor George Yeardley between 1619 and 1621. Simultaneously, he received 85 acres of land in Archer's Hope (6), to the west of Archer's Hope (later, College) Creek. On February 16, 1624, John Johnson I, wife Ann I, and their two children, Ann II and John II, were living on their rural land in the eastern part of Jamestown Island. In 1624 John Johnson I made three appearances before the General Court. On April 12th he acknowledged a debt to John Hall for some clothing he had purchased and for Hall's serving as his substitute in a march against the Indians. On August 16th Johnson was ordered to put a new roof on the dwelling of his neighbor, the late Ensign William Spence, and to repair Spence's

fence. Then, on December 13th he went to court, alleging that John Hall had killed his hog. However, it was determined that Johnson previously had slain four of Hall's swine. When a muster was taken of Jamestown Island's inhabitants on January 24, 1625, John Johnson I, wife Ann I, daughter Ann II (age 4), and son John II (age 1) were living in a household that included maidservant Ann Kean. When a list of patented land was sent back to England in May 1625, John Johnson I was credited with 200 acres. A contemporary document indicates that he had received his acreage on the basis of a court order. In January and March 1629 John Johnson I served on juries, and on April 8, 1629, he was sued by Edward Waller. Johnson died sometime prior to January 25, 1638, at which time his son and daughter were described as his legitimate heirs. Ultimately, John Johnson I's property on Jamestown Island descended to his son, John II, who on March 25, 1654, repatented it and then sold it to brother-in-law Edward Travis I on August 8, 1659. This transaction gave rise to the Travis plantation on Jamestown Island (CBE 38, 56; Patent Book 1 Pt. 1:15, 55, 130; Pt. 2:531; 3:27; 5:242; 7:228-229; VCR 4:474, 551, 556; MCGC 19, 35, 184, 190, 195; DOR 1:35-36; 2:357-358).

ANN JOHNSON I
(MRS. JOHN JOHNSON)

On February 16, 1624, Ann I and her husband, John Johnson I, were living in the eastern end of Jamestown Island (1). In their household were their two young children, Ann II and John II. On January 24, 1625, the muster-taker recorded the children's ages but failed to note the ages of their parents. On February 13, 1629, when Jamestown merchant Thomas Warnett made his will, he made a bequest to Mrs. John Johnson, which suggests that Ann was still alive. The Johnson couple died sometime prior to January 25, 1638, at which time their children were identified as their legitimate heirs (CBE 38, 56; PB 1 Pt. 1:15; Pt. 2:531; SH 11-12; DOR 1:35-36).

ANN JOHNSON II
(MRS. EDWARD TRAVIS I)

Ann II, the daughter of John Johnson I and his wife, Ann I, was living on Jamestown Island (1) with her parents and baby brother on February 16, 1624. She was still there on

January 24, 1625, at which time she was described as 4 years old. Her brother, John II, was age 1. The Johnsons lived in the eastern part of Jamestown Island, somewhat outside of the urbanized area. Ann Johnson II and her brother, John Johnson II, reached maturity and became their parents' heirs. Sometime prior to January 25, 1638, she married Edward Travis I, who in 1659 purchased her brother's interest in their late parents' land on Jamestown Island (CBE 38, 56; PB 1 Pt. 2:531; DOR 1:35-36; 2:357-358).

JOHN JOHNSON II

John Johnson II, the son of Ann and John Johnson I of Jamestown Island (1), was attributed to his parents' household on February 16, 1624, as was his sister, Ann II. On January 24, 1625, when a muster was taken of the colony's inhabitants, John II was listed as age 1. His parents died sometime prior to January 25, 1638, at which time John II and his sister, Ann II, were described as their legitimate heirs. It is uncertain how long John II's mother, Ann I, survived, although she was mentioned in Jamestown merchant Thomas Warnett's February 13, 1629, will. On June 5, 1653, John Johnson II, who identified himself as a James City County planter, disposed of 450 acres of land in Upper Chippokes, property he seems to have inherited from his parents. Then, on March 25, 1654, he repatented his late father's 15 acres in eastern Jamestown Island. He also repatented his father's 135 acres in Archer's Hope (6), on the west side of Archer's Hope (College) Creek, renewing his claim in 1662. On August 8, 1659, John Johnson II sold his parents' Jamestown Island farmstead to his brother-in-law Edward Travis I, who by that date already owned several other parcels on the north side of Passmore Creek. John Johnson II appears to have been a staunch supporter of the rebel Nathaniel Bacon, for in February 1677 he was among those exempted from the king's pardon. He also suffered at the hands of Governor William Berkeley's most zealous supporters, some of whom seized the personal property of suspected rebels. In May 1677 Johnson told the king's commissioners that he and James Barrow had been imprisoned for 17 days by William Hartwell and were only freed when they promised their captor 10,000 shingles. In 1704 John Johnson II paid quitrent on 260 acres in James City County and 350

acres in Surry (CBE 38, 56; Surry County Deeds, Wills &c. 1652-1672:30; PB1 Pt. 2:531; 3:27; 5:242; 7:228-229: HEN 2:370; CO 1/40 ff 22-24; DOR 1:35-36; 2:357-358; SMITH 49).

***

***

JOSEPH JOHNSON

In July 1617 Joseph Johnson was deemed "an incorrigible rogue" when the justices of Middlesex decided that he would be transported to Virginia. He arrived in the colony on the *William and Thomas* and on February 16, 1624, was living in Archer's Hope (6). In October 1624, when Thomas Bransby, the commander of Archer's Hope, warned Joseph Johnson about venturing too far from home and placing himself in danger, Johnson brandished his firearm and threatened to shoot. When a muster was taken of Archer's Hope's inhabitants on February 4, 1625, Joseph headed a household that included his wife, Margaret (Margarett), and a servant. The Johnsons had an ample supply of stored food and defensive weaponry. Joseph Johnson, who appears to have been very volatile, was summoned to court on August 1625 and charged with beating his wife and threatening community commander Thomas Bransby, who tried to intervene. Bransby commented that he was weary of separating "Newgate birds" and "Bridewell whores," a probable reference to Joseph Johnson's being a former jailbird. Joseph was ordered to post a bond, guaranteeing his good behavior. In November 1628 Joseph Johnson, who was identified as an Archer's Hope planter, was fined for disobeying the law requiring householders to plant corn. He and Arthur Avelin also were obliged to post a bond, guaranteeing that they would not disturb Thomas Farley, a neighbor; however, Farley was ordered to pay Johnson and Avelin for the damage his hogs had done to their corn (CBE 8, 41, 58; MCGC 70, 178; DOR 1:38).

MARGARET (MARGARETT) JOHNSON (MRS. JOSEPH JOHNSON)

On February 4, 1625, Margaret (Margarett), the wife of Joseph Johnson, was living in Archer's Hope (6) in a household headed by her husband. The muster-taker noted that Margaret had come to Virginia on the

Abigail. On August 29, 1625, the justices of the General Court learned that Margaret Johnson often was beaten and abused by her husband. He was required to post a bond as a guarantee that he would cease. A statement made by Thomas Bransby about separating "Newgate birds" and "Bridewell whores" suggests that Margaret Johnson, like her husband, was a former prison inmate and perhaps had been incarcerated at Bridewell (CBE 58; MCGC 70).

***

***

JOSEPH JOHNSON

On February 16, 1624, Joseph Johnson was living at Hog Island (16). On June 19, 1635, he patented 400 acres on the Nansemond River (29), using as headrights his wife, Elizabeth, and seven indentured servants (CBE 41; PB 1 Pt. 1:252).

ELIZABETH JOHNSON (MRS. JOSEPH JOHNSON)

On June 19, 1635, when Joseph Johnson patented 400 acres on the Nansemond River (29), he used the headright of his wife, Elizabeth, and seven indentured servants (PB 1 Pt. 1:252).

***

RICHARD JOHNSON

Richard Johnson came to Virginia in 1622 on the *Southampton* and on February 16, 1624, was living at Jordan's Journey (46). On January 21, 1625, when a muster was made of the community's inhabitants, Richard was described as a 22-year-old servant in the household headed by William Farrer and Mrs. Cisley Jordan (CBE 36, 51).

RICHARD JOHNSON

Richard Johnson came to Virginia on the *Hopewell* in 1628 at the expense of Adam Thorogood, who used his headright when patenting some land on June 24, 1635 (PB 1 Pt. 1:179).

ROBERT JOHNSON

When William Andrews patented some land on June 25, 1635, he used Robert Johnson's headright (PB 1 Pt. 1:182).

ROBERT JOHNSON

On May 1, 1612, Robert Johnson prepared a report in which he described the settlement of Henrico (63) and mentioned the activities of George Percy and Captain Davis at Old Point Comfort (17) (HAI 560-562).

STEVEN JOHNSON

In 1629 Steven Johnson testified in court in a slander suit involving Goodwife Gray and Mrs. William Carter of Elizabeth City (18) (MCGC 198).

THOMAS JOHNSON

Thomas Johnson came to Virginia on the *Hopewell* in 1628 at the expense of Adam Thorogood, who used his headright when patenting some land on June 24, 1635 (PB 1 Pt. 1:179).

WILLIAM JOHNSON

William Johnson, a laborer, was one of the first Virginia colonists and arrived in Jamestown (1) in May 1607 (CJS 1:209; 2:142).

WILLLIAM JOHNSON

William Johnson, a goldsmith, came to Virginia in 1608 as part of the 2nd Supply of new settlers. He would have resided in Jamestown (1) (CJS 1:222; 2:162).

WILLIAM JOHNSON

In 1628 William Johnson, captain and master of the *Anne*, sued the estate of ship owner Humphrey Rastall in the General Court, in an attempt to recover several months' back pay. The justices ordered Lancellot Barnes, the Virginia representative of Rastall's heir, to compensate Johnson (MCGC 174).

EDWARD JOLBY

On March 22, 1622, when the Indians attacked Warresqueak (26), Edward Jolby was killed (VCR 3:571).

***

WILLIAM JONAS ALIAS PINKE
(SEE WILLIAM PINKE)

MARY JONAS ALIAS PINKE
(SEE MARY PINKE)

***

[NO FIRST NAME] JONES

On February 16, 1620, the Virginia Company authorized Captain Jones, master of the *Falcon*, to set sail for Virginia "at the first fair wind." On January 4, 1626, he returned to Virginia in order to procure some supplies. He had just captured a Spanish frigate in the West Indies while sailing under the authority of a commission the Low Countries had granted to Captain Powell (VCR 1:312; 4:567-570).

ALICE (ALSE) JONES

Alice (Alse) Jones, one of the young maids sent to Virginia to become colonists' wives, was born at Kidderminster in Woostershire, England. In September 1621 she set out for Virginia on the *Warwick*. Prior to the time Alice came to the colony, she was a servant in Mr. Binneon's home in Bishopsgate. On March 22, 1622, when the Indians attacked Warresqueak (26), Alice Jones was killed (FER 309; VCR 3:571).

ANTHONY JONES

Anthony Jones reportedly came to Virginia on the *Temperance* in 1620 and on February 16, 1624, was living at Flowerdew Hundred (53), where he was listed among Sir George Yeardley's servants. By January 24, 1625, Jones had moved to urban Jamestown (1), where he was identified as a 26-year-old servant in the Yeardley household. On February 4, 1625, when Anthony Jones testified in court, he was identified as a *Duty* boy, thereby raising the possibility that he did not arrive on the *Temperance*. He appeared in court again on February 4, 1626, repeating some of the statements that Peter Marten made against the government while at Edward Fisher's house on Jamestown Island. In a court record dating to 1637–1639 Anthony Jones described himself as a Virginia planter when he received an admiralty commission authorizing him to settle the estate of William Hutchinson, who died at Warresqueak (26). However, the appointment came too late, for the General Court already had made other arrangements (CBE 37, 54; MCGC 93; EAE 73).

CHADWALLADER (CADWALLADER) JONES

Chadwallader (Cadwallader) Jones came to Virginia on the *Marmaduke* in 1623. When a muster was made of Archer's Hope's (6) inhabitants on February 4, 1625, he was identified as a 22-year-old servant in Thomas Bransby's household. On August 29, 1625, when Chadwallader testified about the domestic disputes between Joseph Johnson and his wife, Margaret, he identified Mr. Bransby as his master. By March 15, 1630, Chadwallader Jones had obtained his freedom. It was then that he was identified as a Virginia planter who had exported some Virginia tobacco (CBE 58; MCGC 70; SR 3784).

CHRISTOPHER JONES

On July 7, 1627, Christopher Jones was brought in from Moorgate and taken to the justices of Bridewell, who decided that he would be sent to Virginia (CBE 78).

CLEMENT JONES

On July 15, 1631, Clement Jones, a Virginia planter, asked for relief from customs duties. According to shipping records, his hogsheads of tobacco were marked *CF* (G&M 165).

DAVID JONES

David Jones came to Virginia on the *Truelove* in 1622 and on January 21, 1625, was living alone at Chaplin's Choice (56). He was then age 22. On July 4, 1635, David patented 300 acres of land in Charles City, acquiring his property on the basis of six headrights (CBE 51; PB 1 Pt. 1:206; DOR 1:21).

EDWARD JONES

Edward Jones died sometime after February 16, 1624, but before February 4, 1625, on the lower side of the James River, within the corporation of James City at one of the plantations east of Gray's Creek (10-16) (CBE 60).

EDWARD JONES

On June 24, 1635, when Adam Thorogood patented some land, he used the headright of Edward Jones, whom he said he had transported to Virginia in 1629 in a French ship (PB 1 Pt.1:179).

ELIZABETH JONES

Elizabeth Jones died sometime after February 16, 1624, but before January 20, 1625, at Flowerdew Hundred (**53**) (CBE 51).

GEORGE JONES

George Jones, who lived at Martin's Hundred (**7**), was killed during the March 22, 1622, Indian attack (VCR 3:570).

GEORGE JONES

George Jones died in Elizabeth City (**17, 18**) sometime after April 1623 but before February 16, 1624 (CBE 45).

***

GILES (GYLES) JONES (JOONES)

On December 14, 1619, Giles (Gyles) Jones (Joones), a yeoman, received a patent for 150 acres of land in Warresqueak, near the easternmost edge of Warresqueak (Burwells) Bay, at Day's Point (**28**). By that time Giles had married Elizabeth, an ancient planter who received some acreage on the east side of the Hampton River, within a tract set aside for the Virginia Company's (**17**) use. In May 1625, when a list of patented land was sent back to England, Giles Jones's acreage at Day's Point was described as seated. However, in early 1625 his wife, Elizabeth, was living in Elizabeth City (**18**), in Thomas Dunthorne's home. Also present in the Dunthorne home was the Jones couple's 5-year-old daughter, Sara. In October 1628 Giles Jones disposed of 100 of his 150 acres of land in Warresqueak, retaining the 50 acres that contained his "late mansion house." Simultaneously, the General Court awarded Elizabeth Jones a 100-acre tract on Old Point Comfort Island. Later, she and Giles exchanged her 100 acres for 300 acres on the Back River (**19**) in Elizabeth City. Sergeant Giles Jones testified in court on February 11, 1629. However he died before May 1638, by

which time the widowed Elizabeth had remarried (VCR 4:556; MCGC 138, 187; PB 1Pt. 1:60; Pt. 2:564; 2:140; Isle of Wight Deed Book A:102; BOD 530).

ELIZABETH JONES (JOONES) (MRS. GILES JONES [JOONES], MRS. RICHARD POPELEY)

Elizabeth, an ancient planter, came to Virginia in 1609 on the *Patience*, a vessel built by the men in Sir Thomas Gates's and Sir George Somers' party after being shipwrecked and stranded in Bermuda. On December 16, 1619, Elizabeth, who by that date had wed yeoman Giles (Gyles) Jones (Joones), received a patent for 50 acres of land in Elizabeth City (**17**) on the east side of the Hampton River. The couple later sold Elizabeth's land to Thomas Flint, who was given other acreage after the land he had purchased was confiscated and assigned to the Virginia Company. The Jones family moved to Warresqueak and established a plantation at Day's Point (**28**) on some acreage Giles had acquired in December 1619. In early 1625 Elizabeth Jones, who was 30 years old, was living in Elizabeth City (**18**) in Thomas Dunthorne's household, as was Elizabeth's 5-year-old daughter, Sara Jones. Although Elizabeth was described as a servant, she could have been one of Dunthorne's tenants. On December 12, 1625, Elizabeth Jones appeared before the General Court, where she testified that Captain John Martin had given some tobacco to Captain Thomas Flint. On February 5, 1627, the General Court recognized that Elizabeth was entitled to her first dividend as an ancient planter and on October 16, 1628, gave her 100 acres on Old Point Comfort Island. Later, she and her husband, Giles Jones, exchanged her acreage for a piece of property on the Back River (**19**) in Elizabeth City. In October 1628 the Joneses sold their acreage at Day's Point, with the exception of the 50 acres containing their house. Giles died sometime after February 11, 1629, and Elizabeth married Richard Popeley by May 1638. After Popeley's death, prior to 1645, she served as his executor (CBE 66; MCGC 81, 138; PB 1 Pt. 1:60; Pt. 2:564; 2:90; Isle of Wight Book A:102; BOD 503).

SARA JONES (JOONES)

In early 1625 Sara Jones (Joones), the 5-year-old, Virginia-born daughter of Giles (Gyles) and Elizabeth Jones, was living in Elizabeth City (**18**) in the home of Thomas

Dunthorne. Sara's mother, Elizabeth, probably was one of the Dunthorne's tenants. It is likely that during the early 1620s Sara Jones and her parents lived in their own home at Day's Point (**28**), where Giles Jones owned 150 acres. It is uncertain how long Sara survived (CBE 66).

***

HENRY (HENERY) JONES

Henry (Henery) Jones came to Virginia in 1622 on the *Southampton* and on February 4, 1625, was living on the lower side of the James River. He was a 25-year-old servant at Samuel Mathews' plantation (**15**) (CBE 59).

JEANE JONES (JOANES)

Jeane Jones (Joanes), a young maid, came to Virginia in September 1621 on the *Warwick* and was the 17-year-old daughter of Elizabeth and Evenes (Evans?) Jones, a hat-maker. Virginia Company records show that Jeane Jones was recommended by Mrs. Gilbert (sometimes known as Mrs. Cuffe) in Holborne, an area of London (FER 309).

JOHANNA JONES

On November 20, 1622, Johanna Jones and a group of fellow inmates at Newgate Prison, were pardoned so that they could be transported overseas. They were being sent away because of a deadly outbreak of jail fever (CBE 29).

JOHN JONES

On September 15, 1619, John Jones, a smith and gardener, set out for Virginia on the *Margaret* of Bristol and was one of the colonists being sent to Berkeley Hundred (**55**) to work under John Woodlief's supervision. Jones was to serve the Society of Berkeley Hundred's investors for eight years in exchange for 30 acres of land. Jones died shortly after his arrival in the colony (CBE 14; VCR 3:198, 213).

JOHN JONES

Sometime after April 1623 but before February 16, 1624, John Jones died at one of the plantations on the lower side of the James River, within the corporation of James City (**8-15**) (CBE 41).

OWEN JONES

On March 22, 1622, when the Indians attacked Henricus Island (**63**), Owen Jones was killed. He was identified as one of Captain John Berkeley's people and therefore probably was involved in the construction of an ironworks at Falling Creek (**68**) (VCR 3:565).

PAUL JONES

On April 8, 1623, Richard Norwood, who came to Virginia on the *Margaret and John,* informed his father that shipboard conditions were horrific and that Paul Jones, who had accompanied him, had died for lack of food. It is unclear whether Jones died aboard ship or shortly after he arrived in Jamestown (**1**) (VCR 4:233).

PETER (PEETER) JONES

Peter (Peeter) Jones came to Virginia on the *Southampton* in 1623 and on January 20, 1625, was living at Flowerdew Hundred (**53**), where he was a 24-year-old servant in Abraham Peirsey's household (CBE 50).

PHILIP (PHILLIP) JONES

Philip (Phillip) Jones died at Warresqueak (**26**) sometime after April 1623 but before February 16, 1624 (CBE 50).

RALPH JONES (JOANES)

On January 22, 1620, the justices of Bridewell decided that Ralph Jones (Joanes), a vagrant from Crutched Friars, would be sent to Virginia (CBE 17).

RICE JONES

In 1623 Francis West paid for the transportation of Rice Jones from Canada to Virginia on the *John and Francis*. On December 2, 1628, Jones, who was identified as a Warwick River (**22**) planter, received a patent for 50 acres on the Warresqueak (Pagan) River in Warresqueak (**26**), land assigned to him by Francis West (PB 1 Pt. 1:66-67).

RICHARD JONES

On February 16, 1624, Richard Jones was living in Elizabeth City (**17, 18**) (CBE 43).

RICHARD JONES

Richard Jones died at Flowerdew Hundred (**53**) sometime after April 1623 but before February 16, 1624 (CBE 37).

THEODORE JONES (JOONES)

Theodore Jones (Joones) came to Virginia on the *Margaret and John* in 1620 and on February 16, 1624, was living in Elizabeth City (**18**) on the west side of the Hampton River. He was still there in early 1625 and was a 16-year-old servant in the household headed by Michael Wilcockes and John Slater (CBE 44, 64).

THOMAS JONES

Thomas Jones, a 25-year-old weaver from Middlesex, England, came to Virginia in 1619 aboard the *Bona Nova* at the expense of the Ferrars, who were major Virginia Company investors. Jones probably was a Company servant or tenant (FER 295).

THOMAS JONES

In 1621 when Thomas Jones and the *Falcon* arrived in Virginia, the men in Elizabeth City (**17, 18**) agreed to let their sassafras be taken to London. On November 21, 1621, the Virginia Company authorized Thomas Jones, then identified as master of the *Discovery*, to take passengers to Virginia and to trade and fish. Three days later, he received permission to sail (EAE 11; VCR 1:553, 562; 3:525).

THOMAS JONES

On March 22, 1622, when the Indians attacked Captain Smith's plantation at Bermuda Hundred (**39**), Thomas Jones was killed (VCR 3:566).

***

THOMAS JONES

On February 16, 1624, Thomas Jones and his wife Margaret were living in Pasbehay (**3**), the mainland just west of Jamestown Island. They were still there on January 30, 1625, and reportedly had come to Virginia on the *London Merchant*. At the time of the 1625 muster, they had an ample supply of stored food and defensive weaponry. The Joneses appear to have been rowdy and

volatile. Thomas ran afoul of the law twice during August 1626 by becoming publicly drunk and disorderly and a couple months later, Margaret attacked a neighbor with a tobacco stalk. Thomas Jones made a complaint against merchant Humphrey Rastall, claiming that he was owed some money, and on September 11, 1626, he testified against Joan Wright, who was accused of practicing witchcraft (CBE 39, 57; MCGC 85, 107-108, 111-112, 119; DOR 1:25).

MARGARET JONES (MRS. THOMAS JONES)

Margaret and Thomas Jones came to Virginia on the *London Merchant*. It is uncertain when or where they were married. On February 16, 1624, the Joneses were living in Pasbehay (**3**) and they were still residing there on January 30, 1625, when a muster was made of that area's inhabitants. During September 1626 Margaret Jones got into a fight with her neighbor, John Butterfield. She reportedly scratched his face and beat him with a tobacco stalk while he was trying to gather peas from his own garden. Afterward, she railed at husband, Thomas, because she failed to come to her aid. A short time later, Margaret was accused of assault and arrested. When summoned, she refused to go to court unless Mrs. Giles Allington accompanied her. Margaret Jones, who was found guilty as charged, was sentenced to be towed behind the stern of a boat, to and from the *Margaret and John*, which was anchored in the James River. The same day sentence was passed, Robert Hutchinson was accused of committing adultery with Mrs. Margaret Jones. Margaret survived her watery punishment, for on July 15, 1631, she was one of the Virginia planters who asked the Crown for relief from customs duties. Her hogsheads of tobacco were marked with her initials, *MJ* (CBE 39, 57; MCGC 119; G&M 165).

***

THOMAS JONES

On February 16, 1624, Thomas Jones was living at the College (**66**) in the corporation of Henrico (CBE 35).

THOMAS JONES

On February 16, 1624, Thomas Jones was living at Warresqueak (**26**) within the corporation of Warresqueak, later Isle of Wight (CBE 42).

THOMAS JONES

Thomas Jones came to Virginia on the *Bona Nova* and on January 30, 1625, was living on the Maine (**3**), just west of Jamestown Island, where he was a 25-year-old servant in surgeon Thomas Bunn's household (CBE 57).

THOMAS JONES

In April 1626 Thomas Jones died while he was in Virginia. Administration of his estate was granted to his principal creditor, Rowland Gold (CBE 71; EEAC 33; MOR 61).

WILLIAM JONES

William Jones died in Elizabeth City (**17, 18**) sometime after April 1623 but before February 16, 1624 (CBE 45).

WILLIAM JONES

On February 27, 1619, it was decided that William Jones, a boy, would be sent to Virginia. He was one of the youngsters rounded up from the streets of London so that they could be sent to the colony (CBE 12).

***

WILLIAM JONES

William Jones, who was from Michmanssell in Herefordshire, arrived in Jamestown (**1**) on September 5, 1623, on the *Ann* and took the oath of supremacy. On February 16, 1624, Jones and his wife were living in the rural part of Jamestown Island, where he was a household head. Sometime after April 1623 but before February 16, 1624, William Jones's servant died (MCGC 6; CBE 39-40).

MRS. WILLIAM JONES

On February 16, 1624, Mrs. William Jones and her husband were living in the rural part of Jamestown Island (**1**), where William was a household head. William had arrived in Jamestown on September 5, 1623, and was a free man (MCGC 6; CBE 40).

***

WILLIAM JONES

William Jones came to Virginia on the *Southampton* in 1623 and on January 20, 1625, was a 23-year-old servant living in Abraham Peirsey's household at Flowerdew Hundred (**53**) (CBE 50).

WILLIAM JONES (GOONES)

On February 3, 1626, when William Eppes patented some land, he used the headright of William Jones (Goones), who came to Virginia on the *Anne* in 1623 (PB 1 Pt. 1:49).

***

WILLIAM JONES ALIAS BROOKS (BROOKES, BROOCKES) ALIAS MORGAN (SEE WILLIAM MORGAN I)

SIBILE JONES ALIAS BROOKS (BROOKES, BROOCKES) ALIAS MORGAN (SEE SIBILE MORGAN)

***

[NO FIRST NAME] JOPE

In January 1620 John Rolfe identified Captain Jope as the man who brought a Dutch man-of-war to Virginia with 20-some Africans and arrived at Old Point Comfort (**17**) in late August 1619 (VCR 3:243).

PETER JORDAN (JORDEN)

On December 31, 1619, officials at Bridewell decided that Peter Jordan (Jorden), who was from Cheapside and was being detained, would be sent to Virginia. Jordan came to Virginia on the *London Merchant* in 1620 and on February 16, 1624, was living at the College (**66**). He was still there on January 23, 1625, when he was identified as a 22-year-old servant in the household of Thomas Osborne (CBE 15, 35, 53).

PETER JORDAN (JORDEN)

When the Indians attacked Powle-Brooke or Merchants Hope (**50**) on March 22, 1622, Peter Jordan (Jorden) was killed. He may have been the same individual who formerly had been incarcerated at Bridewell (VCR 3:569).

ROBERT JORDAN

On December 31, 1619, it was decided that Robert Jordan, who was being detained at Bridewell, would be sent to Virginia. On March 22, 1622, when an Indian attack occurred at Berkeley Hundred (55), Robert Jordan was killed (CBE 15; VCR 3:567).

***

SAMUEL JORDAN (JORDAIN, JORDEN, JERDEN)

Samuel Jordan (Jordain, Jorden, Jerden), an ancient planter, came to Virginia in 1610. His arrival date suggests that he was aboard one of the three ships in the fleet of Thomas West, Lord De La Warre, whose June arrival narrowly averted the abandonment of the colony. Jordan probably resided in the vicinity of Charles (or Bermuda) Hundred (39), where John Rolfe and Sir Thomas Dale also lived, for a patent he received in 1620 indicates that he had a dwelling there. In July-August 1619 Samuel Jordan was one of two men who represented the corporation of Charles City in Virginia's first legislative assembly. He also was among the eight men appointed to review one of the four books of laws that had been sent to Virginia. By December 21, 1620, he had wed a young woman named Cisley and received a patent for 450 acres, his first dividend of land. On account of his service to the colony, he was promised a like amount of acreage as soon as he seated his first claim. In December 1620 Samuel Jordan was credited with property in three locations: 50 acres in Charles Hundred that had a house; 12 acres and a tenement abutting west on Captain John Martin's land (59); and 388 acres in or near Sandys Hundred, on the north side of the James River, a probable reference to Southampton Hundred (44), a plantation in which several Virginia Company officials had invested heavily. Jordan quickly acquired his second dividend of land on the south side of the James River, land he seated and called Beggars Bush or Jordan's Journey (46).

In 1621 the Virginia Company sent Samuel Jordan numerous barrels of cider, which suggests that he was in their employ. One of his servants was identified as an apprentice, which raises the possibility that Jordan had some type of specialized skill. In July 1622 he received from Virginia Company investor Mary Tue a share of Company stock that entitled him to 100 acres in Digges Hundred (43), a tract that lay to the west of West and Shirley Hundred (41) on the north side of the James River. When a list of patented land was sent back to England in May 1625, Samuel Jordan was credited with 450 acres "in the territory of Great Weyanoke" within the Corporation of Charles City, acreage that was described as seated (planted). On March 22, 1622, when Indians attacked the settlements along the banks of the James River, Samuel Jordan was living at Jordan's Journey. According to Captain John Smith, he brought some of the survivors from neighboring plantation to Jordan's Journey, which he fortified and made defensible. Samuel Jordan and his wife, Cisley, produced two daughters, Mary (born around 1621) and Margaret. He died sometime after April 1623 but before November 19, 1623, at which time William Farrar (Ferrar, Ferrer) was ordered to bring in an account of his estate. Farrar, whose plantation on the east side of the Appomattox River (39) had been hard hit in the March 1622 Indian attack, moved to Jordan's Journey and on February 16, 1624, was living in the household of the widowed Cisley Jordan. Court testimony dating to September 12, 1625, reveals that Samuel Jordan sometimes traded with John Pountis and Dictorius Christmas, both of whom were associated with Southampton Hundred and Elizabeth City (17, 18). Joan Vinsone of Bermuda Hundred, a known gossip, claimed that Samuel Jordan had had a romantic relationship with Alice Boyse of Bermuda Hundred, which caused problems in his marriage to wife Cisley (VCR 2:74, 89; 3:65, 154, 159, 612; 4:218-220, 554; PB 8:125; MCGC 8, 31, 70; FER 322; CBE 36, 51; CJS 2:295; DOR 2:363-364).

CISLEY (CICELEY, CECILY, SYSELY, SISLEY) JORDAN (JORDAIN, JORDEN, JERDEN) (MRS. SAMUEL JORDAN [JORDAIN, JORDEN, JERDEN]), (MRS. WILLIAM FARRAR [FERRAR, FERRER])

On January 21, 1625, Cisley Jordan (Jordain, Jorden, Jerden), an ancient planter, reported that she had arrived in Virginia in August 1610 on the *Swan*. As she was 24 years old in 1625, she would have been around 9 or 10 years old when she came to the colony.

Cisley may have wed ancient planter John Bayley and produced a daughter, Temperance, who was age 7 in January 1625 and living in her home. It is certain that Cisley married ancient planter Samuel Jordan sometime prior to December 21, 1620, when he received his first dividend of land, which also included her entitlement as an ancient planter. The Jordans took up residence on the lower side of the James River at a plantation they called Jordan's Journey (46). After the March 22, 1622, Indian attack, the Jordan plantation was strengthened and became a rallying point for the area's survivors. Cisley Jordan was widowed sometime after April 1623, and on November 19, 1623, she was authorized to settle her late husband's estate, with the help of William Farrar. Farrar, who at the time of the Indian attack had been occupying a plantation on the east side of the Appomattox River, somewhat inland from Bermuda Hundred (39), may have taken refuge at Jordan's Journey and stayed on. Three or four days after Samuel Jordan's death, the Rev. Grivell Pooly (Pooley), the local minister, expressed an interest in marrying the recently widowed Cisley. When a third party inquired whether she would consider the match, she said that "she would not marry any man until she was delivered," an indication that she was pregnant at the time of Samuel Jordan's death. Afterward, Pooly and Mrs. Cisley Jordan pledged to wed and purportedly drank a toast. Pooley claimed that Cisley asked that their engagement be kept secret, as her late husband's death was so recent. Cisley Jordan later declared that she intended to marry William Farrar and denied that she ever had been engaged to Grivel Pooly. If a rumor spread by JoanVinsone, a community gossip, was true, Cisley's marriage to Samuel Jordan was an unhappy one on account of his love for Alice Boyse, a married woman and resident of Bermuda Hundred. On February 16, 1624, Mrs. Jordan and Farrar were listed as jointly heading a Jordan's Journey household that included her daughters Mary and Margery Jordan, young Temperance Bayley, and several servants. As the cohabitation of a heterosexual couple was illegal, their living arrangements attracted the attention of their neighbors and, ultimately, the authorities. On January 3, 1625, Nathaniel Causey (then a resident of Jordan's Journey) testified that Mrs. Jordan had had a frightening vision in which she and her child were touched by a pair of ghostly hands and a voice cried "Judgment,

Judgment." He said that he had never seen Mrs. Jordan and Mr. Farrar indulge in unfitting behavior but he had seen them kiss. On the other hand, the spurned Rev. Pooly claimed that Mrs. Jordan's behavior with Farrar was scandalous and publicly accused her of breach of promise. The justices of the General Court, forced to deal with the legal ramifications of breaking a marriage contract, sought advice from officials in England. After the charges against Mrs. Jordan were dismissed, Pooly agreed to release her from their marriage agreement. On January 21, 1625, when a muster was made of Jordans Journey's inhabitants, Cisley Jordan and William Farrar were listed as jointly heading a household that included her daughters Mary and Margaret Jordan, Temperance Bayley, and 10 male servants. By May 1625 Cisley and William Farrar had wed. Probate records indicate that they produced at least three children: Cecily, William, and John (CBE 36, 51; PB 8:125; VCR 2:519; 4:218-220; MCGC 31, 41-42, 57; DOR 1:928; 2:363-364).

MARGARET (MARGERY) JORDAN (JORDAIN, JORDEN, JERDEN)

On February 16, 1624, Margaret (Margery), the infant daughter of Samuel and Cisley Jordan (Jordain, Jorden, Jerden), was living at Jordan's Journey (46) in a household headed by her widowed mother and William Farrer. On January 21, 1625, when a muster was made of the community's inhabitants, Margaret was described as a 1-year-old girl who had been born in Virginia. Her birth occurred somewhat after her father's death (CBE 36, 51).

MARY JORDAN (JORDAIN, JORDEN, JERDEN)

On February 16, 1624, Mary, the daughter of Samuel and Cisley Jordan (Jordain, Jorden, Jerden), was living at Jordan's Journey (46) in the household headed by her widowed mother and William Farrer. On January 21, 1625, when a muster was made of Jordan's Journey's inhabitants, Mary was described as a 3-year-old girl who was born in Virginia. Also living in the Jordan household was Mary's mother, Cisley, Mary's baby sister, Margaret, 7-year-old Temperance Bayley, and William Farrer, who became her stepfather (CBE 36, 51).

***

THOMAS JORDAN (JERDAN)

Thomas Jordan (Jerdan) came to Virginia on the *Diana* and on February 16, 1624, was living on the Maine (**3**) or mainland just west of Jamestown Island. On January 30, 1625, when a muster was made of that area's inhabitants, Thomas, who was age 24, was described as one of the governor's servants. After fulfilling his contract as an indentured servant, Thomas Jordan rose in prominence. In 1629 and 1632 he served as a burgess for the corporation of Warresqueak (later, Isle of Wight County) and as a commissioner of the area's monthly court. On July 2, 1635, Thomas patented 900 acres in Warresqueak on the basis of 18 headrights, an indication that he was a successful planter (CBE 39, 57; HEN 1:154, 169, 179, 187; MCGC 200; PB 1 Pt. 1:233, 278; DOR 2:365).

WILLIAM JORDAN (JOURDEN)

On January 29, 1620, the justices of Bridewell decided that William Jordan (Jourden), who had been brought from Fleet Street, would be sent to Virginia. On March 22, 1622, when the Indians attacked the settlement at the College Land (**66**), William was killed (CBE 18; VCR 3:566).

JOHN JORNALL

John Jornall came to Virginia in 1623 on the *Ann* and on February 16, 1624, was living in Elizabeth City (**18**). When a muster was made of that area's inhabitants in early 1625, John was identified as a 20-year-old servant in the household of Michael Wilcocks and John Slater on the west side of the Hampton River (CBE 43, 64).

ASHER JOY

On December 4, 1634, when Hugh Cox received a court order entitling him to a patent, he listed Asher Joy as a headright (PB 1 Pt. 1:282).

JOHN JOYCE (JOYSE)

In early August 1626 John Joyce (Joyse) was hauled before the General Court and charged with being a thief and a runaway. Court testimony reveals that Joyce, who was one of Ensign Francis Eppes's servants and lived at West and Shirley Hundred (**41**), had fled from his master, taking along two guns, powder, shot, and a canoe that he had stolen from Simon Sturgis (Turgis). After two witnesses testified, the justices decided that John Joyce's master had neither mistreated him nor deprived him of food and other necessities. Therefore, they sentenced him to a severe whipping and decided that after he fulfilled his original commitment to Francis Eppes, plus an additional six months, he would be made to serve the colony for five years. He was said to be stubborn and have a foul and unruly disposition. Eppes used John Joyce as a headright when patenting some land on August 26, 1635 (MCGC 105; PB 1 Pt. 2:280).

WILLIAM JOYCE (JOY, JOYNES)

William Joyce (Joy, Joynes) came to Virginia on the *Abigail* in 1621 and on February 16, 1624, was living in Elizabeth City. In early 1625 he was still there and was residing on the east side of the Hampton River on the Virginia Company's land (**17**). Joyce was then a 26-year-old servant or tenant in the household of William Barry. On January 12, 1627, when the tenants of the defunct Virginia Company were distributed among high-ranking public officials, William Joyce was assigned to Surveyor William Claiborne, who had property in Elizabeth City on the west side of the Hampton River (**18**) (CBE 43, 68; MCGC 136).

JOHN JOYNER

On January 29, 1620, the justices of Bridewell decided that John Joyner, who had been brought in from London's Fleet Street, would be sent to Virginia. He probably was one of the children rounded up from the streets so that they could be sent to the colony (CBE 18).

MADDAR JULIAN (JULYAN)

In 1619 it was decided that Maddar Julian (Julyan), a thief from Middlesex who was being detained in Newgate Prison, would be reprieved and transported overseas (CBE 12).

MEDARTUS JULIAN (JULYAN)

On November 20, 1622, Medartus Julian (Julyan), who was being detained in Newgate Prison, was pardoned and deemed suit able for transportation to the colonies. This decision was made during an outbreak of jail fever (CBE 29).

ROBERT JULIAN

On January 24, 1625, Robert Julian, who came to Virginia on the *Jacob*, was a 20-year-old servant in Thomas Passmore's household, in the eastern end of Jamestown Island (1) (HOT 227).

***

WILLIAM JULIAN

William Julian, an ancient planter, came to Virginia on the *Hercules* in 1608–1609. Virginia Company records reveal that Deputy Governor Samuel Argall (1617–1618) assigned Julian some land in Elizabeth City on the east side of the Hampton River (17) and that he had built a house there prior to the arrival of Governor George Yeardley in mid-April 1619. When 3,000 acres of land were set aside for the Virginia Company's use in Elizabeth City, William Julian was evicted from the property he and his four servants had been occupying. On February 16, 1624, when a census was made of the colony's inhabitants, William Julian and his wife were living in Elizabeth City (18) but had moved to the west side of the Hampton River. On September 20, 1624, Julian received a patent for 150 acres of land in Elizabeth City, which included the 100 acres to which he was entitled as an ancient planter. He was then identified as a yeoman. In early 1625 43-year-old William Julian and his wife, Sara, were living in a household that included two servants and four other adults who were free. The Julian household had use of a dwelling, a palisade, an ample supply of stored food and defensive weaponry, and some livestock. On January 3, 1625, William Julian delivered a petition to the governor in which he sought compensation for the acreage he had developed within what became the Virginia Company's land in Elizabeth City. He also requested some back pay the defunct Company owed him. In November 1625 William was told that he would receive compensation from the Company's assets. When a list of patented land was sent back to England in May 1625, William Julian was credited with 150 acres of land in Elizabeth City, acreage that had been seated, most

likely the property he had patented in September 1624 (CBE 43, 64; VCR 2:44; 4:558; PB 1 Pt. 1:31-32; MCGC 41, 76; DOR 1:54).

SARA JULIAN (MRS. WILLIAM JULIAN)

In 1618 Sara, who wed William Julian, came to Virginia on the *Neptune*, the vessel on which Lord Delaware had set sail. On February 16, 1624, Sara and William Julian were living in Elizabeth City (18), where he was a household head. They were still there a year later and were sharing their home with two servants and four other adults. Sara Julian was then 25 years old and her husband was 43 (CBE 43, 64).

***

RICE JUSTINE

On July 31, 1622, the Virginia Company noted that Rice Justine had gone to Virginia on the *James* with John Cornish (FER 400).

K

JOHN KADON

On January 20, 1634, John Kadon owned some land in Elizabeth City (19) adjacent to Gilbert Symond's leasehold on the Old Poquoson River (PB 1 Pt. 1:156).

ALICE KEAN (KEEN, KEENE)

On February 16, 1624, Alice Kean (Keen, Keene) was a servant in the Jamestown Island (1) home of John Hall and his wife. By January 24, 1625, she had joined the household of John Johnson I, who also lived on Jamestown Island. Alice Kean may have been related to Lieutenant Richard Kean, who died during the March 22, 1622, Indian attack on Martin's Hundred (7), for the survivors were evacuated to Jamestown Island (CBE 40, 56).

GEORGE KEAN (KEEN, KEENE)

In September 1620 George Kean (Keen, Keene), a gentleman, set sail from Bristol, England, on the ship *Supply* and accompanied William Tracy, who was bound for Berkeley Hundred (**55**). Kean was supposed to serve the Society of Berkeley Hundred's investors for three years and, in exchange, was to receive 50 acres of land. Governor George Yeardley informed the Virginia Company that George Kean arrived at his destination on January 29, 1621. However, he returned to England a year or so later (CBE 20; VCR 3:396, 426).

***

RICHARD KEAN (KEEN, KEENE)

On September 11, 1621, the Society of Martin's Hundred's investors placed Richard Kean (Keen, Keene) in charge of the new people who were setting out for Virginia. Kean, who was designated a lieutenant, was given Robert Limborough (a metalworker) and four apprentices and was sent a barrel of powder. In December 1621 Virginia Company officials wrote to William Harwood, who was already in Virginia and serving as the leader of Martin's Hundred (**7**), asking him to accommodate Lieutenant Kean and provide him with support. On the other hand, the Society told Kean that it was in his best interest to form good relationships with William Harwood, Sir George Sandys (the colony's treasurer), and Sir Francis Wyatt (the incoming governor). Lieutenant Richard Kean died at Martin's Hundred during the March 22, 1622, Indian attack. A few months later, his father and brother arrived in Virginia (FER 113, 322, 339 VCR 3:506, 570; 4:60).

[NO FIRST NAME] KEAN (KEEN, KEENE)

The father of Lieutenant Richard Kean (Keen, Keene) came to Martin's Hundred (**7**) at Christmastime (January 1623), a few months after the March 1622 Indian attack had claimed Richard's life. Richard's father and brother lived in the home of the settlement's headman, William Harwood, and died there sometime prior to late March or early April 1623 (VCR 4:60).

[NO FIRST NAME] KEAN (KEEN, KEENE)

The brother of Lieutenant Richard Kean (Keen, Keene) arrived at Martin's Hundred (**7**) at Christmastime (January 1623), a few months after the March 1622 Indian attack had claimed Richard's life. Richard's father and brother lived in the home of the settlement's leader, William Harwood, where they died sometime prior to late March or early April 1623 (VCR 4:60).

***

WILLIAM KEDWELL

On January 12, 1627, William Kedwell, a sailor on the *Marmaduke*, testified before the justices of the General Court at Jamestown (**1**). He said that one of William Capps's young male servants went ashore at Cowes and later returned to the ship. Capps was a resident of Elizabeth City (**18**) (MCGC 134).

THOMAS KEELING

Thomas Keeling came to Virginia in 1628 aboard the *Hopewell* at the expense of Adam Thorogood, who used his headright when patenting some land on June 24, 1635. On November 18, 1635, Keeling himself patented 100 acres of land on the lower side of the James River, in what was then Elizabeth City (**20 a**) (PB 1 Pt. 1:179, 313, 315).

***

REV. GEORGE KEITH (KETH, KEYTH, KITH, SKIFFE, CISSE)

The Rev. George Keith (Keth, Keyth, Kith, Skiffe, Cisse), a Scottish clergyman, went to Bermuda in 1612 and stayed until 1615. He set out for Virginia on the *George* in 1617 and took up residence in Elizabeth City (**18**), where he was living when a census was taken on February 16, 1624. Sometime prior to October 10, 1624, the Rev. Keith voluntarily moved to Martin's Hundred (**7**), where he stayed briefly. His wife, Susan, was then the guardian of Sara Spence, a young orphan and landowner. On January 24, 1625, one of the Rev. Keith's servants and Mrs. Susan Keith were listed among the dead at Jamestown (**1**). Around that time, the Rev. Keith, who was age 40, returned to Elizabeth City where he headed a relatively well-provisioned household that included his 11-year-old son, John, and another boy. When a list of patented land was sent back to England in May 1625, the Rev. George Keith was credited with 100 acres in Elizabeth City, land that already had been planted. On

May 2, 1625, the General Court summoned Keith and his neighbor, Susan Bush, to appear on May 16th. By April 3, 1627, George Keith had become responsible for the late Sara Spence's estate, against which a lawsuit was pending. On the same day, he sold the 100 acres he owned adjacent to Elizabeth City's glebe, agreeing to surrender his land title to the purchaser as soon as he had been paid in full. On March 4, 1629, the justices of the General Court noted that the Rev. George Keith, who had vacated his parish in Elizabeth City and gone to England, had returned to Virginia. As his old position as rector of Elizabeth City had been filled, he was assigned to a new parish that included the plantations between Marie's Mount (24) and Water's Creek. Sometime prior to July 29, 1635, the Rev. George Keith became the minister of Chiskiack (30-38). He then patented 850 acres of land on the York River, acreage that he had received by means of a February 26, 1634, court order. Keith used the headrights of his wife, Martha, and his son, John (CBE 44, 56, 64; LEF 706; MCGC 22, 28, 57, 76, 146-147, 189; VCR 4:557; PB 1 Pt. 1:266; DOR 1:55).

SUSAN KEITH (KETH, KEYTH, KITH, SKIFFE, CISSE) (MRS. GEORGE KEITH [KETH, KEYTH, KITH, SKIFFE, CISSE])

On November 1, 1624, the General Court ordered Mrs. Susan Keith (Keth, Keyth, Kith, Skiffe, Cisse), the wife of the Rev. George Keith of Elizabeth City (18), to see that the late Ensign William Spence's acreage in Archer's Hope (6) was surveyed. Mrs. Keith was then guardian of the orphaned Sara Spence, whose parents died in late 1623 or early 1624. On January 24, 1625, Mrs. Keith was listed among those who had died on Jamestown Island (1). Meanwhile, little Sara Spence was living in the Elizabeth City household of Mrs. Susan Bush, a young widow who seems to have been the Keiths' neighbor and may have been a kinswoman (MCGC 28, 57; CBE 56).

MARTHA KEITH (KETH, KEYTH, KITH, SKIFFE, CISSE) (MRS. GEORGE KEITH [KETH, KEYTH, KITH, SKIFFE, CISSE])

On July 29, 1635, when the Rev. George Keith patented some land at Chiskiack (30-

38), he used his wife, Martha, as a headright (PB 1 Pt. 1:266).

JOHN KEITH (KETH, KEYTH, KITH, SKIFFE, CISSE)

John Keith (Keth, Keyth, Kith, Skiffe, Cisse), son of the Rev. George Keith, came to Virginia in 1617 on the *George*. Early in 1625, he was living in Elizabeth City (18), in a household headed by his father, who was the parish rector. John Keith was then age 11. On July 29, 1635, when the Rev. George Keith patented some land in Chiskiack, he used his son, John, as a headright (CBE 64; PB 1 Pt.1:266).

***

WILLIAM KELLOWAY

William Kelloway, a 20-year-old husbandman from Portsmouth, England, arrived in Jamestown on September 5, 1623, on the *Ann* (MCGC 6).

WALTER KELY

On June 5, 1632, Walter Kely was identified as the owner of some land in Elizabeth City (17-18) on the Hampton River, adjoining that of Nicholas Brown (MCGC 201).

ARTHUR KEMIS

On September 3, 1620, Arthur Kemis, a gentleman, was among those who set sail from Bristol, England, on the ship *Supply* and accompanied William Tracy, who was bound for Berkeley Hundred (55). Kemis was supposed to serve the Society of Berkeley Hundred's investors for four years in exchange for 50 acres of land. Arthur Kemis and his fellow passengers arrived at Berkeley Hundred on January 29, 1621, but he died within a short time (CBE 20-21; VCR 3:396, 427).

THOMAS KEMIS

On September 3, 1620, Thomas Kemis, a gentleman, set sail from Bristol, England, on the ship *Supply*, which was bound for Berkeley Hundred (55). He was among those accompanying the settlement's leader, William Tracy. Kemis, a surveyor, was supposed to demarcate Berkeley Hundred's bounds as soon as he arrived and had agreed to serve the Society of Berkeley Hundred's investors for four years, in exchange for 50 acres of land. Surveyor Thomas Kemis arrived at his destination on January 29, 1621. In August 1622 he was identified as Berkeley Hundred's leader, having succeeded the late William Tracy (CBE 20-21; VCR 3:396, 398-400, 426).

***

RICHARD KEMP

Richard Kemp, a native of Gilling in Norfolk, England, was named a councilor and Secretary of the Colony in August 1634. A month later he asked the king for some office land, indentured servants, and livestock. Secretary Richard Kemp's official correspondence reveals that he was fiercely loyal to Governor John Harvey, but clashed with the Rev. Anthony Panton, who subjected him to public ridicule and made fun of his coiffeur. After Governor Harvey was ousted from office, Kemp continued to serve as secretary. In 1636 he proposed the establishment of a customhouse in Virginia and after Harvey regained his governorship, he made Kemp customs officer, a position that yielded handsome fees. On November 14, 1637, Secretary Richard Kemp obtained a patent for 600 acres of land in Archer's Hope (6), part of his stipend as secretary. During February 1638 he sought to obtain the 20 indentured servants and the cattle he claimed were his due as secretary. On January 3, 1638, Kemp purchased George Menefie's 1,200-acre plantation called Littletown. He changed its name to Rich Neck and acquired 100 acres near the Middle Plantation palisade. Two months later Kemp patented 840 acres of contiguous land called The Meadows. These land acquisitions gave him a massive amount of acreage. On August 1, 1638, Secretary Richard Kemp patented a half-acre parcel in urban Jamestown (1), where by January 18, 1639, he had constructed a brick house that Governor John Harvey described as "the fairest ever known in this country for substance and uniformity." In early April 1639 Kemp wrote Secretary Windebank that he wanted to go to England and that a new governor, Sir Francis Wyatt, was expected daily. When Wyatt arrived and a new council took office, Kemp was suspended as secretary. He slipped away to England, where he arrived on August 1640. He an-

gered Wyatt and other Virginia officials by absconding with some of the colony's official records. Kemp asked Lords Baltimore and Maltravers (two of the king's favorites) to help him defend himself against allegations made by the controversial Rev. Anthony Panton. Richard Kemp was married to Elizabeth, the daughter of Christopher Wormeley I and niece of Ralph Wormeley, one of Virginia's wealthiest and most influential planters.

In 1643, after Governor William Berkeley took office, Richard Kemp again became a councilor and secretary of the colony. On April 17, 1643, he repatented Rich Neck and his other holdings and laid claim to an additional 2,192 acres. This gave him an aggregate of 4,332 acres. In June 1644, only two months after a major Indian attack claimed nearly 400 lives, he was named acting governor. In February 1645 Kemp sent word to Governor Berkeley that forts or surveillance posts had been built on the fringes of the frontier to restrict the Indians' access to the colonized area. After Berkeley returned to Virginia, he granted Secretary Kemp the privilege of appointing all county clerks of court, as well as the right to set their pay. As Kemp drew part of his compensation from clerks' fees, this privilege was a potentially lucrative one. In 1649 he acquired 3,500 acres on Mobjack Bay from Ralph Wormeley I. On January 4, 1649, when Richard Kemp of Rich Neck made his will, indicating that he was "sick and weak," he instructed his executrices (his wife and daughter, both of whom were named Elizabeth) to sell Rich Neck and to confirm his sale of 50 acres in the nearby Barren Neck to George Read, a longtime friend and his choice for deputy-secretary. Kemp told his widow to dispose of his house in Jamestown and asked her to take their daughter and leave Virginia. Richard Kemp died sometime prior to October 24, 1650, by which date his widow had married Sir Thomas Lunsford, a Royalist. However, Kemp's will did not reach authorities in England until December 6, 1656 (CO 1/8 ff 90, 166-169; 1/9 ff 209, 228ro, 242ro, 289; 1/10 ff 59, 124, 160; HLOP 104; SAIN 1:191, 207, 232, 263-264, 268, 274, 287-289, 293, 309-311, 314; MCGC 473, 481-483, 491-492, 495-496, 501, 510, 562-563; AMB 2, 3, 4, 34; Lower Norfolk County Book A:178, 246; B:6, 37, 70, 87, 112; WITH 323; MCGH 775; STAN 15, 21, 32; NUG 1:75, 143, 160, 182, 229, 242, 282, 294, 298, 428, 465, 473; JHB 1619-

1660:126; EEAC 34; PB 1 Pt.2:496, 587-588; MHS 131-152; SH 28; NEI 142).

ELIZABETH WORMELEY KEMP (MRS. RICHARD KEMP, MRS. THOMAS LUNSFORD, MRS. ROBERT SMITH)

Elizabeth Kemp, the daughter of Christopher Wormeley and niece of Ralph Wormeley I, married Secretary Richard Kemp and produced a daughter named Elizabeth. After Richard's death in ca. 1650 she married Sir Thomas Lunsford, a hotheaded Royalist and friend of Sir William Berkeley. Elizabeth Kemp Lunsford retained Rich Neck until at least July 1654 and became known as Lady Lunsford. Richard and Elizabeth Kemp's daughter, Elizabeth, who was alive in January 1649, died prior to December 6, 1656, at which time Elizabeth Kemp Lunsford informed English probate officials that she was the surviving executrix. Later, she married Robert Smith (NUG 1 Pt. 1:229, 282, 294, 298, 428; Pt. 2:465, 473; MCGH 775; WITH 323; EEAC 34; SR 3995).

ELIZABETH KEMP II

Elizabeth Kemp, the daughter of Richard and Elizabeth Wormeley Kemp, outlived her father, who in January 1650 named her as an heir. She died prior to December 6, 1656 (WITH 323; EEAC 34; MCGH 775).

***

WILLIAM KEMP

William Kemp came to Virginia on the *William and Thomas* and arrived in the colony in 1618. On May 22, 1622, he sent a list of grievances to the king on behalf of some people who had been living on the east side of the Hampton River in Elizabeth City **(17)** and were evicted when that area was designated the Virginia Company's land. On February 16, 1624, Kemp was living in Elizabeth City **(18),** and early in 1625 he was still there, residing in William Julian's household. He was then age 33. On May 2, 1625, William Kemp was ordered to pay a debt to Mr. Green on behalf of Mr. Leech, a merchant, thereby raising the possibility that he was serving as an attorney or factor. A year later he was identified as one of the

late Ensign William Spence's administrators. In April 1627 Kemp was described as a yeoman when he filed a claim against the Rev. George Keith in an attempt to recover a sum owed to the estate of Sara Spence. William Kemp apparently was a respected member of the community, for in March 1629 he was named a commissioner of Elizabeth City's monthly court and a year later he was elected a burgess for the upper part of Elizabeth City. He was functioning in an official capacity as late as September 1632, at which time he was paid for some shot (MCGC 57, 122, 147, 193; VCR 2:44; 4:185; CBE 43, 64; HEN 1:132, 149, 171, 196).

WILLIAM KEMP

On September 5, 1623, William Kemp, a gentleman from Howes in Leistershire, arrived in Jamestown **(1)** on the *Ann* and took the oath of supremacy (MCGC 6).

***

WILLIAM KEMP

William Kemp came to Virginia on the *George*, and on February 16, 1624, he and his wife were residing on the Maine **(3)** just west of Jamestown Island. On January 30, 1625, William and his wife, Margaret, were still there, along with their infant, Anthony. The Kemp household was relatively well supplied with provisions and defensive weaponry (CBE 39, 57; DOR 1:25).

MARGARET KEMP (MRS. WILLIAM KEMP)

Margaret, the wife of William Kemp, came to Virginia on the *George* and on February 16, 1624, was living on the Maine **(3)**. On January 30, 1625, when a muster was made of the colony's inhabitants, Margaret Kemp was living in a household headed by her husband, William. They shared their home with their 7-week-old son, Anthony (CBE 39, 57; DOR 1:25).

ANTHONY KEMP

On January 30, 1625, Anthony Kemp, the 7-week-old son of William and Margaret Kemp, was sharing a home with his parents on the Maine **(3)** (CBE 57).

***

WILLIAM KEMP

William Kemp came to Virginia on the *John and Dorothy* in 1634. On June 24, 1635, Adam Thorogood used his headright when patenting some land and claimed that he had covered the cost of Kemp's transportation to Virginia (PB 1 Pt. 1:179).

KEMPS

Kemps, an Indian who befriended the English and spent a lot of time in Jamestown (1), sustained abuse at the colonists' hands. Captain John Smith said that Kemps and Tassore, another Indian, were detained as fettered prisoners in 1609 and were forced to show the colonists how to plant fields. Later, both men were released (CJS 2:212).

[NO FIRST NAME] KEMYE

On May 21, 1621, Virginia Company officials decided to place Mr. Kemye in charge of the Company's magazine (or store of supplies) while Edward Blaney was away (VCR 4:448-449).

GEORGE KENDALL

George Kendall, one of the first Jamestown (1) colonists, was among the councilors who on June 22, 1607, sent a letter to officials in England, reporting on the status of the colony. Shortly thereafter, he incurred the wrath of President Edward Maria Wingfield, who claimed that he caused dissention. Kendall was ousted from the council and imprisoned on a pinnace. Later in the year, he was tried in a martial court and executed for mutiny (HAI 99, 124-126, 186, 192, 194).

JOHN KENDALL

On July 21, 1627, the Bridewell Court decided that John Kendall, who had been brought in from Cheapward, would be sent to Virginia as a servant. He was to serve for a term of 8 years (CBE 79).

***

ALLEN KENISTON (KEINNSTON, KINASTON, KNISTON)

Allen Keniston (Keinnston, Kinaston, Kniston) came to Virginia on the *Margaret*

and John and on January 30, 1625, was living alone in Pasbehay (3). He was relatively well provisioned and had a suit of armor. In January 1625 Keniston asked Richard Peirce to allow him to purchase the time remaining on his contract. On March 13, 1626, the justices of the General Court decided that his freedom dues could be deducted from the amount of corn that he needed to buy his freedom. On October 11, 1627, the General Court noted that Allen Keniston had hired Steven Tailor, one of Mrs. John Pott's servants. Two months later, however, after Tailor became lame, Keniston returned him and offered to pay for his cure. Allen Keniston may have moved to what became Surry County, where his wife was residing in 1629 (CBE 57; MCGC 96-97, 155).

MRS. ALLEN KENISTON (KEINNSTON, KINASTON, KNISTON)

On March 25, 1629, Mrs. Allen Keniston (Keinnston, Kinaston, Kniston) was identified as one of the women who had physically examined Thomas Hall, a servant found to be a hermaphrodite (MCGC 155).

***

ELLIS KENISTON (KINISTON, KINASTON)

According to George Percy, Ellis Keniston (Kiniston, Kinaston), one of the first colonists, died on September 18, 1607. He reportedly was "starved with cold" (HAI 100).

THOMAS KENISTON (KEINNSTON, KNISTON)

On February 16, 1624, Thomas Keniston (Keinnston, Kniston) was listed among those who had died in Elizabeth City (17, 18) sometime after April 1623 (CBE 45).

THOMAS KENISTON (KEINNSTON, KNISTON)

Thomas Keniston (Keinnston, Kniston) came to Virginia on the *George* in 1623. By January 30, 1625, he was living on the Maine (3) just west of Jamestown Island, where he shared a home with his partner, Robert Scotchmore, and a male servant. The three men were relatively well provi-

sioned and supplied with defensive weaponry. Thomas may have been the same man
who had been reported dead in Elizabeth
City in February 1624 (CBE 58; DOR 1:28).

PATRICK KENNEDE (KENNEDY)

On January 11, 1627, Patrick Kennede
(Kennedy), a mariner, presented Edmund
Pritchard's will to the General Court at
Jamestown (1). He was ordered to pay
Pritchard's debts to William Claiborne and
George Menefie and to compensate Edward
Waters of Elizabeth City (William Capps's
attorney) for the loss of a young male servant at Cowes. On February 19, 1627,
Patrick Kennede, who was identified as
purser of the *Marmaduke*, testified about a
sexual encounter that allegedly occurred in
James Slight's house at Captain John
Martin's plantation (59). The General Court
ordered him to give Philamon Powell some
casks of wine, as the *Marmaduke's* sailors
had consumed part of Powell's shipment.
Patrick Kennede apparently returned to sea,
for on December 12, 1629, he was aboard
the *Friendship* of London when he witnessed John Rayment's will (MCGC 133-
135, 139; SH 12).

JOHN KENNELL

On April 4, 1625, the General Court ordered Mr. Palmer to return John Kennell (a
servant) to Rice Hoe, in accord with Mr.
Besse's written instructions. Hoe was then
residing at West and Shirley Hundred (41),
whereas William Besse was associated with
Jordan's Journey (46) (MCGC 51).

***

SAMUEL (SAMMUEL) KENNELL

Samuel (Sammuel) Kennell came to Virginia in 1621 on the *Abigail* and on February 16, 1624, was living in Elizabeth City
on the east side of the Hampton River (17),
on the Virginia Company's land. He was
still there in early 1625 and was a 30-year-
old member of John Lauckfield's household. By October 13, 1627, Samuel Kennell
was dead and his widow had married John
Barnett of Jamestown (1). The decedent left
behind some debts, one of which was owed
to Mr. Peirsey (CBE 45, 67; MCGC 156).

MRS. SAMUEL (SAMMUEL)
KENNELL (MRS. JOHN BARNETT)

Sometime prior to October 13, 1627, the
widowed Mrs. Samuel (Sammuel) Kennell
married John Barnett of Jamestown (1). She
ran afoul of the law because she had disposed of her late husband's estate before
satisfying his debt to Mr. Peirsey. The General Court decided that John Barnett was
not culpable (MCGC 156).

***

EZEKAELL KENNINGTON

Ezekaell Kennington, a 20-year-old chandler from Essex, England, came to Virginia
in 1619 on the *Bona Nova* (FER 295).

RICHARD KENSHAM

On January 9, 1624, Richard Kensham,
who was then in Virginia, was identified as
master of the *Mary Prood* (MCGC 10).

***

HUMPHREY KENT

On March 18, 1607, 5-year-old Humphrey
Kent, the son of John Kent, a merchant tailor, was admitted to Christ Church Hospital
from St. Sepulcher. On October 17, 1618,
officials decided that Humphrey should be
sent to his mother, who already was in Virginia. He was put aboard the *George*, which
arrived in the colony in 1619. By January 20,
1625, Humphrey Kent was living at Flowerdew Hundred (53), where he headed a
household that included his wife, Joan, 9-
year-old Margaret Arundell, and one male
servant. The Kents were relatively well supplied with provisions and defensive weaponry. In May 1625 Humphrey Kent was
identified as the patentee of 50 acres of land
on the Appomattox River (39) in the corporation of Charles City. However, two legal
documents executed during the early to mid-
1650s, after Humphrey Kent was deceased,
indicate that he had owned and occupied 60
acres of land at Weyanoke (52) (CH 11; CBE
50; VCR 4:554; DOR 1:22, 417-418).

JOAN KENT
(MRS. HUMPHREY KENT)

Joan Kent came to Virginia on the *Tiger* in
1621. This raises the possibility that she
was one of the marriageable young women

sent to the colony as wives. On January 20, 1625, Joan Kent was living at Flowerdew Hundred (**53**) with her husband, Humphrey, 9-year-old Margaret Arundell, and one male servant. Joan was then age 21 (CBE 50; FER 309).

***

ELIZABETH KENYTHORPE (SEE ELIZABETH KENYTHORPE DELKE [DILKE])

THOMAS KERFITT

Thomas Kerfitt came to Virginia on the *Hopewell*. On January 24, 1625, he was a 24-year-old servant in Thomas Passmore's household in rural Jamestown Island (**1**) (HOT 227).

JOHN KERILL

John Kerill died in Elizabeth City (**17, 18**) sometime after April 1623 but before February 16, 1624 (CBE 42).

THOMAS KERRIDGE

On July 3, 1622, Thomas Kerridge, commander of the East India Company's fleet, received some land from the Virginia Company of London. Shortly thereafter, his land grant was confirmed (VCR 2:73, 89).

THOMAS KERSIE

On August 22, 1625, Thomas Kersie testified that Christopher Hall, who resided on Jamestown Island (**1**), rarely worked a full day. Kersie may have lived there too (MCGC 69).

HENRY KERSLY

On February 16, 1624, Henry Kersly was living in Elizabeth City (**17, 18**). In February 1637 he received a bequest from his friend, William Angell, who indicated that Kersly was still in Virginia (CBE 43; WITH 41-42; EEAC 2).

WILLIAM KERTON

On January 15, 1620, officials at Bridewell decided that William Kerton, a vagrant born in Lincolnshire and incarcerated in Old Bailey, would be sent to Virginia. Kerton died in Jamestown (**1**) sometime after April

1623 but before February 16, 1624 (CBE 17, 39).

[NO FIRST NAME] KETTLEBY

On July 2, 1621, Mr. Kettleby informed the Virginia Company that he wanted to go to Virginia at his own expense and said that he would like to be recommended to the governor (VCR 1:502).

HENRY KETTLIN

On July 31, 627, Henry Kettlin shipped goods from London to Virginia on the *Hopewell* (CBE 79).

***

THOMAS KEY (KEIE, KEYES)

Thomas Key (Keie, Keyes) came to Virginia on the *Prosperous* and arrived in June 1619. Virginia Company records dating to April 1, 1620, indicate that his passage was paid by Thomas Astley. On January 21, 1625, Thomas Key was living at Chaplin's Choice (**56**), where he was a 30-year-old household head sharing a home with his wife, Sarah. Although the Keys had no servants, they were well supplied with provisions and defensive weaponry and had a boat. By December 2, 1628, Thomas Key had married a woman named Martha, who was identified as an ancient planter when she patented some land on the lower side of the James River, bordering the Warresqueak (Pagan) River in Warresqueak (**26**). On March 24, 1630, Thomas Key served as a burgess representing the settlers at Denbigh (**23**) (CBE 51; FER 162; PB 1 Pt. 1:66; HEN 1:148; DOR 1:21).

SARAH KEY (KEIE, KEYES) (MRS. THOMAS KEY [KEIE, KEYES])

Sarah, the wife of Thomas Key (Keie, Keyes), came to Virginia in 1622 on the *Truelove* and probably was part of the group known as Truelove's Company, many of whom settled at Chaplin's Choice (**56**). On January 21, 1625, Sarah and Thomas were living at Chaplin's Choice, where he was a household head. She died prior to December 2, 1628, by which time Thomas had remarried (CBE 51; PB 1 Pt. 1:66).

MARTHA KEY (KEIE, KEYES)
(MRS. THOMAS KEY
[KEIE, KEYES])

Martha, the wife of Thomas Key (Keie, Keyes), was an ancient planter. She married him sometime after January 21, 1625, but before December 2, 1628, when she patented some land on the lower side of the James River, bordering the Warresqueak (Pagan) River. On February 13, 1629, Mrs. Thomas Key was one of Jamestown **(1)** merchant Thomas Warnett's legatees (PB 1 Pt. 1:66; SH 11-12).

***

RICHARD KEYES

On December 19, 1617, Richard Keyes was identified as one of Captain Robert Smalley's (Smallay's) servants at Bermuda Hundred **(39)**. When Smalley made his will, he bequeathed Keyes five yards of kersey cloth and two barrels of Indian corn (SR 3112; SH 4).

BENOMY KEYMAN

On March 22, 1622, when the Indians attacked Lieutenant Gibbs's plantation at Berkeley Hundred **(55)**, Benomy Keyman was killed (VCR 3:567).

NICHOLAS KEYS

Virginia Company records indicate that in 1619 the Ferrars, who were important Company investors, paid Nicholas Keys's transportation to Virginia (FER 296).

ROGER KID (KIDD)

Roger Kid (Kidd) came to Virginia on the *George* in 1623 and on February 16, 1624, was living on the Maine **(3)**, just west of Jamestown Island. On January 30, 1625, when a muster was made of the colony's inhabitants, he was still there. Roger, who was age 24, was a servant in the household headed by Robert Scotchmore and Thomas Kniston. Although it is uncertain when and where he moved after his term of indenture had expired, he died sometime prior to February 9, 1633, at which time Francis Poythress was granted a letter of administration for his estate (CBE 39, 58; MCGC 202).

***

SARAH KIDALL
(KILDALE, KILLDALE?)
(MRS. [NO FIRST NAME] KIDALL
[KILDALE, KILLDALE?],
MRS. EDWARD FISHER)
(SEE SARAH FISHER)

On February 16, 1624, the widowed Sarah Kidall (Kildale, Killdale?) and her two young children were living on the Maine **(3)**, to the west of Jamestown Island. By January 30, 1625, she had married Edward Fisher and was living on the Maine (or Pasbehay) with her 6-year-old son, Edward Kidall, and Clare Ren, who was age 10. Sarah's infant, who had been alive in early 1624, apparently had died. On February 4, 1626, Sarah testified before the General Court that she was in her own home when she heard Peter Marten say that Richard Cornish alias Williams had been wrongfully executed. This was at a time when criticizing the government often resulted in severe punishment (CBE 39, 57; MCGC 93).

[NO FIRST NAME] KIDALL
(KILDALE, KILLDALE?)

On February 16, 1624, an infant belonging to Sarah Kidall (Kildale, Killdale?) was living in a household on the Maine **(3)**, which also included Edward Kidall. The infant appears to have died sometime prior to January 30, 1625 (CBE 39).

EDWARD KIDALL
(KILDALE, KILLDALE?)

On February 16, 1624, Edward Kidall (Kildale, Killdale?) was living on the Maine **(3)** with his widowed mother, Sarah, and a young infant. On January 30, 1625, Edward, who was 6 years old, resided in a household headed by his stepfather, Edward Fisher. Also sharing the Fisher family home were young Edward's mother, Sarah Fisher, and 10-year-old Clare Ren, whose connection with the family is uncertain. Missing was the infant who had been in the Kidall household in mid-February 1624 (CBE 39, 57).

***

THOMAS KIDDAR II

On July 12, 1620, Thomas Kiddar I. asked Virginia Company officials to see that his son, Thomas II, was returned. The elder man claimed that young Thomas had been apprenticed to a London haberdasher for seven years, but had been persuaded by Edward Cross to go to Virginia (VCR 1:401).

EDWARD KIDDER

In 1621 Nicholas Norber sent a firkin to Edward Kidder, who was in Virginia (FER 322).

HUGH KIDDERMASTER

On September 6, 1628, it was decided that Hugh Kiddermaster, who had been imprisoned at Bridewell for a long period of time, would be sent to Virginia at the expense of Henry Dormer (CBE 84).

WILLIAM KILDRIGE

On February 16, 1624, William Kildridge was living in Elizabeth City (**18**) (CBE 44).

WILLIAM KILLDALE (KILDALE?, KIDALL?)

On February 4, 1623, the General Court heard testimony about William Killdale (Kildale?, Kidall?) shooting a dog belonging to Nicholas and Bridget Root. Nicholas Root and Richard Craven reportedly were poised to strike Killdale, whereupon Thomas Hethersall's dog bit Root, who commenced beating it with a stick. The justices ordered Richard Craven to pay for William Killdale's medical treatment, and Craven and Nicholas Root were required to post a bond, guaranteeing their good behavior. As the Roote couple, Richard Craven, and Thomas Hethersall were residing on the Maine (**3**), just west of Jamestown Island, it is probable that William Killdale lived there too. He may have been the husband of Sarah Kidall (Kildale, Killdale), who by February 16, 1624, had been widowed. If so, he would have been the father of Edward Kidall (MCGC 3; CBE 39).

THOMAS KILLSON

In 1623 Thomas Killson came to Virginia on the *Truelove*, and in early 1625 he was residing in Elizabeth City (**18**) in a household headed by Susan Bush, a widow. Thomas Killson was then age 21 (CBE 64).

[NO FIRST NAME] KING

On March 15, 1620, Virginia Company officials noted that Mr. King and 50 people were to go to Virginia on the *Francis Bonaventure* and set up an ironworks in the colony (VCR 1:322).

ELIZABETH KING (KINGE)

On July 19, 1633, the justices of Bridewell decided that Elizabeth King (Kinge), who had been brought in from Whitefriars, would be sent to Virginia. She reportedly expressed her willingness to go (CBE 108).

HENRY KING (KINGE)

On January 22, 1620, officials decided that Henry King (Kinge), a vagrant who was being detained in Bridewell Prison, would be sent to Virginia. He arrived in the colony later in the year on the *Jonathan*. On February 4, 1625, Henry was 22 years old and living on Hog Island (**16**), where he was one of Sir George Yeardley's servants. In 1629 Henry King, who was then living in Stanley Hundred Parish (**22, 23**), was brought before the General Court and accused of having sex with John Jackson's wife. He was ordered to leave the Jackson premises until John Jackson returned (CBE 17, 61; MCGC 200).

JAMES KING (KINGE)

On January 22, 1620, the Bridewell Court decided that James King (Kinge), a vagrant brought in from the Bridge, would be sent to Virginia (CBE 17).

JOHN KING (KINGE)

On October 3, 1618, Bridewell officials noted that John King (Kinge), who was supposed to be transported to Virginia, had been discharged and was given the option of staying in England or going to the colony (CBE 10).

LETTICE KING

In 1621 Lettice King, a young maid born at Newberry, Barkshire (Berkshire), went to Virginia on the *Marmaduke*. She was then 23 years old and her parents were dead. Lettice's late father was a husbandman and her brother was an attorney in Newberry.

One of her uncles was Sir William Udall and another was Edward Colton of the Chart House (FER 306, 309).

NATHANIEL KING (KINGE)

On September 19, 1618, the justices of Bridewell court decided to send Nathaniel King (Kinge), a vagrant born at Radcliffe and brought in from Tower Street, to Virginia (CBE 9).

ROBERT KING (KINGE)

On August 8, 1618, the justices of Bridewell decided to send Robert King (Kinge), a vagrant, to Virginia (CBE 9).

WILLIAM KINGSLEY

William Kingsley came to Virginia on the *Marmaduke* in 1623 and on February 4, 1625, was living at Captain Samuel Mathews' plantation (15) on the lower side of the James River. William was then age 24 (CBE 60).

***

RICHARD KINGSMILL

Richard Kingsmill, an ancient planter, came to Virginia on the *Delaware*, probably in 1610. He was present in 1619 when Governor George Yeardley made a treaty with the Chickahominy Indians. Kingsmill was a prominent member of the Jamestown (1) community and served as its burgess in the assemblies of 1623–1624, 1625, and 1629. He also was churchwarden of the James City Parish and was especially diligent in reporting inebriates. He and his family resided in the northwest part of Jamestown Island, where he occupied a 120-acre tract that abutted the Back River and the west side of Kingsmill Creek. In 1624 Richard Kingsmill was among those who signed *Tragicall Relation*, a document that described conditions in Virginia during the government of Sir Thomas Smith. He appeared in court regularly, where he served on juries, presented wills and inventories, and testified. He was involved in settling the estates of several prominent citizens, including cape merchant Abraham Peirsey, Vice Admiral John Pountis, Captain John Martin, and the Rev. Richard Buck. When Buck and his wife died (in late 1623 or

early 1624) Kingsmill was named one of their minor children's guardians and overseer of the deceased clergyman's will. Kingsmill moved his family to the Buck property on the Neck O'Land (5), where they lived for at least two years. By seeing that it was seated, he secured the Buck orphans' inheritance and would have been entitled to keep a portion of the profits he reaped from the land. On February 16, 1624, Richard Kingsmill, his wife, a son, a daughter, and four servants (one of whom was African) were residing in the Neck O'Land behind Jamestown Island, on the late Richard Buck's land, directly across the Back River from the Kingsmill plantation on Jamestown Island.

On February 4, 1625, the Kingsmill household was still living in the Neck O'Land. Richard and Jane Kingsmill shared their home with their children, Susan (age 1) and Nathaniel (age 5), both of whom were Virginia-born. The Kingsmills had four servants, one of whom was Edward, an African, five houses, a boat, some livestock, and an ample supply of provisions and weaponry. By that time, Captain Ralph Hamor had assigned 100 acres of land to Richard Kingsmill, acreage to which Hamor was entitled for transporting two men to the colony in 1617. On May 8, 1626, Kingsmill received a court order entitling him to Hamor's 100 acres and a like amount he had acquired from ancient planter Thomas Carter, an aggregate of 200 acres in Archer's Hope (6). When a list of patented land was sent to England in May 1625, Kingsmill was credited with 500 acres in Archer's Hope, land that had not been seated. In 1626 Richard and Jane Kingsmill took Peleg Buck into their home after the death of his guardian, Thomas Allnutt. In 1628 Richard Kingsmill was arrested for indebtedness by Jamestown merchant Richard Stephens, and later in the year Kingsmill and John Jackson of Jamestown (another Buck guardian) were sued. In July 1630 Kingsmill informed the General Court that Dr. John Pott had stolen some cattle. Pott, in turn, declared that Kingsmill was a hypocrite. Pott's comment may have been made in reference to Kingsmill's management of the Buck orphans' inheritance, which Governor John Harvey termed self-serving. After Richard Kingsmill's death, which occurred prior to July 25, 1638, his widow, Jane, married Ambrose Harmer. She appears to have gotten a 40-acre dower share of her late husband's land on Jamestown Island, whereas his daughter, Elizabeth Kingsmill Taylor (Tayloe, Tayler) Bacon, inherited the remainder (MCGC 9, 17, 24, 33, 38-39, 44, 54-55, 58, 86, 102-103, 117, 143-144, 150, 160-161, 173, 183-184, 190, 470, 479; FER 113; VCR 4:551, 556; HEN 1:128-129, 138, 145; STAN 53-54; CBE 46, 58; MEY 36, 385; CO 1/10 ff 65-66; PB 1 Pt.2:648; HAI 915; AMB 11, 12; SH 7; WITH 80; DOR 1:36, 419-420).

JANE KINGSMILL
(MRS. RICHARD KINGSMILL, MRS. AMBROSE HARMAR [HARMER])

Jane Kingsmill, an ancient planter, came to Virginia on the *Susan* and sometime prior to February 1625 married ancient planter, burgess, and churchwarden Richard Kingsmill, owner of a 120-acre plantation on Jamestown Island (**1**). Because he was one of the guardians for Rev. Richard Buck's orphans, he and Jane moved to the Buck property in the Neck O'Land (**5**), probably to seat it on the orphans' behalf and reap a profit from the land. In 1626 Richard and Jane Kingsmill took Peleg Buck into their home after the death of his former guardian, Thomas Allnutt. On February 16, 1624, Jane Kingsmill, husband Richard, son Nathaniel, daughter Susan, and four servants (one of whom was African) were residing in the Neck O'Land on the Buck orphans' property. They were still there on February 4, 1625. Mrs. Jane Kingsmill appeared in court in June 1624 to testify in a breach of promise suit involving one of the late Rev. Buck's servants. Richard Kingsmill died sometime after July 7, 1630, but before July 1638. His widow, Jane, married burgess and councilor Ambrose Harmar (Harmer), who immediately sought custody of the Buck estate. The Harmers resided on Jamestown Island and probably occupied a home located on Jane's dower share of her late husband's estate. Jane Kingsmill Harmar and husband Ambrose provided care to the orphaned Benomi Buck, who was mentally impaired and died while he was living with them. In 1652, Mrs. Jane Kingsmill Harmar patented 2,000 acres of land in Northumberland County. She died or sold her Jamestown Island land sometime prior to June 5, 1657 (STAN 34, 53-54, 64; MCGC 17, 33, 38-39, 55, 58, 86, 103, 117, 143, 150, 160, 183, 190, 479; FER 113; MEY 36, 385; WITH 80; HEN 1:145, 289; CO 1/10 ff 65-66; AMB 11; PB 1 Pt. 1:196; 2:742; 3:184; 4:196-197; CBE 46, 58; NUG 1:125).

ELIZABETH KINGSMILL
(MRS. WILLIAM TAYLOR [TAYLOE, TAYLER], MRS. NATHANIEL BACON)

Elizabeth, Richard and Jane Kingsmill's daughter, was born in 1624, if the date on her tombstone is correct. Her name was omitted from the 1624 census and when a muster was taken of the Neck O'Land's inhabitants (**5**) in February 4, 1625, perhaps because she was misidentified as "Susan." Elizabeth Kingsmill outlived her brother, Nathaniel, and sometime prior to September 1638 inherited 80 acres, the bulk of her late father's Jamestown Island (**1**) plantation. By that date she had married William Taylor (Tayloe, Tayler), who in 1640 he purchased the Kings Creek plantation (**30**) in Chiskiack from John Uty's son and heir. The Tayloes, who resided on their Kings Creek property, may have placed Elizabeth's Jamestown Island land in the hands of a tenant or put their servants on it. By 1647 William Taylor (Tayloe, Tayler) had become a York County burgess, and in 1651 he was named to the Council of State. When he died in 1655, he left the Kings Creek plantation to his widow, Elizabeth. Elizabeth became the second wife of Colonel Nathaniel Bacon, who took up residence with her at the Kings Creek plantation. Nathaniel was a councilor from 1656 to 1658 and from 1661 to 1692, and he served as auditor general. In 1671 he purchased a bay in a rowhouse on Jamestown Island. When the rebel Nathaniel Bacon (cousin of the colonel) built a trench across the isthmus leading into Jamestown Island in 1676, Elizabeth Kingsmill Taylor (Tayloe, Tayler) Bacon was one of the women he reportedly placed on the ramparts to shield his men from an attack by Governor Berkeley's loyalists. On November 6, 1661, Elizabeth and her husband, Nathaniel, sold 80 acres of her late father's Jamestown Island plantation to Nicholas Meriwether. Elizabeth predeceased Nathaniel, who became her heir and later remarried (AMB 11, 12; NUG 1:125, 394; MCGH 159; FOR 1:9:8; MEY 385; STAN 36, 66; DOR 1:419-420).

NATHANIELL KINGSMILL

On February 16, 1624, Nathaniel Kingsmill, who was born in Virginia, was living in the Neck O'Land (5) with his parents, Richard and Jane Kingsmill, He was still there on February 4, 1625, and was 5 years old. Nathaniel shared the family home with his parents and 1-year-old sister, Susan (CBE 46, 58; DOR 1:419).

SUSAN KINGSMILL

On February 16, 1624, Richard and Jane Kingsmill's Virginia-born daughter, Susan, was living in the Neck O'Land (5). She was still there on February 4, 1625, at which time she was described as age 1. The census-taker may have mistakenly identified Elizabeth Kingsmill as "Susan," for she was Richard and Jane Kingsmill's daughter and was born in 1624 (CBE 46, 58; DOR 1:419).

***

THOMAS KINGSTON (KINGSTONE)

On October 16, 1629, Thomas Kingston (Kingstone) was serving as a burgess for Martin's Hundred (7). On August 10, 1635, when John Dennett patented some land, his acreage was said to adjoin that of Thomas Kingston, near Martin's Hundred (HEN 1:139; PB 1 Pt. 1:271).

EDWARD KINGSWELL

Edward Kingswell of St. Sepulcher, in Newgate, London, set plans to establish a plantation in Carolina and made an agreement with Samuel Vassall, a mariner, to take his people there in October 1633. However, Vassall brought the Kingswell group as far as Virginia and then abandoned them. The group was stranded until May 1634. By September 1634 Kingswell had made progress toward his goal of establishing a new settlement, but ill health intervened and on January 30, 1635, he made his will. He designated his brother, Roger Wingate, and Wingate's wife, Dorothy, as his executors and made reference to his old servant, James Cooke, who was then in Virginia. Edward Kingswell bequeathed his overseas goods to his heirs but made no reference to any land he may have owned (CBE 118-119; EEAC 34; WAT 1316).

JOHN KINTON

John Kinton died at Jordan's Journey (46) sometime after April 1623 but before February 16, 1624 (CBE 37).

EDWARD KIRBY (KERBY)

In June 1619 Edward Kirby (Kerby), a gentleman, set sail for Virginia on the *Bona Nova*, which arrived in November. William Weldon, who was responsible for the men the Virginia Company sent to the colony, paid for Kirby's passage, the cost of which was supposed to be borne by Mr. Hansbie. In exchange, Weldon assigned George Eden to the Society of Smith's (Southampton) Hundred (44). Edward Kirby probably was sent to the College (66) with the group of Virginia Company tenants entrusted to the care of William Weldon. On July 18, 1620, Kirby sent a letter to the Virginia Company, asking to be freed of his obligation. He added that he would like to bring more people to the colony (VCR 1:407; 3:254).

THOMAS KIRKEHAM

On February 27, 1619, the Bridewell court identified Thomas Kirkeham as a boy who was to be sent to Virginia (CBE 13).

KISSACOMAS

In November 1624 Edward Grindon said that Sir Thomas Dale gave a gun to an Indian named Kissacomas, and that Kissacomas often came to Jamestown (1) to get powder and shot. Interpreter Robert Poole said that Kissacomas killed both fowl and deer and that Dale furnished him with ammunition (MCGC 28).

[NO FIRST NAME] KITCHEN

According to Ralph Hamor's narrative, which was written around 1614, men named Kitchen and Cole and three others were involved in a plan to flee from the colony in 1611. They intended to go to Ocanahowan, where they had heard some Spanish were living (HAI 822).

PHILLIP (PHILIP) KITHLY (KYTELEY, KYTELY, KUTELY)

In 1622 Phillip (Philip) Kithly (Kyteley, Kytely, Kutely) came to Virginia on the

Furtherance and on February 4, 1625, was one of several men living together at the Treasurer's Plantation (11). On December 12, 1625, Phillip agreed to stay on there in exchange for crop shares. He appears to have been one of Treasurer George Sandys' tenants (CBE 60; MCGC 80).

FRANCIS KNARESBURY

On December 31, 1619, it was decided that Francis Knaresbury, who was being detained in Bridewell Prison, would be sent to Virginia (CBE 15).

BENJAMIN (BENIAMINE, BENNANINE) KNIGHT

Benjamin (Beniamine, Bennanine) Knight came to Virginia on the *Bona Nova* in 1620 and on February 16, 1624, was living on the Eastern Shore. In early 1625, when a muster was made of the colony's inhabitants, Knight was still living there and was a 28-year-old servant on Captain Francis Eppes's plantation (74) (CBE 46, 68).

MORDECAY KNIGHT

On February 4, 1625, Mordecay Knight, who came to Virginia on the *William and John*, was living on Hog Island (16), where he was one of Ralph Hamor's servants (CBE 61).

RICHARD KNIGHT

Richard Knight died in Jamestown (1) sometime after April 1623 but before February 16, 1624 (CBE 39, 41). His name was listed twice in the records that were compiled.

ROBERT KNIGHT

Robert Knight, a sawyer, set out for Virginia on the *Garland* in 1619 and appears to have been part of a group heading to Southampton Hundred (44) (FER 137).

THOMAS KNISTON
(SEE THOMAS KENISTON)

CHRISTOPHER KNOLLINGE

On December 5, 1625, Christopher Knollinge testified in Jamestown (1) about a conversation he had had with Jeffrey Cornish (MCGC 78).

JAMES KNOTT

In September 1617 James Knott, who was being detained at Newgate Prison and had been convicted of a felony, was reprieved so that he could be delivered to Sir Thomas Smith and transported overseas. James went to Virginia on the *George* in 1617 and on February 16, 1624, was living on the Eastern Shore. When a muster was made of the colony's inhabitants early in 1625, he was still residing there and was a member of Charles Harmer's household. Harmer, who was one of Lady Elizabeth Dale's overseers, was responsible for some land on the lower side of Old Plantation Creek (73). In early 1625 James Knott was age 23, and he appears to have been a free man. On March 12, 1632, he was identified as a planter and resident of Accomack when he obtained a 21-year lease for a 50-acre tract of land at the mouth of the Hampton River in Elizabeth City (17) and indicated that he wanted to keep a house of entertainment on his land. On March 24, 1635, James Knott secured a patent for 1,200 acres of land on the east side of the Nansemond River, within Elizabeth City (20 c). He apparently took up residence there, for on July 25, 1638, he identified himself as a planter "of Mausanum [Nansemond]" in New Norfolk County, and said that he had resided there for 10 years. Knott then testified about the years during which the colony was governed by Sir Thomas Dale and discussed the 1622 Indian attack. His name was mentioned in Accomack/Northampton records through February 1643, suggesting that he carried on trade with the Eastern Shore. He moved to Maryland, where he died prior to May 13, 1653 (CBE 46, 69; PB 1 Pt.1:133, 334; SH 32; AMES 1:78; 2:263; SR 4525, 10876; DOR 1:421-422).

THOMAS KNOWLER

Thomas Knowler came to Virginia from Bermuda on the ship *Tiger*. On December 4, 1624, when Treasurer George Sandys patented some land, he listed Thomas as a servant and headright (PB 1 Pt. 1:16).

ISRAEL (ISRAELL) KNOWLES

Israel (Israell) Knowles died in Elizabeth City (17, 18) sometime after April 1623 but before February 16, 1624. On April 19, 1625, the General Court learned that he had named John Southern of Jamestown Island (1) as his executor. Afterward, the justices designated him administrator of the decedent's estate (CBE 45; MCGC 55).

JOHN KULLAWAY (HULLAWAY)

On February 16, 1624, John Kullaway was a servant in Dr. John Pott's household in urban Jamestown (1) (CBE 38).

THOMAS KYLES

On August 18, 1629, Thomas Kyles was identified as master of the ship *Friendship,* which was undertaking a voyage from London to Virginia (CBE 88).

L

MARY LACON

Mary Lacon died sometime after April 1623 but before February 16, 1624, at one of the communities on the lower side of the James River (8-15) and within the corporation of James City (CBE 41).

HENRY LACTON

Henry Lacton came to Virginia in 1623 on the *Hopewell.* On January 24, 1625, he was living in urban Jamestown (1) and was an 18-year-old servant in the household of Captain Roger Smith (CBE 55).

DANIEL LACY (LACYE, LACEY, LUCY, LUCYE)

On December 21, 1624, Daniel Lacy (Lacye, Lucy, Lucye) served on the jury that investigated the drowning death of a young child, George Pope II, a resident of Jamestown Island (1). Although Daniel Lacy's name was not included in the 1625 muster, on January 24, 1625, he was in Virginia and reportedly purchased a sow from Robert Marshall of Jamestown Island. On April 19, 1625, Mr. Daniel Lacy was assigned 4 acres on Jamestown Island by means of a court order. The land he received lay adjacent to that of Richard Kingsmill, who voiced his approval. On

May 21, 1627, Daniel Lacy came into court to prove Thomas Grubb's will. Lacy himself died sometime prior to February 8, 1628, at which time John Southern, merchant Thomas Mayhew, and Anthony Warren were named his administrators (MCGC 38, 44, 54, 148, 165, 173).

JOHN LACY (LASEY)

John Lacy (Lasey) died at West and Shirley Hundred (41) sometime after April 1623 but before February 16, 1624 (CBE 56).

THOMAS LACY

In 1619 the Ferrars, who were major Virginia Company investors, paid the cost of Thomas Lacy's transportation to Virginia (FER 296).

***

WILLIAM LACY (LASEY)

William Lacy (Lasey) came to Virginia in 1624 with his wife, Susan, on the *Southampton.* On January 24, 1625, the Lacys were living on Jamestown Island (1) in a household William headed. The Lacys had an ample supply of provisions, defensive weaponry, and livestock (CBE 56; DOR 1:34).

SUSAN LACY (LASEY) (MRS. WILLIAM LACY [LASEY])

Susan Lacy (Lasey) and her husband, William, came to Virginia in 1624 on the *Southampton.* On January 24, 1625, the Lacys were living on Jamestown Island (1) in a household he headed (CBE 56; DOR 1:34).

***

[NO FIRST NAME] LAKE

On February 16, 1624, a Mr. Lake was living at Martin's Hundred (7) (CBE 42).

ALEXANDER LAKE

On July 31, 1622, Alexander Lake left England on the *James* with two men he brought to Virginia. He may have been the Mr. Lake who was residing at Martin's Hundred (7) in mid-February 1624 (FER 400).

ROBERT LAMB

Robert Lamb left England on the *James* on July 31, 1622, and accompanied William Rowley to Virginia (FER 400).

THOMAS LAMBE

On January 29, 1620, the justices of Bridewell Court decided that Thomas Lambe would be sent to Virginia (CBE 18).

WILLLIAM LAMBE

On March 20, 1617, William Lambe, a prisoner in Newgate, was reprieved and delivered to Sir Thomas Smith so that he could be transported to Virginia. Lambe probably was a skilled worker (CBE 8; SR 425; PC 2/29).

[NO FIRST NAME] LAMBERT

On March 10, 1618, Mr. Lambert asked Virginia Company officials to send some cord to the colony, for he had discovered that tobacco cured more successfully when suspended from lines rather than piled in heaps (VCR 3:92).

HENRY LAMBERT

Woollen draper Henry Lambert and his wife were among the Walloons and French who indicated their willingness to go to Virginia. In August 1621 the Virginia Company agreed that they could immigrate (CBE 24).

ROBERT LAMBERT ALIAS DITCHFIELD

In January 1620 Robert Lambert alias Ditchfield was reprieved by the justices of Middlesex so that he could be sent to Virginia. He was detained in Newgate Prison, and in February 1620 officials noted that he was being transported to the colony (CBE 16, 19).

SAMUEL (SAMMUEL) LAMBERT

Samuel (Sammuel) Lambert died in Elizabeth City (17, 18) sometime after February 16, 1624, but before early 1625 (CBE 67).

THOMAS LAMBERT

On December 29, 1608, Thomas Lambert went to Werowocomoco with Captain John Smith on the *Discovery* (CJS 1:244).

THOMAS LAMBERT

On June 1, 1635, Thomas Lambert patented 100 acres on the east side of the James River in Elizabeth City (20 a) and received his land on the basis of two headrights (PB 1 Pt. 1:171).

WILLIAM LAMBERT

William Lambert died at the College (66) sometime after February 16, 1624, but before January 23, 1625 (CBE 67).

JOHN LAMOYNE

In late November 1624, John Lamoyne, a merchant, testified that Simon Tuchin (Tuching) admitted to having been banned from Ireland. On December 27, 1624, Lamoyne made arrangements to rent a store from John Chew, a merchant who owned a lot in urban Jamestown (1) and a plantation at Hog Island (16). On January 3, 1625, Lamoyne testified about Edward and Simon Tuchin's tobacco and was censured for some defamatory remarks he had made about Captain Ralph Hamor (MCGC 33, 37, 39).

JOHN LAMPKIN

On October 15, 1618, John Lampkin testified against Captain Edward Brewster, who was tried in a court martial hearing in Jamestown (1). Lampkin claimed that Brewster was guilty of mutiny because he had opposed Deputy Governor Samuel Argall's orders. Argall, like his predecessors, favored martial law (VCR 1:362).

HENRY LANCASTER

Henry Lancaster, a carpenter, set out for Virginia on the *Garland* in 1619 and appears to have been part of a group of settlers heading to Southampton Hundred (44) (FER 137).

JOHN LANDMAN

On February 16, 1624, John Landman was living at Flowerdew Hundred (53) (CBE 37).

DANIEL LANE

On August 17, 1635, Daniel Lane was occupying Thomas Harwood's land near Mulberry Island (21) (PB 1 Pt. 1:271).

HENRY LANE

Henry Lane came to Virginia on the *Southampton* in 1623. On January 21, 1625, he was living at Jordan's Journey (**46**), where he was a servant in the household headed by Christopher Safford and John Gibbs (CBE 51).

RACHELL LANE

Rachell Lane came to Virginia on the *Hopewell* in 1628 at the expense of Adam Thorogood. On June 24, 1635, when Thorogood patented some land, he used Rachell's headright (PB 1 Pt. 1:179).

***

THOMAS LANE

Thomas Lane came to Virginia on the *Treasurer* in 1613 and was an ancient planter. On February 16, 1624, he was living in Elizabeth City (**18**) in the household of Edward Waters. In early 1625 Thomas Lane was identified as a free man who was 30 years old. He and his wife, Alice, were residing in the Waters home (CBE 43, 66).

ALICE LANE
(MRS. THOMAS LANE)

Alice, who married ancient planter Thomas Lane, came to Virginia on the *Bona Nova* in 1620. By early 1625 the Lanes, who were free, were living in the household of Edward Waters in Elizabeth City (**18**). Alice was then age 24 (CBE 66).

***

SAMUEL LANGHAM

Between May 1629 and April 1630 Samuel Langham and Thomas Phillips were involved in a suit that involved shipping some tobacco from Virginia to Weymouth (EAE 19-20).

***

JOHN LANGLEY (LANGLY)

In 1620 Captain John Smith identified John Langley (Langly) as an investor in the Virginia Company. On July 17, 1622, Langley, then master of the *Margaret and John*, agreed to take passengers to Virginia.

Among those he transported were William Crakeplace and his five servants. Langley's son, Richard, served as bridge-master on the voyage. John Langley died sometime after August 1622 but before April 24, 1623. William Douglas took command of the ship. Trouble arose because Douglas refused to pay the vessel's crew, including bridge-master Richard Langley. On April 26, 1623, Virginia Company officials noted that John Loyde had agreed to be John Langley's apprentice for three years but was to be freed if his master died. Loyde also had invested with Langley in trade goods. In January 1624 the General Court identified John Langley as former master of the *Margaret* (CJS 2:279; VCR 2:99; 4:96-97, 127-128, 274; SH 13; MCGC 10; HOT 196; CBE 28).

RICHARD LANGLEY (LANGLY)

During a 1622 voyage to Virginia, Richard Langley, the son of John Langley (Langly), was bridge-master of the *Margaret and John*. On the way to the colony, the elder man died. In 1629 Richard was identified as one of his father's heirs and reference was made to Richard's marriage to Alice Leicester in 1617. Mariner Richard Langley was 32 years old in 1620 (VCR 4:274; SH 13).

***

RICHARD LANGLEY

According to records maintained by the Drapers Company in London, Richard Langley, who was associated with the Custom House, settled in Virginia in 1620. He may have been John Langley's son, Richard, a mariner (SR 879).

ROBERT LANGLEY (LANGLY)

Mr. Robert Langley (Langly) became ill and died at Isabell Perry's house in urban Jamestown (**1**) sometime prior to December 19, 1625. He was unable to finish the will he had begun making. Witnesses said that Langley wanted John Pountis and William Perry to serve as overseers of his will and said that he had given Robert Tokeley (then in England) his power of attorney. Tokeley, in that capacity, nominated Jamestown merchant Abraham Peirsey as Langley's administrator. On December 19, 1625, the General Court noted that the Rev. David Sandys had delivered Robert Langley's funeral sermon and that the decedent owed money to Sandys, a representative of the Society of Southampton Hundred (**44**). Court records for January 9, 1626, indicate that Edward Waters, Thomas Flint, and Captain Whitakers were indebted to Robert Langley's estate. Other debtors also were identified in Langley's account books. Robert Langley appears to have been a merchant (MCGC 10, 82, 83-84, 87).

SARAH LANGLEY

On February 16, 1624, Sarah Langley was a servant in the household of Captain Ralph Hamor in urban Jamestown (**1**) (CBE 38).

***

PETER (PEETER) LANGMAN (LANGDEN, LANGDON)

Peter (Peeter) Langman (Langden, Langdon) came to Virginia on the *William and Thomas* and on February 16, 1624, was living at Basses Choice (**27**). On January 3, 1625, Langman was ordered to post a bond guaranteeing that he would pay his debt to John Cooke. Henry Watkins, who served as security, agreed to become Cooke's servant if Langman failed to fulfill his obligation. On January 24, 1625, Peter Langman and his wife, Mary, the widow of Peter Ascam, were living in urban Jamestown (**1**), where Peter headed a household that included his two stepchildren (the Ascam youngsters, Abigail and Peter II) and two of the Rev. Richard Buck's orphans. Goodman Peter Langman was credited with a house, two servants, and some livestock. On March 13, 1625, Peter served on a jury that conducted a coroner's inquest. On January 3, 1626, he was identified as one of the Buck orphans' guardians when he was asked to post a bond on their behalf. By August 21, 1626, Peter Langman was dead (CBE 46, 55; MCGC 41, 53, 86, 108; DOR 1:32).

MARY ASCAM (ASCOMB, ASCOMBE) LANGMAN (LANGDEN, LANGDON) (MRS. PETER ASCAM [ASCOMB, ASCOMBE]; MRS. PETER [PEETER] LANGMAN [LANGDEN, LANGDON])

Mary Langman's (Langden's, Langdon's) former husband, Peter Ascam (Ascomb, Ascombe), died in Jamestown (**1**) sometime after August 4, 1623, but before February

16, 1624. On the latter date she was residing in urban Jamestown, where she was the head of a household that included her daughter, Abigail (Abigall), and perhaps her newborn son, Peter Ascam II. When testifying in court on October 4, 1624, Mary gave her age as 40. By January 24, 1625, the widowed Mary Ascam had married Peter Langman, with whom she was living in Jamestown. With the Langmans were Mary's children and two of the late Rev. Richard Buck's orphans. In May 1626 Mary Langman testified that Richard Buck owed money to John Dyos and vouched for the authenticity of Thomas Alnutt's will. By August 21, 1626, Mary had been widowed again (CBE 46, 55; MCGC 102-103, 108).

***

***

JOHN LANKFIELD (LAUCKFILD, LANKFEILD, LANKFORD)

John Lankfield (Lauckfild, Lankfeild, Lankford) came to Virginia in 1621 on the *Bona Nova*. On February 16, 1624, he was living with his wife in Elizabeth City on the east side of the Hampton River (**17**). In early 1625 24-year-old John Lankfield and his wife, Alice, were still living on the Virginia Company's land in Elizabeth City. With them was Samuel Kennell, an older male who appears to have been free. The household that John headed was relatively well provisioned and outfitted with defensive weaponry. On January 12, 1627, when the General Court gave the defunct Virginia Company's tenants to various public officials, John Lankfield was assigned to Governor George Yeardley (CBE 43, 67; MCGC 136; DOR 1:65).

ALICE LANKFIELD (LAUCKFILD, LANKFEILD, LANKFORD) (MRS. JOHN LANKFIELD [LAUCKFILD, LANKFEILD, LANKFORD])

Alice Lankfield (Lauckfild, Lankfeild, Lankford) came to Virginia on the *Abigail* in 1621. On February 16, 1624, she was living in Elizabeth City (**17**) with her husband, a Virginia Company tenant. When a muster was made of the colony's inhabitants in early 1625, Alice and John Lankfield were living on the Virginia Company's land in Elizabeth City. Alice was age 24 (CBE 43, 67; MCGC 136).

WILLIAM LANSDEN

On June 3, 1624, William Lansden, an ancient planter associated with Kecoughtan, later known as Elizabeth City, received 100 acres of land on the west side of the Hampton River (18), adjacent to property owned by William Claiborne (PB 1 Pt. 1:40).

MICHAEL LAPWORTH

On June 26, 1621, Michael Lapworth, who was in Virginia, was told to give the Ferrars a progress report on the establishment of Southampton Hundred (44), a plantation that had been seated by January 1620. Governor George Yeardley promised to inform Virginia Company treasurer, Sir Edwin Sandys, about Michael Lapworth's wellbeing. Lapworth was admired and respected by Company officials, who named him to the Council of State. On July 25, 1621, Yeardley's replacement, Governor Francis Wyatt, was ordered to find good land for Michael Lapworth, who was described as a worthy gentleman. It is uncertain how long Lapworth survived after reaching the colony (FER 268; VCR 3:463, 483, 487).

MICHAEL LAPWORTH

Michael Lapworth, an indentured servant, came to Virginia on the *Southampton* in 1622. On February 4, 1625, he was living on Samuel Mathews' plantation (15), on the lower side of the James River, and was identified as a 16-year-old servant. He may have been a kinsman of the Virginia Company investor Michael Lapworth, who was involved in the establishment of Southampton Hundred (CBE 60).

ROBERT LAPWORTH

Robert Lapworth came to Virginia on the *Abigail*. On January 23, 1625, he was living alone at the College (66), where he was a household head and had an ample supply of provisions and defensive weaponry. Robert died sometime prior to July 3, 1627. Because Robert had failed to make a will, Captain Samuel Mathews was named the administrator of his estate (CBE 56; MCGC 150; DOR 1:7).

WILLIAM LARRATT (LARATT, LORATT)

On August 24, 1618, the justices of Bridewell Court decided that William Larratt (Laratt, Loratt), a vagrant boy born in Hounsditch, would be sent to Virginia. William said that his mother was living in the country, at Westminster. On February 27, 1619, William Larratt was listed among the youngsters who had been rounded up from the streets of London so that they could be transported to the colony (CBE 9, 13).

JACOB LARBEE

Jacob Larbee died at Flowerdew Hundred (53) sometime after February 16, 1624, but before January 20, 1625 (CBE 51).

JAMES LARIMOURE

On March 20, 1626, James Larimoure, who said that he was old and sick, asked the Council of State's permission to return to England (MCGC 98).

JOHN LARKIN

On March 22, 1622, when the Indians attacked the Swinehowe plantation (47), John Larkin was killed (VCR 3:568).

WILLIAM LARKIN (LARKUN)

William Larkin (Larkun) was killed at Southampton Hundred (44) when the Indians attacked on March 22, 1622 (VCR 3:569).

URSULA LARSON

In 1621 Ursula Larson, one of the young marriageable women who came to Virginia to become wives for the colonists, arrived aboard the *Marmaduke* (FER 309).

ROBERT LATCHETT

Robert Latchett came to Virginia on the *George* in 1621 at the expense of Captain William Peirce. Sometime prior to September 9, 1632, William Spencer purchased Latchett's headright from Peirce and used it when patenting some land (PB 1 Pt. 1:120).

ROBERT LATHOM (LUNTHORNE)

Robert Lathom (Lunthorne) came to Virginia on the *George* in 1620. On February 16, 1624, he was listed with some of William Peirce's servants on the Maine (3) just west of Jamestown Island. When a muster was made of the colony's inhabitants on January 30, 1625, Robert was 20 years old and lived on Mulberry Island (21). He was identified as one of Peirce's servants (CBE 39, 56).

JOHN LATHROP

John Lathrop came to Virginia on the *Southampton* in 1623. Although his name was omitted from the 1624 census, on January 20, 1625, he was living at Flowerdew Hundred (53), where he was a servant in Abraham Peirsey's household. John Lathrop was then age 25 (CBE 50).

[NO FIRST NAME] LAUNCE

On July 3, 1622, the Virginia Company awarded land in the colony to Mr. Launce (VCR 2:74).

WILLIAM LAURELL (LAWRELL)

On February 16, 1624, William Laurell (Lawrell) was living on the Maine (3), just west of Jamestown Island (CBE 39).

WILLIAM LAUDSDELL

In May 1625 William Laudsdell was credited with 100 acres in Elizabeth City (17, 18) that had been planted (VCR 4:558).

NATHANIEL (NETHANIEL) LAWE (LAINE)

Sometime after April 1623 but before February 16, 1624, Nathaniel (Nethaniel) Lawe (Laine) died at Warresqueak (26). The 1624 census indicates that he was killed (CBE 42).

HELEN LAWLESSE

On November 20, 1622, Helen Lawlesse, an inmate at Newgate Prison, was pardoned so that she could be transported overseas. This occurred during an outbreak of jail fever (CBE 29).

THOMAS LAWLEY

In mid-March 1627 the General Court heard testimony about Thomas Lawley's fighting while aboard the ship *Plantation.* Lawley reportedly came to blows with Thomas Hittall, a member of the ship's crew, and Robert Cooke tried to separate them. According to several witnesses, Lawley received a hard blow to his chest and was badly hurt. As he already owed money to the ship's surgeon for treatment of ague, he declined medical attention. A short time after Thomas Lawley reached Shirley Hundred (41), he died, presumably from the injuries he had received at the hands of Robert Cooke (MCGC 144-146).

CHRISTOPHER LAWNE

Christopher Lawne, who was from Blandford in Dorset, England, set sail for Virginia in March 1619. Virginia Company records indicate that he transported 15 Company people to the colony instead of the 20 he had agreed to take. He also took the people he intended to seat on his own land. According to Captain John Smith, Lawne arrived on the ship *Marigold* in mid-May 1619. He and his fellow adventurers intended to establish a plantation on a neck of land on the east side of the mouth of what became known as Lawne's Creek (25). Virginia officials expressed concern for Lawne's safety, but he assured them that his settlement, which included 110 people, was near enough to those of Lieutenant Nathaniel Basse and Ensign Washer, who were seated in the territory known as Warresqueak (26). In July 1619 Captain Christopher Lawne represented his plantation in the colony's assembly, and he served as foreman of the jury that tried Captain William Eppes for killing Edward Stallings. During the summer of 1619, Lawne and many of the inhabitants of his plantation became ill. By November 1619 the survivors abandoned their property and withdrew to Charles City (39), where Lawne himself died. In March 1620 the Lawne plantation was credited with a population of 89 men, 12 women, and 9 children, although the acreage itself had been vacated. In June 1620 William Willis was named Christopher Lawne's administrator because the decedent's sons, Lovewell and Symon Lawne, were then underage. Later, Willis and Lawne's fellow adventurers asked for a patent because they had invested so heavily in the settlement that had failed. They said that they wanted their property to be called the Isle of Wight Plantation. They also requested compensation for two people they had sent to Virginia. On February 13, 1622, administrator William Willis asked the Virginia Company to reimburse Lawne's estate for the cost of his transporting 15 Company men to Virginia in 1619 (FER 138, 139; CJS 2:266; VCR 1:255-256, 268, 381, 414, 600; 3:154, 162, 217, 226-229, 242, 246; 4:94; CBE 20; MCGC 90; EEAC 36).

WILLIAM LAWRENCE

On September 19, 1625, the purser of the ship *Elizabeth* assigned William Lawrence and two others to Abraham Peirsey, since three of the servants being brought to Peirsey fled before reaching Virginia (MCGC 71).

ELLICE (ELLIS) LAWRY

On July 29, 1627, Ellice (Ellis) Lawry, master of the ship *Elizabeth* of Saltash, set sail from Plymouth, England, with William Lucas's goods, which he was transporting to Virginia (CBE 83).

ANNE LAWSON (LAWSONE)

On February 27, 1619, the justices of Bridewell decided that Anne Lawson (Lawsone), a young wench, would be sent to Virginia (CBE 13).

***

CHRISTOPHER LAWSON

Christopher Lawson and his wife were living in Captain Roger Smith's household in urban Jamestown (1) on February 16, 1624. By February 4, 1625, Christopher and Alice Lawson had moved to Smith's plantation (10) on the lower side of the James River, where Christopher was a household head. On January 13, 1627, Christopher Lawson was described as a Virginia Company tenant who had been assigned to Smith, a member of the Council of State. By 1639 he was free and was serving as the tobacco viewer for Jamestown and the mainland (3) just west of Jamestown Island, which included Pasbehay, the Governor's Land, and Thomas Harvey's plantation. On January 6, 1640, Lawson still was holding that position (CBE 38, 59; MCGC 136; BRU 120; DOR 1:39).

ALICE LAWSON (MRS. CHRISTOPHER LAWSON)

On February 16, 1624, Mrs. Christopher Lawson and her husband were living in Captain Roger Smith's household in urban Jamestown (1). Alice Lawson moved to Smith's plantation (10) on the lower side of the James River, sometime prior to February 4, 1625. Christopher was then a household head. Official records reveal that he was a Virginia Company tenant who had been assigned to Roger Smith (CBE 38, 59; MCGC 136).

***

THOMAS LAWSON

Thomas Lawson came to Virginia with Thomas West, Lord Delaware, arriving in Jamestown (1) on June 10, 1610. Two days later Delaware commissioned Lawson captain of a company. In May 1611 Sir Thomas Dale made Captain Thomas Lawson responsible for seeing that a stable was built in Jamestown (CJS 2:234; HAI 433, 523).

THOMAS LAWSON

Thomas Lawson, who lived in one of the settlements on the lower side of the James River within the corporation of James City (8-15), died sometime after April 1623 but before February 16, 1624. He may have been the colonist and military leader who arrived in Virginia in June 1610 (CBE 41).

BARTHOLOMEW LAWTON

Bartholomew Lawton, a 31-year-old goldsmith from London, arrived in Virginia in 1619 on the *Bona Nova* and was supposed to be a Virginia Company tenant. However, on April 3, 1620, a Mr. Deverell offered to reimburse the Company for Lawton's transportation costs and send one or two men as his replacement. Company officials agreed but stipulated that Deverell must first find an able man to replace Lawton (FER 295; VCR 1:334).

MARGARET LAXON

On February 27, 1619 the justices of Bridewell decided that Margaret Laxon, a young wench, would be sent to Virginia.

She was one of the children rounded up from the streets of London so that they could be sent to the colony (CBE 13).

WILLIAM LAXON

William Laxon, a carpenter, came to Virginia in 1607 and was one of the first Jamestown (1) settlers. In 1609, during the infamous "starving time," Laxon, who was then identified as an ensign, was sent to the mouth of the James River with 60 to 80 other men to subsist on oysters and other shellfish (CJS 1:208, 263; 2:142, 212).

***

JOHN LAYDON (LAYDEN, LEYDON, LAYTON)

John Laydon (Layden, Leydon, Layton), a laborer/carpenter and ancient planter who arrived in Virginia in 1607 and was one of the first Jamestown (1) settlers, married Anne (Ann) Burras (Buras) in December 1608. She was one of the first two women to arrive in the colony. On February 16, 1624, John and Anne and their daughters Alice, Katherine, and Virginia were living in Elizabeth City (18), where he was a household head. In early 1625 the Laydons were still there. John Laydon, who was then 44 years old, was in possession of two dwellings, a palisade and an ample supply of corn and defensive weaponry. Although he was credited with 200 acres in Coxendale (64) in May 1625, his patent reportedly had not been seated. On December 2, 1628, he traded half of his land in Coxendale and Henricus Island (63) for a 100-acre tract on the east side of Blunt Point Creek (22). When securing a patent for his new property, he acknowledged that he had abandoned his original acreage because it was in an unsafe area. On April 18, 1635, John Laydon's land in Elizabeth City (18) was mentioned in an adjacent patent. During the 1630s he continued to acquire land, some of which was in the vicinity of the Old Poquoson (19) in Warwick River (later, Warwick) County. John Laydon was alive as late as March 1640, at which time he testified about Thomas Sheffield's death in the March 1622 Indian attack (CJS 1:192, 209; 2:142, 242; CBE 43, 63; VCR 4:552; PB 1 Pt. 1:69, 95, 163, 343; Pt. 2:620; SR 11329; DOR 1:51; 2: 431).

ANNE (ANN) BURRAS (BURAS) LAYDON (LAYDEN, LEYDON, LAYTON) (MRS. JOHN LAYDON [LAYDEN, LEYDON, LAYTON])

Anne (Ann) Burras (Buras), a maidservant employed by Mrs. Thomas Forrest, arrived in Virginia on the *Mary Margaret* in 1608, in the 2nd Supply of new settlers. Anne and her mistress were the first two women to arrive in the colony. In December 1608 Anne Burras married laborer/carpenter John Laydon (Layden, Leydon, Layton) in the first wedding ceremony held in the colony. On February 16, 1624, the Laydons were living in Elizabeth City (18) with their three young daughters: Alice, Katherine, and Virginia. They were still there in early 1625 but had added a fourth daughter to their family: Margaret. Anne was then age 30. Court testimony taken in May 1625 reveals that during the years Sir Thomas Dale was deputy governor (1611–1616), Anne Burras Laydon and another woman, who were making shirts, were whipped because their work was deemed faulty. Anne reportedly had a miscarriage as a result of the flogging she received (CJS 1:184, 238, 242; 2:191-192; CBE 43, 63; MCGC 62).

ALICE LAYDON (LAYDEN, LEYDON, LAYTON)

Alice, the daughter of ancient planters John and Anne (Ann) Burras (Buras) Laydon (Layden, Leydon, Layton), was born in Virginia. On February 16, 1624, she and her sisters, Virginia and Katherine, were living in Elizabeth City (18) with their parents. By early 1625 another Laydon daughter (Margaret) had been added to the household (CBE 43, 63).

KATHERINE LAYDON (LAYDEN, LEYDON, LAYTON)

Katherine, who was born in Virginia, was the daughter of ancient planters John and Anne (Ann) Burras (Buras) Laydon (Layden, Leydon, Layton). On February 16, 1624, she and her sisters, Virginia and Alice, were living in Elizabeth City (18) with their parents. By early 1625 another Laydon daughter, Margaret, had been added to the household (CBE 43, 63).

MARGARET LAYDON (LAYDEN, LEYDON, LAYTON)

Margaret, the daughter of ancient planters John and Anne (Ann) Burras (Buras) Laydon (Layden, Leydon, Layton), was born in Virginia sometime after February 16, 1624, but before early 1625. She joined a household that included her parents and her older sisters, Alice, Virginia, and Katherine. The Laydons were living in Elizabeth City (**18**) (CBE 43, 63).

VIRGINIA LAYDON (LAYDEN, LEYDON, LAYTON)

Virginia, the daughter of ancient planters John and Anne (Ann) Burras (Buras) Laydon (Layden, Leydon, Layton), was born in Virginia. On February 16, 1624, she and her sisters, Alice and Katherine, were living in Elizabeth City (**18**) with their parents. By early 1625 another Laydon daughter, Margaret, had been added to the household (CBE 43, 63).

***

KATHERIN LAYDON (LAYDEN, LEYDEN)

On January 22, 1625, seven-year-old Katherin Laydon (Layden, Leyden) was living on West and Shirley Hundred Island (**41**) in the household of the widowed Mrs. Mary Madison. Katherin apparently was free, for she was not listed among Mrs. Madison's servants. Katherin may have been the orphaned daughter of Nathaniel Laydon (Layden, Leyden), who had been killed at nearby Powle-Brooke (Merchant's Hope) (**50**) in the March 22, 1622, Indian attack (CBE 52).

NATHANIEL LAYDON (LAYDEN, LEYDEN)

On March 22, 1622, when the Indians attacked Powle-Brooke (Merchant's Hope) (**50**), Nathaniel Laydon (Layden, Leyden) was killed (VCR 3:569).

[NO FIRST NAME] LEACH (LEECH)

Mr. Leach (Leech), whose given name is unknown, was the Earl of Pembroke's agent. In July 1621 he was authorized to explore the territory to the south of the James River, where Pembroke was entitled to 30,000 acres. A month later he was sent food, a hand-mill, saws, shovels, and other supplies from England. In December 1621 he was named to the Council of State. On May 2, 1625, the General Court noted that William Kemp was indebted to Mr. Leach (STAN 30; VCR 1:520, 571; 3:480, 482; FER 308; MCGC 57).

JAMES LEADING

James Leading came to Virginia on the *Hopewell* in 1628 at the expense of Adam Thorogood, who on June 24, 1635, used his headright when patenting some land (PB 1 Pt. 1:179).

***

AUGUSTINE LEAK (LEAKE, LEEKE)

On February 4, 1625, Augustine Leak (Leake, Leeke) was living in Martin's Hundred (**7**) with his wife, Winifred. Both were free and were members of Robert Adams' household. Augustine reportedly had come to Virginia on the *Bona Nova* and was Robert Adams' partner. On February 12, 1628, the General Court named Augustine Leak administrator of the estate of the late Henry Ganey (Gainy) of Elizabeth City (**18**) (CBE 62; MCGC 167).

WINIFRED LEAK (LEAKE, LEEKE) MRS. AUGUSTINE LEAK (LEAKE, LEEKE)

Winifred, who became the wife of Augustine Leak (Leake, Leeke) came to Virginia on the *George* in 1623. On February 4, 1625, she was living in Martin's Hundred (**7**), where she and husband, Augustine, were members of Robert Adams' household and were free (CBE 62).

***

JOHN LEAK (LEAKE, LEEKE)

John Leak (Leake, Leeke) came to Virginia in 1628 on the *Hopewell* at the expense of Adam Thorogood, who used him as a headright when patenting some land on June 24, 1635 (PB 1 Pt. 1:179).

MARMION LEAK (LEAKE, LEEKE)

Sometime prior to February 27, 1628, Marmion Leak (Leake, Leeke) died at sea while going to or from Virginia. His will was witnessed by William Southey of the *Samuel* (MCGC 168).

SIMON (SYMOND) LEAK (LEAKE, LEEKE)

On November 21, 1621, Simon (Symond) Leak (Leake, Leeke) and his associates, were taking 100 people to Virginia, obtained a patent. Leake was identified as a planter, so he probably had some previous experience in the colony. On December 4, 1621, Virginia Company officials noted that Captain Simon Leak would be going to Virginia soon and recommended that he be made a member of the Council of State and a colonel. Two weeks later Company officials withdrew their recommendation that he be given a military appointment. On June 10, 1622, Simon Leak was identified as owner of a particular (private) plantation. On January 20, 1623, officials in England learned that he was dead, and that he had died before his people had become well acquainted with him (VCR 1:553-554, 561-562, 569, 571; 3:643; 4:9).

ANTHONY LEANE

Sometime prior to May 10, 1629, Anthony Leane agreed to serve Virginia merchant Thomas Mayhew for a year and work on his boat. In exchange, Mayhew agreed to pay him £20. After Thomas Mayhew's death, the General Court assigned Anthony Leane to his brother, Edward Mayhew, for a year but stipulated that he was not to do fieldwork. The Mayhews seem to have conducted business in Jamestown (1) and in Elizabeth City (17, 18) (MCGC 197).

ROBERT LEANER (LEAVER)

Robert Leaner (Leaver) died in Elizabeth City (17, 18) sometime after April 1623 but before February 16, 1624 (CBE 45).

WILLIAM LEAT (LEETE, LEATE)

The Rev. William Leat (Leete, Leate) immigrated to Virginia in 1622 and was outfitted by the Virginia Company of London. He was supposed to stay with the governor until he found a ministerial position, but on February 16, 1624, was living in the Jamestown Island (1) household of Christopher Stokes (VCR 1:575, 581, 591; 3:651; CBE 40).

JAN LECA

Jan Leca, his wife, and five children were among the Walloons and French who indicated their willingness to go to Virginia. In August 1621 the Virginia Company agreed that they could immigrate (CBE 24).

***

CHRISTOPHER LEE (LEES)

Christopher Lee (Lees) came to Virginia in 1623 on the *Southampton*. On January 24, 1625, he was identified as a 30-year-old servant in Abraham Peirsey's household in urban Jamestown (1). Christopher and his wife apparently lived at Peirsey's (Flowerdew) Hundred (53) plantation during at least part of 1624, for she died there sometime after February 16, 1624, but before January 20, 1625. On November 28, 1625, Christopher Lee was ordered to deliver Mr. Peirsey's 44 bushels of corn to a ship's purser, who was expecting the delivery (CBE 51, 55; MCGC 77).

MRS. CHRISTOPHER LEE (LEES)

Mrs. Christopher Lee (Lees) and her husband apparently lived at Abraham Peirsey's plantation, Peirsey's (Flowerdew) Hundred (53), during at least part of 1624, for she died there sometime after February 16, 1624, but before January 20, 1625 (CBE 51).

***

HENRY LEE (LEIGH, LEY)

Henry Lee (Leigh, Ley), a gentleman and Virginia Company investor, came to Virginia in 1608 in the 2nd Supply of Jamestown (1) colonists. According to Captain John Smith, Lee died in 1609, sometime prior to the winter of 1609–1610, the infamous "starving time" (CJS 1:241, 265; 2:190, 214, 279).

LAWRENCE LEE (LEIGH, LEY)

In April 1625, when the will of Lawrence Lee (Leigh, Ley) was proved, probate officials noted that he had land in Virginia (CBE 19).

ROBERT LEE

On April 25, 1626, the General Court identified Robert Lee as one of John Howe's creditors (MCGC 101).

***

THOMAS LEE (LEA)

In 1634 Thomas Lee (Lea) and his wife, Joane, came to Virginia on the *James*. Among their shipmates were William Pennington, John and Elizabeth Yarworth, Bartholomew Hoskins and his wife, and John Woodcock. Depositions taken in 1639 indicate that by that date Thomas Lee was dead and his widow had married John Carter (SH 34).

JOANE LEE (LEA) (MRS. THOMAS LEE [LEA], MRS. JOHN CARTER)

Joan Lee (Lea) and her husband, Thomas, went to Virginia in 1634 on the *James*. He died in the colony sometime prior to 1639, by which time she had married John Carter (SH 34).

***

THOMAS LEE (LEA)

Thomas Lee (Lea) came to Virginia on the *Southampton* in 1623 and on February 16, 1624, was living at Flowerdew Hundred (**53**). He was still there on January 20, 1625, at which time he was identified as a 50-year-old servant in Abraham Peirsey's household (CBE 37, 50).

THOMAS LEE (LEY, LEG)

On February 16, 1624, Thomas Lee (Ley, Leg) was living at Chaplin's Choice (**56**) (CBE 37).

THOMAS LEE (LEA) ALIAS SINGLETON

On September 15, 1625, when the Rev. William Pindar, rector of Mottisfount, Hampshire, made his will, he identified Thomas Lee (Lea) alias Singleton as an heir and kinsman and said that he was in Virginia. The testator also made reference to Thomas's brother, John, who was a carpenter (CBE 77; EEAC 45-46; WAT 469).

WILLIAM LEE (LEA)

William Lee (Lea), who from March through May 1630 was associated with the ship *Sun*, a leaky vessel, died in Virginia (EAE 21-22).

WILLIAM LEE (LEIGH)

On June 20, 1632, William Lee (Leigh), William Dawkes's uncle, was identified as an adventurer (or investor) in Virginia (PB 1 Pt. 1:107).

WILLIAM LEECH

On February 27, 1619, the justices of Bridewell decided that William Leech, a boy, would be detained and sent to Virginia. He was one of the youngsters rounded up from the streets of London so that they could be transported to the colony (CBE 12).

WILHOPE LEECHE

On December 31, 1619, Wilhope Leeche was detained by the authorities until he could be sent to Virginia (CBE 15).

TIMOTHY LEEDS

Timothy Leeds, a gentleman, came to Virginia in 1608 in the 1st Supply of Jamestown (**1**) colonists (CJS 1:222; 2:161).

PONTUS LE GEAN

Bolting cloth weaver Pontus Le Gean, his wife, and their three children were among the Walloons and French who indicated their willingness to go to Virginia. In August 1621 the Virginia Company agreed that they could immigrate (CBE 24).

ELIAS (ELLIS) LEGARDO (LAGEURD, LAGARD, LA GUARD, LA GEURD)

Elias (Ellis) Legardo (Lageurd, Lagard, La Guard, La Geurd), a French vigneron, came to Virginia in 1621 on the *Abigail*. On February 16, 1624, he was living at Buckroe in Elizabeth City (**17**) on land owned by the Virginia Company. When a muster was taken of the colony's inhabitants in early 1625, Elias was identified as a 38-year-old indentured servant in the household of Anthony Bonall, who also was French. Both men were residing on the Company Land in Elizabeth City. By March 14, 1628, Elias Legardo, who was still identified as a vigneron, obtained a leasehold for 100 acres on the west side of Harris Creek in Elizabeth City (19). When he renewed his land claim on May 8, 1633, he received a 21-year lease. Elias Legardo also secured a lease for 12 acres of land at Buckroe, a parcel that previously belonged to his former master, Anthony Bonall, and his successor, John Arundell. On March 7, 1629, the justices of the General Court learned that Richard Stephens, a Jamestown merchant, had sued Elias Legardo. Sergeant Coleman of Elizabeth City was supposed to arrest him but failed to do so; therefore, Captain Purfoy was ordered to bring Elias in and was told to post a bond, guaranteeing the performance of his responsibility (CBE 45, 68; PB 1 Pt. 1:99, 140-141; MCGC 193).

WILLIAM LEGINE (LEGUINE)

On February 26, 1620, it was decided that William Legine (Leguine), who was being detained at Newgate Prison, would be sent to Virginia (CBE 19).

ROBERT LEISTER (LESTER, LEYSTER)

On January 3, 1625, Simon Tuchin's administrator acknowledged that Robert Leister (Lester, Leyster) was among those who had satisfied debts to the decedent's estate. On December 30, 1625, Lawrence Peele testified that in August 1622 Robert Leister, when leaving Jamestown (1), said that he had been insulted by Captain William Tucker of Elizabeth City (17, 18) and would seek revenge if he could. By January 3, 1626, Robert Leister was dead. John Heney of Elizabeth City, who alleged that Captain Tucker's words had caused Leister's death, was punished for slandering Tucker (MCGC 40, 83, 85).

THOMAS LEISTER (LESTER, LEYSTER)

On February 16, 1624, Thomas Leister (Lester, Leyster), one of Dr. John Pott's servants, was living on the physician's property in urban Jamestown (1). By January 24, 1625, Leister, who was age 33, had moved to Pott's farm on the Maine (3), west of Jamestown Island. On February 8, 1625,

Leister testified about a debt someone incurred at Elizabeth City (17, 18), and on May 9th he was summoned to court again, where he admitted that his master, Dr. Pott, had four hogs killed, three of which were marked. He also indicated that Pott had sent him to Captain Powell's house to complain that his hogs were getting into Pott's corn. On February 19, 1626, Leister was back in court and stood accused of fighting with Roger Stanley and cutting his arm. A couple months earlier, Lawrence Peale testified that in August 1622 Thomas Leister made threats against Captain William Tucker, who had spoken to him sternly (CBE 38, 58; MCGC 46-47, 59, 83, 94-95).

GREGOIRE LE JEUNE

Shoemaker Gregoire Le Jeune, his wife, and their four children were among the Walloons and French who indicated their willingness to go to Virginia. In August 1621 the Virginia Company agreed that they could immigrate (CBE 24).

JOSEPH LENING (LENINGE, LEMINGE)

On November 21, 1621, the Virginia Company gave Mr. Joseph Lening (Leninge, Leminge) a patent, for he and his associates were planning to take 100 people to Virginia. Since he was identified as a planter, he already may have been in the colony. On June 10, 1622, Lening was described as holder of a patent for a particular (private) plantation (VCR 3:643).

JAN LE ROU

Printer Jan Le Rou and his wife and six children were among the Walloons and French who indicated their willingness to go to Virginia. In August 1621 the Virginia Company agreed that they could immigrate (CBE 24).

JEROME LE ROY

Cloth weaver Jerome Le Roy and his wife and four children were among the Walloons and French who indicated their willingness to go to Virginia. In August 1621 the Virginia Company agreed that they could immigrate (CBE 25).

CHRISTOPHER LEU

On November 20, 1622, Christopher Leu of Sherburne in Dorsett County, who was planning to take 100 people to Virginia, asked the Virginia Company for a patent (VCR 2:132).

ARTHER LEUELLIS

On February 5, 1623, Arthur Leuellis received a patent from the Virginia Company of London (VCR 2:262).

MICHEL LEUSIER

Cloth weaver Michel Leusier and his wife and child were among the Walloons and French who indicated their willingness to go to Virginia. In August 1621 the Virginia Company agreed that they could immigrate (CBE 25).

THOMAS LEVESON (LEGISON)

On March 20, 1622, Thomas Leveson (Legison) asked for a commission to take passengers to Virginia, as he already had a patent for a particular (private) plantation (VCR 1:622).

GEORGE LEVETT (LEVET)

George Levett (Levet) came to Virginia in 1619 on the *Bona Nova* and on February 16, 1624, was living at Flowerdew Hundred (53), Abraham Peirsey's plantation. By early 1625 he had relocated to Elizabeth City (18), where he was a servant in the household of Reynold Booth. George was then age 29 (CBE 37, 66).

HENRY LEWIS

In November 1624 Henry Lewis was described as having been one of Sir George Yeardley's servants at Flowerdew Hundred (53), where he worked under the supervision of Sergeant Simon Fortesque (MCGC 27).

JOHN LEWIS (LEWES)

John Lewis (Lewes), a cooper, arrived in Virginia in January 1608. He was in the 1st Supply of new settlers and would have lived in Jamestown (1) (CJS 1:223; 2:162).

JOHN LEWIS

Virginia Company records dating to May 17, 1622, indicate that John Lewis was paid to go to Virginia. He probably was a skilled worker (FER 376).

RICHARD LEWIS

When the Indians attacked Edward Bennett's plantation (26) on March 22, 1622, Richard Lewis was killed (VCR 3:571).

ROGER LEWIS (LEWES)

Roger Lewis (Lewes) came to Virginia on the *Edwin* in May 1617 and on February 16, 1624, was living on West and Shirley Hundred (now Eppes) Island (41). On January 22, 1625, when a muster was taken of the inhabitants of West and Shirley Hundred and the island, Roger Lewis was described as the 19-year-old servant in the employ of Mrs. Mary Madison, who lived on the island (CBE 36, 52).

RICHARD LICHFIELD (LITCHFEILD?)

On June 23, 1627, the justices of Bridewell described Richard Lichfield (Litchfeild?) as a vagrant who had been brought in from Coleman Street. Court records indicate that his father was alive and living in a rural area. Richard indicated that he was willing to go to Virginia. He may have been the individual named Richard Litchfeild, who went to the colony in 1629 (CBE 78).

PETER LIGHBORROW

Peter Lighborrow was killed when the Indians attacked Martin's Hundred (7) on March 22, 1622 (VCR 3:570).

JOHN LIGHTFOOT (LIGHTFOOTE, LYTEFOOT, LYTEFOOTE)

John Lightfoot (Lightfoote, Lytefoot, Lytefoote), an ancient planter and yeoman, left England with Sir Thomas Gates in 1609 on the *Seaventure*. He was stranded with Gates in Bermuda and did not arrive in Virginia until 1610. On April 16, 1622, John Lightfoot was described as a resident of Jamestown (1) and a free man, who in 1618 sold corn to Edward Brewster for the men who came to Virginia on the *Neptune*. On February 16, 1624, he was living in urban Jamestown in the home of Captain William Peirce. On August 14, 1624, John Lightfoot patented 12 acres in the eastern end of Jamestown Island, a narrow ridge of land between two marshes. However, he continued to reside in urban Jamestown, and when a muster was made of the colony's inhabitants on January 24, 1625, he was listed among the indentured servants in Ralph Hamor's household. This raises the possibility that Lightfoot lost his freedom temporarily on account of indebtedness or another infraction of the law. Sometime prior to December 13, 1624, he came into possession of a house and some land in urban Jamestown that he intended to rent or sell, perhaps because he intended to develop his property in eastern Jamestown Island. On January 21, 1629, John Lightfoot, who was mortally ill, summoned William Spencer, Nicholas Atwell, and Edward Willmoth to witness his will. He bequeathed his entire estate (which included some cattle and tobacco) to William Spencer, his neighbor in the eastern end of Jamestown Island (CBE 38, 55; C 24/490; PB 1 Pt. 1:10; MCGC 36, 41, 43, 181).

FRANCIS LIMBRECK (LIMBRECKE, LEMBRI)

In 1611 an English pilot named Francis Limbreck (Lembrecke, Lembri) arrived at Old Point Comfort (**17**) in the ship that brought Diego de Molina, a Spanish spy. Limbreck, Molina, and Antonio Pereos were quickly taken into custody and sent up to Jamestown (**1**), where they were kept prisoner aboard some ships anchored there. When Molina sent a letter to one of his superiors in 1613, he said that some people thought that Limbreck was English, but he claimed to be from Aragon, and nobody would think of him as a foreigner. When Sir Thomas Dale set sail for England in 1616, he took Limbreck with him. However, as soon as they came within sight of the English coast, Dale had him hanged (HAI 515-516, 750).

***

ROBERT LIMBROUGH (LYMBROUGH, LINBOROUGH)

In December 1621 Robert Limbrough (Lymbrough, Linborough), his family, and four young male apprentices were sent to Martin's Hundred (**7**) by the Society of Martin's Hundred's investors. Robert, who was then a 40-year-old metalworker, was to be one of the Society's tenants. He was under the supervision of Lieutenant Richard Keane, who was in charge of all newcomers to the settlement. When Robert Limbrough went to Virginia, he was accompanied by his wife, Constance, daughters, Barbara and Ann, and son, Edward, and he was outfitted with the tools of his trade. Although the fate of Robert Limbrough's wife and children is uncertain, Robert survived the March 1622 Indian attack and on June 7, 1622, was ordered to assist Martin's Hundred's headman, William Harwood (FER 339, 391, 343).

CONSTANCE LIMBROUGH (LYMBROUGH, LINBOROUGH) (MRS. ROBERT LIMBROUGH [LYMBROUGH, LINBOROUGH])

In December 1621 Constance, the wife of Robert Limbrough (Lymbrough, Linborough), who was age 35, accompanied her husband to Virginia. The Limbrough family was headed for Martin's Hundred (**7**), where Robert was to be a tenant and metalworker (FER 343).

ANN LIMBROUGH (LYMBROUGH, LINBOROUGH)

Ann, the infant daughter of Constance and Robert Limbrough (Lymbrough, Linborough), went to Virginia in December 1621. The Limbrough family was sent to Martin's Hundred (**7**), where Robert was to be a tenant and metalworker (FER 343).

BARBARA LIMBROUGH (LYMBROUGH, LINBOROUGH)

Barbara, the 15-year-old daughter of Robert Limbrough (Lymbrough, Linborough), went with her family to Virginia in December 1621. The Limbrough family was sent to Martin's Hundred (**7**), where Robert was to be a tenant and metalworker (FER 343).

EDWARD LIMBROUGH (LYMBROUGH, LINBOROUGH)

Edward, the 10-year-old son of Robert Limbrough (Lymbrough, Linborough), went to Virginia with his family in December 1621. The Limbroughs went to Martin's Hundred (**7**), where Robert was to be a tenant and metalworker (FER 343).

***

***

ROBERT LIMPANIE

On February 27, 1622, Robert Limpanie, who was in England, filed a petition with the Virginia Company on behalf of his son, asking that his son be freed. The youth had been entrusted to the care of cape merchant Abraham Peirsey, a resident of Jamestown (**1**) (VCR 1:608).

[NO FIRST NAME] LIMPANIE

Robert Limpanie's son, whose first name is unknown, went to Virginia with Abraham Peirsey. On February 27, 1622, Robert filed a petition with the Virginia Company, asking that he be freed. It is probable that Limpanie's son was in Jamestown (**1**), where Peirsey had a residence and a store, although by early 1624 he may have moved to Peirsey's plantation, Flowerdew Hundred (**53**) (VCR 1:608).

***

ROBERT LINCE

Robert Lince came to Virginia on the *Treasurer*. On January 30, 1625, he was residing on the Maine (**3**), where he was a solitary household head who had defensive attire and some weaponry (CBE 58).

HENRY LINCH

On July 31, 1622, Henry Linch, a servant, set out for Virginia on the *James* with his master, Leonard Allenson (FER 400).

ANN LINCOLN (LINKON)

On February 16, 1624, Ann Lincoln (Linkon) was living at Jordan's Journey (**46**) (CBE 36).

[NO FIRST NAME] LINCOLNE

Captain Lincolne, whose first name is unknown, died in Elizabeth City (**17, 18**) sometime after April 1623 but before February 16, 1624 (CBE 45).

ROBERT LINDSEY

On February 16, 1624, Robert Lindsey was living on the lower side of the James River, within the corporation of James City and west of Gray's Creek (**8, 9**). By February 4, 1625, he had moved to Martin's Hundred (**7**). In April 1626 Robert Lindsey was among the men captured and taken to the Pamunkey Indians' village, where they were detained. He sent word that if he wasn't freed, he would like for his goods and locked chest to be given to Sara Snow in Jamestown (**1**). Sometime prior to January 8, 1627, the Governor's Council noted that Robert Lindsey had been taken to Pamunkey by the Indians the past spring. His fate is uncertain (CBE 40; MCGC 128).

ANNE LINSEY (LYNSEY)

On February 12, 1620, the justices of Bridewell decided that Anne Linsey (Lynsey) would be sent to Virginia (CBE 18).

JOHN LINSEY (LINZEY, LINSLEY)

On September 18, 1620, Virginia Company officials noted that John Linsey (Linzey, Linsley) was among the 56 people going to Berkeley Hundred (**55**) with William Tracy in the *Supply*. Linsey was supposed to serve the Society of Berkeley Hundred's investors for a certain number of years in exchange for some acreage. Virginia Company records contain conflicting information—one document states that Linsey disembarked and stayed in Ireland, whereas another says that he arrived at Berkeley Hundred on January 29, 1621 (CBE 21; VCR 3:397, 427).

ROGER LINSEY (LINZEY, LINSLEY)

Virginia Company records indicate that on September 18, 1620, Roger Linsey (Linzey, Linsley) was among the 56 people going to Virginia with William Tracy on the *Supply*. Linsey, who was headed for Berkeley Hundred (**55**), had agreed to serve the Society of Berkeley Hundred's investors for a certain number of years in exchange for a certain amount of land. Virginia Company records provide conflicting information, for one document states that Linsey disembarked and stayed in Ireland, whereas another says that he arrived at Berkeley Hundred on January 29, 1621 (CBE 21; VCR 3:397, 426).

HENRY LINGE

On February 16, 1624, Henry Linge was living at Flowerdew Hundred (**53**) (CBE 37).

JOHN LINGE

John Linge was living at Flowerdew Hundred (**53**) on February 16, 1624 (CBE 57).

JOHN LINICKER

John Linicker died at Flowerdew Hundred (**53**) sometime after February 16, 1624, but before January 20, 1625 (CBE 51).

JOHN LIPPS

John Lipps came to Virginia on the *London Merchant* in 1621. Although he was not included in the 1624 census, on January 20, 1625, he was living at Flowerdew Hundred (**53**), where he was a household head. Lipps was well supplied with provisions and defensive weaponry (CBE 50; DOR 1:23).

GEORGE LISLE

On September 13, 1626, George Lisle claimed that his late uncle had bequeathed him some cattle that were in Virginia. The governor was asked to investigate (CBE 73).

GEORGE LISTE

In May 1609 George Liste, John Woodall's servant, came to Virginia with a chest of surgical equipment. He would have lived in Jamestown (**1**) (VCR 3:23).

EDWARD LISTER

On March 22, 1622, when the Indians attacked Macock's Divident, Samuel Macock's plantation (**48**), Edward Lister was killed (VCR 3:568).

GEORGE LISTON

On August 12, 1620, the justices of Bridewell decided that George Liston, who was described as a lewd vagrant from Carter's Lane, would be sent to Virginia (CBE 20).

RICHARD LITCHFEILD

Richard Litchfeild came to Virginia in a Spanish frigate in 1629. Captain Francis

Eppes used him as a headright in 1638 when patenting some land (PB 1 Pt. 2:537).

RICHARD LITTLEFRERE

When Richard Littlefrere, one of Edward Grindon's servants, testified before the General Court on February 6, 1628, he indicated that he was 30 years old and had been born in the Bishopric of Durham. Littlefrere said that on the night of January 14, 1628, after everyone had retired, he was awakened by some commotion and had seen William Mills leaving the tobacco house at Grindall's Hill, part of the Treasurer's Plantation (**11**). On January 21, 1628, one of Littlefrere's fellow servants described him as a knave (MCGC 159, 162).

JAMES LITTLEJOHN (LITTLE JOHN)

On June 25, 1635, William Andrews used James Littlejohn (Little John) as a headright when patenting some land on the Eastern Shore (PB 1 Pt. 1:182).

JOHN LITTON

Sometime after April 1623 but before February 16, 1624, John Litton died at Warresqueak (**26**), the Bennett plantation (CBE 42).

WILLIAM LITTON

On November 13, 1620, William Litton assigned his bill of adventure to Captain John Harvey, thereby making him eligible for some Virginia land (VCR 1:418-419).

MATHEW LIVEING (LYVING)

On March 5, 1628, Samuel Mathews claimed that he had paid for Mathew Liveing's (Lyving's) transportation to Virginia on the *Neptune* in 1618 and was given Mathew's headright. He subsequently transferred it to Zachariah Cripps. The *Neptune* was the ship on which Thomas West, Lord Delaware, set sail when returning to Virginia (MCGC 190; PB 1 Pt. 1:174).

EDWARD LLOYD (LOYD)

On February 16, 1624, Edward Lloyd (Loyd) was living in Elizabeth City (**17, 18**). On March 30, 1636, he patented 400 acres on the Elizabeth River (20 a) and served as a Lower Norfolk County justice in 1645 and 1646. In 1649 Lloyd was fined for failing to attend church. He took up some land in Maryland in 1650, where he became part of the Puritan community (CBE 43; PB 1 Pt. 1:359; DOR 2:432).

JOHN LLOYD (LOYD, LOYDE)

On April 26, 1623, Virginia Company officials acknowledged that John Lloyd (Loyd, Loyde) had agreed to serve as John Langley's apprentice for three years, but he was to be freed if Langley died. Lloyd and Langley together invested in trade goods, thereby suggesting that they hoped to be involved in commerce with the Indians. On February 16, 1624, John Lloyd was living in Elizabeth City, in Buckroe (17). He died sometime prior to August 1653, at which time the administration of his estate was granted to his daughter, Mary. The decedent was described as a poor man (CBE 45; VCR 4:128; EEAC 36).

MATHEW (MATTHEW) LLOYD (LOYD)

On February 16, 1624, Mathew (Matthew) Lloyd (Loyd) was a servant in Edward Blaney's household in urban Jamestown (1) (CBE 38).

MORICE LLOYD (LOYD)

On February 16, 1624, Morice Lloyd (Loyd) was living on the lower side of the James River, within the corporation of James City. He resided on one of the plantations east of Gray's Creek (10-15) (CBE 40).

NATHANIEL LLOYD (LOYD)

On February 16, 1624, Nathaniel Lloyd (Loyd) was living on the lower side of the James River, within the corporation of James City, at one of the plantations east of Gray's Creek (10-15) (CBE 40).

JOHN LOCKE

John Locke, who came to Virginia on the *Warwick* in 1621 at the expense of John Sipsey, probably was an indentured servant. Locke died in Elizabeth City (17, 18) sometime after April 1623 but before February 16, 1624 (CBE 45; PB 1 Pt. 1:46).

JOHN LOCKE

Adam Thorogood paid for John Locke's transportation to Virginia on the *Truelove* in 1628. On June 24, 1635, when Thorogood patented some land, he used Locke as a headright (PB 1 Pt. 1:179).

ROBERT LOCKE

Robert Locke came to Virginia on the *Warwick* in 1621 and on February 16, 1624, was living in Elizabeth City (18). When a muster was taken in early 1625, Robert was identified as an 18-year-old servant in the household of Percival Ibbotson, who had a 50-acre tract at Blunt Point (22) (CBE 44, 66; VCR 4:557).

JOYCE LODGE

On June 13, 1621, Joyce Lodge, a widow, asked the Virginia Company for 50 acres of land as her own personal adventure and dower from her late husband. Instead, they gave her 100 acres because the decedent had left goods in Virginia. Company records fail to disclose Mrs. Lodge's husband's identity (VCR 1:497).

***

ROWLAND (ROLAND) LOFTIS (LOTTIS)

On January 3, 1621, Rowland (Roland) Loftis (Lottis) admitted that he was indebted to surgeon Christopher Best and Lieutenant George Harrison, both of whom resided in Jamestown (1). On February 16, 1624, Loftis and his wife were living in Archer's Hope (6) (MCGC 38-40; CBE 41).

MRS. ROWLAND (ROLAND) LOFTIS (LOTTIS)

On February 16, 1624, Mrs. Rowland (Roland) Loftis (Lottis) and her husband were living in Archer's Hope (6) (CBE 41).

***

GEORGE LONDON

George London set sail for Virginia on April 17, 1619, on the *Garland*. He was a freemason who probably was bound for Southampton Hundred (44) (FER 107).

ALICE LONG

On March 25, 1629, Alice Long testified that she had been among the women visiting Nicholas Eyres's (Eyros's) house at the Treasurer's Plantation (11) when an attempt was made to resolve the issue of Thomas Hall's indeterminate gender (MCGC 195).

ANN LONG

Ann Long came to Virginia on the ship *Africa*. On June 24, 1635, when Adam Thorogood secured a patent, he indicated that he had paid for Ann's transportation and used her headright (PB 1 Pt. 1:179).

ELIAS (ELLIAS) LONG (LONGE)

Elias (Ellias) Long (Longe) came to Virginia in 1620 on the *Bona Nova*. On May 8, 1622, when he was ordered to send Ursula French 100 pounds of tobacco, he was identified as a Virginia Company servant and Ursula French's apprentice. Four years later the Company acknowledged that Elias had put the tobacco aside for Mrs. French, who was a widow. On February 16, 1624, he was a servant at West and Shirley Hundred (41). On April 26, 1624, Ursula French sought to have Elias Long freed, as he had fulfilled his four-year contract. By February 4, 1625, he had moved to the Treasurer's Plantation (11), where he may have been a tenant. Also present was Jane Long (Longe), perhaps one of Elias's relations. On June 6, 1625, Elias Long and Thomas Swift witnessed a memorandum executed by merchant Humphrey Rastell, acknowledging a debt to Treasurer George Sandys. Long and Swift made their signature marks, which suggests that they were illiterate. On December 12, 1625, Elias testified that he was present on December 2nd when Mr. Swift made his nuncupative will. Elias apparently was considered a responsible citizen, for he and another man were ordered to see that Robert Wright appeared in court. On November 13, 1626, Elias Long testified that he had been present when John Parsons made a nuncupative will around the end of July 1626 (CBE 36, 60; VCR 1:634; 2:529; 4:562-567; MCGC 79-81, 86, 123).

JANE LONG (LONGE)

On February 4, 1625, Jane Long (Longe) was living at the Treasurer's Plantation (11) and appears to have been free (CBE 60).

JANE LONG

Jane Long came to Virginia in a Spanish frigate in 1629. Captain Francis Eppes used her as a headright in 1638 when patenting some land (PB 1 Pt. 2:537).

JOHN LONG (LONGE)

John Long (Longe) died at Hog Island (16) sometime after April 1623 but before February 16, 1624 (CBE 42).

NICHOLAS LONG (LONGE)

On August 8, 1618, the justices of Bridewell decided that Nicholas Long (Longe), a vagrant from Lombard Street in Bridewell, would be sent to Virginia. On February 16, 1624, he was living on Hog Island (16) (CBE 9, 42).

***

RICHARD LONG (LONGE) I

On February 16, 1624, Richard Long (Longe) I was living at Basses Choice (27) with his wife and infant. When a muster was taken of the community's inhabitants on February 7, 1625, Richard was 33 years old and listed as a household head. Sharing the family home was his wife, Alice, and their 2-year-old son, Robert. Richard Long was in possession of a dwelling and was relatively well supplied with stored food and defensive weaponry (CBE 46, 63; DOR 1:49).

ALICE LONG (LONGE) (MRS. RICHARD LONG [LONGE] I)

Alice, who married Richard Long (Longe), came to Virginia in 1620 on the *London Merchant*. On February 16, 1624, she and her husband were living at Basses Choice (27) with their infant son. A year later, when a muster was taken on February 7, 1625, Alice was described as age 23, and her son was age 2. The Longs lived in a home of their own and had no indentured servants (CBE 46, 63).

ROBERT LONG (LONGE)

Robert Long (Longe), the infant son of Richard and Alice Long, was living with his parents at Basses Choice (**27**) on February 16, 1624. On February 7, 1625, young Robert and his parents were still residing at Basses Choice. He was then age 2 (CBE 46, 63).

***

ROBERT LONG (LONGE)

On September 3, 1620, Robert Long (Longe), a gentleman, left Bristol, England, on the ship *Supply* and was one of the people who went to Berkeley Hundred (**55**) with William Tracy. Long was supposed to serve the Society of Berkeley Hundred's investors for three years and, in exchange, was to receive 50 acres of land. In a letter to the Virginia Company, Governor George Yeardley indicated that Robert Long arrived at his destination on January 29, 1621. However, he apparently died shortly thereafter, for his name was listed among the dead (CBE 20-21; VCR 3:396, 426).

WILLIAM LONG (LONGE)

William Long (Longe) came to Virginia on the *Providence* in 1623 and on February 16, 1624, was living in Elizabeth City (**18**). On February 7, 1625, when a muster was taken of the settlers living in Newportes News (Marie's Mount) (**24**), William Long was identified as a 19-year-old servant in the household of Daniel Gookin (CBE 43, 63).

PETER LONGMAN

On February 16, 1624, Peter Longman was living on Virginia's Eastern Shore (**72-78**). It is uncertain precisely where he was residing (CBE 46).

WILLIAM LOVE

William Love, a tailor, came to Virginia in 1607 and was one of the first Jamestown (**1**) settlers. Captain John Smith identified Love as one of the soldiers who accompanied him to the Pamunkey Indians' territory on December 29, 1608 (CJS 1:209, 243; 2:142, 193).

WILLIAM LOVELL

On February 5, 1627, Peter Stafferton testified before the General Court that he had witnessed an agreement between William Lovell, master of the ship *Aid*, and John Williams, a merchant (MCGC 139).

JOHN LOVETT

In 1619 it was decided that John Lovett, a thief from London, would be transported from Newgate Prison to "foreign parts," probably Virginia (CBE 12).

RICHARD LOWE (LOOE, LOW)

Richard Lowe (Looe, Low) made several appearances before the General Court during 1626. On September 5, 1626, he and Nathaniel Causey were ordered to see that the late James Carter's goods were shipped home. Lowe acknowledged that he had witnessed Carter's will and stated that the decedent had deeded some property to him. On December 11, 1626, Lowe testified that in 1625, when the *Anne* of London made its last voyage, John Trehern's tobacco was aboard. A week later he stated that, in his presence, Thomas Gates admitted owing some tobacco to George Riddle. On July 8, 1627, Richard Lowe was among those shipping goods from London to Virginia on the *Anne*. He returned to Virginia prior to July 2, 1628, when London merchant Richard Perrye authorized him to collect his debts in the colony. In September 1655 Jane Allen alias Lowe, who was identified as the mother of Richard Lowe, a Virginia bachelor, was granted administration of his estate. The decedent may have been the same man who was in the colony during the late1620s (WAT 1016-1017; MCGC 114, 126-128; CBE 78-79; SH 11; EEAC 37).

ROBERT LOWE

On September 26, 1618, it was decided that Robert Lowe, a cooper and vagrant from Garlickehithe, would be sent to Virginia (CBE 10).

MICHAEL LOWICK

Michael Lowick, a gentleman, came to Virginia in 1608 in the 2nd Supply of new colonists. He would have resided in Jamestown (**1**) (CJS 1:241; 2:190).

KATHERINE LOWMAN (LEMAN, LEMON)

Katherine Lowman (Leman, Lemon) came to Virginia on the *Southampton* in 1623 and on January 20, 1625, was residing at Flowerdew Hundred (**53**), where she was one of Abraham Peirsey's servants. On October 10, 1627, Katherine, who was still in Peirsey's employ, ran afoul of the law for allegedly behaving lewdly with William Garrett, a fellow servant (CBE 50; MCGC 154).

MRS. BRIDGET LOWTHER

On January 23, 1629, the General Court learned that the late Nathaniel Jeffreys' servants were in the custody of Mrs. Bridget Lowther. She was ordered to surrender them to the decedent's executor and to account for the service they had provided to her. Jeffreys, who died sometime after March 1626, lived in Jamestown (1). On March 16, 1632, Bridget Lowther, who was described as a widow and resident of Pasbehay (3), received a 21-year lease for 250 acres of land on the west side of the Chickahominy River, opposite the land of Bridges Freeman. The name of Bridget Lowther's late husband is unknown (MCGC 182; PB 1 Pt. 1:137).

THOMASINE LOXMORE

On February 16, 1624, Thomasine Loxmore was living in Elizabeth City (17, 18) (CBE 44).

WILLIAM LUCAS

In mid-May 1625 Captain William Tucker of Elizabeth City (18) offered to pay merchant Walter Williams, on Captain Michael Marshatt's behalf, for Mr. William Lucas's use on the homeward voyage of Marshatt's ship, the *Supply*. This suggests that Lucas was a gentleman but also an indentured servant that Captain Marshatt wanted to employ. On July 29, 1628, William Lucas was in England and shipped goods on the *Elizabeth* of Saltash from Plymouth to Virginia (CBE 83; MCGC 190).

WILLIAM LUCOTT

William Lucott died at Elizabeth City (17, 18) sometime after April 1623 but before February 16, 1624 (CBE 45).

PHILIP LUGGER

Phillip Lugger, a 22-year-old silk-twiner from London, came to Virginia in 1619 aboard the *Bona Nova* (FER 295).

JOHN LULLETT

John Lullett died in Jamestown (1) sometime after April 1623 but before February 16, 1624 (CBE 39).

THOMAS LUM

On January 30, 1626, the General Court heard testimony about Thomas Lum and another man who drowned during some New Year's Eve revelry. According to several men who had been aboard the *Grace*, Adam Thorogood and some others took the ship's boat and cast off. Later, the men heard cries for help when Thomas Lum and John Foster's man fell overboard and drowned. The incident appears to have occurred in Elizabeth City (17, 18) in the James River (MCGC 91-92).

***

ALBIANO (ALIANO) LUPO

Albiano (Aliano) Lupo, an ancient planter, came to Virginia in 1610 on the *Swan*. On March 29, 1620, he sent word to the Virginia Company that he had been in Virginia for nine years and wanted his freedom and 100 acres of land. On February 16, 1624, when a census was compiled of the colony's inhabitants, Lieutenant Albiano Lupo was living in Elizabeth City (18) and was a married man. On September 1, 1624, when Lupo patented 350 acres, he indicated that his land lay adjacent to that of his wife, Elizabeth, and that he was acquiring the property on the basis of his own personal adventure and the headrights of five servants. When a muster was compiled in Elizabeth City in early 1625, Albiano Lupo was described as a 40-year-old household head, who shared his home with his wife, Elizabeth, daughter Temperance, and two male servants. Albiano Lupo's household was well supplied with stored food and defensive weaponry. In May 1625, when a list of patented land was sent back to England, he was credited with 350 acres in Elizabeth City, acreage that (unlike his wife's) was not described as planted. Albiano Lupo died sometime prior to October 9, 1626, at which time his will was presented to the General Court and proved by John Slaughter and Thomas Spellman. In 1628 Captain William Tucker was appointed overseer of Lupo's will. The Rev. Roland Graine was ordered to post a bond, as he was taking custody of the decedent's goods (CBE 43, 63; VCR 1:330; 4:558; MCGC 116, 173; PB 1 Pt. 1:31, 33-34; DOR 1:52; 2:496-497).

ELIZABETH LUPO
(MRS. ALBIANO [ALIANO] LUPO)

Elizabeth, who became the wife of Albiano (Aliano) Lupo, came to Virginia on the *George* in 1616 and was an ancient planter. On February 16, 1624, she was living in Elizabeth City (**18**) with her husband. When a muster was taken of Elizabeth City's inhabitants in early 1625, Elizabeth Lupo and her husband, Albiano, a household head, were sharing their home with their 4-year-old daughter, Temperance, and two male servants. Elizabeth was then age 28. In September 1624 Elizabeth Lupo received a patent for 50 acres of land in Kecoughtan (Elizabeth City) adjacent to the acreage her husband owned. She acquired her patent by means of a court order from England. In May 1625, when a list of patented land was compiled, Elizabeth Lupo was credited with 50 acres, which were described as seated (CB 43, 63; PB 1 Pt. 1:33-34; VCR 4:558).

TEMPERANCE LUPO

Four-year-old Temperance Lupo, who was Virginia-born, was living in Elizabeth City (**18**) in early 1625 with her parents, Elizabeth and Albiano Lupo (CBE 63; DOR 2:496).

PHILIP (PHILLIP) LUPO

Philip (Phillip) Lupo, the brother of Albiano Lupo, came to Virginia on the *George* in October 1621 and on February 16, 1624, was living in Elizabeth City (**18**). He was still residing there when a muster was taken of the area's inhabitants in early 1625. Philip, who was 42 years old at that time, lived alone in a home of his own and was well supplied with stored food and defensive weaponry. He reportedly returned to England after Albiano's death (CBE 43, 64; DOR 1:55; 2:496-497).

***

WILLIAM LUPO

William Lupo died in Elizabeth City (**17, 18**) sometime after April 1623 but before February 16, 1624. He probably was one of Philip and Albiano Lupo's brothers and came to Virginia with them in 1621. Years later, Sir Francis Wyatt used William Lupo's headright when patenting some land (CBE 45; PB 1 Pt. 2:916).

WILLIAM LUSAM

William Lusam came to Virginia on the *Charles* in 1621 and on February 4, 1625, was living on the lower side of the James River on Captain Samuel Mathews' plantation (**15**). At that time, William Lusam was a 27-year-old indentured servant in Mathews' employ (CBE 60).

THOMAS LUSCAM

In January 1624 Thomas Luscam and Supra Clark were identified as former captains of the ship *Furtherance*, a vessel that made many trips to Virginia (MCGC 9).

GEORGE LUXON

On November 1, 1631, George Luxon was identified as master of the ship *Exchange* of Bideford, which was going to Virginia (CBE 96).

PHILIP LUXON

In July 1637 Philip Luxon, captain of the *Blessing*, ran afoul of the law when he and some crew members helped themselves to some "strong waters" that William Harris of Jamestown (**1**) had imported. The incident occurred while the ship was anchored in Jamestown (HCA 13/53 f 249; SR 5862).

SUSANNA LYALL

On October 12, 1627, Susanna Lyall witnessed the will that Sir George Yeardley made in his house in Jamestown (**1**) (SR 3119).

JOHN LYFORD

John Lyford, who in 1624 was a clergyman at the New Plymouth plantation in Massachusetts, arrived in Virginia in 1629 and became the minister of Martin's Hundred (**7**). Because the Rev. Lyford made a salary agreement that was too costly with the settlement's leader, William Harwood, the General Court ordered Harwood to provide a third of Lyford's pay. On April 9, 1629, the Rev. John Lyford presented the will of Robert Adams of Martin's Hundred to the General Court (CJS 2:472; MCGC 196).

JOHN LYNGWOOD

John Lyngwood came to Virginia on the *Abigail*. On April 8, 1623, Richard Norwood informed the Virginia Company that Lyngwood was deceased (VCR 4:233).

ELIZABETH LYON

On February 27, 1619, Elizabeth Lyon was identified as a wench who was being transported to Virginia. She was among the children rounded up from the streets of London so that they could be sent to the colony. On February 16, 1624, Elizabeth was a member of Sir George Yeardley's household in urban Jamestown (1) (CBE 13, 38).

M

EDWARD MABIN

On February 16, 1624, Edward Mabin was living on the Bennett plantation in Warresqueak (26) (CBE 42).

OWEN MACAR

When the Indians attacked Owen Macar's home near Westover (54) on March 22, 1622, Owen and two other people were killed (VCR 3:568; CJS 2:301).

RICHARD MACHINN

On July 15, 1631, Richard Machinn and other Virginia planters sought relief from English customs on tobacco, claiming that the charges were very burdensome. Machinn indicated that his hogsheads of tobacco were marked *RM* (G&M 165).

ROGER MACKER

Roger Macker came to Virginia on the *Marmaduke* in 1621. On September 1, 1628, his headright was used by George Pace, the son and heir of Richard Pace, the

Paces Paines (9) settlement's original patentee (PB 1 Pt.1:64).

***

SAMUEL MACOCK (MAYCOCK, MACOCKE, MORECOCK)

Samuel Macock (Maycock, Macocke, Morecock)—the son of Roger Macocke, a Northampshire, England, husbandman—attended Cambridge University. He went to Virginia sometime prior to March 10, 1618. Deputy Governor Samuel Argall then asked the Virginia Company to allow Macock to function as a clergyman due to the extreme scarcity of ordained ministers. In 1619, while Governor George Yeardley was in office, Samuel Macock became a councilor and in that capacity heard Henry Spellman's testimony about a treaty made with the Indians. Macock lived at Bermuda Hundred (39) in 1620 and 1621 and was described as Governor Yeardley's chief strength. In July 1621 he was again appointed to the council. Samuel Macock had a patent for 2,000 acres of land on the east side of the mouth of Powell's Creek, adjacent to Flowerdew Hundred (53), and called his plantation "Macock's Divident" (48). On March 22, 1622, when the Indians attacked many of the settlements within the James River basin, Samuel Macock was slain at his plantation. He was survived by an infant daughter, Sara (Sarah), his sole heir. On May 8, 1626, it was reported that Samuel Macock had brought four servants to the colony aboard the *Abigail* in 1622. He probably intended to seat them on his plantation (VCR 3:92, 118-119, 482, 554-555, 568, 588; 4:554; CJS 2:266, 301; FER 113; CBE 38; MCGC 102; MEY 416; DOR 2:501-502).

SARA (SARAH) MACOCK (MAYCOCK, MACOCKE, MORECOCK) (MRS. GEORGE PACE)

On February 16, 1624, Sara (Sarah) Macock (Maycock, Macocke, Morecock), the orphaned daughter of councilor Samuel Macock (who was killed in the March 22, 1622, Indian attack), was living in urban Jamestown (1) in the household of Captain Roger Smith and his wife, Jane, John Rolfe's widow. On January 24, 1625, Sara, who was still a member of the Smith household, was described as age 2 and Virginia-born. On May 8, 1626, the General Court noted that Sara Macock was eligible to receive 200 acres of land as her late father's heir, for he had brought four servants to the colony aboard the *Abigail*. The property young Sara inherited probably was part of the Charles City plantation known as Macock's (48), which was on the east side of the mouth of Powell's Creek. Sara Macock eventually married George Pace, the son of ancient planter Richard Pace I, owner of Paces Paines (9) on the lower side of the James River. Together, they produced a son and heir, Richard Pace II. In August 1650 George Pace patented the land his wife, Sara, had inherited from her father (CBE 38, 55; MCGC 102; VCR 3:568; 4:554; PB 2:252; MEY 417, 472-473; DOR 2:501-502).

***

THOMAS MADDOX

On November 13, 1620, Thomas Maddox reportedly gave a bill of adventure to Mr. Stubbs. Maddox came to Virginia and apparently was associated with Edward Bennett's plantation, for he died at Warresqueak (26) sometime after April 1623 but before February 16, 1624 (VCR 1:418-419; CBE 42).

***

ISAAC (ISACK) MADISON (MADDESON, MADDISON)

Isaac (Isack) Madison (Maddeson, Maddison) came to Virginia with Sir Thomas Dale in 1611 and was an ancient planter. In May 1616 Dale placed him in command of West and Shirley Hundred (41). When Captain Madison began making plans to clear and seat at West and Shirley Hundred (Eppes) Island, the citizens of nearby Bermuda Hundred (39) objected because they considered that land to be part of their territory. Court testimony reveals that Madison was present when Deputy Governor Samuel Argall tried Edward Brewster in a martial court in 1618. Isaac Madison was among those who complained on March 15, 1620 that Governor George Yeardley was too lenient. In December 1620, when asking permission to return to England, Madison stated that he had been in Virginia for 12 years, had served Sir Thomas Dale, and had explored the colony on the Virginia Company's behalf. He sent a petition to

England on May 9, 1621, criticizing Captain William Powell. In July 1621 the Company rewarded Captain Isaac Madison by agreeing to provide his wife and him with free transportation to and from the colony, as well as two shares of land and two boys as apprentices. Captain John Smith indicated that Madison was among those he trusted to deal firmly with the Indians. He said that Madison captured the King of Potomac and his son, and that for a time he lived with the Potomac Indians. On April 16, 1622, Edward Brewster claimed that Deputy Governor Samuel Argall had commandeered 42 of Lord Delaware's men and sent them to West and Shirley Hundred to work on his own behalf, placing them under the supervision of Isaac Madison. After the March 22, 1622, Indian attack, Governor Francis Wyatt gave Captain Isaac Madison a commission to go to the Potomac River and assist the King of Potomac in fighting the Potomacs' and the colonists' common enemies. Madison and 30 men went to see Opechancanough sometime prior to October 23, 1622, to demand the return of the colonists captured during the March 1622 attack. Their attempt appears to have been futile. In November Madison and Robert Bennett of the *Samuel* were authorized to trade with the Indians in the Chesapeake Bay, and Madison was given the right to serve as sole truck master or trader.

On January 24, 1623, George Harrison incorrectly reported that Isaac Madison was dead and identified him as Lieutenant Craddock's brother. In June and November 1623 Madison gave testimony about the marriage contract between Cisley Jordan and the Rev. Grivel Pooley, an agreement that led to a breach of promise suit. In July 1623, when Madison was ordered to lead an attack against the Great Weyanoke Indians, he was told to recruit men from Flowerdew Hundred (53) and the plantations that lay to its west, and to see that the men were armed and brought to Jamestown by November 3rd. He also was authorized to collect corn and tobacco as fines levied against those who failed to gather sassafras. On January 9, 1624, Madison was ordered to produce witnesses on behalf of Lieutenant John Gibbs, a casualty of the 1622 Indian attack. Isaac and his wife, Mary, were living at their plantation on West and Shirley Hundred Island on February 16, 1624. Four days later, he was among those who signed a document complaining about conditions in the colony. Captain Isaac Madison died sometime prior to January 22, 1625. In May 1625 he was credited with 250 acres of land in Charles City, acreage that was seated (BRO 782; FER 245; VCR 1:434, 508; 317; 2:115-116; 3:76, 444, 654-655, 700; 4:218-220, 250, 292, 400, 554; CJS 2:309, 312-314; C 24/489; 24/490; SAIN 1:36; CBE 31, 33, 36, 53; SR 1207; MCGC 11; HAI 915).

MARY MADISON (MADDESON, MADDISON) (MRS. ISAAC [ISACK] MADISON [MADDESON, MADDISON])

Mary, who wed Isaac (Isack) Madison (Maddeson, Maddison), came to Virginia in 1618 on the *Treasurer*. In June 1623 Mrs. Mary Madison appeared before the General Court, where she testified in the breach of promise suit the Rev. Grivel Pooley brought against the widowed Cisley Jordan. On November 17, 1623, Mary's testimony in the case was mentioned in official communications with English authorities. On February 16, 1624, Isaac and Mary Madison were living on West and Shirley Hundred Island (**41**). He died sometime prior to January 22, 1625. When a muster was made of the community's inhabitants, Mary was identified as a 30-year-old widow, who headed a household that included two young male servants and Katherine Laydon, a 7-year-old girl who appears to have been orphaned. Mrs. Mary Madison was credited with two dwellings, and her household was well supplied with stored food, defensive weaponry, and livestock. She also had a boat. After January 22, 1625, Mary Madison's name disappeared from public records (CBE 33, 36, 53; VCR 4:218-220; DOR 1:14).

***

CHARLES MAGNOR (MAGNER)

Charles Magnor (Magner) came to Virginia on the *George* in 1623. On January 20, 1625, he was residing at Flowerdew Hundred (**53**), where he was a 16-year-old servant in the Rev. Grivel Pooley's household (CBE 50).

CHARLES MAGNOR (MAGNER)

When a list of patented land was sent back to England in May 1625, Charles Magnor (Magner) was credited with 650 acres on the Appomattox River. He may have been a kinsman of the 16-year-old servant Charles Magnor, then living at nearby Flowerdew Hundred (**53**) (VCR 4:554).

FRANCIS (FRANCISCO) MAGUEL (MIGUEL)

On July 1, 1610, Francis (Francisco) Maguel (Miguel), who reportedly was Irish but spying on behalf of Spain, prepared a written description of the Virginia colony, where he had lived for eight months. He appears to have left Virginia on April 19, 1608, when Captain Christopher Newport returned home. Maguel said that the fort in Jamestown (**1**) was well entrenched. He also described the natural resources that the colonists had found in Virginia. Maguel's report was enclosed in a letter that Don Alonso de Velasco, the Spanish ambassador in London, sent to the King of Spain. Francis Maguel may have used aliases such as Magill or Maguire (HAI 447-453; BRO 394).

MAGDALENE MAINWARINGE (MANWARINGE)

On November 20, 1622, Bridewell Court officials decided that Magdalene Mainwaringe (Manwaringe), a prisoner at Newgate, would be transported overseas, probably to Virginia (CBE 29).

RANDALL MAINWARINGE (MANWARINGE)

On August 20, 1634, Randall Mainwaringe (Manwaringe) reportedly shipped goods from London to Virginia on the *John and Dorothy* (CBE 118).

WILLIAM MAKEPEACE

On November 21,1618, the justices of Bridewell decided that William Makepeace, a vagrant and young rogue, would be transported to Virginia (CBE 11).

JOHN MALDMAN (MALTMAN)

Sometime prior to March 22, 1622, Lieutenant James Harrison of Warresqueak (**26**) purchased John Maldman's (Maltman's) indenture from John Cheesman of Elizabeth City (**18**). On February 16, 1624, John Maldman was living in Warresqueak. Harrison's acquisition of Maldman's contract was mentioned in testimony heard by the General Court in November 1624. (CBE 42; MCGC 35).

PERCIVALL MAN (MANN)

Percivall Man (Mann) died at Martin's Hundred (7) sometime after April 1623 but before February 16, 1624 (CBE 42).

THOMAS MAN (MANN)

Thomas Man (Mann) came to Virginia in 1621 on the *Temperance* at the expense of Sir George Yeardley. Man's headright later was transferred to Thomas Flint (MCGC 166; PB 1 Pt. 1:59).

JOHN MANBY

John Manby came to Virginia on the *Furtherance*. He died in Jamestown (1) sometime after April 1623 but before February 16, 1624 (CBE 39; HOT 196).

JOHN MANING

Sometime after April 1623 but before February 16, 1624, John Maning died on the lower side of the James River, within the corporation of James City (8-15) (CBE 39).

MANGOPEESOMON (SEE OPECHANCANOUGH)

DAVID (DAVY) MANSFIELD (MAINSFIELD, MANSELL, MONSELL)

David (Davy) Mansfield (Mainsfield, Mansell, Monsell) came to Virginia in 1619 on the *Bona Nova*. On February 16, 1624, he was living on the lower side of the James River on the Treasurer's Plantation (11), to the east of Gray's Creek. On February 4, 1625, when a muster was made of that area's inhabitants, he was identified as a hired man and one of Treasurer George Sandys' men. A David Mansell (probably Mansfield) witnessed Mr. Swifte's nuncupative will, which was made at the Treasurer's Plantation on December 12, 1625. On February 1, 1633, David Mansfield was a burgess for Martin's Hundred (7). On July 22, 1635, he renewed his patent for 500 acres in Martin's Hundred, acreage that lay adjacent to his own land and that of Mr.

Barham (CBE 41, 60; HEN 1:203; MCGC 80; PB 1 Pt. 1:259).

[NO FIRST NAME] MANSELL

Captain Mansell died sometime prior to December 15, 1621, at which time he was identified as Peter Arondell's (Arundell's) son-in-law. He was supposed to hunt and fish for Arondell (VCR 3:534).

HENRY MANSELL

On March 29, 1620, the Virginia Company noted that Henry Mansell, a Virginia colonist, had gone to England to see who was planting tobacco there. Nearly two years later, he submitted a claim for compensation for the six or seven years of service he had provided to the Company. Mansell was ordered to substantiate his claim, and on February 27, 1622, his petition was forwarded for consideration. It is probable that some of his service was performed in Virginia (VCR 1:326, 582, 591, 608).

ROBERT MANSTRIDGE (MANSTEED)

On April 25, 1625, the will of Robert Manstridge (Mansteed) of Taunton, Somerset, was proved in Virginia by Richard Brewster of Archer's Hope (6). In February 1630 English officials noted that Robert had died overseas and left goods in Virginia (MCGC 56; CBE 89).

ROBERT MANUELL

Robert Manuell came to Virginia in 1621 on the *Charles* and on February 16, 1624, was living in Virginia at Jordan's Journey (46). On January 21, 1625, when a muster was taken of the community's inhabitants, Robert was identified as a 25-year-old servant in the household of William Farrar and Cisley Jordan (CBE 36, 51).

GILBERT MARBURIE

Gilbert Marburie came to Virginia on the *Southampton* in 1622. In early 1625 he was residing in Elizabeth City (18), where he was a 32-year-old servant in Susan Bush's household (CBE 64).

***

SAMUEL MARCH

On February 16, 1624, Samuel March, who came to Virginia on the *William and Thomas*, was living at Martin's Hundred (7). Samuel and his wife, Collice, were still there on February 4, 1625, and he was a household head. Samuel and Collice March had lost a child during the past year (CBE 42, 62; DOR 1:46) .

COLLICE MARCH
(MRS. SAMUEL MARCH)

Collice, who married Samuel March, came to Virginia in 1623 on the ship *Ann*. On February 4, 1625, she was living at Martin's Hundred (7) with her husband, a household head. The March couple had recently lost a child (CBE 62).

[NO FIRST NAME] MARCH

Sometime after February 16, 1624, but before February 4, 1625, Samuel and Collice March's child died at Martin's Hundred (7). The child's name, age, and gender are unknown (CBE 62).

***

ANN MARCHANT

On January 22, 1620, the justices of Bridewell Court decided that Ann Marchant would be sent to Virginia (CBE 17).

MARGARET

Margaret, an old, blind maidservant, was killed at Richard Owen's household near Westover (54) during the March 22, 1622, Indian attack (VCR 3:567).

MARGARET

On February 16, 1624, an African named Margaret was living at Warresqueak (26), the Bennett plantation (CBE 42).

[NO FIRST NAME] MARKHAM

On January 29, 1629, Mr. Markham asked the Virginia Company for compensation for his service, the nature of which was not described (VCR 1:437).

ELIZABETH MARKHAM

Elizabeth Markham, a young maid, came to Virginia in September 1621 on the *Warwick*. She was the 16-year-old daughter of Jervis Markham. Her parents reportedly approved of her going to the colony (FER 309).

RICHARD MARKHAM

On March 27, 1622, Richard Markham received some shares of Virginia land from Francis Carter, shares that formerly had belonged to the late Thomas West, Lord Delaware (VCR 1:625).

ROBERT MARKHAM

On May 20, 1607, Robert Markham, a sailor who came to Virginia in the first group of Jamestown (1) colonists, accompanied Captain Christopher Newport when he explored the James River (HAI 102).

ROBERT MARKHAM (MARCUM)
ALIAS MOUTAPASS

In 1621 Captain John Smith identified Robert Markham (Marcum) alias Moutapass of the Eastern Shore as a fugitive who had lived among the northerly Indians for five years (CJS 2:289-290).

THOMAS MARKHAM

In June 1621 the justices of Bridewell decided that Thomas Markham, a "lewd boy" whom his parents could not control, would be transported to Virginia (CBE 23).

WALGRAVE (WALDEGRAVE)
MARKS (MARKES)

Walgrave (Waldegrave) Marks (Markes) came to Virginia on the *Margaret and John* and seems to have been a resident of Jamestown Island (1). On December 21, 1624, he served on the jury that conducted young George Pope's inquest, and on January 14, 1625, he testified that he had witnessed an agreement between Thomas Passmore and John Hall (Haul), both of whom were residents of Jamestown. On January 24, 1625, Walgrave Marks and John Jefferson jointly headed a household in urban Jamestown. They were relatively well supplied with provisions and defensive weaponry. On April 18, 1625, Walgrave witnessed an agreement made by Nathaniel Bass of Basses Choice (**27**) (CBE 56; MCGC 90-92; DOR 1:33).

THOMAS MARLET (MARLETT, MARLOTT, MARLOE)

Thomas Marlet (Marlett, Marlott, Marloe), a 30-year-old grocer from Sussex, England, came to Virginia in 1619 on the *Bona Nova*. On February 16, 1624, he was residing at the College (**66**). He was representing the community in the assembly when he signed a rebuttal to the Virginia Company's claim that conditions in the colony had been tolerable earlier on. He also signed the assembly's rebuttal to Captain Nathaniel Butler's allegations. By January 30, 1625, Thomas Marlet had moved to the Maine (**3**), just west of Jamestown Island. On March 14th he testified about John Roe's last illness and nuncupative will. He again appeared in court on June 1, 1625, and testified that Lieutenant Thomas Osborne (of Henrico)—not Treasurer George Sandys— had taken custody of the East India School's goods. Thomas Marlet appeared twice in court during 1626. On one occasion he indicated that Thomas Bunn (a surgeon and resident of the Maine) had hired John Smith after Christmas 1624 (that is, January 1625). Later, he testified about the nuncupative will that William Atkins had made at Bunn's house. In 1628 Marlet, who was identified as a planter, stated under oath that William Enry, who was gravely ill, had asked him to write out his will. However, Enry's condition grew worse and he declared his last wishes via a nuncupative will. Thomas Marlet's role in community affairs suggests that he was considered a trustworthy, responsible citizen who also was literate (FER 295; CBE 35, 46, 57; HAI 915; HEN 1:128-129; MCGC 50, 64, 89, 98, 174; DOR 1:27).

JOHN MARON

On May 27, 1631, Captain John Maron shipped lead shot to Virginia on the *Warwick* (CBE 95).

CHARLES MARSHALL

Charles Marshall died in Elizabeth City (**17, 18**) sometime after April 1623 but before February 16, 1624 (CBE 45).

EDWARD MARSHALL

Edward Marshall came to Virginia in 1621 on the *Abigail* and on February 16, 1624, was living in Buckroe, on the east side of the Hampton River in Elizabeth City (**17**). In early 1625, when a muster was taken of the colony's inhabitants, Edward was identified as a 26-year-old servant in Sergeant William Barry's household on the Virginia Company's land in Elizabeth City. On January 24, 1625, Edward Marshall testified that he was unaware of a bargain purportedly made by John Craddock and Captain Wilcox. On January 12, 1627, when Virginia's governing officials distributed the defunct Virginia Company's tenants and servants among themselves, Edward Marshall, who was described as a Company tenant, was assigned to Sir George Yeardley (CBE 45, 68; MCGC 44, 136).

MICHAEL MARSHALL

In August 1627 Michael Marshall, a 39-year-old merchant from London and owner of the ship *Return*, testified that he had hired Giles Smith to serve as steward on a voyage from Portsmouth, England, to Virginia. Smith returned to England with a shipment of Virginia tobacco and died a short time after going ashore (EAE 18).

***

ROBERT MARSHALL

Robert Marshall came to Virginia in May 1619 on the *George*, a vessel under the command of Captain John Bargrave. Marshall's transportation to the colony was paid by Samuel Jordan, who on December 10, 1620, used Marshall's headright when patenting some land. On February 16, 1624, Robert Marshall was living on the Governor's Land (**3**) just west of Jamestown Island, where he was a member of John Carter's household. In June 1624, Marshall, who was free, became engaged to Eleanor Sprad, the maidservant of Edward Blaney, a resident of urban Jamestown (**1**). Eleanor broke the law by simultaneously agreeing to marry two men, a decision that led to her being brought before the General Court. Robert Marshall quickly found another marriage partner. On January 24, 1625, when a muster was made of Jamestown Island's inhabitants, he and his wife, Ann, were living there, probably on a rural parcel that he and Thomas Grubb were leasing. As Grubb was obliged to serve Treasurer George Sandys until March 1, 1625, he may not have invested much labor in improving the leasehold, for on April 24, 1625, Marshall asked the General Court to partition their land. The break with Grubb may have impelled Robert Marshall to strike out on his own; during 1626 he commenced leasing a nearby 10-acre parcel, which he patented on September 20, 1628. During the mid- to late 1620s Robert Marshall made several appearances before the General Court. On January 24, 1625, he sold a sow to Daniel Lacy (a resident of urban Jamestown). He also sued Richard Allford, one of Captain Roger Smith's servants, who owed him 11 days of work. In 1628 and 1629 he had his neighbor, Robert Wright, arrested and was himself jailed for indebtedness. He was sued by Gabriel Holland and merchants Thomas and Edward Mayhew, who had him incarcerated (CBE 39, 56; MCGC 17, 44, 56, 108, 153, 158, 182-183, 188; PB 1 Pt. 1:92; 8:125; DOR 1:35).

ANN MARSHALL
(MRS. ROBERT MARSHALL)

Ann, Robert Marshall's wife, reportedly came to Virginia aboard the *George*. On January 24, 1625, she and Robert were living in the eastern end of Jamestown Island (1) (CBE 56).

***

MICHAEL MARSHOTT
(MARSHATT, MARSHARTT, MARSHALL)

Michael Marshott (Marshatt, Marshartt, Marshall), a merchant and sea captain, came to Virginia on business sometime prior to September 27, 1624, when he had a dispute with Luke Eden over some goods imported from Canada and the poor quality of tobacco used to pay for them. Court records reveal that over the years, Marshott was involved in many lawsuits, sometimes as plaintiff and sometimes as defendant. Late in 1624 he was ordered to pay merchant Humphrey Rastall on behalf of Captain John Martin. In May 1625, when Marshott set out for England as captain of the *Supply*, Captain William Tucker of Elizabeth City (17, 18) paid him for trans-

porting William Lucas, who was supposed to work during the transatlantic crossing. On March 27, 1626, Michael Marshott was summoned to court because he failed to pay a debt to Jamestown (1) merchant John Gill. Court testimony reveals that Marshott had some indentured servants in Virginia. On April 1, 1626, he was authorized to go north to trade with the Indians for corn and furs. Like many other merchants, he sometimes had to sue to collect debts. Captain Francis West made a mortgage agreement with him, a document held by Nathaniel Basse, who seems to have been serving as West's trustee. In March 1627 Virginia's assembly asked Captain Michael Marshott to bring 16 field carriages to the colony on the *London Merchant*. He returned to England and on August 16, 1627, shipped some goods from London to Virginia on the *Truelove*. He was supposed to bring two servants to Simon Turgis and was obliged to pay Turgis because the men fled before reaching Virginia. However, on October 16, 1629, Marshott was paid for the field carriages he had transported, and in March and September 1632 he was compensated from public funds for services he had performed (MCGC 20-21, 24, 32, 99, 124, 127, 160, 185, 190; CBE 79; JHB 1619-1660:53; HEN 1:171, 196; BL: Wyatt Register Book 1621-1626).

THOMAS MARSON

On March 30, 1623, Treasurer George Sandys, when queried by Thomas Marson's brother, told him that Thomas probably had returned to England or was on a plantation (VCR 4:72).

***

NICHOLAS MARTIAU (MARTEU, MARTEAW, MARTEAU)

Nicholas Martiau (Marteu, Marteaw, Marteau), a French Protestant who was naturalized in England, came to Virginia in 1620 aboard the *Francis Bonaventure*. After the 1622 Indian attack, Captain Martiau was among those who visited the Falling Creek ironworks (68) in Henrico. He apparently lived in Jamestown (1) for a while, for on June 24, 1623, he testified that while he was on sentry duty at the fort, he did not see anyone break into cape merchant Abraham Peirsey's storehouse. On February 16, 1624, Martiau was living in Elizabeth City

(18) in Captain William Tucker's household and represented that area in the colony's assembly. As a burgess he was among those who signed the assembly's rebuttal of the claims the Virginia Company made about living conditions in the colony between 1607 and 1619. On March 7, 1624, Martiau testified in court about Edward Giften's (Gibson's) treating the sick at Falling Creek and Weyanoke (52). In early 1625 Captain Nicholas Martiau's residence was Elizabeth City, where he and two other men headed a household. He was then age 33. On January 16, 1625, Martiau received an apology from John Downman, a man he himself had slandered. In May 1625 he got into a heated discussion with Mr. Mayhew at Kecoughtan and almost came to blows. At issue was the superiority of the kings of England and France. When the matter was aired in court in October, Nicholas Martiau took the oath of supremacy. In March 1629 it was noted that he was supposed to receive a young manservant from Edward Bennett. Martiau was among the first to settle in Chiskiack, and in 1640 he obtained a patent for 1,300 acres that included the 600 acres to which he was entitled for seating himself, his wife Jane, his son Nicholas, daughter Elizabeth, and several others on his property. His property became known as York Plantation (36, 37). Nicholas Martiau's first wife, whose identity is unknown, was the mother of his daughter, Elizabeth, who was born in 1625. Sometime prior to July 5, 1627, he married his second wife, Jane, the widow of Lieutenant Edward Barkeley of Hog Island. Later, he married a third time, wedding Captain Robert Felgate's widow, Isabella. Nicholas Martiau served as a burgess for Chiskiack and the Isle of Kent (in what became Maryland) in 1632 and 1633. He died in 1657 (CBE 43, 64; HAI 915; HEN 1:128-129, 154, 179, 203; MCGC 11, 15, 43, 156, 187; PB 1 Pt. 1:369, Pt. 2:709; MEY 417-419; DOR 1:56; 2:503-505).

JANE MARTIAU (MARTEU, MARTEAW, MARTEAU) (MRS. EDWARD BARKLEY, MRS. NICHOLAS MARTIAU [MARTEU, MARTEAW, MARTEAU])

On July 5, 1627, Mrs. Jane Martiau (Marteu, Marteaw, Marteau), who had married Nicholas Martiau, delivered the inventory of her former husband, Lieutenant Edward Barkley (Bartley), to the General

Court and gave her oath that it was accurate. Martiau used her headright and that of her daughter, Jane Barkley, when he patented some acreage in 1640. Jane died sometime prior to November 5, 1646 (MCGC 151; PB 1 Pt. 1:369, Pt. 2:707; MEY 419; DOR 2:504).

ISABELLA MARTIAU (MARTEU, MARTEAW, MARTEAU) (MRS. ROBERT FELGATE, MRS. GEORGE BEACH [BEECH], MRS. NICHOLAS MARTIAU [MARTEU, MARTEAW, MARTEAU])

Sometime prior to November 5, 1646, Nicholas Martiau (Marteu, Marteaw, Marteau) married the twice-widowed Isabella, who had wed Robert Felgate and then George Beach (Beech). Martiau helped her settle Beach's estate (MEY 419; DOR 2:504).

ELIZABETH MARTIAU (MARTEU, MARTEAW, MARTEAU)

Elizabeth, the daughter of Nicholas Martiau (Marteu, Marteaw, Marteau) and his first wife, was born in 1625. Around 1641 she married George Read, with whom she was buried at Grace Church in Yorktown, Virginia (DOR 2:505).

***

[NO FIRST NAME] MARTIN (MARTYN)

In May or June 1623 a man named Martin sent a petition to the king, claiming that he had been evicted from his houses when Sir George Yeardley set aside the Virginia Company's tract of Company Land in Elizabeth City (17). This individual may have been Captain John Martin (VCR 4:185).

ANTOINE MARTIN

Antoine Martin and his wife and child were among the Walloons and French who indicated their willingness to go to Virginia. In August 1621 the Virginia Company agreed that they could immigrate (CBE 24).

GILES MARTIN

Giles Martin came to Virginia on the *Truelove* in 1623. On January 30, 1625, he was living in Pasbehay (**3**), where he was a servant in the home of John Moone. On March 6, 1633, when John Moone patented some land, he used Giles Martin's headright and indicated that he had paid for his transportation to the colony (CBE 57; PB 1 Pt. 1:127).

GEORGE MARTIN

George Martin, a gentleman, came to Virginia in 1607 and was one of the first Jamestown (**1**) settlers (CJS 1:208).

JEANNE MARTIN

Jeanne Martin, a young girl, was among the Walloons and French who indicated their willingness to go to Virginia. In August 1621 the Virginia Company agreed that they could immigrate (CBE 24).

***

JOHN MARTIN I

Captain John Martin I, the son of Sir Richard Martin, master of the mint and lord mayor of London, arrived in Virginia in 1607 and was one of the first settlers. He also was one of the colony's first councilors. His son, John Martin II, accompanied his father to Virginia. During Captain John Martin's first few months in Virginia, he went with Captain John Smith on a voyage to the Chickahominy River, and he visited the Pasbehay Indians twice to obtain corn. Martin and his son became ill during the summer of 1607, when many of the Jamestown (**1**) settlers died. The elder man gradually recovered his health but the younger one died. Captain John Martin was highly opinionated and clashed with several of his fellow councilors, including Captain John Smith. At various times he also became embroiled in political intrigue. In 1608 Martin and his manservant, Anias Todkill, explored the Monacan Indians' country and the territory above the falls of the James River. He was supposed to bring cedar but instead returned with what he wrongly assumed was gold. In 1609, when food shortages were critical, George Percy sent Captain John Martin and a group of men to the Nansemond River (**29**) so that they could subsist. However, Martin returned to Jamestown and the Indians attacked the settlers he left behind. He went to England but came back to Virginia with

Captain Ratcliffe in the fleet that brought Sir Thomas Gates. Martin again was appointed to the Council, and when Lord Delaware arrived in June 1610, he designated Martin the master of the battery works for steel and iron.

According to George Percy, when Captain John Martin accompanied Sir Thomas Dale in an offensive against the Nansemond Indians in 1611, he was shot in one of his extremities, but survived. According to Ralph Hamor, Martin succeeded in making good, strong silk from native plant materials. Captain John Martin served as a judge in 1618 when Deputy Governor Samuel Argall tried Edward Brewster in a martial court. When the assembly convened in July 1619, he was appointed master of ordnance for the colony. Martin's controversial agreement with the Virginia Company, which he interpreted as making his plantation, Martin's Brandon (**59**), exempt from the colony's laws, led to its delegates being refused a seat at the first assembly. Moreover, as an investor in the Virginia Company, he claimed that he was entitled to 500 acres per share, not 100 acres, like everybody else. Captain John Martin claimed that an area called the King's Forest (centered on Jamestown) had been laid out during Sir Thomas Dale's government, an assertion Governor George Yeardley denied. Martin also alleged that Yeardley had wronged him by not allowing him free trade in the bay. In March 1620 there were 21 people living at Martin's Brandon, but Martin himself probably was at Bermuda Hundred (**39**), where he had tenure of Samuel Jordan's 12 acres and a house. In March 1621 Captain John Martin exported some tobacco from Virginia on Mr. Felgate's ship, on which he secured passage for himself and a servant. While he was in London in 1621, he became embroiled in a dispute with John Bargrave, who objected to Martin's special privileges and trading charter. Martin, in turn, presented the Virginia Company with a list of grievances. When the Company asked him to surrender his old patent for Martin's Brandon, he refused. Ultimately, the Virginia Company decided that Martin's patent and mastership of the ordnance had not been approved, and at first they denied him a new patent, since he would not agree to obey the law. Although they eventually gave him a patent, it was for less land than he thought he should have. On August 28, 1622, when Martin testified in an English court, he gave his age as 55 and said that he resided at Martin's Brandon.

In the wake of the 1622 Indian attack, Captain John Martin prepared a written proposal for subjugating the Indians. He also proffered that Virginia would be better off as a royal colony. In December 1623 Virginia Company officials noted that Captain John Martin was returning to the colony with some servants. The Privy Council ordered Virginia's incumbent governor to assist him, as his plantation had gone to ruin while he was detained in England. Martin and five servants arrived in Virginia in 1624 on the *Swann*, Humphrey Rastall's ship. Throughout the year he sparked controversy by claiming that he had been mistreated by Governor Yeardley and that threats had been made against his life. He also alleged that the planters at Kecoughtan had been wronged and that Edward Sharpless had been unjustly punished. On the other hand, Virginia's governing officials claimed that they had not assisted him because he was undeserving.

In early 1625 Captain John Martin and four of the men who came with him on the *Swann* were living in Elizabeth City on the east side of the Hampton River (17). They were relatively well supplied with food and defensive weaponry. Later in the year, Martin brought suit against Sir George Yeardley, making many wild-sounding allegations, and he claimed that the Virginia Company had been plotting against him. Some detractors claimed that Martin's plantation was a refuge for debtors and outlaws. Others claimed that he exaggerated his own success by bragging about his fine home, whereas he lived in a simple, windowless blockhouse at Martin's Brandon. As Martin's anger mounted, he slandered several people and enhanced his reputation as a troublemaker. Despite his shortcomings, in 1626 he was named a commissioner of Elizabeth City's monthly court. However, he was forced to pay some of his creditors and to lease some of his Martin's Brandon acreage to people who had worked for him. Captain John Martin made his last recorded appearance in court on January 9, 1629, when he was in his early 60s (CJS 1:xlii, 35, 37, 61, 205, 207, 220-221, 268, 609-611; 2:140; HAI 99, 124-126, 186, 188, 199, 279, 431, 433, 459, 503, 505-506, 514, 828-829, 895, 897; VCR 1:491, 522, 550, 560, 570, 594, 613, 635; 2:10, 40-42, 78, 119-120, 126-127, 215-216, 262, 344; 3:13, 153, 156-158, 164, 435-436, 444, 598-602, 704-710; 4:443-444, 507-508, 510, 513-518, 554-555, 559-567; C 24/489; PB 8:125; FER 138, 571; CBE 33-34, 67, 69; MCGC 21-22, 25, 31, 33, 37, 46, 58, 61-62, 81, 106, 125-126, 129, 132, 150-151; DOR 1:64).

JOHN MARTIN II

John Martin II, the son of Captain John Martin, arrived in Virginia in 1607 and was one of the first settlers in Jamestown (1). Captain John Smith described him as a gentleman. According to George Percy, John Martin II died on August 18, 1607 (CJS 1:20, 208; 2:141; HAI 99).

***

JOHN MARTIN (MARTEN)

John Martin (Marten), who arrived in Virginia in August 1618 on Lord Delaware's ship, became one of Governor George Yeardley's most trusted servants and was associated with his household in urban Jamestown (1). Official testimony that Martin gave in England in 1622 and 1630 sheds a great deal of light on his personal history and business dealings. He said that he attended Yeardley as his personal servant and often worked closely with Edward Rossingham, Yeardley's factor and overseer. Martin said that in 1619 Yeardley sent him into the Chesapeake to trade for corn and in 1620 dispatched him to Newfoundland, where he procured fish that were sold in Virginia. In 1621 he went to Holland to sell tobacco on Yeardley's behalf. On April 13, 1622, John Martin, who was then lodging with Captain Harlstone of Ratcliffe, in Stepney Parish, Middlesex, England, testified at an inquiry about the disposition of Lord Delaware's goods in Virginia. He stated that he was age 29 and was identified as a gentleman. Martin said that he was well acquainted with Lord and Lady Delaware and had been his personal servant while they were in England. He indicated that he was with Delaware at the time of his death in 1618 aboard the *Neptune*, on the way to Virginia. Martin described the contentious relationship between Deputy Governor Samuel Argall and Edward Brewster and its impact on Delaware's men. John Martin said that for a time, he had lived at Kecoughtan (17). He added that Argall had sent him and some of Delaware's other men to the West Indies on the *Treasurer.* This voyage resulted in the capture of an Angola ship on which some of the very first Africans were brought to Virginia.

In May 1622 John Martin, who intended to return to Virginia with servants, asked Virginia Company officials not to consider him a "foreigner," which increased the customs rates he was obliged to pay. He reminded them that he was a Company investor and told them that although he had been born in Persia, he had been baptized. On April 2, 1630, when John Martin testified in London in a chancery suit involving Sir George Yeardley's estate, he mentioned some of the duties he and Rossingham had performed for the decedent while members of his household. Martin then identified himself as a resident of All Hallows on the Wall Parish and gave his age as 45. Two other witnesses said that John Martin was commonly known as "the Persian," although some people thought that he was Armenian (Iranian). On March 24, 1637, John Martin inherited some clothing from John Parry, a cooper living in Virginia who had connections to Jamestown (EEAC: 44; C 24/486; 24/489; 24/490; 24/560 Pt. 2 f 34; HCA 13/44 ff 106vo-108vo; VCR 1:633; 2:13-14; EAE 12-13; SH 29; SR 9946-9947).

JOHN MARTIN

On May 8, 1626, the General Court heard testimony that John Martin, Adam Dixon's servant, came to Virginia on the *Margaret and John* at Dixon's expense. On September 8, 1627, when Dixon patented some land, he used Martin's headright and noted that he had come to the colony in 1622 (MCGC 103; PB 1 Pt. 1:53).

***

LAZARUS MARTIN

In March 1629, the Rev. Lazarus Martin, who recently had arrived in Virginia aboard the *London Merchant*, was appointed the minister of Bermuda Hundred (39) and the College tract (66), even though both places were sparsely populated. The Council of State told Martin that if the population was too small to support him, his salary would have to be supplemented with government revenues (MCGC 189).

MARY MARTIN (MARTYN)

On February 26, 1620, it was decided that Mary Martin (Martyn), an inmate in Newgate Prison, would be sent to Virginia (CBE 19).

PETER (PETTER) MARTIN (MARTTIN)

Peter (Petter) Martin (Marttin) died in Jamestown (1) sometime after April 1623 but before February 16, 1624. On January 3, 1625, Richard Kingsmill presented his will to the court. Peter Martin reportedly described Richard Cornish (an executed man) as a good mariner (CBE 39; MCGC 39, 93).

RALPH MARTIN

Ralph Martin, a husbandman, arrived in Jamestown (1) on September 12, 1623, aboard the *Bonny Bess* and took the oath of supremacy. He was from Bachain in Somershire (MCGC 6).

ROBERT MARTIN

Robert Martin came to Virginia on the *George* sometime prior to February 4, 1625, at which time he was Edward Barkley's servant at Hog Island (16). In 1629 Martin testified that the previous January, when he was leaving John Mills's house, he saw Thomas Stroud and accused him of stealing poultry from William White. It is unclear where the incident took place. Martin was required to post a bond. On July 24, 1632, Robert Martin obtained a 21-year lease for 30 acres of land in Archer's Hope (6), acreage he received for clearing the land and erecting buildings on it (CBE 61; MCGC 200; PB 1 Pt. 1:130-131).

RUTH MARTIN

In 1621 Ruth Martin, an indentured servant, was sent to Dr. John Pott, a resident of Jamestown (1), by the Company of Mercers (FER 297).

ROBERT MARVEL

On March 22, 1622, when the Indians attacked Captain Smith's plantation at Bermuda Hundred (39), Robert Marvel was slain (VCR 3:566).

MARY

On March 22, 1622, when the Indians attacked William Farrar's plantation (39) on the east side of the Appomattox River, Mary, one of Hendricke Peterson's maidservants, was killed (VCR 3:566).

MARY

Mary, an African woman, came to Virginia in 1622 on the *Margaret and John*. On February 7, 1625, she was living at Warresqueak (**26**) and was one of Edward Bennett's servants. Anthony (Antonio), another Bennett servant, may have become her husband (CBE 62).

MARY

A woman named Mary was living in Elizabeth City (**18**) on February 16, 1624 (CBE 44).

MARY

On February 16, 1624, a maid named Mary was living at Warresqueak (**26**) (CBE 42).

ANN MASON

Ann Mason came to Virginia on the *Marmaduke* in 1621. On September 1, 1628, when George Pace patented some land, he used Ann's headright (PB 1 Pt. 1:64).

ELIZABETH MASON

Elizabeth Mason died in Elizabeth City (**17, 18**) sometime after April 1623 but before February 16, 1624 (CBE 45).

***

FRANCIS MASON I

Francis Mason I, an ancient planter, came to Virginia on the *John and Francis* in 1613. On February 16, 1624, he and his wife, Mary, were residing in Elizabeth City (**18**). In early 1625 he was still there, heading a household that included his new wife, Alice, their young son, Francis II, and five servants. Although he was said to be 40 years old, he may have been somewhat younger, for in 1638 he deposed that he was age 42, and in 1641 he said that he was age 46. When a list of patented land was sent back to England in May 1625, Francis Mason was credited with 50 acres in Charles City, land that had not been seated. On October 13, 1626, Virginia's governing officials authorized him to make a trip to England. He returned to Virginia and sometime prior to November 19, 1635, patented some land in Elizabeth City, on the lower side of the James River near the Elizabeth River

(**20 a**). In August 1642 Lieutenant Francis Mason patented 1,250 acres on the basis of headrights, one of which was that of his wife, Mary. He played an active role in community life, serving as a court justice, sheriff, and churchwarden. Francis Mason I died intestate sometime after August 10, 1648, but before November 7, 1648 (CBE 44, 65; VCR 4:553; MCGC 121; PB 1 Pt. 1:312; Pt. 2:816; DOR 1:58, 2:569-570).

MARY MASON
(MRS. FRANCIS MASON I)

On February 16, 1624, Francis and Mary Mason, who were husband and wife, were living in Elizabeth City (**18**). In late August 1642, when Lieutenant Francis Mason patented some land on the lower side of the James River in Elizabeth City (**20 a**), he used his own headright and that of his wife, Mary, long since deceased. It is uncertain when they wed (CBE 44; PB 1 Pt. 2:816).

ALICE MASON
(MRS. FRANCIS MASON I)

Alice, who married ancient planter Francis Mason sometime after February 16, 1624, came to Virginia on the *Margaret and John* in 1622. In early 1625 she was living in Elizabeth City (**18**) with her husband and his young son, Francis II, who had been born in Virginia. Together Alice and Francis Mason I produced several children. She was still alive in 1653 (CBE 65; DOR 2:569-570).

FRANCIS MASON II

When a muster was made of the colony's inhabitants in early 1625, Francis Mason II was living in Elizabeth City (**18**) with his father, Francis Mason I, and his mother or stepmother, Alice. Young Francis had been born in Virginia (CBE 65).

***

JOHN MASON

On March 22, 1622, when the Indians attacked the settlers at Martin's Hundred (**7**), John Mason was killed (VCR 3:570).

PETER MASON

Peter Mason came to Virginia on the *Temperance* in 1621, at the expense of Sir George

Yeardley. Yeardley or his widow assigned Mason's headright to Thomas Flint, who used it when patenting some land on September 20, 1628 (MCGC 166; PB 1 Pt. 1:59).

ROBERT MASON

On November 20, 1622, Bridewell officials decided that Robert Mason, a Newgate prison inmate, would be transported to Virginia (CBE 29).

THOMAS MASON

Sometime after April 1623 but before February 16, 1624, Thomas Mason died on the lower side of the James, within the corporation of James City (8-15) (CBE 41).

WALTER MASON

On February 16, 1624, Walter Mason was living in Elizabeth City (17, 18) (CBE 43).

WYATT MASON (MASONN)

Wyatt Mason (Masonn) came to Virginia on the *Ann* in 1623. In early 1625 he was living in Elizabeth City (18), where he was a servant in William Julian's household. Wyatt was then age 16 (CBE 64).

GILBERT MASSIE

On August 12, 1620, the justices of Bridewell decided that Gilbert Massie, a vagrant, would be sent to Virginia (CBE 20).

JOHN MATHEMAN (MATHEYMAN)

John Matheman (Matheyman) came to Virginia on the *Jonathan* in 1619 and on February 16, 1624, was a servant in Sir Francis Wyatt's household in urban Jamestown (1). On January 24, 1625, when a muster was compiled, John was identified as a 19-year-old servant in the Wyatt household. He probably was the youth known as John Matheyman whom, on January 29, 1620, Bridewell's justices decided to send to Virginia. If so, the year recorded by the muster-taker in 1625 referred to the Old Style calendar (CBE 18, 38, 54).

MATHEW

On March 22, 1622, when the Indians attacked Edward Bennett's plantation at Warresqueak (26), a woman named Mathew was killed (VCR 3:571).

MATHEW

Mathew was killed at Thomas Sheffield's plantation (69) during the March 22, 1622, Indian attack (VCR 3:565).

MATHEW

A Polish man named Mathew was killed at Martin's Brandon (59) during the March 22, 1622, Indian attack (VCR 3:569).

ROWLAND MATHEW

On May 26, 1623, Rowland Mathew of St. Clement Danes, Westminster, testified in the suit that the Earl of Warwick undertook against Edward Brewster concerning the ships *Treasurer* and *Neptune*. Mathew, a 43-year-old gentleman, vouched for the authenticity of Sir Samuel Argall's affidavit (HCA 13/44 f 145ro; EAE 13).

WALTER MATHEW

In August 1624 Walter Mathew, a boatswain on the ship *Ambrose* at the time Richard Williams alias Cornish allegedly raped William Couse, testified before the General Court in Jamestown (1). On January 3, 1625, he returned to court and continued his testimony (MCGC 34, 41).

PRUDENCE MATHEWS

On September 28, 1628, it was decided that Prudence Mathews would be delivered to the Rev. Lewis Hughes, who would see that she was sent to Virginia (CBE 84).

ROBERT MATHEWS

Robert Mathews came to Virginia in 1622 on the *Southampton*. On February 16, 1624, he was living on the lower side of the James River at Captain Samuel Mathews' plantation (15). On February 4, 1625, when a muster was compiled of that settlement's population, Robert was identified as a 24-year-old servant (CBE 40, 59).

***

SAMUEL MATHEWS I

Samuel Mathews I came to Virginia sometime prior to 1618 as a servant to Sheriff

Johnson of London. By his own admission, Mathews lived in Jamestown (1) for a while and then went to Shirley Hundred (41) to oversee some of his employer's men. Later, he went to Arrohattock (66) after Deputy Governor Samuel Argall (1617–1618) made him a captain and placed him in charge of a group of men. In mid-November 1619, when William Weldon and some Virginia Company servants went to Arrohattock to seat the land set aside for the College, they found that Mathews already was established there and had built two houses. Virginia Company records indicate that he had seated the land on behalf of Sir Thomas Middleton. In April 1622, when 32-year-old Samuel Mathews testified in an English court, he said that he was from Arrohattock. However, he withdrew from the property and in November 1622 asked the Virginia Company to give him a patent, as he was taking 100 people to Virginia. He returned to Virginia, arriving in December 1622 on the *Southampton*, a few months after the Indian attack. In 1623, Captain Samuel Mathews received a commission to lead an offensive against the Tanx Powhatan Indians. That same year he served as a burgess for the Warwick River area. In April 1623 Treasurer George Sandys criticized Samuel Mathews for being preoccupied with the cultivation of tobacco. That summer Mathews led a march against the Indians in the Chickahominy River basin, and later in the year he and three others were instructed to obtain information on Virginia on behalf of the king. He also signed the rebuttal to Alderman Johnson's claims about the colony's wellbeing between 1607 and 1619.

By February 16, 1624, Samuel Mathews had seated himself on the lower side of the James River, across from Jamestown. In August 1624 he was added to the Council of State. When a list of patented land was sent back to England in May 1625, he was credited with some acreage on the lower side of the James River, just west of Hog Island's neck (15), and some land at Blunt Point, near the mouth of the Warwick River. It was the latter tract that he developed into his plantation called Denbigh or Mathews Manor (23). On February 4, 1625, when Samuel Mathews was living on his property near Hog Island, he was in possession of three storehouses, a dwelling, and 23 servants. He was well supplied with corn and defensive weaponry and had two boats at his disposal. Treasurer George Sandys' brother, the Rev. David Sandys, shared Samuel Mathews' home. Mathews made several appearances in court during 1625. He asked Hugh Crowther to exchange his acreage at Hog Island for some land at the College or at Martin's Hundred (7). He said that he had seated part of Captain William Powell's land (14) at Hog Island at the request of Powell's widow, and that he had cleared part of that acreage. In December 1625 Mathews asked for more land at Blunt Point. Within two years, he had sold his acreage near Hog Island and focused his attention on his Blunt Point plantation, Mathews Manor.

In 1626 Samuel Mathews was authorized to trade for corn with the Indians of the Chesapeake Bay, a privilege that was renewed three years later. He went to court from time to time, to give testimony or to assist in the settling of estates. In January 1627, when the colonists were warned about the possibility of foreign invasion, orders were given for all women, children, and cattle from the lower peninsula to be brought up to Mathews Manor if enemy ships were sighted. Captain Mathews was authorized to raise an army of volunteers to lead a march against the Pamunkey Indians or other natives considered enemies of the colony. He also led an offensive against the Warresqueak Indians and in 1629 was among those who agreed to seat on the York River within the Chiskiack Indians' territory. Around 1628 Samuel Mathews I married the twice-widowed Frances Grenville, who had outlived Nathaniel West and cape merchant Abraham Peirsey.

In May 1630 Samuel Mathews was given the responsibility of building a fort at Old Point Comfort. In compensation, he was given a year's monopoly on Indian trade in the Chesapeake Bay. During the mid-1630s, while Mathews was a councilor, he had many disagreements with Governor John Harvey and ultimately was highly instrumental in Harvey's ouster. By that time Mathews had married the daughter of Sir Thomas Hinton, whom Harvey had dismissed from his council. Samuel Mathews, as a result of his overt opposition to Harvey, was summoned to England and placed on trial for mutiny. When he was released on bail, he protested against Harvey's actions and illegal seizure of his opponents' personal property, which Mathews alleged had been given to one of Harvey's favorites. Samuel Mathews spent three years in England because of his problems with Sir John Harvey and returned to Virginia around 1637. Dutch mariner David Devries stayed briefly at Mathews' plantation, Mathews Manor, in March 1633 and described it as elaborately developed. In the 1640s the plantation was said to have "a fine house and all things answerable to it." His workers included weavers, flax makers, tanners, shoemakers, and other craftsmen. His agricultural operations were so extensive that he sold substantial quantities of wheat, barley, and beef to other colonies. Lieutenant Colonel Samuel Mathews, who sided with the Commonwealth government, continued to support the Virginia colony's interests. He served on the Council of State until his death sometime after November 1657 but before March 1658 (MEY 444, 480; VCR 1:601-604; 2:132; 3:226-229, 262-265; 4:111, 250, 464-465, 501, 555, 557; SAIN 1:58, 116, 193, 212, 217, 252, 281, 314; 9:170; CO 1/5 ff 199-200; 1/8 ff 178-180; 1/9 ff 132-134, 289-290; 1/10 ff 73-74, 190; PC 2/50 ff 543, 572; C 24/490; MHS 107, 112, 131; STAN 16, 31, 36, 71; HAI 915; CBE 40, 71, 120; CJS 2:215; MCGC 16, 53, 63, 65-66, 83, 128; 135-136, 150-151, 155, 180, 190, 192-193, 479, 498, 505; PB 1 Pt. 1:50, 74; EAE 21-22, 89; HEN 1:137, 140, 150, 153, 171, 175, 177, 196, 178, 187, 202, 221, 386-387; DEV 33; WITH 195; G&M 217-218, 233; FOR 2:7:6; 2:8:14; Lower Norfolk County Book A:121, 191, 331; B:87, 112, 140, 204; DOR 1:40; 2:636-639).

FRANCES GRENVILLE (GREVILL, GREVELL) WEST PEIRSEY MATHEWS (MRS. NATHANIEL WEST, MRS. ABRAHAM PEIRSEY, MRS. SAMUEL MATHEWS I) (SEE FRANCES GRENVILLE, MRS. NATHANIEL WEST, MRS. ABRAHAM PEIRSEY)

Frances Grenville, the widow of Nathaniel West and later of Abraham Peirsey, came to Virginia in 1620 on the *Supply* with William Tracy's family. She married Samuel Mathews I sometime after March 24, 1628, and by 1633 was dead (CBE 21, 40, 67; VCR 3:396, 426; MEY 444, 480; DOR 2:638).

[NO FIRST NAME] HINTON MATHEWS (MRS. SAMUEL MATHEWS I)

Around 1634 Samuel Mathews I married the daughter of Sir Thomas Hinton, a mem-

ber of Virginia's Council of State (FOR 2:8:14-15; DOR 2:639).

FRANCIS MATHEWS

Francis Mathews, the son of Samuel Mathews I and his wife, the twice-widowed Frances Grenville, was born sometime after March 24, 1628 but before 1634. He served as a captain of militia and York County justice (DOR 2:640).

SAMUEL MATHEWS II

Samuel Mathews II, the son of Samuel Mathews I, was born around 1629. His mother was the twice-widowed Frances Grenville, whom Samuel Mathews I married sometime after March 24, 1628. Samuel II represented Warwick River County in the 1652, 1653 and 1654 sessions of the assembly and was a local justice and a councilor. In 1657 Samuel Mathews II was elected governor of Virginia and held office until his death in January 1660 (MEY 445; MCGC 505; STAN 16, 36; DOR 2:639-640).

***

WILLIAM MATHEWS

On July 13, 1630, William Mathews, Henry Booth's servant, was found guilty of treason. He was drawn and then hanged, probably in Jamestown (1), where Booth resided (MCGC 479; HEN 1:146).

MATHUSALEM (METHUSALEM)

Mathusalem (Methusalem) was killed at Thomas Sheffield's plantation (69) during the March 22, 1622, Indian attack (VCR 3:565).

PHILIPPE MATON

Dyer Philippe Maton, his wife, five children, and two servants were among the Walloons and French who indicated their willingness to go to Virginia. In August 1621 the Virginia Company agreed that they could immigrate (CBE 25).

THOMAS MATTERDY

Thomas Matterdy, who came to Virginia in 1617 at the expense of Samuel Jordan, had been Jordan's apprentice while they were in England. On December 10, 1620, when Jordan patented some land, he listed Thomas Matterdy as a headright (PB 8:125).

ROBERT MATTSON

In 1621 and 1622 Robert Mattson was described as a sawyer for the Company of Shipwrights. While in Virginia, he worked under the supervision of master shipwright Thomas Nunn. Like others in Nunn's group, Mattson would have resided on Jamestown Island (1) (FER 378, 381).

EDWARD MAUNDER

In February 1626 the General Court heard testimony about the debts of Edward Maunder, a self-described poor man who came to Virginia as purser on the *Sparrow*, exchanging his labor for his passage and supplies. On January 11, 1627, the General Court learned that Maunder, who was then in England, was indebted to Thomas Weston, a merchant and owner of the *Sparrow*. Court testimony reveals that during Maunder's absence from Virginia, John Bainham erred by giving his tobacco to James Carter instead of Weston. As a result, Maunder's debt to Weston was unpaid (MCGC 132-133).

THOMAS MAXES

Thomas Maxes, a gentleman, came to Virginia in 1608 in the 2nd Supply of new settlers. He would have resided in Jamestown (1) (CJS 241; 2:190).

CHARLES MAXEY

On June 4, 1627, Charles Maxey was found guilty of a sex offense against 7-year-old Dorothy Harris. As punishment, Maxey was sentenced to be whipped in Jamestown (1) and again at Shirley Hundred (41), where the offense occurred. He also was ordered to execute Thomas Hale, who had been found guilty of raping four children (MCGC 149).

[NO FIRST NAME] MAY

On September 6, 1634, officials in England noted that Mr. May, master of the ship *Revenge*, was making a voyage from London to Virginia (CBE 119).

***

CORNELIUS MAY (MAYE)

Cornelius May (Maye), an ancient planter, came to Virginia on the *Providence* in 1616. According to Captain John Smith, he was among the men who came to the colony with Captain Nathaniel Butler, one-time governor of Bermuda. In 1622–1623, May was on a trading ship at Kecoughtan when the vessel was blown across the James to the opposite side of the river. He managed to make his way back and saw that his companions were rescued. On February 16, 1624, Cornelius May, his wife, Elizabeth, and child, Henry, were living in Elizabeth City (18). When a muster was taken in early 1625, Cornelius was listed as a 25-year-old household head who was relatively well supplied with stored food and defensive weaponry. Neither Cornelius's wife nor his son was listed. In May 1625 Cornelius May was credited with a 100-acre patent at Blunt Point (22). On March 5, 1631, when Joseph May of St. Mary Strand, Middlesex, made his will, he identified Cornelius May as his cousin who had a Virginia-born son (CBE 44, 65; CJS 2:318-320; VCR 4:557; EEAC 38; DOR 1:53).

ELIZABETH MAY (MAYE) (MRS. CORNELIUS MAY [MAYE])

On February 16, 1624, Elizabeth, the wife of ancient planter Cornelius May (Maye), was living in Elizabeth City (18) with her husband and son or stepson, Henry May (CBE 44).

HENRY MAY (MAYE)

On February 16, 1624, Henry, the son of ancient planter Cornelius May (Maye), was living in Elizabeth City (18). His mother may have been Cornelius's wife, Elizabeth (CBE 44).

***

JOHN MAY

On June 5, 1632, the General Court learned that John May and John Cumber had gone by boat to Thomas Farley's house in Archer's Hope (6) to get tobacco on January 25, 1632, and were told that Farley's tobacco already had been loaded aboard Tobias Felgate's ship, the *Defense* (MCGC 201).

LAWRENCE MAY

On August 6, 1623, the Virginia Company noted that Lawrence May was to be assisted by Virginia's governor and council and that he was to be paid what he was owed. However, May's compensation apparently was not forthcoming, for on November 21, 1625, the General Court determined that he was to be paid out of the Virginia Company's assets. On December 29, 1625, Lawrence May gave a receipt to Lieutenant William Barry of Elizabeth City (17), signifying that the Virginia Company had paid him in full. Court records dating to January 30, 1626, indicate that he had been the master of the ship *Elizabeth*. He probably had transported Company servants or supplies to Virginia (VCR 4:269; MCGC 76, 90-92).

WILLIAM MAY

William May, a laborer, came to Virginia in 1608 as part of the 1st Supply of new settlers and would have lived in Jamestown (1) (CJS 1:223; 2:162).

EDWARD MAYBANK

Edward Maybank came to Virginia on the *John and Francis* in 1622. On February 7, 1625, he was residing in Warresqueak (26), where he was an indentured servant in Edward Bennett's household (CBE 62).

WILLIAM MAYDEN

William Mayden, a 25-year-old cloth worker from Shropshire, England, came to Virginia in 1619 on the *Bona Nova* (FER 295).

***

EDWARD MAYHEW (MAHEW)

Edward Mayhew (Mahew) and his brother, Thomas, were merchants who did business in Virginia. Sometime prior to January 23, 1629, Edward, who was in Virginia, had some tobacco packed for shipment to his brother. Because Robert Marshall opened the hogshead and removed part of the tobacco, Edward Mayhew went to court to recover what was missing. In late January 1629 the General Court decided that Edward Mayhew was entitled to some tobacco from Captain Wilcock's estate for the use of Nicholas Clements. Lieutenant Edward Waters was supposed to deliver it, which suggests that the dealings were taking place in Elizabeth City (17, 18). On May 10, 1629, Thomas Mayhew went to court to transfer Anthony Leane's contract to his brother, Edward. Leane, an indentured servant, was to serve Edward Mayhew for a year aboard his boat, but was not to be used as a field hand (MCGC 182-183, 197).

THOMAS MAYHEW (MAHEW)

Thomas Mayhew (Mahew) came to Virginia sometime prior to May 1626, when he became indebted to John Orchard, a merchant. On May 21, 1627, the General Court decided that Orchard should be repaid out of Mayhew's goods. When Thomas Mayhew was made administrator of Daniel Lacy's estate in 1628, he was identified as a merchant. In November 1628 he was summoned to court, where he agreed to pay Martin Peale the wages he was owed for service on the *Gift*; Edward Grindon appeared as a witness. In January 1629 Thomas Mayhew went to court in an attempt to recover some tobacco that Robert Marshall had misappropriated. Thomas was in Jamestown (1) in 1629 and served on a jury. On May 10, 1629, he went to court in order to transfer Anthony Leane's contract to his brother, Edward Mayhew, who was planning to have the servant work aboard his boat for a year (MCGC 149, 165, 173, 177, 182-184, 197).

***

JOHN MAYOR

John Major died at Flowerdew Hundred (53) sometime after April 1623 but before February 16, 1624 (CBE 37).

JAMES MAYRO

On February 16, 1624, James Mayro was living on West and Shirley Hundred Island (41) (CBE 36).

THOMAS MEARE

In January 1622 Thomas Meare was identified as a servant whom Thomas Crispe brought to Virginia on the *Abigail* (MCGC 50).

WILLIAM MEAKINS

On March 22, 1622, when the Indians attacked Powle-Brooke or Merchants Hope (**50**), William Meakins was killed (VCR 3:569).

***

REV. WILLIAM MEASE (MACE, MAYS)

The Rev. William Mease (Mace, Mays) was the minister at Kecoughtan (**17**) in 1616, when John Rolfe described conditions in the colony. On April 30, 1623, when Mease rebutted Captain Nathaniel Butler's allegations about conditions in the colony, he said that he had been a minister in Virginia for ten years. He returned to England and on January 22,1625, testified in litigation involving settlement of the late John Pountis's estate. Mease, who then identified himself as a 40-year-old schoolmaster from All Hallows Parish in London, said that when he was in Virginia he lived around 40 miles from Pountis's residence. He added that he was a preacher and was busy tending to his parishioners' needs, and therefore had little knowledge of Pountis's business affairs. Pountis usually resided in Jamestown (**1**) (BRO 782; VCR 2:385; HAI 874; SR 9951; C 24/511 Part 1:19).

MARGERY (MARGRY) MEASE (MACE, MAYS) (MRS. WILLIAM MEASE [MACE, MAYS])

On January 22, 1625, Margery (Margry), the wife of the Rev. William Mease (Mace, Mays), testified before chancery officials in England in the settlement of the late John Pountis's estate. She indicated that she was 22 or 23 years old. Margery said that she had married her present husband while living in Virginia and that Pountis had given her away. She stated that Pountis had been in possession of 10 milk cows approximately two years before she had returned to England (SR 9951; C 24/511 Part 1:20).

***

JOAN MEATHERST

On October 11, 1627, the General Court heard testimony about Joan Meatherst, a maidservant brought to Virginia by Benjamin Sims (Syms), who had intended to marry her. As it turned out, Joan and Benjamin found that they disliked each other intensely. Therefore, she was assigned to Jamestown (**1**) merchant John Gill, whom she was to serve for two years, and Gill was to pay Sims for her work. Benjamin Sims was living at Basses Choice (**26**) in 1624 and 1625 but later moved to Elizabeth City (**19**) (MCGC 154-155).

***

GEORGE MEDCALFE (MEDCALF)

On February 16, 1624, George Medcalfe (Medcalf) was living in Elizabeth City on the east side of the Hampton River (**17**), on the Virginia Company's land. He was still there in early 1625 and shared his home with his wife, Sara, and daughter, Joane. George Medcalfe was then age 46 and probably was a Virginia Company tenant, for he was free. The household was relatively well supplied with stored food and defensive weaponry but lacked servants. In January 1626 George went to court, where he admitted owing tobacco to Mr. Rastall, a merchant. He returned a month later and made arrangements to get an indentured servant from John Hayes. At that time it was decided that he would receive John Dennis. On January 24, 1629, George Medcalfe had Obedience Robins (a resident of the Eastern Shore) arrested (CBE 43, 67; MCGC 87, 95, 183; PB 1 Pt. 1:81; DOR 1:64).

SARA MEDCALFE (MEDCALF) (MRS. GEORGE MEDCALFE [MEDCALF])

Sara, the wife of George Medcalfe (Medcalf) came to Virginia on the *Hopewell* in 1624. In early 1625 she and her husband were living on the east side of the Hampton River on the Virginia Company's land (**17**). They shared their home with George's child, Joane (CBE 67).

JOANE MEDCALFE (MEDCALF)

In early 1625 Joane Medcalfe (Medcalf), who probably was the daughter of George Medcalfe, was living with him and his wife, Sara, on the east side of the Hampton River on the Virginia Company's land (**17**). It is uncertain whether Joane was born in Virginia or had immigrated to the colony (CBE 67).

***

GEORGE MEE

George Mee came to Virginia on the *Hopewell* in 1633 at the expense of Adam Thorogood, who used Mee's headright when patenting some land on June 24, 1635 (PB 1 Pt. 1:179).

THOMAS MELLING

In June 1619 Thomas Melling, a London merchant and member of the Virginia Company, informed Company officials that he currently had people in Virginia. On March 13, 1622, Company officials learned that Melling had obtained his land from Captain Ralph Hamor. Although its location is uncertain, Hamor is known to have had land at Warresqueak (**26**), on Jamestown Island (**1**), at Hog Island (**16**), at Blunt Point (**22**), and in Archer's Hope (**6**) (EAE 8; VCR 1:619).

WILLIAM MELLRICKES

William Mellrickes was among those sent to Captain John Woodlief's plantation (**49**) in September 1619. Later it was noted that he had died after being in Virginia for four years (CBE 14).

CLEMENT MELTON (METTON)

In May 1622 Clement Melton (Metton), a servant being sent to Virginia on the *Furtherance*, set sail from Isle of Wight. In June 1622 it was noted that he had left England before Virginia Company officials had received word of the March 22, 1622, Indian attack (VCR 3:618-619; CBE 28).

GEORGE MELTON (METTON)

On August 1, 1622, the Virginia Company noted that George Melton (Metton) set sail for Virginia on the *Furtherance* in June 1622 (VCR 3:674).

THOMAS MELTON

Thomas Melton came to Virginia on the *Hopewell* in 1628. His transportation costs were paid by Adam Thorogood, who used Melton's headright when patenting land on June 24, 1635 (PB 1 Pt. 1:179).

WILLIAM MELTON

On February 27, 1619, the justices of Bridewell decided that William Melton, a boy, would be sent to Virginia (CBE 12).

***

GEORGE MENEFIE (MENIFY)

George Menefie (Menify) immigrated to Virginia on the *Samuell* in 1622 and resided in urban Jamestown (**1**). In 1623 he was accused of illegally purchasing sack (a wine) from Sir George Yeardley. Menefie's name appeared in official records numerous times during the 1620s. He served on juries and participated in inquests, and in January 1624 he acted as the attorney of Thomas Hamor of Warresqueak (**26**), the brother of his neighbor, Ralph Hamor. On February 4, 1624, Menefie received a patent for a Jamestown lot, the property on which his house was situated. At that time he identified himself as a merchant and said that he had been in Virginia for three years. On February 16, 1624, George Menefie was listed as a household head. Later in the year, Margery Mutch, the wife of one of Dr John Pott's servants, made reference to Menefie's house in testimony she gave before the General Court. In 1624 George Menefie agreed to pay a debt to Captain Roger Smith, another Jamestown resident, and he testified about some inflammatory statements Captain John Martin had made. He served as the administrator of Lt. James Harrison of Warresqueak and agreed to pay a debt Mr. Bennett owed to Menefie's neighbor and fellow Jamestown merchant John Chew. He failed to pay provost marshal Randall Smallwood's fee on time, which resulted in his being summoned to court. In April 1624 George Menefie sent a letter to George Harrison's brother, John, to report his death from a wound received in a duel. As overseer of the decedent's estate, he also sought John Harrison's advice about the estate's disposition. The working relationship between George Menefie and the Bennetts and Harrisons of Warresqueak raises the possibility that he was tied into their London-based trading network. He also had business dealings with Jamestown merchants John Pountis and Edward Blaney and the Blands, who were important London merchants.

On January 24, 1625, George Menefie was credited by the muster-taker with two houses, some livestock, a boat, and two servants. He was well supplied with stored food and defensive weaponry. On at least one occasion he was called on to settle a debt of John Ferrar's, and in 1627 he was named Ralph Hamor's administrator. In August 1626 George Menefie was identified as the official merchant and factor for the corporation of James City, which spanned both sides of the James River and extended from Skiffs Creek westward to a point above the Chickahominy River. As the territory's official merchant, he drew a 12 percent commission. In October 1629 George Menefie was a burgess for Jamestown. Court testimony taken in August 1626 reveals that he had an operational forge in Jamestown, a structure that may have been on his urban lot. Because he was functioning as the corporation's official merchant, he may have used a storehouse that was on public property rather than on land he owned personally.

In July 1635 George Menefie patented 1,200 acres at Rich Neck, which he developed into a plantation known as Littletown, and confirmed its title on February 23, 1636. He also acquired land in Charles City County, a plantation he called Buckland, which he developed into a family seat. On August 3, 1640, Menefie patented a second lot in Jamestown, a parcel he was required to use or lose. During the early 1640s he secured a patent for 3,000 acres on the north side of the York River, part of which later became the plantation known as Rosewell. George Menefie was one of Virginia's most highly successful merchants and planters and was a member of the Council of State from 1635 to 1644. When Dutch mariner David Devries visited George Menefie's Littletown plantation in March 1633, he described its elaborate gardens and said that his host was a great merchant. The Council convened at Littletown on May 11th. In December 1633 George Menefie and Dr. John Pott made arrangements for the Rev. Anthony Panton to come to Virginia. Panton soon alienated Governor John Harvey and Secretary Richard Kemp. In April 1635, when Menefie was a councilor, the disagreements between Harvey and his council became extremely intense. On one occasion the dialogue became so heated that Harvey struck Menefie on the shoulder, accused him of treason, and ordered his arrest. The other councilors refused to take Menefie into custody and, instead, turned Harvey out of office. Menefie refused to charge Harvey with high treason but detained him at Littletown until he could be transported back to England. In mid-January 1637, when Sir John Harvey returned to Virginia, his governorship restored, he had George Menefie and several other councilors sent to England as prisoners and confiscated their goods. Menefie professed his innocence and was released after two months' detention. When he returned to Virginia he reportedly brought many servants. He again served as a councilor.

George Menefie probably was living at Buckland during the mid-1630s when he took a Tappahanna Indian boy into his home and reared him in the Christian faith. According to law, Menefie received a stipend for doing so. In 1640 Menefie had in his custody two runaway servants, one of whom belonged to the Governor of Maryland. In February 1645 he and Richard Bennett were authorized to purchase powder and shot for use in defending the colony from the Indians. In December 31, 1645, when George Menefie made his will, he mentioned his third wife, Mary, and daughters Mary and Elizabeth. He bequeathed his land in Jamestown to his daughter, Elizabeth, who by that date had married her stepbrother, Henry Perry. He also made reference to his ships, the *Desire* and the *William and George*. He left a sum of money to Jamestown merchant John White, if White agreed to collect his debts, and asked his executors to see that he was buried in the cemetery at Westover Church. George Menefie died shortly after making his will, which was presented for probate in London on February 25, 1646. Nearly 30 years later, a dispute arose over the ownership of Buckland involving the Perry heirs (MCGC 4-5, 9-10, 20-21, 30, 37, 45, 47, 53, 55, 57-58, 81-82, 107, 109, 117-118, 121-122, 128, 133, 157, 165, 170, 187, 383, 466, 477, 480, 491, 498; PB 1 Pt. 1:5-6, 199; Pt. 2:704, 730; 4:199; CBE 38, 47, 56; CO 1/3 ff 63-64, 210; 1/9 f 134; 1/10 f 190; 1/32 f 7; SAIN 1:61, 207, 212, 217, 252, 256, 264, 281, 314; HEN 1:138, 297; STAN 33, 54; DEV 34; EAE 44, 50, 78; SH 29; Lower Norfolk County Book A:59, 246; EEAC 39; WITH 180-181; SR 3994; MHS 150; DOR 1:33; 2:649-650).

ELIZABETH MENEFIE (MENEFY) (MRS. GEORGE MENEFIE [MENEFY])

Sometime before 1635, George Menefie (Menefy) married a woman named Elizabeth, who died before 1637. She produced a daughter named Elizabeth, who married Henry Perry (MEY 448-449; WITH 180-181; DOR 2:650-651).

ISABELL (IZABELLA) PACE PERRY MENEFIE (MENEFY) (MRS. RICHARD PACE, MRS. WILLIAM PERRY, MRS. GEORGE MENEFIE [MENEFY]) (SEE MRS. WILLIAM PERRY, MRS. RICHARD PACE]

After August 1637, Isabell (Izabella), who had outlived husbands Richard Pace and Captain William Perry, married George Menefie (Menefy) of Jamestown (1) and Buckland, in Charles City County. She was Menefie's second wife. Isabell (Izabella) and William Perry had a son, Henry, who married George Menefie's daughter and heir, Elizabeth (MEY 473, 486-487; DOR 2:650; PB 1 Pt. 2:702).

MARY MENEFIE (MENEFY) (MRS. GEORGE MENEFIE [MENEFY])

After Isabell (Izabella) Pace Perry Menefie's death, George Menefie married a woman named Mary, whose surname is unknown. When he made his will, he named her his executrix and guardian of his daughter, Elizabeth (MEY 449; WITH 180-181; DOR 2:650).

ELIZABETH MENEFIE (MENEFY) (MRS. HENRY PERRY)

Elizabeth Menefie (Menefy), the daughter of George Menefie and his first wife, Elizabeth, married her stepbrother, Henry Perry, sometime after 1646. The couple made their home at Buckland, the Menefie plantation in Charles City County, which Elizabeth inherited along with her father's lot in urban Jamestown (1). The Perrys disposed of Elizabeth's late father's lot in Jamestown sometime prior to 1656 (MEY 449; AMB 27; PB 4:228; DOR 2:650-651).

***

THOMAS MENTIS (MEUTIS)

On February 16, 1624, Thomas Mentis or Meutis was a servant in the household of Edward Blaney, a merchant living in urban Jamestown (1) (CBE 38).

JOHN MERIDAY (MEREDIE, MERIDIEN)

John Meridien or Meriday died in Jamestown (1) sometime after April 1623 but before February 16, 1624. His name was listed twice in the accounting of the dead (CBE 39, 41).

[NO FIRST NAME] MERIWETHER

A butcher named Meriwether immigrated to Virginia, departing from England on April 17, 1619 (FER 107).

***

EDWARD MERIWETHER (MERRIWETHER)

Around 1619 Edward Meriwether (Merriwether) and his wife went to Virginia on the *Garland* and were among the settlers heading for Southampton Hundred (44) (FER 137).

MRS. EDWARD MERIWETHER (MERRIWETHER)

Mrs. Edward Meriwether (Merriwether) and her husband went to Virginia on the *Garland* around 1619 and were bound for Southampton Hundred (44) (FER 137).

***

THOMAS MERRES (SEE THOMAS NEARES)

JOHN MERRITT

John Merritt, who in 1621 was identified as one of the passengers on the *Falcon*, went to Jamestown (1) (EAE 11).

WILLIAM METHOWLD

On July 6, 1627, it was noted that William Methowld was shipping goods on the *Golden Lion* of Dundee from London to Virginia (CBE 78).

METHUSALEM
(SEE MATHUSALEM)

WILLIAM METTICKS

William Metticks was among those sent to Berkeley Hundred (55) in September 1619. Later it was noted that he had died after being in Virginia for four years (VCR 3:198).

MICHAELL (MICHAEL)

A man known as Michaell (Michael), a laborer, came to Virginia in 1608 in the 1st Supply of new Jamestown (1) colonists (CJS 1:223; 2:162).

ANN MICHAELL
(MIGHILL, MICHELL)

On February 27, 1619, the officials at Bridewell decided that Ann Michaell (Mighill, Michell), whom they identified as a wench, would be sent to Virginia. She probably was one of the children rounded up from the streets of London so that they could be sent to the colony. In 1619 Ann was transported to the colony on the *George*. On February 16, 1624, she was living at Chaplin's Choice (56). She was still residing there on January 21, 1625, and was identified as a servant in Isaac Chaplin's household (CBE 13, 37, 51).

FRANCIS MICHAELL (MICHELL)

Sometime prior to the March 22, 1622, Indian attack, Francis Michaell (Michell) purchased six acres at Bermuda Hundred (39) from Joseph Chard. On September 20, 1624, he patented some land in Kecoughtan (17) adjacent to John Taylor's property (MCGC 79-80; PB 1 Pt. 1:26).

JOHN MICHAELL (MICHELL)

In 1619 the justices of Bridewell decided that John Michaell (Michell), a thief from London who was imprisoned at Newgate, would be transported overseas. On January 22, 1625, he was listed among the dead at West and Shirley Hundred (41). A notation was made that he had been killed by Indians (CBE 12, 53).

REMEMBER MICHEL
(MICHAELL?)

On March 22, 1622, Remember Michel (Michaell?) was killed when the Indians at-tacked Edward Bennett's plantation in Warresqueak (26) (VCR 3:571).

THOMAS MICHELL

Thomas Michell, a 21-year-old brewer from Yorkshire, England, came to Virginia in 1619 aboard the *Bona Nova*. The cost of his transportation was paid by the Ferrars, who were major Virginia Company investors (FER 295, 296).

WILLIAM MICKLEWOOD

On January 29, 1620, the justices of Bridewell Court decided that William Micklewood, who was from Baynards Castle, was to be sent to Virginia. He was still imprisoned on May 6, 1620, and was described as a longtime inmate (CBE 17, 20).

ANTHONY MIDDLETON

Anthony Middleton set sail for Virginia on the ship *Jonathan* in March 1620. His transportation costs were paid by his father, David Middleton. On February 16, 1624, Anthony was living in Elizabeth City (18) (EAE 11; CBE 43).

DAVID MIDDLETON

David Middleton, a Virginia Company investor, sent two people (Lewknor and Arthur Middleton) to Virginia on the *Jonathan*, which set sail in March 1620. David also came to the colony and was supposed to become a member of the Council of State. According to official records, David Middleton, who was the father of Anthony Middleton, was a large, corpulent man with gray hair. He died soon after reaching Virginia (EAE 11; CJS 2:283; VCR 1:379, 479).

HENRY MIDDLETON
(MIDDELLTON)

Henry Middleton (Middellton) died in Elizabeth City (17, 18) sometime after February 16, 1624, but before early 1625 (CBE 67).

LEWKNOR MIDDLETON

Lewknor Middleton was one of two people whom Virginia Company investor David Middleton sent to Virginia on the *Jonathan*, which set sail in March 1620 (EAE 11).

LODOWICK MIDDLETON (MIDLETON)

On January 22, 1620, the justices of Bridewell decided to send Lodowick Middleton (Midleton) to Virginia. He was from Cheapside, (CBE 17).

ROBERT MIDDLETON

On April 3, 1627, when Robert Middleton, a resident of Virginia, made his will, he indicated that he was a bachelor. He bequeathed most of his belongings to his brother, William, who was in Yorkshire, and gave him all of his possessions at his plantation, which he had entrusted to the care of Peter Andrews. It is uncertain where Middleton's plantation was located (EEAC 39; SH 8; WITH 175-176; SR 3116; CBE 38).

THOMAS MIDDLETON

On July 13, 1617, Thomas Middleton, a prisoner in Oxford's jail, was reprieved and delivered to Sir Thomas Smith so that he could be transported to Virginia (SR 4525; PC 2/29).

THOMAS MIDDLETON

In October–November 1635, Thomas Middleton was sued by Edward Wigg, who had sent a shipment of tobacco from Virginia on the *Robert Bonaventure*. The ship went to Holland instead of London, and Wigg's tobacco was seized (EAE 55).

FRANCIS MIDWINTER

Francis Midwinter, a gentleman, came to Virginia in 1607 and was one of the first colonists. According to George Percy, he died in Jamestown (1) on August 14, 1607 (CJS 1:20; 2:142; HAI 99).

JOHN MILEMAN

John Mileman was buried in Elizabeth City (17, 18) on April 28, 1624 (CBE 67).

[NO FIRST NAME] MILMAN

Master Milman, whom Captain John Smith described as a boy, came to Virginia in 1608 in the 2nd Supply of new settlers. Therefore, he would have lived in Jamestown (1) (CJS 1:242; 2:191).

JOHN MILLER

In 1619 when John Miller came to Virginia, his transportation costs were paid for by the Ferrars, who had heavily invested in the Virginia Company (FER 296).

ROBERT MILLER

Virginia Company records dating to April 26, 1624, indicate that Garrett Weston paid for transporting Robert Miller and Francis Weston (Garrett's brother) to Virginia. Miller was one of Garrett Weston's servants (VCR 2:532).

WILLIAM MILLER

William Miller died sometime after April 1623 but before February 16, 1624. He resided on the lower side of the James River within the corporation of James City (8-15) (CBE 41).

FRANCIS (FRANCES) MILLETT

Francis (Frances) Millett, who resided on the lower side of the James River within the corporation of James City (8-15), died sometime after April 1623 but before February 16, 1624 (CBE 41).

JOHN MILLS

When Robert Martin testified in 1629 against Thomas Stroud, an accused chicken thief, he made reference to John Mills's house, which appears to have been on the lower side of the James River, within the corporation of James City (8-16) (MCGC 200).

SUSAN MILLS

Susan Mills came to Virginia on a Spanish frigate in 1629. Captain Francis Eppes used her as a headright when patenting some land in 1638 (PB 1 Pt. 2:537).

WILLIAM MILLS

When William Mills, an indentured servant, testified before the General Court on January 21, 1628, he indicated that he was age 21 and had been born in Purton, in Wiltshire. William—who in 1628 was in the employ of Edward Grindon of Grindon's Hill, a component of the Treasurer's Plantation (11)—admitted that he had stolen from his master on several occasions and had taken the purloined goods to the home of John Tios and Thomas Hall. When the General Court's justices convened on February 6th, two witnesses testified that they had seen William Mills sneaking out of the Grindon plantation's storehouse in the middle of the night. Among the items he removed were shoes, currants, and sugar. On at least one occasion, he stole some of his master's chickens. On February 7, 1628, William Mills was sentenced to be whipped "at the cart's tail" from urban Jamestown (1) to the gallows and back. The location of the gallows in Jamestown was most likely at a site on the edge of town, overlooking Pitch and Tar Swamp. (MCGC 159, 162-164).

RICHARD MILMER

Richard Milmer, a laborer, came to Virginia in 1608 in the 1st Supply of new settlers. Therefore, he resided in Jamestown (1) (CJS 1:223; 2:162).

ROBERT MILNER (MILVER)

Robert Milner (Milver) came to Virginia on the *Francis Bonaventure* in August 1620 and was a free man. On February 16, 1624, he was living at West and Shirley Hundred (41). He was still there on January 22, 1625, when a muster was made of the community's inhabitants. Robert, was then age 24 and free, shared his home with three other men. They were relatively well supplied with stored food and defensive weaponry and had a modest amount of livestock (CBE 36, 53; DOR 1:15).

JOHN MILNHOUSE (MILNEHOUSE)

John Milnhouse (Milnehouse) came to Virginia on the *London Merchant*. On January 30, 1625, he was living on the Governor's Land (3) in Pasbehay and was described as one of the Governor's men. Milnhouse was then 36 years old. On December 11, 1626, John Milnhouse agreed to continue occupying his home in Pasbehay, using as much land as he wanted and paying a modest annual rent to the governor. However, by July 24, 1632, he had acquired a 21-year lease for 40 acres in Archer's Hope (6), acreage

that he had cleared and seated (CBE 57; MCGC 126; PB 1 Pt. 1:131).

RICHARD MILTON

On September 3, 1620, Richard Milton left Bristol, England, on the ship *Supply* with William Tracy, who was bringing a group of settlers to Berkeley Hundred (55). He was to serve a certain number of years and, in exchange, was to receive a quantity of land. The Virginia Company learned that Tracy's group arrived at their intended destination on January 29, 1621. In August 1622 Richard Milton, despite his association with the Society of Berkeley Hundred, was described as a Virginia Company servant. On June 28, 1624, he testified before the General Court about the late George Thorpe's debt to a Mr. Dade. Thorpe, who had been one of Berkeley Hundred's leaders, had been killed in the March 22, 1622, Indian attack. On January 17, 1625, Richard Milton was ordered to live at Shirley Hundred (41), so that he could take care of Berkeley Hundred's cattle. By January 21, 1625, he had relocated to Jordan's Journey (46), where he was living alone in a home of his own. He was relatively well supplied with stored food and defensive weaponry and had some livestock in his possession. On April 25, 1625, he was ordered to appear before the General Court as a representative of Berkeley Hundred, so that he could testify about some cattle that Sir Samuel Argall was trying to claim. In 1630 Richard Milton prepared a memorandum about the cattle that had been in his custody, animals that belonged to John Smyth and Richard Berkeley, members of the Society of Berkeley Hundred. In 1632 when the Society of Berkeley Hundred's investors considered reviving their plantation, they noted that Richard Milton and John Gibbs had asked for a much larger number of servants than they had been given (CBE 21, 28, 43, 52; VCR 3:396-397, 426, 674; MCGC 17-18, 55; S of N 40, 41; DOR 1:19).

***

HENRY MILWARD

On March 22, 1622, when the Indians attacked the plantations near Bermuda Hundred (39), Henry Milward was killed. Also slain were Henry's wife, child, and sister. When a list of patented land was sent back to England in May 1625, Henry Milward was credited with 250 acres on the Appomattox River. His land on the Appomattox would have been near Bermuda Hundred (VCR 3:566; 4:554).

MRS. HENRY MILWARD

During the March 22, 1622, Indian attack, Mrs. Henry Milward, her husband, child, and sister-in-law were killed at a plantation near Bermuda Hundred (**39**) (VCR 3:566).

[NO FIRST NAME] MILWARD

Mr. and Mrs. Henry Milward's child was killed during the March 22, 1622, Indian attack. The family lived near Bermuda Hundred (**39**) (VCR 3:566).

[NO FIRST NAME] MILWARD

Henry Milward's sister was killed at a plantation near Bermuda Hundred (**39**) when the Indians attacked on March 22, 1622 (VCR 3:566).

***

JOHN MILWARD

According to Virginia Company records, John Milward was sent to Virginia by the Company of Mercers. On March 10, 1622, he witnessed the will made by John Rolfe, a resident of Jamestown. When Dr. John Pott patented some land on September 1, 1632, he claimed to have transported John Milward to Virginia and used him as a headright (FER 297; PB 1 Pt. 1:113; SH 5; MCGH 861).

THOMAS MIMES

On February 16, 1624, Thomas Mimes was living at Flowerdew Hundred (**53**) (CBE 37).

WILLIAM MINNS

On January 30, 1626, William Minns was ordered to sell his tobacco and post a bond with Captain Eppes, as a guarantee that he would serve Captain Ward for the time remaining on his 12-month contract (MCGC 91).

***

RICHARD MINTER

On August 14, 1622, Virginia Company officials identified Richard Minter as Dr. Lawrence Bohunn's tenant. However, Minter was a tenant associated with the physician general's office land, not with Bohunn personally. Minter's wife, Ann, reminded Company officials that Mintner had paid for his own provisions and transportation to the colony and was supposed to be given 50 acres of land. In July 1635 Richard Minter was identified as the late father of Edward and John Minter (VCR 2:101; PB 1 Pt. 1:259).

ANN MINTER
(MRS. RICHARD MINTER)

Ann Minter was the wife of Richard Minter, a tenant assigned to the land of the colony's physician general, Dr. Lawrence Bohunn. On June 19, 1622, and again on July 14, 1622, she sent petitions to Virginia Company officials requesting that her husband be freed and insisting that he had paid for his own transportation to the colony. Later, she came to the colony herself. On July 22, 1635, when Edward Minter patented some land, he indicated that he was the son of Richard and Ann Minter and was entitled to their personal adventures or headrights (VCR 2:50, 101; PB 1 Pt. 1:259).

EDWARD MINTER

When Edward Minter patented some land on July 22, 1635, he indicated that he was the son and heir of Richard and Ann Minter and was using their headrights. He also used the headrights to which his late father was entitled for transporting him and his brother, John, to the colony (VCR 2:50, 101; PB 1 Pt. 1:259).

JOHN MINTER

Sometime prior to July 22, 1635, Richard Minter paid for the transportation of his son, John, to Virginia. Richard also brought John's mother, Ann, and his brother, Edward, to the colony (PB 1 Pt. 1:259).

***

DAVID MINTON (MYNTON)

On January 22, 1629, David Minton (Mynton) accused Bridges Freeman of beating and wounding him. He asked the General Court to require Freeman to pay his medical bills, but the justices rejected his proposal because Minton had insulted Freeman, prompting the assault (MCGC 182).

JOHN MINTERNE
(SEE JOHN MYNTERNE
[MINTRENE?])

***

RICHARD MINTRENE I

Richard Mintrene I came to Virginia on the *Margaret and John* in 1620 and was accompanied by his son, Edward. On February 16, 1624, when a census was taken of the colony's inhabitants, Richard Mintrene I was living in Elizabeth City (18) with his son, Richard II. When a muster was made in early 1625, Richard Mintrene I was described as age 40. He shared his home with his 12-year-old son, Edward, and four other males, none of whom were servants. Mintrene had an ample supply of stored food and defensive weaponry (CBE 44, 65; DOR 1:56).

EDWARD MINTRENE

Edward Mintrene came to Virginia in 1620 on the *Margaret and John*, the ship that brought his father. In early 1625 he was identified as a resident of Elizabeth City (18) and the 12-year-old son of Richard Mintrene I. The Mintrenes shared their home with four other males, none of whom were servants (CBE 65).

RICHARD MINTRENE II

On February 16, 1624, Richard Mintrene II reportedly was living in Elizabeth City (18) with his father, Richard I. He may have been the same youth identified as Edward Mintrene in the 1625 muster (CBE 44).

***

***

FRANCIS (FRANCES)
MITCHELL (MICHELL)

Francis (Frances) Mitchell (Michell) came to Virginia in 1618 on the *Neptune*, the vessel that brought Lord Delaware to the colony. On February 16, 1624, he was living in Elizabeth City (18). When a muster was made of that area's inhabitants in early 1625, Francis, who was age 38, was sharing a dwelling with his wife, Maudlin, and their 1-year-old son, John, who had been born in Virginia. Francis Mitchell and his partner,

Miles Prickett, an ancient planter and saltmaker, jointly headed the household. They had an ample supply of stored food and defensive weaponry, and their home was defended by a palisade (CBE 44, 63; DOR 1:52).

MAUDLIN MITCHELL (MICHELL)
(MRS. FRANCIS [FRANCES]
MITCHELL [MICHELL])

Maudlin, the wife of Francis (Frances) Mitchell (Michell), came to Virginia on the *Bona Nova* in 1620. In early 1625 she was living in Elizabeth City (18) in a home she shared with her husband, their 1-year-old son, John, and her husband's partner, Miles Prickett. Maudlin was then age 21 (CBE 63).

JOHN MITCHELL (MICHELL)

In early 1625 John Mitchell (Michell), who was age 1, was living in Elizabeth City (18) with his parents, Francis and Maudlin Mitchell, in a home they shared with his father's partner, Miles Prickett (CBE 63).

***

JOHANNA MITCHELL

On November 20, 1622, it was decided that Johanna Mitchell, a prisoner at Newgate, would be transported overseas (CBE 29).

RICHARD MITTON

On February 5, 1623, the Virginia Company authorized Richard Mitton of Abraham to take a shipload of passengers to Virginia and then go on a fishing voyage (VCR 2:262).

TIMOTHY MOISE (MOSES)

On March 22, 1622, when the Indians attacked Martin's Hundred (7), Timothy Moise (Moses) was slain (VCR 3:570).

ESTINIEN [ETIENNE, STEPHEN]
MOLE (MOLL)

In 1621 Estinien (Etienne, Stephen) Mole (Moll), a Frenchman, accompanied John Pory on a journey to the Eastern Shore (CJS 2:288).

GEORGE MOLE (MOLL)

On March 27, 1622, the Virginia Company acknowledged that George Mole (Moll) had acquired two shares of land from Lady Delaware. He also received from Francis Carter some shares that formerly belonged to Lord Delaware (VCR 1:622, 625).

SAMUEL MOLE (MOLL)

On March 15, 1620, Samuel Mole (Moll), a surgeon, leased some land and a house from Sir George Yeardley in urban Jamestown (1) for a term of 60 years. On April 4, 1623, when Mole began making plans to return to England, he asked incumbent Governor Francis Wyatt for permission to sell or sublet his leasehold to someone else. He stated that he had spent a great deal "repairing & amending of wch mesuage or tenement" and would like to get the best profit he could by leasing or selling his house. Mole's petition was granted. In 1643 Mole's land was in the possession of Robert Hutchinson. On April 30, 1623, before Samuel Mole left Virginia, he signed a document refuting the allegations Captain Nathaniel Butler had made about conditions in the colony. He departed from Virginia shortly thereafter and by June 11th was back in England, where he testified in court. He then indicated that he was 41 years old and a native of Rochelle, France. He said that he had been living in Jamestown in January 1623 when Thomas Hamor died, and stated that Nathaniel Jeffreys, with whom Mole shared his home, had made Hamor's coffin (VCR 2:386; 4:97-98; EAE 14; HCA 13/44 f 147ro; SR 5860; PB 1 Pt. 2:944).

DIEGO DE MOLINA (MALINOS)

In 1611 Diego de Molina (Malinos), Antonio Pereos, and a renegade English pilot named Limbreck were aboard a Spanish ship that entered the mouth of the James River and paused near Old Point Comfort. The men went ashore and were captured and kept prisoner for several years because they were considered Spanish spies. Colonist John Clarke, who was captured by Molina's shipmates, was spirited away to Havana. On May 28, 1613, Molina wrote a letter to Spanish ambassador Alonso de Velasco, who was then in London, and smuggled it out of Virginia in the sole of a shoe. He described conditions in the colony as he knew them, including the extent of Virginia's fortifications, which he claimed were low level, fragile, and vulnerable. He spoke disdainfully of the military skills of Dale and Gates, the colony's principal leaders, despite their ex-

perience in the Low Countries. He said that although he had not visited the peninsula on which the colonists had placed their main settlement, Jamestown (1), he had heard that approximately 150 settlers were living there. Molina said that the colonists' forts, which were wooden, were surrounded with earthworks and equipped with artillery. He added that the death rate was extremely high and that the colonists had little food or apparel to sustain them. He indicated that Sir Thomas Gates wanted him to urge the Spanish to release John Clarke, a captured Englishman. Molina wrote another letter to Velasco on July 8, 1613, reiterating many of the same points. In an April 30, 1614, letter to Gondomar, the Spanish ambassador to England, he said that he had been sick for 17 months but was being treated kindly. Two months later he indicated that he was being moved to another location. In 1616 Molina was freed in a carefully orchestrated prisoner exchange (HAI 515-516, 533-541, 751, 783-791; BRO 649, 652, 659, 744).

RICHARD MOLINEUX (MULLINAX, MOLYNEUX)

Richard Molineux (Mullinax, Molyneux), a gentleman, came to Virginia in 1608 and was in the 1st Supply of new settlers. He would have resided in Jamestown (1) (CJS 1:222; 2:161).

SAPCOTT MOLINEUX (MOLYNEUX, MULLINAX)

On June 13, 1617, Sapcott Molineux (Molyneux, Mullinax), a prisoner in the Oxford jail, was reprieved and delivered to Sir Thomas Smyth so that he could be transported to Virginia (CBE 9; PC 2/29; SR 4525).

THOMAS MOLTON

Thomas Molton, a cook and gardener, went to Virginia on the *Margaret* of Bristol in September 1619 and accompanied Captain John Woodlief, whose plantation (49) was on the lower side of the James River, within the corporation of Charles City. In August 1622 Thomas Molton was said to be living in Virginia (CBE 14, 28).

ANN MOMFORD

On November 22, 1620, the justices of Bridewell decided to send Ann Momford, to

Virginia. She was described as an "old guest," or longtime prisoner, and was said to have led an incontinent life. That description suggests that Ann was a prostitute (CBE 17).

THOMAS MOMFORD

In 1608 Thomas Momford, whom Captain John Smith described as a gentleman, accompanied him on his second exploratory voyage on the Chesapeake Bay. Momford was the co-author of an account that Smith used in his writings. Momford would have lived in Jamestown (1) (CJS 1:197, 224, 230; 2:163, 169-170).

ROGER MONROE

Roger Monroe came to Virginia on the *James*, which left England on July 31, 1622. Richard Quaile, a sea captain, paid for his transportation to the colony (FER 400).

PETER (PEETER) MONTECUE (MONTAGUE, MOUNTEGUE)

Peter (Peeter) Montecue (Montague, Mountegue) came to Virginia on the *Charles* in 1621. On February 4, 1625, he was described as a 21-year-old servant living at Captain Samuel Mathews' plantation (15) on the lower side of the James River. He apparently returned to England, for on July 19, 1627, he shipped some goods from London to Virginia on the *James*. By March 1632 he had returned to the colony and witnessed a will in what became York County. Montecue obtained a patent for land on the lower side of the James River in August 1637, land that abutted the Elizabeth River (20 a). In 1647 he acquired 100 acres in Nansemond County, which he represented in assembly in 1652 and 1653 (CBE 60, 79; York County Deeds, Orders, Wills &c. 1 [1633-1694]:33; PB 1 Pt. 2:463; 2:73, 130; DOR 2:652-653).

WILLIAM MONTEFORT

On March 22, 1622, when the Indians attacked the settlers living at Southampton Hundred (44), William Montefort was killed (VCR 3:569).

OLIVER MONTELL

On January 29, 1620, the justices of Bridewell decided that Oliver Montell, who was from Cripplegate, would be sent to Virginia (CBE 18).

[NO FIRST NAME] MOONE

Captain John Smith said that Captain Moone, who brought the 3rd Supply of new colonists to Virginia in 1610, was very capable (CJS 1:270; 2:219, 222).

***

JOHN MOON (MOONE, O'MOON, OMOONCE)

John Moon (Moone, O'Moon, Omoonce) was born at Berry (near Gosport) in Stoak Parish, Hampshire, England. On April 30, 1621, he asked the Virginia Company of London for the right to his late brother Nicholas's bill of adventure, which would have enabled him to claim the land to which Nicholas was entitled as a Company investor. Disposition of the Moon request is uncertain. In 1623 John Moon came to Virginia on the *Return*. By January 30, 1625, he had seated acreage in Pasbehay, on the Governor's Land (3). With him were three young male servants who reportedly had come to the colony on the *Truelove*, right after the March 22, 1622, Indian attack. The household was relatively well supplied with stored food and defensive weaponry. Little is known about John Moon's activities during this period, except that in early January 1626 he was ordered to pay a debt he owed to Captain William Peirce of Jamestown (1). Moon's identification as "Mr." indicates that he was considered a gentleman.

By early 1629 John Moon had moved to Warresqueak (26) (later, Isle of Wight), which he made his permanent home. In February 1629 he was summoned to appear before the General Court, which attempted to settle his dispute with Mrs. Rachel Polentine, whose land was on the west side of Pagan Creek in Warresqueak. Court testimony reveals that Moon had ordered Mrs. Polentine's servants to work in his tobacco field without seeking her permission. The General Court responded by partitioning Mrs. Polentine's land and awarding Moon a three-year lease for half of her acreage. Therefore, it appears that she or her late husband, John, was indebted to Moon or had been his partner. On the other hand, Moon was ordered to compensate Mrs. Polentine and to allow her to possess the dwelling and tobacco house on the property he was to lease. On March 7, 1629, Moon ran afoul of the law by insulting Warresqueak's militia commander, Captain Nathaniel Basse of Basses Choice (**27**). On March 6, 1633, John Moon, a planter, patented 200 acres in Warresqueak, securing his land on the basis of four headrights: his own and the three male servants with whom he had been living on the Governor's Land in January 1625. In October 1635 he patented an additional 900 acres in Warresqueak, by then Isle of Wight County, using his wife, Susan, as one of his headrights. Two years later he acquired an additional 550 acres adjacent to his previous patent.

By January 1639 John Moon had begun representing Isle of Wight County in the colony's assembly. He also served as a burgess in 1640. Moon was re-elected to the assembly as one of Isle of Wight's delegates in 1652 and 1654. By the time of his death in 1655, he had attained the rank of captain in the militia. It may have been during the years John Moon served as an Isle of Wight burgess that he acquired a lot in Jamestown's New Town, for when patenting a lot on March 1, 1655, Mrs. Ann Talbott made reference to "the path leading to Captain Moone's house" and the Back Street, which formed her property's northern boundary line. When Captain John Moon made his will sometime during the 1650s, he instructed his executors to sell his "Brew House and Land belonging to it at James Town," using the proceeds to cover his debts. He left his beloved wife, Prudence, a fourth of his personal estate, noting that the remainder was to be divided among his three daughters. Daughter Sarah was to inherit his dwelling called Bethlehem and some land on Pagan Creek, whereas daughter Susanna was to receive his acreage called Bethsaida, on the east side of Bethlehem Creek. Daughter Mary was to receive his land at Red Point. John Moon also made bequests to his stepdaughter, Joan Wilson Garland, and her husband, Peter, and to his stepson, William Wilson. He indicated that he was entitled to 900 acres of new land and that he wanted his widow, Prudence, to have a third. He noted that he had mortgaged his land in England, near Berry and Alvenstoak, and instructed his executors to sell it and distribute the proceeds among his three daughters. Moon made philanthropic bequests to his home parishes in England and in Isle of Wight

County. Captain John Moon's will was entered into the records of Isle of Wight County on August 12, 1655. His land in Jamestown probably was sold within a relatively short time, for there is no evidence that his heirs retained the property (Isle of Wight County Deeds, Wills, Guardian Accounts Book A:81; VCR 1:452, 461; CBE 57; MCGC 87, 186, 192, 465; PB 1 Pt. 1:127, 291; 3:331; STAN 61, 68, 71; HEN 1:386-387; MCGH 158, 207-209; AMB 59, 114; DOR 1:26; 2:677-678).

SUSAN MOON (MOONE, O'MOON, OMOONCE) (MRS. JOHN MOON [MOONE, O'MOON, OMOONCE])

On October 21, 1635, when John Moon (Moone, O'Moon, Omoonce) patented some land, he used the headright of his wife, Susan, and indicated that it was for her own personal adventure (PB 1 Pt. 1:291).

PRUDENCE WILSON MOON (MOONE, O'MOON, OMOONCE) (MRS. JOHN MOON [MOONE, O'MOON, OMOONCE])

By the 1650s, Prudence, a widow, had married Captain John Moon of Isle of Wight County. He left her a fourth of his personal estate and a third interest in his 900 acres of newly patented land. Captain John Moon's will was entered into the records of Isle of Wight County on August 12, 1655. Prudence Moon died intestate without having remarried, and on March 9, 1663, her son, William Wilson, was appointed her administrator. She was the mother of Joan Wilson Garland (Isle of Wight County Deeds, Wills, Guardian Accounts Book A:81; Administrations and Probates:7; MCGH 158, 208; DOR 2:678).

***

WILLIAM MOORES (MORRIS?)

William Moores (Morris?) set out for Virginia in September 1619 and was bound for Berkeley Hundred (**55**), where he was to be under the supervision of Captain John Woodlief. Moores died within four years of his arrival in the colony (VCR 3:198; CBE 14).

NATHANIEL MOPER

On February 16, 1624, Nathaniel Moper was living at Basses Choice (**27**) (CBE 46).

MORASSANE

In November 1624 interpreter Robert Poole said that while Samuel Argall was deputy-governor, six men were slain by Natives who carried their firearms to Pamunkey, where they were used by Indians named Morassane and Nemattanew (Jack of the Feather). Governor George Yeardley sent Poole to Pamunkey to steal the guns' firing mechanisms so that the Indians would return the guns to Jamestown (1) to be repaired (MCGC 28).

GEORGE MORDANT

On December 31, 1627, when George Mordant made his will, he identified himself as a gentleman and mariner of Fellingham or Flemington in Norfolk, England. He left his interests in Virginia to his son, Henry Mordant, and made bequests to his other sons and his friends in Virginia. George Mordant's will was presented for probate on November 2, 1633 (SH 9; EEAC 40; CBE 108; SR 3967).

OLIVER MORDEN

On February 13, 1622, the Virginia Company transferred one share of land from Francis Carter to Oliver Morden, noting that it formerly had belonged to Lord Delaware (VCR 1:604).

[NO FIRST NAME] MORE (MOORE)

On September 18, 1626, Mr. More (Moore) of Kecoughtan (17, 18) testified that Mrs. Joan Wright, an accused witch, had put a curse on his poultry, which died (MCGC 114).

GERARD MORE

Gerard More, Esquire, a 32-year-old gentleman from Middlesex, England, came to Virginia in 1619 on the *Bona Nova* (FER 295).

HENRY MORE (MOORE)

On February 27, 1619, the justices of Bridewell sent Henry More (Moore), a boy, to Virginia. On March 22, 1622, he was killed during the Indian attack at Warresqueak (26) (CBE 12; VCR 3:571).

HENRY MORE (MOORE)

On December 22, 1628, the General Court decided that Henry More (Moore), a merchant, owed money to Hugh Hawkridge, as did Henry Bagwell and John Crosse (MCGC 180).

HUMPHREY MORE (MOORE)

In November 1628 Humphrey More (Moore) brought suit against John Palmer. However, More failed to appear in court to prosecute his case, so he was fined and the case against Palmer was dismissed (MCGC 178).

JAMES MORE (MOORE)

James More (Moore) died in Elizabeth City (17, 18) sometime after April 1623 but before February 16, 1624 (CBE 67).

JARRAT MORE (MOORE)

On March 22, 1622, when the Indians attacked the College (66), Jarrat More (Moore) was slain (VCR 3:566).

JOHN MORE

John More, a 25-year-old gentleman from Hartfordshire, England, came to Virginia in 1619 on the *Bona Nova*. His transportation costs were paid by the Ferrars, who had invested heavily in the Virginia Company. On June 13, 1621, Company officials noted that More was entitled to two shares of land that formerly had belonged to Richard Hakluyt's son, Edward (FER 295, 296; VCR 1:497).

***

JOHN MORE (MOORE)

John More (Moore) came to Virginia on the *Bona Nova* in 1620. On February 16, 1624, he was living in Elizabeth City with his wife. In early 1625 John and his wife, Elizabeth, were living on the east side of the Hampton River in Elizabeth City (17), on the Virginia Company's land, and John was a household head. The Mores had a fortified dwelling and a storehouse and were well supplied with provisions and defensive weaponry. On July 3, 1635, John More was in possession of some land in Elizabeth

City on Little Poquoson Creek (**19**) (CBE 43, 67; PB 1 Pt. 1:202; DOR 2:685).

ELIZABETH MORE (MOORE) (MRS. JOHN MORE [MOORE])

Elizabeth, who became the wife of John More (Moore), came to Virginia in 1622 and on February 16, 1624, was living in Elizabeth City (**17**) with her husband. The Mores were still there in early 1625 and were occupying a home on the Virginia Company's land (CBE 43, 67).

***

JOHN MORE (MOORE)

In June 1621 John More (Moore) was tried at Middlesex and sentenced to be transported overseas (CBE 23).

JOHN MORE (MOORE)

On February 5, 1628, the General Court's justices noted that John More (Moore), a gentleman, was supposed to bring five male servants to Edward Sharpless on the *Thomas and John*. He failed to do so, so Sharpless sued and More was ordered to provide him with the servants (MCGC 160-161).

JOSEPH MORE (MOORE)

Joseph More (Moore) came to Virginia in 1622 on the *Margaret and John*. On September 7, 1632, when John Robins Sr. patented some land, he used Joseph as a headright (PB 1 Pt. 1:116).

LAWRENCE MORE (MOORE)

On November 20, 1622, the justices of Bridewell decided that Lawrence More (Moore), an inmate in Newgate prison, would be transported overseas (CBE 29).

LEONARD MORE (MOORE)

Leonard More (Moore), a 20-year-old gentleman from London, came to Virginia in 1619 on the *Bona Nova* at the expense of the Ferrars, who were major Virginia Company investors. His time and means of arrival suggests that he was one of the Virginia Company servants and tenants that William Weldon seated on the College Land at Arrohattock in late November 1619. On February 16, 1624, Leonard More was living at the College (**66**). On January 23, 1625, when a muster was taken, he was still there and was listed as a household head. Although he lived alone, he was relatively well provided with stored food and protective weaponry. On March 13, 1626, he testified in court about a transaction between John Watson and merchant Edward Blaney at Arrohattock. On March 21, 1633, Leonard Moore secured a 21-year lease for 100 acres of land on the north side of the James River, within the corporation of Henrico and west of Four Mile Creek. Even though he was then identified as a Bermuda Hundred planter, the land he commenced leasing was relatively close to Arrohattock, where he had been seated earlier (FER 295, 296; CBE 35, 53; MCGC 97; PB 1 Pt. 1:146; DOR 1:8).

NICHOLAS MORE (MOORE)

On September 2, 1631, Nicholas More (Moore), a boy being detained at Bridewell, was sent to Virginia by a merchant (CBE 96).

ROBERT (ROBART) MORE (MOORE)

Robert (Robart) More (Moore) came to Virginia on the *Providence* in 1622 and on February 16, 1624, was living in Elizabeth City on the east side of the Hampton River (**17**). When a muster was made in early 1625, Robert was described as a 50-year-old indentured servant in the household of William Tyler (CBE 43, 67).

SARA MORE (MOORE)

On February 16, 1624, Sara More (Moore) was living in Chaplin's Choice (**56**) (CBE 37).

THOMAS MORE (MOORE)

On May 31, 1620, Thomas More (Moore) presented the Virginia Company with a proposal for making soap ashes and potashes and raising flax. Three years later, on May 7, 1623, he and his associates received a patent because they were planning to transport 100 people to Virginia. The patent was confirmed a week later (VCR 1:364-365; 2:412, 428).

WILLIAM MORE (MOORE)

William More (Moore), a 30-year-old gentleman from London, came to Virginia in 1619 on the *Bona Nova* at the expense of the Ferrars, who were major Virginia Company investors. William most likely was one of the Virginia Company servants and tenants that William Weldon seated on the College Land (66) at Arrohattock in late November 1619, for on February 16, 1624, he was listed among the dead at the College (FER 295, 296; CBE 35).

***

REGINOLD (REVOLL) MORECOCK (MORECOCKE, MOORECOCK)

Reginold (Revoll) Morecock (Morecocke, Moorecock) came to Virginia on the *Jonathan*. On February 16, 1624, he and his wife were living on the Maine (Pasbehay) (3). On January 30, 1625, when a muster was made of that area's inhabitants, Reginold was identified as the head of a household that included his wife, Elizabeth, and son, Thomas. The Morecock household was relatively well supplied with stored food and defensive weaponry. On April 8, 1629, Reginald Morecock's wife, Elizabeth, who was age 30, testified in court (CBE 39, 57; MCGC 194; DOR 1:25).

ELIZABETH MORECOCK (MORECOCKE, MOORECOCK) (MRS. REGINOLD [REVOLL] MORECOCK [MORECOCKE, MOORECOCK])

On February 16, 1624, Elizabeth, the wife of Reginold (Revoll) Morecock (Morecocke, Moorecock), was living with her husband on the Maine (Pasbehay) (3), just west of Jamestown Island. On January 30, 1625, she and her husband were still there and were sharing their home with their 1-year-old son, Thomas. On August 21, 1626, Elizabeth Morecock appeared before the justices of the General Court, where she named three men in her community who had been drunk and disorderly. On April 8, 1629, Elizabeth, who was 30 years old, testified that the baby to which George Unwin's maidservant gave birth was stillborn (CBE 39, 57; MCGC 108, 194).

THOMAS MORECOCK (MORECOCKE, MOORECOCK)

On January 30, 1625, when a muster was made of the residents of the Maine (Pasbehay) (3), Thomas Morecock (Morecocke, Moorecock), who was age 1, was living with his parents, Reginold (Revoll) and Elizabeth Morecock (CBE 57).

***

THOMAS MORELAND

Thomas Moreland came to Virginia in 1621 on the *Abigail*. In early 1625 he was living on the east side of the Hampton River on the Virginia Company's land in Elizabeth City (17). Thomas, who was age 19, was a servant in the household headed by John Haney and Nicholas Rowe (CBE 68).

THOMAS MOREMAN

Thomas Moreman, a 30-year-old grocer from Warwickshire, England, came to Virginia in 1619 on the *Bona Nova*. On July 12, 1620, he informed the Virginia Company that although he had come to the colony as a Company servant to work under the supervision of Captain Samuel Mathews, he had repaid the cost of his transportation and wanted his freedom and some land. Thomas Moreman's petition was approved (FER 295; VCR 1:402).

RICHARD MOREWOOD

On February 16, 1624, Richard Morewood was living on West and Shirley Hundred (Eppes) Island (41) (CBE 36).

[NO FIRST NAME] MORGAN

In early 1622 a Native known as Jack of the Feather or Nemattanew, who was reputed to have magic powers, killed a Mr. Morgan. Afterward, two of Morgan's young male servants, who saw Nemattanew with some of their master's goods, executed him and reported the incident to George Thorpe at the College (66). Some people claimed that the slaying of Nemattanew, a favorite of the Powhatan Indians' paramount chief Opechancanough, sparked the March 22, 1622, Indian attack (CJS 2:293).

ANN MORGAN

On February 27, 1619, the justices of Bridewell decided that Ann Morgan, a wench, would be sent to Virginia (CBE 13).

EDWARD (EDMOND) MORGAN (MORGAINE, MORGON)

Edward (Edmond) Morgan (Morgaine, Morgon) came to Virginia on the *Providence* in 1623 and on February 16, 1624, was living in Elizabeth City (**18**). On February 7, 1625, Morgan was residing in Newportes News (**24**), Daniel Gookin's settlement, and was described as a 22-year-old servant in the Gookin household (CBE 43, 63).

JOHN MORGAN

In March 1620, when demographic records were compiled for the Virginia colony, John Morgan was said to be on a trading voyage to Accomac and Acohanock. On May 29, 1635, when John Parrott patented some land on the south side of the James River, he listed a John Morgan (perhaps the same man) as a headright (FER 159; PB 1 Pt. 1:170).

JONE (JANE) MORGAN

On August 8, 1618, officials at Bridewell was decided that Jone or Jane Morgan, a vagrant from Lombard Street in Bridewell, would be sent to Virginia (CBE 9).

ROBERT MORGAN (MORGAINE)

Robert Morgan (Morgaine) came to Virginia in 1621 on the *Flying Hart* and on February 16, 1624, was listed among those who died in Elizabeth City (**17, 18**) sometime after April 1623. On September 2, 1624, when John Sipsey patented some land using Robert Morgan's headright, he indicated that he had paid for Morgan's transportation to Virginia (CBE 45; PB 1 Pt. 1:46).

THOMAS MORGAN (MORGAINE)

Thomas Morgan (Morgaine) died at one of the communities on the lower side of the James River west of Gray's Creek (**8, 9**), within the corporation of James City. In May 1625, when a list of patented land was sent back to England, Morgan was credited with 150 acres of land within the corporation of Henrico. His acreage was located on the lower side of the James River, east of the falls (CBE 41; VCR 4:552).

***

WILLIAM MORGAN ALIAS BROOKS (BROOKES, BROOCKES) ALIAS JONES

Ancient planter William Morgan alias Brooks (Brookes, Broockes) alias Jones arrived in Virginia in 1610 on the *Starr*. On February 16, 1624, he was living in Elizabeth City (**18**) with his wife, Sibile, and was known as William Brooks. In early 1625 he was still living in Elizabeth City, where he was a 30-year-old household head. However, wife Sibile was dead. The couple's son, identified as William Morgan, was then age 2. The elder William Morgan's household was well supplied with stored food and defensive weaponry and had some livestock. In May 1625 when a list of patented land was sent back to England, the elder William Morgan was credited with 100 acres in Elizabeth City, acreage that was planted. On November 18, 1635, Morgan's land was used as a reference point when Thomas Keeling patented some acreage in Elizabeth City. In a May 2, 1638, patent William Morgan was identified as William Morgan alias Brookes. Finally, in August 1642, when he patented some land, he was called William Morgan alias Brookes alias Jones. Official records fail to disclose why he repeatedly changed his name (CBE 44, 64; PB 1 Pt. 1:313; Pt. 2:564, 795; VCR 4:558; DOR 1:54).

SIBILE MORGAN ALIAS BROOKS (BROOKES, BROOCKES) ALIAS JONES (MRS. WILLIAM MORGAN ALIAS BROOKS [BROOKES, BROOCKES] ALIAS JONES)

On February 16, 1624, Sibile, the wife of William Morgan alias Brooks (Brookes, Broockes) alias Jones, was living with her husband in Elizabeth City (**18**). She died there and was buried on July 18, 1624. Sibile Morgan was survived by her husband, William, and 2-year-old son, William (II) (CBE 44, 67).

WILLIAM MORGAN ALIAS BROOKS, BROOKES, BROOCKES ALIAS JONES II

Although William II, the son of William Morgan alias Brooks (Brookes, Broockes) alias Jones, was described as a 2-year-old child when a muster was made of the inhabitants of Elizabeth City (18) in early 1625, his name was not included in the February 16, 1624, census. His mother probably was Sibile Morgan, who was buried on July 18, 1624 (CBE 64, 67).

***

[NO FIRST NAME] MORLEY (MORELL)

In 1608 a laborer named Morley or Morrell came to Virginia in the 2nd Supply of new settlers and would have landed in Jamestown (1) (CJS 2:191).

HENRY MORRELL

Sometime prior to December 1635, Henry Morrell was sent to Virginia by his master, Charles Dawson of Flushing (EAE 59).

EDWARD MORRIS (MORISH)

Edward Morris or Morish, a gentleman, came to Virginia in 1607 and was one of the first settlers. According to George Percy, he died suddenly in Jamestown (1) on August 14, 1607. He was identified as a corporal (CJS 1:20, 2:141; HAI 99).

ELIZABETH MORRIS

On November 20, 1622, it was decided that Elizabeth Morris, an inmate at Newgate, would be transported overseas (CBE 29).

EMANUEL MORRIS

On December 31, 1629, the justices at Bridewell decided that Emanuel Morris, who had been brought in by the marshal of Middlesex, would be sent to Virginia (CBE 14).

MARY MORRIS (MORRICE)

Mary Morris (Morrice), a young maid, came to Virginia aboard the *Warwick* in 1621. She was then 20 years old and had been highly recommended by Mr. Webb, one of the Virginia Company's suppliers (FER 309).

JOHN MORRIS

John Morris, a 20-year-old draper from Somersetshire, England, came to Virginia in 1619 on the *Bona Nova*. On February 16, 1624, he was living in Elizabeth City (18). He was still there in early 1625 and was living in the household of Captain William Tucker. John Morris, who was free, was then 24 years old. Also living in the Tucker household was 22-year-old Mary Morris, who may have been John's wife or kinswoman. In October 1628 the General Court noted that John Morris was indebted to merchant George Downes, whom Captain William Tucker was told to pay after recovering the funds from Morris's attorney (FER 295; CBE 43, 63; MCGC 175).

MARY MORRIS (MRS. JOHN MORRIS?)

Mary Morris came to Virginia on the *George* in 1623. In early 1625 she was living in Elizabeth City (18), where she was a member of Captain William Tucker's household. She was then age 22 and free. Mary Morris may have been the wife or sister of John Morris, who also lived in the Tucker household and was free (CBE 63).

RICHARD MORRIS

Sometime after April 1623 but before February 16, 1624, Richard Morris died on the lower side of the James River, within the corporation of James City (8-15) (CBE 41).

ROBERT MORRIS

On December 4, 1634, when Hugh Cox received a court order entitling him to a patent, he listed Robert Morris as a headright (PB 1 Pt. 1:282).

SAMUEL MORRIS

Samuel Morris came to Virginia on the *Abigail* and on February 16, 1624, was residing on the Maine (3), just west of Jamestown Island. By January 25, 1625, he had moved to Mulberry Island **(21)**, where he was identified as one of William Peirce's servants. Samuel was then age 20 (CBE 39, 57).

THOMAS MORRIS (MORIS, MORYS)

On November 22, 1625, Thomas Morris (Moris, Morys), who was age 22, testified that his master, Captain Whitaker, had sent him to Francis Mason's house to let Mrs. Ganey know that Whitaker was waiting at her home to collect a debt. Thomas signed his written testimony with an *X*, thereby revealing his illiteracy (MCGC 32).

WILLIAM MORRIS

William Morris came to Virginia on the *George* in 1621 at the expense of William Claiborne. On June 3, 1624, when Claiborne patented some land, he used William Morris as a headright (PB 1 Pt. 1:41).

MATHEWE MORTON

On January 6, 1635, Mathewe Morton witnessed Thomas Whaplett's will while both men were in Virginia (WITH 77).

RALPH (RALFE) MORTON (MOORTON, MURTON)

Ralph (Ralfe) Morton (Moorton, Murton), a gentleman who came to Virginia in 1608 in the 1st Supply of new settlers, accompanied Captain John Smith on an exploratory voyage of the Chesapeake Bay. Morton was appointed to the Council and in 1620 was identified as an investor in the Virginia Company. Morton would have lived in Jamestown **(1)** (CJS 1:222, 224; 2:160, 163, 279).

RICHARD MORTON (MORRETON)

On November 15, 1620, Virginia Company officials received a petition from Richard Morton (Morreton), who said that he had been in Virginia for almost three years and wanted some land. Company officials responded that before he could receive land, he had to complete his three years of service to the colony or find someone else to do so (VCR 1:426).

STEPHEN MORTON

On July 17, 1627, Stephen Morton shipped goods on the *Robert and John* from London to Virginia (CBE 79).

WILLIAM MORTON (MORTEN)

William Morton (Morten) came to Virginia in 1620 on the *Margaret and John* and on February 16, 1624, was living in Elizabeth City **(18)**. In early 1625 he was still there and was a 20-year-old servant in the household headed by John Banam (Bainham) and Robert Sweete. In 1628 the justices of the General Court, on learning that William Morton was dead, gave a letter of administration to a man named John whose surname is not included in extant court records (CBE 44, 64; MCGC 174).

***

JOHN MOSELEY I

On April 9, 1628, the justices of the General Court learned that Captain John Preene had delivered the late John Moseley I's belongings to Captain Smyth. They also were informed that Preene had left two of Moseley's servants in the West Indies. In October 1628, John Moseley's widow, Anne, who was then in England, authorized Francis Baldwin and Edward Grindon to serve as her attorneys in Virginia and to see that her late husband's estate was settled. The decedent's eldest son, John II, also signed the document (MCGC 171, 176).

ANNE MOSELEY (MRS. JOHN MOSELEY)

In October 1628, Anne Moseley authorized Francis Baldwin and Edward Grindon to serve as her attorneys and see that the Virginia estate of her late husband, John Moseley I, was settled. The decedent's son, John II, also signed the document. On December 9, 1628, the General Court authorized Captain Smyth to use the tobacco he had received from Nathaniel Causey on behalf of Mrs. Anne Moseley (MCGC 176, 179).

JOHN MOSELEY II

In October 1628 John Moseley II was identified as the eldest son of the late John Moseley I, who had immigrated to Virginia. John II co-signed a document authorizing Francis Baldwin and Edward Grindon to settle his father's estate (MCGC 176).

***

JOSEPH MOSELEY (MOSLEY)

Joseph Moseley (Mosley) came to Virginia on the *Providence* in 1623 and on February 16, 1624, was living in Elizabeth City (**18**). On February 7, 1625, Joseph, who was identified as a 21-year-old indentured servant, was living in Newportes News (**24**), in a household headed by Daniel Gookin (CBE 44, 63).

JOSEPH MOSES (MOYSES, MOYES, MOYSES, MOISES)

On October 3, 1618, the justices of Bridewell decided that Joseph Moses (Moyses, Moyes, Moyses, Moises), a vagrant from Bread Street, would be transported to Virginia (CBE 10).

THEODORE MOSES (MOYES, MOYSES, MOISES, MOSSES)

On February 16, 1624, Theodore Moses (Moyes, Moyses, Moises, Mosses), who came to Virginia on the *London Merchant* and may have been a Virginia Company tenant, was residing at the College (**66**). On January 23, 1625, he was still there and was living alone. He was well supplied with defensive weaponry. By February 9, 1628, Moses had moved to Archer's Hope (**6**). It was then that he testified in court about separating two of his neighbors, Amy Hall and William Harman, who were engaged in fisticuffs. During 1628, 1629, and 1630 Theodore Moses served as a burgess for Archer's Hope. In 1640 Ann Belson, a young indentured servant who was unhappy with the way Theodore Moses had treated her, asked to be freed. She claimed that he had promised to teach her to read and to treat her as a daughter but had failed to do so. Ann also tried to recover her inheritance, which was in Moses' hands. By 1640 he had patented land on the west side of the Chickahominy River, abutting what became

known as Moses Creek (CBE 35, 53; MCGC 166, 465; STAN 54-55; HEN 1:138, 148; DOR 1:8).

RICHARD MOSSE

On March 22, 1622, when the Indians attacked the Swinhow Plantation (**47**) in the corporation of Charles City, Richard Mosse was killed at Mr. Thomas Swinhowe's house (VCR 3:568).

ROBERT MOSTON (MOSTEN)

On March 27, 1622, the Virginia Company gave Robert Moston (Mosten) a patent, as he was planning to transport 100 people to Virginia. On June 10, 1622, Moston was identified as the holder of a patent for a particular (private) plantation (VCR 1:624; 3:643).

***

JOHN MOTT I

In 1621 John Mott I and his son, John II, came to Virginia on the *George* at the expense of George Sandys. Sandys later transferred the Motts's headrights to John Bainham, who used them on December 1, 1624, when patenting some land. On January 3, 1625, the General Court acknowledged that Sandys had brought the Motts to Virginia (PB 1 Pt. 1:17; MCGC 39).

JOHN MOTT II

John Mott II and his father, John I, came to the colony on the *George* in 1621. Their transportation was paid for by George Sandys. Sandys later transferred the Motts's headrights to John Bainham, who used them on December 1, 1624, when patenting some land. On January 3, 1625, the General Court acknowledged that Sandys had brought the Motts to Virginia (PB 1 Pt. 1:17; MCGC 39).

***

BENJAMIN MOULSON

In April or May 1629, Benjamin Moulson, a 25-year-old mariner from Wapping in Middlesex, testified about tobacco that he had transported from Virginia to England on the *Anne* of London (EAE 19).

THOMAS MOULTON (MOULTONE, MOLTON, MOULSTON)

On September 15, 1619; Thomas Moulton (Moultone, Molton, Moulston), a cook and gardener, set sail for Virginia on the *Margaret* of Bristol, whose passengers were bound for Berkeley Hundred (**55**). Moulton, who was to work under John Woodlief's supervision, was supposed to serve for four or five years in exchange for 25 acres of land. On February 16, 1624, Thomas Moulston was a servant in Captain William Peirce's household in urban Jamestown (**1**). Sometime prior to January 3, 1625, however, Moulton was sent to Shirley Hundred (**41**), where he was employed on Berkeley Hundred's behalf. This raises the possibility that he was employed as a cow keeper, since Berkeley's livestock was taken to Shirley for safekeeping. By February 4, 1625, Moulton had been shifted to the plantation of Captain Roger Smith (**10**), who had married John Rolfe's widow. He was then identified as a 25-year-old servant and had an ample supply of stored food and defensive weaponry. On October 12, 1626, Thomas Moulton testified before the General Court in the suit that John Butterfield brought against Margaret Jones. Butterfield and Jones both lived in Pasbehay (**3**) (VCR 3:198, 213; CBE 38, 59; MCGC 41, 119; DOR 1:39).

RICHARD MOUNFORD (MUMFORD)

On June 24, 1624, Richard Mounford (Mumford) testified that on the night he stood watch at the fort in Jamestown (**1**), he did not see anyone break into Mr. Peirsey's storehouse. On January 24, 1625, Mounford was listed among the dead at Jamestown (MCGC 15; CBE 56).

THOMAS MOUNSLIE

According to George Percy's narrative, Thomas Mounslie, one of the first Jamestown (**1**) colonists, died on August 17, 1607 (CJS 1:20; HAI 99).

SIR WILLIAM MOUNSON (MOUSON)

On July 7, 1620, Sir William Mounson (Mouson) and his associates received a patent for the rights to two new commodities they hoped to discover in Virginia. Eleven days later they received a patent for a particular plantation, a grant that was confirmed on May 2, 1621 (VCR 1:397, 407, 468).

PETER MOUNTAGUE (SEE PETER [PEETER] MONTECUE [MONTAGUE, MOUNTEGUE])

WILLIAM MOUNTAGUE (MONTAGUE)

On August 16, 1627, William Mountague (Montague) shipped some goods from London to Virginia on the *Truelove* (CBE 79).

***

ALEXANDER MOUNTNEY

Alexander Mountney, an ancient planter, came to Virginia on the *Mary James* in 1610 and on February 16, 1624, was living in Elizabeth City (**18**). On September 20 1624, when he patented 100 acres of land in Kecoughtan (Elizabeth City), Mountney was identified as a yeoman. In early 1625 he was 33 years old and still living in Elizabeth City. He headed a household that included five men, none of whom were servants. One was 21-year-old Leonard Mountney, perhaps a kinsman. Alexander Mountney's household had use of two dwellings, a palisade, and an ample supply of stored food and defensive weaponry. When a list of patented land was sent back to England in May 1625, Mountney was credited with 100 acres in Elizabeth City, acreage that had been seated. By 1635 Alexander Mountney had moved to Accomack and had taken possession of nearly 300 acres of land. He was appointed to the parish vestry and was nominated as a sheriff, indications that he was a man of good social standing. Over time, he made numerous court appearances. He married the twice-widowed Hanna (Hannah) Boyle Hill Spellman. On behalf of his orphaned stepdaughters, Elizabeth Hill and Mary Spellman, he sold their land in Elizabeth City, converting the proceeds to cattle. Alexander Mountney died sometime prior to February 1644 (CBE 44, 66; PB 1 Pt. 1:37; VCR 4:558; DOR 1:63; 2:357-358; AMES 1:39, 58; 2:15-16, 212-213, 326).

HANNA (HANNAH) BOYLE HILL SPELLMAN MOUNTNEY (MRS. EDWARD HILL, MRS. THOMAS SPELLMAN [SPILLMAN, SPELMAN, SPILMAN], MRS. ALEXANDER MOUNTNEY) (SEE MRS. EDWARD HILL, MRS. THOMAS SPELLMAN [SPILLMAN, SPELMAN, SPILMAN])

Hanna (Hannah), the daughter of Richard Boyle, came to Virginia in 1620 on the *Bona Nova*. She married Edward Hill of Elizabeth City, who was buried in Virginia on May 15, 1624. Afterward, Hanna wed Thomas Spellman (Spillman, Spelman, Spilman), whom she also outlived. At Spellman's death in March 1627, she inherited his Virginia property. She married Alexander Mountney of Accomack sometime prior to 1638 and moved to the Eastern Shore prior to February 1644. When testifying in court in 1655, Hanna said that she was age 53. She died sometime after February 1658 but before November 1659 (CBE 44, 65; SR 3115, 3118; AMES 2:212-213, 326; MEY 225-226; DOR 1:357-358).

***

LEONARD (LENORD) MOUNTNEY

Leonard (Lenord) Mountney came to Virginia in 1620 on the *Bona Nova*. In early 1625 he was living in Elizabeth City (18) in the all-male household of Alexander Mountney, perhaps a kinsman. Leonard, who was age 21, appears to have been free (CBE 66).

ROBERT MOUTAPASS ALIAS ROBERT MARKHAM (MARCUM) (SEE ROBERT MARKHAM [MARCUM] ALIAS MOUTAPASS)

THOMAS MOUTON

Thomas Mouton, a gentleman, came to Virginia in 1607 and was one of the first settlers. According to George Percy, Mouton died on August 17, 1607, in Jamestown (1) (CJS 1:21; 2:141; HAI 100).

FRANCIS MOYE (MOYNES)

When Francis Moye (Moynes), the purser of the *Peter and John*, appeared before the General Court on March 12, 1627, he testified that George Sandys had brought seven servants aboard the ship but only paid for the passage of six. Moye returned to court on March 29, 1628, by which time he was purser of the ship *Samuel*. He testified that there was contention over the payment for the passage of Thomas Day, who had been brought to Virginia on the *Indeavor*. Captain Francis Moye made another appearance in court on December 22, 1628. This time he claimed that Captain William Saker owed Captain Preene for the passage of Thomas Gregory (MCGC 144, 169, 180).

JOHN MOYER

John Moyer came to Virginia in 1621 on the *Temperance* at the expense of Sir George Yeardley, who later transferred his headright to Thomas Flint (MCGC 166; PB 1 Pt. 1:59).

JOHN MOYSE

John Moyse came to Virginia on the *Hopewell* in 1628 at the expense of Adam Thorogood, who used his headright when patenting some land on June 24, 1635 (PB 1 Pt. 1:179).

GEORGE MULESTON

On February 13, 1629, when Jamestown (1) merchant Thomas Warnett made his will, he named George Muleston as one of his beneficiaries (SH 11-12).

WILLIAM MULLINS

In July 1621 William Mullins made his will, indicating that he was a resident of Virginia. He died overseas, perhaps in New England (North Virginia) (CBE 23).

VALENTINE MUMFORD

In January 1636 Valentine Mumford, a 39-year-old sailor from Ratcliffe in Middlesex, testified that he had gone to Virginia on the *John and Dorothy* (EAE 61).

MARY MUNDAY (MOUNDAY)

On February 16, 1624, Mary Munday (Mounday) was living in Captain William Tucker's household in Elizabeth City (18). In the same household was Robert Munday (Mounday), perhaps a kinsman (CBE 43).

ROBERT MUNDAY (MOUNDAY)

Robert Munday (Mounday) came to Virginia on the *George* in 1623 and on February 16, 1624, was living in Elizabeth City (**18**) in Captain William Tucker's household. In the same household was Mary Munday (Mounday), perhaps a kinswoman. In early 1625 Robert, who was 18 years old, was still living with Captain Tucker and appears to have been free (CBE 43, 63).

FRANCIS MUNDEN

Between May 1630 and July 1631 Francis Munden, a 22-year-old mariner from Limehouse, Middlesex, testified that he was not in Virginia when the *Gift of God* arrived. He said, however, that he knew that it had departed for England with passengers and tobacco. Munden himself returned home on the *Hopewell* (EAE 23).

WILLIAM MUNNES (MUNS, MONES)

William Munnes (Muns, Mones) came to Virginia on the *Sampson* in 1619. On December 20, 1624, he and Henry Wilson asked the General Court's permission to plant their own ground, stating that they had almost fulfilled their contractual obligation to their master, Captain John Ward, who was then in England and unable to give them their freedom dues. The General Court ordered both men to post a bond guaranteeing that they would complete their term of service if they were freed and found to owe time. By early 1625 William Munnes was residing on the Eastern Shore, where he was a servant in Captain William Eppes's household (**74**). On February 5, 1627, he testified before the General Court about Captain Eppes's actions at Captain John Ward's plantation (**61**) before and after the March 1622 Indian attack. He said that Eppes took a barrel of powder from Ward's plantation shortly before the onslaught. Afterward, Eppes returned with his brother, Peter Eppes, and took Ward's servants to his own plantation. William Munnes indicated that no crops were harvested on Ward's plantation in the wake of the Indian attack and said that he was unsure how productive the property was the following year, despite the fact that Ward's four servants, Eppes and his five servants, and three Dutchmen were situated there.

William Munnes was living on the Eastern Shore in the late 1630s when he sold a cow to another man, and he was among those who inventoried the late Daniel Cugley's estate on May 4, 1641 (CBE 68; MCGC 138-139; AMES 1:147; 2:66, 78, 81).

JOHN MUREY (MURRAY?)

On January 29, 1620, the justices of Bridewell decided to send John Murey (Murray?) to Virginia (CBE 17).

ANNE MURRELL

On February 27, 1619, the Bridewell Court decided to send Anne Murrell to Virginia (CBE 19).

WILLIAM MUSGRAVE

On June 14, 1632, William Musgrave was indicted for murder. However, he was absolved from guilt after a jury determined that the deceased man's death was accidental. On October 9, 1640, William Musgrave testified on behalf of Ann Belson, an indentured servant in the employ of Theodore Moses, who asked to be assigned to another master (MCGC 465, 480).

WILLIAM MUSICK

On April 8, 1629, William Musick aired a dispute with Richard Bennett before the General Court. At issue was a lease for some land in Warresqueak (**26**), the Bennett plantation. The General Court referred the matter to Captain Nathaniel Basse for disposition (MCGC 193-194).

RICHARD MUSSELL ALIAS WILLIAMS (SEE RICHARD WILLIAMS ALIAS MUSSELL) ROGER MUTCH (MUDGE, MUCH)

Roger Mutch (Mudge, Much) died at Jordan's Journey (**46**) sometime after April 1623 but before February 16, 1624 (CBE 37).

***

WILLIAM MUTCH (MUDGE, MUCHE)

On February 16, 1624, William Mutch (Mudge, Muche), who came to Virginia on the *Jonathan,* was living in the urban Jamestown (1) household of provost marshal Randall Smallwood. On December 21, 1624, William was a member of a jury that investigated the drowning death of little George Pope. By January 24, 1625, William was heading a household of his own, which he shared with his wife, Margery. The couple had a modest supply of stored food. On January 31, 1625, William Mutch testified that he formerly was Captain John Harvey's servant and that Harvey had refused to give him his freedom dues. Court records also reveal that when Mutch asked for what he was owed, Harvey struck him on the head with his truncheon. On May 9, 1625, William Mutch appeared in court to testify about the will and assets of the late William Cobb, who married Elizabeth Dagg, a maidservant the Virginia Company had sent to Virginia. In 1638 Captain Samuel Mathews listed William Mutch among those who owed him tobacco (CBE 38, 56; EAE 89; MCGC 38, 46, 58-59; DOR 1:33).

MARGERY MUTCH (MUDGE, MUCHE) (MRS. WILLIAM MUTCH [MUDGE, MUCHE])

Margery, who wed William Mutch (Mudge, Muche), came to Virginia on the *George* in 1623. She married William sometime prior to December 27, 1624, when she testified that Mrs. Ralph Hamor was illegally selling bottles of alcoholic beverages in Jamestown (1). On January 24, 1625, Margery Mutch was living in urban Jamestown in a household headed by her husband, William (CBE 56; MCGC 37).

***

RICHARD MUTTON

In 1607 a youth named Robert Mutton came to Virginia in the first group of settlers and would have lived in Jamestown (1) (CJS 1:209; 2:142).

[NO FIRST NAME] MYNNARD

On March 2, 1629, Rev. Mynnard, the minister of Martin's Hundred (7), brought suit against his parishioners because they did not pay him. The General Court ordered Martin's Hundred's inhabitants to compensate Mr. Mynnard, even though he had been replaced by the Rev. John Lyford (MCGC 188).

DAVID MYNTON (MINTON)

On January 22, 1629, David Mynton (Minton) accused Bridges Freeman of beating and wounding him. He asked the General Court to require Freeman to pay his medical bills. The justices declined because Mynton had insulted Freeman, prompting the assault (MCGC 182).

***

JOHN MYNTERNE (MINTERNE, MINTRENE?)

On March 15, 1617, when John Mynterne (Minterne, Mintrene?) made his will, he indicated that he was a resident of Manigo, in Virginia, and bequeathed clothing to several other colonists. When the decedent's will was presented for probate in January 1619, administration was granted to his wife, Alice Mynterne (CBE 12; EEAC 40).

ALICE MYNTERNE (MINTERNE) (MRS. JOHN MYNTERNE [MINTERNE])

In January 1619 Alice, the widow of John Mynterne (Minterne, Mintrene?), who had died in Virginia, was authorized to serve as his administrator. Court records suggest that she was then in England (CBE 21; EEAC 40).

N

NAMONTACK

When the English colonists visited Powhatan at Werowocomoco in 1608, Powhatan gave them Namontack, an Indian youth, as a token of goodwill. Later, Namontack was present when Powhatan and Captain Christopher Newport exchanged gifts at the paramount chief's coronation (CJS 1:79; 2:235-237).

NANTICOS

In November 1624 Edward Grindon said that an Indian named Nanticos was the first Native he met who knew how to use firearms. He added that he did not know who had taught him how to shoot (MCGC 28).

WILLIAM NARSLAKE

William Narslake, who stole a mare in Middlesex, England, and was incarcerated in Newgate Prison, was reprieved in 1619 so that he could be transported overseas (CBE 12).

HENRY NASFIELD

In 1624 Henry Nasfield came to Virginia on the *Swan*. In early 1625 he was living in Elizabeth City (18), where he was a servant in the household of Faroah (Farrar) Flinton, whose home was on the west side of the Hampton River (CBE 65).

JOHN NASH

On November 20, 1622, John Nash, an inmate in Newgate Prison, was pardoned but sentenced to transportation overseas. He was freed on account of an outbreak of jail fever (CBE 29).

NATHANIEL

Sometime after February 16, 1624, but before February 7, 1625, Nathaniel, one of Edward Bennett's African servants, died at Warresqueak (26) (CBE 62).

PRUDENCE NATION

On February 27, 1619, Prudence Nation was identified by the justices of Bridewell Court as one of the wenches being sent to Virginia. She was one of the youngsters rounded up from the streets of London so that they could be transported to the colony (CBE 13).

WILLIAM NAYLE (NAILE)

William Nayle (Naile) came to Virginia on the *Ann* in 1623, when he was around 13 years old. On February 16, 1624, he was residing on the lower side of the James River in the Proctor household at Paces Paines (9), to the west of Grays Creek. He was summoned to court on October 10, 1624, to testify at an investigation into the death of Elizabeth Abbott, a deceased servant. Under oath, he stated that he had whipped Elizabeth—who had belonged to his master, John Proctor—using stout cord that contained fish hooks. He said that Proctor had told him to beat Elizabeth on several other occasions while he (Proctor) stood by and watched. Other witnesses corroborated Nayle's statements. On February 4, 1625, William Nayle, who was then age 15, was still living in John Proctor's Paces Paines household (CBE 40, 59; MCGC 23-24).

THOMAS NAYLOR

Thomas Naylor, a 25-year-old smith from Lancastershire, England, arrived in Virginia in November 1619 aboard the *Bona Nova*. He died at the College (66) sometime after April 1623 but before February 16, 1624. He probably was a Virginia Company servant or tenant (FER 295; CBE 35).

JOHN NEALE

On January 14, 1630, John Neale received a 50-acre leasehold at the Strawberry Banks in Elizabeth City (17), a gift from his friend Lionell Roulston. On February 12, 1632, when Neale renewed the title to his land, he was identified as a merchant. His acreage was said to have formerly belonged to Dictoris Christmas, who had conveyed it to Lionell Roulston (PB 1 Pt. 1:134-135).

RAPHAEL NEALE

On December 31, 1619, Raphael Neale, who was brought in by the Marshal of Middlesex, was sentenced by the justices of Bridewell Court to be transported to Virginia (CBE 14).

THOMAS NEARES (MERRES)

Thomas Neares (Meeres) came to Virginia in 1620 on the *Francis Bonaventure*. On February 16, 1624, he was living at Buckroe (17). In early 1625 he was still residing on the east side of the Hampton River on the Virginia Company's land and was a member of Thomas Flint's household. Thomas, who was then 21 years old, was free (CBE 45, 67).

JOHN NEEDOME (NEEDOM)

John Needome (Needom) came to Virginia in 1621 on the ship *Tiger*. On December 4, 1624, when George Sandys patented some land, he used Needome as a headright and noted that he was one of the servants he had brought in from Bermuda. On February 16, 1624, John Needome was living on the lower side of the James River, to the east of Grays Creek, probably on the Sandys property known as the Treasurers Plantation (**11**) (PB 1 Pt. 1:16; CBE 40).

JOHN NEEDLES

On March 12, 1627, John Needles, a sailor, testified before the General Court in Jamestown (**1**) about an incident that had taken place in the West Indies involving the ship *Saker* (MCGC 143).

PETER NEIMANT (NEIMART, NEWMART)

When a list of patented land was sent to England in May 1625, Peter Neimant (Neimart, Newmart) was credited with two tracts of land on the south side of the James River within the corporation of Henrico: 40 acres at Coxendale (**64**) and 110 acres at The Falls (**67**). Neither of Neimant's properties was described as planted (VCR 4:552).

CHRISTOPHER NELME (NELMES)

Christopher Nelme (Nelmes), a shoemaker, set sail for Virginia in September 1619 on the *Margaret* of Bristol. He was heading for Berkeley Hundred (**55**), where he was to be under the supervision of Captain John Woodlief. Nelme, who was given two years' wages in advance, was supposed to serve the Society of Berkeley Hundred's investors for three years and, in exchange, was to receive 20 acres of land. Christopher Nelme's wife, who remained behind in England, was supposed to receive annual support from the Society of Berkeley Hundred. Christopher Nelmes died shortly after he reached Virginia (CBE 13-14; VCR 3:187, 197, 199, 213-215).

[NO FIRST NAME] NELSON

In a May 16, 1621, letter Sir George Yeardley briefly mentioned a Mr. Nelson, who was then in Virginia (VCR 3:452-453).

FRANCIS NELSON

Francis Nelson, captain of the *Phoenix*, arrived in Jamestown (**1**) in early April 1608,

with part of the 1st Supply of new settlers. Captain John Smith described Captain Nelson as a good mariner and an honest man. He said that because Nelson's ship had encountered a hurricane in the West Indies and had been driven ashore, he was late in reaching Virginia. Smith said that Nelson had refused to have his vessel and crew spend extra time in the colony unless they were compensated. On May 20, 1608, Captain Francis Nelson accompanied Captain Christopher Newport on an exploratory voyage of the James River. When Nelson left Virginia on June 2, 1608, he carried a cargo of cedar wood. Nineteenth-century historian Alexander G. Brown surmised that Captain Francis Nelson probably transported the so-called Velasco map back to England. On November 9, 1612, Francis Nelson, who was preparing to set sail for Virginia and intended to search for the Northwest Passage, made his will. He indicated that he was from St. Katherine's Precinct in London and identified himself as a mariner. Nelson named as heirs his mother, Annie Handley of Sadbery in County York, his sisters Elizabeth Nelson and Anne Sherwood, and his cousin Daniel Nelson (CJS 1:83, 85, 97, 214, 219; 2:154, 158; 3:92; HAI 102; SH 3; BRO 184).

GEORGE NELSON

George Nelson came to Virginia on the *Francis Bonaventure* and on February 16, 1624, was a servant in the home of Governor Francis Wyatt in urban Jamestown (**1**). By January 30, 1625, Nelson had moved to the Governor's Land (**3**). He was then identified as a 19-year-old servant to the governor (CBE 38, 57).

ROWLAND NELSTROP

Rowland Nelstrop, a laborer who arrived in Virginia in 1608, was part of the 1st Supply of new colonists in Jamestown (**1**) (CJS 1:223; 2:162).

NEMATTANEW (NEMETENEW, NENEMACHANEW)

Nemattanew (Nemetenew, Nenemachanew), sometimes known as Jack of the Feather because of his feathered battle attire, was a great warrior and one of paramount chief Opechancanough's favorites. Some Indians believed that he possessed magical powers that made him impervious to gunfire. Sometime prior to Governor Francis Wyatt's arrival in Virginia in 1621, Nemattanew killed a colonist named Morgan. Later, a couple of Morgan's servants, who encountered the Indian wearing the dead man's cap, captured him and put him to death. Nemattanew's demise at the hands of the English preceded the 1622 Indian attack. In fact, some people considered it an underlying cause. In November 1624 interpreter Robert Poole said that while Samuel Argall was deputy-governor (1617–1618), six men were slain by Natives who carried their firearms to Pamunkey, where they were used by Indians named Morassane and Nemattanew. Poole said that incoming Governor George Yeardley sent him to Pamunkey to steal the guns' firing mechanisms so that the Indians would return them to Jamestown (1) to be repaired (VCR 4:11; MCGC 28).

EDWARD NEVELL

On December 5, 1625, Edward Nevell brought suit against his employer, merchant and mariner Thomas Weston, in the General Court. Two weeks later Nevell was ordered to pay Weston for some damaged tobacco, and on February 20, 1626, he was obliged to post a bond guaranteeing that he would fulfill his obligation to Weston. On January 3, 1626, Edward Nevell incurred the wrath of Virginia's governing officials by reportedly making an ill-advised comment to someone while he was in Canada. According to court testimony, when Nevell was asked about the execution of sea captain Richard Cornish for forcing his attentions on a young male crew member, he said that the deceased man had been wrongfully punished. For daring to criticize a decision made by the Council of State, Edward Nevell was ordered to stand in the pillory in the marketplace in Jamestown (1). He also was to lose his ears and to serve the colony for a year. He was declared incapable of ever being free. Some (or perhaps all) of Nevell's punishments may have been suspended, for on February 20, 1626, he appeared before the General Court, where he filed a complaint against three men who allegedly stole some sack (a wine) from the cabin of the ship he was on (MCGC 78, 82, 85, 95).

THOMAS NEVES

On October 16, 1618, the Bridewell Court decided that Thomas Neves, a vagrant from Bishopsgate, should be transported to Virginia (CBE 11).

JOHN NEWARKE

John Newarke came to Virginia in 1628 aboard the *Hopewell* at the expense of Adam Thorogood, who on June 24, 1635, used his headright when acquiring some land (PB 1 Pt. 1:179).

ALICE NEWBERRY

Alice Newberry came to Virginia on the *James* with William and Elizabeth Rowley (Rowsley) and left England on July 31, 1622. The Rowley household, which included a large group of servants, resided on Jamestown Island (1). A census of the colony's inhabitants reveals that William and Elizabeth Rowley died sometime after April 1623 but before February 16, 1624. One of the Rowleys' maidservants also perished, perhaps Alice Newberry (FER 400; CBE 39).

WILLIAM NEWCOME

On February 16, 1624, William Newcome was living in Elizabeth City (18) (CBE 44).

CHRISTOPHER NEWGENT

Christopher Newgent came to Virginia in 1634 aboard the *John and Dorothy* at the expense of Adam Thorogood, who on June 24, 1635, used his headright when acquiring some land (PB 1 Pt. 1:179).

ROBERT NEWLAND

Virginia Company records dating to August 11, 1619, suggest that Robert Newland, a merchant who had assisted Captain Lawne (most likely planter and mariner Christopher Lawne), probably was then in England. However, on June 27, 1622, officials noted that Newland, who was from the western part of England, was ready to set sail for Virginia with Captain Barwick (VCR 3:190, 660-661).

FRANCIS NEWMAN

On April 8, 1620, some of colonist Francis Newman's friends informed Virginia Company officials that he was a free man who had been made a servant by former Deputy Governor Samuel Argall. Incumbent Governor George Yeardley, who investigated the matter, reported that Newman died at Henrico (**63**) sometime prior to Yeardley's April 1619 arrival (VCR 1:337; 3:121, 452-453).

JOHN NEWMAN

On June 5, 1623, John Newman, Robert Watson, and Richard Perry (a London merchant) were identified as co-owners of the ship *Abigail*, which made frequent trips to Virginia (VCR 2:455).

ROBERT NEWMAN

Robert Newman came to Virginia on the *Neptune* in 1618. By February 16, 1624, he was living in Elizabeth City (**18**) on the west side of the Hampton River. In early 1625 he was still there and was sharing a home with a partner, William Gayne. Newman was then age 25. Newman and Gayne had possession of an ample supply of stored food and defensive weaponry. On November 21, 1625, Robert Newman appeared before the General Court, where he testified in a complicated court case that involved Edward Nevell, who owed Thomas Crispe and him a quantity of tobacco and had refused to pay. Newman indicated that he had tried to collect the tobacco from Nevell and his employer, mariner-and-merchant Thomas Weston, while all of them were in Canada. The justices decided that Weston had to pay Newman for the work done by Arthur Avelinge, his servant. On December 5, 1625, Robert Newman again appeared in court to make a complaint against Thomas Weston. When Newman returned to court on December 19, 1625, he testified that Weston had promised to bring him two or three servants from Canada. Weston, on the other hand, said that he had failed to do so because he knew that Newman's partner would not provide for them adequately. Robert Newman was literate, for he reviewed a certificate that was presented in court. He also testified about the ship *Swan's* voyage to Canada. Sometime prior to February 9, 1629, Robert Newman sold some livestock to Mr. Wheeler, whose 19-year-old son, John, confirmed the sale and the resulting debt. On June 26, 1635, Robert Newman patented some land on the Nansemond River adjacent to the property of Robert Bennett (MCGC 75-76, 78, 81-82, 185; PB 1 Pt. 1:188; DOR 1:59).

ROBERT NEWMAN

On February 27, 1619, Robert Newman was identified as one of a group of boys and wenches being sent to Virginia. He probably was one of the poor children rounded up from the streets of London and sent to the colony (CBE 12).

WILLIAM NEWMAN

William Newman came to Virginia in 1622 on the *Furtherance* and on February 16, 1624, was living at Basses Choice (**27**) within the corporation of Warresqueak. On January 3, 1625, he was fined for failing to attend church, despite having been ordered to do so by the settlement's commander, Captain Nathaniel Basse. When demographic records were compiled at Basses Choice on February 7, 1625, William Newman was described as age 35. He and his partner, John Army, jointly headed a household and occupied one dwelling. In their possession was an adequate supply of stored food and defensive weaponry. On February 26, 1627, William Newman appraised the goods of the late Margaret Byard (Biard), which were in the custody of Captain Nathaniel Basse, and made an inventory of her estate. Court records indicate that she died aboard the *Furtherance* around August 3, 1622, while on the way to Virginia (CBE 46, 62; MCGC 39, 141; DOR 1:49).

***

CAPTAIN CHRISTOPHER NEWPORT

Captain Christopher Newport, who was born between 1560 and 1570, made several voyages to the West Indies before going to Virginia. He was known as a skillful mariner, experienced in sailing along the North American coast. In December 1606 the Virginia Company selected Newport to bring the first colonists to Virginia. When they arrived at Cape Henry on April 26, 1607, he and some others went ashore. On May 20, 1607, he set off to explore the James River and planted a cross at the falls. He left Virginia on June 22, 1607. Newport made a return voyage to the colony with the 1st Supply of new immigrants, arriving in Jamestown (**1**) in January 1608. Although the fort burned shortly after the newcomers' arrival, Newport and his crew helped the colonists rebuild. He brought some presents for Powhatan and in return received some turkeys. Newport and Captain John Smith explored the Pamunkey River and traded with the Indians' paramount chief, Powhatan, for corn. Captain Christopher Newport returned to Virginia in 1609, traveling with Sir Thomas Gates and Sir George Somers, with whom he was shipwrecked in Bermuda. In June 1610 Lord Delaware designated Newport a vice admiral and in July named him to his council. According to Captain John Smith, in 1611 Sir Thomas Dale became so frustrated with Christopher Newport that he yanked his beard and threatened to hang him because the colonists were so poorly supplied. Newport and his men constructed a wharf in Jamestown while Dale was having improvements built there. He returned to England in a fleet that included other Virginia ships. In 1612 Captain Christopher Newport, a Virginia Company investor, was employed by the East India Company. He died in 1617 and was survived by a widow and son, his heirs (CJS 1:7, 33, 61, 204-205, 214, 234; 2:12, 137-138, 154, 181, 218, 280; HAI 98, 101, 109, 130, 133, 184, 196-197, 433, 459, 523, 907; BRO 956-957; SP 14/28 f 34; FOR 1:7:13).

MRS. CHRISTOPHER NEWPORT

On July 10, 1621, Mrs. Christopher Newport was awarded land in Virginia for having paid for the transportation of six men on the *Jonathan* in 1619 (VCR 1:509).

[NO FIRST NAME] NEWPORT

On November 17, 1619, Captain Christopher Newport's son and heir asked Virginia Company officials for land on behalf of his late father's £400 adventure (VCR 1:274).

***

THOMAS NEWSON

Thomas Newson came to Virginia in 1621 on the *Temperance* at the expense of then-governor Sir George Yeardley. Later, Newson's headright was assigned to Thomas Flint, who used it on September 20, 1628, when patenting some land (PB 1 Pt. 1:59).

FRANCIS NEWTON

In 1628 Francis Newton came to Virginia on the *Hopewell* at the expense of Adam

Thorogood, who on June 24, 1635, used his headright when acquiring some land (PB 1 Pt. 1:179).

JONE (JOAN) NEWTON

On February 27, 1619, Jone (Joan) Newton was identified by the Bridewell Court as one of the wenches being sent to Virginia. She was part of a group of boys and girls who were rounded up from the streets of London so that they could be sent to the colony (CBE 13).

NICHOLAS

Nicholas was killed in Elizabeth City (**18**) sometime after April 1623 but before February 16, 1624 (CBE 45).

NICHOLAS

On March 4, 1629, the General Court decided that a servant identified only as Nicholas was to serve Thomas Willoughby for four years. He probably resided in Elizabeth City (**18**), where Willoughby's household was located, or on the lower side of the James River near the Elizabeth River (**20 a**), where Willoughby also owned land (MCGC 190).

RICHARD NICHOLAS

In 1629 Richard Nicholas, an ironmonger and the partner of Joshua Foote, sold ironware to Sir John Harvey, who as late as March 1636 still owed him £45 for those goods. Harvey was then residing in Jamestown (**1**) (SAIN 1:225).

AGNES NICHOLLS

On March 29, 1620, Agnes Nicholls was identified as the mother and executrix of the late Henry Davies, who went to Virginia in 1617 with Lord Delaware. Mrs. Nicholls most likely was in England when she drafted her petition to Virginia Company officials (VCR 1:331).

ANDREW (ANDREWE) NICHOLLS

On February 19, 1620, the Bridewell Court decided that Andrew Nicholls, who was brought in by the churchwardens of St. Brides, would be sent to Virginia. He probably was a vagrant (CBE 19).

JAMES NICHOLLS

On January 29, 1620, the justices of Bridewell Court decided that James Nicholls, one of several men brought in from Ludgate Hill, would be sent to Virginia. He probably was a vagrant (CBE 17).

JOHN NICHOLLS

John Nicholls, a youth, was among the group of boys and wenches whom the justices of Bridewell Court decided—at their February 27, 1619 session—to send to Virginia (CBE 12).

JOHN NICHOLLS (NICHOLS)

John Nicholls (Nichols), a gentleman, came to Virginia in 1608 in the 1st Supply of new Jamestown (1) colonists (CJS 1:222; 2:161).

MARY NICHOLLS

On January 22, 1620, the justices of Bridewell Court decided that Mary Nicholls, who was described as a lewd vagrant from the Bridge, would be sent to Virginia (CBE 17).

THOMAS NICHOLLS (NICHOLAS)

On September 19, 1618, Thomas Nicholls (Nicholas) was identified by the justices of Bridewell Court as a vagrant found begging on the streets. A London native, he was among those selected to be sent to Virginia (CBE 9).

THOMAS NICHOLLS (NICHOLS)

On January 1, 1620, Thomas Nicholls (Nichols) was identified by Virginia Company officials as the clerk (or record-keeper) of Captain Roger Smith's company of men and the clerk of Smith's storehouse, which was on the Governor's Land (3). Company officials noted that Nichols, who was a Virginia Company servant, would be outfitted with apparel, furniture, and equipment and that his ground rent would be paid. On September 9, 1622, the Society of Martin's Hundred asked the Virginia Company to free Thomas Nichols, who apparently had some knowledge of surveying. Company officials agreed, and Nichols was given the task of surveying the Society of Martin's Hundred's plantation (7) and sub-dividing it into parcels. The Virginia Company sent him instruments and books so that he could perform his duty, and promised him some land. On April 2, 1623, Thomas Nichols sent a letter to Sir John Wolstenholme, informing him that the settlers at Martin's Hundred were starving. He said that out of the group of 56 tenants of which he was part, only 14 were left. He also said that female colonists were relatively useless, for they consumed food but did little work. He also complained about how costly it was to get a woman to do his laundry. On February 16, 1624, Thomas Nichols was listed among those who had died at Martin's Hundred sometime after April 1623 (FER 216; VCR 2:102-103; 4:231-232; CBE 42).

WILLIAM NICHOLLS (NICHOLLAS)

William Nicholls or Nichollas arrived in Virginia in May 1619 on the *Duty*, raising the possibility that he was one of the "Duty boys"—young male servants brought to the colony as a group. On February 16, 1624, William was residing in West and Shirley Hundred (41). By January 21, 1625, he had moved to Jordan's Journey (46), where he was identified as ancient planter John Clay's servant. William Nicholls was then age 26 (CBE 36, 51).

WILLIAM NICHOLLS (NICHOLS)

William Nicholls (Nichols) was an investor in the Virginia Company of London. On September 26, 1627, three years after the company's demise, he sent goods from London to Virginia on the *Samuell* (VCR 3:86; 4:358-361; CBE 80).

HUGH NICKMOTT (NICHCOTT, HICKMOTT?)

Hugh Nickmott (Nichcott) died in Elizabeth City (17, 18) sometime after April 1623 but before February 16, 1624 (CBE 45).

NICHOLAS NORBER

In 1621 Nicholas Norber sent goods to Mr. Bland, Richard Keene (Keane) of Martin's Hundred (7), Thomas Gilbert, and Edward Kidder. Bland may have been Edward Bland of Westover (54) (FER 322).

EDWARD NORINGTON

On February 26, 1621, Edward Norington, an inmate of Newgate Prison, was brought before the justices of Bridewell Court, who decided that he would be sent to Virginia (CBE 19).

WILLIAM NORMAN

William Norman, a 40-year-old laborer from Berkshire, England, came to Virginia in 1619 on the *Bona Nova*. He may have been a Virginia Company servant or tenant (FER 295).

EDWARD NORMANSELL

Edward Normansell died in Jamestown (1) sometime after April 1623 but before February 16, 1624 (CBE 39).

THOMAS NORMANTON

In 1635 Thomas Normanton patented 50 acres of land in Elizabeth City (19), adjacent to Harris Creek. Normanton purchased his land from John Ward, who had acquired it by means of a headright (PB 1 Pt. 1:334-335).

JOHN NORRIS

On February 12, 1620, John Norris was among those chosen by the justices of Bridewell Court to be sent to Virginia (CBE 18).

CHARLES NORTH

On November 21, 1621, Sir Charles North and his associates, who were taking 100 people to Virginia, received a patent for a particular (private) plantation. Although North expressed interest in becoming a planter, it is uncertain whether he ever came to Virginia (VCR 1:553-554, 561-562; 3:643).

THOMAS NORTH

On February 16, 1624, Thomas North was living in Elizabeth City. As he was a Virginia Company tenant who had come to Virginia with Captain Thomas Nuce around 1620, it is probable that he was residing on the lower side of the Hampton River on the Virginia Company's land (17). Court records dating to December 19, 1625, indi-cate that Thomas North was supposed to serve a seven-year apprenticeship before being set free. In 1627 he was identified as a Company tenant when he was assigned to William Farrar, who was associated with Jordan's Journey (46) and Henrico or Farrar Island (63) (CBE 43; MCGC 81, 136).

THOMAS NORTON

Thomas Norton, a gentleman who arrived in Jamestown (1) in 1608 as part of the 2nd Supply of new colonists, was an investor in the Virginia Company of London (CJS 1:241; 2:190, 280).

CAPTAIN WILLIAM NORTON

Captain William Norton came to Virginia at the expense of the Virginia Company of London. He was supposed to take six foreign glassmakers to the colony and was authorized to bring ten people to seat his own acreage. In 1621 the Company outfitted Norton with three millstones, supplies, and several other pieces of equipment. When he set sail for Virginia in mid-July, he brought along four Italian glassworkers, their wives and children, and only two servants of his own. Norton was to see that the glass furnace was set up within three months and that the glassworkers produced glass and beads. They were supposed to instruct apprentices and were entitled to a moiety of the glass and other commodities they fabricated. Norton indicated that he wanted a 7-year monopoly on the glass furnace, at half shares, that is, half of the furnace's profits for 7 years. As it turned out, the cost of outfitting the workers and their families and purchasing tools and supplies proved much too costly. As a result, the Adventurers for the Glasshouse released Captain William Norton from his contract. When the Italian glassworkers first arrived in Virginia, they were accommodated in Jabez Whittaker's guesthouse on the Company Land in James City (4). As soon as they had recovered their health, they moved to Glasshouse Point (2). In August 1621 Treasurer George Sandys was authorized to take over management of the glasshouse project in the event of Captain Norton's death. Norton died in late summer 1622, and in 1625 his goods were appraised. One person to whom Norton was in debt was John Burland, a Virginia Company servant and vintner who had been in his employ. Another was tailor

Thomas Wilson, a servant in Dr. John Pott's Jamestown household (1). On the other hand, Thomas Swyfte (one of George Sandys' employees) was indebted to Norton. Captain John Smith described Captain William Norton as a valiant and industrious gentleman who also was a skillful physician and surgeon (FER 294, 295, 322, 477; VCR 1:477, 484, 486, 493, 498-499, 503, 507, 510-513; 3:468, 477, 485, 489, 492, 494-495, 587; 4:22, 104; MCGC 60-61, 72, 74; CJS 2:304).

RICHARD NORWOOD (NOREWOOD, MOREWOOD)

On April 30, 1621, Virginia Company officials decided to send Richard Norwood (Norewood, Morewood), an experienced surveyor, to Virginia to lay out particular (or privately sponsored) plantations. On May 21, 1621, Company officials noted that Norwood had been highly recommended by Captain William Tucker for his expertise as a surveyor and stated that he had expressed an interest in going to Virginia. Plans were made to meet with Norwood to discuss how he would be compensated. On April 8, 1623, Richard Norwood informed his father that he had arrived in Virginia on April 1st on the *Margaret and John*, which had met up with the *Abigail*. Norwood said that he was half-starved when he landed and that many people were sick. On April 24, 1623, he and some of his fellow passengers on the *Margaret and John* sent a petition to the governor, complaining about the shipboard conditions they had endured on the voyage to Virginia. On May 7, 1623, the Virginia Company awarded Richard Norwood and his associates a patent for bringing 100 people to Virginia. Their land grant was confirmed on May 14, 1623. Richard Norwood may be the same individual whom the Bermuda Company sent to Bermuda and who produced a highly accurate map of the islands in 1622 and died in Bermuda around 1675 (VCR 1:458, 472; 2:412, 428; 4:127-128, 233; CJS 1:xliv).

ROBERT NORWOOD

In March 1623 Robert Norwood, who was identified as a skillful engineer, was to spend a few weeks in Holland before being sent to Virginia (CBE 32).

ANDREWE (ANDREW) NOTTING

On January 22, 1620, the justices of Bridewell Court decided that Andrewe (Andrew) Notting, a vagrant brought in from the Bridge, was to be sent to Virginia (CBE 17).

ELIZABETH NOVILL

Elizabeth Novill, a young maid, came to Virginia in September 1621 on the *Warwick* and was one of the marriageable women sent to the colony as prospective wives for the colonists. Virginia Company records indicate that in 1621 Elizabeth Novill was 19 years old and that she had been born in Westminster. Her father was described as a gentleman of worth, and her mother was identified as Francis (Frauncis) Travis (FER 309).

JOHN NOWELL

John Nowell came to Virginia on the *Margaret and John*. On January 25, 1625, he was living on Mulberry Island (21) where he was a household head. Nowell had in his possession an adequate supply of food and defensive weaponry (CBE 57; DOR 1:47).

THOMAS NOWELL

By January 2, 1630, Thomas Nowell was in possession of some land on the east side of Skiffs Creek, probably within Martin's Hundred (7). Although Nowell's patent is no longer extant, his acreage was described as being near Dr. John Pott's property and across from the land of Jacob Averie and the Rev. Willis Hely of Mulberry Island Parish (PB 1 Pt. 1:102, 113, 144, 271).

GEORGE NUCE

On February 16, 1624, George Nuce was living in Elizabeth City (18) on the west side of the Hampton River (CBE 43).

***

THOMAS NUCE (NEWCE)

On May 17, 1620, Thomas Nuce (Newce) was made deputy of the Virginia Company's land in Virginia, and within a month he was given a contract for his services. Nuce was responsible for all of the Virginia Company's tracts of Company Land and was to oversee the Company's tenants. Nuce, who was allocated 50 tenants of his own, was to get 1,200 acres of land distributed among the colony's four corporations (600 acres in Elizabeth City, 400 acres in Charles City, 100 acres in Henrico, and 100 acres in James City). He also was to receive a salary and was named to the Council of State. Thomas Nuce reportedly left Ireland, where he had been living, and settled in Elizabeth City. In April 1621, when Company officials learned that Thomas Nuce then had only 40 tenants, they decided to give him another 10 so that he would have his full complement. Captain Thomas Nuce's brother, William Nuce, also came to Virginia, where he served as marshal. On May 27, 1621, Captain Thomas Nuce, who was living in Elizabeth City (**17**) on Company-owned land, sent a letter to Sir Edwin Sandys, treasurer of the Virginia Company. He described agricultural practices in the colony, mentioned the shortage of cattle and food, and discussed the need for changes in the way the colony was managed. Virginia Company officials apparently heeded some of his advice, for they sent some supplies to him in August 1621 and gave him an additional 300 acres. However, they tabled his recommendations about modifying Company tenants' agreements. In September 1621 Nuce was told that he would receive two French youths in the spring. One of those males, Peter Arundell, later claimed that he had not received as much assistance as he expected from Nuce or from the Virginia Company. In a March 27, 1622, communiqué, Thomas Nuce again recommended that the Company alter the terms under which their tenants worked, a measure he believed would improve revenues. According to Captain John Smith, Thomas Nuce was a good manager and prior to the March 22, 1622, Indian attack, had a large corn crop planted in Elizabeth City. Nuce also obtained supplies for his men from William Harwood of Martin's Hundred (**7**) and accompanied Ralph Hamor on a trading voyage. After the Indian assault, Nuce reportedly fortified his house in Elizabeth City, provided shelter to his neighbors, and built two houses for the reception of newly arrived immigrants. He also built a brick-lined well in an attempt to provide a good supply of drinking water. John Smith said that Thomas Nuce was a good man who shared whatever he had. Nuce became mortally ill and died in 1622; he was survived by his wife and baby. One writer said that Nuce's people had perished in such large numbers that he was heartbroken and that only three of his 50 servants were alive (VCR 1:349, 375, 379, 454-458, 479, 624; 3:240, 472, 534, 588, 647, 699; 4:99, 106-107, 185, 270; CJS 2:283, 304, 309-312; FER 184, 307, 322; SH 5; CBE 31; MCGC 57; SAIN 1:36).

MRS. THOMAS NUCE (NEWCE)

On May 27, 1621, Virginia Company officials were informed that Mrs. Thomas Nuce (Newce), who was living with her husband in Elizabeth City (**17**), had just given birth to a baby boy. Thomas Nuce died in 1622, leaving a widow and baby. On August 6, 1623, Vice-Admiral John Pountis approached the Virginia Company on behalf of the widowed Mrs. Nuce, asking that she be given the moiety of her late husband's tenants until his position was filled. Pountis said that she and her late husband had helped many colonists and that she was deserving of support. He indicated that Thomas Nuce, though deputy of the Company's land in Virginia, had died poor. Company officials decided that Mrs. Nuce could have use of the decedent's tenants' labor for a year (VCR 2:466; 3:458; 4:270; CJS 2:311).

CAPTAIN WILLIAM NUCE (NEWCE)

Captain William Nuce (Newce) and his wife came to Virginia in 1620. William Nuce and his brother, Thomas, left Ireland and settled in Elizabeth City. Governor George Yeardley later noted that the Nuces and their people were living on the Company's Land in Elizabeth City (**17**), a tract located on the east side of the Hampton River. On April 21, 1621, William Nuce offered to bring 1,000 people to Virginia by summer 1625 and asked Virginia Company officials to designate him Virginia's new marshal. They did so on May 2, 1621, and also gave him a patent for a particular plantation. William Nuce of Newcetown, Ireland, an associate of Daniel Gookin's, was said to have had a considerable amount of military experience in Ireland and was knowledgeable in the construction of fortifications. He was authorized to serve as marshal for three years, and as part of his stipend, he was to be given 50 tenants who were to be put to work on his 1,500 acres of office land. Nuce offered to outfit the tenants on the marshal's land at a charge of £8 per person and said that he would establish his own people on a particular plantation and be their leader. Governor George Yeardley had high praise for Captain Nuce and his wife. On June 11, 1621, he was named to the Council of State, and it was noted that he was to be knighted by the king. By January 21, 1623, William Nuce was dead, having survived the reading of his patent by only two days (VCR 1:446-447, 452-454, 468, 475, 477-479, 482-483; 3:699; 4:78, 99, 106-107, 185, 231-232, 270).

MRS. WILLIAM NUCE (NEWCE)

On June 5, 1623, the widowed Mrs. William Nuce (Newce) asked the Virginia Company for the pay her late husband was supposed to receive (VCR 2:456).

***

THOMAS NUNN

In 1621 the Company of Shipwrights signed a five-year contract with Thomas Nunn, a boat builder, whereby he was to receive a salary and be provided with five helpers. After Nunn fulfilled his contractual agreement, he was to be given 25 acres of land at a low rent. In 1622 Nunn received money and was promised a moiety of his earnings for the first two years of his contract; afterward he was to get a larger percentage. Plans were made for Thomas Nunn, his wife, a maidservant named Amy Gamsby, and Nunn's workmen (3 sawyers, 2 carpenters, and a smith) to come to Virginia on the *Furtherance*. It was agreed that Nunn and his men would be paid for building their own houses. Nunn and his party appear to have left England in May 1622. On April 8, 1623, they were sent to Elizabeth City (17, 18) to repair a vessel. While Nunn was there, his wife died. Treasurer George Sandys, who was in charge of the artisans and tradesmen sent to the colony by Virginia Company investors, claimed that Thomas Nunn and his crew (which consisted of 20 men and boys) were incompetent. Although Nunn was supposed to set up shop at Martin's Hundred (7), he settled in Jamestown (1), most likely because he arrived a few months after the March 1622 Indian attack. In December 1623 Thomas Nunn testified about certain goods that Captains Barwick and Wilcocks had ob-

tained for the shipwrights' use. He said that he saw tools, nails, pitch, and tar being packed for shipment to Virginia, but added that those commodities were sold as soon as they reached the colony. Nunn also testified about some tobacco that was ruined in wet weather and a man who was taken from Salford's Creek (in Elizabeth City) to Warresqueak (26). While Thomas Nunn and his men were living on Jamestown Island, they built a small shallop for Thomas Barwick. They were identified as workers in the employ of the Company of Shipwrights (FER 373, 378, 382, 385; VCR 4:106, 144; 4:144; MCGC 8, 44-46, 99-100; CBE 45).

MRS. THOMAS NUNN

On May 18, 1622, when the Company of Shipwrights made an agreement with boat builder Thomas Nunn, who was coming to Virginia, they stated that if his wife performed household chores (defined as cooking, cleaning, mending, and laundry) for his workers, she would be paid. Mrs. Nunn accompanied her husband, his workers, and a maidservant (Amy Gamsby) to Virginia. She died in Elizabeth City (17, 18) sometime after April 1623 but before February 16, 1624 (FER 378; CBE 45).

***

THOMAS NUSON

On March 22, 1622, Thomas Nuson was slain during the Indian attack on Flowerdew Hundred (53), which then belonged to Sir George Yeardley (VCR 3:568).

ANDREW NUTTING

On August 8, 1618, the justices of Bridewell Court decided that Andrew Nutting, a vagrant brought in from Fleet Street in London, would be sent to Virginia (CBE 9).

O

***

THOMAS OAGE (OAGUE, OAYNE, OGE)

In 1617 Thomas Oage (Oague, Oayne, Oge), who came to Virginia on the *Starr*, was living in Bermuda Hundred (**39**) where he was a servant in Captain Robert Smalley's household. Oage stayed on after Smalley's death and on February 16, 1624, was identified as head of a household that included his wife and their child. When a muster was taken on January 24, 1625, 40-year-old Thomas Oage of Bermuda Hundred was credited with a dwelling that he shared with his wife, Ann, and 2-year-old son, Edward. The Oage family was relatively well provisioned and equipped with defensive weaponry. In May 1625 Thomas Oage was credited with 100 acres in the corporation of Charles City, the jurisdiction in which Bermuda Hundred was located. This land allotment, combined with the fact that Oage arrived on the *Starr*—a ship in Sir Thomas Dale's fleet—indicates that he was an ancient planter (SR 3112; SH 4; CBE 36, 54; VCR 4:553; DOR 1:10).

ANN OAGE (OAGUE, OAYNE, OGE) (MRS. THOMAS OAGE [OAGUE, OAYNE, OGE])

Ann, who became the wife of Thomas Oage (Oague, Oayne, Oge), went to Virginia on the *Neptune*, which arrived in the colony in August 1618. On February 16, 1624, Mr. and Mrs. Thomas Oage and their infant were living in Bermuda Hundred (**39**) in a household that Thomas headed. On January 24, 1625, when a muster was made of Bermuda Hundred's inhabitants, Ann and Thomas Oage were residing there with their 2-year-old son, Edward (CBE 36, 54).

EDWARD OAGE (OAGUE, OAYNE, OGE)

On February 16, 1624, Edward Oage (Oague, Oayne, Oge), an infant, was living in Bermuda Hundred (**39**) in the household of his parents, Mr. and Mrs. Thomas Oage. On January 24, 1625, Edward was described as 2 years old and was residing at Bermuda Hundred with his parents (CBE 36, 54).

***

RICHARD OAKLEY (OKELEY)

On August 8, 1628, Richard Oakley (Okeley), who had been arrested in St. Sepulchre's and brought before the Court of

Bridewell, indicated his willingness to go to Virginia (CBE 83).

MARGERY OCKLEY

On November 20, 1622, Margery Ockley, an inmate in Newgate Prison where jail fever was rampant, was pardoned so that she could be put to work or transported overseas (CBE 29).

ROBERT OKEY

On June 7, 1615, Robert Okey, the 12-year-old son of Francis Okey, a waterman, was admitted to Christ Church Hospital at the request of the Recorder of London. He was assigned to the Virginia Company on August 12, 1619, so that he could be sent to Virginia (CH 11).

ROBERT OKLEY (OKELEY)

In September 1618 the justices of Bridewell Court decided that Robert Okley (Okeley), a vagrant from Cheap Ward, would be sent to Virginia. Shortly thereafter, he set sail on the *William and Thomas*. On February 16, 1624, Okley was living in Flowerdew Hundred (**53**), where he was a servant in Abraham Peirsey's household. He was still in the Peirsey home on January 20, 1625, and was identified as a 19-year-old servant (CBE 10, 37, 50).

WILLIAM OLBERY

On August 16, 1627, William Olbery shipped goods from London to Virginia on the *Truelove*. He may have been one of the investors known as Truelove's Company, whose settlers arrived in Virginia in the wake of the March 22, 1622, Indian attack (CBE 79).

SUSAN OLD

Susan Old, who on January 22, 1625, was identified as a 10-year-old maidservant in Richard Biggs's household in West and Shirley Hundred (**41**), came to Virginia on the *Marigold* in 1616 and reportedly was Biggs's cousin (CBE 52).

JOHN OLDHAM

John Oldham, a merchant, testified about some imported cloth goods when he appeared before the General Court in Jamestown (1) on October 13, 1626 (MCGC 121).

THOMAS OLDIS

On November 7, 1634, Thomas Oldis was among those attesting to the accuracy of a list of the goods that the late Thomas Lee had brought to Virginia (CBE 208).

VALENTINE OLDIS

On November 19, 1627, merchant Valentine Oldis testified before the General Court in Jamestown (1) in an attempt to recover a debt. He claimed that he had loaned £20 to Benjamin Brown, a sick mariner who had given him a legal interest in his ship's cargo (MCGC 157-158).

ARNOLD OLDESWORTH (OULDSWORTH, OLDISWORTH)

In September 1620 Arnold Oldesworth (Ouldsworth, Oldisworth) Esq. set sail from Bristol, England, with William Tracy, the chosen leader of Berkeley Hundred (55). Although some Virginia Company records imply that Oldesworth died on the way to Virginia, he survived the voyage and on January 29, 1621, arrived at Berkeley Hundred. On April 21, 1621, Virginia Company officials received word that Mr. Oldesworth, who was then living in Virginia, wanted to be named to the Council of State. He received the appointment but died sometime prior to July 16, 1621 (CBE 20-21, VCR 1:448, 467-468, 479, 520; 3:396, 426).

ROBERT OLDESWORTH (OULDSWORTH, OLDISWORTH)

On September 24, 1620, Robert Oldesworth acquired a portion of George Thorpe's legal interest in Berkeley Hundred (55) (VCR 3:412-415).

JOHN OLIVE

John Olive, an indentured servant, arrived at Martin's Hundred (7) at Christmastime 1623, that is, in early January 1623. By early March he was dead. Virginia Company records indicate that Olive was a servant in the household of William Harwood, the Society of Martin's Hundred's principal representative in Virginia and the settlement's leader (VCR 4:60).

EDWARD OLIVER (OLLIVER)

In January 1624 Virginia Company officials noted that a Mr. Tomlyns had given Edward Oliver (Olliver) a share of Virginia land. On February 16, 1624, when a census was taken of the colony's inhabitants, Edward Oliver was living on the Maine (3), the mainland just west of Jamestown Island. As that area was part of the Governor's Land, Oliver would have been renting the land he occupied. In 1639 Edward Oliver was designated to view the crop of tobacco produced on Jamestown Island (1) and on the Maine and nearby Pasbehay, the territory that stretched westward to the mouth of the Chickahominy River (VCR 2:497; CBE 39; BRU 120).

JOHN OLIVER (OLIVES)

John Oliver (Olives) was living at Flowerdew Hundred (53) on February 16, 1624 (CBE 37).

***

ANNE (ANNA) OLIFFE (OLIFE) (MRS. JAMES HARRISON, MRS. JUSTINIAN COOPER [COWPER, COUPER]) (SEE MRS. JUSTINIAN COOPER [COWPER, COUPER])

ROBERT OLIFFE (OLIFE)

Robert Oliffe (Olife), Captain Christopher Lawne's stepson, invested ?27 in Lawne's colonization venture (25) and probably accompanied him to Virginia. Robert's sister, Anne (Anna), also was an investor and came to the colony. On March 16, 1642, when Anne's husband, Justinian Cooper, secured a patent for some land in Isle of Wight County, he made use of Robert's and Anne's personal adventures and investments (PB 1 Pt. 2:874).

***

[NO FIRST NAME] OMEROD

On November 20, 1619, Mr. Omerod reportedly died of the flux in Jamestown (1) (VCR 3:246).

JOHN OMOONCE
(SEE JOHN MOON [MOONE, O'MOON])

***

GEORGE ONION
(SEE GEORGE UNGWIN [UNGWINE, ONION, UNION, UNWYN, VINON, VINOYN])

ELIZABETH ONION I
(MRS. GEORGE UNGWIN)
(SEE ELIZABETH UNGWIN [UNGWINE, ONION, UNION, UNWYN, VINON, VINOYN] I)

KATHERINE ONION I
(MRS. GEORGE UNGWIN)
(SEE KATHERINE UNGWIN [UNGWINE, ONION, UNION, UNWYN, VINON, VINOYN] I)

ELIZABETH ONION II
(SEE ELIZABETH UNGWIN [UNGWINE, ONION, UNION, UNWYN, VINON, VINOYN] II)

KATHERINE ONION II
(SEE KATHERINE UNGWIN [UNGWINE, ONION, UNION, UNWYN, VINON, VINOYN] II)

***

OPECHANCANOUGH
(ABOCHANCANO, MANGOPEESOMON)

Opechancanough (Abochancano, Mangopeesomon), also known as Mangopeesomon, was one of Powhatan's brothers and a powerful war captain. He became the Powhatan Chiefdom's paramount leader soon after Powhatan's death around 1619. Opechancanough began visiting Jamestown (1) shortly after the first colonists' arrival. In early April 1614, when Pocahontas and John Rolfe were married in the church in Jamestown, one of the bride's uncles, perhaps Opechancanough, gave her away. In 1617 Opechancanough returned to Jamestown to receive a gift from Deputy-Governor Samuel Argall. Two years later interpreter Henry Spellman led the Native chief to believe that Governor George Yeardley would be replaced by Lord Rich, a more forceful leader. Some public officials thought that Opechancanough and Powhatan conspired to disrupt the colonists' treaty with the Chickahominy Indians. On at least one occasion Opechancanough sought justice from the colonial government after Captain John Martin's men forcibly seized some of the Indians' corn. Immediately after Powhatan's death, Opitchapam (Itoyatin, Otiotan, Sasawpen, Iotan), his brother, succeeded him as Great King even though Opechancanough was far stronger a leader and eventually replaced him. In 1621 Opechancanough asked George Thorpe for religious instruction and convinced Thorpe to have an English-style house built for him. Opechancanough had a brass plate attached to an oak tree as a tangible symbol of peace and agreed that some of his people should live near the colonists to learn their religion. But despite these gestures, he quietly tried to obtain poisonous plants from the Eastern Shore that he could use to destroy the colonists. When that attempt failed, he led the carefully orchestrated March 22, 1622, attack that claimed more than a third of the colonists' lives. The Indians also took prisoners and in early 1623 offered to return them in exchange for being allowed to plant their crops. In the aftermath of the 1622 attack, a reward was offered for Opechancanough's capture. The King of the Potomac Indians joined the English in an offensive against the powerful Pamunkey leader, but it fell short of their objective. On December 15, 1622, Opechancanough was said to be residing on an island in the Pamunkey River, a position from which he ruled his 32 kingdoms and territory that extended from the Roanoke River to the Pamunkey (York) River. A map made around 1662 reveals that Opechancanough's village, Menmend, was on or near Goddin's Island at the mouth of Manquin Creek in King William County. On April 18, 1644, Opechancanough, who was then very old and infirm but revered as a god, led a second Indian attack. Afterward, he was captured and brought to Jamestown, where he was shot in the back by a guard who acted without orders (VCR 2:115-116, 404-405; 3:73-74, 128-129, 157, 229, 436-438,

462, 549-550, 552, 670, 704-710; 4:98-103, 118, 231-232, 507-508; FER 113; FOR 2:8:1; HAI 845; BEV 60-61).

OPITCHAPAM (ITOYATIN, OTIOTAN, SASAWPEN, IOTAN)

Opitchapam (Itoyatin, Otiotan, Sasawpen, Iotan), Powhatan's immediate successor as paramount chief, came to power in 1618. He briefly ruled the Indian people in the region between the Pamunkey (York) and Roanoke Rivers. His successor was Opechancanough, a much stronger leader (VCR 3:229; CJS 2:247).

JOHN ORCHARD

Sometime prior to May 21, 1627, John Orchard, a merchant, sold some commodities to Thomas Mayhew (Mahew) on credit. The General Court decided that Orchard was entitled to take the payment he was due out of Mayhew's goods (MCGC 149).

MARMADUKE ORDE

On December 31, 1619, officials at Bridewell decided that Marmaduke Orde, an inmate who had been transferred there from the Middlesex House of Correction, would be sent to Virginia (CBE 14).

GEORGE OSBORNE (OSBORN, OSBOURN)

In June 1621 the Bridewell Court decided that George Osborne (Osborn, Osbourn), who had been sentenced to prison at Middlesex, would be transported overseas (CBE 23).

HUMPHREY OSBORNE (OSBORN, OSBOURN)

In July 1619 Humphrey Osborne (Osborn, Osbourn) was identified as an indentured servant employed by the Society of Berkeley Hundred. He had agreed to serve for three years under the supervision of Captain John Woodlief in exchange for 30 acres of land at Berkeley Hundred (**55**). On September 15, 1619, Humphrey set sail from England on the *Margaret* of Bristol but died shortly after arriving in the colony (CBE 13-14; VCR 3:187, 197, 213).

JENKIN OSBORNE (OSBORN, OSBOURN)

Jenkin Osborne (Osborn, Osbourn) came to Virginia in 1617 on the *George*. On February 16, 1624, he was a resident of West and Shirley Hundred (**41**) and lived on West and Shirley Hundred (now Eppes) Island. On January 22, 1625, when a muster was made of West and Shirley Hundred's inhabitants, Jenkin Osborne and his partner, Robert Milner, jointly headed an all-male household that included two others. Osborne was then age 24. The men occupied a solitary dwelling and were well supplied with provisions and defensive weaponry. They also had some livestock. Jenkin Osborne may have stayed on in the area, for on July 9, 1635, he was awarded a patent for 400 acres of land within Charles City, the corporation in which West and Shirley Hundred was located. Osborne obtained his land, which adjoined that of William Bayly and Captain Woodley, on the basis of eight headrights, an indication that he was a successful planter who succeeded in accumulating enough disposable income to purchase headrights or to pay for others' transportation to the colony (CBE 36, 53; PB 1 Pt 1:214; DOR 1:15).

***

JOHN OSBORNE (OSBORN, OSBOURN)

On February 16, 1624, John Osborne (Osborn, Osbourn) was living on Jamestown Island (**1**), where he headed a household that included his wife. On December 31, 1624, the Osbornes testified in court about the accidental drowning of George Pope II, a little boy entrusted to Mrs. Osborne's care. On January 24, 1625, when a muster was taken of Jamestown Island's inhabitants, John Osborne and his wife, Mary, were still residing there in a home located in the eastern end of the island. In March 1626 the General Court ordered John to repay a debt to Allen Kenistone, and in August he was fined for being drunk and disorderly. By January 1627 he had moved to the mainland west of Jamestown Island and established a home on the Governor's Land (**3**). John Osborne, a free man, quickly discovered that the soil there was infertile and sought permission to move. In February 1627 he was identified as the governor's former cow-keeper and the man who had been responsible for the cattle sent to the colony by Virginia Company investor John Woodall. In June 1627 John Osborne was found guilty of negligence while on sentry duty at the Jamestown fort. As punishment, he was fined and made to clear the nearby woods. However, he apparently was considered a respectable citizen, for in January 1629 he was chosen to serve on a jury trying a capital case. In 1643 he patented some acreage on the mainland directly behind the western end of Jamestown Island, within the territory known as the Neck O'Land (5). His property was on Jamestown Island, just west of Robert Hutchinson's (CBE 40, 56; MCGC 38, 97, 107-108, 129, 141, 150, 183-184, PB 1 Pt 2:944).

MARY OSBORNE (OSBORN, OSBOURN) (MRS. JOHN OSBORNE [OSBORN, OSBOURN])

On February 16, 1624, Mrs. John Osborne (Osborn, Osbourn) was living on Jamestown Island (1) in a household headed by her husband, John, a free man. On December 31, 1624, she testified at the inquest held after little George Pope II tumbled into an open well and drowned. Mrs. Osborn admitted that while she was taking care of the youngster, she had sent him to the well to fetch water and that he had fallen in. On January 24, 1625, Mrs. Mary Osborne and her husband, John, were still residing on Jamestown Island (CBE 40, 56; MCGC 38).

***

RALPH (RALFE) OSBORNE (OSBORN, OSBOURN)

Ralph Osborne (Osborn, Osbourn) came to Virginia in 1619 on the *Bona Nova*, a ship that brought a hundred of the Virginia Company's indentured servants and tenants to the colony. On February 16, 1624, he was living on the Company's land in Elizabeth City or Kecoughtan (17), on the lower side of the Hampton River, and was a servant in Lieutenant William Barry's household. When a muster was made of the colony's inhabitants in early 1625, Ralph, who was age 22, was still a servant in the Barry household. On January 12, 1627, he was identified as a Virginia Company servant when he was assigned to Captain Francis West. This occurred after the Virginia Company's third and final charter had been revoked (CBE 43, 68; MCGC 136).

THOMAS OSBORNE (OSBORN, OSBOURN)

Thomas Osborne (Osborn, Osbourn), a 32-year-old silk man from Essex, England, came to Virginia on the *Bona Nova*, which arrived in mid-November 1619. He probably was among the 25 men promptly sent up to the College Land or Arrohattock (66) in the corporation of Henrico. In the wake of the March 1622 Indian attack, those who were living within the upper reaches of the James River were evacuated to positions of greater safety. The College men went to live on the lower side of the James River, across from Jamestown, on William Ewen's plantation (13), near what became known as College Creek. However, a few months later they were sent back to the College Land in Henrico, where Thomas Osborne was living on February 16, 1624. On January 23, 1625, when a muster was made of the College's inhabitants, Lieutenant Thomas Osborne headed a household that included three male servants. He and his men were relatively well armed and provisioned and were equipped with a boat and a canoe. During May and June 1625, Osborne testified before the General Court about events that took place while he and the College men were living at William Ewen's plantation. A few months later he returned to court to testify about a business transaction that occurred at Arrohattock, where the College men were living. Thomas Osborne may not have been a religious man, for in January 1626 the Rev. Grivel Pooley, minister for the upper James River settlements, reported that Osborne was frequently absent from church, an infraction of moral law at that time. In July 1627 Lieutenant Thomas Osborne was put in command of the men at the College and Bermuda Hundred (39), who were preparing to undertake an expedition against the Tanx (that is, Little) Powhatan Indians. Two years later he was named commander of the settlers at the College and Bermuda Hundred and was ordered to appoint a deputy for the College. In October 1629 he commenced serving in the General Assembly, representing the freeholders living on the College property. In 1630 he attained the rank of captain and by 1633 was serving as a burgess for several neighboring communities, notably the College Land (Arrohattock), Henricus (63), Curles (42), and Bermuda Hundred. In 1632 he was named a commissioner or justice in the local court serving Henrico and Charles City. One of the public duties Captain Thomas Osborne performed was procuring buff coats and lead for use by the militia (FER 295; CBE 35, 53; MCGC 60, 64, 88-89, 151, 192-193; HEN 1:138, 147, 154, 168, 171, 178, 196, 202; DOR 1:7).

THOMAS OSBORNE (OSBORN, OSBOURN)

Thomas Osborne (Osborn, Osbourn) came to Virginia on the *Francis Bonaventure*. On February 16, 1624, he was living on the Governor's Land (3), part of the mainland just west of Jamestown Island. On January 30, 1625, when a muster was taken of the Governor's Land's inhabitants, Thomas was described as an 18-year-old servant in the employ of Governor Francis Wyatt (CBE 39, 57).

VALENTINE OSSERBY

Valentine Osserby came to Virginia in 1623 as an indentured servant to Mathew Brockbanke, who died on the way to the colony. Because Osserby had three years left to serve at the time of his master's death, carpenter Thomas Passmore purchased Osserby's remaining time in mid-1623. Osserby promptly dispatched a protest to the Virginia Company, voicing his objections to serving his new master. When Valentine Osserby became mortally ill in October 1623, he was still living with Passmore, whose farmstead was located in the eastern end of Jamestown Island (1) (VCR 4:95-96, 286-287).

JAMES OSTIN (OSTEN)

On September 5, 1626, the justices of the General Court awarded one of the late James Carter's indentured servants, James Ostin (Osten), a year of his time, which Carter had bequeathed him. Carter, who had been master of the *Truelove*, owned some land in Shirley Hundred (41) and in the lowlands (WAT 1016-1017).

WILLIAM OSTIN (OSTEN)

William Ostin (Osten), a 22-year-old carpenter from Gloucestershire, England, came to

Virginia in 1619 on the *Bona Nova*, a ship that brought a hundred Virginia Company servants and tenants to the colony (FER 295).

OTIOTAN (SEE OPITCHAPAM) THOMAS OTLEY

On August 8, 1618, Thomas Otley, a vagrant brought in from London's Cheap Ward, appeared before the court at Bridewell, whose justices decided that he would be sent to Virginia (CBE 9).

THOMAS OTTWAY (OTTAWAY, OTTAWELL, OTTOWELL, ATTOWELL)

Thomas Ottway (Ottaway, Ottawell, Ottowell, Attowell) came to Virginia on the *Bona Nova* and on February 16, 1624, was a servant in Edward Blaney's household in urban Jamestown (1). Simultaneously, Ottway's name was listed among the men living on Blaney's plantation (14) on the lower side of the James River, property Blaney held on account of his marriage to William Powell's widow. On February 4, 1625, Ottway was identified as a 40-year-old servant residing on Edward Blaney's plantation. He eventually obtained his freedom and on August 18, 1627, was occupying some land on the lower side of the Warwick River, within the corporation of Elizabeth City (18). He and Nathaniel Floyd most likely were Captain Samuel Mathews' tenants (CBE 38, 40, 59; PB 1 Pt 1:50).

BENJAMIN OWEN (OWIN)

Benjamin Owen (Owin) came to Virginia in 1623 on the *Swann* and on February 16, 1624, was residing on the lower side of the James River, across from Jamestown Island and east of Grays Creek (10-15). By early 1625 he had relocated to Elizabeth City (17) or Kecoughtan and was living on the east side of the Hampton River on land that belonged to the Virginia Company. Benjamin Owen was then an 18-year-old servant in the household of Francis West. Benjamin's presence on the Company Land in Kecoughtan suggests that he was a Virginia Company servant (CBE 40, 67).

DAVID OWEN (OWIN)

On March 22, 1622, David Owen (Owin), who was residing on John West's plantation at Westover (**54**), was killed by the Indians (VCR 3:567).

RICHARD OWEN (OWIN)

Richard Owen (Owin), a gentleman who had established a settlement in the corporation of Charles City near Westover (**54**), was killed in his own home when the Indians attacked on March 22, 1622. Also slain were five of Owen's servants (VCR 3:567).

THOMAS OWEN (OWIN)

Thomas Owen (Owin), an indentured servant, came to Virginia in 1632 on the *Susan* of London. On June 24, 1635, when Hannibal Fletcher obtained a patent for some land just west of Lawnes Creek, in what became Surry County, he used Thomas as a headright (PB 1 Pt 1:176).

JOHN OWYLE (OWLY, OWLES)

Sometime prior to May 1625, John Owyle (Owly, Owles) secured patents for 50 and 150 acres in the corporation of Charles City. Neither parcel reportedly had been planted (VCR 4:553).

ROBERT OWYLE (OWLY, OWLES)

Robert Owyle (Owly, Owles) came to Virginia in 1622 on the *Southampton* at the expense of William Farrar. On March 3, 1629, Farrar came into court and transferred Owyle's headright to William Andrewes, a resident of Accomac, who used it on March 14, 1629, when patenting some land on the Eastern Shore (MCGC 188; PB 1 Pt 1:71).

P

***

RICHARD PACE

Richard Pace, a carpenter from Wapping, Middlesex, England, married Isabell (Izabella) Smythe on October 8, 1608, at St. Dunstan's, Stepney, in Middlesex. The Paces, who were ancient planters, immigrated to Virginia sometime prior to 1616.

They produced a son, George, who by 1628 had come of age. On December 5, 1620, the Paces were granted 200 acres of land on the lower side of the James River, developing it into a plantation they called Paces Paines (**9**). Later, Richard acquired an additional 300 acres in the same vicinity, using the headrights of six people he brought to Virginia on the *Marmaduke* in 1621. Richard Pace invested in the Virginia Company's plan to bring a group of marriageable young women to Virginia in 1621, for which the Company rewarded him. The night before the March 22, 1622, Indian attack, a native youth, probably Chanco, who was living in the Pace household and had been converted to Christianity, told Richard Pace about the natives' plan to assault the colonists' settlements the next day. Thanks to the young Indian's timely warning, Pace crossed the James River and alerted the authorities in Jamestown (**1**). As a result, many lives were spared that otherwise might have been lost. After the onslaught, Richard Pace and his household withdrew to Jamestown Island, where they lived for several months. In a petition written between October 1622 and January 1623, Richard Pace asked permission to return to his own plantation. He said that he had gone to great expense developing it, and that he intended to make it defensible. Official records reveal that Pace had a financial interest in a plantation that Captain William Powell intended to establish on the Chickahominy River and that he had served as overseer of Powell's plantation on the lower side of the James River before going forth to seat his own land. Richard Pace died between January and April 1623. He was survived by his widow, Isabell, and their son, George. Afterward, Isabell married William Perry (VCR 3:494, 554-555, 682; 4:555; CJS 2:297-298; MCGC 63, 65; PB 1 Pt. 1:62, 64; DOR 2:764-765).

ISABELL (IZABELLA) SMYTHE PACE (MRS. RICHARD PACE, MRS. WILLIAM PERRY, MRS. GEORGE MENEFIE [MENEFY) (SEE MRS. WILLIAM PERRY, MRS. GEORGE MENEFIE [MENEFY])

On October 8, 1608, Isabell (Izabella) Smythe married Richard Pace, a carpenter from Wapping, Middlesex, England, at St. Dunstan's, Stepney, in Middlesex. Together, they immigrated to Virginia sometime prior to 1616. Isabell and Richard Pace produced a son, George, who by 1628 had come of age. On December 5, 1620, the Paces, as ancient planters, were allocated 200 acres of land on the lower side of the James River that they developed into their plantation, Paces Paines (9). In the wake of the March 22, 1622, Indian attack, the Paces moved to Jamestown Island (1), where they lived for several months. Later, they received permission to return to their own plantation so that they could protect their investment. By February 16, 1624, the widowed Isabell Smythe Pace had married ancient planter William Perry and was living in Jamestown with an infant, probably their son, Henry. In 1628 Isabell exercised her legal interest in Paces Paines, the 100 acres—which formed the westernmost part of Paces Paines and abutted Burrows Hill (8)—to which she was entitled personally as an ancient planter. She then combined it with the 100 acres she purchased from Richard Richards and Richard Dolphenby, whose land lay on the east side of the 100 acres that had belonged to her late husband, Richard Pace. Isabell outlived William Perry and sometime after August 1637 married Jamestown merchant George Menefie (VCR 3:555, 682; PB 1:Pt 1:62, 64; MCGC 58, 62-63, 65, 83, 111; CBE 38; MCGC 159; DOR 2:650, 765).

GEORGE PACE

George Pace, the son of ancient planters Richard and Isabell Smythe Pace of Paces Paines (9), may not have been living in the colony when a census of its inhabitants was compiled on February 16, 1624. He also was not among those counted at the time of the 1625 muster. In September 1628 George, as his late father's primary heir, received a patent for "the plantation called Paces Paines." His property—which included the 100 acres granted to his father on December 5, 1620, and 300 acres to which his father was entitled on the basis of six headrights—abutted west on the 100 acres that belonged to his mother as an ancient planter, and east on the land she had purchased from Richard Richards and Richard Dolphenby. George married Sarah (Sara) Macock (Maycock, Macocke, Morecock) and in August 1650 patented 1,700 acres in Charles City County, on the east side of Powell's Creek, the land known as

Macock's (48). An apparently successful planter, George Pace acquired an additional 507 acres in 1652, in the same area. Together George and Sarah Macock Pace produced a son, Richard, who became their heir (PB 1 Pt. 1:64; 2:252; 3:170; DOR 2:765-766; Charles City County Order Book 1655-1658:3; 1658-1661:179).

SARAH (SARA) MACOCK (MAYCOCK, MACOCKE, MORECOCK) PACE (MRS. GEORGE PACE) (SEE SARA [SARAH] MACOCK [MAYCOCK, MACOCKE, MORECOCK])

Sarah (Sara), the daughter and heir of Samuel Macock (Maycock, Macocke, Morecock), married George Pace. Together they produced a son and heir, Richard Pace. In August 1650 George patented the land Sarah had inherited, called Macock's (48) (PB 3:170; DOR 2:765-766; Charles City County Order Book 1655-1658:3; 1658-1661:179).

***

FRANCES (FRANCIS) PACK (PARK)

On January 29, 1620, officials at Bridewell decided that Frances (Francis) Pack (Park), a young person brought in from Old Bailey, would be detained until he or she could be sent to Virginia (CBE 18l; HUME 23).

RICHARD PACKE

Richard Packe came to Virginia in 1621 on the *Warwick* and on February 16, 1624, was living in Elizabeth City (18). He was still there in early 1625, at which time he was living in a household headed by William Gayne and Robert Newman. Packe was 23 years old and appears to have been free (CBE 44, 65).

***

THOMAS PACKER (PARKER)

Thomas Packer (Parker) came to Virginia on the *Neptune* and on February 16, 1624, was living in West and Shirley Hundred (41). By January 23, 1625, he had relocated to the College Land (66), where he lived alone but headed one of the households under Captain Thomas Osborne's command. Sometime prior to March 15, 1632, Thomas Packer patented some land on the north side of the James River in the corporation of Charles City, next to two other planters' leaseholds. They may have been renting part of the land that formerly belonged to the Virginia Company (62). By February 12, 1635, Thomas had married Elizabeth, the widow of Sergeant William Sharpe (Sharp). Thomas Packer's arrival on the *Neptune* and his presence at West and Shirley Hundred raises the possibility that he was one of the late Lord Delaware's men (CBE 36, 53; PB 1 Pt. 1:138, 147, 373; MEY 554-555; DOR 1:8).

ELIZABETH SHARPE (SHARP) PACKER (PARKER) (MRS. WILLIAM SHARPE [SHARP], MRS. THOMAS PACKER (PARKER), MRS. WILLIAM BAUGH) (SEE MRS. WILLIAM SHARPE [SHARP], MRS. WILLIAM BAUGH)

On February 12, 1635, Elizabeth, who identified herself as the widow of Sergeant William Sharpe (Sharp), patented 200 acres in the Varina area, just east of Henricus Island (63) and within Henrico County, acquiring her land on the basis of headrights. Later, Elizabeth and her new husband, Thomas Packer (Parker), enhanced the size of her holdings. She outlived him and married William Baugh (PB 1 Pt. 1:330, 373; MEY 554-555).

***

GEORGE PACY

George Pacy, a grocer from London, arrived in Jamestown (1) on September 12, 1623, on the *Bonny Bess* and took the oath of supremacy (MCGC 6).

***

CALEB PAGE

On December 5, 1625, Caleb Page testified in a suit involving John Pickernell and the purser of the *Elizabeth*. The General Court ordered Caleb, brother of the late Richard Page, to pay the decedent's debt of aquavitae and ginger to William Brewer.

Caleb also was ordered to take custody of the goods and tobacco of Thomas Page, another brother, presenting an inventory to the General Court. Caleb Page became ill and died on April 2, 1627. On the following day, Lieutenant Giles Allington, who lived between Blunt Point (22) and Newportes News (24), was named administrator of Caleb's estate and was ordered to make an inventory. Robert Adams of Martin's Hundred (7) agreed to serve as Allington's guarantor. Witnesses testified that shortly before Caleb Page died, he freed his servant, Henry Hart, from two years of service. On October 15, 1627, John Upton of Jamestown Island (1), who described himself as the late Caleb Page's partner, said that he and Caleb often received goods from Jamestown merchant George Menefie and that Caleb usually worked off whatever debt he incurred as a result of making purchases. Upton said, however, that when Caleb Page died, he owed him four ounces of silver and that Caleb had given some silver spoons to Menefie. This raises the possibility that Caleb Page was a silversmith or that he was procuring silverware that he was trading for merchandise (MCGC 79, 147, 257).

RICHARD PAGE

In May–June 1621, Richard Page, a 26-year-old mariner from St. Katherine's in London, testified in court about a voyage made by the *Falcon,* which was authorized to go to Jamestown (1), Newfoundland, and Malaga before returning to its home port. Sometime prior to May 21, 1622, Richard married Elizabeth—the widow of mariner James Brett, who died in Virginia—and became master of the *Elizabeth.* Richard Page died sometime prior to November 28, 1625. The justices of the General Court ordered his brother, Caleb Page, to inventory his estate and pay his debt to William Brewer, to whom he owed some aquavitae and ginger (MCGC 77-78; EAE 11; SR 9947).

ELIZABETH GREENE PAGE (MRS. JAMES BRETT, MRS. RICHARD PAGE) (SEE ELIZABETH BRETT)

Sometime prior to May 21, 1622, Elizabeth, the widow of mariner James Brett, married Richard Page. Elizabeth was the sister of William Greene (SR 9947; C 24/489).

THOMAS PAGE

On November 28, 1625, Thomas Page was represented by his brother, Caleb, in the General Court. Caleb Page was then ordered to make an inventory of Thomas's goods (MCGC 77).

***

***

JOHN PAGE

In September 1620 John Page and his wife, Francis, were among those who set sail from Bristol, England, on the *Supply* and accompanied William Tracy to Berkeley Hundred (**55**). Although one official report states that John Page disembarked in Ireland and never went on to Virginia, another account indicates that he was among those arriving at Berkeley Hundred on January 29, 1621 (CBE 21; VCR 3:396, 426).

FRANCIS PAGE
(MRS. JOHN PAGE)

In September 1620 Francis Page and her husband, John, set sail from Bristol, England, on the ship *Supply*. They were among those accompanying William Tracy, who was bound for Berkeley Hundred (**55**). One official report states that John got off the ship in Ireland instead of continuing on to Virginia, but another account states that he landed at Berkeley Hundred on January 29, 1621. It is likely that Francis Page joined her husband in whatever choice he made (CBE 21; VCR 3:396-397, 426).

***

JOSEPH PAGE

In March 1630 Joseph Page, a merchant and part owner of the *Sun*, rode the vessel from Canada to Virginia. Because the ship had become leaky, he tried to sell it in Virginia but was unable to find a buyer. Page returned to England on the *London Merchant* (EAE 21-22).

ROBERT PAGE

On December 24, 1634, Robert Page witnessed the will made by Tobias Felgate of Westover (**54**) (SH 19).

ANTHONY PAGITT (PAGETT)

Anthony Pagitt (Pagett) came to Virginia on the *Southampton* in 1623 and on January 20, 1625, was living at Flowerdew Hundred (**53**), where he was a 35-year-old servant in Abraham Peirsey's household. In October 1629 Anthony Pagitt served as Flowerdew Hundred's burgess (CBE 50; HEN 1:138).

JOHN PAINE

On February 16, 1624, John Paine was living in the Neck O'Land (**5**) within the corporation of James City (CBE 35).

RICHARD PAINE

On December 31, 1619, the justices of Bridewell Court decided that Richard Paine would be detained until he could be sent to Virginia (CBE 15).

THOMAS PAINE

Thomas Paine, an 18-year-old tailor from Hertfordshire, England, set sail for Virginia in 1619 on the *Bona Nova*. He was killed at Richard Owen's house near Westover (**54**) during the March 22, 1622, Indian attack (FER 295; VCR 3:567).

EDWARD PAINTER (PAYNTER)

On September 15, 1619, Edward Painter (Paynter) set sail for Virginia on the *Margaret* of Bristol and was one of the people being sent to Berkeley Hundred (**55**) to work under Captain John Woodlief's supervision. Painter was supposed to serve the Society of Berkeley Hundred's investors for seven years in exchange for 30 acres of land. On March 22, 1622, when the Indians attacked Berkeley Hundred, Edward Painter was slain (CBE 14; VCR 3:198, 213).

ELLEN (ELIN) PAINTER
(PAYNTER)

On February 16, 1624, Ellen (Elin) Painter was a maidservant in Henry Soothey's Jamestown Island (**1**) household (CBE 38).

ROLAND (ROWLAND)
PAINTER (PAYNTER)

On September 15, 1619, Roland (Rowland) Painter (Paynter) set sail for Virginia on the

Margaret of Bristol and was one of the people being sent to Berkeley Hundred (**55**) to work under Captain John Woodlief's supervision. Roland was appointed sergeant and clerk of the kitchen. He was supposed to serve the Society of Berkeley Hundred's investors for three years in exchange for 50 acres of land. On June 1, 1620, John Smyth of Nibley, a member of the Society of Berkeley Hundred, complained that he had heard nothing from Roland Painter. By that time, Roland probably was dead (CBE 13-14; VCR 3:184, 197, 210, 213, 293).

DANIEL PALMER

Daniel Palmer came to Virginia in 1621 on the *Warwick* at the expense of Albiano Lupo and was one of his servants. On September 1, 1624, when Albiano Lupo of Elizabeth City (**18**) patented some land, he acknowledged that he had paid for Daniel Palmer's passage, which originally had been the responsibility of John Downman (PB 1 Pt. 1:33).

EDWARD PALMER

When Edward Palmer of Leamington in Gloucestershire made his will in December 1624, he bequeathed his Virginia land and investment to his son, Richard, along with his interest in New England (CBE 48; EEAC 43; WAT 982).

EDWARD PALMER

Edward Palmer came to Virginia in 1629 in a French ship at the expense of Adam Thorogood, who used his headright when securing a patent on June 24, 1635 (PB 1 Pt. 1:179).

JOHN PALMER

On November 6, 1622, John Palmer and his associates asked the Virginia Company for a patent because they were planning to take 100 people to Virginia. They repeated their request on November 20, 1622 (VCR 2:122, 132).

JOHN PALMER

In November 1628 John Palmer, a Virginia colonist, was sued by Humphrey Moore, who failed to appear in court to prosecute his case. As a result, Moore was fined and the case against Palmer was dismissed (MCGC 178).

***

THOMAS PALMER

Thomas Palmer arrived in Virginia in November 1621 on the *Tiger* and was accompanied by his wife, Joan, and daughter, Priscilla. The following year he inventoried the estate of the late George Thorpe, who was killed in the March 22, 1622, Indian attack on Berkeley Hundred (**55**). On February 16, 1624, Thomas Palmer and his household, which included a young male servant, were living at Jordan's Journey (**46**). They were still there on January 21, 1625, at which time they had an abundant supply of stored provisions and defensive weaponry. In January 1625 Thomas Palmer testified that he expected to receive a servant from Rice Hoe, and that in exchange he would give Hoe his servant John Kendle. In 1629 Palmer was named commander of the Shirley Hundred (**41**) mainland and a commissioner for the monthly court serving the settlements near the head of the James River. At the end of the year, he was elected burgess for Shirley Hundred Maine. These connections with Shirley Hundred during the late 1620s raise the possibility that he and his family had relocated. Although Thomas Palmer was elected Shirley Hundred's burgess and was supposed to represent the community in the March 1630 session of the assembly, he became mortally ill while enroute to England and died on December 29, 1629. Thomas Palmer's will, which was written on December 9, 1629, and witnessed by Thomas Williams and Thomas Jones, reveals that he had several children, some of whom may have been in England. He left a gold ring and some tobacco to his eldest son and bequeathed tobacco to his second and third sons and to his daughters, Joan, Elizabeth, Dorothy, and Mary. He bestowed on Captain Gardner a spit, andirons, pan, tongs, and a flesh hook and gave the rest of his estate to his executor, George Jerman of London (S of N #431; CBE 36, 51; MCGC 44, 51, 192-193; HEN 1:138, 147; SR 3959).

JOAN PALMER
(MRS. THOMAS PALMER)

Joan Palmer came to Virginia in 1621 on the *Tiger* and was accompanied by her husband, Thomas, and their daughter, Priscilla. On February 16, 1624, the Palmers were living at Jordan's Journey (**46**). They were still there on January 21, 1625, and Thomas was a household head. On January 3, 1625, Joan Palmer testified in the breach of promise suit that the Rev. Grivel Pooley brought against the widowed Cisley Jordan of Jordan's Point. She said that Mrs. Jordan spoke of dreaming about Judgment Day (CBE 36, 51; MCGC 41).

PRISCILLA PALMER

Priscilla Palmer and her parents, Joan and Thomas Palmer, came to Virginia on the *Tiger* in 1621. On February 16, 1624, she was living with her parents at Jordan's Journey **(46)**. The Palmer family was still there on January 21, 1625. Priscilla was then identified as age 11. Virginia Company records make note of the fact that a Palmer child went to Virginia on the *Tiger* in September 1621 (CBE 36, 51; FER 309).

***

THOMAS PALMER

On July 15, 1631, Thomas Palmer, a Virginia planter, was among those who asked English officials for relief from customs fees on tobacco exported to England. On February 21, 1632, he was named a commissioner of the local court serving the "upper parts," that is Henrico and Charles City (G&M 165; HEN 1:168).

THOMAS PALMER

In court records spanning the period from December 1635 to July 1637, Thomas Palmer of St. Giles Cripplegate in London, a merchant tailor, indicated that he was sending his son and a servant to Virginia on the *Constance* (EAE 58).

WILLIAM PALOWE

On November 7, 1633, William Palowe shipped goods from Barnstable to Virginia on the *Phoenix* (CBE 108).

JOHN PALY

John Paly was killed at Lieutenant John Gibbs's dividend at Westover **(54)** during the March 22, 1622, Indian attack (VCR 3:567).

ANTHONY PANTON

The Rev. Anthony Panton, an Anglican clergyman, came to Virginia sometime prior to February 1634 at the expense of Dr. John Pott and George Menefie, both of whom were residents of Jamestown **(1)**. He became rector of both York and Chiskiack parishes. Panton openly ridiculed Secretary Richard Kemp, a staunch supporter of Governor John Harvey, and he spoke against Harvey himself. As a result of his inflammatory remarks, Panton was arrested, charged, convicted of mutiny, and fined. He also was ordered to apologize publicly in every parish in the colony before being banished from Virginia. Panton and his supporters sent protests to the Privy Council, claiming that he had been expeditiously tried and sentenced with Kemp serving as the only judge. Ultimately the case against Panton was dismissed. His goods and parish fees were restored, and he regained his parish. Afterward, Harvey and Kemp were censured for what was considered an illegal trial (MCGC 481, 483, 492, 496; HLOP:104).

[NO FIRST NAME] PARAMORE

On June 11, 1621, a Mr. Paramore was mentioned as a possible candidate for secretary of the colony (VCR 1:478).

JOHN PARAMORE (PARRAMORE)

John Paramore (Parramore) came to Virginia in 1622 on the *Bona Venture*, probably the *Francis Bonaventure*, and in early 1625 was living on the Eastern Shore, where he was a 17-year-old servant in John Blower's household on Old Plantation Creek **(73)**. On February 19, 1625, he was ordered by the justices of the local court to pay a debt to John Graves. On January 1, 1637, John Paramore filed suit against Richard Cooke in the Accomack monthly court. However, he himself was entangled by debt and was sued by several people, including one man who charged him for supplying food to Paramore's wife. In July 1638 John Paramore was punished for coming to court drunk. He continued to run afoul of the law by using abusive language and fighting with his neighbors. By 1640 Paramore had married a woman named Jane. In an August 1642 court document, he was identified as a cow-keeper at Lady Elizabeth Dale's livestock pen. In 1654 he purchased some land on Occahannock Creek (CBE 60; AMES 1:164, 70, 114; 2:3-4, 313; DOR 2:776-777).

ROBERT PARAMORE (PARAMOUR, PARRAMORE)

Robert Paramore (Paramour, Parramore) came to Virginia on the *Swann* and on February 16, 1624, was living at Hog Island (**16**). By January 30, 1625, he had moved to the Governor's Land (**3**), where he was a solitary household head. On June 25, 1627, the General Court fined Robert Paramore for being negligent while on sentry duty in Jamestown (**1**) (CBE 41, 57; MCGC 150; DOR 1:25).

EDWARD PARISH

Edward Parish came to Virginia in 1628 on the *Hopewell* at the expense of Adam Thorogood, who on June 24, 1635, listed him as a headright when securing a patent (PB 1 Pt. 1:179).

FRANCES PARK

On February 29, 1620, the Bridewell Court decided that Frances Park, a young person brought in from Old Bailey, would be detained and sent to Virginia (HUME 23).

THOMAS PARKE

On February 16, 1624, Thomas Parke was living on the Eastern Shore in one of the homesteads along Old Plantation Creek (**73**). He died sometime prior to January 31, 1625. Two of Parke's neighbors testified that he had not made a will before leaving Accomack, but that he had named as heirs his partner, William Bibby, and his mother, who was in England (CBE 46; MCGC 46).

WILLIAM PARKE

William Parke made his November 13, 1633, will while he was in Virginia and died sometime prior to August 1634. Since the will was witnessed by John Felgate, Adam Thorogood, and Thomas Key, all of whom were residents of Elizabeth City (**17, 18**), Parke probably was associated with that area. William Parke made bequests to his wife, who was in England, and to his sons, Daniel and William. He also left funds to Daniel Boucher (purser of the *Blessing*), Adam Thorogood, James Stone (a London merchant), and Thomas Key (SH 15; WITH 121-122; CBE 118; SR 3969).

ANN PARKER

Ann Parker, who was born at Chayton in Hampshire, set sail for Virginia on the *Warwick* in September 1621. She was 20 years old and was one of the young, marriageable women being sent to Virginia to become colonists' wives. Virginia Company records indicate that Ann Parker had been a servant for Mr. Emmons, a scrivener near the Exchange (FER 309).

JAMES PARKER

On May 8, 1626, the justices of the General Court decided that James Parker should be given his freedom because he had brought goods and servants to Virginia. On February 12, 1628, the court's justices ordered Thomas Delamajor to compensate Parker for the servant Parker brought Delamajor on the *Gift*. Only partial payment was due because the servant died shortly after Delamajor took custody of him (MCGC 103, 167).

ROBERT PARKER

On July 31, 1622, Robert Parker set sail for Virginia on the *James* (FER 400).

THOMAS PARKER (SEE THOMAS PACKER)

WILLIAM PARKER

Around 1611 William Parker was captured by the Indians and taken to Powhatan, who detained him. On June 18, 1614, Sir Thomas Dale sent word to England that he wanted to recover Parker but that the Indians claimed he was dead. Ralph Hamor, in his 1614 account, said that Parker had been taken prisoner by the Indians while working in Elizabeth City (**17**) near Fort Henry. Hamor added that when he encountered Parker at the native village called Matchcot, he scarcely recognized him, as he looked more like an Indian than an Englishman. Parker told Hamor that he wanted to go home. Hamor claimed that ultimately he was able to convince Powhatan to release Parker (CJS 2:250; HAI 825-826, 836, 844).

WILLIAM PARKER

William Parker, an ancient planter, came to Virginia on the *Charles* in 1616 and on February 16, 1624, was living in Elizabeth City

(18) in John Bush's household. On December 1, 1624, when Bush patented some land, he used William Parker as a headright, stating that he had come on the *Charles* in 1620. John Bush died, and in early 1625 Parker, who was a 20-year-old servant, was living in the Elizabeth City household of Susan Bush, the late John Bush's widowed sister-in-law. After becoming a free man, William Parker moved to Merry Point, where he had a house of his own. In March 1629 he testified that while Thomas Godby and six other men were drinking at his home, William Bentley's boat ran aground. He said that Bentley became quite irate because nobody came to his assistance and that Bentley and Thomas Godby exchanged insults, then fought, and Godby was killed. At that time, William Parker said that he was 22 years old (CBE 45, 64; PB 1 Pt. 1:31; MCGC 190-191).

WILLIAM PARKER

On September 26, 1618, officials at Bridewell decided that William Parker, a vagrant from Cripplegate Without, would be transported to Virginia (CBE 10).

WILLIAM PARKER

On September 15, 1619, William Parker set sail for Virginia on the *Margaret* of Bristol and went to Berkeley Hundred **(55)** to work under Captain John Woodlief's supervision. Parker was supposed to serve the Society of Berkeley Hundred's investors for six years in exchange for 30 acres of land. On March 22, 1622, when the Indians attacked Lieutenant John Gibbs's dividend at nearby Westover **(54)**, William Parker was killed. Virginia Company records indicate that he died before he had fulfilled his contractual obligation to the Society of Berkeley Hundred (CBE 14; VCR 3:198, 213; MCGC 42, 73-74).

***

ANDREW PARKES

On July 2, 1628, Andrew Parkes, a London haberdasher, made his will on the eve of his departure for Virginia on the *Hopewell*. He left all of his money to his brother, John, who already was in the colony, and he made a bequest to his aunt, Sewzan (probably Susan or Suzanne) Parkes of London. Andrew Parkes died in Virginia sometime prior to February 1630, at which time his aunt, Ellen Warden of Christ Church Hospital, London, was named his administrator (EEAC 44; SR 3957; CBE 89-90).

JOHN PARKES

John Parkes, the brother of London haberdasher Andrew Parkes, went to Virginia sometime prior to July 2, 1628. It was then that Andrew made his will, leaving John all of his money (EEAC; CBE 89-90; SR 3957).

***

JOHN PARKHURST

On May 20, 1622, John Parkhurst, a citizen and grocer of London, acquired part of the late Lord Delaware's Virginia land by purchasing it from Lord Delaware's widow, Lady Cisley (VCR 2:17, 25).

ELIZABETH PARKINS

On February 27, 1619, the Bridewell Court decided that Elizabeth Parkins, a wench from St. Faith's, would be sent to Virginia. She was part of a large group of young people rounded up from the streets of London so that they could be dispatched to the colony (CBE 13).

RICHARD PARKINS

On November 20, 1622, it was decided that Richard Parkins, who was being detained in Newgate Prison, would be pardoned and transported to Virginia due to an outbreak of jail fever (CBE 29).

THOMAS PARKINS (PERKINS)

Thomas Parkins (Perkins) died in Elizabeth City **(17, 18)** sometime after April 1623 but before February 16, 1624 (CBE 45).

DOROTHY PARKINSON

On February 16, 1624, Dorothy Parkinson was listed among those who had died in Elizabeth City **(17, 18)** since April 1623 (CBE 45).

ELIZABETH PARKINSON (PERKINSON)

On February 16, 1624, Elizabeth Parkinson (Perkinson) was living at Bermuda Hundred **(39)** (CBE 45).

MARMADUKE PARKINSON (PERKINSON)

Sometime prior to March 22, 1622, Lieutenant Marmaduke Parkinson (Perkinson) went on a voyage of discovery to the head of the Potomac River. On January 20, 1623, Virginia Company officials learned that he already had gone down to Martin's Hundred (**7**) (VCR 3:547; 4:9).

MARY PARNE

On November 20, 1622, it was decided that Mary Parne, who was being detained in Newgate Prison, would be pardoned and transported to Virginia due to an outbreak of jail fever (CBE 29).

PARNEL

On March 22, 1622, when the Indians attacked Edward Bennett's plantation at Warresqueak (**26**), a woman named Parnel was killed. It is unclear whether "Parnel" was the woman's first or last name (VCR 3:571).

WALTER PARNELL

On February 16, 1624, Walter Parnell was living in one of the settlements on the lower side of the James River, east of Gray's Creek (**11-16**) and within the corporation of James City (CBE 40).

WILLIAM PARNELL

In 1622 William Parnell came to Virginia on the *Southampton* and on February 16, 1624, was living in one of the settlements on the lower side of the James River, east of Gray's Creek (**11-16**) within the corporation of James City. By early 1625 William Parnell had moved to Elizabeth City and was living on the east side of the Hampton River, on the Virginia Company's land (**17**). He was then an 18-year-old servant in the household of Francis West (CBE 40; 67).

[NO FIRST NAME] PARR

In August 1621 Virginia Company officials sent many items to a Mr. Parr who was then living in Virginia (FER 308).

***

JOHN PARROTT (PARRETT, PARRATT)

John Parrott (Parrett, Parratt) came to Virginia on the *Providence* in 1623 and on February 16, 1624, was living in Elizabeth City (**18**). On February 7, 1625, he was identified as a 36-year-old servant in Daniel Gookin's household at Newportes News (**24**). On May 29, 1635, when John Parrott patented 450 acres on the Nansemond River (**20 c**), he listed himself, wife Prunella, and seven others as headrights (CBE 40, 63; PB 1 Pt. 1:170).

PRUNELLA PARROTT (PARRETT, PARRATT) (MRS. JOHN PARROTT [PARRETT, PARRATT])

On May 29, 1635, when John Parrott (Parrett, Parratt) patented some land on the Nansemond River (**29**), he used his wife, Prunella, as a headright (PB 1 Pt. 1:170).

***

THOMAS PARRISH

Thomas Parrish came to Virginia in 1622 on the *Charity* and on February 16, 1624, was living in Elizabeth City. In early 1625 he was identified as a 26-year-old servant in Thomas Spelman's (Spilman's) Elizabeth City (**18**) household (CBE 45, 65).

THOMAS PARRISH

On February 16, 1624, Thomas Parrish was living in Elizabeth City (**17, 18**). He may have been listed twice in the 1624 census (CBE 45).

EDWARD PARREY

Edward Parrey came to Virginia in 1618 on the *Neptune,* the ship that brought Lord Delaware to Virginia. On August 18, 1627, when Gilbert Peppett of Blunt Point (**22**) patented some land, he listed Edward Parrey as a headright and indicated that he had acquired Parrey's headright from Samuel Mathews (PB 1 Pt. 1:179).

SAMUELL (SAMUEL) PARSON

Samuell (Samuel) Parson came to Virginia on the *Hopewell* and on February 4, 1625, was living at Hog Island **(16)**, where he was a servant in John Chew's household (CBE 61).

JOHN PARSONS

John Parsons came to Virginia on the *Marigold* in 1619 and on February 16, 1624, was living on the Eastern Shore, perhaps on the Virginia Company's land **(76)**. By February 4, 1625, he had moved to the Treasurer's Plantation **(11)**, a community of settlers seated on land belonging to the colony's treasurer, George Sandys. On December 12, 1625, John Parsons testified before the General Court, describing an agreement Philip Kytely had made with three other men. On January 3, 1626, he returned to testify about some of John Evins' corn that had been put into George Sandys' loft in the "old fort." By July 1626 John Parsons had become gravely ill. When he made his nuncupative will, he left his bedding and corn to Ismael Hill's wife, Barbara; bequeathed his clothing to William Rookins; and left the remainder of his estate to his partner, William Pilkinton. John Parsons died sometime prior to November 13, 1626, and on January 11, 1627, William Pilkinton presented the General Court with an inventory of his estate (CBE 46, 60; MCGC 80, 86, 123, 133).

THOMAS PARTER (PARKER?)

On February 16, 1624, Thomas Parter (Parker?) was living in Elizabeth City **(17, 18)** (CBE 44).

***

ROBERT PARTIN I

Robert Partin I, an ancient planter, came to Virginia in June 1609 on the *Blessing*. Although nothing is known about his first years in the colony, on July 15, 1620, he was described as one of Richard Domelawe's (Domelow's) debtors and was also mentioned in Alexander Winchelsey's will. In February 1620 Robert Partin received a patent for 100 acres within the corporation of Henrico. Virginia Company officials sent him large quantities of supplies during 1621, thereby suggesting that he was in their employ. On February 16, 1624, Robert Partin was living at West and Shirley Hundred **(41)** with his wife, Marga-

ret, and daughters, Rebecca and Avis. The family was still there on January 22, 1625, at which time Robert was described as a 36-year-old household head. The family had grown with the addition of little Robert Partin II, then 4 months old. The Partin household had an ample supply of stored food and defensive weaponry, as well as some cattle, swine, and poultry. When a list of patented land was sent back to England in May 1625, Robert Partin was credited with 50 acres of undeveloped land in the corporation of Charles City and another 100 acres that had been planted. On May 23, 1625, Partin claimed an unmarked cow that had been pastured on Jamestown Island **(1)**, stating that his calf had matured. On January 9, 1626, Robert Partin and his wife testified in a dispute between the Rev. Grivel Pooley and Thomas Paulett (Pawlett). The Partin family was still living at Shirley Hundred on July 3, 1627, when the General Court decided that Robert's wife, Margaret, and daughter, Avis, should be punished because of a sexual offense committed by Thomas Hale, a Partin servant (WITH 69-70; FER 322; PB 2:95; CBE 36, 52; VCR 4:553; MCGC 59-60, 88-89, 150; DOR 1:13).

MARGARET PARTIN
(MRS. ROBERT PARTIN I)

Margaret, who married ancient planter Robert Partin, came to Virginia on the *George* in 1617 and on February 16, 1624, was living at West and Shirley Hundred **(41)** with her husband and daughters Rebecca and Avis. When a muster was made of the community on January 22, 1625, Margaret Partin, who was age 36, was sharing a home with her husband and three children: 5-year-old Avis, 3-year-old Rebecca, and 4-month-old Robert II. Also living with the Partins were two servants. Sometime prior to June 4, 1627, Thomas Hayle (Hale), a Partin servant, raped four little girls in the community, one of whom was 7-year-old Avis Partin. Margaret Partin was sentenced to a whipping because she did not report the crime (CBE 36, 52; MCGC 149-150).

AVIS PARTIN

On February 16, 1624, Avis Partin, the daughter of Robert and Margaret Partin, was living with her parents and sister, Rebecca, at West and Shirley Hundred **(41)**. When a muster was made of that community on January 22, 1625, Avis, who was Virginia-born, was 5 years old. Her sister, Rebecca, was age 3 and her brother, Robert II, was 4 months old. Also sharing the Partin home were two servants, Ellen Cook and Thomas Hayle (Hale). Sometime prior to June 4, 1627, Avis Partin and Ann Usher, two of the four little girls raped by the Partins' servant, Thomas Hayle, were sentenced to receive 40 stripes at the whipping post in the fort in Jamestown (1). This punishment, termed "correction," was intended to address any part the girls had played in the incidents. Avis was then only 7 years old. Her mother, Margaret, also was whipped for failing to report what happened (MCGC 149; CBE 36, 52).

REBECCA PARTIN

On February 16, 1624, Rebecca, the daughter of Robert and Margaret Partin, was living with her parents and sister, Avis, at West and Shirley Hundred (41). On January 22, 1625, when a muster was made of that community, Rebecca was 3 years old. Her baby brother, Robert II, was 4 months old and her sister, Avis, was age 5. All three Partin children were Virginia-born (CBE 36, 52).

ROBERT PARTIN II.

On January 22, 1625, Robert Partin II, the son of Margaret and Robert Partin I, was living with his parents and sisters, Avis and Rebecca, at West and Shirley Hundred (41). Young Robert was then only 4 months old. He and both of his sisters had been born in Virginia. On April 13, 1642, Robert Partin II sold the 100 acres his late father had owned in the corporation of Henrico (CBE 52; PB 2:95).

***

[NO FIRST NAME] PARTRIDGE

In 1609–1610 Captain John Smith described Master Partridge as one of his "old soldiers," but failed to mention his first name. He would have lived in Jamestown (1) (CJS 1:270; 2:222).

CHARLES PARTRIDGE

In February 1620 members of the Society of Berkeley Hundred identified Charles Partridge as one of the men who went to Virginia on their behalf on the *London Merchant*. On January 3, 1625, Partridge was identified as one of the men placed at Shirley Hundred (41) on behalf of Berkeley Hundred (55) (VCR 3:260-261; MCGC 42).

RICHARD PARTRIDGE

On March 27, 1619, Richard Partridge, one of George Thorpe's servants, went with him to Virginia on the *London Merchant*. He was one of the Society of Berkeley Hundred's servants and was bound for Berkeley Hundred (55). Richard Partridge reportedly died prior to February 1620 (VCR 3:178, 199, 260-261; CBE 14).

THOMAS PARTRIDGE

On September 4, 1619, Thomas Partridge, who was then in Virginia, was appointed bailiff of husbandries for Berkeley Hundred (55) (VCR 3:210).

ROBERT PASSITT

On December 31, 1619, officials at Bridewell decided that Robert Passitt, who had been brought in by the marshal of Middlesex, would be sent to Virginia (CBE 14).

JOHN PASSMAN (PASSEMAN)

John Passman (Passeman) came to Virginia on the *Jonathan* in May 1620 and was a free man. On January 22, 1625, he was living in Robert Milner's household at Shirley Hundred (41) and was age 29. On July 21, 1627, John Passman delivered Hugh Hilton's will to the General Court and verified its authenticity. Hilton had been living at nearby Bermuda Hundred (39) (CBE 53;MCGC 151).

***

THOMAS PASSMORE (PASMORE, PARSEMORE)

On August 14, 1624, Thomas Passmore (Pasmore, Parsemore), a carpenter who came to Virginia on the *George* sometime prior to 1618, patented 12 acres in the eastern end of Jamestown Island (1). He also owned an additional 16-acre parcel that was nearby. Passmore resided on one of his patents and probably placed one or more indentured servants or a tenant on the other.

On May 23, 1620, Thomas Passmore testified in court about Captain Edward Brewster's court martial hearing, held by Deputy Governor Samuel Argall (Argol) in 1618. In 1623 Passmore twice sought Governor Francis Wyatt's assistance in resolving problems that involved his purchasing an indentured servant named Valentine Osserby from a dying man's estate. One of the merchants with whom Thomas dealt was William Holmes. On February 16, 1624, Thomas Passmore was living in urban Jamestown in a household headed by John Southern, an experienced artisan whom the Society of Southampton Hundred sent to Virginia to establish an ironworks and oversee their plantation. By June 23, 1624, Passmore had married, for his wife was mentioned in a court case. In August 1624 Thomas Passmore testified in court, and in late December 1624 he and several other residents of eastern Jamestown Island participated in an inquest held in response to a local youngster's drowning death. On January 24, 1625, when a muster was made of Jamestown Island's inhabitants, Thomas Passmore and his wife, Jane, were residing in the rural part of the island in a household that included three male servants in their early 20s. Thomas, a household head, was credited with a dwelling, some stored food, and livestock. In August 1625 Thomas Passmore and Christopher Hall aired a dispute before the General Court involving the division of their tobacco crop. Passmore indicated that instead of a larger share of the crop, he would prefer an additional piece of ground. On January 30, 1626, Thomas Passmore went to court to recover a debt from John Hall, perhaps a kinsman of his partner, Christopher Hall, with whom he clashed from time to time. During late August 1626 Thomas Passmore's wife, Joanne, went to court to confirm a servant's indenture and ownership. Thomas Passmore was still alive on January 24, 1629, and was appointed to a jury (VCR 1:360-364; 4:95-96, 286-287; EAE 89; CBE 38, 56; PB 1 Pt. 1:10-11, 55, 92; 3:158; MCGC 18-19, 38, 50, 69, 92-93, 110, 153, 183-184; DOR 1:34).

JANE PASSMORE (PASMORE, PARSEMORE) (MRS. THOMAS PASSMORE [PASMORE, PARSEMORE])

Jane, who married carpenter Thomas Passmore (Pasmore, Parsemore), came to Virginia on the *George*. Thomas arrived in the colony sometime prior to 1618 and was living alone in urban Jamestown (1) on February 16, 1624. However, he wed prior to June 23, 1624. It was then that some night watchmen informed the General Court that Mrs. Thomas Passmore had been seen near the Jamestown fort. By January 24, 1625, Jane and Thomas Passmore were living in rural Jamestown Island in a household he headed. Jane died prior to August 28, 1626, unless the General Court's clerk mistakenly listed her given name as Joanne (MCGC 15, 110; CBE 56; VCR 1:360-364).

JOANNE PASSMORE (PASMORE, PARSEMORE) (MRS. THOMAS PASSMORE [PASMORE, PARSEMORE])

On August 28, 1626, Mrs. Joanne Passmore, Thomas Passmore's wife, appeared before the General Court. She said that she preferred Jeremy White, a servant then living in the Passmores' Jamestown Island (1) household, over the maidservant whom Mrs. Margaret West (Edward Blaney's widow) had taken from her (MCGC 110).

***

JAMES PASCOLL

James Pascoll came to Virginia on the *Warwick* in 1621 and in early 1625 was living in Elizabeth City (18), where he was a 20-year-old servant in the household headed by John Bainham and Robert Sweet (CBE 64).

JAQUES (JACQUES) PASTALL

On February 9, 1629, Jaques (Jacques) Pastall proved the will of John Bainham, a resident of Elizabeth City (18). Pastall's name suggests that he was French, raising the possibility that he was one of the vignerons sent to Virginia to make wine and raise silkworms (MCGC 185).

THOMAS PATCHE

On September 15, 1619, Thomas Patche set sail for Virginia on the *Margaret* of Bristol and was among those being sent to Berkeley Hundred (55) to work under Captain John Woodlief's supervision. Thomas was supposed to serve the Society of Berkeley

Hundred's investors for six years in exchange for 30 acres of land. Virginia Company records indicate that Thomas Patche died before he had fulfilled his contractual obligation to the Society of Berkeley Hundred (CBE 14; VCR 3:188, 198, 213).

WILLIAM PATCHE

On September 15, 1619, William Patche set sail for Virginia on the *Margaret* of Bristol and was one of the people being sent to Berkeley Hundred (**55**) to work under Captain John Woodlief's supervision. William was supposed to serve the Society of Berkeley Hundred's investors for six years in exchange for 30 acres of land. Virginia Company records indicate that William Patche died before he had fulfilled his contractual obligation to the Society of Berkeley Hundred (CBE 14; VCR 3:188, 198, 213).

HENRY PATTISON

On December 4, 1634, when Hugh Cox received a court order entitling him to a patent, he listed Henry Pattison as a headright (PB 1 Pt. 1:282).

***

JOHN PATTISON

John Pattison and his wife were killed at Martin's Hundred (**7**) in early 1624 (CBE 42).

MRS. JOHN PATTISON

Mrs. John Pattison and her husband were killed at Martin's Hundred (**7**) in early 1624 (CBE 42).

***

***

FRANCIS PAUL (PALL, PAULE) I

Francis Paul (Pall, Paule) I came to Virginia sometime prior to 1616 and on May 25, 1637, was identified as an ancient planter when his son Thomas patented some land in James City County as his late father's heir. Francis Paul and his wife, Mathew, also had a daughter, Frances, and another son, Francis II (PB 1 Pt. 1:430; CBE 56).

MATHEW PAUL (PALL, PAULE) (MRS. FRANCIS PAUL [PALL, PAULE])

Mathew Paul (Pall, Paule) was the wife of Francis Paul I, an ancient planter. On May 25, 1637, when the Paul couple's son, Thomas, patented land on the Chickahominy River in James City County, he did so utilizing his late father's headright and his mother's and sister's personal adventures. Mathew and Francis Paul's daughter was named Frances, and they also had a son named Francis (PB 1 Pt. 1:430; CBE 56).

FRANCES PAUL (PALL, PAULE)

On May 25, 1637, when Thomas Paul patented some land in James City County, he did so utilizing the headright of his late father, Francis Paul, an ancient planter, and the personal adventures of his mother, Mathew, and sister, Frances (PB 1 Pt. 1:430).

FRANCIS PAUL (PALL, PAULE) II

On January 24, 1625, Francis Paul (Pall, Paule) II, a 4-year-old boy, was living in rural Jamestown Island (**1**) in the household of George Unguin (Union, Onion). Also present was Francis's brother, Thomas, age 6. On May 25, 1637, when Thomas Paul patented land in James City County, he identified his father, Francis I, as an ancient planter and utilized the personal adventures of his mother, Mathew, and sister, Frances. No mention was made of the brother named Francis, perhaps because he was Virginia-born (CBE 56; PB 1 Pt. 1:430).

THOMAS PAUL (PALL, PAULE)

On January 24, 1625, 6-year-old Thomas Paul (Pall, Paule) was living in rural Jamestown Island (**1**) in the household of George Unguin (Union, Onion). Also living in the Union home was 4-year-old Francis Paul, Thomas's brother. On May 25, 1637, when Thomas Paul patented some land in James City County, he did so utilizing the headright of his late father, Francis Paul I, an ancient planter, and the personal adventures of his mother, Mathew, and sister, Frances. On September 20, 1643, Thomas patented a one-acre lot in the eastern end of Jamestown Island, near the Back River. He had six months in which to develop his land or face forfeiture (CBE 56; PB 1 Pt. 1:430; Pt. 2:890).

***

GEORGE PAUL (PALL, PAULE)

On March 24, 1623, Virginia Company officials noted that George Paul (Pall, Paule), who had been living with Sir George Yeardley, was dead. It is unclear whether he was living in Jamestown (1) or Flowerdew Hundred (53) (VCR 4:233-234).

ROBERT PAWLETT (PAULETT, PAULETTE)

On September 15, 1620, the Rev. Robert Pawlett (Paulett, Paulette), a clergyman and surgeon, was among those who set sail from Bristol, England, on the ship *Supply* and accompanied William Tracy, who was bound for Berkeley Hundred (55). Pawlett asked the Society of Berkeley Hundred to furnish him with items that would be useful in physic and surgery. He arrived at his destination on January 29, 1621, and on July 16, 1621, was chosen a provisional councilor. He was named to the Council of State on July 24th. On June 10, 1622, before word of a major Indian attack had reached England, Virginia Company officials decided to send the Rev. Robert Pawlett to Martin's Hundred (7). He did not go, unless he did so when the settlement was reoccupied (CBE 20-21; VCR 1:520; 3:290, 396, 401-402, 426, 482, 646, 651).

THOMAS PAWLETT (PAULETT, PAWLETTE)

Thomas Pawlett (Paulett, Pawlette) came to Virginia with Lord Delaware on the *Neptune*, which arrived in Jamestown (1) in mid-August 1618. On May 5, 1622, when Pawlett was queried by English chancery officials, he said that he did not know who Delaware had authorized to take custody of his goods, but that when the *Neptune* landed in Jamestown, Edward Brewster took over. Pawlett, who said that he was 34 years old and from Pawlton in Hampshire, described the *Neptune's* voyage and said that he had helped Delaware's men get settled in Virginia. By February 16, 1624, Thomas Pawlett had returned to Virginia and was living at West and Shirley Hundred (41). He was still there on January 22, 1625, at which time he headed a household that included one male servant. On April 7, 1625, Pawlett, who was identified as a gentleman, testified that he had witnessed Andrew Dudley's death at the hands of the

Indians and on September 10, 1625, he witnessed the will made by his Shirley Hundred neighbor, Richard Biggs. Thomas Pawlett continued to rise in prominence. In August 1626 he was made a commissioner of the monthly court that served the "upper parts," which included Henrico and Charles City, and he was reappointed in February 1632. In July 1627 Pawlett was given the responsibility of leading an expedition against the Indians, and on March 7, 1629, he was named commander of Westover (54). In February 1633 he served as burgess for Westover and Flowerdew (53) (SR 9947; C 24/489; VCR 3:154; CBE 36, 52; SH 6; MCGC 51, 106, 151, 192; HEN 1:168, 202; DOR 1:14).

WILLIAM PAWMET (PAWLETT?)

William Pawmet (Pawlett?) was killed at Martin's Hundred (7) during the March 22, 1622, Indian attack. He probably was the "Mr. Pawlett" who represented Argall's Gift or Argall Town in the July 1619 assembly meeting, for Deputy Governor Samuel Argall wrongfully seated the Society of Martin's Hundred's colonists on part of the Governor's Land (3) in a settlement he named after himself (VCR 3:154, 570).

HENRY PAULSTEAD

On March 27, 1622, Henry Paulstead, a merchant tailor, acquired part of the late Lord Delaware's Virginia land by purchasing it from Francis Carter, who had obtained it from Delaware's widow (VCR 1:625).

SUSAN (SUZAN) PAYNE

On February 27, 1619, the Bridewell Court decided that Susan (Suzan) Payne, a wench, would be sent to Virginia. She was part of a large group of children rounded up from the streets of London so that they could be dispatched to the colony (CBE 13).

HENRY PAYTON

Henry Payton died in Elizabeth City (17, 18) sometime after April 1623 but before February 16, 1624 (CBE 45).

NATHANIEL PEACOCK (PECOCK)

According to Captain John Smith, Nathaniel Peacock (Pecock), a boy, came to Virginia in 1607 and was one of the first Jamestown (1) settlers. He later identified Peacock as both a soldier and a sailor who accompanied Smith on a voyage to the Pamunkey Indians' territory (CJS 1:244; 2:142, 193).

WILLIAM PEACOCKE

On August 16, 1627, William Peacocke shipped goods from London to Virginia on the *Truelove* (CBE 79).

***

JOHN PEAD (PEED, PEEDE) I

John Pead (Peed, Peede) I came to Virginia on the *Southampton* in 1622 and on February 16, 1624, was living at Jordan's Journey (46). He was still there on January 21, 1625, and was described as a 35-year-old servant in the household headed by William Farrar and Ciseley Jordan. John Pead eventually married and produced a son and a daughter. After Pead's death, his wife, Mary wed Joseph Ham, who prepared his will on March 3, 1638, and made bequests to his underage stepchildren, Catherine and John Pead II. John and Mary Pead's son, John II, patented some land on September 21, 1652, using his parents' headrights (CBE 36, 51; PB 3:127; DOR 2:796).

MARY PEAD (PEED, PEEDE) I (MRS. JOHN PEAD [PEED, PEEDE] I)

Mary, who became the wife of John Pead (Peed, Peede) I sometime after January 21, 1625, produced two children, Catherine and John Pead II. After John Pead's death, Mary remarried sometime prior to March 3, 1638. Her new husband, who predeceased her, was Joseph Ham (DOR 2:796).

CATHERINE PEAD (PEED, PEEDE) I

Catherine, the daughter of John Pead (Peed, Peede) I and his wife, Mary, was orphaned while still a minor. In March 1638 her stepfather, Joseph Ham, named her as an heir (DOR 2:796).

JOHN PEAD (PEED, PEEDE) II

John Pead (Peed, Peede) II, the son of John Pead I and his wife, Mary, was orphaned while still a minor. In March 1638 his stepfather, Joseph Ham, named him as an heir. In September 1652, when John Pead II patented some land in what is now Mathews County, he used his parents' headrights (DOR 2:796).

***

ROBERT PEAKE

Robert Peake came to Virginia on the *Margaret and John* in 1623 and on February 16, 1624, was living on Yeardley's plantation, Flowerdew Hundred (53). By January 24, 1625, he had moved to urban Jamestown (1), where he was an indentured servant in the household of Sir George Yeardley (CBE 37, 54).

LAWRENCE PEAL (PEALE, PEELE)

Lawrence Peal (Peale, Peele) came to Virginia in 1620 on the *Margaret and John* and on February 16, 1624, was living in Elizabeth City (18). He was still there in early 1625 and was identified as a 23-year-old household head who shared his home with his partner, William Smith. On December 30, 1625, Peal testified that around August 1622 he had been present when Robert Leister of Jamestown (1), one of Dr. John Pott's servants, criticized Captain William Tucker and made threats against him (CBE 44, 64; MCGC 83; DOR 1:53).

MARTIN PEAL (PEALE, PEELE)

In November 1628 Martin Peal (Peale, Peele) brought suit against mariner Thomas Mayhew in an attempt to recover the wages he was owed for service on the *Gift*. On December 9, 1628, Peal appeared before the General Court, where he proved Edward Grindon's will (MCGC 177, 179).

GREGORY PEARL (PEARLE)

On April 30, 1623, Gregory Pearl (Pearle), who identified himself as a master's mate, was among those rebutting Captain Nathaniel Butler's claims about conditions in Virginia. Gregory, who was then in Jamestown (1), stated that he had been in the colony for 16 months (VCR 2:386).

***

LODOWICK (LODWICK) PEARL (PEARLE)

On January 30, 1626, Lodowick (Lodwick) Pearl (Pearle) testified before the General Court. He said that on New Year's Eve he was aboard the ship *Grace*, which was anchored at the mouth of the James River, but did not hear any commotion caused by some men accused of being drunk and disorderly. In early 1626, while Pearl was commander of Bennett's Welcome (26), in Warresqueak, the General Court ordered him to give the Rev. Bolton the two years' back pay he was owed by the community's settlers. On October 13, 1626, Pearl was told to take custody of Mr. Richard Bennett's goods and servants, making an account of them, and to collect the decedent's debts and handle his business affairs. A month later the General Court ordered Pearl to ask Edward Bennett, who was then in England, to send over Richard Stubb's indenture and to inform Bennett that the decedent's chest had been lost or destroyed by those who had custody of it. Lodowick Pearl died sometime prior to March 3, 1628, at which time his widow, Alice, presented an inventory of his estate (MCGC 91-92, 98, 120, 124, 168).

ALICE PEARL (PEARLE) (MRS. LODOWICK (LODWICK) PEARL [PEARLE])

On March 4, 1628, Alice, the widow of Lodowick (Lodwick) Pearl (Pearle), presented the General Court with an inventory of her late husband's estate. The decedent had lived at Bennett's Welcome (26) (MCGC 168).

***

[NO FIRST NAME] PEARNS

Mr. Pearns's servant, William, died in Jamestown (1) sometime after April 1623 but before February 16, 1624 (CBE 39).

CUTBERT (CUTHBERT) PEARSON (PEIRSON, PEERSON, PERSON, SEIRSON)

In 1619 Cutbert (Cuthbert) Pearson (Peirson, Peerson, Person, Seirson) came to Virginia on the *Bona Nova*. On February 16, 1624, he was living in the Indian Thicket on the east side of the Hampton River in Elizabeth City (17). He was still there in early 1625 and was identified as a 22-year-old servant in William Barry's household on the Virginia Company's land. On August 21, 1626, Cutbert informed the General Court that Thomas Jones, Robert Hutchinson, and John Osborne, residents of the Governor's Land (3) and Jamestown Island (1), had been drunk and disorderly. When Cutbert Pearson was assigned to the governor on January 12, 1627, he was identified as a tenant of the defunct Virginia Company (CBE 43, 68; MCGC 136, 168).

ELIZABETH PEARSON (PEERSON)

In September 1621 Elizabeth Pearson (Peerson), a young maid, came to Virginia on the *Warwick* and was one of the marriageable women sent to the colony as prospective wives. Elizabeth, who was 19 years old, was born in Oxenford and was the daughter of William Pearson, a plasterer. Both of her parents were dead. A Mr. Ryder had recommended Elizabeth to the Virginia Company (FER 309).

ABRAHAM PEATE

Abraham Peate was living in Virginia on January 6, 1635, when he witnessed the will made by Thomas Whaplett, a Jamestown (1) merchant and planter. The testator left half of his plantation to his sister, Rebecca Whaplett, and the other half to Abraham Peate, whom he asked to manage Rebecca's share of the property. Peate also was to pay all of the decedent's debts in Virginia. Whaplett died sometime prior to November 13, 1636 (SR 3975; SH 20; WITH 77; EEAC 62).

RICHARD PECK

On March 14, 1625, Richard Peck was identified as one of three servants who arrived in the colony in December 1621 aboard the *Warwick*, having been transported by Thomas Crispe. In March 1629 Peck, who said that he was 25 years old, testified about an event that had occurred at William Parker's house at Merry Point in Elizabeth City (18) on February 8, 1629. At issue was a heated dispute between William

Bentley and Thomas Godby, which culminated in Godby's death (MCGC 50, 190-191).

THOMAS PECK

On January 3, 1625, Thomas Peck was identified as one of the men placed at Shirley Hundred (41) on behalf of the Society of Berkeley Hundred (55) (MCGC 42).

ELIZABETH PECON

On January 22, 1620, the justices of Bridewell Court decided that Elizabeth Pecon, who was from Christchurch Parish, would be sent to Virginia (CBE 17).

ELIZABETH PEDDOCK (PEDOCK, PEDOCKE)

On July 15, 1631, Elizabeth Peddock (Pedock, Pedocke) was among the Virginia planters who exported tobacco from the colony and asked for relief from customs fees (G&M 166).

LEONARD PEDDOCK (PEDOCK, PEDOCKE)

On March 12, 1627, Leonard Peddock (Pedock, Pedocke) testified before the General Court about an incident in the West Indies that involved the ship *Saker*. On February 10, 1629, he was described as a merchant when he was named administrator of the estate of John Beard, who died in Accomack. On January 12, 1634, Mr. Peddock was identified in Accomack's monthly court as an assignee of planter Stephen Charleton (MCGC 143, 186; AMES 1:10).

PEDRO (PETER)

On February 16, 1624, an African named Pedro (Peter) was living at Warresqueak (26), the Bennett plantation, which was known as Bennett's Welcome (CBE 42).

JOHN PEDRO

John Pedro, an African, came to Virginia on the *Swann* in 1623. In early 1625 he was living on the east side of the Hampton River on the Virginia Company's land (17) in Elizabeth City and was a 30-year-old servant in the home of Francis West. John Pedro's surname suggests that he had been associated with Spanish-occupied territory, perhaps in the West Indies or Africa (CBE 67).

PETER (PEETER)

On February 7, 1625, a 19-year-old man named Peter (Peeter), who came to Virginia on the *Margaret and John* in 1620, was living in Warresqueak (26), where he was a servant in Henry Woodward's household (CBE 62).

PETER (PEETER)

Peter (Peeter) died in Elizabeth City (17, 18) sometime after February 16, 1624, and was buried on May 16, 1625 (CBE 67).

MARY PETERS (PEETERS)

Mary Peters (Peeters) came to Virginia in 1620 on the *London Merchant* and on February 16, 1624, was living at Shirley Hundred (41). She was still there on January 22, 1625, at which time she was identified as a 16-year-old servant in the household headed by Richard Biggs (CBE 36, 52).

WILLIAM PETERS (PEETERS)

On March 4, 1628, William Peters (Peeters) was identified as master of the ship *Pleasure* of Bideford, which undertook a journey from Barnstable to Virginia (CBE 82).

JOHN PEGDEN

John Pegden, a gentleman from London, arrived in Jamestown (1) on September 12, 1623, on the *Bonny Bess* and took the oath of supremacy. He died sometime prior to February 16, 1624 (MCGC 6; CBE 39).

ELIZABETH PEERCE

In July 1624 the General Court's justices noted that Elizabeth Peerce had been engaged to John Phillimore (Philmore, Philmott, Filmore) at the time of his death, which occurred "over the water," that is, across from Jamestown Island and east of Gray's Creek (10-16). Although Phillimore's will was lost, witnesses agreed that Elizabeth was entitled to his land and belongings. Her father-in-law (i.e., stepfather) was Thomas Bennett (MCGC 27; CBE 60).

EDWARD PEIRCE (PIERCE)

Edward Peirce (Pierce) was killed at William Bikar's plantation (57) during the March 22, 1622, Indian attack (VCR 3:568).

HENRY PEIRCE (PIERCE, PERSE, PEERSE, PEERS)

Henry Peirce (Pierce, Perse, Peerse, Peers) —who set sail for Virginia on the *Margaret* of Bristol on September 15, 1619—was one of the people sent to Berkeley Hundred (55) to work under Captain John Woodlief's supervision. On September 4th, shortly before his departure from England, Henry was appointed usher for Berkeley Hundred's hall. He was supposed to serve the Society of Berkeley Hundred's investors for 4 years in exchange for 25 acres of land. Virginia Company records indicate that Henry Peirce died before he had fulfilled his contractual obligation to the Society of Berkeley Hundred (CBE 13-14; VCR 3:197, 210, 213).

JOHN PEIRCE (PIERCE)

On February 16, 1620, when John Peirce (Pierce) and his associates were asked to train Indian children in Virginia, they declined and Peirce indicated that he did not intend to go to the colony for another two or three months. On July 16, 1621, Virginia Company officials noted that because John Peirce had patented land in the northern colony, he stood to forfeit his Virginia land unless he seated it. He may have been connected with the plan to educate young Indians at College (66) or the East India School (VCR 1:310-312, 515).

NICHOLAS PEIRCE (PIERCE, PERSE)

In 1619 Nicholas Peirce (Pierce, Perse) came to Virginia on the *Faulcon* and on February 4, 1625, was living in Samuel Mathews' plantation (15) on the lower side of the James River. Nicholas was then a 23-year-old servant in the Mathews household (CBE 60).

NICHOLAS PEIRCE (PIERCE, PERSE)

On January 29, 1620, Bridewell officials identified Nicholas Peirce (Pierce, Perse) as one of the people to be sent to Virginia. On February

16, 1624, he was living at the College (66) in the corporation of Henrico. However, by January 3, 1625, he had been moved to Shirley Hundred (41), where he was employed on behalf of the Society of Berkeley Hundred (55) (CBE 18, 35; MCGC 42).

***

RICHARD PEIRCE (PIERCE, PERSE, PERCE, PEERCE)

Richard Peirce (Pierce, Perse, Perce, Peerce) and his wife came to Virginia on the *Neptune*. He became a planter and in 1624 had some business dealings with William Holmes, a Jamestown (1) merchant. On February 16, 1624, Peirce and his wife were living in the Neck O'Land (5). When the General Court heard testimony in a breach of promise suit on June 24, 1624, Richard Peirce said that he had overheard Robert Marshall and maidservant Eleanor Sprad discuss their plans to marry. On February 4, 1625, when demographic records were compiled on Archer's Hope's (6) inhabitants, Richard Peirce headed a well-supplied household that included his wife, Elizabeth. Peirce made several appearances in court during the mid-1620s. In May 1625 he indicated that he had delivered some documents to John Pountis of Jamestown (1), and he testified about some business dealings between John Osborne and his servant, Allen Kenistone. He apparently was fond of veal, for he was ordered to replace Mr. Woodall's calf, which he had killed and eaten, and he was said to have butchered a calf that John Osborne kept. In 1626 he was ordered to pay Dr. John Pott some corn and tobacco. In September 1636 Richard Peirce patented 600 acres of land on the east side of the Chickahominy River on the basis of 12 headrights. Thus, he seems to have been a relatively successful planter (EAE 89; CBE 35, 58; MCGC 17, 58-59, 96-97, 111-112, 141; PB 1 Pt. 1:379; DOR 1:37).

ELIZABETH PEIRCE (PIERCE, PERSE, PERCE, PEERCE) (MRS. RICHARD PEIRCE [PIERCE, PERSE, PERCE, PEERCE])

Elizabeth, who married Richard Peirce (Pierce, Perse, Perce, Peerce) came to Virginia on the *Neptune* and on February 16, 1624, was living in the Neck O'Land (5)

with her husband. On February 4, 1625, Elizabeth and Richard Peirce were living in Archer's Hope (**6**), where he headed a household (CBE 35, 58).

***

***

THOMAS PEIRCE (PIERCE, PERSE, PERCE, PEERCE)

When Virginia's first assembly convened in July 1619, Thomas Peirce (Pierce, Perse, Perce, Peerce), who appears to have been a kinsman of Captain William Peirce, was appointed sergeant-at-arms. Thomas Peirce, his wife, and their child were killed at Mulberry Island (**21**) during the March 22, 1622, Indian attack. On October 7, 1622, Virginia Company officials noted that Thomas Peirce's estate was to be inventoried and that his brother, Edward Peirce, a London merchant tailor, was to serve as administrator. On April 19, 1625, the Rev. Richard Buck and William Peirce presented the General Court with a partial inventory of Thomas Peirce's goods in Virginia. The decedent was credited with a case of bottles, pewter, guns, and some bedding (VCR 2:106; 3:153-154, 570; CJS 2:302; MCGC 55; DOR 2:799).

MRS. THOMAS PEIRCE (PIERCE, PERSE, PERCE, PEERCE)

Mrs. Thomas Peirce (Pierce, Perse, Perce, Peerce), her husband, and their child were killed at Mulberry Island (**21**) during the March 22, 1622, Indian attack (VCR 3:570; CJS 2:302).

[NO FIRST NAME] PEIRCE (PIERCE, PERSE, PERCE, PEERCE)

During the March 22, 1622, Indian attack, a child of unknown age and gender was killed at Mulberry Island (**21**) along with his parents, Thomas Peirce (Pierce, Perse, Perce, Peerce) and his wife (VCR 3:570; CJS 2:302).

***

THOMAS PEIRCE (PIERCE, PERSE, PERCE, PEERCE)

On September 15, 1619, Thomas Peirce (Pierce, Perse, Perce, Peerce) set sail for Vir-

ginia on the *Margaret* of Bristol and was among those being sent to Berkeley Hundred (**55**) to work under Captain John Woodlief's supervision. Peirce was brought to Berkeley Hundred to produce hops and oad (ingredients used in producing beer), but he asked to be trained in carpenter's work, a trade his father also favored. Thomas Peirce agreed to serve the Society of Berkeley Hundred's investors for 7 years in exchange for 30 acres of land. Virginia Company records indicate that he died sometime before he had fulfilled his contractual obligation to the Society of Berkeley Hundred (CBE 13-14; VCR 3:195-197, 213).

***

WILLIAM PEIRCE (PIERCE, PEARSE, PERSE, PERCE, PEERCE)

William Peirce (Pierce, Pearse, Perse, Perce, Peerce) left England in 1609 on the *Seaventure*, the vessel bringing Sir Thomas Gates to Virginia. Like Gates and John Rolfe, who later became his son-in-law, he was shipwrecked in Bermuda and reached Virginia in 1610. While Deputy Governor Thomas Dale was in office (1611–1616), Peirce was among those who taught natives how to use firearms, something that drew criticism in the wake of the 1622 Indian attack. William Peirce was made captain of the guard in Jamestown (**1**) and was mentioned in the will made by Captain Robert Smallay of Bermuda Hundred (**39**) on December 19, 1617. Court testimony taken in 1622 indicates that when Lord Delaware's skilled workers arrived in Jamestown in 1618, Peirce and some of the island's other inhabitants offered to hire them so that they could become self-supporting. Lieutenant William Peirce was present in 1619 when Governor George Yeardley made a treaty with the Chickahominy Indians, and he had some involvement in business dealings that involved Berkeley Hundred (**55**). In late summer 1619 Governor Yeardley sent William Peirce, William Ewen, and John Rolfe to meet the incoming ship *Treasurer* (a vessel that brought some of the colony's first Africans) at Old Point Comfort (**17**). Peirce later had in his household a black woman named Angelo, who reportedly came to Virginia on the *Treasurer*. George Sandys, the colony's treasurer, lived in the Peirce home in Jamestown and raised silkworms in one room of the dwelling. In December 1619 Captain William Peirce received a patent for 650 acres on Mulberry Island (**21**), plus another 1,450 acres. Later, the people of Martin's Hundred (**7**) claimed that he had encroached on their property. Peirce tried to collect some money that cape merchant Abraham Peirsey owed his son-in-law, John Rolfe. On March 10, 1621, when Rolfe made his will, he designated William Peirce as guardian of his children and left him some oxen and defensive weaponry.

George Sandys apparently had ambivalent feelings about William Peirce. Sandys said that Peirce, who was the lieutenant governor, captain of the governor's guard, and the commander of Jamestown Island and its blockhouses, tried very hard to fulfill his responsibilities but was not very adept at doing so. He added that Peirce was a close friend of Governor Francis Wyatt. During July 1623 William Peirce led an expedition against the Indians in the Chickahominy River drainage. Later in the year he was ordered to collect the tobacco levied in support of building the new fort at Warresqueak (**26**). Taxpayers were supposed to bring their tobacco to Peirce's new house in Jamestown, which in April 1623 was described as "one of the fairest in Virginia" and was located on a large urban lot. In January 1624 William Peirce and William Powell were named the *Furtherance's* new captains. On February 16, 1624, William Peirce and his wife, Joan, were living in Jamestown. He was elected Jamestown's burgess in 1624 and signed the rebuttal to Alderman Johnson's claim that the colony thrived under martial law. Lieutenant William Peirce obtained four servants and some goods from Mr. Franck in England, workers he placed on his outlying property. On January 24, 1625, the Peirce household was living in Jamestown but William then had servants on his Mulberry Island property.

During the mid-1620s Captain William Peirce made several appearances in court. He served as Nicholas Elford's administrator, inventoried the late Thomas Peirce's estate, and testified about some statements Captain John Martin made while visiting his home. He also went to court to obtain compensation from Peter Stafferton, and he was released from his obligation to pay Mr. Woolridge. The court agreed to see that William Peirce was compensated for the loss of his shallop, and in May 1625 it was noted that Thomas Edwards owed him a

hogshead of beer. Others with whom Peirce had business dealings included John Moone and Thomas Roper. Peirce also presented Robert Austen's will for probate, served as Abraham Porter's administrator, and testified about conditions at Martin's Hundred, which he visited right after the 1622 Indian attack. He had a disagreement with Captain Gire, a mariner, and sought intervention by the General Court, and he also brought suit against the estate of Roger Peirce. In 1627 he was given three men who had been tenants of the defunct Virginia Company.

In 1629 Captain William Peirce wrote a descriptive account of conditions in the colony, drawing on his 20 years of experience. His narrative received wide distribution in England. He was a highly successful planter and entrepreneur who had a store in Jamestown. In 1635 he patented 2,000 acres of land on Lawnes Creek, and during the early 1640s he acquired 1,170 acres in James City County and a 27-acre leasehold on the Governor's Land (**3**). Peirce was designated a tobacco inspector for Stanley Hundred and Denbigh Parish in January 1640, the same year that six of his runaway servants were tried before the General Court. He was a member of the Council of State from 1632 to 1643 and was instrumental in ousting Governor John Harvey from office. When Harvey regained the upper hand, Peirce was summoned to England and detained, and his personal estate was seized. He later returned to Virginia, where he resided until at least June 1643. William Peirce died after 1644 but before June 22, 1647 (CBE 38, 53, 55, 95; SH 4-5; FER 113; VCR 1:399, 485, 497; 2:108; 3:118, 186, 243, 616; 4:106, 108, 110-111, 209, 250, 401, 556; SR 1207; PB 1 Pt. 1:75, 212, 255; Pt. 2:927; C 24/490; CO 1/5 ff 69-71; 1/9 ff 132-134, 155; 1/10 f 190; PC 2/50 f 572; MCGC 9, 28, 40, 44, 55, 61, 63, 65, 87, 115, 130-131, 134, 137, 141, 151, 156-157, 180, 187-188, 199, 467, 495; EAE 23, 89; EEAC 48; JHB 1619-1659:41; HAI 915; HEN 1:128-129, 140, 153, 171, 178, 196, 202; WITH 487; SAIN 1:100, 217, 252, 314; STAN 32; G&M 217-218, 223; AMB 4; DOR 1:31, 46-47; 2:797-800).

JOAN (JONE) PEIRCE (PIERCE, PEARSE, PERSE, PERCE, PEERCE) (MRS. WILLIAM PEIRCE [PIERCE, PEARSE, PERSE, PERCE, PEERCE])

Joan, who married ancient planter William Peirce (Pierce, Pearse, Perse, Perce,

Peerce), came to Virginia on the *Blessing* in 1609. On February 16, 1624, the Peirces were living in urban Jamestown (1) and shared their home with four servants. On January 24, 1625, Joan and William were still residing in Jamestown, where they had a lot that adjoined the Back Street. Court testimony dated May 9, 1625, reveals that Mrs. Edward Blaney came to the Peirce dwelling and asked Joan Peirce to obtain some pork from Dr. John Pott, her next-door neighbor. Mrs. Blaney, who was pregnant, later had a miscarriage and blamed it on Pott's refusal to share his pork. As a result of Mrs. Blaney's allegations, the matter was aired before the General Court. In 1629 Mrs. Joan Peirce, whom Captain John Smith termed "an honest and industrious woman" who had lived in the colony for nearly 20 years, had a large garden in Jamestown from which she reportedly gathered nearly 100 bushels of figs a year. Mrs. Peirce was quoted as saying that she could "keep a better house in Virginia for 3 or 4 hundred pounds than in London," even though she had gone to the colony "with little or nothing." When colonist Anthony Barham made his will in 1641, he made a bequest to Mrs. Joan Peirce, which suggests that she was still alive (CBE 38, 55; MCGC 58; CJS 3:218; SR 3989; DOR 2:799-800).

JOAN (JOANE, JONE) PEIRCE (PIERCE, PEARSE, PERSE, PERCE, PEERCE) II (MRS. JOHN ROLFE, MRS ROGER SMITH) (SEE MRS. JOHN ROLFE, MRS. ROGER SMITH)

Joan (Joane, Jone) Peirce (Pierce, Pearse, Perse, Perce, Peerce) II, who came to Virginia on the *Blessing*, probably in 1609, married the twice-widowed John Rolfe after his May 1617 return to Virginia. John and Joan Peirce Rolfe most likely lived on one of the two parcels in urban Jamestown (1) that were owned by her parents, William and Joan Peirce. The Rolfes had a daughter, Elizabeth, who was born around 1621. When John Rolfe died in 1622, he left Joan an interest in his land at Mulberry Island (21). Joan married Captain Roger Smith of Jamestown and moved into his home. She was living there with daughter, Elizabeth Rolfe (age 3), when a census was taken on

February 16, 1624. On January 24, 1625, when new demographic records were compiled, she was still there. In the Smith household in 1625 were two other children: the orphaned Sara Macock (age 2) and Elizabeth Salter (age 7) (CBE 38, 55; MCGH 861; SH 5; DOR 2:799-800).

***

WILLIAM PEIRCE (PEIRS)

In September 1620 William Peirce (Peirs), the elder, set sail from Bristol, England, on the ship *Supply*. He was one of the people who accompanied William Tracy and was bound for Berkeley Hundred (55) (CBE 21).

WILLIAM PEIRCE (PIERCE)

On January 14, 1624, William Peirce (Pierce), master of the *Return*, was given a commission to go to Virginia (VCR 2:497).

HENRY PEIRCY

On November 6, 1622, Henry Peircy received some shares of Virginia land from Sir Henry Rich and his wife, Isabella, the daughter of Sir Walter Cope (VCR 2:122).

JOHN PEIRCY

In 1619 John Peircy, a burglar from Middlesex who was being detained at Newgate Prison, was sentenced to transportation overseas and most likely was sent to Virginia (CBE 12).

RICHARD PEIRSBY

On February 16, 1624, Richard Peirsby was living at Buckroe (17) in the corporation of Elizabeth City (CBE 45).

THOMAS PIERSMAN

According to Richard Frethorne, Thomas Piersman, a young servant, arrived at Martin's Hundred (7) around Christmastime, that is, in early January 1623. He died sometime prior to March 1623 at the home of William Harwood, the settlement's leader (VCR 4:60).

***

ABRAHAM PEIRSEY (PERSEY, PERSEYE, PEARSEY)

Virginia Company investor Abraham Peirsey (Persey, Perseye, Pearsey) of Maidstone in Kent, England, came to Virginia in 1616 on the *Susan,* the colony's first magazine ship. As Virginia's cape merchant, he was supposed to sell the magazine's goods profitably in exchange for tobacco and sassafras, but he also was authorized to trade freely. Peirsey escorted the *Susan* back to England and returned the following year on the *George,* another magazine ship. Afterward, he made Virginia his permanent residence. He served as vice-admiral during Deputy Governor Samuel Argall's government (1617–1618), and in 1622 he testified about the disposition of Lord Delaware's goods when the Neptune arrived in Jamestown (1) in August 1618. In July 1619 Peirsey participated in the colony's first assembly, representing his position as cape merchant. He sent word to England that many of the commodities he was supposed to sell to the colonists were relatively useless and that plows and other necessities were badly needed.

In August 1619 Abraham Peirsey accompanied Governor George Yeardley to Old Point Comfort (17), where they traded food for some Africans who had just arrived in a Dutch man-of-war. In November 1619 the Virginia Company rewarded Peirsey for his faithful service by giving him 200 acres. This land became part of the 1,150 acres called Peirseys Toile, which was located on the upper side of the Appomattox River near Swift's Creek and Bermuda Hundred (39). Abraham Peirsey went to England in March 1620 and returned with some servants, eight of whom were women. In April 1620 he was accused of price-gouging and wrongfully detaining the *George.* One of the men with whom Peirsey had business dealings was John Rolfe of Jamestown. In a May 24, 1621, letter, Peirsey said that he had sent Virginia Company Treasurer Sir Edwin Sandys some sturgeon and that the *George* had gone to Newfoundland for fish. He also dispatched a shipment of tobacco to the Netherlands.

On March 22, 1622, when the Indians attacked the Peirsey plantation on the Appomattox River, four people were killed. In May 1622 Abraham Peirsey testified against Captain John Martin, whom he accused of harboring debtors at his plantation and drawing arms against the provost marshal. On the other hand, Peirsey himself was accused of selling 10 cows that belonged to the Society of Martin's Hundred. When testifying in England in 1622, he identified himself as a 45-year-old "citizen and dyer of London but by profession Cape Merchant to the Virginia Company." Abraham Peirsey set sail from England on July 31, 1622, on the *James.* Afterward, he sent a shipment of Virginia sturgeon to Company officials in England. In 1623 he was one of the men selected to compile information on the Virginia colony, on the king's behalf.

When a census was made of the colony's inhabitants on February 16, 1624, Abraham Peirsey's name was omitted, perhaps because he was not then in Virginia. By that date he had purchased from Sir George Yeardley and his wife, Lady Temperance, the 1,000-acre Flowerdew Hundred (53) plantation and 2,200 acres across the James at Weyanoke (52). Peirsey also had use (and perhaps ownership) of some property in urban Jamestown, the focal point of his mercantile operations. On June 24, 1624, court testimony made reference to Peirsey's storehouse near the fort, and when a muster was taken on January 24, 1625, he was credited with a dwelling, two storehouses, and some livestock. Peirsey, who had been named to the Council of State, was then living in urban Jamestown with his daughters Mary (age 11) and Elizabeth (age 15), and his new wife, Frances Grenville (the widow of Nathaniel West). Four servants were part of the Peirsey household in Jamestown, and an additional 27 servants—including four who were black—were residing on his property at Peirsey's (formerly Flowerdew) Hundred,. Throughout this period Peirsey was identified as the colony's cape merchant. Abraham Peirsey's business dealings resulted in his frequently appearing before the General Court, for he brought suit against those who owed the Company (or him) funds and he was sued by his own creditors. He also was among those called to testify about the personal property attributable to the estates of people slain during the 1622 Indian attack. In May 1625 he was credited with 1,150 on the Appomattox River; 1,000 acres at Flowerdew Hundred; and 2,000 acres at Weyanoke. Among the

Jamestown people with whom Peirsey did business were Sir George Yeardley, Sir Samuel Argall, and Vice Admiral John Pountis. In 1626 he was named Robert Langley's administrator, and in 1627 he witnessed Sir George Yeardley's will. He also was among those who arbitrated disputes on behalf of the General Court. Peirsey occasionally was accused of selling overpriced commodities, and in October 1626 he was ordered to settle his debt to the magazine's adventurers. In April 1626 John Upton was ordered to serve Abraham Peirsey for eight months. Peirsey had problems with some of his servants at Peirsey's Hundred—Alice Chambers became pregnant, and later some of his servants were accused of lewd behavior.

In October 1626, when officials were concerned about a possible Indian attack, Abraham Peirsey was ordered to impale (fence in) all of the unsecured houses on his plantation at Peirseys Hundred. He was a successful planter and, according to Captain John Smith, planned to sow 200 acres of English wheat and an equal amount of barley, enough to feed 60 people. On March 1, 1627, Abraham Peirsey, who was living at Flowerdew Hundred, made his will and requested a simple burial in his plantation's garden. He left his widow, Frances, her dower third of his estate and made a bequest to his stepson, Nathaniel West. His principal heirs were his daughters Elizabeth and Mary Peirsey. He named Richard Kingsmill and the Rev. Grivel Pooley as overseers of his Virginia estate and asked London merchant Delyonel (Delyonell) Russell to take charge of his business affairs in England. Abraham Peirsey died in Virginia around January 16, 1628, and his will was presented to the General Court on February 8th. The widowed Frances Peiresy submitted an inventory of his estate on March 24, 1628, a document that was found to be accurate. By May 10, 1633, when the late Abraham Peirsey's will was presented to English probate officials, the widowed Frances Peirsey (who later married Samuel Mathews) was dead, and Abraham's daughter Mary Peirsey Hill was named administrator (STAN 24, 31; WITH 80-81, 133; VCR 1:240, 261, 263, 273, 331-333, 364-365, 400, 504-505, 608; 2:43, 132; 3:153, 162, 243, 454; 4:464-465, 501, 554, 556; CJS 2:280, 301; 3:216; FER 253, 400; C 24/486, 24/489, 24/490; CO 1/8 ff 15-18; SR 3966, 9946; SAIN 1:58, 176; MCGC 15, 27, 36, 38-39, 47, 54-55, 71, 73-74, 76-78, 84-85, 87, 117-118, 120, 132, 134, 136, 144, 154, 156-157, 165, 168; PB 1 Pt. 1:19; Pt. 2:484; CBE 55, 70-71, 73, 107, 113; EEAC 19, 45; SH 7; G&M 189; EAE 89; DOR 1:23-24, 31; 2:801-803).

ELIZABETH DRAPER PEIRSEY (PERSEY, PERSEYE, PEARSEY) (MRS. ABRAHAM PEIRSEY [PERSEY, PERSEYE, PEARSEY])

Elizabeth, the daughter of Elizabeth and Clement Draper of St. Clement in London, married cape merchant Abraham Peirsey (Persey, Perseye, Pearsey). In November 1619 she asked the Virginia Company to grant her husband some land on account of his lengthy service to the colony. Abraham Peirsey and Elizabeth produced two surviving children, Mary and Elizabeth, and probably accompanied them to Virginia in 1623 on the *Southampton*. Mrs. Elizabeth Peirsey died in Jamestown (1) sometime after February 16, 1624, but before January 24, 1625 (CBE 19, 56; VCR 1:263, 334; WITH 133; SR 3966; DOR 1:31; 2:803).

FRANCES (FRANCIS) GRENVILLE PEIRSEY (PERSEY, PERSEYE, PEARSEY) (MRS. ABRAHAM PEIRSEY [PERSEY, PERSEYE, PEARSEY]) (SEE FRANCES GRENVILLE, MRS. NATHANIEL WEST, MRS. SAMUEL MATHEWS)

Frances Grenville came to Virginia on the *Supply* in 1620 with the family of William Tracy, who were headed for Berkeley Hundred (55). She married Lord Delaware's brother, Nathaniel West of West and Shirley Hundred (41), whom she outlived. Afterward, she joined the household headed by her brother-in-law John West. Sometime after February 16, 1624, but before early 1625, Frances moved to Elizabeth City (17), where she and her son shared Captain Francis West's home. The widowed Frances Grenville West wed Abraham Peirsey (Persey, Perseye, Pearsey) of Flowerdew Hundred (53) later in the year. She outlived him and on March 24, 1628, informed the General Court that she had inventoried his estate accurately. Later, she married Samuel Mathews I of Denbigh (23). She died sometime prior to May 10, 1633 (CBE 40, 67; MCGC 168; DOR 1:31; 2:803).

ELIZABETH PEIRSEY (PERSEY, PERSEYE, PEARSEY) (MRS. RICHARD STEPHENS, MRS. JOHN HARVEY) (SEE MRS. RICHARD STEPHENS, MRS. JOHN HARVEY)

Elizabeth Peirsey (Persey, Perseye, Pearsey) came to Virginia in 1623 with her sister, Mary, on the *Southampton*, a vessel owned by Captain John Harvey. The girls were the daughters of Abraham Peirsey and his wife, the former Elizabeth Draper. On January 24, 1625, Elizabeth was 15 years old and living in urban Jamestown (1) with her recently widowed father and her sister, Mary. Later in the year she and her sister probably accompanied their father to Flowerdew Hundred (53), the plantation he had purchased from Sir George Yeardley. Around 1628 Elizabeth married Richard Stephens, a Jamestown merchant, with whom she produced a son, Samuel. After the death of Richard Stephens in 1636, Elizabeth married Governor John Harvey of Jamestown, a titled nobleman many years her senior and one of her late husband's enemies. After Sir John Harvey fell on hard times and was replaced as governor, he and Elizabeth returned to England. She died there sometime prior to September 15, 1646, when Sir John Harvey made his will (CBE 55; SH 7; SR 3966; PB 1 Pt. 2:484; DOR 1:31; 2:804-805).

MARY PEIRSEY (PERSEY, PERSEYE, PEARSEY) (MRS. THOMAS HILL, MRS. THOMAS BUSHROD)

Mary, the daughter of Abraham and Elizabeth Draper Peirsey (Persey, Perseye, Pearsey), was born around 1614 and came to Virginia in 1623 with her mother and older sister, Elizabeth, on the *Southampton*. On January 24, 1625, Mary was living in her father's household in urban Jamestown (1) and was age 11. Later in the year she and her sister probably accompanied their father to Flowerdew Hundred (53), the plantation he had purchased from Sir George Yeardley. By May 1633 Mary Peirsey had married Captain Thomas Hill of Stanley Hundred (22) in what became Warwick County. She was named administrator of her late father's estate in 1635, by which time her stepmother, Frances, was de-

ceased. Controversy ensued, for it was alleged that her stepmother's widower, Samuel Mathews I, had depleted the late Abraham Peirsey's estate. After Thomas Hill's decease in 1657, Mary Peirsey Hill married Thomas Bushrod of York County, who outlived her (CBE 55; SH 7; SR 3966; DOR 1:31; 2:805-806).

JOHN PEIRSEY (PERSEY, PERSEYE, PEARSEY)

On June 30, 1633, John Peirsey (Persey, Perseye, Pearsey), the brother of the late Abraham Peirsey, claimed that he was unable to collect a debt from the decedent's widow, Frances, who had married Samuel Mathews I of Denbigh (23) (G&M 189).

***

HENRY PELHAM

On June 10, 1622, Captain Henry Pelham and his associates were identified as holders of a patent for a particular plantation. On November 12, 1622, the Virginia Company confirmed the Pelham group's patent (VCR 1:404; 3:643).

THOMAS PELLITARY

On August 10, 1622, officials at Bridewell decided that Thomas Pellitary, a vagrant from Lime Street, would be transported to Virginia (CBE 28).

SAMPSON PELSANT

Sampson Pelsant died in Elizabeth City (17, 18) sometime after April 1623 but before February 16, 1624 (CBE 45).

WOLSTON PELSANT

Wolston Pelsant died in Elizabeth City (17, 18) sometime after April 1623 but before February 16, 1624 (CBE 45).

ABRAHAM PELTEARE (PELTERRE)

Abraham Pelteare (Pelterre) came to Virginia on the *Swann* in 1624 and in early 1625 was living in Elizabeth City (18), where he was a servant in John Hazard's household. On August 28, 1626, Sir George Yeardley presented the General Court with a petition submitted by Abraham's widowed mother, Margaret Pelteare, of St. Mary Stayning Parish, England. It stated that although Abraham had gone to Virginia to serve as Humphrey Rastall's apprentice for 7 years and was not an indentured servant, Rastall had sold Abraham's contract to John Hazard, who later transferred it to Robert Thresher. The General Court ordered Hazard and Thresher to pay Abraham Pelteare for his service. Afterward, the youth was entrusted to Sir George Yeardley's care. He may have lived in the Yeardley home in Jamestown (1) or on one of Sir George's outlying properties (CBE 64; MCGC 109).

GEORGE PELTON ALIAS STRAYTON

George Pelton alias Strayton went to England on the *Furtherance* in May or June 1622, setting sail from Isle of Wight before word of the 1622 Indian attack reached England. On February 4, 1625, Pelton was living at Burrows Hill (8), where he headed his own household, which had a modest supply of stored food. In 1649, when *A New Description of Virginia* was published, the writer stated that Mr. George Pelton alias Strayton, an ancient planter who had been in Virginia for 25 years, was a beekeeper and maker of Matheglin, a liquor. Significantly, although Pelton had been in Virginia more than 25 years, he was not an "ancient planter" in the legal sense (CBE 28; VCR 3:618-619, 674; FOR 2:8:5; DOR 1:38).

[NO FIRST NAME] PEMBERTON

On July 3, 1622, the Virginia Company assigned Mr. Pemberton, a minister, some Virginia land (VCR 2:74).

THOMAS PEMBIE

On February 27, 1622, Hiddlebrand Preiwsen assigned to Thomas Pembie a share of Virginia land. Virginia Company officials updated their records accordingly (VCR 1:608).

EARL OF PEMBROKE

In January 1622 Virginia Company officials noted that the Earl of Pembroke was interested in land that lay to the south of the colonized area, probably in the territory that became known as Carolina (VCR 3:587).

[NO FIRST NAME] PENECELL

On March 20, 1620, Virginia Company learned that Mr. Penecell, a mariner employed on the *Treasurer*, was being detained in Bermuda. He reportedly wanted to be returned to Virginia (VCR 1:323).

RICHARD PENN

On April 26, 1633, officials at Bridewell decided that Richard Penn, a vagrant brought in from Candlewick Ward, would be sent to Virginia (CBE 107).

ROBERT PENN

Robert Penn came to Virginia on the *Abigail* in 1620 and on February 4, 1625, was living on the lower side of the James River on Captain Samuel Mathews' plantation (15), where he was a 22-year-old servant. On May 6, 1629, when Robert Penn testified before the General Court in a case involving William Ewen, he identified himself as a Virginia planter and said that he was age 25. He also stated that he had known Ewen for nine years and had worked for him. Robert Penn's testimony concerned the *Saker*'s bringing an African to the Ewen's plantation (13), which was close to the Mathews property (CBE 60; EAE 19).

WILLIAM PENNINGE

In July 1623, William Penninge of St. Boltoph Aldgate, London, made his will when preparing to depart for Virginia (CBE 33).

JEREMY PENNINGTON

Jeremy Pennington set sail from England on July 31, 1622, on the *James* and was among those accompanying William Cradock to Virginia (FER 400).

JOHN PENNINGTON (PENINGTON)

John Pennington (Penington) came to Virginia in 1607 and was one of the first Jamestown (1) colonists (CJS 2:141).

MATHEWE PENNINGTON

On February 27, 1619, the Bridewell Court decided that Mathewe Pennington, a boy, would be sent to Virginia. He was part of a large group of children rounded up from the streets of London so that they could be transported to the colony (CBE 12).

ROBERT PENNINGTON (PENINGTON)

Robert Pennington (Penington) came to Virginia in 1607 and was one of the first colonists. He died in Jamestown (1) on August 18, 1607. In 1620 he was identified as a Virginia Company investor (CJS 1:20; 2:280; HAI 99).

JOHN PENNY

John Penny came to Virginia in 1621 on the *Temperance* at the expense of Sir George Yeardley. Afterward, Yeardley assigned Penny's headright to Thomas Flint, who used it when patenting some land on September 20, 1628 (MCGC 166; PB 1 Pt. 1:59).

JOHN PENRISE (PENRICE)

In early September 1623, John Penrise (Penrice) sent a petition to the governor, requesting permission to trade for corn in the Chesapeake Bay. He said that he had authorization from his superiors in Southampton Hundred (44) and wanted to trade even though Captain Isaac Madison was doing so. On February 16, 1624, John Penrise was living in Elizabeth City (18). On January 30, 1626, he was among the several Elizabeth City men accused of going aboard the *Grace* without permission to do so. For breaking the law, he was fined and made to post a bond guaranteeing his good behavior. On January 12, 1627, John Penrise was identified as a Virginia Company tenant who was being assigned to Captain William Tucker. Two weeks later, his year-old peace bond was revoked because of his good behavior (VCR 4:275-277; MCGC 91-92, 137).

ROBERT PENRISE (PENRICE)

Robert Penrise (Penrice) came to Virginia on the *Bona Nova* in 1620 and in early 1625 was identified as a 12-year-old servant in the Elizabeth City (18) household of Edward Waters (CBE 66).

HENRY PENRY

On August 18, 1619, Henry Penry was identified as master of the ship *Margaret* of Bristol, which was leaving England on September 15th (VCR 3:193-195).

WILLIAM PENRYN

In August 1635 it was reported that William Penryn and others who had been in England in May had received some tobacco from Richard Bennett, who was associated with Warresqueak (26) (EAE 54).

JOHN PENTON

John Penton came to Virginia in 1628 on the *Hopewell* at the expense of Adam Thorogood, who used his headright when patenting some land on June 24, 1635 (PB 1 Pt. 1:179).

EDWARD PEPPETT

In November 1625 Lieutenant Edward Peppett testified that Simon Tuching had been diligent about sounding the depths of the James River and other tributaries of the Chesapeake Bay. He also said that Tuching had admitted to being banished from Ireland and England and claimed to care nothing for his kindred (MCGC 33-34).

***

GILBERT PEPPETT (PEPPER)

Gilbert Peppett (Pepper) came to Virginia sometime prior to May 12, 1623, when he was authorized to trade for corn within the Chesapeake Bay area. He was living at Sir George Yeardley's plantation, Flowerdew Hundred (53), on February 16, 1624, and married Alice, a woman Yeardley brought to the colony in 1619. On December 27, 1624, Lieutenant Gilbert Peppett testified before the General Court in a matter involving Yeardley and Captain John Martin. In February 1625 Virginia Company officials decided to have Peppett questioned by Yeardley. Later, he was summoned by the General Court whose justices wanted to know why he had rejected some of Yeardley's tobacco, which he claimed was of poor quality. Three months later Gilbert Peppett testified that he had been at Captain William Tucker's house in Elizabeth City (18) when he witnessed an agreement between two men. When a list of patented land was sent back to England in May 1625, Peppett was credited with 50 acres at

Blunt Point (**22**), land he had seated and to which he was entitled on account of his personal adventure. In August 1627 he patented 250 acres in the same vicinity, using several headrights that he had procured from other people. In November 1628 Lieutenant Gilbert Peppett testified about some inflammatory statements made by Lieutenant Thomas Flint at Robert Poole's house. By that time Gilbert's wife, Alice, was dead, and he had wed a woman named Lucy. Gilbert Peppett died sometime prior to March 4, 1629, when Zachary Cripps and George Woodcocke proved his will. Afterward, Cripps bought his land at the mouth of the Warwick River (VCR 4:189, 517, 557; MCGC 37, 46, 130, 151, 177, 189-190; PB 1 Pt. 1:50).

ALICE PEPPETT (PEPPER) (MRS. GILBERT PEPPETT [PEPPER])

Alice, the wife of Lieutenant Gilbert Peppett (Pepper), came to Virginia in 1619 on the *Jonathan* at the expense of Sir George Yeardley. Yeardley later transferred Alice's headright to Peppett, who used it on August 18, 1627, when patenting some land on the Warwick River (PB 1 Pt. 1:50).

LUCY PEPPETT (PEPPER) (MRS. GILBERT PEPPETT [PEPPER])

In November 1628 Lucy, the wife of Lieutenant Gilbert Peppett (Pepper), testified that when she was at Robert Poole's house, she heard Lieutenant Thomas Flint criticize the governor (MCGC 177).

***

BARTHOLOMEW PERAM (PERRAM)

Bartholomew Peram (Perram) was killed at Falling Creek (**68**), Captain Berkeley's plantation, during the March 22, 1622, Indian attack (VCR 3:565).

GILES PERAM (PERRAM)

Giles Peram (Perram) was killed at Falling Creek (**68**) at Captain Berkeley's plantation during the March 22, 1622, Indian attack (VCR 3:565).

GEORGE PERCY

George Percy, a gentleman and brother of the Earl of Northumberland, was one of the first Jamestown (**1**) colonists. He left London on December 20, 1606, and arrived in Virginia in late April 1607. Thanks to Percy, there is a written description of the colonists' first few weeks and the hardships they experienced. He wrote about interaction with the Indians and the first fort the settlers built. He chronicled some of the colonists' explorations and accompanied Captain John Smith on visits to Werowocomoco and Pamunkey. He also had dealings with the Pasbehay and Chickahominy Indians. Percy was president of the Virginia colony from September 1609 to May 1610, vacating office as soon as Sir Thomas Gates arrived. Thus, he presided over the colony during the infamous "starving time," when many colonists perished for lack of nourishment. Gates surrendered the reins of government to Lord Delaware, and when Delaware left the colony in March 1611, Percy became deputy governor. He served in that capacity until Sir Thomas Dale's arrival in May 1611. George Percy left Virginia in late April 1612 on the *Trial* and reached England during the summer. After publication of Captain John Smith's *General History*, which Percy viewed as unjustly critical, he wrote *A Trewe Relacyon,* which described conditions and events in the colony from 1609 to 1612. In that account Percy mentioned his dwelling in Jamestown, spoke of participating in a march against the Chickahominy and Pasbehay Indians, and said that one Indian who was slain was brought to the fort and buried. He described how Sir Thomas Gates and Sir George Somers were marooned in Bermuda and said that when Gates's fleet was seen approaching Jamestown in August 1611, the colonists mistook it for Spanish ships and began preparing for an attack. Because Sir Thomas Dale thought the settlers might flee if their fort came under fire, he ordered them aboard ships so that they would be compelled to defend the colony. George Percy died in England in 1632 (HAI 85, 90-94, 98-99, 102, 199, 354, 418-419, 433, 459, 499-519, 558-559, 899; CJS 1:128, 193-194, 208, 239, 243, 251-252, 263, 432; 2:140, 181, 186, 189, 192-193, 210, 213, 216, 220, 255; 3:285; STAN 13, 28; FOR 1:7:13).

JOHN PERCY (PERCIE)

John Percy (Percie) came to Virginia in 1628 on the *Hopewell* at the expense of

Adam Thorogood, who used his headright when securing a patent on June 24, 1635 (PB 1 Pt. 1:179).

ANTONIO PEREOS (PEREZ)

In June 1611 Antonio Pereos (Perez), Diego de Molina (Malinos), and a renegade English pilot named Limbreck were aboard a Spanish ship when it entered the mouth of the James River and paused near Old Point Comfort (**17**). They were captured and detained. In May 1613 Molina said that Pereos, whom he termed a good soldier, had died from hunger after he was in the colony a few months (HAI 515-516, 750).

WILLIAM PERIGO

William Perigo was killed at Henricus Island (**63**) during the March 22, 1622, Indian attack (VCR 3:565).

FRANCIS PERIN

On September 28, 1628, Francis Perin was delivered to the Rev. Lewis Hughs so that he could be sent to Virginia (CBE 84).

RICHARD PERIN (PERRIN)

Richard Perin (Perrin), a Virginia planter who was in England between June 1638 and February 1639, stated that he had land in the colony and intended to stock it from the *Elizabeth*. Perin indicated that he was age 26 and was from All Hallows, Barking, London (EAE 90).

THOMAS PERIN (PERYN)

On November 20, 1622, officials at Bridewell decided that Thomas Perin (Peryn), who was being detained at Newgate, would be transported overseas (CBE 29).

***

FRANCIS PERKINS I

Francis Perkins I and his son, Francis II, left Gravesend, England, on October 8, 1607, and arrived in Jamestown (**1**) on January 4, 1608, in the 1st Supply of new settlers. In a letter Francis I sent to a friend in England on March 28, 1608, he said that on January 7th a fire had consumed all but three buildings in the fort and that he and his son lost all of their possessions onshore. Francis asked for some clothing, as his had burned, and he also expressed his desire to be appointed to the Council. In his *General History* Captain John Smith described Francis Perkins I as a gentleman (CJS 1:161; 2:223; HAI 131-133, 131, 135).

FRANCIS PERKINS II

Francis Perkins II, the son of Francis Perkins I, came to Virginia in the 1st Supply of new colonists and arrived in Jamestown (**1**) in January 1608. According to Captain John Smith, the younger Francis Perkins was a laborer (CJS 1:223; 2:161).

***

WILLIAM PERKINS

On August 16, 1627, William Perkins shipped goods from London to Virginia on the *Truelove* (CBE 79).

DANIEL PERMAN

Virginia Company records indicate that on December 17, 1622, meal was sent to Daniel Perman at Martin's Hundred (**7**) (FER 435).

[NO FIRST NAME] PERRY

After April 1628 but before October 1628, the justices of the General Court decided that Mr. Perry's shallop should be repaired at Edmund Barker's expense and returned to its proper owner. Court minutes suggest that Barker sold the shallop to Humphrey Rastall's men without the legal right to do so. It is likely that the Mr. Perry whose shallop was wrongfully sold was John or William Perry (MCGC 173).

ALEXANDER PERRY

On September 30, 1627, officials at Bridewell decided that Alexander Perry, who had been brought in from Cripplegate, would be sent to Virginia (CBE 80).

GEORGE PERRY

When a list of patented land was sent from Virginia to England in May 1625, George Perry was credited with 100 acres of land in Archer's Hope (**6**) (VCR 4:556).

JOHN PERRY

On July 8, 1627, John Perry, a London merchant, shipped cloth goods and footwear from London to Virginia on the *Ann Fortune*. By June 22, 1628, he had gone to Virginia and was at Perry's (later, Swann's) Point (**9**) within the corporation of James City. It was then that he made his will, indicating that he was from St. Antholin's Parish in London. The testator made bequests to several people in England and identified London merchant Richard Perry as his brother when naming him as executor. John Perry died in Jamestown (**1**) sometime prior to December 1628, when William Perry, a gentleman, presented John's will to the General Court and vouched for its authenticity (CBE 45, 78-79, 87; SH 10; MCGC 173; EEAC 45; SR 3482; SH 10).

JOHN PERRY

John Perry was killed at the College (**66**) during the March 22, 1622, Indian attack and probably was one of the Virginia Company's servants or tenants (VCR 3:566).

RICHARD PERRY

On June 5, 1623, Richard Perry, John Newman, Robert Watson, and John Bland were identified as owners of the *Abigail* and on July 7, 1628, Richard was identified as someone who had shipped goods from London to Virginia on the *Ann Fortune*. He claimed that he was defrauded after the ship's master, James Carter, became ill. In July 1635 Richard Perry was described as a London merchant and the former master of John Davis and John Rishton. When John Davis patented 50 acres of land on July 4, 1635 on the east side of Jockey's Neck, in Archer's Hope (**6**), he noted that the land was being transferred to him by his former master, Richard Perry, in accord with a covenant they had made. Likewise, on July 7, 1635, when John Rishton patented 50 acres on the lower side of the James River, he cited a similar covenant. Rishton's land was on the "great creek" opposite Jamestown, probably Gray's Creek, where members of the Perry family owned land in the immediate vicinity of Paces Paines (**9**) and the promontory known as Perry's (or Swann's) Point (VCR 2:455; CBE 78-79; PB 1 Pt. 1:204, 211).

SAMUEL PERRY

On November 7, 1634, Samuel Perry was among those in Virginia certifying a list of goods that the newly arrived but deceased Thomas Lee had brought to the colony (CBE 208).

***

WILLIAM PERRY

William Perry, an ancient planter, immigrated to Virginia in 1611. He patented 100 acres on the south side of the James River, within the corporation of Henrico and below The Falls (**67**), but seems to have withdrawn to Jamestown Island (**1**) in the wake of the March 1622 Indian attack. In April 1622 Captain William Perry was identified as one of four people who had cleared acreage at Hog Island (**16**). During 1623 he married the recently widowed Isabell Smythe Pace of Paces Paines (**9**). He was among those who went to England in early 1624 to ask the Virginia Company for tax relief because of the losses sustained during the March 1622 Indian attack. William Perry, who was accompanied by an Indian boy, also asked for funds that could be spent rearing the boy in the Christian faith. In February 1624 Mrs. Isabell Perry and her infant son were living in urban Jamestown, perhaps because her husband was abroad. In 1627 Isabell Pace Perry patented a 100-acre tract adjacent to the 100 acres she already owned at Paces Paines, land to which she was entitled as an ancient planter. William and Isabell Perry probably resided at Paces Paines until they moved to Charles City during the 1630s.

Over the years, William Perry made numerous appearances before the General Court, often testifying about local events. He was a witness in a lawsuit involving some Hog Island acreage for which William Powell and Samuel Mathews filed conflicting claims, and he also testified against Samuel Argall in April 1625. Perry blamed his Paces Paines neighbor, John Proctor, for losing his shallop and demanded compensation. He was chosen to oversee the wills made by Robert Langley and Alexander George. He also made an inventory of Francis Weekes's estate, and he proved the will of London merchant John Perry, who in 1628 was at Perry's (later, Swann's) Point. Sometime prior to 1629 William

Perry was placed in command of the settlers living in the vicinity of Paces Paines and Smith's Mount (Burrows Hill) **(8)**, a neighboring plantation, and he served as the area's burgess in the assemblies of 1629, 1630, and 1632. In 1632 the territory he represented extended from Paces Paines downstream to Hog Island.

Lieutenant William Perry was named to the Council of State in 1632 and held office until 1637. On September 19, 1633, he was granted some land in the corporation of Charles City, acreage on which he established a plantation called Buckland. He may have been looking ahead to the time when his stepson, George Pace, would take possession of his late father's acreage at Paces Paines. Captain William Perry made his will on August 1, 1637, and died five days later. He named as heirs his wife, Isabell, their son, Henry (his primary heir), and his brother-in-law, William Mercer, a London haberdasher. William Perry was interred in the graveyard at Westover Church in Charles City County. In 1641 George Menefie filed a claim on behalf of the late William Perry's estate, noting that for a decade he and the decedent had reared a Tappahannah Indian boy as a Christian and therefore were entitled to compensation (MCGC 51-52, 63, 65, 78, 83, 87, 151-152, 158-159, 173, 192, 477-478; NUG 1:120; PB 1 Pt 1:62; Pt 2:702; HEN 1:138, 148, 150, 153-154, 178, 202; CJS 2:297; VCR 2:519, 532, 538; 4:552, 555; STAN 32, 54-56; WITH 184; DOR 2:815-816; SH 10).

ISABELL (IZABELLA) SMYTHE PACE PERRY (MRS. WILLIAM PERRY, MRS. GEORGE MENEFIE [MENEFY])
(SEE MRS. RICHARD PACE, MRS. GEORGE MENEFIE [MENEFY])

In October 1608, Isabell (Izabella) Smythe married Richard Pace, with whom she immigrated to Virginia sometime prior to 1616. Ancient planters Isabell and Richard had a son, George, who in 1628 was described as Richard's heir apparent. On December 5, 1620, the Paces patented 200 acres of land on the lower side of the James River, developing it into their plantation, Paces Paines **(9)**. After the March 22, 1622, Indian attack, the Paces moved to Jamestown Island **(1)**, where they lived for several months. However, they went back to

their own plantation as soon as they were allowed to return. By February 16, 1624, Isabell Pace was widowed and married her neighbor, ancient planter William Perry. She returned to Jamestown with her infant, perhaps their son, Henry Perry. In May 1625 Mrs. Isabell Perry went to court to testify about an incident in Jamestown that involved Mrs. Margaret Blaney and Dr. John Pott. She also described certain events that had transpired during Sir Thomas Dale's government, and she repeated some potentially libelous comments that Captain John Martin of Martin's Brandon **(59)** had made in her presence. In January 1626 Isabell testified that Robert Langley, who became ill, died in her home on the lower side of the James River. Later in the year she offered testimony about Mrs. Margaret Wright, a woman accused of practicing witchcraft.

In October 1627 Mrs. Isabell Smythe Pace Perry was assigned some land on Jamestown Island, acreage she was obliged to develop within three years or forfeit. Three months later she obtained a 100-acre tract from Richard Richards and Richard Dolphenby, a parcel that adjoined the east side of the late Richard Pace's portion of Paces Paines. In September 1628 Isabell repatented her newly purchased acreage and her original 100-acre share of Paces Paines, which abutted west on Burrows Hill **(8)**. Her parcels flanked the 400-acre riverfront tract that her eldest son, George Pace, had inherited from his father, ancient planter Richard Pace. It is probable that Isabell and William Perry occupied the Paces Paines property until they became established at Buckland in the early 1630s. When Isabell Perry testified in August 1629 about the last wishes of London merchant, John Riley, who died at her husband's home in Virginia, she said that she was 40 years old. After Captain William Perry's death in August 1637, Isabell married Jamestown merchant George Menefie (Menefy), whom she predeceased (VCR 3:55, 682; NUG 1:10; PB 1:Pt 1:62, 64; MCGC 58, 62-63, 65, 83-84, 111-112, 155, 159; CBE 38; EAE 21; DOR 2:815-816).

[NO FIRST NAME] PERRY

On February 16, 1624, Mrs. Isabell Pace Perry was living in Jamestown **(1)** with her infant, perhaps her son Henry Perry (CBE 38).

HENRY PERRY

Henry Perry was the son of Captain William Perry and his wife, the former Isabell (Izabella) Smythe, the widow of Richard Pace of Paces Paines (**9**). In 1633 William Perry, who was named to the Council of State in 1632 and served until 1637, was granted some land in the corporation of Charles City, acreage on which he established a plantation called Buckland. William Perry made his will on August 1, 1637 and died five days later. He made a bequest to his wife, Isabell, but named their son, Henry, as his primary heir. Henry Perry inherited his late father's 2,000-acre plantation called Buckland, which he repatented in August 1637. The twice-widowed Isabell Pace Perry married Jamestown merchant George Menefie (Menefy), who took up residence at the Perry home, Buckland. Henry Perry eventually married his stepsister, Elizabeth Menefie (Menefy), heir to her late father's property in Jamestown (**1**). The Perrys made their home at Buckland. Henry was named to the Council of State in 1655 and died sometime after April 1663 (MEY 487-488; PB 1 Pt. 2:510; WITH 180-181; STAN 36; DOR 2:816-818).

ELIZABETH MENEFIE PERRY (MRS. HENRY PERRY) (SEE ELIZABETH MENEFIE [MENEFY])

Elizabeth Menefie, the daughter of George Menefie (Menefy) and his first wife, Elizabeth, married her stepbrother, Henry Perry, sometime after 1646. The couple made their home at Buckland, the Perry plantation in Charles City County. Elizabeth inherited her late father's lot in urban Jamestown (**1**). The Perrys disposed of it sometime prior to 1656 (MEY 449; AMB 27; PB 4:228; HEN 1:516; DOR 2:817-818).

***

EDWARD PERSE (PERCE)

On January 29, 1620, the Bridewell Court decided that Edward Perse (Perce) would be sent to Virginia (CBE 17).

WILLIAM PERSE (PERCE)

According to Captain John Smith, William Perse (Perce), a laborer, came to Virginia in the 1st Supply of new colonists. Therefore, he was one of the first Jamestown (**1**) settlers (CJS 1:223; 2:161).

ELIZABETH PERSONS (MRS. THOMAS POWELL)

On November 26, 1609, Elizabeth Persons, Mrs. Horton's maid, married Thomas Powell in Bermuda, where they were stranded. They were part of the 3rd Supply of new settlers and had accompanied Sir Thomas Gates and Sir George Somers on their voyage to Virginia (HAI 413).

***

HENRICK PETERSON

Henrick Peterson, his wife, Alice, and their son, William, were killed at William Farrar's house on the east side of the Appomattox River near Charles City (**39**) during the March 22, 1622, Indian attack (VCR 3:566).

ALICE PETERSON (MRS. HENRICK PETERSON)

Alice Peterson, her husband, Henrick, and their son, William, were killed at William Farrar's house on the east side of the Appomattox River near Charles City (**39**) during the March 22, 1622, Indian attack (VCR 3:566).

WILLIAM PETERSON

William Peterson and his parents, Alice and Henrick Peterson, were killed at William Farrer's house on the Appomattox River near Charles City (**39**) during the March 22, 1622, Indian attack. William was a child (VCR 3:566).

***

JOHN PETERSON

In May 1625, when a list of patented land was sent from Virginia to England, John Peterson was credited with 100 acres on the south side of the James River, below The Falls (**67**) and within the corporation of Henrico (VCR 4:552).

ARTHUR PETT

Arthur Pett, master of the *Unity* and a Virginia Company member, made his will on

August 30, 1609. He became ill on the way to Virginia with Sir George Somers and died aboard the *Blessing* while it was anchored in Jamestown (1). Pett's will was presented for probate on March 10, 1611. The testator made bequests to his wife, Florence, and 10-year-old daughter, Elizabeth, who were in England (WITH 47; CBE 4).

ELIZABETH PETT

On November 20, 1622, it was decided that Elizabeth Pett, who was being detained in Newgate Prison, would be pardoned and sent overseas because of an outbreak of jail fever (CBE 29).

ARON PETTER

On February 5, 1620, officials at Bridewell decided that Aron Petter, who had been brought in, would be sent to Virginia (CBE 18).

JOHN PETTIE (PETTEY)

John Pettie (Pettey), who on May 8, 1622, identified himself as a 47-year-old citizen and barber surgeon of St. Olave's Parish, Southwark, in London, testified in a suit that Lord Delaware's heirs brought against Sir Samuel Argall. The plaintiffs claimed that Argall had seized Delaware's goods and had put Edward Brewster (one of Lord Delaware's men) on trial in a court martial hearing. They also asserted that Delaware's men had been put aboard Argall's ship, the *Treasurer*, and sent to the West Indies. Pettie, who appears to have been an eyewitness, sided with Argall. He said that Brewster was disliked by most of those aboard the *Neptune* and that after Lord Delaware's people arrived in Jamestown (1), they would have perished had it not been for Argall's timely intervention. Pettie also contended that Brewster had asked Argall to put Delaware's men on the *Treasurer* and that those who remained on land died while trying to fend for themselves. When John Pettie testified a second time in 1624, he identified himself as a resident of Walthamstow, in Essex (SR 9947; EAE 13).

ROBERT PETTUS (PETTIS)

On December 31, 1619, officials at Bridewell decided that Robert Pettus (Pettis),

who had been brought in by the marshal of Middlesex, would be sent to Virginia (CBE 14).

THEODORE PETTUS

Theodore Pettus, a gentleman from Norwich, arrived in Jamestown (1) on September 12, 1623, on the *Bonny Bess* and took the oath of supremacy. On November 6, 1626, he testified about mariner James Carter's statements with regard to the tobacco belonging to John Trehern of Chaplin's Choice (56) (MCGC 6, 126-127).

THOMAS PHELPS

According to Captain John Smith, Thomas Phelps, a tradesman, came to Virginia in 1608 as part of the 2nd Supply. Therefore, he resided in Jamestown (1) (CJS 1:241; 2:191).

[NO FIRST NAME] PHETIPLACE

In 1609–1610, when Captains Phetiplace and Ratcliffe set out from Jamestown (1) on a trading voyage, they visited Powhatan. Ratcliffe was ambushed and killed at Powhatan's behest. Phetiplace may have suffered a similar fate (HAI 504).

THOMAS PHILDUST

Thomas Phildust, one of Sir George Yeardley's servants, came to Virginia in 1620 aboard the *Temperance* and on January 24, 1625, was living in the Yeardley household in urban Jamestown (1). Thomas was then described as age 15 (CBE 54).

PHILLIP

On February 16, 1624, a man known as Phillip was living on the Eastern Shore (CBE 46).

ELEANOR PHILIPS

On September 5, 1622, Eleanor Philips, who was in England, agreed to underwrite the cost of Daniel Franck's transportation to Virginia. He was a convicted criminal, and after he had been living in the colony for a short time, he was found guilty of theft. On February 16, 1624, Franck was listed among those who had died at West and

Shirley Hundred (41) sometime after April 1623. On June 5, 1633, Elmer Phillips used Daniel Franck as a headright and indicated that both of them had come to Virginia on the *Southampton* in 1622. This raises the possibility that there was a familial relationship between Eleanor and Elmer Philips (CBE 27, 36; VCR 2:102; MCGC 4-5; PB 1 Pt. 1:123).

ELMER PHILIPS (PHILLIPS)

Elmer Philips (Phillips) came to Virginia in 1622 on the *Southampton*. On August 21, 1626, Elmer, a former resident of West and Shirley Hundred (41) who was living on Jamestown Island (1), testified that he heard Richard Allford, one of Captain Roger Smith's servants, admit that he owed work to Robert Marshall. A month later Philips testified about an event that occurred at Jordan's Point (46), and in September 1627 he certified John Crannidge's will. By September 20, 1628, Elmer Philips had patented some land on Jamestown Island. He apparently was residing there in January 1629 when he served on a jury twice and certified that the will of Abraham Porter (also of Jamestown) was authentic. By June 5, 1633, Elmer had moved to Elizabeth City. It was then that he patented 100 acres near Fox Hill (19), using himself and the late Daniel Franck as headrights (MCGC 108, 113-114, 153, 184, 187, 190; PB 1 Pt. 1:92, 123).

HENRY PHILLIPS

On February 16, 1624, Henry Phillips was living at Warresqueak (26), the Bennett plantation (CBE 42).

JOHN PHILLIPS

John Philips died in Elizabeth City (17, 18) sometime after April 1623 but before February 16, 1624 (CBE 45).

JOHN PHILIPS (PHILLIPS)

John Philips (Phillips) came to Virginia in 1621 on the *Temperance* at the expense of Sir George Yeardley, who later assigned his headright to Thomas Flint. On March 22, 1622, when the Indians attacked Flowerdew Hundred (53), John reportedly was killed (VCR 3:568; MCGC 166; PB 1 Pt. 1:59).

JOHN PHILIPS (PHILLIPS)

On October 11, 1627, John Philips (Phillips) was found guilty of having a sexual relationship with Joan White, who gave birth to a child. John and Joan were sentenced to a whipping and Abraham Peirsey, their master and then-owner of Flowerdew Hundred (53), was ordered to keep them apart. Unless there were two men named John Philips at Flowerdew Hundred, it is probable that the man purportedly killed in the March 1622 Indian attack had, in fact, survived (MCGC 155).

***

THOMAS PHILIPS (PHILLIPS, PHILLIPES)

Thomas Philips (Phillips, Phillipes) came to Virginia on the *William and Thomas* in 1618 and on February 7, 1625, was living in Basses Choice (27), where he headed a well-provisioned household that he shared with his wife, Elizabeth, who had arrived on the *Seaflower*. In early 1625 Thomas was 26 years old. In 1629 he presented William Barnes's inventory to the General Court and received a letter of administration. Between May 1629 and April 1630 he and Samuel Langham were plaintiffs in a suit that involved shipping tobacco from Virginia to Weymouth. On July 10, 1635, Thomas Philips was identified as Rowland Chambers' former master when he gave Rowland a covenant for land. Thomas secured a patent for 300 acres of land on the Chickahominy River, using his own headright and those of his wife and daughter and three other people. He also claimed some land on the lower side of the James River (CBE 62; MCGC 200; EAE 19-20; PB 1 Pt. 1:216, 287; DOR 1:48).

ELIZABETH PHILIPS (PHILLIPS, PHILLIPES) I (MRS. THOMAS PHILIPS [PHILLIPS, PHILLIPES])

Elizabeth I, the wife of Thomas Philips (Phillips, Phillipes), came to Virginia on the *Seaflower* with her daughter, Elizabeth II. On February 7, 1625, the elder Elizabeth and her husband were living at Basses Choice (27). She was then age 23. On July 9, 1635, when Thomas Philips patented some land on the Chickahominy River, he used his wife and daughter as headrights (CBE 62; PB 1 Pt. 1:216).

ELIZABETH PHILIPS (PHILLIPS, PHILLIPES) II

On July 9, 1635, when Thomas Philips (Phillips, Phillipes) patented some land, he used his daughter, Elizabeth, as a headright and indicated that she and her mother had come to Virginia on the *Seaflower* (PB 1 Pt. 1:287).

***

THOMAS PHILIPS (PHILLIPS)

In December 1619 officials at Bridewell decided that Thomas Phillips (Phillips) would be detained so that he could be sent to Virginia (CBE 15).

THOMAS PHILIPS (PHILLIPS)

Thomas Philips (Phillips) went to the colony on the *Bona Nova*, a vessel that brought many Virginia Company servants and tenants in November 1619. On February 16, 1624, he was living at Hog Island **(16)**. He was still there on February 4, 1625, and was a servant in Edward Barkley's house. On August 28, 1626, Thomas Philips testified against an accused thief, Henry Woodward, in a case aired before the General Court. By December 18, 1626, Thomas Philips had obtained his freedom. He was then identified as a Hog Island planter who wanted to move to Captain Samuel Mathews' plantation, Denbigh **(23)**, on the upper side of the James River, (CBE 15, 40, 61; MCGC 110, 128).

THOMAS PHILIPS (PHILLIPS)

Thomas Philips (Phillips) was killed at a settlement in Charles City, opposite Flowerdew Hundred **(53)**, during the March 22, 1622, Indian attack (VCR 3:568).

THOMAS PHILIPS (PHILLIPS)

On July 31, 1622, Thomas Philips (Phillips) went to Virginia on the *James* with William Felgate (FER 400).

THOMAS PHILIPS (PHILLIPS)

On February 16, 1624, Thomas Philips (Phillips) was living in Elizabeth City **(17, 18)** (CBE 43).

THOMAS PHILIPS (PHILLIPS)

On February 16, 1624, Thomas Philips (Phillips) was living at Chaplin's Choice **(56)** (CBE 37).

JOHN PHILLIMORE (PHILMOTT, FILMORE)

On November 1, 1624, the General Court noted that the late John Phillimore (Philmott, Filmore) had left his land and belongings to Elizabeth Peerce, to whom he had been engaged. He also made bequests to Mr. Constable and Thomas Sully of Jamestown **(1)**. On February 4, 1625, the muster-taker indicated that John was among those who had died "over the water," that is, on the lower side of the James River, across from Jamestown and east of Gray's Creek **(10-16)** (MCGC 27; CBE 60).

HENRY PHILPOT

In 1608 Henry Philpot, a gentleman, arrived in Jamestown **(1)** as part of the 2nd Supply. In 1620 he was identified as a Virginia Company investor (CJS 1:241; 2:190, 280).

PHINLOE

Phinloe died in Jamestown **(1)** sometime after February 16, 1624, but before January 24, 1625 (CBE 56).

PHAROW PHLINTON (SEE PHAROAH [FARROW, FARRAR] FLINTON [FINTON])

JOHN PIDDOX

On April 8, 1620, John Piddox sent a petition to the Virginia Company, which forwarded it to the colony's governor (VCR 1:337).

JOHN PICKERNELL

On October 3, 1625, the General Court's justices were informed that John Pickernell was dead. On December 5, 1625, it was determined that the decedent owed money to William Webster, purser of the *Elizabeth*. Therefore, it was necessary to set a rate at which Pickernell's goods would be valued (MCGC 72, 78).

DRUE (DRU) PICKHOUSE (PIGGASE)

Drue (Dru) Pickhouse (Piggase), a gentleman, arrived in Virginia in 1607 and was one of the first Jamestown (1) colonists. He died there on August 19, 1607. In 1608 Edward Maria Wingfield commented that he had found Mr. Pickhouse agreeable and disinclined to revile him (CJS 1:20, 208; 2:141; HAI 99, 199).

ROBERT PIDGEON (PIDGION)

Robert Pidgeon (Pidgion) died on the lower side of the James River, within the corporation of James City (8-15), sometime after April 1623 but before February 16, 1624 (CBE 41).

***

WILLIAM PILKINTON (PILKINGTON)

William Pilkinton (Pilkington) came to Virginia in 1620 on the *Bona Nova* and on February 4, 1625, was living on the Treasurer's Plantation (11) with his wife, Margaret, in a portion of the property seated by Edward Grindon. On April 11, 1625, William testified at the inquest held after John Verone's death. On October 13, 1626, he was identified as the partner and heir of William Parsons, whose inventory he presented to the General Court on January 11, 1627. The next day William Pilkinton was identified as a Virginia Company tenant who had been assigned to Abraham Peirsey. On July 10, 1635, he patented 300 acres on Lawnes Creek, claiming the land on the basis of six headrights, including wife Margaret and himself. Then, on November 16, 1635, he patented 200 acres on the west side of Lower Chippokes Creek in James City County, land later claimed by Sir John Harvey. William Pilkinton died in Virginia sometime prior to October 1641, at which time the administration of his estate was granted to his brother, Sir Arthur Pilkinton (CBE 20, 60; MCGC 53, 123, 133, 137; PB 1 Pt. 1:219, 308; EEAC 45).

MARGARET PILKINTON (PILKINGTON) (MRS. WILLIAM PILKINTON [PILKINGTON])

On February 4, 1625, Margaret Pilkinton (Pilkington) and her husband, William,

were living on the Treasurer's Plantation (11). On July 10, 1635, when William patented some land on Lawnes Creek, he identified Margaret as his wife and used her as a headright (CBE 60; PB 1 Pt. 1:219).

***

HENRY PINCKE

Henry Pincke came to Virginia on the *London Merchant* in 1619 and on January 24, 1625, was reported to the authorities for refusing to serve as a substitute for John Bennett as sentinel at the Warresqueak fort. On February 7, 1625, when a muster was made of Warresqueak or Bennett's Welcome (26), Henry Pincke was identified as a servant in Edward Bennett's household (MCGC 44; CBE 62).

WILLIAM PINDAR

William Pindar, the rector of Mottisfount in Hampshire, died sometime prior to February 1627. The decedent's kinsman, Thomas Singleton alias Lea (Lee), who was then in Virginia, was appointed his administrator (CBE 77).

***

WILLIAM PINKE ALIAS JONAS

Sometime prior to 1623, William Pinke, an ancient planter sometimes known as William Jonas, acquired a 12-acre parcel near Black Point in the eastern end of Jamestown Island (1). He and his wife, Mary, made their home on the property, and at his death she inherited his 100-acre dividend of land, which included their 12-acre homestead (PB 1:11).

MARY PINKE ALIAS JONAS (MRS. WILLIAM PINKE ALIAS JONAS, MRS. GABRIEL HOLLAND) (SEE MARY PINKE ALIAS JONAS HOLLAND)

Mary Pinke alias Jonas and her husband, William, an ancient planter, acquired and occupied a 12-acre homestead in the eastern end of Jamestown Island (1) sometime prior to 1623. When William died, she inherited his property and promptly repatented it, securing the title in her own name. On August

14, 1624, Mary indicated that she had married Gabriel Holland, a yeoman. Mary Pink alias Jonas Holland died between August 14, 1624, and January 24, 1625, at which point her land (which she owned outright) descended to her new husband, Gabriel (Patent Book 1:11; CBE 56).

***

WILLIAM PINSEN

On February 16, 1624, William Pinsen was living in Elizabeth City (**17, 18**) (CBE 43).

JOHN PIPPS

John Pipps came to Virginia on the *Tiger* in 1621 at the expense of William Claiborne, who used his headright on June 3, 1624 when patenting some land (PB 1 Pt. 1:41).

ROBERT PIRES

On December 9, 1628, Robert Pires and Nathaniel Causey were fined for going aboard the *William and John* without permission (MCGC 179).

EDWARD PISING

Edward Pising, a carpenter, came to Virginia in 1607 and was one of the first Jamestown (**1**) settlers. On July 20, 1607, he was among those who accompanied Captain John Smith on a voyage of discovery in the Chesapeake Bay. In 1608 he went with Smith on a second journey into the bay. In late December 1608 Pising and Smith went to Werowocomoco (on the York River) and to the Pamunkey Indians' territory, staying at the Kecoughtan Indians' village (near Old Point Comfort) on the way. In his narratives, Captain John Smith referred to Edward Pising as a carpenter, a soldier, a gentleman, and a sergeant. He appears to have been alive in January 1609 (CJS 1:208, 230, 243-244, 2:142, 170, 193-194).

WILLIAM PISSE (PIFF, PIFFS)

In September 1620 William Pisse (Piff, Piffs) was among those who set sail from Bristol, England, on the *Supply* and accompanied William Tracy, who was bound for Berkeley Hundred (**55**). Pisse was supposed to serve the Society of Berkeley Hundred's investors for a certain number of years in exchange for some land. Virginia Company records reveal that when the *Supply* reached Ireland, William Pisse disembarked and seemingly never returned to the ship (CBE 21; VCR 3:397).

EDWARD PITCHANDE (PITCHARD)

On January 3, 1625, Edward Pitchande (Pitchard) testified before the General Court about an incident that had occurred on the *Little Hopewell*. He said that he had witnessed a verbal agreement between two Jamestown (**1**) residents, John Cooke and Peter Langman, who had come aboard. On June 7, 1625, the General Court noted that Edward Pitchande had returned to England and that he and Nicolas Ferrar were authorized to collect the debt that Simon Withe owed to the orphaned Sarah Templeman (MCGC 41, 74).

CHRISTOPHER PITMAN

Christopher Pitman died on the lower side of the James River, within the corporation of James City (**8-15**), sometime after April 1623 but before February 16, 1624 (CBE 41).

JOHN PITTMAN

John Pittman, a sawyer sent to Virginia by the Company of Shipwrights, came to Virginia in 1621 to work under the supervision of Thomas Nunn, a master shipwright. Pittman and his fellow workers built homes on Jamestown Island (**1**) (FER 378).

EDWARD PITTS

Edward Pitts came to Virginia in 1628 on the *Hopewell* at the expense of Adam Thorogood. On June 24, 1635, when Thorogood secured a patent, he used Pitts's headright (PB 1 Pt. 1:179).

FRANCIS PITTS

On February 16, 1624, Francis Pitts was living in Elizabeth City (**17, 18**) (CBE 43).

HUMPHREY PLANT

On September 15, 1619, Humphrey Plant, a carpenter/sawyer, set sail for Virginia on the

Margaret of Bristol. He was one of the people being sent to Berkeley Hundred (**55**) to work under Captain John Woodlief's supervision. Plant was supposed to serve the Society of Berkeley Hundred's investors for three years in exchange for 30 acres of land. Virginia Company records indicate that Humphrey Plant reached Virginia but died before he had fulfilled his contractual obligation to the Society of Berkeley Hundred (CBE 13-14; VCR 3:186-187, 197, 213).

WILLIAM PLANT

William Plant died sometime after February 16, 1624, but before February 4, 1625, at one of the plantations on the lower side of the James River west of Gray's Creek (**8, 9**), within the corporation of James City (CBE 60).

***

[NO FIRST NAME] PLATT

Richard Platt's brother was killed near Bermuda Hundred (**39**) during the March 22, 1622, Indian attack (VCR 3:566).

RICHARD PLATT

Richard Platt and his brother were killed near Bermuda Hundred (**39**) during the March 22, 1622, Indian attack (VCR 3:566).

***

JAMES PLAYSE (PLAICE)

On March 13, 1626, James Playse (Plaice) testified before the General Court about a wager Thomas Allnutt made with his servant, Roger Roeds, on March 7, 1625, in his presence. At issue was the date on which Easter occurred. Allnutt agreed to free Roedes a year early if he won the bet (MCGC 96-97).

JOHN PLAYSE (PLAICE)

In late 1634 John Playse (Plaice) purchased some of the late Thomas Lee's goods, which were sold by Bartholomew Hopkins (CBE 208).

THOMAS PLUMER (PLOMER)

In October 1628 Thomas Plumer (Plomer) testified before the General Court that

Jamestown Island (**1**) carpenter Richard Tree worked on the new church at Hog Island (**16**) for a week or so after the assembly adjourned but left when planting season commenced. Tree was censured for not finishing construction of the church (MCGC 175).

JOHN PLUMLEY

On September 20, 1627, John Plumley was identified as master of the *Parramore* (CBE 80).

WILLIAM PLUNKETT

On February 27, 1619, the Bridewell Court decided that William Plunkett, a boy, would be sent to Virginia. He was part of a large group of young people who were to be sent to the colony (CBE 12).

POCAHONTAS (MATOAKA, REBECCA) (MRS. JOHN ROLFE) (SEE REBECCA [POCAHONTAS, MATOAKA] ROLFE)

Pocahontas (Matoaka), Powhatan's favorite daughter, was taken hostage by the English in 1611. Afterward, she converted to Christianity and adopted the English name Rebecca. John Rolfe, a widower and secretary of the colony, fell in love with her and in early April 1614 the two were married in the church in Jamestown (**1**). The union had Powhatan's consent and one of Pocahontas's uncles, probably Opechancanough, gave her away. In May 1616 Pocahontas and her husband accompanied Sir Thomas Dale when he returned to England. She was introduced at court and treated as a native princess. She also encountered her old friend, Captain John Smith. In March 1617, when the Rolfes and their little son were in Gravesend awaiting the ship that would take them back to Virginia, Pocahontas developed consumption (tuberculosis) and died. She was buried in the yard of St. Mary le Bow Church, in Gravesend (VCR 2:105-106; 3:70; HAI 809, 820, 850-856, 887-890; MEY 508; SP 14/87 ff 67, 146; CJS 2:245-246, 255, 261-262).

ROBERT PODDY

Robert Poddy, a 38-year-old sailor and ships' carpenter from Ratcliffe, Middlesex, testified during the summer of 1630 that while the *Susan* was in Virginia, it was caulked, as was the *Friendship* of London. He said that all but one of the *Susan*'s passengers made it to Virginia safely, the exception being a man who fell overboard one night (EAE 25).

ROBERT POLAND

On February 8, 1625, Robert Poland and several other individuals presented claims against the late George Thorpe's estate (MCGC 47).

***

JOHN POLENTINE (POLLENTIN)

In July 1619 John Polentine (Pollentin) served as burgess for the city of Henricus (**63**). On July 24, 1621, Virginia Company officials noted that he had a debt to Richard Topping of London, a brown-baker. By February 16, 1624, John had moved to Warresqueak (**26**) where he was sharing a home with his wife, Rachel, and Margaret Polentine. On February 20, 1624, John, who was then serving as a Warresqueak burgess, signed the General Assembly's rebuttal to Alderman Johnson's claims that the colony thrived during its early years. When a list of patented land was sent back to England in May 1625, John Polentine was credited with 600 acres of land in Warresqueak. On July 6, 1626, he testified that the purpose of the *Peter and John's* going to Virginia was to transport passengers. His date of death is uncertain (VCR 1:522; 3:154; 4:556; HAI 915; CBE 42, 72; HEN 1:128-129).

RACHEL POLENTINE (POLLENTIN) (MRS. JOHN POLENTINE [POLLENTIN])

On February 16, 1624, Rachel Polentine (Pollentin) was living in Warresqueak (**26**) with her husband, John, and Margaret Polentine, who may have been their daughter. In June 1628 Rachel was listed among the planters exporting tobacco from Virginia. On February 10, 1629, Mrs. Rachel Polentine was involved in a dispute with her Warresqueak neighbor, John Moone (Omoonce), over a share of the year's tobacco and corn crops. The General Court decided that she was entitled to a share of

the house she then occupied, a tobacco house, half of the crops, and half of the land. In return, she was to lease Moone the remaining half of the land and the other houses on the property (CBE 42; MCGC 186; SR 3784a).

MARGARET POLENTINE (POLLENTIN)

On February 16, 1624, Margaret Polentine (Pollentin) was living in Warresqueak (**26**) with John and Rachel Polentine. As her name is listed immediately after theirs, she may have been their daughter (CBE 42).

***

***

DANIEL POOLE

On February 4, 1625, Daniel Poole, who was described as a Frenchman in the employ of Virginia treasurer George Sandys, was living at the Treasurer's Plantation (**11**) with his wife and young child. Daniel may have been related to David Poole, a French vigneron (CBE 60).

MRS. DANIEL POOLE

Mrs. Daniel Poole and her young child were living at the Treasurer's Plantation (**11**) on February 4, 1625, with her husband, Daniel, a Frenchman employed by George Sandys (CBE 60).

[NO FIRST NAME] POOLE

On February 4, 1625, Mr. and Mrs. Daniel Poole were living at the Treasurer's Plantation (**11**) with their young child. Neither the youngster's name nor gender is known (CBE 60).

***

DAVID POOLE

On December 12, 1627, David Poole, a French vigneron, leased 60 acres of land at Buckroe (**17**) from his master, James Bonall of London. David's land was near that of James Bonall and John Arundell. He may have come to Virginia around 1621, when Bonall and Arundell arrived (PB 1 Pt. 1:80-81, 84).

JONAS POOLE

Jonas Poole, a sailor, came to Virginia with the first group of settlers who seated Jamestown Island (1). On May 20, 1607, he accompanied Captain Christopher Newport on an exploratory voyage of the James River (HAI 102).

NATHANIEL POOLE
(SEE NATHANIEL POWELL)
RICHARD POOLE

Richard Poole came to Virginia in 1634 on the *John and Dorothy* at the expense of Adam Thorogood. On June 24, 1635, when Thorogood secured a patent, he listed William Edwards as a headright (PB 1 Pt. 1:179).

***

ROBERT POOLE I

Robert Poole I, an ancient planter, came to Virginia with Sir Thomas Dale on the *Starr* with his sons, Robert II and John. By September 8, 1627, Robert Poole I and his son John were dead. It was then that Robert Poole II, one of the Virginia government's Indian interpreters, patented 300 acres of land on the Warwick River (22), using his headright and those of both decedents (PB 1 Pt. 1:51).

JOHN POOLE

John Poole, an ancient planter, came to Virginia with Sir Thomas Dale on the *Starr* and accompanied his father, Robert Poole I, and brother, Robert Poole II. By September 8, 1627, John and Robert Poole I were deceased. It was then that Robert Poole II patented 300 acres of land on the Warwick River (22) using his headright and those of his father and brother (PB 1 Pt. 1:51).

ROBERT POOLE II

Robert Poole II came to Virginia with Sir Thomas Dale on the *Starr* and was an ancient planter. He was accompanied by his brother, John, and their father, Robert Poole I. Robert Poole II became fluent in the Algonquian language and served as one of the government's official interpreters. However, Captain John Smith considered him treacherous and in 1618 claimed that Poole may have aroused the Indians against the colonists. In July 1619 Robert Poole II made formal accusations against Henry Spellman, another interpreter, whom he confronted in the presence of the assembly. In November 1624 Robert testified that he had lived with Opechancanough during Sir Thomas Dale's government (1611-1616) and that Captain John Smith had taught some Indians how to use firearms. He also said that he had had 10,000 to 20,000 beads for use in trading with the Indians for corn. In December 1624 Robert Poole II was among those who took part in an inquest concerning George Pope II's death. In February 1624 Robert requested compensation as an interpreter. He was residing in urban Jamestown (1) on January 24, 1625, and headed a household of which he was the sole occupant. In late January he testified that he heard master shipbuilder Thomas Nunn talk about some tobacco that was spoiled. In May 1625, when Robert Poole II requested permission to go to England, he was described as a longtime interpreter. He returned to Virginia, and in January 1627 reference was made to his land on the Blunt Point (Warwick) River (22), where he had a dwelling. He patented his 300 acres on September 8, 1627, using the headrights of his father and brother (both deceased) and himself. In November 1628 Robert Poole II, who was identified as a gentleman, testified against Lieutenant Thomas Flint, who was under house arrest. On March 5, 1629, he told the General Court's justices about an event that had occurred in mid-May 1625 in Elizabeth City (17, 18). In April 1629 the Court's justices determined that Robert Poole II owed some tobacco and corn to George Whitfield (Whitefield). Simultaneously, they gave Poole a commission to go on a trading expedition to the Eastern Shore (CJS 2:268, 312-314; FER 113; VCR 3:174-175, 242, 244-245, 249-253; 4:98-101, 457-458; MCGC 28-29, 38, 45-46, 57, 130, 176, 190, 193; CBE 55; PB 1 PT. 1:50-51; DOR 1:31).

***

THOMAS POOLE

Thomas Poole was killed at Thomas Sheffield's plantation (69), three miles from Falling Creek, during the March 22, 1622, Indian attack (VCR 3:565).

THOMAS POOLE

In May 1625 when a list of patented land was sent back to England, Thomas Poole was credited with 100 acres in Warresqueak (26) (VCR 4:556).

WILLIAM POOLE

William Poole, who was from Preton in Andernesse in Lankeshire, arrived in Jamestown (1) on September 5, 1623, on the *Ann* and took the oath of supremacy (MCGC 6).

GRIVEL (GRIVELL) POOLEY

The Rev. Grivel (Grivell) Pooley left England on July 31, 1622, and came to Virginia with Abraham Peirsey on the *James*. The Virginia Company appointed Pooley the minister for Flowerdew Hundred (53), Chaplin's Choice (56), Jordan's Journey (46), and Shirley Hundred (41). He apparently fulfilled his ministerial obligations, for he was authorized to collect church taxes from the residents of the communities he served. Sometime prior to June 4, 1623, Pooley proposed to Cisley, Samuel Jordan's widow, only three or four days after Jordan's death, and according to witnesses they drank a toast to their engagement. However, Cisley Jordan later changed her mind, which prompted Pooley to sue her for breach of promise. As no legal precedent for such suits had been established in the colony, the General Court sought the Virginia Company's advice. On February 16, 1624, the Rev. Grivel Pooley was living at Flowerdew Hundred. He continued to pursue his lawsuit against Mrs. Jordan, and because William Farrar had moved into her home, Pooley accused them of immoral conduct. Finally, in January 1625, Pooley agreed to release Cisley from her marriage contract. On January 20, 1625, Pooley was living at Flowerdew, where he headed a household that included two servants. On January 9, 1626, he appeared before the General Court where he was accused of insulting Mr. Pawlett. The Rev. Pooley witnessed the wills made by Abraham Peirsey and James Carter, and in August 1626 he testified about John Joyse, a runaway servant. He was summoned to court in March 1629 on account of a dispute with Edward Auborne (FER 400; VCR 2:519; 4:402, 218-220; SR 1207; CBE 37, 50; MCGC 41-42, 89, 105, 165, 189, 192; SH 7; WAT 1016-1017; DOR 1:22).

INNOCENT (INOCENT) POORE (POWER)

Innocent (Inocent) Poore (Power) came to Virginia on the *Southampton* in 1622 at the expense of John Cheeseman. She died in Elizabeth City (18) sometime after April 1623 but before February 16, 1624. On September 2, 1624, when John Cheeseman patented some land, he identified Innocent as his servant and used her as a headright (CBE 45; PB 1 Pt. 1:47).

STEPHEN POORE

On June 7, 1625, the General Court's justices reviewed the documents collected in response to an April 12, 1624, court order in Stephen Poore's suit against the estate of Simon With, who allegedly owed funds to Sara Templeman, an orphan. Although the records presented were somewhat illegible, the justices decided that With's tobacco would be sent to England, where two of the court's representatives would see that Sara was given what she was owed (MCGC 64).

WILLIAM POORE

On August 8, 1618, officials at Bridewell decided that William Poore, a vagrant brought in from Fleet Street, would be sent to Virginia (CBE 9).

[NO FIRST NAME] POPE

On February 4, 1625, a man named Pope, who had been a cook on Sir George Yeardley's ship, was tentatively identified as Captain John Martin's servant (VCR 4:511).

EDWARD POPE

Edward Pope came to Virginia with John Hitch on the *James*, departing from England on July 31, 1622 (FER 400).

ELIZABETH POPE

Elizabeth Pope came to Virginia on the *Abigail* in 1621 and on February 16, 1624, was living in Elizabeth City (18). She was still there in early 1625 and was identified as an 8-year-old servant in William Ganey's household (CBE 44, 66).

***

GEORGE POPE I

George Pope I came to Virginia on the *London Merchant* in 1622, accompanied by his wife and son. On February 16, 1624, he was living in a Jamestown Island (1) household headed by John Osborne. In late 1624 George Pope I's 4-year-old son, George II, drowned when he fell into an open well. An inquest was held on December 31, 1624 (CBE 40; MCGC 38).

MRS. GEORGE POPE I

The wife of George Pope I came to Virginia in 1622 on the *London Merchant* with her husband and son, George Pope II, and lived in Jamestown (1). Mrs. Pope died there sometime after April 1623 but before February 16, 1624 (MCGC 38; CBE 40).

GEORGE POPE II

George Pope II, who resided with his father, George Pope I, on Jamestown Island (1), came to Virginia with his parents in 1622 on the *London Merchant*. He was then age 2. On December 30, 1624, he fell into an open well and drowned. Margaret Osborne, who was taking care of 4¹/₂ -year-old George II when the mishap occurred, said that she often sent him to the well to fetch water, which he scooped up with a dish and poured into a rundlet or small barrel. The 5-year-old son of Christopher Stokes, a neighbor, said that he saw George II kneel to scoop up water and then throw it away because it was muddy. When he leaned forward to "take up cleerer" water, he fell in. On December 31, 1624, when an inquest was held to determine the cause of little George Pope II's death, it was ruled accidental (MCGC 38).

***

JOHN POPE

John Pope came to Virginia with William Rowley aboard the *James* and left England on July 31, 1622 (FER 400).

PHILIP POPE

Phillip Pope came to Virginia with William Ewins on the *James* and left England on July 31, 1622 (FER 400).

THOMAS POPE

Thomas Pope died at Martin's Hundred (7) sometime after April 1623 but before February 16, 1624 (CBE 42).

***

RICHARD POPELEY

Richard Popeley came to Virginia on the *Bona Nova* in 1620 and on February 16, 1624, was living in Elizabeth City (18). He was still there in early 1625 and resided in the household headed by the Rev. Jonas Stockton. Richard, who was then age 26, was free. On December 18, 1626, he proved William Foster's will and was ordered to inventory his estate and serve as administrator. By October 10, 1628, Richard Popeley had been given the rank of lieutenant. One of his responsibilities was to attend Governor Francis West, who had long been associated with Elizabeth City and probably was a personal acquaintance. On March 4, 1629, Popeley was ordered to pay a sum to John Army who was indebted to Thomas Flint. He also was told to deliver one of his five new male servants to Roger Saunders, from whom he had accepted payment. By 1638 Richard Popeley had married Elizabeth, the widow of Giles Jones of Day's Point (28). He also had acquired some land in Middle Plantation and appears to have moved there. On June 30, 1640, he was accused of killing a bull that belonged to his neighbor, John White. Richard Popeley died sometime prior to 1645, at which time his widow, Elizabeth, served as his executrix (CBE 43, 66; MCGC 128, 154, 189, 471; PB 1 Pt. 2:564; PB 2:59).

ELIZABETH JONES POPELEY (MRS. GILES JONES, MRS. RICHARD POPELEY) (SEE ELIZABETH JONES [JOONES])

***

WILLIAM POPHAM

On July 8, 1627, William Popham shipped some goods from London to Virginia on the *Ann* (CBE 78-79).

THOMAS POPKIN

Thomas Popkin came to Virginia on the *George* in 1621, at the expense of Dr. John Pott and on February 16, 1624, was living in the Neck O'Land (5). However, he apparently moved to Jamestown Island (1), for on January 24, 1625, he was listed among those who had died there since February 16, 1624. On September 1, 1632, when Dr. John Pott patented some land, he used Thomas Popkin's headright (CBE 35, 56; PB 1 Pt. 1:113).

WILLIAM POPLETON (POPPLETON, POPKTON)

On July 31, 1622, William Popleton (Poppleton, Popkton) set sail from England on the *James* and was brought to Virginia by Michael Marshall (Marshott), a merchant and sea captain. On November 30, 1624, William Emmerson told the General Court that the past Christmas (that is, in early January 1624) he and John Davis had purchased two years of William Popleton's time from Lieutenant John Gibbs. On January 21, 1625, Popleton was living at Jordan's Journey (**46**) and was a servant in the home of Davis and Emmerson. By October 1629 he had gained his freedom and was elected a burgess for Jordan's Journey. When William Popleton's will was proved in July 1631, he was said to be from St. Giles Cripplegate, in London. He left his Virginia land to William Emmerson, William Thorogood, and Richard Buffington (FER 400; CBE 52, 103; EEAC 46; WITH 159; MCGC 34).

ABRAHAM (ABRAM) PORTER

Abraham (Abram) Porter came to Virginia in December 1622 at the Rev. Richard Buck's expense. On February 16, 1624, he was residing in urban Jamestown (**1**) in a household headed by Peter Ascomb, whose wife, Mary, had custody of Benomi, one of the Rev. Buck's orphans. On December 13, 1624, Abraham Porter testified that when he had been at William Cluch's house a year ago, he had witnessed the slaughter of a hog that lacked an earmark. He added that Cluch claimed to have traded a gun for it. On January 3, 1625, Abraham Porter indicated that he had sold a sow to Captain Nathaniel Basse and was awaiting payment. On January 24, 1625, when a muster was made of Peter Langman's household in urban Jamestown, Abraham Porter was identified as a 36-year-old servant. As the widowed Mary Ascomb recently had wed Langman, she probably brought Porter (a servant) to the marriage as part of the Buck estate. On January 3, 1626, Abraham Porter testified that he had complained to Richard Kingsmill (overseer of the Rev. Richard

Buck's will) about how poorly Thomas Allnutt was maintaining the Buck orphans' cattle, and said that one cow was allowed to get stuck in the mud. On May 8, 1626, he said that John Dyus (Dyas) had "drenched" Buck's cattle (that is, he had given them an oral medication). By March 1629 Abraham Porter was dead, and Elmer Philips, a resident of Jamestown Island, proved Porter's will. Reference was then made to Abraham Porter's house and to the fact that he had waived his claim to a debt John Rodis owed (MCGC 35, 40, 86, 103, 175, 187-188; CBE 38, 55).

JAMES PORTER

On May 8, 1626, James Porter testified that Edward Dade had agreed to serve Robert Gyer (Guyar, Geyer, Gier, Gire) for 5 years (MCGC 103).

PETER PORTER

Peter Porter came to Virginia on the *Tiger* in 1621 and on February 16, 1624, was living on the Eastern Shore. He was still there in early 1625 and was identified as a 19-year-old servant in Captain William Eppes's household (**74**). He may have been the same individual who reportedly was living in Elizabeth City (**18**), an area with which settlers on the Eastern Shore had much commerce (CBE 46, 68).

PETER PORTER

In 1621 Peter Porter came to Virginia on the *Tiger*. By early 1625 he was living in Elizabeth City (**18**) where he was a 20-year-old servant in Captain William Tucker's household (CBE 63).

JOHN PORY (POREY, PORYE)

John Pory (Porey, Porye) was named secretary of state in 1619, as soon as Sir Edwin Sandys became treasurer of the Virginia Company. He accompanied Governor George Yeardley to Virginia and arrived in April 1619. In July and August 1619, when the first session of the Virginia assembly was held, John Pory served as speaker and took minutes. Thanks to his efforts, the transactions of the New World's first legislative assembly have been preserved. During 1619 John Pory went on a trading voyage in search of corn in the Chesapeake Bay. On September 30, 1619, he informed Virginia Company officials that 11 ships had arrived during his five months in the colony. He said that former Deputy Governor Samuel Argall had turned privateer and that Governor George Yeardley was a skilled military man with experience in the Low Countries. Pory indicated that in 1619 the summer heat had claimed many people's lives, and he told Company officials that agricultural equipment and cattle were badly needed. He said that vineyards could be expected to thrive, and thanks to the marketability of tobacco, many colonists were prospering. He added that in Jamestown (1) even the cow-keeper wore flaming silk and the wife of a former collier (coal dealer) sported a fine beaver hat. In January 1620 John Pory was among those who signed a letter sent to Company officials stressing the economic importance of tobacco. In a personal letter, he said that the colonists were on good terms with the Indian leader Opechancanough. Pory witnessed a treaty Governor Yeardley made with the Chickahominy Indians and commented on interpreter Henry Spellman's reaction.

In 1620 John Pory went on a fishing voyage to Newfoundland aboard the *Temperance*, a ship owned by Governor George Yeardley. In May 1620 Virginia Company officials decided that, as part of his stipend, Secretary Pory should have 500 acres as office land and 20 servants. They later decided that 10 men would suffice. Like George Thorpe, John Pory favored converting the Indians to Christianity. In 1621 he went to Holland to sell tobacco, and in February 1622 he made a voyage to the south, visiting what became Carolina. He sent word to incoming governor Sir Francis Wyatt, recommending that he visit every plantation. Treasurer George Sandys disliked John Pory and considered him to be a dull and unsatisfactory secretary. Although Pory was replaced, he was respected by many of his superiors and in October 1623 was among those selected to compile information about the colony on the king's behalf. Therefore, on March 2, 1624, several questions were posed to Governor Francis Wyatt and the assembly. John Pory angered Virginia officials by sending a letter to England in which he said that Edward Sharples' punishment had been excessive. Governor Wyatt and his council retaliated

by informing their superiors that Pory had betrayed them. In March 1630, when John Pory testified in an English court, he gave his age as 56 and stated that he had served as secretary for three years. Pory reportedly died in England in 1636 (STAN 21, 51; POR 72; VCR 1:340, 342, 349, 369, 371, 375, 478, 488-489; 3:153-177, 253, 300, 305, 445-447, 549, 641, 647; 4:64, 110, 480-481, 500; SAIN 1:58; CJS 2:56, 266, 288-291; MHS 4; PRO 30/15/2:290; C 24/560 Pt. 2 f 84; FER 113, 143, 244; MCGC 14, 148).

PETER PORY

Peter Pory, a gentleman, came to Virginia in 1608 as part of the 1st Supply and resided in Jamestown (1) (CJS 1:222; 2:161).

CHRISTOPHER POTLEY

On July 13, 1617, Christopher Potley, a prisoner being detained in the Oxford jail, was reprieved and delivered to Sir Thomas Smyth so that he could be transported to Virginia (CBE 9; SR 4525; PC 2/29).

***

FRANCIS POTT

Francis Pott, the brother of Dr. John Pott, came to Virginia sometime prior to March 1629 when Dr. Pott, who was then deputy-governor, appointed him captain of the fort at Old Point Comfort (17). He held that position until February 1633. In 1629 he received a bequest from Thomas Warnett, a Jamestown merchant. According to Secretary Richard Kemp, Francis Pott constantly tried to undermine Governor John Harvey and his policies. As a result, Harvey stripped him of his command in early 1635 and appointed a replacement, Captain Francis Hook. No doubt Francis Pott's loss of his lucrative position at Old Point Comfort fueled his hostility toward Harvey. In April 1635 Francis Pott was instrumental in ousting Governor Harvey from office, and he was among those who accompanied him to England. Harvey quickly turned the tables, however, for he had Pott arrested and thrown into prison. Francis Pott petitioned the Privy Council for the right to post a bond so that he could get out of jail, and he claimed that Sir John Harvey owed him money. Although Pott was tried for attempting to depose the governor, he apologized and was released. By that time he had been detained in Fleet Prison for two years. When Dr. John Pott died (sometime after May 1635), his 12-acre lot in urban Jamestown (1) and 500 acres in the Great Barren Neck near Middle Plantation descended to his brother, Francis, who seems to have retained the Jamestown property until at least August 1640. During the latter part of his life, Francis Pott moved to the Eastern Shore, where in 1647 he was living with his wife, Susanna. He patented 2,000 acres in Northampton County in February 1653, and another 1,000 acres in 1657 (MCGC 84; SH 11-12; SAIN 1:207, 212, 218, 234; CO 1/8 ff 193-194; 1/10 f 190; PB 1 Pt. 2:730; 4:101; AMES 2:354).

DR. JOHN POTT

Dr. John Pott, the colony's physician-general, came to Virginia in 1621 on the *George* with his wife, Elizabeth, and incoming governor, Sir Francis Wyatt. Pott was accompanied by two servants and two surgeons. Dr. Pott, who was described as an expert in the distillation of waters and was "well practiced in surgery and physics," replaced the late Dr. Lawrence Bohun (Bohune, Bohunne). The Virginia Company furnished Dr. Pott with a chest of medicines, medical books, and some of the provisions and equipment he needed to become established in the colony. Pott was named a provisional councilor and, as physician, was supposed to receive 500 acres of office land and 20 tenants, who were to help him build a house as soon as possible. As no office land had been laid out for the colony's physician, on August 11, 1624, Pott patented a 3-acre lot in urban Jamestown (1), where he built a home. He placed some of his servants on his land in Jamestown and seated the rest on his leasehold on the Governor's Land (3).

Treasurer George Sandys made some scathing comments about Dr. John Pott, whom he described as a "pitiful counselor" and unintelligent. Sandys said that Pott enjoyed the company of his inferiors, who clung to him as long as his good liquor lasted. Pott had some serious ethical problems. In 1626 he was sued by Richard Townsend, an indentured servant, who claimed that Pott had agreed to teach him the apothecary's art but refused to. Jane Dickinson of Martin's Hundred (7), who was captured during the 1622 Indian attack and detained for nearly a year, claimed that although Dr. Pott had redeemed her with some glass beads, he kept her in greater slavery than the Indians had. Some indentured servants got into trouble for killing a calf and dressing it in a house belonging to Dr. Pott, seemingly with his knowledge.

In 1624 Dr. John Pott was described as unfit to serve as a councilor because he was implicated in poisoning a group of Indians who had gathered to sign a peace treaty. As a result of this transgression, he was removed from office. When a census was made on February 16, 1624, Dr. John Pott headed a Jamestown household that included his wife, Elizabeth, and six servants, including Jane Dickinson (the widow from Martin's Hundred) and Fortune Taylor (a young, marriageable maid who came to the colony in 1621). On January 24, 1625, the Pott household in Jamestown included Dr. and Mrs. Pott and four servants. Dr. Pott was credited with two houses and a herd of livestock that included cattle, swine, and goats. The family also had a better-than-average supply of provisions and defensive weaponry. Dr. John Pott made several appearances in court during 1624 and 1625. He testified in lawsuits, and from time to time he had to defend himself from the accusations of his neighbors. In 1624 he was obliged to resolve a dispute with Captain William Holmes, from whom he had agreed to buy three chests of physic, and in May 1625 he had to address the allegations of his neighbor, Mrs. Margaret Blaney, who claimed that he had killed one of her hogs and then refused to share the meat. Pott justified his actions by saying that his neighbors' hogs had damaged his approximately 12 acres of corn, even though they were enclosed with a fence.

During 1624 Dr. Pott was given an opportunity to lease part of the College Land (66) at Henrico for five years but declined to do so, and he tried to resolve a dispute between two people over a rental house in eastern Jamestown Island. He also testified about Roger Dilke, Thomas Wilson, and a confrontation between Captain John Harvey and an indentured servant. Pott went to court in an attempt to force Randall Holt I, one of his own servants, to stay a little longer. Pott provided medical treatment to the sick and injured and sometimes had difficulty collecting payment. In July 1625 he had Jamestown merchant John Chew imprisoned for indebtedness, and he went to court to recover corn and tobacco from Richard Peirce, also of the capital city.

One member of the Pott household during 1628 was boat-builder William Bennett, who agreed to construct a vessel for Dr. Pott in exchange for room, board, and the materials he needed. On September 10, 1627, Dr. Pott was authorized to add 9 acres to his Jamestown lot and received a patent for 12 acres on September 20, 1628. He apparently had problems obtaining (and perhaps retaining) the cattle to which he was entitled as part of his official stipend. In 1626, after the dissolution of the Virginia Company, he was required to procure written verification from Treasurer George Sandys or former Governor Francis Wyatt that he was entitled to all of the cattle in his possession. He also learned that if he resigned his position as physician-general or died, his estate would be liable for replacing the animals.

In March 1629 Pott's fellow councilors elected him deputy governor. He sent William Claiborne into the Chesapeake on a voyage of exploration and authorized him to trade with the Dutch and other English colonies. He also placed Claiborne in command of the forces sent out against the Indians. Pott appointed local commissioners to try minor court cases, and he attempted to strengthen the colony's defenses. He patented 200 acres on Skiffs Creek and some acreage in Harrop (**6**), seven miles from Jamestown. However, when Sir John Harvey arrived in the colony to assume the governorship, he promptly placed Dr. John Pott under house-arrest at Harrop for pardoning a known murderer and because he was accused of stealing some cattle. Two months later, Harvey asked the king to pardon Dr. Pott because he was "skilled in epidemical diseases." Meanwhile, Mrs. Elizabeth Pott, steadfastly loyal to her husband, went to England to assert his innocence. During the early 1630s Dr. Pott's relationship with Governor Harvey continued to deteriorate. According to Secretary Richard Kemp, Pott was angry because Harvey had removed his brother, Francis, as commander of the fort at Old Point Comfort. In April 1635, when Harvey was arrested by his councilors, Dr. John Pott was one of the prime movers. Richard Kemp's eyewitness account of Governor Harvey's arrest in Pott's presence reveals that he was alive in April 1635. The date of his death is uncertain (CJS 2:286; 3:215, 217; HEN 1:128-129, 131-132, 137, 140, 145, 147, 171, 196; STAN 14, 30; FER 299, 308, 322; MCGC 3-4, 7, 12-13, 25, 36-37, 39-40, 46, 58, 61, 66, 84, 97-98, 108, 115-115, 117-118, 128, 136, 147, 152, 157-158, 161-162, 182-183, 190, 479-480, 484; VCR 1:512, 515-516, 523; 2:481; 3:482-483, 485, 565, 588, 695; 4:67, 110, 185, 473; CBE 38, 55, 71, 88, 91, 96; HAI 915; SH 11-12; CO 1/3 f 94; 1/5 ff 85-86, 203-210; 1/6 ff 36-37; 1/8 ff 166-1681/39 ff 114-115, 118; PB 1 Pt. 1:8-9, 61-62, 113; SAIN 1:116-118, 133, 207, 212; MHS 150; DOR 1:28, 30).

ELIZABETH POTT (MRS. JOHN POTT)

Elizabeth, the wife of Dr. John Pott, came to Virginia on the *George* in 1620 and on February 16, 1624, lived in urban Jamestown (**1**) in a household her husband headed. On January 24, 1625, the Pott household included John, Elizabeth, and four servants. Mrs. Elizabeth Pott testified before the General Court in May 1625 and October 1627. On one occasion she said that she had given a hog to her servants to dine on, and on another, she said that she allowed Allen Kineston to hire her servant, Stephen Tailor, and that Kineston returned him for medical treatment after he became lame. On December 24, 1627, Mrs. Pott said that she had provided timber and boards to boat-builder William Bennett so that he could construct a vessel for her husband. The Potts apparently were friends of Jamestown merchant Thomas Warnett, who named them in his will. Around 1630, when Dr. John Pott was accused of stealing cattle, Elizabeth went to England to assert his innocence. On July 15, 1631, she was among the Virginia planters asking for relief from the customs duties imposed on imported tobacco (CBE 38, 55, 92, 96; MCGC 58, 155, 158; SH 11-12; CO 1/5 f 234; G&M 165).

***

RICHARD POTTS

Richard Potts, a gentleman, came to Virginia in the 2nd Supply of new colonists and reached Jamestown (**1**) in 1608. Captain John Smith identified him as clerk of the council and credited him with coauthoring a narrative that he included in his *Proceedings* (CJS 1:200, 222, 275; 2:136, 227).

ANTHONY POTTER

Anthony Potter, a 28-year-old glover from Darbyshire, England, came to Virginia in

1619 on the *Bona Nova*, a vessel that carried Virginia Company servants and tenants (FER 295).

HENRY POTTER

On October 20, 1617, Virginia Company officials noted that Henry Potter, who was in the colony, had been pardoned for stealing a calf. Afterward, he fled to the Indians (VCR 3:74).

***

HENRY (HENRIE) POTTER

Henry (Henrie) Potter came to Virginia on the *London Merchant* and on February 16, 1624, was living in Elizabeth City. In early 1625 he was living on the east side of the Hampton River on the Virginia Company's land (**17**). Henry, who was age 50 and free, was living in John Ward's household and may have been a Virginia Company tenant (CBE 43, 67).

ANN POTTER (MRS. HENRY [HENRIE] POTTER)

Ann, the wife of Henry (Henrie) Potter, came to Virginia on the *London Merchant*. In early 1625 the Potters, who were free, were living in John Ward's household on the east side of the Hampton River, on the Virginia Company's land (**17**). It is uncertain whether the Potters were married when they came to the colony (CBE 67).

***

WILLIAM POTTS

On May 6, 1620, officials at Bridewell decided that William Potts, a vagrant brought in from Fleet Street, would be sent to Virginia (CBE 20).

JOHN POUNTIS (PONTIS, POUNTES, POUNTIS, PONTES)

John Pountis (Pontis, Pountes, Pountis, Pontes), a mariner, citizen of London, and cloth worker, made his will in December 1618, probably on the eve of his departure for Virginia. He had an economic interest in the northern fisheries and was an investor in the Virginia Company. In late 1619 or early 1620, he brought 40 passengers to Virginia and then went on a voyage in order to procure sturgeon. Virginia Company officials noted in January 1620 that Pountis wanted to build cellars and special houses in Virginia where sturgeon could be processed. Later in the year he was named to the Council of State and was among those signing a letter stressing the economic importance of tobacco. Virginia Company officials noted that John Pountis wanted to go on another fishing voyage on behalf of the colony. They sent him some books and other supplies for his use while in Virginia and designated him vice-admiral for a year. In 1621 he brought a dozen young, marriageable women to the colony to become wives for the settlers.

In November 1621 the Virginia Company extended John Pountis's appointment as vice-admiral and gave him a stipend of 300 acres and 12 tenants. In January 1622 he obtained a newly arrived indentured servant, who had been his apprentice in England. Pountis informed the Council that a Dutch mariner, Cornelius Johnson, had offered to bring some men to the colony who were capable of building wind-propelled sawmills. On March 22, 1622, when the Indians attacked Warresqueak (**26**), two of John Pountis's men (John Scotchmore and Edward Turner) were killed. In June 1622 Pountis asked Virginia Company officials for permission to return to England, but they denied his request because he was so useful to the colony. They sent him six young male servants in 1622 and promised to send six more the following year. Pountis was treasurer of Southampton Hundred (**44**), and in June 1622 he submitted a petition on the surviving settlers' behalf. In August 1622 he reported that there was much sickness in the colony, especially at Southampton Hundred and Newportes News (**24**), and a great shortage of corn. In January 1623 he told Company officials that in 1622 the King of the Eastern Shore Indians had warned the colonists about a potential attack. He also sent a report on the status of the young maids he had brought to the colony and made an account of John Woodall's cattle. Later in the year, when Pountis went on a trading voyage in the Potomac River, the Indians overran his pinnace and killed several men. In February 1623 Pountis came into court to witness an agreement between two men, and in 1624 he signed a document describing conditions in the colony.

Treasurer George Sandys, so often critical of his fellow officials, said that John Pountis was well intentioned and honest. Pountis played an active role in the colony's affairs, and on February 16, 1624, he was living in Jamestown (1), where he was a household head. He assisted in settling at least three prominent men's estates, and he testified about some corn that had been obtained from the Eastern Shore. Shortly thereafter, he set sail for England as a representative of the Council of State to plead the colony's case. However, he died at sea and his will was proved on March 18, 1624. Because John Pountis's business affairs were intertwined with those of Southampton Hundred, his cow-keepers were summoned to court and appraisers were appointed. When Pountis's assets and liabilities were compared, it was evident that he had not done everything for which he had been paid. Therefore, some funds that ordinarily would have been accruable to his estate were rescinded. Most of Pountis's debts were associated with Southampton Hundred (EEAC 46; WAT 1089-1090; VCR 1:379, 382, 392, 479, 506, 545-550, 558; 2:75, 90-91, 466; 3:118, 243, 482, 486, 492-495, 526-528, 533, 571, 586, 588, 649, 652, 657; 4:9, 41, 89, 108, 110, 183, 185, 450, 453, 474-475, 559-567, 580; FER 138, 139, 308, 322, 436, 437; CJS 2:283; PRO 30/15/2 f 90; CO 1/3 ff 207-208; 5/1354 f 277; SH 5; MCGC 7-8, 10-11, 17, 48-49, 55, 58, 68-70, 77-78, 81-83, 87, 100, 141; HAI 915; CBE 38, 46-48, 70, 73, 77; HEN 1:128-129; G&M 108-109).

ELIZABETH POWELL (POMELL)

On February 16, 1624, Elizabeth Powell (Pomell) was living in urban Jamestown (1) in the home of Sir Francis Wyatt (CBE 38).

HENRY POWELL

Henry Powell, a tradesman, came to Virginia in 1608 in the 2nd Supply of new settlers and resided in Jamestown (1). In late December 1608, he accompanied Captain John Smith on a trading voyage to the Pamunkey Indians' territory. Smith later said that Henry Powell accepted presents from the Indians on his behalf and had protected him when it appeared that he might be ambushed. In 1610 Captain John Smith described Henry Powell as one of his old soldiers and said that he had served as a councilor (CJS 1:241, 244, 251, 252-253, 270; 2:191, 193, 200, 202).

HUGH POWELL

On December 4, 1634, when Hugh Cox received a court order entitling him to a patent, he listed Hugh Powell as a headright (PB 1 Pt. 1:282).

JOHN POWELL

John Powell, a tailor, came to Virginia in the 1st Supply of new settlers and arrived in Jamestown (1) in 1608. Later in the year he accompanied Captain John Smith on an exploratory voyage of the Chesapeake Bay (CJS 1:223-224; 2:162-163).

***

JOHN POWELL I

John Powell I came to Virginia on the *Swallow* in 1609 and was an ancient planter. On June 19, 1622, he claimed that Deputy Governor Samuel Argall had given him some land on the east side of the Hampton River in Elizabeth City (17) and that incoming Governor George Yeardley had confiscated it on behalf of the Virginia Company. In April 1625 Powell was compensated for clearing and building on what had been designated the Company Land in Elizabeth City. By February 16, 1624, he had moved to the west side of the Hampton River but was still living in Elizabeth City (18) and headed a household that included his wife, Catherene (Katherin). On September 20, 1624, when John Powell patented 150 acres of land in Elizabeth City, he was described as a yeoman. On November 1, 1624, interpreter Robert Poole II told the General Court that Powell had been Captain George Webb's servant during Sir Thomas Dale's government and that he had taught Indians how to shoot firearms. A week later John Powell appeared in court to report on an agreement that he and some other men had made with Daniel Gookin for some men and supplies. In early 1625 John Powell I, a 29-year-old household head, was living in Elizabeth City with his wife, Catherene (Katherin), and their young son, John II. The family, which included a male servant, was well provisioned and adequately prepared to defend themselves. In May 1625, when a list of patented land was sent back to England, John Powell was credited with 150 acres in Elizabeth City, acreage that had been planted. In April 1625 he testified about some cattle that were in Lieutenant Shepherd's possession. On November

21, 1625, the General Court acknowledged that the defunct Virginia Company owed some money to John Powell and agreed that he should be compensated from the Company's assets. In September 1632 John Powell served as a burgess for the settlements between Waters Creek and Marie's Mount **(24)** (VCR 2:44; 4:557; CBE 43, 64; PB 1 Pt. 1:26-27; MCGC 28, 30, 52, 56, 76; HEN 1:179; DOR 1:52).

CATHERENE (KATHERIN) POWELL (MRS. JOHN POWELL I)

Catherene (Katherin), who married ancient planter John Powell I, came to Virginia on the *Flying Hart* in 1622 and on February 16, 1624, was living in Elizabeth City **(18)** with her husband, a household head. In early 1625 the Powell family included John, his wife, Catherene (Katherin), who was age 22, and their young son, John II (CBE 43, 64).

JOHN POWELL II

In early 1625, John II, the Virginia-born child of John and Catherene (Katherin) Powell, was living with his parents in Elizabeth City **(18)** (CBE 64).

***

JOHN POWELL

In October 1617 Virginia Company officials were informed that Stephen Sparrow had sent John Powell to Virginia on the *George* (VCR 1:330).

JOHN POWELL

On January 22, 1620, officials at Bridewell decided that John Powell, who had been brought in from Christchurch Parish, would be sent to Virginia (CBE 17).

JOHN POWELL

On July 20, 1625, the General Court noted that Captain John Powell was captain of the *Black Bess* of Flushing (MCGC 66).

***

CAPTAIN NATHANIEL POWELL

Nathaniel Powell, a gentleman, came to Virginia in 1607 and was one of the first Jamestown **(1)** colonists. In 1608 he accompanied Captain John Smith on an exploratory voyage in the Chesapeake Bay, and he went with Anas Todkill on a southward journey to the territory of the Mangoags to search for the Roanoke colonists. In late December 1608 Nathaniel went to Powhatan's York River village, Werowocomoco, with Captain John Smith, who later identified him as a coauthor of the *Proceedings*. Powell was appointed sergeant major general on October 20, 1617, during Deputy Governor Samuel Argall's administration, and in 1618 was present when Edward Brewster was tried in a court martial hearing. Later he witnessed interpreter Henry Spellman's statements about an Indian treaty made while Sir George Yeardley was governor. In April 1619 while Nathaniel Powell was living in the corporation of Charles City, he was named acting governor and served from April 9–19, 1619, stepping aside when Sir George Yeardley arrived. In July he became a burgess and in 1621 was named to the Council of State. On January 21, 1620, Nathaniel Powell was among those who signed a letter to Virginia Company officials stressing the importance of tobacco in the colony's economy. On March 22, 1622, Captain Nathaniel Powell and his wife, Joyce, the daughter of Berkeley Hundred leader William Tracy, were killed at his plantation called Powell-Brooke **(50)**. Captain John Smith described Powell as a valiant soldier and said that he had been beheaded by the Indians. In May 1625, when a list of patented land was sent back to England, he was credited with 600 acres in Charles City within the territory of Great Weyanoke **(52)**. In July 1626 the late Nathaniel Powell's older brother, Thomas Powell, obtained letters of administration that authorized him to take custody of the decedent's estate, which had been wrongfully entrusted to William Powell, a Virginia colonist who reportedly was not related to the decedent or his siblings (CJS 1:208, 230, 265; 2:141, 170, 180, 215, 258, 266. 295, 302; C 24/289; PRO 30/15/2:290; FER 113, 437; VCR 2:107; 3:119, 435-436, 482, 555, 569, 588; CBE 20, 72; G&M 103-104; PB 1 Pt. 1:151).

JOYCE TRACY POWELL (MRS. NATHANIEL POWELL)

In September 1620 Joyce Tracy left Bristol, England, on the *Supply* with her parents,

William and Mary Tracy, and brother, Thomas. On the way to Virginia she married Captain Nathaniel Powell. Joyce and her family arrived at Berkeley Hundred (**55**) on January 29, 1621. Her father died shortly thereafter and her mother and brother decided to return to England. On March 22, 1622, when the Indians attacked Powle-Brooke (Merchants Hope) (**50**), Captain Nathaniel Powell's plantation, Joyce Tracy Powell and her husband were slain (CBE 20-21; VCR 3:396, 426, 555).

THOMAS POWELL

Thomas Powell came to Virginia on the *Seaflower* and on February 16, 1624, was living at Hog Island (**16**). He was still there on February 4, 1625, and was a servant in Ralph Hamor's household. On July 21, 1626, Thomas Powell sent a petition to the Privy Council in an attempt to recover the estate of his younger brother, Captain Nathaniel Powell. He said that the decedent's estate had been handed over to William Powell, even though he was not related to him and his siblings. Thomas Powell noted that after William Powell's death, his widow, Margaret, married Edward Blaney, who then took custody of the late Nathaniel Powell's estate (SR 4530; SAIN 1:81; CBE 42, 61, 72).

***

PHILEMON POWELL

On January 10, 1627, Philemon Powell of Jamestown (**1**) sued Captain John Harvey in an attempt to recover a debt Harvey owed to London merchant John Sharples. The General Court decided to give Powell legal possession of Harvey's real estate in Jamestown so that funds generated from its rental could satisfy his debt to Sharples. In February Powell sought the General Court's assistance in recovering a shipment of wine sent to him on the *Marmaduke*. By September 1627 Philemon Powell was dead. At that time he was identified as a Jamestown merchant who had been serving as John Sharples' factor. Powell died intestate (MCGC 130-131, 139, 152).

RICHARD POWELL

In November 1628 Richard Powell, the assignee of Nathaniel Jeffreys' executors, was ordered to appear before the General Court so that he could respond to John Southern's suit (MCGC 178).

ROGER POWELL

On July 13, 1617, Roger Powell, a prisoner in the Oxford Jail, was reprieved and delivered to Sir Thomas Smyth so that he could be sent to Virginia (SR 4525; CBE 9).

ROWLAND POWELL

On January 23, 1629, merchants Rowland Powell and John Cheseman—who were functioning as the attorneys of John Jeffreys, the late Nathaniel Jeffreys' executor—were ordered to take custody of Nathaniel Jeffreys' servants, who were in Mrs. Bridget Lowther's custody. Jeffreys, who died sometime after March 1626, had lived in Jamestown (**1**). In April–May 1629 Rowland Powell was identified as purser of the *Anne* of London when he wrote a bill of lading for some tobacco being exported from Virginia (MCGC 182; EAE 19).

***

THOMAS POWELL

On November 26, 1609, Thomas Powell, Sir George Somers' cook, married Elizabeth Persons, Mrs. Horton's maid. The couple wed in Bermuda, where they were shipwrecked on the way to Virginia (HAI 413).

ELIZABETH PERSONS POWELL (MRS. THOMAS POWELL)

Elizabeth Persons, Mrs. Horton's maid, married Thomas Powell, Sir George Somers' cook, on November 26, 1609, while in Bermuda but enroute to Virginia (HAI 413).

***

THOMAS POWELL

Thomas Powell came to Virginia on the *Sampson* in 1618. On February 16, 1624, he and his wife were living on the Eastern Shore. He was still there in early 1625 and was identified as a solitary household head, who was well provisioned and supplied with defensive weaponry. Sometime prior to January 1626 Powell testified before the

General Court, stating that Captain Ward had reduced James Blackbourne's term of service by a year. In early February 1627 Thomas Powell's leasehold near the Company Land (76) was mentioned in a patent. Accomack County court records dating to the 1630s suggest that Powell was still alive (CBE 46, 68; PB 1 Pt. 1:76; MCGC 91; DOR 1:69).

[NO FIRST NAME] POWELL (MRS. THOMAS POWELL)

On February 16, 1624, Gody (Goodwife) Powell was living with her husband, Thomas, on the Eastern Shore. They may have been living on his leasehold near the Company Land (76) (CBE 46).

***

THOMAS POWELL

On February 5, 1628, Thomas Powell was identified as the servant of Edward Sharples of Jamestown (1) (MCGC 160-161).

WALTER POWELL

On December 24, 1619, officials at Bridewell decided that Walter Powell would be transported to Virginia (CBE 14).

WILLIAM POWELL

On January 22, 1620, William Powell was among those Bridewell officials decided to send to Virginia (CBE 17).

***

WILLIAM POWELL

Captain William Powell, a Virginia Company investor and gentleman, came to Virginia in 1609 in the 3rd Supply of Jamestown (1) settlers. In 1610 he served as George Percy's ensign and in October 1617 he was appointed captain of Deputy Governor Samuel Argall's guard, commander of Jamestown and its blockhouses, and lieutenant governor. He was present in 1618 when Edward Brewster (one of Lord Delaware's men) was tried in a martial court. Sometime prior to January 1620 William Powell accompanied John Rolfe on a visit to Opechancanough and later in the year he lived briefly at Bermuda Hundred (39). After the 1622 Indian attack, he was criticized for having taught Indians how to use firearms. In 1619 Captain William Powell served as a burgess for James City, and in the assembly's first session accused his servant, Thomas Garnett, of behaving lecherously with a maidservant and of trying to get him killed. Deputy Governor Argall had Powell and his men clear land in Pasbehay (3) for occupancy by some settlers the Society of Martin's Hundred sent to Virginia. Later, Powell tried to force the Martin's Hundred colonists to pay him for the work his men had done, even though Argall had seated them in the wrong location.

In April 1620 Captain William Powell made formal complaints about Governor George Yeardley. However, they later reconciled and took communion together, publicly signifying that they had made amends. Powell, sometimes described as Jamestown's gunner, seems to have favored a return to marital law. Early in 1620 he and a fellow colonist named John Smith took possession of some acreage on Hog Island (16), sharing its use with Samuel Mathews. Powell and his wife, Margaret, had a house in urban Jamestown and he sometimes squabbled with Dr. John Pott, his neighbor. Immediately after the March 1622 Indian attack Captain William Powell went to Martin's Hundred (7) to evacuate survivors and supplies. However, he took custody of the estate of the late Captain Nathaniel Powell, a casualty of the Indian attack, even though he was not a kinsman, a misdeed that escaped notice until after his own death. Late in 1622 Captain Powell led an expedition against the Chickahominy Indians, an offensive that claimed his life. Afterward, his widow, Margaret, married merchant Edward Blaney, who took up residence on the Powell property in Jamestown. Blaney also tried to protect Powell's orphans' interest in his property at Hog Island. William Powell reportedly had a financial interest in a voyage made by the *Furtherance* and in May 1625 when a list of patented land was sent back to England, he was credited with a total of 750 acres of land across from Jamestown but east of Gray's Creek (10-16), acreage that had been settled and was on the west side of Lower Chippokes Creek (CJS 2:222, 280, 310, 318, 482; HAI 512; VCR 1:126, 146, 308, 336; 3:74-75, 87, 118-119, 153, 159, 169, 175-176, 244-245, 332, 436-438, 444; 4:9, 22-26, 104, 365, 551, 555, 566; C 24/489;

STAN 52; FER 244, 437; MCGC 9, 28, 40, 59, 63, 65-66, 80, 130-131; SAIN 1:36; CBE 31, 72; G&M 103-104; PB 2:81; DOR 2:40).

MARGARET POWELL
(MRS. WILLIAM POWELL,
MRS. EDWARD BLANEY,
MRS. FRANCIS WEST)
(SEE MRS. EDWARD BLANEY,
MRS. FRANCIS WEST)

Around 1623 Margaret, Captain William Powell's widow and a resident of Jamestown (1), married cape merchant Edward Blaney, who moved into her home. He placed servants on Captain Powell's acreage at Hog Island (16) and at Lower Chippokes Creek in an attempt to protect the decedent's heirs' legal interest in the property. Margaret Powell Blaney was widowed again and sometime prior to February 6, 1626, wed Captain Francis West. She died before March 1628, when West (then acting governor) married Sir George Yeardley's widow, Lady Temperance (MCGC 58, 93, 110; MEY 656; DOR 2:31, 40).

GEORGE POWELL

George, the orphan of William Powell, inherited his late father's property on the lower side of the James River at Lower Chippokes Creek. George died without heirs—the property he had inherited escheated to the Crown and in 1646 was patented by another (PB 2:81).

***

POWHATAN (WAHUNSUNACOCK)

When the first colonists arrived in Virginia in 1607, much of the coastal plain's native population was under the sway of a paramount chief named Powhatan or Wahunsunacock. He ruled 32 districts that encompassed more than 150 villages whose inhabitants supported him in times of war and paid him tribute. Captain John Smith described Powhatan as a monarch to whom many lesser kings (or werowances) were subservient. He reportedly was tall and well proportioned and had gray hair and a thin beard. Powhatan, despite his age, was described as strong and hardy and his intelligence was well known to the English, who considered him crafty. Although he was presented with a crown and some gifts from King James, symbolically making him an English subject, he refused to kneel for the crown to be placed on his head. Some political leaders believed that Powhatan and Opechancanough plotted to see that the colonists' treaty with the Chickahominy Indians was broken. Around the first of April 1614, Powhatan's daughter, Pocahontas, married John Rolfe in the church in Jamestown (1). The union had Powhatan's consent. By 1617 Powhatan's influence over his people may have begun to wane. In June he went to visit the King of the Potomac Indians. Powhatan died in 1618, a year after the death of his daughter, Pocahontas. The taking up of Powhatan's bones is thought to have coincided with the March 1622 Indian attack against the settlements along the James River (VCR 3:70-74; 4:9, 111; HAI 179, 281-282, 299, 615, 809).

THOMAS POWES (POWIS)

Thomas Powes (Powis) came to Virginia in 1621 on the *Temperance* at the expense of Sir George Yeardley. In 1628 Thomas's headright was transferred to Thomas Flint, who used it when patenting some land (MCGC 166; PB 1 Pt. 1:59).

JOHN POYNE (POYNES)

In mid-May 1620 the Virginia Company assigned a patent to John Poyne (Poynes) and his associates (VCR 1:341, 345).

FRANCIS POYTHRESS

On February 9, 1633, the General Court gave Francis Poythress two letters of administration, at his request. One was for Roger Kidd's estate and the other for Thomas Hall's. On July 13, 1637, Francis patented some land in Charles City County, near Jordan's Point (46), using himself and others as headrights (MCGC 202; PB 1 Pt. 1:439).

GEORGE PRAN

On February 16, 1624, George Pran was living in Archer's Hope (6) (CBE 41).

THOMAS PRATER (PRATT)

In 1622 Thomas Prater (Pratt) came to Virginia on the *Marie Providence* and in early 1625 was living in Elizabeth City (18), where he was a 20-year-old servant in the household of John Powell. On November 20, 1636, Thomas Pratt witnessed the will made by the Rev. Thomas Butler of Elizabeth City (CBE 64; WITH 49).

ISABELL PRATT

Isabell Pratt came to Virginia on the *Jonathan* and on February 16, 1624, was living in the Neck O'Land (**5**). She was still there on February 4, 1625, at which time she was identified as a servant in the household of Richard Kingsmill (CBE 35, 58).

JOHN PRATT

John Pratt, a gentleman and tradesman, came to Virginia in 1608 in the 2nd Supply of new colonists and lived in Jamestown (**1**). In late December 1608 Pratt was among those who went with Captain John Smith to the Pamunkey Indians' territory. In 1620 Pratt was identified as a Virginia Company investor (CJS 1:244; 2:191, 193, 280).

RICHARD PRATT (PRATE)

In May 1625, when a list of patented land was sent back to England, Richard Pratt (Prate) was credited with 150 acres of land in Great Weyanoke (**52**), acreage that was unplanted (VCR 4:554).

JOHN PREEN (PREENE, PRYNN, PRINN)

On June 23, 1623, John Preen (Preene, Prynn, Prinn) of the *London Merchant*, an experienced mariner and merchant, received a patent from the Virginia Company. Throughout the next decade he made numerous trips to Virginia. In July 1626 he brought passengers on the *Peter and John* and was given a warrant for some powder he transported. Official records dating to March 1627 indicate that he brought some of George Sandys' servants to the colony. He was identified as captain of the *Samuel* of Newcastle when he brought the *Saker*'s purser, Thomas Gregory, to the colony. Eventually he sued Captain William Saker's estate to recover the cost of Gregory's passage. John Preen charged Edward Bennett for transporting two male servants to Virginia on the *Hopewell* in 1623, even though he failed to deliver them. Bennett brought suit and in March 1628

Preen was fined by the General Court and ordered to replace the servants. He also was told to deliver some barrels of raisins to the Bennetts, owners of the plantation known as Bennett's Welcome (**26**). Preen ran afoul of the law on another occasion when he left the late John Moseley's servants in the West Indies instead of bringing them to Captain Smith in Virginia. As captain of the *Friendship* of London, Preen brought incoming governor John Harvey to Virginia. Simultaneously, his ship, the *Trial* of London, made a transatlantic crossing. Preen also seems to have had a financial interest in the *Indeavor*. In 1630 he successfully sought the release of the *Trial* and was allowed to proceed to Virginia with passengers. He had purchased the ship from Captain William Smith, who had it detained and tried to have Preen's license revoked. Captain John Preen died sometime prior to February 9, 1633 (VCR 2:449; SAIN 1:81; CBE 72-73, 77-78, 83, 87, 92; MCGC 144, 169-171,173, 180, 201-202; G&M 136).

HELEN PRESCOTT

On November 20, 1622, officials at Bridewell decided that Helen Prescott, who was being detained in Newgate Prison, would be transported overseas (CBE 29).

ROGER PRESTON

Roger Preston came to Virginia in March 1621 on the *Discovery* and on February 16, 1624, was living in Jordan's Journey (**46**). He was still there on January 21, 1625, and was identified as a 21-year-old servant in the household headed by William Farrar and Cisley Jordan (CBE 36, 51).

GEORGE PRETTY

George Pretty, a gentleman and Virginia Company investor, came to Virginia in the 1st Supply of new colonists and reached Jamestown (**1**) in early 1608 (CJS 1:222; 2:161, 280).

[NO FIRST NAME] PRICE

According to Captain John Smith, in 1607 Mr. Price and a man named Webb, who were part of the first group of Jamestown (**1**) colonists, allegedly hatched some sort of plot. Smith referred to their scheme as "evil plans" (CJS 2:240; HAI 822).

DAVID PRICE

On December 31, 1629, officials at Bridewell decided that David Price, who had been brought in by the marshal of Middlesex, would be sent to Virginia (CBE 14).

EDWARD PRICE

Edward Price died on the lower side of the James River within the corporation of James City (8-15) sometime after April 1623 but before February 16, 1624 (CBE 41).

***

EDWARD PRICE (PRISE)

Edward Price (Prise) came to Virginia on the *George* in 1623 and on February 16, 1624, was living in urban Jamestown (1). On January 24, 1625, he was still there and was identified as a servant in Richard Stephens' household. Price eventually married Eleanor, Robert Brittin's (Brittaine's) widow. He died sometime prior to April 9, 1629, and was survived by his wife, Eleanor, who was ordered to inventory his estate (CBE 38, 56; MCGC 196).

ELEANOR PRICE (PRISE) (MRS. ROBERT BRITTIN [BRITTAINE], MRS. EDWARD PRICE [PRISE]) (SEE MRS. ROBERT BRITTIN [BRITTAINE])

Sometime prior to April 9, 1629, Eleanor, Robert Brittin's (Brittaine's) widow, married Edward Price (Prise). She outlived him too, and on April 9, 1629, the General Court ordered her to make an inventory of both men's estates (MCGC 196).

***

HENRY PRICE

Henry Price was killed at Warresqueak (26) during the March 22, 1622, Indian attack. In 1620 Captain John Smith identified him as an investor in the Virginia Company (VCR 3:571; CJS 2:280).

HUGH PRICE (PRYSE)

According to Captain John Smith, during the "Starving Time" (the winter of 1609–

1610), Jamestown (1) settler Hugh Price (Pryse)—who was delirious, ranting blasphemously, and walking around in the settlement's marketplace—was killed by Indians. When slain, he was with a butcher who reportedly was obese (HAI 507).

***

HUGH PRICE

Hugh Price came to Virginia on the *William and John* in January 1618. On February 16, 1624, he was living at Bermuda Hundred (39) with his wife and their child. On January 24, 1625, Hugh Price, a 35-year-old household head, was sharing his home in Bermuda Hundred with his wife, Judith, and their 2-year old son, John. The Prices were amply supplied with stored food and defensive weaponry and had some cattle and poultry (CBE 36, 54; DOR 1:11).

JUDITH PRICE (MRS. HUGH PRICE)

Judith, who married Hugh Price, came to Virginia on the *Marigold* in May 1619. On February 16, 1624, she, her husband, and their child were living in Bermuda Hundred (39). On January 24, 1625, Judith Price was 24 years old and her husband, Hugh, was 35. Their son, John, was age 2 (CBE 36, 54; DOR 1:11).

JOHN PRICE

On February 16, 1624, John Price, an infant, was living with his parents, Hugh and Judith Price, in their home at Bermuda Hundred (39). The Prices were still there on January 24, 1625, at which time John was 2 years old (CBE 36, 54; DOR 1:11).

***

***

JOHN PRICE I

In 1625 the muster-taker noted that John Price I came to Virginia on the *Starr* in May. As the *Starr* brought Sir Thomas Dale to Virginia in May 1611, Price probably reached the colony at that time and was an ancient planter. On February 20, 1620, he received a patent for 150 acres in the corporation of Henrico. John Price I and his wife were living in Bermuda Hundred (39) on

February 16, 1624. They were still there on January 24, 1625, and John, who was age 40, headed a household that included his wife, Ann, and the couple's 3-month-old daughter, Mary. The Prices also had a son named Mathew, whose name was omitted from the census and muster. The Price household was amply supplied with stored food and defensive weaponry and had some cattle and poultry. In May 1625, when a list of patented land was sent back to England, John Price I was credited with his 150 acres on the south side of the James River, within the corporation of Henrico. On May 12, 1625, he appeared before the General Court, where he testified about some statements Captain John Martin had made about a trip to Canada. He died in 1628, leaving his widow, Ann, and at least two children, John II and Mathew (CBE 35, 54; VCR 4:552; MCGC 61-62; DOR 1:10; 2:828-829).

(MRS. JOHN PRICE I, MRS. ROBERT HALAM [HOLLAM, HALLOM] I, MRS. DANIEL LLEWELYN) (SEE MRS. ROBERT HALAM [HOLLAM, HALLAM])

Ann, the wife of John Price I, came to Virginia on the *Francis Bonaventure* in August 1620. On February 16, 1624, the Prices were living at Bermuda Hundred (39). They were still there on January 24, 1625, at which time Ann was described as age 21. Ann and John Price had a 3-month-old daughter, Mary. Ann Price, who was widowed in 1628, married Robert Hallom around 1630, and they had three children together. Ann was widowed again by May 1638, when she repatented the Hallom land. Ann married Daniel Llewelyn and died sometime prior to 1666 (CBE 35, 54; DOR 1:10; 2:231-232, 828-829, 849).

JOHN PRICE II

John Price II, the youngest son of John Price I and his wife, Ann, was born sometime after January 24, 1625, and died sometime prior to 1662, by which time his widow had remarried (DOR 1:10; 2:829).

MARY PRICE

On January 24, 1625, Mary, the 3-month-old daughter of John and Mary Price, was living with her parents in the family home in Bermuda Hundred (39) (CBE 54; DOR 1:10).

MATHEW PRICE

On May 23, 1638, Mathew Price, who identified himself as the heir of John Price I and his wife, Ann, patented some land in Henrico County. His name apparently was omitted from the 1625 muster (PB 1 Pt. 2:558; DOR 2:828-829).

***

JOHN PRICE

On February 5, 1620, officials at Bridewell decided that John Price, who was from Aldgate, would be detained until he could be sent to Virginia (CBE 18).

JOHN PRICE

On July 11, 1629, John Price shipped some goods from London to Virginia on the *Hopewell* (CBE 87).

RICHARD PRICE

In November 1630 the will of Richard Price, who had died in Virginia, was presented for probate. He was described as a citizen and vintner of London and former resident of St. Margaret, Westminster, in Middlesex. Price was survived by his wife, Margaret, who was authorized to settle his estate (CBE 92-93; EEAC 47).

ROBERT PRICE (PRISE)

Robert Price (Prise) died at Flowerdew Hundred (53) sometime after April 1623 but before February 16, 1624 (CBE 37).

WALTER PRICE (PRIEST)

Walter Price (Priest) came to Virginia on the *William and Thomas* in 1618 and on February 16, 1624, was living at Chaplin's Choice (56). He was still there on January 21, 1625, at which time he and Henry Turner headed a household that included one servant. Testimony taken before the General Court on January 17, 1625, reveals that Walter Price was a member of Truelove's Company and that Nathaniel Causey, as the Truelove group's agent, had agreed to furnish three men to seat their plantation if Ensign Isaac Chaplin would permit Price, Henry Turner, and their servant to stay on his land. In October 1629 Walter Price served as a burgess for Chaplin's Choice, and in March 1630 he represented Chaplin's Choice and Jordan's Journey (46) (CBE 37, 51; MCGC 43; HEN 1:138, 148; DOR 1:21).

WILLIAM PRICE

William Price came to Virginia on the *Starr*. On February 16, 1624, he was living at the College (66). He was still there on January 23, 1625, and was described as a household head who lived alone. William Price's arrival on the *Starr*, the vessel that brought Sir Thomas Dale to Virginia in May 1611, suggests strongly that he was an ancient planter (CBE 35, 53; DOR 1:8).

[NO FIRST NAME] PRITCHARD

In 1619 a man whose surname was Pritchard came to Virginia on the *Garland* at the expense of John Ferrar and Thomas Sheppard. Thus, he probably was associated with the Virginia Company (EAE 9).

EDMUND PRITCHARD

Edmund Pritchard, purser of the *Marmaduke*, died sometime prior to January 11, 1627. It was then that Patrick Kennede (Kennedy) presented his will and inventory to the General Court. The decedent's will was provided by Robert Dennys (Dennis), another mariner (MCGC 133).

ELIZABETH PRITCHARD

Because of an outbreak of jail fever, Elizabeth Pritchard, who was being detained at Newgate Prison, was reprieved on November 20, 1622 so that she and some fellow inmates could be transported overseas (CBE 29).

HENRY PRITCHARD

On February 16, 1624, Henry Pritchard was living in Elizabeth City (17, 18) (CBE 44).

JOHN PRITCHARD

John Pritchard, a carpenter for the Company of Shipwrights, came to Virginia in 1622. On May 18, 1622, Virginia Company officials told his supervisor, master boatbuilder Thomas Nunn, that he was to have 5 acres of land when his term of indenture expired. Pritchard, like Nunn and the others who came to the colony under the sponsorship of the Company of Shipwrights, arrived in the wake of the 1622 Indian attack and built homes on Jamestown Island (1) (FER 378).

ROGER PRITCHARD

Roger Pritchard died during 1629, at which time John Dansey presented an inventory of his estate to the General Court. On June 5, 1632, Jeremy Clements was named the decedent's administrator and given the responsibility of distributing his estate among his creditors. Dansy and Clements were residents of the corporation of James City, raising the possibility that Pritchard was as well (MCGC 200-201).

THOMAS PRICHARD

Thomas Pritchard came to Virginia on the *Abigail* in 1620 and on February 16, 1624, was living on the Maine (3) just west of Jamestown Island. On January 30, 1625, when a muster was made of that area's inhabitants, Thomas Pritchard was identified as a 28-year-old servant in Dr. John Pott's household. On January 20, 1626, he testified before the General Court about a fight between two of Pott's servants that took place on February 19, 1625 or 1626 (CBE 39, 58; MCGC 94-95).

THOMAS PRICHARD

Thomas Prichard died on the lower side of the James River, within the corporation of James City (8-15) sometime after April 1623 but before February 16, 1624 (CBE 41).

***

JOHN PRICKETT (PRICHETT)

On November 30, 1626, John Prickett (Prichett), brother of the late Miles Prickett, was named his brother's executor and heir. He inherited Miles's 200 acres in Elizabeth City (18), near Salford's Creek (WAT 206).

MILES PRICKETT (PRICHETT)

Miles Prickett (Prichett) came to Virginia on the *Starr* in 1610 (actually, 1611) and was an ancient planter. During his first years in the colony, he reportedly made salt. This raises the possibility that he was among those Sir Thomas Dale sent to the Eastern Shore to establish a salt works on Smith's Island **(72)**. Miles Prickett returned to England, but on September 11, 1621, the Virginia Company decided to send him back to the colony as a salt-maker. He was obliged to serve until Allholllantide 1622, that is, November 1, 1622. Virginia Company records dating to January 1622 reveal that Maurice Berkeley was given the responsibility of building a salt works and that Miles Prickett was supposed to work under his supervision. On February 16, 1624, Prickett was living in Elizabeth City **(18)**, and by September 20, 1624, he was in possession of some land adjacent to Robert Salford's. In early 1625 Miles Prickett, who was age 36, shared a home with Francis Mitchell and his family. In May 1625, when a list of patented land was sent back to England, Miles Prickett was credited with 150 acres in Elizabeth City, land that had been seated. When he made his will on November 30, 1626, he described himself as an adventurer in Virginia and a baker of St. Cross near Canterbury, in Kent. Miles Prickett left his 200 acres in Elizabeth City near Salford's Creek to his brother, John, and named him executor of his estate (CBE 44, 63, 78; VCR 3:507, 586; 4:558; PB 1 Pt. 1:30; EEAC 47; WAT 206; DOR 1:52).

***

MARGERY PRICKETT (PRICHETT)

On February 16, 1624, Margery Prickett (Prichett) was living in Elizabeth City **(17, 18)** (CBE 44).

THOMAS PRICKETT (PRICHETT)

Thomas Prickett (Prichett) died at Warresqueak **(26)** sometime after April 1623 but before February 16, 1624 (CBE 42).

WILLIAM PRICKETT (PRICHETT)

On December 1, 1624, William Prickett (Prichett) was in possession of some land adjacent to John Bush's property in Elizabeth City **(18)** (PB 1 Pt. 1:31).

JOHN PRIEST

John Priest, a tailor from Langport in Somersetshire, England, arrived in James-town on September 12, 1623, aboard the *Bonny Bess* and took the oath of supremacy (MCGC 6).

ALICE PRIESTLEY

On November 20, 1622, officials at Bridewell decided that Alice Priestly, an inmate at Newgate, would be transported overseas (CBE 29).

ANN PRINCE

Ann Prince left England on July 31, 1622, on the *James*, accompanying William Rowley and his family to Virginia. The Rowleys lived in Jamestown **(1)** (FER 400).

EDWARD PRINN

On June 25, 1623, the Virginia Company decided that Edward Prinn would receive a patent because he was taking 100 people to Virginia (VCR 2:457).

MARTIN PRINN

On July 3, 1622, Captain Martin Prinn of the *Royal James* was given land by the Virginia Company (VCR 2:73).

WILLIAM PRIOR (PRYOR)

On October 3, 1625, William Prior (Pryor) and Robert Saben were summoned before the General Court, and Prior was ordered to bring a copy of their covenants. In 1635 William Prior secured a patent for 600 acres on the York River between Ballard Creek and Bracken Pond, receiving part of his land for seating his plantation **(34)** while it was on the colony's frontier. When William made his will in 1647, he left his interest in the *Honor* to his eldest daughter, Margaret, and some land to his daughter, Mary. He also made monetary bequests to several people, including the children of his brother-in-law, Jasper Playton (MCGC 72, SR 3995; EEAC 47; WITH 107-108; PB 1 Pt. 1: 223, 427, 447).

[NO FIRST NAME] PRISEMAN

On January 3, 1625, a man named Priseman was living at Shirley Hundred **(41)** on behalf of the Society of Berkeley Hundred's **(55)** investors (MCGC 42).

[NO FIRST NAME] PROBY

On September 5, 1626, James Carter, who had acquired some Virginia land from the late Lord Delaware's widow, gave Mr. Proby, a clergyman, 50 acres in Shirley Hundred (now Eppes) Island (**41**). The acreage was to be used as a glebe in perpetuity by Proby and the clergy who succeeded him (WAT 1016-1017).

***

JOHN PROCTOR

Even though the 1625 muster states that John Proctor, an ancient planter, reached Virginia in 1607 on the *Seaventure*, it is much more likely that he came to the colony in 1609-1610 in one of the vessels that comprised part of Sir Thomas Gates's fleet. In December 1617 Proctor was identified as a debtor in the will made by Robert Smalley of Bermuda Hundred (**39**). Sometime after 1621 he wed Alice (Allis, Allice), whom Captain John Smith described as a proper gentlewoman. By early 1622 the Proctor couple had established a plantation (**70**) on the lower side of the James River within the corporation of Henrico. According to Captain John Smith, on March 22, 1622, when the Indians attacked the sparsely scattered settlements along the banks of the James River, Mrs. Alice Proctor single-handedly defended the family home, which was adjacent to what became known as Proctor's Creek. In the wake of the Indian attack, the Proctors, like other colonists living near the head of the James River, were ordered to withdraw to positions of greater safety. As soon as the Proctors abandoned their home, the Indians returned and destroyed it. In 1623 John Proctor, who said that he had been in Virginia for 14 years, was among those who refuted Captain Nathaniel Butler's allegations about the colony. On June 25, 1623, the Virginia Company agreed to give John Proctor a patent for transporting 100 people to Virginia. He, in turn, agreed to serve as the attorney for two London merchants so that he could recover funds they were owed by the late Hugh Crowder. Proctor also was supposed to send the two merchants' surplus goods to Virginia. On February 16, 1624, John and Alice Proctor and their servants were living at Paces Paines (**9**) on land they were renting. They were still there on February 4, 1625, and were well provi-

sioned and outfitted with defensive weaponry. The Proctors apparently had become hardened to life, for in October 1624 they were brought before the authorities and accused of causing the death of a servant girl they had ordered flogged with stout cord and fishhooks. Court testimony provided by some of the Proctors' servants suggests that they were guilty and that they also were responsible for the death of another servant. Moreover, the Proctors were accused of detaining another planter's servant. In May 1625 John Proctor was credited with 100 acres within the corporation of Henrico, the plantation he and his wife had seated prior to the 1622 Indian attack. By July 3, 1627, John Proctor was dead, at which time his widow, Alice, presented the justices of the General Court with an inventory of his estate and was designated his administrator. Among the debts Alice was authorized to collect on her late husband's behalf were sums owed by a Dutch carpenter and a man who had lost Proctor's small boat (SR 3112; SH 4; VCR 2:385, 457; 3:611; 4:245-246, 466-467, 552; CBE:40, 59; CJS 2:303; MCGC 12-13, 22-24, 54, 62, 78, 150; DOR 1:38).

ALICE (ALLIS, ALLICE) PROCTOR (MRS. JOHN PROCTOR)

Alice (Allis, Allice), who became the wife of ancient planter John Proctor, came to Virginia in 1621 on the *George*. By 1622 the Proctors had established a home (**70**) on the lower side of the James River within the corporation of Henrico. According to Captain John Smith, on March 22, 1622, when the Indians attacked the settlements thinly scattered along the banks of the James River, Mrs. Proctor, "a proper, civill, modest Gentlewoman," stoutly fended off her attackers and successfully preserved her home, which was adjacent to what became known as Proctor's Creek. The Proctors, like other colonists living near the head of the James River, were ordered to withdraw to positions of greater safety. They may have moved temporarily to Jamestown (**1**), for in April 1625 Alice and another colonist were accused of killing a hog that belonged to George Graves, a resident of the capital city until at least 1629. By February 16, 1624, John and Alice Proctor and their servants were living at Paces Paines (**9**), a plantation across the river from Jamestown. They apparently had a cruel streak, for they were summoned before the authorities and accused of causing the death of a maidservant they had had flogged and a man servant they had caused to be brutally beaten. In May 1625 Alice Proctor appeared before the General Court as a witness against Captain John Martin of Martin's Brandon **(59)**. On July 3, 1627, Mrs. Alice Proctor informed the General Court that her husband, John, was dead and presented an inventory of his possessions. She was designated his administrator (VCR 2:375; 3:611; CBE 40, 59; CJS 2:303; MCGC 22-24, 54, 62, 150).

***

THOMAS PROCTOR

Thomas Proctor, a servant, came to Virginia in 1623 on the *Mary Providence* at the expense of Captain Richard Shepperd. Later, Proctor's headright was sold to John Powell, who used it when patenting some land. On October 9, 1624, Thomas Proctor, who had returned to England, made his will. He indicated that he was from Stepney, Middlesex, and was a citizen and haberdasher of London. He said that he had some goods in Virginia, and he designated his wife, Jane Proctor alias Squires, and his uncle, William Gray, as his executors. The testator also made reference to his son, Samuel Proctor, then a minor (PB 1 Pt. 1:27; WITH 70-72; CBE 48; EEAC 47).

RICHARD PRODGET

Richard Prodget, a gentleman, arrived in Virginia in early 1608 in the 1st Supply of new colonists. He would have resided in Jamestown **(1)** (CJS 1:222; 2:161).

JONAS PROFIT (PROPHETT)

Jonas Profit (Prophett), a sailor, came to Virginia in 1607 and was one of the first to arrive in Jamestown **(1)**. According to Captain John Smith, Jonas accompanied him on two exploratory voyages of the Chesapeake Bay, and in late December 1608 he went with Smith on a visit to Werowocomoco, Powhatan's York River village. Besides describing Jonas Profit as a sailor, Smith also identified him as a soldier and fisherman (CJS 1:209, 224, 230; 2:142, 163, 170, 193).

JACOB PROFIT (PHROPHETT)

Jacob Profit (Prophett) died in Jamestown **(1)** sometime after April 1623 but before February 16, 1624 (CBE 39).

JANE PROSSER

Jane Prosser came to Virginia in 1628 on the *Hopewell* at the expense of Adam Thorogood, who used her headright on June 24, 1635, when securing a patent (PB 1 Pt. 1:179).

THOMAS PROSSER

On April 30, 1623, when Thomas Prosser signed a document rebutting Captain Nathaniel Butler's allegations about the conditions in the colony, he said that he had made three trips to Virginia as a master's mate and had stayed in the colony for nine months (VCR 2:386).

WALTER PROSSER

In September 1620 Walter Prosser set sail from Bristol, England, on the ship *Supply* and was among those who went with William Tracy to Berkeley Hundred **(55)**. Prosser was supposed to serve the Society of Berkeley Hundred's investors for a period of years in exchange for some land. Governor George Yeardley later indicated that Walter Prosser arrived at his destination on January 29, 1621, but died within a relatively short time (CBE 21; VCR 3:397, 426).

[NO FIRST NAME] PROWSE (PROUSE)

Mr. Prowse (Prouse) was killed at Warresqueak **(26)** during the March 22, 1622, Indian attack (VCR 3:571).

GEORGE PROWSE (PROUSE)

George Prowse (Prouse) came to Virginia on the *Diana* and on February 16, 1624, was living at Hog Island **(16)**. By February 4, 1625, he had moved to Archer's Hope **(6)** and was living in a household headed by Joseph Johnson. On August 29, 1625, when Prowse testified before the General Court, he said that he had gone with Mr. Thomas Bransby to Joseph Johnson's house to investigate a domestic dispute and that he had returned later on to retrieve Bransby's hat and hat band. George Prowse, when testifying, identified Bransby as his master. In November 1628 Prowse was fined for disobeying a law that required all householders to plant corn (CBE 41, 58; MCGC 70, 178).

WILLIAM PROWSE (PROUSE)

William Prowse (Prouse) came to Virginia on the *Temperance* in 1624. On August 18, 1627, Gilbert Peppett used him as a headright when patenting some land (PB 1 Pt. 1:50).

HENRY PRUST

On January 8, 1631, English officials noted that Henry Prust, master of the *Friendship* of Bideford, was going from Barnstaple to Virginia (CBE 94).

JOHN PRYNN (SEE JOHN PREEN, PREENE, PRINN)

FRANCES (FRANCIS) PUDEVANT (PUDERANT)

On February 27, 1619, the Bridewell Court decided that Frances (Francis) Pudevant (Puderant), a boy brought in from All Hallows, would be sent to Virginia. He was part of a large group of children rounded up from the streets of London so that they could be transported to the colony (CBE 12).

CHRISTOPHER PUGGETT (PUGETT)

On February 16, 1624, Christopher Puggett (Pugett) was living at Flowerdew Hundred (53) (CBE 37).

CESAR PUGGETT (PUGETT)

Cesar Puggett (Pugett) came to Virginia on the *Diana* in 1619 and on February 16, 1624, was living at Flowerdew Hundred (53). By February 4, 1625, he had moved to Hog Island (16), at which time he was described as a 20-year-old servant in Sir George Yeardley's household (CBE 37, 61).

BENNETT PULLE (PULLEY?)

Bennett Pulle (Pulley?) came to Virginia on the *Marmaduke* in 1621. On September 1, 1628, George Pace used his headright when patenting his late father's acreage at Paces Paines (9) (PB 1 Pt. 1:64).

RICHARD PULLEY (PULLE)

On May 26, 1623, Richard Pulley (Pulle) of Staples Inn, London, who was 32 years old, affirmed the authenticity of an affidavit signed by Sir Samuel Argall. He testified in the Chancery suit that the Earl of Warwick brought against Edward Brewster, one of the late Lord Delaware's men, involving the *Neptune* and the *Treasurer*. Pulley's familiarity with the case suggests that he was in Virginia in 1618–1619 (HCA 13/44 ff 114vo-145ro; EAE 13).

RICHARD PULLIPEN

In 1621 Richard Pullipen came to Virginia on the *Elizabeth* at the expense of John Sipsey, who used his headright when patenting some land. Pullipen had been brought to the colony from Newfoundland (PB 1 Pt. 1:46).

HENRY PUMRY

Henry Pumry indicated that he had been present on January 30, 1630, when Lyonell Roulston transferred 50 acres at Strawberry Banks (17) to his friend John Neal (PB 1 Pt. 1:135).

***

THOMAS PURFOY (PUREFOY, PURFRAY, PURFREY, PURFURY, PURIFOY, PURIFIE, PURIFYE, PURRIFIE)

Thomas Purfoy (Purefoy, Purfray, Purfrey, Purfury, Purifoy, Purifie, Purifye, Purrifie) came to Virginia on the *George* in 1621 and on February 16, 1624, was living on the lower side of the James River to the east of Gray's Creek (10-16), within the corporation of James City. By early 1625 Purfoy, who was age 43, had moved to Elizabeth City (18), where he headed a well-equipped household that he shared with Daniel Tanner, Christopher Calthrope, and two servants. By August 1626 Thomas Purfoy had become a lieutenant and was named a commissioner of Elizabeth City's monthly court. In July 1627 he was authorized to lead an expedition against the Nansemond Indians. In September 1628 Thomas patented 100 acres in Elizabeth City near the fields called Fort Henry. Later that year he testified before the General Court on Captain John Stone's behalf. In March 1629 Captain Thomas Purfoy was instructed to have a local man arrested or post a bond on account of his indebtedness. By that time

Purfoy had been named principal commander of Elizabeth City. He continued to serve as a commissioner of the area's monthly court. In March 1630 Thomas Purfoy served as a burgess for the lower (eastern) part of Elizabeth City. In that capacity he was ordered to inspect the site selected for the construction of a fort at Old Point Comfort (**17**). In 1631 he obtained a 500-acre leasehold in Elizabeth City on the Back River (**19**), and a year later he was named to the Council of State. Thomas Purfoy's wife, Lucy, identified herself as a resident of Back River when testifying that William Claiborne had given her husband some cattle and then reclaimed them. In April 1635 Thomas Purfoy confirmed his patents for 2,000 acres of land in Elizabeth City, half of which was on the Poquoson River. Several months later he acquired an additional 100 acres that originally had been assigned to Captain Thomas Grayes, an ancient planter. Purfoy died between September 1638 and October 1639 (CBE 40, 65, 208; MCGC 106, 151, 179, 193; PB 1 Pt. 1:88, 163, 323; Pt. 2:601, 680; HEN 1:131-132, 149-150, 153, 170, 178, 187, 202; SR 11330; DOR 1:54; 2:863-864).

LUCY PURFOY (PUREFOY, PURFRAY, PURFREY, PURFURY, PURIFOY, PURIFIE, PURIFYE, PURRIFIE) (MRS. THOMAS PURFOY [PURFRAY, PURFREY, PURFURY, PURIFOY, PURIFIE, PURIFYE, PURRIFIE])

Sometime prior to 1629 Lucy, the wife of Thomas Purfoy (Purefoy, Purfray, Purfrey, Purfury, Purifoy, Purifie, Purifye, Purrifie), identified herself as a resident of the Back River area (**19**) when she testified that William Claiborne had given her husband some cattle. In June 1648 Lucy Purfoy was mentioned as the occupant of some neighboring land (SR 11330; PB 2:139; DOR 2:864).

***

EDWARD PURQUITE

On January 3, 1625, Edward Purquite was identified as one of the men who were living at Shirley Hundred (**41**) on behalf of the Society of Berkeley Hundred's (**55**) investors (MCGC 42).

WILLIAM PUSSETT (PUFFET)

William Pussett (Puffet) was killed at Weyanoke (**52**) during the March 22, 1622, Indian attack and was identified as one of Sir George Yeardley's people (VCR 3:569).

[NO FIRST NAME] PUTTOCK (PUTTOCKE)

In 1610 a man named Puttock (Puttocke), who was described as a lieutenant or captain, was in charge of the blockhouse in Jamestown (**1**). Contrary to orders, he ventured out and was ambushed, then stabbed to death, by a Pasbehay Indian (HAI 512-513).

WILLIAM PYLGRYM

On November 20, 1622, William Pylgrym was among the Newgate inmates who were pardoned because of an outbreak of jail fever and then sentenced to transportation overseas (CBE 29).

Q

ANN QUAILE (MRS. RICHARD QUAILE [QUAYLE]?)

Ann Quaile (Quayle) died in Jamestown (**1**) after April 1623 but before February 16, 1624. She may have been the wife of Richard Quaile (Quayle) (CBE 39).

RICHARD QUAILE (QUAYLE)

Captain Richard Quaile (Quayle), who in 1622 paid for Roger Monroe's transportation to Virginia aboard the *James,* was master of the *Ann.* In February 1623 the Virginia Company authorized him to take passengers to Virginia and then go on a fishing voyage. In March 1624, while Sir Francis Wyatt was governor, Quaile was found guilty of making slanderous speeches against high-ranking officials. As a result, he was was pilloried and lost his ears, and he was demoted to the status of a carpenter. Quaile promptly asked the governor for a pardon, claiming that he was sick, poor, and deeply in debt. He also indicated that both his wife and servant were dead. Richard Quaile appears to have been pardoned, for he returned to sea. In November 1632, when his death was reported, he was identified as the captain of the *Great Seahorse*, a vessel that made regular trips from the plantations to the West Indies (FER 400; VCR 2:262; 4:468; MCGC 12; CBE 104).

WILLIAM QUERKE

William Querke came to Virginia in 1621 on the *Marmaduke* and on February 16, 1624, was living in Elizabeth City (**18**), where he was a servant in the household of Francis Mason. In early 1625 Querke was 30 years old and still a servant in the Mason household (CBE 44, 65).

PIERRE QUESNEE

Brewer Pierre Quesnee, an unmarried man, was among the Walloons and French who indicated their willingness to go to Virginia. In August 1621 the Virginia Company agreed that he could immigrate (CBE 24).

[NO FIRST NAME] QUINEY

In 1621 a Captain Quiney sent a barrel of seeds to Virginia by means of a ship that belonged to the Virginia Company of London (FER 322).

RICHARD QUINEY (QUEYNING)

In November 1635 Richard Quiney (Queyning), John Sadler, and William Barker patented 1,250 acres of land in Charles City, adjacent to the plantation known as Merchants Hope (**50**), which was owned by Barker and his associates. Quiney and his partners received their acreage on the basis of 25 headrights. Probate records associated with the January 1657 settlement of Richard Quiney's estate reveal that he was from St. Stephen Wallbrook, London. His son, Richard, was named executor (PB 1 Pt. 1:320; EEAC 47).

WILLIAM QUICKE

William Quicke, a citizen and grocer of Christ Church, London, was a member of the Virginia Company of London, investing in 1609 after the Company had received its second charter. He had a legal interest in land in Virginia and Bermuda. In October 1614 when William Quicke made his will, he named his wife, Elizabeth, and his business associate, Roger Harris, as his executors. Quicke's will was proved in January 1615, at which time he was identified as the owner of some land in Virginia (CBE 7; EEAC 47; WITH 147-148; WAT 20).

THOMAS QUIGLEY

On January 21, 1624, Thomas Quigley testified that Sir Samuel Argall, Virginia's deputy governor, had forced Quigley to relinquish the compensation to which he was entitled. This statement indicates that Quigley had been in Virginia during 1617–1618, while Argall was deputy governor (FER 524).

R

THOMAS RABENETT (RAVENETT)

In May 1621 Thomas Rabenett (Ravenett) was named administrator of the estate of Alexander Winchelsey of Limehouse, Middlesex, England, a Virginia planter who appears to have been associated with Shirley Hundred (**41**). In his July 1620 will, Winchelsey, who had tobacco in Virginia, made bequests to several people in Shirley Hundred and London, and named Rabenett his executor (EEAC 65; WITH 69-70).

THOMAS RABEY

On November 20, 1622, Thomas Rabey, a Newgate inmate, was among those pardoned because of an epidemic of jail fever and sentenced to transportation overseas, probably to Virginia (CBE 29).

WILLIAM RABNETT (RAVENETT)

On February 16, 1624, William Rabnett (Ravenett) was a servant living in Captain William Peirce's household in urban Jamestown (**1**). In March 1626 he was identified as one of the late John Rolfe's servants. Rabnett's presence in the Peirce home most likely was attributable to the fact that Peirce had been Rolfe's father-in-law and one of his heirs. In 1634 William Rabnett was described as owner of a plantation on Skiff's Creek, within the Martin's Hundred (7) Parish of James City County. He received a patent for his land in November 1635 and simultaneously was assigned some land bordering Mr. Heley's acreage in Warwick (or Denbigh) County (CBE 38; MCGC 99; PB 1 Pt. 1:154, 305, 318).

ROGER RACE

On April 24, 1632, Roger Race, Walter Floyd, Thomas Smith, and carpenter Silvester Tatnam received a 21-year lease that entitled them to 400 acres in Martin's Hundred (7). Their land extended toward Skiff's Creek. The men may have been granted a lease instead of a patent because the Society of Martin's Hundred still had a legal claim on the property (PB 1 Pt. 1:130).

JOHN RADISH (REDDISH)

John Radish (Reddish), a feather-maker from Northamptonshire, England, came to Virginia in 1619 on the *Bona Nova*. Virginia Company records dated April 7, 1623, indicate that Radish, an indentured servant, became ill after the March 1622 Indian attack, and that his master had provided him with food, clothing, and shelter. On February 16, 1624, Radish was residing on Jamestown Island (1) in Robert Fitts's home. On November 1, 1624, Radish testified about the late John Phillimore's nuncupative will, and on January 3, 1625, he presented Peter Martin's will to the General Court. Both decedents, like Radish, were associated with Jamestown Island. On January 24, 1625, John Radish conveyed some land in the eastern end of Jamestown Island at Black Point (acreage he had purchased from David Ellis) to Sir George Yeardley. At the time of the transaction, Radish, a free man, was living alone in the Neck O'Land (5). John Radish ran afoul of the law in May 1625 by allowing Robert Fitts and some of Sir George Yeardley's servants to get drunk while they were guests in his home. Radish, for his role in this infraction of church law, had the choice of paying a fine or making a good pair of stocks for the court's use. In May 1637 John Radish purchased a 16-acre tract located to the north of Goose Hill Marsh in the eastern

end of Jamestown Island (FER 295; VCR 4:104-106; CBE 40, 58; MCGC 27, 38-39, 44, 58; PB 1 Pt. 1:423; DOR 1:37).

ROBERT RAFFE (RASSE?)

Robert Raffe (Rasse?) died in Jamestown (1) sometime after April 1623 but before February 16, 1624 (CBE 39).

ANDREW RAILEY (RALYE, RAWLEIGH, REILY)

Relatively little is known about Andrew Railey (Ralye, Rawleigh, Reily) except that on February 16, 1624, he and Thomas Passmore were living in urban Jamestown (1) in a household headed by John Southern, an experienced artisan whom the Society of Southampton Hundred sent to Virginia in 1620 to set up an ironworks and oversee their plantation. On January 24, 1625, Andrew Railey was listed as a resident of rural Jamestown Island. In 1627 he and Robert Wright (a carpenter and ancient planter) inherited from Thomas Grubb a leasehold in the eastern end of the island. They secured a 10-year lease of their own in October 1628. These parcels appear to have been Andrew Railey's only acreage. In January 1628 Andrew and Jonas Railey (perhaps a kinsman) were arrested because of their indebtedness to Mr. John Gill, a Jamestown merchant (CBE 38, 46; FER 449; MCGC 73, 148, 154, 158).

JAMES RAILEY (RALELEY, RYLEI, RAYLEY, RYALY, RYLEI, REILY)

On June 24, 1624, James Railey (Raleley, Rylei, Rayley, Ryaly, Rylei, Reily) testified that on the night of June 23rd, when he was on watch at the fort in Jamestown (1), he did not see anyone break into Abraham Peirsey's store. He said, however, that he saw two men "close under the Countrie howse," a public building. The men claimed that they were unable to enter Sir George Yeardley's dwelling because the door was locked (MCGC 15).

JOHN RAILEY

John Railey immigrated to Virginia with Richard English aboard the ship *James*, which left England on July 31, 1622 (FER 400).

JONAS RAILEY (RALELEY, RYLEI, RAYLEY, RYALY, RYLEI, REILY)

Jonas Railey (Raleley, Rylei, Rayley, Ryaly, Rylei, Reily), an indentured servant, was living at West and Shirley Hundred (41) on February 16, 1624. On January 3, 1625, Abraham Peirsey of urban Jamestown (1) purchased his contract from Sir George Yeardley and John Pountis, who also were residents of the capital city. Railey, who was eager to obtain his freedom, agreed to pay Peirsey outright or compensate him with work as a sawyer. On March 12, 1627, Jonas Railey, who was identified as a Jamestown Island planter, was fined for failing to perform sentry duty. In January 1628 he and Andrew Railey (perhaps a kinsman) were arrested by merchant John Gill because of indebtedness (CBE 36; MCGC 15, 38-39, 143, 158).

JOSEPH RAILEY (RALELEY, RYLEI, RAYLEY, RYALY, RYLEI, REILY)

On January 30, 1625, Joseph Railey (Raleley, Rylei, Rayley, Ryaly, Rylei, Reily) was living alone on the Maine (3), west of Jamestown Island. He came to Virginia on the *William and Thomas* (CBE 57).

THOMAS RAMSHAW (RAMSHAWE, RAMSHEE, RAMSHEER)

Thomas Ramshaw (Ramshawe, Ramshee, Ramsheer) was residing in Elizabeth City (18) on February 20, 1626, when he testified about Mr. Weston, owner of the ship *Sparrow*. He was a successful planter, who by early 1632 had become a burgess for the Warwick River area in the corporation of Elizabeth City. In July 1635 Thomas Ramshaw patented two tracts of land: one in Elizabeth City County and one in Denbigh (actually, Warwick) County on the Warwick River (23). He acquired his land on the basis of six headrights, an indication of his ability to accumulate wealth (MCGC 96; HEN 1:154; PB 1 Pt. 1:262, 264).

***

WILLIAM RAMSHAW (RAMSHAWE, RAMSHEE, RAMSHEER, RANSHAW)

William Ramshaw (Ramshawe, Ramshee, Ramsheer, Ranshaw), who came to Virginia on the *Francis Bonaventure,* was living on Hog Island (16) on February 16, 1624. In August he testified before the Council of State about ownership of some tobacco grown at Hog Island fort and also about some insults exchanged by Hog Island residents John Uty and William Tyler. On February 4, 1625, William Ramshaw, a free man, was still living on Hog Island. He was identified as a blacksmith in November 1626 when he was ordered to ply his trade at Mathews Manor (23) until he had paid his debts to Michael Marshott and provost marshal John Uty. On July 1, 1635, William Ramshaw acquired 200 acres on the Elizabeth River (20 a), on the lower side of the James within Elizabeth City County, using himself, his wife, Katherine, and two other people as headrights (CBE 41, 61; MCGC 18-19, 124; PB 1 Pt. 1:193).

KATHERINE RAMSHAW (RAMSHAWE, RAMSHEE, RAMSHEER, RANSHAW) (MRS. WILLIAM RAMSHAW)

On July 1, 1635, when William Ramshaw (Ramshawe, Ramshee, Ramsheer, Ranshaw) patented 200 acres on the Elizabeth River (20 a), in what was then Elizabeth City County, he used the headright of his wife, Katherine, but failed to indicate when she came to the colony (PB 1 Pt.1:193).

***

WILLIAM RAND

In December 1619 officials at Bridewell decided that William Rand, an inmate, would be detained until he could be sent to Virginia (CBE 15).

ANTHONY RANDALL

On November 19, 1623, Anthony Randall was mentioned in connection with a court case that involved Dr. John Pott and his wife, Elizabeth, residents of urban Jamestown (1). Sybil Royall, who lived in Captain Ralph Hamor's household and was the Potts's neighbor, testified about the disposition of some items stored in a trunk in the Potts's house. Thus, Randall may have been a resident of Jamestown too (MCGC 7).

RICHARD RANKE

On February 16, 1624, Richard Ranke was listed among those who had died at Flowerdew Hundred (53) after April 1623 (CBE 37).

ABRAHAM (ABRAM) RANSACK

Abraham Ransack, a refiner, arrived in Virginia in 1608 in the 1st Supply of new Jamestown (1) settlers (CJS 1:222; 2:162).

RICHARD RAPIER (RAPER)

On February 16, 1624, Richard Rapier (Raper) was living in Elizabeth City in a community known as the Indian Thicket (17), part of the Virginia Company's land on the east side of the Hampton River. In January 1627 Raper testified that around Easter 1624, Captain Douse reduced by two years the amount of time his servant, Robert Todd, was supposed to serve (CBE 43; MCGC 131).

***

HUMPHREY RASTALL (RASTELL, ROISTALL)

Court testimony dating to 1624 indicates that Humphrey Rastall (Rastell, Roistall), a London merchant, was master of the ship *Unity*, which brought John Martin to Virginia. In January and April 1625, he testified before the General Court in the suit between Abraham Porter and Nathaniel Basse. Rastall regularly transported indentured servants to the colony and agreed to supply young male servants to Nathaniel Basse, William Barry, and John Ward. In June 1625 he was sued by George Sandys, to whom he was in debt, and Rastall, in turn, sued William Ganey, one of his own debtors. In 1626 Humphrey Rastall made several appearances in court in suits that involved disagreements about the procurement of servants. He went to Canada sometime prior to January 1627 and by 1628 was dead. His brother, Thomas Rastall (also a London merchant) served as executor. Documents associated with the settlement of Humphrey Rastall's estate reveal that he owned the ship *Anne Fortune* and that he sometimes transported tobacco from Virginia to Newfoundland. Rastall's factor in

Virginia was William Webster, purser of the ship *Elizabeth* (MCGC 25, 40, 84, 86-87, 109, 131, 134, 173-175, 185).

THOMAS RASTALL (RASTELL, ROISTALL)

In July 1627 Thomas Rastall (Rastell, Roistall), a London merchant and Humphrey Rastall's brother, reportedly shipped goods to Virginia aboard the *Anne Fortune* and the *Golden Lion* of Dundee. In March 1629 the justices of Virginia's General Court decided to send Rastell a letter about alleged irregularities in the conduct of his business affairs in the colony (CBE 78; MCGC 192).

***

ELKINTON RATCLIFE (RATLIFFE)

On February 16, 1624, Elkinton Ratclife (Ratliffe) was living in Captain Ralph Hamor's household in urban Jamestown (1). By February 4, 1625, he had relocated to Hamor's property on Hog Island (16). He was then identified as an indentured servant who had come to the colony on the *Seaflower* (CBE 38, 61).

***

JOHN RATCLIFFE ALIAS SICKLEMORE

John Ratcliffe alias Sicklemore, a Virginia Company investor, set sail for Virginia in December 1606 as captain of the *Discovery*, which brought some of Virginia's first colonists. The Virginia Company appointed him to the colony's council, and in June 1607 he was among the officials in Jamestown (1) who sent a letter describing the status of the colony. In September 1607 John Ratcliffe was elected council president after Edward Maria Wingfield was deposed. Captain John Smith later said that he and Ratcliffe shared the task of rebuilding Jamestown after it burned (in January 1608) and saw that the year's harvest was gathered in. Within a few months John Ratcliffe alienated his fellow council members, including Smith, by his arbitrary rule and liberal use of the colony's provisions. In July 1608 he was deposed and arrested for mutiny; afterward he was replaced by Smith, who sarcastically referred to the ex-president's home as his "palace." Ratcliffe was released from detention and restored to his council seat, but left Virginia in December 1608 with Captain Christopher Newport. On June 1, 1609, when Captain John Ratcliffe of the *Diamond* was preparing to set sail for Virginia in the fleet carrying the 3rd Supply of new settlers, he made his will, leaving his entire estate to his wife, Dorothy, and naming her and his friend, Richard Percivall, as co-executors. When they reached Virginia in late summer 1609, Captains Ratcliffe and Christopher Newport campaigned to have President John Smith ousted from office. When Sir Thomas Gates arrived in Virginia, he placed Ratcliffe in charge of Algernon Fort at Old Point Comfort (**17**). On October 4, 1609, Ratcliffe sent a letter to the Earl of Salisbury describing conditions in the colony. While on a 1609–1610 trading voyage, he was ambushed and killed at Powhatan's behest. According to George Percy, Ratcliffe was bound to a tree and tortured. The will of John Ratcliffe alias Sicklemore was presented for probate in England on April 25, 1611 (CJS 1:20, 33, 35, 128, 205, 207, 210, 229, 232-233, 268, 271-272, 275; 2:13, 138, 140, 158, 162, 169, 180, 182, 186, 188-189, 222, 231-232, 244; WITH 485; HAI 100, 124-126, 141, 158, 162, 182, 188, 354-355, 441, 504, 806; SH 1; EEAC 52; CO 1/1 ff 66-67; VCR 3:13, 22; SR 3105).

DOROTHY RATCLIFFE ALIAS SICKLEMORE (MRS. JOHN RATCLIFFE ALIAS SICKLEMORE)

On June 1, 1609, when Captain John Ratcliffe alias Sicklemore made his will, he named his wife, Dorothy, as his sole heir and designated her co-executor. She and fellow executor Richard Percivall saw that the will was proved on April 25, 1611 (WITH 485).

***

***

ROGER RATCLIFFE (RATLIFE, RATLIFFE)

In May 1619 Roger Ratcliffe (Ratlife, Ratliffe) came to Virginia on the *George*, a ship that belonged to newly arrived Governor George Yeardley. On February 16, 1624, Ratcliffe and his wife, Ann, were living in West and Shirley Hundred (**41**). On January 22, 1625, when a muster was made of the colony's inhabitants, Roger Ratcliffe was described as the 40-year-old head of a West and Shirley Hundred household that included his wife, Ann, and their 9-month-old son, Isaac (CBE 36, 53; DOR 1:15).

ANN RATCLIFFE (RATLIFE, RATLIFFE) (MRS. ROGER RATCLIFFE [(RATLIFE, RATLIFFE])

On February 16, 1624, Ann Ratcliffe (Ratlife, Ratliffe) was living in West and Shirley Hundred (**41**) in a household headed by her husband, Roger. On January 22, 1625, the Ratcliffes were residing in West and Shirley Hundred with their 9-month-old son, Isaac (CBE 36, 53).

ISAAC RATCLIFFE (RATLIFE, RATLIFFE)

On January 22, 1625, Isaac Ratcliffe (Ratlife, Ratliffe), who was 9 months old, was living in the home of his parents, Roger and Ann Ratcliffe, in West and Shirley Hundred (**41**) (CBE 53).

***

THOMAS RATCLIFFE (RATLIFE, RATLIFFE)

On March 22, 1622, Thomas Ratcliffe (Ratlife, Ratliffe) was among those slain in the Indian attack on Westover (**54**). He lived on Lieutenant John Gibbs's dividend of land (VCR 3:567).

***

EZEKIAH (ISIAS) RAUGHTON

On February 16, 1624, Ezekiah (Isias) Raughton, who came to Virginia on the *Bona Nova*, was living on the College Land (**66**) at Arrohattock, in the corporation of Henrico. He probably was one of the Virginia Company servants or tenants sent there in November 1619 and placed under the command of Captain William Weldon. If Raughton was living at the College at the time of the March 1622 Indian attack, he would have been evacuated to the safety of William Ewen's plantation (13), across the river from Jamestown Island. On January 23, 1625, when a muster was made of the College's inhabitants, Ezekiah Raughton was identified as a household head who shared his home with his wife, Margaret (CBE 35, 53; DOR 1:8).

MARGARET RAUGHTON (MRS. EZEKIAH [ISIAS] RAUGHTON)

On January 22, 1625, Margaret Raughton and her husband, Ezekiah (Isias), were living on the College Land (66) in Henrico. She reportedly came to Virginia on the *Warwick* (CBE 53).

***

REBECCA RAVENING (SEE REBECCA RAVENING TAYLOR)

HENRY RAVENS

Henry Ravens, who set sail for Virginia in the fleet that brought the 3rd Supply of Jamestown (1) settlers, was shipwrecked in Bermuda with Sir Thomas Gates and Sir George Summers. Afterward, Ravens, cape merchant Thomas Whittingham, and six sailors set out for Virginia in a longboat outfitted like a pinnace. They may have been lost at sea, for they never were heard from again. However, Powhatan later claimed that his people killed Ravens and his men (HAI 401-402, 418).

ANDREW RAWLEY

On February 16, 1624, Andrew Rawley was living at Basses Choice (27) (CBE 46).

RICHARD RAWSE

Richard Rawse was living in Bermuda Hundred (39) on February 16, 1624, when a census was made of the colony's inhabitants (CBE 35).

CHRISTOPHER RAWSON

Christopher Rawson was among those who died at Warresqueak (26) sometime after April 1623 but before February 16, 1624 (CBE 42).

***

NICHOLAS RAYBERD (RAINBERTE, RAYNEBERDE, RAYNBEARE, REYNEBERD)

Nicholas Rayberd (Rainberte, Rayneberde, Raynbeare, Reyneberd), an indentured servant employed by Captain William Eppes, came to Virginia in 1624 on the *Swann*. On November 23, 1624, he was in Jamestown (1) and testified against Captain John Martin. When a muster was made of the colony's inhabitants in early 1625, Rayberd was a 22-year-old servant in Eppes's household on the Eastern Shore (74). In February 1626, when William Eppes obtained a patent for some land, he used Rayberd's headright and indicated that he had paid for Rayberd's transportation to Virginia. In 1633 Nicholas Rayberd appeared in the Accomack/Northampton court, where he admitted that his taxes were in arrears. In May 1635 he was in England, where he reportedly received some tobacco from merchant Richard Bennett. Nicholas Rayberd returned to Virginia and in January 1637 brought suit against one of his own debtors. He died sometime prior to November 1637 (CBE 68; MCGC 28; PB 1 Pt. 1:49; EAE 54; AMES 1:4, 63, 66, 95, 136).

MRS. NICHOLAS RAYBERD (RAINBERTE, RAYNEBERDE, RAYNBEARE, REYNEBERD)

In November 1637 Farmar Jones testified before the Accomack/Northampton court that shortly before Nicholas Rayberd (Rainberte, Rayneberd, Raynbeare, Reyneberd) died, his wife inquired what he intended to bequeath her toward her own support. The dying man reportedly admitted that he had nothing to leave her until he had satisfied his debt to Obedience Robins (AMES 1:95).

***

JOHN RAYMENT

On December 2, 1629, John Rayment of Poole, who had set sail for Virginia aboard the *Friendship* of London, prepared his will, which was witnessed by mariner Patrick Kennede (Kennedy). Rayment instructed Kennede and Humphrey Barrett to sell his goods in Virginia and to send his tobacco to his wife, Mary Graves alias

Rayment, then in England. Rayment named as heirs his wife, his mother and sisters in Poole, and a kinsman in Wapping. In September 1630 John Rayment's widow, Mary, was granted administration of his estate. As the decedent had goods and tobacco in Virginia, it is likely that in 1629 he was returning to the colony. He may have been the colonist named John Raymond (Raimond) (SH 12; WAT 316; EEAC 48; EAE 26; CBE 91).

MARY GRAVES RAYMENT (MRS. JOHN RAYMENT)

On December 2, 1629, when John Rayment of Poole made his will, he named his wife, Mary Graves alias Rayment, as one of his principal heirs and noted that she was then in England. In September 1630 Mary was named administrator of her late husband's estate (SH 12; WAT 316; EEAC 48; EAE 26; CBE 91).

***

JOHN RAYMOND (RAIMOND)

On January 4, 1623, John Raymond, one of Captain Nathaniel Butler's men, reportedly sailed into the Chickahominy River on the *Adam and Eve*. He was later accused of killing one of Lady Elizabeth Dale's cattle while he was there. By November 17, 1623, John Raymond had returned to England. He testified that he had been in Virginia in May when the Indian leader Iotan (Itoyatin or Opitchapam) promised to see that 10–12 English prisoners were returned to Governor Francis Wyatt and offered to assist in the capture of Opechancanough (VCR 2:383; 4:8).

WILLIAM RAYMONT

On January 25, 1625, William Raymont, who came to Virginia on the *Neptune*, was living on Mulberry Island (21). He was a household head and adequately supplied with corn and defensive weaponry (CBE 57; DOR 1:47).

***

ADAM RAYNER

Adam Rayner, who had set sail from Bristol on the *Supply* on September 10, 1620, and was bound for Berkeley Hundred (55), married Isabell Gifford while they were at sea.

In March 1622 she was killed in the Indian attack on Powle Brooke (50) (VCR 3:396, 426; CBE 21).

ISABELL GIFFORD RAYNER (MRS. ADAM RAYNER)

On September 10, 1620, Isabell Gifford left Bristol, England, on the *Supply* with William Tracy and his party, who were heading for Berkeley Hundred (55) to join Mrs. Joyce Tracy. While at sea, Isabell married Adam Rayner. On January 29, 1621, Adam and Isabell Gifford Rayner arrived at Berkeley Hundred. When the Indians attacked on March 22, 1622, Isabell Gifford Rayner was killed at Powle Brooke (50), a neighboring plantation (CBE 21; VCR 3:569, 426).

***

MARMADUKE RAYNER

On September 30, 1619, Marmaduke Rayner was identified as the pilot of a Flemish man-of-war that accompanied the ship *Treasurer* to Virginia. Four months later John Rolfe indicated that 20-some Africans had been aboard Rayner's vessel, which had arrived at Old Point Comfort (17) in late August. Thus, he was instrumental in bringing some of the first Africans to the colony. In March 1620 Governor George Yeardley recommended that the Virginia Company commission Rayner to make a map of the colony. Two years later, when reporting about conditions in Virginia, he was identified as owner of the *Marmaduke*. In April 1623 Marmaduke Rayner was among those refuting Captain Nathaniel Butler's derogatory claims about Virginia. He said that he had lived in the colony for 16 months and had made three trips to Virginia as the master of ships. In 1623 he offered to send supplies to the colony and in 1624 made plans to transport goods and passengers. Rayner was in Virginia in December 1624 and made claims against the late Captain George Thorpe's estate. In 1626 he was identified as the former master of the ships *Deal* and *Temperance*, the latter a vessel once owned by Sir George Yeardley. Marmaduke Rayner was in Virginia in March 1629 and served on a jury (VCR 1:326, 605-606; 2:326, 385, 529; 3:222, 243; 4:245-246; MCGC 36, 47, 59-60, 95, 192; CBE 73, 77; G&M 105-106).

***

WASSILL (WASSELL, WATSALL) RAYNER (RAYNOR, ROYNER)

Wassill (Wassell, Watsall) Rayner (Raynor, Royner), a distiller, set sail for Virginia on April 17, 1619. On February 16, 1624, he and his wife, who were indentured servants, were living in the urban Jamestown (1) household of merchant Richard Stephens. Wassill, who was age 28, and his wife, Joan (Joane), were still living with Stephens in Jamestown on January 24, 1625. Wassill and Joan Rayner testified in court that John Bath, a gentleman and leather-seller who became ill while living in the Stephens home, had asked Richard Stephens to serve as his administrator. On July 15, 1631, Wassill Rayner was identified as a Virginia planter when he joined those asking for relief from the customs fees paid on tobacco exported from Virginia. Rayner indicated that his hogsheads of tobacco bore the mark *WR* (FER 107, 109; CBE 38, 56; MCGC 45; G&M 165).

JOAN (JOANE) RAYNER (RAYNOR, ROYNER) (MRS. WASSILL [WASSELL, WATSALL] RAYNER [RAYNOR, ROYNER])

On February 16, 1624, Joan (Joane), the wife of distiller Wassill (Wassell, Watsall) Rayner (Raynor, Royner), was living in the urban Jamestown (1) household of Richard Stephens. The Rayners, who were servants, were still residing in the Stephens home in Jamestown on January 24, 1625. They testified that John Bath, a houseguest, asked Richard Stephens to serve as his administrator (FER 109; CBE 38, 56; MCGC 45).

***

ANTHONY READ

Anthony Read was living in Warresqueak (26) on February 16, 1624, and appears to have been one of Edward Bennett's servants (CBE 42).

***

GEORGE READ (READE)

George Read (Reade), who was born on October 25, 1608, was the son of Robert and Mildred Windebank Reade of England. He came to Virginia with the reinstated Governor John Harvey in 1637 and resided in Harvey's dwelling in urban Jamestown (1). Read greatly appreciated the assistance he obtained from Governor Harvey and Secretary Richard Kemp, and in February 1638 he informed his brother, Robert, that he would not have survived without their numerous favors. George Reade asked his brother to send him money and servants, adding that Jerome Hawley had failed to do so. In April 1640 George asked Robert to send two men completely outfitted for life in the colony. After Sir John Harvey was removed from office, George Reade, who anticipated Richard Kemp's departure, asked his brother, Robert, to use his influence to see that George was named Secretary of the Colony. Robert Read apparently followed through, for on August 27, 1640, George Reade succeeded Kemp. Shortly thereafter he married Elizabeth, the daughter of Nicholas Martiau of Elizabeth City (17) and later Chiskiack (36, 37). In 1649 when Richard Kemp made his will, he left George Reade a 50-acre James City County tract called the Barren Neck, where Reade then lived. In 1648 George Reade was made clerk of the Council of State, and in 1658 he became a councilor. He served as a burgess for James City in 1649 and for York in 1656. When George Reade made his will in September 1670, he left his home tract, the Martiau land in York County, to his eldest sons, George II and Robert, with reversionary rights to sons Francis and Benjamin. However, the late George Reade's wife, Elizabeth, had life-rights in the property, part of which became the site of Yorktown. The will was presented for probate in November 1671 (CO 1/9 ff 188ro, 209ro-210vo; 1/10 f 176; SAIN 1:264, 309, 311, 314; MCGC 473; HEN 1:358-359; WITH 323; MCGH 775; CBE 34).

ELIZABETH MARTIAU READ (READE) (MRS. GEORGE READ [READE]) (SEE ELIZABETH MARTIAU [MARTEU, MARTEAW, MARTEAU])

***

HARRY READ (READE)

On February 3, 1619, Harry Read (Reade), a highway robber from Middlesex, England, who was incarcerated in Newgate Prison, was identified as someone suitable for transportation to Virginia (CBE 12).

HENRY READ (READE)

In June 1619 Ferdinando Sheppard testified that Henry Read (Reade), who was bound for Virginia, drew his sword against Captain William Wye, a mariner, who had threatened to duck him. This individual may be Harry Reade, the Newgate prisoner and robber (EAE 9).

HUMFREY READ (READE, REEDE)

Humfrey Read (Reade, Reede), who was shipwrecked in Bermuda with Sir Thomas Gates and part of the 3rd Supply of Virginia colonists being brought to Jamestown (1), told Gates that Stephen Hopkins had tried to pervert the Scriptures and use them for his own purposes, in disobedience of the law (HAI 406).

JAMES READ (READE)

James Read (Reade), a blacksmith, was one of the first Jamestown (1) settlers. Sometime after September 17, 1607, he was struck by John Ratcliffe alias Sicklemore, then-president of the colony, and retaliated by returning the blow. According to Edward Maria Wingfield, Read was sentenced to hanging but was reprieved after he accused councilor George Kendall of mutiny. In 1608 James Read accompanied Captain John Smith on a voyage to explore the Chesapeake Bay. Then, in late December 1608, Smith sent him overland to Werowocomoco, on the York River, to build a house for Powhatan. Smith, who also went to the paramount chief's principal village, referred to James Read as a soldier (CJS 1:224, 244; 2:142, 163, 193; HAI 193).

***

JAMES READ (READE)

On March 13, 1622, officials of the Virginia Company were informed that James Read (Reade) had died in Virginia and that his widow, Isabelle, wanted his house and 100 acres in the colony. His daughter, Joan, stood to inherit his goods, which were in the possession of Captain John Martin of Martin's Brandon (59). It is possible that this James Read was the blacksmith who had come to Virginia in 1607 and was one of the first colonists. He also may have been an ancient planter (VCR 1:618).

ISABELLE READ (READE) (MRS. JAMES READ [READE])

On March 13, 1622, James Reade's widow, Isabelle, who was in England, asked the Virginia Company to order Captain John Martin of Martin's Brandon (59) to surrender her late husband's goods. She indicated that her late husband's daughter, Joan, was entitled to his belongings whereas she stood to inherit his house and 100 acres in Virginia (VCR 1:618).

JOAN READ (READE)

Records of the Virginia Company dated March 13, 1622, reveal that Joan, the daughter of James Read (Reade), stood to inherit her late father's goods, which were in the possession of Captain John Martin of Martin's Brandon (59). Joan was then in England (VCR 1:618).

***

JOHN READ (READE)

On August 21, 1624, officials at Bridewell decided that John Read (Reade), a vagrant brought in from London's Bridge Ward, was to be transported to Virginia (CBE 47).

PHILLIP READ (READE)

On September 26, 1618, the justices of Bridewell Court sentenced Phillip Read (Reade), a vagrant from "the Bridge" in London (probably the Bridge Ward), to transportation to Virginia. He was born at Aldgate (CBE 10).

STEPHEN (STEVEN) READ (READE, REEDE, REEDS)

On August 8, 1618, Stephen (Steven) Read (Reade, Reede, Reeds), a young vagrant from Lombard Street in Bridewell, was sentenced to transportation to Virginia. He went to the colony on the *George* in 1619 when he was only 11 years old and probably was one of the street urchins the Mayor of London sent to Virginia around that time. On February 16, 1624, Stephen Read was living in Elizabeth City and was a servant in Edward Waters' household at Blunt Point (22). He was still residing in the Waters home in early 1625 and was age 17. On March 29, 1628, Stephen Read gave his age as 21 when testifying before the General Court. He stated that he had been present when William Capps told Thomas Thorogood that his brother, Adam, was a rogue and thief (CBE 9, 13, 44, 66; MCGC 169).

THOMAS READ (READE)

In July 1622 Virginia Company officials learned that Governor George Yeardley had awarded Thomas Read (Reade) 100 acres in Henrico at Coxendale (**64**)—part of a tract traditionally known as Mount My Lady or Mount Malady—in compensation for his eight years of service to the colony. Virginia Company records note that Read conveyed his acreage to Edward Hurd of London, an ironmonger. On January 25, 1625, Thomas Read was a 65-year-old tenant or servant in Thomas Harwood's household on Mulberry Island (**21**) in Elizabeth City. In May 1625 he was credited with his 100-acre patent in Coxendale, property then described as unseated. On July 7, 1635, when Thomas Harwood patented some land, he listed Thomas Read as a headright (VCR 2:91; 4:552; CBE 57; PB 1 Pt. 1:208).

WILLIAM READ (READE)

On January 24, 1629, William Read (Reade), a 13- or 14-year-old laborer and servant in the home of Benjamin Jackson of Blunt Point (**22**), was indicted for murdering John Burrows of Jamestown (**1**). Read testified in his own defense and claimed that fellow servant John Gay, who was mending a pot, had demanded his knife. When he refused, John Burrows tried to seize it and was mortally wounded in the struggle that ensued. Although a jury found William Reade guilty of manslaughter, ultimately he was given benefit of clergy and freed (MCGC 183-184).

THOMAS REASLY (REASBY)

On January 15, 1620, Thomas Reasly or Reasby, a thief and vagrant born in Hampshire and brought in from Queenhith in London, was sentenced to transportation to Virginia (CBE 17).

REBECCA

On March 22, 1622, when the Indians attacked Edward Bennett's plantation at Warresqueak (**26**), Rebecca was killed (VCR 3:571).

JOHN REDING (REDDING, READING)

John Reding (Redding, Reading) died in Jamestown (**1**) sometime after April 1623 but before February 16, 1624 (CBE 29).

***

CHRISTOPHER REDHEAD

On February 16, 1624, Christopher Redhead, a Virginia Company tenant, was living on the Maine, part of a 3,000-acre tract known as the Governor's Land (**3**). He may have been under the supervision of Captain Roger Smith, who had a company of men on the Governor's Land. By early 1625 Christopher Redhead had relocated to Roger Smith's plantation (**10**) on the lower side of the James River. He was then 24 years old and residing in his own home. In January 1627 Redhead, who was identified as a tenant of the defunct Virginia Company, was assigned to Captain Samuel Mathews, a member of the Council of State (CBE 39, 59; MCGC 136; DOR 1:39).

[NO FIRST NAME] REDHEAD (MRS. CHRISTOPHER REDHEAD?)

On March 22, 1622, Goodwife Redhead, who was living near Bermuda Hundred (**39**), was killed during the Indian attack (VCR 3:566). She may have been the wife of a Virginia Company tenant named Christopher Redhead.

***

JOHN REDMAN

On January 6, 1635, Thomas Whaplett designated as his executor John Redman, a close friend and co-investor in his plantation in Virginia. Abraham Peate, a Virginia planter, was to inherit half of the decedent's interest in the property and Whaplett's sister, Rebecca, was to inherit the other half (WITH 77; SH 20).

MARY REES (REESE)

Mary Rees (Reese) died at Jordan's Journey (**46**) sometime after April 1623 but before February 16, 1624 (CBE 37).

JAMES REEVE

In 1620 James Reeve, an inmate at Newgate Prison in London, was sentenced to be put to work or transported overseas, probably to Virginia. He was among the prisoners being reprieved because of an epidemic of jail fever (CBE 29).

JOHN REEVE

When the Indians attacked on March 22, 1622, John Reeve—who was living at Thomas Sheffield's plantation (**69**), three miles below Falling Creek—was slain (VCR 3:565).

NATHANIEL REEVE

On February 16, 1624, Nathaniel Reeve was residing at Bermuda Hundred (**39**). On March 12, 1624, he gave his age as 40 when testifying that he had refused to sign Mr. White's tobacco note. Later in the month, Reeve identified himself as a boatswain when appearing as a witness in a suit against Captain John Harvey (CBE 35; MCGC 13-14).

RICHARD REEVE (REENE)

Richard Reeve (Reene) came to the colony on the *James* in 1624 at the expense of William Streate, a mariner. Streate assigned Reeve's headright to William Eppes of Accomack (**74**), who utilized it when patenting some land on the Eastern Shore on February 3, 1627 (PB 1 Pt. 1:49).

SAMUEL REEVE

On March 22, 1622, Samuel Reeve was killed when the Indians attacked Thomas Sheffield's plantation (**69**), three miles below Falling Creek (VCR 3:565).

WILLIAM REEVE

William Reeve was killed at Richard Owen's house near Westover (**54**) during the March 22, 1622, Indian attack (VCR 3:567).

ROBERT REEVES

On November 16, 1636, Robert Reeves, a resident of Kecoughtan (**17, 18**), witnessed the will made by Daniel Hopkinson, also of Kecoughtan (SH 28).

LUCY REMNANT

Lucy Remnant, one of the marriageable young maids the Virginia Company sent to the colony in September 1621, set sail for Virginia aboard the *Warwick*. She was described as a 22-year-old orphan, born at Gifford in Surrey. Sir William Russell, Lucy's maternal uncle, signed the documents facilitating her departure from England (FER 309).

CLARE REN

On January 30, 1625, Clare Ren was living in Pasbehay (**3**) in the household headed by Edward and Sarah Kidall (Kildale, Killdale?) Fisher. Clare probably was a child, for in the muster she was listed with Sarah's 10-year-old son, Edward (CBE 57).

WILLIAM RENTER

On October 9, 1624, the justices of Bridewell Court decided that William Renter, a vagrant from the Bridge Ward, was to be sent to Virginia (CBE 48).

THOMAS REY (KEY?)

On November 13, 1633, Thomas Rey (Key?) and John Felgate witnessed the will of Daniel and William Parke's father, William, who died overseas. Thomas Rey actually may have been Thomas Key of Chaplin's Choice (**56**) (SH 15).

[NO FIRST NAME] REYNOLDS

On February 5, 1623, the Virginia Company authorized Mr. Reynolds, master of the *William and John*, to take passengers to Virginia before sailing northward on a fishing expedition (VCR 2:262).

CHRISTOPHER REYNOLDS (REINOLDS)

Christopher Reynolds (Reinolds) came to Virginia in 1622 on the *John and Francis*. On February 16, 1624, he was living in Warresqueak (**26**) and was one of Edward Bennett's servants. On February 7, 1625, Reynolds was still residing in the Bennett household. On March 13, 1626, Christopher Reynolds testified that he had seen the contract of Peter Collins, another Bennett servant (CBE 42, 62; MCGC 97).

EDWARD REYNOLDS

In 1629 Edward Reynolds came to Virginia on a French ship. On June 24, 1635, when Adam Thorogood of Elizabeth City (**20 b**) patented some land, he used Reynolds as a headright (PB 1 Pt. 1:179).

JOHN REYNOLDS (RENNOLDS)

John Reynolds (Rennolds), a 20-year-old husbandman from Hartfordshire, England, arrived in Jamestown (**1**) in 1619 aboard the *Bona Nova* and was one of the Virginia Company's servants or tenants. He died in the capital city sometime after April 1623 but before February 16, 1624 (FER 295; CBE 39).

JOHN REYNOLDS

In 1633 John Reynolds came to Virginia on the *Hopewell*. On June 24, 1635, when Adam Thorogood patented some land in Elizabeth City (**20 b**), he used Reynolds as a headright (PB 1 Pt. 1:179).

NATHANIEL REYNOLDS (REIGNOLDS, REIGHNOLDS)

In 1623 Nathaniel Reynolds (Reignolds, Reighnolds) served on a jury and as a James City Parish churchwarden, both signifying that he was a respected member of the community. On February 16, 1624, he was identified as a gentleman living in urban Jamestown (**1**) in the home of John Pountis. Reynolds was summoned to court in March 1625 because his sow had damaged corn belonging to Adam Dixon, another resident of Jamestown Island. On April 3, 1626, the General Court noted that Nathaniel Reynolds had appraised the estate of the Rev. Richard Buck, who died in late 1623 or early 1624 (MCGC 4-5, 8, 64, 100; CBE 38).

NICHOLAS REYNOLDS

On April 24, 1623, Nicholas Reynolds, who had come to Virginia on the *Margaret and John,* sent a petition to the governor (VCR 4:127-128).

PAUL (PAULE) REYNOLDS (RENALLES)

Paul (Paule) Reynolds (Renalles) came to Virginia in 1619 on the *Tryall* and on Feb-

ruary 16, 1624, was residing on the lower side of the James River. On February 4, 1625, he was a servant in the household of Hugh Crowder (**12**). On April 11, 1625, he was identified in the General Court's records as a Crowder servant (CBE 40, 60; MCGC 53).

ROBERT REYNOLDS

Robert Reynolds, who lived on the lower side of the James River (**8-15**), died sometime after April 1623 but before February 16, 1624 (HOT 192).

HENRY RICE

Henry Rice, one of Sir George Yeardley's manservants, was killed at Weyanoke (**52**) during the March 22, 1622, Indian attack (VCR 3:569).

MARGARET RICH (RICHE)

In December 1621 Margaret Rich or Riche was identified as one of the three servants brought to Virginia by Thomas Crispe of Elizabeth City (**18**) (MCGC 50).

ROBERT RICH

On November 21, 1621, Robert Rich, the Earl of Warwick, and his associates received a patent for taking 100 people to Virginia. He was an important Virginia Company investor and believed that a military-style government was critical to the colony's success (VCR 1:561-562).

THOMAS RICH

On August 23, 1631, officials at Bridewell decided that Thomas Rich, a boy from Langborne, in London, would be sent to Virginia (HUME 36).

RICHARD

On March 22, 1622, when the Indians attacked Edward Bennett's plantation at Warresqueak (**26**), a man named Richard was killed (VCR 3:571).

RICHARD

On March 22, 1622, when the Indians attacked Bermuda Hundred (**39**), a boy named Richard was killed (VCR 3:566).

RICHARD

Richard, one of surgeon Thomas Bunn's servants, died at his home in Pasbehay (3) sometime after February 16, 1624, but before January 30, 1625 (CBE 57).

RICHARD

In early 1625 Richard, a 15-year-old boy who came on the *Swan* in 1624 and appears to have been free, was living in the Elizabeth City (18) household headed by Bartholomew Wethersby and Richard Bolton (CBE 65).

ANN RICHARDS

Ann Richards, one of the young, marriageable women sent to Virginia to become wives, was born in St. Sepulcher's Parish. She arrived in 1621 on the *Warwick* and was described as a 25-year-old widow who had been recommended to the Virginia Company by her parish minister and clerk (FER 309).

RICHARD RICHARDS

Richard Richards came to Virginia in 1620 on the *London Merchant*. Sometime after December 5, 1620, but before January 21, 1621, he and Richard Dolphenby purchased a 100-acre tract from Francis Chapman and sold it to Isabell Pace Perry. The Richards-Dolphenby land that changed hands was part of the community known as Paces Paines (9). On June 24, 1624, Richards testified that he did not intend to marry Mara Buck, the young and somewhat slow-witted orphan of the late Rev. Richard Buck of Jamestown Island (1). In October 1624 he appeared as a witness in a court case involving the physical abuse of Elizabeth Abbott, one of John and Alice Proctor's maidservants. On January 24, 1625, Richard Richards and his partner, Richard Dolphenby, were living at Burrows Hill (8), a settlement just west of Paces Paines. They were in possession of a dwelling and a tobacco house and were relatively well armed and supplied with provisions. In May 1625 Richard Richards testified that he had assisted Richard Pace in clearing Captain William Powell's land (14) and that he was entitled to a share of the ground he had cleared. By 1632 Richards had been elected a burgess representing the territory from Captain William Perry's plantation (at Swann's Point) (9) to Hog Island (16). He was still serving as a burgess in 1641, at which time he represented part of James City County (CBE 59; MCGC 15, 23, 63; PB 1 Pt. 1:62; HEN 1:154, 178, STAN 61; DOR 1:38).

WILLIAM RICHARDS

William Richards died in Elizabeth City (17, 18) sometime after April 1623 but before February 16, 1624 (CBE 45).

HENRY RICHARDSON

On December 19, 1617, Henry Richardson witnessed the will made by Captain Robert Smalley (Smallay), a resident of Bermuda Hundred (39) (SH 4; 3112).

JAMES RICHARDSON

James Richardson, a 28-year-old cloth worker from Yorkshire, England, came to Virginia in 1619 aboard the *Bona Nova*. His transportation costs were covered by the Ferrars, who were Virginia Company investors. Thus, Richardson probably was one of their indentured servants or tenants (FER 295).

THOMAS RICHARDSON ALIAS ARNOLD

On August 12, 1620, it was decided that Thomas Richardson alias Arnold, a vagrant being detained in Bridewell Prison, would be sent to Virginia (CBE 20).

WILLIAM RICHARDSON

William Richardson came to Virginia on the ship *Edwin* sometime prior to February 16, 1624, at which time he was living on the lower side of the James River, west of Grays Creek (8, 9). By January 25, 1625, he had moved to Mulberry Island (21), where he was living in his own house and was adequately supplied with food and defensive weaponry. On October 27, 1630, William Richardson was in England when he testified that Ralph Yeardley accused Edmund Rossingham of mismanaging the late Sir George Yeardley's estate (CBE 40, 60; SR 9963; DOR 1:47).

FRANCIS RICHBILL

On August 23, 1634, Francis Richbill, a planter, was leasing some acreage from William Stafford, whose property was on the east side of Skiffs Creek in what was then Warwick County but is now the city of Newport News. Richbill's leasehold lay north of the land occupied by Stafford (PB 1 Pt. 1:154).

JOHN RICHMOND ALIAS SHEAPHEARD

On January 9, 1624, ship captain John Richmond alias Sheapheard was accused of neglecting Daniel Gookin's vessel, the *Mary Prood,* to the point where it had become unserviceable. Because Gookin had used the ship as collateral when securing a debt, he sued the mariner for damages. As a result Richmond was obliged to pay Gookin's debt (MCGC 10).

WILLIAM RICHMOND

On March 22, 1622, when the Indians attacked, William Richmond was among those killed at Ensign William Spence's house in Archer's Hope **(6)** (VCR 3:570).

SARA RIDDALL (RUDDELL)

On February 16, 1624, Sara Riddall (Ruddell) was living in the household of Mr. and Mrs. Hickmore in urban Jamestown **(1)**. She may have been a servant (CBE 38).

GEORGE RIDDLE (RIDDELL)

On December 18, 1624, Thomas Gates, a former Virginia Company servant, acknowledged in the presence of the General Court's justices that he owed tobacco to George Riddle (MCGC 128).

PETER RIDLEY

On October 9, 1624, the justices of Bridewell Court decided that Peter Ridley, an inmate at Bridewell Prison, would be detained until he could be sent to Virginia. Ridley appears to have been a vagrant (CBE 48).

THOMAS RIGLEE

On January 29, 1620, the justices of Bridewell Court decided to send Thomas

Riglee to Virginia. Riglee, who was being detained at Bridewell, was from Fleet Street and appears to have been a vagrant (CBE 17-18).

JOHN RILY (RILEY, RYLYE, RAILEY?)

On July 8, 1627, John Rily (Riley, Rylye, Railey?), a London merchant, shipped goods from London to Virginia aboard the *Ann.* He later came to Virginia and stayed in the home of William Perry, who then lived at Paces Paines **(9)**. On August 26, 1629, shortly before he died, Rily asked Perry to see that his hogsheads of tobacco were marked properly and sent to his mother and to John Holland. Rily's trading partners in London were William Crowther and Charles Wichcote (CBE 78-79; EAE 21).

JENNET RIMMER

Jennet Rimmer, one of the young, marriageable maids sent to Virginia to become colonists' wives, came to Virginia in 1621 on the *Warwick* at age 20. Virginia Company records reveal that she was born at North Mills in Lancashire and that she had been given letters of recommendation by the clerk of Blackfriars Parish and by her uncle, Allen Morrice, who lived near Moorgate (FER 309).

ADAM RIMWELL (RUMELL)

Adam Rimwell (Rumell) came to Virginia in 1619 on the *Bona Nova,* a ship that transported 100 Virginia Company servants and tenants to the colony. On February 16, 1624, he was living on the east side of the Hampton River in an area known as the Indian Thicket **(17)**, part of a 3,000-acre tract of land reserved for the Virginia Company's use. Rimwell was still residing there in early 1625 and was 24 years old. He was a member of John Ward's household (CBE 67).

JOHN RING

On August 31, 1636, when John Ring, a London yeoman, set sail for Virginia on the *Great Hopewell,* he made a bequest to his friend Thomas Fluelling (Llewelyn), who already was in the colony and lived at Potash Quarter, near Samuel Mathews' plantation **(23)**. Ring also left part of his personal estate to Richard and Abigail Atkins, residents of Mulberry Island (**21**), and to Robert Burnett's wife, Margaret. John Ring, a bachelor, died abroad and his will was proved on April 19, 1637 (EEAC 48; SR 3977; WITH 152).

CHRISTOPHER RIPPING (RIPEN)

Christopher Ripping or Ripen came to Virginia on the *Francis Bonaventure*. On February 16, 1624, he was residing on the Maine, part of the Governor's Land (**3**). When a muster was made of the area's inhabitants on January 30, 1625, Ripping, who was age 22, was still living on the Governor's Land and was one of the governor's servants (CBE 39, 57).

ELLIS RIPPING

Ellis Ripping came to Virginia on the *Return* in 1624. On January 22, 1625, he was living in Shirley Hundred (**41**), where he was a 23-year-old servant in John Throgmorten's household (CBE 53).

THOMAS RISBY

On February 16, 1624, Thomas Risby was living in Elizabeth City at Buckroe (**17**), part of a 3,000-acre tract owned by the Virginia Company of London. This raises the possibility that Risby was a Company servant or tenant (CBE 45).

JOHN RISHTON

On July 7, 1635, John Rishton patented 50 acres on the "great creek" across the James River from Jamestown, receiving his land from an agreement he had made with his late master, Richard Perry, a London merchant. Since Gray's Creek is directly across from the western end of Jamestown Island, and the Perrys owned land in the immediate vicinity of Paces Paines (**9**) and the promontory known as Swann's Point, it is probable that John Rishton's property was in that area (PB 1 Pt. 1:211).

MARGARET ROADES (RHODES)

On February 16, 1624, Margaret Roades or Rhodes was living across from Jamestown, to the east of Grays Creek but west of Hog Island (**8-15**) (CBE 40).

GEORGE ROADS

On February 16, 1624, George Roads was living in Elizabeth City on the east side of the Hampton River (**17**), on land owned by the Virginia Company of London. He probably was a Virginia Company servant or tenant (CBE 43).

JOHN ROBBINS

On February 2, 1626, when William Eppes patented some land in Accomack (**74**) on the Eastern Shore, he used the headright of John Robbins, who came to Virginia on the *Returne* in 1625 (PB 1 Pt. 1:49).

ROBERT

When writing about life in the colony in 1616, Captain John Smith made reference to Robert, a Polish man. He would have been one of the first Jamestown (**1**) settlers (CJS 2:257).

ROBERT

On March 22, 1622, when the Indians attacked Edward Bennett's plantation at Warresqueak (**26**), a man named Robert was killed (VCR 3:571).

ROBERT

On March 22, 1622, when the Indians attacked Powle-Brooke or Merchants Hope (**50**), a man named Robert was killed (VCR 3:569).

ROBERT

Robert, Mr. Ewin's servant, who lived at one of the plantations on the lower side of the James River (**8-15**), died sometime after April 1623 but before February 16, 1624 (CBE 41).

[NO FIRST NAME] ROBERTS

On April 7, 1623, Governor Francis Wyatt informed the Virginia Company that a Company servant named Roberts had been rented to a colonist named Gates. The given names of both individuals were omitted from surviving records (VCR 4:104).

CHRISTOPHER ROBERTS

Christopher Roberts died in Elizabeth City (Kecoughtan) **(17, 18)** sometime after April 1623 but before February 16, 1624 (CBE 45).

ELIAS ROBERTS

On December 23, 1619, Elias Roberts acquired 100 acres of Virginia land by purchasing it from the Virginia Company of London (VCR 1:289).

JAMES ROBERTS

James Roberts, a servant, was living in Ensign William Spence's household on Jamestown Island **(1)** on February 16, 1624 (CBE 40).

JEREMY ROBERTS

On November 8, 1624, Jeremy Roberts testified before the General Court that Mr. Gayne sent a Dutchman onto a ship. He probably was referring to William Ganey of Kecoughtan **(18)** (MCGC 30).

KENDRICK ROBERTS

Kendrick Roberts, a 22-year-old servant from Denbighshire, England, came to Virginia in 1619 aboard the *Bona Nova*, which carried a substantial number of Virginia Company servants and tenants. He may have been the Company servant named Roberts whom Governor Francis Wyatt said on April 7, 1623, was in the possession of a planter named Gates (FER 295; VCR 4:104).

THOMAS ROBERTS

Thomas Roberts died at West and Shirley Hundred **(41)** sometime after April 1623 but before February 16, 1624 (CBE 36).

WILLIAM ROBERTTS

William Robertts died in Elizabeth City **(17, 18)** sometime after April 1623 but before February 16, 1624 (CBE 36).

JAMES ROBESON

On January 30, 1625, 35-year-old James Robeson, who came to Virginia on the *Swann*, was living on the Maine **(3)**, part of

the Governor's Land. He was a servant in surgeon Thomas Bunn's household (CBE 57).

EDWARD ROBINS

According to testimony given in August 1635, Edward Robins had been in England in May when he and others received tobacco from Richard Bennett, whose plantation was in Warresqueak **(26)** (EAE 54).

***

JOHN ROBINS I
(SEE JOHN ROBINSON I)
JOHN ROBINS II
(SEE JOHN ROBINSON II)

***

***

OBEDIENCE ROBINS

On January 21, 1628, Obedience Robins, a surgeon living on the Eastern Shore **(72-78)**, testified that Captain John Wilcox had agreed to give Walter Scott three shares of his tobacco crop as compensation for overseeing his men. A year later George Medcalf, a planter, sued Robins and summoned him to court; however the case was dismissed because Medcalf failed to appear. In March 1630 Obedience Robins commenced serving as a burgess for Accomack, and by 1632 he had become a commissioner of the local court and a vestryman. Two years later he became the county's deputy lieutenant. Sometime after September 10, 1630, he married Grace, the widow of Edward Waters. Obedience Robins was alive in 1645 (MCGC 159, 183; HEN 1:149, 170, 187; MEY 461, 651; AMES 1:4-6, 18, 39, 44, 66; 2:39-41, 54, 86, 88, 141, 453).

GRACE WATERS ROBINS
(MRS. EDWARD WATERS,
MRS. OBEDIENCE ROBINS)
(SEE GRACE WATERS
[WATTERS, WALTERS])

Sometime after September 10, 1630, but before 1634, Edward Waters' widow, Grace, who came to Virginia in 1619 on the *Diana*, married Obedience Robins, probably in England. On March 22, 1638, when Obedience Robins received a court order that enabled him to patent some additional land, he used the headrights of Mrs. Grace Robins and Margaret Waters (CBE 65; PB 2:639; MEY 461-462, 651; AMES 1:146).

***

CHRISTOPHER ROBINSON

On July 21, 1627, Christopher Robinson agreed to go to Virginia as Rowland Truelove's servant and serve for ten years. Although Truelove sent groups of indentured servants to Virginia and was entitled to a patent, the precise location of his land (58) is uncertain. However, because Nathaniel Causey of Causey's Care (45) took charge of Truelove's Company's goods, and because some of Truelove's people were at Chaplin's Choice (56) in 1625, his land probably was nearby (CBE 79).

JAMES ROBINSON

James Robinson came to Virginia on the ship *Catherine* in 1621 and was an indentured servant. Testimony given before the General Court in 1629 indicates that William Spencer of Jamestown Island (1) was entitled to use Robinson as a headright. Spencer's September 8, 1632, patent for some land on Lawnes Creek in Warresqueak (25), in which James Robinson is listed as a headright, reveals that he had paid Mr. Weston, merchant of the *Charitie,* for his passage (MCGC 200; PB 1 Pt. 1:120).

JOHN ROBINSON

John Robinson, a gentleman and investor in the Virginia Company of London, arrived in Virginia in 1607 in the first group of Jamestown (1) settlers. When Edward Maria Wingfield was tried in September 1607, Robinson was fined £100 for slander. Later in the year he joined Captain John Smith and Thomas Emry in exploring the Chickahominy River. According to Smith's account, Robinson was slain by the Indians while he was sleeping beside a canoe. Smith later claimed that some members of the Council wanted to punish him because of John Robinson's death (CJS 1:21, 45, 47, 208; 2:141, 146, 152, 280; HAI 195).

JOHN ROBINSON

In 1619 John Robinson, a thief from Middlesex who was detained in Newgate Prison, was sentenced to transportation to "foreign parts," probably Virginia (CBE 12).

***

JOHN ROBINSON (ROBINS) I

Between January and April 1623 John Robinson (Robins) I, who was related to planter William Ganey, set sail for Virginia on the *Margaret and John* with his son, John II, and four servants: Henry West, Peter Asheley, Joseph Moore, and William Davis. He also brought along some goods. John Robinson I died at sea. Because the ship's master, Captain Douglas, refused to give the decedent's goods to his son and heir, John Robinson II filed a complaint with the Virginia government and Virginia Company officials. A September 1632 patent reveals that John II, when patenting some land on the Back River in Elizabeth City (19), used the headrights to which his late father was entitled (VCR 4:5-6, 127-128; PB 1 Pt. 1:116).

JOHN ROBINSON (ROBINS) II

John Robinson (Robins) II came to Virginia in 1623 on the *Margaret and John.* He accompanied his father, John I, who brought goods and four male servants. The elder man died while crossing the Atlantic, so on April 24, 1623, John II took legal steps in an attempt to recover his late father's belongings, which the ship's master, Captain Douglas, refused to relinquish. On February 16, 1624, John Robinson II was living in Elizabeth City, where he was a servant in the household of Francis Mason (18). He was still there in early 1625 and was 21 years old. He may have returned to England, for on July 19, 1627, a John Robinson shipped goods from London to Virginia on the *James.* In September 1632 John Robinson II, who identified himself as a Virginia planter and his father's son and heir, patented 300 acres on the Back River in Elizabeth City (19), using six headrights: those of his father and himself and the four servants they had transported to Virginia. On January 3, 1633, he witnessed a document in which Francis Hough conveyed the late Christopher Windmill's leasehold to Henry Coleman. In 1634 John Robinson II purchased some of the late Thomas Lee's goods, which were sold by Bartholomew Hopkins. On March 21, 1634, when Adam

Thorogood patented some land on the Back River in Elizabeth City County, his property was said to abut John Robinson's (VCR 4:5-6, 127-128; CBE 44, 65, 79, 208; PB 1 Pt. 1:116, 148, 160).

***

MARGARET ROBINSON

On February 27, 1619, Margaret Robinson, who was described as a wench, was among those chosen to be sent to Virginia. She appears to have been one of the children rounded up from the streets of London so that they could be sent to the colony (CBE 13).

MARY ROBINSON

In 1618 Mary Robinson, a gentlewoman who resided in England, bequeathed money to the church in Virginia. In February 1628 Virginia officials noted that she had donated a communion cup, chalices, and other liturgical items to be used in the church that would serve the settlers at Southampton Hundred (44). The items had been entrusted to the care of Sir George Yeardley, the plantation's local manager, whose widow, Lady Temperance, surrendered them to Virginia's Council of State shortly after his death (CBE 16; MCGC 167).

MATHEWE ROBINSONN

Mathewe Robinsonn, an indentured servant, came to Virginia on the *Great Hopewell* in 1623. In early 1625 he was living in Elizabeth City on the west side of the Hampton River (18), where he was a 24-year-old servant in Captain William Tucker's household (CBE 63).

RICHARD ROBINSON

Richard Robinson came to Virginia in 1620 aboard the *Bona Nova* and on February 16, 1624, was living in the corporation of Elizabeth City, on the east side of the Hampton River in a community known as the Indian Thicket (17). This suggests strongly that he was a Virginia Company servant or tenant. In early 1625 Richard Robinson, who was then age 22, was a servant in the household of John Bainham and Robert Sweete. He eventually obtained his freedom and on April 21, 1635, received a

patent for 100 acres on the north side of the Great Poquoson River (19) in Elizabeth City (CBE 43, 64; PB 1 Pt. 1:167).

ROWLAND ROBINSON

On February 27, 1619, Rowland Robinson, a boy, was among those the Bridewell Court chose for transportation to Virginia. He was one of the children rounded up from the streets of London so that they could be sent to the colony (CBE 12).

THOMAS ROBINSON

Thomas Robinson, an apprentice and mason from Waser in Stafford County, England, was sent to Virginia in 1622 at age 29. He was to serve for six years, at the end of which time he was to have 25 acres of land (FER 380).

WILLIAM ROBINSON

William Robinson, who was sent to Virginia by Edward Bennett, left England on July 31, 1622, aboard the *James*. On February 16, 1624, he was listed among those who had died at Warresqueak (26), the Bennett plantation, since April 1623 (FER 400; CBE 42).

GEORGE ROCKE

On July 18, 1628, George Rocke asked the Privy Council to release the *George*, which was bound to Virginia and St. Christopher's (CBE 83).

RALPH ROCKLEY

Ralph Rockley died in the corporation of Elizabeth City (17, 18) sometime after April 1623 but before February 16, 1624 (CBE 45).

CHRISTOPHER RODES

Christopher Rodes, a laborer, arrived in Virginia in January 1608 as part of the 1st Supply of new settlers (CJS 1:223; 2:161).

DOROTHY RODES

On March 25, 1629, Dorothy Rodes testified before the governor's council that she had been among a group of women visiting at Nicholas Eros's house when Thomas

Hall's gender was discussed. On February 4, 1625, Eyros was residing in Tappahannah, at the Treasurer's Plantation (11) (MCGC 195; CBE 60).

ROGER RODES (REDES, ROEDS)

Roger Rodes (Redes, Roeds), Mr. Fitzjeffrey's servant, arrived in Jamestown (1) aboard the *Bonny Bess* on September 12, 1623. When he took the oath of supremacy he indicated that he was around 19 years old and was from Dowton in Wilshire. On February 24, 1624, Roger Rodes was living in the household of Thomas Allnutt in the Neck O'Land (5) behind Jamestown Island. By January 24, 1625, he had moved to urban Jamestown, where he was identified as a 20-year-old servant in the Allnutt home. On March 7, 1626, the General Court added an additional year of service onto Roger Rodes's contract with Thomas Allnutt due to a bet they had made about the date of Easter. Court testimony reveals that Rodes and Allnutt had wagered a year of Rodes's time, and Rodes had lost (MCGC 6, 96-97; CBE 35, 55).

WILLIAM RODES (ROODS)

Diarist George Percy indicated that William Rodes (Roods), one of the first Virginia planters, died in Jamestown (1) on August 27, 1607 (HAI 99).

JOHN RODIS

According to minutes of the General Court for March 2, 1629, John Rodis became indebted to Abraham Porter of Jamestown Island (1), who forgave Rodis's debt when on his deathbed (MCGC 188).

EDWARD ROECROFT ALIAS STALLINGS (SEE EDWARD STALLINGS ALIAS ROECROFT)

BRYAN ROGERS

Bryan Rogers came to Virginia in 1621 on the ship *Elizabeth*. In early 1625 he was living in ancient planter Alexander Mountney's household in Elizabeth City (18), on the west side of the Hampton River. He was then age 18 and appears to have been free (CBE 66).

EDWARD ROGERS (ROGERES)

Edward Rogers or Rogeres arrived in Jamestown (1) on September 5, 1623, aboard the *Ann* and took the oath of supremacy. He was identified as a carpenter from Porbery in Somershire, England. When a muster was made of the colony's inhabitants in early 1625, Edward was living on the Eastern Shore in the household of William Eppes (74), where he was a servant. Rogers was then age 26. On February 3, 1626, when Eppes patented some land, he used Edward Rogers as a headright and noted that he had come to Virginia in 1623 on the *Ann* (MCGC 6; CBE 68; PB 1 Pt. 1:49).

EDWARD ROGERS

On March 22, 1622, Edward Rogers was killed at Martin's Hundred (7) during the Indian attack (VCR 3:570).

FRANCIS (FRANCES) ROGERS

In September 1636 Francis (Frances) Rogers, who was living in Virginia, received a bequest from John Bigge of Whitechapel in Middlesex, England. She was identified as a minor and spinster, who was to receive her bequest at age 21 (EEAC 7; WAT 628).

GEORGE ROGERS

On February 16, 1624, George Rogers, who came to Virginia on the *Bona Nova*, was living in the corporation of James City, on the lower side of the James River (8-15). On February 4, 1625, he was still there and was identified as one of Edward Blaney's servants then residing on the late Captain William Powell's plantation (14) in Tappahannah. Rogers was age 23 (CBE 40, 59).

JOHN ROGERS

On November 20, 1622, John Rogers, an inmate in Newgate Prison, was among those pardoned because of an epidemic of jail fever and chosen to be transported overseas, probably to Virginia (CBE 29).

LAWRENCE ROGERS

In April 1625 Lawrence Rogers informed the General Court that he had inspected Sir George Yeardley's tobacco after it had been loaded aboard the ship. He later testified that much of the crop was bad (MCGC 51, 60).

RALPH ROGERS

Ralph Rogers died at Martin's Hundred **(7)** sometime after April 1623 but before February 16, 1624 (CBE 42).

RICHARD ROGERS

Richard Rogers of St. Michael Crooked Lane, London, controller of the king's mint, owned some land in Virginia. In September 1636 he bequeathed a life interest in his acreage, which already had been seated, to his son Edward Rogers and named his grandson, Richard Rogers, as reversionary heir. Also mentioned in Richard Rogers' will were his daughter, Ann Draper, and son Jasper Draper. A May 1636 patent for some land in Warresqueak **(26)** refers to the adjacent property of Edward Rogers, perhaps the land the testator left to his son (EEAC 48; WAT 642-644; PB 1 Pt. 1:346).

ROBERT ROGERS

On July 21, 1627, Robert Rogers agreed to go to Virginia as a servant (CBE 79).

STEPHEN ROGERS

In April 1617 Stephen Rogers, a convicted killer who was identified as a carpenter, was sent to Virginia by Sir Thomas Smith, treasurer of the Virginia Company of London (CBE 8).

WILLIAM ROGERS

In 1619 when William Rogers was sent to Virginia, his transportation costs were borne by the Ferrars, who were major Virginia Company investors (FER 296).

HENRY ROLFE

On April 30, 1621, Henry Rolfe submitted an account to the Virginia Company's auditors on behalf of his brother, John, who was then in Virginia (VCR 1:461-462).

JAMES ROLFE

On March 22, 1622, James Rolfe, one of Lieutenant John Gibbs's men, was killed in the Indian attack on West and Shirley Hundred **(41)** (VCR 1:461-462).

***

JOHN ROLFE

John Rolfe and his pregnant wife (whose identity is uncertain) left England in June 1609 with Sir Thomas Gates and Sir George Somers on the *Seaventure*, which wrecked in Bermuda. While stranded, Mrs. Rolfe gave birth to a daughter they named Bermuda. Afterward, mother and infant died. John Rolfe resumed his journey to Virginia and arrived in May 1610. A month later, Lord Delaware's fleet came in and a military form of government was instituted. During those years (1610–1616), John Rolfe conducted the tobacco experiments for which he gained fame. His efforts led to the development of a palatable and marketable strain that became the colonists' money crop. Rolfe, a member of the Council of State, served as the colony's secretary of state from 1614 to 1619, and in 1614 he wrote a descriptive account of life in the colony.

Around April 1, 1614, John Rolfe married the Indian princess Pocahontas, by then converted to Christianity. Two years earlier he had sought the advice of Sir Thomas Dale about the propriety of marrying a Native. In May 1616 the Rolfes and their infant son, Thomas, set sail for England. Pocahontas died in England while waiting for the ship that would transport them back to Virginia. John Rolfe entrusted his son, Thomas, to the care of his brother, Henry, and returned to Virginia. On June 8, 1617, when John dispatched a letter to officials in England reporting on conditions in the colony, he asked for an official post and land that would provide an inheritance for his son. Within a year or two the twice-widowed John Rolfe had married Joane Peirce, Captain William Peirce's daughter. The Rolfes resided in urban Jamestown **(1)**, probably on the Peirce property, for John seemingly had no acreage of his own on the island. In January 1620 John Rolfe informed Virginia Company Treasurer Edwin Sandys that in late August a Dutch man-of-war had arrived at Old Point Comfort and traded "20 and odd negroes" (the first Africans that reached the Virginia colony) for much needed provisions. Three or four days later, a ship called the *Treasurer* arrived and

Governor Yeardley sent Rolfe, William Peirce, and William Ewins to meet it. The vessel carried some Africans, one of whom (a woman named Angelo) was living in the Peirce home in urban Jamestown in 1624 and 1625. Virginia Company records indicate that John Rolfe and his father-in-law, William Peirce, often collaborated in business dealings, and Rolfe had some involvement in the late Lord Delaware's financial affairs.

On March 10, 1622, when John Rolfe of Jamestown made his will, he described himself as sick and weak. He left his land on the lower side of the James River (what became known as Surry County's Rolfe-Warren Plantation, located just east of Paces Paines [9]) to son, Thomas, and his heirs or, if Thomas died without heirs, to daughter, Elizabeth. He bequeathed to wife Joan Peirce Rolfe life rights in his property on Mulberry Island (21), naming their daughter, Elizabeth, as reversionary heir. Rolfe's personal property was to be divided into thirds and distributed among his wife and children. His father-in-law, William Peirce, whom he named as administrator, was to inherit three oxen and Rolfe's sword, armor, and girdle; he also was to manage the children's inheritance. John Rolfe left his wife, Joan (Joane, Jone), the time remaining on their three servants' contracts, and he bequeathed a sum of money to servant Robert Davys. John died sometime prior to October 1622, when his brother, Henry Rolfe, asked that an inventory be made of John's Virginia estate. However, the decedent's will was not presented for probate in England until May 21, 1630. Land records postdating John Rolfe's death reveal that he had owned 400 acres on the lower side of the James River at the head of Gray's Creek, plus a half interest in the 1,700 acres at Mulberry Island that he shared with his father-in-law, William Peirce. Both tracts were planted. Rolfe also had owned some land in Charles City at Bermuda Hundred (39) (LEF 1:47; HAI 413, 808-809, 820, 845, 856, 865-877 887-890; CJS 2:245-246, 249-251, 255, 261-262; MEY 507-509; PRO 30/15/2 ff 208, 290; C 24/490; STAN 21, 28; VCR 1:399-400, 459-460, 477, 625, 629; 2:103, 105-106; 3:70-72, 153, 170, 241-248, 482; 4:551, 555-556; FER 113; CBE 49, 91; SR 3960; SH 5; MCGH 861; PB 1:Pt 1:59, 125; EEAC 48).

[NO FIRST NAME] ROLFE (MRS. JOHN ROLFE)

Mrs. John Rolfe and her husband left England in June 1609 on the *Seaventure*, which ran aground in Bermuda. While stranded there, Mrs. Rolfe gave birth to a daughter they named Bermuda. The infant lived long enough to be christened but died shortly thereafter, as did her mother (LEF 1:47; HAI 413).

REBECCA (POCAHONTAS, MATOAKA) ROLFE (MRS. JOHN ROLFE) (SEE POCAHONTAS MATOAKA, [REBECCA])

Pocahontas or Matoaka, Powhatan's favorite daughter, was taken hostage by the colonists in 1611. Afterward, she converted to Christianity and adopted the English name Rebecca. John Rolfe, a widower and secretary of the colony, fell in love with her and the two were married around April 1, 1614, in the church in Jamestown (1). The union had Powhatan's consent and one of Pocahontas's uncles, probably Opechancanough, reportedly gave her away. In May 1616 Pocahontas, her husband, and their infant son accompanied Sir Thomas Dale when he returned to England, where she was introduced at court and treated as a Native princess. She also encountered her old friend Captain John Smith. In March 1617, when the Rolfes and their little son were in Gravesend awaiting the ship that would take them back to Virginia, Pocahontas contracted consumption (tuberculosis) and died. She was buried in the yard of St. Mary le Bow Church, in Gravesend (VCR 2:105-106; 3:70; HAI 809, 820, 850-856, 887-890; MEY 508; SP 14/87 ff 67, 146; CJS 2:245-246, 255, 261-262).

JOAN (JOANE, JONE) PEIRCE ROLFE (MRS. JOHN ROLFE, MRS. ROGER SMITH) (SEE JOAN PEIRCE II, MRS. ROGER SMITH)

Joan (Joane, Jone) Peirce, who came to Virginia on the *Blessinge*, married John Rolfe after the death of Pocahontas and Rolfe's May 1617 return to Virginia. John and Joan

Peirce Rolfe most likely lived on one of the two parcels in urban Jamestown (1) that were owned by her parents, William and Joan Peirce. The Rolfes produced a daughter, Elizabeth, around 1621. When John Rolfe died in 1622, he left his wife, Joan, an interest in his land at Mulberry Island (21). Sometime prior to 1623, Joan Peirce Rolfe married Captain Roger Smith of Jamestown and moved into his home. She was living there with daughter Elizabeth Rolfe (then age 3) on February 16, 1624, when a census was taken, and on January 24, 1625, when the population was tabulated again. In the Smith household in 1625 were two other children: the orphaned Sara Macock (age 2) and Elizabeth Salter (age 7) (CBE 38, 55; MEY 416, 478; MCGH 861; SH 5).

BERMUDA ROLFE

Bermuda Rolfe, the infant daughter of John Rolfe and his wife, whose identity is unknown, was born on the island for which she was named. On February 1610, when she was christened there, Christopher Newport, William Strachey, and a Mrs. Horton served as witnesses. The infant died a short time later (LEF 1:47; HAI 413).

ELIZABETH ROLFE

Elizabeth Rolfe was the daughter of John and Joan (Joane, Jone) Peirce Rolfe, who resided in urban Jamestown (1), probably on the property owned by Captain William Peirce, Elizabeth's maternal grandfather. Elizabeth inherited land at Mulberry Island (21) from her father under the terms of his March 10, 1622, will. Joan Peirce Rolfe, after being widowed, married Captain Roger Smith, whose land in Jamestown was next door to that of her parents, the Peirces. On February 16, 1624, Elizabeth Rolfe was living with her mother and stepfather, Roger Smith, in his house in Jamestown. On January 24, 1625, Elizabeth, who was still in the Smith household, was described as age 4 and Virginia-born. Two other children were in the Smith household: the orphaned Sara Macock (age 2) and Elizabeth Salter (age 7) (SH 5; MCGH 861; MEY 508; CBE 38, 55).

THOMAS ROLFE

Thomas Rolfe, who was born in 1615, was the son of John Rolfe and his wife, Poca-

hontas (Rebecca), and accompanied them on their May 1616 trip to England. After Pocahontas's death in March 1617, John decided to leave Thomas in England temporarily and entrusted him to the care of his brother, Henry Rolfe. After John Rolfe returned to Virginia, he married Joan (Joane, Jone), the daughter of Captain William Peirce, a resident of urban Jamestown (1). Rolfe became ill and on March 10, 1622, when he prepared his will, left his son, Thomas, 400 acres of land on the lower side of the James River on Grays Creek, in what became Surry County. The acreage includes the site of a fort that Captain John Smith built in 1608. In 1618 Virginia Company officials heard a rumor that the Indians had given their country to Thomas Rolfe and were reserving it for him until he came of age. Thomas returned to Virginia and married a woman with whom he produced a daughter named Jane. In 1635 Thomas Rolfe was listed among the headrights of his stepgrandfather, Captain William Peirce, and sometime prior to March 1640 he took possession of his father's land on the lower side of the James River. On October 6, 1646, Thomas Rolfe agreed to build a fort at Moysenac—on the west side of Diascund Creek's mouth, within what is now New Kent County—promising to see that it was manned and maintained for three years. In exchange for doing so, he received 400 acres. A blockhouse or fortified stronghold was built at the site to maintain surveillance over the Indians (VCR 2:52; 3:70; HAI 887-890; CJS 2:262; SH 5; MEY 508-509; MCGH 861; PB 3:13).

***

GEORGE ROOKE

On April 3, 1622, George Rooke acquired two shares of the late Lord Delaware's Virginia land from Francis Carter. It is uncertain whether Rooke made any attempt to seat his land in the colony. On September 30, 1630, Rooke was identified as a London merchant when he and John Barnabee, a Virginia planter, sought permission to trade in the king's dominions (VCR 1:630; CBE 92).

RALPH ROOKE

In August 1618 Ralph Rooke, who was described as an incorrigible rogue and vagabond from Middlesex, England, was sentenced to transportation to Virginia (CBE 9).

WILLIAM ROOKINGS
(ROOKINS, ROOKINGE)

William Rookings (Rookins, Rookinge), a 21-year-old cook from Essex, England, came to Virginia in 1619 on the *Bona Nova*, a vessel that brought a large number of Virginia Company servants and tenants to the colony. On February 16, 1624, he was living at Buckroe, on the east side of the Hampton River in Elizabeth City (**17**) on the Virginia Company's land. In early 1625, when a muster was made of the colony's inhabitants, William Rookings was still there and was identified as a 26-year-old servant in Sergeant William Barry's household. Barry, like Rookings, had come to Virginia in 1619 on the *Bona Nova*. On November 13, 1626, William Rookings was described in court as John Parsons' heir, and on January 7, 1653, John Hacker referred to him as a planter when bequeathing him some cattle (FER 295; CBE 45, 68; MCGC 123; WAT 878).

ABRAHAM ROOT (ROOTE)

On August 13, 1634, Abraham Root (Roote), a planter and resident of Hog Island (**16**), obtained a 21-year-lease for 50 acres on the Hog Island mainland. His leasehold was known as "the Rocks" (PB 1 Pt. 1:153).

JOHN ROOT (ROOTE)

On February 4, 1625, John Roote was residing on Hog Island (**16**) on property that belonged to Sir George Yeardley. Little is known about Root except that he came to Virginia on the *Gifte* (CBE 61).

***

NICHOLAS ROOT (ROOTE)

On February 4, 1623, Nicholas Root (Roote) and his wife, Bridget, were among several people involved in an altercation that was aired before the justices of the General Court. At issue was William Killdale's threatening to shoot a seemingly aggressive dog that belonged to Thomas Hethersall. Nicholas Root and Richard Craven reportedly were poised to strike Killdale when Hethersall's dog bit Root, who commenced beating it with a stick. The justices ordered Richard Craven to pay for

William Killdale's medical treatment, and Craven and Nicholas Root were required to post bonds guaranteeing their good behavior. On February 16, 1624, Nicholas Root was residing on the Maine (**3**) just west of Jamestown Island. Since Richard Craven and Thomas Hethersall lived there too, it is likely that the episode occurred there (MCGC 3; CBE 39).

BRIDGET ROOT (ROOTE)
(MRS. NICHOLAS ROOT [ROOTE])

On February 4, 1623, Bridget Root (Roote) and her husband, Nicholas, testified before the General Court that William Killdale had threatened to shoot Thomas Hethersall's dog. Afterward, Nicholas Root and Richard Craven attacked Killdale with a stick, and Bridget Root and Craven seized his gun. Since Nicholas Root and Richard Craven were residents of the Maine (**3**) in February 1624, it is likely that the incident occurred there (MCGC 3).

***

CLEMENT ROPER

On January 20, 1625, Clement Roper was living at Flowerdew Hundred (**53**), where he was a 25-year-old servant in Abraham Peirsey's household. Roper and many of Peirsey's other servants reportedly came to Virginia on the *Southampton* in 1623 (CBE 50).

THOMAS ROPER

Thomas Roper, a gentleman from Malden in Bedfordshire, England, arrived in Jamestown (**1**) on September 12, 1623, on the *Bonny Bess* and took the oath of supremacy. In April and May 1623, he and Mr. Fitzjeffries (Fitz-Jeffry, Fitz-Jefferys, Fitzjeffreys), who were planning to bring 100 people to Virginia, requested and then received a patent for some land. Roper apparently became ill within months of his arrival, for he died on Jamestown Island sometime prior to February 16, 1624. When preparing his will, which was undated, he bequeathed two of his servants (Alexander Gill and John West) their freedom, noting that Gill was then in the employ of William Peirce of Jamestown. He specified that if Peirce refused to free Alexander, he was to compensate him for his work. Roper bequeathed a pair of linen breeches to William Smith of Jamestown, and he left some money to the Rev. Haute Wyatt, whom he identified as the minister there. He left his tobacco crop and some money then in the hands of his father-in-law (that is, stepfather) to his brother, John Roper, who was then in England, and asked George Fitzjeffries (Fitz-Jeffry, Fitz-Jefferys, Fitzjeffreys) of Jamestown to see that he received it. Thomas Roper's will was presented for probate in England on February 5, 1627, at which time his brother, John, was given letters of administration. His appointment superceded that of Thomas Shepherd of Moine in Bedfordshire, who had served as administrator during the minority of John, Elizabeth, and Constance Shepherd, the decedent's maternal half-brother and half-sisters (MCGC 6; CBE 39, 77; VCR 2:345, 428; EEAC 49-50; WITH 487-488).

[NO FIRST NAME] ROSE

According to Captain John Smith, a male laborer whose surname was Rose arrived in Virginia in 1608 in the 2nd Supply of new settlers. He would have lived in Jamestown (1) (CJS 1:242; 2:191).

JOHN ROSE

On February 16, 1624, John Rose was living on the Maine (3) to the west of Jamestown Island (CBE 39).

JOHN ROSE (ROSSE)

On July 29, 1626, John Rose or Rosse, an inmate at Bridewell Prison, was selected for transportation to Virginia (CBE 72).

***

REBECCA (REBECKA) HILL ROSE (ROSSE)

On February 16, 1624, Mrs. Rebecca (Rebecka) Hill Rose (Rosse), a widow, was living on the mainland in West and Shirley Hundred (41) with her two children, listed as her sons. On January 22, 1625, when a muster was made of the colony's inhabitants, Mrs. Rose was identified as a 50-year-old widow and household head, who had come to Virginia on the *Marigold* in 1619.

In 1625 she was sharing her home with two children, Marmaduke (age 11) and Jane Hill (age 14), perhaps the youngsters previously described as her sons. In court testimony taken on March 5, 1627, Goodwife Rose, a midwife, was identified as the mother of Jane Hill, who stood accused of having sex with John Ewins. Since Marmaduke and Jane Hill came to Virginia on the *Marigold*, the same ship that brought Rebecca Rose, they probably were offspring from a prior marriage. On September 10, 1625, when Richard Biggs of West and Shirley Hundred made his will, he indicated that Rebecca Rose was his sister and bequeathed her 6 acres of land, part of his plantation (CBE 36, 52; MCGC 142; SH 6; WITH 53-54; DOR 1:14).

[NO FIRST NAME] ROSE (HILL?)

On February 14, 1624, a child whose surname was Rose was identified as one of Mrs. Rebecca Rose's two sons and attributed to her household in West and Shirley Hundred (41). Because Marmaduke Hill (age 11) and his sister Jane (age 14) were living in Mrs. Rose's home on January 22, 1625, and later were identified as her children, the census-taker may have erroneously assumed that they shared their mother's surname (CBE 36, 52; MCGC 142).

[NO FIRST NAME] ROSE (HILL?)

The census-taker attributed a boy named Rose to Mrs. Rebecca Rose's household in West and Shirley Hundred (41) on February 14, 1624. Because Marmaduke Hill (age 11) and his sister Jane (age 14) were living in Mrs. Rose's home on January 22, 1625, and later were identified as her children, the census-taker may have assumed that they shared their mother's surname (CBE 36, 52; MCGC 142).

***

THOMAS ROSE (REES)

On February 16, 1624, Thomas Rose (Rees) was living on the Maine or Governor's Land (3) and was one of Captain William Peirce's servants. On January 25, 1625, he was residing on Mulberry Island (21), where he again was identified as one of Peirce's servants. He was then 35 years old and reportedly came to Virginia on the *Jonathan*. In May 1625 Thomas Rose was credited with 100 acres in Charles City, land that was patented but not planted (CBE 39, 57; VCR 4:553).

HILL ROSSE (ROSE)

On December 31, 1619, the justices of Bridewell Court decided that Hill Rosse (Rose), a detainee, would be sent to Virginia (CBE 15).

HULL ROSSE (ROFFE)

On February 26, 1620, the justices of Bridewell Court decided that Hull Roffe, a prisoner at Newgate, would be sent to Virginia. This may have been the same individual previously identified as Hill Rosse (CBE 19).

JOHN ROSIER

On June 26,1637, John Rosier, a 34-year-old cleric from Warresqueak (**26**), testified before the justices of Isle of Wight County that he had buried William Hutchinson, who had died three or four years earlier. He stated that Hutchinson had designated Richard Bennett (owner of Bennett's Welcome), as overseer of his estate. Thus, Rosier would have been in Virginia in 1633 or 1634 (EAE 73; BOD 1:93-94).

EDMUND ROSSINGHAM (ROFFINGHAM)

Edmund Rossingham (Roffingham), Sir George Yeardley's nephew, accompanied Yeardley to Virginia, leaving England in December 1618 and arriving in April 1619. In the July and August 1619 assembly meeting, Rossingham served as a burgess for Yeardley's plantation, Flowerdew Hundred (**53**). He later testified in court that in 1619 Yeardley sent him on a trading voyage on the Chesapeake Bay and in January 1620 had given him a power of attorney and sent him to Newfoundland to trade. He said that Yeardley also dispatched him to Holland in 1621 and 1623 to serve as his factor. Edmund Rossingham, on Sir George Yeardley's behalf, sought relief from indebtedness to the Virginia Company of London and the Society of Southampton Hundred. While Captain Rossingham was in England, he spoke against Captain John Martin, a fellow colonist and one of Sir George Yeardley's detractors. In May or June 1623,

Virginia Company officials asked Rossingham about conditions in Virginia. After Sir George Yeardley's death in early November 1627, Edmund Rossingham sought to recover funds from Yeardley's estate—payment for services he had performed on Sir George's behalf. When the decedent's brother and administrator, Ralph Yeardley, refused to pay him, Rossingham sent a petition to the Privy Council, which ordered a payment of £200. Ralph Yeardley refused to comply, and Rossingham initiated a chancery suit that dragged on until at least November 1630 (VCR 2:43; 3:154; 4:185; C 24/560 Pt. 2:84; CO 1/5:51-54, 120; SR 626, 10406; CBE 87, 90; SAIN 1:98, 107).

[NO FIRST NAME] ROSWELL

On February 16, 1624, Mr. Rosswell was listed among those residing in Elizabeth City (**17, 18**) (CBE 43).

THOMAS ROTLINGHAM

On September 26, 1618, the justices of Bridewell Court decided that Thomas Rotlingham, a vagrant from Cheapside, was to be transported to Virginia (CBE 10).

LIONELL (LYONELL) ROULSTON (ROWLSTON, ROWLSTONE)

Lionell (Lyonell) Roulston (Rowlston, Rowlstone) came to Virginia in 1623 on the *Gift of God*. Although it is uncertain where he was living on February 16, 1624, when a census was taken of the colony's inhabitants, in early 1625 he was living in Elizabeth City on the west side of the Hampton River (**18**). At that time he was a 30-year-old indentured servant in the household of Francis Chamberlin. Lionell Roulston apparently accumulated some wealth by the time he obtained his freedom, for on July 7, 1627, he dispatched a shipment of goods from London to Virginia aboard the *Ann Fortune*. On September 29, 1628, he was identified as an Elizabeth City planter when he obtained from Dictoris Christmas a lease for 50 acres of land at the Strawberry Banks (**17**). During 1629 Lionell Roulston was named a justice of Elizabeth City's monthly court, and he was elected a burgess for Elizabeth City. In October 1629 he was among the assembly members given the responsibility of finding men to plant at

Chiskiack (**30-38**) by November 1630, in exchange for an allotment of land. On January 14, 1630, he transferred his 50-acre leasehold at Strawberry Banks to his friend John Neal. Later in the year he was among those named as an heir in the will of Edward Waters, an Elizabeth City gentleman. Lionell Roulston represented the York River plantations in the September 1632 and February 1633 sessions of the colony's assembly, an indication that he then owned property in that area (CBE 66, 78; PB 1 Pt. 1:134; MCGC 193; HEN 1:132, 139-140, 179, 203; SH 13).

[NO FIRST NAME] ROUSLIE (ROWSLEY?)

In January 1638 Captain Samuel Mathews testified that in 1624 he had received some tobacco from Captain William Holmes of Jamestown (**1**). Mathews admitted that at the time he accepted the tobacco, he still owed Holmes for the house he had purchased from him, a structure that formerly belonged to Holmes's brother, Rouslie (Rowsley?) (EAE 89; MCGC 143).

ANDREW ROWE (ROW, ROE)

On July 20, 1625, Andrew Rowe (Row, Roe), who was from Holt in Northfolk (probably Norfolk), England, informed the General Court that he had landed in Virginia on July 11, 1625, having set out from Flushing with Captains Powell and Jones on the *Black Bess*. He said that Powell and Jones picked up victuals in Isle of Wight and then headed out to sea. They arrived at the Western Islands and then continued on to the West Indies, capturing a frigate that they took with them on the remainder of their journey. Because Captain Powell refused to give the men adequate food and water and forced them to sign a document in which they promised to fight any vessels they encountered, there was considerable unrest. Finally, Powell allowed some of his crew to leave in the frigate. After some misadventures and being lost at sea, they arrived in Virginia. In late October 1628 Andrew Rowe testified that in August 1627 he saw carpenter Richard Tree and his servant working on the construction of a church at Hog Island (**16**) and that they were using some dubbed (finished) boards that had been left there (MCGC 66-68, 175).

*** *

JOHN ROWE (ROW, ROE)

John Rowe (Row, Roe), who was identified as "the parson's man," came to Virginia in 1619 on the *Bona Nova*, a ship that brought a large number of Virginia Company servants and tenants. In 1621 he told Sir Edwin Sandys that he had been very ill during the transatlantic crossing and that Sir George Yeardley and his wife had been extremely kind to him. He said that he was then living in Pasbehay (**3**) with his wife and his son-in-law (stepson?), John Smyth (Smith). He also reported that progress was being made on building the Southampton Hundred (**44**) iron works. In September 1624 John Rowe, who was still living in Pasbehay, was fined for being drunk and boisterous. In January 1625 he and surgeon Thomas Bunn (another Pasbehay resident) testified about some crops that had been destroyed by swine. On March 11, 1625, while John Rowe was at Captain Mathews' house (**15**) on the lower side of the James River, he became extremely sick and prepared his will, making bequests to his mother, a resident of Yorkshire, and to Thomas Bunn, who was providing him with medical care. At the time of his death, John Rowe was in possession of some goods that belonged to deceased planter Henry Wentworth, whose belongings were to be sent to England (FER 295; VCR 3:464; MCGC 20, 46, 50).

MRS. JOHN ROWE (ROW, ROE)

On May 27, 1621, the husband of Mrs. John Rowe (Row, Roe) sent a letter to Sir Edwin Sandys saying that Sir George Yeardley and his wife had been very kind to him and his wife, and that they were residing in Pasbehay (**3**). In July 1621 the Rowe couple was still living there with son-in-law (stepson?) John Smith. Mrs. Rowe may have died prior to March 11, 1625, for her husband failed to name her as one of his heirs, and her name was missing from the demographic records compiled in 1624 and 1625 (VCR 3:462-464).

***

NICHOLAS ROWE (ROE)

According to Virginia Company records, on April 1, 1620, Thomas Astley paid for the passage of Nicholas Rowe (Roe) who came to Virginia on the *Elizabeth* in 1621. On February 16, 1624, when a census was taken of the colony's inhabitants, Rowe was living at Buckroe, on the east side of the Hampton River (**17**), the Virginia Company's land in Elizabeth City. In early 1625 Nicholas Rowe and his partner, John Haney, jointly headed a household that included their wives and two servants. Rowe and Haney had possession of a palisaded dwelling and three storehouses, and they were well supplied with food and defensive weaponry. On December 5, 1625, Nicholas Rowe was one of several men who testified before the General Court about a shipboard discussion that took place at Dambrells Cove, Canada. At issue was whether Jeffrey Cornish's brother had been executed wrongfully. On December 19th Nicholas returned to court to testify about a ship that had been damaged because it was anchored in shallow water. At the same court session, he was granted use of the two servants then in his possession. In July 1627 John Giles, one of Nicholas Rowe's servants, sued for his freedom, but in February 1628 the General Court's justices ordered Giles to serve an additional six months, two of which were to cover Rowe's court costs. On December 2, 1628, Nicholas Rowe was granted a 43-acre leasehold in Elizabeth City on the east side of the Hampton River, adjoining Old Point Comfort Creek. Thus, the land he was allocated was part of the Virginia Company's tract of Company Land (CBE 45, 68; FER 162; MCGC 78, 82, 165; PB 1 Pt. 1:96; DOR 1:68).

MARY ROWE (ROE)
(MRS. NICHOLAS ROWE [ROE])

Mary, the wife of Nicholas Rowe (Roe), came to Virginia on the *London Merchant* in 1620. In early 1625 Mary and Nicholas Rowe, John Haney (Rowe's partner), and others were sharing a home on the east side of the Hampton River, part of the Virginia Company's tract of Company Land in Elizabeth City (**17**) (CBE 68).

***

HENRY ROWEN

According to General Court records, Henry Rowen was brought to Virginia by Sir George Yeardley on the *Temperance* in 1621. On September 20, 1628, when Thom-

as Flint patented some land, he used Rowen as a headright and repeated the same information contained in the General Court records. Rowen may have been the individual listed in demographic records as Henry Rowlinge, an indentured servant, who in 1624 and 1625 was living at Flowerdew Hundred (**53**), formerly the Yeardley plantation, and reportedly arrived on the *Temperance* in 1621 (MCGC 166; PB 1 Pt. 1:59).

JOHN ROWES (ROSE?, ROSSE?)

On February 16, 1624, a man named John Rowes (perhaps Rose or Rosse) was living in Elizabeth City (**18**), on the west side of the Hampton River (CBE 43).

JOHN ROWLES (ROLLES)

John Rowles (Rolles), a 37-year-old weaver from Gloucestershire, England, came to Virginia in 1619 on the *Bona Nova* and was killed at Berkeley Hundred (**55**) during the March 22, 1622, Indian attack (FER 295; VCR 3:567).

***

RICHARD ROWLES (ROLLES)

On September 10, 1620, Richard Rowles (Rolles), who had agreed to go to Virginia to seat at Berkeley Hundred (**55**), left England in the first group of settlers heading to the plantation. As a tenant, he was supposed to receive a share of land in exchange for working a certain number of years. Richard, his wife, Jane, and their child were accompanied by his married son, Benedict, and daughter-in-law, Francys (Frances). All were entrusted to the care of headman William Tracy, who was on the same ship. Richard Rowles and his family arrived at Berkeley Hundred on January 29, 1621, and were slain there during the March 22, 1622, Indian attack (VCR 3:397, 426, 567; CBE 21).

JANE ROWLES (ROLLES)
(MRS. RICHARD ROWLES [ROLLES])

Jane Rowles (Rolles) and her husband, Richard, a tenant of the Society of Berkeley Hundred, were among those who by September 10, 1620, had agreed to go to Virginia to settle at Berkeley Hundred (**55**).

The Rowles couple, their child, and other family members arrived at Berkeley Hundred on January 29, 1621. Jane Rowles, her husband, and their underage child were slain at Berkeley during the March 22, 1622, Indian attack (VCR 3:397, 426, 567; CBE 21).

[NO FIRST NAME] ROWLES (ROLLES)

On March 22, 1622, when the Indians attacked Berkeley Hundred (55), the underage child of Richard and Jane Rowles (Rolles) was among those slain (VCR 3:567).

BENEDICT ROWLES (ROLLES)

Benedict Rowles (Rolles) was among those who set out for Berkeley Hundred (55) on September 10, 1620. He, like his father, Richard Rowles, was to receive a share of land in exchange for working a certain number of years. When Benedict Rowles arrived at Berkeley Hundred on January 29, 1621, he was accompanied by his wife, Francys (Frances). It is unclear whether the couple had wed before setting sail for Virginia or after their departure. Benedict Rowles and several members of his family were slain at Berkeley Hundred in the March 22, 1622, Indian attack. It is unclear whether Benedict's wife, Francys, escaped harm (VCR 3:397, 426, 567; CBE 21).

FRANCYS (FRANCES) ROWLES (ROLLES) (MRS. BENEDICT ROWLES [ROLLES])

On January 29, 1621, Francys (Frances) Rowles (Rolles), the wife of Richard Rowles's son, Benedict, arrived at Berkeley Hundred (55), having come to Virginia with William Tracy. Although Benedict Rowles and the rest of his family were slain at Berkeley Hundred during the March 22, 1622, Indian attack, Francys' life may have been spared, for she was not listed among those who were killed (VCR 3:427, 567).

***

WILLIAM ROWLEY (ROWSLEY)

William Rowley (Rowsley), a surgeon, and his wife, Elizabeth, came to Virginia on the *James* with their ten male servants and left

England on July 31, 1622. On April 3, 1623, Rowley, who was in Jamestown (1), informed Virginia Company officials that his wife wanted to return to England. He said that there was much famine and death in Jamestown and that all of his servants were dead. He added, however, that he and his wife fared as well as the best people there. William Rowley said that the colonists' livestock were depleted and that they needed help from England. He indicated that he had purchased a cow for an exorbitant price and that the woods were very dangerous because of the Indians. William and Elizabeth Rowley died at their home in urban Jamestown sometime prior to February 16, 1624, and their maidservant also perished (FER 400; VCR 4:228, 235, 238; CBE 39; MCGC 80).

ELIZABETH ROWLEY (ROWSLEY) (MRS. WILLIAM ROWLEY [ROWSLEY])

Elizabeth Rowley (Rowsley) came to Virginia on the *James*, accompanied by her husband, William, and ten servants. They departed from England on July 31, 1622. On April 3, 1623, William Rowley informed Virginia Company officials that Elizabeth was eager to return to England, as there was much famine and death in Jamestown (1), where they lived. William and Elizabeth Rowley died there sometime prior to February 16, 1624. On December 12, 1625, several people testified that Mrs. Rowsley made a nuncupative will while she lay ill in her late husband's house in urban Jamestown. She then freed Anthony West, one of the Rowleys' servants (FER 400; VCR 4:228, 235, 238; CBE 39; MCGC 80).

***

HENRY ROWLINGE

Henry Rowlinge came to Virginia aboard the *Temperance* in 1621 and on February 16, 1624, was living at Flowerdew Hundred (53). On January 20, 1625, when a muster was made of the settlement's inhabitants, he was still there and was identified as a 25-year-old servant in Abraham Peirsey's household. He may have been the man later identified as Henry Rowen, who was transported to Virginia by Sir George Yeardley on the *Temperance* in 1621 and whose headright was used in September 1628 by Thomas Flint (CBE 37, 50).

THOMAS ROWLSON

In the 1625 muster Thomas Rowlson was listed among those who died at one of the plantations on the lower side of the James River, within the corporation of James City **(8-15)** (CBE 60).

JOSEPH ROYALL

Joseph Royall arrived in Virginia in July 1622, having crossed the Atlantic on the *Charitie*. On February 16, 1624, he was living in Bermuda Hundred **(39)**. He was still there on January 24, 1625, when he was identified as a 22-year-old servant in Luke Boise's household. Court testimony reveals that Joseph Royall was a tailor, who on February 25, 1625, had signed a contract with Luke Boise. On January 11, 1627, the General Court ordered Royall to continue serving Boise's widow, Alice, and to make clothing for her and all the members of her household (CBE 35, 53; MCGC 132; DOR 1:25).

ROGER ROYALL

Roger Royall was killed at Bermuda Hundred **(39)** during the March 22, 1622, Indian attack (VCR 3:566).

SIBIL (SYBIL, SYBILL) ROYALL

On November 19, 1623, Sybil (Sybil, Sybill) Royall, a widow, testified in court about some items stored in a trunk at Dr. John Pott's house in urban Jamestown **(1)**. She died sometime prior to October 4, 1624, at which time the widowed Mary Ascomb, a resident of Jamestown, testified that while Mrs. Royall lay on her deathbed, she asked for assistance in writing her will. Mrs. Ascomb said that Mrs. Royall had left her everything, with the exception of a gift that was intended for her goddaughter in England. Elizabeth Hamor of Jamestown, who also was queried about Mrs. Royall's final wishes, said that the decedent, when very ill, had come to her house and said that she wanted Mrs. Ascomb to have all her possessions, with the exception of 50 pounds of tobacco that she wanted to give her goddaughter in London. On January 24, 1625, Mrs. Sibil Royall was listed among those who had died in Jamestown sometime after February 16, 1624. Although the identity of Mrs. Royall's late husband is uncer-

tain, he may have been Roger Royall, who perished at Bermuda Hundred **(39)** in the March 22, 1622, Indian attack (MCGC 7-8, 21; CBE 56).

WILLIAM ROYLY

William Royly, a servant John Harrison sent to his brother, Lieutenant George Harrison, in Virginia, went ashore at St. Christopher's in the West Indies and never was heard from again. This was reported to the General Court on March 12, 1624 (MCGC 13).

THOMAS ROYSTON

On January 8, 1620, the marshal of Middlesex brought Thomas Royston and several other men before the Bridewell Court, which decided that they would be sent to Virginia (CBE 16).

RUBEN

On February 4, 1625, Virginia Company officials were informed that Ruben and another one of Captain Whittaker's servants had used their seed corn for food (VCR 4:511).

ROGER RUCE (RUESE, RUSE)

On February 16, 1624, Roger Ruce (Ruese, Ruse) was a servant in Captain William Peirce's household in urban Jamestown **(1)**. By January 25, 1625, he had been transferred to Captain Peirce's property on Mulberry Island **(21)**, where he was a servant. It was then noted that he had come to the colony on the *Charles* (CBE 38, 57).

RICHARD RUDDERFORD

In December 1635 Richard Rudderford was identified as a 40-year-old Virginia planter who had sent seven servants to the colony on the *Constance* at his own expense and also had paid for his own transportation. His entitlement to land was mentioned in English court documents in July 1637 (EAE 56, 59).

CLINTON RUSH

Clinton Rush came to Virginia on the ship *Truelove* in 1623. On January 30, 1625, he was identified as a 13-year-old servant in the household of John Moon, whose residence was on the Maine (3), just west of Jamestown Island (CBE 57).

GEORGE RUSHMORE

On February 16, 1624, George Rushmore was residing in Warresqueak (26), on Edward Bennett's plantation, where he probably was a servant (CBE 42).

[NO FIRST NAME] RUSSELL

In July 1620 Mr. Russell, an English chemist or alchemist, presented Virginia Company officials with a proposal for the manufacture of artificial wine, which he felt would be beneficial to the colony. Company records fail to disclose Russell's first name or whether he went to Virginia (VCR 3:365-367).

ANN RUSSELL

On October 31, 1618, Ann Russell, an inmate in Newgate Prison, was reprieved. She was to be sent to Sir Thomas Smith, Virginia Company treasurer, so that she could be transported to Virginia (CBE 11; PC 2/29; SR 429).

BRIDGET RUSSELL

On January 22, 1620, Bridget Russell, who was brought in from Christchurch Parish, was among the vagrants the court of Bridewell decided to send to Virginia (CBE 17).

DELYONEL (DELYONELL) RUSSELL

On March 1, 1626, when Abraham Peirsey of Flowerdew Hundred (53) made his will, he named London merchant Delyonel (Delyonell) Russell as an overseer of his estate and identified him as a friend to whom he was bequeathing £30 (SH 7; SR 3966).

DENNIS RUSSELL

Dennis Russell was transported to Virginia in 1628 on the *Hopewell* by Adam Thorogood, who was then living in Elizabeth City (19) near the Back River. On June 24, 1635,

Thorogood used Russell as a headright when acquiring some land on the lower side of the James River (PB 1 Pt. 1:179).

JOHN RUSSELL

John Russell, a gentleman who came to Virginia in 1608 in the 2nd Supply of new Jamestown (1) settlers, descended the James River with Captain John Smith and was among those taught how to cut down trees and make clapboard. Russell accompanied Smith on a voyage to the Pamunkey Indians' territory, and he also paid a visit to Powhatan from whom he helped Smith escape. In January 1609 Russell and Smith went to Werowocomoco on the York River. Captain John Smith said that the weather was very cold at the time they made the trip and that John Russell, who was obese, over-exerted himself onshore and became ill. In 1620 Smith identified Russell as a Virginia Company investor (CJS 1:238, 241, 243, 245, 251, 255; 2:185, 190, 192, 194, 198, 200, 280).

JOHN RUSSELL

On February 16, 1624, John Russell was living on the lower side of the James River, opposite Jamestown and east of Gray's Creek. He was a servant on Captain William Powell's plantation (14), which was then in the hands of Edward Blaney, who had married Powell's widow. By January 24, 1625, John, who was age 19 and reportedly had come to Virginia on the *Bona Nova*, was residing in urban Jamestown (1), where he was a servant in the Blaney household. On June 24, 1635, John Russell patented 250 acres on Lower Chippokes Creek, using himself and four others as headrights. Russell's land was located in the immediate vicinity of the Powell acreage, on which he had resided during the mid-1620s (CBE 40, 55; PB 1 Pt. 1:177).

MAXIMILIAN RUSSELL

Virginia Company records indicate that Maximilian Russell came to Virginia in September 1621 aboard the *Warwick* and accompanied his granddaughter-in-law, Mary Ellyott, one of the young maids being sent to the colony to be wives. Maximilian Russell was killed at Martin's Hundred (7) on March 22, 1622, when the Indians attacked (FER 309; VCR 3:570).

RICHARD RUSSELL

Richard Russell, master of the *Hopewell,* made trips to Virginia in July 1627 and July 1628. In court documents spanning the period May 1630 to July 1631, he was identified as the 39-year-old captain of the *Hopewell.* Russell, who indicated that he was a mariner from Ratcliffe in Middlesex, England, testified that he had loaded tobacco onto the *Gift of God* but had come home on the *Hopewell* (CBE 79, 87; EAE 23).

THOMAS RUSSELL

On April 24, 1623, Thomas Russell, who had been a passenger on the *Margaret and John,* sent a petition to the governor, complaining about shipboard conditions (VCR 4:127-128).

WALTER RUSSELL

Walter Russell, a doctor of physic, reportedly came to Virginia in 1608 in the 1st or 2nd Supply of new settlers in Jamestown **(1)**. He accompanied Captain John Smith on an exploratory voyage within the Chesapeake Bay and was co-author of an account of their travels. When Smith was stung by a stingray, Dr. Russell gave him first aid and offered medical assistance (CJS 1:122, 224, 229; 2:161, 163, 168-169, 222, 228).

WILLIAM RUSSELL

William Russell, a gentleman who came to Virginia in 1608 in the 2nd Supply of colonists, was captured by Powhatan but escaped and, according to Henry Spellman, reached Jamestown **(1)** (CJS 1:241; 2:190; HAI 485).

RUTH

On September 1, 1632, when Dr. John Pott of Jamestown **(1)** patented some land, he listed a maidservant named Ruth as a headright (PB 1 Pt. 1:113).

JOHN RUTHERFORD

John Rutherford came to Virginia on the *Warwick* in 1621 at the expense of Robert Sweete of Elizabeth City **(18)**, who used him as a headright when patenting some land on March 14, 1628 (PB 1 Pt. 1:70).

RICHARD RUTHERFORD

On January 3, 1633, Richard Rutherford witnessed a document in which Francis Hough conveyed the late Christopher Windmill's leasehold to Henry Coleman. The land being transferred was in Elizabeth City on the east side of the Hampton River **(17)**, perhaps the area in which Rutherford lived (PB 1 Pt. 1:148).

THOMAS RUTLINGHAM

On February 27, 1619, Thomas Rutlingham was identified as a boy who was to be sent to Virginia. He was among the poor children rounded up from the streets of London so that they could be shipped to the colony (CBE 12).

ELIZABETH RUTTEN

On February 16, 1624, Elizabeth Rutten was living at one of the plantations on the lower side of the James River and to the east of Gray's Creek **(10-15)**, within the corporation of James City (CBE 41).

JAMES RYALY
(SEE JAMES RAILEY)
JONAS RYALY
(SEE JONAS RAILEY)
JOSEPH RYALE (RYLEI)
(SEE JOSEPH RAILEY)

EDWARD RYDER (RIDER)

On November 21, 1621, Edward Ryder (Rider) and his associates received a patent from the Virginia Company because they were planning to take 100 people to the colony. On June 10, 1622, Ryder was identified as the holder of a patent for a particular (private) plantation in Virginia. Its location is unknown (VCR 1:553-554, 561-562; 3:643).

FERDINAND RYDER

Virginia Company records dating to 1621 indicate that the Company sent a large quantity of supplies to Mr. Ferdinand Ryder, who was then in Virginia (FER 308).

S

ROBERT SABIN (SABYN, SAVIN)

Robert Sabin (Sabyn, Savin) came to Virginia on the *Margaret and John* in 1622 and on February 16, 1624, was residing in Elizabeth City (**18**). In early 1625, Robert, who was 30 years old and free, was living in the household headed by John Waine (Wayne). In October 1625 the governor summoned Robert Sabin about an agreement he had made with William Pryor. Two months later he testified about Arthur Avelin's failure to obey a summons and about a conversation between Robert Newman and Mr. Weston that taken place in his home. Sabin served as a burgess for Warresqueak (**26**) in 1629, 1630, and 1633 and in July 1631 was one of the Virginia planters who asked the king for relief from customs duties. His hogsheads of tobacco bore the initials *RS*. In 1637 Robert Sabin, who was in England to testify before the Admiralty Court, identified himself as a 45-year-old tallow chandler from Maides Mill, in Herts. At that time he and Richard Bennett and Anthony Jones were plaintiffs in a suit brought by Hutchinson and Company (CBE 44, 65; MCGC 72, 81-82; EAE 74; G&M 165; HEN 1:139, 149, 203).

JOHN SABINE

On March 24, 1621, Virginia Company officials noted that John Sabine had returned to England on Mr. Felgate's ship, which also transported Sabine's tobacco (VCR 3:435-436).

JOHN SACKER

John Sacker came to Virginia in 1623 on the *Margaret and John*. In early 1625 he was living on the east side of the Hampton River in Elizabeth City (**17**), on the Virginia Company's land, and was a 20-year-old servant in a household headed by Robert Thrasher and Rowland Williams (CBE 68).

[NO FIRST NAME] SACHIVERELL

Virginia Company records dating to July 24, 1621, indicate that a Mr. Sachiverell, who had gone to Virginia, had reimbursed the Company for the cost of his passage and had been freed (VCR 1:522).

JOHN SADDOCKE

When court testimony was heard about the ship *Constance*'s voyage to Virginia in December 1625, Christopher Dawson of Flushing (in the Netherlands) said that he had arranged for the passage of Mr. Harwood's servant, John Saddocke. Christopher Boyce, who identified himself as a Virginia planter, said that he had made an agreement with the *Constance*'s purser for the transportation of his own servants and two others, one of whom was Saddocke (EAE 58-59).

JOHN SADLER I

On November 26, 1635, John Sadler I, Richard Queyning, and William Barker patented 1,250 acres in Charles City County, adjacent to Merchant's Hope (**50**). Sadler eventually acquired acreage in Merchant's Hope and nearby Martin's Brandon (**59**). In September 1655 he was identified as the father (probably father-in-law) of John Westhope, to whom he gave some cattle. On December 11, 1658, when Sadler made his will, he left his Virginia land to his son, John Sadler II of St. Stephen Wallbrook, London (PB 1 Pt. 1:320; WITH 186; EEAC 50; WAT 621).

***

CHRISTOPHER SAFFORD

Christopher Safford, an ancient planter, came to Virginia on the *Treasurer* in 1613. On February 16, 1624, he and his wife were living at Jordan's Journey (**46**). Christopher was still there on January 21, 1625, and shared a home with his partner, John Gibbs, and one servant (CBE 36, 51; DOR 1:18).

MRS. CHRISTOPHER SAFFORD

On February 16, 1624, Mrs. Christopher Safford was living at Jordan's Journey (**46**) with her husband (CBE 36).

***

JAN SAGE

Serge maker Jan Sage, his wife, and their six children were among the Walloons and French who indicated their willingness to go to Virginia. In August 1621 the Virginia Company agreed that they could immigrate (CBE 24).

JOHN SAKEN

On August 22, 1628, officials at Bridewell noted that John Saken, a vagrant from Fleet Street who was to be sent to Virginia, had been returned to his master (CBE 84).

WILLIAM SAKER

In 1625 Captain William Saker of Lambeth in Surrey, England, was owner of the *Temperance*, which went to Newfoundland and then continued on to Virginia, where it stayed for six or seven months. Marmaduke Rayner, the *Temperance's* master, reportedly sold Saker's goods. Court testimony taken in June 1627 reveals that Saker was obliged to post a bond, as he had threatened to kill Rayner. The nature of the men's dispute is unknown. On December 1, 1627, William Saker made his will, indicating that he had a servant, Thomas Gregory, and some goods in Virginia. When the testator's will was proved on December 7, 1627, the responsibility of settling his estate was assigned to Sir Thomas Jay and Nathaniel Finch. The General Court determined that Captain Preen of the *Samuel* was to be paid for transporting Thomas Gregory to Virginia and that the decedent also owed money to Mr. Buldham (CBE 73, 80; MCGC 174, 180; SR 7217, 9958, 10851; EEAC 50; WITH 194; WAT 207).

***

ROBERT SALFORD

Robert Salford, a yeoman and ancient planter, came to Virginia in 1611 on the *John and Francis*. On February 16, 1624, Robert, his son, John, Mary Salford (probably John's wife), and two servants were living in Elizabeth City (**18**). In September 1624 Robert Salford patented 100 acres of land in Elizabeth City, noting that he intended for the parcel to descend to his son, John. Robert also indicated that his wife, Joan (Joane), an ancient planter, was deceased. In early 1625 Robert Salford, who was age 56, was identified as head of an Elizabeth City household that had four houses and a palisade and was well supplied with stored food and defensive weaponry. In May 1625 Salford was credited with two tracts of 100 acres each in Elizabeth City, both of which had been planted. In August 1626 Mr. Robert Salford was made a commissioner of Elizabeth City's monthly court (CBE 44, 65; PB 1 Pt. 1:21, 30; VCR 4:557; DOR 1:57).

JOAN (JOANE) SALFORD (MRS. ROBERT SALFORD)

Joan (Joane), an ancient planter and the wife of yeoman Robert Salford, died sometime prior to September 20, 1624, probably in Elizabeth City (**18**) where other family members were living. The 100 acres to which Joan was entitled descended to her husband, Robert, and then to their son, John (PB 1 Pt. 1:30).

JOHN SALFORD

John Salford, the son of ancient planters Robert and Joan (Joane) Salford and brother of Sara (Sarah) Salford, came to Virginia on the *George* in 1616. On February 16, 1624, he was living in his father's household in Elizabeth City (**18**), where Mary Salford also resided. In early 1625 John Salford was 24 years old, the same age as Mary Salford, who may have been his wife. On December 1, 1624, when John Salford patented the land to which his late sister, Sara (Sarah), was entitled, he was identified as a yeoman. The property he acquired was between Blunt Point (**22**) and Newportes News (**24**). On May 1625, when a list of patented land was sent back to England, John Salford was credited with 50 acres of acreage in Elizabeth City (property that had been planted or seated) and 100 acres below Blunt Point (CBE 44, 65; PB 1 Pt. 1:21, 30; VCR 4:557).

MARY SALFORD (MRS. JOHN SALFORD?)

Mary Salford came to Virginia on the *Bona Nova* in 1620 and on February 16, 1624, was living in Elizabeth City (**18**) in a household headed by ancient planter Robert Salford. Mary, who was 24 years old, was still there in early 1625. She may have been the wife of Robert Salford's son, John, who also was age 24 (CBE 44, 65).

SARA (SARAH) SALFORD

Sara (Sarah), the daughter of Robert Salford and the sister of John Salford, was an ancient planter. She died at Flowerdew Hundred (**53**) sometime after April 1623 but before February 16, 1624. Afterward, her brother inherited and patented the land to which she was entitled. It is unclear why she was at Flowerdew at a time when the rest of her family was in Elizabeth City **(18)** (PB 1 Pt. 1:21; CBE 37).

***

WILLIAM SALISBURY

Between April 1623 and February 16, 1624, William Salisbury died at one of the plantations on the lower side of the James River, within the corporation of James City **(8-15)** (CBE 41).

JOHN SALMON

On April 13, 1622, when John Salmon testified in the suit Lady Delaware undertook against Sir Samuel Argall, he said that he was 40 years old and lodged at Queenes Head in Southwark. He stated that he had been one of Lord Delaware's servants and had gone to Virginia with him on the *Neptune* in 1618. He said that he had lived in Jamestown **(1)** for around 5 months, until Argall, as deputy governor, sent him to sea on the *Treasurer* in 1619. Salmon said that he had disembarked in Bermuda and returned to England, although the *Treasurer* continued on to the West Indies. He commented that Argall provided Lord Delaware's men (many of whom were tradesmen) with meager rations and gave them neither clothes nor lodging, nor the means to earn a living. Salmon said that he had shared accommodations with Henry Tawney, the first man entrusted with the key to the store in which Lord Delaware's goods were kept. According to Salmon, Argall's man, Twyne, later was put in charge of Delaware's goods and sold some of them. John Salmon testified about the animosity between Edward Brewster and Deputy Governor Argall, which culminated in Brewster's being tried in a martial court and banished from Virginia (C 24/486, 24/490; SR 9946).

ELIZABETH SALTER

On February 16, 1624, Elizabeth Salter, who came to Virginia on the *Seaflower,* was living in Captain Roger Smith's household in urban Jamestown **(1)**. When a muster was made of Jamestown Island's inhabitants on January 24, 1625, Elizabeth was still living in the Smith household and was described as age 7. She may have been entrusted to the care of Roger Smith's wife, Joane, who was John Rolfe's widow (CBE 38, 55).

JOHN SALTER

On February 16, 1624, John Salter was living in Elizabeth City **(17, 18)** (CBE 44).

JOHN SALTMAN

John Saltman left England on July 31, 1622, and came to Virginia aboard the *James* with Edward Grindon (FER 400).

WILLIAM SAMBAGE

William Sambage, a gentleman, arrived in Jamestown **(1)** in 1608 as part of the 2nd Supply of new colonists (CJS 1:241; 2:190).

ANNE SAME

On February 26, 1620, officials at Bridewell decided that Anne Same, who was being detained in Newgate Prison, would be sent to Virginia (CBE 19).

JOHN SAMON

On March 22, 1622, when the Indians attacked Mulberry Island **(21)**, John Samon was killed (VCR 3:570).

JOSEPH SAMON

On July 14, 1635, Joseph Samon received a patent for 150 acres on the Nansemond River **(20 c)** adjacent to George Fawdon's land (PB 1 Pt. 1:329).

MARGARET SAMON

On November 20, 1622, Margaret Samon, who was being detained at Bridewell, was sentenced to transportation overseas (CBE 29).

KATHERINE SAMPSON

On October 3, 1618, the Bridewell Court decided that Katherine Sampson would be sent to Virginia (CBE 10).

WILLIAM SAMPSON ALIAS EDEN

Captain William Sampson alias Eden, a mariner, made several trips to Virginia and seems to have worked closely with Virginia Company officials. In 1622, while he was master of the *Furtherance*, he made a wager with Thomas Hamor concerning Nicholas Elford's authorization to set sail on the *Tiger*. Although Sampson lost the bet, he refused to pay Hamor, who promptly brought suit. In October 1622 the Virginia Company authorized Captain Sampson to trade with the Indians. In December 1623, when he was in Virginia and still captain of the *Furtherance*, he testified before the General Court that Captain Barwick had custody of some Virginia Company goods. In February 1627 Captain Sampson was questioned about two oxen that he had procured from John Pountis, animals that really were supposed to be used for John Woodall's benefit. Later in the year Sampson arrived in Jamestown (1) with some Indians he had brought from the Carib Islands. They were considered dangerous, and because they had fled into the forest, perhaps to the native population, the General Court decided that they should be captured and hanged (VCR 3:695, 698-699; MCGC 8-9, 141, 155).

SAMUEL

According to Captain John Smith, a Dutchman named Samuel, one of the first Jamestown (1) colonists, gave some firearms to the Indians in 1608. He said that in 1609 Samuel was living with Powhatan at Werowocomoco, a village that was located on the York River (CJS 1:250; 2:200, 217).

[NO FIRST NAME] SANCÉ

During the first part of 1629 the Baron de Sancé told the Privy Council that he would like to take a group of French Protestants to Virginia, where they could plant vines and olives and make silk and salt. He also requested denization. Later in the year the Baron said that he would like to take 100 men to plant on the St. Jacques River, to the south of Virginia (SR 626; CO 1/5 ff 50, 150-151).

JOHN SANDERFORD

In March or April 1623 Richard Frethorne of Martin's Hundred (7) sent word to England that John Sanderford, who had come to the settlement at Christmastime (that is, in early January 1623), had died while living at William Harwood's house (VCR 4:60).

ALEXANDER SANDERS (SAUNDERS)

Alexander Sanders (Saunders) came to Virginia in 1623 on the *Truelove* and on February 4, 1625, was living on Hog Island (16), where he was one of Sir George Yeardley's servants. Alexander was then age 24. He may have been the man identified as Alexander Sanderson in the 1624 census (CBE 61).

EDWARD SANDERS (SAUNDERS)

On April 30, 1623, Edward Sanders (Saunders), who was among those rebutting Captain Nathaniel Butler's allegations about conditions in Virginia, testified that he had been in the colony for three years. He admitted that he lacked knowledge of any ordnance or fortifications to the west of Jamestown (1) (VCR 2:386).

EDMUND SANDERS (SAUNDERS)

On May 3, 1621, Virginia Company officials noted that Lieutenant Edmund Sanders (Saunders) had custody of 17 cattle whose ownership was disputed by Captain John Martin of Martin's Brandon (59) and John Bargrave, who also had a plantation (60). On March 22, 1622, when the Indians attacked Martin's Brandon, Edmund Sanders was killed. When Captain John Martin's suit against Sir George Yeardley was aired before the General Court in December 1624, Martin was ordered to provide proof that Yeardley had taken goods from Captain Sanders' house. Ensign Isaac Chaplin also testified in the case and denied that Sanders had promised him two cattle in satisfaction for Captain John Martin's debt (VCR 3:444, 569; MCGC 37).

HENRY SANDERS (SAUNDERS)

Henry Sanders (Saunders) came to Virginia on the *Southampton* in 1623 and on January 20, 1625, was living at Flowerdew Hundred (53), where he was a 20-year-old servant in Abraham Peirsey's household (CBE 50).

HUMPHREY SANDERS (SAUNDERS)

On November 20, 1622, Humphrey Sanders (Saunders), an inmate at Newgate Prison, was sentenced to transportation overseas, probably to Virginia (CBE 29).

RICHARD SANDERS (SAUNDERS)

Richard Sanders (Saunders) came to Virginia on the *Francis Bonaventure* sometime prior to February 16, 1624, and took up residence on the Governor's Land (**3**). On January 30, 1625, Richard, who was age 25, was identified as one of the governor's servants. On August 28, 1644, Richard Sanders patented a 1-acre lot in the western end of Jamestown Island (**1**), near the isthmus that led to the mainland (CBE 39, 57; PB 2:11).

***

ROGER SANDERS (SAUNDERS)

On January 20, 1626, Roger Sanders (Saunders) testified before the General Court about an incident that had occurred on New Year's Eve and involved some inebriated men who illegally boarded a vessel called the *Grace* in Elizabeth City (**17, 18**). A month later he was identified as one of George Medcalfe's servants. By March 14, 1628, Roger Sanders had become a free man. He married Francis (Frances), the widow of John Blore (Bloar, Blower), and was identified as a mariner of Accomack when he obtained a 50-acre leasehold on Old Plantation Creek (**73**). In 1629 he brought suit against Richard Popeley but acknowledged his own debt to John Army. By February 1632 Roger Sanders had become a commissioner of Accomack's monthly court. Soon after, he patented a 300-acre tract in Accomack known as the Indian Field, acreage that was to be doubled after it was seated. In February 1633 he commenced serving as a burgess for Accomack. Roger Sanders died sometime prior to October 20, 1634 (MCGC 91-92, 95, 189; PB 1 Pt. 1:98, 106, 157; HEN 1:170, 187, 203; AMES 1:1-2, 27, 98, 118).

FRANCIS (FRANCES) BLORE (BLOAR, BLOWER) SANDERS (SAUNDERS) (MRS. ROGER SANDERS [SAUNDERS]) (SEE FRANCIS [FRANCES] BLORE [BLOAR, BLOWER])

***

ALEXANDER SANDERSON

On February 16, 1624, Alexander Sanderson was living at Chaplin's Choice (**56**). He may have been the individual identified as Alexander Sanders in the 1625 muster (CBE 37).

JOHN SANDERSON

John Sanderson died in Elizabeth City (**17, 18**) sometime after April 1623 but before February 16, 1624 (CBE 45).

GEORGE SANDES

In 1619 George Sandes, who had been found guilty of stealing a gelding in Middlesex and was being detained at Newgate Prison, was reprieved and sentenced to transportation overseas, most likely to Virginia (CBE 12).

THOMAS SANDFORD

On September 15, 1619, Thomas Sandford set sail for Virginia on the *Margaret* of Bristol and was among those being sent to Berkeley Hundred (**55**) to work under Captain John Woodlief's supervision. Sandford was supposed to serve the Society of Berkeley Hundred's investors for six years in exchange for 30 acres of land. Virginia Company records indicate that he died prior to fulfilling his obligation to the Society of Berkeley Hundred (CBE 14; VCR 3:198, 213).

THOMAS SANDS

Thomas Sands, a gentleman, came to Virginia in 1607 and was one of the first Jamestown (**1**) colonists (CJS 1:208; 2:141).

WILLIAM SANDS

On February 16, 1624, William Sands was living on the lower side of the James River (**8, 9**) in the corporation of James City. He died there sometime prior to February 4, 1625 (CBE 40, 61).

***

DAVID SANDYS (SANDS, SANDERS)

The Rev. David Sandys (Sands, Sanders), Treasurer George Sandys' brother, came to Virginia in 1622 on the *Bonaventure*. On February 16, 1624, he was living on Hog Island (**16**). In June 1624 he was accused of trying to take advantage of Mara Buck, a

12-year-old orphan and heiress, by trying to "lure her away." Afterward, Thomas Allnutt of Jamestown (1), who made the allegations, was accused of slander and then fined by the General Court, probably because the minister's brother was an influential justice. On February 4, 1625, the Rev. Sandys was living at Samuel Mathews' plantation (15) on the neck of Hog Island. He died around August 1, 1625, shortly after he became minister to the community of settlers living at Martin's Hundred (7). His parishioners were ordered to pay the remainder of his salary as a clergyman, even though he died before fulfilling a year of service. His estate also was to be compensated out of the estate of Robert Langley, whose funeral sermon he preached, and reimbursed by the Society of Southampton Hundred's investors. He was among those to whom the late George Thorpe owed money. The Rev. David Sandys died indebted to John Pountis (CBE 41, 59; MCGC 15, 18, 36, 47, 72, 77, 82; VCR 4:489-490).

GEORGE SANDYS
(SANDS, SANDERS)

George Sandys (Sands, Sanders), the youngest son of the Archbishop Sandys, was born in 1577 and attended Oxford University. He was widely traveled and invested in the colonization of Bermuda and Virginia. He was named treasurer of the Virginia colony in 1621, arriving during Sir Francis Wyatt's first term, and held office until 1625. Throughout that period he was a member of the Council of State. Among Sandys' numerous responsibilities were collecting duties and rents and seeing that commodities were produced by Virginia Company investors' artisans. After the death of the men responsible for overseeing the skilled workers sent to the colony to make glass, build boats, and produce iron, Sandys was given oversight of all three projects. While George Sandys was in Virginia, he resided in urban Jamestown (1) in the home of Captain William Peirce, where he translated the *Ovid* and tried to raise silkworms. Since Sandys was supposed to receive 50 tenants as part of his official stipend as treasurer, he offered to treat the Italian glassworkers as his servants until the Virginia Company could take charge of them. He was authorized to take up 1,500 acres as office land. George Sandys asked for a 7-year patent for the glassworks, but

his proposal was rejected. In 1621 and 1622 he corresponded with Virginia Company officials on a regular basis and received a relatively steady supply of instructions, commodities, and equipment for use by Company-sponsored workers.

In January 1622 Sandys informed Company officials that he had purchased 200 acres for his servants because he lacked office land, and that he was building a watermill on his property. Later in the year he asked for five men from the late Captain William Nuce's estate. He was among those who sent letters about the March 1622 Indian attack and the food shortages and disease that occurred in its aftermath, thanks to the influx of refugees in Jamestown. Sandys reported on the glassworks and promised to prepare an account of the shipwrights' business. He said that although he had rebuilt the glass furnace, no glass had been produced and the Italian glassworkers, clamoring to return to England, were determined to see the project fail. He said that he had given worm seed to the Frenchmen sent to make silk and produce wine, and that the colony should have a large, two-storey house where silkworms could be raised. Sandys said that conditions in Virginia were harsh and that Sir George Yeardley had lost two-thirds of his investment. He described the colonists as starving and poor and said that he had sent the shipwrights to Elizabeth City (17, 18) for that reason. In his opinion, the settlers' plantations were too thinly dispersed to be safe from Indian attacks. During early 1623 he asked for some English sand that could be used in glassmaking. He approved of building a fort at Warresqueak but complained about mariners unloading goods in Jamestown near the high water mark. He mentioned that he had bought a one-sixth interest in a ship.

On February 16, 1624, George Sandys was still living in Jamestown, in Captain William Peirce's home. Although he signed a document critical of conditions in Virginia, he defended the colony against the allegations made by Captain Nathaniel Butler. Like other colonists, Sandys sought justice from the General Court on matters that ranged from problems with his servants to collecting debts. At times he also was forced to acknowledge his own debts. In July 1624 Sandys was among those who attacked the Pamunkey Indians in their stronghold. When he appeared in court to testify about Sir George Yeardley's holdings in April 1625, he identified himself as a merchant. On December 4, 1624, Treasurer George Sandys patented 300 acres on the lower side of the James River, three adjacent parcels that became known as the Treasurer's Plantation (**11**). Conditions were harsh there. One of Sandys' servants said that Sandys was mean and so stingy that he allowed his men to starve. Some of the people he put to work on his plantation had been brought in from Bermuda. Sandys received 400 acres in Archer's Hope (**6**), which he sold to Edward Grindon in December 1624. By January 17, 1625, Sandys had chosen 500 acres of land in Upper Chippokes on the lower side of the James and opposite Sandy Point, receiving the acreage as his office land. In 1625, after the Virginia Company's dissolution, George Sandys rendered an account of the glassworks project, the labor of the Company's tenants, and the shipwrights project, and claimed that he had given financial support to the glassworks. He continued to play an active role in the colony's affairs and tried to see that debts that had been incurred while he was the colony's treasurer were settled. By October 12, 1626, George Sandys had returned to England. However, in 1627 he procured six servants at Gravesend and returned to Virginia. In 1639 the Virginia government sent him to England to present a petition opposing the re-establishment of the Virginia Company. Sandys duplicitously reversed course and urged that the Company be reinstituted. As soon as the burgesses learned what he had done, they strongly voiced their objections. George Sandys died in England in March 1644 (CJS 2:281, 286, 297, 371; VCR 1:323, 448, 450, 468, 477-479, 498-500, 512-513, 591; 2:481; 3:128, 240, 467-468, 471-472, 482, 485, 495, 548, 554, 585-588, 650, 670, 690, 699; 4:9, 22-26, 64-75, 105, 108-110, 183, 185, 239, 555, 562-567; FER 113, 308, 322; STAN 24, 30; LEF 1:264; CO 1/2 ff 147-148; HAI 915; CBE 38, 60, 71, 73, 82, 94; HEN 1:128 129; MCGC 11, 24, 34, 36, 43, 47, 51, 53, 86-87, 98-100, 118, 144, 161, 167, 179, 472; PB 1 Pt. 1:12, 16; FOR 2:6:3).

CHRISTOPHER SANFORD

On January 3, 1625, Christopher Sanford was identified as one of the men who worked as a cow-keeper on Jamestown Island (**1**) after the March 1622 Indian attack (MCGC 39-40).

JOHN SAUER

In 1619 John Sauer came to Virginia at the expense of the Ferrars, who were major Virginia Company investors (FER 296).

RICHARD SAVAGE

Richard Savage, a laborer, arrived in Jamestown (**1**) in 1608 as part of the 1st Supply of new settlers. In late December 1608 he accompanied Captain John Smith on a trip to the Pamunkey Indians' territory and to Werowocomoco, Powhatan's village. Smith later said that Richard Savage and another man saw the Dutchmen give some weapons to the Indians, and he tried to reach Jamestown to report it to the authorities (CJS 1:223, 244, 250; 2:162, 193, 200).

ROBERT SAVAGE (SAVADGE, SALVAGE)

Robert Savage (Savadge, Salvage) came to Virginia in 1621 on the *Elizabeth*. On February 16, 1624, he was living at Buckroe (**17**), part of the Virginia Company's land in Elizabeth City. He was still there in early 1625, at which time he was identified as an 18-year-old servant in the household of Thomas Flint (CBE 45, 67).

***

THOMAS SAVAGE (SAVADGE, SALVADGE)

Thomas Savage (Savadge, Salvadge), a young laborer, came to Virginia on the *John and Francis*, leaving England in 1607. He arrived in Jamestown (**1**) in 1608 in the 1st or 2nd Supply of new colonists. According to Captain John Smith, Captain Christopher Newport gave Thomas Savage to Powhatan in exchange for an Indian he took back to England. During the three years Thomas spent with the Indians, he became fluent in their language. In 1614 when Sir Thomas Dale sent Ralph Hamor to visit Powhatan, Thomas Savage accompanied him and served as interpreter. In March 1620 when a census was taken of the colony's inhabitants, interpreter Thomas Savage was on a trading voyage to Accomack and Acohanock, having returned and left again. In July 1621 Virginia Company officials were informed that Thomas Savage had learned that the French were carrying on a great fur trade within Chesapeake Bay. Captain John Smith later said that Thomas had served the public well and that as a result of a quarrel with an Indian leader on the Eastern Shore, he was wounded by an arrow shot into his back. In 1624 Thomas Savage traded actively on behalf of Virginia's governing officials. He purchased corn at Machepongo with Captain Ralph Hamor's beads, and he was involved in trade with Captain William Holmes (a mariner), Samuel Mathews, cape merchant Abraham Peirsey, and the governor. He hired John Vaughan, a Virginia Company tenant or servant, from Captain Jabez Whittaker for a year and took him on a trading voyage. In early 1625 Thomas Savage, his wife, Hannah (Ann), and two servants were living on his acreage on the Eastern Shore (**77**), land that he had been given by the region's Native leader, known as the Laughing King. Thomas and Hannah Savage had a son, John, whose name was omitted from the 1625 muster. In February 1625 Governor George Yeardley said that when he hired Thomas Savage as a public interpreter, he was unaware that he was one of Captain John Martin's servants, even though Thomas had been living at Martin's Brandon (**59**). In March 1625 Ensign Thomas Savage was appointed interpreter for Accomack, but was ordered not to interact with the Indians without Captain William Eppes's permission. In May 1625, when a list of patented land was sent back to England, Thomas was credited with a dividend on the Eastern Shore, and in March 1632 he obtained a 21-year lease for 100 acres on Old Plantation Creek (**73**). He died sometime prior to September 1633, at which time Hannah was identified as a widow. His land descended to his son, John (CJS 1:216, 223; 2:162, 248, 289-290; HAI 830-831; FER 159; VCR 1:504; 4:513, 559; EAE 89; MCGC 10-11, 48; CBE 46, 68; PB 1 Pt. 1:57, 137, 275; DOR 1:69).

HANNAH (ANN) SAVAGE [SAVADGE, SALVADGE] (MRS. THOMAS SAVAGE [SAVADGE, SALVADGE], MRS. DANIEL CUGLEY)

In 1621 Hannah (Ann), who became the wife of Thomas Savage (Savadge, Salvadge), came to Virginia on the *Seaflower* at her own expense, accompanying Captain Ralph Hamor. In early 1625 she was living in her husband's household on the Eastern

Shore (**77**). In December 1627, when Hannah patented 50 acres in Accomack (her own personal dividend), she mentioned her arrival on the *Seaflower* in 1621. Ensign Thomas Savage died sometime after March 1632 but before September 1633, at which time Hannah was described as his widow. Their son, John, born around 1624, was Thomas's heir. By 1638 Hannah had married Daniel Cugley, with whom she had a daughter, Margery (CBE 68; PB 1 Pt. 1:56-57, 188, 275; MEY 534; AMES 1:5, 29, 37-38, 107-108, 127, 158).

JOHN SAVAGE (SAVADGE, SALVADGE)

John Savage (Savadge, Salvadge), the son of Ensign Thomas Savage and his wife, Hannah (Ann), was born around 1624. In July 1643 he violated moral law by having sexual relations with a maidservant. In 1677 John Savage stated that he was 53 years old (MEY 534; PB 1 Pt. 1:275; 2:291-292).

***

THOMAS SAVAGE (SAVADGE, SALVADGE)

Thomas Savage (Savadge, Salvadge) came to Virginia on the *Ambrose* in 1623. In early 1625 he was living in Elizabeth City (**18**), where he was an 18-year-old servant in William Ganey's household. In July 1626, when Thomas waded into the water at Mr. English's house at Kecoughtan in an attempt to recover Anthony Afton's canoe, he became stuck in the mire and drowned. When the cause of Thomas Savage's death was discussed by the General Court in October 1626, he was described as one of merchant Humphrey Rastall's young servants whom William Ganey had hired for a year. A few months later Anthony Afton was fined because the General Court concluded that he could have waded into the water and prevented Thomas Savage's drowning death (CBE 66; MCGC 122, 131-132).

WILLIAM SAVAGE (SAVIGE)

William Savage (Savige), a 21-year-old leather dresser from Somersetshire, England, came to Virginia in 1619 aboard the *Bona Nova*. He probably was a Virginia Company servant or tenant (FER 295).

DANIELL SAVEWELL

Daniell Savewell died in Elizabeth City **(17, 18)** sometime after February 16, 1624, but before early 1625 (CBE 45).

WILLIAM SAVILL

On March 20, 1623, the Virginia Company transferred two shares of Virginia land to William Saville. He had obtained it from Sir Anthony Pell and his wife, Lady Judith, who had inherited it from her former husband, Aldram Rotheram (VCR 1:622).

ROBERT SAVIN
(SEE ROBERT SABIN)

THOMAS SAWELL

Thomas Sawell came to Virginia on the *George* in 1619 and on February 16, 1624, was living at Flowerdew Hundred **(53)**. He was still residing there on January 20, 1625, at which time he was identified as a 26-year-old servant in Abraham Peirsey's household (CBE 37, 57).

JOHN SAWYER

On March 22, 1622, when the Indians attacked Captain John Berkeley's plantation **(68)** at Falling Creek, where an ironworks was being built, John Sawyer was killed (VCR 3:565).

THOMAS SAWYER (SAWIER)

On February 16, 1624, Thomas Sawyer (Sawier) was living at the Bennett plantation in Warresqueak **(26)**. However, by January 24, 1625, he had moved to Jamestown **(1)**, where he was a 23-year-old servant in Peter Langman's household. In January 1628 two Jamestown merchants, Edward Sharples and Mr. Gill, arrested Sawyer for indebtedness. The following month he and two other men received permission to move to Warresqueak (CBE 42, 55; MCGC 158, 165).

WILLIAM SAWYER (SAWIER)

William Sawyer (Sawier) came to Virginia on the *Hopewell*. On February 16, 1624, he was attributed both to Edward Blaney's household in urban Jamestown **(1)** and to Blaney's land on the lower side of the

James River **(14)**. This probably occurred because Blaney shifted his servants from one property to the other. On February 4, 1625, William Sawyer was identified as an 18-year-old servant who lived on the Blaney plantation on the lower side of the river (CBE 38, 40, 59).

ROBERT SAXON

Robert Saxon, a 30-year-old husbandman from Yorkshire, came to Virginia in 1619 on the *Bona Nova* at the expense of the Virginia Company. He probably was a Company servant or tenant (FER 295).

[NO FIRST NAME] SAYRE

On March 21, 1632, the Virginia assembly decided to pay Captain Sayre out of public funds. It is unclear what service he had performed (HEN 1:171).

***

EDMUND (EDMOND) SCARBOROUGH (SCARBURGH) I

Edmund Scarborough (Scarburgh) I came to Virginia sometime prior to March 1630, when he commenced serving as a burgess for Accomack. He held office until at least 1633, and he also served as a commissioner of the local court. Scarborough died sometime prior to November 28, 1635, at which time his son and heir, Edmund Scarborough II, patented some land using his parents as headrights (HEN 1:149, 154, 170, 187, 203; PB 1 Pt. 1:322–323; AMES 1:30).

HANNAH SCARBOROUGH (SCARBURGH) (MRS. EDMUND [EDMOND] SCARBOROUGH [SCARBURGH] I)

On February 19, 1635, Mrs. Hannah Scarborough (Scarburgh), who identified herself as Edmund Scarborough's widow, appeared before Accomack's monthly court to document the sale of a cow she had disposed of on January 9, 1635. When Hannah's son, Edmund Scarborough II, patented some land in November 1635, he used his parents' headrights (AMES 1:30; PB 1 Pt. 1:322–323).

***

RICHARD SCARBOROUGH (SCARBURGH)

In 1621 Richard Scarborough (Scarburgh) was identified as one of the workers associated with the East India School (FER 272).

JOHN SCARPE (SEE JOHN SHARPE)

JOHN SCOTCHMORE

On March 22, 1622, when the Indians attacked Edward Bennett's plantation (26) in Warresqueak, John Scotchmore was killed (VCR 3:571).

ROBERT SCOTCHMORE (SCOTSMORE, SCOTTESMORE)

Robert Scotchmore (Scotsmore, Scottesmore) came to Virginia in 1623 on the *George* and on February 16, 1624, was living on the mainland or Governor's Land (3) just west of Jamestown Island. He was still there on January 30, 1625, in a well-provisioned household that he shared with partner Thomas Kniston and servant Roger Kidd. However, by February 4th Scotchmore and his household had moved to Martin's Hundred (7). He was still residing there on October 31, 1626, when he presented Ellis Emerson's will to the General Court. In 1630, 1632, and 1633 he served as a burgess and represented the Martin's Hundred community in the assembly. In July 1631 Robert Scotchmore was among the Virginia planters who asked the king for relief from customs duties. Some of the hogsheads of tobacco that his household produced were marked *TC* (CBE 39, 58, 62; MCGC 123; HEN 1:148, 179, 203; G&M 165-166; DOR 1:28, 46).

[NO FIRST NAME] SCOTT (SCOT)

In 1608 a laborer identified only as Master Scott (Scot) arrived in the 2nd Supply of Jamestown (1) colonists (CJS 1:242; 2:191).

ANTHONY SCOTT (SCOT)

When Thomas West, Lord Delaware, arrived in Jamestown (1) on June 10, 1610, his ensign, Anthony Scott (Scot), read his commission aloud (HAI 432).

GEORGE SCOTT (SCOT)

On February 12, 1620, officials at Bridewell decided to send George Scott (Scot) to Virginia (CBE 18).

GEORGE SCOTT (SCOT)

On July 4, 1623, Virginia Company officials noted that George Scott (Scot) of London was going to send his surplus goods to Martin's Hundred (7). When he made his will on May 8, 1645, Scott noted that he was a bachelor and left his land and possessions in Martin's Hundred to the children of his brother, Edmund Scott. He also made a bequest to his brother Richard, who was then in New England. George Scott's will was proved on February 22, 1648 (VCR 4:245-246; EEAC 51).

HENRY SCOTT (SCOT)

On February 16, 1624, Henry Scott (Scot) was a servant in Captain William Holmes's household in urban Jamestown (1). He died on the mainland (3), just west of Jamestown Island, sometime prior to January 30, 1625 (CBE 38, 58).

NICHOLAS SCOTT (SCOT)

Nicholas Scott (Scot), a drummer, came to Virginia in 1607 and was one of the first Jamestown (1) colonists (CJS 1:209; 2:142).

***

WALTER SCOTT (SCOT)

Walter Scott (Scot) came to Virginia on the *Hercules* in 1618 and on February 16, 1624, was living on the Eastern Shore (72-78) with his wife, Aphia. Walter was a planter and in 1624 was among those who gave Captain Samuel Mathews a tobacco note in payment for a debt. In early 1625 Walter and Aphia Scott and their child, Pervis (Percis), still were living on the Eastern Shore. In September 1626 Walter sent goods from London to Virginia on the ship *Plantation*. In October 1627 John Wilcocks, whose property was on the upper side of Old Plantation Creek (73), offered to let Walter Scott (then his tenant) have three shares of his tobacco crop, or more if he agreed to oversee Wilcocks' servants. Scott declined. In 1633 Walter Scott publicly admitted that his taxes were in arrears and that he was indebted to others. However, he apparently was considered a man of integrity, for in 1634 he was named provost marshal. By 1635 he appears to have made some economic progress, for he acquired a land certificate after proving that he had brought six people to Virginia. When he testified in court in January 1636, he gave his age as 50. When William Smith made his will the following year, he named Walter Scott as executor. In late January 1638 Captain Samuel Mathews testified that Walter Scott had been poor at the time of his death and that he (Mathews) had provided for Walter's widow. In 1642 Samuell (Samuel) Scott was identified as Walter's orphan (EAE 89; CBE 46, 68, 74; MCGC 159; AMES 1:4, 8, 10-11, 36, 45, 62; 2:28, 222-223; DOR 1:69).

APHIA SCOTT (SCOT) (MRS. WALTER SCOTT [SCOT])

Aphia, who married Walter Scott, came to Virginia in 1618 on the *Gift*. On February 16, 1624, she and her husband were living on the Eastern Shore (**72-78**). In early 1625 they were still there and shared their home with their child, Pervis (Percis), who was born in Virginia. When Walter Scott's orphan, Samuell (Samuel), obtained a land certificate in 1642, he listed Africa (perhaps Aphia) as a headright (CBE 46, 68; AMES 2:222-223).

PERVIS (PERCIS) SCOTT (SCOT)

When a muster was made of the inhabitants of the Eastern Shore (**72-78**) in early 1625, Pervis (Percis) Scott (Scot), the child of Walter and Aphia Scott, was described as Virginia-born. In 1642, when Walter Scott's surviving child, Samuell (Samuel), obtained a land certificate, he listed Pervis Scott as a headright (CBE 68; AMES 2:222-223).

SAMUELL (SAMUEL) SCOTT (SCOT)

On November 28, 1642, the Accomack County court granted a land certificate to Samuell (Samuel) Scott, the orphan of Walter Scott. As Samuell was then an adult, he would have been born in the 1620s or perhaps earlier (AMES 2:222-223).

***

MATHEW SCRIVENER (SCRIVENOR)

Mathew Scrivener (Scrivenor), a gentleman and Virginia Company investor, arrived in Virginia in January 1608 in the 1st Supply of new Jamestown (**1**) colonists. He was named a member of the Council of State, eventually serving as secretary. Scrivener was keenly interested in exploration and accompanied Captains John Smith and Christopher Newport on several voyages of discovery, visiting Werowocomoco, Nansemond, the Pamunkey River, and Cape Henry. In time Mathew Scrivener and John Smith allied themselves against John Ratcliffe alias Sicklemore, Captain John Martin, and Captain Christopher Newport. After Newport and Martin left Virginia, only Ratcliffe posed a threat to the Scrivener-Smith political alliance. As soon as Ratcliffe was overthrown, Mathew Scrivener became acting president, serving from the time of Ratcliffe's July 1608 ouster until September 1609, when Smith was elected president. During part of that time Scrivener was sick with a fever. He eventually became disenchanted with Smith. In early 1609 Mathew Scrivener and Captain Waldo set out for Hog Island (**16**) but were caught in a winter storm—their boat sunk and Scrivener drowned. Captain John Smith described Scrivener as a wise and understanding man and said that he had been helpful in rebuilding the Jamestown fort after it burned in January 1608 (CJS 1:61, 63, 69, 77, 79, 87, 215, 218, 221-222, 229, 233, 239-240, 242, 254; 2:55, 154, 157-158, 160, 162, 169-170, 180, 182, 184, 187, 191, 203, 224, 281; HAI 196; VCR 3:12-13).

FRANCIS (FRANCES) SEABORNE

In 1618 officials at Bridewell decided that Francis (Frances) Seaborne, a young male vagrant from Canning Street who had been born in Surrey, would be sent to Virginia. In 1619 plans were still being made to transport him to the colony (CBE 10, 12).

BRIDGETT SEARLE

Bridgett Searle died on the Maine (**3**) sometime after April 1623 but before February 16, 1624 (CBE 45).

THOMAS SEARLE

Thomas Searle, a 27-year-old husbandman from Hartfordshire, came to Virginia in 1619 aboard the *Bona Nova* at the expense of the Virginia Company and probably was a Company servant or tenant (FER 295).

EDWARD SEARLES

Edward, the 3-year-old son of Gregory Searles, a bricklayer from St. Sepulcher, was admitted to Christ Church Hospital on April 5, 1606. On August 18, 1618, he was assigned to the Virginia Company so that he could be sent to the colony (CH 11).

JOHN SEAWARD

On July 1, 1635, John Seaward received patents for two pieces of property in Warresqueak or Isle of Wight County, obtaining them on the basis of headrights (PB 1 Pt. 1:191, 194).

HENRY SEAWELL

In September 1632 Henry Seawell served as a burgess for the upper parish of Elizabeth City (**18**) (HEN 1:179).

THOMAS SEAWELL (SAYWELL, SEYWELL)

Thomas Seawell (Saywell, Seywell) came to Virginia on the *Tiger* in 1623. In early 1625 he was described as a 20-year-old servant in the Elizabeth City (**18**) household of ancient planter Reynold Booth. In April 1635 Thomas patented 400 acres of his own in Elizabeth City (**19**) (CBE 66; PB 1 Pt. 1:164, 292).

JOSEPH SEDGEWICK

Joseph Sedgewick came to Virginia in 1634 on the *John and Dorothy* at the expense of Adam Thorogood. On June 24, 1635, when Thorogood secured a patent, he listed Joseph as a headright (PB 1 Pt. 1:179).

CHRISTOPHER SELBY

On October 9, 1624, the Bridewell Court decided that Christopher Selby, who was from Cheap Ward, would be sent to Virginia (CBE 48).

ROBERT SELBY (SELBEY)

On July 31, 1622, Robert Selby (Selbey) set sail from England on the *James*, accompanying Anthony Banham. He may have been the same individual James Knott used as a headright when patenting some land in 1635 (FER 400; PB 1 Pt. 1:334).

***

THOMAS SELBY

In 1619 Thomas Selby went to Virginia with Captain Christopher Lawne, who established a plantation (**25**) on the east side of Lawnes Creek, in Warresqueak. On July 12, 1620, Thomas's wife, Joan, who had remained behind in England, asked Virginia Company officials to see that he was returned (VCR 1:400).

JOAN SELBY (MRS. THOMAS SELBY)

On July 12, 1620, Joan Selby was identified as the wife of Thomas Selby, who had gone to Virginia with Captain Christopher Lawne (VCR 1:400).

***

J. SELLOAN

On May 15, 1622, a man known as J. Selloan was described as an employee of the Company of Shipwrights who had worked with Thomas Nunn. Nunn and his men built homes on Jamestown Island (**1**) (FER 378).

JOHN SELLEY

John Selley died in Warresqueak (**26**) sometime after February 16, 1624, but before February 7, 1625 (CBE 62).

CUTBERT (CUTHBERT) SEIRSON (SEE CUTBERT [CUTHBERT] PEIRSON [PEIRSON, PEERSON, PERSON])

JOHN SENIOR (SENEOR)

Sometime prior to 1624 John Senior (Seneor) patented 12 acres in the eastern end of Jamestown Island (**1**), an area where many ancient planters had homesteads. He eventually moved to the lower side of the James River, to what later became Surry County, making it his permanent home. Senior surveyed Secretary Richard Kemp's property in 1643 and shortly thereafter surveyed the Governor's Land (**3**) and Greenspring Plantation, Governor William Berkeley's estate. Between 1644 and 1652 John Senior patented three tracts of land in Surry County (two of which were opposite Jamestown), and he acquired some acreage along the north side of the Piankatank River, in what is now Mathews County. For a time, he owned the Glasshouse tract (**2**) on the mainland adjacent to Jamestown Island. The quantity of acreage Senior owned suggests that he was a very successful planter. On November 5, 1654, Edward Travis I bought 150 acres from Senior on Jamestown Island, on the north side of Passmore Creek, a parcel that included Senior's original 12 acres (PB 1 Pt. 1:158; 2:49, 207, 346; 3:158, 207; 7:228-229; AMB 78; Surry County Deeds and Wills 1652-1672:112).

JOHN SERE

Between February 16, 1624, and February 4, 1625, John Sere died at one of the plantations on the lower side of the James River, within the corporation of James City (**8-16**) (CBE 60).

RICHARD SERJEANT (SERIEANT)

Richard Serjeant (Serieant) came to Virginia on the *Southampton* in 1623. On January 24, 1625, he was living in urban Jamestown (**1**), where he was a 36-year-old servant in cape merchant Abraham Peirsey's household (CBE 55).

JOHN SEWARD (SEAWARD)

John Seward (Seaward) came to Virginia on the *Gift* in 1622 and on February 16, 1624, was living in Elizabeth City (**18**). He was still there in early 1625 and was a 30-year-old servant in Susan Bush's household. On July 1, 1635, John Seward patented 300 acres in Warresqueak (or Isle of Wight) County and acquired additional land there in 1636 and 1638. On September 16, 1651, when John Seward made his will, he identified himself as a Bristol merchant who had land in Isle of Wight, Virginia, but was then living in England. Probate was granted to the decedent's widow, Sarah (CBE 44, 64; PB 1 Pt. 1:191; Pt. 2:470, 544; WITH 142, EEAC 52).

THOMAS SEXTON

Thomas Sexton, a 17-year-old youth from London who formerly had lived at Christ Church's Hospital, arrived in Jamestown (**1**) on the *Bonny Bess* on September 12, 1623. He died in Jamestown sometime prior to February 16, 1624 (MCGC 6, CBE 39; CH 7).

THOMAS SEYWELL
(SEE THOMAS SEAWELL)

SHACROW (CHACROW)

In November 1624 Edward Grindon said that during Sir Thomas Dale's government (1611–1616), an Indian named Shacrow (Chacrow), who lived with Lieutenant Skarse (John Sharpe), the commander of Jamestown (**1**), often used firearms. Interpreter Robert Poole added that Shacrow had lived with Skarse and also with Captains William Pierce and William Powell, and that he routinely used a gun (MCGC 28).

THOMAS SHAMBROOK

On February 27, 1619, the Bridewell Court decided that Thomas Shambrook, a boy, would be sent to Virginia. He was part of a large group of children rounded up from the streets of London so that they could be sent to the colony (CBE 12).

GEORGE SHARKS (SHURKE)

George Sharks (Shurke) reportedly died on Jamestown Island (**1**) after April 1623 but before February 16, 1624. At the same time, however, he was identified as a member of Ensign William Spence's household (CBE 39-40).

GEORGE SHARPE

On March 22, 1622, when the Indians attacked Berkeley Hundred (**55**), Captain George Sharpe, one of the king's pensioners, was killed (VCR 3:567).

JOHN SHARPE
(SKARFE, SCARPE)

John Sharpe (Skarfe, Scarpe), a Virginia Company investor, came to Virginia sometime prior to 1614, when Captain Francis West, Lord Delaware's brother, designated him a lieutenant and placed him in command of Jamestown (1). When Sir Thomas Dale left Virginia in May 1616, he placed Lieutenant Sharpe in charge at Jamestown. Sharpe was later identified as one of those who had taught Indians how to shoot firearms (HAI 827, 874; MCGC 28).

JUDITH SHARPE

Judith Sharpe died in Jamestown (1) after April 1623 but before February 16, 1624 (CBE 39).

***

SAMUEL SHARPE (SHARP)

Samuel Sharpe (Sharp) set sail for Virginia in 1609 on the *Seaventure*, which was wrecked in Bermuda. While marooned in the islands, he told Sir Thomas Gates that Stephen Hopkins (a known religious dissenter) had encouraged disobedience of the law, using the Holy Scriptures as the basis of his arguments. In July 1619 Samuel Sharpe represented Charles City or Bermuda City (40) in the assembly. Later, he was among those who inventoried the estate of George Thorpe, who died at nearby Berkeley Hundred (55) during the March 22, 1622, Indian attack. On March 24, 1623, Samuel Sharpe sent word to England that sickness and death were prevalent in the colony, making it difficult for anyone to plant crops or conduct business. He said that most of the men who came to Virginia on the *Abigail* had died, noting that George Paul, whose help he had sought from Sir George Yeardley, was deceased. In 1624 Sharpe was among the burgesses signing a rebuttal to Alderman Johnson's claims about conditions in the Virginia colony. On February 16, 1624, he and his wife were living at Flowerdew Hundred (53). Samuel and Elizabeth Sharpe were still there on January 20, 1625, and shared their amply supplied home with a young male servant. When a list of patented land was sent back to England in May 1625, Samuel Sharpe was credited with 100 acres on the Appomattox River (39). In 1625 he had a disagreement with merchant Edward Blaney over the ownership of some cattle. Later in the year Richard Biggs of West and Shirley Hundred (41) identified Samuel Sharpe as his loving friend and named him as overseer of his estate. In early 1626 Sharpe testified in court about a disagreement between the Rev. Grivel Pooley and Mr. Thomas Pawlett. Later he went to England on the *Temperance* to see that Richard Biggs's estate was presented for probate. In July 1626 Sharpe was identified as a gentleman when he and a dozen others testified that when the *Temperance* arrived in Cowes, in Isle of Wight, England, their goods and tobacco had been wrongfully detained because of a dispute between the ship's master and its owner (CBE 37, 50, 72; HAI 406, 915; VCR 3:154; 4:233-234, 554; S of N 43; MCGC 39-40, 88-89, 100-101; SH 6; G&M 104-105; DOR 1:22).

ELIZABETH SHARPE (SHARP) (MRS. SAMUEL SHARPE [SHARP])

Elizabeth, who married Samuel Sharpe (Sharp), came to Virginia on the *Margaret and John* in 1621. On January 20, 1625, she was living in the Flowerdew Hundred (53) household headed by her husband (CBE 50).

***

THOMAS SHARPE (SHARP)

On March 22, 1622, when the Indians attacked Berkeley Hundred (55), Thomas Sharpe (Sharp) was killed (VCR 3:571).

***

WILLIAM SHARPE (SHARP)

William Sharpe (Sharp), an ancient planter, came to Virginia on the *Starr*, probably in May 1611, and on February 16, 1624, he and his wife were living at Bermuda Hundred (39). On January 20, 1625, Sharpe was identified as a 40-year-old household head. He and his wife, Elizabeth, shared their amply supplied home with their sons, Isack (age 2 months) and Samuell (age 2). In May 1625, when a list of patented land was sent back to England, William Sharpe was credited with 40 acres within the corporation of Charles City, the area in which Bermuda Hundred was located. On September 18, 1626, some remarks Sergeant Sharpe had made while he was inebriated were discussed by his superiors. Sharpe reportedly had complained about a government decision that eliminated individual plantations' right to trade with incoming ships and gave that privilege to official merchants. In January 1629 William Sharpe and several others allegedly prevented Richard Taylor from taking possession of some land to which he held a patent. In October 1629 Sergeant Sharpe was elected a burgess for Bermuda Hundred. He died sometime prior to February 12, 1635 (CBE 35, 54; VCR 4:553; MCGC 113-114, 180-181; HEN 1:138; DOR 1:12).

ELIZABETH SHARPE (SHARP) (MRS. WILLIAM SHARPE [SHARP]), MRS. THOMAS PACKER [PARKER], MRS. WILLIAM BAUGH (SEE MRS. THOMAS PACKER [PARKER], MRS. WILLIAM BAUGH)

In August 1620, Elizabeth, who married ancient planter William Sharpe (Sharp), went to Virginia on the *Francis Bonaventure*. On February 16, 1624, she and her husband were living at Bermuda Hundred **(39)**. Elizabeth, who was age 25, was still there on January 20, 1625. Also present were the couple's sons, Isack (age 2 months) and Samuell (age 2). Elizabeth was widowed sometime after October 1629 but before February 12, 1635, when she patented some land in the Varina area, just east of Henricus Island **(63)**, in Henrico County. Later, she married Thomas Packer (Parker) but by July 12, 1636, had been widowed again. Finally, she married William Baugh (CBE 35, 54; PB 1 Pt. 1:330, 373; MEY 556-557).

ISACK SHARPE (SHARP)

On January 20, 1625, 2-month-old Isack Sharpe (Sharp) was living at Bermuda Hundred **(39)** in the household of his parents, William and Elizabeth Sharp. Isack's brother, Samuell, was age 2 (CBE 54).

SAMUELL SHARPE (SHARP)

On January 20, 1625, Samuell Sharp (Sharp), who was age 2, was living at Bermuda Hundred **(39)** with his parents, William and Elizabeth Sharp, and his 2-month-old brother, Isack (CBE 54).

***

WILLIAM SHARPE

In 1619 court officials decided that William Sharpe, a burglar from Middlesex who had

broken into Lord Paggett's house and was being detained in Newgate Prison, would be sent to the colonies (CBE 12).

WILLIAM SHARPE

On July 19, 1633, officials at Bridewell decided that William Sharpe, a vagrant from Greenwich, would be sent to Virginia. William, who had been born in Putney, indicated that he would willingly go to the colony (CBE 108).

***

EDWARD SHARPLES

On February 16, 1624, Edward Sharples, the brother of English merchant John Sharples, was living in a Jamestown **(1)** household headed by Christopher Davison's widow, Alice. He, like the late Mr. Davison, was clerk of the Council of State. Although it is uncertain when Sharples arrived in the colony, he is known to have witnessed John Atkins' September 3, 1623, will. By May 10, 1624, Edward Sharples had been found guilty of insubordination, for he had surreptitiously sent some government documents to the king and Privy Council. As a result, he was sentenced to having his ears nailed to the pillory and then cut off, and was ordered to serve Jamestown Island resident Clement Dilke for seven years. On April 11, 1625, Sharples appealed his sentence, but Governor Francis Wyatt and the council rejected his request. In June 1625 the Council of State sent word to Virginia Company officials that Sharples had lost only a piece of one ear. Within a couple years Edward Sharples apparently regained his freedom, for in September 1627 he served as merchant Philamon Powell's administrator and in January 1628, while he and Mr. John Gill were conducting business as merchants, he had four debtors arrested: Thomas Sawyer of Jamestown Island, Stephen Barker of Hog Island **(16)**, and Edward Wigg and Wassil Webling of Warresqueak **(26)**. In February 1628 Sharples sued mariner John Moore of the *Thomas and John* in an attempt to take delivery of the five servants for whom he had paid. In December he sued the estate of Captain Wilcocks of the Eastern Shore. Edward Sharples had a boat built by William Bennett of Jamestown Island and probably used the vessel in his trading ventures. Almost all of Sharples' political, legal, and business transactions suggest that he lived on Jamestown Island while he was in Virginia (WITH 35-36; CBE 38; MCGC 14, 52, 152, 158, 160-161, 180; VCR 4:559-562).

JOHN SHARPLES

London merchant John Sharples was the brother of Edward Sharples, who served briefly as secretary of the Council of State. In January 1627 Sharples brought suit against John Harvey of Jamestown (1), one of his debtors, and was represented by Philemon Powell, who served as his attorney. In late July 1627 John Sharples sent some goods from London to Virginia on the *Thomas and John* (MCGC 130-31; CBE 79).

***

PHILIP (PHILLIP) SHATFORD

Philip (Phillip) Shatford, a 20-year-old baker from Gloucestershire, England, came to Virginia in 1619 aboard the *Bona Nova*. He was killed at Henrico Island (63) during the March 22, 1622, Indian attack (FER 295; VCR 3:565).

ANNIS SHAW

Annis Shaw came to Virginia in 1623 on the *Southampton* and on January 24, 1625, was a maidservant in Abraham Peirsey's Jamestown (1) household (CBE 55).

JOHN SHAW

When the will of John Shaw of Surbiton, in Surrey, England, was proved in March 1628, officials noted that he had land in Virginia (CBE 82).

MICHAEL SHAWE

On December 31, 1619, officials at Bridewell decided that Michael Shawe, who was from London, would be sent to Virginia or Bermuda (CBE 15).

WALTER SHAWE

On March 22, 1622, when the Indians attacked Captain Henry Spellman's (Spillman's) house (51) in Charles City, Walter Shawe was killed (VCR 3:569).

WILLIAM SHAWE

On February 16, 1620, William Shawe, master of the *London Merchant*, was authorized to go to Virginia at the first favorable wind (VCR 1:312).

WILLIAM SHAWE

When William Shawe of Wapping, Middlesex, prepared to go to Virginia, he made his will. When his will was proved in October 1620, his widow, Martha, was ordered to settle his estate (EEAC 52; CBE 21).

ARTHUR SHEERES

On September 26, 1626, Arthur Sheeres sent goods from London to Virginia on the ship *Plantation* (CBE 74).

***

THOMAS SHEFFIELD

On March 22, 1622, when the Indians of the Powhatan Chiefdom tried to drive the colonists from their land, Thomas Sheffield's plantation (69) was one of the settlements attacked. Thirteen people at the Sheffield plantation lost their lives, including Thomas and his wife, Rachel. However, Thomas's 2-year-old son, Samuel, who was mute, survived. In August 1622, when the late Thomas Sheffield's estate commenced the probate process, the decedent's father, William Sheffield, agreed to allow his own grandson, Lawrence Rutt, to serve as administrator. When a list of patented land was sent back to England in May 1625, Thomas Sheffield was credited with 150 acres in Henrico, property that was classified as unseated (undeveloped). In 1639 Samuel Mathews estimated that in 1622 Thomas Sheffield's personal estate (which included corn, cattle, and tobacco) was worth around £250 (VCR 1:161; 3:446-447, 565; 4:552; EEAC 52; CJS 2:301; CBE 28; SR 4126, 8634, 11329; PB 1 Pt. 1:155; MOR 96).

RACHEL SHEFFIELD (MRS. THOMAS SHEFFIELD)

On March 22, 1622, when the Indians attacked the Sheffield plantation (69) in the corporation of Henrico, Mrs. Rachel Sheffield and her husband, Thomas, were slain (VCR 3:565).

SAMUEL SHEFFIELD

On March 22, 1622, when the Indians attacked Thomas Sheffield's plantation (69), Thomas and his wife, Rachel, were killed but their 2-year-old son, Samuel, survived. Court testimony given by the late Thomas Sheffield's father, William Sheffield, on August 16, 1622, reveals that young Samuel was his father's heir. Samuel Mathews, who was familiar with the Sheffield plantation in Henrico, later said that in 1622 Samuel Sheffield was present when the Indians attacked but lived. A March 28, 1623, letter described the youngster as mute (VCR 1:166; 2:93; 3:565; EEAC 52; SR 4126, 8634, 11329).

***

AARON SHELL

On August 2, 1628, officials at Bridewell decided that Aaron Shell, a vagrant from Cornhill who was being detained, would be sent to Virginia if a warrant could be obtained (CBE 83).

MATHEWE SHELLA ALIAS DAWES

On January 22, 1620, the Bridewell court decided that Mathewe Shella alias Dawes, a detainee, would be sent to Virginia (CBE 17).

JOHN SHELLEY (SHULE, SHELLY)

John Shelley (Shule, Shelly) came to Virginia on the *Bona Nova*. On February 16, 1624, when a census was taken of the colony's inhabitants, he was attributed to Edward Blaney's household in urban Jamestown (1) and to Blaney's plantation on the lower side of the James River (14), which actually belonged to the orphans of the late William Powell. Shelley probably was listed twice because Edward Blaney, like many other planters who possessed more than one piece of property, shifted their servants from place to place as needed. On February 4, 1625, John Shelley was identified as a 23-year-old servant on Edward Blaney's property on the lower side of the James River. On June 4, 1627, Shelley was brought before the General Court, where he and Nathaniel Floyd (Floid) were found guilty of stealing a maidservant from Captain Francis West. As punishment, they were ordered to return her and were made to sit in the stocks (CBE 38, 40, 59; MCGC 149).

JOHN SHELLY (SELLEY)

On February 16, 1624, John Shelly (Selley) was living at Basses Choice (27). He died there sometime prior to February 7, 1625 (CBE 46, 62).

WALTER SHELLY (SHELLEY)

In July 1619 Walter Shelly (Shelley) was a burgess representing Southampton or Smyth's Hundred (44) in the general assembly. He died in Jamestown (1) on August 1, 1619, while the assembly was in session (VCR 3:154, 162).

JOHN SHEPHAM

On December 17, 1622, John Shepham, a boy, was identified as one of the Society of Martin's Hundred's (7) servants. His contract required him to serve for five years (FER 435).

COSEN SHEPP

Cosen Shepp, a butcher, left England on April 17, 1619, enroute to Virginia (FER 107).

[NO FIRST NAME] SHEPPARD

On February 16, 1624, the son of a man identified only as "Old Sheppard" was living at the Glasshouse (2) (CBE 41).

[NO FIRST NAME] SHEPPARD

On February 16, 1624, Lieutenant Sheppard, whose first name is unknown, was living in Elizabeth City (17, 18). He was identified as Daniel Gookin's agent in Virginia when ordered to pay John Clarke's widow what Gookin owed her late husband. On April 11, 1625, the General Court noted that Captain Francis West was to present proof that Lieutenant Sheppard had conveyed some cattle to Captain Croshaw (VCR 4:456-457; CBE 43; MCGC 52).

FERDINANDO SHEPPARD

In June 1619 Ferdinando Sheppard identified himself as a 22-year-old gentleman from Rollright in Oxfordshire, and as the brother of Thomas Sheppard and brother-in-law of John Ferrar. He testified that he had set out for Virginia on the *Bona Nova* but had been transferred to the *Garland*, which was carrying 130 passengers to the colony, including 40 carpenters, sawyers, and bricklayers. Sheppard said that on the way to Virginia, four people died and many others became ill (EAE 9).

***

ROBERT SHEPPARD (SHEAPARD)

Robert Sheppard (Sheapard) came to Virginia on the *George* in 1621 and on February 16, 1624, was living on the lower side of the James River, east of Gray's Creek and within the corporation of James City **(10-16)**. On February 4, 1625, Robert was living at the Treasurer's Plantation **(11)** and appears to have been free. On July 19, 1635, he patented 300 acres of land near the head of Chippokes Creek, using himself and his wife, Pricilla, as headrights. In 1646 and 1647 Captain Robert Sheppard served as a burgess for James City County, which then included the lower side of the James River (CBE 40, 60; PB 1 Pt. 1:250; STAN 65-66; HEN 1:322, 339).

PRISCILLA SHEPPARD (SHEAPARD) (MRS. ROBERT SHEPPARD [SHEAPARD])

On July 19, 1635, when Robert Sheppard (Sheapard) patented 300 acres of land near the head of Chippokes Creek, he used his wife, Priscilla, as a headright (PB 1 Pt. 1:250).

***

ROBERT SHEPPARD (SHEPHEARD)

Robert Sheppard (Shepheard) came to Virginia on the *Hopewell* and on February 16, 1624, was living in Edward Blaney's household in urban Jamestown **(1)**. On February 4, 1625, he was residing on the lower side of the James River, at the Blaney/Powell **(14)** plantation. Robert was then age 20 and was one of Blaney's servants (CBE 38, 59).

THOMAS SHEPPHARD

On March 22, 1622, when the Indians attacked Edward Bennett's plantation **(26),** Thomas Shepphard was killed (VCR 3:571).

THOMAS SHEPPARD (SHEPHERD)

On February 1, 1633, Thomas Sheppard served as a burgess for the upper parish of Elizabeth City (HEN 1:203).

THOMAS SHEPPY (SHEEPY, SHIPPEY)

In September 1620 Thomas Sheppy (Sheepy, Shippey), a gentleman, was among those who set sail from Bristol, England, on the ship *Supply* and accompanied William Tracy to Berkeley Hundred **(55)**. Thomas was supposed to serve the Society of Berkeley Hundred's investors for a certain number of years in exchange for some land. He arrived at Berkeley Hundred on January 29, 1621, but by February 16, 1624, had relocated to Bermuda Hundred **(39)**. He was still living there on January 24, 1625, at which time he was identified as a 22-year-old household head who lived alone. On November 14, 1635, Thomas Sheppy patented 250 acres of land opposite Bermuda Hundred (CBE 21, 35, 54; VCR 3:396-397, 426; PB 1 Pt. 1:307; DOR 1:11).

HUMFREY (HUMPHREY) SHERBROOKE

On March 22, 1622, when the Indians attacked Edward Bennett's plantation **(26),** Humfrey (Humphrey) Sherbrooke was killed (VCR 3:571).

STRENGTH (STRENGHT, STEPHEN) SHERE (SHEERE)

Strength (Strenght, Stephen) Shere (Sheere) came to Virginia on the *Eleanor (Ellins)* in 1621. On February 16, 1624, he was living in Elizabeth City **(18)**, where he was a member of Captain William Tucker's household. He was still there in early 1625 and was identified as a 23-year-old servant. In 1628 when Captain Tucker patented some land, he used Strength Shere as a headright, indicating that he had paid for his transportation to the colony (CBE 43, 63; MCGC 173; PB 1 Pt. 1:61).

***

RICHARD SHERIFE (SHERIFFE) I

According to Virginia Company records, on September 15, 1619, Richard Sherife (Sheriffe) I, a carpenter, and his son, Richard II, a cooper, set sail for Virginia on the *Margaret* of Bristol and went to Berkeley Hundred (55) to work under Captain John Woodlief's supervision. Richard I was supposed to serve the Society of Berkeley Hundred's investors for three years in exchange for 30 acres of land. However, a conflicting account that also is included in Virginia Company records, indicates that the elder Richard and several other Berkeley Hundred servants went to the colony on the *London Merchant* with George Thorpe, who was obliged to designate three of them Company servants. On January 3, 1625, Richard Sherife I was identified as one of 16 Berkeley Hundred men who had been living in West and Shirley Hundred (41) prior to the March 22, 1622, Indian attack. George Thorpe owed church dues for all 16 of these men at the time of his death (CBE 13-14, 28; VCR 3:187, 197, 199, 213, 260-261, 674; MCGC 42).

RICHARD SHERIFE (SHERIFFE) II

On September 15, 1619, Richard Sherife (Sheriffe) II, a cooper, set sail for Virginia on the *Margaret* of Bristol and went to Berkeley Hundred (55) to work under Captain John Woodlief's supervision. Richard II, like his carpenter father, Richard I, was supposed to serve the Society of Berkeley Hundred's investors for three years in exchange for 30 acres of land. Richard Sherife II died at Jordan's Journey (46) sometime after April 1623 but before February 16, 1624, prior to fulfilling his obligation to the Society of Berkeley Hundred (CBE 13-14; VCR 3:187, 197, 213).

***

[NO FIRST NAME] SHERLEY

On March 22, 1622, when the Indians attacked Martin's Brandon (59), Ensign Sherley, whose first name is unknown, was killed (VCR 3:569).

DANIELL SHERLEY (SHIRLEY, SHURLEY)

Daniel Sherley (Shirley, Shurley), a 21-year-old grocer from London, came to Virginia on the *Bona Nova* in 1619, at the expense of the Ferrars, who were major Virginia Company investors. On February 16, 1624, he was living in Henrico at the College (66). He was still there on January 23, 1625, at which time he was identified as a 30-year-old servant in Thomas Osborne's household. On April 12, 1633, Daniel Sherley obtained a 21-year lease for 50 acres in Bermuda Hundred (39), and by May 1634 he had acquired some acreage in Henrico (FER 295, 296; CBE 35, 53; PB 1 Pt. 1:143, 148).

HENRY SHERLEY

On December 4, 1617, English authorities noted that Henry, the son of Sir Henry Sherley, had been jailed on account of debt but had escaped from the King's Bench prison. Thomas West, Lord Delaware, asked that the absconded prisoner not be allowed to go to Virginia as he purportedly intended (SR 425; PC 2/29).

LIDIA SHERLEY

Lidia Sherley came to Virginia on the *George* in 1623. She died at Jordan's Journey (46) sometime after February 16, 1624, but before January 21, 1625 (CBE 52).

SUSAN SHERLEY

Susan Sherley, an infant, died at Jordan's Journey (46) sometime after February 16, 1624, but before January 21, 1625. She probably was Lidia Sherley's daughter (CBE 52).

PEACEABLE (PECEABLE) SHERWOOD

On February 16, 1624, Peaceable (Peceable) Sherwood was residing in the urban Jamestown (1) household headed by Captain William Holmes and Mr. Calker. On December 8, 1624, Sherwood, who was age 26, testified before the General Court in a case that involved some legal documents that had floated out of a trunk that had fallen into the water. On February 5, 1625, Peaceable Sherwood was listed among those who had died on the lower side of the James River (**10-16**), within the corporation of James City (CBE 38, 61; MCGC 29).

PETER (PEETER) SHERWOOD (SHEREWOOD)

Peter (Peeter) Sherwood (Sherewood) came to Virginia in 1621 on the *Flying Hart*. In early 1625 he was identified twice as a servant and member of Daniel Gookin's household: once in Elizabeth City (**18**) and once in Newportes News (**24**). It is probable that Gookin, like many other Virginia colonists, moved his servants from property to property (CBE 63, 66).

THOMAS SHERWOOD (SHERWARD, SHERWOUD)

On February 16, 1624, Thomas Sherwood (Sherward, Sherwoud) was living at Basses Choice (**26**). He died there sometime prior to February 7, 1625 (CBE 46, 62).

THOMAS SHIERS

On April 30, 1623, the Virginia Company noted that Thomas Shiers and his associates were planning to send the *William and Thomas* to Virginia with passengers (VCR 2:388-389).

JOHN SHIPPY (SIPPEY)

John Shippy (Sippey) came to Virginia on the *Treasurer* in 1617 at the expense of William Ganey, who used him as a headright when patenting some land (PB 1 Pt. 1:39).

JOHN SHIPWARD (SHIPWAY)

On February 23, 1623, Lieutenant John Shipward (Shipway), Daniel Gookin's overseer in Newportes News (**24**), signed a promissory note acknowledging Gookin's debt to Captain Raleigh Croshaw. On April 25, 1625, he was identified as Captain John Shipway when mentioned in connection with some dealings with John Cheeseman on Daniel Gookin's behalf (MCGC 48-49, 56).

THOMAS SHIPWAY

On August 1, 1622, Thomas Shipway was identified as one of the people sent to the colony as a Virginia Company servant (CBE 28; VCR 3:674).

JOHN SHORT

John Short, a gentleman, arrived in Virginia in 1607 and was one of the first Jamestown (**1**) colonists. In 1608 Edward Maria Wingfield referred to him as "old Short," a bricklayer. Winfield said that Short visited with him and other colonists and was among those who did not revile him (CJS 2:141; HAI 199).

GEORGE SHORTON

On March 3, 1629, the General Court decided that the goods of the late George Shorton would be sold at auction by Ensign Thomas Willoughby, who would deliver the proceeds to the decedent's administrator and debtors (MCGC 188).

JEFFREY SHORTRIDGE

Jeffrey Shortridge, a tradesman, came to Virginia in 1608 as part of the 2nd Supply of new settlers to Jamestown (**1**). In late 1608, when Shortridge accompanied Captain John Smith on a voyage to Werowocomoco on the York River, and to the Pamunkey Indians' territory, Smith referred to him as a soldier (CJS 1:241, 243; 2:190, 193, 243).

NICHOLAS SHOTTEN

Nicholas Shotten came to Virginia on the *Ann* in 1623 and on February 16, 1624, was living in Archer's Hope (**6**). He was still there on February 4, 1625, at which time he was identified as a 40-year-old servant in Thomas Farley's household (CBE 41, 58).

THOMAS SHOWELL

On October 16, 1618, officials at Bridewell decided that Thomas Showell, a vagrant, would be transported to Virginia. On July 7, 1619, Virginia Company officials noted that a man named Showell, who had been sent to Virginia to assist the cape merchant, had committed some misdemeanors (CBE 11; VCR 1:240).

MARGARETT SHRAWLEY

Margaret Shrawley died in Jamestown (**1**) sometime after April 1623 but before February 16, 1624 (CBE 39).

GEORGE SHURKE
(SEE GEORGE SHARKS)

ANDREW SHUTTER

On January 20, 1621, officials at Bridewell decided that Andrew Shutter, who was being detained at Newgate Prison, would be sent to Virginia or Bermuda (CBE 23).

THOMAS SIBERG (SIBERY)

On February 16, 1624, Thomas Siberg (Sibery) was living at Martin's Hundred (7) (CBE 42).

JOHN SIBLEY (SIPSEY, SIPSE, SYPSEY)

On February 16, 1624, John Sibley (Sipsey, Sipse, Sypsey) was living in Elizabeth City (18). When he patented 250 acres of land on the basis of the headright system on September 2, 1624, Sibley was identified as a yeoman and resident of Kecoughtan. However, when a list of patented land was sent back to England in May 1625, Sibley was credited with 250 acres on the south side of the James River in Elizabeth City (20 a). On April 4, 1629, he was brought before the General Court, where he was fined for failing to attend church as required by law. He apparently was considered a responsible and respected citizen, for he served as a burgess for the upper parish of Elizabeth City in 1632 and 1633. In June 1635 John Sibley received a patent for 1,500 acres of land on the Elizabeth River adjoining his other patent. In 1639 he was identified as part owner of the ship *America* (CBE 44; VCR 4:558; MCGC 194; HEN 1:179, 203; PB 1 Pt. 1:46, 172-173; SR 4007).

JOHN SICKLEMORE ALIAS RATCLIFFE
(SEE JOHN RATCLIFFE)

MICHAEL SICKLEMORE

Michael Sicklemore, a gentleman, came to Virginia in 1608 in the 1st or 2nd Supply of new Jamestown (1) settlers. He accompanied Captain John Smith on two exploratory voyages on the Chesapeake Bay and went with him on a visit to Powhatan's village, Werowocomoco, on the York River. Smith described Michael Sicklemore as an honest, valiant, and conscientious soldier when he sent him into the territory on the south side of the James River to search for survivors of Sir Walter Raleigh's colonization venture (the Roanoke colonists). He also was to look for silk grass. In 1609 Smith noted that Sicklemore had returned from Chawonock without learning anything about the fate of the "lost colonists." In 1609 Captain John Martin placed Michael Sicklemore in charge of a group of men he left on an island in the Nansemond River (29). He was killed there in an Indian attack (CJS 1:222, 224, 230, 243-244, 265; 2:161, 163, 170, 193, 215; HAI 501).

THOMAS SIDES

On February 16, 1624, Thomas Sides was living in the Neck O'Land (5). He died in Jamestown (1) sometime prior to January 24, 1625 (CBE 35, 56).

GILBERT SIMMONS (SYMONDS)

On October 20, 1634, when Gilbert Simmons (Symonds) obtained a 21-year lease for some land on the Old Poquoson River (19), he was identified as a planter (PB 1 Pt. 1:156).

JOHN SIMMONS (SYMONS)

On December 31, 1619, officials at Bridewell decided that John Simmons (Symons), who had been brought in by the marshal of Middlesex, would be sent to Virginia. He died in Warresqueak (26) sometime prior to February 16, 1624 (CBE 14, 42).

MARGERY SIMMONS (SYMMONS)

On February 27, 1619, Margery Simmons (Symmons) was identified as a wench who was being sent to Virginia. She probably was one of the London street urchins rounded up and sent to the colony (CBE 13).

MARTHA SIMMONS (SYMONCE)

On February 4, 1625, Martha Simmons (Symonce) testified in the suit Captain John Martin brought against Sir George Yeardley and Captain John Bargrave (CBE 69).

RICHARD SIMMONS

According to George Percy, Richard Simmons, who was one of the first Jamestown (1) planters, died on September 18, 1607 (HAI 100).

RICHARD SIMMONS
(SYMONDS, SYMONS)

In May 1625 Richard Simmons (Symonds, Symons) was credited with 100 acres of land on the Appomattox River. He may have been an ancient planter or Virginia Company investor (VCR 4:554).

JOHN SIMNELL

When Captain John Harvey patented some land on January 12, 1625, he used John Simnell as a headright and said that he had come to Virginia in 1624 on the *Southampton*, Harvey's ship. Simnell died in Elizabeth City (**17, 18**) sometime prior to early 1625 (PB 1 Pt.1:7; CBE 67).

WILLIAM SIMON

William Simon, a laborer, came to Virginia in 1608 in the 1st Supply of new settlers to Jamestown (**1**) (CJS 1:223; 2:161).

[NO FIRST NAME] SIMONS

In 1614 a colonist named Simons reportedly was in the hands of the Indians. Sir Thomas Dale wanted to recover him but learned that he had fled to Nandtaughtacund, an Indian village on the Rappahannock River (HAI 844).

ROBERT SIMPSON (SYMPSON)

Robert Simpson (Sympson), a 34-year-old husbandman from Buckinghamshire, England, came to Virginia in 1619 aboard the *Bona Nova* at the expense of the Ferrars, who were major Virginia Company investors (FER 295).

THOMAS SIMPSON (SYMPSONE)

On February 16, 1624, Thomas Simpson (Sympsone) was living at Hog Island (**16**). On August 16, 1624, he testified that he had carried some tobacco to Ralph Hamor's house (CBE 42; MCGC 19).

ANDREW SIMS

On June 25, 1635, when William Andrews patented some land, he used Andrew Sims as a headright (PB 1 Pt. 1:182).

***

BENJAMIN (BENIAMINE) SIMS
(SYMES, SIMES, SIMMES)

On February 16, 1624, Benjamin (Beniamine) Sims (Symes, Simes, Simmes) was living in Basses Choice (**27**). He was still there on February 7, 1625. Benjamin, who was age 33 and free, was living in Thomas Bennett's household. His wife, Margaret, was recently deceased. On January 3, 1625, Sims was ordered to pay Nathaniel Hawkworth's debts and bequests, including one to the Rev. Francis Bolton. On October 11, 1627, a dispute between Benjamin Sims and Joan Meatherst was aired before the General Court. Testimony reveals that Benjamin had paid for Joan's transportation to the colony with the intention of marrying her. However, in May 1627 they had a dispute that led to a permanent rift. Although Joan agreed to serve Benjamin for two years to reimburse him for the cost of her transportation, the General Court ordered her to serve merchant John Gill for two years. He, in turn, was told to pay Sims for her transportation. In February 1629 Benjamin Sims was identified as one of Jamestown merchant Thomas Warnett's beneficiaries. On April 20, 1635, Sims's land near the Old Poquoson (**19**) was mentioned in another's patent. According to a 1649 account, when Benjamin Sims made his will, he left his house, 200 acres in Elizabeth City, and 40 cattle to local authorities for the purpose of establishing a free school. It is believed to be the first such institution of its kind in the United States (CBE 476, 62; MCGC 39,154-155; SH 11-12; PB 1 Pt. 1:164; FOR 2:8:15).

MARGARET SIMS (SYMES, SIMES, SIMMES) (MRS. BENJAMIN (BENIAMINE) SIMS [SYMES, SIMES, SIMMES])

On February 7, 1625, Margaret, the wife of Benjamin (Beniamine) Sims (Symes, Simes, Simmes) of Basses Choice (**27**), was listed among those who died in Warresqueak (later known as Isle of Wight) (CBE 62).

***

JOHN SINGER

On September 15, 1619, John Singer, a surgeon, set sail for Virginia on the *Margaret* of Bristol and headed for Berkeley Hundred **(55)** to work under Captain John Woodlief's supervision. Singer was furnished with a surgeon's chest and was to be paid for his services to the Society of Berkeley Hundred's settlers (CBE 14; VCR 3:186, 199, 213).

THOMAS SINGLETON ALIAS LEE (LEA)

In February 1627 administration of the estate of William Pindar, rector of Mottisfount, Hampshire, was granted to his kinsman, Thomas Singleton alias Lee (Lea), who was then in Virginia (CBE 77).

THOMAS SISSON

Thomas Sisson, a haberdasher from London, arrived in Jamestown **(1)** on the *Ann* on September 5, 1623, and took the oath of supremacy (MCGC 6).

MATHEW SIZEMORE

On July 18, 1620, the Virginia Company received a petition from Mathew Sizemore, a woman who claimed that she had paid the cost of her own transportation to Virginia and wanted compensation (VCR 1:407).

***

WILLIAM SIZEMORE (SISMORE, SEYMORE, SYSMORE)

On February 16, 1624, William Sizemore (Sismore, Seymore, Sysmore) and his wife, Martha, were living on West and Shirley Hundred Island **(41)**. In May 1625 he was credited with 100 acres on the west side of the Appomattox River **(40)**. His patent probably gave rise to the name of Sizemores Creek and the place named Sizemores, in what became Chesterfield County (CBE 36; VCR 4:554; PB 1 Pt. 2:590, 689, 839; 5:139).

MARTHA SIZEMORE (SISMORE, SEYMORE, SYSMORE) (MRS. WILLIAM SIZEMORE [SISMORE, SEYMORE, SYSMORE])

On February 16, 1624, Martha, the wife of William Sizemore (Sismore, Seymore,

Sysmore), was living with her husband on West and Shirley Hundred Island **(41)**. On May 23, 1625, she was mentioned by Mrs. Elizabeth Hamor, who was testifying in a slander suit involving Captain John Martin. Mrs. Hamor claimed that Martin told her that he encountered Martha Sizemore when he was in London's Newgate Market and that one of his companions had inquired whether she was one of his Virginia whores, inasmuch as she had made so many trips from Virginia to England. Mrs. Hamor said that on another occasion, Martin told her that someone had informed Martha Sizemore that he had called her a whore (CBE 36; MCGC 61-62).

***

RICHARD SKARCOROW

According to court testimony taken on June 1, 1625, Richard Skarcorow reached Virginia but died before he went to Arrohattock **(66)** (MCGC 64).

JOHN SKARFE (SEE JOHN SHARPE)

ROBERT SKEETE

On February 27, 1619, the Bridewell Court decided that Robert Skeete, a boy, would be sent to Virginia. He was part of a large group of children rounded up from the streets of London so that they could be sent to the colony (CBE 13).

FRANCIS SKILPINE

On September 26, 1627, Francis Skilpine was among the several men shipping goods from London to Virginia on the *Samuell* (CBE 80).

JOHN SKINNER (SKINER, SKYNNER)

John Skinner (Skiner, Skynner) came to Virginia in 1621 on the *Marmaduke* and on February 16, 1624, was living on the lower side of the James River in the settlement known as Paces Paines **(9)**. On October 10, 1624, when Skinner testified before the General Court, he said that he was age 16 and one of John Proctor's servants. He admitted that he and William Nayle, another young male servant, had flogged fellow servant Elizabeth Abbott on their master's orders, and that she had died. Ann Wood also testified that Skinner and Nayle had whipped Abbott. On February 4, 1625, John Skinner was living at Paces Paines, where he was then a servant in the household headed by Daniel Watkins and Phettiplace Close. On September 1, 1628, when George Pace (Richard and Isabella Pace's son) patented some land, he used John Skinner as a headright (CBE 40, 59; MCGC 23-24; PB 1 Pt. 1:64).

NICHOLAS SKINNER

On February 16, 1624, Nicholas Skinner was living in Warresqueak (26). On April 4, 1625, he informed the General Court that he had inspected Sir George Yeardley's tobacco after it had been loaded aboard ship and that Yeardley had paid him for doing so. On April 20, 1626, Nicholas Skinner sought to recover some money he was owed by the late John Bate (Bates) (CBE 42; MCGC 51, 60, 101).

THOMAS SKINNER (SKYNNER)

On May 20, 1607, Thomas Skinner (Skynner), a sailor who came to Virginia with the first Jamestown (1) colonists, accompanied Captain Christopher Newport on an exploratory voyage of the James River (HAI 102).

***

JOHN SLATER

In October 1617 John Slater came to Virginia on the *George* at the expense of Stephen Sparrow. In early 1625 John and his wife, Ann, were living in Elizabeth City (18), where he and Michael Wilcocks headed a well-equipped household that included three servants. John Slater was then age 22 (VCR 1:330; CBE 64).

ANNE SLATER (MRS. JOHN SLATER)

Anne, who became the wife of John Slater, went to Virginia on the *Gift* in 1622. By early 1625 she had married John and was living in Elizabeth City (18). Anne was then age 17 (CBE 64).

***

JOHN SLAUGHTER

John Slaughter came to Virginia on the *George* in 1617 and was a servant to Albiano Lupo, who used him as a headright when patenting some land on September 1, 1624. On October 9, 1626, John Slaughter and Thomas Spellman proved Lieutenant Lupo's will. On May 30, 1635, Slaughter patented 200 acres of land on the Elizabeth River (20 a). Two months later he and Percival Champion reportedly were occupying Captain John Smith's land in Denbigh (Warwick) County (18), near Nutmeg Quarter (22) (PB 1 Pt. 1:33, 169, 212; MCGC 116).

JOHN SLAUGHTER

On March 22, 1622, when the Indians attacked one of the plantations across the James River from Flowerdew Hundred (53), John Slaughter was killed (VCR 3:568).

JOHN SLAUGHTER

On November 16, 1635, John Slaughter was identified as a servant transported by Roger Bagnall, who used him as a headright when patenting some land in Warresqueak (26) (later Isle of Wight) County (PB 1 Pt. 1:308).

MARTIN SLAUGHTER

Martin Slaughter, a young servant, came to Virginia on the *Swann*, after spending some time in Canada. On February 4, 1625, he was identified as a 20-year-old servant in Ellis Emerson's household at Martin's Hundred (7) (CBE 62).

JAMES SLEIGHT (SLIGHT)

James Sleight (Slight) came to Virginia in 1610 on the *Tryall* and on February 16, 1624, was living in Elizabeth City (18). He was still there in early 1625 and was heading a household he shared with Francis Huff. Sleight was then age 42. Sometime prior to February 19, 1627, James Sleight and Bridges Freeman moved to Martin's Brandon (59), where they shared a dwelling. Sleight, who described himself as a yeoman, testified in a case that involved Captain John Huddleston's statements about the immoral conduct of Alice Boyce and Captain William Eppes. On May 21, 1627, James Sleight and Bridges Freeman received permission to leave Martin's Brandon and move to a more secure position. However, on July 4, 1627, the two men agreed to continue leasing some land at Martin's Brandon until Christmas 1628, that is, early January 1629. At that point they seem to have gone their separate ways (CBE 43, 65; MCGC 139-140, 149, 151).

WILLIAM SLEIGHT (SLIGHT)

In May 1625 William Sleight (Slight) was identified as heir to the bulk of Henry Wilkinson's estate (MCGC 64).

HUMPHREY SLEYNEY

On September 20, 1627, Humphrey Sleyney shipped some goods from London to Virginia on the *Parramore* (CBE 80).

ROBERT SMALDON

On July 16, 1632, Robert Smaldon, master of the *Blessing*, received permission to go to Virginia and Bermuda (CBE 103).

HUGO SMALE (SMALLEY?)

Between April 1623 and February 16, 1624, Hugo Smale (Smalley?) died in Elizabeth City (**17, 18**) (CBE 45).

LAWRENCE SMALEPAGE (SMALLPAGE, SMALPAGE)

Lawrence Smalepage (Smallpage, Smalpage) came to Virginia on the *Abigail* and on February 16, 1624, was living on the Maine or Governor's Land (**3**). He was still there on January 30, 1625, and was identified as a 20-year-old servant in Thomas Swinhow's household. When Swinhow, who was mortally ill, made a nuncupative will on March 18, 1626, he said that if he were to die before receiving payment for his servant, Lawrence, then Lawrence was to be freed. When the General Court heard the terms of Swinhow's will, they decided that Lawrence Smalepage would be freed until further instructions were forthcoming from the decedent's heir in London. On December 11, 1626, the General Court decided that Lawrence Smalepage could remain in the house he was occupying in Pasbehay, paying rent to the governor. This suggests that Lawrence had obtained his freedom and would continue to live on the Governor's Land (CBE 36, 57; MCGC 98-99, 126).

ROBERT SMALL

Robert Small, a carpenter, came to Virginia in 1607 and was one of the first Jamestown (**1**) colonists. In 1608 he accompanied Captain John Smith on an exploratory voyage on the Chesapeake Bay. At that time Smith identified Robert Small as a soldier (CJS 1:208, 224; 2:142, 163).

***

ROBERT SMALLEY

Robert Smalley most likely came to Virginia in the 3rd Supply of new colonists and therefore spent time in Jamestown (**1**). Sir Thomas Dale (1611–1616) reportedly placed Captain Robert Smalley in command at Henrico (**63**). When Smalley made his will on December 19, 1617, he and his wife, Elizabeth, were living at Bermuda Hundred (**39**). He left his house and land at Bermuda Hundred and some cattle to his widow, and he named Deputy Governor Samuel Argall as his executor. He made bequests to several other people, some of whom were his servants, and noted that some prominent officials (including Sir Thomas Dale) were indebted to him. On July 12, 1620, the widowed Elizabeth Smalley testified under oath that her late husband had served in Virginia for 11 years. When Smalley's will was presented for probate on November 15, 1621, Elizabeth Smalley was named executor, as Sir Samuel Argall declined to serve. Afterward Mrs. Smalley brought suit against Argall. The litigation spanned several years (BRO 782; EEAC 53; WITH 78; SH 4; FER 483; SR 3112; CBE 25).

ELIZABETH SMALLEY (MRS. ROBERT SMALLEY, MRS. RANDALL CREW) (SEE ELIZABETH SMALLEY CREW)

On December 12, 1617, when Robert Smalley of Bermuda Hundred (**39**) made his will, he left his house, land, livestock, and personal belongings to his wife, Elizabeth. On July 12, 1620, Elizabeth Smalley asked the Virginia Company for a widow's pension, noting that her late husband had served in the colony for 11 years. She also claimed that Sir Samuel Argall had taken the house, oxen, and belongings that her husband had bequeathed to her. On October 31, 1621, Mrs. Smalley pressed her case by sending a petition to the king. Shortly thereafter, she was appointed substitute executor of her late husband's estate. Then, on February 27, 1622, she was given a commission and authorized to inquire into what happened to his real and personal property. On May 8, 1622, Elizabeth Smalley was told that she could have her late husband's Virginia land and could sell the oxen that she had inherited. In June she made some allegations against Sir Samuel Argall but then withdrew them. In January 1623 the Virginia Company rejected her petition and complaints against Argall, noting that the matter should be settled by the court in Virginia. Elizabeth headed for the colony and by December 1624 had reached New England. She took up residence in Virginia and by January 11, 1627, had married Randall Crew, who pursued her case against Sir Samuel Argall (FER 483; VCR 1:401, 543, 608, 633; 2:50-51, 78; 4:507-508; MCGC132).

***

MATHEW SMALLWOOD

On February 9, 1633, Mathew Smallwood, factor of the late Captain John Prynn, was ordered to give some tobacco to Richard Cooke, a planter. Later, Smallwood, acting on the decedent's behalf, sent some tobacco to England on the *Unicorn*, a vessel on which Henry Cantrell was a passenger. On March 30, 1634, when Mathew Smallwood received a 21-year lease for 500 acres in Charles City County on Bicknes (Bickers or Tar) Bay, he was identified as a merchant (MCGC 201; EAE 41; PB 1 Pt. 1:151).

RANDALL SMALLWOOD (SMALWOOD, SMALEWOOD)

Randall Smallwood (Smalwood, Smalewood), a resident of urban Jamestown (1), came to Virginia sometime prior to August 4, 1623, when it was noted that some of his goods had been stolen. In 1623 he and the Rev. Buck made an inventory of Henry Jacob's estate. On February 16, 1624, Smallwood and two male servants were living in Jamestown. In June 1624 he testified in court about conversations he overheard at John Burrows' house, and a few months later he returned to court concerning William Julian's petition to the governor. On January 24, 1625, Randall Smallwood still was residing in Jamestown, where he was a solitary household head. As the corporation of James City's provost marshal, he received a salary of 200 pounds of tobacco a year and some corn. In an official capacity, he warned Jamestown merchant George Menefie to appear in court, and he inventoried the estate of the late John Pountis, another local merchant. He also reported to the court about some funds that were owed to Elizabeth Fox, and he testified about a land transaction that took place at Bermuda Hundred (39) a few days before the March 1622 Indian attack. On January 30, 1626, provost marshal Randall Smallwood testified that he had taken a muster of the colony's inhabitants in the presence of Governor George Yeardley. A couple months later Smallwood was given temporary custody of the goods of the late Thomas Swinehow, who died at a house on the Governor's Land (3). Smallwood also testified that he and Nathaniel Reignolds had inventoried and appraised the late Rev. Richard Buck's estate. In May 1626 the General Court decided that Randall Smallwood, as the late Thomas Swinhowe's administrator, was obliged to fulfill some of the decedent's obligations. One was seeing that a palisade was built around Dr. John Pott's house at Harrop. Later in the year Smallwood summoned Richard Allford to court, and he appraised the late Captain Ralph Hamor's goods. When the provost marshal's compensation was set in January 1627, Randall Smallwood was assigned Reignold Godwin, a Virginia Company servant. During 1627 and 1628 Randall Smallwood, as provost marshal, continued making appearances in court. He arbitrated a dispute between John Upton and his partner, Caleb Page, both of whom were residents of Jamestown Island. He also appraised the late Captain John Martin's goods and was named John Croodick's administrator. In 1632 Randall Smallwood and another person were supposed to appraise estates and, in compensation, were to divide a 10 percent fee. Sometime prior to June 1639, Smallwood acquired some land in Warwick County near Skiff's Creek. In March 1640 Smallwood testified about the Indians' attack on Thomas Sheffield's plantation (69) in March 1622, noting that Sheffield's child was spared despite the fact that the Natives burned the family home

(MCGC 4-5, 15-16, 41, 45, 55, 57, 72-73, 79, 91, 99-100, 103, 107, 117, 124, 130, 137, 144, 150, 152, 164, 480; PB 1 Pt. 2:654; SR 11329; CBE 38, 55; DOR 1:32).

WILLIAM SMETHES

William Smethes, a gentleman, came to Virginia in 1607 and was one of the first Jamestown (1) colonists (CJS 2:141).

[NO FIRST NAME] SMITH

On June 11, 1621, Virginia Company officials noted that a Mr. Smith was a possible candidate for secretary (VCR 1:478).

[NO FIRST NAME] SMITH

Mrs. Smith died in Jamestown (1) sometime after April 1623 but before February 16, 1624 (CBE 39).

AMBROSE SMITH

In mid-June 1618, officials at Bridewell decided that Ambrose Smith, an able-bodied felon being detained in Newgate Prison, would be reprieved. He was to be delivered to Sir Thomas Smith so that he could be transported to Virginia (CBE 8; SR 425; PC 2/29).

ARTHUR SMITH

Arthur Smith came to Virginia on the *Margaret and John* in 1622 and on February 16, 1624, was living in Elizabeth City (18). He was still there in early 1625 and was a 25-year-old servant in Pharaoh Flinton's household. On March 12, 1627, Smith, who was then a free man, brought suit against his former master, who had posted a bond guaranteeing that he would deliver a servant to him (CBE 44, 65; MCGC 145).

AUSTEN (OSTEN) SMITH

Austen (Osten) Smith, a carpenter, arrived in Jamestown on September 12, 1623, aboard the *Bonny Bess* and took the oath of supremacy. On February 16, 1624, he was living in urban Jamestown (1) in the household of merchant Richard Stephens (CBE 38; MCGC 6).

CHRISTIAN SMITH (SMYTH)

In 1621 Christian Smith (Smyth), a marriageable young maid and orphan who was

born at Newberry in Berkshire, came to Virginia on the *Warwick*. Virginia Company records indicate that 19-year-old Christian had been in service to Mr. Newton of Mile End, who gave her a good recommendation (FER 309).

CHRISTOPHER SMITH

Christopher Smith came to Virginia on the *Return* in 1624. In early 1625 he was living in Elizabeth City (18) in a household headed by Thomas Godby. Christopher, who was age 23, was free (CBE 65).

EDWARD SMITH

When the ship *Falcon* undertook a voyage to Jamestown (1) in 1621, Edward Smith was identified as a member of the crew (EAE 11).

EDWARD SMITH

Edward Smith came to Virginia on the *George* in 1621 and on February 16, 1624, was living on the lower side of the James River at Paces Paines (9). He was still there on February 4, 1625, at which time he was identified as a 30-year-old servant in John Proctor's household (CBE 40, 59).

EDWARD SMITH

On September 2, 1631, officials at Bridewell noted that Edward Smith, a boy, was being sent to Virginia by a merchant (CBE 65).

ELIZABETH SMITH

On November 20, 1622, officials at Bridewell decided that Elizabeth Smith, who was being detained in Newgate Prison, would be transported overseas (CBE 29).

JACOB SMITH

In 1625 Jacob Smith bequeathed money to a merchant who was supposed to transport him and his son to Virginia. Jacob stipulated that if his son was not sent to the colony, he was to be apprenticed (SH 7).

JOHN SMITH

Captain John Smith, one of Virginia's best-known early settlers, was born in 1579 in

Lincolnshire, England. In his youth he traveled and fought in the Low Countries and throughout Europe. John Smith came to Virginia in 1607 in the first group of colonists. Because he was implicated in a mutiny, he was kept in irons from February to June 1607, despite the fact that the Virginia Company had designated him a councilor. He was admitted to the Virginia Council on June 10, 1607. In September 1607, after Edward Maria Wingfield had been deposed as president and been replaced by John Ratcliffe alias Sicklemore, John Smith served as cape merchant. He undertook several exploratory voyages, venturing up the James River and into the Chickahominy and Pamunkey Rivers, and he was captured and detained briefly by the Indians. He also made two lengthy voyages on the Chesapeake Bay. In September 1608 Smith became president of the Virginia colony. During his time in office he rebuilt and strengthened Jamestown (1) and its fortifications and forced the colonists to work toward their own support. He also interacted extensively with the Natives. When the colonists were confronted with starvation, he divided them into three groups and sent them out to seek subsistence. Smith was arrested a year later and sent to England, where he stayed from December 1609 to March 1614. Afterward, he went to New England. Captain John Smith's accounts of the colonization of Virginia, though based on the work of others and embellished with self-aggrandizing statements, shed a considerable amount of light on people and events that otherwise would have escaped notice. In May 1621 Smith asked the Virginia Company for a reward, stating that he had rebuilt Jamestown twice, explored the countryside, and risked his life in service to the colony. Company officials referred his request to a committee, which apparently ignored it. In 1629 he interviewed some Virginia colonists then visiting England and included their information in his narrative. Captain John Smith died in England on June 21, 1631, and was buried in London. His published works, though largely drawn from the writings of others, provide many insights into the early years of colonization and his perspective on Native American life (STAN 13, 27; CJS 1:61, 127, 233; 2:138, 180; 3:377-378, 390; HAI 102, 117, 124-126, 188, 195-196, 200, 895; VCR 1:319-320, 471; 3:13; 4:144; CO 1/1 ff 129-131).

***

JOHN SMITH (SMYTH)

John Smith (Smyth) came to Virginia in 1611 on the *Elizabeth* and was an ancient planter. On February 2, 1620, he and Captain Powell asked the Virginia Company for 400 acres on the lower side of the James River, near Chippokes Creek, and 300 acres at Hog Island (16). Sometime prior to February 16, 1624, John Smith, his wife, and their child moved to Burrows Hill (8). In July 1624 John told the justices of the General Court that he was familiar with John Phillimore's intended bequests. Later in the year he testified about some business dealings that involved Captain John Martin and merchant Humphrey Rastell. On February 4, 1625, John Smith was living at Burrows Hill with his wife, Susanna, and 1-year-old son, Francis. In August 1626 he testified that he had offered two capons to John Burrows as ground rent, but Burrows refused to accept them. In October 1629 John Smith served as a burgess for the area then generally known as Paces Paines (9), and in 1632 and 1633 he represented the settlers living in the same vicinity, which included Burrows Hill (or Smith's Mount) and Perry's (Swann's) Point (CBE 40, 59; MCGC 25, 27, 89; HEN 1:138, 178, 203; DOR 1:38).

SUSANNA SMITH (SMYTH) (MRS. JOHN SMITH [SMYTH])

Susanna, who married ancient planter John Smith (Smyth), came to Virginia in 1619 on the *Bona Nova*. On February 16, 1624, she, her husband, and their Virginia-born infant, Francis, were living at Burrows Hill (8). Susanna Smith and her family were still there on February 4, 1625 (CBE 40, 59).

FRANCIS SMITH

On February 16, 1624, Francis, the Virginia-born infant of John and Susanna Smith (Smyth), was living at Burrows Hill (8). He was still there on February 4, 1625, and was described as age 1 (CBR 40, 59).

***

JOHN SMITH (SMYTH)

On February 3, 1619, John Smith (Smyth) of Nibley was identified as one of the Society of Berkeley Hundred's investors who held a patent for Berkeley Hundred (**55**). On August 18, 1619, he was among those shipping supplies to the Society's plantation. By September 24, 1620, John Smith and Arnold Oldesworth had purchased part of George Thorpe's interest in Berkeley Hundred. Smith was well known to high-ranking Virginia Company officials, and on June 27, 1621, Governor George Yeardley was told to keep Company treasurer Sir Edwin Sandys informed about how the Berkeley Hundred settlement was faring. On July 4, 1623, Virginia Company officials noted that John Smith had agreed to send his surplus goods to Virginia (VCR 3:110, 130-134, 187, 193-195, 412-415, 464; 4:245-246; MCGC 179).

JOHN SMITH

On January 29, 1620, officials at Bridewell decided that John Smith, who was being detained, would be sent to Virginia (CBE 17).

JOHN SMITH (SMYTH)

In July 1621 John Smith (Smyth) was living in Pasbehay (**3**), where his in-laws, Mr. and Mrs. John Rowe, also resided. In August 1621 the Virginia Company identified him as a carpenter and sent a box to him. When John Smith was assigned to Governor George Yeardley on January 12, 1627, he was identified as a tenant of the defunct Virginia Company (VCR 3: 464; FER 308; MCGC 136).

JOHN SMITH (SMYTH)

John Smith (Smyth) came to Virginia on the *Swann* in 1624. In early 1625 he was living on the Virginia Company's land in Elizabeth City (**17**), on the east side of the Hampton River, and was a 31-year-old servant in Captain John Martin's household (CBE 67).

JOHN SMITH (SMYTH)

John Smith (Smyth) came to Virginia on the *Abigail* and on February 16, 1624, was living on the Maine (**3**), just west of Jamestown Island. He was still there on January 30, 1625, at which time he was described as a 30-year-old servant in Thomas Bunn's household. In January 1626 there was a dispute over how long Smith was supposed to

serve. One witness stated that Bunn told him that Smith was to serve for a year, commencing on Christmas 1624 (that is, early January 1625). The General Court responded by ordering John Smith to serve Thomas Bunn until February 1, 1626 (CBE 39, 57; MCGC 89).

JOHN SMITH (SMYTH)

John Smith (Smyth) came to Virginia on the *Bonaventure* and on February 16, 1624, was living in the Neck O'Land (**5**). He was still there on February 4, 1625, and was a solitary household head who had an adequate supply of stored food and defensive weaponry and some swine (CBE 35, 58; DOR 1:37).

JOHN SMITH (SMYTH)

On May 23, 1625, John Smith (Smyth), one of Mr. Giles Beaumont's servants, testified before the General Court about an event that occurred in the Downes. He said that when he and another man went ashore, seeking servants to transport to Virginia, they found a baker. However, Beaumont turned the baker away because he was reputed to be one of the king's men (MCGC 59-60).

JOHN SMITH (SMYTH)

On August 21, 1626, John Smith (Smyth), one of Francis Fowler's servants, was found guilty of making false accusations against Mr. Bunn, Mr. Woolridge, Mr. Harwood, and several other people. Smith was made to apologize and was punished by being made to serve Fowler for an extra three days and the public for three months. This individual may have been Thomas Bunn's former servant, John Smith (MCGC 108).

OSBORNE SMITH

On February 16, 1624, Osborne Smith was living in Elizabeth City (**17, 18**) (CBE 43).

OSMOND SMITH

In 1620 Osmond Smith, an indentured servant, came to Virginia on the *Bona Nova*. On January 24, 1625, he was a 17-year-old indentured servant in the urban Jamestown (**1**) household of Dr. John Pott (CBE 55).

NICHOLAS SMITH

Nicholas Smith came to Virginia in 1621 on the *Bona Nova* and on February 16, 1624, was living on the lower side of the James River. On February 4, 1625, he was still there and was identified as an 18-year-old servant at Hugh Crowder's plantation (**12**). On April 11, 1625, Nicholas testified at the inquest held in connection with John Verone's death (CBE 40, 60; MCGC 53).

PHILIP SMITH

On February 9, 1628, the General Court noted that Philip Smith came to Virginia on the *Temperance* in 1621 at the expense of Sir George Yeardley. When Thomas Flint patented some land on September 20, 1628, he used Philip Smith as a headright, indicating that he had been transported to the colony by Yeardley (MCGC 166; PB 1 Pt. 1:59).

***

RICHARD SMITH (SMYTH)

In September 1620 Richard Smith, a gardener, set sail from Bristol, England, on the *Supply* and accompanied William Tracy to Berkeley Hundred (**55**). Smith was accompanied by his wife, Joan, and sons, Anthony and William. He was supposed to serve the Society of Berkeley Hundred's investors as a tenant at half-shares, although at first he was to receive support from the Society (CBE 21; VCR 3:393-394, 398).

JOAN SMITH (SMYTH) (MRS. RICHARD SMITH [SMYTH])

In September 1620 Joan, the wife of gardener Richard Smith, set sail from Bristol, England, on the *Supply*. She, her husband, and their sons, Anthony and William, were among those who accompanied William Tracy to Berkeley Hundred (**55**) (CBE 21; VCR 3:393-394).

ANTHONY SMITH (SMYTH)

Anthony Smith (Smyth) left England in September 1620 on the *Supply* with his parents, Richard and Joan Smith, and his brother, William. The Smiths were accompanying William Tracy to Berkeley Hundred (**55**) where Richard was to be a tenant at half-shares (CBE 21; VCR 3:393-394).

WILLIAM SMITH (SMYTH)

William Smith (Smyth) left England in September 1620 on the *Supply* with his parents, Richard and Joan Smith, and his brother, Anthony. The Smiths, who accompanied William Tracy, were headed for Berkeley Hundred (**55**) (CBE 21; VCR 3:393-394).

***

RICHARD SMITH

Richard Smith came to Virginia on the *George* in 1623 and arrived at Martin's Hundred (**7**) around Christmas, that is, in January 1624. On November 8, 1624, he testified that he was one of Robert Adams' servants at Martin's Hundred and that he had never wrongfully gathered any of Mr. William Harwood's corn. On February 4, 1625, Richard Smith was still living at Martin's Hundred, where he was a 24-year-old servant in the household headed by Robert Adams and Augustine Leake (CBE 57; VCR 4:60; MCGC 30).

RICHARD SMITH

Richard Smith came to Virginia on the *London Merchant* and on February 16, 1624, was living on the Maine (**3**). He was still there on January 30, 1625, and was a solitary household head whose possessions were very modest (CBE 39, 62).

RICHARD SMITH (SMYTH)

In September 1632 the Virginia assembly determined that Richard Smith would be paid from public funds. It is unclear what type of goods or services he had provided to the colony (HEN 1:196).

***

ROBERT SMITH

Robert Smith, a London merchant tailor, acquired two shares of Virginia land from Francis Carter. On July 31, 1622, Smith, his wife, Ellen, and son, John, set sail from England on the *James* (FER 400; VCR 2:56).

ELLEN SMITH (MRS. ROBERT SMITH)

Ellen Smith, her husband, Robert, and their son, John, set sail from England on the *James* on July 31, 1622 (FER 400).

JOHN SMITH

John Smith and his parents, Robert and Ellen, set sail from England on the *James* on July 31, 1622 (FER 400).

***

ROBERT SMITH

In July 1623, when Robert Smith of St. Michael, Bassishaw, London, prepared his will, he made reference to his land in Virginia. His wife, Judith, was to serve as his executor (EEAC 54; CBE 33).

ROBERT SMITH

On February 16, 1624, Robert Smith was living at Flowerdew Hundred (53) (CBE 37).

ROBERT SMITH

Robert Smith came to Virginia on the *Providence* in 1624. On February 16, 1624, he was living in Elizabeth City (18). He was still there on February 7, 1625, at which time he was identified as a 22-year-old servant in Daniel Gookin's household (CBE 44, 63).

ROBERT SMITH

In December 1631 Robert Smith, who was then in Virginia, received a bequest from his brother, Peter Chambrelan Sr. of St. Dionis Backchurch, in London (WITH 175; EEAC 12; CBE 97).

***

ROGER SMITH

Captain Roger Smith, who served in the Netherlands for a dozen years and was commander of an infantry company, was associated with Thomas West, Lord Delaware. He came to Virginia sometime prior to 1616 and was an ancient planter. Because Smith was convinced that the colony needed strong leadership, he disapproved of Governor George Yeardley's more lenient management style. In 1619 he went to England, where he voiced his concerns. Roger Smith was eager to return to the colony and by December 1620 had persuaded Virginia Company officials to outfit him and put him in charge of 50 tenants to be placed on the Company's land. He was accompanied by

Thomas Bunn, a surgeon, but also had wanted to take along a young preacher. As soon as Captain Roger Smith reached Virginia, he began serving on the Council of State. According to Captain John Smith, during the March 22, 1622, Indian attack, five people were killed at Captain Roger Smith's plantation near Charles City (39). This raises the possibility that at the time of the assault, he and the Virginia Company's tenants had been living on the Company Land (62) within the corporation of Charles City. Shortly after the Indian attack, Captain Roger Smith was ordered to evacuate the inhabitants of Henrico Island (63) and Coxendale (64), and he was given absolute power over those residing in Charles City. In May 1622 he was placed in command of the settlers living in Pasbehay (3). Later, he was ordered to take over part of the Company's land in Elizabeth City (17).

Roger Smith's military expertise was highly valued, for he was given the means and authority to build a fort on the lower side of the James River in Warresqueak (26). By April 1623 construction had gotten underway and was going well. Although Treasurer George Sandys informed Company officials that Smith's deeds were more valuable than his words, he conceded that Smith was doing a good job on the Warresqueak fort. During 1624 and 1625 Captain Roger Smith played an active role in the Virginia government. In 1624 he was among those who signed a document highly critical of how the colony was managed during Sir Thomas Smith's government. Then, in July 1624 he led an expedition against the Pamunkey Indians, one of the retaliatory marches undertaken each summer for the purpose of destroying the Natives' food supply. He also testified against Captain John Martin, who was considered a controversial figure. In October 1624 Captain Roger Smith, Dr. John Pott, and surgeon Thomas Bunn (all of whom had possession of parcels on the Governor's Land) were given permission to seat part of the acreage in Henrico that had been set aside for the College (66). There is no evidence, however, that they did. By late 1624 Smith had begun receiving the compensation to which he was entitled for building the Warresqueak fort.

On February 16, 1624, when a census was made of Jamestown Island's inhabitants, Captain Roger Smith headed a household in urban Jamestown (1) that included his wife, three young children (Elizabeth Rolfe, Sarah Macocke, and Elizabeth Salter), and four Virginia Company servants. On January 24, 1625, the Smith household, which had an abundance of supplies, included Roger Smith and his wife, Joan (Joane, Jone), who was the daughter of William Peirce and the widow of John Rolfe. Also present were the same three children. By February 4, 1625, two of Roger Smith's Company servants had been moved to his plantation (10) on the lower side of the James River. Sometime prior to January 3, 1626, one of Smith's servants, Henry Booth, was injured by a weapon that Jamestown gunsmith John Jefferson had repaired inadequately. Booth was described as "a poore man and A Tenant to the Company." On December 12, 1625, Captain Roger Smith patented 4 acres in urban Jamestown, land he already had developed. In May 1625, when a list of patented land was sent back to England, he was credited with 100 acres in Archer's Hope (6), acreage that he had received as an ancient planter and already had seated. Smith and his father-in-law, Captain William Peirce, also owned some acreage near Blunt Point (22).

On January 10, 1627, Smith and Peirce informed the General Court that if the acreage Governor George Yeardley wanted intruded on their holdings, they would be content to have some land elsewhere. In late January 1627, when the defunct Virginia Company's tenants and servants were assigned to government officials until their contracts expired, Captain Roger Smith received three men who already were employed on his plantation on the lower side of the James River. In December 1628 he sued Nathaniel Causey's estate on behalf of John Moseley's widow, Anne. In March 1629 Roger Smith testified that Captain William Peirce, the overseer of Abraham Porter's estate, had arranged for gunsmith John Jackson to take over that duty. The date of Smith's death is uncertain, but he was still alive in June 1629 (BRO 1011; VCR 1:429, 433-434, 520; 2:16, 481; 3:231-232, 482, 609, 611, 623; 4:111, 129-130, 188, 222, 228-229, 481, 551, 556; FER 215, 571; CJS 2:301; EAE 89; HAI 915; HEN 1:128-129, 137-138, 178, 196, 203; CBE 38, 55, 70-71; MCGC 20-21, 25, 30-32, 36, 45, 79, 84, 89, 115, 130, 136, 176, 179, 187; PB 1 Pt. 1:3-4; STAN 30; MOR 98; DOR 1:30, 39).

JOAN (JOANE, JONE) PIERCE ROLFE SMITH (MRS. JOHN ROLFE, MRS. ROGER SMITH) (SEE JOAN PEIRCE II, MRS. JOHN ROLFE)

Joan (Joane, Jone) Peirce, who came to Virginia on the *Blessing* in 1609, married Pocahontas's widower, John Rolfe, after his May 1617 return to Virginia. John and Joan Peirce Rolfe probably lived on the urban Jamestown (1) property of her parents, William and Joan Peirce, and perhaps shared their home. The Rolfes produced a daughter, Elizabeth, around 1621. When John Rolfe died in 1622, he left Joan an interest in his land at Mulberry Island (21). Sometime prior to 1623, she married Captain Roger Smith and moved into his home in Jamestown, where she was residing on February 16, 1624, and on January 24, 1625, when demographic records were compiled. In the Smith household were Elizabeth Rolfe (age 4) and two other children, Sara Macock (age 2) and Elizabeth Salter (age 7) (CBE 38, 55).

***

SOLOMON SMITH

On December 24, 1634, Solomon Smith witnessed the will made by Tobias Felgate of Westover (54) (SH 19).

THOMAS SMITH (SMYTH)

Sir Thomas Smith (Smyth), first treasurer of the Virginia Company, was born around 1558 and was educated at Oxford. He was a member of the Turkey Company and the East India Company and invested in Sir Walter Raleigh's colonization efforts at Roanoke Island. Smith was knighted for gallantry during the late 1590s and was knighted again by King James in 1603. In 1604 he was made ambassador to Russia. Sir Thomas Smith invested heavily in the Virginia Company and served as its treasurer for 12 years. He and some fellow investors received a large tract of Virginia land, which they developed into the plantation known as Smith's (Smyth's) Hundred (44), later renamed Southampton Hundred. When Virginia Company members began squabbling among themselves and factional differences emerged, the Smith government was criticized for allowing the colony to gain the reputation of a death trap. Sir Thomas Smith made his will on January 30, 1621, and added a codicil to it on September 4, 1624. Both documents were presented for probate on October 12, 1625 (WITH 47; BRO 1013-1015).

THOMAS SMITH (SMYTH)

On December 31, 1619, officials at Bridewell decided that Thomas Smith (Smyth), a boy who had been brought in by the marshal of Middlesex, would be sent to Virginia (CBE 14).

THOMAS SMITH (SMYTH)

According to Virginia Company records, William Weldon was credited for paying for Thomas Smith's (Smyth's) transportation to Virginia, because one of the men Weldon actually brought was assigned to the Society of Smith's (Southampton) Hundred. Therefore, it is probable that Thomas Smith came to the colony in 1619, when Weldon did. He may have returned to England, for he reportedly carried a letter from Weldon letter to Company officials (VCR 3:254, 266).

THOMAS SMITH

On November 21, 1621, Thomas Smith of the *Hopewell* received the Virginia Company's permission to go on a fishing voyage (VCR 1:554, 562; 3:513).

THOMAS SMITH (SMYTH)

On July 31, 1622, Thomas Smith (Smyth) set sail for Virginia on the *James* with Alexander Lake (FER 400).

THOMAS SMITH (SMYTH)

Thomas Smith (Smyth) came to Virginia on the *Abigaile* and on February 16, 1624, was living in urban Jamestown (1) in the household headed by Captain William Peirce. On January 24, 1625, Thomas was identified as a 17-year-old servant in the Peirce household (CBE 38, 55).

THOMAS SMITH (SMYTH)

Thomas Smith (Smyth) died in Elizabeth City (17, 18) sometime after April 1623 but before February 16, 1624 (CBE 45).

THOMAS SMITH (SMYTH)

Thomas Smith (Smyth) died in Warresqueak (26) sometime after April 1623 but before February 16, 1624 (CBE 42).

THOMAS SMITH (SMYTH)

Thomas Smith (Smyth) came to Virginia on the *Abigail* and on February 16, 1624, was living on the Maine (3). He was still there on January 30, 1625, and was a 16-year-old servant in the household of surgeon Thomas Bunn (CBE 39, 57).

THOMAS SMITH (SMYTH)

On May 5, 1624, Thomas Smith (Smyth), a soldier, testified in the Earl of Warwick's suit against Edward Brewster. The litigation involved the ships *Neptune* and *Treasurer*, which were in Virginia in 1618. Smith testified at Lady Delaware's request (EAE 14; HCA 13/44 f 296vo).

THOMAS SMITH (SMYTH)

On December 2, 1628, the General Court ordered John Burland to pay Thomas Smith (Smyth) for providing him with two male servants (MCGC 178).

THOMAS SMITH (SMYTH)

On April 24, 1632, Thomas Smith (Smyth) and three other men received a 21-year lease for 400 acres in Martin's Hundred (7) adjoining Skiff's Creek. In July 1635 Smith received a patent for part of the land he had been leasing and had developed into a plantation (PB 1 Pt. 1:130, 257-258, 268).

THOMAS SMITH (SMYTH)

Thomas Smith (Smyth) came to Virginia in 1634 on the *John and Dorothy* at the expense of Adam Thorogood. On June 24, 1635, when Thorogood secured a patent, he listed Smith as a headright (PB 1 Pt. 1:179).

WARREN (WARRIN) SMITH

The will of Warren (Warrin) Smith of Holborn in Middlesex, an adventurer in Virginia, was proved in May 1615 (EEAC 54; CBE 7; WITH 264-265).

WILLIAM SMITH

William Smith came to Virginia on the *Sampson* in 1618 and on February 16, 1624, was living on the Eastern Shore **(72-78)**. In early 1625 he was still there and was identified as a 26-year-old household head with an adequate supply of stored food and defensive weaponry. On October 15, 1629, Smith was identified as a planter when he obtained a 100-acre leasehold for some land bordering the Chesapeake Bay. This raises the possibility that he was leasing part of the acreage formerly attributed to the Virginia Company **(76)**. He appears to have survived until 1636 and continued to reside in Accomack (CBE 46, 68; PB 1 Pt. 1:100; AMES 1:61-63; DOR 1:69).

WILLIAM SMITH

William Smith, a smith by trade, left England on April 17, 1619, and was bound for Virginia. On April 7, 1623, Virginia Company officials noted that Smith, a Company servant, had been assigned to Governor Francis Wyatt's guard. Therefore, he would have resided in Jamestown **(1)** or on the Governor's Land **(3)**. In February 1627 William Smith of Jamestown was identified as one of Thomas Roper's heirs. Roper, a gentleman who died sometime prior to February 16, 1624, left Smith a pair of linen breeches (FER 107; VCR 4:104-106; WITH 487).

WILLIAM SMITH

William Smith came to Virginia in 1621 on the *Flying Hart* and on February 16, 1624, was living in Elizabeth City **(18)**. On February 7, 1625, he was described as a 23-year-old servant in Daniel Gookin's household at Newportes News **(24)** (CBE 43, 63).

WILLIAM SMITH

William Smith came from Bermuda on the *Tiger* in 1621 at the expense of George Sandys, who used him as a headright on December 4, 1624 (PB 1 Pt. 1:12).

WILLIAM SMITH

William Smith died at Flowerdew Hundred **(53)** sometime after April 1623 but before February 16, 1624 (CBE 37).

WILLIAM SMITH

William Smith came to Virginia on the *Jacob* in 1624 and in early 1625 was living in Elizabeth City **(18)**, where he was a 30-year-old servant in Lawrence Peale's household (CBE 64).

WILLIAM SMITH

On April 11, 1625, William Smith was one of the men to be summoned to court to testify in some litigation involving the ownership of some cattle that Lieutenant Shephard, Daniel Gookin's agent, transferred to Captain Raleigh Croshaw of Elizabeth City **(17, 18)**. This raises the possibility that William Smith also was associated with that area (MCGC 52).

WILLIAM SMITH

On September 30, 1630, Captain William Smith, a mariner, asked that Captain John Preen's license be revoked (CBE 92).

HENRY SMOOTE

On February 26, 1620, officials at Bridewell decided that Henry Smoote, who was being detained in Newgate Prison, would be sent to Virginia (CBE 19).

TIMOTHY SNAPE

Timothy Snape, a yeoman from London who was preparing to go to Virginia, made his will on September 10, 1624. He indicated that he was a bachelor and the son of Edmond Snape, clerk of St. Savior's Parish in Southwark, Surrey. Timothy Snape died in Virginia sometime prior to July 1629, when probate was granted to his brother, Samuel Snape, and his sister, Hannah Barker alias Snape (EEAC 54; WAT 20; CBE 87).

THOMAS SNAPP

On February 16, 1624, Thomas Snapp was living in Elizabeth City **(17, 18)** (CBE 45).

FRANCIS SNARSBROUGH

Francis Snarsbrough, a gentleman, came to Virginia in 1607 and was one of the first Jamestown **(1)** colonists (CJS 1:208; 2:141).

JOHN SNEAD (SNEDE, SNADE, SNODE, SNOADE)

On April 30, 1623, when John Snead (Snede, Snade, Snode, Snoade) rebutted Captain Nathaniel Butler's allegations about conditions in the colony, he said that he had been in Virginia for three-and-a-half years. On November 28, 1625, Snead verified the accuracy of the late John Clarke's inventory. On January 30, 1626, he and four other Elizabeth City men were accused of going aboard the ship *Grace*, contrary to law. A year later the peace bond he had been required to post was revoked because of his good behavior. In March 1627 John Snead sued Pharaoh Flinton, who had agreed to bring him a 17-year-old servant but failed to do so. Sometime prior to April 20, 1635, John Snead patented some land at the Old Poquoson (**19**) (VCR 2:386; MCGC 77, 91-92, 137, 145; PB 1 Pt. 1:164).

***

SAMUEL SNEAD

On August 4, 1635, when Samuel Snead patented some James City County acreage at the head of Skiff's Creek, he used himself, his wife, Alice, his son, William, and a servant as headrights (PB 1 Pt. 1:268).

ALICE SNEAD (MRS. SAMUEL SNEAD)

When Samuel Snead patented some James City County acreage on August 4, 1635, he used his wife, Alice, as a headright (PB 1 Pt. 1:268).

WILLIAM SNEAD

When Samuel Snead patented some James City County acreage on August 4, 1635, he used his son, William, as a headright (PB 1 Pt. 1:268).

***

THOMAS SNEADE

In 1619 Thomas Sneade came to Virginia at the expense of the Ferrars, who were major investors in the Virginia Company of London. Sneade probably was a Company servant or tenant (FER 296).

WILLIAM SNEADE

In 1619 William Sneade set sail for Virginia in 1619. The cost of his transportation was borne by the Ferrars, who were major investors in the Virginia Company of London. He probably was a Company servant or tenant (FER 296).

NATHANIEL SNELL

On July 19, 1627, Nathaniel Snell shipped goods from London to Virginia on the *James* (CBE 79).

ANDREW SNELLING

On February 20, 1626, Andrew Snelling testified before the General Court about the cargo of the ship *Deal* (MCGC 95).

ANN SNOAD (SNOADE)

On July 3, 1627, the General Court learned that Ann Snoad (Snoade) had been pregnant when she fought with Alice Thornbury and had lost the baby she was carrying. Ann and Alice were told that they would be whipped if they fought again (MCGC 150).

HANNAH SNODE

On July 15, 1631, Hannah Snode was identified as one of the planters who exported tobacco from Virginia and wanted relief from customs (G&M 166).

ARTHUR SNOW (SNOWE)

On November 20, 1622, officials decided that Arthur Snow (Snowe), an inmate of Newgate Prison, would be reprieved and sent overseas because of an outbreak of jail fever (CBE 29).

***

ELEANOR (ELINOR, ELLENOR) SNOW (SNOWE) (MRS. [JOHN?] SNOW [SNOWE]; MRS. GEORGE GRAVES [GRAVE]) (SEE MRS.GEORGE GRAVES [GRAVE])

On February 16, 1624, Eleanor (Elinor, Ellenor), whose late husband's surname was Snow (Snowe), was living in urban

Jamestown (1) with her current husband, George Graves (Grave) and her daughters, Rebecca and Sara Snow. Eleanor was still residing there on January 24, 1625. She may have been the widow of John Snow (Snowe) who perished at Weyanoke (52) during the March 22, 1622, Indian attack (CBE 38, 55).

REBECCA SNOW (SNOWE)

On February 16, 1624, Rebecca Snow (Snowe) was living in urban Jamestown (1) in the household headed by her stepfather, George Graves (Grave), and her mother, Eleanor (Elinor, Ellenor). Also part of the Graves household was Sara Snow, Rebecca's sister. Rebecca may have been the daughter of John Snow (Snowe), who was killed at Weyanoke (52) during the March 22, 1622, Indian attack (CBE 38, 55).

SARAH SNOW (SNOWE)

On February 16, 1624, Sara Snow was living in urban Jamestown (1) in the household headed by her stepfather, George Graves (Grave). Also in the Graves household was Sara's mother, Eleanor (Elinor, Ellenor), and Rebecca, Sara's sister. Sara and her family were still residing in Jamestown when a muster was made on January 24, 1625. In 1626 Robert Lindsey of Martin's Hundred (7), who was among the several men captured and detained by the Pamunkey Indians, sent word that if he was not freed, he wanted his locked chest and personal possessions to be given to Sara Snow. She may have been the daughter of John Snow (Snowe), who was killed at Weyanoke (52) during the March 22, 1622, Indian attack (CBE 38, 55; MCGC 128).

***

***

JOHN SNOW (SNOWE)

On March 22, 1622, when the Indians attacked Weyanoke (52), John Snow (Snowe), one of Sir George Yeardley's people, was killed, as was his son. In November 1624 John Snow was identified as one of Yeardley's former servants who had lived at Flowerdew (53) and was under Sergeant Henry Fortesque's supervision. John may have been the husband of Eleanor (Elinor, Ellenor) Snow and the father of Rebecca

and Sara Snow, who were living in Jamestown (1) in 1624 and 1625 (VCR 3:569; MCGC 27).

[NO FIRST NAME]
SNOW (SNOWE)

When the Indians attacked Weyanoke (52) on March 22, 1622, John Snow's (Snowe's) son was killed (VCR 3:569).

***

THOMAS SNOW

On February 16, 1624, Thomas Snow was living on the Maine (3) (CBE 39).

JOHN SNOWOOD

In early 1625 John Snowood was living in Elizabeth City (18) where he was a 25-year-old servant in Joseph Cobb's household (CBE 64).

SARES SOALE (SOASE)

Sares Soale (Soase) left England on April 17, 1619, and immigrated to Virginia (FER 107).

[NO FIRST NAME] SOAME

On March 12, 1624, the General Court noted that Mr. Bennett was in debt to Mr. Soame and three others known to have been merchants (MCGC 13).

WILLIAM SOANE

William Soane came to Virginia in 1621 or 1622 on the *George* at the expense of John Southern, who used Soane as a headright when patenting some land in November 1627 (MCGC 103; PB 1 Pt. 1:55).

GEORGE SOLDAN

On March 22, 1622, when the Indians attacked the settlers living on the College Land (66), George Soldan was killed (VCR 3:566).

***

SIR GEORGE SOMERS

Sir George Somers, who was born in Lyme Regis, Dorsetshire, and was knighted at

Whitehall in 1603, was around 30 years old in early June 1609 when he set sail for Virginia with Sir Thomas Gates. They were shipwrecked in Bermuda but arrived in the colony on May 23, 1610. Gates designated Somers one of his councilors. On June 15, 1610, Somers wrote a letter in which he described his experiences in Bermuda and the famine he and Gates encountered in Virginia. When Lord Delaware arrived in Jamestown (1), he appointed Sir George Somers an admiral and sent him to Bermuda to bring back food for the colonists. However, Somers became ill and died in Bermuda in November 1610. The will Sir George Somers made on April 23, 1609, in preparation for his voyage to Virginia, was proved on August 16, 1611. Probate was granted to Sir George's brother, John. The decedent's nephews later tried to claim the Virginia land to which he was entitled on account of his service to the colony (WAT 460-461; CO 1/1 ff 84-85; WITH 52; BRO 401; FOR 3:1:20; CJS 1:129, 268, 276-277; HAI 415, 433-434, 445-446, 459-460, 509, 896; SH 1; EEAC 54; VCR 1:414; 3:13).

MATHEW SOMERS

In November 1620 Mathew Somers and his brother, Nicholas, who were Sir George Somers' nephews and heirs, asked the Virginia Company to give them the 30,000 acres of land in Virginia that Sir George was supposed to receive (VCR 1:462-463).

NICHOLAS SOMERS

In November 1620 Nicholas Somers and his brother, Mathew, Sir George Somers' nephews and heirs, asked the Virginia Company to give them the 30,000 acres in Virginia that Sir George was supposed to receive in compensation for his service to the colony (VCR 1:462-463).

***

THOMAS SOMERSALL

Thomas Somersall died on Jamestown Island (1) sometime after April 1623 but before February 16, 1624 (CBE 39).

HENRY SONEY

In 1629 James City Parish churchwarden John Jackson reported Henry Soney and three others to the General Court because their church dues were in arrears. Each man was required to post a bond guaranteeing that he would pay what he owed. On September 6, 1632, Henry Soney's bond was nullified at his request. He would have been a resident of the corporation of James City, which had its church in Jamestown (1) (MCGC 200).

ELIZABETH SOOTHALL (SOUTHE)

On February 27, 1619, officials at Bridewell decided that Elizabeth Soothall (Southe), a young wench, would be sent to Virginia. She was one of the children rounded up from the streets of London and sent to the colony (CBE 13).

***

HENRY SOOTHEY (SOUTHEY, SOTHEY) I

On January 16, 1622, Virginia Company officials noted that Henry Soothey (Southey, Sothey) I, a gentleman from Rimpton, in Somerset, England, had asked for a patent because he and his associates were planning to bring 100 people to Virginia to establish a particular plantation. On June 10, 1622, Soothey received a patent for 900 acres, a grant subject to the governor's approval. Henry Soothey and his wife, Elizabeth, came to Virginia on the *Southampton* in 1622, accompanied by their six children and ten servants. However, between April 1623 and February 16, 1624, while the Sootheys were residing in urban Jamestown (1), Henry and all but one of his children (daughter Ann) died. In early May 1626 the General Court, apparently unaware that Henry Soothey I's son and primary heir, Henry II, was deceased, authorized Henry II to take up 900 acres, the quantity of land to which his late father was entitled on the basis of 18 headrights. In September 10, 1627, after the justices of the General Court learned that Henry Soothey II was dead, they awarded Mrs. Elizabeth Soothey a parcel of land on behalf of her late son, acreage in the east-central portion of Jamestown Island (VCR 1:575, 579; 3:643; MCGC 102, 152; CBE 39).

ELIZABETH SOOTHEY (SOUTHEY, SOTHEY) (MRS. HENRY SOOTHEY [SOUTHEY, SOTHEY] I)

Elizabeth, the wife of Henry Soothey (Southey, Sothey) I, came to Virginia on the *Southampton* in 1622 with their six children and ten servants. Mr. Soothey and his associates intended to establish a particular plantation and received a patent for 900 acres. However, between April 1623 and February 16, 1624, while the Sootheys were residing in urban Jamestown (1), Mr. Soothey and all but one of his children became ill and died. Mrs. Elizabeth Soothey and daughter Ann were still living in Jamestown when a muster was made of the community's inhabitants on January 24, 1625. The Soothey household had an ample supply of stored food and a hog. In May 1626 the General Court, apparently unaware that Henry Soothey I's son and heir, Henry II, had died, authorized Henry II to take up 900 acres, the quantity of land to which his late father was entitled on the basis of 18 headrights. In September 10, 1627, after it had become known that Henry Soothey II was dead, the General Court awarded Mrs. Elizabeth Soothey a parcel of land on behalf of her late son. The acreage (of unknown size) reportedly was near the late Rev. Richard Buck's house, in the east-central portion of Jamestown Island. On September 18, 1626, the General Court heard testimony about an event witnessed by Roger Dilke, who was residing at Mrs. Soothey's house in August 1626 (CBE 38, 56; MCGC 113, 115, 152; DOR 1:33).

ANN SOOTHEY (SOUTHEY, SOTHEY)(MRS. CHARLES HARMAR [HARMOR, HARMER, HARMAN] MRS. NATHANIEL LITTLETON) (SEE MRS. CHARLES HARMAR [HARMOR, HARMER, HARMAN])

Ann Soothey (Southey, Sothey) and her parents, Henry I and Elizabeth, came to Virginia on the *Southampton* in 1622 with her five siblings and ten servants. Mr. Soothey (a gentleman from Rimpton, Somerset, England) and some associates planned to establish a particular plantation, and he received a patent. However, between April 1623 and February 16, 1624, while the Sootheys were residing in urban Jamestown (1), Mr. Soothey and all but one of his children (Ann) became ill and died. She and her mother, Mrs. Elizabeth Soothey, were still living in Jamestown when a muster was made of the community's inhabitants on January 24, 1625. In May 1626 the General Court, apparently unaware that Ann's brother, Henry Soothey II, had died, authorized him to take up 900 acres, the quantity of land to which his late father was entitled on the basis of 18 headrights. But on September 10, 1627, after it became known that Henry II also was dead, the General Court awarded Mrs. Elizabeth Soothey a parcel of land in right of her late son: acreage in the east-central portion of Jamestown Island. When Ann Soothey reached maturity, she married Charles Harmar (Harmor, Harmer, Harman), Lady Elizabeth Dale's overseer in Accomack. Their union was mentioned by Accomack's justices in November 1635. After Charles Harmar's death, Ann wed Nathaniel Littleton, who also lived in Accomack and was one of the Eastern Shore's most prominent citizens. On October 20, 1643, Ann Soothey Harmar was issued a certificate that entitled her to 900 acres on behalf of her late parents, Elizabeth and Henry Soothey I, and brother, Henry II. Ann was still alive in 1645 and residing on the Eastern Shore (CBE 38, 56; WITH 573; EAE 27; AMES 1:xxx, 42; 2:xi, 42, 309-310, 398, 437).

HENRY SOOTHEY (SOUTHEY, SOTHEY) II

Henry Soothey (Southey, Sothey) II and his parents, Henry I and Elizabeth, came to Virginia on the *Southampton* in 1622 with his five siblings and ten servants. The elder Henry Soothey and some associates received a patent and planned to establish a particular plantation. Between April 1623 and February 16, 1624, while the Sootheys were residing in urban Jamestown (1), Henry Soothey II, his father, and all but one of his siblings became ill and died. In May 1626 the justices of the General Court, apparently unaware that Henry Soothey II was dead, authorized him to take up 900 acres, the quantity of land to which his late father was entitled on the basis of 18 headrights. On September 10, 1627, after it had become known that Henry II was deceased, the General Court awarded Mrs. Elizabeth Soothey a parcel of land on behalf of her late son. It was located in the east-central portion of Jamestown Island (CBE 39; MCGC 102, 152).

MARY SOOTHEY
(SOUTHEY, SOTHEY)

Mary Soothey (Southey, Sothey) and her parents, Henry I and Elizabeth, came to Virginia on the *Southampton* in 1622 with her five siblings and ten servants. Between April 1623 and February 16, 1624, while the Sootheys were residing in urban Jamestown (**1**), Mary, her father, and all but one of her siblings became ill and died (CBE 39; MCGC 102).

THOMAS SOOTHEY
(SOUTHEY, SOTHEY)

Thomas Soothey (Southey, Sothey) and his parents, Henry I and Elizabeth, came to Virginia on the *Southampton* in 1622 with his five siblings and ten servants. Between April 1623 and February 16, 1624, while the Sootheys were residing in urban Jamestown (**1**), Thomas, his father, and all but one of his siblings became ill and died (CBE 39; MCGC 102).

[NO FIRST NAME] SOOTHEY
(SOUTHEY, SOTHEY)

Henry Soothey (Southey, Sothey) I and his wife, Elizabeth, came to Virginia on the *Southampton* in 1622 with their six children and ten servants. Between April 1623 and February 16, 1624, while the Sootheys were residing in urban Jamestown (**1**), all but one of the Soothey children became ill and died. Two of the Soothey children's first names are unknown (CBE 39; MCGC 102).

[NO FIRST NAME] SOOTHEY
(SOUTHEY, SOTHEY)

Henry Soothey (Southey, Sothey) I and his wife, Elizabeth, came to Virginia on the *Southampton* in 1622 with their six children and ten servants. Between April 1623 and February 16, 1624, while the Soothey couple was living in urban Jamestown (**1**), all but one of their children became ill and died. Two of the Soothey children's first names are unknown (CBE 39; MCGC 102).

***

WILLIAM SOUTH

William South, a 22-year-old husbandman from Cheshire, England, came to Virginia in 1619 aboard the *Bona Nova*. He probably was a Virginia Company servant or tenant (FER 295, 296).

HENRY SOUTHERN
(SOUTHERNE, SAERTHORE)

On June 1, 1633, Henry Southern (Southerne, Saerthore) was in possession of some land on the Back River in Elizabeth City (**19**). In February 1639 he was identified as a resident of Kecoughtan (PB 1 Pt. 1:122; AMES 1:142).

JOHN SOUTHERN (SOTHERNE)

John Southern (Sotherne) of Tichfield, in Southampton County, England, was an experienced artisan. In 1620 he was sent to Virginia on the *George* by the Society of Southampton Hundred to take charge of the plantation the Society's investors intended to establish. Southern brought along the men and equipment needed to erect an ironworks at Southampton Hundred (**44**). However, when Southern arrived in the colony the governor sent him to the ironworks at Falling Creek (**68**), where he was wounded. Southern urged Virginia Company officials to support the construction of an ironworks in Virginia. On February 16, 1624, John Southern was residing in urban Jamestown (**1**), where he headed a household that included two other males. He was still there on January 24, 1625, sharing his well-supplied home with a manservant. However, in August 1624 the adventurers of the Society of Southampton Hundred asked the Virginia's governing officials to allow John Southern, whom they described as "old and weak," to return to his wife and children in England. Southern may have begun developing his property in the eastern end of Jamestown Island by spring 1625 because several months later he went to court several times to testify about events that had occurred in his neighborhood. John Southern, who was literate and respected, frequently was called on to serve as an attorney, juror, or administrator, and sometimes he was ordered to inventory people's estates or to testify as a witness. He represented the corporation of James City as a burgess from 1623 to 1624, and in 1630 and 1632.

During the mid- to late 1620s John Southern recorded Sir George Yeardley's testimony, worked with Mrs. Rowsley's accounts while she was ill, testified in court, managed the accounts attributable to the Rev. Richard Buck's estate, arbitrated disputes between two Jamestown Island residents, appraised the goods of Captains Ralph Hamor and John Martin, and served as Daniel Lacey's administrator. Most of those whom John Southern assisted were residents of Jamestown Island. He also paid people's bills, served as an attorney, took a turn at jury duty, proved wills, and testified in court. The only suggestion of wrongdoing was when he was accused of drunkenness (an infraction of moral law) during late August 1626. On May 8, 1626, the General Court awarded John Southern 50 acres of land under the headright system because he had transported a manservant to the colony in 1622. Southern indicated that he intended to take 10 of his 50 acres on Jamestown Island, using the remainder of his allotment for 40 acres at Blunt Point (**22**) in Elizabeth City. By November 1, 1627, Southern had patented two 12-acre tracts in the eastern end of Jamestown Island. A March 1629 reference to John Southern's dwelling in urban Jamestown indicates that it was situated near the stocks, which were located close to (or perhaps within) the fort. Therefore, it is likely that he had placed indentured servants on his rural property or leased it to tenants. The date of John Southern's death is uncertain (FER 449, 321; MCGC 8, 13, 40-41, 48-49, 55-56, 65, 69, 73-74, 79, 100-103, 115, 117, 126, 144, 150, 157-158, 165, 176, 178, 182, 184, 190, 198; VCR 4:9, 262, 504, 513-517, 556-557; STAN 53, 55-56; HAI 915; CBE 38, 55; HEN 1:128-129, 148, 154; PB 1 Pt. 1:55; SH 11-12; DOR 1:31).

ROGER SOUTHERN (SOTHERNE, SOTHERN)

On October 3, 1618, officials at Bridewell decided that Roger Southern (Sotherne, Sothern), a vagrant youth, would be sent to Virginia. His transportation was delayed but on February 27, 1619, was reinstated. He was among the youngsters rounded up on the streets of London so that they could be sent to the colony (CBE 10, 12).

WILLIAM SOUTHEY (SOUTHEREE)

On February 27, 1628, William Southey (Southeree), who was a surgeon on the ship *Samuel*, was in Jamestown (**1**). He informed the General Court that he had witnessed the wills made by Samuel Gilpin and Marmion Leake while they were aboard the *Samuel* (MCGC 168).

HENRY SOUTHWELL

On November 18, 1635, Henry Southwell was in possession of land in Elizabeth City (**19**) near the Back River (PB 1 Pt. 1:313).

RICHARD SOWRY

On February 5, 1620, officials at Bridewell decided that Richard Sowry would be sent to Virginia (CBE 18).

ELIZABETH SOWTHERTON

On July 8, 1627, Elizabeth Sowtherton shipped goods from London to Virginia on the *Ann* (CBE 78-79).

EDMUND (EDMOND) SPALDEN

On February 16, 1624, Edmund (Edmond) Spalden was living in Elizabeth City (**17, 18**) (CBE 44).

***

EDWARD SPALDING

On February 16, 1624, Edward Spalding, his wife, a son, and a daughter were living in urban Jamestown (**1**), in Mr. Cann's household (CBE 38).

MRS. EDWARD SPALDING

Mrs. Edward Spalding was living with her husband and a son and daughter in urban Jamestown (**1**) and on February 16, 1624, was a member of Mr. Cann's household (CBE 38).

[NO FIRST NAME] SPALDING

On February 16, 1624 Mr. and Mrs. Edward Spalding's son was living in urban Jamestown (**1**) in Mr. Cann's household (CBE 38).

[NO FIRST NAME] SPALDING

On February 16, 1624, Mr. and Mrs. Edward Spalding's daughter was living in urban Jamestown (**1**) in Mr. Cann's household (CBE 38).

***

ANN SPARK

Ann Spark came to Virginia in 1628 on the *Hopewell* at the expense of Adam Thorogood. On June 24, 1635, when Thorogood secured a patent, he listed her as a headright (PB 1 Pt. 1:179).

GEORGE SPARKE

On February 16, 1624, George Sparke was living on one of the plantations on the lower side of the James River, within the corporation of James City **(10-16)** (CBE 41).

JOHN SPARKES

Between April 1623 and February 16, 1624, John Sparkes died in Elizabeth City **(17, 18)** (CBE 45).

JOHN SPARKES (SPARKS)

John Sparkes (Sparks) came to Virginia on the *George* in 1621. On February 4, 1625, he was living at the Treasurer's Plantation **(11)**, where he was a servant in Treasurer George Sandys' household. Sometime prior to April 25, 1625, he witnessed Robert Mansteed's will. John Sparkes apparently became a successful planter, for on June 3, 1635, he patented 750 acres of land in Isle of Wight on the basis of 15 headrights. He may have been erroneously reported dead in 1624 (CBE 60; MCGC 56; PB 1 Pt. 1:239).

ROBERT SPARKES

Robert Sparkes came to Virginia sometime prior to 1611. He accompanied John Rolfe on the visit to Powhatan when the paramount chief was told that the colonists were detaining Pocahontas. In January 1613 Captain Samuel Argall left Robert Sparkes and four other men and boys as hostages when trading with the Indians for corn in the Potomac River (CJS 2:245; HAI 753, 808).

THOMAS SPARKES

Thomas Sparkes, an ancient planter, came to Virginia on the *Susan* in 1616. In early 1625 he was living on the Eastern Shore **(72-78)**, where he and William Bibbie jointly headed a well-supplied household. Thomas Sparkes was then age 24. During the early 1930s, when the late Nell M. Nugent prepared the first volume of her seminal work on Virginia Land Office Records, Thomas Sparkes was incorrectly identified as William Sparkes (CBE 69; DOR 1:71; NUG 1:xxxiii).

THOMAS SPARKES

On February 9, 1633, Thomas Sparkes was identified as one of Edward Hurd's servants when Thomas Harwood, as Hurd's agent, was ordered to pay Sparkes his freedom dues. When Edmund Scarborough patented some land in Accomack on February 21, 1638, he used Thomas Sparkes as a headright. By 1643 Sparkes had obtained his freedom and brought suit against Edmund Carter in Accomack's monthly court (MCGC 202; PB 1 Pt. 2:615; AMES 2:269).

WILLIAM SPARKES
(SEE THOMAS SPARKES)

WILLIAM SPARKES

On December 31, 1619, officials at Bridewell decided to send William Sparkes, a boy, to Virginia. He was among the youngsters rounded up from the streets of London so that they could be sent to the colony (CBE 15).

STEPHEN SPARROW
(SPARROWS)

On June 24, 1619, Stephen Sparrow (Sparrows) informed the Virginia Company that he had sent four men to Virginia and wanted headrights for them. On January 26, 1620, Virginia Company officials noted that Sparrow had given his share of Company stock to John Hope, a mariner. At the end of March 1620, Sparrow asked that Albiano Lupo be freed from his contract with the Virginia Company and given 100 acres. He asked for 150 acres on his own behalf and stated that he had sent three men to Virginia: John Slater and John Powell in 1617 and William Thisselton in 1618 (VCR 1:235, 300, 330).

***

EDWARD SPARSHOTT

Edward Sparshott came to Virginia on the *Seaflower* in 1621 and on February 16, 1624, was living on West and Shirley Hundred (Eppes) Island **(41)**. On January 22, 1625, Edward was identified as a 31-year-old servant in John Throgmorton's household. He eventually gained his freedom and on November 20, 1635, patented 100 acres in Charles City on Merchants Hope Creek, using the headrights of his wife, Maudelin, and a servant. In July 1638 Edward Sparshott patented some additional land in the same vicinity (CBE 36, 53; PB 1 Pt. 1:314; Pt. 2:581).

MAUDELIN CANE (CAVE) SPARSHOTT (MRS. EDWARD SPARSHOTT)

On November 20, 1635, when Edward Sparshott patented some land in Charles City, he used his wife, the former Maudelin Cane or Cave, as a headright (PB 1 Pt. 1:314).

***

JOHN SPEARMAN

John Spearman, a laborer, arrived in Jamestown (1) in early 1608 as part of the 1st Supply of new settlers (CJS 1:223; 2:161).

JOHN SPEDING

On August 23, 1631, officials at Bridewell decided that John Speding, a boy from Langborne, would be sent to Virginia (HUME 36).

HENRY SPEED (SPEEDE)

On May 30, 1625, Henry Speed (Speede), a sailor on the *Temperance*, testified before the General Court about how the late Henry Wilkinson disposed of his personal effects. Speed was in Jamestown (1) again on March 12, 1627, at which time he testified about an incident in the West Indies involving the ship *Saker* (MCGC 64, 143-144).

WILLIAM SPEED

William Speed came to Virginia in 1633 on the *Hopewell* at the expense of Adam Thorogood. On June 24, 1635, when Thorogood secured a patent, he listed Speed as a headright (PB 1 Pt. 1:179).

HENRY SPELLMAN (SPILLMAN, SPILMAN, SPELMAN)

Henry Spellman (Spillman, Spilman, Spelman), who was around 15 years old, arrived in Virginia in August 1609 aboard the *Unity*, a vessel in the fleet that carried Sir Thomas Gates, Sir George Somers, and the 3rd Supply of new colonists to Virginia. When he reached Jamestown (1) Spellman found only 80 men, who were then under the leadership of Captain John Smith. Smith sold Spellman to the Little Powhatan Indians, with whom he lived for a time. He escaped an attack by Powhatan and fled to the King of the Patomeck and stayed there until Captain Samuel Argall ransomed him for some copper. Henry Spellman wrote a narrative in which he described Virginia's Natives, the colony's fauna and flora, and some of the events that had occurred. Virginia Company officials and some of his contemporaries considered him the colony's most skillful linguist. Spellman left Virginia with Lord Delaware in 1611 but by 1616 had returned to the colony and again began serving as an interpreter. He made another trip to England in 1618 but returned on the *Treasurer* and was present when Edward Brewster, one of Lord Delaware's men, was tried in a martial court by Deputy Governor Samuel Argall. During the late spring or early summer 1619, Captain Henry Spellman angered high-ranking officials with statements he allegedly made to the Indian leader, Opechancanough. Robert Poole, a rival interpreter, claimed that Spellman had described Governor George Yeardley as a weak leader who soon would be replaced by Lord Rich—whom he likened to Lord Delaware—and that Rich would plant Chiskiack. Incumbent officials felt that Spellman's ill-advised remarks undermined their ability to deal with the Indians from a position of strength. Therefore, when the assembly met in July and August 1619, Captain Henry Spellman was censured and his rank was reduced from captain of the troop to Company servant. He also was ordered to serve the governor for seven years as a public interpreter. According to Captain John Smith, on March 22, 1622, when the Indians attacked Spellman's plantation (51) on March 22, 1622, two people were killed. His property, identified in 1637 as Speilmans, was located on the lower side of the James River, on the west side of Ward's Creek, and extended toward Flowerdew Hundred (53). Henry Spellman met with a violent death in March 1623 when he was killed by the Anacostan Indians while serving as an interpreter. Henry Spellman was the brother of Thomas Spellman, a gentleman who immigrated to Virginia in 1616. When a list of patented land was sent back to England in May 1625, Captain Henry Spellman, an ancient planter, was credited with some acreage in Charles City. In April 1625 the General Court's justices made note of a debt to his estate (HAI 481-495; POR 163 ftnt.; CJS 1:161, 271; 2:57, 232, 236, 257, 302, 320-321; EEAC 51; WITH 211-212; CBE 7, 13; FER 113, 143, 322; VCR 1:309-310; 3:174-175, 242, 244-245; 4:88-89, 230, 450, 554; MCGC 56; CO 24/489; PB 1 Pt. 2:485).

***

THOMAS SPELLMAN (SPILLMAN, SPILMAN, SPELMAN)

Thomas Spellman (Spillman, Spilman, Spelman), an ancient planter, came to Virginia on the *George* in 1616, at his own expense. On February 16, 1624, he was living in Elizabeth City (**18**). In December 1624 he was identified as a gentleman when he patented some land in that area. By early 1625 Thomas, who was age 24, had married Hanna (Hannah), the widow of Edward Hill. Also sharing the family home was Hanna's daughter, Elizabeth Hill. When a list of patented land was sent back to England in May 1625, Thomas Spellman was credited with 50 acres in Elizabeth City, acreage that had been seated (developed). Court testimony that he gave in April 1625 reveals that he was the brother of interpreter Henry Spellman, who was slain by the Indians in 1623. In September 1625 the General Court ordered Thomas to transfer a servant boy named Whiffe to Mr. Wooldridge in exchange for a servant who had run away. When the estate of Luke Aden was being settled in February 1626 in accord with his nuncupative will, one witness stated that Aden had claimed on his deathbed that Thomas Spellman, without authorization, had left a servant boy at Chaplin's Choice (**56**) in exchange for a barrel of corn. Thomas Spellman appeared before the General Court three times during October 1626: once to demand payment of a debt, another to prove Albano Lupo's will, and a third time to obtain a pass authorizing him to return to England. On January 10, 1627, Thomas Spellman was still in Virginia, at which time he posted a bond and agreed to administer the estate of the late Edward Hill, whose widow he had married two

years earlier. At issue was the protection of the assets of the decedent's orphan, Elizabeth Hill, Thomas Spellman's stepdaughter. Shortly thereafter Thomas went to England, where he became ill. He died in Truro in March 1627. When making a nuncupative will, Thomas Spellman indicated that he was from Truro, Cornwall, and Virginia, and stated that he wanted his wife, Hanna, to have his property in Virginia and wanted his daughter, Mary (Marie), to have his land in England (CBE 45, 65, 77; PB 1 Pt. 1:35; VCR 4:558; MCGC 56, 71, 94, 116, 121-122; EEAC 54; SH 10; SR 3115, 3118; DOR 1:58).

HANNA (HANNAH) SPELLMAN (SPILLMAN, SPILMAN, SPELMAN) (MRS. THOMAS SPELLMAN [SPILLMAN, SPILMAN, SPELMAN], MRS. ALEXANDER MOUNTNEY) (SEE MRS. EDWARD HILL, MRS. ALEXANDER MOUNTNEY)

Hanna (Hannah), who wed Thomas Spellman (Spillman, Spilman, Spelman), an Elizabeth City (**18**) gentleman, came to Virginia on the *Bona Nova* in 1620 and was the daughter of Richard Boyle of Blackfriars in London. On February 16, 1624, Hanna was living in Elizabeth City with her husband, Edward Hill. He died and was buried on May 15, 1624. By early 1625, 23-year-old Hanna had married her neighbor, Thomas Spellman. Also living in the Spellman household was Hanna's daughter, Elizabeth Hill. Thomas Spellman went to England sometime between January and March 1627. He became ill and died in Truro, leaving his real and personal property in Virginia to his wife, Hanna. Hanna Spellman later married Alexander Mountney of Accomack, with whom she had four children. She was still living on the Eastern Shore in 1645 but was dead by 1659 (CBE 44, 65; PB 1 Pt. 1:35; SH 10; EEAC 54; MEY 225-226; AMES 2:326, 353-354, 356-357, 361, 375-378, 386, 410-411).

MARY (MARIE) SPELLMAN (SPILLMAN, SPILMAN, SPELMAN)

In April 1627 when Thomas Spellman (Spillman, Spilman, Spelman) made a nuncupative will, he left his real and personal property in England to his daughter, Mary (Marie), indicating that she was then in Virginia. Mary probably resided in Elizabeth

City (**18**) in Thomas's household (EEAC 54; SH 10; SR 3115, 3118).

***

THOMAS SPELLMAN (SPILLMAN, SPILMAN, SPELMAN)

Thomas Spellman (Spillman, Spilman, Spelman) came to Virginia on the *George* in 1623 and on February 16, 1624, was living in the household of Richard Stephens, a Jamestown (**1**) merchant. He was still there on January 24, 1625, and was identified as a 28-year-old servant (CBE 38, 56).

***

WILLIAM SPENCE (SPENSE)

William Spence (Spense), an ancient planter, arrived in Jamestown (**1**) in 1608 in the 1st Supply of new settlers. Captain John Smith variously described him as a laborer, farmer, and gentleman, who was an honest and valiant man. While the colony was under the leadership of Sir Thomas Dale (1611–1616), Ensign William Spence reportedly was the first farmer to go forth to his own land, which was located in the eastern end of Jamestown Island, abutting the Back River. According to Edward Brewster, Ensign Spence was among those who in 1618 offered to employ the late Lord Delaware's workers so that they could be self-supporting. In July 1619 Ensign William Spence and Captain William Powell represented Jamestown in Virginia's first legislative assembly. Later in the year Ensign Spence served as a tobacco-taster; that is, he sampled portions of the tobacco crop to evaluate its quality. In January 1619 or 1620 William Spence and his partner, John Fowler, secured a patent for 300 acres between Glebe and Archer's Hope (College) Creeks, in Archer's Hope (**6**). However, Spence continued to reside on Jamestown Island and probably placed indentured servants on his Archer's Hope acreage, perhaps in a household headed by his partner, John Fowler. During the March 22, 1622, Indian attack, five people at Spence's house in Archer's Hope were slain, including John Fowler. Spence himself was in England at the time and set sail for Virginia on the *James* on July 31, 1622. In May 1625, when a list of Virginia land patents was sent back to England, Ensign William Spence was credited with 300 acres in Archer's Hope.

When a census was made of the colony's inhabitants on February 16, 1624, Spence, his wife, and their daughter, Sara (Sarah), were said to be residing on Jamestown Island. At the same time, however, Spence and his wife were reported as "lost" and, like two others with whom they were grouped, were listed among those who had died since February 1623. By early 1625 the Spence couple's 4-year-old daughter, Sara, had been entrusted to the care of a guardian, Mrs. Susan Bush, a 20-year-old widow and resident of Elizabeth City (**18**). In August 1624 John Johnson I was ordered to replace the roof of the late Ensign Spence's house and to repair his fences. Three months later the General Court ordered Sara Spence's guardians to have her Archer's Hope property surveyed. Tenant Thomas Farley was in residence there by late November 1625. Sara's guardians apparently were slow to respond, for in October 1626 they were told that they would be fined if they failed to survey the land. By April 3, 1627, 6-year-old Sara Spence was dead and her legal guardians were ordered to inventory her estate. Ensign William Spence should not be confused with William Spencer, who also lived on Jamestown Island (CJS 1:223; 2:161, 247, 302; STAN 52; C 24/490; VCR 3:153, 228, 443-444; 4:556; MCGC 4-5, 19, 27, 122; CBE 39-40; PB 1 Pt. 1:15; FER 400).

MRS. WILLIAM SPENCE (SPENSE)

On February 16, 1624, when a census was made of the colony's inhabitants, Ensign William Spence (Spense), his wife, and their daughter, Sara (Sarah), were residing on Jamestown Island (**1**). At the same time, however, Spence and his wife were reported dead, having been "lost." The Spence couple's daughter, Sara, was entrusted to the care of a guardian, Mrs. Susan Bush, a 20-year-old widow and resident of Elizabeth City (**18**) (CBE 39-40, 64; MCGC 42).

SARA (SARAH) SPENCE (SPENSE)

On February 16, 1624, when a census was made of the colony's inhabitants, Ensign William Spence, his wife, and their Virginia-born daughter, Sara (Sarah), were residing on Jamestown Island (**1**). Simultaneously, however, Spence and his wife were reported "lost," and their names were included among those who had died since

April 1623. The Spence couple's daughter, Sara, survived and was entrusted to the care of a guardian, Mrs. Susan Bush, a young widow, who was partially responsible for the orphan's inherited assets. In early 1625 Sara, who was then 4 years old, was living with Mrs. Bush in Elizabeth City (18). In August 1624 John Johnson I was ordered to make repairs to the late Ensign Spence's house and property, probably rendering it tenantable. Three months later the General Court ordered Sara Spence's guardians to have her Archer's Hope (6) property—a tract on which renter Thomas Farley was residing in late November 1625—surveyed. Sara's guardians were slow to respond and in October 1626 were ordered to proceed or be fined. By April 3, 1627, Sara Spence was dead and the Rev. George Keith of Elizabeth City was ordered to inventory her estate and pay her debts (CBE 40, 64; MCGC 42, 76, 147).

***

KATHREN SPENCER (SPENSER)

On February 16, 1624, Kathren Spencer (Spenser) was a servant in Governor Francis Wyatt's urban Jamestown (1) household (CBE 38).

PETER SPENCER (SPENSER)

On July 3, 1634, Peter Spencer (Spenser) testified against Jeremy Blackman, stating that he tortured a ship's boy on a voyage to Virginia (CBE 117).

RICHARD SPENCER

On October 3, 1618, officials at Bridewell decided that Richard Spencer, who had been born on Fenchurch Street, would be sent to Virginia (CBE 10).

THOMAS SPENCER

On February 16, 1624, Thomas Spencer was living in Warresqueak (26), probably at Bennett's Welcome (CBE 42).

***

WILLIAM SPENCER (SPENSER) I

William Spencer (Spenser) I, an ancient planter and yeoman, came to Virginia on the *Sarah* or *Susan Constant*. On August 14, 1624, he secured a patent for a narrow ridge of land on Jamestown Island (1), fronting on the James River. William Claiborne later made an official survey of the Spencer property. On January 24, 1625, William Spencer was residing on his property in rural Jamestown Island, sharing a well-supplied home with his wife and 4-year-old daughter, both of whom were named Alice (Allice). Son William II had died sometime after February 16, 1624. In January 1625 William Spencer I was credited with two houses, some cattle, swine and goats, and a boat. He later inherited the property of his neighbor John Lightfoot. From 1620 until at least 1626 William Spencer served as overseer of the servants whom Captain William Peirce had on his leasehold in the Governor's Land (3) and—after the late John Rolfe's death—on his plantation on the lower side of the James River. In 1622 Rolfe's, Peirce's, and Spencer's servants were living together on Rolfe's holdings. In 1633 William Spencer served as a burgess for Mulberry Island (21), another area in which Peirce had an extensive investment. In 1629 Spencer patented 290 acres of land using the headright of his current wife, Dorothy, who came to Virginia on the *Neptune* in 1619. During the early 1630s he patented 1,350 acres of land abutting Lawnes Creek, and in 1640 he served as official tobacco viewer for the territory that extended from Lawnes Creek to Hog Island. Spencer retained his Jamestown Island property until around 1637-1638. He conducted business on Captain William Peirce's behalf as late as January 1655 (CBE 40, 56; MCGC 99, 181, 200; EAE 89; PB 1 Pt. 1:9, 120, 249, 255; Pt. 2:501; HEN 1:203; Surry County Deeds and Wills 1652-1672:116; MEY 581-582; DOR 1:35).

ALICE (ALLICE) SPENCER (SPENSER) I (MRS. WILLIAM SPENCER [(SPENSER] I)

On January 24, 1625, Alice (Allice) I, the wife of William Spencer (Spenser) I, was living on Jamestown Island (1) with her husband and 4-year-old daughter, Alice (CBE 56).

DOROTHY SPENCER (SPENSER) (MRS. WILLIAM SPENCER [SPENSER] I)

In 1629, when William Spencer (Spenser) I patented 290 acres of land, he used his wife

Dorothy as a headright and said that she had come to the colony on the *Neptune* in 1619. It is unclear whether William married Dorothy before or after he wed wife Alice, with whom he was living in January 1625 (MCGC 200).

ALICE (ALLICE) SPENCER (SPENSER) II

Alice (Allice) Spencer (Spenser) II, the daughter of William and Alice Spencer, was living in Jamestown (1) with her parents on January 24, 1625. She was then age 4 and probably was born in Virginia (CBE 56).

ANNE SPENCER (SPENSER) (MRS. WILLIAM COCKERAM)

William Spencer (Spenser) I and his wife produced a daughter named Anne. A note that the Spencers' daughter Elizabeth sent to William Cockerham in 1654 reveals that he was married to her sister, Anne (MEY 583; PB4:72).

ELIZABETH SPENCER (SPENSER) (MRS. ROBERT SHEPPARD, MRS. THOMAS WARREN, MRS. JOHN HUNNICUTT)

Elizabeth, William Spencer (Spenser) I's daughter, wed three times in succession, marrying Robert Sheppard, Thomas Warren, and John Hunnicutt (MEY 581-582).

WILLIAM SPENCER (SPENSER) II

William Spencer (Spenser) II, the young son of William Spencer I, died on Jamestown Island (1) between February 16, 1624, and January 24, 1625 (CBE 56).

***

GREGORY SPICER

Gregory Spicer came to Virginia on the *Trial* in 1618. In early 1625 he was living on Captain Samuel Mathews' plantation (15), where he was a 22-year-old servant (CBE 60).

JOHN SPILTIMBER

On July 7, 1635, when Thomas Harwood patented some land on Skiffs Creek in Warwick County, he used John Spiltimber as a headright (PB 1 Pt. 1:208).

ELEANOR (ELINOR) SPRAD (SPRADD, SPRADE, SPRAGE)

On February 16, 1624, Eleanor (Elinor) Sprad (Spradd, Sprade, Sprage) was living in urban Jamestown (1), where she was a servant in merchant Edward Blaney's household. In June she became engaged to Robert Marshall, but before the marriage bans were posted in the parish church, she accepted another man's proposal. Eleanor was made to apologize to the congregation of the church in Jamestown for this infraction of the law. Eleanor later testified that she overheard Mr. and Mrs. Alnutt talk about how the Rev. David Sandys tried to entice the 12-year-old orphan Mara Buck into an inappropriate relationship (MCGC 15-17; CBE 35).

RUDOLPH (RUDALPH, RADOLPH, RADULPH) SPRAGGON (SPRAGON, SPRAGLING)

On June 23, 1635, Rudolph (Rudalph, Radolph, Radulph) Spraggon (Spragon, Spragling) set sail for Virginia on the *America*, which was under the command of Captain William Barker, a mariner who lived in Jamestown (1). All of the men and women aboard the ship had been given a certificate by the minister of Gravesend attesting to their conformity to the Church of England's precepts, and all probably were indentured servants. On August 18, 1644, Rudolph Spraggon received a patent for a 1-acre lot in the western end of Jamestown Island, a parcel he seems to have occupied. Rudolph Spraggon "of James City" was identified as a debtor in the April 17, 1649, court minutes of what became Surry County in 1652 (CBE 152; PB 2:11; Surry County Deeds, Wills, &c. 1652-1672:108).

ROBERT SPRING

Robert Spring came to Virginia in 1634 on the *John and Dorothy* at the expense of Adam Thorogood. On June 24, 1635, when Thorogood secured a patent, he listed Spring as a headright (PB 1 Pt. 1:179).

RICHARD SPURLING

On February 16, 1624, Richard Spurling was living at Flowerdew Hundred (53) (CBE 37).

BARNABUS SQUIRES

In 1619 Barnabus Squires, a carpenter and millwright, went to Virginia on the *Garland*. He appears to have been one of the settlers going to Southampton Hundred **(44)** (FER 137).

PETER STABER (STAVER)

On February 16, 1624, Peter Staber (Staver) was living in the Neck O'Land **(5)** (CBE 35).

OLIVER ST. JOHN

On June 24, 1619, Virginia Company officials learned that two people had given Oliver St. John their shares of Virginia land (VCR 1:235).

[NO FIRST NAME] STACIE (STACY)

According to Captain John Smith, in 1610 Master Stacie (Stacy) and some other men sought revenge against the Pasbehay Indians. He was one of the first Jamestown **(1)** settlers (CJS 2:236).

[NO FIRST NAME] STACIE (STACY)

On March 25, 1629, the General Court learned that Mr. Stacie (Stacy) had told John Atkins that his (Atkins') servant, Thomas Hall, was a hermaphrodite (MCGC 195).

ROBERT STACIE (STACY)

In July 1619 Robert Stacie (Stacy) was chosen as a burgess for Martin's Brandon **(59)**, Captain John Martin's plantation. However, the community ultimately was denied seat and voice in the assembly (VCR 3:154).

THOMAS STACIE (STACY, STACEY)

In September 1619 Thomas Stacie (Stacy, Stacey) of Maidstone in Kent, England, bequeathed his Virginia land to his nephew, William Joye. When the decedent's will was proved, probate was granted to Robert Joye. In 1620 Thomas Stacie was identified as a Virginia Company investor (EEAC 55; WITH 148; CJS 2:282).

***

PETER STAFFERTON (STASSERTON)

On September 3, 1623, Peter Stafferton (Stasserton), a gentleman, witnessed the will of John Atkins of Warresqueak **(26)**, who bequeathed him his household furnishings. On February 16, 1624, Stafferton and his wife, Mary, were living on the Maine or Governor's Land **(3)**. On December 21, 1624, Stafferton was a juror, participating in the inquest held to investigate the drowning death of George Pope II, a child who lived on Jamestown Island **(1)**. A month later Stafferton was ordered to pay his debt to Captain Peirce. On February 5, 1627, Peter Stafferton testified that he had witnessed the agreement made by merchant John Williams and William Lovell, master of the *Aid*. Several months later Stafferton shipped goods from London to Virginia on the *Thomas and John*. In December 1628 Stafferton was sued by Thomas Flint. Although the General Court postponed the case, Captain Samuel Mathews was ordered to take custody of Stafferton's tobacco until a decision could be made. On July 15, 1631, Peter Stafferton was among the Virginia planters who asked the king for relief from customs duties. In 1635 and 1638 he patented land in Elizabeth City **(18, 19)** (WITH 35-36; MCGC 38, 40, 139, 180; CBE 39, 79; G&M 165; PB 1 Pt. 1:306; Pt. 2:557).

MRS. PETER STAFFERTON (STASSERTON)

On February 16, 1624, Mrs. Peter Stafferton (Stasserton) and her husband were living on the Maine **(3)** (CBE 39).

***

RICHARD STAFFORD

On June 3, 1620, Richard Stafford of Staplehurst, Kent, a 25-year-old gentleman, testified that in 1619 the *Treasurer*, which went to the West Indies in consort with a Dutch vessel, brought 25 Africans to Bermuda. Stafford, who appears to have been aboard the *Treasurer* and an eyewitness to the events he described, testified that the ship left Bermuda in February 1620 (EAE 81).

WILLIAM STAFFORD

William Stafford came to Virginia on the *Furtherance*. In early 1625 he was living in

Elizabeth City (**18**) in the household headed by Nicholas Martiau and was described as a 17-year-old servant (CBE 64).

WILLIAM STAFFORD

William Stafford came to Virginia on the *Furtherance* in 1622. In early 1625 he was living in Elizabeth City (**18**) in the household headed by Francis Mason and was described as a 16-year-old servant. William may have been the same youth simultaneously attributed to Nicholas Martiau's household (CBE 65).

***

WILLIAM STAFFORD

On August 23, 1634, William Stafford, a Warwick County planter, acquired a 100-acre leasehold on Skiffs Creek. In 1635 he patented 300 acres there, using the headright of his wife, Rebecca. William probably was one of the young male servants who lived in Elizabeth City (**18**) in early 1625 (PB 1 Pt. 1:154, 305).

REBECCA STAFFORD (MRS. WILLIAM STAFFORD)

On November 12, 1635, when William Stafford patented some land on Skiffs Creek, he used the headright of his wife, Rebecca, stating that she was entitled to 50 acres on account of her personal adventure (PB 1 Pt. 1:305).

***

[NO FIRST NAME] STAGG (STEGG?)

In June 1635 Mr. Stagg (perhaps Stegg) was identified as Captain John Prynn's factor in Virginia (EAE 53-54).

DANIEL STALLINGS

Daniel Stallings, a jeweler, arrived in Jamestown (**1**) in 1608 in the 1st Supply of new colonists (CJS 1:222; 2:162).

EDWARD STALLINGS ALIAS ROECROFT

In 1615 Edward Stallings alias Roecroft was in New England with Captain John

Smith and co-authored an account of their adventures. Smith later called Stallings a gallant soldier and gentleman. Stallings returned to New England in December 1619, having been hired to undertake a fishing voyage. He captured a French vessel in New England and then cruised down the coast, intending to spend the winter in Virginia. Shortly after he arrived in the colony, Edward Stallings had a heated dispute with Captain William Eppes and fought a duel with him at Southampton (Smyth's) Hundred (**44**). Stallings, who received a blow to the head from Eppes's sheathed sword, collapsed and died. Afterward, Governor George Yeardley assigned the use of Stallings' ship, which was in poor condition, to Southampton Hundred and entrusted Stallings' men to Captain John Martin. The captain of Stallings' vessel later allowed it to run aground at Newportes News (**24**). However, Edward Stallings' personal property was saved for his widow, who was in England (CJS 1:351, 356; 2:266, 428, 431, 440; VCR 1:274; 3:121, 242; 4:511; MCGC 37).

JOHN STAMFORD

John Stamford died in Elizabeth City (**17, 18**) and was buried on April 20, 1624 (CBE 67).

NATHANIEL STANBRIDG

Nathaniel Stanbridg died at Warresqueak (**26**) sometime after April 1623 but before February 16, 1624 (CBE 58).

JAMES STANDISH

On January 30, 1625, James Standish was living on the Maine (**3**) in a household he shared with Robert Cholme. James came to Virginia on the *Charitie* (CBE 58).

MATHEW STANELING (STAVELING)

Mathew Staneling (Staveling) died at Martin's Hundred (**7**) sometime after April 1623 but before February 16, 1624 (CBE 42).

SYMON (SIMON) STANFEILD

Symon (Simon) Stanfeild came to Virginia in 1634 on the *John and Dorothy* at the expense of Adam Thorogood. On June 24,

1635, when Thorogood secured a patent, he listed Symon as a headright (PB 1 Pt. 1:179).

HENRY STANLEY

On January 15, 1620, officials at Bridewell decided that Henry Stanley, a vagrant born in Lancashire who had been brought in from Millbrook, would be sent to Virginia (CBE 17).

MORRIS STANLEY

Morris Stanley came to Virginia on the *Hopewell* in 1624. In early 1625 he was living on the Virginia Company's land in Elizabeth City (**17**), on the east side of the Hampton River. Stanley was then a 26-year-old servant in William Barry's household (CBE 68).

ROGER STANLEY

Roger Stanley came to Virginia on the *Abigail* in 1620. On January 30, 1625, he was living on the Maine (**3**) and was a 27-year-old servant in Dr. John Pott's household. On February 20, 1626, Thomas Pritchard informed the General Court that when Roger Stanley told Thomas Lister (Leyster) that Dr. Pott owed him some tobacco, Lister disputed the amount. Both men grabbed swords, then abandoned them and fought with their bare hands. Lister seized Stanley's sword, broke it, and then inflicted a wound to Stanley's arm (CBE 58; MCGC 94-95).

JOHN STANTON

John Stanton died at Flowerdew Hundred (**53**) sometime after April 1623 but before February 16, 1624 (CBE 37).

***

RICHARD STAPLES

Although Richard Staples, his wife, and their child were among those reportedly killed at Martin's Hundred (**7**) during the March 22, 1622, Indian attack, he in fact survived. Afterward, William Peirce went to the plantation to retrieve Staples' corn, which had escaped destruction. In February 1624 Richard Staples was among the burgesses who signed the General Assembly's rebuttal to Alderman Johnson's claims that

conditions in the colony were good between 1607 and 1619. In May 1625 Richard Staples was credited with 150 acres of land in Archer's Hope (**6**). His brother, Robert, had been Martin's Hundred's minister (VCR 1:535; 3:570; 4:556; HAI 915; MCGC131).

MRS. RICHARD STAPLES

On March 22, 1622, when the Indians attacked Martin's Hundred (**7**), Mrs. Richard Staples and her child were killed (VCR 3:570).

[NO FIRST NAME] STAPLES

When the Indians attacked Martin's Hundred (**7**) on March 22, 1622, Mr. and Mrs. Richard Staples' child was killed (VCR 3:57).

ROBERT STAPLES

In October 1621 Virginia Company officials learned that the Rev. Robert Staples, who had a brother in Virginia, was willing to become the minister at Martin's Hundred (**7**). On May 8, 1622, before Company officials received word of the March 22nd Indian attack, they noted that Staples wanted an allowance and that he planned to take his wife and child to the colony (VCR 1:535, 544, 635).

***

RICHARD STARKES (STORKS)

On March 22, 1622, when the Indians attacked a settlement across the river from Sir George Yeardley's plantation, Flowerdew Hundred (**53**), Richard Starkes (Storks) was killed. In November 1624 Richard was identified as having been one of Yeardley's servants at Flowerdew who had been under the supervision of Sergeant Henry Fortesque. Starkes may have died at Weyanoke (**52**), which was across the James River from Flowerdew Hundred and also was owned by Yeardley (VCR 3:568; MCGC 27).

ELIZABETH STARKEY

Elizabeth Starkey, a young maid, came to Virginia in 1621 on the *Warwick*. She was the daughter of Frauncis (Francis) Starkey, a tailor at Three Cranes in Vitney. On February 16, 1624, Elizabeth was living in urban Jamestown **(1)**, where she was a member of merchant Edward Blaney's household (FER 309; CBE 38).

JOHN STARR

In Spring 1630 officials in England learned that John Starr, master of the *Sun*, had died in Virginia. They also were informed that the *Sun* was a leaky ship (EAE 21-22).

THOMAS STARRE

On December 31, 1619, the Bridewell Court decided that Thomas Starr, who was being detained in the Middlesex House of Correction, would be sent to Virginia (CBE 14).

ELIZABETH STAYNER (STAYMER)

On February 26, 1620, officials at Bridewell decided that Elizabeth Stayner (Staymer), who was being detained at Newgate Prison, would be sent to Virginia (CBE 19).

JANE STECKIE

Sometime prior to September 19, 1625, Jane Steckie became one of cape merchant Abraham Peirsey's servants. He received her from the purser of the *Elizabeth* in exchange for another servant whom he had been promised. It is probable that Jane resided in the Peirsey home at Flowerdew **(53)** or in Jamestown **(1)**, where Abraham Peirsey also had a residence (MCGC 71).

THOMAS STEED

Thomas Steed, one of Samuel Jordan's servants, arrived in Virginia in July 1620 on the *Falcon*. On December 10, 1620, when Jordan patented some land, he used Steed as a headright (PB 8:125).

WILLIAM STENT

On June 23, 1627, when John Throgmorton of Shirley Hundred **(41)** made a nuncupative will, he bequeathed his servant, William Stent, two years of his time (MCGC 153).

STEPHEN

According to Captain John Smith, on May 20, 1607, Stephen, a sailor, accompanied Captain Christopher Newport on an exploratory voyage up the James River. Therefore, Stephen would have spent time in Jamestown **(1)** (HAI 102).

STEPHEN

A man named Stephen came to Virginia on the *Furtherance* and died in Jamestown **(1)** sometime after April 1623 but before February 16, 1624 (CBE 39).

JOHN STEPHENS (STEEVENS, STEVENS)

John Stephens (Steevens, Stevens) came to Virginia on the *Warwick* sometime prior to October 1622, when he and Ralph Baylie asked the Virginia Company to see that the colony's governor gave them some land. In 1623 Stephens reportedly purchased some sack (wine) from Sir George Yeardley, contrary to law. Even so, he apparently was considered a respectable citizen, for in August 1623 he served on a jury. On February 16, 1624, John Stephens was living in bricklayer John Jackson's household at Martin's Hundred **(7)**. He was still there on February 4, 1625, and was age 35. Although he was listed among Jackson's servants, he probably was one of the Society of Martin's Hundred's tenants. John Stephens died sometime prior to April 25, 1625. His will was witnessed by William Green, a surgeon who had attended him while at sea, and was presented to the General Court by mariner Toby Felgate. Jamestown **(1)** merchant Richard Stephens, probably a kinsman, agreed to allow John's estate to be inventoried. John Stephens reportedly brought Andrew Waters to Virginia as a servant (VCR 2:107; MCGC 4-5, 56, 65; CBE 42, 62).

RICHARD STEPHENS

Richard Stephens died at Martin's Hundred **(7)** sometime after April 1623 but before February 16, 1624 (CBE 42).

***

RICHARD STEPHENS

Richard Stephens, a painter-stainer and investor in the Virginia Company, obtained a share of land from Lady Cecily Delaware in 1622. He also acquired some acreage from

Francis Carter, who had procured the land from Lady Delaware. Shortly thereafter, Stephens outfitted two servants, John and Hastings Bateman, and assembled 21 hogsheads of goods, sending both the men and supplies to Virginia on the *James*, which left England on July 31, 1622. Richard Stephens himself came to the colony on the *George* in 1623. As a merchant, he had agreed to contribute toward the relief of the colony and, in collaboration with John Hart, was supposed to decide where a bloomery should be built. As soon as Richard Stephens arrived in Jamestown (**1**), he secured a patent for a small urban lot on the waterfront and quickly developed his property. He also became a burgess, representing the community's merchants. On February 16, 1624, when a census was made of the colony's inhabitants, Richard and seven servants were residing together in Jamestown. Some of Richard Stephens' mercantile activities involved the Bennett family, London merchants who had established a plantation in Warresqueak (**26**). In 1624 Richard Stephens and George Harrison fought a duel, which resulted in Harrison's death. When a muster was taken on January 24, 1625, Stephens and his servants comprised a household in urban Jamestown. He was credited with three houses and a boat. One of Richard's servants, Wassell Rayner, was a distiller, who came to the colony in 1619. Two others, Francis Fowler and Austen Smith, were carpenters. During the 1620s Richard Stephens made several appearances before the General Court. He participated in an inquest, inventoried estates of the deceased, and sued to collect debts from Richard Kingsmill and others. During 1625 John Bath (a gentleman) died in the Stephens home, and Richard served as his administrator. On another occasion, Richard agreed to have John Stephens' estate inventoried. He also paid for medical treatment given to Andrew Stephens, who in 1626 was a servant in Richard's home.

Around 1628 Richard Stephens married Elizabeth, the daughter of cape-merchant Abraham Peirsey. She eventually inherited her father's plantation, Flowerdew Hundred (**53**), and repatented it in her own name. The couple produced two sons: Samuel and William. In 1630, during Sir John Harvey's administration, Richard Stephens was named to the Council of State, on which he served until 1636. In 1632 he was made a commissioner of the local court that settled minor disputes in what became Warwick County. By that time he had patented some land on the Back River in Elizabeth City. Richard clashed openly with Governor John Harvey and was among those who sought to have him ousted from office. In 1635 the two men came to blows, and the enraged Harvey knocked out some of Stephens' teeth. Richard Stephens died ca. 1636, leaving to his wife, Elizabeth, his 500-acre Warwick River plantation called Boldrup (VCR 1:622, 625; 4:245-247, 257, 262-269; PB 1 Pt. 1:1, 5, 7, 116, 160; Pt. 2:484; FER 400; STAN 32, 53; HEN 1:128-129, 178, 187; CBE 38, 47, 56, 103; MCGC 38, 45, 56, 89, 101, 117-118, 160, 164, 193; EAE 24; MEY 587-588; NEI 135; DOR 1:33).

ELIZABETH PEIRSEY STEPHENS (MRS. RICHARD STEPHENS, MRS. JOHN HARVEY) (SEE ELIZABETH PEIRSEY STEPHENS HARVEY)

Elizabeth, the daughter of cape merchant Abraham and Elizabeth Peirsey of Jamestown (**1**), came to Virginia in 1623 with her sister, Mary, on the *Southampton*, a vessel owned by Captain John Harvey. Around 1628 Elizabeth, who was age 18, married Jamestown merchant Richard Stephens, with whom she produced sons Samuel and William. Elizabeth Peirsey Stephens, as her father's heir, inherited Flowerdew Hundred (**53**), which she patented on September 20, 1636, and repatented a month later. Richard Stephens died in 1636, leaving her Boldrup, 500 acres in Warwick County, which she patented on September 23, 1637. Afterward, she married incumbent Governor John Harvey, a titled nobleman many years her senior and one of her late husband's enemies. The Harveys lived in Jamestown, probably in the residence that sometimes served as the colony's statehouse. After Sir John Harvey fell on hard times and was replaced as governor, Elizabeth returned with him to England. She died there sometime prior to September 15, 1646, when Sir John made his will (PB 1 Pt. 1:387, 395; Pt. 2:484; MEY 481-482, 588-589).

SAMUEL STEPHENS

Samuel Stephens, the son of Richard and Elizabeth Peirsey Stephens, was born around 1629. As his father's primary heir, he stood to inherit his home lot in urban Jamestown **(1)**. After Richard Stephens' death in 1636, two pieces of land—2,000 acres in Elizabeth City and 500 acres in Warwick County—were transferred to Samuel's name, although Samuel's mother, Elizabeth, enjoyed life-rights in a dower third of both parcels. When Samuel matured he married Frances Culpeper. On January 1, 1653, they signed a marriage contract in which Samuel agreed to give Frances the plantation known as Boldrup if he died without producing an heir. In October 1662 Samuel Stephens was made commander of Albemarle (in Carolina), and five years later he commenced serving a three-year term as its governor. It is uncertain whether Samuel retained his father's Jamestown lot after his interests shifted to Carolina, but it was while he was there that the western part of his lot was used for the construction of a turf fort. Samuel Stephens died sometime prior to March 1670, without having produced a living heir. In accord with his 1653 marriage contract, Boldrup descended to his widow, Frances, who in June 1670 married Sir William Berkeley (PB 1 Pt. 1:387; HEN 2:321-325; MEY 587; NEI 341-342).

WILLIAM STEPHENS

William Stephens, the son of Richard and Elizabeth Peirsey Stephens and the brother of Samuel Stephens, was born around 1630. He stood to inherit his mother's land in Warwick County. Around 1656, when William Stephens died, he was identified as a cooper (MEY 588-589; PB 4:97).

***

THOMAS STEPHENS

On February 27, 1619, the Bridewell Court decided that Thomas Stephens, a boy, would be sent to Virginia. He was part of a large group of young people rounded up from the streets of London and sent to the colony. On March 22, 1622, when the Indians attacked Weyanoke **(52)**, Thomas Stephens was killed. He was identified as one of Sir George Yeardley's people (CBE 12; VCR 3:569).

THOMAS STEPNEY

Thomas Stepney came to Virginia on the *Swan* in 1610 and was an ancient planter. In early 1625 he was living in Elizabeth City **(18)**, where he was a 35-year-old household head. Thomas lived alone and had an ample supply of stored food and defensive weaponry (CBE 66; DOR 1:62).

ADAM STEVELY

Adam Stevely, John Slaughter's servant, came to Virginia sometime prior to May 30, 1635, when Slaughter used him as a headright (PB 1 Pt. 1:169).

JOHN STEVENSON

John Stevenson, a gentleman, came to Virginia in 1607 and was one of the first Jamestown **(1)** colonists (CJS 2:141).

THOMAS STEVENSON

On December 31, 1619, officials at Bridewell decided that Thomas Stevenson, who had been brought in by the marshal of Middlesex, would be sent to Virginia (CBE 14).

AUGUSTINE (AUGUSTIN) STEWARD

Augustine (Augustin) Steward went to Virginia on the *Neptune* in 1618 with Lord Delaware. When he testified in the suit undertaken by the Earl of Warwick against Edward Brewster in May 1622, he identified himself as a 37-year-old gentleman and resident of Hoxton, in Middlesex. He said that Brewster had behaved harshly toward Lord Delaware and others. He also described the *Neptune's* encounter with the *Treasurer* while both ships were at sea and their subsequent arrival in Jamestown **(1)**. When Steward testified again in April 1623, he said that he was from St. Leonard in Shoreditch and was age 38. He testified a final time in 1624 (SR 9947; C 24/489; HCA 13/44; EAE 13).

JAMES STEWARD

On November 20, 1622, James Steward of Buckham, Scotland, asked Virginia Company officials to give him a patent because he intended to take 100 people to the colony (VCR 2:132).

JOHN STEWARD

On December 31, 1619, officials at Bridewell decided that John Steward, who had been brought in by the marshal of Middlesex, would be sent to Virginia (CBE 14).

EDWARD STOCKDELL

On February 14, 1624, Edward Stockdell was living in Elizabeth City (**18**) (CBE 44).

WILLIAM STOCKER

William Stocker came to Virginia on the *Bonny Bess* in 1623 and was John Uty's servant. On February 16, 1624, he was living on the Maine (**3**), just west of Jamestown Island. When John Uty patented some land on November 3, 1624, he used Stocker's headright and said that he had transported Stocker to the colony. On February 4, 1625, William Stocker was living at Hog Island (**16**) and was identified as one of Uty's servants (CBE 39, 61; PB 1 Pt. 1:14).

JAMES STOCKTON

On September 10, 1622, James Stockton was in Elizabeth City (**18**) and witnessed Captain John Wilcocks' will (SH 5).

JOHN STOCKTON (STOGDEN, STOCKDEN)

According to testimony taken before the General Court in March 1624, John Stockton (Stogden, Stockden) gave a tobacco note to John Roe (Row), who passed it along to surgeon Thomas Bunn. Since Roe and Bunn were residents of the Governor's Land (**3**), James Stockton may have lived there, too (MCGC 50).

***

JONAS STOCKTON (STOGDEN, STOCKDEN)

The Rev. Jonas Stockton (Stogden, Stockden) came to Virginia in 1620 on the *Bona Nova*. On July 25, 1621, the Virginia Company noted that he was going to be replaced as Elizabeth City's minister by the Rev. Francis Bolton, who was accompanying Captain Nuce to the colony. On February 16, 1624, Stockton was living on the west side of the Hampton River in Elizabeth City (**18**). In October 1624 he was appointed minister for that area, replacing the late Rev. William White. The area he served lay between the Hampton River and Tucker's Creek. In early 1625 the

Rev. Jonas Stockton, who was age 40, headed a well-provisioned household that included four free males and two indentured servants. Timothy Stockton, age 14 and part of the household, probably was a kinsman, perhaps the clergyman's son. During the 1620s the Rev. Jonas Stockton made numerous appearances before the General Court. He testified against Captain John Martin, and he went to court to prove wills and collect debts. However, he also was sued as a debtor. In September 1625 the General Court's justices learned that Stockton's house had burned. The fire destroyed a receipt that proved he had satisfied a debt to John Pountis (one of Southampton Hundred's officers), from whom he had obtained two men. In August 1626 the Rev. Stockton was made a commissioner of Elizabeth City's monthly court. In March 1628 he was accused of wrongfully detaining William Ellet as a servant. He acquired part of what had been the Virginia Company's land (**17**) in September 1627, but he died within a year (VCR 3:485; CBE 44, 66; MCGC 21-22, 70, 77, 87, 106, 123, 146, 171; PB 1 Pt. 1:79, 90-91, 147; DOR 1:62).

TIMOTHY (TIMOTHEY, TIMOTHEE) STOCKTON (STOGDEN, STOCKDEN)

Timothy (Timothey, Timothee) Stockton (Stogden, Stockden) came to Virginia on the *Bona Nova* in 1620. On February 16, 1624, he was living in Elizabeth City (**18**) in a household headed by the Rev. Jonas Stockton. In early 1625 Timothy was identified as age 14 and free. He may have been the minister's son (CBE 44, 66).

***

THOMAS STOCKTON (STOGDEN, STOCKDEN)

Thomas Stockton (Stogden, Stockden) left England on the *James* on July 31, 1622, accompanying John Cornish (FER 400).

PETER STOFFORD

On July 31, 1627, Peter Stofford was identified as having shipped goods from London to Virginia on the *Thomas and John* (CBE 79).

WILLIAM STOGDILL

On April 26, 1631, the General Court decided to hold an inquest into the suspected suicide of William Stogdill (MCGC 480).

[NO FIRST NAME] STOKES

On May 12, 1619, Lieutenant Stokes requested some Virginia land in compensation for his lengthy service to the colony (VCR 1:217).

[NO FIRST NAME] STOKES

On February 4, 1624, Virginia Company officials learned that someone named Stokes was a crew member on the ship that belonged to Edward Stallings and Sir Fernando Gorges, a vessel that ran aground at Newportes News (24). Afterward, Stokes decided to stay in Virginia as a servant of the colony. He may have been one of Stallings' men who remained behind with Captain John Martin (VCR 4:513).

***

CHRISTOPHER STOKES (STOAKS, STOCKS, STOIKS, STOAKES)

On July 31, 1622, Christopher Stokes (Stoaks, Stocks, Stoiks, Stoakes) and his wife, Mary, set sail for Virginia on the *James*, at the expense of merchant Edward Bennett. Their young son, William Stokes, who was then age 3, probably accompanied them. The Virginia Company sent Christopher Stokes some bedding, a saw, and several containers of goods on behalf of the Society of Southampton Hundred, which suggests that he was to go to their plantation, Southampton Hundred (44). Although the Stokes family was not included in the February 16, 1624, census, they appear to have been residents of Jamestown Island (1), where the family's presence is well documented. In late December 1624 Christopher Stokes served on the jury that conducted an inquest following a Jamestown Island child's drowning death, and 5-year-old William Stokes was a witness in the case. By 1630 Christopher Stokes had moved to what later became Warwick County and represented the Denbigh (23) area as a burgess. In 1635 he patented some land in Elizabeth City (18) (FER 321, 322, 400; MCGC 38; HEN 1:139, 148; STAN 55; PB 1 Pt. 1:223, 264-265).

MARY STOKES (STOAKS, STOCKS, STOIKS, STOAKES) (MRS. CHRISTOPHER STOKES [STOAKS, STOCKS, STOIKS, STOAKES])

Mary, the wife of Christopher Stokes (Stoaks, Stocks, Stoiks, Stoakes), left England on the *James* on July 31, 1622, and went to Virginia at the expense of merchant Edward Bennett. They brought along their 3-year-old son, William. The Stokes family most likely resided on Jamestown Island (1) (FER 321, 322, 400; MCGC 38).

WILLIAM STOKES (STOAKS, STOCKS, STOIKS, STOAKES)

On July 31, 1622, Christopher Stokes (Stoaks, Stocks, Stoiks, Stoakes) and his wife, Mary, set sail for Virginia on the *James*, probably bringing along their young son, William. In 1624 the Stokes most likely lived on Jamestown Island (1), where William, who was then 5 years old, witnessed the drowning death of George Pope II, a local youngster. Christopher and William Stokes were among those who testified at a coroner's inquest (FER 400; MCGC 38).

***

***

JOHN STOKES (STOAKS, STOCKS, STOIKS, STOAKES)

John Stokes (Stoaks, Stocks, Stoiks, Stoakes) and his wife, Ann, came to Virginia on the *Warwick*. On February 16, 1624, they were living in the rural part of Jamestown Island (1) with their infant. On January 24, 1625, the Stokes couple was still there and had a very modest supply of stored food. Their baby apparently died during the year (CBE 40, 56; DOR 1:34).

ANN STOKES (STOAKS, STOCKS, STOIKS, STOAKES) (MRS. JOHN STOKES) (STOAKS, STOCKS, STOIKS, STOAKES)

Ann, who wed John Stokes (Stoaks, Stocks, Stoiks, Stoakes), came to Virginia on the *Warwick*. They were living in the rural part of Jamestown Island (1) on February 16, 1624, with their baby. On January 24, 1625, the Stokes were still there, but their infant apparently had died (CBE 40, 56).

[NO FIRST NAME] STOKES (STOAKS, STOCKS, STOIKS, STOAKES)

John and Ann Stokes (Stoaks, Stocks, Stoiks, Stoakes) and their infant were living in the rural part of Jamestown Island (1) on February 16, 1624. By January 24, 1625, the child apparently had died, for no youngsters were attributed to Stokes household (CBE 40, 56).

***

ROBERT STOKES (STOAKS, STOCKS, STOIKS, STOAKES)

On December 24, 1619, the Bridewell Court decided that Robert Stokes (Stoaks, Stocks, Stoiks, Stoakes) would be sent to Virginia (CBE 14).

JOHN STOKELEY ALIAS TAYLOR (SEE JOHN TAYLOR ALIAS STOKELEY)

RICHARD STON

Richard Ston died at Martin's Hundred (7) sometime after April 1623 but before February 16, 1624 (CBE 42).

***

ANDREW STONE

Captain John Stone, one of Andrew Stone's brothers, began trading on the Eastern Shore sometime prior to 1626. On June 4, 1635, when Andrew's brother William Stone patented a large tract of land between Hungers and Mattawomans Creek, he used Andrew's personal adventure as a headright (PB 1 Pt. 1:244; AMES 1:xxxi).

JOHN STONE

John Stone came to Virginia sometime prior to 1623 and settled at Martin's Hundred (7). Although Virginia Company officials claimed that he left Martin's Hundred, he was still living there on February 16, 1624, when a census was taken of the colony's inhabitants. Stone, a mariner, was authorized to trade with the Indians of the Eastern Shore. Because Stone and merchant-mariner Humphrey Rastell had agreed to provide Henry Woodward with four male servants but had failed to do so, the General Court assigned three of Stone's servants to Woodward and allowed Woodward to take them to Warresqueak (26). Stone was supposed to provide a fourth servant on his return from England. In September 1626 the General Court determined that Martin's Hundred's leader, William Harwood, had evicted Captain John Stone from the house he had built there at his own expense, and ordered Harwood to pay Stone. In March 1628 the General Court learned that Captain John Stone had offloaded some meal in the West Indies that Edward Hurd (an English merchant) had sent to Thomas Harwood. According to Dutch mariner David Devries, Captain Stone, a mariner, was in a group that had dinner at Governor John Harvey's home in urban Jamestown (1) on March 12, 1633. Later in the year, when Stone was transporting grain and cattle to Boston, he was killed by Indians on the Connecticut River. His heir was William Stone, a resident of the Eastern Shore, who brought suit against Stephen Charlton, the decedent's trading partner on the *Virginia*, which undertook voyages to the island of St. Christopher (FER 572; CBE 42; MCGC 104, 114, 134, 170-171; DEV 35; AMES 1:xxxi, xxxvi, xlvii, 23-24).

WILLIAM STONE

On September 15, 1619, William Stone set sail for Virginia on the *Margaret* of Bristol and was one of the people being sent to Berkeley Hundred (55) to work under Captain John Woodlief's supervision. William was supposed to serve the Society of Berkeley Hundred's investors for six years in exchange for 30 acres of land. Sometime prior to February 9, 1629, he received a tobacco bill from Richard Wheeler. By June 4, 1635, William had patented 1,800 acres in Accomack (72-78). Local court records reveal that he was the brother of Andrew Stone and Captain John Stone, who had been trading on the Eastern Shore since 1626. By 1634 William Stone had become a commissioner of the county court. Sometime prior to February 1636 he married Verlinda, the daughter of ancient planter Thomas Graves. William went on to become a sheriff and vestryman. In 1645 he was residing on the Eastern Shore, in what had become Northampton County. By 1648 he had become the third proprietary governor of Maryland (CBE 14; VCR 3:188, 198,

213; MCGC 185; PB 1 Pt. 1:244; AMES 1:8, 17-18, 49; 2:xii-xiii, 444).

***

FRANCIS STONE

On December 18, 1626, Francis Stone informed the General Court that Thomas Gates had acknowledged owing George Riddle some tobacco (MCGC 128).

JAMES STONE

On February 13, 1629, James Stone was designated the overseer of Jamestown (1) merchant Thomas Warnett's will (SH 11-12).

JOHN STONE

John Stone came to the Virginia on the *George* in 1621. He was brought to the colony from Bermuda at the expense of Treasurer George Sandys, who used him as a headright when patenting some land in December 1624. On February 16, 1624, Stone was living on the lower side of the James River at the Treasurer's Plantation (11). He was still there on February 4, 1625, and was identified as a young male servant in one of Sandys' households. On December 9, 1628, John Stone, who indicated that he could prove that he was over the age of 21, said that George Sandys was supposed to train him in a trade but had failed to do so. Lieutenant Thomas Purfoy testified on Stone's behalf, stating that the young man's friends had paid the bulk of his passage. The General Court ordered Sandys to see that John Stone was trained by the end of his year's term of service. Otherwise, he was obliged to pay Stone for his work (CBE 41, 60; PB 1 Pt. 1:16; MCGC 179).

***

JOHN STONE

John Stone came to Virginia on the *Swan*, and on February 4, 1625, he and his wife, Sisley, were living on Hog Island (16). On August 28, 1626, he testified about an incident that occurred on Hog Island at a site known as Powell's Hole, near the location of his dwelling. On January 10, 1627, John Stone was identified as a blacksmith when he presented the General Court with an inventory of Walter Blake's estate (CBE 61; MCGC 110, 130).

SISLEY STONE (MRS. JOHN STONE)

Sisley, who married John Stone, came to Virginia on the *Seaflower*. On February 4, 1625, she and her husband were living on Hog Island (16) (CBE 61).

***

***

MAXIMILLIAN STONE I

Maximillian Stone I came to Virginia on the *Temperance* in 1620 or 1621 at the expense of Sir George Yeardley. On February 4, 1625, he was living on Hog Island (16) with his wife, Elizabeth, and their 9-month-old son, Maximillian II. Maximillian Stone I was then a 36-year-old servant. On January 3, 1626, the General Court decided that he was to serve Lady Temperance Yeardley until February 1627. However, on January 11, 1627, he was identified as a resident of Martin's Hundred (7) when he testified against Richard Crocker, who was accused of saying that some public officials were price-gouging. Stone said that he had been at Mr. William Harwood's house in August 1626 when the inflammatory statements were made. On September 20, 1628, Thomas Flint used the headrights of Elizabeth and Maximillian Stone I when he patented some land, but noted that he had acquired the headrights from Sir George Yeardley (CBE 61; MCGC 83, 132, 166; PB 1 Pt. 1:59).

ELIZABETH STONE (MRS. MAXIMILLIAN STONE I)

Elizabeth, the wife of Maximillian Stone I, came to Virginia on the *Temperance* in 1620 or 1621 at the expense of Sir George Yeardley. On February 4, 1625, Elizabeth, who was a Yeardley servant, was living on Hog Island (16) with her husband and their 9-month-old son, Maximillian II. On September 20, 1628, Thomas Flint used Elizabeth and Maximillian Stone I as headrights when he patented some land, indicating that he had acquired the headrights from Sir George Yeardley (CBE 61; MCGC 166; PB 1 Pt. 1:59).

MAXIMILLIAN STONE II

On February 4, 1625, Maximillian Stone II, the 9-month-old child of Maximillian and

Elizabeth Stone, was living with his parents on Hog Island **(16)**, in Sir George Yeardley's settlement (CBE 61).

***

MOSES (MOYSES) STONE (STONES, STON)

Moses (Moyses) Stone (Stones, Ston), who was from Longworth in Berkshire, arrived in Jamestown **(1)** on September 12, 1623, on the *Bonny Bess*. When he took the oath of supremacy, he said that he was 18 years old. On February 16, 1624, Moses was residing in urban Jamestown in merchant George Menefie's household, where he was a servant. By early 1625 he had moved to Elizabeth City **(18)**, where he was living in a household headed by John Downman. Moses was then said to be age 16 (MCGC 6; CBE 38, 63).

ROBERT STONE

On April 26, 1622, Robert Stone, who was in England, testified that he had been in Virginia in August 1618 when the *Neptune* arrived. He said that there had been a dispute between Edward Brewster and Richard Beamond, the *Neptune's* master. Stone said that he had given Brewster some boxes in which the late Lord Delaware's goods could be stored. He said that those who arrived on the *Neptune* were in need of provisions but that the Virginia planters refused to supply them because of Brewster's attitude. Robert Stone said that he had been present in Jamestown **(1)** when Edward Brewster was tried in a martial court (SR 9947; C 24/489).

***

[NO FIRST NAME] STONE (MRS. [NO FIRST NAME] STONE) MRS. ROBERT GODWIN (GODWYN)

Sometime prior to February 9, 1633, Theophilus Stone's widowed mother married Robert Godwin (Godwyn), who assumed responsibility for the orphan's inheritance. As Godwin was associated with Elizabeth City **(17, 18)**, his wife probably was living there, too (MCGC 202).

THEOPHILUS STONE

On February 9, 1633, the justices of the General Court noted that the late Theo-philus Beristone had bequeathed 1,000 pounds of tobacco to Theophilus Stone, an orphan. In accordance with the decedent's will, Zachary Cripp retained the orphan's inheritance but wanted to transfer it to Robert Godwin (Godwyn), his stepfather. Cripps was supposed to deliver a cow to Godwin for the orphan's use before May 1st. Godwin, in turn, was supposed to post a bond as part of his fiduciary responsibility. Cripps and Godwin were associated with Elizabeth City **(17, 18)**, raising the possibility that Theophilus Stone lived there too (MCGC 202).

***

THOMAS STONE

On August 28, 1628, Thomas Stone shipped goods from London to Virginia on the *London Merchant* (CBE 84).

***

ALEXANDER STONER (STOMER, STOMMER, STONAR, STONNAR)

Alexander Stoner (Stomer, Stommer, Stonar, Stonnar) came to Virginia sometime prior to June 22, 1635, when he patented 350 acres that abutted the James City Parish glebe in Archer's Hope **(6)**. By that time he had married Jane, the widow and heir of John Cooke, a Virginia Company servant. The patent Alexander received noted that on June 20, 1620, John Cooke had received a certificate from Governor George Yeardley entitling him and his heirs to 100 acres when he fulfilled his term of indenture. Alexander Stoner claimed the 100 acres that wife Jane had inherited and acquired some additional acreage on the basis of headrights. In February 1638 Alexander mortgaged his 350 acres to Jamestown merchant John Chew but eventually was able to redeem his property and regain an unencumbered title. On August 23, 1637, Alexander was identified as a brick-maker when he received a patent for a 1-acre lot on the isthmus then connecting Jamestown Island **(1)** to the mainland. He also had 27 acres contiguous to the Governor's Land **(3)** and Glasshouse Point **(2)**, plus some acreage on the Chickahominy River. Eventually he was obliged to forfeit his 27 acres on the mainland, and he disposed of his acreage on the Chickahominy. In 1638 John Jackson and Richard Kingsmill's daughter, Elizabeth, listed

Alexander Stomer as a headright, raising the possibility that they had paid for his transportation to the colony (PB 1 Pt. 1:254, 306, 379; Pt. 2:466-467, 595, 600, 616; 2:150).

JANE COOKE STONER
(MRS. JOHN COOKE,
MRS. ALEXANDER STONER
[STOMER, STOMMER, STONAR,
STONNAR])
(SEE JANE COOKE)

Sometime prior to by June 22, 1635, Jane, the widow of John Cooke, a Virginia Company servant, married brick-maker Alexander Stoner (Stomer, Stommer, Stonar, Stonnar). Alexander patented 350 acres that abutted the James City Parish glebe, claiming the 100 acres to which Jane was entitled as her late husband's heir. Stoner's patent noted that on June 20, 1620, John Cooke had received a certificate from Governor George Yeardley entitling him and his heirs to 100 acres when he fulfilled his term of indenture (PB 1 Pt. 1:254).

***

JOHN STONER

In May 1635 John Stoner, a Virginia planter, was in England. In August 1635 he was identified among those receiving tobacco from Richard Bennett of Warresqueak (26) (EAE 54).

***

JOHN STORER

John Storer of St. Andrew by the Wardrobe, London, died in Virginia sometime prior to May 5, 1632. His widow, Mary, renounced administration of his will (CBE 101).

MARY STORER
(MRS. JOHN STORER)

On May 5, 1632, Mary Storer, who lived in England, was identified as the widow of John Storer, who died in Virginia. She declined the right to administer his will (CBE 101).

***

ROBERT STORY (STORYE)

According to court testimony given by Richard Brewster on May 4, 1622, in the suit involving the disposition of the late Lord Delaware's estate, Robert Story (Storye) took his room and board in Deputy Governor Samuel Argall's house in Jamestown (1). In late April 1622 Story, who identified himself as a 36-year-old gentleman from St. Benet Finck in London, said that he went to Virginia with Argall and departed with him in spring 1619. He was a witness in the suit Lady Cecily Delaware undertook against Sir Samuel Argall (C 24/489; 24/490; SR 9946).

WILLIAM STRACHEY

William Strachey, a minor Virginia Company investor, set sail from England in June 1609 on the *Seaventure*, the vessel transporting Sir Thomas Gates and Sir George Somers, which ran aground in Bermuda. Later, Strachey's description of his shipmates' adventures in Bermuda became the basis of Shakespeare's play, *The Tempest*. William Strachey and his companions arrived in Jamestown (1) on May 23, 1610. When Lord Delaware reached the colony in early June, he designated Strachey, a member of the Council of State, as the colony's secretary. Strachey held that position until his departure from Virginia in 1611. A letter Strachey wrote in mid-July 1610 describes the Jamestown fort's size and appearance at that time. He also recounted the colonists' temporary abandonment of Jamestown and the unexpected arrival of Lord Delaware. When William Strachey left Virginia during the late summer of 1611, he took to England a copy of the *Lawes Divine and Martiall*, compiled sequentially by Sir Thomas Gates and Sir Thomas Dale. Strachey died in England around 1634 (CJS 1:193; 2:27-28, 281; HAI 27, 381, 383, 418-419, 427-430, 433, 440-441, 459, 594-689; STAN 21, 28; FOR 3:2:2-62).

WILLIAM STRACHEY

William Strachey came to Virginia on the *Temperance* in 1620 and on February 16, 1624, was living at Flowerdew Hundred (53). He was still there on January 20, 1625, and was identified as a 17-year-old servant in the household of Sir George Yeardley (CBE 37, 61).

[NO FIRST NAME] STRANGE

On October 25, 1629, an orphaned boy named Strange reportedly approached officials at Bridewell and offered to go to Virginia with Captain Turber (HUME 35).

WILLIAM STRANGE (STRAINGE, STRAUNGE)

In 1619 the Bridewell Court decided that William Strange (Strainge, Straunge), a boy who was being detained, would be sent to Virginia. He set sail shortly thereafter on the *George*. On February 16, 1624, Strange was living at Flowerdew Hundred (**53**). By January 24, 1625, he had moved to Jamestown (**1**), where he was an 18-year-old servant in Sir George Yeardley's household (CBE 13, 37, 54).

JOSEPH STRATTON

Joseph Stratton came to Virginia sometime prior to March 1630, when he began serving as a burgess for Nutmeg Quarter, in what was then Elizabeth City (**18**) but later became Warwick County. In July 1631 he was one of the Virginia planters who asked the king for relief from customs and indicated that his hogsheads of tobacco bore the initials *JS*. In September 1632 Joseph Stratton became the burgess for the territory between Waters Creek and Marie's Mount (**24**). In July 1635 he patented some land that he purchased from Sir Francis Wyatt's attorney, William Pierce, most likely not his first land acquisition. Warwick County records indicate that Joseph Stratton was still alive in 1656 (HEN 1:148, 179; G&M 164; PB 1 Pt. 1:212; DUNN 567).

GEORGE STRAYTON ALIAS PELTON (SEE GEORGE PELTON ALIAS STRAYTON)

WILLIAM STREETS

On September 12, 1626, William Streets testified before the General Court about Captain Thomas Dowse's abandonment of his wife in Kinsale. He said that Dowse became involved with a married woman, with whom he fled to Ireland (MCGC 113).

SAMUEL STRINGER

Samuel Stringer, a 27-year-old merchant tailor from Cheshire, England, came to Virginia in 1619 aboard the *Bona Nova*. He was killed during the March 22, 1622, Indian attack on the settlers living at the College (**66**). On October 7, 1622, Virginia Company officials noted that Governor George Yeardley was having Stringer's estate inventoried and planned to send that compilation to England with John Tuke on the *Abigail*. Samuel Stringer's sisters, Jane Glover and Bridgett Hubbard, who were in England, were named the decedent's administrators (FER 295; VCR 2:106; 3:566).

THOMAS STROUD

Court testimony taken in 1629 reveals that Thomas Stroud, with the assistance of Gyles (Giles) Harrod, stole two hens from William White. Afterward, Stroud privately admitted to Robert Martin what they had done. The General Court decided that Thomas Stroud had persuaded Gyles Harrod to steal. Therefore, as punishment, Stroud was to be tied to the gallows and whipped by Harrod. All of the men involved in this incident lived on the lower side of the James River, within the corporation of James City (**8-16**) (MCGC 200).

RICHARD STUBBS

Richard Stubbs was supposed to serve Edward Bennett for four years. However, because Bennett's men broke open Stubbs's chest and lost his indentures, it was unclear how much time (if any) was left on his contract. On November 13, 1626, the justices of the General Court decided to free Stubbs unless Bennett (then in England) could send over a duplicate copy of his contract and prove that he had longer to serve (MCGC 124).

THOMAS STUDLEY (STOODIE)

Thomas Studley (Stoodie), a gentleman, came to Virginia in 1607 and was one of the first Jamestown (**1**) colonists. According to George Percy, Studley served briefly as cape merchant and died on August 28, 1607. He was co-author of an account that Captain Smith included in his *Proceedings* (CJS 1:20, 203, 208, 214, 221; 2:141, 153, 160; HAI 99).

SIMON (SYMON) STURGIS (TURGIS)

Simon (Symon) Sturgis (Turgis) came to Virginia in 1618 on the *William and Thomas*. On February 16, 1624, he was living at West and Shirley Hundred (**41**). He was still there on January 22, 1625, and headed a well-supplied household with his partner, Henry Bagwell. Simon was then 30 years old. In 1625 Simon Sturgis informed the General Court that he had been present when Andrew Dudley was attacked by Indians at West and Shirley Hundred and was slain. Sturgis made another appearance before the General Court in August 1626. This time he testified about John Joyse, a runaway servant who allegedly stole a canoe. In 1628 Sturgis brought suit against Michael Marshall, a merchant, who failed to deliver two indentured servants for whom Sturgis's brother had paid. In July 1631 Simon Sturgis was among the Virginia planters who asked the king for relief from customs duties. He indicated that his hogsheads of tobacco bore the mark *SS*. Two years later Sturgis signed another petition, this time claiming that he and other Virginia planters would suffer if Maurice Thompson was given a monopoly on the colony's shipping. In 1636 he and two others who identified themselves as London merchants purchased the plantation known as Martin's Brandon (59) from Captain John Martin's heirs. Simon Sturgis was still alive in 1639–1640 and dispatched a shipment of tobacco from Virginia (CBE 36, 52, 115-116; MCGC 51, 105, 160, 165; G&M 187-188; SR 3506; E 190/44/1; PB 1 Pt. 1:415; Pt. 2:910).

JOHN STURLING

On July 21, 1627, officials at Bridewell indicated that John Sturling was going to Virginia as a servant (CBE 79).

JOHN STURT

On January 8, 1631, it was reported that John Sturt had shipped blankets from Barnstaple to Virginia on the *Friendship* of Bideford (CBE 94).

JOHN SUERSBY

On March 22, 1622, when the Indians attacked Weyanoke (52), John Suersby, one of Sir George Yeardley's people, was killed (VCR 3:569).

ALEXANDER SUFFAMES (SUSSAMES)

Alexander Suffames (Sussames) died at Warresqueak (26) sometime after April 1623 but before February 16, 1624 (CBE 42).

***

THOMAS SULLY (SULLEY)

Thomas Sully (Sulley), an ancient planter, came to Virginia in 1611 on the *Sarah*. When a census was made of the colony's inhabitants in March 1620, Sully was on a trading voyage to Accomack and Acohanock. On February 16, 1624, Sully and his wife were living in the Neck O'Land (5). On August 14, 1624, when he patented 6 acres in the extreme western end of Jamestown Island (1), he was identified as a yeoman. Thomas already owned a parcel at Black Point, in the eastern end of Jamestown Island, which he sold to Sir George Yeardley on January 24, 1625. In November 1624 Thomas Sully appeared twice before the General Court: once when he testified that he and his wife had witnessed the will of John Phillimore, who left Sully a barrel of corn, and another time when he was censured (and fined) for hunting on Sunday. By early 1625, 36-year-old Thomas Sully and his wife, Maudlyn, had moved to Elizabeth City (18), where they were residing in the household of William Julian. On November 30, 1628, Thomas Sully was described as an Elizabeth City planter when he patented 94 acres near the head of the Hampton River; at the same time, his 6-acre patent on Jamestown Island was to be doubled (CBE 35, 64; FER 159; MCGC 27, 33, 45; PB 1 Pt. 1:12, 65).

MAUDLYN SULLY (MRS. THOMAS SULLY [SULLEY])

Maudlyn, who married ancient planter Thomas Sully (Sulley), came to Virginia on the *London Merchant* in 1620. On February 16, 1624, Maudlyn and her husband, Thomas, a Jamestown Island landowner (1), were living in the Neck O'Land (5). In July she witnessed the will of John Phillimore, who lived on the lower side of the James River in what became Surry County. By early 1625 Maudlyn and Thomas Sully had moved to Elizabeth City (18). Maudlyn was then 30 years old (CBE 35, 64; MCGC 27).

***

JOHN SUMMERFIELD (SUMMFIL, SUNNFIL)

On February 16, 1624, John Summerfield (Summfil, Sunnfil) was living on the Eastern Shore (72-78) (CBE 46).

NICHOLAS SUMMERFIELD (SUMERFILD)

Nicholas Summerfield (Sumerfild) came to Virginia on the *Sampson* in 1619. In early 1625 he was living on the Eastern Shore and was a 15-year-old servant on the plantation of Captain William Eppes (**74**) (CBE 68).

JOHN SUMNER

On September 1, 1631, John Sumner, a boy being detained at Bridewell, was identified as someone a merchant was sending to Virginia (CBE 96).

SUSAN

In early 1625 a 12-year-old girl named Susan, who came to Virginia in 1624 on the *Swan*, was living in Elizabeth City (**18**) in Richard Yonge's household (CBE 63).

EDWARD SUTTON

On November 20, 1622, Edward Sutton was one of the detainees in Newgate Prison who was pardoned because of an outbreak of jail fever and sent overseas (CBE 29).

NICHOLAS SUTTON

On July 31, 1622, Nicholas Sutton left England on the *James* with William Felgate. On February 16, 1624, he was living at Chaplin's Choice (**56**). He was killed there by the Indians sometime prior to January 21, 1625 (FER 400; CBE 37, 51).

WILLIAM SUTTON

On February 16, 1624, William Sutton was living in one of the communities on the lower side of the James River (**8-15**) within the corporation of James City (CBE 40).

ARTHUR SWAINE (SWAYNE)

On November 21, 1621, the Virginia Company issued a patent to Arthur Swaine (Swayne) and his associates, who were planning to take 100 people to Virginia. In July 1622 he was identified as master of the *Flying Hart*. Apparently the plans made by Swaine and his fellow investors fell apart, for in October 1624 Company officials were still discussing Swaine's intention to take people to the colony. The voyage eventually took place but not until after the Virginia Company's charter had been revoked. Governor Francis Wyatt sent word to England that the *Flying Hart* of Flushing (in the Netherlands), sent out by Arthur Swaine and William Constable on the authority of the Virginia Company, had arrived in Jamestown (**1**) in December 1625. Wyatt said that half of the ship's passengers (which included servants) were poorly provisioned and were famished when they came ashore (VCR 1:534, 553-554, 561-562; 2:74; 3:643; CBE 71).

STEPHEN SWAINE

Stephen Swaine came to Virginia on the *Bonaventure* in 1634 at the expense of Adam Thorogood. On June 24, 1635, Thorogood used Swaine as a headright when patenting some land (PB 1 Pt. 1:179).

WILLIAM SWANDAL

On March 22, 1622, when the Indians attacked Captain John Berkeley's plantation at Falling Creek (**68**), William Swandal was killed (VCR 3:570).

ANN SWANN

On March 20, 1630, Ann Swann testified in the suit involving Edward Rossingham and Ralph, Sir George Yeardley's administrator. She said that she had been living in Virginia 12 years earlier, when Rossingham and Captain John Martin arrived from England, and knew that around 1621 Rossingham had undertaken a fishing voyage on Sir George's behalf (SR 9962, 9963; C 24/560, 24/419).

RICHARD SWANN

On January 22, 1619, officials at Bridewell decided that Richard Swann, a boy who had been brought in, would be detained until he could be sent to Virginia (HUME 19).

***

WILLIAM SWANN (SWAN)

William Swann (Swan) and his wife, Judith, immigrated to Virginia sometime prior to November 1635, when he patented 1,200 acres of land on the south side of the James

River, directly across from Jamestown Island's western end. His acreage abutted west on Burrow's or Smith's Mount (**8**), later known as Four Mile Tree, and extended eastward, taking in Paces Paines (**9**) and Halfway Neck, formerly Perry's Point. Swann acquired his patent on the basis of 24 headrights, each of which entitled him to 50 acres of land. It is uncertain to what extent Swann developed his property, but in time it became his family seat, Swann's Point. William Swann also laid claim to a 300-acre parcel near Upper Chippokes Creek. A genealogical account compiled by William's grandson, Samuel Swann, in 1707 reveals that William resided on the eastern part of his acreage near the promontory known as Swann's Point. William Swann and his wife, Judith, had a son, Thomas, who was born in 1616 and became their principal heir (PB1 Pt 1:293; WITH 535).

JUDITH SWANN (SWAN) (MRS. WILLIAM SWANN [SWAN])

Judith, who married William Swann (Swan) and had a son, Thomas Swann, died in February 1636 and was buried at Swann's Point. She was age 47 (WITH 534).

THOMAS SWANN (SWAN)

Thomas Swann (Swan), the son of William and Judith Swann, was born in May 1616. His name first appeared in official records in November 1635, when he repatented 1,200 acres that had belonged to his father, a plantation that formerly had been Captain William Perry's (**9**) but became known as Swann's Point. By 1640 Thomas had been appointed the official tobacco viewer for the area on the lower side of the James River between Smith's Fort and Grindon Hill, and during the 1640s and 50s served as a burgess. Over the years he married five times. In 1652, when Surry County was formed, he became high sheriff, an indication that he already was a county justice. In March 1655 Swann was held responsible for the death of his servant Elizabeth Buck, although her demise was ruled an involuntary act. In 1656 and 1658 he patented two large tracts of land in Surry, and in 1668 he claimed 500 acres in James City County. Colonel Thomas Swann I made his home at Swann's Point in Surry and had a tavern at Wareneck. He made numerous appearances before the Surry County court and from time to time undertook action

in the General Court. He occasionally was sued, and in March 1660 he was fined for failing to collect some of the tobacco owed as taxes. In 1672 Swann had a dispute with Colonel Nathaniel Bacon. Occasionally Swann was called on to audit accounts and arbitrate disputes. He lost a suit against William Momford, from whom he had accepted an expensive necklace as collateral, and he was sued by Thomas Rabley of Jamestown (**1**). However, he also won suits from time to time. Thomas Swann was named to the Council of State in 1659 and served through the late 1660s. In 1661, when the assembly decided that tan houses were to be built in each county, the vestries of Southwark and Lawnes Creek parishes agreed that Surry County's should be built on Colonel Swann's land. In 1671 Swann purchased part of a Jamestown rowhouse from his son-in-law, Henry Randolph, and a year later was named to the commission given the task of building a brick fort in Jamestown. He acquired two pieces of land in Jamestown (**1**), one urban and one rural, and erected a tavern on his urban lot. Although Swann reportedly was sympathetic to Bacon's views and his daughter-in-law was the daughter of executed rebel William Drummond, his popular house of entertainment was torched on September 19, 1676, when the rebel Nathaniel Bacon burned the capital city. Some of Colonel Thomas Swann's detractors dubbed him "ye great toad." In 1677 the Special Commissioners sent by the king to investigate the causes of Bacon's Rebellion stayed in the Swann home at Swann's Point. After Governor Berkeley left office, Swann regained his Council seat and rebuilt his tavern in Jamestown. Colonel Thomas Swann died on September 16, 1680, and was buried at Swann's Point (WITH 534-535; PB 1 Pt. 1:293; HEN 1:298, 358-359, 406, 547; 2:568; Surry County Deeds and Wills 1652-1672:6, 32, 117, 168, 197, 315; 1672-1684:27, 82, 304; Order Book 1671-1691:3, 9, 114, 179-180, 189, 210-211, 227, 314, 327, 358; MCGC 205, 230, 237, 259, 271, 302, 306, 328-329, 340, 342, 360, 403, 405-406, 415-416, 419, 421, 484, 486, 488, 490-491, 503, 514; CO 1/39 f 65; 5/1371 f 268; AMB 53; STAN 38).

***

JOHN SWARBECK (SWARBROOKE, SWARTBRICK)

On April 7, 1623, John Swarbeck (Swarbrooke, Swartbrick), a Virginia Company servant, was identified as a cow keeper for Governor Francis Wyatt and Captain William Powell, both of whom were residents of Jamestown Island (1). In early January 1625 Swarbeck informed the General Court that he had served as Captain Powell's cow keeper for several months after the March 22, 1622, Indian attack. However, he ceased being responsible for the Powell herd after Powell's widow married Edward Blaney. Swarbeck also stated that he was no longer responsible for the cattle belonging to Mr. Sharpe, perhaps a reference to Lieutenant John Sharpe of Jamestown, an ancient planter. On January 24, 1625, John Swarbeck was living in Pasbehay, on the Governor's Land (3), where he was a solitary household head (VCR 4:104-106; MCGC 39-40; CBR 57; DOR 1:26).

ROBERT SWEET (SWEETE, SWEAT)

Robert Sweet (Sweete, Sweat) came to Virginia on the *Neptune* in 1618, at his own expense. In 1622 he identified himself as an ancient planter and adventurer in New England when asking the king for relief from customs duties. On February 16, 1624, Robert was living in Elizabeth City (18). In October 1624 he informed the Council of State that Captain Nathaniel Butler wanted a list of Treasurer George Sandys' wrongdoings, and he testified against Captain John Martin concerning his activities in Kecoughtan. In early 1625 Robert Sweet, who was age 42, was still living in Elizabeth City, where he and John Bainham headed a well-provisioned household. In September 1626 he and Richard Lowe were asked to see that James Carter's goods, which were in the Low Countries, were shipped home. In March 1628 Robert Sweet was identified as the administrator of Thomas Hebb, one of Captain Ralph Hamor's creditors, and he also patented some land in Elizabeth City, east of Waters Creek, using his own headright. On February 9, 1629, Sweet presented an inventory of John Bainham's estate but renounced executorship so that Elizabeth, the decedent's widow, could serve as administrator. During spring 1630 Robert Sweet went to England on the *London Merchant*, afterward stating that he was afraid to go on the *Sun* because of its reputation as a leaky ship. He returned to Virginia sometime prior to October 17, 1640, at which time he ran afoul

of the law by getting a black woman servant pregnant. For this infraction of moral law he was ordered to do penance in the Jamestown church (CBE 29, 44, 64; VCR 3:580; MCGC 22, 24, 170, 185, 477; PB 1 Pt. 1:70; WAT 1016-1017; EAE 21-22).

JAMES SWIFT

James Swift, who was in Bermuda in 1609 with Sir Thomas Gates and Sir George Somers, served as godfather to Edward Eason's baby boy, who was born there. Swift continued on to Virginia, and in January 1613 Captain Samuel Argall left him and four other males with the Indians as hostages while trading for corn in the Potomac River basin. Ensign James Swift was with Argall in March 1613 when Pocahontas was captured. In 1620 Swift was among those who petitioned for the removal of Sir George Yeardley as governor (HAI 413, 753-754; VCR 3:231-232).

THOMAS SWIFT (SWIFTE, SWYFT, SWYFTE)

Thomas Swift (Swifte, Swyft, Swyfte) came to Virginia on the *Tiger* in 1622 and on February 16, 1624, was living on the lower side of the James River in Treasurer George Sandys' household. On February 4, 1625, Thomas, who was free, was living on the Treasurer's Plantation (11). In May 1625 he was ordered to inventory the estate of Captain William Norton, who was associated with the glassworks, and shortly thereafter, he and Elias Longe witnessed a legal document. Later in the year Swift was identified as a gentleman when he testified that John Burland was owed money and wanted to be paid out of Captain Norton's estate. Mr. Thomas Swift became ill and died sometime prior to December 12, 1625. He made a nuncupative will, leaving his estate to his brother-in-law, Robert Lee of Gravesend, for the benefit of his children. On his deathbed he asked Zachariah Crispe and Edward White to see that his estate was settled in accordance with his wishes. In January 1626 the late Thomas Swift was identified as one of George Sandys' servants. At the time of his death, he owed debts to Captain Norton, Thomas Delamajor, and Vicentia Castillian. A month or so later, the General Court learned that the decedent had allowed Thomas Hall to keep William Bancks's corn and that he had accepted some money from Thomas Hitchcok on behalf of Treasurer George Sandys (CBE 40, 60; MCGC 60, 73, 80-81, 86, 90, 94, 96, 101-102).

***

THOMAS SWINHOW (SWINEHOWE) I

Thomas Swinhow (Swinehowe) I came to Virginia on the *Diana* sometime prior to 1621. He patented and seated 300 acres of land in Charles City, the plantation called Swinehowe's or Swinyards (**47**), from which Swinyards Creek got its name. In 1621 Thomas Swinhow received supplies from the Virginia Company. When the Indians attacked his plantation on March 22, 1622, Mrs. Swinhow, the couple's sons (George and Thomas II), and four others were slain. Thomas Swinhow was incorrectly listed among the dead. On February 16, 1624, he was living on the Maine or Governor's Land (**3**). He was still there on January 30, 1625, and was sharing his home with Lawrence Smalepage, a servant. Thomas Swinhow became ill and on March 18, 1626, made a nuncupative will. He bequeathed his clothing and other personal effects to John Carter, asking him to see that his just debts were paid. He left money for rings to Carter, David and Margaret Ellis, and their child, and identified David Ellis as his brother (probably his brother-in-law). Thomas Swinhow asked that his servant, Lawrence, be freed, and said that he wanted Mr. Gill to sell his tobacco and send the proceeds to his (the testator's) brother in London. On March 27, 1626, provost Marshal Randall Smallwood was ordered to make an inventory of Thomas Swinhow's estate. Then, on May 8, 1626, the General Court ordered Smallwood to see that Dr. John Pott's house was palisaded because Swinhow had agreed to do so but had died before the job was complete. The dwelling presumably was Pott's house on the Governor's Land (FER 322; VCR 3:568; 4:553; CJS 2:302; CBE 39, 57; MCGC 98-99, 103; DOR 1:27).

MRS. THOMAS SWINHOW (SWINEHOWE) I

On March 22, 1622, when the Indians attacked the Swinehow plantation (**47**), Mrs. Thomas Swinhow (Swinehowe) I and her sons, George and Thomas II, were killed (VCR 3:568).

GEORGE SWINHOW (SWINEHOWE)

On March 22, 1622, when the Indians attacked the plantation owned by Thomas Swinhow (Swinehowe) (**47**), Swinhow's wife and sons, George and Thomas II, were killed (VCR 3:568).

THOMAS SWINEHOW (SWINEHOWE) II

On March 22, 1622, when the Indians attacked the plantation owned by Thomas Swinhow (Swinehowe) (**47**), Swinhow's wife and sons, Thomas II and George, were killed (VCR 3:568).

***

JOHN SWYE

On September 15, 1619, Virginia Company officials noted that John Swye, a major, was leaving for Virginia on the *Margaret* of Bristol and was being sent to Berkeley Hundred (**55**) by the Society of Berkeley Hundred's investors (VCR 3:213).

PETER SWYER (SAWYER?)

On December 24, 1634, when Tobias Felgate of Westover (**54**) made his will, he mentioned Peter Swyer [Sawyer?] (SH 19).

GEORGE SYBERRY (SYBERRYE)

George Syberry (Syberrye), a tallow-chandler from London, arrived in Jamestown (**1**) on September 12, 1623, on the *Bonny Bess* and took the oath of supremacy (MCGC 6).

HENRY SYBERRY (SYBERRYE)

Henry Syberry (Syberrye), a chandler from London, arrived in Jamestown (**1**) on September 12, 1623, on the *Bonny Bess* and took the oath of supremacy (MCGC 6).

FRANCIS SYEN

On September 26, 1627, Francis Syen was identified as someone who had shipped goods from London to Virginia on the *Samuel* (CBE 80).

HUGH SYMFTER

On September 19, 1626, Hugh Symfter, who was preparing to leave England on the *Elizabeth*, was identified as a carpenter and servant of Abraham Peirsey (MCGC 71).

SYMON

Sometime after April 1623 but before February 16, 1624, Symon, an Italian, died at Warresqueak **(26)** (CBE 42).

GILBERT SYMONDS
(SEE GILBERT SIMMONS)
RICHARD SYMONDS (SYMONS)
(SEE RICHARD SIMMONS)
JOHN SYMONS
(SEE JOHN SIMMONS)
MARGERY SYMMONS
(SEE MARGERY SIMMONS)
MARTHA SYMONCE
(SEE MARTHA SIMMONS)

T

MRS. PERYUE TABERLEN

On May 23, 1625, Mrs. Peryue Taberlen and Vencentia (Vicentia) Castine (Castillian) testified that Captain John Clever died in August 1622 at the Treasurer's Plantation **(11)**, and that they saw he was laid out properly for burial (MCGC 61).

SAMUEL TALBOTT

On March 12, 1624, Samuel Talbott, one of Captain John Stone's servants, became indebted to Mr. Bennett. In June 1626 Captain William Tucker, Elizabeth City's **(17, 18)** commander, ordered Samuel to go to Warresqueak **(26)**, the Bennett plantation, with Henry Woodward. Samuel was to stay there until Captain Stone returned to Virginia and decided where he should go (MCGC 134).

RICHARD TABORER

On February 16, 1624, Richard Taborer was living at the Glasshouse **(2)** (CBE 41).

JOHN TAINTER

On November 21, 1618, officials decided that John Tainter, a vagrant boy and young rogue, would be detained at Bridewell and kept at work until he could be transported to Virginia (CBE 11).

ANN TANNER

Ann Tanner, a marriageable young maid, set sail for Virginia in August 1621 on the *Marmaduke*. Virginia Company records indicate that she was born at Chelmsford in Essex and was the daughter of Clement Tanner, a husbandman. Ann was the cousin of Thomas Tanner, a Newgate saddler, and had been recommended to Company officials by John Plummer of Rosemary Lane. Ann Tanner had a number of useful domestic skills—she could spin, sew in blackwork, brew, bake, make butter and cheese, and do embroidery (FER 306, 309).

DANIEL TANNER

Daniel Tanner came to Virginia on the *Sampson* in 1618 and on February 16, 1624, was living in Elizabeth City **(18)**. He was still there in early 1625 and was identified a 40-year-old free man who lived in a household headed by Lieutenant Thomas Purfoy. The all-male Purfoy household included three free men and two servants. They had a relatively abundant supply of stored food and defensive weaponry, and their home was defended by a palisade (CBE 43, 64).

JOSIAS TANNER

On January 24, 1625, Josias Tanner, who was age 24, was residing in the eastern part of Jamestown Island **(1)** (CBE 56).

STEPHEN TARFET

Stephen Tarfet set out for Virginia on the *Margaret* of Bristol on September 15, 1619, and came to the colony at the expense of the Society of Berkeley Hundred's investors. He was bound for their plantation, Berkeley Hundred **(55)** (VCR 3:213).

NATHANIEL TATAM (TATTAM)

On February 27, 1619, Nathaniel Tatam (Tattam), a boy, was identified as part of a group of youngsters brought in from the streets of London so that they could be sent to the colony. He arrived in Virginia in May 1619 on the *George* and on February 16, 1624, was living at West and Shirley Hundred (**41**). When a muster was taken of the community's inhabitants on January 22, 1625, Nathaniel Tatam was identified as a 20-year-old man who lived alone (CBE 12, 36, 53; DOR 1:16).

RICHARD TATEM

On July 31, 1622, Richard Tatem and two companions went to Virginia on the *James*. On July 4, 1623, the Virginia Company identified him as a subscriber for the relief of the colony (FER 400; VCR 4:245-246).

WILLIAM TATEMAN

On February 15, 1620, the justices of Bridewell decided that William Tateman, a boy who had been brought in, would be detained until he could be sent to Virginia (HUME 27).

WILLIAM TATHILL (TOTLE)

William Tathill (Totle) came to Virginia in 1623 on the *George* and on February 16, 1624, was living on West and Shirley Hundred (now Eppes) Island (**41**). He was still there on January 22, 1625, at which time he was identified as an 18-year-old servant in Christopher Woodward's household (CBE 36, 52).

SILVESTER TATNAM (TOTNAM)

On April 24, 1632, carpenter Silvester Tatnam (Totnam) and four other men obtained a 21-year lease for 400 acres of land in Martin's Hundred (**7**), close to Skiff's Creek. On July 21, 1635, Silvester secured a patent for 100 acres of land in Martin's Hundred, acquiring it on the basis of two headrights. Earlier in the month Thomas Harwood, who lived on the east side of Skiff's Creek, used Silvester Tatnam's headright and indicated that he had paid for Silvester's transportation to Virginia (PB 1 Pt. 1:130, 208, 257).

HENRY TAVERNER

In 1633–1634 Henry Taverner, master of the *George*, was supposed to go from London to Carolina but failed to do so. Port records dating from November 1634 to April 1635 indicate that Taverner, a 32-year-old mariner from All Hallows, Barking, in London, was to go to Virginia as master of the *Thomas*. He may have been the individual identified as Hilary Taverner in the following year's shipping records (CBE 119; EAE 50).

HILARY TAVERNER

Between Christmas 1634 and Christmas 1635 Hilary Taverner, master of the *Thomas*, brought 58 passengers to Virginia (EXC 157/20 ff 58v-59; SR 3466).

JOHN TAVERNER (TAVERNOR)

John Taverner (Tavernor), a gentleman and Virginia Company investor, came to Virginia in 1608 in the 1st Supply of new colonists and, therefore, lived in Jamestown (**1**). In 1608 Tavernor accompanied Captain Christopher Newport on a journey to Werowocomoco. In May 1609 he was identified as the former cape merchant of the fort and store, whose replacement had been Thomas Wittingham. John Tavernor's friends submitted a petition to the Virginia Company asking that he be allowed to return to England (CJS 1:216, 222; 2:161, 282; VCR 3:23).

HENRY TAVIN

Henry Tavin, a laborer, came to Virginia in 1607 and was one of the first Jamestown (**1**) colonists (CJS 1:209; 2:142).

HENRY TAWNEY
(TAWNY, TOWNEY)

Henry Tawney (Tawny, Towney), a barber surgeon from Winchcombe or Wingham in Gloucester, set sail for Virginia in 1618 on the *Neptune*—the ship transporting Thomas West, Lord Delaware, to the colony. Delaware became ill and died on the way to Virginia, but his men continued on to Jamestown (**1**). Henry Tawney lived in Virginia for a year or so and then returned to England. During the early 1620s he testified in a series of lawsuits that involved the disposition of Lord Delaware's goods. Testimony taken in mid-April 1622 reveals that Captain Edward Brewster, one of Delaware's most trusted men, gave Tawney the key to the storehouse in which the decedent's belongings were kept. However, Deputy Governor Samuel Argall insisted on taking custody of the key even though he continued to hold Tawney accountable for Delaware's goods. When Tawney refused to cooperate, Argall assigned the duty to another man. Captain John Martin attested to these events, basing his statements on the recollections of John Salmon, with whom Tawney had shared sleeping accommodations. On July 11, 1623, after Henry Tawney had returned to England, he testified in a suit that Robert Rich, the Earl of Warwick, an Argall supporter, brought against Edward Brewster, whom Argall had tried in a martial court. In 1624 Tawney gave his age as 29 when he spoke on Lady Delaware's behalf. A year later, when testifying in a suit that involved Captain Nathaniel Butler, Henry Tawney said that he was 31 (C 24/490; HCA 13/44 ff 156ro-158ro; EAE 14-15).

[NO FIRST NAME] TAYLOR

On February 16, 1624, Mrs. Taylor was living at Martin's Hundred (**7**), perhaps alone (CBE 42).

EDWARD TAYLOR

On September 19, 1618, the Bridewell court decided that Edward Taylor, a vagrant from Smithfield, would be sent to Virginia (CBE 9).

EDWARD TAYLOR

On February 27, 1619, Edward Taylor, a boy from St. Sepulcher's, was identified as one of the children rounded up from the streets of London so that they could be sent to Virginia (CBE 13).

FORTUNE TAYLOR

Fortune Taylor, a young marriageable maid, came to Virginia in September 1621 on the *Warwick* when she was 18 years old. Her uncles—Mr. Barbor from East Summerfield, England, and Mr. Baker from East Smithfield—vouched for her character. On February 16, 1624, Fortune was a servant in the urban Jamestown (**1**) household of Dr. John Pott (CBE 38; FER 309).

JAMES TAYLOR (TAYLOUR)

On March 6, 1620, James Taylor (Taylour) was identified as one of the servants Lieu-

tenant George Harrison had brought to Virginia. On March 6, 1621, when Harrison was granted 200 acres in Charles City, he used James Taylor's headright (CBE 19; SAIN 1:25; VCR 3:432-433).

JASPER TAYLOR

Jasper Taylor died in Elizabeth City (**17, 18**) sometime after April 1623 but before February 16, 1624 (CE 45).

***

JOHN TAYLOR

John Taylor, an ancient planter, came to Virginia in 1610 on the *Swann*. When he patented some land in Elizabeth City (**18**) on September 20, 1624, he was identified as a yeoman and resident of Newportes News (**24**). In early 1625 John Taylor and his wife, Rebecca, were living in Elizabeth City, where they were members of a household headed by William Gayne and Robert Newman. John was then age 34. When a list of patented land was sent back to England in May 1625, John Taylor was credited with 50 acres of land in Elizabeth City, acreage that already had been planted. On November 28, 1633, Taylor relinquished the patent he had received in September 1624 and asked for 150 acres. He tried to use his dividend as an ancient planter and the headright of his wife, the former Rebecca Ravening, whom he claimed to have brought to Virginia in 1623 on the *Bonny Bess*. He was ordered to prove that he had paid for her passage (CBE 65; VCR 4:557; PB 1 Pt. 1:26).

REBECCA RAVENING TAYLOR (MRS. JOHN TAYLOR)

Rebecca Ravening came to Virginia on the *Margaret and John* in 1623. By September 20, 1624, she had become the wife of ancient planter and yeoman John Taylor of Newportes News (**24**), who attempted to use her headright when patenting some land in Elizabeth City (**18**). John Taylor was ordered to prove that he had paid for Rebecca's passage to the colony. In early 1625 Rebecca Ravening Taylor was living in Elizabeth City (**18**) with her husband, John, in a household headed by William Gayne and Robert Newman. She was age 22 (CBE 65; PB 1 Pt. 1:26; EEAC 57).

***

JOHN TAYLOR ALIAS STOKELEY

On September 15, 1619, John Taylor alias Stokeley set sail for Virginia on the *Margaret* of Bristol and was among those sent to Berkeley Hundred (**55**) to work under Captain John Woodlief's supervision. Taylor was supposed to serve the Society of Berkeley Hundred's investors for six years in exchange for 25 acres of land. On January 3, 1625, John Taylor was identified as one of 16 Berkeley Hundred men who had been living in West and Shirley Hundred (**41**) prior to the March 22, 1622, Indian attack. He seems to have worked as a cow keeper during that period. On June 23, 1625, John, a 37-year-old resident of Elizabeth City (**18**), testified that while he was at Shirley Hundred he had given two of Lady Elizabeth Dale's cattle to George Thorpe, who had died during the Indian attack. Virginia Company records indicate that John Taylor perished before he had fulfilled his obligation to the Society of Berkeley Hundred (CBE 14; VCR 3:198, 213; MCGC 42, 73-74).

***

JOHN TAYLOR

John Taylor and his wife were killed at Martin's Brandon (**59**) during the March 22, 1622, Indian attack (VCR 3:569).

MRS. JOHN TAYLOR

Mrs. John Taylor and her husband were killed at Martin's Brandon (**59**) during the March 22, 1622, Indian attack (VCR 3:569).

***

PAUL TAYLOR

On February 27, 1619, Paul Taylor, a boy, was identified as one of the children rounded up from the streets of London so that they could be sent to Virginia (CBE 12).

***

RICHARD TAYLOR (TAILOR)

Richard Taylor (Tailor), an ancient planter, arrived in Virginia in September 1608 on the *Mary Margaret*. He was living at Bermuda Hundred (**39**) on December 11, 1623, when he testified that Captain Thomas Barwick—who was responsible for the men the Company of Shipwrights sent to the colony—had sold him some goods. On February 16, 1624, Richard Taylor and his wife were living at Bermuda Hundred. On January 24, 1625, they were still there, and Richard was described as a 50-year-old head of household. The household included his 21-year-old wife, Dorothy, who had come to Virginia aboard the *London Merchant* in May 1620, and their 3-month-old daughter, Mary. The Taylors shared their home with a servant and were amply supplied with stored food and defensive weaponry and had some livestock. In May 1625, when a list of patented land was sent back to England, Richard Taylor was credited with 100 acres in Charles City, acreage that was planted. Over the next several years Taylor made several court appearances. On March 6, 1626, he testified about a slanderous statement made by Joane Vincent, a Bermuda Hundred resident. Then, on September 18, 1626, he ran afoul of the law by making statements against the government while inebriated. In early 1627 Taylor accused three men of planting on his land at Bermuda Hundred, even though he had earlier signed a lease allowing them use of the acreage if they cleared it. He lost his case. Richard Taylor claimed that Luke Boise of Bermuda Hundred had possession of another man's cow, and in January 1629 he successfully brought suit against William Sharpe and others, whom he claimed had kept him from making use of the land to which Governor George Yeardley had given him a patent. Taylor's last known court appearance occurred on January 24, 1629, at which time he served on a jury (CBE 36, 54; MCGC 8-9, 96, 113-114, 129, 180-181, 184; VCR 4:553; DOR 1:10).

DOROTHY TAYLOR (TAILOR) (MRS. RICHARD TAYLOR [TAILOR])

Dorothy, the wife of Richard Taylor (Tailor) came to Virginia in May 1620 on the *London Merchant* and on February 16, 1624, was living at Bermuda Hundred (**39**) in a household headed by her husband. On January 24, 1625, Richard and Dorothy Taylor and their 3-month-old daughter, Mary, were still at Bermuda Hundred. Dorothy Taylor was then age 21. Her husband was more than twice her age (CBE 36, 54).

MARY TAYLOR (TAILOR)

On January 24, 1625, when a muster was made of Bermuda Hundred's (39) inhabitants, Mary Taylor (Tailor), a 3-month-old infant, was living in the home of her parents, Richard and Dorothy Taylor (Tailor) (CBE 54).

***

ROBERT TAYLOR

Robert Taylor, one of the Society of Berkeley Hundred's (55) men under the command of Captain John Woodlief, came to Virginia in September 1619 on the *Margaret* of Bristol. He died within four years of the time he arrived in the colony (CBE 14; VCR 3:198).

ROBERT TAYLOR

On October 31, 1621, Virginia Company officials learned that Robert Taylor, who was then in Virginia, wanted to be free. He offered to reimburse the Company for the cost of his transportation to the colony and his provisions. Company officials agreed to his proposal (VCR 1:544).

ROBERT TAYLOR

Robert Taylor was killed at Flowerdew Hundred (53) during the March 22, 1622, Indian attack (VCR 3:568).

ROBERT TAYLOR

Sometime after April 1623 but before February 16, 1624, Robert Taylor died at one of the plantations on the lower side of the James River, within the corporation of James City (8-15) (CBE 41).

STEVEN TAYLOR (TAILOR)

On October 11, 1627, Steven Taylor (Tailor) testified in court that he was a servant of Mrs. John Pott, a Jamestown (1) resident. He said that he had been hired out to Allen Keniston and that he became lame while in Keniston's employ. Taylor was returned to Mrs. Pott's household so that he could be cured (MCGC 155).

THOMAS TAYLOR

When a list of patented land was sent back to England in May 1625, Thomas Taylor was credited with 50 acres in Elizabeth City (17, 18), acreage that already had been planted (VCR 4:557).

THOMAS TAYLOR

During the March 22, 1622, Indian attack, Thomas Taylor was killed at Thomas Sheffield's plantation (69), which was located three miles from Falling Creek, within the corporation of Henrico (VCR 3:565).

VINCENT TAYLOR

Sometime prior to 1624 Vincent Taylor was sent to Virginia by the Company of Mercers (FER 297).

WILLIAM TAYLOR (TALER)

William Taylor (Taler), a laborer, came to Virginia in 1608, in the 2nd Supply of Jamestown (1) colonists (CJS 1:242; 2:191).

***

WILLIAM TAYLOR (TAYLOE, TAYLER)

Captain William Taylor (Tayloe, Tayler), who wed Elizabeth, the daughter and heir of ancient planter Richard Kingsmill of Jamestown Island (1), purchased the 1,200-acre Kings Creek plantation (30) from John Uty's son, John II, on April 8, 1640. The Uty property abutted the York River and extended from Queens Creek (on the west) to Utimaria Point on the west side of Kings Creek's mouth. In November 1647, the year William Taylor first was elected a York County burgess, his plantation was designated as one of the points at which Indians could enter the James-York peninsula on official business. In 1651 Taylor, a merchant, was named to the Council of State. When he died sometime after 1655, he left his Kings Creek plantation (minus 150 acres he had already sold) to his widow, Elizabeth, who later married Colonel Nathaniel Bacon (STAN 36, 66; Lower Norfolk County Book B:204; HEN 1:348; MCGH 159; York County Deeds, Orders, Wills 1:71, 153; 9:113; NUG 1:22, 90-91, 122).

ELIZABETH KINGSMILL TAYLOR (TAYLOE, TAYLER) (MRS. WILLIAM TAYLOR [TAYLOE, TAYLER], MRS. NATHANIEL BACON) (SEE ELIZABETH KINGSMILL)

***

JAMES TEALLER (TAYLOR?)

On January 15, 1620, the Bridewell court decided that James Tealler (Taylor?), a vagrant from Aldgate, would be sent to Virginia (CBE 17).

EDWARD TEMPLE

Edward Temple came to Virginia in May 1622 on the *Margaret* and on February 16, 1624, was living on West and Shirley Hundred Island (**41**). When a muster was taken of the community's inhabitants on January 22, 1625, Temple was identified as a 20-year-old servant in the household of Richard Briggs (CBE 36, 52).

EDWARD TEMPLE

Edward Temple died at Flowerdew Hundred (**53**) sometime after April 1623 but before February 16, 1624 (CBE 37).

EDWARD TEMPLE

Court testimony given on February 6, 1628, reveals that Edward Temple, a servant, stole sugar and currants from his master, Edward Grendon, and took them to John Tios's house. Grendon and Tios were inhabitants of the Treasurer's Plantation (**11**) (MCGC 163).

SARA TEMPLEMAN

On April 12, 1624, Sara Templeman, an orphan, was represented by Stephen Poore in a suit against Symon Withe, a bricklayer who died in Elizabeth City (**17, 18**) (MCGC 64).

PARNELL TENTON

Parnell Tenton, a young maid, set sail for Virginia in September 1621 on the *Warwick*. Virginia Company records reveal that she was 20 years old and was born in London. Parnell was recommended to the Virginia Company by Mr. Hobson of the Company of Drapers. Her father was dead and her mother reportedly brought her to the ship. Parnell Tenton may have been the female identified only as "Parnell" who was killed at Edward Bennett's plantation in Warresqueak (**26**) during the March 22, 1622, Indian attack (FER 309; VCR 3:571).

RICHARD TERRELL

On February 27, 1619, the Bridewell court decided that Richard Terrell, a boy, would be sent to Virginia. He was one of the youngsters rounded up from the streets of London and sent to the colony (CBE 12).

NICHOLAS THIMBLEBY

Nicholas Thimbleby, who lived on the lower side of the James River within the corporation of James City (**8-15**), died sometime after April 1623 but before February 16, 1624 (CBE 41).

WILLIAM THAMES

On July 31, 1627, William Thames, a London merchant, shipped goods to Virginia on the *Hopewell* and on the *Thomas and John* (CBE 79).

WILLIAM THISSELTON

In August 1618 Stephen Sparrow sent William Thisselton to Virginia on the *William and Thomas* (VCR 1:330).

THOMAS

Thomas died in Elizabeth City (**17, 18**) sometime after April 1623 but before February 16, 1624 (CBE 45).

THOMAS

On February 16, 1624, a boy known only as Thomas was living in Warresqueak (**26**) (CBE 42).

THOMAS

On February 16, 1624, an Indian boy named Thomas was living in Elizabeth City (**18**) in Thomas Dunthorne's household (CBE 44).

THOMAS

Sometime after February 16, 1624, but before February 7, 1625, Thomas, one of Edward Bennett's servants, died at Warresqueak **(26)**. He may have been the boy who had been living there on February 16, 1624 (CBE 62).

THOMAS

Thomas, a servant in Thomas Willoughby's household in Elizabeth City **(18)**, died sometime after February 16, 1624, but before early 1625 (CBE 64).

EDWARD THOMAS

Edward Thomas was sent to Virginia by Mr. Hutchinson and left England on July 31, 1622, on the *James* (FER 400).

HENRY THOMAS

Henry Thomas set out for Virginia with William Felgate, leaving England on July 31, 1622, aboard the *James* (FER 400).

JOHN THOMAS

John Thomas came to Virginia in 1622 on the *Southampton* and on February 16, 1624, was living on the lower side of the James River at Captain Samuel Mathews' plantation **(15)**. He was still there on February 4, 1625, and was described as an 18-year-old servant (CBE 40, 60).

JOHN THOMAS

On May 18, 1622, John Thomas, a sawyer sent to Virginia by the Company of Shipwrights, set sail for Virginia with Thomas Nunn on the *Furtherance*. Like Nunn, he probably lived and died on Jamestown Island **(1)** (FER 378).

JOHN THOMAS

John Thomas, an indentured servant in the household of William Harwood, the leader of Martin's Hundred **(7)**, arrived at the plantation around Christmas 1623. Fellow servant Richard Frethorne indicated that Thomas died relatively soon after arriving in Harwood's home (VCR 4:60).

MARY THOMAS

Mary Thomas, a young maid, came to Virginia in 1621 aboard the *Warwick*. Virginia Company records indicate that she was born in London and reared there by her grandfather, Roger Tudor, a cloth-worker reputed to be an honest man. In 1621 Mary was 18 years old (FER 309).

NATHANIEL (NATHANIELL) THOMAS

In 1621 Nathaniel (Nathaniell) Thomas came to Virginia on the *Temperance* at the expense of Sir George Yeardley, and on February 16, 1624, was living at Flowerdew Hundred **(53)**. When a muster of that community's inhabitants was made on January 20, 1625, Thomas was identified as a 23-year-old servant in Abraham Peirsey's household. On February 9, 1628, the General Court noted that Yeardley had brought Nathaniel Thomas to Virginia on the *Temperance*. Later in the year, when Thomas Flint patented some land, he indicated that he had acquired Thomas's headright from Yeardley (CBE 37, 50; MCGC 166; PB 1 Pt. 1:59).

RICHARD THOMAS

On July 4, 1635, when John Davis patented some land east of Jockey's Neck **(6)**, he used the headright of his servant, Richard Thomas (PB 1 Pt. 1:204).

THOMAS THOMAS

On February 27, 1619, the Bridewell court decided that Thomas Thomas, a boy, would be transported to Virginia. He was one of the youngsters rounded up from the streets of London so that they could be sent to the colony (CBE 13).

HUMPHREY TOMPKINS

On January 12, 1620, Humphrey Tompkins received one share of Virginia Company stock in a lottery. On May 4, 1624, he testified on behalf of Edward Brewster, who was being sued by the Earl of Warwick. At that time Tompkins indicated that he was 46 years old and a resident of Ratcliffe, in Surrey, England (VCR 3:60; HCA 13/44 ff 294vo-296ro).

[NO FIRST NAME] THOMPSON (THOMSON, TOMSON)

Mr. Thompson (Thomson, Tomson) died in Elizabeth City (18) sometime after February 16, 1624, but before early 1625 (CBE 67).

FREDERICK THOMPSON

On September 26, 1618, it was decided that Frederick Thompson, a vagrant from Cripplegate who had been born in Thames Street, would be sent to Virginia (CBE 10).

***

GEORGE THOMPSON (THOMSON)

George Thompson (Thomson) came to Virginia in 1623 on the *George*. He also had made a trip to the colony sometime prior to March 4, 1621, at the expense of his elder brother, prominent merchant and mariner Maurice Thompson. On February 16, 1624, George Thompson was living in Elizabeth City (18). When Captain William Tucker patented some land on September 20, 1624, he used the headright of George Thompson, whom Tucker identified as the brother of his wife, Mary. When a muster of Elizabeth City's inhabitants was made in early 1625, George Thompson was identified as a 17-year-old servant in the Tucker household. Also present were George's brothers, Paul and William Thompson, who had accompanied him to Virginia. On October 15, 1627, George Thompson, by then an ensign, testified about an incident he had witnessed in Elizabeth City in May 1626. He said that Captain Nicholas Martiau and Mr. Mayhew (probably Thomas or Edward Mayhew) had argued so vehemently about the superiority of the kings of France and England that they almost had come to blows. In March 1629 Lieutenant George Thompson was named a commissioner of Elizabeth City's monthly court, and he was made commander of the area from Lieutenant Lupo's Creek to Chamberlaine's Creek. In October 1629 he served as one of Elizabeth City's burgesses (CBE 43, 63; PB 1 Pt. 1:20, 29; MCGC 156, 193; HEN 1:132, 139).

MAURICE (MORRIS) THOMPSON (THOMSON)

In December 1619 Maurice (Morris) Thompson (Thomson), captain of the *Jona-*

than, was authorized to take 200 men to Virginia for the Virginia Company. On April 8, 1620, Company officials decided that Thompson's charter would become null and void two weeks after he reached Jamestown (1). When Maurice Thompson, a gentleman, secured a patent on March 4, 1621, for 150 acres of land between Newportes News (24) and Blunt Point (22), he was identified as a new planter. He indicated that he had been in Virginia for four years and had paid for his own transportation to the colony and that of two others. His sister was Mary, the wife of his business partner, Captain William Tucker. On April 30, 1623, Maurice Thompson was among the colonists signing a written rebuttal of Captain Nathaniel Butler's allegations about conditions in Virginia. Thompson stated that he had been in Virginia for six years but knew nothing about the amount of ordnance on hand at Henrico (63), Charles City (40), or Flowerdew Hundred (53). On July 4, 1623, Maurice Thompson was among those who provided supplies as relief to the colony. He appeared before the General Court twice during spring 1625: once to complain about shipboard food shortages and another time to testify about Robert Bennett's account book. When a list of patented land was sent back to England in May 1625, Thompson was credited with 150 acres of land that was east of Blunt Point and a quarter mile from some acreage owned by Sir Francis Wyatt. On December 29, 1626, Maurice Thompson, who was then in London, asked to be reimbursed for paying a man to bring a Virginia Indian to England. He reported that Sir Francis Wyatt and Mr. Sandys were in good health and awaiting news from England. During 1627 Thompson shipped goods from London to Virginia on the *Golden Lion* of Dundee. He returned to Virginia prior to March 21, 1628, when he made a claim on the estate of Jamestown merchant Ralph Hamor. However, he was back in England in 1630 to testify in a lawsuit involving Sir George Yeardley's estate. In 1632 Maurice Thompson, William Felgate, and some other London merchants lost a shipment of tobacco that was aboard a vessel that went down at sea. In May 1633 several Virginia planters protested about an agreement Maurice Thompson and his associates made with Governor John Harvey whereby they would become the sole exporters of Virginia tobacco. During 1633 and 1634 Thompson and his group sent passengers to Virginia on the *Expedition*, and a year later he and two other men sent vessels to the Caribbean. In 1649 he was a member of the Guinea Company, which was involved in trade to the Gold Coast that included the acquisition and sale of Africans. Thompson's trading activities were extensive, and in 1650 he reportedly wrote a description of China (VCR 1:277-278, 288-289, 337; 2:386; 4:245-246, 557; PB 1 Pt. 1:20-21; MCGC 54, 60, 103, 170; FER 606; SR 9963; EAE 31, 42; G&M 187-188; CBE 57, 110-112).

PAUL THOMPSON (TOMPSON)

Paul Thompson (Tompson) came to Virginia in 1623 on the *George* and on February 16, 1624, was living in Elizabeth City (**18**). He was still there in early 1625, at which time he was identified as a 14-year-old servant in Captain William Tucker's household. A patent Tucker secured on September 20, 1624, reveals that his wife, Mary, was the sister of Paul Thompson and his brothers George and William. Paul's eldest brother was prominent merchant and mariner Maurice Thompson (CBE 43, 63; PB 1 Pt. 1:29).

WILLIAM THOMPSON (TOMPSON)

William Thompson (Tompson) came to Virginia in 1623 on the *George* and on February 16, 1624, was living in Elizabeth City (**18**). He was still there in early 1625 and was an 11-year-old servant in Captain William Tucker's household. A patent Tucker secured on September 20, 1624, reveals that his wife, Mary, was the sister of William Thompson and his brothers George and Paul. Prominent merchant and mariner Maurice Thompson was William's eldest brother (CBE 43, 63; PB 1 Pt. 1:29).

***

HATHER THOMPSON (THOMSON)

Hather Thompson (Thomson) came to Virginia in 1623 on the *Ambrose* and in early 1625 was an 18-year-old servant in the home of William Ganey in Elizabeth City (**18**) (CBE 66).

LAWRENCE THOMPSON

On August 21, 1624, the justices of Bridewell Court decided that Lawrence

Thompson would be detained until he could be transported to Virginia (CBE 47).

NICHOLAS THOMPSON (TOMPSON)

Nicholas Thompson (Tompson) came to Virginia in 1621 on the *George* and on February 16, 1624, was living on the lower side of the James River, within the corporation of James City but east of Gray's Creek. On February 4, 1625, he was identified as one of George Sandys' servants who resided on the Treasurer's Plantation (**11**). On December 12, 1625, Nicholas Thompson testified before the General Court that Mr. Swifte made a nuncupative will in Thompson's presence. When he returned to court on January 21, 1629, Nicholas gave his age as 25. He stated that John Burland had asked Richard Bennett for three male servants, whom Bennett's uncle was supposed to deliver. Later, when Bennett gave Burland three young men who were age 17, Burland rejected them because they were too young (CBE 40, 60; MCGC 80-81, 181).

***

ROGER THOMPSON (THOMSON)

Roger Thompson (Thomson), who was born in Bishopsgate Street, London, was a vagrant in Leadenhall when he was brought to Bridewell. On January 15, 1620, court officials decided that Roger would be sent to Virginia. He arrived in the colony on the *London Merchant* later that year. When a census was compiled on February 16, 1624, Roger was living at Flowerdew Hundred (**53**). By January 24, 1625, he had moved to urban Jamestown (**1**), where he and his wife, Ann, were servants in Sir George Yeardley's household. Roger Thompson was then 40 years old. On February 26, 1627, he testified about some cattle he had delivered to John Pountis of Jamestown on behalf of John Woodall. He also gave an estimate of how many of Sir George Yeardley's cattle had been killed and reported that Richard Peirce (another local resident) had slain a calf (CBE 17, 37, 54; MCGC 141).

ANN THOMPSON (THOMSON) (MRS. ROGER THOMPSON [THOMSON])

On January 24, 1625, Ann, the wife of Roger Thompson (Thomson), was living in urban Jamestown (**1**), where she and her husband were servants in Sir George Yeardley's household. On February 13, 1629, when Jamestown merchant Thomas Warnett made his will, Mrs. Roger Thompson was one of his beneficiaries (CBE 54; SH 11-12).

***

WILLIAM THOMPSON

William Thompson came to Virginia on the *Southampton* in 1622 at the expense of John Sibley (Sipsey, Sipse, Sypsey) of Elizabeth City (**18**). Thompson died sometime after April 1623 but before February 16, 1624. Sibley used Thompson's headright in 1625 when patenting some land on the lower side of the James River, within Elizabeth City (**20 a**) (CBE 45; PB 1 Pt. 1:46).

WILLIAM THOMSON (TOMSON)

William Thomson (Tomson) came to Virginia on the *Swan* in 1624 and in early 1625 was living in Elizabeth City (**18**), where he was a 22-year-old servant in Thomas Dunthorne's household (CBE 66).

RICHARD THORGLAND

Richard Thorgland set sail for Virginia in December 1621 and was one of the four young men being sent to Martin's Hundred (**7**) as apprentices to metalworker Robert Limborough. Thorgland was to serve as an apprentice for three years and then work for the Society of Martin's Hundred for four years as a servant at half-shares (FER 339).

JAMES THORLEY

On March 22, 1622, when the Indians attacked Martin's Hundred (**7**), James Thorley was killed (VCR 3:570).

ALICE THORNBURY

On July 3, 1627, the justices of the General Court heard testimony about Alice Thornbury's physical fight with Anne Snoade, which led to Anne's miscarriage. Alice was sentenced to a whipping but both women, who appear to have lived in Elizabeth City (**17, 18**), were told they would be flogged if they ever fought again (MCGC 150).

THOMAS THORNBURY (THORNEBURY, THORNBURROW)

Thomas Thornbury (Thornebury, Thornburrow), an ancient planter, came to Virginia on the *George* in 1616. When demographic records were compiled in March 1620, Thornbury was on a trading voyage to Accomack and Acohannock. He returned but left again shortly thereafter. In early 1625 Thomas, who was age 20 and free, was living in Elizabeth City (**18**) in the household of Edward Waters. On January 9, 1626, he brought Waters' boat up to Jamestown (**1**) in order to transport Waters back to Elizabeth City. At the end of that month, Thornbury ran afoul of the law when he and four other Elizabeth City men, who were drinking heavily on New Year's Eve, boarded Waters' ship, the *Grace*, took a small boat or tender, and sailed away, eventually losing a man overboard. Thomas Thornbury was fined and made to post a bond guaranteeing his good behavior. His peace bond was revoked a year later because he had fulfilled his obligation. On December 30, 1626, when John Gundry sold 150 acres in Elizabeth City to Adam Thorogood, he noted that Thomas Thornbury was leasing a portion of the property. By 1634 Thomas had patented some land of his own in Elizabeth City on the Back River (**19**) (FER 159; CBE 66; MCGC 89, 91-92, 137; PB 1 Pt. 1:152, 161, 477).

HENRY THORNE

Henry Thorne came to Virginia in 1622 on the *James* and on February 16, 1624, was living in Chaplin's Choice (**56**). He was still there on January 21, 1625, at which time he was identified as an 18-year-old servant in Isaac Chaplin's household (CBE 37, 51).

***

ADAM THOROGOOD (THOROWGOOD, THORUGOOD)

Adam Thorogood (Thorowgood, Thorugood), the seventh son of William and Anne Edwards Thorogood of Norwich, England, came to Virginia on the *Charles* in 1621 and on February 16, 1624, was living in Elizabeth City (**18**). When a muster was taken in early 1625, Adam was identified as an 18-year-old servant in Edward Waters' household. In early 1626 he ran afoul of the law when he and four other Elizabeth City men, who were drinking heavily on New Year's Eve, went aboard Waters' ship, the *Grace*, took a boat, and sailed away, losing a man overboard in the process. By December 30, 1626, Adam Thorogood had gained his freedom and purchased a 150-acre tract in Elizabeth City, land that was in the hands of tenants. Afterward he returned to England, where he married Sarah Offley. On July 31, 1627, two weeks after his marriage, he shipped some goods from London to Virginia on the *Hopewell*, the same vessel on which he and his wife traveled to Virginia in 1628. On March 29, 1628, he incurred the wrath of William Capps, who confronted him in court and called him a rogue and thief, claiming that he was in possession of stolen goods. Capps (known for being hotheaded) wanted to have Thorogood's flesh branded with the emblem of thievery, if it was legally permissible. Capps's accusations apparently did little to deter Adam Thorogood from rising in the ranks of society, for only a year after he was accused of wrong-doing, he was named a commissioner of Elizabeth City's monthly court. In October 1629 he was elected to the first of successive terms in the assembly and eventually was named to the Council of State. In 1630 he was among those willing to help colonize the York River frontier at Chiskiack (**30-38**). On November 13, 1633, William Parke of Virginia made a bequest to Adam Thorogood. In 1634 Captain William Button asked the Privy Council to give Thorogood some land on the lower side of the James River because he was taking so many new settlers to the colony. Thorogood purchased some land in Elizabeth City on the Back River (**19**) in March 1634. Thorogood also mentioned another trip that he had made in 1634 on the *Dorothy*. On June 24, 1635, he acquired 5,350 acres on the Chesapeake Bay, using his own headright and that of his wife, Sarah. As time went on, Adam Thorogood added to his holdings in the vicinity of Lynnhaven Bay. In 1637 he was a member of the Lower Norfolk County Court, and he served on the Lynnhaven Parish vestry. Thorogood made his will on February 17, 1640, and died sometime prior to April 27, 1640. He was survived by his wife, Sarah; son, Adam; and daughters, Ann, Sarah, and Elizabeth (CBE 44, 66, 79 118; MCGC 91-92; 169, 193; HEN 1:139-140, 149, 170, 179, 187; SH 15; G&M 204-205; PB 1 Pt. 1:160, 179, 315, 327, 477; MEY 607-608).

SARAH OFFLEY THOROGOOD (THOROWGOOD, THORUGOOD) (MRS. ADAM THOROGOOD [THOROWGOOD, THORUGOOD], MRS. JOHN GOOKIN, MRS. FRANCIS YEARDLEY)

Sarah Offley married Adam Thorogood (Thorowgood, Thorugood) at St. Anne's Church, Blackfriars, London, on July 18, 1627, and came to Virginia on the *Hopewell* in 1628. On June 24, 1635, when Adam patented some land, he used Sarah as a headright and indicated that he had paid for her transportation to Virginia, as well as his own. Together they produced four children: Adam, Ann, Sarah, and Elizabeth. After Adam Thorogood's death in 1640, Sarah quickly married John Gookin. She was widowed again and in 1647 wed Captain Francis Yeardley (PB 1 Pt. 1:179; MEY 607-609, 727; DOR 2:103).

THOMAS THOROGOOD (THOROWGOOD, THORUGOOD)

On February 16, 1624, Thomas Thorogood (Thorowgood, Thorugood), who was Adam Thorogood's kinsman, was living in Elizabeth City (**18**). He appears to have gone to England and returned with Adam on the *Hopewell* in 1628. On March 29, 1628, Thomas Thorogood testified before the General Court that his kinsman, Adam, had sent him to question Mr. William Capps about whether Capps had called Adam a rogue and a thief. On June 24, 1635, when Adam Thorogood patented some land, he used Thomas Thorogood's headright, indicating that he had paid for his passage to Virginia on the *Hopewell* in 1628 (CBE 43; MCGC 169; PB 1 Pt. 1:179).

***

THOMAS THOROGOOD (THOROWGOOD, THORUGOOD)

On February 16, 1624, Thomas Thorogood (Thorowgood, Thorugood) was living on the Mainland (**3**) just west of Jamestown Island. On January 24, 1625, he was identified as a 17-year-old servant in John Burrows' household in the eastern part of Jamestown Island (**1**) (CBE 39, 56).

ALICE THOROWDEN

Alice Thorowden came to Virginia in 1623 on the *Southampton*. On January 20, 1625, when a muster was made of Flowerdew Hundred's (**53**) inhabitants, Alice was identified as one of Abraham Peirsey's servants (CBE 50).

GEORGE THORPE

George Thorpe, the son of Nicholas Thorpe of Wanesell Court, was a gentleman pensioner and a gentleman of the king's Privy Chamber. In 1614 he was a member of Parliament for Portsmouth, as well as a member of the Virginia Company and an investor in Bermuda. In 1618 Thorpe and his cousin, Sir William Throgmorton, joined Sir George Yeardley and several other investors in forming a partnership known as the Society of Berkeley Hundred, the purpose of which was to establish a private plantation in Virginia—the settlement called Berkeley Hundred (**55**). The Society received its patent, and on February 18, 1619, George Thorpe informed Sir George Yeardley that the patent had been written out by his Indian boy. After preparing carefully for the voyage, Thorpe set sail for Virginia with Captain John Woodlief on the *Margaret* of Bristol on September 16, 1619. Virginia Company officials noted that Thorpe, who was named to Virginia's Council of State, was supposed to serve as deputy for the College Land (**66**); in compensation, he was to receive 300 acres there and ten male servants. Thorpe returned to England briefly but in September 1620 went back to Virginia, this time with William Tracy, with whom he jointly governed Berkeley Hundred. Thorpe still was responsible for the servants at the College, and he did what he could to advance the Falling Creek (**68**) ironworks and other Virginia Company projects. He spoke optimistically about the colony's economic future but, as a deeply religious man, felt that it was important to convert the Indians to Christianity. On June 22, 1621, George Thorpe informed Company officials that he was going to visit the Indians' principal leader, Opechancanough, whom he hoped to convert. Contemporary accounts reveal that he went to great lengths in an effort to win the Indians' trust and that he had an English-style house built for Opechancanough. However, between January and March 1622

relations between the Indians and colonists deteriorated after an Indian (one of Opechancanough's favorites) killed a settler and was slain in reprisal. On March 22, 1622, when the Indians attacked the settlements sparsely scattered along the James River, George Thorpe and ten others were killed at Berkeley Hundred. According to Captain John Smith, the Natives mutilated Thorpe's corpse. On January 9, 1624, the General Court ordered Sir George Yeardley to see that George Thorpe's estate was inventoried. That document, compiled by three of his neighbors, is the earliest known inventory of a Virginia colonist's estate. On August 14, 1634, a copy of the inventory was presented to officials in England, in response to legal action undertaken by Thorpe's son, William. A tabulation of debts owed by the late George Thorpe reveals that he had many creditors, including Sir George Yeardley, to whom he owed payment for having Opechancanough's house built (CJS 2:282-283, 287, 293-295, 370; VCR 1:332, 336, 347, 371, 375, 379-380, 479; 3:109, 124, 130-134, 138-139, 148, 151, 187, 193-195, 240, 305, 374-380, 397-400, 412-415, 417-418, 435-436, 445, 446-449, 452, 462, 489, 495, 552, 555, 583, 588, 670; 4:185; CBE 22, 113, 118; FER 244, 322; MCGC 11, 17-18, 40, 47-48, 73-74; S of N 43; BRO 1005, 1031).

WILLIAM THORPE

On August 14, 1634, William Thorpe of Bristol, the son of the late George Thorpe, made inquiries about the estate of his father, who had been killed at Berkeley Hundred (**55**) during the March 1622 Indian attack. He asked when his father had arrived in Virginia and when he had died (S of N 44; CBE 118).

***

MATHEW THORPE

On November 20, 1622, Mathew Thorpe, an inmate in Newgate Prison, was pardoned during an outbreak of jail fever so that he could be sent to Virginia (CBE 29).

THOMAS THORPE

On September 15, 1619, Thomas Thorpe set out for Virginia on the *Margaret* of Bristol and was one of the colonists being sent to Berkeley Hundred (**55**) to work under John

Woodlief's supervision. He was to serve the Society of Berkeley Hundred's investors for seven years in exchange for 30 acres of land. Thomas Thorpe died shortly after his arrival in the colony. Since the name "Thomas" was recurrent in George Thorpe's family, Thomas and George may have been kinsmen (CBE 14; VCR 3:198, 213).

ROBERT THRASHER (THRESHER)

Robert Thrasher (Thresher) came to Virginia in 1620 on the *Bona Nova* and probably was a Virginia Company tenant. On February 16, 1624, he was living in Elizabeth City (17) on the east side of the Hampton River, on the Company's land. When a muster was made of that area's inhabitants in early 1625, Thrasher and his partner, Roland Williams (Williames), were heading a household that was amply supplied with stored food and defensive weaponry and included one servant. Robert was then age 22. On November 21, 1625, Robert Thrasher successfully sued Thomas Weston, a merchant and mariner, who was supposed to bring him a servant. He also testified in a suit involving Captains John Martin and William Tucker, and a month later he was called on to discuss Thomas North's status. On August 28, 1626, Robert Thrasher informed the General Court that John Hassarde had illegally sold him four years of Abraham Pelterre's time. A month later he testified against Mrs. John Wright, who stood accused of witchcraft. By June 17, 1635, Robert Thrasher had acquired some land of his own in Elizabeth City (CBE 43, 68; MCGC 76, 81-82, 109, 112, 114; PB 1 Pt. 1:309; DOR 1:67).

THOMAS THRASHER (THRESHER)

On February 27, 1619, officials at Bridewell decided that Thomas Thrasher (Thresher), a boy, would be sent to Virginia. He was one of the children rounded up from the streets of London so that they could be transported to the colony (CBE 12).

NICHOLAS THREDDER

Nicholas Thredder came to Virginia on the *Katherine* in 1623 and in early 1625 was living in Elizabeth City (18), where he was a 30-year-old servant in the household

jointly headed by John Banum (Bainham) and Robert Sweet. In 1628 the General Court learned that Nicholas Thredder was dead. Because Thredder was intestate, John Hill and Robert Brittaine were given letters of administration (CBE 64; MCGC 174).

***

EDWARD THRENORDEN (TRAMORDEN)

Edward Threnorden (Tramorden) came to Virginia on the *Diana* in 1619 and on February 16, 1624, was living at Flowerdew Hundred (53). When a muster was made of that area's inhabitants on January 20, 1625, Edward was heading a household that he shared with his wife, Elizabeth. They had a modest supply of provisions and defensive weaponry (CBE 37, 50; DOR 1:23).

ELIZABETH THRENORDEN (TRAMORDEN) (MRS. EDWARD THRENORDEN [TRAMORDEN])

Elizabeth, the wife of Edward Threnorden (Tramorden), came to Virginia on the *George* in 1619. On January 20, 1625, she and her husband were living at Flowerdew Hundred (53), where he was a household head (CBE 50).

***

WILLIAM THRINNE

On March 12, 1627, William Thrinne, a sailor, testified before the General Court about an incident in the West Indies involving the ship *Saker* (MCGC 143).

HENRY THROGMORTON

Henry Throgmorton and his cousin, John Throgmorton, began sharing a home at Shirley Hundred (41) sometime after January 22, 1625, when a muster was compiled of the community's inhabitants. On June 23, 1627, when the Indians attacked the plantation, John was severely injured but lived long enough to express his last wishes. He freed Henry Throgmorton, whom he identified as his servant, and bequeathed him all of his possessions except half of his house and land, which he left to another man. On September 17, 1627, the General Court designated Henry Throgmorton administrator of John Throgmorton's estate and ordered him to make an inventory, a compilation he presented to the court on October 9, 1627. On March 7, 1629, Henry Throgmorton was placed in command of Shirley Hundred Island and was named a commissioner for the monthly court serving the "upper part," that is, the settlements near the head of the James River (MCGC 153-154, 192-193).

JOHN THROGMORTON

On July 26, 1618, John Throgmorton, a convicted felon and prisoner in Newgate, was reprieved and was to be delivered to Sir Thomas Smith for employment in Virginia. Although the nature of his crime is uncertain, official records disclose that he was able-bodied and had not been found guilty of murder, rape, burglary, or witchcraft. According to demographic records, John Throgmorton came to Virginia in 1618 on the *William and Thomas*. By February 16, 1624, he was living on the Eastern Shore (**72-78**). Sometime prior to January 22, 1625, he moved to Shirley Hundred (**41**), where he and Cheney Boise headed a household that included three male servants, one of whom was his cousin. The men were amply supplied with stored food and defensive weaponry and had some livestock. John Throgmorton was then 24 years old. On June 23, 1627, when the Indians attacked Shirley Hundred, John Throgmorton was mortally wounded while working in a field near a wooded area. He lived long enough to make a nuncupative will. He freed his cousin, servant Henry Throgmorton, and bequeathed him everything he owned except half of his house and ground, which he left to Edward Albourne. He left William Edes and Thomas Stent two years of their time and gave a year of his African servant's service to Mrs. Oliver Jenkins. He bequeathed Richard Andrews, "the old cooper," his (the testator's) share of Andrews time for the coming year. On September 17, 1626, Henry Throgmorton was named administrator of his late cousin's estate and was ordered to compile an inventory of his goods, a document that was presented to the General Court on October 9, 1627 (SR 4525; PC 2/29; CBE 46, 53; MCGC 153-154; DOR 1:15).

KENELM (KENELME) THROGMORTON

Kenelm (Kenelme) Throgmorton, a gentleman, came to Virginia in 1607 and was one of the first Jamestown (**1**) colonists. According to George Percy, he died on August 26, 1607 (CJS 1:20, 208; 2:141; HAI 99).

SIR WILLIAM THROGMORTON

On February 3, 1619, Sir William Throgmorton of Clowerwall in Gloucestershire was identified as an investor in the Society of Berkeley Hundred, which intended to establish the plantation known as Berkeley Hundred (**55**). Two of Throgmorton's cousins, George Thorpe and William Chester, also were partners and investors. The Society received its patent in late summer 1619. Sir William Throgmorton prepared a shipment of supplies to transport on the *Margaret* of Bristol and on September 16, 1619, set sail for Virginia with Captain John Woodlief and a group of settlers. In March 1620 there reportedly were 50 people at Berkeley Hundred. On May 11, 1620, Sir William Throgmorton indicated that one of the Indian maids whom Sir Thomas Dale brought to England in 1616 had become a servant to a merchant in Cheapside. He said that she had contracted consumption and was receiving medical care (VCR 1:338; 3:130-134, 138-139, 187, 193-195; FER 138).

CLEMENT THRUSH

Clement Thrush came to Virginia on the *Returne* of London in 1623 at the expense of his master, John Moone, who used his headright when patenting some land on March 6, 1633. Moone owned a lot in urban Jamestown (**1**) and acreage in the corporation of Warresqueak (**26**), later known as Warresqueak (then Isle of Wight) County (PB 1 Pt. 1:127).

JOHN THURLEBY

On September 12, 1626, John Thurleby, a gentleman, testified before the General Court in support of Mrs. Ann Dowse, a former resident of Elizabeth City (**17, 18**). Thurleby and other witnesses said that after Mrs. Dowse and her husband, Thomas, returned to England and took up residence in Kinsalle, he became involved with Charity Lovell, a married woman, with whom he fled to Ireland. Although Ann Dowse had her husband's power of attorney and had been given the right to his property in Virginia when he abandoned her in Kinsalle, she was destitute. She was forced to depend on the charity of local merchants, who paid her way to Virginia. She sought the General Court's help in recovering her husband's real and personal estate and was given the right to use it as she pleased toward her own maintenance (CBE 43; MCGC 113).

JAMES THURSBY

Sometime after April 1623 but before February 16, 1624, James Thursby died at one of the plantations on the lower side of the James River, within the corporation of James City (**8-15**) (CBE 41).

MRS. [NO FIRST NAME] TINDALL

On February 16, 1624, Mrs. Tindall, a widow, was living on the Maine (**3**), just west of Jamestown Island. She may have been the widow of the Thomas Tindall who had died a short time earlier (CBE 39).

ROBERT TINDALL (TYNDALL)

Robert Tindall (Tyndall), a gunner, came to Virginia in 1607 in the first party of colonists to settle on Jamestown Island (**1**). He made a second voyage to Virginia between May and November 1609 and a third trip between April 1610 and June 1611, as captain of Lord Delaware's ship, the *Delaware*. On June 17, 1610, Delaware sent Tindall into the Chesapeake Bay on a fishing expedition and on July 7, 1610, dispatched him to Capes Henry and Charles. On June 22, 1607, Robert Tindall wrote a letter to Prince Henry from Jamestown, describing the discoveries made thus far. He is best known for the map he prepared of Virginia in 1608, a schematic representation that identifies the location of Jamestown and some of the sites at which the Natives were living (HAI 102, 128, 434, 460; BRO 1035).

THOMAS TINDALL (TYNDALL)

Thomas Tindall died in Jamestown (**1**) sometime after April 1623 but before February 16, 1624. In May 1625 he was credited with 100 acres of land in Coxendale (**64**) in the corporation of Henrico. He may have been an ancient planter (CBE 39; VCR 4:552).

THOMAS TINDALL (TYNDALL)

On March 25, 1631, Thomas Tindall was pilloried for threatening Lord Baltimore and calling him a liar (MCGC 480; HEN 1:552).

HENRY TIREMAKER ALIAS GIBBINS
(SEE HENRY GIBBINS ALIAS TIREMAKER)

***

JOHN TIROS
(SEE JOHN TYROS)
JANE TIROS
(MRS. JOHN TIROS)
(SEE JANE TYROS)

***

ROBERT TODD

Robert Todd came to Virginia in 1622 on the *Hopewell* and in early 1625 was living on the east side of the Hampton River, on the Virginia Company's land in Elizabeth City (**17**). Todd was then a 20-year-old servant in William Tyler's (Tiler's) household. On January 10, 1627, Robert Todd told the General Court that he had come to Virginia with Captain Prince and was supposed to serve Captain Thomas Dowse for seven years. He said that Dowse later agreed to reduce his term of service by two years and that because neither pen nor ink was available, Christopher Windmill and Richard Raper (Rapier) served as witnesses to the verbal agreement. The justices of the General Court upheld Robert Todd's claim and agreed to count his seven years of service from the time of his arrival in Virginia, thereby making him eligible to be freed (CBE 67; MCGC 131).

ANAS TODKILL

Anas Todkill, a carpenter, came to Virginia in 1607 and was one of the first colonists in Jamestown (**1**). He co-authored an account of the settlers' first year. Todkill, whom Captain John Smith described as a soldier, accompanied Smith to the Pamunkey Indians' territory while on a second voyage of discovery on the Chesapeake Bay. While Smith's vessel was in the Rappahannock River, Anas Todkill went ashore to look around. He was captured by the Indians but was rescued. In 1608 Todkill accompanied

Nathaniel Powell and some Indian guides on an expedition into the countryside south of the James River. Their goal was to find the so-called "lost colonists," who were thought to be living with Indians known as the Mangoags. On December 29, 1608, Todkill went with Smith to Werowocomoco, Powhatan's principal seat. He also made two trips to the Pasbehay Indians' village with Captain John Martin, later identifying himself as one of Martin's servants (CJS 1:199, 203, 203, 208, 216, 221, 224, 229-230, 258, 265-266; 2:142, 160, 163, 169-170, 173-174, 193, 207, 215).

ROBERT TOKELEY

On January 3, 1626, the General Court's justices learned that the late Robert Langley, a Jamestown (1) merchant, had given a power of attorney to Robert Tokeley, who was then in England. Tokeley, as Langley's attorney, nominated Abraham Peirsey of Jamestown to serve as the decedent's administrator in Virginia and authorized him to collect Langley's debts. Six days later the justices of the General Court decided to require Robert Tokeley to produce a copy of the letters of administration that gave him authority over Langley's estate (MCGC 84, 87).

THOMAS TOLLING

Thomas Tolling was killed at Martin's Hundred (7) during the March 22, 1622, Indian attack (VCR 3:570).

GILBERT TOMLINSON

Gilbert Tomlinson, who came to Virginia on the *Garland* in 1619, was sent tools by the Virginia Company. He appears to have been headed for Southampton Hundred (44) and probably was a skilled worker (FER 137).

JAMES TOOKE (TOOK, TUKE)

James Tooke (Took, Tuke) came to Virginia on the *George* in 1621, at the expense of William Dum, the ship's carpenter. On February 16, 1624, Tooke was a servant in William Spence's household in the eastern end of Jamestown Island (1). By January 30, 1625, he had moved to the Governor's Land (3), where he headed a household that was amply supplied with stored food and defensive weaponry. On January 12, 1627, James Tooke was given permission to move from

the Governor's Land to Mulberry Island (21). When William Spencer patented some land on September 9, 1632, he used Tooke's headright, indicating that he had acquired it from William Dum (CBE 40, 58; MCGC 89, 133; PB 1 Pt. 1:120; DOR 1:27).

JOHN TOOKE (TOOK, TUKE)

On November 12, 1619, John Tooke (Took, Tuke), mate on the ship *George*, was appointed a tobacco taster. On May 30, 1625, he testified in the General Court about the delivery of some sack (a wine) to Robert Bennett of Warresqueak (26). The justices considered it a just debt and required John Carter of Warresquake to post a bond guaranteeing that he would pay Tooke by November (VCR 3:228; MCGC 63-64).

JOHN TOPLIFFE

On October 15, 1629, the justices of Bridewell decided that John Topliffe, a boy, would be sent to Virginia (HUME 35).

STEPHEN TORSET

On September 15, 1619, Stephen Torset set out for Virginia on the *Margaret* of Bristol and was one of the colonists sent to Berkeley Hundred (55) to work under John Woodlief's supervision. He was supposed to serve the Society of Berkeley Hundred's investors for four years in exchange for 25 acres of land. However, Stephen Torset died soon after he arrived in the colony (CBE 14; VCR 3:198, 213).

FRANCIS TOWERS

On April 21, 1635, Francis Towers, a gentleman, patented 200 acres of land on the Elizabeth River, in Elizabeth City (20 a). An adjacent patent reveals that his acreage was next to that of John Sibley (Sipsey, Sipse, Sypsey) (PB 1 Pt. 1:165, 173).

HENRY TOWNSEND

Henry Townsend set out for Virginia in February 1620 on the *London Merchant*, the ship that transported George Thorpe to Berkeley Hundred (55). Thorpe had the right to choose three men (including Townsend) to be his servants. Henry Townsend died shortly after reaching the colony (VCR 3:199, 260-262).

RICHARD TOWNSEND (TOWNSHEND)

In 1620 Richard Townsend (Townshend) came to Virginia on the *Abigaile* and on February 20, 1621, signed a contract with Dr. John Pott, who agreed to teach him the apothecary's art in exchange for his labor. On February 16, 1624, Townsend was living in urban Jamestown (1) in Pott's household. He was still there on January 24, 1625, at which time he was identified as a 19-year-old servant. In 1626 Dr. Pott, whose servants had killed some of Captain William Powell's hogs that had gotten into Pott's corn, ordered Richard Townsend to take some of the pork to Powell. Townsend said that Pott always had his servants kill hogs that got into his cornfield and that four or more trespassing swine had been slaughtered and consumed. On October 10, 1626, Richard Townsend testified in court that although he was Dr. Pott's apprentice and had been promised instruction as an apothecary, Pott had failed to do so. Townsend produced their agreement as proof of his allegations. The General Court sided with the plaintiff and ordered Pott to train Townsend as an apothecary or pay for his services. In October 1629 Richard Townsend served as a burgess for the territory between Archer's Hope (6) and Martin's Hundred (7), and in 1637 he was named to the Council of State. He died in Virginia in 1645 (CBE 38, 55; MCGC 58-59, 117; HEN 1:138; STAN 34).

THOMAS TOWNSEND (TOWNSON)

In March 1629 when galley-pot maker Christian Whithelme I made his will in England, he identified Thomas Townsend (Townson) as his son-in-law and one of his principal heirs and executors. Townsend was then married to the testator's daughter, Mary. Whithelme, who had invested in one of Governor John Harvey's entrepreneurial schemes, also named as an heir his own son, Christian Whithelm II, who was then in Virginia. On January 2, 1635, Thomas Townsend, who was age 26, came to Virginia on the *Bonaventure*. He was accompanied by another Thomas Townsend, who was age 14 and perhaps a kinsman. Christian Whithelme I's son-in-law, Thomas Townsend, eventually returned to England and carried on the family tradition of manufacturing delftware (WITH 159; SR 3958; CBE 122).

THOMAS TOWNSEND (TOWNSON)

On January 2, 1635, Thomas Townsend (Townson), who was age 14, came to Virginia on the *Bonaventure* and may have been a kinsman of 26-year-old potter Thomas Townsend, who also was on the ship (CBE 122).

EDWARD TOWSE

Edward Towse was killed at Edward Bennett's plantation, Warresqueak (26), during the March 22, 1622, Indian attack (VCR 3:571).

LAWRENCE TOWTALES

Lawrence Towtales, a tailor, came to Virginia in 1608 as part of the 1st Supply of new settlers and therefore would have lived in Jamestown (1) (CJS 1:223; 2:162).

***

WILLIAM TRACY

On January 26, 1620, William Tracy of Gloucestershire, a Virginia Company investor, asked Company officials for a patent because he and Robert Heath planned to take 500 people to Virginia to establish a plantation. The Virginia Company agreed but urged Tracy not to focus on the cultivation of tobacco when planting his land. William Tracy stayed on in England and apparently decided to pursue another strategy. On April 15, 1620, he sent a letter to John Smyth of Nibley, a member of the Society of Berkeley Hundred, asking for some land, cattle, and horses if a smithery or bloomery were to be built. Within a month, Sir William Throgmorton of Clowerwall in Gloucester, a member of the Society, assigned Tracy some land in Berkeley Hundred (55). On June 1, 1620, Virginia Company officials learned that Lady Elizabeth Dale's people were going to loan William Tracy some goats and give him some silkworms, and they had promised him some kine (cows). Tracy was to be made a member of the Council of State when he reached Virginia. In a July 5, 1620, letter William Tracy said that when he went to Virginia he was going to take his wife, son, daughter, four female servants, and six male servants. He said that he would have preferred to take

20 to 30 men with him but had only found a dozen. A week later, Tracy, who was at Bristol, received a commission authorizing him to go to Virginia on the *Supply* with 65 passengers. Because the ship was not available, however, Tracy was left with the burden of providing food and shelter to his people. Finally, at the end of August 1620 it was agreed that William Tracy and his group would go to Virginia with George Thorpe, the governor of Berkeley Hundred, who was leaving Bristol with 54 people. The *Supply* set sail in September 1620. Aboard were William Tracy and his wife, Mary, daughter, Joyce, and son, Thomas. A list prepared on September 18, 1620, includes the names of the people going to Virginia on behalf of Berkeley Hundred, along with their terms of service and the number of acres they stood to receive. Some of the people William Tracy hoped to bring to the plantation were left behind because the ship was overcrowded. His group arrived at Berkeley Hundred on January 29, 1621. William Tracy died sometime prior to April 8, 1621, leaving behind a substantial amount of debt (VCR 1:296-297, 382, 404, 479, 512, 520, 535-536; 3:118, 134, 260-261, 266, 271-274, 289-291, 293, 367-370, 373-380, 395-396, 397-400, 405-406, 410-411, 426; CJS 2:283; CBE 20-21; S of N 45).

MARY TRACY
(MRS. WILLIAM TRACY)

In September 1620 Mary, William Tracy's wife, set sail from Bristol, England, on the *Supply* with her husband, daughter, Joyce, and son, Thomas. They were heading for Berkeley Hundred (**55**), a plantation in which William Tracy had invested heavily. The group arrived at Berkeley Hundred on January 29, 1621. By that time Joyce Tracy had married Captain Nathaniel Powell. William Tracy died sometime prior to April 8,1621. Shortly thereafter, his widow, Mary, and son, Thomas, returned to England (VCR 3:396, 426; CBE 20-21).

JOYCE TRACY
(MRS. NATHANIEL POWELL)

In September 1620 Joyce Tracy left Bristol, England, on the *Supply* with her parents, William and Mary Tracy, and brother, Thomas. On the way to Virginia, she married Captain Nathaniel Powell. Joyce and her family arrived at Berkeley Hundred

(**55**) on January 29, 1621. Her father died shortly thereafter and her mother and brother decided to return to England. On March 22, 1622, when the Indians attacked Powle-Brooke (Merchants Hope) (**50**), Captain Nathaniel Powell's plantation, Joyce Tracy Powell and her husband were slain (CBE 20-21; VCR 3:396, 426, 555).

THOMAS TRACY

Thomas Tracy left Bristol, England, on the *Supply* in September 1620 and was accompanied by his parents, William and Mary Tracy, and sister, Joyce. The Tracys arrived at Berkeley Hundred (**55**) on January 29, 1621. William Tracy died shortly thereafter and his wife, Mary, decided to take Thomas and return to England. Meanwhile, the newly married Joyce Tracy and her husband, Captain Nathaniel Powell, took up residence at nearby Powle-Brooke (Merchants Hope) (**50**), where they were slain during the March 22, 1622, Indian attack. In May 1625, when a list of patented land was sent back to England, Thomas Tracy was credited with 100 acres of land in the corporation of Henrico. His patent was located on the lower side of the James River, below The Falls (**67**) (CBE 20-21; VCR 3:396, 426, 555; 4:552).

***

JOHN TRANEERE

On May 29, 1635, when John Parrott patented some land, he used John Traneere as a headright (PB 1 Pt. 1:170).

GEORGE TRAVELLOR
(TRAVELLER)

On January 10, 1627, George Travellor (Traveller) of Accomack was identified as one of Captain John Martin's servants. George was given the choice of paying Martin for a year's service or continuing to live on Martin's land as a tenant. Although it is uncertain what decision George Travellor made, sometime after March 14, 1628, he came into possession of a 50-acre leasehold on Old Plantation Creek (**73**), which he assigned to another man on October 20, 1634. On June 18, 1636, when Travellor patented 500 acres on the creek, he used his own headright and that of his wife, Alice. The Travellor couple made their home on the property and continued to live in Accomack. When George Travellor made his will on February 3, 1643, he made bequests to his wife, Alice, son, George II, and daughter, Elizabeth (MCGC 131; PB 1 Pt. 1:157; AMES 2:246-246).

RICHARD TRAVERSE

On September 12, 1618, the justices of Bridewell decided that Richard Traverse, a vagrant from Leadenhall who had been born in Montgomeryshire, would be sent to Virginia (CBE 9).

ANN JOHNSON TRAVIS
(MRS. EDWARD TRAVIS I)
(SEE ANN JOHNSON II)

AMBROSE TREE

Ambrose Tree, a miller, set sail for Virginia on April 17, 1619, at the expense of the Virginia Company (FER 107).

***

RICHARD TREE

Richard Tree, a free man and a carpenter, was an ancient planter and therefore arrived in Virginia sometime prior to Sir Thomas Dale's departure in May 1616. Since he reportedly came to the colony with cape merchant Abraham Peirsey on the *George*, which arrived in 1618, he apparently went back to England and then returned. On August 14, 1624, Tree patented an 8-acre ridge of land in the eastern end of Jamestown Island (1) near the road to Black Point, and he acquired 42 acres about a mile below Blunt Point (22). On January 24, 1625, Richard Tree was residing in rural Jamestown Island with his 12-year-old son, John, and an adult male servant. Tree was credited with two houses and some livestock and his household was well provisioned and outfitted with military equipment. He apparently was a successful farmer, for he had excess corn to sell. He had owned a boat that some men borrowed and then lost. Richard Tree apparently was a respected member of the Jamestown Island community, for he served on juries, participated in an inquest, and was church warden of James City Parish in 1626. One of his servants had some animal husbandry skills and treated a Jamestown resident's cow in 1625. When a list of patented land was sent back to England in May 1625, Richard Tree was credited with 50 acres

at Blunt Point. However, by October 1628 he had moved to the lower side of the James River and had been hired to build a frame church for the parishioners of Hog Island (16). A year later he began serving as that area's burgess. Richard Tree retained his Jamestown Island property until at least February 1638, for it was used as a reference point at that time. By August 1638 he had acquired a half-acre lot in urban Jamestown, land that he was obliged to develop or forfeit. Tree apparently was a successful planter, for he sold some headrights to another individual (PB 1 Pt. 1:19-20, 88; Pt. 2:521, 587-588, 621; MCGC 35-36, 38, 85, 107-108, 175; CBE 56; VCR 4:556-557; STAN 54, 57; HEN 1:138, 140, 179; DOR 1:34).

JOHN TREE

On January 24, 1625, John Tree, Richard Tree's 12-year-old son, was living in his father's household on Jamestown Island (1) (CBE 56).

***

JOHN TREHEARNE
(TRACHERN, TRAHORNE)

John Trehearne (Trachern, Trahorne) came to Virginia in 1622 on the *Truelove*, the ship that brought the people whom Rowland Truelove and his fellow investors (known as Truelove's Company) had sent to the colony. On February 16, 1624, Trehearne was living at Chaplin's Choice (56). When a muster was made of that settlement's inhabitants on January 21, 1625, Trehearne was described as a 33-year-old household head who lived alone and had armor and a firearm. On December 11, 1626, he asked the General Court's justices to help him recover the value of some tobacco he had sent to his brother in England. He said that he had shipped the crop with James Carter, master of the *Anne* of London, who disposed of the tobacco after learning of Trehearne's brother's death. John Trehearne said that he hoped to receive what the tobacco was worth so that he could pass the proceeds along to his brother's widow. One witness said that James Carter, acting as a factor, had sold the tobacco and purchased commodities for Trehearne. John Trehearne survived until at least March 24, 1630, at which time he served as a burgess for the territory around Weyanoke (52) (CBE 37, 51; MCGC 126-127, HEN 1:148; DOR 1:21).

WILLIAM TREMITHON

A Virginia Company document dated April 1, 1620, indicates that William Tremithon was being sent to Virginia at the expense of Thomas Astley (FER 162).

JAMES TRENTRAM

On September 26, 1618, the justices of Bridewell decided that James Trentram, a vagrant, would be sent to Virginia (CBE 10).

RICHARD TRESSELL

On February 27, 1618, Richard Tressell, a boy, was detained at Bridewell until he could be sent to Virginia. He was one of the youngsters rounded up from the streets of London so that they could be sent to the colony (HUME 11).

EDWARD TREW

On November 15, 1620, William Potterton informed Virginia Company officials that his apprentice, Edward Trew, had gone to Virginia with Thomas West, Lord Delaware, and was still in the colony as a Company servant. Potterton was told to discuss the matter with Lady Delaware (VCR 1:426).

THOMAS TRIGGS

Between April 1623 and February 16, 1624, Thomas Triggs died at one of the plantations on the lower side of the James River, within the corporation of James City **(8-15)** (CBE 41).

JOHANNA TROTT

Because of an outbreak of jail fever, Johanna Trott, an inmate at Newgate Prison, was pardoned on November 20, 1622, so that she could be transported to the colonies (CBE 29).

NICHOLAS TROTT

Nicholas Trott, an inmate at Newgate Prison, was pardoned on November 20, 1622, due to an outbreak of jail fever. He and his fellow inmates were to be transported to the colonies (CBE 29).

RICHARD TRUBBE

On September 8, 1626, the justices of Bridewell decided that Richard Trubbe, a vagrant from Farrington Without, would be sent to Virginia. He was identified as "a common nipper" or pickpocket (CBE 73).

ROWLAND TRUELOVE

On July 24, 1621, the Virginia Company noted that Rowland Truelove, a London cloth-worker, had obtained two shares of Virginia land from Francis Carter, who had procured them from the widowed Lady Cecily (Ceciley, Cecelia, Cisley) Delaware. Three months later Truelove and his associates obtained some additional shares of her land. On November 21, 1621, when Rowland Truelove and his associates received a patent and authorization to establish a particular (private) plantation, they reported that they were taking 100 people to Virginia. Despite the March 1622 Indian attack, Truelove and his group—who in June 1622 were identified as patentees—resolved to proceed with their plans. Shortly thereafter the ship *Truelove* of London set out for Virginia with supplies and 25 new immigrants. Because of the Indian attack, the people who came on the *Truelove* were placed on plantations that had been strengthened and were being retained. Some were placed at West and Shirley Hundred **(41)** and some at Chaplin's Choice **(56)**, where they were still living in early 1625. The settlement that Rowland Truelove and his fellow investors intended to establish probably never became a reality, for in January 1625 the General Court ordered Nathaniel Causey of Jordan's Journey **(46)** to take custody of the goods belonging to the Truelove plantation. On December 4, 1626, Rowland Truelove and Company indicated that William White was handling their business in Virginia and that they wanted their servant, John Brown, to be released, as he already had served five of the seven years on his contract. As late as July 31, 1627, Rowland Truelove was still shipping goods to Virginia, although it appears that he and his associates had abandoned hope of establishing a plantation of their own (VCR 1:523, 553-554, 561-562; 2:93; 3:643; 4:245-246; MCGC 126; CBE 79).

[NO FIRST NAME] TRUNSTON

On January 29, 1620, officials at Bridewell decided to transfer Trunston, an old prisoner being kept so that he could be sent to Virginia, to a person willing to retrieve him (CBE 18).

JOHN TRUSSELL

On February 16, 1624, John Trussell was living at West and Shirley Hundred (41). When a muster was made of that community's inhabitants on January 22, 1625, he was identified as a servant in Thomas Pawlett's household. In late 1634 Trussell purchased some of the late Thomas Lee's goods, which were sold by Bartholomew Hopkins (CBE 52, 208).

JOHN TRYE

John Trye came to Virginia on the *Abigail* in 1620. On January 30, 1625, he was living on the Maine (3), just west of Jamestown Island, where he was one of Dr. John Pott's servants (CBE 58).

***

EDMUND TUCHING (TUTCHIN)

On January 10, 1625, the Virginia Company noted that a charter had been granted to Edmund Tuching (Tutchin), authorizing him to make a voyage to Virginia on the *Due Return*. Edmund died shortly thereafter, having turned his responsibilities over to his brother, Simon Tuching (VCR 4:509-510).

SIMON (SYMON) TUCHING (TUTCHIN)

In late November 1624 the General Court heard testimony from a man who had been aboard a ship that had captured a Spanish vessel. One of the passengers on the Spanish ship was a Spanish lady, and some of the Spanish persuaded Simon (Symon) Tuching (Tutchin), who was in another ship, to go to Spain to fetch ransom money for the lady. Another witness testified that Tuching had openly declared that he had been banished from England and Ireland, despite being from a good family. Tuching also allegedly referred to Protestants as Lutherans and claimed that he did not care whether all of his kin were hanged. Two men verified the witnesses' testimony, and one witness indicated that Tuching claimed he was respected in Madeira. All of these issues were aired before the General Court shortly before the December 29th arrival in Virginia of Simon Tuching's ship, the *Due Return*. They raised the possibility that

Simon Tuching was sympathetic to Rome. However, Lieutenant Edward Peppett testified that Simon Tuching had been diligent about sounding the depths of Virginia's rivers and the Chesapeake Bay. He also said that Simon—as skipper of the ship that his late brother, Edmund Tuching, had captained—took the oath of allegiance. When Simon was queried about his banishment, he claimed that it had been repealed. On January 3, 1625, Simon Tuching appeared before the General Court and collected some of the debts that were owed to him and his brother (MCGC 33-34, 37, 39-40; VCR 4:509-510).

BARTHOLOMEW TUCKER

On July 29, 1626, the Bridewell court decided that Bartholomew Tucker, a prisoner, would be sent to Virginia (CBE 72).

***

DANIEL TUCKER (TOOKER)

According to Captain John Smith, Daniel Tucker (Tooker), a gentleman and investor in the Virginia Company, came to Virginia in 1608 in the 2nd Supply of new colonists and was living in Jamestown (1) while Smith was president of the colony. George Percy said that Tucker was highly instrumental in having a large boat built at a time when one was badly needed. When Thomas West, Lord Delaware, arrived in Virginia in June 1610, he designated Daniel Tucker as provost marshal, truck-master, vice-admiral, and clerk of the store. Tucker also served on the Council of State. He acquired some shares of land in Bermuda and in 1616 became Bermuda's governor, holding office until 1619. On April 28, 1619, Daniel Tucker, who was highly critical of Governor George Yeardley even though he had just taken office, informed the Virginia Company that he (Tucker) had spent five years in Virginia and identified himself as an associate of Lord Delaware. In November 1620, when he asked the Company for compensation for the services he had performed during Delaware's administration, they gave him some shares of land. In March 1622 Company officials noted that Tucker was to receive a patent because he was transporting 100 people to the colony. His patent was confirmed on July 3, 1622. In May 1622 he identified himself as a 43-

year-old resident of Milton, in Kent, when he testified about Captain Edward Brewster's court martial. He gave false testimony, for he claimed to have witnessed certain events that occurred in Virginia at a time when he was known to have been elsewhere. Captain Daniel Tucker was in Virginia in November 1624 and served as an attorney. However, he returned to Bermuda and died there in February 1625 (CJS 1:241; 2:57-58, 190, 282, 362-369, 371, 373-374; LEF 1:82, 706; HAI 433, 459, 506; VCR 1:214, 421, 426-427, 624; 2:74, 90; 3:231-232; STAN 29; MCGC 30; SR 9947; C 24/489).

WILLIAM TUCKER (TOOKER, TUKER) I

Ancient planter William Tucker (Tooker, Tuker) I, a Virginia Company investor, came to Virginia on the *Mary and Thomas* in 1610 and probably was in the fleet that brought Lord Delaware to the colony. Although nothing is known of Tucker's first decade in the colony, in 1619 he served as a burgess, representing Kecoughtan (Elizabeth City) (**17, 18**). In 1621 he made an agreement with Thomas Jones of the *Falcon* to transport sassafras to London. On December 23, 1621, Captain William Tucker of the *Eleanor* received the Virginia Company's permission to trade in the Chesapeake Bay. After the March 22, 1622, Indian attack, Tucker was placed in command of Elizabeth City's inhabitants. Later in the year, he and Henry Gates were ordered to account for the Virginia Company's goods entrusted to their care. Like his brother, Daniel, Captain William Tucker had a distinguished military and political career and in 1623 was named to the Council of State. With the governor's authorization, he undertook important trading voyages on the Chesapeake and the Pamunkey and Potomac River basins. In May 1623 he led an expedition against the Indians on the lower side of the James River and was sent to the Potomac to rescue some male colonists the Indians were detaining. Tucker also was actively involved in Dr. John Pott's infamous scheme of serving poisonous wine to Natives signing a peace treaty. Tucker and a work crew—including carpenter Ambrose Griffin, who had worked on the Jamestown (**1**) fort in 1622—were sent to Warresqueak (**26**) to help Captain Roger Smith build fortifications there. Treasurer George Sandys described Tucker

as an industrious man. As a military leader, he headed expeditions against the Nansemond and Warresqueak Indians. He also was considered a great merchant.

On December 6, 1623, the Virginia Company ordered Captain William Tucker to compile a list both of the living and those who had died or were slain in Elizabeth City since the 1622 Indian attack. Governor Francis Wyatt also instructed him to board all departing ships, and he was authorized to detain debtors and others attempting to leave the colony without a pass. Captain William Tucker resided in Kecoughtan throughout the 1620s and 30s. He patented 150 acres there in 1624, a year after he had been designated to collect the tobacco levied as taxes, and he also received a patent for 680 acres on the lower side of the James, within Elizabeth City (**20 a**). On February 16, 1624, Captain William Tucker and his wife were living in Elizabeth City (**18**), and they were still there in early 1625. William was then age 36 and headed a household that included his wife, Mary, and their infant daughter, Elizabeth, plus 18 servants. The Tucker household had use of three dwellings and a palisade. From 1625 through 1629, Captain William Tucker, as Kecoughtan's commander, made many appearances before the General Court and often implemented its decisions on a local level. He also settled disputes, presented wills, and saw that debs were collected and suits settled. In 1630 Tucker testified that he left Virginia on the *Grace* on December 8, 1628, and arrived in Plymouth, England, on February 2, 1629. It was while he was in London that Captain John Smith interviewed him about conditions in the colony. In 1633 Tucker enhanced the quantity of land under his control by acquiring some property on the Back River in Elizabeth City (**19**), and in 1636 he patented some additional acreage. When Captain William Tucker testified before an English court in 1634, he identified himself as age 44 and a native of Redriffe, Surrey, England. He said that he had been involved in Virginia trade for 23 years, had lived there, and had been a member of the Council. In August 1639 he said that he had been detained in England for three years because of charges made by Sir John Harvey. When Captain William Tucker prepared his will on October 12, 1642, he left his Virginia land to his son, William II. Tucker's will was presented to English probate officials in February 1644 (VCR 2:104, 383; 3:154, 535, 623, 664; 4:6-9, 111, 129-130, 190, 221, 250, 284-286, 292, 407, 441-447, 511-512, 557-558; MCGC 11, 41, 49, 58, 62, 73-75, 77, 81, 83-86, 105-106, 115-118, 130, 134, 137, 145, 156-157, 170-175, 190, 196; HAI 915; CJS 2:282; 3:215; EAE 11, 22, 43; STAN 31; CBE 43, 63, 69-71, 90; PB 1 Pt. 1:29, 46, 122-123, 231; HEN 1:128-129, 153, 170, 187, 202; WITH 367; PC 2/50 f 572; HCA 13/49; SR 4001; DOR 1:51).

MARY THOMPSON TUCKER (TOOKER, TUKER) (MRS. WILLIAM TUCKER [TOOKER, TUKER])

In 1623, Mary, who became the wife of William Tucker (Tooker, Tuker), came to Virginia on the *George* and was accompanied by her brothers, George, Paul, and William Thompson. On February 16, 1624, the Tuckers were living in Elizabeth City **(18)**. Mary and William Tucker were still there in early 1625, along with their daughter, Elizabeth, who was born in August 1624. The household included 18 servants, three of whom were Mary's brothers. Mary Tucker may not have been alive when her husband prepared his will in October 1642, naming their son, William II, as principal legatee (CBE 43, 63; PB 1 Pt. 1:29).

ELIZABETH TUCKER (TOOKER, TUKER)

Elizabeth, the daughter of William and Mary Thompson Tucker (Tooker, Tuker), was born in August 1624 and in early 1625 was living in Elizabeth City **(18)** with her parents. She and her mother may not have been alive in October 1642 when her father prepared his will (CBE 63).

***

BARTHOLOMEWE TURBER

On July 29, 1626, the justices of Bridewell decided that Bartholomewe Turber, a boy, would be sent to Virginia (HUME 31).

SIMON (SYMON) TURGIS (SEE SIMON [SYMON] STURGIS)

THOMAS TURNBRYDG (TURNBRIDGE)

On May 20, 1607, Thomas Turnbrydg (Turnbridge), a sailor, accompanied Captain

Christopher Newport on an exploratory voyage of the James River (HAI 102).

ALEXANDER TURNER

On January 29, 1620, officials at Bridewell decided to detain Alexander Turner, who was brought in from Cheap Ward so that he could be sent to Virginia (CBE 18).

CHRISTOPHER TURNER

Christopher Turner was killed at Mr. John West's plantation, Westover **(54)**, during the March 22, 1622, Indian attack (VCR 3:567).

EDWARD TURNER

Edward Turner, John Pountis's manservant, was killed at Edward Bennett's plantation, Warresqueak **(26)**, during the March 22, 1622, Indian attack (VCR 3:571).

GEORGE TURNER (TURNOR)

George Turner (Turnor) came to Virginia on the *Swan* in 1624. In early 1625 he was identified as a 27-year-old servant in Thomas Dunthorne's household in Elizabeth City **(18)** (CBE 66).

HELEN TURNER

On November 20, 1622, Helen Turner, an inmate in Newgate Prison, was pardoned so that she could be sent overseas. She was among those pardoned due to an outbreak of jail fever (CBE 29).

HENRY TURNER

Henry Turner, an ancient planter, came to Virginia in 1615 on the *John and Francis* and on February 16, 1624, was living at Chaplin's Choice **(56)**. He was still residing there on January 21, 1625, at which time he and his partner, Walter Price, headed a household that included one servant. On January 17, 1625, when the General Court ordered Nathaniel Causey to take custody of the goods that belonged to Truelove's Company, they asked Causey to inquire whether Ensign Isaac Chaplin would be willing to provide land and housing to Henry Turner, Walter Price, and their servant. If so, Causey was to provide three men in their place to strengthen Truelove's plantation (CBE 37, 51; MCGC 43; DOR 1:21).

HENRY TURNER

Henry Turner came to Virginia on the *London Merchant* and on February 16, 1624, was living on the Maine (**3**), just west of Jamestown Island. He was still there, living alone, when a muster was made of that area's inhabitants on January 30, 1625 (CBE 39, 57).

HUGH TURNER

In 1619 Hugh Turner was sent to Virginia at the expense of the Ferrars. It is likely that he was being sent to Martin's Hundred (**7**) or Southampton Hundred (**44**), plantations in which the Ferrars had invested heavily (FER 296).

JOSEPH TURNER

Joseph Turner died at Martin's Hundred (**7**) sometime after April 1623 but before February 16, 1624 (CBE 42).

MARTIN (MARTTIN) TURNER (TOURNER)

Martin (Marttin) Turner (Tourner) came to Virginia on the *George* in 1621, having spent time in Bermuda. On February 16, 1624, he was a servant living on the Treasurer's Plantation (**11**), on the lower side of the James River. He was still there on February 4, 1625, and was identified as a servant in Treasurer George Sandy's household. In November 1624 Sandys acknowledged that he had freed Martin Turner from two years of service but said that Turner still had five years to serve. On December 4, 1624, when Sandys patented some land, he listed Martin Turner as a headright and indicated that he had brought him from Bermuda. On February 20, 1626, Turner testified about a bargain he witnessed two men make. One of these men was joiner Thomas Delamajor of Jamestown Island (**1**). On May 5, 1626, Turner testified about a matter that involved two other men who lived on the lower side of the James River. Minutes of the General Court, dating to August 14, 1626, indicate that Martin Turner was missing and presumed dead. George Bourcher testified that approximately a month earlier, when he was at George Menefie's forge in Jamestown, he heard William Carter (a Menefie servant) tell Martin Turner that Mr. Harmar

had come to take his bed. Turner reportedly told Carter not to allow anyone to take it, for he lodged wherever he worked, and said that when he died he wanted Carter to have his bed. The court justices ordered Rice Watkins (one of Edward Blaney's servants, who lived on the lower side of the James River) to make an inventory of Martin Turner's belongings. They indicated that if Turner was not heard from in ten days, they would grant letters of administration to Watkins so that he could settle Turner's estate (CBE 41, 60; PB 1 Pt. 1:16; MCGC 34, 94, 101-102, 107).

ROBERT TURNER

Robert Turner came to Virginia on the *Trial* in June 1619 and on February 16, 1624, was a servant at Bermuda Hundred (**39**). By January 21, 1625, he had moved to Jordan's Journey (**46**), where he was a servant in the household headed by Cicely Jordan and William Farrer (CBE 35, 51).

ROGER TURNER (TURNOR)

Roger Turner (Turnor) died on Jamestown Island (**1**) sometime after April 1623 but before February 16, 1624 (CBE 39).

SAMUEL TURNER

Samuel Turner, a prisoner at Norwich, ran afoul of the law because he stole a horse. In November 1620 Sir Thomas Smith was authorized to have him sent to Virginia. However, in September 1621, officials noted that Samuel Turner, who had gone to the colony, had been sent back to England (CBE 22).

THOMAS TURNER

Thomas Turner came to Virginia on the *Marigold* in 1616 and on February 16, 1624, was living in the household of his cousin, Richard Biggs, at West and Shirley Hundred (**41**). He was still there on January 22, 1625, and was identified as an 11-year-old servant (CBE 36, 52).

WILLIAM TURNER

On July 15, 1631, William Turner was identified as a Virginia planter who exported tobacco from the colony and sought relief from customs duties. The mark on his hogsheads of tobacco was *WT* (G&M 165).

ZACHARIAS (ZACHEUS, ZACHIAS, ZACHARY) TURNER

On June 25, 1635, when William Andrews of Accomack patented some land, he used Zacharias (Zacheus, Zachias, Zachary) Turner as a headright. On August 3, 1640, Turner testified before the justices of Accomack's monthly court about a manservant allegedly abused by his master. In November 1640 Zacharias Turner and others acknowledged owing some taxes. On September 20, 1641, he was among those receiving compensation from the estate of Elias Taylor, and in April 1642 he received payment from another individual. Zacharias Turner's name was mentioned again in a court record dating to November 28, 1642 (PB 1 Pt. 1:181; AMES 2:24-25, 41, 122, 159, 223).

JOHN TWINE (TWYNE)

In 1618 Deputy Governor Samuel Argall placed John Twine (Twyne) in charge of the late Lord Delaware's store of goods, which had been on the *Neptune*, the vessel that brought Delaware's body to Virginia. Captain John Martin and others later testified that Twine was given custody of the goods after Delaware's man, Henry Tawney, refused to be held accountable for them. Although Twine accepted responsibility for Delaware's goods, Argall kept the only key to the storeroom. Martin claimed that after Edward Brewster was condemned at a martial court, Argall had Twine sell some of Lord Delaware's beer, wine, and vinegar. In July and August 1619 John Twine served as clerk of Virginia's first assembly (VCR 3:154; C 24/490).

***

WILLIAM TYLER (TILER)

William Tyler (Tiler) came to Virginia on the *Francis Bonaventure* in 1620, and on February 16, 1624, he and his wife were living on Hog Island (16). William's outspokenness got him into trouble with the authorities during the summer of 1624. On one occasion he said that he would not be a member of the Council of State, even if he could. On another, he called councilor John Uty a thief and claimed that he had stolen some of the Virginia Company's tobacco

and given it to Captain Ralph Hamor and Captain William Holmes. He also said that Uty was pretentious. Ultimately William Tyler was fined for slandering John Uty and the government, and he was ordered to apologize to the community of settlers at Hog Island. By early 1625 William Tyler and his wife, Elizabeth, had moved to Elizabeth City and were living on the east side of the Hampton River on the Virginia Company's land (17). Since the Tylers appear to have been free and had six servants in their household, William may have been a Virginia Company tenant (CBE 41, 67; MCGC 18-20; DOR 1:65).

ELIZABETH TYLER (TILER) (MRS. WILLIAM TYLER [TILER])

Elizabeth, the wife of William Tyler (Tiler), came to Virginia with her husband in 1620 on the *Francis Bonaventure*. On February 16, 1624, she and her husband were living on Hog Island (16). By early 1625 the Tylers and their six servants were living on the east side of the Hampton River (17) in Elizabeth City, on the Virginia Company's land (CBE 41, 67).

***

***

WILLIAM TYLER (TILER) I

On March 22, 1622, when the Indians attacked Thomas Sheffield's plantation (69) in the corporation of Henrico, William Tyler (Tiler) I was slain. Also killed were his sons, Robert and William II (VCR 3:565).

ROBERT TYLER (TILER)

When the Indians attacked Thomas Sheffield's plantation (69) in the corporation of Henrico on March 22, 1622, Robert Tyler (Tiler) was slain along with his father, William I, and brother, William II (VCR 3:565).

WILLIAM TYLER (TILER) II

William Tyler (Tiler) II died at Thomas Sheffield's plantation (69) in the corporation of Henrico during the March 22, 1622, Indian attack. Also slain were his father, William I, and brother, Robert (VCR 3:565).

***

JOHN TYROS (TYERS, TYAS, TIROS, DYOS?)

John Tyros (Tyers, Tyas, Tiros, Dyos?), who was born in Lowe Layden in Essex, came to Virginia on the *Bona Nova* in 1620 and was a Virginia Company tenant. On February 16, 1624, he was living on the Eastern Shore, perhaps on the Company's Land (76). By February 4, 1625, John had moved to the Treasurer's Plantation (11) on the lower side of the James River, where he was identified as one of Treasurer George Sandy's servants. In March 1626 John Tyros testified in a case being aired before the General Court, and in early 1627 he was identified as a Virginia Company tenant assigned to Abraham Peirsey. On January 21, 1628, John Tyros and his wife, Jane, were questioned about a theft that occurred at the Treasurer's Plantation. Although John denied that there were stolen goods in his house, some purloined sugar and currants were discovered when the premises were searched. On February 7, 1628, John Tyros, who was age 26, was sentenced to a whipping because he was considered an accessory to the crime committed by William Mills, a thief. He admitted that he had accepted some poultry brought to him by Mills at Christmastime and that he had sold some of the shoes Mills had given him. On May 30, 1634, John Tyros obtained a 21-year lease for 50 acres in James City County, near the Chickahominy River's mouth (CBE 46, 60; MCGC 96, 136-137, 159, 162-164; PB 1 Pt. 1:142, 150).

JANE TYROS (TYERS, TYAS, TIROS, DYOS?) (MRS. JOHN TYROS [TYERS, TYAS, TIROS, DYOS?])

On January 21, 1628, the justices of the General Court were informed that Jane, the wife of Virginia Company tenant John Tyros (Tyers, Tyas, Tiros, Dyos?), who lived on the Treasurer's Plantation (11), had received and made use of some stolen goods. When she testified in court on February 6 and February 7, 1628, Jane indicated that she was 22 years old and had been born at Wombarne in Staffordshire. She said the sugar and currants that the authorities found in her home had been purchased from a Frenchman and from Edmond Doggatt. She testified that William Mills, who was ac-

cused of chicken-stealing, had brought poultry to her house at various times and also had brought sugar and currants there. Although the General Court decided that John Tyros was a thief and therefore deserved to be punished, Jane was not punished, for it was felt that she had been drawn into a scheme by her husband (MCGC 159, 162-164).

U

CASANDER UNDERWOOD

Casander Underwood came to Virginia on the *Africa* at the expense of Adam Thorogood, who used Underwood's headright on June 24, 1635, when patenting some land (PB 1 Pt. 1:179).

***

GEORGE UNGWIN (UNGWINE, UNGUIN, UNWINE, ONION, UNION, UNWYN, VINON, VINOYN)

George Ungwin (Ungwine, Unguin, Unwine, Onion, Union, Unwyn, Vinon, Vinoyn) came to Virginia on the *Francis Bonaventure* and on February 16, 1624, was residing on Hog Island (16). Ungwin had stood watch at the Jamestown (1) fort on the night Abraham Peirsey's storehouse was robbed, and on June 24, 1624, he testified about what he had seen. George Ungwin and his wife, Elizabeth, were living in the eastern end of Jamestown Island (1) on January 24, 1625. The household he headed had a very modest amount of stored food and defensive weaponry. On January 14, 1628, Ungwin was arrested by Edward Wigg for indebtedness and was summoned to court. On April 8, 1629, he made another court appearance because one of his maidservants, Dorcas Howard, was pregnant. At that time he described himself as a 30-year-old planter and married man. On May 25, 1637, George Ungwin patented 250 acres on the Chickahominy River, using his wife Katherine and daughters Elizabeth and Katherine as headrights. He sold that property in August 1646 but may have had some other acreage in the vicinity, for as late as

1653 his Chickahominy River plantation, near Checroes (now Gordon's) Creek, was considered a local landmark (CBE 41, 56; MCGC 15, 158, 194; PB 1 Pt. 1:430, Pt. 2:684-685, 846, 868, 939; 2:96, 260; 3:31; DOR 1:35).

ELIZABETH UNGWIN (UNGWINE, UNGUIN, UNWINE, ONION, UNION, UNWYN, VINON, VINOYN) I (MRS. GEORGE UNGWIN (UNGWINE, UNGUIN, UNWINE, ONION, UNION, UNWYN, VINON, VINOYN)

Elizabeth, who became the wife of planter, George Ungwin (Ungwine, Unguin, Unwine, Onion, Union, Unwyn, Vinon, Vinoyn), came to Virginia on the *Francis Bonaventure*. On January 24, 1625, the Ungwins were living on Jamestown Island (1), outside of the urbanized area. On April 8, 1629, when George Ungwin testified in court, he described himself as a 30-year-old married man. It is uncertain whether he was then wed to Elizabeth or to Katherine, the wife he listed as a headright in a May 1637 patent (CBE 41, 56; MCGC 158, 194; PB 1 Pt. 1:430).

KATHERINE UNGWIN (UNGWINE, UNGUIN, UNWINE, ONION, UNION, UNWYN, VINON, VINOYN) I (MRS. GEORGE UNGWIN (UNGWINE, UNGUIN, UNWINE, ONION, UNION, UNWYN, VINON, VINOYN)

On May 25, 1637, Mrs. Katherine Ungwin (Ungwine, Unguin, Unwine, Onion, Union, Unwyn, Vinon, Vinoyn) was named as a headright in her husband George's patent for land on the Chickahominy River. Also listed were daughters Elizabeth and Katherine Ungwin (PB 1 Pt. 1:430).

ELIZABETH UNGWIN (UNGWINE, UNGUIN, UNWINE, ONION, UNION, UNWYN, VINON, VINOYN) II

On May 25, 1637, Elizabeth II, the daughter of George Ungwin (Ungwine, Unguin, Unwine, Onion, Union, Unwyn, Vinon, Vinoyn), was named as a headright in his patent for land on the Chickahominy River.

Also listed were George's wife and another daughter, both of whom were named Katherine. Elizabeth may have been the daughter of George's previous wife, who was named Elizabeth (PB 1 Pt. 1:430).

KATHERINE UNGWIN (UNGWINE, UNGUIN, UNWINE, ONION, UNION, UNWYN, VINON, VINOYN) II

On May 25, 1637, Katherine II, the daughter of George Ungwin (Ungwine, Unguin, Unwine, Onion, Union, Unwyn, Vinon, Vinoyn), was named as a headright in his patent for land on the Chickahominy River. Also listed were George's wife Katherine and daughter Elizabeth (PB 1 Pt. 1:430).

***

JAMES UPSALL

On March 22, 1622, when the Indians attacked the plantation of Lieutenant Gibbs at Westover (54), John Upsall was slain (VCR 3:567).

***

JOHN UPTON (UPTONE)

John Upton (Uptone) immigrated to Virginia in 1622 on the *Bona Nova* as a servant to cape merchant Abraham Peirsey. On February 16, 1624, he was identified as a servant in Peirsey's household at Flowerdew Hundred (53). He was still living there on January 20, 1625, at which time he was age 26. By April 19, 1625, Upton had gained his freedom, doing so by paying Peirsey for the eight months that remained on his contract. It was then noted that Upton had been away for an extended period after the 1622 Indian attack. He may have been living on Jamestown Island (1) in 1626 when he made arrangements to purchase some corn from Richard Tree. In April 1626 John Upton approached Kelinet Hitchcock (one of Sir George Yeardley's servants) about renting some of Yeardley's land at Black Point, at the eastern tip of Jamestown Island. At the January 13, 1627, session of the General Court, Hitchcock testified that Upton had asked to rent the house and ground at a reasonable fee, for the dwelling and fence were in need of repairs. In September 1627 John Upton was one of several people required to post a bond guaranteeing his good behavior. A year later his peace bond was canceled. The court record, though cryptic, implies that Upton had been quarreling with someone and perhaps had become unruly. In 1627 John Upton and his partner, Caleb Page, had business dealings with Jamestown merchant George Menefie. Court testimony suggests that they were buying items from Menefie and reselling them. By February 1629 John had wed. He had acquired some land in 1633 in Warresqueak (**26**), or Isle of Wight, an area he represented as a burgess through 1647. He continued to patent land there, and in 1637 he laid claim to 1,650 acres. Later in the year he patented another 850 acres. Upton attained the rank of captain and led an expedition against the Indians in 1637. He also served as a local justice of the peace. When he went to England in April 1641, he found a man to replace him in the militia. John Upton made his will on January 16, 1651, and it was presented for probate in the monthly court of Isle of Wight County on December 6, 1652. He was survived by his wife, the former Margaret Underwood, and a son, John II (VCR 1:608; CBE 37, 50; MCGC 54, 112, 137, 153, 157, 159, 200, 474; HEN 1:149, 169, 187; 203; STAN 59-61, 65-66; MCGH 156, 212; PB 1 Pt. 1:210; Pt. 2:471, 482).

MRS. JOHN UPTON (UPTONE)

On February 13, 1629, Mrs. John Upton (Uptone) was named in Thomas Warnett's will as one of his beneficiaries. Warnett was a Jamestown merchant (**1**) (SH 11-12).

MARGARET UNDERWOOD UPTON (UPTONE) (MRS. JOHN UPTON [UPTONE])

When John Upton made his will on January 16, 1651, which was presented for probate in Isle of Wight County on December 6, 1652, he named as a beneficiary his wife, the former Margaret Underwood, and a son named John (II) (SH 11-12).

***

WILLIAM UPTON (UPTONE)

On April 25, 1626, William Upton was ordered to see that John Howe posted a bond to secure his debt to Robert Lee (MCGC 101).

ANN USHER

On January 22, 1625, Ann Usher, who was 8 years old, was living in West and Shirley Hundred (**41**) in John and Susan Collins' household. Ann, who was free, was Virginia-born. On June 4, 1627, Ann, who was still living in West and Shirley Hundred and was age 10, was sentenced to a whipping in the fort in Jamestown (**1**). She and another young girl were punished because they had been raped by Thomas Hayle, a young male servant (CBE 52; MCGC 149).

BENJAMIN USHER

Benjamin Usher died on Jamestown Island (**1**) sometime after April 1623 but before February 16, 1624. At the same time he was listed among the dead at one of the plantations on the lower side of the James River, east of Gray's Creek (**10-15**), within the corporation of James City (CBE 39, 41).

JAMES USHER (USHUR)

When a list of patented land was sent back to England in May 1625, James Usher (Ushur) was credited with 100 acres of land in the corporation of Charles City, acreage that had not been seated (VCR 4:553).

***

JOHN UTY (UTIE, UTEY) I

John Uty (Utie, Utey) I came to Virginia on the *Francis Bonaventure* and was associated with the Society of Southampton Hundred's settlement (**44**) in Charles City. On February 14, 1623, Uty was living on Hog Island (**16**), an area to which some of Southampton Hundred's settlers had withdrawn in the wake of the 1622 Indian attack. Uty had been ordered to see that sassafras was collected so that it could be sent back to England. On February 16, 1624, he and his wife, Ann, and their young son were living on Hog Island. They still were in residence there a year later. On February 20, 1624, John Uty, a burgess, was among the men who signed a document describing the harsh conditions in Virginia. In August 1624 he sued William Tyler for slander, after Tyler called him a thief and a fiddler. Tyler, on the other hand, accused Uty of stealing some of the Virginia Company's tobacco and taking it to Captain William Holmes in Jamestown (**1**). Tyler also claimed that Uty had been a musician in England and had played a violin aboard the ship that had brought them to Virginia. Ultimately, Uty was made to apologize. In November 1624 John Uty returned to court to testify about how John Southern obtained corn for Southampton Hundred, a settlement in which Southern had been an officer. He also patented 100 acres across from Jamestown at the neck of Hog Island, using the headrights of two servants he had brought to Virginia in 1623. When securing his patent, Uty was identified as an ensign, a gentleman, and a resident of Hog Island. His acreage, which he called "Utopia," was credited to him in May 1625 when a list of patented land was compiled. On February 4, 1625, John, his wife, Ann, and son, John II, were living on Hog Island with their three servants.

John Uty made several appearances in court during 1625 and 1626. He testified in litigation involving John Lamoyne and the Tuchin brothers, who were merchants and ship captains. He hired Bryan Cawt to build a shallop, and he testified about supplies he had obtained for Southampton Hundred, purchasing them from William Harwood of Martin's Hundred (**7**). He also gave testimony about some of the servants associated with Southampton Hundred. In 1626 he claimed that Henry Woodward was a habitual thief who had stolen some corn. Uty owed money to Luke Aden's estate but claimed that William Ranshaw was indebted to him. In 1627 Ensign John Uty reported to the authorities one man who refused to perform military duty and another who was drunk. In 1628 he was granted 250 acres in Archer's Hope (**6**), land that formerly was owned by John Jefferson but had escheated to the Crown. In March 1629 John Uty was placed in command of the plantations between Martin's Hundred and Archer's Hope, and he served as that area's burgess. In 1630 he became a burgess for Hog Island and was ordered to inspect the fort being built at Old Point Comfort. He also agreed to plant a settlement in Chiskiack, at King's Creek (**30**), and received a patent for 1,250 acres for so doing. Uty's patent on the York River extended from Queens Creek eastward to what became known as Utimaria Point, at the mouth of Kings Creek. In 1632 John Uty was named to the Council of State. Like most of his fellow councilors, he had irrec-

oncilable differences with Governor John Harvey and was among those who helped thrust Harvey from office and send him back to England. One issue over which Uty and Harvey clashed was the ownership of some cattle. As soon as Harvey was back in power, he had Uty and some of his fellow councilors arrested and sent to England to stand trial. Harvey also seized Uty's estate but later was ordered to return it. John Uty I died in 1639 at his home, Kings Creek plantation or "Utimaria" (VCR 4:21, 555; HAI 915; CBE 41, 61; MCGC 18-20, 69, 39, 55, 77, 110, 117-118, 124, 147-149, 173, 192-193, 479; STAN 32, 54; HEN 1:138, 148, 150, 153, 202; CO 1/32 f 7; 1/9 ff 132-134; PB 1 Pt. 1:14, 123, 174; SAIN 1:252; G&M 217-218; York County Deeds, Orders, Wills 1633-1646:4; DOR 1:43).

ANN UTY (UTIE, UTEY) (MRS. JOHN UTY [UTIE, UTEY] I)

On February 16, 1624, Ann Uty (Utie, Utey) and her husband, John I, were living on Hog Island (**16**) with their infant son. Ann and her son, John II, had come to Virginia on the *Seaflower*. The Utys were still there on February 4, 1625 (CBE 41, 61).

JOHN UTY (UTIE, UTEY) II

John II, the son of Ann and John Uty (Utie, Utey) I, was living on Hog Island (**16**) with his parents on February 16, 1624. On February 4, 1625, he was still there and was said to have come to Virginia with his mother on the *Seaflower* (CBE 41, 61).

V

JOHN VALES

On February 27, 1618, it was decided that John Vales, a boy being detained at Bridewell, would be kept until he could be sent to Virginia (HUME 8).

THOMAS VARLEY

On August 20, 1634, Thomas Varley was identified as the master of the ship *John and Dorothy* (CBE 118).

SAMUEL VASSALL

On July 4, 1628, Samuel Vassall, a ship captain, sent some goods from London to Virginia on the *Ann*. In 1629 he chartered the *Susan* in order to take a group of passengers to the colony. In 1633-1634 Captain Samuel Vassall promised Edward Kingswell to take a group of colonists to Carolina on the *George*. He later vacated their agreement and abandoned Kingswell and his people in Virginia (CBE 83, 91, 119).

JOHN VAUGHAN (VAGHAN)

John Vaughan (Vaghan), an 18-year-old cutler from Devonshire, set sail for Virginia in 1619 on the *Bona Nova* and arrived in November. Court testimony given on March 7, 1624, reveals that he was a Virginia Company servant whom Captain Jabez Whitaker had loaned to Ensign Thomas Savage for a year, during which time Vaughan and Savage had gone on a trading voyage. When a muster was made of the colony's inhabitants in early 1625, John Vaughan was identified as a 19-year-old servant in Sergeant William Barry's household on the lower side of the Hampton River, on the Virginia Company's land (**17**) (FER 295; CBE 68; MCGC 10-11).

RICHARD VAUSE

Richard Vause came to Virginia on the *Jonathan* in 1620. On January 24, 1625, he was living in Bermuda Hundred (**39**), where he was one of William Sharp's servants. Richard Vause was then age 20 (CBE 54).

JOHN VAVES

In 1619 it was decided that John Vaves, a boy from Billingsgate, would be sent to Virginia (CBE 12).

SIR HORATIO VEERE

On May 11, 1620, Sir Nathaniel Rich indicated that Sir Horatio Veere was willing to assist in finding an engineer to build fortifications in Virginia (VCR 1:339).

DON ALONSO DE VELASCO

Don Alonso de Velasco, who was appointed ambassador to England in January 1610, sent a June 14, 1610, letter to the King of Spain providing intelligence information on the Virginia colony. He said that the Indians had killed the majority of the English settlers and that the survivors were holed up in a stronghold they had built. He claimed that famine had driven the settlers to cannibalism and that it would be easy to extinguish the colony because it was so weak. On January 16, 1611, Velasco informed King Philip III that within a month four ships would transport 300 men to Virginia, 60 of whom were bringing their wives. The ships also were transporting eight clergymen and a substantial quantity of weapons, ammunition, and defensive attire. He said that the colonists intended to fortify themselves and build ships, making use of the abundance of good oak and pitch. On March 22, 1611, Velasco sent another letter to the King of Spain. This time, he said that two forts had been built near Old Point Comfort (**17**) and that England's undesirables were being sent to the colony. He enclosed a copy of a chart prepared by a surveyor sent to Virginia in 1610 to make a sketch map for King James I. In time, that drawing became known as the Velasco map (BRO 392, 442-443, 455-458; CJS 1:123, 129).

NICHOLAS VEN

Nicholas Ven, a laborer, came to Virginia in 1608 in the 1st Supply of new colonists. He would have lived in Jamestown (**1**) (CJS 1:223; 2:161).

JOHN VERIN (VERONE)

John Verin (Verone) came to Virginia on the *George* in 1623. On February 4, 1625, he was living on the lower side of the James River, where he was a servant on Hugh Crowder's (Crowther's) plantation (**12**). Sometime prior to April 11, 1625, Verin withdrew into the loft of a building on the Crowder plantation and hanged himself. When an inquest was held to investigate the cause of his death, witnesses testified that John Verin had not been mistreated by his master and had committed suicide. The justices of the General Court agreed (CBE 60; MCGC 53).

JOHN VERNIE

On February 16, 1624, John Vernie was living on the Maine (**3**), just west of Jamestown Island (CBE 39).

EM. VESIE

On November 6, 1622, the Virginia Company noted that Em. Vesie, a gentleman from Grays Inn, England, had received some shares of Virginia land from his uncle, Henry Reynolds. It is uncertain whether Vesie ever attempted to patent and seat land in the colony (VCR 2:122).

JOHN VICARS

John Vicars died sometime after April 1623 but before February 16, 1624, at one of the plantations on the lower side of the James River, within the corporation of James City (8-15) (CBE 41).

BODWINE VICTORY

In September or October 1623, Bodwine Victory, a mariner, asked Governor Francis Wyatt to see that the master of his ship paid him the wages he was owed (VCR 4:275).

HENRY VINCENT

On August 4, 1635, Henry Vincent was identified as one of Samuel Snead's servants. Snead had used Vincent's headright when patenting some land (PB 1 Pt. 1:268).

***

WILLIAM VINCENT (VINCENE)

William Vincent (Vincene) came to Virginia on the *Mary and James* sometime prior to January 11, 1622. On February 16, 1624, he and his wife were living in Bermuda Hundred (39), where he was a household head. They were still residing there on January 24, 1625. William was then 39 years old and his wife, Joan, was 42. William Vincent's household was relatively well supplied with stored food and defensive weaponry, and he occupied a dwelling of his own. When a list of patented land was sent back to England in May 1625, William Vincent was credited with 100 acres of land in Charles City, acreage that had been seated. On March 13, 1626, he brought suit against Thomas Harris and his wife but was fined for failing to appear in court to present his case. On January 9, 1627, he was accused of planting part of Richard Taylor's land in Bermuda Hundred; how-

ever, he was given 5 acres as compensation for clearing part of Taylor's land and the charges were dropped. On February 9, 1628, William Vincent got into another land dispute, this time with his neighbor, John Dodds. The General Court decided that each man would have half of the acreage in question and a portion of the house Vincent had been sharing with Dodds. Vincent was ordered to pay Dodds for his efforts in clearing and seating the land. Sometime prior to 1638, William Vincent came into possession of some land on 4 Mile Creek in Henrico County (CBE 35, 54; MCGC 97, 129, 166; VCR 4:553; DOR 1:9; PB 1 Pt. 2:551).

JOAN VINCENT (VINCENE) (MRS. WILLIAM VINCENT [VINCENE])

On February 16, 1624, Joan, the wife of William Vincent (Vincene), was living in Bermuda Hundred (39). She apparently was an habitual gossip, for in November 1624 the General Court decided to have her punished for slandering her neighbor Alice Boyse (Boise), whom she accused of bastardry and causing problems between Samuel Jordan and his wife, Cisley. By March 1626 Joan Vincent again had run afoul of the law. This time she was found guilty of slandering several women in her community's church, whom she termed Thomas Harris's whores. Interestingly, Joan's husband, William Vincent, was then suing Harris in an attempt to recover a debt. On January 24, 1625, Joan Vincent and her husband were still living at Bermuda Hundred, where he was a household head. She was then age 42 (CBE 35, 54; MCGC 31, 96; DOR 1:9).

***

***

VINCENCIO (VICENTIO) (SEE VINCENCIO [VICENTIO] CASTINE [CASTILLIAN]) MRS. VINCENCIO (VICENTIO) (SEE MRS. VINCENCIO [VICENTIO] CASTINE [CASTILLIAN])

***

***

GEORGE VINON (VINOYN) (SEE GEORGE UNGWIN [UNGWINE, ONION, UNION, UNWYN])

ELIZABETH VINON (VINOYN) I (MRS. GEORGE VINON [VINOYN]) (SEE ELIZABETH UNGWIN [UNGWINE, ONION, UNION, UNWYN] I)

KATHERINE VINON (VINOYN) I (MRS. GEORGE VINON [VINOYN]) (SEE KATHERINE UNGWIN [UNGWINE, ONION, UNION, UNWYN] I)

ELIZABETH VINON (VINOYN) II (SEE ELIZABETH UNGWIN [UNGWINE, ONION, UNION, UNWYN] II)

KATHERINE VINON (VINOYN) II (SEE KATHERINE UNGWIN [UNGWINE, ONION, UNION, UNWYN] II)

***

DANIEL VIRGO (VERGO, VIERO)

On February 16, 1624, Daniel Virgo (Vergo, Viero) came to Virginia on the *George* in 1623 and on February 16, 1624, was living at West and Shirley Hundred (41). He died there sometime before a muster was compiled on January 22, 1625 (CBE 36, 53).

***

JOHN VIRGO (VERGO)

John Virgo (Vergo) came to Virginia on the *Treasurer*. On February 16, 1624, he was living on the lower side of the James River, within the corporation of James City but west of Gray's Creek (8, 9). On January 24, 1625, Virgo was identified as one of William Peirce's indentured servants residing on Mulberry Island (21). He shared a home with his wife, Susan, who also was a Peirce servant. On March 5, 1629, John Virgo was fined for refusing to assist the provost marshal in carrying out his official duties. He posted a bond guaranteeing that he would appear in court when summoned. However, on April 8, 1629, he failed to comply and, as a result, forfeited his bond (CBE 40, 57; MCGC 190, 196; DOR 1:47).

SUSAN VIRGO (VERGO) (MRS. JOHN VIRGO [VERGO])

On January 24, 1625, Susan Virgo, one of William Peirce's indentured servants, was living on Mulberry Island (21) with her husband, John. John and Susan came to Virginia on the *Treasurer* (CBE 57).

***

WILLIAM VOLDAY (VOLDA)

William Volday (Volda), a Swiss citizen, came to Virginia in 1607 and was one of the first Jamestown (1) colonists. Captain John Smith considered him villainous, for when he was sent to retrieve some Dutchmen who had fled from the settlement, he purportedly furnished them with everything they needed to destroy the colony. Volday, on the other hand, claimed that when he caught up with the Dutch fugitives, they were angry and uncooperative (CJS 1:266-267; 2:215-216).

PHILIIP VRANGE

Philip Vrange was among the colonists sent to Berkeley Hundred (55). He apparently died a short time after his January 29, 1621, arrival, for his name was marked off a list of people sent to establish the plantation (VCR 3:426).

W

JOHN WADE

When Thomas Crispe testified before the General Court on November 21, 1625, he said that he witnessed an agreement between Edward Nevell and Robert Newman. According to Crispe, Nevell gave Newman a tobacco bill signed by John Wade and promised to deliver some tobacco to Newman when they arrived in Canada (MCGC 75-76).

WILLIAM WADFORD

On April 11, 1625, the justices of the General Court ordered William Wadford and several others to appear on April 25th to testify in a case that involved some cattle that Lieutenant Shephard signed over to Captain Croshaw (MCGC 52).

THOMAS WADLAND

On December 19, 1631, Thomas Wadland received permission to ship some goods from Barnstable to Virginia or New England on the *Pleasure* (CBE 98).

WILLIAM WADLAND

William Wadland was authorized on December 19, 1631, to ship some goods from Barnstable to Virginia or New England on the *Pleasure* (CBE 98).

THEODORE WADSWORTH

Theodore Wadsworth received a commission from the Virginia Company on January 16, 1622, authorizing him to take 60 passengers to Virginia on the *George* (VCR 3:591).

THOMAS WADSWORTH

On January 16, 1622, Thomas Wadsworth of the *George* asked the Virginia Company for permission to take 60 passengers to Virginia (VCR 1:574-575).

WILLIAM WADSWORTH

William Wadsworth came to Virginia in 1621 on the *Flying Hart*. On February 7, 1625, he was living in Newportes News (**24**) and was one of Daniel Gookin's servants. William, who was then 26 years old, also was identified as a Gookin servant in Elizabeth City (**18**), which suggests that he alternated between the two locations (CBE 63).

WAHUNSUNACOCK (SEE POWHATAN)

***

JOHN WAINE (WAYNE)

John Waine (Wayne) came to Virginia in 1618 on the *Neptune*, the ship that transported Lord Delaware to Virginia. On February 16, 1624, John and his wife, Amity (Amyte, Ann), an ancient planter, were living in Elizabeth City (**18**) in a household that included George and Mary Ackland.

The Waines were still there in early 1625 and shared their home with the Acklands, who were young Virginia-born children. Also present were three adult males who appear to have been free. The Waine household, which was headed by 30-year-old John, was relatively well supplied with stored food and defensive weaponry and had two buildings and a palisade. In December 19, 1625, a reference was made to the Waine house in court testimony involving Thomas Crispe and Captain William Tucker. On March 16, 1627, John Waine informed the General Court that while he was aboard the *Plantation*, he saw a fight between Thomas Lawley and Thomas Hittal, who were separated by Robert Cooke. By April 25, 1628, John Waine had attained the rank of sergeant. He then testified that the Rev. Rowland Graine of Elizabeth City had refused to allow his boat to be used for public service, despite a warrant from Captain William Tucker (CBE 44, 65; MCGC 81-82, 145, 172; DOR 1:57).

AMITY (AMYTE, ANN) WAINE (WAYNE) (MRS. JOHN WAINE [WAYNE])

Amity (Amyte, Ann), the wife of John Waine (Wayne), was an ancient planter who came to Virginia in 1610 on the *Swan*. On February 16, 1624, she was living with her husband in Elizabeth City (**18**). The Waines shared their home with George and Mary Ackland, two young children. In early 1625 Amity Waine was age 30; George Ackland was age 7 and Mary was age 4. As both Ackland youngsters were Virginia-born, they may have been Amity's children from a prior marriage. When Jamestown (**1**) merchant Thomas Warnett made his will on February 13, 1629, he named Mrs. John Waine as one of his beneficiaries (CBE 44, 65; SH 11-12).

***

RICHARD WAINHAM

When the Indians attacked Lieutenant Gibbs'd dividend at Westover (**54**) on March 22, 1622, Richard Wainham was slain (VCR 3:567).

THOMAS WAINMAN

In June 1619 John Woodlief (Woodliffe, Woodlase) I, an ancient planter and Virginia

Company investor, asked for a patent, indicating that he had invested in the Company in 1608 and had lived in the colony for 11 years. He said that he and his associates would seat 200 people on their land within six years. Virginia Company officials, who approved John Woodlief's request in July 1619, stipulated that the patent was to be listed under the name of Sir Thomas Wainman and associates. The property eventually became known as Woodlief's plantation **(49)** (VCR 1:232, 252).

THOMAS WAINWRIGHT

On June 19, 1622, Thomas Wainwright, a London fishmonger, received a share of Virginia land from Francis Carter, who had purchased some of Lady Delaware's land rights (VCR 2:56).

RICHARD WAKE

On November 5, 1624, John Woodall, in anticipation of surgeon Richard Wake's setting sail for Virginia, authorized Wake to take custody of certain containers of goods and letters that Woodall had sent to his servant, Christopher Best, on the *Margaret*, if Best was no longer alive. Wake was to sell some of the items for the best price he could get and to return the letters and specific containers to Woodall unopened. When Richard Wake arrived in Virginia and learned that Christopher Best was dead, he presented Woodall's letter to the justices of the General Court. They decided to buy the surgical chest and other medical paraphernalia because the colony had such great need of them. Later in the year Richard Wake was listed among those to whom the late Thomas Clarke owed money at the time of his death aboard the *Elizabeth*; it appears that Wake had provided him with medical care. On January 30, 1626, Richard Wake presented the General Court with a copy of a bill of lading for goods he was sending on the *Margaret* to Elizabeth Page in London. On April 9, 1628, Wake, who was still a practicing surgeon, informed the General Court about a man that Captain John Preen was supposed to deliver to Richard Bennett in 1623. Wake, who had been aboard Preen's ship, realized that the man was too sick to survive the voyage and therefore had him put ashore. Richard Wake was still alive on May 26, 1633, at which time he joined a group of Virginia planters who claimed that

Governor John Harvey and his council were trying to make Maurice Thompson the sole exporter of Virginia tobacco (MCGC 71-72, 92, 171, 199; G&M 187-188).

JOHN WAKEFIELD

John Wakefield, a boy being detained at Bridewell, was pardoned on July 12, 1633, so that he could be sent to Virginia. He came to the colony in 1634 on the *Bonaventure*. Adam Thorogood covered the cost of his passage and used him as a headright when patenting some land on June 24, 1635 (HUME 38; PB 1 Pt. 1:179).

THOMAS WALCHDER

Thomas Walchder, a 23-year-old gardener from Kent, England, left England in 1619 aboard the *Bona Nova*. He probably was a Virginia Company servant or tenant (FER 295).

HUMPHREY WALDEN

Humphrey Walden came to Virginia on the *Warwick* and on February 16, 1624, was living at Martin's Hundred **(7)**. He was still there on February 4, 1625. He and his partner, Stephen Barker, headed a household that was relatively well supplied with stored food and defensive weaponry (CBE 42, 62; DOR 1:46).

ROBERT WALDEN

When the Indians attacked Martin's Hundred **(7)** on March 22, 1622, Robert Walden was slain (VCR 3:570).

RICHARD WALDO (WALDOE)

Richard Waldo (Waldoe), a gentleman, came to Virginia in 1608 in the 2nd Supply of new settlers. Shortly after he arrived in Jamestown **(1)**, he became a member of the governor's council. Waldo accompanied Captain John Smith on an exploratory voyage to the territory of the Monacan Indians. Smith later sent him to Powhatan with a crown. He also went to Hog Island **(16)** with Smith, who described Waldo as a valiant gentleman, an "old soldier," and someone who was attentive to his responsibilities. Waldo accompanied Captain John Smith to Powhatan's York River village, Werowocomoco, and was second in command when Smith went to the territory of the Pamunkey Indians in December 1608. Sir Thomas Gates designated Waldo master of the works in May 1609 (CJS 1:235, 239-240, 243, 254; 2:182, 184, 188, 190-192, 203; VCR 3:13).

ROBERT WALDRON

On April 9, 1628, the General Court heard testimony about two manservants whom Captain John Preen was supposed to bring to Richard Bennett of Warresqueak (**26**) in 1623. Preen said that one of the servants was too ill to survive the voyage and therefore was put ashore at the Downes. The other man, Robert Waldron, was a gentleman and merchant whom Bennett had told Preen to treat well. For that reason, Captain Preen said that he did nothing to prevent Waldron from going ashore (MCGC 171).

[NO FIRST NAME] WALKER

Master Walker, a tradesman, came to Virginia in 1608, in the 2nd Supply of new settlers. Therefore, he would have lived in Jamestown (**1**) (CJS 1:242; 2:191).

GEORGE WALKER

George Walker, a Virginia Company investor and a gentleman, came to Virginia in 1607 and was one of the first Jamestown (**1**) settlers. According to George Percy's narrative, Walker died on August 24, 1607, and was buried the same day (CJS 2:141, 283; HAI 99).

JOHN WALKER

John Walker came to Virginia on the *Furtherance* and died on Jamestown Island (**1**) sometime after April 1623 but before February 16, 1624 (CBE 39).

JOHN WALKER

On September 2, 1631, officials at Bridewell decided that John Walker, a boy who was being detained, would be sent to Mr. Drake, if Drake agreed to send him to Virginia (HUME 37).

RICHARD WALKER

Richard Walker died on Jamestown Island (**1**) sometime after April 1623 but before February 16, 1624 (CBE 39).

RICHARD WALKER

On September 25, 1624, officials at Bridewell decided that Richard Walker, a vagrant from Cordwainer Ward who was being detained, would be sent to Virginia (CBE 48).

ROGER WALKER

Roger Walker came to Virginia in 1623 on the *Providence* and on February 16, 1624, was living in Elizabeth City (**17, 18**). By February 7, 1625, he had moved to Newportes News (**24**), where he was a 22-year-old servant in Daniel Gookin's household (CBE 43, 63).

WILLIAM WALKER

When William Walker, a boy, was brought to Bridewell on January 22, 1619, it was decided that he would be sent to Virginia (HUME 21).

WILLIAM WALKER

On March 22, 1622, when the Indians attacked Weyanoke (**52**), William Walker was slain (VCR 3:569).

WILLIAM WALKER

William Walker was living at the College (**66**) on February 16, 1624. He may have been the boy who had been detained at Bridewell in 1619 (CBE 35).

CHARLES WALLER

Charles Waller came to Virginia in 1620 aboard the *Abigail* and on February 16, 1624, was living in urban Jamestown (**1**) in the household of Captain Roger Smith. On January 24, 1625, he was described as a 22-year-old servant in the Smith household. Charles Waller and some others ran afoul of the law in March 1629 when they refused to help the provost marshal place an unruly person in the stocks. Because Waller ignored a summons to appear in court, the bond he had posted was forfeited to the government (CBE 38, 55; MCGC 190, 196).

EDWARD WALLER

On April 8, 1629, Edward Waller brought suit against John Johnson I. He claimed that Johnson took his gun and a sow and promised to replace them, but never did. Johnson, on the other hand, said that he had sent Edward Waller a pig and that Richard Dolphenby had brought him a gun. The General Court's justices decided to postpone their decision until they could hear from Dolphenby (MCGC 195).

JOHN WALLER

John Waller, a gentleman and Virginia Company investor, came to Virginia in 1607 and was one of the first Jamestown (1) colonists. According to George Percy, Waller seized the King of the Pasbehay Indians and stabbed him with his sword (CJS 1:208; 2:141, 283; HAI 512).

JOHN WALLER

John Waller, who identified himself as a resident of St. Edmundsbury, in Suffolk, England, gave his age as 40 in early May 1622 when he testified in Chancery proceedings. He said that he had been aboard the *Neptune*, which was bringing the late Lord Delaware to Virginia in 1618, and knew that John Rolfe was supposed to take custody of Delaware's goods. Waller had witnessed Edward Brewster's attack on George Perrin and also had been present when Brewster struck George Percy, the Earl of Northumberland's younger brother, and called him a vile name. John Waller indicated that he was in Virginia when Edward Brewster was tried at a court martial hearing (SR 9947; C 24/489).

JOHN WALLER

On November 22, 1622, Virginia Company officials noted that John Waller, an ancient planter and Company investor, wanted the land to which he was entitled. He may have been the same man who came to Virginia in 1607 (VCR 2:145-146).

JEFFREY (JEFFRY) WALLET

Jeffrey (Jeffry) Wallett set sail for Virginia on April 17, 1619. He may have been a Virginia Company servant or tenant (FER 107).

EDMUND WALLIS

Edmund Wallis came to Virginia on the *Hopewell* in 1628 at the expense of Adam Thorogood, who used Wallis as a headright

when patenting some land on June 24, 1635 (PB 1 Pt. 1:179).

EDWARD WALLIS

On May 29, 1630, officials in England were informed that Deputy-Governor John Pott, a physician, had freed Edward Wallis, a convicted murderer and resident of Archer's Hope (6) (CBE 91; SAIN 1:117).

WILLIAM WALLIS

William Wallis set sail from England on July 31, 1622, aboard the *James* and was sent to Virginia by William Ewins, whose plantation (13) was on the lower side of the James River (FER 400).

JOHN WALMSLEY

John Walmsley died at one of the settlements on the lower side of the James River, within the corporation of James City (8-15), sometime after April 1623 but before February 16, 1624 (CBE 41).

THOMAS WALSINGHAM

On November 21, 1618, Thomas Walsingham, a vagrant and "young rogue" who was being detained at Bridewell, was sentenced to transportation to Virginia (CBE 11).

WILLIAM WALTER

William Walter, a 19-year-old shoemaker from Penbrookshire, set sail from England in 1618 or 1619 aboard the *Bona Nova*. On February 4, 1625, he was living on Captain Samuel Mathews' plantation (15), where he was a 27-year-old servant (CBE 60; FER 295).

JOHN WALTHAM

John Waltham, a 32-year-old sailor from London, testified before the High Court of the Admiralty that he was part of the crew of the *Faulcon*, which was going to Jamestown (1) to pick up a large quantity of sassafras that was to be transported to Boyers Bay and sold. He said that when the ship reached Virginia, the sassafras was not ready, and as a result, there was a three-month delay. Also, a much smaller quantity of sassafras was provided than had been promised by the Virginians who were selling it (EAE 11; HCA 13/43 ff 201ro-201vo; SR 3807).

JOHN WALTON
(WALTONN, WALTUN)

John Walton (Waltonn, Waltun) came to Virginia on the *Elizabeth* in 1621 and on February 16, 1624, was living in Elizabeth City (**18**). He was still there in early 1625 and was a member of Alexander Mountney's household. Walton, who was age 28, was free. On August 28, 1626, John Walton asked the General Court's permission to make a voyage to Canada, taking along Peter Smith and some others. He was authorized to do so but had to provide the names of the men accompanying him. On February 11, 1629, Sergeant Giles Jones testified that he had witnessed an agreement between John Walton and Captain Wilcocks, who had agreed to transport Walton's servants and goods to Wilcocks' plantation in Accomack (**72-78**). During the 1630s Walton's name frequently appeared in Accomack court records. On September 16, 1640, John Walton made his will, indicating that he was sick and weak. He was survived by his wife, Grace, and young son, John Jr., who inherited his father's 300-acre plantation (CBE 44, 66; CGC 110, 187; AMES 1:30, 78, 135-136, 144, 158; 2:46-49).

WILLIAM WALTON

In January 1627 William Walton was tried at the Middlesex Sessions, found guilty of false impersonation, and sentenced to transportation to Virginia (CBE 77).

WILLIAM WANERTON

William Wanerton died on Jamestown Island (**1**) sometime after February 16, 1624, but before January 24, 1625 (CBE 56).

JOHN WARD (WARDE)

Virginia Company records indicate that in 1619 John Ward (Warde) was issued a patent because he and his associates had transported people to Virginia that year. In July 1619 Ward represented his plantation (**61**) in the assembly even though Speaker John Pory claimed that Ward had seated his land illegally. In October 1619 Captain John Ward sent his ship into the Potomac River to trade with the King of the Patawo-mack Indians. When he returned to Jamestown (**1**) in December, he claimed that he had been cheated. In March 1620 there were 26 men living at Ward's plantation in the corporation of Charles City. When Ward went to England, he entrusted his plantation and servants to a tenant, Captain William Eppes. On May 17, 1620, the Virginia Company confirmed the patent assigned to Ward and his fellow investors. While in England, Ward asked the Company to free Luke Burden, who was being detained by the Virginia colony's governing officials.

In 1621 Ward set sail on the *Elizabeth* but apparently did not reach Virginia until after the March 22, 1622, Indian attack. Several years later three of his servants, who were about to be freed, were queried about the amount of tobacco and corn they had raised the summer following the Indian attack, while Captain William Eppes was still in possession of the plantation. Eppes himself, when asked, stated that shortly after the Indians attacked, he went to the Ward plantation, rescued the survivors, and took them to his plantation (**74**) on the Eastern Shore so that they could find shelter.

Captain John Ward moved to Elizabeth City (**17**) after he returned to Virginia and on February 16, 1624, was living at the Indian Thicket, part of the Virginia Company's land. When a muster was made of that area's inhabitants in early 1625, Ward was described as head of a household that included seven other people. The two dwellings in his possession were located on the east side of the Hampton River on Company property. The Ward household was well supplied with stored food and defensive weaponry. Captain John Ward's name was mentioned several times in General Court records from 1626 and 1627, in relation to settling and collecting debts. Some of his business dealings involved merchant Humphrey Rastall and John Darker, whom he paid with a tobacco note from Captain William Eppes. In February 1627 Captain John Ward was back in England (VCR 1:345, 400; 3:118, 154, 155-156, 244, 247; FER 138, 139; CBE 43, 67; MCGC 43, 87, 96, 119, 138-139; DOR 1:66).

JOHN WARD (WARDE)

On January 12, 1627, John Ward (Warde) was identified as a Virginia Company tenant who was being assigned to the incumbent governor (MCGC 136).

JOHN WARD (WARDE)

On March 21, 1633, John Ward (Warde) of Varina, a planter, received a 21-year lease for 25 acres of land near the property already in his possession (PB 1 Pt. 1:147).

ROGER WARD

In 1619 Roger Ward, a convicted thief from London who was being detained in Newgate Prison, was sentenced to transportation overseas (CBE 12).

ROGER WARD

Roger Ward came to Virginia on the *John and Dorothy* in 1634 at the expense of Adam Thorogood, who used him as a headright when patenting some land on June 24, 1635 (PB 1 Pt. 1:179).

SETH WARD (WARDE)

On May 30, 1634, Seth Ward (Warde) of Varina, a planter, received a 21-year lease for 60 acres of land in the territory that became Henrico County. He may have been renting some land that had belonged to the Virginia Company (PB 1 Pt. 1:148).

THOMAS WARD

Thomas Ward set sail from England in 1619 aboard the *Warwick*. He and his master, bricklayer John Jackson, were among the approximately 266 people whom the Society of Martin's Hundred sent to Virginia in 1618–1619 to establish a plantation on land the Society had been assigned. In January 1620 John Rolfe reported that the Martin's Hundred settlers were residing in Pasbehay, on what officially had become the Governor's Land (3). By March they had gone forth to the vast tract that had been set aside for the establishment of the Martin's Hundred plantation (7). In January 1622 the residents of Martin's Hundred reportedly were weakened by sickness and malnutrition. When Indians attacked the settlement on March 22, 1622, many lives were lost. Thomas Ward survived and on February 16, 1624, was in the household of John Jackson at Martin's Hundred. Ward was still in the Jackson household on February 4, 1625, at which time he was described as a 47-year-old servant.

On May 20, 1625, when Thomas Ward and his master sent a letter to the Society of Martin's Hundred's treasurer, complaining about conditions in their plantation, Ward, who was literate, identified himself as a "pottmaker." He indicated that he and the other settlers the Society had sent to Virginia had not been furnished with the tools of their trade, adequate clothing and shoes, or the arms and ammunition they needed to protect themselves. The name of Thomas Ward appeared in the General Court's minutes on several occasions during the mid- to late 1620s, by which time Virginia had become a Crown colony. Ward stayed on at Martin's Hundred and on January 12, 1627, testified about conditions there. He was a resident of Martin's Hundred on January 20, 1634, when he witnessed the will of his neighbor, John Creed. Archaeological excavations undertaken by the Colonial Williamsburg Foundation at Martin's Hundred during the 1970s led to the discovery of a potter's pond and shed, potter's tools, and locally made earthenware vessels. Potter Thomas Ward is the earliest identifiable practitioner of his trade in English North America (CBE 42, 62; MCGC 135; FER 569; SH 15; WITH 80; SR 3971).

WILLIAM WARD (WARDE)

William Ward (Warde), a tailor and Virginia Company investor, came to Virginia in 1608 in the 2nd Supply of new settlers in Jamestown (1). In July 1608 he accompanied Captain John Smith on a voyage of discovery on the Chesapeake Bay, and in late December 1608 he went with Smith to Pamunkey and to Werowocomoco. Captain John Smith categorized William Ward as a soldier (CJS 1:223, 230; 2:170, 193, 243, 283).

WILLIAM WARD (WARDE)

On January 22, 1619, William Ward (Warde), a boy born in Yorkshire who had been brought in from Old Bailey, was detained at Bridewell until he could be sent to Virginia (CBE 18).

WILLIAM WARD (WARDE)

William Ward (Warde) came to Virginia on the *Jonathan* and on February 16, 1624, was living in urban Jamestown (1) in Edward Blaney's household. However, he was attributed at the same time to the Blaney plantation on the lower side of the James River (14). On February 4, 1625, William Ward was still living at the latter location and was described as a 20-year-old indentured servant. Ward may have been the boy sent to Virginia by officials at Bridewell (CBE 38, 40, 59).

THOMAS WARDEN

On September 5, 1623, Thomas Warden, a husbandman from Ely in Hampshire, arrived in Jamestown on the *Ann* and took the oath of supremacy. By early January 1625 he had moved to the Eastern Shore, where he was living in the household of Captain William Eppes (74). Warden was then described as a 24-year-old indentured servant. On February 3, 1626, when Captain William Eppes patented some land, he used Thomas Warden as a headright and stated that he had come to the colony on the *Ann* in 1623 (MCGC 6; CBE 68; PB 1 Pt. 1:49).

RICHARD WARE

On May 26, 1634, Richard Ware and other planters whose families had been in Virginia for several years, said that they feared they would sustain major losses if Maurice Thompson was appointed sole shipper (supplier) to the colony (CBE 115-116).

JOHN WAREHAM

John Wareham, a merchant, came to Virginia sometime prior to January 21, 1629. It was then that he testified that Mrs. Adams' husband, probably Robert Adams of Martins Hundred (7), had bought a servant but failed to pay for him. On May 10, 1629, when Wareham testified before the General Court, he indicated that he was age 25. He said that Andrew Leane had agreed to serve Thomas Mayhew for a year and work on his boat. In September 1632 John Wareham served as a burgess for Mounts Bay, an area in the eastern part of Archer's Hope (6). In February 1633 he represented the settlements from Harrop to Martin's Hundred, territory that stretched from the east side of Archer's Hope (now College) Creek to Skiffs Creek (MCGC 181, 197; HEN 1:179, 203).

AUGUSTINE WARNER

Augustine Warner came to Virginia on the *Hopewell* in 1628 at the expense of Adam Thorogood, who used him as a headright when patenting some land on June 24, 1635. On October 12, 1635, Warner patented some land in his own right, securing 250 acres in the New Poquoson (19) in Elizabeth City (PB 1 Pt. 1:179, 298).

***

THOMAS WARNET (WARNETT)

Thomas Warnet (Warnett), a merchant and mariner from Southwark, in London, England, made his will in Jamestown (1) on February 13, 1629, and identified himself as a local resident. His will was presented for probate in London by his executrix and widow, Thomasine, on November 8, 1630. The testator made bequests to several Jamestown Island residents and to people who lived in Elizabeth City (17, 18) and Martin's Hundred (7) (SR 3965; SH 11-12; EEAC 61; CBE 93).

THOMASINE WARNET (WARNETT) (MRS. THOMAS WARNET [WARNETT])

Thomasine Warnet (Warnett) of London was the widow and executrix of Jamestown (1) merchant and mariner, Thomas Warnet (Warnett), as well as one of his heirs (SR 3965; SH 11-12; EEAC 61; CBE 93).

***

ANTHONY WARREN

On February 8, 1628, Anthony Warren was identified as the co-administrator of Daniel Lacey's estate. Lacey was a gentleman and resident of Jamestown Island (1) (MCGC 165).

ELIZABETH WARREN

On July 27, 1632, Elizabeth Warren, a girl described as a "common pilferer" and longtime prisoner at Bridewell, escaped from jail. She was to be sent to Virginia at her own request (HUME 37).

***

THOMAS WARREN

On November 20, 1635, when Thomas Warren patented some land on Bailey's

Creek in Charles City County, he used the headright of his wife, Susan, whom he identified as the widow of ancient planter Robert Greenleaf (PB 1 Pt. 1:314).

SUSAN GREENLEAF WARREN (MRS. ROBERT GREENLEAF, MRS. THOMAS WARREN) (SEE SUSAN GREENLEAF [GREENLEAFE])

Sometime prior to November 20, 1635, Susan, the widow of ancient planter Robert Greenleaf, married Thomas Warren, who used her as a headright when patenting some land (PB 1 Pt. 1:314).

***

WILLIAM WARREN

On April 12, 1633, William Warren had tenure of 50 acres in Elizabeth City's Indian Thicket (**17**), part of a 100-acre leasehold that had been transferred to Lancelot Barnes. The property the men were renting was land that belonged to the defunct Virginia Company (PB 1 Pt. 1:142).

WILLIAM WAS

William Was came to Virginia on the *Hopewell* in 1633 at the expense of Adam Thorogood, who used him as a headright when patenting some land on June 24, 1635 (PB 1 Pt. 1:179).

JOHN WASHBORNE

John Washborne came to Virginia in 1619 on the *Jonathan*. In early 1625 he was living in Elizabeth City (**18**), where he was a 25-year-old servant in Alexander Mountney's household (CBE 66).

JOHN WASHBORNE (WASBORNE)

John Washborne (Wasborne) came to Virginia on the *Jonathan* in 1620 and on February 16, 1624, was living on the Eastern Shore. In early 1625 he was still there and was a 30-year-old servant in Thomas Savage's household in Savages Neck (**77**). Washborne witnessed a bill of sale in the Accomack court on March 22, 1634, and another one the following month (CBE 46, 68; AMES 1:15, 36).

[NO FIRST NAME] WASHER

When Virginia's first assembly convened in July 1619, Ensign Washer, whose first name is unknown, served as burgess for Captain Christopher Lawne's plantation (**25**). On November 11, 1619, Virginia Company officials were informed that Ensign Washer and Captain Lawne would secure the neck of land they were occupying on Warresqueak Bay (VCR 3:154, 226-229).

WILLIAM WASKEY (WASKY)

On January 22, 1620, officials at Bridewell decided that William Waskey (Wasky), a vagrant, would be sent to Virginia (CBE 17).

EDWARD WATERHOUSE

On June 11, 1621, Virginia Company officials noted that Mr. Edward Waterhouse was a possible candidate for secretary. He later wrote a lengthy narrative in which he recounted the history of the colony and described the March 22, 1622, Indian attack (VCR 1:478).

JOHN WATERHOUSE

On March 22, 1622, when the Indians attacked Abraham Peirsey's plantation on the upper side of the Appomattox River (**39**), John Waterhouse was slain (VCR 3:566).

JULIAN WATERMAN

On July 27, 1632, Bridewell officials described Julian Waterman as a boy and common pilferer who tried to break out of jail. He was to be sent to Virginia at his own request (HUME 37).

THOMAS WATERMAN

On April 20, 1624, Ralph Hamor of Jamestown (**1**) asked William Harwood of Martin's Hundred (**7**) to return his manservant, Thomas Waterman, who reportedly was at Harwood's plantation (MCGC 52).

ANDREW WATERS

The General Court's minutes for April 25, 1626, note that surgeon Thomas Bunn provided medical treatment to Andrew Waters, one of Richard Stephens' servants in urban Jamestown (**1**). The minutes also state that

Waters was a servant who had been brought to Virginia by John Stephens (MCGC 56, 101).

***

EDWARD WATERS
(WATTERS, WALTERS)

Ancient planter Edward Waters (Watters, Walters) left England in 1609 on the *Seaventure,* the ship that was bringing Sir George Somers and Sir Thomas Gates to Virginia and then wrecked in Bermuda. Afterward, the survivors constructed the *Patience* and the *Deliverance* from the native cedar wood and continued on to Virginia. Edward Waters arrived in Jamestown (1) on the *Patience* in April 1610. A few months later he accompanied Sir George Somers on a return trip to Bermuda to procure hogs and other food stuffs for the surviving Virginia colonists. Somers died, and Waters and a few other men were left in Bermuda to stake England's claim. During their explorations, they discovered a large, valuable piece of ambergris and began squabbling over it. According to Captain John Smith, Waters killed Edward Samuell, another sailor. Waters escaped execution and later was pardoned; some sources blame the crime on another man. Smith stated that after the Bermuda Company was formed and the ambergris was sent to England, Edward Waters was one of six men named to Bermuda's council of governors. In 1615 he and several others set sail for the West Indies but landed in the Canary Islands. They made another attempt to reach the West Indies but almost drowned. An English pirate or privateer who saved their lives took them to England. Waters eventually returned to Bermuda, and in 1617 Governor Daniel Tucker sent him to Virginia to procure goats and hogs. He and his men were unsuccessful in returning to Bermuda, so they went back to Virginia, where Waters stayed. During the March 22, 1622, Indian assault, the Waters home in Elizabeth City (18) came under attack. Although Edward Waters, his wife, and other members of his household were listed among the dead, the Waters family actually had been captured by the Indians and transported across the James River to Nansemond (20 c), where they were kept prisoner. They eventually found a canoe and escaped across the river to Kecoughtan.

On February 16, 1624, Edward Waters and his wife, Grace, and son, William, were living in Elizabeth City near Waters Creek, the stream now dammed to create Lake Maury. On August 14, 1624, Waters was termed a gentleman when he patented some additional Elizabeth City acreage adjacent to Waters Creek. In early 1625 Edward and Grace Waters were living on their plantation near Blunt Point (22). The household included their son, William, daughter, Margaret, six servants, and five other adults, including two married couples. Edward Waters, who was age 40, was in possession of four dwellings, a palisade, a boat, and an ample supply of stored food and defensive weaponry. In May 1625 he was credited with 100 acres at Blunt Point. On January 5, 1626, Edward Waters was obliged to post a bond guaranteeing that he would pay a just debt to Mr. Langley, a merchant. At the same General Court session, Waters testified that he had been the pilot of a Dutch ship that was brought up to Jamestown and that Thomas Thornbury (a member of Waters' household) brought up Waters' own boat so that he could return to Elizabeth City. In August 1626 Edward Waters was named a justice of Elizabeth City's monthly court. On November 21, 1626, he testified that he had witnessed a contract between Captain John Wilcocks and William Claiborne—an agreement to outfit a shallop.

On January 9, 1627, Edward Waters received permission to lease 50 acres at the Strawberry Banks in Elizabeth City (17), land that belonged to the then-defunct Virginia Company. Functioning as a justice of Elizabeth City's local court, he presented the late Thomas Hunter's will to the General Court's justices. In 1628 he presented an inventory of Captain John Wilcocks' estate and was named administrator because he was the decedent's greatest creditor. In January 1629 he transferred part of Wilcocks' estate to another creditor. Waters also compiled and presented Captain Crotias's inventory to the General Court, and he delivered the late Thomas Hunter's estate to Patrick Canada's attorney, Richard Cocke. In March 1629 Lieutenant Edward Waters' appointment as a court justice was reaffirmed, and he was placed in command of the Elizabeth City plantations from the east side of the Hampton River to Fox Hill (19). Captain Edward Waters made a trip to England sometime prior to August 20, 1630, when he made his will at Great

Nornemead in Hertfordshire. He left his son, William, all of his Virginia land and his goods in England and Ireland. He also made bequests to his wife, Grace; to his daughter, Margaret; to his brother, John Waters of Middleham in Yorkshire; and to his friend Lionel Rawlston of Elizabeth City. The testator made reference to the tobacco in his cellar in Elizabeth City, which was to go to Mr. Pennyton at Cheapside. Edward Waters died prior to September 11, 1630, at which time his brother, John, presented his will for probate (HAI 412; CJS 2:301, 308-309, 350-352, 358-359, 368; VCR 3:571; 4:557; CBE 44, 65, 92; PB 1 Pt. 1:18, 77-78, 93, 135; MCGC 87, 89, 106,125, 129-130, 159, 173, 183, 186, 193; HEN 1:131-132; SH 13; EEAC 61; SR 3964; DOR 1:59).

GRACE WATERS
(WATTERS, WALTERS)
(MRS. EDWARD WATERS
[WATTERS, WALTERS],
MRS. OBEDIENCE ROBINS)
(SEE GRACE WATERS ROBINS)

Grace, who married ancient planter Edward Waters (Watters, Walters), came to Virginia in 1618 on the *Diana*. During the March 22, 1622, Indian assault, when the Waters home in Elizabeth City (**18**) came under attack, Grace and her husband, Edward, and their son, William, were listed among those slain. However, they actually were captured by the Indians and spirited across the James River to Nansemond (**20 c**), where they were kept prisoner. They found a canoe and managed to escape to Kecoughtan. On February 16, 1624, Grace and her family were living in Elizabeth City, near Blunt Point (**22**), and they were still there in early 1625. Grace was then 21 years old, almost half her husband's age. On March 23, 1630, while Grace and Edward Waters were in England, Grace testified in a chancery suit involving the disposition of Sir George Yeardley's estate. She gave her age as 28 and said that she had been in Virginia for ten years. Grace Waters indicated that she had been living in Sir George Yeardley's household in 1621 and was aware that one of the litigants had some of Yeardley's cattle in his possession. On August 20, 1630, when Edward Waters made his will, he named his wife, Grace, as one of his heirs. Edward died prior to September 11, 1630. Later, the widowed Grace Waters

married Obedience Robins and moved to the Eastern Shore (**72-78**) (VCR 3:571; CJS 2:301, 308-309; CBE 44, 65; C 24/560 Pt. 2:84; SH 13).

WILLIAM WATERS
(WATTERS, WALTERS)

William Waters (Watters, Walters), the son of ancient planter Edward Waters, was presumed to have been killed in the March 22, 1622, Indian attack on the family home. However, he survived and on February 16, 1624, was living with his parents in Elizabeth City (**18**). He was still there in early 1625 and was described as Virginia-born. In September 1630 William Waters was identified as the minor son and primary heir of Edward Waters of Elizabeth City, who died at Hormead in Hertfordshire. After the widowed Grace Waters married Obedience Robins, William Waters and his sister, Margaret, moved to the Eastern Shore (**72-78**). He was still alive in October 1644 (VCR 3:571; CBE 44, 65; EEAC 61; MEY 461-462; AMES 2:105, 187, 198, 270, 281, 322, 390, 440).

MARGARET WATERS
(WATTERS, WALTERS)

In early 1625 Margaret Waters (Watters, Walters), the daughter of Edward and Grace Waters, was living in Elizabeth City (**18**) with her parents and brother, William. Margaret was born in Virginia and in August 1630 was named as one of her late father's heirs. After the widowed Grace Waters married Obedience Robins, Margaret Waters and her brother, William, moved to the Eastern Shore (**72-78**). Robins used Margaret as a headright when patenting some land in 1639 (CBE 65; MEY 461-462; PB 2:364).

***

EDWARD WATERS

On October 10, 1624, the General Court noted that Edward Waters was dead. His executor was to present an account of the decedent's estate to Captain William Tucker, the commander of Kecoughtan (**18**) (MCGC 22).

JOHN WATERS
(WATTERS, WALTERS)

John Waters (Watters, Walters) came to Virginia on the *Hopewell* in 1628 at the expense of Adam Thorogood, who used him as a headright when patenting some land on June 24, 1635 (PB 1 Pt. 1:179).

WILLIAM WATERS
(WATTERS, WALTERS)

On February 5, 1620, William Waters (Watters, Walters) from Holborn was detained at Bridewell until he could be sent to Virginia (CBE 18).

DANIEL WATKINS (WATTKINS)

Daniel Watkins (Wattkins) came to Virginia on the *Charles* in 1621 and on February 16, 1624, was living on the Eastern Shore (72-78). By October 10, 1624, he had moved to Paces Paines (9). It was then that he testified before the General Court, stating that he had seen John and Alice Proctor's maidservant, Elizabeth Abbott, punished numerous times. On February 4, 1625, Daniel Watkins and Phettiplace Close were living at Paces Paines, where they headed a household that included two servants and was relatively well supplied with provisions and defensive weaponry. On September 11, 1626, Daniel Watkins testified that Mrs. Joane Wright (a woman accused of witchcraft) had predicted Elizabeth Arundel's death (MCGC 23, 112; CBE 46, 59).

EVAN WATKINS

On March 22, 1622, when the Indians attacked Warresqueak, Edward Bennett's plantation (26), Evan Watkins was slain (VCR 3:571).

GIFFORD (GIFFARD)
WATKINS (WATKIN)

On June 28, 1634, Gifford (Giffard) Watkins (Watkin), a London merchant who was preparing to go to Virginia, made his will, which was witnessed by his brother, Arthur, and several others. When Gifford's will was presented for probate on June 27, 1637, he was said to have died in Virginia (SR 3979; SH 18).

HENRY WATKINS

Henry Watkins came to Virginia sometime prior to March 22, 1622. In September 1623 he was identified as the overseer of Lady Elizabeth Dale's property (72), servants, and cattle on the Eastern Shore; he served in that capacity until mid-1625. On February 16, 1624, while Watkins was living on the Eastern Shore, he represented that area in the February–March 1624 assembly session. As a burgess, he endorsed the assembly's rebuttal to Alderman Johnson's claim that conditions in the colony were not harsh prior to Governor George Yeardley's arrival in 1619. On January 3, 1625, Henry Watkins posted security for Peter Langman of Jamestown (1); Langman, in turn, agreed to serve Watkins for a year if he defaulted on his debt. Court testimony dating to June 23, 1625, mentioned that Watkins loaned two of Lady Dale's cattle to her cousin, George Thorpe of Berkeley Hundred (55), who perished in the March 1622 Indian attack. The animals probably were pastured at West and Shirley Hundred Island (41), where Lady Dale had some acreage. By April 3, 1627, Charles Harmar (Harmor, Harmer, Harman) had replaced Henry Watkins as overseer. Harmar then informed the General Court that he had taken custody of Lady Dale's cattle, crops, and other property, which Watkins had delivered to him (MCGC 11, 41, 48, 73-74, 146; CBE 46; HEN 1:128-129; HAI 915).

JAMES WATKINS

James Watkins, a laborer, came to Virginia in 1608 in the 2nd Supply of Jamestown (1) colonists. He accompanied Captain John Smith on two exploratory voyages on the Chesapeake Bay. Watkins was among those sent overland to build a house for Powhatan, and in June 1608 he journeyed overland to the King of Potomac's village on the Potomac River. Smith described James Watkins as an "old soldier" and said that Watkins killed an Indian during an ambush (CJS 1:223-224, 227, 230; II:161, 163, 170, 173, 193).

PEREGRIM (PEREGREE)
WATKINS (WATTKINS)

Peregrim (Peregree) Watkins (Wattkins) came to Virginia in 1621 on the *George* and on February 16, 1624, was living on the Eastern Shore (72-78). He was still there in early 1625 and was a 24-year-old household head (CBE 46, 69; DOR 1:71).

RICE (RYS) WATKINS

Rice (Rys) Watkins came to Virginia on the *Francis Bonaventure* and on February 16, 1624, was living on Hog Island (**16**), where he was one of Edward Blaney's servants. He was still there on February 4, 1625, at which time he was described as age 30. On August 14, 1626, Rice Watkins was ordered to inventory the goods of Martin Turner, a servant on the Treasurer's Plantation (**11**). He also was to serve as Turner's administrator, since he was the decedent's principal heir. On April 21, 1628, Rice Watkins was appointed administrator of the late Hugh Crowder's estate (**12**) (CBE 41, 59; MCGC 19-20, 107).

HENRY WATSON

In 1639 Henry Watson, age 29, testified in a lawsuit involving the late Thomas Lee's estate and the sale of the decedent's goods by Bartholomew Hopkins of Elizabeth City (**17**). Lee and his wife came to Virginia in 1634, and he died shortly thereafter (CBE 208).

JAMES WATSON (WATTSON)

James Watson (Wattson) came to Virginia on the *George* in 1623 and on February 16, 1624, was living on West and Shirley Hundred Island (**41**). He was still there on January 22, 1625, and was identified as a 20-year-old servant in the household headed by Mrs. Mary Madison, Isaac Madison's widow (CBE 52).

JOHN WATSON (WATTSON)

John Watson (Wattson) came to Virginia on the *William and Thomas* and on February 16, 1624, was living at the College (Arrohattock) (**66**). He was still residing there on January 23, 1625, when a muster was made of that area's inhabitants. Watson lived alone and headed a household that had an ample supply of provisions and defensive weaponry. Court testimony on March 13, 1625, indicates that John Watson, who was living at Arrohattock, purchased several yards of cloth from Edward Blaney, a Jamestown (**1**) merchant, and delivered it to Mathew Edlow (CBE 35, 53; MCGC 97; DOR 1:7).

***

JOHN WATSON (WATTSON)

John Watson (Wattson) came to Virginia on the *Swann* in 1624 and in early 1625 was living in Elizabeth City (**18**), where he was a 24-year-old servant in the Rev. Jonas Stockton's household. On July 11, 1635, John Watson patented some land in the New Poquoson (**19**), using himself and his wife, Elizabeth, as headrights. He may have purchased a lot in urban Jamestown in 1643 (CBE 66; PB 1 Pt. 1:225, 265; PB 1 Pt. 2:889).

ELIZABETH WATSON (WATTSON) (MRS. JOHN WATSON [WATTSON])

On June 11, 1635, when John Watson (Wattson) patented some land in the New Poquoson (**19**), he used his wife, Elizabeth, as a headright (PB 1 Pt. 1:225).

***

ROBERT WATSON

On June 5, 1623, Robert Watson, John Bland, John Newman, and Richard Perry were identified as owners of the ship *Abigail* (VCR 2:455).

JOHN WATTON

John Watton died on Jamestown Island (**1**) sometime after April 1623 but before February 16, 1624 (CBE 39).

***

LAWRENCE WATTS (WATS)

On March 22, 1622, when the Indians attacked Martin's Hundred (**7**), Lawrence Watts (Wats) and his wife were slain (VCR 3:570).

MRS. LAWRENCE WATTS (WATS)

Mrs. Lawrence Watts (Wats) and her husband were slain on March 22, 1622, when the Indians attacked Martin's Hundred (**7**) (VCR 3:570).

***

THOMAS WATTS

Thomas Watts came to Virginia on the *Treasurer* and on February 16, 1624, was living at Flowerdew Hundred (**53**). By February 4, 1625, he had relocated to Hog Island (**16**), where he was listed as one of Sir George Yeardley's tenants (CBE 37, 61).

THOMAS WATTS

On June 1, 1633, Thomas Watts was in possession of some land on the Back River in Elizabeth City (**19**). When he secured a 50-acre leasehold in the same area on May 30, 1634, he was described as a planter. Watts may have been the same Thomas Watts who was Sir George Yeardley's former tenant (PB 1 Pt. 1:122, 149).

THOMAS WATTSON

On February 16, 1624, Thomas Wattson was living on West and Shirley Hundred Island (**41**) (CBE 36).

GEORGE WAUTRE

Musician George Wautre, his wife, and their four children were among the Walloons and French who indicated their willingness to go to Virginia. In August 1621 the Virginia Company agreed that they could immigrate (CBE 24).

WILLIAM WAYCOME

William Waycome died at Flowerdew Hundred (**53**) sometime after April 1623 but before February 16, 1624 (CBE 37).

JOHN WAYNE
(SEE JOHN WAINE)

SAMUEL WEAVER

Samuel Weaver of London, who was 18 years old, arrived in Jamestown on September 12, 1623, aboard the *Bonny Bess* and took the oath of supremacy. On February 16, 1624, he was living at Martin's Hundred (**7**). When a muster was taken of the community on February 4, 1625, he was identified as a 20-year-old servant in the household of William Harwood, Martin's Hundred's leader. On July 2, 1635, Samuel Weaver patented 650 acres of land in York County, adjacent to Thomas Smith's plantation in Martin's Hundred, which was in James City County (MCGC 6; CBE 42, 61; PB 1 Pt. 1:198, 258).

WILLIAM WEAVER

William Weaver came to Virginia on the *John and Francis* in 1623 at the expense of Robert Sweete, who used Weaver as a headright when patenting some land on March 14, 1628 (PB 1 Pt. 1:70).

[NO FIRST NAME] WEBB

On February 16, 1624, Goodman Webb, whose first name is unknown, headed a household in the eastern half of Jamestown Island (**1**) (CBE 38).

ELIZABETH WEBB
(WEB, WEBBE)

Elizabeth Webb (Web, Webbe) left Bristol, England, on the *Supply* in September 1620. She was one of the settlers accompanying William Tracy, who intended to seat at Berkeley Hundred (**55**). Elizabeth reportedly arrived at Berkeley on January 29, 1621. On August 1, 1622, Virginia Company officials noted that Elizabeth was a Company servant and stated that she had married; however they failed to record her husband's name (CBE 28; VCR 3:396, 426, 674).

GEORGE WEBB

George Webb was captain of a ship that brought the 3rd Supply of new colonists to Jamestown (**1**). According to Captain John Smith, Webb was an astute man and, soon after his arrival in 1610, quickly sized up the situation. On June 12, 1610, Lord Delaware selected Captain George Webb to be sergeant-major of the fort. In January 1613 Captain Samuel Argall, who was trading for corn in the Potomac River, arranged an exchange of hostages. He swapped some Indian boys he had captured for Captain George Webb and some other men who were being detained by the Indians. In 1614 Webb was named commander of Forts Henry and Charles in Kecoughtan (**17**). He still held that post in May 1616, when Sir Thomas Dale departed for England. In 1624, when Virginia's governing officials reviewed the events that led up to the 1622 Indian attack, Captain George Webb was criticized for having allowed his servant, John Powell, to teach Indians how to use firearms (CJS 2:219, 222; HAI 433, 459, 753, 827; MCGC 28).

JOHN WEBB

On February 20, 1626, John Webb, a mariner, testified before the General Court about George Medcalfe's attempt to purchase a newly arrived servant from Mr. Hayes. Later in the day Webb and two other men were ordered to pay for some sack and other items they took from Edward Neville's cabin. On December 13, 1627, John Webb patented 50 acres on the Eastern Shore (72-78). His land abutted that of George Medcalfe (MCGC 95; PB 1 Pt. 1:85).

ROGER WEBB

On February 9, 1625, Roger Webb informed the General Court that Captain Crowshaw had hired Hugh Brett and agreed to take him to England the following year (MCGC 47).

STEPHEN WEBB

On February 16, 1624, Stephen Webb was living on the Governor's Land (3) in a household headed by George Fryer. By February 4, 1625, Webb had been moved to the lower side of the James River, where he was a 25-year-old servant on the plantation of Captain Roger Smith (10), a Jamestown (1) resident. On January 3, 1625, George Fryer informed the General Court that when William Hening was dying, he made a nuncupative will and bequeathed to Stephen Webb the debt he was owed by Thomas Farley. On October 12, 1626, Stephen Webb testified before the General Court about Margaret Jones's attack on John Butterfield—both Jones and Butterfield were residents of the Governor's Land. Webb also said that Jones indicated that she refused to go to Jamestown without her husband, Thomas. Court testimony on January 13, 1627, reveals that Stephen Webb was a Virginia Company tenant who had been assigned to Captain Roger Smith after the Company was defunct. On June 30, 1635, Stephen Webb patented 300 acres at the mouth of Lower Chippokes Creek, in what was then James City County but eventually became Surry. In June 1638 Webb, who identified himself as a 39-year-old James City County planter, said that he and his wife and children were passengers on

the *Elizabeth* when it was captured and taken to Cadiz. He said that he was kept prisoner and forced to work as a slave for eight months and that he lost his goods and three servants. On February 18, 1642, Stephen Webb made an agreement with George Powell, William Powell's son and heir, to lease 300 acres of land on Lower Chippokes Creek. He also agreed to build a house with a cellar on the property and to plant a one-acre orchard. Stephen Webb served as one of James City's burgesses in 1643 and 1644, probably representing the territory on the lower side of the James River (CBE 40, 59; MCGC 40, 119, 136-137; PB 1 Pt. 1:190; EAE 90; HEN 1:239; STAN 63; Surry County Court Record Book 1:175-176; DOR 1:39).

THOMAS WEBB

In 1607 Thomas Webb came to Virginia and was one of the first Jamestown (1) colonists. Captain John Smith described him appreciatively as a carpenter and a gentleman, but said that Webb and a man named Prise (Price) undertook a plot shortly after their arrival. In 1608 Smith identified Webb as one of his "old soldiers." In May 1610 Sir Thomas Gates called on Thomas Webb and John Ratcliff to settle a dispute that occurred during Ratcliff's government (CJS 1:208; 2:141, 240).

THOMAS WEBB

On February 27, 1619, Thomas Webb, a boy, was among the youngsters rounded up from the streets of London so that they could be sent to the colony (CBE 12).

THOMAS WEBB (WEBBE)

In 1620 Captain John Smith identified Thomas Webb (Webbe) as a Virginia Company investor. On July 10, 1621, Webb received three shares of land from the Company, whose officials noted that Webb was going to Virginia (CJS 2:282; VCR 1:509).

WILLIAM WEBB

In June 1619 William Webb, a 55-year-old London merchant, was identified as the Virginia Company's "husband" or supplier. He reportedly had agreed to serve for seven years and had sent out the *Garland* with 103 passengers. On May 17, 1620, he requested compensation for his duties. On November 15, 1620, Company officials noted that Webb had custody of two Virginia Indian girls, whom he intended to hire out as servants so that they would be self-supporting. On June 5, 1623, William Webb and John Cuffe were authorized to sell sassafras in order to recover what the Virginia Company owed them. Webb continued to do business with the Virginia colony. On September 7, 1626, he sent a shipment of goods to Virginia on the *Peter and John,* and on July 19, 1627, he dispatched another cargo on the *James* (EAE 8; VCR 1:347, 427; 2:455; CBE 73, 79).

WILLIAM WEBBE

On January 22, 1620, William Webbe, a vagrant from Langborne Ward, was among those chosen to be sent to Virginia (CBE 17).

JOHN WEBBER

On June 24, 1635, when John Russell patented some land, he used John Webber as a headright (PB 1 Pt. 1:177).

WASSELL (WESSELL) WEBLIN (WEBLING)

On September 25, 1622, Wassell (Wessell) Weblin (Webling), the son of London brewer Nicholas Weblin, signed a contract with Edward Bennett, who underwrote the cost of Weblin's transportation to Virginia and agreed to provide him with adequate food, shelter, and clothing. In exchange, Weblin agreed to serve as an apprentice for three years. At the end of his term of service, Wassell Weblin was to be given his freedom dues, a house, and 50 acres of land in exchange for 50 shillings and two days' work a year. Shipping records indicate that Weblin set out for Virginia in 1621 on the *James,* which arrived in Jamestown (**1**) in July 1622. On February 16, 1624, he was living at Warresqueak (**26**), the Bennett plantation. He was still there on February 7, 1625, at which time he was identified as a servant in Edward Bennett's household. On November 13, 1626, the General Court reviewed a copy of Weblin's contract, and Edward Bennett was ordered to uphold his end of the bargain. On January 14, 1628, Wassell Weblin and Stephen Barker were arrested by Jamestown merchant Edward Sharples for debt. Weblin apparently relocated for a time, for on Febru-

ary 8, 1628, he and two other men were ordered to live in Warresqueak (MCGC 123-124, 158, 165; CBE 42, 62).

***

ROGER WEBSTER

Roger Webster came to Virginia sometime prior to February 16, 1624, at which time he was living on Hog Island (**16**). On June 18, 1624, he appeared before the General Court, where he testified about how many tobacco plants the Virginia Company's men set out at Hog Island. On February 4, 1625, Roger and his wife, Joan, were living on Hog Island. Later in the month he and John Uty were summoned to court to testify on behalf of the Society of Southampton Hundred (**44**), whose investors claimed that Sir Samuel Argall had taken some of their cattle. This raises the possibility that Webster had been associated with Southampton Hundred, where Uty was an officer. Webster and Uty also would have been familiar with the Society's moveable property, which had been transferred to Hog Island after the March 1622 Indian attack. On August 28, 1626, Roger Webster testified that Henry Woodward, one of the Society of Southampton Hundred's tenants and an accused thief, had been seen near Webster's cornfield. In late May 1627 Webster himself ran afoul of the law when he was found guilty of public drunkenness and fined; the man who reported him was Ensign John Uty. On February 9, 1628, Roger Webster of Hog Island testified that while visiting Archer's Hope (**6**), he had witnessed a fight between Amy Hall and William Harman. In September 1632 and February 1633 Roger Webster served as the burgess for the settlers living in the vicinity of the James City Glebe and Archer's Hope (**6**) (CBE 41, 61; MCGC 19, 55, 110, 149, 166; HEN 1:178; STAN 57-58).

JOAN WEBSTER (MRS. ROGER WEBSTER)

On February 4, 1625, Joan, Roger Webster's wife, was sharing a home with him on Hog Island (**16**) (CBE 61).

***

WILLIAM WEBSTER

On December 5, 1625, William Webster was identified as purser of the *Elizabeth.*

He informed the General Court that Thomas Clark, who had died aboard the ship while it was on the way to Virginia, was indebted to him. On February 9, 1628, Webster presented mariner John Hinsley's will to the General Court. In October 1628 he was identified as a factor when he presented an account of the *Anne Fortune's* voyage to Newfoundland and his agreement with Humphrey Rastall. The justices of the General Court decided that William Webster should be compensated out of Rastall's estate (MCGC 78, 166, 175, 199).

THOMAS WEEKES

On November 28, 1625, Thomas Weekes testified that while he was aboard the *Elizabeth*, a boy being sent to Virginia by Thomas Page assisted the boatswain in performing whatever tasks he was asked to undertake. In an unrelated matter, the late Thomas Clark, who died aboard the *Elizabeth* enroute to Virginia, was found to owe money to Thomas Weekes (MCGC 77, 199).

VALENTINE WEEKES

The Ferrars, who were major Virginia Company investors, underwrote the cost of transporting Valentine Weekes to Virginia in 1621 (FER 296).

JOHN WELCHMAN

On February 16, 1624, John Welchman was living in Elizabeth City (**17, 18**) (CBE 43).

LEWIS WELCHMAN

On February 16, 1624, Lewis Welchman was living in Elizabeth City (**17, 18**) (CBE 43).

WILLIAM WELDON (WELDER)

On August 10, 1619, William Weldon (Welder), a 22-year-old tanner from Northamptonshire, set sail from England on the *Bona Nova*. As an employee of the Virginia Company, he had agreed to escort to Virginia 50 men—Company servants and tenants who would be seated at the College (Arrohattock) (**66**) in Henrico. He also brought along the men's supplies and some goods he hoped to sell. William Weldon arrived in Jamestown (**1**) on November 4, 1619. Although he had originally planned to go to the College Land on November 15th to seat

with Captain Samuel Mathews at Arrohattock, Virginia's governing authorities decided that because the newcomers were inexperienced and it was too late in the year to plant crops, it was best to send only 25 men to the College and place the remainder with planters already acclimated to frontier life. On January 14, 1620, William Weldon informed Virginia Company officials that they had given him passage for two gentleman and two servants who belonged to Mr. Whitaker and Mr. Hansby, but had not sent George Eden. Then, on March 6, 1620, Weldon sent another letter via one of his own servants, this time asking the Company for more men. He also said that his people's provisions were inadequate and that Samuel Mathews and Thomas Dowse were seated on some of the most fertile ground within the territory assigned to the College. Therefore, he asked Company officials not to confirm the land grants Mathews and Dowse had been given by Deputy-Governor Samuel Argall. In June 1621 Governor George Yeardley sent word to Virginia Company officials that the College project was proving too costly. Shortly thereafter, Captain William Weldon decided to vacate his contract, despite the fact that he had served less than half of the seven-year term for which he was obligated. He claimed that the Company had failed to provide the men he had been promised and the only income he had received was from tobacco he had raised or from sale of the goods he had brought to Virginia. He also stated that instead of being the College men's governor and commander, as he had expected, he was a mere bailey (bailiff). In Weldon's view, his duties ended when George Thorpe was made deputy of the College Land. Virginia Company officials disagreed and concluded that William Weldon was guilty of breach of contract. They refunded the bond he had posted but claimed that he still owed them £11. Virginia Company records dated June 10, 1622, indicate that William Weldon held a patent for a particular (private) plantation, but on February 16, 1624, he was still living at the College. He was still there when a muster was made of the College's population on January 23, 1625, at which time he was identified as a solitary household head. Thus, the Virginia Company seemingly refused to release him from his contract (FER 261, 295; VCR 1:593-594, 601-604, 606; 3:226-229, 246, 254, 262-265; CBE 35, 53; DOR 1:8).

ELIZABETH WELLE

On July 19, 1633, officials at Bridewell learned that Elizabeth Welle, a girl who was being detained, was willing to go to Virginia (HUME 38).

JOHN WELLS

On February 27, 1619, John Wells, a boy, was selected as one of the children who were going to be sent to Virginia (CBE 12).

JONE (JANE) WENCHMAN

On August 8, 1618, it was decided that Jone (Jane) Wenchman, a vagrant from Fleet Street in Bridewell, would be sent to Virginia (CBE 9).

HENRY WENTWORTH

On May 8, 1622, Henry Wentworth acquired from Francis Carter a share of the late Lord Delaware's land in Virginia. Wentworth apparently began making preparations to establish a plantation in the colony, for he sent over some goods and spoke of going there personally. On March 11, 1624, when a Virginia colonist named John Roe was on his deathbed, attending surgeon Thomas Bunn suggested that Roe make disposition of his estate and that of Mr. Henry Wentworth. Roe, who was at Captain Samuel Mathews' house (15) on the lower side of the James River, asked Bunn to see that Wentworth's goods were sent to Wentworth in England unless he already had come to the colony. In fact, Henry Wentworth arrived in Virginia sometime prior to April 21, 1624. He described himself at that time as a poor planter when asking for tax relief because of the 1622 Indian attack (VCR 1:635; 2:519; MCGC 50).

NICHOLAS WESSELL (WEASELL, WEASLE)

Nicholas Wessell (Weasell, Weasle), a Virginia Company tenant, came to the colony on the *Abigail* in 1621. On February 16, 1624, he was living in Elizabeth City (17) on the east side of the Hampton River. He was still there in early 1625 and was a member of William Barry's household. Nicholas Wessell was then age 28. Sometime prior to January 3, 1626, he ran afoul of the law by borrowing Henry Geney's boat without permission and allowing it to be damaged. Wessell was ordered to serve Geney for the rest of the year and whip two other men, who had been sentenced to corporal punishment. Afterward, Wessell himself was to be whipped in Elizabeth City. On January 12, 1627, when the defunct Virginia Company's tenants were distributed among the colony's governing officials, Nicholas Wessell was assigned to Governor George Yeardley (CBE 43, 68; MCGC 86, 136).

ALICE WEST

On December 16, 1631, the General Court decided that because Edward Grimes (Grymes) had been sexually involved with Alice West , he could not marry anyone without the approval of the governor and his council. Grimes was in possession of land in the western part of the corporation of Elizabeth City (18) (MCGC 480).

ANTHONY WEST

Anthony West came to Virginia in 1622 on the *James* and was one of Mr. and Mrs. William Rowsley's servants. On February 16, 1624, West was residing in urban Jamestown (1) in Captain Holmes's household. By February 4, 1625, Anthony West had relocated to the lower side of the James River, where he was a servant at the Treasurer's Plantation (11). On December 12, 1625, John Southern testified that shortly before Mrs. Elizabeth Rowsley died, she said that she intended to give Anthony West his freedom. She also told Southern that she had asked Captain Sampson to take West back to England. Therefore, the General Court freed West and gave him permission to leave Virginia. Anthony West stated that he wanted to nullify an agreement he had made with Zachary Crisp, from whom he had agreed to purchase 1,500 tobacco plants in exchange for some labor. West also mentioned an agreement he had made with Philip Kytely. On January 19, 1626, Anthony West testified that George Sandys borrowed tobacco from some of the men at the Treasurer's Plantation. West finally returned to England. On March 10, 1634— when he announced his plans to marry Anne, the widow of Anthony Huffe—he identified himself as a 28-year-old surgeon and bachelor from Stepney Parish in Middlesex. Anthony West returned to Virginia with his wife, Anne, and was living in Northampton County when he made his will, which was proved on May 25, 1652 (CBE 38, 67; MCGC 79-80, 90; MEY 662).

***

FRANCIS WEST I

In 1608 Francis West I, the brother of Thomas West, the third Lord Delaware, arrived in Jamestown (1) on the *Mary Ann Margaret* with part of the 2nd Supply of new settlers. He was an investor in the Virginia Company and, later, in Bermuda. In late December 1608 Francis West accompanied Captain John Smith on a voyage to Powhatan's village, Werowocomoco, and to the Pamunkey Indians' homeland. He also went with Captain Christopher Newport and others to explore the Monacan Indians' territory, and in January 1609 he was involved in rescuing Smith from Opechancanough. West was named to the Council of State and in 1609 went on an expedition to The Falls (67) of the James River, where he and some of the people from the 3rd Supply built a fort. However, some of his men were slain by the Indians at Arrohattock (66). He later set off on a trading voyage on the Potomac River, but the Natives attacked and killed half of his men. When Captain John Smith was removed as chief executive in September 1609, Council president Francis West served as acting governor for two weeks. In 1611 the Nansemond Indians shot West in the thigh while he was on an expedition with Sir Thomas Dale. He recovered and in 1612 was designated commander of Jamestown. In 1617 Captain Francis West received a lifetime appointment as "maker of Ordnance," and in 1622 he was named admiral of New England. He was present in 1618 when Deputy-Governor Samuel Argall had Edward Brewster tried in a court martial hearing. West was among those who petitioned for the removal of Governor George Yeardley. He claimed that Yeardley had placed the Berkeley Hundred (55) settlers on Lord Delaware's land and later stated that the estate of the deceased George Thorpe of Berkeley Hundred owed him money.

On February 16, 1624, Francis West was residing at West and Shirley Hundred Island (41), in the household of Captain Isaac Madison. By early 1625, however, he had moved to Elizabeth City, where he headed a household on the Company Land (17). He shared a home with his widowed sister-in-law, Frances West, and her son, Nathaniel, as well as six servants, one of whom was an African male. Francis West, who was then age 36, had two dwellings, a palisade, a boat, an abundance of stored food and defensive weaponry, and a herd of goats. When a list of patented land was sent back to England in May 1625, Captain Francis West was credited with 500 acres at Westover (54), and he also had a legal claim to some ground on Lower Chippokes Creek. During the mid-1620s West witnessed legal agreements, inventoried estates, and functioned as a member of the General Court. He also saw that court orders were obeyed in Elizabeth City. On one occasion he tried to mediate a domestic dispute between Thomas Flint and his wife. West became acting governor on November 14, 1627, and held office for two years. When he visited England in the late 1620s, he saw Captain John Smith, who interviewed him about conditions in the colony. West said that by 1628 the population had increased by 1,000 people. He continued to be associated with the Hampton River area and in 1632 obtained a lease for 50 acres at Buckroe. He married three times in rapid succession. His first wife, Margaret, was the widow of Captain William Powell and cape merchant Edward Blaney, both of whom resided in Jamestown. Francis and Margaret Powell Blaney West produced a son, Francis II.

After Margaret died, Francis West married Lady Temperance Flowerdew Yeardley, Sir George's widow, in late March 1628. She died intestate in December 1628, and in February 1629 when West was asked to account for Sir George Yeardley's estate in Virginia, he refused. On February 1, 1630, West went to England as the colony's representative. While there he brought suit against substitute-executor Ralph Yeardley, in an attempt to recover Lady Temperance's dower third of Sir George Yeardley's substantial estate. Francis West made his November 17, 1629, will immediately prior to setting sail for England and authorized his brother, John West, and Dr. John Pott to act as his attorneys during his absence. Councilor Francis West died in Virginia in 1633–1634, possibly in a drowning accident. He was survived by his third wife, Jane, Sir Henry Davye's daughter, whom he wed in England. West's will was presented for probate in England on April 28, 1634 (WITH

52; CJS 1:163, 169-170, 241, 243, 255, 263, 275, 432; 2:184, 190, 193, 200, 210, 220-221, 223, 231-232, 266, 282, 370; 3:215, 217; STAN 14, 28; HAI 431, 482-483, 503-505, 514, 827, 895; VCR 3:75, 231-232, 248-249, 482, 580; 4:554; C 24/489, 24/490; SR 3968, 9947, 10376; CBE 29, 36, 67, 71, 80, 82, 113; MCGC 11, 20-21, 36-37, 42, 46, 49, 52, 62, 84, 93, 97, 110, 121-123, 127, 136, 149, 151-152, 156-157, 176-177, 186-187; SH 6-7; HEN 1:128-129, 153, 178, 202; G&M 149-150; PB 1 Pt. 1:133, 136; DOR 1:64; MEY 656).

JANE DAVYE WEST
(MRS. FRANCIS WEST I)

Jane, the daughter of Sir Henry Davye, married Francis West I in England after the death of his second wife, Temperance Flowerdew Yeardley. Jane outlived Francis, and on December 12, 1629, she was authorized to sell his land in Virginia (WITH 52; SH 7; SR 3968).

MARGARET POWELL BLANEY
WEST (MRS. WILLIAM POWELL,
MRS. EDWARD BLANEY,
MRS. FRANCIS WEST I)
(SEE MRS. WILLIAM POWELL,
MRS. EDWARD BLANEY)

Margaret, Captain William Powell's widow and a resident of Jamestown (1), married cape merchant Edward Blaney prior to April 1623. She was widowed again by late 1625 or early 1626, for by February 6, 1626, she had wed Captain Francis West I. Margaret died sometime prior to March 1628, at which time West (then acting governor) married Sir George Yeardley's widow, Lady Temperance. Margaret and Francis West produced a son, Francis II (MCGC 58, 93, 110; MEY 656).

TEMPERANCE FLOWERDEW
YEARDLEY WEST
(MRS. GEORGE YEARDLEY,
MRS. FRANCIS WEST I)
(SEE TEMPERANCE
FLOWERDEW YEARDLEY
[YARDLEY])

Lady Temperance Flowerdew Yeardley, Sir George Yeardley's widow and a resident of Jamestown (1), married acting-governor Francis West I in late March 1628. She died

intestate in December 1628. Because she had not finished settling Sir George's estate, Ralph Yeardley, George's brother, became administrator. On February 1, 1630, Francis West, as Temperance's widower and heir, brought suit against Ralph Yeardley in an attempt to recover her dower third of Sir George's estate. He contended that Temperance's share was worth at least £3,000 and claimed that when Sir George's estate was liquidated, his administrator had kept all of the proceeds (MCGC 161, 187; MEY 656; G&M 149-150).

FRANCIS WEST II

When Francis West I made his will on November 17, 1629, he made provisions for his widow, Jane, but stipulated that his son, Francis II, was to have half of his estate at age 21. Francis West II was the son of Francis West I and his wife, Margaret, the widow of William Powell and Edward Blaney (SR 3968; SH 7; EEAC 62).

JOHN WEST I

John West I was born in 1590 in Hampshire, England, and was the son of Thomas West, the second Lord Delaware. He also was the brother of Francis West I, Nathaniel West I, and Thomas West, Virginia's governor and the third Lord Delaware. John West I attended Magdalene College at Oxford. He was an investor in the Virginia Company and in 1618 went to Virginia, where he established the plantation known as Westover (54). Two people were killed at Westover during the March 22, 1622, Indian attack, and afterward, West led a company of men on a retaliatory raid against Tanx Powhatan. One of John West I's debtors was George Thorpe, headman at Berkeley Hundred (55), who died during the Indian attack. On February 16, 1624, West was living on the lower side of the James River, within the corporation of James City and east of Gray's Creek (10-16). Sharing his home briefly were his nephew, Nathaniel West II, and sister-in-law Frances, the widow of his late brother, Nathaniel West I. On January 13, 1627, Captain John West, as a councilor, was assigned one of the defunct Virginia Company's tenants. He apparently continued to live on his plantation east of Gray's Creek, for on March 7, 1629, he was placed in command of the settlements between Paces Paines (9) and Hog Island

(16), and he also represented that area as a burgess. In October 1630, when a decision was made to extend settlement northward to Chiskiack, Colonel John West I was among the first to patent land there. His York River property was seated by 1632 and called the Indian Field plantation (32), though eventually it became known as Bellfield. In 1631 West returned to the Council of State and held office until 1659. In 1634 he became a justice of York County. When Governor John Harvey was thrust from office in May 1635, John West (as senior council member) was elected governor. After Governor Harvey was reinstated, he had West arrested on a charge of mutiny and sent him to England, where he was detained until he could be placed on trial. In West's absence, Governor Harvey seized his property. When John West returned to Virginia, his confiscated belongings were restored and he was designated muster-master. In 1652 he received a patent for 3,000 acres at the tip of Pamunkey Neck, where the Pamunkey and Mattaponi Rivers join to form the York. John West I died in the colony in 1659. His son and heir, John II, was born around 1632 (STAN 15, 32; CJS 2:282, 301, 371; VCR 3:567; 4:9; WITH 52; MCGC 11, 136-137, 192, 279, 481, 491; HEN 1:138, 148, 153, 178; CBE 40; CO 1/8 f 166; 1/9 f 13, 132-134; 1/10 f 190; PC 2/50:572; SAIN 1:207-208, 217, 231, 252, 314; G&M 217-218).

JOHN WEST II

John West II, who was born around 1632, lived on his father's plantation at West Point. He served in succession as a captain, major, and lieutenant colonel of militia from 1652 to 1673. He was staunchly loyal to Governor William Berkeley and was among those who participated when some accused rebels were tried in a court martial hearing. By 1664 he had married Unity Croshaw, with whom he produced several children. He also had a child with Cockacoeske, Queen of the Pamunkey Indians, who was widowed in 1656. In 1677 that child, who was tall and slender and known as "Captain John West," participated in the ceremony in which the treaty of Middle Plantation was signed. In 1680 West was a New Kent County justice of the peace, and he served several terms in the assembly during the 1680s and 90s (MEY 222, 659; FOR 1:8:14).

NATHANIEL WEST I

Nathaniel West I was born in 1592 and was the son of Thomas West, the second Lord Delaware. He was the brother of John West I, Francis West I, and Thomas West, the third Lord Delaware and Virginia's governor. On October 20, 1617, the Virginia Company designated Nathaniel West captain of the Lord General's Company. He came to Virginia around 1618. Three years later he married Frances Grenville, who went to Virginia on the *Supply* in 1621, heading for Berkeley Hundred (55). In March 1622 two people were killed at Westover (54), Nathaniel West's family's plantation in Charles City. In July 1623 West embarked on an expedition against the Appomattox and Tanks Weyanoke Indians. He died at West and Shirley Hundred (41) sometime prior to February 16, 1624, by which time his widow, Frances, and their little son, Nathaniel II, had taken up temporary residence at the plantation of her brother-in-law, Captain John West, on the lower side of the James River (10-16). By early 1625 Francis and her son, Nathaniel II, were living in Elizabeth City (17) in a household headed by another brother-in-law, Captain Francis West. Around 1626 she married cape merchant Abraham Peirsey (VCR 3:75-76; 4:250; MCGC 11; CJS 2:301; CBE 36, 40, 67; MEY 480, 658).

FRANCES (FRANCIS) GRENVILLE WEST I (MRS. NATHANIEL WEST I, MRS. ABRAHAM PEIRSEY, MRS. SAMUEL MATHEWS I) (SEE FRANCES GRENVILLE, MRS. ABRAHAM PEIRSEY, MRS. SAMUEL MATHEWS I)

Frances Grenville came to Virginia on the *Supply* in 1621 with the family of William Tracy, which was headed for Berkeley Hundred (55). She married Lord Delaware's brother, Nathaniel West of West and Shirley Hundred (41), who died in late 1623 to early 1624. Sometime prior to February 16, 1624, she moved into the household headed by brother-in-law John West I, whose plantation was across from Jamestown (10-16). Before early 1625, however, she relocated to Elizabeth City (17), where she and her little son, Nathaniel II, shared Captain Francis West I's home. The widowed Frances Grenville West wed Abraham Peirsey of Flowerdew Hundred (53) later in the year. She outlived him and on March 24, 1628, informed the General Court that she had inventoried his estate accurately. She later married Samuel Mathews I of Denbigh (23) (CBE 40, 67; MEY 480; MCGC 168).

NATHANIEL WEST II

Nathaniel West II, the son of Nathaniel and Frances Grenville West, was born in Virginia around 1622. His father died at West and Shirley Hundred (41) sometime after July 1623 but before February 16, 1624. Young Nathaniel and his mother moved to the lower side of the James River, within the corporation of James City and east of Gray's Creek (10-16), where they temporarily resided with John West I. By early 1625 mother and son had moved to Elizabeth City (17), where they lived in the household of Francis West I. The widowed Frances Grenville West married Abraham Peirsey, who in March 1626 made a bequest to his young stepson, Nathaniel West II. During his childhood, Nathaniel II was sent to England to live with one of his West first cousins (CBE 40, 67; SH 7; MEY 659).

THOMAS WEST, LORD DELAWARE

Sir Thomas West, the third Lord Delaware, was born in 1577 and was the eldest surviving son of Thomas West, the second Lord Delaware. His brothers were John West I, Francis West I, and Nathaniel West I, all of whom went to Virginia. Thomas West attended Queens College at Oxford, served as a member of Parliament, and married Cecily Sherley in 1596. He was knighted in 1599 and in 1602 succeeded to his father's peerage as Lord Delaware. He became a member of the Privy Council and was a member of the Virginia Company's Council. Thomas West was the first Lord Governor and Captain General of Virginia, receiving that title on February 28, 1610. In April he set sail for Virginia in a fleet of three ships (including the *Blessing* and the *Delaware*) that carried 250 people, a considerable number of whom were skilled workers. Almost half of the people Delaware brought were experienced soldiers, and a few knights accompanied him as well. The instructions Virginia Company officials gave him closely resembled those provided to Sir Thomas Gates, who was named Lieutenant Governor. When Lord Delaware entered the James River on June 9, 1610, he encountered the small fleet of Sir George Somers and Sir Thomas Gates, which was evacuating the surviving Jamestown colonists to Newfoundland, where they could secure passage home. If not for Delaware's timely arrival, the surviving colonists—who had endured the infamous "starving time" in the winter of 1609–1610—might have abandoned the colony. When he arrived in Jamestown (1) on June 10, 1610, Delaware found the settlement's fort and buildings in disrepair. He stayed aboard ship, as there were no suitable accommodations on shore, and devoted his energies to placing the colony on a much firmer footing.

On June 12, 1610, Lord Delaware put into operation the military code of justice that Sir Thomas Gates devised, and he set the men to work cleansing the town, cutting down the vegetation near the palisades, planting crops, fishing, and making coals for the forges. He had the settlers repair their houses or build new, more weatherproof ones, and he implemented a number of other projects. He dispatched Sir George Somers to Bermuda to bring back food. As governor, he chose officers to serve as masters of the ordnance and the battery works for steel and iron, and he selected a sergeant major for the fort and clerks for the store. In October 1610 he sent some of his men to the head of the James River to search for gold and silver, and he had two forts built at Old Point Comfort and one at The Falls of the James. However, more than half of Lord Delaware's 250 men died after they arrived in Virginia, and after 10 months sickness forced Delaware himself to withdraw to the West Indies. He left behind 200 healthy men and a ten-month supply of food, and he designated George Percy as deputy-governor until Sir Thomas Dale's arrival.

After returning to England, Lord Delaware continued to promote the Virginia colony. By 1613 he had begun making plans to return to Virginia, where his brothers already were living. However, it was not until March 1618, however, that he had accumulated the goods and supplies he needed and actually set sail on the *Neptune*. En route to the colony, Lord Delaware became ill. He died at sea, and according to John Martin, one of his attendants aboard the *Neptune*, his remains were brought to Jamestown and interred. Delaware's goods and men were entrusted to the care of Edward Brewster, one of the decedent's principal subordinates. According to a lawsuit undertaken by Lord Delaware's heirs in 1622, Deputy-Governor Samuel Argall misappropriated the decedent's goods and servants. Between 1619 and 1623 Lady Cecily (Ceciley, Cecelia, Cisley) West and her son, Henry, the fourth Lord Delaware, gradually disposed of the late Lord Delaware's more than 65 shares of Virginia land. The plantation in which Lord Delaware had a personal investment was West and Shirley Hundred **(41)**, which also included West and Shirley (now Eppes) Island (WITH 52; CJS 1:68, 128-130, 276-277; 2:234-235, 237; 3:272; STAN 13; VCR 1:224, 381, 360-364; 3:24-25; HAI 427, 432, 454-466, 475, 510-511, 525-532, 898, 905; FOR 1:7:11, 15; 3:1:18, 20; 3:2:7; 3:3:14; AP 71-73; CO 1/1 f 85; C 24/290).

CECILY (CECILEY, CECELIA, CISLEY) SHERLEY WEST, LADY DELAWARE (MRS. THOMAS WEST, LADY DELAWARE)

Cecily (Ceciley, Cecelia, Cisley) Sherley married Thomas West, Lord Delaware, who was designated Lord Governor and Captain of Virginia in February 1609 and left England in April 1610. When Sir Thomas Dale brought Pocahontas (then Mrs. John Rolfe) to England in 1616, Lord and Lady Delaware reportedly befriended her and introduced her at court. After her husband's death during the summer of 1618, Lady Cecily tried to recover the debts and back pay accruable to her late husband's estate. In July 1620 she accused Sir Samuel Argall of misappropriating his servants and goods, and she claimed that some of his personal property was in John Rolfe's hands. A year later she was still trying to settle the estate. In August 1619 Virginia Company officials told Lady Cecily that if she would unite her settlement with the settlements of Lady Dale and Captain John Bargrave, the three plantations would have the special privileges reserved to hundreds. A few months later Lady Cecily sought—and received—a pension from the Virginia Company. In January 1622 she and Edward Brewster, who had been Lord Delaware's principal commander in Virginia, sued Sir Samuel Argall, whom she claimed took some of her husband's men and went on a piratical voyage on the *Treasurer*, an allegation supported by fact. In May 1622 Lady Cecily Delaware began assigning some of her late

husband's shares of land to others. Although she gradually disposed of his interest in West and Shirley Hundred **(41)**, she and her son, Henry, the fourth Lord Delaware, obtained some land a short distance downstream, near Westover **(55)**. In June 1634 Lady Delaware, who had been granted a pension of £500 a year for 31 years, asked that her allowance be renewed, as she had five daughters to support. Lady Cecily died in 1662 (CJS 2:261; VCR 1:168, 219, 299,333, 397, 425-426, 459-460, 507; 2:17; 3:290; CBE 116; SR 10376; MEY 655).

***

FRANCIS WEST

On September 19, 1618, officials at Bridewell decided that a vagrant named Francis West would be sent to Virginia (CBE 9).

FRANCIS (FRANCES) WEST

On February 27, 1619, it was decided that Francis (Frances) West, a boy from Hounsditch, would be sent to Virginia. He was part of a group of children brought in from the streets of London and detained at Bridewell so that they could be transported to the colony (CBE 13).

HENRY WEST

Henry West came to Virginia on the *Margaret and John* in 1622 at the expense of John Robins I. Later, Robins' son, John Robins II, used Henry West's headright. West died in Elizabeth City **(17, 18)** sometime after April 1623 but before February 16, 1624 (PB 1 Pt. 1:116; CBE 45).

JOHN WEST

John West, a husbandman from Witley, in Surrey, England, arrived in Jamestown on September 12, 1623, aboard the *Bonny Bess* and took the oath of allegiance. On February 16, 1624, he and Thomas West (perhaps his kinsman), who also came on the *Bonny Bess* in 1623, were residing on Jamestown Island **(1)** in the household of John Grevett. On January 24, 1625, John West and Thomas Crompe headed a household together on Jamestown Island. They were credited with a house and were well supplied with stored food and defensive weaponry (MCGC 6; CBE 40, 56; DOR 1:34).

JOHN WEST

Sometime prior to February 5, 1627, John West, an indentured servant living in Virginia, was freed by his master, Thomas Roper (WITH 487).

THOMAS WEST

Thomas West, a cooper from London, arrived in Jamestown (1) on September 12, 1623, on the *Bonny Bess* and took the oath of allegiance. On February 16, 1624, he and John West (perhaps a kinsman), a fellow passenger on the *Bonny Bess*, were residing in the Jamestown Island household of John Grevett. Thomas West died sometime prior to January 24, 1625 (MCGC 6; CBE 40, 56).

WILLIAM WEST (WESTE)

Around 1610 William West (Weste), a gentleman from Dedsham in Slinfold, Sussex, Canterbury, England, prepared a nuncupative will shortly before he set sail for Virginia. He named Mary, Richard Blunt's wife, as his sole heir. After reaching the colony, William West accompanied George Percy on a trip to the Pasbehay Indians' village at the mouth of the Chickahominy River; he was supposed to stand guard. Later, West and Captain Edward Brewster went to The Falls (67) of the James. The Indians killed West, although Brewster managed to escape. William West's will was proved by witnesses on June 1, 1616 (HAI 509, 513; SH 2; SR 3110; EEAC 62; CBE 7).

ANN WESTCOTE

Ann Westcote, a young marriageable maid, came to Virginia in September 1621 on the *Warwick*. She was 20 years old and was said to be a young woman of good character. She was recommended by Mr. Collingwood, the Virginia Company's secretary, and was presented by her father, a victualer in St. Martin's (FER 309).

JANE WESTERFIELD

Jane Westerfield came to Virginia on the *Hopewell* in 1628 at the expense of Adam Thorogood, who used her headright when he patented some land on June 24, 1635 (PB 1 Pt. 1:179).

[NO FIRST NAME] WESTON

On March 22, 1622, when the Indians attacked Henrico Island (63), a person named Weston was slain (VCR 3:565).

***

FRANCIS WESTON

Francis Weston came to Virginia sometime prior to February 2, 1624, at the expense of his brother, Garrett, who asked for an allotment of land. Garrett also covered the transportation costs of three servants. In May 1625 Francis Weston was credited with 300 acres of land on the south side of the James River, at The Falls (67). Francis Weston may have been the individual named Weston who was killed on March 22, 1622, when the Indians attacked Henrico Island (63) (VCR 2:511, 532; 4:552).

GARRETT WESTON

On February 2, 1624, Garrett Weston asked the Virginia Company for 300 acres of land: 100 acres for his own adventure plus an additional 200 acres for transporting four people to the colony. Company officials insisted that he substantiate his claim. On April 26, 1624, Weston presented the required proof that he had paid for the transportation of his brother, Francis, and three servants (VCR 2:511, 532).

***

HUGH WESTON

Hugh Weston, master of the ship *Merchants Hope*, brought 75 people to Virginia in July 1635. On July 14, 1637, he was identified as master of the *Flower de Luce*, which had transported tobacco to England (SR 3466, 3498).

JOHN WESTON

On June 3, 1620, John Weston, a 22-year-old gentleman from Oxford, England, testified that he had known Daniel Elfirth for 18 months. He also indicated that the ship *Treasurer*, after leaving some Africans in Virginia, had arrived in Bermuda in September 1619 with the remaining Africans (EAE 181).

THOMAS WESTON

Thomas Weston came to Virginia on the *George* in 1623. On January 22, 1625, he was listed among those who had died in West and Shirley Hundred (41) (CBE 53).

THOMAS WESTON

Thomas Weston, a merchant and owner of the *Sparrow*, was an adventurer in New England before he undertook trading activities in Virginia. He was involved in transporting and selling servants and cargoes of fish and made regular trips to Canada. Sometimes he carried Virginia tobacco to Canada and returned with servants, although he voiced his objections to indentured servitude. The General Court ordered Thomas Weston, who had transported some of Thomas Crispe's tobacco, to compensate Crispe because the tobacco had arrived in a damaged condition. Weston was involved in commercial activities in Newportes News **(24)** and in Elizabeth City **(17, 18)**, and in 1626 he was authorized to sell fish in Jamestown **(1)**. On February 8, 1628, he appeared before the General Court and testified in the case of John Giles, a servant trying to obtain his freedom. Sometime prior to July 2, 1635, Thomas Weston patented some land in York County, which he sold to Samuel Weaver. Weston eventually moved to Maryland and finally returned to England (CJS 1:lii; MCGC 10, 81-82, 95-96, 109, 132-133, 165; PB 1 Pt. 1:198).

WILLIAM WESTON

William Weston came to Virginia on the *Jonathan* in May 1620 and on February 16, 1624, was living at Chaplin's Choice **(56)**. By January 22, 1625, he had moved to Shirley Hundred **(41)**, where he shared a well-provisioned household with Robert Milner and two other men. William Weston, a free man, was age 25 (CBE 37, 53).

ROBERT WESTWELL

Robert Westwell came to Virginia on the *Merchants Hope* in 1634 at the expense of Adam Thorogood, who used him as a headright when patenting some land on June 24, 1635 (PB 1 Pt. 1:179).

SACKFORD WETHERELL

Sackford Wetherell came to Virginia on the *Swann* in 1624. On October 15, 1624, he testified before the General Court in a suit that involved Captain John Martin and Humphrey Rastall, a merchant. In early 1625 Wetherell was living in Captain John Martin's household in Elizabeth City **(17)**, on part of the Virginia Company's land. He was then age 21 and appears to have been free (CBE 26, 67).

[NO FIRST NAME] WETHEREDG (WETHERIDGE)

On November 21, 1625, Mr. Wetheredg (Wetheridge) agreed to post a bond for Thomas Crispe of Elizabeth City **(18)**, who was involved in a lawsuit (MCGC 75).

[NO FIRST NAME] WETHERSBY

A person named Wethersby died in Elizabeth City **(17, 18)** on August 8, 1624 (CBE 67).

ALBIANO WETHERSBY (WETHERSBIE)

On February 16, 1624, Albiano Wethersby (Wethersbie) was living in Elizabeth City **(17, 18)**. He may have been the person named Wethersby who died there on August 8, 1624 (CBE 43).

***

BARTHOLOMEW (BARTHOLMEW) WETHERSBY (WETHERSBIE)

Bartholomew (Bartholmew) Wethersby (Wethersbie) came to Virginia on the *Providence* in 1616 and on February 16, 1624, was living in Elizabeth City **(18)**. Wethersby was still there in early 1625, at which time he and his wife, Dorothy, were sharing a home with Robert Bolton. Bartholomew and Dorothy Wethersby were 30 years old and free. On March 3, 1629, Bartholomew Wethersby was designated the administrator of the late Thomas Godby's estate. Wethersby's land, which was near Salford's Creek in Elizabeth City, was mentioned in patents dated 1638 and 1648 (CBE 43, 65; MCGC 188; PB 1 Pt. 2:629; 2:138).

DOROTHY WETHERSBY (WETHERSBIE) (MRS. BARTHOLOMEW [BARTHOLMEW] WETHERSBY [WETHERSBIE])

Dorothy, who married Bartholomew (Bartholmew) Wethersby (Wethersbie), came to Virginia on the *London Merchant* in 1620. By early 1625 the Wethersbys were living in Elizabeth City (**18**), where they shared their home with Richard Boulton. Dorothy Wethersby was then age 30 and free (CBE 65).

***

FERDINANDO WEYMAN (WEYNMAN, WAYNEMAN)

Sir Ferdinando Weyman (Weynman, Wayneman), an investor in the Virginia Company, went to Virginia with incoming Governor Thomas West, Lord Delaware, and arrived in Jamestown (**1**) on June 10, 1610. Two days later Delaware appointed Ferdinando Weyman master of the ordnance. By July 7, 1610, he had been named to Lord Delaware's council. Sir Ferdinando Weyman died later that year. According to George Percy, Weyman was an honest and valiant gentleman whose death was much lamented (CJS 2:234; HAI 427, 433, 459, 509; VCR 1:381).

SIR THOMAS WEYMAN (WEYNMAN, WAYNEMAN)

On July 7, 1620, Sir Thomas Weyman (Weynman, Wayneman) and his associates were awarded a patent by the Virginia Company (VCR 1:397).

THOMAS WHAPLETT

On January 6, 1635, when Thomas Whaplett, a Virginia planter, made his will, he referred to a plantation in which he and his friend, John Redman, had invested, but he failed to disclose its name. He bequeathed half of his portion of the plantation to Abraham Peate and the other half to his sister, Rebecca Whaplett, but asked Peate to manage Rebecca's share of the property. Abraham Peate also was to pay all of the decedent's bills in Virginia. Thomas Whaplett died sometime prior to November 13, 1636. Rebecca Whaplett's share of the plantation later descended to widower Ralph Gregg (SR 3975; SH 20; WITH 77; EEAC 62).

JAMES WHARTON

On August 12, 1622, James Wharton of Norfolk, England, who was being detained at Bridewell Prison, was reprieved and selected for transportation to Virginia (CBE 28).

GEORGE WHEATLEY

On September 7, 1626, George Wheatley was listed among those who had sent goods to Virginia on the *Peter and John* (CBE 73).

DOROTHY WHEELER

Dorothy Wheeler came to Virginia on the *Africa* at the expense of Adam Thorogood, who used her as a headright when patenting some land on June 24, 1635 (PB 1 Pt. 1:179).

HENRY WHEELER

Henry Wheeler came to Virginia on the *Trial* in 1620 and on February 16, 1624, was living in Buckroe, on the east side of the Hampton River in Elizabeth City (**17**). Wheeler was still there in early 1625 and was residing in the household of Thomas Flint, who occupied part of the Virginia Company's land. Henry Wheeler, who was age 20, seems to have been a free man. He probably was a Virginia Company tenant (CBE 45, 67).

HESTER WHEELER

On February 27, 1619, Hester Wheeler, a young wench, was listed among the children being detained at Bridewell Prison until they could be sent to Virginia. On September 1, 1624, when Albiano Lupo patented some land, he used Hester as a headright and indicated that he had underwritten the cost of her transportation to the colony on the *George* in 1619 (CBE 13; PB 1 Pt. 1:33).

JOHN WHEELER

On February 9, 1629, John Wheeler, who was age 19, testified before the General Court. He stated that Robert Newman had sold some livestock to Mr. Richard Wheeler (MCGC 185).

RICHARD WHEELER

In February 1629 the General Court heard Daniel Cugley's testimony about a bundle of stockings that Mr. Richard Wheeler had purchased from Captain William Stone and brought to Cugley's house on Old Plantation Creek (**73**) in May 1628. Wheeler, when making his purchase, gave Stone a tobacco bill. Reference was made to Wheeler's purchase of some swine from Robert

Newman, whom he never paid. On February 3, 1656, when Richard Wheeler made his will, he identified himself as a citizen and inn holder of London. He made bequests to his grandchildren, Richard and John Moye, and said that they were living in Virginia in the Lynnehaven area (MCGC 185-186; SH 47; WITH 150; EEAC 63).

JEREMY WHINIARD (WHIMARD)

On January 22, 1620, the Bridewell Court decided that Jeremy Whiniard (Whimard), who had been brought in from Newgate Market, would be sent to Virginia. By March 6, 1621, his transportation to the colony had been arranged by George Harrison of Charles City, who used Whiniard as a headright when receiving a patent from Governor George Yeardley (CBE 17, 19; VCR 3:432-433; SAIN 1:25).

[NO FIRST NAME] WHITAKER

On June 19, 1622, Virginia Company officials were informed that Sir John Bourchiers wanted his son-in-law, a colonist named Whitaker, to return to England, where he had a wife and child (VCR 2:50).

***

ALEXANDER WHITAKER (WHITTAKER, WHITAKERS)

The Rev. Alexander Whitaker, son of the Rev. William Whitaker of St. Ann, in Black Friars, obtained a degree from Cambridge University about 1604. He made his will on February 16, 1610, and in 1611 accompanied Sir Thomas Dale to Virginia, where he intended to serve as a missionary for three years. He became minister of the community of settlers in Henrico and in 1612–1614 lived on the lower side of the James River at Coxendale (**64**), the location of his parsonage, Rock Hall. In 1611 the Rev. Alexander Whitaker wrote a treatise called *Good News from Virginia*, in which he described the colony's natural advantages. He also dispatched letters to England in which he promoted the colonization of Virginia. On June 18, 1614, he sent word to his cousin, the Rev. Gorge of Black Friars in London, that Pocahontas had converted to Christianity and had married John Rolfe. Prior to May 1616, when Sir Thomas Dale left Virginia, the Rev. Whitaker became minister of

the Bermuda Nether Hundred (**39**) community. He accidentally drowned in 1617, and his will was presented for probate on August 4, 1617. One of his heirs was his brother Jabez Whitaker, an employee of the Virginia Company who lived in Virginia and was responsible for the Company's servants and tenants at the College (**66**) (CJS 2:242, 251, 298; WITH 29; HAI 548-551, 695-745, 825, 848-849; CBE 8; VCR 4:511).

ISAAC WHITAKER (WHITTAKER, WHITAKERS)

Isaac Whitaker (Whittaker, Whitakers) came to Virginia sometime prior to April 7, 1623, at which time Governor Francis Wyatt indicated that he had placed him on some of the most fertile ground available. In late October 1623 Captain Isaac Whitaker was commissioned to raise 20 men so that he could lead an attack on the Indians, a raid in retaliation for the March 22, 1622, assault. Isaac Whitaker and his wife, Elizabeth, were residents of Elizabeth City (**17**) on February 16, 1624, and probably were living there earlier on. Official records reveal that Whitaker purchased corn from William Capps in 1623, and that prior to January 9, 1626, he became indebted to Mr. Langley, a merchant. On February 23, 1627, Thomas Flint patented 50 acres of land located on the east side of the Hampton River, a parcel known as the Indian Thicket, which was said to have formerly been occupied by Captain Isaac Whitaker (VCR 2:524-525; 4:104, 292; CBE 43; MCGC 87; PB 1 Pt. 1:77).

ELIZABETH WHITAKER (WHITTAKER, WHITAKERS) (MRS. ISAAC WHITAKER [WHITTAKER, WHITAKERS])

On February 16, 1624, Elizabeth, the wife of Isaac Whitaker (Whittaker, Whitakers), was living on the east side of the Hampton River in Elizabeth City (**17**), on part of the Virginia Company's land (CBE 43).

JABEZ WHITAKER (WHITTAKER, WHITAKERS)

In November 1619 Jabez Whitaker (Whittaker, Whitakers), the Rev. Alexander Whitaker's brother, was placed in charge of the 50 newly arrived Virginia Company tenants and servants who were sent to the colony to live on the tracts of land set aside for the Company's use. However, because the men reached Virginia in the winter and had no experience with frontier living conditions, the decision was made to place half of them on the Company Land in James City (**4**) and to entrust the remainder to the care of experienced planters. In January 1620 John Rolfe reported that 25 men were living at that time with Mr. Whitaker on the Company Land at the mouth of the Chickahominy River. Six months later Company officials commended Jabez Whitaker for keeping them informed about the status of their men. In May 1621 Whitaker informed the Virginia Company's leaders that he had provided for three groups of newly arrived servants. He also said that he had built a guesthouse on the Company Land in James City to provide shelter to newcomers while they underwent the seasoning process. He added that his men had planted vines and fenced in a hundred acres of land. Among those to whom Whitaker provided care were the Company servants who arrived on the *Jonathan*, the *Trial*, and the *London Merchant*. He also gave shelter to Captain William Norton's glassworkers. The Virginia Company awarded Whitaker the use of two servants in appreciation for his efforts. On February 20, 1624, Jabez Whitaker was among the burgesses who signed the General Assembly's rebuttal to Alderman Johnson's claim about conditions in the colony between 1607 and 1619. By February 16, 1624, he and his wife, Mary, had moved to Elizabeth City (**17**), where his brother Isaac was living. On March 4, 1626, Jabez Whitaker was appointed to the Council of State (WITH 29; VCR 1:369, 508; 3:226-229, 246; 3:441-443, 494; HAI 915; HEN 1:128-129; CBE 46, 71).

MARY WHITAKER (WHITTAKER, WHITAKERS) (MRS. JABEZ WHITAKER [WHITTAKER, WHITAKERS])

On February 16, 1624, Mary, the wife of Captain Jabez Whitaker (Whittaker, Whitakers), was living in Elizabeth City (**17**). On November 19, 1624, she testified before the General Court about some derogatory statements that Captain John Martin allegedly had made about the Virginia Company while visiting the home she and her husband shared (CBE 43; MCGC 28).

WILLIAM WHITAKER (WHITTAKER, WHITAKERS)

The Rev. William Whitaker (Whittaker, Whitakers), an English clergyman and the father of the Rev. Alexander Whitaker, is believed to have put Captain John Smith in touch with William Symonds, who helped Smith get his writings published (CJS 1:122).

***

JOHN WHITAKER (WHITTAKER, WHITAKERS)

The General Court was informed that John Whitaker (Whittaker, Whitakers) was a servant who had been brought to Virginia by Thomas Crispe in January 1622 (MCGC 50).

RICHARD WHITBY

On February 16, 1624, Richard Whitby was living at Hog Island (**16**) (CBE 41).

BENJAMIN WHITE

On May 20, 1607, Benjamin White, a sailor, accompanied Captain Christopher Newport on an exploratory voyage up the James River (HAI 102).

EDWARD (EDMOND) WHITE (WHITT)

Edward (Edmond) White (Whitt), a yeoman, came to Virginia in 1620 on the *Bona Nova* and on February 16, 1624, was living on the lower side of the James River at the Treasurer's Plantation (**11**), where he probably was a tenant. He was still there on February 4, 1625, and was well supplied with stored food and defensive weaponry. On May 30, 1625, White testified that he had helped clear part of the ground belonging to Captain William Powell (**14**), and that he and Zachariah Cripps had understood that temporary use of the acreage would belong to those who had cleared it. In June 1625 Anthony West testified that Edward White and Zachariah Cripps had loaned Treasurer George Sandys some tobacco. On December 12, 1625, White and Cripps were appointed administrators of Mr. Thomas Swift's estate. Two weeks later both men acknowledged owing tobacco to the estate of Luke Eden (Aden). On January 8, 1627,

White and Cripps purchased some acreage from Captain Ralph Hamor. Edward White died sometime prior to January 22, 1629, at which time his partner, Zachariah Cripps, was named administrator of his estate (MCGC 63, 80-81, 90, 94, 128, 182; CBE 40, 60; DOR 1:42).

GEORGE WHITE

On October 20, 1617, George White was pardoned for having fled to the Indians with weaponry (VCR 3:74).

GEORGE WHITE

On June 3, 1635, the Rev. George White patented 200 acres on the Nansemond River (**20 c**), using four headrights. The location of his land was mentioned in a patent that was awarded several months later (PB 1 Pt. 1:240, 310).

JEREMY (JEREME) WHITE (WHITT)

Jeremy (Jereme) White (Whitt) came to Virginia on the *Tyger* and on February 16, 1624, was living on the lower side of the James River. He was still there on February 4, 1625, and was a 20-year-old servant in Edward Blaney's household on the Powell plantation (**14**). On August 28, 1626, Thomas Passmore's widow, Joanne, informed the General Court that she preferred Jeremy White—a servant then living in the Passmore household on Jamestown Island (**1**)—to the maidservant Mrs. Margaret West (Edward Blaney's widow) had taken from her. Jeremy White was supposed to serve Mrs. Passmore until December 1, 1627, as he was part of Thomas Passmore's estate (CBE 40, 56; MCGC 110).

JOAN WHITE

On October 11, 1627, Joan White, one of Abraham Peirsey's servants at Flowerdew (**53**), was found guilty of having a sexual relationship and a child with fellow servant John Philips. White and Philips were sentenced to a whipping, and Peirsey was ordered to keep them separated (MCGC 155).

JOHN WHITE

John White, who set sail from England on July 31, 1622, aboard the *James*, went to

Virginia with William Cradock. He may have been a kinsman of the Rev. Robert White, who also was aboard (FER 400).

JOHN WHITE

In March 1624, John White, master's mate of the *Southampton*, brought suit against the ship's owner, Captain John Harvey. White claimed that Harvey had failed to pay him and then released him from his employ. On March 24, 1625, Nathaniel Reeve, boatswain of the *Southampton*, testified that 18 sailors had left the ship because Captain Harvey had refused to honor his agreement with them. Reeve also said that on the way to Virginia, he had seen Harvey and John White arguing heatedly and that Harvey had threatened to take the matter to the governor (VCR 4:459-461; MCGC 13-14).

JOSEPH WHITE

On February 5, 1620, Joseph White, who had been brought to Bridewell Prison from White Tower Street, was sentenced to transportation to Virginia (CBE 18).

***

ROBERT WHITE

The Rev. Robert White, who set sail from England on July 31, 1622, aboard the *James*, went to Virginia with William Cradock. White's wife, Mary, accompanied him. Mr. White may have been related to the John White who also was aboard (FER 400).

MARY WHITE (MRS. ROBERT WHITE)

Mary, the wife of the Rev. Robert White, set sail from England on July 31, 1622, aboard the *James*. She went to Virginia with her husband and William Cradock (FER 400).

***

THOMAS WHITE

On September 11, 1621, Virginia Company officials agreed to pay for the passage of the Rev. Thomas White if he was willing to go to a particular (privately sponsored) plantation. In January 1622 the Council of State informed Company officials that they were very pleased that the Rev. White was being sent to the colony (VCR 3:506, 583).

WILLIAM WHITE

William White, a laborer, came to Virginia in 1607 in the first group of Jamestown (1) colonists. He lived with the Natives for a time and later reported on their customs. He also described George Casson's death. Captain John Smith referred to Mr. William White as one of his "old soldiers" (CJS 1:209, 270; 2:142, 222; HAI 138, 140-141).

WILLIAM WHITE

When William White, a linen-draper from London, made his will on August 20, 1622, he indicated that he had become a planter and had both land and servants in Virginia. White died in the colony, and on June 26, 1627, his brother, John, was named administrator of his estate (EEAC 63; WAT 206).

WILLIAM WHITE

On February 16, 1624, William White was living at Chaplin's Choice (56). He died sometime prior to January 17, 1625, at which time he was identified as the overseer of the goods and servants belonging to Truelove's Company. The General Court ordered Nathaniel Causey to inventory the Truelove's Company's goods and servants and report back. Since William White had bequeathed Causey three servants, Causey was allowed to keep them as long as he provided replacements to Ensign Isaac Chaplin. On December 4, 1626, Nathaniel Causey testified that William White had written to the Truelove's Company's investors and requested that servant John Browne be granted his freedom because he had completed his term of indenture. Causey was named William White's replacement as overseer of the Truelove's Company's belongings (CBE 37; MCGC 43, 126).

WILLIAM WHITE (WHITT)

The Rev. William White (Whitt) moved to Elizabeth City (17, 18), where he replaced the Rev. George Keith, who had gone elsewhere. Mr. White died in Elizabeth City and was buried there on September 12, 1624. When his will was proved in June 1627, it was learned that he had land in Virginia at the time of his death (MCGC 22; CBE 67, 78).

WILLIAM WHITE

In 1629 Thomas Stroud admitted stealing poultry from William White. Both men appear to have lived on the lower side of the James River (8-16), across from Jamestown Island (MCGC 200).

GEORGE WHITEHAND

George Whitehand came to Virginia in 1620 on the *Temperance* at Sir George Yeardley's expense. On February 4, 1625, he was living at Hog Island (16), where he was identified as one of Yeardley's servants. George Whitehand was then age 25. On February 9, 1628, the General Court was informed that Whitehand had been brought to the colony by Sir George Yeardley on the *Temperance* in 1621. (Note that there is a discrepancy in the date that Whitehand reportedly came to Virginia. Either the General Court or the muster-taker got the date wrong *or* one made reference to the Old Style calendar and the other to the New Style calendar.) By September 20, 1628, George Whitehand's headright had been assigned to Thomas Flint, who used it when patenting some land (CBE 61; MCGC 166; PB 1 Pt. 1:59).

GEORGE WHITEHEAD

George Whitehead came to Virginia on the *John and Dorothy* in 1634 at the expense of Adam Thorogood, who used him as a headright when patenting some land on June 24, 1635 (PB 1 Pt. 1:179).

ROBERT WHITEHED (WHITEHEAD?)

On April 4, 1625, it was reported that Robert Whitehed (Whitehead?) was deceased and that Nathaniel Jeffreys of Jamestown (1) had been one of his servants. By that date, Jeffreys and Edward Cadge were sharing a dwelling in urban Jamestown (MCGC 51).

ANN WHITETHORNE

Ann Whitethorne came to Virginia at the expense of Adam Thorogood, who used her as a headright when patenting some land on June 24, 1635 (PB 1 Pt. 1:179).

GILBERT WHITFIELD (WHITFILD)

Gilbert Whitfield (Whitfild) came to Virginia on the *Flying Hart* in 1621 and on

February 16, 1624, was living in Elizabeth City (**17, 18**). By February 7, 1625, he had moved to Newportes News (**24**), where he was a 23-year-old servant in Daniel Gookin's household. In November 1628, when the justices of the General Court heard testimony about Lieutenant Thomas Flint's behavior while being detained at Robert Poole's house, Poole said that Flint drew his knife and threatened Gilbert Whitfield, one of the men posted as guards. Another guard rushed to his aid and Whitfield helped subdue Flint by giving him a blow on the head (CBE 43, 63; MCGC 176-177).

***

CHRISTIAN WHITHELME (WHITEHELM, WITHELM) I

Christian Whithelme (Whitehelm, Withelm) I, a Dutch vinegar-maker, moved to England around 1605 with his wife and child. After being widowed, he married a Dutch immigrant named Neelkin, who was then in England. By 1618 Whithelme was describing himself as a galley-potmaker (delftware potter) and distiller of aquavitae. He and his household lived in St. Olave's Parish in Southwark, where he had a workshop. In July 1628 he obtained a royal grant of privilege as the sole manufacturer of galley ware (delftware) for 14 years. He also asked for the sole right to make smalt (the cobalt blue pigment used in decorating tin-glazed pottery and in starch), despite another man's patent. Because Christian Whithelme's request was denied, and he needed smalt to decorate his pottery, he had to either purchase it from a supplier who had a 31-year monopoly, procure it from abroad, or produce his own, despite risk of prosecution. Christian Whithelme I's will—prepared March 8, 1629—reveals that he decided to cut his losses by investing in the production of potashes, one of the principal compounds used in smalt-making. The testator described himself as "a great Adventurer into Virginia and other parts" and said that he had invested with Sir John Harvey of Jamestown (**1**) and others in the production of soap ashes, pot ashes, and other commodities. Whithelme specified that his estate be divided equally between his son, Christian Whithelme II, who was then in Virginia, and his son-in-law, Thomas Townsend. He said that if Christian II re-

turned from Virginia in disrepute, he was to receive an inheritance of only £200. Christian Whithelme I named his daughter, Mary, and her husband, Thomas Townsend, as his executors. Whithelme died within a month of making his will, which was presented for probate on April 9, 1629. His son-in-law (and perhaps his son) continued the tradition of manufacturing delftware. Examples of Whithelme pottery still survive in museum collections (WITH 159; SR 3958; CBE 90; EEAC 63).

CHRISTIAN WHITHELME (WHITEHELM, WITHELM) II

Christian Whithelme (Whitehelm, Withelm) II was the son of galley-potmaker Christian Whithelme I, a Dutch artisan living in England. When the elder Whithelme made his will in March 1629, he indicated that young Christian, who was living in Virginia, was to get half of his estate unless he returned from overseas "lewd, bad and not obedient" (WITH 159; SR 3958; CBE 90; EEAC 63).

***

JAMES WHITINGE

James Whitinge came to Virginia on the *George* in 1617 and in early 1625 was living in Elizabeth City (**18**), where he was a member of the household headed by the Rev. George Keith. Whitinge was then age 16 and appears to have been free (CBE 64).

ROBERT WHITMORE

Robert Whitmore, who was brought in from the streets of London, was taken to Bridewell Prison, where on December 24, 1619, officials decided that he would be sent to Virginia. He went to the colony on the *Duty* and on February 16, 1624, was a servant in the urban Jamestown (**1**) household of merchant Edward Blaney. By February 5, 1625, Whitmore had relocated to Blaney's plantation (**14**) on the lower side of the James River, where he was a 22-year-old indentured servant (CBE 14, 38, 59).

***

[NO FIRST NAME] WHITNEY

Mr. Whitney and his son set sail for Virginia on April 16, 1619 (FER 107).

[NO FIRST NAME] WHITNEY

The son of Mr. Whitney, whose first name is unknown, set sail for Virginia on April 16, 1619 (FER 107).

***

KATHERINE WHITNEY

On November 20, 1622, officials decided that Katherine Whitney, who was being detained at Newgate Prison, would be sent to Virginia (CBE 29).

SAMUEL WHITNEY

According to records maintained by the Drapers Company in London, Samuel Whitney, a point-maker, settled in Virginia in 1625 (SR 879).

ROBERT WHITT

Robert Whitt died at Warresqueak (26) sometime after April 1623 but before February 16, 1624 (CBE 42).

JOHN WHITTON

On April 30, 1621, the Virginia Company noted that John Whitton, whose passage to Virginia had been paid by his stepfather, Leonard Dansby, had been awarded land in Virginia. Company records also indicate that John's mother wed Thomas Harteastle after Leonard Dansby's death (VCR 4:461-462).

ALICE WHITWOOD

On November 20, 1622, officials at Newgate decided that Alice Whitwood, a woman found guilty of killing her infant, would be pardoned and transported overseas, probably to Virginia (CBE 29).

MARGARET WICHERING

In late February 1619, it was decided that Margaret Wichering, a girl brought to Bridewell from Ardens Alley, would be detained until she could be sent to Virginia (HUME 23).

JAMES WICKHAM

On February 24, 1623, James Wickham, a 25- or 26-year-old servant in Dr. John Pott's household in urban Jamestown (1), was involved in killing and dressing a stolen calf (MCGC 3-4).

WILLIAM WICKHAM

On March 10, 1618, Deputy Governor Samuel Argall said that he would like Mr. William Wickham to be ordained. He added that Wickham's eyesight was poor and that he needed someone to read to him. William Wickham was a councilor during Governor George Yeardley's first term, which began in spring 1619 (VCR 3:92; CJS 2:266).

RICHARD WIFFE (WISSE)

Richard Wiffe (Wisse) died in Elizabeth City (17, 18) and was buried on April 26, 1624 (CBE 67).

RICHARD WIFFIN (WYFFING, WYFFIN)

Richard Wiffin (Wyffing, Wyffin), a gentleman and Virginia Company investor, came to Virginia in early 1608 in the 1st Supply of new settlers to reach Jamestown (1). Later in the year he accompanied Captain John Smith on a voyage to Pamunkey. Smith authorized Richard Wiffin and Sergeant Jeffrey Abbott to capture and kill the Dutchmen who had fled to the Indians. Wiffin also risked his life in order to get a message to Smith. He was coauthor of a verse that accompanied Smith's *Proceedings* (CJS 1:216, 222; 2:13, 55, 136, 160, 203, 206-207, 216, 254, 258, 282).

***

EDWARD WIGG

Edward Wigg came to Virginia on the *Abigail* in 1621 and on February 7, 1625, was living at Basses Choice (27) in the household headed by Nathaniel Basse. Wigg was age 22 and appears to have been free. On January 14, 1628, he was among those summoned to court and identified as one of merchant Edward Sharples' debtors. On March 2, 1629, Wigg testified about a bequest Abraham Porter of Jamestown (1) made while on his deathbed. The General Court ordered Edward Wigg to compensate John Jackson because he had borrowed his canoe without permission and allowed it to be damaged. Wigg sued Robert Hutchinson, a debtor, and he had George Ungwin (Ung-wine, Unguin, Onion, Union, Unwyn, Vinon, Vinoyn) arrested. In 1629 Edward Wigg married one of Stephen Barker's maidservants. He failed to compensate Barker, a resident of Martin's Hundred (**7**) and, later, the Neck O'Land (**5**), even though he had agreed to do so. In October and November 1635 Edward Wigg, a Virginia planter, sued Thomas Middleton. The complaint centered on the low value that Thomas Middleton had assigned to the tobacco that Wigg had shipped to his brother, William Wigg of St. Benet Sherehog, London—a 36-year-old grocer (CBE 62; MCGC 158, 188, 197; EAE 55).

MRS. EDWARD WIGG

In 1629 Edward Wigg married a maidservant who belonged to Stephen Barker, a resident of Martin's Hundred (**7**) who later moved to the Neck O'Land (**5**). Barker sued Wigg, who had agreed to pay him for the maidservant but had failed to do so. Mrs. Edward Wigg's given name is unknown (MCGC 197).

***

VALENTINE WIKE

Valentine Wike, a 30-year-old gentleman from Shropshire, set sail from England in 1619 aboard the *Bona Nova*. He may have been related to fellow passenger William Wike (FER 295).

WILLIAM WIKE

William Wike, a 29-year-old gentleman from Shropshire, set sail from England in 1619 aboard the *Bona Nova*. He may have been related to Valentine Wike, a passenger on the same ship (FER 295).

***

JOHN WILCOCKE (WILCOCKS, WILCOX, WILCOCKES)

John Wilcocke (Wilcocks, Wilcox, Wilcockes), who was from Plymouth, England, came to Virginia on the *Bona Nova* in 1620. Captain John Smith (who was quoting John Pory) said that Wilcocke established a plantation on Virginia Company's land (**76**) on the Eastern Shore shortly after his arrival. On September 10,

1622, when Wilcocke was in Elizabeth City (**17**) and preparing to go on an expedition against the Indians, he made his will, which was witnessed by the Rev. Jonas Stockton and Peter Arundell. He made bequests to his wife and executrix, Temperance, to his sisters, Katherin and Susana Wilcocke, and to his stepdaughter, Grace Burges. He named Captain Thomas Nuce and John Pountis as overseers. Captain John Wilcocke survived the march against the Indians. Court testimony given on December 11, 1623, by boat builders Thomas Nunn and Bartholomew Blake suggests that Wilcocke may have purchased some goods that Captain John Barwick misappropriated from the Virginia Company. In 1624 Wilcocke reportedly gave a tobacco note to William Holmes, a merchant and mariner, who passed it along to Samuel Mathews and cape merchant Abraham Peirsey.

When a census was taken of the colony's inhabitants on February 16, 1624, Captain John Wilcocke was living on the Eastern Shore. He represented that area as a burgess and was among those who refuted Alderman Johnson's claim that conditions in the colony were good prior to Sir George Yeardley's arrival in 1619. In early 1625 Wilcocke was still living on the Virginia Company's land on the Eastern Shore and headed a household that included another free white male. During the year the General Court questioned whether Wilcocke had made a bargain with John Crowdeck. On November 21, 1625, Wilcocke agreed to outfit and deliver a shallop to William Claiborne at Kecoughtan within two weeks, a vessel that Claiborne was planning to sell to Thomas Harwood of Mulberry Island (**21**). Claiborne sued Wilcocke because he failed to deliver the shallop on time. As late as 1627 John Wilcocke was occupying part of the Virginia Company's land in Accomack. In March 1627, however, he asked for 500 acres on the upper side of Old Plantation Creek (**73**); the General Court's approval was dependent on whether Wilcocke could prove that he had brought ten servants to the colony. In October 1627 Wilcocke agreed to let Walter Scott, his tenant, have three shares of their tobacco crop, or more if Scott agreed to oversee Wilcocke's servants. Scott declined. By January 21, 1628, Captain John Wilcocke was dead, having perished while crossing the Chesapeake Bay. An inventory of his estate was presented by Edward Waters, who was designated the decedent's administrator in Virginia. At the time of his death, Captain Wilcocke was indebted to several people, notably Edward Waters, Edward Sharples, Edward Mayhew, and Nicholas Clements. He apparently was planning to acquire some additional servants, for he had arranged for John Walton to transport them to Virginia. On June 20, 1628, the widowed Temperance Wilcocke, who was in England, presented her late husband's will for probate. It was noted that he had property in Plymouth, England; Accomack, Virginia; and in New England (CJS 2:228; SH 5; MCGC 8-9, 44, 124-125, 146, 159, 173, 180, 183, 187; EAE 89; CBE 46, 68, 83; HAI 915; HEN 1:128-129; PB1 Pt. 1:76, 85; EEAC 64; WAT 3; SR 3117; DOR 1:69).

TEMPERANCE WILCOCKE (WILCOCKS, WILCOX, WILCOCKES) (MRS. JOHN WILCOCKE [WILCOCKS, WILCOX, WILCOCKES])

On September 10, 1622, when John Wilcocke (Wilcocks, Wilcox, Wilcockes) made his will shortly before leaving on an expedition against the Indians, he named his wife, Temperance, as his executrix and noted that she was then in London. He specified that if Temperance died before his will was presented for probate, he wanted his stepdaughter, Grace Burges, to serve as sole executrix (SR 3117; SH 5).

***

MANDLIN WILCOCKS

On February 16, 1624, Mandlin Wilcocks was living in Elizabeth City (**17, 18**) (CBE 44).

***

MICHAEL (MIHELL) WILCOCKE (WILCOCKS, WILCOX, WILCOCKES)

Michael (Mihell) Wilcocke (Wilcocks, Wilcox, Wilcockes), an ancient planter, came to Virginia on the *Prosperous* in 1610. In late 1623-early 1624 he filed a complaint with Governor Francis Wyatt, acknowledging that he had agreed to serve William Ganey of Elizabeth City (**18**) for a year. In exchange, Ganey was to build a 20-foot by 15-foot house for his use and pay him five barrels of corn and some tobacco. Wilcocke said that Ganey had failed to finish the house and had not paid him the amount of corn on which they agreed. He also said that Ganey had insisted that Wilcocke provide him with six deer, and that he had. On February 16, 1624, Michael Wilcocke was living in Elizabeth City. In early 1625 he was still residing there and jointly headed a household with his partner, John Slater. Also living there were Elizabeth Wilcocke (Michael's wife), John Slater's wife, and three servants. Michael Wilcocke was then age 31. The Wilcocke-Slater household had a dwelling and an ample supply of stored food and defensive weaponry. On January 3, 1625, Michael Wilcocke was summoned to court, where it was determined that he owed money to Simon Tuchin, a merchant and mariner. On April 3, 1627, he was fined because he went aboard the *Charitie* without proper authorization and purchased some sugar. During the 1630s Michael Wilcocke appears to have moved to the lower side of the James River, in what was then Upper Norfolk County (CBE 44, 64; VCR 4:288; MCGC 40, 147; PB 1 Pt. 2:739; DOR 1:53).

ELIZABETH WILCOCKE (WILCOCKS, WILCOX, WILCOCKES) (MRS. MICHAEL [MIHELL] WILCOCKE [WILCOCKS, WILCOX, WILCOCKES])

Elizabeth, who married ancient planter Michael [Mihell] Wilcocke (Wilcocks, Wilcox, Wilcockes), came to Virginia on the *Concord* in 1621. In early 1625 she was living in Elizabeth City (**18**) in a household headed by her husband. Elizabeth was then age 23 (CBE 64).

***

JOHN WILDE

In 1621 John Wilde was identified as a man associated with the East India School. Although he was among those taken to William Ewen's plantation (**13**) in the wake of the March 22, 1622, Indian attack, he and two other men were sent to Arrohattock (**66**) in February 1623. John Wilde reportedly died there before the end of August 1623. The General Court noted his death on May 23 and June 1, 1625 (FER 272; MCGC 60, 64).

ROBERT WILDE

On June 12, 1610, Lord Delaware appointed Robert Wilde as master of the store in Jamestown (1), a job that gave him the responsibility of distributing provisions and supplies. On July 7, 1610, Wilde was still serving in that position. He apparently left Virginia, for on July 31, 1622, he returned to the colony with Anthony Barham on the *James* (HAI 433, 459; FER 400).

JEAN WILDMAN

Jean Wildman, a young maid, came to Virginia in September 1621 on the *Warwick*. She was brought to the colony by Mr. J. Eaton (FER 309).

BISHOP WILES

Bishop Wiles, a laborer, came to Virginia in 1608 in the 1st Supply of new settlers. He would have lived in Jamestown (1) (CJS 1:223; 2:162).

GILES WILKINS

Giles Wilkins left Bristol, England, on the *Supply* in September 1620 and was one of the settlers accompanying William Tracy, who intended to seat at Berkeley Hundred (55). Wilkins reportedly arrived at Berkeley on January 29, 1621. He was among those slain at the settlement during the March 22, 1622, Indian attack (CBE 21; VCR 3:426, 567).

***

JOHN WILKINS (WILKINES)

John Wilkins (Wilkines) came to Virginia on the *Marigold* in 1618 and on February 16, 1624, was living on the Eastern Shore with his wife, Bridgett. In early 1625 the Wilkinses were still there and John was identified as a 26-year-old household head who was in possession of a dwelling, a storehouse, and an ample supply of stored food and defensive weaponry. The Wilkins home was part of the community of settlers on Old Plantation Creek (73). On January 31, 1625, John Wilkins and another man testified about Thomas Parke's refusal to make a will before leaving the Eastern Shore. John Wilkins became a commissioner of the Accomack monthly court in

1633, and two years later he became a vestryman. He patented 1,300 acres on the Nansemond River (20 c) in 1636, which he repatented a year later and then sold. He also patented 500 acres of land in Accomack near King's Creek (75) in 1637 and within three years had added another 600 acres to his holdings. Over the years John Wilkins made numerous appearances in the Accomack monthly court, sometimes responding to suits and sometimes suing to collect debts. He had an altercation with an indentured servant, who threatened him with a blow to the head. Wilkins apparently had an explosive temper and on at least one occasion was fined for swearing. In 1634 his wife allegedly committed adultery. By September 1637 John Wilkins had remarried, taking as his bride a woman named Anne. He served as a burgess for the Eastern Shore in 1641. Wilkins returned to England a couple times and made a trip to Amsterdam and Hamburg in 1649. In 1642 John Wilkins and Obedience Robins hired Anthony Lynney and his crew to build a windmill on their newly acquired property on King's Creek. Wilkins' will—which was made on December 23, 1649, and was proved on January 29, 1651—indicates that he was preparing to make another a trip to England. Wilkins named his wife, Anne, and his children as his heirs (CBE 46, 69; MCGC 46; PB 1 Pt. 1:378, 420; Pt. 2:539, 948; MEY 677; AMES 1:5-7, 9-10, 13, 19-20, 41-42, 53-54, 59, 67, 77, 83, 96, 98-100, 118, 122-123, 139, 143, 154-155, 163, 165-166, 171, 178, 182, 202, 210, 275-276, 301, 325-326, 407; 2:5, 19, 77, 118, 202, 275-276, 325-326, 412-413, 453; DOR 1:71).

BRIDGETT CROSSE (CRAFT) WILKINS (WILKINES) (MRS. JOHN WILKINS [WILKINES])

Bridgett, who married John Wilkins (Wilkines), came to Virginia on the *Warwick* in 1621. On February 16, 1624, Bridgett and John were living on the Eastern Shore (72-78). They were still residing there in early 1625 and Bridgett was described as age 20. Accomack-Northampton County records suggest that she lived until the early to mid-1630s. A slander suit aired in 1634 raises the possibility that she committed adultery with Thomas Butler, a married man. It is probable that Bridgett Wilkins was the former Bridgett Crosse

(Craft), one of the marriageable young maids who came to Virginia on the *Warwick* in September 1621. If so, she was born in Burford, Wiltshire, and was the orphaned daughter of John Crosse (CBE 46, 69; FLEE 1:12; FER 309).

ANNE WILKINS (WILKINES) (MRS. JOHN WILKINS [WILKINES])

Sometime after 1634 but before September 1637, John Wilkins (Wilkines) married a woman named Anne, who served as his attorney in 1644 when he made a trip to England. Together, they had several children. In 1651 Anne Wilkins served as her late husband's executrix (AMES 2:326; MEY 677).

***

JOHN WILKINS

When the Indians attacked Warresqueak, Edward Bennett's plantation (**26**), on March 22, 1622, John Wilkins was slain (VCR 3:571).

JOHN WILKINS (WILKINES)

In early 1625 John Wilkins (Wilkines) was living on the Eastern Shore and was a servant in John Blore's household on Old Plantation Creek (**73**) (CBE 69).

[NO FIRST NAME] WILKINSON

In late 1634 Mr. Wilkinson, whose first name is unknown, purchased some of the late Thomas Lee's goods, which were sold by Bartholomew Hopkins, probably in Elizabeth City (**17, 18**) (CBE 208).

HENRY WILKINSON (WILKINSONE)

Henry Wilkinson (Wilkinsone) came to the colony as a free man. On May 30, 1625, the justices of the General Court learned that he died in Newportes News (**24**) after a three-week illness and that he left the bulk of his estate to William Slight (MCGC 64).

JOHN WILKINSON

On February 1, 1633, John Wilkinson served as a burgess representing the settlers in Accomack (**72-78**) (HEN 1:203).

MARGERY WILKINSON

On November 30, 1622, Margery Wilkinson, a woman being detained at Newgate, was pardoned due to an outbreak of jail fever. She was among those being sent to Virginia (CBE 29).

MILDRED WILKINSON

Mildred Wilkinson, a woman being detained at Newgate, was pardoned on November 30, 1622, due to an outbreak of jail fever. She was among those being sent to Virginia (CBE 29).

PHILLIP WILKINSON

On February 27, 1619, Phillip Wilkinson, a boy, was among the children rounded up from the streets of London so that they could be sent to Virginia (CBE 13).

WILLIAM WILKINSON

William Wilkinson, a surgeon, came to Virginia in 1607 in the first group of Jamestown (**1**) colonists (CJS 1:209; 2:142).

***

WILLIAM WILKINSON

On November 20, 1635, when the Rev. William Wilkinson patented a tract of land in the Lynnehaven (**20 b**) area, he used his wife, Naomy, as a headright (PB 1 Pt. 1:315).

NAOMY WILKINSON (MRS. WILLIAM WILKINSON)

When the Rev. William Wilkinson patented some land in the Lynnehaven (**20 b**) area on November 20, 1635, he used his wife, Naomy, as a headright (PB 1 Pt. 1:315).

***

HUGH WILLASTONE (WILLESTON, WOOLESTON)

On June 29, 1608, Hugh Willastone (Willeston, Wooleston), a gentleman, invested funds with the Virginia Company and obtained the right to an "adventure" or share of land. He arrived in the colony in 1608 in the 2nd Supply of new settlers and therefore lived in Jamestown (**1**). On February 2,

1624, Virginia Company officials noted that Hugh Willastone had died in Virginia. As he had neither wife nor children, his nephew and heir, Richard Willaston, asked for the Virginia land to which the decedent had been entitled and one servant (CJS 1:241; 2:190, 282; MCGC 49; VCR 2:511).

RICHARD WILLASTONE (WILLESTON, WOOLESTON)

On February 2, 1624, Richard Willastone (Willeston, Wooleston), Hugh Willastone's nephew and legal heir, asked the Virginia Company for the Virginia land to which his late uncle had been entitled and one servant (VCR 2:511).

WILLIAM WILLASTONE (WILLESTON, WOOLESTON)

In 1620 Captain John Smith identified William Willastone (Willeston, Wooleston) as an investor in the Virginia Company (CJS 2:283).

THOMAS WILLER

Thomas Willer died within the corporation of James City, at one of the plantations on the lower side of the James River and east of Gray's Creek (**10-15**), sometime after April 1623 but before February 16, 1624 (CBE 41).

WILLIAM

Mr. Pearns's servant, William, died in Jamestown (**1**) sometime after April 1623 but before February 16, 1624. William was not identified as an African (CBE 39).

WILLIAM

On February 16, 1624, an African named William was living at Flowerdew Hundred (**53**) (CBE 37).

WILLIAM

In early 1625, William, an African child, was living in Elizabeth City (**18**) in Captain William Tucker's household with his parents, servants Anthony and Isabella. William, like his parents, had been baptized (CBE 43, 63; DOR 1).

[NO FIRST NAME] WILLIAMS

In 1608 Master Williams, a laborer, came to Virginia in the 2nd Supply of new Jamestown (**1**) settlers (CJS 1:242; 2:191).

DAVID WILLIAMS

David Williams, a 26-year-old felt maker from Brecknockshire, set sail from England in 1619 aboard the *Bona Nova*. The cost of his passage was paid by the Ferrars, who were major Virginia Company investors. On February 16, 1624, David Williams was living at the College (**66**). However, by early 1625 he had moved to the lower side of the James River, within the corporation of James City (**10-16**), where he died sometime prior to February 4, 1625 (FER 295; CBE 35, 60).

EDWARD WILLIAMS

On August 18, 1619, Edward Williams, a merchant from Bristol, was identified as the owner of the ship *Margaret* (VCR 3:193).

EDWARD WILLIAMS

Edward Williams came to Virginia in 1624 on the *William and John*. On January 24, 1625, he was a 26-year-old servant in the urban Jamestown (**1**) household of George Menefie (CBE 56).

ELIZABETH WILLIAMS

On February 16, 1624, Elizabeth Williams was living on the lower side of the James River, within the corporation of James City and east of Gray's Creek (**10-16**) (CBE 40).

***

HENRY WILLIAMS

Henry Williams, an ancient planter, came to Virginia on the *Treasurer* in 1613, and on February 16, 1624, he and his wife were residing at Jordan's Journey (**46**). Henry and Susan Williams were still there when a muster was taken of the settlement's inhabitants on January 21, 1625. Williams headed a household that was well supplied with provisions and defensive weaponry. On January 3, 1626, Luke Boyse and Thomas Harris were summoned to appear in the General Court to testify on Henry Williams' behalf, probably regarding a suit in which

Williams was involved. On September 6, 1635, Henry Williams patented 150 acres in Accomack on Old Plantation Creek (**73**). He used his dividend as an ancient planter and acquired 50 acres on behalf of Susan Andrews, perhaps his wife. Henry Williams moved to Accomack and was still alive in 1645 (CBE 37, 51; MCGC 86; PB 1 Pt. 1:375; AMES 1:429; DOR 1:18).

SUSAN WILLIAMS
(MRS. HENRY WILLIAMS)

Susan, who married ancient planter Henry Williams, came to Virginia on the *William and Thomas* in 1618. On February 16, 1624, the Williams couple was living at Jordan's Journey (**46**). Susan and Henry were still there when a muster was made of the colony's inhabitants on January 21, 1625 (CBE 37, 51).

***

HUGH WILLIAMS (WINGE)

Hugh Williams (Winge) came to Virginia in 1620 on the *George*. On February 16, 1624, he was an indentured servant in the urban Jamestown (**1**) household of William Peirce. By January 25, 1625, he had moved to Mulberry Island (**21**), where he was a 30-year-old servant in the Peirce household (CBE 38, 56).

JOHN WILLIAMS

On August 10, 1622, officials at Bridewell decided that John Williams, a vagrant brought in from Lime Street, would be detained until he could be sent to Virginia (CBE 28).

JOHN WILLIAMS

On August 12, 1626, John Williams, a merchant, shipped goods from London to Virginia on the *Marmaduke*. On February 5, 1627, Virginia colonist Peter Stafferton informed the General Court that he had witnessed the agreement John Williams made with William Lovell, master of the ship *Aid* (CBE 73; MCGC 139).

KATHERINE WILLIAMS

On January 29, 1620, it was decided that Katherine Williams would be detained at Bridewell until she could be sent to Virginia (CBE 17).

LEWIS WILLIAMS

On March 22, 1622, when the Indians attacked Captain John Berkeley's plantation at Falling Creek (**68**), Lewis Williams was slain (VCR 3:565).

PIERCE WILLIAMS

Pierce Williams came to Virginia on the *Southampton* in 1623. On January 20, 1625, Williams was living at Flowerdew Hundred (**53**), where he was a 23-year-old servant in Abraham Peirsey's household (CBE 50).

RICE WILLIAMS

On October 9, 1624, the Bridewell Court decided that Rice Williams would be detained until he could be sent to Virginia (CBE 48).

RICHARD WILLIAMS ALIAS CORNISH
(SEE RICHARD CORNISH)

RICHARD WILLIAMS ALIAS MUSSELL

On November 20, 1622, it was decided that Richard Williams alias Mussell, who was incarcerated at Newgate, would be detained until he could be sent to Virginia (CBE 29).

***

ROBERT WILLIAMS

On March 22, 1622, when the Indians attacked the settlers at Falling Creek (**68**), Robert Williams, his wife, and their child were slain (VCR 3:565).

MRS. ROBERT WILLIAMS

On March 22, 1622, when the Indians attacked the settlers at Falling Creek (**68**), Mrs. Robert Williams, her husband, and their child were slain (VCR 3:565).

[NO FIRST NAME] WILLIAMS

Mr. and Mrs. Robert Williams' child was slain on March 22, 1622, when the Indians attacked the settlers at Falling Creek (**68**) (VCR 3:565).

***

ROBERT WILLIAMS

Sometime after April 1623 but before February 16, 1624, Robert Williams died at one of the plantations on the lower side of the James River, within the corporation of James City (**10-15**). He may have been the same individual reportedly slain in the 1622 Indian attack (CBE 40).

ROBERT WILLIAMS

On February 16, 1624, Robert Williams was living on the lower side of the James River, within the corporation of James City and west of Gray's Creek (**8, 9**) (CBE 40).

ROGER WILLIAMS

Roger Williams came to Virginia on the *Southampton* in 1622. On February 4, 1625, he was living at Captain Samuel Mathews' plantation (**15**), where he was a 20-year-old servant. On June 17, 1625, Williams—who gave his age as around 23—testified in court in litigation involving Captain Mathews and Captain William Powell's heirs. The dispute involved a portion of the late Captain Powell's property that Captain Mathews' servants had cleared and seated. Roger Williams said that Mathews had intended to send some goods and servants to Powle-Brooke (**50**), but had not. Ultimately, Roger Williams remained on the Powell property (**14**) that he had cleared (CBE 59; MCGC 65-66).

ROLAND (ROWLAND) WILLIAMS (WILLIAMES)

In 1623 Roland (Rowland) Williams (Williames) came to Virginia on the *Jonathan* and appears to have been a Virginia Company employee or tenant. Court testimony taken on December 11, 1623, indicates that Williams, then identified as a sergeant, had received some powder, shot, spices, and other items from Captain John Wilcocks—goods that belonged to the Virginia Company. On February 16, 1624, Roland Williams was living at Buckroe, on the east side of the Hampton River, part of the Virginia Company's land (**17**). He was still there in early 1625 and headed a household that included his partner, Robert Thrasher, and a male servant. Williams was then described as age 20. The two men were in possession of a dwelling, some stored food, and defensive weaponry. On January

3, 1625, Sergeant Roland Williams, at his own request, was compensated for having cleared some of the Virginia Company's land at Kecoughtan and built houses there (CBE 45, 68; MCGC 9, 41).

SIDRACK WILLIAMS

On July 8 1627, it was noted that Sidrack Williams was among those who had shipped goods from London to Virginia on the *Ann* (CBE 78-79).

THOMAS WILLIAMS

Thomas Williams came to Virginia on the *Duty* in May 1618. On February 16, 1624, he was living at Jordan's Journey (**46**) in the household of William Farrar and Cisley Jordan. He was still there on January 21, 1625, at which time Williams was identified as a 24-year-old servant (CBE 36, 51).

WALTER WILLIAMS

Walter Williams, a merchant, was at Captain William Tucker's house in Elizabeth City (**18**) when Tucker, acting on Captain Michael Marshatt's behalf, offered to pay Williams for the use of his servant, Mr. William Lucas. Marshatt was then captain of the *Supply*, which was going to return to England. On March 5, 1629, the General Court's justices discussed this bargain (MCGC 190).

***

WILLIAM WILLIAMS

On February 16, 1624, William Williams and his wife were living on the Eastern Shore (**72-78**). He later patented some land there (CBE 46; AMES 2:14).

MRS. WILLIAM WILLIAMS

On February 16, 1624, William Williams' wife was sharing a home with him on the Eastern Shore (**72-78**) (CBE 46).

***

JAMES WILLIAMSON

On January 29, 1620, officials at Bridewell Prison decided that James Williamson from Bishopsgate would be sent to Virginia (CBE 18).

MARY WILLINS

On July 27, 1632, Bridewell's officials learned that a girl named Mary Willins, who was an "old prisoner" and common pilferer, had escaped from jail. She was supposed to be sent to Virginia, at her own request (HUME 37).

ANN WILLIS

Ann Willis came to the colony in 1620 on the *Temperance*. On January 24, 1625, she was identified as a maidservant living in Sir George Yeardley's household in urban Jamestown (1) (CBE 54).

RICHARD WILLIS

In May 1622 Richard Willis was identified as a servant who was being sent to Virginia on the *Furtherance*, which was expected to depart from Isle of Wight, England. Virginia Company records dated August 1, 1622, indicate that Willis set sail in June 1622, before word had been received of the March 22nd Indian attack (VCR 3:618-619, 674; CBE 28).

WILLIAM WILLIS

On February 13, 1622, William Willis made a claim against the late Captain Christopher Lawne's estate. Lawne's plantation (25) was located on the lower side of the James River, on the east side of Lawnes Creek (VCR 1:600).

EDWARD WILLMOTH

Sixteen-year-old Edward Willmoth testified on January 21, 1629, that when John Lightfoot was on his deathbed, he told Nicholas Spencer that he wanted William Spencer to have his tobacco and cattle. Willmoth may have lived in the eastern end of Jamestown Island (1), where Lightfoot resided (MCGC 181).

***

THOMAS WILLOUGHBY (WILLOBY, WILLOWBY, WILLOWBYE) I

Thomas Willoughby (Willoby, Willowby, Willowbye) I, an ancient planter, came to Virginia in 1610 on the *Prosperous*. In 1617–18, deputy-governor Sir Samuel Argall gave Willoughby some land in Eliza-

beth City (17) on the east side of the Hampton River, acreage on which he built a home. When Governor George Yeardley arrived in April 1619 and commenced implementing the Virginia Company's instructions, the territory in which Thomas Willoughby and his neighbors had become established was designated Company Land. On June 19, 1622, Willoughby claimed that Yeardley had evicted him from his homestead and that he had received no compensation. When a census was made of the colony's inhabitants on February 16, 1624, Thomas Willoughby was still living in Elizabeth City (18) but had moved to the west side of the Hampton River. He was still there in early 1625 and headed a household that included four servants. Ensign Thomas Willoughby was then age 23 and was in possession of three houses, a palisade, and an abundant supply of stored food and defensive weaponry. When a list of patented land was sent back to England in May 1625, Thomas Willoughby was credited with 100 acres within the corporation of Elizabeth City, but on the south side of the James River in the vicinity of the Elizabeth River (20 a). Also attributed to him were 200 acres located two miles inland from the mouth of the Pamunkey (later, York) River. However, neither tract was planted. In December 1625 Willoughby received a court order confirming his 200 acres on the Pamunkey River, which he had seven years to seat. He went to England in 1626 and made plans to bring goods and passengers to Virginia on the *Peter and John*. When Willoughby returned in 1627, he led an expedition against the Chesapeake Indians. In mid-November 1628 he claimed 50 acres on the north side of the James River and west of the Hampton River, bordering Salford's Creek—land that Captain William Tucker previously had owned.

In March 1629 Lieutenant Thomas Willoughby was made commander of the area from Marie's Mount or Newportes News (24) to Captain William Tucker's (18), and he was named a commissioner of Elizabeth City's monthly court. In that capacity he ordered the auctioning of the late George Shorton's goods. Willoughby also appeared before the General Court so that he could settle a dispute with one of his own servants. In April 1629 he was among those who asked that their parish, which had been subdivided, be restored to its former size. He became a burgess for the upper part of Elizabeth City and in that capacity inspected the fort built at Old Point Comfort. Two years later he served as burgess for the area from Water's Creek (now Lake Maury) to the limits of the upper parish of Elizabeth City. In 1634 Thomas Willoughby was among the Virginia planters who sent word to England that they feared financial losses if Maurice Thompson was given a monopoly on Virginia's tobacco trade. By November 1635 Willoughby had built a home on his property on the south side of the James River and had acquired some adjacent acreage. He went to England around 1644–47, and when his son, Thomas II, was admitted to the Merchant Taylor's School, the elder Thomas identified himself as a merchant of Red Lyon Alley, St. Botolph, London. However, he made Lower Norfolk County, Virginia, his permanent home, calling his plantation "Willoughby's Hope." When Thomas Willoughby was deposed in November 1650, he indicated that he was age 52 and had lived in Virginia for 39 years. A patent he secured in 1654 used the headrights of his son, Thomas; daughter, Elizabeth; and Alice Willoughby, probably Thomas's wife. Willoughby died while visiting All Hallows, Barking, in London, and in April 1657 his nephew, Thomas Middleton, was named administrator. Willoughby Spit, in Norfolk, was named for Thomas Willoughby (VCR 2:45; 4:558; CBE 44, 64, 72, 115-116; MEY 688-690; MCGC 173, 188, 190, 193; PB 1 Pt. 1:61, 311; 3:321; HEN 1:149-150, 154, 170, 179, 187; EAE 123; SR 4213; EEAC 64; DOR 1:55).

ALICE WILLOUGHBY (WILLOBY, WILLOWBY, WILLOWBYE) I (MRS. THOMAS WILLOUGHBY [WILLOBY, WILLOWBY, WILLOWBYE] I)

When Thomas Willoughby secured a patent for 2,900 acres in Lynnhaven Parish on October 7, 1654, he listed as headrights his son, Thomas II, daughter, Elizabeth, and Alice Willoughby, who probably was his wife (PB 3:321; MEY 689-690).

ELIZABETH WILLOUGHBY (WILLOBY, WILLOWBY, WILLOWBYE)

Elizabeth Willoughby (Willoby, Willowby, Willowbye), the daughter of Virginia planter Thomas Willoughby I, was a minor at the time of her father's death in the 1650s and was one of his heirs (EEAC 64).

THOMAS WILLOUGHBY (WILLOBY, WILLOWBY, WILLOWBYE) II

Thomas Willoughby (Willoby, Willowby, Willowbye) II, the son of Virginia planter Thomas Willoughby I, was a minor at the time of his father's death in the 1650s and was one of his heirs (EEAC 64).

***

WILLIAM WILLOUGHBY (WILLOBY, WILLOWBY, WILLOWBYE)

On May 26, 1634, William Willoughby (Willoby, Willowby, Willowbye) and some other well-established Virginia planters expressed their concern that they would sustain major losses if Maurice Thompson was appointed sole shipper (supplier) to the colony (CBE 115-116; G&M 187-188).

ANTHONY WILLS

On July 15, 1631, Anthony Wills was among the Virginia planters exporting tobacco from the colony who asked for relief from customs duties. He indicated that his hogsheads of tobacco bore the mark *AW*. Wills testified before the General Court on June 5, 1632, when an inquiry was held into the mistreatment of Edmund Clark's orphaned child, who was in England (G&M 165; MCGC 201).

GEORGE WILMER

On May 8, 1622, the Virginia Company noted that George Wilmer had received two shares of land from Clement Wilmer (VCR 1:635).

JOHN WILMORE (WILMOSE)

On February 16, 1624, John Wilmore (Wilmose) was living on the Maine (**3**), the mainland west of Jamestown Island (CBE 39).

CLEMENT WILSON

Clement Wilson died at Warresqueak (**26**) sometime after April 1623 but before February 16, 1624 (CBE 42).

FRANCIS WILSON

On November 21, 1618, officials at Bridewell decided that Francis Wilson, a vagrant and young rogue, would be sent to Virginia (CBE 11).

GEORGE WILSON

When a census was taken of the colony's inhabitants in March 1620, George Wilson was among those on a trading voyage to Accomack and Acohanock. He returned but almost immediately went out again (FER 159).

HENRY WILSON (WILLSON)

Henry Wilson (Willson) came to Virginia in 1619 on the *Sampson* and most likely was living at Captain John Ward's plantation (**61**) at the time of the March 22, 1622, Indian attack. Christopher Barker, one of Captain Ward's former servants, said that Captain William Eppes took Captain Ward's servants to his plantation (**74**) in Accomack in the summer of 1622. He indicated that Ward's houses were burned and nothing remained. On February 16, 1624, Henry Wilson was living on the Eastern Shore in Captain William Eppes's household. He was still there in early 1625 and was described as a 24-year-old servant. On January 30, 1626, Henry Wilson and his fellow servant, William Munn (Minns), were authorized to sell their tobacco crop. However, they were obliged to post a bond guaranteeing that they would serve the amount of time Captain John Ward could prove he was owed. On February 5, 1627, Henry Wilson and William Munn asked the General Court to set them free, for Captain Ward had returned to England without giving either of them the 50 acres of land, food, and clothing to which they were entitled. Both said that they wanted to plant for themselves and that their terms of service were almost finished. Since Ward was not available to appear on his own behalf, the General Court's justices agreed to free Henry Wilson and William Munn if they posted a bond. In 1635 Wilson patented 50 acres on Old Plantation Creek (**73**). He died prior to September 10, 1638, at which time his will was proved in Accomack County court (CBE 46, 68; MCGC 91, 138–139; AMES 1:120).

HENRY WILSON

Henry Wilson came to Virginia on the *Truelove* in 1622 and on February 16, 1624, was among those living at Chaplin's Choice (**56**). He died there sometime prior to January 21, 1625 (CBE 37, 51).

JAMES WILSON (WILSONN)

James Wilson (Wilsonn) came to Virginia on the *Hopewell* in 1633 at the expense of Adam Thorogood, who used him as a headright when patenting some land on June 24, 1635 (PB 1 Pt. 1:179).

JOHN WILSON

On February 16, 1624, John Wilson was living at Flowerdew Hundred (**53**) (CBE 37).

SUSAN WILSON

On October 11, 1627, Susan Wilson testified that Mrs. John Pott of Jamestown (**1**) had hired out her servant, Steven Taylor, to Allen Kineston. She said that when Taylor became lame, Kineston returned him to Mrs. Pott so that she could cure him. Susan may have been the wife of Thomas Wilson, a Pott servant (MCGC 155).

***

THOMAS WILSON

Thomas Wilson reportedly came to Virginia in 1620 aboard the *Abigail* and on January 24, 1625, was a 27-year-old servant living in urban Jamestown (**1**) in Dr. John Pott's household. Wilson was a tailor who sometimes "worked abroad at his trade." In October 1625 Mrs. Pierce Bernardo (the wife of one of the Italian glassmakers) indicated that Thomas Wilson had been employed long-term for Captain William Norton, original overseer of the glassworks, but had never been paid. Wilson later testified in court about a man associated with the Treasurer's Plantation (**11**), where the glassworkers lived after abandoning the Glasshouse (**2**). By August 1626 Thomas Wilson had married and become Dr. John Pott's tenant. He may have lived on Pott's leasehold in the Governor's Land (**3**). In August 1626 Thomas Wilson was hauled into court, where he was charged with getting drunk and beating his wife. As punishment, he was put into the stocks, fined, and required to post a peace bond. Two months later Dr. John Pott came into court and testified that Wilson was behaving himself. This enabled him to be released from the peace bond that he had posted (MCGC 72-73, 79-80, 108, 116; CBE 55).

MRS. THOMAS WILSON

Sometime after January 24, 1625, but before August 21, 1626, tailor Thomas Wilson, one of Dr. John Pott's former servants, married. He was found guilty of getting drunk and beating his wife and was obliged to post a bond guaranteeing his good behavior. The Wilsons may have lived on the Governor's Land (3), where Dr. John Pott had a leasehold. Mrs. Wilson's given name may have been Susan (MCGC 108, 116).

***

WILLIAM WILSON

In May 1609 Virginia Company officials decided that William Wilson, who was then in Virginia, would be allowed to return to England to tell the officials what the colonists needed in the way of medical supplies and equipment. Those items were to be sent to John Woodall's man, George Liste, who had medical skills (VCR 3:23).

FRANCIS WILTON

On November 21, 1618, officials decided that Francis Wilton, a vagrant and young rogue being detained at Bridewell, would be transported to Virginia. Wilton went to the colony on the *Jonathan* and on January 23, 1625, was living at the College (66), where he was a household head (CBE 11, 53; DOR 1:8).

JOHN WILTON

On February 19, 1620, officials decided that John Wilton, who was apprehended in St. Sepulchre's and detained at Bridewell Prison, would be placed with an artisan or sent to Virginia (CBE 19).

ALEXANDER WINCHELSEY

On July 15, 1620, when Alexander Winchelsey, a Virginia planter, made his will, he indicated that he was from Limehouse in Middlesex. He bequeathed Mrs. Ravelin a gold ring and mentioned Thomas Jarvis's wife. He indicated that Robert Partin of Shirley Hundred (41) had custody of his tobacco, some of which was owed to Shirley Hundred resident Richard Domelaw. Alexander Winchelsey's will was proved in May 1621 by Thomas Rabenett (Ravenett), who was named administrator (EEAC 65; WITH 69-70).

EDWARD WINDAM

Edward Windam came to Virginia on the *John and Dorothy* in 1634 at the expense of Adam Thorogood, who used him as a headright when patenting some land on June 24, 1635 (PB 1 Pt. 1:179).

GEORGE WINDE

On February 22, 1620, officials decided that George Winde, a vagrant brought in from Langborne Ward and detained at Bridewell Prison, would be sent to Virginia (CBE 17).

FRANCIS WINDER

On March 22, 1622, when the Indians attacked Edward Bennett's plantation in Warresqueak (26), Francis Winder was killed (VCR 3:571).

***

EDWARD WINDOR

Edward Windor died at Martin's Hundred (7) sometime after April 1623 but before February 16, 1624 (CBE 42).

ANN WINDOR
(MRS. EDWARD WINDOR)

Ann, Edward Windor's widow, was living at Martin's Hundred (7) on February 16, 1624 (CBE 42).

***

CHRISTOPHER WINDMILL
(WENDMILE, WYNWILL, WENDMILL)

Christopher Windmill (Wendmile, Wynwill, Wendmill) came to Virginia on the *Bona*

Nova in 1619 and on February 16, 1624, was living at the Indian Thicket in Elizabeth City (**17**), the Virginia Company's land. In early 1625, 26-year-old Christopher Windmill was part of John Ward's household and a free man. On January 10, 1627, he testified before the General Court that around Easter 1624 he and Richard Raper were present when Captain Douse agreed to reduce Robert Todd's seven-year term of service by two years. In January 1627 Christopher was identified as a Virginia Company tenant who was being assigned to Governor George Yeardley. On September 20, 1628, Windmill received a lease for 60 acres in Elizabeth City, near the Indian Thicket, and two months later he received another lease for 50 acres in the same area. He died prior to October 20, 1632, by which time his widow had married Francis Hough (CBE 43, 67; MCGC 131, 136; PB 1 Pt. 1:90, 93, 145, 147).

MRS. CHRISTOPHER WINDMILL (WENDMILE, WYNWILL, WENDMILL) (MRS. FRANCIS HUFF [HOUGH])

Sometime prior to October 20, 1632, Christopher Windmill's widow married Francis Huff (Hough). Both men were residents of Elizabeth City (**17, 18**) (PB 1 Pt. 1:145, 147).

***

[NO FIRST NAME] WINGATE

In 1633–1634 Mrs. Wingate and her maid, Margaret Dalton, went from England to Virginia on the *Mayflower* (CBE 119).

RICHARD WINGER

In 1621 Richard Winger sent meal, bedding, and containers to Virginia (FER 322).

EDWARD MARIA WINGFIELD

In 1607 Edward Maria Wingfield, a Virginia Company investor, came to Virginia in the first group of Jamestown (**1**) colonists. He was the eldest son of Thomas Maria Wingfield, a member of Parliament for Huntington. Wingfield served as a soldier in Ireland and the Netherlands and was one of the grantees of the Virginia Company's 1606 charter. He was selected as a member of the colony's first council; on May 14, 1607, the council's members chose Wingfield as president, the first chief executive. During Wingfield's time in office, disease and food shortages caused severe problems and the colonists began to die in droves. On September 10, 1607, he was removed from office and incarcerated. He also was summoned to court to answer a complaint by John Robinson. The fact that Edward Maria Wingfield's family was Roman Catholic most likely aroused suspicions that he was sympathetic to Spain, which at that time was viewed as an enemy. He was released and sent back to England with Captain Christopher Newport, arriving there in May 1608. Edward Maria Wingfield was author of a document entitled *A Discourse of Virginia,* which largely defended his activities in the colony. He said that he had expected trouble from Captain Gosnold and Gabriel Archer. He claimed that while he was president, he had lived in a tent and raised poultry for his own consumption, and had not horded the Company's supplies, as had been alleged. He also claimed that some items had been stolen from his trunk. Wingfield retained an interest in the Virginia Company and in 1609 was one of the grantees of its second charter. In 1613 he was living in Stoneley, Huntingtonshire, England. The year of his death is uncertain (CJS 1:20, 27, 33, 35, 193, 205, 207, 219; 2:138, 140, 158, 282; HAI 100, 124-126, 183-184, 188-189, 192, 194-195, 198-199).

ROBERT WINGFIELD

In June 1621 Robert Wingfield was sentenced at Middlesex and detained until he could be transported overseas (CBE 23).

GRIFFIN WINNE

Griffin Winne came to Virginia on the *Francis Bonaventure.* On January 30, 1625, he was living in Pasbehay (**3**), where he was one of Governor Francis Wyatt's servants. Griffin Winne was then age 28 (CBE 57).

JOAN WINSCOMB (WINCOMB)

Joan Winscomb (Wincomb) came to Virginia on the *George* in 1618 and on January 21, 1625, was living at Jordan's Journey (**46**), where she was a 20-year-old servant in Nathaniel Causey's household (CBE 52).

JOHN WINSELEY

On January 29, 1620, officials at Bridewell decided that John Winseley would be detained until he could be sent to Virginia (CBE 18).

***

THOMAS WINSLOWE

Thomas Winslowe, who was sent to Virginia by Edward Bennett, set sail from England on July 31, 1622, on the *James*, accompanied by his wife, Elizabeth. Between April 1623 and February 16, 1624, the Winslowe couple died at the Bennett plantation in Warresqueak (**26**) (FER 400; CBE 42).

ELIZABETH WINSLOWE (MRS. THOMAS WINSLOWE)

Elizabeth, the wife of Thomas Winslowe, set sail from England on July 31, 1622, on the *James*, and went to Virginia with her husband, who was being sent to the colony by Edward Bennett. Sometime between April 1623 and February 16, 1624, Elizabeth Winslowe and her husband died at the Bennett plantation in Warresqueak (**26**) (FER 400; CBE 42).

[NO FIRST NAME] WINSLOWE

Thomas Winslowe's child died at Warresqueak (**26**) sometime after April 1623 but before February 16, 1624 (CBE 42).

***

ROBERT WINTER

Robert Winter died at Jordan's Journey (**46**) sometime after April 1623 but before February 16, 1624 (CBE 37).

THOMAS WINTER

When a list of patented land was sent back to England on May 1625, Thomas Winter was credited with 100 acres of land in Warresqueak (**26**) (VCR 4:556).

THOMAS WINTERFALL (WINTERSALL)

Thomas Winterfall (Wintersall), a 21-year-old goldsmith from Sussex, set sail from England in 1619 aboard the *Bona Nova*. He died in Elizabeth City (**17, 18**) sometime after April 1623 but before February 16, 1624 (FER 295; CBE 45).

WILLIAM WISE

When William Wise came to Virginia in 1619, the Ferrars, who were major investors in the Virginia Company, covered the cost of his transportation. He probably was a Company tenant or servant (FER 296).

RICHARD WISEMAN

On November 21, 1621, Richard and Thomas Wiseman and their associates received a patent for Virginia land because they were planning to take 100 new settlers to the colony (VCR 1:561-562).

THOMAS WISEMAN

On November 21, 1621, the Virginia Company awarded Richard and Thomas Wiseman and their associates a patent for some Virginia land because they were planning to take 100 new settlers to the colony (VCR 1:561-562).

GABRIEL WISHER

On November 13, 1620, the Virginia Company noted that Gabriel Wisher had offered to procure men from Poland and Sweden to go to Virginia to produce marketable commodities (VCR 1:420).

SIMON (SYMON) WITHE (WITH)

Simon (Symon) Withe (With), a bricklayer from London, arrived in Jamestown (**1**) on September 5, 1623, aboard the *Ann* and took the oath of supremacy. Withe died in Elizabeth City (**17, 18**) sometime after April 1623 but before February 16, 1624. On June 7, 1625, the General Court decided that the proceeds of his estate—which was being sued by Sara Templeman's representative, Stephen Poore—would be sent back to England to Nicholas Ferrar (MCGC 6, 64; CBE 45).

RICHARD WITHER (WITH)

Richard Wither (With) died in Elizabeth City (**17, 18**) sometime after April 1623 but before February 16, 1624 (CBE 45).

MARGARET WITHERING

On January 29, 1620, officials at Bridewell decided that Margaret Withering, a vagrant from Bishopsgate, would be sent to Virginia (CBE 18).

ANTHONY WITHERS

On July 24, 1621, the Virginia Company noted that Anthony Withers had procured a "rich commodity" from the Low Countries, utilizing an agricultural product of some sort. Withers reportedly planned to have it planted in Virginia and had found men who knew how to grow it (VCR 1:521).

EDWARD WITHERS

On May 11, 1622, Edward Withers of Goodworth, Clatforde, in Hampshire, testified in a lawsuit that the Earl of Warwick undertook against Edward Brewster. Withers identified himself as a 26 year old and said that he went to Virginia in 1618 on the *Neptune*, Lord Delaware's ship. He testified that Brewster had sold one of Delaware's men, Cartwright, to an old planter named Peirce. Withers also described some of Edward Brewster's other actions and his court martial hearing, held by Deputy-Governor Samuel Argall. On January 29, 1623, when Edward Withers testified again, he gave his age as 25 and identified himself as a resident of St. Katherine's. This time, he indicated that he had been one of Lord Delaware's attendants and was a passenger on the *Neptune* when it had an encounter with the *Treasurer*. He also said that Argall had prepared a storehouse in Jamestown (1) to hold provisions for the *Treasurer*, which was expected to go on a fishing voyage. This "fishing voyage" resulted in the arrival of some of Virginia's first Africans (SR 9947; C 24/489; HCA 13/44 ff 73vo-75ro; EAE 12).

JOHN WITHERS

John Withers came to Virginia in 1634 on the *John and Dorothy* at the expense of Adam Thorogood, who used him as a headright when patenting some land on June 24, 1635. John was accompanied by Stephen Withers, who may have been a kinsman (PB 1 Pt. 1:179).

STEPHEN WITHERS

In 1634 Stephen Withers came to Virginia on the *John and Dorothy* at the expense of Adam Thorogood, who used him as a headright when patenting some land on June 24, 1635. Also aboard the *John and Dorothy* was John Withers, who may have been a kinsman (PB 1 Pt. 1:179).

JOHN WITTERS (WRITTERS)

When a list of patented land was sent back to England in May 1625, John Witters (Writters) was credited with 100 acres in the corporation of Charles City (39-62) (VCR 4:553).

THOMAS WITTINGHAM

In May 1609 Thomas Wittingham was appointed cape merchant of the Jamestown (1) fort and store. He was John Tavernor's replacement (VCR 3:23).

THOMAS WITTON

On September 17, 1630, officials at Bridewell decided that Thomas Witton, a vagrant boy from St. Sepulcher, would be sent to Virginia (CBE 92).

[NO FIRST NAME] WITTS

Goodman Witts, whose first name is unknown, died on Jamestown Island (1) sometime after April 1623 but before February 16, 1624 (CBE 39).

THOMAS WITTS

According to records maintained by the Drapers Company in London, Thomas Witts, a silk-weaver, settled in Virginia in 1625 (SR 879).

ALICE WOAD (WAD)

Alice Woad (Wad) came to Virginia in 1619 on the *George*. On December 10, 1620, when Samuel Jordan patented some land, he used Alice as a headright and said that she was one of his servants. Alice may have been the Alice Wood who was one of the children rounded up from the streets of London so that they could be sent to the colony (PB 8:125).

WILLIAM WOOLEY

On February 27, 1619, officials at Bridewell decided that William Wooley, a boy, would be sent to Virginia. He was one of the children rounded up from the streets of London so that they could be transported to the colony (CBE 12).

SIR JOHN WOLSTENHOLME

On July 21, 1619, Sir John Wolstenholme asked his fellow Virginia Company officials for a share of land for every £12.10.0 the Society of Martin's Hundred spent on developing its plantation, Martin's Hundred (**7**). His request was denied. In November 1632 Sir John Wolstenholme and William Claiborne asked the king for the right to enjoy free trade in Kent Island (VCR 1:248-249; CBE 104).

[NO FIRST NAME] WOOD

Captain John Smith identified Captain Wood as one of his "old soldiers." He was identified as a member of Sir Thomas Gates's group when he was named to the Council of State in May 1609 and was captain of a ship that brought part of the 3rd Supply of new colonists to Jamestown (**1**). Captain John Smith said that Captain Wood was astute and after his arrival had quickly assessed conditions in the colony (CJS 1:270; 2:219, 222; VCR 3:13).

ABRAHAM (ABRAM) WOOD

Abraham (Abram) Wood, who came to Virginia in 1620 on the *Margaret and John*, had a lengthy and remarkable life. On February 16, 1624, he was living at Captain Samuel Mathews' plantation (**15**) on the lower side of the James River, within the corporation of James City and east of Gray's Creek. When a muster was made of that settlement on February 4, 1625, Wood, who was only 10 years old, was identified as one of Mathews' servants. Although very little is known about his early life, by 1636 he had become a Virginia planter. On December 31, 1636, he and two other men leased a tract of land on the west side of the Appomattox River, in what was then Henrico County (now Chesterfield). Less than two years later, Abraham Wood patented 400 acres on the east side of the Appomattox, within what was then Charles City County but is now Prince George. He added to his acreage on the west side of the Appomattox and consolidated his holdings in 1642. In the wake of the 1644 Indian attack, when a decision was made to con-

struct fortified garrisons at the heads of the lower Tidewater's major rivers, Captain Abraham Wood agreed to build Fort Henry at the falls of the Appomattox River. He received 600 acres in exchange for seeing that the fortified blockhouse was manned and maintained. The acreage Wood was awarded was included in a 1,557-acre patent he received in June 1653. By that date he had attained the rank of major and was placed in command of the Charles City and Henrico militia. He became a county justice, a burgess, and finally a member of the Council of State. In 1650 he joined four other men on a journey of discovery beyond the head of the Appomattox River. By April 1676 Abraham Wood, who was then in his early 60s, had begun having medical problems. However, in 1680 he apparently was well enough to help negotiate a treaty with the Indians, an expansion of the 1677 peace agreement known as the Treaty of Middle Plantation. Major-General Abraham Wood died sometime prior to 1682, having witnessed the maturation of the colony, two major Indian attacks, Bacon's Rebellion, and other pivotal events (CBE 40, 60; PB 1 Pt. 2:557, 590, 653, 839; 3:77; HEN 1:315, 325-326; MEY 695-697).

ALICE WOOD

On February 27, 1619, officials at Bridewell decided that Alice Wood, a young wench, would be sent to Virginia. She was one of the children rounded up from the streets of London so that they could be sent to the colony. Alice Wood may be the same individual as Alice Woad (Wad), who came to the colony in 1619 and was one of Samuel Jordan's servants (CBE 13).

ALICE WOOD

On November 20, 1622, officials at Newgate Prison decided that Alice Wood would be sent to Virginia (CBE 29).

***

AMBROSE WOOD

On June 13, 1621, Ambrose Wood of Tattingstone, Sussex County, England, the heir of his brother, Thomas, received five shares of Virginia land. On April 3, 1622, Ambrose Wood, a gentleman, conveyed those shares to Nathaniel Etherington (VCR 1:497, 630).

THOMAS WOOD

On November 13, 1620, Thomas Wood told Virginia Company officials that he wanted to be paid a larger sum if they wanted him to transport cattle from Ireland to Virginia. Two days later he agreed to do so. By June 13, 1621, Thomas Wood was dead. His brother and heir, Ambrose Wood of Tattingstone, Sussex County, England, received five shares of Thomas's Virginia land (VCR 1:420, 423, 497).

***

GEORGE WOOD

On September 26, 1626, George Wood sent some goods from London to Virginia on the *Plantation* (CBE 74).

HENRY WOOD

In 1621 Henry Wood, who formerly had been in Bermuda, came to Virginia on the *Tiger*. On February 16, 1624, he was living on the Treasurer's Plantation (**11**) on the lower side of the James River. On December 4, 1624, when Treasurer George Sandys patented some land, he used Henry Wood's headright (CBE 40; PB 1 Pt. 1:16).

HENRY WOOD

Henry Wood came to Virginia in 1634 on the *John and Dorothy* at the expense of Adam Thorogood, who used him as a headright when patenting some land on June 24, 1635 (PB 1 Pt. 1:179).

JOHN WOOD

In January 1620 officials in Middlesex Sessions reprieved John Wood and decided that he would be sent to Virginia (CBE 16).

JOHN WOOD

On July 12, 1620, John Wood asked for a patent on the Elizabeth River (**20 a**) in exchange for eight shares of Virginia land and said that he wanted to establish a shipyard. If he ever received his land, he may not have developed it (VCR 1:402).

JOHN WOOD

Sometime after April 1623 but before February 16, 1624, John Wood died at the College (**66**) (CBE 35).

JOHN WOOD

John Wood, a 50-year-old sailor from Wapping in Middlesex, testified in 1624 in a lawsuit that involved Lord Delaware's heirs and Sir Samuel Argall. Wood said that after the ship *Treasurer* sailed from Bermuda to Virginia in 1619, it overturned in a creek (EAE 13).

***

PERCIVAL (PERCIVALL, PERCIVELL) WOOD

Percival (Percivall, Percivell) and Ann Wood came to Virginia on the *George* and on February 16, 1624, were residing on the lower side of the James, to the west of Gray's Creek (**8, 9**). By January 25, 1625, they had relocated to Mulberry Island (**21**). It was then that the Woods sold a house and 12 acres of land on Jamestown Island (**1**), at Black Point, to Sir George Yeardley. On April 25, 1625, the General Court authorized Percival Wood to collect some tobacco from a debtor, Francis Chamberlayne. On February 21, 1632, Wood served as a burgess for Archer's Hope (**6**), but on September 4, 1632, he represented the settlers living in Martin's Hundred (**7**) (CBE 40, 57; MCGC 45, 56; HEN 1:154, 179; DOR 1:47).

ANN WOOD (MRS. PERCIVAL [PERCIVALL, PERCIVELL] WOOD)

Ann Wood and her husband, Percival (Percivall, Percivell) came to Virginia on the *George* and on February 16, 1624, were residing on the lower side of the James, to the west of Gray's Creek (**8, 9**). In October 1624 Mrs. Ann Wood appeared before the General Court, where she testified that she had seen the late Elizabeth Abbott—one of John and Alice Proctor's maidservants at Paces Paines (**9**)—flogged by two of the Proctors' male servants. By January 25, 1625, the Woods had relocated to Mulberry Island (**21**) and disposed of their house and 12 acres on Jamestown Island (**1**). On April 4, 1625, Alice Wood, who brought suit against Francis Chamberlayne, was summoned to court (CBE 40, 57; MCGC 23-24, 45, 51).

***

PHILIP WOOD

On March 13, 1622, Philip Wood obtained a share of Virginia land from Francis Carter, who had purchased it from the widow of Thomas West, Lord Delaware (VCR 1:619).

THOMAS WOOD

Thomas Wood came to Virginia on the *George* in 1620 and on February 16, 1624, was living on the Maine (**3**), where he was one of William Peirce's servants. Sometime prior to January 25, 1625, Peirce moved Wood to his plantation on Mulberry Island (**21**). He was identified at that time as a 35-year-old servant (CBE 39, 57).

THOMAS WOOD

On March 22, 1622, when the Indians attacked the settlers at Captain John Berkeley's plantation at Falling Creek (**68**), Thomas Wood was slain (VCR 3:565).

HENRY WOODALL

On February 16, 1624, Henry Woodall was living at the Indian Thicket, part of the Virginia Company's land in Elizabeth City (**17**) (CBE 43).

JOHN WOODALL

In May 1609 John Woodall, a Virginia Company investor, sent a chest of surgical equipment to George Liste, one of his servants. Woodall may have been hotheaded, for in 1620 he was accused of slandering the Company and in 1621 he was warned about making scandalous speeches. By that time he already had sent some servants to the colony, as well as some cattle that were entrusted to the care of John Pountis. John Woodall dispatched his servant Christopher Best, a surgeon, to Virginia. On April 1, 1623, Best, who was living in urban Jamestown (**1**) in the household of John Pountis, informed Woodall that many of his cattle were dead. On November 5, 1624, John Woodall authorized surgeon Richard Wake, who was preparing to set sail for Virginia, to take custody of some medical supplies and letters he had sent to Christopher Best on the *Margaret*, if Wake discovered that Best was dead. In that event, the items were to be returned to Woodall. As it turned out, Best died sometime prior to September 19, 1625. Shortly thereafter, Richard Wake presented John Woodall's letter to the justices of the General Court, who decided to purchase Woodall's surgical chest and other medical paraphernalia on behalf of the colony. John Woodall's cattle may have been kept on Jamestown Island or the Governor's Land (**3**), for the governor's former cow-keeper, John Osborne, was responsible for them. In September 1626 Richard Peirce was censured for killing one of John Woodall's calves and was ordered to replace it. As time went on, Woodall, as an absentee owner, continued to have problems with the people to whom he had entrusted his real and personal property in Virginia. In 1634 Woodall asked Virginia's governor to intervene on his behalf because his servants had failed to give him an account of his goods and livestock. Woodall's problems stemmed in part from his purchase of land from the estate of Sir Samuel Argall, whose property was then the object of a lawsuit. In June 1636 John Woodall asked that his goods and cattle in Virginia be put into the custody of his new agent, John Convers. He also asked for a monopoly on apiculture—what he termed "the commodity of bees." On July 31, 1638, John Woodall thanked the Privy Council for helping him recover his property in Virginia and requested a patent for the Virginia land he had purchased from Sir Samuel Argall's heirs. Three months later Woodall's request was forwarded to incumbent governor, Sir John Harvey. If a patent was issued to John Woodall, it has not survived. Likewise, no patents apparently exist for land claimed by Sir Samuel Argall (VCR 1:407, 437; 3:23; 4:238; MCGC 72, 112, 141; CBE 95, 116; SR 4539, 4541, 4544; PC 2/44:84; 2/46:283; SAIN 1:238; G&M 224, 237).

GEORGE WOODCOCKE

On March 4, 1629, George Woodcocke proved the will of Gilbert Peppitt, a resident of Blunt Point (**22**) (MCGC 189).

ANN WOODLEY (WOODLASE, WOODLIEF?, WOODLIFFE?)

On February 16, 1624, Ann Woodley (Woodlase, Woodlief?, Woodliffe?) was living in Bermuda Hundred (**39**) in Thomas Harris's household. When a muster was taken of that settlement's inhabitants on January 24, 1625, Ann was identified as a

7-year-old kinswoman of Thomas and Adria Harris, whose home she shared. She may have been the daughter of John Woodlief I (CBE 35, 54; MEY 706).

[NO FIRST NAME] WOODLEY

On July 9, 1635, Captain Woodley was in possession of some land in Charles City adjacent to that of Jenkin Osborne (PB 1 Pt. 1:214).

***

JOHN WOODLIEF (WOODLIFFE, WOODLASE) I

In June 1619 John Woodlief (Woodliffe, Woodlase) I, a merchant and gentleman from Prestwood in Buckingham, asked Virginia Company officials for a patent, indicating that he had been an investor since 1608. He said that he had gone to Virginia around that time and remained there for 11 years, and therefore he was an ancient planter. Woodlief indicated that he and his associates would seat 200 people on their land within six years. Company officials, who approved Woodlief's request in July 1619, stipulated that the patent was to be listed under the name of Sir Thomas Wainman and associates, not Woodlief's name. However, the property soon became known as Woodlief's plantation (**49**), the name it retained. In 1618, a year before John Woodlief sought land of his own, he and several other investors had formed a partnership known as the Society of Berkeley Hundred, with the goal of establishing the plantation known as Berkeley Hundred (**55**). As soon as the Society received its patent, its members began preparations for their colonizing venture. Because Woodlief was an experienced colonist, he was chosen as Berkeley's captain and governor. He was supposed to take a group of settlers to the plantation, along with some goods that he was to sell before returning to England. Captain John Woodlief sent four men to Berkeley in April 1619, and it appears that his wife and children also went on ahead. Woodlief himself set sail from England on the *Margaret* of Bristol on September 16, 1619, and arrived in Virginia ten weeks later. With him were 35 to 38 colonists headed for Berkeley Hundred. When they arrived at their destination, the settlers commemorated their safe arrival with a day of thanksgiving, in accord with the instructions they had received from their sponsors. It was America's first celebration of its kind. In January 1620 Governor George Yeardley, a Berkeley Hundred investor, informed the Virginia Company that he had assigned the Society of Berkeley Hundred's colonists to a good location that did not impinge on the late Lord Delaware's landholdings. By June 1620 some of the Society of Berkeley Hundred's investors had become disenchanted with John Woodlief, whom they claimed was uncommunicative. This culminated in the revocation of his commission in August 1620. However, Woodlief seems to have been successful in his own right and by December 10, 1620, had received a patent for 550 acres near Jordan's Point (**46**). In May 1625 he was credited with 550 acres of unplanted land in the territory of Great Weyanoke, the tract known as Woodlief's plantation. By 1637, he was dead. His son was John Woodlief II (CJS 2:268; VCR 1:232, 252; 3:110, 185, 188, 193-197, 199, 207, 212, 247-249, 292-294, 374-375; 4:554; PB 1 Pt. 2:467, 788; 8:125; MEY 705-706).

JOHN WOODLIEF (WOODLIFFE, WOODLASE) II

John Woodlief (Woodliffe, Woodlase) II, the son of ancient planter John Woodlief I, was born around 1615, for on March 17, 1666, he stated that he was age 51. In August 1637 he identified himself as the son and heir of the late John Woodlief when patenting the decedent's 550-acre plantation (**49**) in what is now Prince George County. A year later he acquired an additional 200 acres on the basis of headrights. When he repatented his landholdings in 1642, he noted that 20 of his 750 acres were at Bermuda Hundred (**39**). John Woodlief II served as a burgess in 1652, representing Charles City County. In 1661 he was placed in command of a company of militia, which served under Colonel Abraham Wood (PB 1 Pt. 2:467, 580, 778; MEY 706).

***

THOMAS WOODLIEF (WOODLIFFE)

Thomas Woodlief (Woodliffe), a Virginia colonist, died sometime prior to July 2, 1621. Thomas Jadwin told Virginia Company officials that he wanted to recover the money the decedent owed him (VCR 1:501).

ROBERT WOODS

Robert Woods died at Jordan's Journey (46) sometime after April 1623 but before February 16, 1624 (CBE 37).

JAMES WOODSHAW

On March 22, 1622, when the Indians attacked the settlers at William Farrar's house on the Appomattox River (40), James Woodshaw was slain (VCR 3:566).

THOMASIN WOODSHAW

Between October 1622 and January 1623, Thomasin Woodshaw, a Virginia colonist who had been found guilty of manslaughter, was sentenced to death. She later apologized to the governor for her "horrid crime." She was reprieved and eventually was pardoned because of her good behavior (VCR 3:681-682).

FRANCES (FRANCIS) WOODSON

On February 16, 1624, Frances (Francis) Woodson was living at Warresqueak (26), the Bennett Plantation. He was still there on January 24, 1625, and reportedly took a turn as sentinel at the Warresqueak Fort (CBE 42; MCGC 44).

***

JOHN WOODSON

Doctor John Woodson, a surgeon, came to Virginia on the *George* in 1619 with incoming governor, Sir George Yeardley. On February 16, 1624, Woodson and his wife, Sarah, were living at Flowerdew Hundred (53), where they were still residing on January 20, 1625 (CBE 37, 50; DOR 1:23).

SARAH WOODSON (MRS. JOHN WOODSON)

Sarah came to Virginia with her husband, Dr. John Woodson, in 1619 on the *George,* which brought incoming governor, Sir George Yeardley, to the colony. On February 16, 1624, the Woodsons were living at Flowerdew Hundred (53). They were still there on January 20, 1625 (CBE 37, 50).

***

CHRISTOPHER WOODWARD

In June 1620 Christopher Woodward came to Virginia on the *Trial*, a ship that brought some of the Society of Martin's Hundred's settlers to Virginia. On January 22, 1625, he was living at West and Shirley Hundred (41), where he shared a home with two partners and three servants. Woodward was then 30 years old. The household was relatively well supplied with stored food and defensive weaponry. On September 10, 1625, Christopher Woodward's land at Shirley Hundred was described as being adjacent to that of Richard Biggs. In October 1629 Woodward served as a burgess for Westover. In November 1635 he patented some acreage on the Appomattox River (40), near the land of William Farrar (CBE 52; SH 6; HEN 1:138; PB 1 Pt. 1:301; DOR 1:13).

CHRISTOPHER WOODWARD

Christopher Woodward reportedly died at Martin's Hundred (7) sometime after April 1623 but before February 16, 1624. He may have been the same man who in January 1625 was living at West and Shirley Hundred (41) (CBE 42).

HENRY WOODWARD

On February 16, 1624, Henry Woodward, a free man, was living at the Bennett plantation in Warresqueak (26). On June 18, 1624, he testified in the John Uty's lawsuit against William Tyler. At issue was a disagreement over ownership of a hook and some insulting remarks that the two men exchanged. On February 7, 1625, Henry Woodward was still living in Warresqueak, where he and his partner, John Browninge, headed a household that included two servants. In the two men's possession were two houses and an ample supply of stored food and defensive weaponry. In January 1627 Henry Woodward sued Captain John Stone and merchant Humphrey Rastall, claiming that he had paid for four servants but received only three. Stone and Rastall were ordered to see that Woodward was provided with the additional servant (CBE 42, 62; MCGC 18-19, 134; DOR 1:49).

***

HENRY WOODWARD

Henry Woodward came to Virginia on the *Diana* and on February 16, 1624, was living on Hog Island (16). He was still there on February 4, 1625, and was sharing a home with his wife, Jane, and several other people. On August 28, 1626, Roger Webster testified that Henry Woodward—one of the Society of Southampton Hundred's (44) tenants who had been moved to Hog Island after the March 1622 Indian attack—was a possible thief who had been seen near his cornfield. Several other witnesses said that Woodward had been seen in that vicinity, and one man described him as a "pilfering fellow." Although Henry Woodward denied that he had been stealing corn and tobacco, he was ordered to post a bond with the provost marshal guaranteeing his good behavior (CBE 41, 61; MCGC 110, 114).

JANE WOODWARD
(MRS. HENRY WOODWARD)

Jane, Henry Woodward's wife, came to Virginia on the *Swann*. On February 4, 1625, the Woodwards were living on Hog Island (16) (CBE 61).

***

MARY WOODWARD

On February 16, 1624, Mary Woodward was a servant in Governor Francis Wyatt's household in urban Jamestown (1) (CBE 38).

RICHARD WOODWARD

On March 22, 1622, when the Indians attacked the settlers at Edward Bennett's plantation in Warresqueak (26), Richard Woodward was slain (VCR 3:571).

THOMAS WOOLCHER

On March 22, 1622, Thomas Woolcher was slain when the Indians attacked the settlers at Powle-Brooke (Merchant's Hope) (50) (VCR 3:569).

JOHN WOOLEY (WOOLLEY)

On February 16, 1624, John Wooley (Woolley) was living in Elizabeth City (17, 18). On April 11, 1625, he was among the several men from that area who were summoned before the General Court to testify about some cattle that Captain Croshaw had signed over to Lieutenant Shepherd (CBE 43; MCGC 52).

SAMUEL WOOLVES

On February 8, 1628, Samuel Woolves and Robert Brown were asked by Thomas Graves, the commander of Accomack (72-78), whether they had ever sold glass bottles to the Indians. The concern was serious because the Natives sometimes fashioned projectile points from glass. Samuel may have been the Samuel Wools who was living on the Eastern Shore in the 1630s and 40s (MCGC 165; AMES 1:104, 149; 2:335).

JOHN WOOTEN

John Wooten set sail from England on July 31, 1622, on the *James* and went to Virginia with Mr. Spencer (FER 400).

THOMAS WOOTEN (WOTTON)

Thomas Wooten, a surgeon and gentleman, came to Virginia in 1607 in the first group of Jamestown (1) colonists. On May 20, 1607, he was among those who accompanied Captain Christopher Newport on a voyage of discovery toward the head of the James River. Captain John Smith said that Thomas Wooton was a skillful surgeon and saved many lives during the summer sicknesses. However, Edward Maria Wingfield disliked him because Wooten wanted to live aboard the pinnace instead of moving to Jamestown Island, where many men were sick and wounded (CJS 1:208; 2:141, 143, 153; HAI 102, 200).

RICHARD WORLEY (WORLIE)

Richard Worley (Worlie), a gentleman, arrived in Jamestown (1) in 1608 and was in the 2nd Supply of new settlers. On December 29, 1608, he accompanied Captain John Smith on a trip to the territory of the Pamunkey Indians and two days later went with him to Werowocomoco, Powhatan's village on the York River (CJS 1:222, 243; 2:161, 192).

***

JOHN WOLRICH (WOOLRICH, WOOLRIDGE)

On February 16, 1624, John Wolrich (Woolrich, Woolridge) and his wife, Joan, were living on the Maine (3) or Governor's Land, where he was a household head. The following month he was listed among those owing funds to William Bennett. On June

13, 1625, Wolrich, a gentleman, received a warrant from England authorizing him to recover some money from William Peirce and Mr. Edward Blaney. On September 19, 1625, ship's purser William Webster was obliged to relinquish Mr. Wolrich's tobacco note, payment he had accepted for an indentured servant who ran away before he could be delivered. Thomas Spillman was ordered to give Wolrich a young male servant known as Whiffie. On February 27, 1626, John Wolrich went to court, where he testified that he had received a sick servant named George Allen from Thomas Dunthorne of Elizabeth City (**18**), and that Dunthorne had purposefully concealed the man's illness; Allen verified that claim. Sometime prior to August 21, 1626, Wolrich, who was among several men slandered by John Smith, received an apology. On December 24, 1627, John Wolrich testified in court about a shipment of servants. He said that Mr. Moore had indicated that he was sending only ten male servants on the *Thomas and John* (CBE 39; MCGC 65, 71, 96, 108, 158).

JOAN WOLRICH (WOOLRICH, WOOLRIDGE) (MRS. JOHN WOLRICH [WOOLRICH, WOOLRIDGE])

On February 16, 1624, Joan, the wife of Mr. John Wolrich (Woolrich, Woolridge), a gentleman, was living on the Maine (**3**), just west of Jamestown Island, and was sharing a home with her husband (CBE 39).

***

WILLIAM WORLDIGE (WORLIDGE, WOOLRICH)

William Worldige (Worlidge, Woolrich) came to Virginia on the *Bona Nova* and arrived in 1622. On February 16, 1624, he was living in Elizabeth City (**18**) in Francis Chamberlin's household. He was still there in early 1625 and was identified as an 18-year-old indentured servant. On June 17, 1635, William Worldige received a patent for 400 acres of land in Elizabeth City (CBE 44, 66; PB 1 Pt. 1:309).

CHRISTOPHER WORMELEY I

Christopher Wormeley I, who was governor of Tortuga from 1632 to 1635, served as Virginia's Secretary of State from 1635 to 1649. In 1638 Wormeley, one of Governor John Harvey's supporters, was appointed captain of the fort at Old Point Comfort (**17**). He patented 1,420 acres fronting on the York River, on the east side of what already was known as Wormeley Creek, and established a plantation (**38**) there. Christopher Wormeley, a county justice, sometimes hosted local court meetings in his home. He died in 1656, leaving a son, Christopher Wormeley II, and a daughter, Elizabeth, who married Secretary of the Colony Richard Kemp of Jamestown (**1**) (MCGH 775; SAIN 1:244; STAN 34; MCGC 498; WITH 323; EEAC 34; HLOP 104; PB 1 Pt. 2:607).

BOWYER WORSLEY (WORSLEEP)

On April 3, 1622, Sir Bowyer Worsley (Worsleep), who was planning to send some settlers to Virginia, received a patent from the Virginia Company. On June 10, 1622, he was identified as the holder of a patent for a particular (private) plantation (VCR 1:629; 3:643).

RICHARD WORSLEY (WORSLEEP)

On November 4, 1620, Sir Richard Worsley (Worsleep), one of Christopher Lawne's fellow adventurers, wanted the Virginia Company to confirm his patent. Worsley and his associates planned to call their settlement the Isle of Wight plantation. On May 2, 1621, Sir Richard Worsley's patent was confirmed (VCR 1:414, 468).

PHILIP WORTH

On March 22, 1622, when the Indians attacked the settlers at Edward Bennett's plantation in Warresqueak (**26**), Philip Worth was slain (VCR 3:571).

THOMAS WORTHALL

Thomas Worthall came to Virginia in 1621 on the *Marmaduke*. In early 1625 he was living in Elizabeth City (**18**), where he was a 14-year-old servant in Francis Mason's household (CBE 65).

NATHANIEL WORTON

In May 1625 Nathaniel Worton was credited with a 100-acre patent at The Falls (**67**), on the south side of the James River (VCR 4:552).

WILLIAM WRAXHALL

On September 3, 1629, William Wraxhall of London, a joiner, made his will. He indicated that he intended to go to Virginia and named as his beneficiaries his wife, Anne, and daughter, Mabell. Sometime prior to June 17, 1630, William Wraxhall reached Virginia, where he died. His will was proved in London, and his widow was granted probate privileges (SR 3961; SH 12; WITH 54-55; EEAC 65; CBE 91).

JAMES WRAY

On June 23, 1627, officials at Bridewell decided that James Wray, a vagrant brought in from Coleman Street, would be detained until he could be sent to Virginia (CBE 78).

JOHN WRAY

On February 9, 1628, the General Court learned that Sir George Yeardley had brought John Wray to Virginia in 1621 on the *Temperance*. Wray's headright was assigned to Thomas Flint, who used it when patenting some land on September 20, 1628 (MCGC 166; PB 1 Pt. 1:59).

[NO FIRST NAME] WRIGHT

Mr. Wright, who came to Virginia on the *Margaret and John*, died in Jamestown (1) sometime after April 1623 but before February 16, 1624 (HOT 196).

HORTEN WRIGHT

Horten Wright came to Virginia on the *Susan* and on February 4, 1625, was living in the Neck O'Land (5). He was a 20-year-old servant in the household of Richard Kingsmill, who was then occupying the late Rev. Richard Buck's property (CBE 58).

JOHN WRIGHT

On March 22, 1622, when the Indians attacked the settlers at Captain Nathaniel West's plantation in Westover (54), John Wright was slain (VCR 3:567).

JOHN WRIGHT

John Wright came to Virginia on the *Ambrose* in 1623. In early 1625 he was living in Elizabeth City (18), where he was a 20-year-old servant in William Ganey's household (CBE 66).

***

JOHN WRIGHT

John Wright died in Elizabeth City (17, 18) sometime after April 1623 but before February 16, 1624, and was survived by his wife (CBE 45).

MRS. JOHN WRIGHT

On February 16, 1624, Mrs. John Wright was living in Elizabeth City (17, 18). She had been recently widowed (CBE 45).

***

ROBERT WRIGHT

Robert Wright, an ancient planter and sawyer, came to Virginia in 1609 aboard the *Swan* and married his wife, Joane (Joan, Jane), in 1610. On February 16, 1624, the Wrights were living in Elizabeth City (17) with their daughter. In early 1625 the muster-taker noted that the Wrights and their two Virginia-born children were members of the household of Anthony Bonall, a French vigneron who resided on the lower side of the Hampton River, on the Virginia Company's land. Robert Wright was then age 45. He was pursued by creditors, whom he was forced to repay, often with labor. When he did some work for George Fryer of Jamestown Island (1), he appears to have had the assistance of a male servant. In September 1626 Robert Wright's wife, Joane, was accused of being a witch. By that time the Wrights had moved from Elizabeth City to the area west of Gray's Creek (9), in what later became Surry County. Because rumors about Jane's supernatural powers persisted, the General Court repeatedly summoned the Wrights to appear. The problems the Wrights had with their neighbors may have given rise to Robert's request on January 13, 1627, for permission to move to Jamestown Island; he also asked for land on which he could build a dwelling. The General Court's justices agreed, and on August 27, 1627, they gave Robert Wright a patent for a 12-acre ridge of land known as *Labour in Vain*, which was located in a rural area in the eastern end of Jamestown Island. His patent was confirmed on September 1, 1627, suggesting that he had seated his acreage. Robert Wright and his partner, Andrew Rawleigh, also received a 10-year lease for a small parcel in eastern Jamestown Island, a tract they had inherited from Thomas Grubb, a joiner. Court testimony from 1628 and 1629 reveals that Robert Wright repeatedly was jailed as a debtor. He died sometime after March 2, 1629 (CBE 43, 68; MCGC 81, 97, 101, 111-112, 137, 152, 154, 158, 188; PB 1 Pt. 1:54-55).

JOANE (JOAN, JANE) WRIGHT (MRS. ROBERT WRIGHT)

Joane (Joan, Jane) Wright, a midwife, was the first Virginia colonist publicly accused of witchcraft. She seems to have aroused suspicion because she was left-handed and thought to be clairvoyant. While the colony was under martial law during Sir Thomas Dale's government, Joane was flogged for hemming a shirt improperly. She and her husband, Robert, a sawyer, were ancient planters who wed in Virginia in 1610. On February 16, 1624, the Wrights and their daughter were residing in Elizabeth City (**17**). The Wrights were still there in early 1625, living in the household of Anthony Bonall with their two young Virginia-born children. By 1626 the Wrights had moved to the lower side of the James River and were living across from Jamestown Island at the Perry plantation, the easternmost part of Paces Paines (**9**). Because rumors persisted about Joane's supernatural powers, the Wrights were repeatedly brought before the General Court. While she lived in Elizabeth City, she was accused of predicting people's deaths and putting a curse on those she disliked. Similar accusations followed her to her new home. One witness claimed that while Joane was living in Hull, England, she had practiced witchcraft. In 1626 Robert Wright testified that he and wife, Joane, had been married for 16 years and that he knew nothing about her practicing witchcraft. It may have been the couple's problems with their neighbors that prompted Robert Wright to request permission in January 1627 to move to Jamestown Island (**1**) and be assigned a plot of land there to build a home. The General Court agreed and on August 27, 1627, gave him a patent for a 12-acre waterfront property in the southeastern end of Jamestown Island, a parcel known as *Labour in Vain*. It is uncertain how long Joane Wright lived (CBE 43, 68; PB 1 Pt 1:54; MCGC 62, 111-114, 137, 152; PB 1 Pt. 1:54).

[NO FIRST NAME] WRIGHT

On February 16, 1624, Robert and Joane (Joan, Jane) Wright were living in Elizabeth City (**17**) with their Virginia-born daughter. In early 1625 she, a sibling, and her parents were members of vigneron Anthony Bonnall's household, which was located on the Virginia Company's land (CBE 43, 68).

[NO FIRST NAME] WRIGHT

In early 1625 Robert and Joane (Joan, Jane) Wright were living in Elizabeth City (**17**) with their two Virginia-born children. The Wrights were members of vigneron Anthony Bonnall's household, which resided on the Virginia Company's land (CBE 43, 68).

***

THOMAS WRIGHT

On August 8, 1628, Thomas Wright shipped goods on the *Thomas* from Bristol, England, to Virginia. Sometime prior to May 30, 1635, he acquired some land on the Elizabeth River (**20 a**) (CBE 88; PB 1 Pt. 1:169).

WILLIAM WRIGHT

On January 29, 1620, officials at Bridewell Prison decided that William Wright would be sent to Virginia (CBE 17).

WILLIAM WRIGHT (RIGHT)

William Wright (Right) came to Virginia on the *Tiger* in 1621, having formerly been in Bermuda. On December 4, 1624, when Treasurer George Sandys patented some land, he used William Wright's headright (CBE 40; PB 1 Pt. 1:16).

JOHN WRITT

John Writt came to Virginia on the *Hopewell* in 1633 at the expense of Adam Thorogood, who used him as a headright when patenting some land on June 24, 1635 (PB 1 Pt. 1:179).

SAMUEL WROTT

In 1630 Samuel Wrott, who was in England, testified that Sir George Yeardley served as governor for approximately three years and also was Receiver General of Southampton Hundred (**44**). Wrott said that Yeardley had sent Edmund Rossingham to England to request that Yeardley be freed from obligation to the Virginia Company and the Society of Southampton Hundred, and that Rossingham had represented Yeardley in court (C 24/560 Pt. 2:84).

EZEKIAGH WROUGHTON

Ezekiagh Wroughton, a 21-year-old smith from Lincolnshire, set sail from England in 1619 aboard the *Bona Nova*. He probably was a Virginia Company servant or tenant (FER 295).

***

FRANCIS WYATT

Francis Wyatt, the eldest son of George Wyatt, was born in 1588 at Boxley in Kent. He attended Oxford and Grays Inn and was knighted on July 7, 1618, around the time he married Sir Samuel Sandys' daughter, Margaret, the niece of Virginia Company Treasurer Sir Edwin Sandys and Virginia Treasurer George Sandys. On January 29, 1621, Sir Francis Wyatt was named Virginia's governor at the recommendation of the Earl of Southampton. The Virginia Company provided him with the funds he needed to become established in the colony, and he obtained a bill of adventure from Captain Edward Brewster, one of the late Lord Delaware's men. Wyatt set sail for Virginia on the *George*, accompanied by his brother, the Rev. Hautt (Haute, Hant) Wyatt, George Sandys, and surveyor William Claiborne. Governor Wyatt's detailed instructions from the Virginia Company included enhancing the colony's economic position through the production of marketable commodities, building fortifications and mills, and compiling demographic data. He was supposed to place the Company's tenants on the Governor's Land (**3**) but was to see that public labor was distributed fairly. He had the authority to use public labor as a mode of punishment but could not take punitive action against his councilors. Governor Francis Wyatt arrived in Virginia on November 18, 1621, only months before the March 22, 1622, Indian attack. He responded to the crisis forcefully and effectively and had the surviving Martin's Hun-

dred (**7**) and Warresqueak (**26**) settlers evacuated to the safety of Jamestown Island (**1**).

While Sir Francis Wyatt was in Virginia serving his first term as governor (November 1621–May 1626), he and his family resided in urban Jamestown, perhaps at first in the "governor's house" built in 1618 but later in a townstead of his own, which he seems to have been occupying by January 1623. In April 1623 Wyatt informed his superiors that he had tried to see that a palisade, guesthouse, and court of guard were built in Jamestown, but that the Indian attack had put a stop to those projects. He said that he was having a fort built in Warresqueak (**26**) and that he had required the colonists to plant a sufficient amount of corn. He had placed Lieutenant William Peirce in command of Jamestown and was making plans to initiate a series of marches against the Indians. Wyatt also issued proclamations against stealing livestock, and he forbade the hoarding of commodities (which fueled inflation and created shortages), public drunkenness, swearing, and theft. He tried to improve the quality and consistency of the tobacco exported from Virginia by having bad leaves burned. Wyatt was furnished with Company servants to work the Governor's Land, but he claimed that their labor had yielded little. On February 16, 1624, when a census was made of the colony's inhabitants, Governor Francis Wyatt was residing in urban Jamestown with his wife, Lady Margaret; his brother, the Rev. Haute Wyatt; and ten servants. On January 24, 1625, Governor Wyatt's household included himself and five male servants. He was credited with a house, a store, and some livestock. In May 1625 Wyatt was credited with 500 acres below Blunt Point (**22**), land that he had received by means of a court order.

Governor Francis Wyatt appears to have been an astute, forward-looking leader. In 1624 he recommended that a palisade be run across the James-York peninsula, a policy that was not implemented for several years, and he authorized Raleigh Crowshaw to trade along the Chesapeake Bay. He also intended to press the offensive against the Indians. Even though Wyatt was in office in August 1624, when the Virginia Company's charter was revoked and the colony came under the Crown's control, the king found him to be an acceptable leader and appointed him royal governor. Wyatt's evenhandedness facilitated Virginia's transition to a Crown colony. He communicated regularly with the Privy Council, which rewarded him by authorizing him to have 20 tenants and 12 boys as servants. He also acquired a Portuguese African man named Brass through a lawsuit. Wyatt saw that prices were set for certain commodities, required the colonists to plant enough corn to feed their families, and tried to control trade by forbidding anyone to go aboard newly arrived ships without official permission. However, he encouraged trade with the Indians. In May 1626 he received a patent for 500 acres in Elizabeth City (18) on Waters Creek, land that was below Blunt Point.

Sometime after May 8, 1626, Sir Francis Wyatt departed for England and was replaced by Governor George Yeardley. In November 1639 Wyatt was appointed the successor to Governor John Harvey. On October 13, 1641, Wyatt received a patent for a lot in urban Jamestown and a 50-acre leasehold on the Governor's Land. Wyatt's second term in office was marred by political factionalism, which eroded his popularity. However, it was during his administration that the Crown officially recognized the Virginia assembly's role in local affairs and stipulated that they should convene once a year. After incoming governor Sir William Berkeley arrived in February 1642, Sir Francis Wyatt became a councilor. Sir Francis Wyatt returned to England sometime prior to July 1644, and authorized William Peirce to act on his behalf. On August 6, 1644, Sir Francis Wyatt prepared his will, which was presented for probate less than three weeks later. He was interred at Boxley Abbey. He and his wife, Margaret, had five children— Henry, Edwin, William, George, and Elizabeth (WITH 625, 632; VCR 1:418-419, 436, 438, 454-455, 497, 509, 516; 2:519; 3:468-482, 485, 489, 541, 549-550, 583, 585, 588, 608-611, 622-623, 654, 658, 678-679, 703; 4:18, 40, 104-106, 129-130, 167-168, 172-173, 185, 188-189, 209, 211-214, 228-229, 236-238, 271, 275-276, 283-284, 292, 399-400-401, 444, 470, 480-481, 551, 556-557, 562-567; CO 1/2 ff 145-146; 1/10 ff 59-60, 144, 160-161; 5/1354 f 212; CJS 2:56, 284, 286, 291, 293, 318, 334; CBE 38, 47-48, 54; HAI 910, 915; HEN 1:3-5, 114, 128-129; FER 113, 539; STAN 14, 35; EAE 89; SAIN 1:58, 69, 286, 310; MCGC 22, 71-72, 83, 93, 103, 116-118, 161, 146, 164, 495, 498-499; PB 1 Pt. 1:212; Pt. 2:730; AMB 3, 4; DOR 1:28).

MARGARET SANDYS WYATT (MRS. FRANCIS WYATT)

Margaret, Sir Samuel Sandys' daughter and the niece of Virginia Company Treasurer Sir Edwin Sandys, married Sir Francis Wyatt around 1618. She also was the niece of Virginia Treasurer George Sandys. Lady Margaret Wyatt, who set sail for Virginia on October 12, 1622, corresponded with her parents and sisters while living in urban Jamestown (1). Her letters reveal that she was an intelligent woman with a keen wit and considerable stamina. She described the misery of her voyage aboard the *Abigail* and spoke with compassion of the women captured during the March 1622 Indian attack. On April 4, 1623, Lady Margaret wrote her sister and mother about the numerous deaths in Jamestown, and in June she told them that provisions in Virginia were expensive and of poor quality. She said that approximately half of her husband's cattle, and nearly a third of his men, had died. Lady Margaret said that she was in the process of starting a garden and asked her mother to send her some malt. On February 16, 1624, Lady Margaret Wyatt was living in Jamestown with her husband and ten servants. By January 24, 1625, she had returned to England (VCR 2:11; 3:690; 4:228-229; CBE 33; WITH 625, 632; MEY 100).

HENRY WYATT

On December 16, 1641, Henry Wyatt, the eldest son of Sir Francis and Lady Margaret Wyatt, secured a lease for 50 acres in the Governor's Land (3) (PB 1 Pt. 2:757).

HAUTT (HAWT) WYATT

The Rev. Haute Wyatt, the younger brother of Sir Francis Wyatt, was born in 1594 at Boxley in Kent and was the son of George Wyatt. Haute Wyatt attended Oxford and Grays Inn. When Francis was chosen governor of Virginia, Haute was selected as minister for the tenants of the Governor's Land (3). The Wyatt brothers came to Virginia in 1621. On February 16, 1624, the Rev. Haute Wyatt was living in urban Jamestown (1) in a household headed by his brother, the governor. The Rev. Haute Wyatt became rector of James City Parish around 1624, after the death of the Rev.

Richard Buck. When Sir Francis Wyatt returned to England in 1626, Haute accompanied him (VCR 1:516; 3:485; CBE 38; WITH 487, 626, 632; MEY 718-719).

***

WILLIAM WYE

On March 20, 1620, the Ferrars sent William Wye to Virginia as master of the *Garland*. He was accompanied by 45 men who were supposed to be employed in the colony's ironworks but instead were left in Bermuda. On October 14, 1622, when the Virginia Company sued Wye for failing to fulfill his contractual obligations, three men spoke against him. By December 9, 1622, the case against William Wye had been dismissed (VCR 1:323; 3:692-695, 701-702).

EDWARD WYNNE

On May 8, 1622, Edward Wynne, an ancient adventurer in the Virginia Company, received a patent. On June 10, 1622, he was identified as the holder of a patent for a particular (private) plantation (VCR 1:632; 3:643).

HUGH WYNNE (WINNE)

In 1608 Hugh Wynne (Winne), a tradesman, came to Virginia in the 2nd Supply of new colonists and, therefore, would have lived in Jamestown (1) (CJS 1:241; 2:191).

HUGH WYNNE (WYNN, WINNE)

Hugh Wynn (Wynne, Winne) came to Virginia on the *George* at the expense of Captain William Peirce, who sold Wynn's headright to William Spencer. Spencer used Wynn's headright when patenting some land on September 9, 1632 (PB 1 Pt. 1:120).

OWEN WYNNE (WYN, WYNN, WINNE)

On January 12, 1609, Owen Wyn (Wynn, Wynne, Winne), a Virginia Company adventurer in Virginia, made his will. It was proved on May 10, 1611 (WITH 91-92).

PETER WYNNE (WINNE)

Peter Wynne (Winne), a gentleman and shareholder in the Virginia Company, came to Virginia in 1608 in the 2nd Supply of new settlers. Shortly after he arrived in Jamestown (1), he became a member of the Council of State. He accompanied Captain John Smith on an exploratory voyage to the territory of the Monacan Indians. Smith later sent him with Captain Christopher Newport to present Powhatan with a crown. Wynne also went to the territory of the Nansemond Indians and with 50 men tried to capture some Dutchmen who had fled to the Natives. Captain John Smith said that Peter Wynne was a valiant gentleman and "old soldier," who was attentive to his duties. On November 26, 1608, Wynne, who was living in Jamestown, wrote a letter to Sir John Egerton, describing the colony's attributes. He said that he had accompanied Captain Christopher Newport on a journey to The Falls (67) of the James River and had visited the country of the Monacans, whose language differed from that of the Powhatans. He said that some of the men in his group thought that the Monacans' language resembled Welch and therefore wanted him to come along as an interpreter. Captain Peter Wynne died in Virginia in 1609. In May 1609 Sir Thomas Gates, who was unaware of Wynne's death, designated him sergeant-major of the fort and lieutenant governor (CJS 1:235, 239-240, 242, 260-261, 265; 2:182, 184, 188, 190-192, 209-210, 214; HAI 203-204, 402-403; VCR 3:13; STAN 28).

FRANCES WYRAN

On July 31, 1622, Francis Wyran set out for Virginia on the *James* on behalf of Lieutenant John Gibbs. He may have been going to Westover (54), where Gibbs's plantation was located (FER 400).

Y

GEORGE YARINGTON

George Yarington, a gentleman, went to Virginia in 1608 in the 2nd Supply of Jamestown (1) colonists. In late December 1608 he accompanied Captain John Smith on a trip to the Pamunkey Indians' territory (CJS 1:241, 244; 2:190, 193).

JOHN YARWORTH

In 1634 John Yarworth, a cloth-worker and citizen of London, went to Virginia on the *James* with Thomas Lee. John, who was age 55, was accompanied by his wife, Elizabeth (SH 34).

ELIZABETH YARWORTH (MRS. JOHN YARWORTH)

Elizabeth, the wife of London cloth-worker John Yarworth, went to Virginia on the *James* in 1634. She was then age 53 (SH 34).

***

WILLIAM YATEMAN

On February 12, 1620, officials at Bridewell Prison decided that William Yateman would be sent to Virginia (CBE 18).

[NO FIRST NAME] YATES

On February 16, 1624, Mr. Yates was living in Elizabeth City (**17, 18**) (CBE 43).

EDWARD YATES

Edward Yates came to Virginia on the *Duty* in 1619 and on February 4, 1625, was living on Hog Island (**16**), where he was an 18-year-old servant in Sir George Yeardley's household. Edward may have been one of the so-called *"Duty* boys" sent to the colony by the Virginia Company (CBE 61).

FERNANDO (FERDINANDO) YATES

On September 4, 1619, Fernando (Ferdinando) Yates, a gentleman, went to Virginia on the *Margaret* of Bristol. He was headed to Berkeley Hundred (**55**), where he was supposed to work under Captain John Woodlief's supervision for three years in exchange for 50 acres of land. Yates, who was designated an ensign, was to receive monetary compensation rather than apparel. Sometime prior to June 1, 1620, he sent a letter to John Smyth of Nibley, in which he described his voyage to Virginia and the colony itself. Smyth characterized Yates's comments as ill advised and perhaps inaccurate. By March 24, 1621, Fernando Yates

had left Virginia, having secured passage to England with Mr. Felgate (VCR 3:109-111, 197, 199, 213, 219, 293, 435-436).

LEONARD YATES (YEATS)

On February 16, 1624, Leonard Yates (Yeats) was living at Flowerdew Hundred (**53**) (CBE 37).

***

SIR GEORGE YEARDLEY (YARDLEY)

George Yeardley, who was born in 1588, joined a company of foot-soldiers in the Low Countries, where he became acquainted with Sir Thomas Gates. In June 1609 he accompanied Gates, Virginia's incoming lieutenant governor, when he set sail on the flagship *Seaventure,* which wrecked off the coast of Bermuda. Yeardley was stranded there with Gates, Sir George Somers, and Christopher Newport, captain of Gates's fleet. George Yeardley finally arrived in Virginia on the *Deliverance* in spring 1610 and was made captain of Sir Thomas Gates's guard, a position of trust. In November he sent word to England that the colony was in great need of men for husbandry as well as supplies, provisions, and agricultural equipment. When Lord Delaware (the colony's governor and captain general) arrived in June 1610, he sent Yeardley and a group of 150 men to search for precious metals. According to Ralph Hamor, in 1611 Sir Thomas Gates made Captain George Yeardley his lieutenant. Yeardley was second in command to Sir Thomas Dale at Bermuda Hundred (**39**), and when Dale left Virginia in May 1616, Yeardley was named acting governor—a position he held until Deputy Governor Samuel Argall arrived in May 1617. In 1613, during Dale's government, Captain George Yeardley married Temperance Flowerdew, who had arrived in the colony in 1609. The Yeardleys left the colony in late 1617, but in October 1618 he was designated Virginia's governor and a month later he was knighted. Plans were made for him to return to Virginia with 300 men and boys, 50 of whom were servants and part of the governor's stipend. Immediately prior to Sir George Yeardley's January 1619 departure from England, he received a lengthy set of instructions and was given the authority to implement the Virginia Company's November 1618 Great Charter, which set many new and important precedents. He was ordered to put the Virginia Company's servants on public property known as the Common Land and to use as an official residence a dwelling that Sir Thomas Gates had erected.

Governor George Yeardley arrived in Jamestown (1) on April 19, 1619, after a difficult crossing. He found that there were severe food shortages and no fortifications against a foreign enemy. He also discovered that Deputy Governor Samuel Argall had seated some people on the Governor's Land (3), a 3,000-acre tract near Jamestown Island that the Virginia Company had set aside toward the incumbent governor's support. Yeardley later claimed that Argall failed to leave behind the full complement of Company servants that the governor was supposed to have. He reportedly spent £3,000 outfitting new people to seat on his own private plantation. Like several Virginia Company members, Yeardley was an investor in the Society of Smythe's (Southampton) Hundred (44), and he agreed to take a role in its management. Within months, Governor George Yeardley led a march against the Chickahominy Indians, which yielded some corn and confirmation of a peace treaty that Sir Thomas Dale had made with the Indians earlier. Yeardley presided over the colony during a pivotal period in its history—when the first representative assembly convened (the first body of its kind in the New World) and the headright system was established. In August 1619 Yeardley procured some Africans from a Dutch mariner who entered Hampton Roads; in all probability they were the first members of their ethnic group to arrive in Virginia. In mid-summer Sir George Yeardley told his superiors that he wanted to resign his governorship in order to pursue personal objectives, for by that time his titles to Weyanoke (52) and Flowerdew Hundred (53) had been confirmed. In 1620 he sent word to England that the colonists were happy with the Great Charter and that men with experience in the Low Countries were needed to build forts in the colony. He indicated that he had bought a ship and dispatched it to Flushing in the Netherlands with some tobacco, and that he was planning to send some walnut planks home on the *Trial*. On behalf of the colony, Yeardley asked for husbandmen, vignerons, and other specialized workers to cultivate and process silk grass and flax.

Because Samuel Argall had seated the Society of Martins Hundred's settlers on the Governor's Land, Yeardley charged them rent, thereby forcing them to acknowledge that they were in the wrong location. This and the eviction of settlers from land he had been ordered to set aside for the Virginia Company's use enraged some colonists, who blamed him personally. Secretary John Pory informed Company officials that Yeardley had invested his own funds in the advancement of the colony and took only enough corn from the common storehouse to feed his guard. He said that Yeardley hoped to recover his expenditures from the profits derived from the Governor's Land, while diverting the remainder toward the construction of a fort at Old Point Comfort (17). Yeardley criticized some of ex-Deputy Governor Samuel Argall's actions and later claimed that Argall had committed piracy when he sent out the *Treasurer*, which returned with some Africans. Like many other colonists, Sir George Yeardley believed that tobacco was extremely important to the Virginia economy. After the first assembly meeting, he asked permission to withdraw into the countryside for three or four weeks so that he could review the laws to be discussed when the assembly reconvened on March 1, 1620. It was perhaps at that assembly meeting—the minutes of which no longer survive—that the March 1620 census was compiled. In June 1620 Yeardley said that the Virginia Company's boatwright was dead, and he asked for blue and white beads that could be used in trade with the Indians. Secretary John Pory said that it was difficult to get the colonists to contribute work toward building an ironworks, and that Yeardley had compelled those on watch in Jamestown, despite their grumbling, to work on building a new bridge (wharf) and gun platforms for the defense of the capital city. In 1621 he informed Company officials that a surveyor was needed and that clothing was in short supply. He and Captain William Powell of Jamestown had a serious disagreement but managed to reconcile their differences. In March 1621 Yeardley made reference to the house he had built in Southampton Hundred, where he was captain, and said that he had planted a vineyard there.

Sir George Yeardley's first term as governor expired on November 18, 1621. As the time approached for Governor Yeardley to vacate his office, he was told to leave 100 men on the Governor's Land for his replacement's use; he later was accused of failing to do so. He also was criticized for evicting people from the acreage they had seated on the east side of the Hampton River, property that Virginia Company officials had selected as Company Land in Elizabeth City. Ultimately he promised to see that the ancient planters, who had made improvements to the Company Land, were compensated.

As soon as Sir Francis Wyatt took office as governor in 1622, Sir George Yeardley channeled his energies into developing his own property, though he also continued to address the colony's needs. He built a windmill at Flowerdew Hundred and received a patent for transporting 300 people to the colony. He later claimed that he had sacrificed two-thirds of his estate in service to the colony. In June 1622, three months after an Indian attack claimed numerous lives, Yeardley was authorized to explore the countryside along the Chesapeake Bay to find a safer site on which the survivors could reside, and he helped to settle the estates of those who died during the March 1622 Indian attack. Although he was criticized for consulting Opechancanough about some land that the paramount chief had given to Pocahontas and John Rolfe's son, Thomas, in 1622 Yeardley led an expedition against Pocahontas's people, who lived within the Pamunkey River drainage. He undertook a trading voyage with William Tucker and, afterward, distributed the corn seized from the Indians. In 1623 Yeardley led a march against the Chickahominy Indians, who allegedly had killed ten colonists. He also served as a member of the Governor's Council during the Wyatt administration and, despite his substantial investment in outlying properties, made Jamestown his primary residence. In 1623 Yeardley was accused of wrongdoing when he purchased a hogshead of sack (a wine) from Mr. Bennett and then resold it to two Jamestown residents, George Menefie and John Stephens.

When a census was compiled on February 16, 1624, Sir George Yeardley, Lady Temperance, their children (Elizabeth and Argoll), and a substantial number of servants were residing in Yeardley's household in urban Jamestown, a 7$\frac{1}{2}$-acre tract that Yeardley patented on December 2, 1624, as

part of his 100-acre personal adventure as an ancient planter. Since Yeardley gave surgeon Samuel Mole a lease for part of his acreage in March 1620, it appears that Yeardley had laid claim to his land at least four years before he secured his patent. By February 1624 Sir George Yeardley sold his Flowerdew Hundred and Weyanoke plantations to cape merchant Abraham Peirsey. After Sir George's death, his widow confirmed both transactions. When demographic information on urban Jamestown was compiled on January 24, 1625, the Yeardley household included Sir George, Lady Temperance, and their three children (Argoll, Elizabeth, and Francis) and 24 servants, eight of whom were African. Sir George Yeardley was credited with three houses, a large herd of cattle, swine, and goats, all of which were associated with his townstead in Jamestown. His watercraft included a barque, a 4-ton shallop, and a skiff. Sir George also was in possession of some land on Hog Island (**16**), where he had a substantial number of servants. In January 1625 the Yeardley couple purchased three parcels of land at Black Point, in the eastern end of Jamestown Island, and in 1627 he patented 1,000 acres near Blunt Point (**22**), a plantation he called Stanley Hundred. He acquired 3,700 acres of land on the Eastern Shore, acreage that bordered the Chesapeake Bay and Hungars Creek. During the years Sir Francis Wyatt was governor, Sir George Yeardley continued to take an active role in government, and when Wyatt left the colony in 1624 Yeardley was designated acting governor. Yeardley testified in court from time to time and conducted business on his own behalf. He led another march against the Pamunkey Indians and reportedly insisted that Indian servants surrender their guns. In June 1625 officials of the defunct Virginia Company noted that Sir George Yeardley was returning to England with an account of the Society of Southampton Hundred's property and a petition to the king. By that time Virginia had become a royal colony. When Sir George Yeardley again became governor in early 1626, he received detailed instructions that mirrored those given to Sir Francis Wyatt in 1621. One task Yeardley faced was to dispose of the property formerly owned by the Virginia Company. He continued to seek new land to be cultivated and in October 1626 made arrangements to lease the orphaned Mary Bayley's Hog Island tract for three years—land that already was in his possession. In January 1627 Governor George Yeardley received 18 indentured servants whose unexpired contracts formerly belonged to the Virginia Company. Then, in October he was given seven years' use of a group of young male servants known as the "*Duty* boys," who had served seven years for the Company and were obliged to serve a like amount of time as tenants at half-shares.

On October 12, 1627, Sir George Yeardley, who described himself as "weak and sicke in body but in perfect minde and memory," made his will. He bequeathed to his wife, Temperance, life-rights to the dwelling they occupied in Jamestown, plus all of its contents. He specified that the rest of his real and personal property should be sold and the proceeds divided into thirds. Lady Temperance was to receive a third; eldest son, Argoll, was to receive a third; and the remaining third was to be divided equally between son Francis and daughter, Elizabeth. On October 29th Sir George added a codicil to his will, instructing his wife to sell their property on Jamestown Island so that whatever income it generated could be added to his estate. He died within two weeks and on November 13, 1627, was interred in Jamestown. His will was presented for probate on February 5, 1628. By February 8, 1628, Lady Temperance Yeardley had begun settling her late husband's estate and making arrangements to sell his property. She remarried before her responsibilities were discharged but died shortly thereafter. At that juncture, Sir George Yeardley's brother, Ralph, became administrator. He was soon at odds with Lady Temperance Yeardley's new husband, Francis West, who tried to recover her dower share of Sir George's estate (HAI 433, 825-826, 898, 904, 907; VCR 1:216, 229, 239-240, 255-257, 268, 310, 318-319, 326, 331-333, 334-336, 419-420, 432, 435, 484, 488, 543, 579, 588; 2:16, 43-44, 94-95, 105-106, 393-397, 481; 3:29-31, 98-109, 101, 118-119, 125-126, 130-134, 146-148, 152-153, 176, 189-190, 212, 216-219, 243, 248-249, 255-258, 298-299, 426-427, 432, 436-438, 444-445, 448-450, 452, 462-464, 471, 482, 526-528, 585-586, 588, 643, 656-657, 678-679, 683-690; 4:6-9, 22, 37, 97-98, 110, 118, 504, 510-517, 554, 556, 559, 562-567; AP 77, 80-81; CJS 2:56, 255-257, 262, 266, 283-284, 302, 310-311, 315; 3:215, 217; STAN 14, 28; POR 40, 72, 80-81, 83; FER 91, 92, 113, 141, 184; EAE 10; PRO 30/15/2:246, 279, 290; CO 1/3 f 226; 1/4 f 88; 5/1354 f 48, 257-258; S of N 43; MCGC 5, 8, 10-11, 15, 18-19, 21, 27-28, 36-37, 40-41, 44-45, 47, 51, 55, 58, 60-62, 64, 73-74, 89-91, 93, 122, 130, 136-137, 148, 154, 156-157, 161, 168, 176; CBE 38, 48, 54, 71, 80, 86-87; HEN 1:128-129; SAIN 1:69, 77; PB1 Pt. 1:3, 15; NEI 68; WITH 156; SH 9; SR 3119; WAT 30; MEY 723-727; MOR 120; AMES 1:166; 2:34; DOR 1:29, 44).

TEMPERANCE FLOWERDEW YEARDLEY (YARDLEY) (MRS. GEORGE YEARDLEY [YARDLEY], MRS. FRANCIS WEST)

Temperance Flowerdew, who arrived in the colony in August 1609 on the *Faulcon*, married Captain George Yeardley in 1613, while Sir Thomas Dale was in Virginia. The Yeardleys went back to England but returned to Virginia in 1619, arriving in mid-April. Since Sir George Yeardley was then Virginia's new governor, the household resided in urban Jamestown (1). On March 10, 1622, Lady Temperance Yeardley witnessed the will made by John Rolfe, who also lived in Jamestown. When a census of the colony's inhabitants was compiled on February 16, 1624, Lady Temperance, Sir George, and two of their children (Argoll and Elizabeth) were residing in Jamestown in a household that included a substantial number of servants. When a muster was compiled on January 24, 1625, the Yeardley household was still residing in urban Jamestown and included the couple's three children (Argoll, Elizabeth, and Francis) and 24 servants, eight of whom were African. Lady Temperance seems to have been a woman of considerable intelligence, for she took a relatively active role in her household's business affairs. In September 1625, when Captain Jones's African servant was a member of her household, the Governor's Council ordered her to pay him 40 pounds of tobacco for his work. In January 1627 one of the Yeardleys' servants negotiated with John Upton (a newly freed indentured servant) about renting Lady Temperance's land at Black Point. Although court records indicate that the land was Lady Temperance's, in fact she and Sir George had purchased it in 1625. This raises the possibility that she was managing his financial affairs because he had become seriously ill. On October 12, 1627, when Sir George Yeardley made his will, he left his wife, Temperance, life-rights to the dwelling they occupied in Jamestown and all of its contents. The rest of his personal and real estate was to be liquidated and divided into three equal shares, with Lady Temperance receiving a third. On October 29, 1627, when Sir George Yeardley added a codicil to his will, he asked that his wife sell his land and houses on Jamestown Island. He died shortly thereafter. On November 16, 1627, Lady Temperance Yeardley renounced her dower interest in Flowerdew Hundred (**53**) and Weyanoke (**52**), properties her late husband had sold to Abraham Peirsey. By February 8, 1628, Lady Temperance had begun settling her late husband's estate and making arrangements to sell his property. Even before she commenced serving as executrix, she sued to collect debts that were owed to Sir George. In February and March 1628 she surrendered the cattle that were part of the governor's stipend and asked for an accounting of Southampton Hundred's finances. Lady Temperance Yeardley married interim Governor Francis West in late March 1628 but died intestate in December 1628. Because she had not finished settling Sir George Yeardley's estate, his brother, Ralph, was named administrator. On February 1, 1630, Francis West, as Temperance's widower and heir, brought suit against Ralph Yeardley in an attempt to recover his late wife's dower share of Sir George Yeardley's estate, which West claimed was worth at least £3,000 and included land, servants, tobacco, and other goods (CBE 38, 54, 87; MCGH 861; SH 5; VCR 3:536; MCGC 72, 83, 137, 157, 159, 166-169; SR 3119; MOR 120).

ARGOLL (ARGALL) YEARDLEY (YARDLEY)

Argoll (Argall) Yeardley (Yardley), the eldest son of Sir George and Lady Temperance Flowerdew Yeardley, was born in Virginia around 1620 and on February 16, 1624, was residing in Jamestown (**1**) with his parents and sister, Elizabeth, and the family's servants. The Yeardleys were still in Jamestown on January 24, 1625, at which time Argoll was age 4. Argoll Yeardley and his siblings lost their father in November 1627; their mother, who remarried in late March 1628, died the following December. Argoll, as the eldest son, stood to inherit a third of his late father's estate, the

bulk of which was in the hands of his uncle, Ralph Yeardley. From 1639 to 1655 Argoll Yeardley served on the Council of State, and in 1642 he became a commissioner of the Accomack Court. In 1649, while on a trip to the Netherlands, he met and married Ann Custis, his second wife, and brought her to Virginia. The Yeardley couple lived on the Eastern Shore in Northampton County, as did his politically powerful brother-in-law, Colonel John Custis of Arlington. Argoll Yeardley's household resided in Old Town Neck, where he patented 2,000 acres. He died sometime prior to October 29, 1655 (CBE 38, 54; MEY 726-728; PB 1 Pt. 2:595; FOR 3:10:49; Lower Norfolk County Book A:59; AMES 2:passim).

ELIZABETH YEARDLEY (YARDLEY)

Elizabeth, the daughter of Sir George and Lady Temperance Flowerdew Yeardley, was born in Virginia around 1619 and on February 16, 1624, was residing in Jamestown (**1**) with her parents, brother Argoll, and the family's servants. The Yeardleys were still in Jamestown on January 24, 1625, at which time Elizabeth was age 6. The Yeardley children lost their father in 1627 and their mother (who had remarried) in December 1628. Elizabeth stood to inherit a sixth of her late father's estate, the bulk of which was in the hands of her uncle, Ralph Yeardley, who lived in England (CBE 38, 54; MEY 726).

FRANCIS YEARDLEY (YARDLEY)

Francis, the youngest son of Sir George and Lady Temperance Flowerdew Yeardley, was born in Virginia around 1624. The Yeardley household then resided in urban Jamestown (**1**). They were still there on January 24, 1625, at which time Francis was age 1. Francis Yeardley and his siblings lost their father in November 1627 and their mother (who had remarried) in December 1628. Francis stood to inherit a sixth of his late father's estate. In January 1643 he received a patent for 3,000 acres of land on the Eastern Shore. Francis Yeardley married the twice-widowed Sarah Offley Thorogood Gookin in 1647 and began residing at Lynnhaven. He served as a Lower Norfolk County justice from 1651–1653 and was a member of the Maryland Council. He also became a burgess for Lower Norfolk

County in 1653. In 1654 he chronicled a trip he made to Roanoke Island, where he visited the site the "Lost Colonists" had occupied, and said that he and his wife, Sarah, had entertained some Natives in their home in Lynnhaven. Francis Yeardley died in 1656 (CBE 38, 54; HEN 1:379; MEY 726-727; AMES 2:passim).

RALPH YEARDLEY (YARDLEY)

On September 30, 1619, Ralph Yeardley, Sir George Yeardley's brother, was described as an apothecary. After Lady Temperance Yeardley West's death in December 1628, Ralph became Sir George Yeardley's administrator. Lady Temperance's widower, Francis West, sued Ralph Yeardley in an attempt to recover her dower share of the late Sir George Yeardley's estate (VCR 3:221; CBE 90; SR 10406).

***

RICHARD YEAW

On March 22, 1622, when the Indians attacked Owen Macar's house at Westover **(54)**, Richard Yeaw was slain (VCR 3:568).

JAMES YEMANSON

On February 16, 1624, James Yemanson, an indentured servant, was living in Captain Ralph Hamor's household in urban Jamestown **(1)** (CBE 38).

ROBERT YEOMAN

Robert Yeoman was killed at Flowerdew **(53)** during the March 22, 1622, Indian attack (VCR 3:566).

JOHN YEOMANS

On September 26, 1618, officials at Bridewell decided that John Yeomans, a vagrant from Aldermanbury who was born on Watling Street, would be sent to Virginia (CBE 10).

[NO FIRST NAME] YOUNG (YOUNGE, YONGE)

On February 16, 1624, there was a servant with the surname Young (Younge, Yonge) in Sir George Yeardley's household in urban Jamestown **(1)** (CBE 38).

ANTHONY YOUNG (YOUNGE)

On February 27, 1619, Anthony Young (Younge), a boy being detained at Bridewell, was among those chosen to be sent to Virginia. He probably was one of the children rounded up from the streets of London so that they could be sent to the colony (CBE 12).

ANTHONY YOUNG (YOUNGE)

Anthony Young (Younge), a grocer and citizen of London, came to Virginia sometime prior to 1636. When he made his will on February 23, 1636, he seems to have been associated with the New Poquoson **(19)** area. He made bequests to his servant Thomas Hunson, Captain Samuel Mathews, the church at Denbigh **(23)**, and the church at New Poquoson, and he forgave the debts of Thomas Downum (probably Downman), Thomas Curtis, William Petty, and John Carter (a surgeon living in the New Poquoson). When Anthony Young's will was presented for probate, he was said to have been from St. Dunstan in east London. Probate officials also noted that he had died in Virginia (EEAC 66; WITH 195).

CHRISTOPHER YOUNG

In late 1634 Christopher Young purchased some of the late Thomas Lee's goods, which were sold by Bartholomew Hopkins in Elizabeth City **(17)** (CBE 208).

HUMPHREY (HUMFREY) YOUNG

On August 23, 1631, officials at Bridewell decided that Humphrey (Humfrey) Young, a boy from Langborne, would be sent to Virginia (HUME 36).

NICHOLAS YOUNG

On October 14, 1622, Nicholas Young was one of three men who testified against William Wye of the *Garland*, a vessel that had made numerous trips to Virginia (VCR 3:692-695).

***

RICHARD YOUNG

Richard Young, an ancient planter, came to Virginia on the *George* in 1616. On February 16, 1624, he and his wife, Joan (Joane, Jone), and young daughter were living in an urban Jamestown (1) household headed by Thomas Gray. By early 1625 the Youngs had moved to Elizabeth City (18), where 31-year-old Richard was a household head. Joan was then age 26 and their daughter, Joan, was only 2. Sharing the Young home was a 12-year-old girl named Susan, whose connection with the family is uncertain. In early 1625 Richard Young's household was in possession of a dwelling and an ample supply of stored food and defensive weaponry (CBE 38, 63; DOR 1:52).

JOAN (JOANE, JONE) YOUNG I (MRS. RICHARD YOUNG)

Joan (Joane, Jone), who became the wife of ancient planter Richard Young, came to Virginia in 1618 on the *Gift*. On February 16, 1624, she and Richard were living in Thomas Gray's household in urban Jamestown (1). By early 1625 the Youngs and their 2-year-old daughter, Joan, had moved to Elizabeth City (18), where he was a household head. The elder Joan Young was then age 26. A 12-year-old girl named Susan also shared their home (CBE 38, 63).

JOAN (JOANE, JONE) YOUNG II

On February 16, 1624, Joan (Joane, Jone) Young II, the Virginia-born the daughter of Richard and Joan Young, was living with her parents in Thomas Gray's household in urban Jamestown (1). By the beginning of 1625, 2-year-old Joan and her parents had moved to Elizabeth City (18), where her father was a household head. A girl named Susan, who was age 12, also shared their home (CBE 38, 63).

***

ROBERT YOUNG

On July 31, 1622, Robert Young set sail for Virginia on the *James* with William Rowley (FER 400).

THOMAS YOUNG (YONGE, YOUNGE)

On September 23, 1632 or 1633, Thomas Young (Yonge, Younge), who was from London, was authorized to undertake a voyage of discovery in Virginia. In April 1634

he dispatched a letter to England's governing officials, which said that he and his nephew, Robert Evelin, wanted to trade in America, especially in Virginia. Sometime prior to July 13, 1634, Thomas Young arrived in Jamestown (1). He then sent a letter home to England in which he said that there was a great deal of tension between Lord Baltimore's supporters and opponents (MHS 81-114).

WILLIAM YOUNG

William Young, a Virginia Company investor, arrived in Jamestown (1) in 1608 in the 1st Supply of new colonists (CJS 1:223; 2:162, 283).

HENRY YORKE

On December 31, 1619, Henry Yorke, who had been incarcerated at Newgate Prison but transferred to Bridewell, was among those chosen to be sent to Virginia (CBE 15).

Z

ZOROBABELL

Zorobabell died at West and Shirley Hundred (41) sometime after April 1623 but before February 16, 1624 (CBE 36).

EDWARD ZOUCH

In December 1617 Sir Edward Zouch of the Castle of Dover, Lord Warden of the Cinque Ports, made an investment with Lord Delaware, who agreed to transport seven men to Virginia on his behalf. On February 15, 1619, Zouch informed the Virginia Company that he was sending his ship, the *Silver Falcon*, to the colony (VCR 3:77, 135; CJS 2:283).

***

JOHN ZOUCH I

Sir John Zouch I of Codnor Castle in Derbyshire was a member of the Virginia Company. He and his wife, Isabel, produced a son (John II) and three daughters (Isabella, Mary, and Elizabeth), who survived to adulthood. On June 26, 1620,

Zouch obtained a patent for some Virginia land but failed to establish a settlement in the colony. On June 23, 1623, Zouch and some associates were given a new patent after indicating that they intended to transport 100 people to Virginia. Later in the year Sir John Zouch and his son, John II, secured some acreage near the head of the James River, at Rochdale Hundred **(65)**, and made elaborate plans to build an ironworks. Sir John sold Codnor Castle and around 1634 moved his son and his daughter Isabella to Virginia. Although he invested heavily in his plantation and the ironworks project, his efforts proved unsuccessful. Shortly after Sir John Zouch I arrived in Virginia, incumbent Governor John Harvey informed the Privy Council that Zouch was unsuitable to serve as a Council member because he was "of the Puritan Sect." Harvey probably was uneasy about Zouch's friendship with councilor Samuel Mathews I, whom he considered an adversary. On August 13, 1636, when Sir John Zouch made his will, he left his Virginia land and the bulk of his personal property (which included his watch, books, armor, quilted coats, and guns) to his son, John Zouch II. The testator expressed his regrets that he was unable to leave more, but noted that he had invested £1,200 in his plantation and that his partners had failed to provide the necessary support. Sir John Zouch I bequeathed to his unmarried daughter, Isabella, his servant, some horses and other livestock, his plate and household goods, and all other personal property not given to her brother. He said that if the bequest to Isabella was worth more than £400, the excess was to be split between her sisters, Elizabeth and Mary. Zouch stated that he did not love Isabella more than her sisters, but that she had "ventured her life in a dangerous voyage." Sir John Zouch died in Virginia, and his will was presented for probate on December 15, 1639. His land eventually escheated to the Crown. Virginia officials noted that in 1639 "Sir John Zouch and his son began upon an iron work wch came to nothing, their ptners. failing them" (VCR 1:375, 381; 2:449, 457; PB 1 Pt. 2:567, 839; 6:84; 7:127; SAIN 1:217; EEAC 66; WITH 67-68; SR 3987; SH 26; MCGC 481; MEY 729).

JOHN ZOUCH II

John Zouch II was the son of Sir John Zouch I, who in June 1623 secured a patent

for some acreage within the vast tract that Sir Thomas Dale delimited and named Rochdale **(65)**. John II, his father, and John II's sister Isabella came to the colony and attempted to establish a plantation and ironworks, but their efforts proved unsuccessful. On May 5, 1635, John Zouch II described the hostile relationship that existed between Governor John Harvey and his Council and Harvey's expulsion from office. On August 13, 1636, when Sir John Zouch made his will, he left his Virginia land and the bulk of his personal property to his son, John Zouch II. He noted that he had invested £1,200 in his plantation and that John II had invested £250. In 1639 a Bishop's Court granted John Zouch II administration of his father's will. By October 1642 John Zouch II had come into possession of some land on the north side of the Appomattox River, and in 1644 he served as a burgess for Henrico County. Genealogical sources indicate that he died without living heirs and that the property he inherited from his father escheated to the Crown (EEAC 66; WITH 67-68; SR 3987; SH 26; CO 1/32 f 7; NEI 118-120; MCGC 481).

ISABELLA ZOUCH

Isabella, the daughter of Sir John Zouch I, accompanied her father and brother to Virginia around 1634 and would have settled with them at Rochdale **(65)**. On August 13, 1636, when Sir John Zouch made his will, he left his unmarried daughter, Isabella, a servant, some horses and other livestock, his plate, household goods, and all of his other goods not given to her brother, John II. He said that if the bequest to Isabella was worth more than £400, the excess was to be split between her sisters, Elizabeth and Mary. He noted that he did not love Isabella more, but that she had "ventured her life in a dangerous voyage" (EEAC 66; WITH 67-68; SR 3987; SH 26).

***

PEDRO DE ZUNIGA

Don Pedro de Zuniga became Spain's ambassador to England in autumn 1605. His reputation was tarnished by the Gunpowder Plot of November 1605, and he remained highly unpopular. His correspondence reveals that he prided himself in passing along intelligence information. On June 16, 1608, Zuniga sent word to Spain that the

Virginia colonists had fortified their settlement and were prepared to become pirates. On September 10, 1608, he sent another letter, plus a sketch map that he had obtained, probably surreptitiously. That chart of Tidewater Virginia, which shows the Jamestown fort, has become known as the Zuniga map. Zuniga said that people were being encouraged to invest in Virginia land and that large numbers of colonists were expected to immigrate. On April 12, 1609, he told his superiors that workmen were being brought to Virginia to build ships and that the colonists were planning to abandon their first settlement and move to a healthier location. Finally, on November 23, 1609, Zuniga reported hearing that Sir Thomas Gates and Sir George Somers' ship was lost and that the cattle previously sent to Virginia were thriving. In May 1610 Velasco replaced Zuniga as ambassador (BRO 172, 184, 258, 265, 272, 332).

INDEX

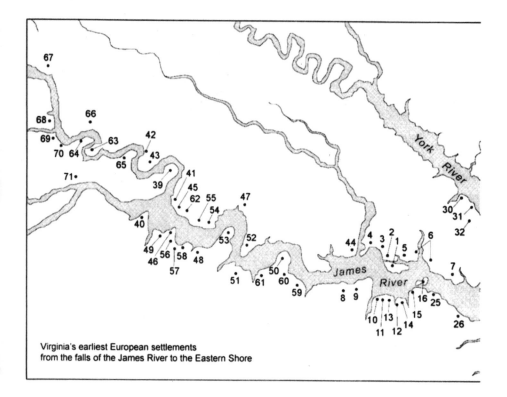

Virginia's earliest European settlements
from the falls of the James River to the Eastern Shore

1. Jamestown Island
2. Glasshouse
3. Governor's Land (The Maine and Pasbehay)
4. Company Land in James City
5. Neck O'Land
6. Archer's Hope
7. Martin's Hundred
8. Burrows Hill (Burrows Mount, Smith's Mount)
9. Paces Paines
10. Captain Roger Smith's Plantation
11. Treasurer's Plantation
12. Hugh Crowder's Plantation
13. William Ewen's Plantation
14. Captain William Powell's Plantation
15. Captain Samuel Mathews' Plantation
16. Hog Island
17. Old Point Comfort, the Company Land, and the Common Land in Elizabeth City
18. Elizabeth City (west side of the Hampton River)
19. Elizabeth City (near the mouth of the York River)
20. Elizabeth City (lower side of the James River):
  20 a: Elizabeth River
  20 b: Lynnhaven area
  20 c: Nansemond River area
21. Mulberry Island
22. Blunt Point and Stanley Hundred
23. Mathews Manor (Denbigh)
24. Newportes News (Marie's Mount)
25. Captain Christopher Lawne's Plantation
26. Bennett's Welcome (Warresqueak)
27. Basses Choice
28. Giles Jones's Plantation at Day's Point
29. Nansemond
30. Kings Creek Plantation
31. Ringfield
32. The Indian Field Plantation
33. Francis Morgan's Plantation
34. William Prior's Plantation
35. Richard Townsend's Plantation
36. Martiau's Plantation
37. York Plantation
38. Wormeley Creek